FUNDAMENTAL PRINCIPLES
OF
FAMILY LAW

Second Edition

LYNN D. WARDLE

Professor of Law
J. Reuben Clark Law School
Brigham Young University
Provo, Utah

&

LAURENCE C. NOLAN

Professor of Law
Howard University School of Law
Washington, D.C.

William S. Hein & Co., Inc.
Buffalo, New York
2006

Library of Congress Cataloging-in-Publication Data

Wardle, Lynn D.
    Fundamental principles of family law / by Lynn D.
Wardle and Laurence C. Nolan.—2nd ed.

        p. cm.
    Includes bibliographical references and index.
    ISBN 0-8377-3832-6 (cloth : alk. paper)
    1. Domestic relations—United States. 2. Parent and
child (Law)—United States. I. Nolan, Laurence C. II. Title.
KF505.W374 2005
346.7301'5—dc22   2005050319

Printed in the United States of America

This volume is printed on acid-free paper
by William S. Hein & Co., Inc.

Preface

How small of all that human hearts endure,
that part which laws or kings can cause or cure.
--Samuel Johnson, Lines Added to Goldsmith's Traveller

Fundamental Principles of Family Law is written for use by law students in the basic Family Law courses taught in American law schools. This casebook is designed especially for use in national and regional law schools where the students come from and expect to be practicing in many different states. It emphasizes the basic general principles of substantive and procedural law that regulate family relations in most American states.

Several qualities distinguish *Fundamental Principles of Family Law* from other Family Law casebooks. First, it provides a simple but comprehensive organizational structure for family law that students find very useful for ordering coherently their study of the subject. Family Law topics after the introduction are organized in six sections in a before-during-after sequence: *Before* concerns the creation of family relations, *During* concerns the regulation of ongoing family relations, and *After* deals with the termination of family relations and post-termination relations. In each section, we examine the two core family relationships: relations between husband and wife (and marriage-like relationships), the "horizontal" relations of family law; and relations between parent and child (and analogous guardian relations), the "vertical relations" of family law. This organizational structure provides a permanent conceptual framework to help the students to rationally organize their study of family law, and to prepare them to give coherence to their family law practice.

Second, the chapter structure is consistent throughout this casebook. Every chapter contains from one to four sub-chapters, each covering a discrete topic of family law relevant to the general subject of the chapter. Each sub-chapter consists of four parts that review the history and background of that area or law; present leading cases, statutes, and doctrinal trends in American family law relating to the topic; raise practical and ethical issues; and provide an introductory bibliography of resource materials.

Third, while *Fundamental Principles of Family Law* provides a thorough overview of the prevailing principles, rules, doctrines and approaches in the United States as a whole, it emphasizes the dominant importance of local, state-specific rules of family law. Thus, the book is intended to be supplemented by 150-200 pages of local family law cases, statutes, regulations and notes. Every chapter can (and should) be supplemented by local family law materials. Since the critical details of family law that family lawyers must master and know how to find and to use effectively are found in *local* cases, statutes, regulations, and administrative materials, this casebook is designed to help students learn the importance of (and how to find) state family law doctrines and resources.

Fourth, this casebook emphasizes the tremendous positive value of families and family relations for individuals and for society. The protection and facilitation of the basic institutions and core relationships of family life are among the most important purposes and social ordering functions of any legal system. Indeed, because the family truly is the fundamental social unit of society, the long-term success and survival of a society, as well as the short-term health, prosperity and happiness of its members, may depend more on whether its family law is successful in transmitting and supporting valid principles of happy, stable, liberating family relations than any other area of law. While this book presents a variety of competing policy perspectives and viewpoints, in the belief that law students should seek to understand the pros-and-cons of family policy issues, we underscore the importance and value of marriage and marriage-based families for the health and happiness of individuals and for the security and prosperity of society.

Fifth, these materials are intended to increase student awareness of practical and ethical considerations that arise in the practice of family law. Every chapter includes some material raising practical and ethical issues. A pervasive theme is that family law should be viewed and practiced as a way of rendering genuine service. Family lawyers have a special opportunity to give meaningful service to persons with very poignant needs, excruciating personal pains, bitter distress, and aching sorrows concerning the most tender, important, intangible relations. The family lawyer can soothe injuries, cool anger, create, repair, or terminate relationships, defend the exploited, and protect the vulnerable, and promote family justice. Practicing family law requires the total professionalism of the attorney -- i.e., knowledge of the law, analytical competency, professional skill, interprofessional acumen, community awareness, patience, sensitivity, understanding, tact, diligence, courage, and compassion. The consequences of the lawyer's service in a family law cases may effect family members for many years in ways that will influence their lives profoundly. This book helps students to prepare to practice family law in the highest service-giving tradition of the legal profession.

Fundamental Principles of Family Law is designed to give the student a complete and balanced introduction to the theories, doctrines, and practice of family law. While a casebook intended for use in a 3-hour survey class obviously cannot cover every detail of family law, we believe that teachers and students alike will find that these materials are well-organized, teach the fundamental principles of family law, raise consciousness of important policy issues, highlight practical skills and ethical considerations, and emphasize service orientation in family law.

19 June 2006	Lynn D. Wardle	Laurence C. Nolan
	Provo, Utah	Washington, D.C.

Dedication

To our students.

Acknowledgments

We appreciate the assistance of many people who have helped us prepare this casebook. We have benefitted from the valuable research and editing assistance of many research assistants, most recently (for Lynn) Genevieve Gribble and Joseph Wright, and (for Laurence) Everett Greene, Rosalyn Roberson, and Erica Bradley. This second edition reflects the work of our former research assistants who helped with the first edition, including (for Lynn) William J. Perkins, Brittany Howick, Amy Smedley, Velvet Poston, Emily Warner, Jose Silva, Bill Duncan, and (for Laurence) Everett Greene, Rosalyn Roberson, Erica Bradley, and Susan Branch. Additionally, over the years many of our students have offered criticisms and suggestions regarding these materials that have contributed to their improvement and refinement. Marcene Mason, Florence Beal, Gina Patch, Heather Witt, and other secretaries at the J. Reuben Clark Law School have provided patient, capable, valuable service, as have many student computer consultants. Stephanie Dyson of the Howard University School of Law Library has provided wonderful service. The editorial and proofreading service of Lisa Hawkins has made a valuable contribution to this second edition. We are grateful to David Wardle and his Anchor Legal Publications for publishing the first version of this casebook (in 2001), and to Sheila Jarrett and Wm. S. Hein & Co. for their decision to publish *Fundamental Principles of Family Law*, to distribute it nationally, for publishing this second edition, and for the grace and courtesy with which they have worked with us over the past five year. We are especially grateful to our own family members who have endured, supported, and encouraged our work as Family Law teachers and authors. We are indebted to them all, but we, alone, take responsibility for the book and its flaws.

LDW & LCN
June 2006

Explanation of Editing and Symbols

For the most part, we have tried to follow the general conventions of legal citation form as established in The Bluebook, A Uniform System of Citation. However, for pedagogical, practical, and aesthetic reasons, we have varied from these forms in a few particulars to simplify or clarify matters for the benefit of the readers, or to avoid unnecessary printing costs. The major deviations from standard legal citation form are listed below:

*	indicates that one or more citation has been omitted.
. . .	indicates that text of less than one paragraph has been omitted
. . . .	indicates that one or more paragraphs of text have been omitted

Case and statutory citations are generally given in standard legal citation form and parallel citations usually are omitted.

Full citations to secondary sources such as monographs, treatises, law review materials, and articles in other periodicals are provided in general legal citation form in the *Bibliography* listing ("4. Bibliography") of each of the sections (Sections A, B, C, etc.) of each Chapter. Elsewhere in the text these sources are cited in short form - usually the last name of the leading author and/or, if needed, the date of publication or a key word from the title of the publication.

One multi-volume family law treatise that is referenced many times in most chapters is generally cited in short form as "Contemporary Family Law, vol. x, ch. y (1988)." The full citation to the treatise is: "Contemporary Family Law, vols. 1-4 (Lynn D. Wardle, Christopher L. Blakesley & Jacqueline Y. Parker eds. 1988)."

Most footnotes have been omitted from the original opinions without any indication of those omissions, except that when footnotes are kept their original footnote number is used.

Some case opinions and other materials have been reformatted for appearance, uniformity, or to use the printed space more efficiently. For example, we have italicized all case names, whether they were italicized in the opinions or not.

FUNDAMENTAL PRINCIPLES OF FAMILY LAW
TABLE OF CONTENTS

PART VII TERMINATION AND POST-DISSOLUTION PARENTS - CHILD RELATIONS

PART I
INTRODUCTION

CHAPTER 1

Introduction:
Definition, Organization, Importance, and Sources of Family Law

A. INTRODUCTION TO FAMILY LAW: DEFINITION AND ORGANIZATION

1. Background

a. History of Family Law as Canon Law and in Ecclesiastical Courts

For centuries during the middle ages, throughout England and Europe, most of the issues that we today would call family law issues were under the jurisdiction of church (canon) law and ecclesiastical courts. In England, from at least the twelfth century until the nineteenth century, authority over marriage and divorce was ceded to the Church and disputes regarding marriage rights, duties, and dissolution were resolved by ecclesiastical courts. Since marriage and procreation were deemed primarily spiritual matters during most of the era of the common law (though not without debate, especially after the time of Martin Luther and the Protestant Reformation), canon law or church doctrine was the source of many rules of law regarding marriage, procreation, child-rearing, and family relations in common law England. Likewise, in America, even among the settlers who came to the new world to find religious tolerance, the family laws also reflected popular religious values of the day.

For purposes of ecclesiastical jurisdiction, England after the Conquest was divided into two provinces (Canterbury and York), and these into dioceses. The Diocesan Courts (sometimes called Consistory Courts) were usually the courts of first instance in suits upon matrimonial causes. Appeals from the Diocesan Courts could be taken to the Provincial Courts, which also could hear some cases in the first instance. Appeals from the Provincial Courts originally were taken to the Pope in Rome, but after the English crown broke with the Roman Catholic Church, appeals were taken to the Crown (in Chancery first, later in Council). The jurisdiction of the ecclesiastical courts eroded somewhat over the centuries, but the distinct jurisdiction of these courts over marriage issues remained until well into Queen Victoria's reign. Rayden's, *infra*, at 1-4. Today, church courts have no secular legal effects, yet the existence of special state tribunals

3

(e.g., juvenile and family courts) for family law cases may reflect in part the ancient notion that family law disputes are unique and should be heard by special courts rather than by courts of general jurisdiction that hear ordinary commercial, tort, and criminal cases.

Family law has long reflected strong values comparable in intensity to and often derived from religious beliefs. Matters of family life have been of central concern to religions throughout the ages, and regulations of family relations still generally reflect prevailing moral and religious beliefs.

b. What Subjects Are Included in Family Law?

Family Law is that branch of law consisting of the substantive and procedural rules that regulate the creation, ongoing relations, termination, and post-termination consequence of family relationships, and the legal rights, privileges, benefits, duties, limits and restrictions pertaining to such relationships. *Direct regulation* of family relations (e.g., rules governing marriage, paternity, adoption, child abuse and neglect, divorce, custody, support, etc.) is the major concern of law school courses and of most family law practice. However, *indirect regulation* of family relations arises in virtually all other subjects in the law school curriculum, also. The addition of the "family factor" to otherwise normal problems of property, evidence, contract, or tort law often creates a new, hybrid dilemma in which the family law issue may overshadow the other issues. Historically, the primary focus of state family law regulation has been (and still is) on the nuclear family, though the regulation of relations between persons in analogous relationships such as extended, quasi-, and alternative families is increasingly arising in the cases and being discussed in the literature.

2. Statutes, Cases, and Doctrines

a. *Braschi v. Stahl*

Miguel Braschi v. Stahl Associates Company
74 N.Y.2d 201, 543 N.E.2d 49, 544 N.Y.S.2d 784 (1989)

TITONE, JUDGE.

In this dispute over occupancy rights to a rent-controlled apartment, the central question to be resolved on this request for preliminary injunctive relief ... is whether appellant has demonstrated a likelihood of success on the merits ... by showing that, as a matter of law, he is entitled to seek protection from eviction under New York City Rent and Eviction Regulations 9 NYCRR 2204.6(d) .... That regulation provides that upon the death of a rent-control tenant, the landlord may not dispossess "either the surviving spouse of the deceased tenant or some other member of the deceased tenant's *family* who has been living with the tenant" (emphasis supplied). ***. Resolution of this question requires this court to determine the meaning of the term "family" as it is used in this context.

I.

Appellant, Miguel Braschi, was living with Leslie Blanchard in a rent-controlled apartment located at 405 East 54th Street from the summer of 1975 until Blanchard's death in September of 1986. In November of 1986, respondent, Stahl Associates Company, the owner of the apartment building, served a notice to cure on appellant contending that he was a mere licensee with no right to occupy the apartment since only Blanchard was the tenant of record. In December of 1986 respondent served appellant with a notice to terminate informing appellant that he had one month to vacate the apartment and that, if the apartment was not vacated, respondent would commence summary proceedings to evict him.

Appellant then initiated an action seeking a permanent injunction and a declaration of entitlement to occupy the apartment. By order to show cause appellant then moved for a preliminary injunction, pendente lite, enjoining respondent from evicting him until a court could determine whether he was a member of Blanchard's family within the meaning of 9 NYCRR 2204.6(d). After examining the nature of the relationship between the two men, Supreme Court concluded that appellant was a "family member" within the meaning of the regulation and, accordingly, that a preliminary injunction should be issued. The court based this decision on its finding that the long-term interdependent nature of the 10-year relationship between appellant and Blanchard "fulfills any definitional criteria of the term 'family.' "

The Appellate Division reversed, concluding that section 2204.6(d) provides noneviction protection only to "family members within traditional, legally recognized familial relationships" .... Since appellant's and Blanchard's relationship was not one given formal recognition by the law, the court held that appellant could not seek the protection of the noneviction ordinance. ... We now reverse.

II.

* * *

It is fundamental that in construing the words of a statute "[t]he legislative intent is the great and controlling principle" ...Indeed, "the general purpose is a more important aid to the meaning than any rule which grammar or formal logic may lay down".... Finally, where a problem as to the meaning of a given term arises, a court's role is not to delve into the minds of legislators, but rather to effectuate the statute by carrying out the purpose of the statute as it is embodied in the words chosen by the Legislature ....

The present dispute arises because the term "family" is not defined in the rent-control code and the legislative history is devoid of any specific reference to the noneviction provision. ...

Rent control was enacted to address a "serious public emergency" created by "an acute shortage in dwellings," which resulted in "speculative, unwarranted and abnormal increases in rents" .... These measures were designed to regulate and control the housing market so as to "prevent exactions of unjust, unreasonable and oppressive rents and rental agreements and to forestall profiteering, speculation and other disruptive practices tending to produce threats to the public health ... [and] to prevent uncertainty, hardship and dislocation" (*id.*). Although initially designed as an emergency measure to alleviate the housing shortage attributable to the end of World War II, "a serious public emergency continues to exist in the housing of a considerable number of persons" (*id.*). Consequently, the Legislature has found it necessary to continually reenact the rent-control laws, thereby providing continued protection to tenants.

To accomplish its goals, the Legislature recognized that not only would rents have to be controlled, but that evictions would have to be regulated and controlled as well (*id.*). Hence, section 2204.6 of the New York City Rent and Eviction Regulations (9 NYCRR 2204.6), which authorizes the issuance of a certificate for the eviction of persons occupying a rent-controlled apartment after the death of the named tenant, provides, in subdivision (d), noneviction protection to those occupants who are either the "surviving spouse of the deceased tenant or some other member of the deceased tenant's family who has been living with the tenant [of record.]" The manifest intent of this section is to restrict the landowners' ability to evict a narrow class of occupants other than the tenant of record....

Respondent argues that the term "family member" as used in 9 NYCRR 2204.6(d) should be construed, consistent with this State's intestacy laws, to mean relationships of blood, consanguinity and adoption in order to effectuate the over-all goal of orderly succession to real property. Under this interpretation, only those entitled to inherit under the laws of intestacy would be afforded noneviction protection (see, EPTL 4-1.1). Further, as did the Appellate Division, respondent relies on our decision in *Matter of Robert Paul P.*, 63 N.Y.2d 233, 481 N.Y.S.2d 652, 471 N.E.2d 424, arguing that since the relationship between appellant and Blanchard has not been accorded legal status by the Legislature, it is not entitled to the protections of section 2204.6(d), which, according to the Appellate Division, applies only to "family members within traditional, legally recognized familial relationships" .... Finally, respondent contends that our construction of the term "family member" should be guided by the recently enacted noneviction provision of the Rent Stabilization Code ..., which was passed in response to our decision in *Sullivan v. Brevard Assocs.* ...and specifically enumerates the individuals who are entitled to noneviction protection under the listed circumstances ....

However, as we have continually noted, the rent-stabilization system is different from the rent-control system in that the former is a less onerous burden on the property owner, and thus the provisions of one cannot simply be imported into the other .... Respondent's reliance on *Matter of Robert Paul P.* is also misplaced, since that case, which held that one adult cannot adopt another where none of the incidents of a filial relationship is evidenced or even remotely intended, was based solely on the purposes of the adoption laws (see, Domestic Relations Law § 110) and has no bearing on the proper interpretation of a provision in the rent-control laws.

We also reject respondent's argument that the purpose of the noneviction provision of the rent-control laws is to control the orderly succession to real property in a manner similar to that which occurs under our State's intestacy laws (EPTL 4-1.1, 4-1.2). The noneviction provision does not concern succession to real property but rather is a means of protecting a certain class of occupants from the sudden loss of their homes. ...

Contrary to all of these arguments, we conclude that the term family, as used in 9 NYCRR 2204.6(d), should not be rigidly restricted to those people who have formalized their relationship by obtaining, for instance, a marriage certificate or an adoption order. The intended protection against sudden eviction should not rest on fictitious legal distinctions or genetic history, but instead should find its foundation in the reality of family life. In the context of eviction, a more realistic, and certainly equally valid, view of a family includes two adult lifetime partners whose relationship is long term and characterized by an emotional and financial commitment and interdependence. This view comports both with our society's traditional concept of "family" and with the expectations of individuals who live in such nuclear units (*see also 829 Seventh Ave. Co. v. Reider*, 67 N.Y.2d 930, 931-932, 502 N.Y.S.2d 715, 493 N.E.2d 939 [interpreting 9 NYCRR 2204.6(d)'s additional "living with" requirement to mean living with the named tenant "in a family unit, which in turn connotes an arrangement, whatever its duration, bearing some indicia of permanence or continuity"]). In fact, Webster's Dictionary defines "family" first as "a group of people united by certain convictions or common affiliation" (Webster's Ninth New Collegiate Dictionary 448 [1984]; *see* Ballantine's Law Dictionary 456 [3d ed. 1969] ["family" defined as "(p)rimarily, the collective body of persons who live in one house and under one head or management"]; Black's Law Dictionary 543 [Special Deluxe 5th ed. 1979]). Hence, it is reasonable to conclude that, in using the term "family," the Legislature intended to extend protection to those who reside in households having all of the normal familial characteristics. Appellant Braschi should therefore be afforded the opportunity to prove that he and Blanchard had such a household.

This definition of "family" is consistent with both of the competing purposes of the rent-control laws: the protection of individuals from sudden dislocation and the gradual transition to a free market system. [Fn3. *We note, however, that the definition of family that we adopt here for purposes of the noneviction protection of the rent-control laws is completely unrelated to the concept of "functional family," as that term has developed under this court's decisions in the context of zoning ordinances....*] Family members, whether or not related by blood, or law who have always treated the apartment as their family home will be protected against the hardship of eviction following the death of the named tenant, thereby furthering the Legislature's goals of preventing dislocation and preserving family units which might otherwise be broken apart upon eviction. This approach will foster the transition from rent control to rent stabilization by drawing a distinction between those individuals who are, in fact, genuine family members, and those who are mere roommates ... or newly discovered relatives hoping to inherit the rent-controlled apartment after the existing tenant's death.

The determination as to whether an individual is entitled to noneviction protection should be based upon an objective examination of the relationship of the parties. In making this assessment, the lower courts of this State have looked to a number of factors, including the exclusivity and longevity of the relationship, the level of emotional and financial commitment, the manner in which the parties have conducted their everyday lives and held themselves out to society, and the reliance placed upon one another for daily family services (*see e.g. Athineos v. Thayer*, N.Y.L.J., Mar. 25, 1987, at 14, col. 4 [Civ. Ct., Kings County], affd. N.Y.L.J., Feb. 9, 1988, at 15, col. 4 [App. Term, 2d Dept.] [orphan never formally adopted but lived in family home for 34 years]; *2-4 Realty Assocs. v. Pittman*, 137 Misc.2d 898, 902, 523 N.Y.S.2d 7 [two men living in a "father-son" relationship for 25 years]; *Zimmerman v. Burton*, 107 Misc.2d 401, 404, 434 N.Y.S.2d 127 [unmarried heterosexual life partner]; *Rutar Co. v. Yoshito*, No. 53042/79 [Civ. Ct., N.Y. County] [unmarried heterosexual life partner]; *Gelman v. Castaneda*, NYLJ, Oct. 22, 1986, at 13, col. 1 [Civ. Ct., N.Y. County] [male life partners]). These factors are most helpful, although it should be emphasized that the presence or absence of one or more of them is not dispositive since it is the totality of the relationship as evidenced by the dedication, caring and self-sacrifice of the parties which should, in the final analysis, control. Appellant's situation provides an example of how the rule should be applied.

Appellant and Blanchard lived together as permanent life partners for more than 10 years. They regarded one another, and were regarded by friends and family, as spouses. The two men's families were aware of the nature of the relationship, and they regularly visited each other's families and attended family functions together, as a couple. Even today, appellant continues to maintain a relationship with Blanchard's niece, who considers him an uncle.

In addition to their interwoven social lives, appellant clearly considered the apartment his home. He lists the apartment as his address on his driver's license and passport, and receives all his mail at the apartment address. Moreover, appellant's tenancy was known to the building's superintendent and doormen, who viewed the two men as a couple.

Financially, the two men shared all obligations including a household budget. The two were authorized signatories of three safe-deposit boxes; they maintained joint checking and savings accounts, and joint credit cards. In fact, rent was often paid with a check from their joint checking account. Additionally, Blanchard executed a power of attorney in appellant's favor so that appellant could make necessary decisions—financial, medical and personal—for him during his illness. Finally, appellant was the named beneficiary of Blanchard's life insurance policy, as well as the primary legatee and coexecutor of Blanchard's estate. Hence, a court examining these facts could reasonably conclude that these men were much more than mere roommates.

Inasmuch as this case is before us on a certified question, we conclude only that appellant has demonstrated a likelihood of success on the merits, in that he is not excluded, as a matter of law, from seeking noneviction protection. Since all remaining issues are beyond this court's scope of review, we remit this case to the Appellate Division so that it may exercise its discretionary powers in accordance with this decision.

Accordingly, the order of the Appellate Division should be reversed and the case remitted to that court for a consideration of undetermined questions. The certified question should be answered in the negative.

BELLACOSA, JUDGE (concurring).

* * *

The application of the governing word and statute to reach a decision in this case can be accomplished on a narrow and legitimate jurisprudential track. The enacting body has selected an unqualified word for a socially remedial statute, intended as a protection against one of the harshest decrees known to the law—eviction from one's home. Traditionally, in such circumstances, generous construction is favored. Petitioner has made his shared home in the affected apartment for 10 years.

The only other occupant of that rent-controlled apartment over that same extended period of time was the tenant-in-law who has now died, precipitating this battle for the apartment. The best guidance available to the regulatory agency for correctly applying the rule in such circumstances is that it would be irrational not to include this petitioner and it is a more reasonable reflection of the intention behind the regulation to protect a person such as petitioner as within the regulation's class of "family". ...

* * *

SIMONS, JUDGE (dissenting) [HANCOCK, J., joins].

I would affirm. The plurality has adopted a definition of family which extends the language of the regulation well beyond the implication of the words used in it. In doing so, it has expanded the class indefinitely to include anyone who can satisfy an administrator that he or she had an emotional and financial "commitment" to the statutory tenant. Its interpretation is inconsistent with the legislative scheme underlying rent regulation, goes well beyond the intended purposes of 9 NYCRR 2204.6(d), and produces an unworkable test that is subject to abuse. The concurring opinion fails to address the problem. It merely decides, ipse dixit, that plaintiff should win.

* * *

Central to any interpretation of the regulatory language is a determination of its purpose. There can be little doubt that the purpose of section 2204.6(d) was to create succession rights to a possessory interest in real property where the tenant of record has died or vacated the apartment .... It creates a new tenancy for every surviving family member living with decedent at the time of death who then becomes a new statutory tenant until death or until he or she vacates the apartment. ... The interests are properly balanced if the regulation's exception is applied by using objectively verifiable relationships based on blood, marriage and adoption, as the State has historically done in the estate succession laws, family court acts and similar legislation .... The distinction is warranted because members of families, so defined, assume certain legal obligations to each other and to third persons, such as creditors, which are not imposed on unrelated individuals and this legal interdependency is worthy of consideration in determining which individuals are entitled to succeed to the interest of the statutory tenant in rent-controlled premises. Moreover, such an interpretation promotes certainty and consistency in the law and obviates the need for drawn out hearings and litigation focusing on such intangibles as the strength and duration of the relationship and the extent of the emotional and financial interdependency .... The plurality's response to this problem is to turn to the dictionary and select one definition, from the several found there, which gives the regulation the desired expansive construction. [FN... For example, the definitions found in Black's Law Dictionary 543 (Special Deluxe 5th ed.) are: "Family. The meaning of word 'family' necessarily depends on field of law in which word is used, purpose intended to be accomplished by its use, and facts and circumstances of each case ... Most commonly refers to group of persons consisting of parents and children; father, mother and their children; immediate kindred, constituting fundamental social unit in civilized society ... A collective body of persons who live in one house and under one head or management. A group of blood-relatives; all the relations who descend from a common ancestor, or who spring from a common root. A group of kindred persons ... Husband and wife and their children, wherever they may reside and whether they dwell together or not" (citations omitted). The term is similarly defined in the other dictionaries cited in the plurality opinion.] I would search for the intended meaning by looking at what the Legislature and the Division of Housing and Community Renewal (DHCR), the agency charged with implementing rent control, have done in related areas. These sources produce persuasive evidence that both bodies intend the word family to be interpreted in the traditional sense.

The legislative view may be found in the "roommate" law enacted in 1983 (Real Property Law § 235-f, L.1983, ch. 403). That statute granted rights to persons living with, but unrelated to, the tenant of record. The statute was a response to our unanimous decision in *Hudson View Props. v. Weiss*, ... In *Hudson View* the landlord, by a provision in the lease, limited occupancy to the tenant of record and the tenant's "immediate family". When the landlord tried to evict the unmarried heterosexual partner of the named tenant of record, she defended the proceeding by claiming that the restrictive covenant in the lease violated provisions of the State and City Human Rights Laws prohibiting discrimination on the basis of marital status. We held that the exclusion had nothing to do with the tenants' unmarried status but depended on the lease's restriction of occupancy to the tenant and the tenant's "immediate family". Implicitly, we decided that the term "immediate family" did not include individuals who were unrelated by blood, marriage or adoption, notwithstanding "the close and loving relationship" of the parties.

The Legislature's response to Weiss was measured. It enacted Real Property Law § 235-f(3), (4) which provides that occupants of rent-controlled accommodations, whether related to the tenant of record or not, can continue living in rent-controlled and rent-stabilized apartments as long as the tenant of record continues to reside there. Lease provisions to the contrary are rendered void as against public policy (subd. [2]). Significantly, the statute provides that no unrelated occupant "shall ...acquire any right to continued occupancy in the event the tenant vacates the premises or acquire any other rights of tenancy" (subd. [6]). Read against this background, the statute is evidence the Legislature does not contemplate that individuals unrelated to the tenant of record by blood, marriage or adoption should enjoy a right to remain in rent-controlled apartments after the death of the tenant ....

... The DHCR promulgates the regulations for both rent-regulation systems, and the eviction regulations in rent control and the exceptions to them share a common purpose with the renewal requirements contained in the Rent Stabilization Code *. In the Rent Stabilization Code, the Division of Housing and Community Renewal has made it unmistakably clear that the definition of family includes only persons related by blood, marriage or adoption. Since the two statutes and the two regulations share a common purpose, it is appropriate to conclude that the definition of family in the rent-control regulations should be of similar scope.

Specifically, the rent-stabilization regulations provide under similar circumstances that the landlord must offer a renewal lease to "any member of such tenant's family ... who has resided in the housing accommodation as a primary resident from the inception of the tenancy or commencement of the relationship" (9 NYCRR 2523.5[b][1]; see also, 2523.5[b][2]). Family for purposes of these two provisions is defined in section 2520.6(o) as: "A husband, wife, son, daughter, stepson, stepdaughter, father, mother, stepfather, stepmother, brother, sister, nephew, niece, uncle, aunt, grandfather, grandmother, grandson, granddaughter, father-in-law, mother-in- law, son-in-law, or daughter-in-law of the tenant or permanent tenant".

All the enumerated relationships are traditional, legally recognized relationships based on blood, marriage or adoption. That being so, it would be anomalous, to say the least, were we to hold that the agency, having intentionally limited succession rights in rent-stabilized accommodations to those related by blood, marriage or adoption, intended a different result for rent-controlled accommodations; especially so when it is recognized that rent control was intended to give way to rent stabilization ....

Finally, there are serious practical problems in adopting the plurality's interpretation of the statute. ... The enumeration of such factors, and the determination that they are controlling, is a matter best left to Legislatures because it involves the type of policy making the courts should avoid ....

* * *

Accordingly, I would affirm the order of the Appellate Division.
WACHTLER, C.J., took no part.

b. *Raum v. Restaurant Associates*

Donald Raum v. Restaurant Associates, Inc.
252 A.D.2d 369, 675 N.Y.S.2d 343 (Supreme Ct, App. Div. 1998)
app. dism'd **704 N.E.2d 229(N.Y. 1998),** *app. dism'd* **734 N.E.2d 761 (N.Y. 2000)**
ROSENBERGER, J.P., WALLACH, RUBIN and TOM, JJ.

[Raum filed a wrongful-death claim for the death of his same-sex partner.]

Order, Supreme Court, New York County (Shelia Abdus-Salaam, J.), entered August 5, 1996, which granted defendants' motions for partial summary judgment dismissing plaintiff executor's individual wrongful-death claims against them, affirmed, without costs.

The IAS court correctly held that the wrongful-death statute (EPTL 5-4.1), which, by its terms (EPTL 1-2.5, 4-1.1, 5- 1.2), does not give individuals not married to the decedent (other than certain blood relatives) a right to bring a wrongful-death action, operates without regard to sexual orientation, in that unmarried couples living together, whether heterosexual or homosexual, similarly lack the right to bring a wrongful-death action, and, as such, the statute does not discriminate against same-sex partners in spousal-type relationships. Nor is there merit to plaintiff's argument that the word "spouse" in EPTL § 5-1.2 should be read to include such same-sex partners (see *Greenwald v. H & P 29th St. Assocs.*, 241 A.D.2d 307, 659 N.Y.S.2d 473 [construing the spousal privilege in CPLR 4502(b) and distinguishing *Braschi v. Stahl Assocs. Co.* (74 N.Y.2d 201, 544 N.Y.S.2d 784, 543 N.E.2d 49) and *Matter of Jacob* (86 N.Y.2d 651, 636 N.Y.S.2d 716, 660 N.E.2d 397)]; *Matter of Cooper*, 187 A.D.2d 128, 592 N.Y.S.2d 797, affg. 149 Misc. 2d 282, 564 N.Y.S.2d 684, appeal dismissed 82 N.Y.2d 801, 604 N.Y.S.2d 558, 624 N.E.2d 696 [construing the right of election in EPTL 5-1.1(c)]). The dissent unduly strains the language of EPTL 5-1.2, defining a husband or wife to be a surviving spouse, to conclude that the statute does not preclude from the classification persons who are other than a husband or wife. Although the dissent would apply a "functional" rather than a "literal" interpretation, that endeavor is contrary to standard canons of statutory construction. Whatever expansion may be given various family-related terms in other statutes and codes, the EPTL 5-1.2 definition in this regard is clear and preclusive. Since it is not within the judicial province to redefine terms given clear meaning in a statute (*Matter of Cooper, supra*), plaintiff's sole recourse lies in legislative action.

For similar reasons, *Braschi v. Stahl Associates* (74 N.Y.2d 201, 544 N.Y.S.2d 784, 543 N.E.2d 49), upon which the dissent relies, does not change the analysis. *Braschi* was a decision propelled by policy considerations not pertinent to the present case. In *Braschi*, involving a non-marital surviving life partner of the deceased rent-controlled tenant, the Court was required to interpret the term "family", within the meaning of the rent-control statute. Preliminarily, an expansive definition for those purposes has no direct bearing on an entirely different statute. Moreover, even for purposes of analogizing similar terms in different statutes, the comparison must fail: "family" is an inherently more expansive classification than "spouse" under New York law, and it is as a spousal-equivalent that plaintiff herein claims standing. Further, the *Braschi* court drew a sharp distinction between rent-control laws, which serve to stabilize living arrangements, and the EPTL, which exists to ensure the orderly succession of property rights among clearly defined classes of persons. Finally, the dispositive point is that the *Braschi* Court found "family" to be undefined in the rent-control statute, thus invoking the judicial role of resolving ambiguities in legislative terms, whereas in EPTL 5-1.2, the Legislature defined the term "spouse". This circumstance should foreclose any further judicial intervention.

All concur except ROSENBERGER, J.P., who dissents in a memorandum.

ROSENBERGER, Justice Presiding (dissenting).

I dissent, and would reverse and remand, on the ground that under the Equal Protection Clause of the State and Federal Constitutions, plaintiff cannot be denied standing to sue for wrongful-death damages pursuant to EPTL 5-4.1. The motion court erred in granting defendants' motion for partial summary judgment dismissing plaintiff's wrongful-death claim.

* * *

Nowhere in the EPTL is a surviving "spouse" limited to a "husband or wife". EPTL 5-1.2 merely states, "A husband or wife is a surviving spouse" unless the parties divorced or separated, or the marriage was void, or the survivor abandoned or refused to support the decedent. Rather than limiting the class of people who could be considered a surviving "spouse," EPTL 5-1.2 provides that a husband or wife will be presumed to be a member of this class unless certain things have occurred. Thus, the statutory language does not foreclose plaintiff's argument that he should be considered a surviving spouse for purposes of bringing a wrongful-death action.

Moreover, precedent exists for preferring a functional over a literal interpretation of a statute whose purpose is to promote the public welfare, so that homosexual couples will not be disadvantaged by their inability to give their relationship a legal status. In *Braschi v. Stahl Associates*, ... the Court of Appeals held that the deceased tenant's life partner could be considered a "family member" with succession rights to the tenant's rent-controlled apartment. The court believed that the applicable statute should be read broadly, because its purpose is to promote the public good and prevent landlords from unjustly exploiting tenants. ...

Accordingly, the court held that a surviving life partner should be given the chance to prove that his household arrangements with the decedent were familial. Factors to be considered would include the duration of the relationship, whether their friends and relatives regarded them as a couple, their shared financial responsibilities for the household and assumption of legal rights and responsibilities such as power of attorney or executor of estate .... All these indicia of familial relations are present in the instant case.

* * *

Finally, an entity may have a different legal status in different contexts for public-policy reasons. ... It makes sense to construe the intestacy statute's definition of "surviving spouse" narrowly when the opposing parties are innocent heirs, and broadly when they are tortfeasors.

Plaintiff argues that it would be unconstitutional to interpret the relevant statutes so as to deny homosexual life partners the right to sue. Under the Equal Protection Clause of the U.S. Constitution, 14th Amendment, and the analogous provision in the New York Constitution, article I, § 11, such an interpretation would amount to an invidious distinction between homosexuals and heterosexuals, which could not survive rational-basis review. This argument has merit.

This court has interpreted both the Federal and the State Constitutions' Equal Protection Clauses to forbid discrimination "on the basis of sexual orientation or affectional preference" .... The "constitutional predicate upon which we rest [ed]" in *Under 21* was that homosexuals were a "significant and insular minority" which had historically been subjected to "immediate and severe opprobrium", and that, therefore, State action, which discriminated on the basis of homosexuality, should be "subjected to strict, or at least heightened, scrutiny" ....

The motion court granted summary judgment dismissing plaintiff's equal protection claim because the statute equally denied wrongful-death benefits to unmarried homosexual couples and unmarried heterosexual couples, an argument which the majority adopts and upon which it partly relies. However, this was not the appropriate comparison. Homosexual life partners, who legally cannot marry, are not similarly situated to unmarried heterosexual couples who have the option to marry and obtain the protection of the statute, yet choose not to. If the Legislature does not allow homosexual couples to marry, or even to enter into an equivalent legally binding commitment, it cannot make marriage a condition precedent to a statutory right that is available to heterosexuals, especially where sexual preference is irrelevant to the purposes of the statute (*see Levy v. Louisiana*, ...).

* * *

Exclusion of homosexual life partners from the class of persons who have standing under EPTL 5-4.1 lacks a rational basis because it is neither rationally related to the interests served by the statute, nor to the state's policy against same-sex marriage, nor even to administrative convenience.

The goals of the wrongful-death statute are to compensate the victim's dependents, to punish and deter tortfeasors and to reduce welfare dependency by providing for the families of those who have lost their means of support. The legal status of the dependents' relationship to the decedent does not affect their need for compensation and support, nor diminish society's interest in preventing tortious behavior.

There is thus no rational basis for excluding a class of injured dependents from recovery, nor for granting a windfall to those who negligently cause death, simply because the dependents did not have a legally-recognized relationship with the decedent.

The fact that New York does not recognize same-sex marriage should be irrelevant for purposes of EPTL 5-4.1. If the state's asserted interest in encouraging marriage must give way to equal protection considerations in the adoption context ..., which directly implicates the child-rearing concerns that motivate the state's policy on marriage, then the state's interest is even weaker and more tangential when only tort damages are at stake.

The Supreme Court articulated this principle in the wrongful-death context in *Levy v. Louisiana* .... Under a rational basis standard, "it is invidious to discriminate against [out-of-wedlock children] when no action, conduct, or demeanor of theirs is possibly relevant to the harm that was done the mother."

The final objective that could be served by a literal legal definition of surviving "spouse" is administrative convenience. ... Nonetheless, courts have not found such fact-based inquiries to be particularly problematic in the past.

While New York has not recognized common-law marriages created in New York since 1933, it will recognize such marriages if they were valid under the laws of the states where contracted .... Accordingly, if a common-law spouse claims workers' compensation death benefits ..., an elective share of the estate ..., or other rights and privileges of a legal spouse in New York, the court will investigate the facts of the relationship—such as the parties' financial and living arrangements, and whether they held themselves out to their acquaintances as a couple—to determine whether the common-law marriage is entitled to full faith and credit in New York. There is no rational basis for concluding that such an inquiry into a party's status and relationship with the decedent is unduly burdensome when the couple is homosexual, but not when the couple is heterosexual.

In applying *Braschi* to homosexual survivors of deceased tenants, this court similarly managed to examine the objective facts of the relationship in question, without undue inconvenience and without opening the door to a vast increase in litigation .... Thus, the asserted inconvenience does not compel a different result in the instant case, especially when, as in *Braschi*, the dependent plaintiff has asserted an important countervailing interest.

Therefore, I would reverse the decision below and reinstate the plaintiff's wrongful-death claim under EPTL 5-4.1.

c. Notes and Questions

1) *Braschi* Notes

What are the characteristics of a "household with normal characteristics"? If three persons lived together in an economically interdependent sexual union would both survivors qualify as family? Why/why not? If the survivor was a minor-lover that the decedent had supported? Why/why not? Is marriage relevant to the purposes of the statute? Why/why not? Is there a separation of powers issue? In *Langan ex rel. Estate of Spicehandler v. St. Vincent's Hosp.*, 765 N.Y.S.2d 411 (Sup. Ct. Nassau County 2003) the court allowed a wrongful death suit by surviving same-sex partner by recognizing the New York party's Vermont civil union as equivalent to a marriage for purposes of wrongful death, but the Appellate Division reversed (3-2) finding that the statute clearly allowed only spouses to bring such claims, that same-sex civil unions are not marriages (even in Vermont), that refusing to treat same-sex couples as married does not violate the state or federal constitution, and inviting plaintiffs to take their case to the legislature. *Langan v. St. Vincent's Hosp.*, 802 N.Y.S.2d 476 (App. Div. 2005). In *Loyoza v. Sanchez,*

66 P.3d 948 (N.M. 2003), the New Mexico Supreme Court held that a loss of consortium claim could be maintained by woman who lived with man for 30 years, bore him three children, jointly bought a home and filed joint tax returns with him, and who married him after the accident for which she sought damages for loss of consortium. The court also noted ". . . no other State in the union currently allows unmarried cohabitants to recover for loss of consortium." *Id.* at 954.

2) *Raum* Notes

Distinguish the statutory from the constitutional analysis in both opinions. Are married couples more likely to be economically and emotionally interdependent than cohabiting couples? Is there a difference in social constitution? *See generally* Culhane, *infra.*

3) Related Cases

Questions about whether persons not legally or biologically related may claim legal benefits provided to family members arise in a wide variety of contexts. "Nonmarital partners are rarely recognized under common law principles determining, for example, who is entitled to recover for wrongful death or loss of consortium." Polikoff, *infra* at 379. *See e.g. Elden v. Sheldon*, 758 P.2d 582, 590 (Cal. 1988) (negligent infliction of emotional harm and loss of consortium claims by nonmarital cohabitant denied); *City of Ladue v. Horn*, 720 S.W.2d 745, 752 (Mo. Ct. App. 1986) (an unmarried couple who shared a bedroom, maintained a joint checking account for household expenses, entertained together, and disciplined each other's children, were not a "family" for zoning purposes); *In re Ray Cummings*, 640 P.2d 1101, 1102 (Cal. 1982) (nonmarital partner of prisoner who shared seven-year-long emotional, psychological, and financial commitment was not "immediate family" entitled to overnight family visitation);*Nieto v. City of Los Angeles*, 188 Cal. Rptr. 31 (Ct. App. 1982) (no wrongful death recovery to engaged, cohabiting woman); *Prince George's County v. Greenbelt Homes, Inc.*, 431 A.2d 745 (Md. App. 1981) (covenant restricting residence to "immediate family" denying unmarried couples does not violate antidiscrimination code); *but see Dunphy v. Gregor II*, 642 A.2d 372 (N.J. 1994) (allowing emotional distress claim to be asserted by woman who saw her fiancé with whom she had been cohabiting for years sustain fatal injuries when struck and thrown 240 feet while changing a tire five feet from her); *Butcher v. Superior Court of Orange County*, 139 Cal. App. 3d 58 (Cal. Ct. App. 1983) (allowing recovery for loss of consortium by nonmarital cohabitant in a stable and significant relationship; overruled by *Hinman, infra*).

Most cases also have rejected claims to "marital" benefits asserted by same-sex couples. In *Hinman v. Department of Personnel Admin.* 167 Cal.App.3d 516, 213 Cal.Rptr. 410 (1985), a California appellate court ruled that it did not violate the equal protection clause of the state Constitution for a state agency to deny to the same-sex cohabitants of a state employee the same dental insurance coverage offered spouses of employees. The denial of coverage was not based on Hinman's sexual orientation because all unmarried employees received identical treatment. Basing coverage on marriage was not improper discrimination because marriage relates to legitimate state and social interests. Likewise, in *Beaty v. Truck Insurance Exchange*, 6 Cal. App. 4th

1455, 8 Cal. Rptr. 2d 593 (1992), *rev. denied* (Aug. 27, 1992), a California appellate court held that an insurer did not violate a state civil rights act by refusing to offer a same-sex cohabiting couple the same insurance policy at the same premium it regularly offered to married couples. The court declined to amend the civil rights act to add "marital status" as a new category of prohibited discrimination, citing the strong public policy in favor of marriage. "[T]he shared responsibilities and the legal unity of interest in a marital relationship—a status not conferred on unmarried couples whatever their sexual orientation—provide a fair and reasonable means of determining eligibility for services or benefits." *Id.* Most courts have denied marital benefits claimed by same-sex partners and held that laws banning sexual orientation discrimination do not mean employers must provide benefits to employees' lifetime same-sex partners. *See Ross v. Denver Dep't of Health & Hosps.*, 883 P.2d 516, 521 (Colo. Ct. App. 1994) (denial of family sick leave to care for same-sex partner upheld); *Lilly v. City of Minneapolis*, 527 N.W.2d 107, 112 (Minn. Ct. App. 1995) (city council resolutions authorizing health care insurance coverage for same sex domestic partners are ultra vires); *Phillips v. Wisconsin Personnel Comm'n*, 482 N.W.2d 121, 127 (Wis. Ct. App. 1992) (denial of health insurance for lesbian partner of state employee upheld); *but see* Baker v. State, 744 A.2d 864 (Vt. 1999) (requiring state to provide same-sex couples with legal status and benefits equivalent to marriage); *Tanner v. Oregon Health Sciences University*, 980 P.2d 186, 188, 189 (Or. Ct. App. 1999) (Oregon Constitution requires state university to give same-sex partners of employees the same benefits provided to employee's spouses). Michigan allows wrongful death recovery by close family members and others who could take under a will. Mich. Comp. Laws Ann. § 600.2922(1)-(3)(c) (West 2004). A few states (including Vermont, California, and New Jersey) have created special statuses for same-sex couples, which includes coverage under wrongful death and related schemes. *See* Culhane, *infra*; *Developments in the Law*, *infra* at 1634; Franklin, *infra*; O'Brien, *infra*; Polikoff, *infra*; Richardson, *infra*; Simerman, *infra*; Treuhart, *infra*; Zielinski, *infra*; Wardle, *infra*; *See infra*, Ch. 8.

4) What Is the Legal Meaning of the Term *Family*?

Traditionally, the term *family* has included persons related by blood, marriage, or adoption. Today, that is still the most common and the default meaning, both in law and in colloquial usage. Thus, the traditional meaning of *family* is mostly synonymous with biological or legal kinship. Anthropologists, sociologists of the family, and historians have noted the importance of such relationships in the development of societies. They trace social organization to the family, then to the broader kinship organization, then to the tribe, and to political society in general. *See generally*, Diamond; Hoebel; Locke.

Historically, the term *family* included the extended family. Indeed, in many societies, the family functioned as a different, allied level of government reciprocally supported by the formal political government. For example, the Roman family consisted of the "paterfamilias," who was the oldest male ancestor of the family members, generally, and those under his control (known as "alieni iuris") consisting of his wife (if the marriage was a "manus" marriage), his children (natural, legitimated, and adopted), all of his descendants through the male line, and his slaves. A wife by "manus" marriage (a type of marriage with the greatest dignity) was the "materfamilias." (A wife by any other form of marriage was called "uxor," and her property and rights remained under the potestas of her former paterfamilias. Recently (perhaps since the Industrial Revolution changed the common or ideal household living arrangements from multi-generational families to one- or two-generational "nuclear families"), *family* quite frequently means the members of the "nuclear family" (husband and wife, parents and children). However, the inclusion of other members of the extended family is still a common usage, especially in subcultures of our society where multi-generational households are still common, or in subcultures in which extended family ties are deliberately fostered. In many Islamic societies, and many African and Asian countries, for example, the head of the extended family until recently had and in some cultures still has tremendous family, personal, cultural, and even legal power. Even in the United States, the tradition of extended families is deep and wide, and the Supreme Court has held unconstitutional a law that interferes excessively with extended family members living together. *Moore v. City of East Cleveland*, 431 U.S. 494 (1977).

5) No Unitary Legal Definition of *Family*

The legal meaning of the term *family* is not unitary—it does not necessarily mean the same thing in every statute or legal context. Rather, it has many meanings and different statutes define it differently. As the search for meaning of legal terms is a search for legislative intent, the multiplicity of meanings of the term *family* is understandable because lawmakers sometimes intend different meanings or levels of meaning when they use the term *family*. For instance, domestic violence laws often cover "family members," defined very broadly to include past and former roommates, while family liability, insurance, or tax dependency exemption laws may define the same term very narrowly. *See* Wardle, *Domestic Violence, infra.*

6) Legal Significance of *Family* Definitions

[O]ur laws bestow great benefits upon families. Consider, for example, marital interests in real property; privileged communications between husband and wife; inheritance rights belonging to family survivors under intestate succession laws; and wrongful death rights in tort law. The Supreme Court has also established several categories of extraordinary constitutional protection for marriage, child-parent relationships, and related interests. These benefits arise from the law's recognition that family relationships are extremely important to individuals. In addition, the law reflects strong social and even political interests in sustaining formal family ties.

The relationships historically protected by American law are limited to those that arise from kinship, adoption, or heterosexual marriage. Thus, unmarried couples are not regarded as families for the many purposes addressed by state and federal laws. American legal institutions—particularly the judiciary—have begun over the last several years to recognize a few exceptions that would once have been denied by a very rigid legal and social policy of reinforcing formal family relationships. Generally, however, the law remains quite certain about what a family is for the most fundamental purposes. There is nonetheless a growing

sense of uncertainty about the place of the formal family in our hierarchy of
national values. . . .

Hafen, *infra* at 454–65. *See also* Zielinski, *infra* at 297 (chart comparing legal benefits
enjoyed by married couples and domestic partners).

7) The Supreme Court Perception of the Family

Until recently, Supreme Court decisions appeared to embrace a perception of *family*
that reflected and supported the "traditional" model of family relations. Eva Rubin has
noted:

> The family accepted by the Supreme Court in these early cases is clearly the ideal
> Victorian family. The family unit is a small government in its own right,
> authoritarian and paternalistic, with women and children in a subordinate position.
> The rearing and education of children is its most important function. Although wives
> and mothers are respected and should be consulted on family matters, there is little
> internal democracy. Parents speak and act for children, discipline them and
> determine what their education will be. Families educate and socialize children.
> When families fail, it is not surprising to find that the children turn out badly, turning
> to antisocial behavior and ultimately to crime.
> ... [In these cases, marriage is monogamous.] The family unit is the basic institution
> of Western society. It is formed by marriage, and it is within the union so arrived at
> that sexual activity, procreation and childbearing take place. The rights to marry and
> have children are basic rights of man. ...
>   The institution of marriage creates a private realm which the state should not enter.
> ...
> Sometimes the Justices have waxed lyrical about marriage and the family,
> institutions that seem to take on an almost mystical aura as they are described in the
> opinions of the Court. ...
>   The Supreme Court also accepts the proposition that the primary function of
> marriage and family life is the bearing and raising of children. The home derives its
> preeminence from the part it plays as the abode of the family. The individual has a
> right to marry and establish a home in order to bring up children. Parents have the
> responsibility for raising and educating their children, and this responsibility brings
> with it the power to control the children's actions. ...

E. Rubin, *infra*, at 16–19. Rubin argues that this family image is "a mythological
construct" based on the Bible, tradition, and personal family experiences of the justices,
and that this model of family patriarchal, oppressive to women, and insensitive to
minorities. Rubin asserts that this old image of the family has undergone significant
change in recent years. There has long been a different family law for the aspirational
middle-class than for the poor who depend on public assistance. Likewise, David Meyer
argues that the Court should defer to "self-definition" of family by individuals as a matter
of constitutional interpretation. Meyer, *infra*.

Generally, claims for constitutional recognition of unwritten rights or relationships
(like family) must pass the objective deeply-rooted-in-the-history-and-traditions-of-our-
people test, or the quasi-objective essential-to-our-concept-of-ordered-liberty test. Should

the test for constitutional purposes be objective or subjective? Do alternative relationships satisfy either test? Do they make marriage-equivalent contributions to meeting social needs and public interests? Why/why not?

8) Changing Social and Legal Definitions of *Family*

Laws regulating family relations generally reflect the image of the family that is prevailing at the time. As social perceptions change, so do the laws. Thus, family law is an especially dynamic area of law. Carl Schneider has written:

> The family law we inherited from the nineteenth century sought not just to regulate family life, but to set a standard of behavior not readily attainable. That law enunciated and sought to enforce an ideal of lifelong marital fidelity and responsibility. ... Divorce was discouraged, was justified primarily by serious misconduct by a spouse, and was available only to the innocent. ... Sexual restraint in various forms was a prominent part of this ideal. Laws prohibiting fornication, cohabitation, and adultery confined sexual relations to marriage; laws declining to enforce contracts based on meretricious consideration and laws giving relief in tort for interference with the marital relationship sought to achieve the same effect indirectly. Sexual relations were confined to monogamous marriage by laws prohibiting polygamy and to exogamous marriage by laws prohibiting incest. ...
>
> Modern family law, as this survey suggests, not only rejects some of the old standards as meaningless, undesirable, or wrong; it also hesitates to set standards that cannot readily be enforced or that go beyond the minimal responsibility expressed in the cant phrase, "Do your own thing, as long as you don't hurt anybody else." The standard embodied in that phrase, with its emphasis on its first clause, is emphatically not aspirational; that standard can instill neither the inspiration nor the empathy to encourage people to anticipate ways in which their conduct might be harmful, much less to shape their conduct so that it is actively helpful.

Schneider, *infra*, at 1820. Should family law be "aspirational" or "accommodating" of non-traditional intimate relationships?

9) Is Family Law Really Law?

As noted above, historically in England (and most other European countries) during the middle ages, many of the issues that we today would call family law issues were subject not to the jurisdiction of the secular lawmakers and courts, but to the jurisdiction of canon law and ecclesiastical courts. Historically, family law was closely linked to moral laws or religious laws. Is family law just an effort to "legislate morality"? Does the trend away from traditional morals in family law reflect that notion? *See Schneider, infra*. If law represents public or common values, does the trend toward the "privatization" of family law—the replacement of public standards about family relations that are legally enforced with privately contracted standards—also show repudiation of family "law" in favor of private agreements?

If *discretion* is distinguished from *law*, may the *law* of family law be questioned because of the tremendous discretion accorded courts by many family law standards? Standards such as "the best interests of the child" are undeniably subjective in the extreme. Yet they typify the kinds of difficult decisions that courts must make in deciding family disputes.

If *law* is the companion and instrument of *justice*, do not some litigants have good cause to challenge the validity of family law? While most judges try earnestly to do their best to decide cases fairly, the obstacles to justice in many family law cases are insuperable. Many litigants lack the resources to obtain the necessary evidence or present it in family cases. Some cannot afford legal representation or can afford only limited legal service. The subjectivity of many standards and the discretion of the court provide a personal element that may interfere with justice. The matters that family courts must decide are sometimes simply beyond human ability to discern (for example, who knows, really, whether a particular child will flourish better in the custody of a particular mother or father?). And often the choices the court must make exclude any good option, and reduce the issue to a matter of choosing among tragic options all entailing suffering and harm.

Philosophers and anthropologists of law have noted the evolution of law out of custom, and of society out of family and tribal roots. There still is much "customary" law in family relations. And those customs vary from family to family, and tribe to tribe, even in our modern and postmodern sophisticated social systems. Professor Fuller suggested that formal law is adept at regulating relations among friendly strangers. As they become intimate (as in the case of family relations), the ability of the law to regulate the relations drops, as it does also as they become less friendly. Nothing could be more unfriendly than a hostile divorce involving former intimates, and in those kinds of situations, the formal law often finds its limits. (Can a judge *really* make an angry 14-year-old child live with his or her mother if he or she does not want to? How good is the law at enforcing child support obligations or visitation rights against angry ex-husbands or ex-wives?) The large element of futility in enforcement of family law orders, judgments and decrees raises questions about the *law* in family law.

3. Practical and Ethical Considerations

a. An Organizational Framework for the Study and Practice of Family Law

Relationships within the family that are subject to legal regulation may be categorized for pedagogical purposes into two types: *spousal* or *spousal-like relations* and *parent-child and analogous relations.* The former involve horizontal relations of status equality and consent; the latter vertical relations of guardianship; all are assumed to be long-term or lifelong, and committed. Moreover, regulations of these relations may be categorized into three categories: *before* (regulating the creation of the spousal or parent-child relationship), *during* (regulating the ongoing relationship), and *after* (regulating the termination of and post-termination incidents of the relationship). There are, of course, many other ways that state regulations of family relations may be categorized (e.g., public law–private law, federal–state, statutory–case law, direct–indirect, constitutional–nonconstitutional law, etc.), but for pedagogical purposes, the six categories involving the before, during, and after regulations of spousal and parent-child relations provide the clearest matrix for understanding and organizing family law. Additionally, topics concerning family laws generally (definition, history, theories, administration, general matters, etc.) may be grouped in a preliminary section. Thus, the subjects of Family Law are organized in this casebook into seven general parts, presented in the following sequence:

	Introduction/General/Theories–I		
	Before	During	After
Husband–Wife	II	IV	VI
Parent–Child	III	V	VII

This organizational structure has the advantages of being simple, comprehensive, and constant. The chapters of this book are organized according to this structure; this models a simple and effective method for organizing further information relating to family law.

b. Notes and Questions

1) Categories

Into which category (for example: H-W, Before = category II, P-C, After = category VII) should the following kinds of legal issues be placed: a) Adoption? b) Failure to return a child after a visitation period? c) Parental liability for damage caused by vandalism committed by their child? d) Same-sex marriage? e) Whether parents can remove their child from certain controversial sex education programs at a public school? f) Whether a husband is liable for the attorney fees of a criminal attorney his wife hired to defend herself against drug possession charges? g) Division of pensions upon divorce? h) Use of DNA testing in paternity cases? i) Legal restrictions on human cloning?

2) Time Periods

Give two examples of legal issues or cases from each of the three time periods (before, during, after) relating to the regulation of marriage.

4. Bibliography

Mary Jo Bane, Here to Stay (1976).
Brigman & Stinnett, *The State of the Family System in America: Perceptions of Family-Life Professionals*, 17 Fam. Perspectives 193 (1983).
Broschart, *Gender and the Definition of the Family and Kinship*, 17 Fam. Perspectives 155 (1983).
W. Buckland, A Textbook of Roman Law from Augustus to Justinian (1921).
John G. Culhane, *Even More Wrongful Death: Statutes Divorced from Reality*, 32 Fordham Urb. L.J. 171 (2005).
Alexis de Tocqueville, Democracy in America (1945 ed.).
Development in the Law, Statutory Protection for Gays and Lesbians in Private Employment, 109 Harv. L. Rev. 1625 (1996).
Stanley Diamond, *The Rule of Law Versus the Order of Custom*, 38 Soc. Res. 42 (1971).
Kris Franklin, *"A Family Like Any Other Family:" Alternative Methods of Defining Family Law*, 18 N.Y.U. Rev. L. & Soc. Change 1027 (1990/1991).
Carol Gilligan, In a Different Voice (1982).
Mary Ann Glendon, The New Family and the New Property (1981).

Bruce C. Hafen, *The Constitutional Status of Marriage, Kinship, and Sexual Privacy*, 81 Mich. L. Rev. 464
    (1983).
E. Adamson Hoebel. The Law of Primitive Man (1954).
Christopher Lasch, Haven in a Heartless World (1979).
John Locke, Second Treatise of Government (1691).
David D. Meyer, *Self-Definition in the Constitution of Faith and Family*, 86 Minn. L. Rev. 791 (2002).
B. Nicholas, An Introduction to Roman Law (1962).
Raymond C. O'Brien, *Domestic Partnership: Recognition and Responsibility*, 32 San Diego L. Rev. 163
    (1995).
Nancy D. Polikoff, *Making Marriage Matter Less: The ALI Domestic Partner Principles Are One Step in the
    Right Direction*, 2004 U. Chi. Legal F. 353 (2004).
David G. Richardson, *Family Rights for Unmarried Couples*, 2 Kan. J.L. & Pub. Pol'y 117 (1993).
Rayden's Practice and Law of Divorce 1–4 (Joseph Jackson, C.F. Turner, & D.R. Ellison, eds., 9th ed. 1964).
Eva Rubin, The Supreme Court and the American Family (1986).
David Sampedro, *When Living As Husband and Wife Isn't Enough: Reevaluating Dillon's Close
    Relationship Test in Light of* Dunphy v. Gregor, 25 Stetson L. Rev. 1085 (1996).
Carl Schneider, *Moral Discourse and the Transformation of American Family Law*, 83 Mich. L. Rev. 1803
    (1985).
Anne E. Simerman, Note, *The Right of a Cohabitant to Recover in Tort: Wrongful Death, Negligent
    Infliction of Emotional Distress and Loss of Consortium*, 32 U. Louisville J. Fam. L. 531 (1993–1994).
Mary Patricia Treuthart, *Adopting a More Realistic Definition of "Family,"* 26 Gonz. L. Rev. 91
    (1990/1991).
Wall St. J., Sep. 25, 1986, at 1, Col. 1, and 26, Col. 1.
Lynn D. Wardle, *Deconstructing Family: A Critique of The ALI's "Domestic Partners" Proposal*, 2001
    B.Y.U. L. Rev. 1189.
Lynn D. Wardle, *Marriage and Domestic Violence in the United States: New Perspectives About Legal
    Strategies to Combat Violence*, 15 St. Thomas L. Rev. 791–805 (Summer 2003).
A. Watson, The Law of Persons in the Later Roman Republic (1967).
Debbie Zielinski, Note, *Domestic Partnership Benefits: Why Not Offer Them to Same-Sex Partners and
    Unmarried Opposite Sex Partners*, 13 J.L. & Health 281 (1999).

B. THE IMPORTANCE OF FAMILY LAW

1. Background

a. Issues of Defining Historical Importance

It is not unlikely that historians in the not-too-distant future will agree that the most important issues of American legal and social policy arising in the present period (turn-of-the-millennium)—the defining issues that shaped the identity of a society and revealed the vision of the nation—were family law issues, issues relating to the structure, status, rights, and responsibilities of family and quasi-family relations. Issues concerning the fundamental policies concerning governmental preferences, permissions, and proscriptions regarding the structure, status, rights, and responsibilities of family and quasi-family relations are still in the formative (or, more precisely, *reformative*) stage. Clearly there have been profound social changes regarding family structures and relations, but whether these are merely transitory (merely the particular style of the "baby boom" generation, which will pass with them) or permanent is not yet clear. Likewise, there have been significant changes in family law policies (including unilateral no-fault divorce, legalized abortion-on-demand, recognition of non-marital cohabitation, "normalization" of illegitimacy, etc.), but, again, whether those changes are merely transitory or permanent is not settled.

Family policy issues are extremely important because their consequences can be far-reaching. Generationally, economically, educationally, socially, morally, and in myriad other ways, family structure and relations have tremendous impact upon (and are often reflective of basic values and aspirations of) individuals and society. They are important because the family is the "basic unit of society," Chesterton, *infra*, at 700, and because our political and legal system (not to mention our economy) is based upon some assumptions about family relations and family functions that are under profound pressure for change. The impact upon the legal and social order of profound, permanent changes in family structure and relations could be substantial.

b. Social Foundations

Sociologist Robert Nisbet observed: "[F]amily, not the individual, is the real molecule of society, the key link of the social chain of being. It is inconceivable ... that either intellectual growth or social order or the roots of liberty can possibly be maintained among a people unless the kinship tie is strong and has both functional significance and symbolic authority." Nisbet, *infra*. Christine Beasley observed: "The family is the very seedbed of democracy. Home is the place where we get our first ideas about ourself, our attitudes toward other people, and our habits of approaching and solving problems." Beasley, *infra*. It is in the home that children learn lessons about cooperation and commitment, sharing and sacrifice, and obedience to the unenforceable that form the foundation for self-government, and both children and parents learn and practice how to make the best of shortages, how to care for others, how to be happy, to love liberty, to fulfill one's duty, and the critical citizenship skills of mutual respect and cooperation. Historically, the family has been the fundamental unit of socialization and the basic economic unit of society. Society has an interest in fostering family forms, practices, and relationships that produce socially beneficial results that avoid lost productivity, reduce tax expenditures for medicines, health services, social security, and prevent and minimize the social costs of dysfunctional behavior of struggling adolescents and adults reflecting the pain and frustration of broken and abusive families. Thus, society has a direct and measurable interest in fostering good, happy marriages, and stable, loving families.

Family law is important because it channels, facilitates, expresses, and defines the structure, boundaries, rights, and duties of the fundamental unit of our society. The health and well-being of individuals and the strength and stability of the nation ultimately depend upon the virtues of citizens nurtured and organized in families that are shaped in part by family law. Because families and family relations contribute to the welfare and success of individuals and of society in such profound ways that are unmatched by any other relationships, they need and deserve special legal status, protection, preference, and deference. Other organizations and institutions, including the government itself, are incapable of adequately and effectively substituting for healthy families or performing as well or as efficiently the functions that families perform. While the government must act to provide assistance or protection to needy or dysfunctional families at times, most attempts of government agencies to act as surrogates for the family, even when necessary, are costly, of limited success, and often produce unanticipated undesirable consequences. One corollary to the great value and importance of families is the great responsibility of family lawyers and lawmakers to constantly remember and respect that importance.

c. Sophisticated Simplicity

Family law is filled with paradoxes and ironies. Typically, family law has been considered a *simple* area of practice; today, with the complexities of qualified domestic relations orders (QDROs), qualified medical child support orders (QMCSOs), tax consequences, bankruptcy considerations, business valuations, and complicated (and changing) rules governing paternity, adoption, child custody, and so forth, the subject can be extremely complex and sophisticated. The stereotype of a family lawyer has been a relatively unskilled practitioner; yet because of the breadth of legal subjects included in family law, the constitutionalization of family law, the enactment of complicated statutory schemes, and because of the volatile emotional dimensions of family law requires more breadth of legal knowledge as well as a higher level of interpersonal legal skills (interviewing, counseling, negotiation, cross-examination of hostile witnesses) than is usually required in most other kinds of legal practice. The practice of family law today is one of the most demanding areas of legal practice.

2. Statutes, Cases, and Doctrines

[Omitted]

3. Practical and Ethical Considerations

a. Bread-and-Butter Law

Family law is the single largest area of law practiced in America. It is regularly reported that one-third of all civil cases filed in American state courts of general jurisdiction are domestic relations cases. *See* DeWitt at 53. In 2000, the National Center for State Courts reported (using complete data from 22 states and only partial data from 27 states) that 5,183,601 domestic relations cases were filed in American state courts—over 25 percent of all civil cases filed in state courts of general or limited jurisdiction that year. Examining the Work, *infra*, at 36; National Court Statistics Project, *infra*. If the additional 2,005,704 juvenile court filings were added, it would represent over 35 percent of all state court cases filed. *Id.* Domestic relations filings were up 79 percent from 1984; the highest increase in court filings in any category reported; not surprisingly, juvenile cases had the second highest increase. *Id.* Compared to 1996, divorce filings in 2000 were down 3 percent, paternity filings down 10 percent, and interstate support filings down 37 percent, while custody case filings were up 15 percent, adoption filings up 14 percent, and domestic violence filings up 12 percent. Examining the Work, *infra*, at 37, 42. Divorce cases still comprise 37 percent of the total domestic relations caseload, with nearly twice as many filings as the next highest categories (custody and domestic violence, about 20 percent apiece). *Id.* at 39. Some reporting disparities exist because classification and counting differences among the states, such as whether custody hearings in divorce cases count as separate cases, and some filings like domestic violence may be reported multiple times because of overlapping jurisdiction of several courts. *Id.* at 39–42.

Every year there are more than 1 million divorces in the United States, most involving multiple family law claims including in addition to divorce, property division, alimony, child custody, visitation, child support, sometimes domestic violence claims, restraining orders, and litigation over interim orders and their modification and enforcement. This does not include the large amount of "post-divorce" litigation involving efforts to modify or enforce divorce-related decrees, or adoption cases, or paternity cases, or cases involving protection of parental or family rights, or many other types of family law cases. Over half of all lawyers report dealing with family law issues every year. Lawyer-referral services report that requests for referrals to lawyers to handle family law issues far exceed referral requests for any other category of law. Even lawyers who try to avoid family law cases find that their relatives, neighbors, friends, and strangers come to them for advice or representation when, for example, a single mother is unable to collect child support, a divorced father is denied visitation, a school forces a child to attend an objectionable sex education program, or a child runs away. Thus, family law is the "bread-and-butter" practice of most small and medium-sized law firms and solo practitioners.

b. Solvency

Like other lawyers, family law practitioners must pay rent, pay bar dues, pay secretarial and research assistants, pay for computers, telephones, and other services, and provide support for their own families. Unfortunately, many people who need family law services are irate at the notion that they should pay for them. Lawyers who practice family law are often besieged by family, friends, neighbors, acquaintances, and strangers who want free legal advice or representation. Clients who sign agreements to pay for legal services cannot always be counted upon to fulfill their obligations. Thus, family lawyers often have more work to do than they can handle, but fewer paying clients than they need to stay solvent.

c. Service

Family lawyers deal with the closest, most precious human relationships. How important family relationships and the disruption of families are to clients who seek the services of a family lawyer, and to their children, spouses, relatives, and friends! As nascent lawyers, the law students who use these materials have the opportunity now to learn how to render real service. Students in Family Law classes must begin to prepare to render compassionate, beneficial, edifying service as well as competent, diligent, effective representation. *Properly done, the practice of family law involves professional service in the highest and most demanding sense.*

Clients with family law problems, and the other parties in family law disputes, are often very vulnerable. The problems they bring to the attorney are of the gravest nature to them. Often the intimate lives and well-being of other adults and of children (the most neglected people in our adult-individual-rights-oriented legal system) are also affected by the client's problems. Usually their problems have profound extralegal dimensions (e.g., emotional, psychological, social, moral, religious, medical, financial, and interpersonal).

Often, they need counsel and assistance from persons trained in other disciplines or callings, yet frequently they cannot even afford to pay fully for all the legal assistance they need. The opportunities for service abound. These materials also are intended to help law students begin to understand how (and how important it is for them) to use their knowledge of family law as a tool for rendering genuine service to their clients and their communities.

4. Bibliography

Christine Beasley, *Democracy in the Home* 25 (1954).

G.K. Chesterton, Eugenics and Other Evils (1922), reprinted in 4 The Collected Works of G.K. Chesterton 291, 398 (James V. Schall ed., 1987), quoted in Dale Ahlquist, *G.K. Chesterton's Uncommonly Sensible Views on the Law*, 3 Ave Maria L. Rev. 685 (2005).

Paula M. DeWitt, Breaking Up is Hard to Do, American Demographics, Oct. 1992, at 53.

National Center for State Courts, Examining the Work of State Courts, 1999–2000—A National Perspective from the Court Statistics Project 42 (Brian J. Ostrom et al. eds. 2001) <http://www.ncsc.dni.us/divisions/research/csp/csp-exam_2001.html>.

National Center for State Courts, National Court Statistics Project, Cases filed in State Courts (2001) <http://www.ncsc.dni.us/divisions/research/csp/csp-stat01.html>.

National Center for State Courts, State Court Caseload Statistics, 2001 (Melissa T. Cantrell, et al., 2001) <http://www.ncsc.dni.us/divisions/research/csp/2001%20Files/Tables5-8.pdf>

Robert Nisbet, The Twilight of Authority (1975), cited in Allan Carlson, *The Family: Where Do We Go From Here?* Society, Vol. 32, No. 5, at 7, 11 (July 17, 1995) (1995 WL 12535265).

See further supra, Part A.4. Bibliography.

C. SOURCES OF FAMILY LAW

1. Background

a. Sources of Family Law

It is imperative that family lawyers know the sources to which they can turn to find the law, to keep up with new developments, to learn of uses and criticisms of the law, and of proposed law reforms. Listed in the Bibliography below (C.4.) are a few general or national secondary sources. However, since most family law is local (state) law, it is important to become familiar with primary sources (statutes, regulations, cases) and secondary sources (treatises, monographs, journals, periodicals) of and for your "homestate"—the state in which you intend (or are mostly likely) to practice law.

2. Statutes, Cases and Doctrines

a. Notes and Questions

Identify the titles or sections of your homestate statutes or codes that deal with the following subjects: (1) marriage; (2) paternity; (3) adoption; (4) divorce; (5) custody and visitation; (6) alimony.

3. Practical and Ethical Considerations

a. Notes and Questions

While it is tempting to assume that the professional ethics one will follow as a practicing lawyer will be learned after graduation, on-the-job, human habits do not so easily conform to convenient compartmentalization. The ethical principles that law students practice in law school will follow them into practice as their habitual personal ethical patterns, tendencies, and norms. The honesty, integrity, dependability, trustworthiness, courtesy, obedience, and moral courage of the law student become the professional ethics of the practicing lawyer.

4. Bibliography

a. A Sample Bibliography

1) A Sample Family Law Journals & Periodicals

Fam. L. Quarterly; Int'l. J. of Law and the Family; J. American Academy Matrimonial Lawyers.

2) A Sample Family Law Reporters and Newsletters

AALS Family Law Section Newsletter Family Law Reporter; Juvenile & Fam. Law Digest.

3) A Sample National Family Law Treatise

Contemporary family Law, vols. 1-4 (Lynn D. Wardle et al. 1988).

4) A Sample of Internet Sources of Family Law Information

Adoption.com Inc. <http://www.adoption.com>; ABA Center on Children and the Law; The Dave Thomas Center for Adoption Law <http://www.capital.edu/adoption/index.htm>; <http://www.abanet.org/child/home.html>; ABA Commission on Domestic Violence <http://www.abanet.org/domviol/home>; ABA Section of family Law Children's Defense Fund <http://www.tmn.com/cdf/>; Cornell University State Family Law Resources <http://www.law.cornell.edu/topics/state_statutes.html#family>; Americans for Divorce Reform <http://www.divorcereform.org>; Academy of Family Mediators <gopher://gopher.igc.apc.org/00/orgs/afm/1>; Divorce Source <http://www.divorcesource.com/>; Family Research Council <http://www.frc.org>; Federal Office of Child Support Enforcement <http://www.acf.dhhs.gov/programs/CSE/index.html>; National Right to Life Committee <http://www.nrlc.org/>; Smart Marriages: <http://archives.his.com/smartmarriages/search/>; U.S. House of Representatives Internet Law Library Domestic Relations—General <http://law.house.gov/97.htm>; Children <http://law.house.gove/318.htm>; Marriage and Divorce <http://law.house.gov/319.htm>.

b. Research Assignment

(1) Identify at least one family law journal, periodical, reporter, or newsletter that emphasizes family law in or of your homestate. (2) Find three internet sites that deal with international adoptions. (3) Find two adoption agencies in your homestate.

CHAPTER 2

The Variety of American Family Laws and Courts; Federalism in Family Law; Constitutionalization; Family Autonomy

A. THE VARIETY AND STRUCTURE OF AMERICAN FAMILY LAWS AND COURTS

1. Background

a. The Variety of American Family Laws

The first fact that students of family laws in the United States must understand is that there is no such thing as *THE* family law of the United States of America. Rather, there are two (or fifty-two, depending on your perspective) sets and systems of family law in the United States, varying tremendously in substance, procedures, and structures from each other.

Second, because the government of the United States of America is bifurcated between the national and the state systems, persons living in the United States are simultaneously subject to two sets of laws: Federal laws (passed by Congress, adopted by federal agencies, or declared by federal courts) and state laws (passed by state legislatures, adopted by federal agencies, or declared by state courts). Both federal and state lawmakers may enact laws affecting family relations, and federal and/or state law may govern family cases. Some family legal issues may be governed by federal law (e.g., due process, full faith and credit, equal protection, federal tax or bankruptcy law), while other issues in the same cases may be governed by state law (e.g., marriage validity, divorce grounds, adoption procedures, paternity claims, custody standards).

Third, no state has developed its family law entirely independently. Such factors as persuasive sister-state judicial opinions, effective or novel legislation enacted in other states, proposals for uniform legislation, national media influences, and lobbying efforts by national organizations have produced many multi-state trends in family law. Federal programs offering incentives for states to adopt specific laws (such as child abuse reporting laws, child custody jurisdictional standards, child support guidelines) also have generated some consistency. Interstate matters such as interstate collection of child support are common subjects of federal regulation. However, despite the similarities and homogenizing influences, the family laws of the American states remain remarkably diverse in policy and practice.

b. Courts That Hear Family Cases

Family law issues can and do arise in any court in the United States of America. But most often, they arise in state courts adjudicating cases asserting typical family law claims (e.g., adoption, paternity, divorce, custody, support).

Because state courts in the United States developed separately within each state, each designed by a different state legislature, the structure and organization of American state courts vary tremendously. There are fifty separate state court systems, each with its own judicial structure, as well as four federal territories with their own separate court systems. However, there are some general similarities. For instance, every state has a court of general civil jurisdiction (sometimes divided into different divisions or jurisdictions along old law-or-equity lines). Typically, family law cases are heard by the courts of general jurisdiction; if the state court structure has separate courts for "law" and "equity" most family court cases may be heard by "equity" or "chancery" courts. (In pre-1776 England, the ecclesiastical courts exercised jurisdiction over much of what today is called family law, and when the secular civil courts were given jurisdiction of civil status and civil claims relating to family relations, a share of the jurisdiction was assumed by equity courts. Ecclesiastical courts were not established in America, so jurisdiction over those claims fell to equity courts.) Often today, there will be a separate division within the courts of general jurisdiction for family law cases; traditionally probate cases were lumped with family cases and often the division was called "Probate." All states have set up special courts to hear and decide certain cases involving minors (usually called Juvenile Courts), especially cases involving alleged delinquency by minors or abuse and neglect of minors. There have been movements to create separate, "unified" or "family courts" in some states, with broad jurisdiction over most family-related cases. The use of "Domestic Relations Commissioners," magistrates, or masters to resolve pretrial motions or specific issues in family law cases is not uncommon. Many states mandate or encourage referral of some family law issues to mediation or ADR.

Most states have intermediate courts of appeal to which family law litigants dissatisfied with the decision of the trial court may appeal. Review by state supreme courts is also possible, but as they often have discretionary jurisdiction in family cases, state intermediate courts of appeal are often the courts of last resort in family law.

2. Statutes, Cases, and Doctrines

a. Notes and Questions

1) Homestate Family Courts

Look up the court structure of your homestate. What courts have jurisdiction of (which type of) family law cases?

3. Practical and Ethical Considerations

a. Notes and Questions

1) Learning and Practicing Family Law in America

The variety of state-based family law systems, structures, rules, and doctrines in the United States has significant consequences for students and practitioners of family law.

First, it means that family law is inherently local; it must be studied and learned at the local level. Second, it means that the study of Family Law in America is really a matter of comparative law; one must separately learn (and may usefully compare) family law as it exists in a given state with family law in other states. Third, practitioners must know and keep abreast of at least two bodies of law—their home state family law and federal laws that significantly influence family law. Fourth, likewise, professional responsibility rules and protocols regarding such things as fees, dual representations, retainer agreements, conflict of interest standards, confidentiality rules, etc., vary from state to state. Fifth, there are no "national" family law firms or lawyers because to become an expert in family law requires mastery of a specific jurisdiction's statutes, cases, rules, judges, practices, and procedures. Some lawyers (particularly in border areas) may be admitted to practice in and become proficient in the family laws of two or even three states, but seldom do they handle family cases outside their own (and perhaps a neighboring) jurisdiction.

4. Bibliography

Want's Federal-State Court Directory. *See also* § 4.d., *infra.*

B. FEDERALISM IN FAMILY LAW AND THE DOMESTIC RELATIONS EXCEPTION TO DIVERSITY JURISDICTION

1. Background

a. Indirect Federal Regulation of Family Law

Article VI of the United States Constitution provides that properly enacted federal law "shall be the supreme Law of the Land." Thus, when federal and state laws conflict, the federal law preempts the countervailing state law. For instance, in *McCarty v. McCarty,* 453 U.S. 210 (1981), the Supreme Court of the United States held that federal law governing military retirement pay, interpreted as vesting ownership in the military member alone, preempted state community property law which gave the spouse an equal ownership interest in the property which could be awarded to her upon divorce. (Later, Congress changed the federal law to protect the interests of the spouses of members of the military services.)

However, there is probably less federal law pertaining to domestic relations than there is pertaining to any other subject of law. The regulation of domestic relations historically has been, and today remains, primarily a matter of state law. Indeed, the Supreme Court of the United States has observed, not infrequently, that the "[r]egulation of domestic relations [is] an area that has long been regarded as a virtually exclusive province of the states." *Sosna v. Iowa,* 419 U.S. 393, 404 (1975); *see also Lehman v. Lycoming County Children's Services Agency,* 458 U.S. 502 (1982); *Moore v. Sims,* 442 U.S. 415 (1979); *Barber v. Barber,* 62 U.S. (21 How.) 582 (1859). Thus, the enforcement of family law is left primarily to state courts, and the bulk of the governing rules are state, not federal, laws.

There are two historical reasons for this deference to state regulation of family relations. First, the powers of the federal government are limited to those specifically enumerated in the Constitution, and the power to regulate family relations is not so enumerated. Thus, while federal legislation and regulations dealing with national matters such as commerce, defense, health, social security, taxes, and federal programs often affect family relations, the direct regulation of family relations historically has been deemed to be beyond the proper scope of the federal lawmaking authority. (*See* The Federalist No. 10 (J. Madison); No. 17 (A. Hamilton); No. 45 (J. Madison).) Second, federal courts historically have declined to exercise diversity jurisdiction over suits involving family relations claims, and even in cases involving federal question jurisdiction they have hesitated to resolve domestic disputes. Behind both of these federalism practices are such strong policy values as a desire to preserve pluralism, belief that laws regulating families should reflect local values, suspicion of concentration of power, principles of comity and "shared sovereignty," respect for the expertise of state courts, federal judges' dislike for family disputes, and a belief that federal government priorities must focus on other national concerns.

Federalism in family law was one of the reasons the Supreme Court declined to decide the pledge of allegiance case. In *Elk Grove Unified School Dist. v. Newdow*, 542 U.S. 1 (2004), the Court explained that, "while rare instances arise in which it is necessary to answer a substantial federal question that transcends or exists apart from the family law issue, see, e.g., *Palmore v. Sidoti*, 466 U.S. 429, 432-434 (1984), in general it is appropriate for the federal courts to leave delicate issues of domestic relations to the state courts." 542 U.S. at 13. *See also United States v. Morrison*, 529 U.S. 598, 615-16 (2000) (protecting federalism in "family law and other areas of traditional state regulation [even though] the aggregate effect of marriage, divorce, and childrearing on the national economy is undoubtedly significant.") *United States v. Lopez*, 514 U.S. 549, 566-68 (1995) (Congress lacks the authority to enact Gun-Free School Zones Act regulating gun possession in school zones); *id.* at 565 ("This analysis would be equally applicable, if not more so, to subjects such as family law . . . ."). Family law is a prime example of the type of regulation which is reserved to the states and beyond the regulatory authority of the national government. *See, generally, Sosna v. Iowa*, 419 U.S. 393 (1975) (upholding state durational residency requirement for divorce); *see further Santosky v. Kramer*, 455 U.S. 745, 770 (1982) (Rehnquist, J., dissenting) ("I believe that few of us would care to live in a society where every aspect of life was regulated by a single source of law, whether that source be this Court or some other organ of our complex body politic. . . . If ever there were an area in which federal courts should heed the admonition of Justice Holmes that 'a page of history is worth a volume of logic,' it is in the area of domestic relations. This area has been left to the States from time immemorial, and not without good reason.").

Notwithstanding the "local" nature of family law in the United States, there is one important area in which federal law has grown enormously and undeniably shaped American family laws since the end of World War II. That is in respect to the definition and protection of constitutional individual liberties interpreted by the courts. In particular, the expansion of equal protection and substantive and procedural due process doctrines has created some significant limits on state regulation and enforcement of domestic relations. Especially since the creation of the privacy doctrine in the late 1960s and the gender equality principles in the early 1970s many state family laws have been invalidated, and state domestic relations rules and statutes today are drafted and enforced with an eye on federal constitutional principles.

2. Statutes, Cases, and Doctrines

a. Jurisdiction over Parties in Family Law Litigation

The types of claims that may be asserted in "family law" litigation are many and varied indeed. The standards for asserting jurisdiction over the parties may also vary, depending on the particular type of claim asserted in a particular case. Of course, in every case the validity of asserting jurisdiction over the parties is determined by a three-step analysis: (1) does a statute (or common law rule) authorize the assertion of jurisdiction? (2) if so, is it (and the application of it) constitutional? and (3) if so, has it been followed?

All states have general long-arm statutes that authorize the assertion of jurisdiction over nonresidents having specified contacts with the forum in cases involving particularly described pecuniary claims. These general long-arm statutes provide a basis for assertion of jurisdiction over nonresidents in many family law cases. However, the statutes are not always drafted with family litigation in mind, and the language may not support jurisdiction in all cases. In addition, all states have some specific jurisdictional statutes applicable to particular family law claims (e.g., divorce, child custody, child support). While most courts are inclined to construe jurisdictional statutes broadly, the wording of the jurisdictional statute is crucial.

Constitutionally, it has long been established that to determine the pecuniary claims or property incidents of family status (e.g., support, alimony, property division) a court must have normal *in personam* jurisdiction over the defendant whose interests are being determined. *Estin v. Estin,* 334 U.S. 541 (1948); *Vanderbilt v. Vanderbilt,* 354 U.S. 416 (1957). The constitutional test for *in personam* jurisdiction over nonresident defendants regarding claims for alimony, support, property division, and child support is whether the defendant had "certain minimum contacts with [the territory of the forum] such that the maintenance of the suit does not offend 'traditional notions of fair play and substantial justice.'" *International Shoe Co. v. Washington,* 326 U.S. 310 (1945).

However, jurisdiction to adjudicate family relationship status itself (e.g., marriage validity, divorce, paternity, custody, adoption), traditionally has not been deemed *in personam* and the jurisdictional standard is different. In *Williams v. North Carolina,* 317 U.S. 287 (1942), the Supreme Court held that domicile of one spouse (whether innocent or deserting) was constitutionally a sufficient basis for assertion of jurisdiction to determine marital status (e.g., grant a valid divorce).

> [T]he decrees in this case like other divorce decrees are more than in personam judgments. They involved the marital status of the parties. Domicil creates a relationship to the state which is adequate for numerous exercises of state power. ... Each state as sovereign has a rightful and legitimate concern in the marital status of persons domiciled within its borders. ... Thus, it is plain that each state by virtue of its command over its domiciliaries and its large interest in the institution of marriage can alter within its own borders the marriage status of the spouse domiciled there, even though the other spouse is absent.

Id. at 298–99. Thus, litigation concerning family status traditionally has been viewed as being in the nature of *in rem,* the status itself (e.g., the marital, custodial, or paternity status) being the fictional "res" whose presence in the forum territory (equated with the domicile there of one of the parties to the family relationship in issue) is necessary to give the court jurisdiction to determine status.

In *Shaffer v. Heitner,* 433 U.S. 186 (1977), involving a shareholder's derivative suit against a corporation, the Supreme Court extended the "minimum contacts" test for determining the constitutionality of the assertion of state court jurisdiction over the interests of nonresident defendants to most *in rem* and *quasi in rem* suits. While the logic and broad language of that opinion could easily embrace family status disputes also, the Court carefully noted that it was not deciding whether "the particularized rules governing adjudication of status, are inconsistent with the standard of fairness." *Id.* at 208, n.30. A year later, the Court held that the "minimum contacts" test for jurisdiction applies in state court actions against nonresident defendants to modify child support—an economic incident of parental status. *Kulko v. Superior Court,* 436 U.S. 84 (1978). However, the Supreme Court has not determined whether the "minimum contacts" jurisdictional standard is constitutionally required in cases determining domestic status.

b. Limited Federal Court Subject Matter Jurisdiction

As noted above, federal courts have no direct jurisdiction over family law cases. The federal government has not been given power to directly regulate family relations, so federal question jurisdiction normally does not apply in divorces, custody disputes, adoptions, etc. Historically, there have been relatively few federal cases of significance in family law. Most of them have been recent and deal with constitutional issues of jurisdiction, due process, Full Faith and Credit, individual constitutional rights, equal protection, or supremacy or application of some federal legislation (ERISA, tax, bankruptcy, etc.). Thus, federal district and court of appeals cases are not often cited in family law litigation, with one exception. The exception is when dealing with federal laws such as tax laws (e.g., who is entitled to the child dependency exemption) or federal bankruptcy law (e.g., is a court-imposed obligation to pay the ex-spouse's attorneys fees dischargeable in bankruptcy). Most such issues arise in state court litigation and go to the U.S. Supreme Court after going through the state court system, but sometimes such claims arise in federal court.

c. *Ankenbrandt v. Richards*

Ankenbrandt v. Richards
504 U.S. 689 (1992)

JUSTICE WHITE delivered the opinion of the Court.

This case presents the issue whether the federal courts have jurisdiction or should abstain in a case involving alleged torts committed by the former husband of petitioner and his female companion against petitioner's children, when the sole basis for federal jurisdiction is the diversity-of-citizenship provision of 28 U.S.C. § 1332.

Petitioner Carol Ankenbrandt, a citizen of Missouri, brought this lawsuit on September 26, 1989, on behalf of her daughters L.R. and S.R. against respondents Jon A. Richards and Debra Kesler, citizens of Louisiana, in the United States District Court for the Eastern District of Louisiana. Alleging federal jurisdiction based on the diversity of citizenship provision of § 1332, Ankenbrandt's complaint sought monetary damages for alleged sexual and physical abuse of the children committed by Richards and Kesler. Richards is the divorced father of the children and Kesler his female companion. On December 10, 1990, the District Court granted respondents' motion to dismiss this lawsuit. Citing In re Burrus, 136 U.S. 586 (1890), for the proposition that "[t]he whole subject of the domestic relations of husband and wife, parent and child, belongs to the laws of the States and not to the laws of the United States," the court concluded that this case fell within what has become known as the "domestic relations" exception to diversity jurisdiction, and that it lacked jurisdiction over the case. The court also invoked the abstention principles announced in Younger v. Harris, 401 U.S. 37 (1971), to justify its decision to dismiss the complaint without prejudice. ...The Court of Appeals affirmed in an unpublished opinion. ...

We granted certiorari limited to the following questions: "(1) Is there a domestic relations exception to federal jurisdiction? (2) If so, does it permit a district court to abstain from exercising diversity jurisdiction over a tort action for damages? and (3) Did the District Court in this case err in abstaining from exercising jurisdiction under the doctrine of *Younger v. Harris*, [*supra*]?" ... We address each of these issues in turn.

The domestic relations exception upon which the courts below relied to decline jurisdiction has been invoked often by the lower federal courts. The seeming authority for doing so originally stemmed from the announcement in *Barber v. Barber*, 21 How. 582 (1859), that the federal courts have no jurisdiction over suits for divorce or the allowance of alimony. In that case, the Court heard a suit in equity brought by a wife (by her next friend) in federal district court pursuant to diversity jurisdiction against her former husband. She sought to enforce a decree from a New York state court, which had granted a divorce and awarded her alimony. The former husband thereupon moved to Wisconsin to place himself beyond the New York courts' jurisdiction so that the divorce decree there could not be enforced against him; he then sued for divorce in a Wisconsin court, representing to that court that his wife had abandoned him and failing to disclose the existence of the New York decree. In a suit brought by the former wife in Wisconsin Federal District Court, the former husband alleged that the court lacked jurisdiction. The court accepted jurisdiction and gave judgment for the divorced wife.

* * *

The [*Barber*] Court ... dismiss[ed] the former husband's contention that the case involved a subject matter outside the federal courts' jurisdiction. In so stating, however, the Court also announced the following limitation on federal jurisdiction: "Our first remark is—and we wish it to be remembered—that this is not a suit asking the court for the allowance of alimony. That has been done by a court of competent jurisdiction. The court in Wisconsin was asked to interfere to prevent that decree from being defeated by fraud. "We disclaim altogether any jurisdiction in the courts of the United States upon the subject of divorce, or for the allowance of alimony, either as an original proceeding in chancery or as an incident to divorce a vinculo, or to one from bed and board." *Barber, supra*, at 584. ...

The statements disclaiming jurisdiction over divorce and alimony decree suits, though technically dicta, formed the basis for excluding "domestic relations" cases from the jurisdiction of the lower federal courts, a jurisdictional limitation those courts have recognized ever since. The *Barber* Court, however, cited no authority and did not discuss the foundation for its announcement. Since that time, the Court has dealt only occasionally with the domestic relations limitation on federal-court jurisdiction, and it has never addressed the basis for such a limitation. Because we are unwilling to cast aside an understood rule that has been recognized for nearly a century and a half, we feel compelled to explain why we will continue to recognize this limitation on federal jurisdiction.

A

Counsel argued in *Barber* that the Constitution prohibited federal courts from exercising jurisdiction over domestic relations cases. ... An examination of Article III, *Barber* itself, and our cases since *Barber* makes clear that the Constitution does not exclude domestic relations cases from the jurisdiction otherwise granted by statute to the federal courts.

Article III, § 2, of the Constitution ... delineates the absolute limits on the federal courts' jurisdiction. But in articulating three different terms to define jurisdiction—"Cases, in Law and Equity," "Cases," and "Controversies"—this provision contains no limitation on subjects of a domestic relations nature. Nor did *Barber* purport to ground the domestic relations exception in these constitutional limits on federal jurisdiction. The Court's discussion of federal judicial power to hear suits of a domestic relations nature contains no mention of the Constitution, *see Barber, supra*, at 584, and it is logical to presume that the Court based its statement limiting such power on narrower statutory, rather than broader constitutional, grounds. ...

Subsequent decisions confirm that *Barber* was not relying on constitutional limits in justifying the exception. In one such case, for instance, the Court stated the "long established rule" that federal courts lack jurisdiction over certain domestic relations matters as having been based on the assumptions that "husband and wife cannot usually be citizens of different States, so long as the marriage relation continues (a rule which has been somewhat relaxed in recent cases), and for the further reason that a suit for divorce in itself involves no pecuniary value." *De La Rama v. De La Rama*, 201 U.S. 303, 307 (1906). Since Article III contains no monetary limit on suits brought pursuant to federal diversity jurisdiction, *De La Rama's* articulation of the "rule" in terms of the statutory requirements for diversity jurisdiction further supports the view that the exception is not grounded in the Constitution.

* * *

Court implicitly has made clear its understanding that the source of the constraint on jurisdiction from *Barber* was not Article III; otherwise the Court itself would have lacked jurisdiction over appeals from these legislative courts. ... We therefore have no difficulty concluding that when the *Barber* Court "disclaim [ed] altogether any jurisdiction in the courts of the United States upon the subject of divorce," 21 How., at 584, it was not basing its statement on the Constitution.

B

That Article III, § 2, does not mandate the exclusion of domestic relations cases from federal-court jurisdiction, however, does not mean that such courts necessarily must retain and exercise jurisdiction over such cases. Other constitutional provisions explain why this is so. Article I, § 8, cl. 9, for example, authorizes Congress "[t]o constitute Tribunals inferior to the Supreme Court" and Article III, § 1, states that "[t]he judicial Power of the United States, shall be vested in one supreme Court, and in such inferior Courts as the Congress may from time to time ordain and establish." The Court's cases state the rule that "if inferior federal courts were created, [Congress was not] required to invest them with all the jurisdiction it was authorized to bestow under Art. III." ...

This position has held constant since at least 1845, when the Court stated that "the judicial power of the United States ... is (except in enumerated instances, applicable exclusively to this court) dependent for its distribution and organization, and for the modes of its exercise, entirely upon the action of Congress, who possess the sole power of creating the tribunals (inferior to the Supreme Court) ... and of investing them with jurisdiction either limited, concurrent, or exclusive, and of withholding jurisdiction from them in the exact degrees and character which to Congress may seem proper for the public good." ... We thus turn our attention to the relevant jurisdictional statutes.

The Judiciary Act of 1789 provided that "the circuit courts shall have original cognizance, concurrent with the courts of the several States, of *all suits of a civil nature at common law or in equity, where the matter in dispute exceeds*, exclusive of costs, the sum or value of *five hundred dollars*, and ... an alien is a party, or the suit is *between a citizen of the State where the suit is brought, and a citizen of another State*." Act of Sept. 24, 1789, § 11, 1 Stat. 73, 78. (Emphasis added.) The defining phrase, "all suits of a civil nature at common law or in equity," remained a key element of statutory provisions demarcating the terms of diversity jurisdiction until 1948, when Congress amended the diversity jurisdiction provision to eliminate this phrase and replace in its stead the term "all civil actions."

* * *

We have no occasion here to join the historical debate over whether the English court of chancery had jurisdiction to handle certain domestic relations matters, though we note that commentators have found some support for the Barber majority's interpretation. Certainly it was not unprecedented at the time for the Court to infer, from what it understood to be English chancery practice, some guide to the meaning of the 1789 Act's jurisdictional grant. ... We thus are content to rest our conclusion that a domestic relations exception exists as a matter of statutory construction not on the accuracy of the historical justifications on which it was seemingly based, but rather on Congress' apparent acceptance of this construction of the diversity jurisdiction provisions in the years prior to 1948, when the statute limited jurisdiction to "suits of a civil nature at common law or in equity." ... Considerations of stare decisis have particular strength in this context, where "the legislative power is implicated, and Congress remains free to alter what we have done." ...

With respect to the 1948 amendment, the Court has previously stated that "no changes of law or policy are to be presumed from changes of language in the revision unless an intent to make such changes is clearly expressed." ...

III

In the more than 100 years since this Court laid the seeds for the development of the domestic relations exception, the lower federal courts have applied it in a variety of circumstances. ... Many of these applications go well beyond the circumscribed situations posed by Barber and its progeny. *Barber* itself disclaimed federal jurisdiction over a narrow range of domestic relations issues involving the granting of a divorce and a decree of alimony, see 21 How., at 584, and stated the limits on federal-court power to intervene prior to the rendering of such orders: "It is, that when a court of competent jurisdiction over the subject-matter and the parties decrees a divorce, and alimony to the wife as its incident, and is unable of itself to enforce the decree summarily upon the husband, that courts of equity will interfere to prevent the decree from being defeated by fraud. The interference, however, is limited to cases in which alimony has been decreed; then only to the extent of what is due, and always to cases in which no appeal is pending from the decree for the divorce or for alimony." *Id.*, at 591.

The *Barber* Court thus did not intend to strip the federal courts of authority to hear cases arising from the domestic relations of persons unless they seek the granting or modification of a divorce or alimony decree. The holding of the case itself sanctioned the exercise of federal jurisdiction over the enforcement of an alimony decree that had been properly obtained in a state court of competent jurisdiction. Contrary to the *Barber* dissenters' position, the enforcement of such validly obtained orders does not "regulate the domestic relations of society" ... And from the conclusion that the federal courts lacked jurisdiction to issue divorce and alimony decrees, there was no dissent. ... *See also Simms v. Simms,* ... (stating that "[i]t may therefore be assumed as indubitable that the Circuit Courts of the United States have no jurisdiction, either of suits for divorce, or of claims for alimony, whether made in a suit for divorce, or by an original proceeding in equity, before a decree for such alimony in a state court").

Subsequently, this Court expanded the domestic relations exception to include decrees in child custody cases. In a child custody case brought pursuant to a writ of habeas corpus, for instance, the Court held void a writ issued by a Federal District Court to restore a child to the custody of the father. "As to the right to the control and possession of this child, as it is contested by its father and its grandfather, it is one in regard to which neither the Congress of the United States nor any authority of the United States has any special jurisdiction." *In re Burrus,* 136 U.S. 586, 594 (1890).

Although *In re Burrus* technically did not involve a construction of the diversity statute, as we understand Barber to have done, its statement that "[t]he whole subject of the domestic relations of husband and wife, parent and child, belongs to the laws of the States and not to the laws of the United States," ... has been interpreted by the federal courts to apply with equal vigor in suits brought pursuant to diversity jurisdiction. ... This application is consistent with *Barber's* directive to limit federal courts' exercise of diversity jurisdiction over suits for divorce and alimony decrees. ... We conclude, therefore, that the domestic relations exception, as articulated by this Court since *Barber*, divests the federal courts of power to issue divorce, alimony, and child custody decrees. Given the long passage of time without any expression of congressional dissatisfaction, we have no trouble today reaffirming the validity of the exception as it pertains to divorce and alimony decrees and child custody orders.

Not only is our conclusion rooted in respect for this long-held understanding, it is also supported by sound policy considerations. Issuance of decrees of this type not infrequently involves retention of jurisdiction by the court and deployment of social workers to monitor compliance. As a matter of judicial economy, state courts are more eminently suited to work of this type than are federal courts, which lack the close association with state and local government organizations dedicated to handling issues that arise out of conflicts over divorce, alimony, and child custody decrees. Moreover, as a matter of judicial expertise, it makes far more sense to retain the rule that federal courts lack power to issue these types of decrees because of the special proficiency developed by state tribunals over the past century and a half in handling issues that arise in the granting of such decrees. ...

By concluding, as we do, that the domestic relations exception encompasses only cases involving the issuance of a divorce, alimony, or child custody decree, we necessarily find that the Court of Appeals erred by affirming the District Court's invocation of this exception. This lawsuit in no way seeks such a decree; rather, it alleges that respondents Richards and Kesler committed torts against L.R. and S.R., Ankenbrandt's children by Richards. Federal subject-matter jurisdiction pursuant to § 1332 thus is proper in this case. We now address whether, even though subject-matter jurisdiction might be proper, sufficient grounds exist to warrant abstention from the exercise of that jurisdiction.

IV

[The Court rejected claims of abstention under *Colorado River Water Conservation Dist. v. United States*, 424 U.S. 800, 813 (1976) as disruptive of federal-state comity because the federal courts have a "virtually unflagging obligation ... to exercise the jurisdiction given them." *Id.*, at 817. They rejected the *Younger v. Harris*, 401 U.S. 37 (1971) abstention because there was no allegation of any pending state proceedings; and they rejected the *Buford* abstention because the status of the domestic relationship had been determined as a matter of state law, and had no bearing on the underlying torts alleged.]

V

We thus conclude that the Court of Appeals erred by affirming the District Court's rulings to decline jurisdiction based on the domestic relations exception to diversity jurisdiction and to abstain under the doctrine of Younger v. Harris, supra. The exception has no place in a suit such as this one, in which a former spouse sues another on behalf of children alleged to have been abused. Because the allegations in this complaint do not request the District Court to issue a divorce, alimony, or child custody decree, we hold that the suit is appropriate for the exercise of § 1332 jurisdiction given the existence of diverse citizenship between petitioner and respondents and the pleading of the relevant amount in controversy. Accordingly, we reverse the decision of the Court of Appeals and remand the case for further proceedings consistent with this opinion.

It is so ordered.

JUSTICE BLACKMUN, concurring in the judgment.

I agree with the Court that the District Court had jurisdiction over petitioner's claims in tort. Moreover, I agree that the federal courts should not entertain claims for divorce, alimony, and child custody. I am unable to agree, however, that the diversity statute contains any "exception" for domestic relations matters. ... In my view, the longstanding, unbroken practice of the federal courts in refusing to hear domestic relations cases is precedent at most for continued discretionary abstention rather than mandatory limits on federal jurisdiction. For these reasons I concur only in the Court's judgment.

* * *

Whether the interest of States remains a sufficient justification today for abstention is uncertain in view of the expansion in recent years of federal law in the domestic relations area. [Fn8 *See e.g.* Victims of Child Abuse Act of 1990, 104 Stat. 4792, 42 U.S.C. § 13001 et seq.; Family Violence Prevention and Services Act, 98 Stat. 1757, 42 U.S.C. § 10401 et seq.; Parental Kidnaping Prevention Act of 1980, 94 Stat. 3568, 28 U.S.C. § 1738A; Adoption Assistance and Child Welfare Act of 1980, 94 Stat. 500, 42 U.S.C. §§ 620–628, 670–679a; Child Abuse Prevention and Treatment and Adoption Reform Act of 1978, 92 Stat. 205, 42 U.S.C. § 5111 et seq.; Child Abuse Prevention and Treatment Act,

88 Stat. 4, 42 U.S.C. § 5101 et seq. Like the diversity statute, the federal-question grant of jurisdiction in Article III of the Constitution limits the judicial power in federal-question cases to "Cases, in Law and Equity." Art. III, § 2. Assuming this limitation applies with equal force in the constitutional context as the Court finds today that it does in the statutory context, the Court's decision today casts grave doubts upon Congress' ability to confer federal-question jurisdiction (as under 28 U.S.C. § 1331) on the federal courts in any matters involving divorces, alimony, and child custody.] ... Absent a contrary command of Congress, the federal courts properly should abstain, at least from diversity actions traditionally excluded from the federal courts, such as those seeking divorce, alimony, and child custody.

Justice STEVENS, with whom Justice THOMAS joins, concurring in the judgment.

This should be an exceedingly easy case. As demonstrated by each of the opinions, whatever belief one holds as to the existence, origin, or scope of a "domestic relations exception," the exception does not apply here. The judgment of the Court of Appeals must be reversed. For that reason, I would leave for another day consideration of whether any domestic relations cases necessarily fall outside of the jurisdiction of the federal courts and of what, if any, principle would justify such an exception to federal jurisdiction.

d. Notes and Questions

1) *Ankenbrandt* Note

Does *Ankenbrandt* hold that Congress constitutionally may enact a statute conferring jurisdiction on federal courts to hear ordinary divorces and other family cases if there is minimum diversity? Why/why not? As a matter of policy, why should/should not federal courts hear family law disputes in addition to or in lieu of state courts? What research or history does the majority cite to support their conclusion that there is no constitutional basis for a limit on federal court jurisdiction over family law issues?

As noted earlier, in *Elk Grove Unified School District v. Newdow*,542 U.S. 1 (2004), the Supreme Court emphasized federalism in family law and respect for state control of domestic relations in holding that a noncustodial parent lacked standing to assert a constitutional claim challenging the state law requiring teachers to lead voluntary grade school students, including his daughter, in reciting the pledge allegiance to the flag each morning. Since the father, who shared physical custody but had no legal custody, lacked legal standing under state law to represent his daughter, the Court held that under the doctrine of federalism in family law, he could not bring suit alleging violation of the Establishment Clause on behalf of his daughter, or for himself since his parental rights had been curtailed by loss of joint legal custody.

A related "probate" exception to federal court jurisdiction has also, in recent years, been curtailed by the Supreme Court. In *Marshall v. Marshall*, __ U.S. __, 126 U.S. 1735 (2006), a very wealthy man, J. Howard Marshall, died without leaving his widow (a.k.a. Anna Nicole Smith) anything in his will. She filed for bankruptcy in federal court. The son of the deceased , who was the ultimate beneficiary of the estate plan, filed a proof of claim in bankruptcy alleging that the widow had defamed him in (she said that he had engaged in forgery, fraud and undue influence to get control of the estate assets). She answered alleging truth as a defense, and counterclaimed for tortious interference with a gift. The son objected on ground that those were probate issues outside the jurisdiction of the federal court. The Bankruptcy Court agreed with the widow, but the federal district court and Ninth Circuit agreed with the son. The U.S. Supreme Court reversed (8+1). Justice Ginsburg, for the Court, noted the similarity between the family law and probate exceptions to federal court jurisdiction, and relied heavily on *Ankenbrandt*. She noted that the Court in *Ankenbrandt* had established that the exception to jurisdiction for family law issues covered a "narrow range of domestic relations issues," and "only 'divorce, alimony, and custody decrees' remain outside federal jurisdictional bounds." 126 U.S. at 1746, quoting *Ankenbrandt*, 504 U.S. at 701-04. Is that statement of the holding in *Ankenbrandt* complete and accurate? Does it define the full scope of the family law exception to federal court jurisdiction?

2) Jurisdictional Questions

(a) Many states authorize divorce jurisdiction when a member of the armed forces or a spouse who has resided in the state for three months brings the suit. Military personnel do not usually acquire domicile in states to which they move for duty. Would assertion of jurisdiction by such a state in a divorce suit by a nondomiciliary serviceman temporarily posted in the state constitutionally be valid if the defendant spouse lived 1500 miles away, had never visited the state, and objected to jurisdiction?

3. Practical and Ethical Considerations

a. Where to file?

What practical (and ethical) factors should influence where (in what jurisdiction and court) a lawyer files a family law case? To what extent should familiarity with local law influence that decision? If the "minimum contacts" test for jurisdiction applied to domestic status cases, would it substantially alter jurisdiction in divorce cases?

4. Bibliography

See infra at § D.4.

C. CONSTITUTIONALIZATION OF FAMILY LAW

1. Background

a. "Constitutionalizing" Family Law

Since the 1920s, the Supreme Court has rendered a significant number of decisions invalidating laws directly or indirectly regulating family relations as violative of the U.S. Constitution. Inasmuch as the Constitution is the supreme law of the land, these decisions effectively established constitutional boundaries for the regulation of family relations by the states as well as by the federal government. Although it is an overstatement to say that family law is now "dominated" by federal constitutional rules, it is fair to say that these decisions have set some general national standards for the regulation of domestic relations and have precipitated the nationwide acceptance of certain substantive and procedural values in family law policy. Two influences have encouraged increased judicial scrutiny of family law under constitutional principles: the acceptance of social substantive due process, and the rejection of stereotyped gender discrimination.

Before the modern "activist Court" era, the Supreme Court rarely decided more than two or three cases dealing with family law issues in any given term or year, and usually just one or two such cases. (For example, from 1945–64, the Court averaged fewer than two family law decisions per term). During the two decades from the mid-1960s through the mid-1980s, however, the Court decided as many as a dozen family law cases in a given year or terms of Court. From 1965–1984, the Court averaged more than 5.5 family law decisions per term. The Rehnquist Court heard significantly fewer family law cases.

2. Statutes, Cases, and Doctrines

a. Substantive Due Process

The Supreme Court did not explicitly extend special constitutional protection to family relations until the twentieth century. However, in 1923, the "heyday" of the doctrine of "substantive due process," the Supreme Court declared that certain family relations were entitled to special constitutional deference. *See Meyer v. Nebraska,* 262 U.S. 390 (1923), *infra* § D.2.a. That was the beginning of a still-important line of cases extending special constitutional protection to certain family relations as fundamental rights. *Infra* § D.2.c. Today, substantive due process is generally discredited, and the Court aspires to some principled basis for determining when rights and relationships not mentioned in the Constitution should be given special judicial protections as unwritten "fundamental" constitutional rights. *See generally Moore v. City of East Cleveland,* 431 U.S. 494 (1977), *infra* § D.2.b.

b. Equal Protection

In its most significant aspects the equal protection doctrine is a substantive constitutional doctrine because the outcome of equal protection analysis will nearly always depend upon which "standard of scrutiny" under which the law or rule creating an inequality will be examined. That determination involves a substantive (policy) question, i.e., whether the discrimination operates to disadvantage any "suspect" classification or the exercise of any "fundamental" rights. In recent years, the Supreme Court has increased the number of the kinds of inequality that it will subject to the very demanding standard of strict judicial scrutiny. Nevertheless, it has attempted to do so cautiously, with some restraint, as explained by Justice White.

> The general rule is that legislation is presumed to be valid under the equal protection clause and will be sustained if the classification drawn by the statute is rationally related to a legitimate state interest. ... When social or economic legislation is at issue, the Equal Protection Clause allows the states wide latitude ... and the Constitution presumes that even improvident decisions will eventually be rectified by the democratic processes.
>
> The general rules gives way, however, when a statute classifies by race, alienage or national origin. These factors are so seldom relevant to the achievement of any legitimate state interest that laws grounded in such considerations are deemed to reflect prejudice and antipathy—a view that those in the burdened class are not as worthy or deserving as others. For these reasons and because such discrimination is unlikely to be soon rectified by legislative means, these laws are subjected to strict scrutiny and will be sustained only if they are suitably tailored to serve a compelling state interest ... Similar oversight by the courts is due when state laws impinge on personal rights protected by the Constitution. ...

Legislative classifications based on gender also call for a heightened standard of review. That factor generally provides no sensible ground for differential treatment. ...A gender classification fails unless it is substantially related to a sufficiently important governmental interest. ... Because illegitimacy is beyond the individual's control and bears "no relation to the individual's ability to participate in and contribute to society," ... official discriminations resting on that characteristic are also subject to somewhat heightened review. Those restrictions "will survive equal protection scrutiny to the extent they are substantially related to a legitimate state interest." ...

We have declined, however, to extend heightened review to differential treatment based on age. ...

The lesson of *Murgia* is that where individuals in the group affected by a law have distinguishing characteristics relevant to interests the state has authority to implement, the courts have been very reluctant, as they should be in our federal system and with respect for the separations of powers, to closely scrutinize legislative choices as to whether, how and to what extent those interests should be pursued. In such cases, the Equal Protection Clause requires only a rational means to serve a legitimate end.

City of Cleburne v. Cleburne Living Center, 473 U.S. 432, 445 (1985). Since many laws regulating family relations are based upon or involve ideas about sex roles, and since the gender-equality movement of the 1970s raised social consciousness about unnecessary, antiquated, or inflexible sex-based stereotypes, the equal protection doctrine has assumed profound significance in determining the boundaries of permissible state-imposed gender-model compulsion and restraint.

3. Practical and Ethical Considerations

a. Constitutionalizing Family Law
Should the Court give more deference and respect to state policy when reviewing family laws than to state commercial laws or tort laws? Why/why not?

4. Bibliography

See infra at § D.4.

D. FAMILY AUTONOMY

1. Background

a. History of Noninterference
The principle of noninterference by the state with internal family matters has a long and distinguished genealogy. "The important western legal tradition of family autonomy and non-interference in the family can be traced to the Judeo-Christian tradition, early Germanic and Anglo-Saxon customary law, and Roman law, all of which had significant impact on modern law in the United States." Blakesley, *infra* at §1.01. Professor Carl Schneider observed, "As family traditions go, this one [family autonomy] . . . is quite old. But it is worth recalling that the view of the family as a haven and a regard for family privacy and autonomy are primarily products of the nineteenth century. Earlier centuries

did not perceive clear boundaries between the family and society, and were willing to intervene directly in families and to use families to carry out the policies of the state." Schneider, *infra* at 1835 n. 120. However, Professor Lee Teitelbaum has challenged the notion that the doctrine of family autonomy developed during the nineteenth century. He explains that classic liberal theory sees the development of the nineteenth century family "as a functional response to industrial capitalism. . .... The family as refuge ... was an essential condition of survival in industrial society." Teitelbaum, *infra* at 1137. Citing nineteenth century poor laws, the development of public education, the reform and refuge movement to protect neglected and dependent children, the origin of juvenile courts, and recognition of equal custodial rights of mothers, he argues "that during the nineteenth and twentieth centuries, when the private sphere of the household is said to have developed (for good or ill), public concern for an involvement in child rearing, and perhaps family relationships more generally, increased dramatically." *Id* at 1146–47 He opines that before the twentieth century the pure family autonomy or total recognition of the complete private sphere of family life was unknown. *Id.*

2. Statutes, Cases and Doctrines

a. *Meyer v. Nebraska*

Meyer v. Nebraska
262 U.S. 390 (1923)

JUSTICE McREYNOLDS delivered the opinion of the Court.

Plaintiff in error was tried and convicted in the district court for Hamilton county, Nebraska, under an information which charged that on May 25, 1920, while an instructor in Zion Parochial School he unlawfully taught the subject of reading in the German language to Raymond Parpart, a child of 10 years, who had not attained and successfully passed the eighth grade. The information is based upon "An act relating to the teaching of foreign languages in the state of Nebraska," approved April 9, 1919 (Laws 1919, c. 249), which follows: "Section 1. No person, individually or as a teacher, shall, in any private, denominational, parochial or public school, teach any subject to any person in any language than the English language. "Sec. 2. Languages, other than the English language, may be taught as languages only after a pupil shall have attained and successfully passed the eighth grade as evidenced by a certificate of graduation issued by the county superintendent of the county in which the child resides. "Sec. 3. Any person who violates any of the provisions of this act shall be deemed guilty of a misdemeanor and upon conviction, shall be subject to a fine of not less than twenty-five dollars ($25), nor more than one hundred dollars ($100), or be confined in the county jail for any period not exceeding thirty days for each offense. "Sec. 4. Whereas, an emergency exists, this act shall be in force from and after its passage and approval."

The Supreme Court of the state affirmed the judgment of conviction of Meyer [for teaching in a parochial school Bible stories in German to a child who had not passed the eighth grade.] ...

The obvious purpose of this statute was that the English language should be and become the mother tongue of all children reared in this state. The enactment of such a statute comes reasonably within the police power of the state. ...

"The problem for our determination is whether the statute as construed and applied unreasonably infringes the liberty guaranteed to the plaintiff in error by the Fourteenth Amendment: "No state ... shall deprive any person of life, liberty or property without due process of law."

While this court has not attempted to define with exactness the liberty thus guaranteed, the term has received much consideration and some of the included things have been definitely stated. Without doubt, it denotes not merely freedom from bodily restraint but also the right of the individual to contract, to engage in any of the common occupations of life, to acquire useful knowledge, to marry, establish a home and bring up children, to worship God according to the dictates of his own conscience, and generally to enjoy those privileges long recognized at common law as essential to the orderly pursuit of happiness by free men. ...The established doctrine is that this liberty may not be interfered with, under the guise of protecting the public interest, by legislative action which is arbitrary or without reasonable relation to some purpose within the competency of the state to effect. Determination by the Legislature of what constitutes proper exercise of police power is not final or conclusive but is subject to supervision by the courts. ...

The American people have always regarded education and acquisition of knowledge as matters of supreme importance which should be diligently promoted. The Ordinance of 1787 declares: 'Religion, morality and knowledge being necessary to good government and the happiness of mankind, schools and the means of education shall forever be encouraged.

Corresponding to the right of control, it is the natural duty of the parent to give his children education suitable to their station in life; and nearly all the states, including Nebraska, enforce this obligation by compulsory laws. Practically, education of the young is only possible in schools conducted by especially qualified persons who devote themselves thereto. The calling always has been regarded as useful and honorable, essential, indeed, to the public welfare. Mere knowledge of the German language cannot reasonably be regarded as harmful. Heretofore it has been commonly looked upon as helpful and desirable. Plaintiff in error taught this language in school as part of his occupation. His right thus to teach and the right of parents to engage him so to instruct their children, we think, are within the liberty of the amendment. The challenged statute forbids the teaching in school of any subject except in English; also the teaching of any other language until the pupil has attained and successfully passed the eighth grade, which is not usually accomplished before the age of twelve. The Supreme Court of the state has held that "the so-called ancient or dead languages" are not "within the spirit or the purpose of the act." ... Latin, Greek, Hebrew are not proscribed; but German, French, Spanish, Italian, and every other alien speech are within the ban. Evidently the Legislature has attempted materially to interfere with the calling of modern language teachers, with the opportunities of pupils to acquire knowledge, and with the power of parents to control the education of their own.

It is said the purpose of the legislation was to promote civic development by inhibiting training and education of the immature in foreign tongues and ideals before they could learn English and acquire American ideals, and "that the English language should be and become the mother tongue of all children reared in this state." It is also affirmed that the foreign born population is very large, that certain communities commonly use foreign words, follow foreign leaders, move in a foreign atmosphere, and that the children are thereby hindered from becoming citizens of the most useful type and the public safety is imperiled. That the state may do much, go very far, indeed, in order to improve the quality of its citizens, physically, mentally and morally, is clear; but the individual has certain fundamental rights which must be respected. The protection of the Constitution extends to all, to those who speak other languages as well as to those born with English on the tongue. Perhaps it would be highly advantageous if all had ready understanding of our ordinary speech, but this cannot be coerced by methods which conflict with the Constitution—a desirable end cannot be promoted by prohibited means.

For the welfare of his Ideal Commonwealth, Plato suggested a law which should provide: "That the wives of our guardians are to be common, and their children are to be common, and no parent is to know his own child, ... nor any child his parent. ... The proper officers will take the offspring of the good parents to the pen or fold, and there they will deposit them with certain nurses who dwell in a separate quarter; but the offspring of the inferior, or of the better when they chance to be deformed, will be put away in some mysterious, unknown place, as they should be." In order to submerge the individual and develop ideal citizens, Sparta assembled the males at seven into barracks and intrusted their subsequent education and training to official guardians. Although such measures have been deliberately approved by men of great genius their ideas touching the relation between individual and state were wholly different from those upon which our institutions rest; and it hardly will be affirmed that any Legislature could impose such restrictions upon the people of a state without doing violence to both letter and spirit of the Constitution. The desire of the Legislature to foster a homogeneous people with American ideals prepared readily to understand current discussions of civic matters is easy to appreciate. Unfortunate experiences during the late war and aversion toward every character of truculent adversaries were certainly enough to quicken that aspiration. But the means adopted, we think, exceed the limitations upon the power of the state and conflict with rights assured to plaintiff in error. The interference is plain enough and no adequate reason therefore in time of peace and domestic tranquility has been shown.

The power of the state to compel attendance at some school and to make reasonable regulations for all schools, including a requirement that they shall give instructions in English, is not questioned. Nor has challenge been made of the state's power to prescribe a curriculum for institutions which it supports. Those matters are not within the present controversy. Our concern is with the prohibition approved by the Supreme Court. ...[One case] pointed out that mere abuse incident to an occupation ordinarily useful is not enough to justify its abolition, although regulation may be entirely proper. No emergency has arisen which renders knowledge by a child of some language other than English so clearly harmful as to justify its inhibition with the consequent infringement of rights long freely enjoyed. We are constrained to conclude that the statute as applied is arbitrary and without reasonable relation to any end within the competency of the state. ...

Reversed.

Mr. Justice Holmes and Mr. Justice Sutherland, dissent.

b. *Moore v. City of East Cleveland*

Moore v. City of East Cleveland
431 U.S. 494 (1977)

MR. JUSTICE POWELL announced the judgment of the Court, and delivered an opinion in which MR. JUSTICE BRENNAN, MR. JUSTICE MARSHALL, and MR. JUSTICE BLACKMUN joined.

East Cleveland's housing ordinance, like many throughout the country, limits occupancy of a dwelling unit to members of a single family. 1351.02. But the ordinance contains an unusual and complicated definitional section that recognizes as a "family" only a few categories of related individuals. 1341.08. [Fn: Section 1341.08 provides: "Family" means a number of individuals related to the nominal head of the household or to the spouse of the nominal head of the household living as a single housekeeping unit in a single dwelling unit, but limited to the following: ... (D) ... a family may include not more than one dependent married or unmarried child ... and the spouse and dependent children of such dependent child. ..."] Because her family, living together in her home, fits none of those categories, appellant stands convicted of a criminal offense. The question in this case is whether the ordinance violates the Due Process Clause of the Fourteenth Amendment.

Appellant, Mrs. Inez Moore, lives in her East Cleveland home together with her son, Dale Moore, Sr., and her two grandsons, Dale, Jr., and John Moore, Jr. The two boys are first cousins rather than brothers; we are told that John came to live with his grandmother and with the elder and younger Dale Moore after his mother's death.

In early 1973, Mrs. Moore received a notice of violation from the city, stating that John was an "illegal occupant" and directing her to comply with the ordinance. When she failed to remove him from her home, the city filed a criminal charge. Mrs. Moore moved to dismiss, claiming that the ordinance was constitutionally invalid on its face. Her motion was overruled, and upon conviction she was sentenced to five days in jail and a $25 fine. The Ohio Court of Appeals affirmed after giving full consideration to her constitutional claims, and the Ohio Supreme Court denied review. We noted probable jurisdiction of her appeal, 425 U.S. 949 (1976).

II

The city argues that our decision in *Village of Belle Terre v. Boraas*, ... requires us to sustain the ordinance attacked here. Belle Terre, like East Cleveland, imposed limits on the types of groups that could occupy a single dwelling unit. ... We sustained the Belle Terre ordinance .... But one overriding factor sets this case apart from *Belle Terre*. The ordinance there affected only unrelated individuals. It expressly allowed all who were related by "blood, adoption, or marriage" to live together, and in sustaining the ordinance we were careful to note that it promoted "family needs" and "family values." ... East Cleveland, in contrast, has chosen to regulate the occupancy of its housing by slicing deeply into the family itself. This is no mere incidental result of the ordinance. On its face it selects certain categories of relatives who may live together and declares that others may not. ... [I]t makes a crime of a grandmother's choice to live with her grandson in circumstances like those presented here.

When a city undertakes such intrusive regulation of the family, neither *Belle Terre* nor *Euclid* governs; the usual judicial deference to the legislature is inappropriate. "This Court has long recognized that freedom of personal choice in matters of marriage and family life is one of the liberties protected by the Due Process Clause of the Fourteenth Amendment." *Cleveland Board of Education v. LaFleur*, 414 U.S. 632, 639–640 (1974). A host of cases, tracing their lineage to *Meyer v. Nebraska*, 262 U.S. 390, 399–401 (1923), and *Pierce v. Society of Sisters*, 268 U.S. 510, 534–535 (1925), have consistently acknowledged a "private realm of family life which the state cannot enter." *Prince v. Massachusetts*, 321 U.S. 158, 166 (1944). *See, e. g., Roe v. Wade*, 410 U.S. 113, 152–153 (1973); *Wisconsin v. Yoder*, 406 U.S. 205, 231–233 (1972); *Stanley v. Illinois*, 405 U.S. 645, 651 (1972); *Ginsberg v. New York*, 390 U.S. 629, 639 (1968); *Griswold v. Connecticut*, 381 U.S. 479 (1965); *id.*, at 495–496 (Goldberg, J., concurring); *id.*, at 502–503 (White, J., concurring); *Poe v. Ullman*, 367 U.S. 497, 542–544, 549–553 (1961) (Harlan, J., dissenting); cf. *Loving v. Virginia*, 388 U.S. 1, 12 (1967); *May v. Anderson*, 345 U.S. 528, 533 (1953); *Skinner v. Oklahoma ex rel. Williamson*, 316 U.S. 535, 541 (1942). Of course, the family is not beyond regulation. See *Prince v. Massachusetts, supra*, at 166. But when the government intrudes on choices concerning family living arrangements, this Court must examine carefully the importance of the governmental interests advanced and the extent to which they are served by the challenged regulation. *See Poe v. Ullman, supra*, at 554 (Harlan, J., dissenting).

When thus examined, this ordinance cannot survive. The city seeks to justify it as a means of preventing overcrowding, minimizing traffic and parking congestion, and avoiding an undue financial burden on East Cleveland's school system. Although these are legitimate goals, the ordinance before us serves them marginally, at best. For example, the ordinance permits any family consisting only of husband, wife, and unmarried children to live together, even if the family contains a half dozen licensed drivers, each with his or her own car. At the same time it forbids an adult brother and sister to share a household, even if both faithfully use public transportation. The ordinance would permit a grandmother to live with a single dependent son and children, even if his school-age children number a dozen, yet it forces Mrs. Moore to find another dwelling for her grandson John, simply because of the presence of his uncle and cousin in the same household. ...

III

The city would distinguish the cases based on *Meyer* and *Pierce*. It points out that none of them "gives grandmothers any fundamental rights with respect to grandsons," Brief for Appellee 18, and suggests that any constitutional right to live together as a family extends only to the nuclear family—essentially a couple and their dependent children.

To be sure, these cases did not expressly consider the family relationship presented here. ... But unless we close our eyes to the basic reasons why certain rights associated with the family have been accorded shelter under the Fourteenth Amendment's Due Process Clause, we cannot avoid applying the force and rationale of these precedents to the family choice involved in this case. Understanding those reasons requires careful attention to this Court's function under the Due Process Clause. Mr. Justice Harlan described it eloquently:

"Due process has not been reduced to any formula; its content cannot be determined by reference to any code. The best that can be said is that through the course of this Court's decisions it has represented the balance which our Nation, built upon postulates of respect for the liberty of the individual, has struck between that liberty and the demands of organized society. If the supplying of content to this Constitutional concept has of necessity been a rational process, it certainly has not been one where judges have felt free to roam where unguided speculation might take them. The balance of which I speak is the balance struck by this country, having regard to what history teaches are the traditions from which it developed as well as the traditions from which it broke. That tradition is a living thing. A decision of this Court which radically departs from it could not long survive, while a decision which builds on what has survived is likely to be sound.

No formula could serve as a substitute, in this area, for judgment and restraint. ... [T]he full scope of the liberty guaranteed by the Due Process Clause cannot be found in or limited by the precise terms of the specific guarantees elsewhere provided in the Constitution. This "liberty" is not a series of isolated points pricked out in terms of the taking of property; the freedom of speech, press, and religion; the right to keep and bear arms; the freedom from unreasonable searches and seizures; and so on. It is a rational continuum which, broadly speaking, includes a freedom from all substantial arbitrary impositions and purposeless restraints, ... and which also recognizes, what a reasonable and sensitive judgment must, that certain interests require particularly careful scrutiny of the state needs asserted to justify their abridgment." *Poe v. Ullman, supra*, at 542–543 (dissenting opinion).

Substantive due process has at times been a treacherous field for this Court. There are risks when the judicial branch gives enhanced protection to certain substantive liberties without the guidance of the more specific provisions of the Bill of Rights. As the history of the *Lochner* era demonstrates, there is reason for concern lest the only limits to such judicial intervention become the predilections of those who happen at the time to be Members of this Court. That history counsels caution and restraint. But it does not counsel abandonment, nor does it require what the city urges here: cutting off any protection of family rights at the first convenient, if arbitrary boundary— the boundary of the nuclear family.

Appropriate limits on substantive due process come not from drawing arbitrary lines but rather from careful "respect for the teachings of history [and] solid recognition of the basic values that underlie our society." *Griswold v. Connecticut*, 381 U.S., at 501 (Harlan, J., concurring). ... Our decisions establish that the Constitution protects the sanctity of the family precisely because the institution of the family is deeply rooted in this Nation's history and tradition. It is through the family that we inculcate and pass down many of our most cherished values, moral and cultural.

Ours is by no means a tradition limited to respect for the bonds uniting the members of the nuclear family. The tradition of uncles, aunts, cousins, and especially grandparents sharing a household along with parents and children has roots equally venerable and equally deserving of constitutional recognition. Over the years millions of our citizens have grown up in just such an environment, and most, surely, have profited from it. Even if conditions of modern society have brought about a decline in extended family households, they have not erased the accumulated wisdom of civilization, gained over the centuries and honored throughout our history, that supports a larger conception of the family. Out of choice, necessity, or a sense of family responsibility, it has been common for close relatives to draw together and participate in the duties and the satisfactions of a common home. Decisions concerning child rearing, which *Yoder, Meyer, Pierce* and other cases have recognized as entitled to constitutional protection, long have been shared with grandparents or other relatives who occupy the same household—indeed who may take on major responsibility for the rearing of the children. Especially in times of adversity, such as the death of a spouse or economic need, the broader family has tended to come together for mutual sustenance and to maintain or rebuild a secure home life. This is apparently what happened here.

Whether or not such a household is established because of personal tragedy, the choice of relatives in this degree of kinship to live together may not lightly be denied by the State. *Pierce* struck down an Oregon law requiring all children to attend the State's public schools, holding that the Constitution "excludes any general power of the State to standardize its children by forcing them to accept instruction from public teachers only." ... By the same token the Constitution prevents East Cleveland from standardizing its children—and its adults—by forcing all to live in certain narrowly defined family patterns.

Reversed.

MR. JUSTICE BRENNAN, with whom MR. JUSTICE MARSHALL joins, concurring.

I join the plurality's opinion. I agree that the Constitution is not powerless to prevent East Cleveland from prosecuting as a criminal and jailing a 63-year-old grandmother for refusing to expel from her home her now 10-year-old grandson who has lived with her and been brought up by her since his mother's death when he was less than a year old. ... The plurality's opinion conclusively demonstrates that classifying family patterns in this eccentric way is not a rational means of achieving the ends East Cleveland claims for its ordinance, and further that the ordinance unconstitutionally abridges the "freedom of personal choice in matters of ... family life [that] is one of the liberties protected by the Due Process Clause of the Fourteenth Amendment." *Cleveland Board of Education v. LaFleur*, 414 U.S. 632, 639–640 (1974). I write only to underscore the cultural myopia of the arbitrary boundary drawn by the East Cleveland ordinance in the light of the tradition of the American home that has been a feature of our society since our beginning as a Nation—the "tradition" in the plurality's words, "of uncles, aunts, cousins, and especially grandparents sharing a household along with parents and children ... ." Ante, at 504. The line drawn by this ordinance displays a depressing insensitivity toward the economic and emotional needs of a very large part of our society.

In today's America, the "nuclear family" is the pattern so often found in much of white suburbia. ... The Constitution cannot be interpreted, however, to tolerate the imposition by government upon the rest of us of white suburbia's preference in patterns of family living. The "extended family" that provided generations of early Americans with social services and economic and emotional support in times of hardship, and was the beachhead for successive waves of immigrants who populated our cities, remains not merely still a pervasive living pattern, but under the goad of brutal economic necessity, a prominent pattern—virtually a means of survival—for large numbers of the poor and deprived minorities of our society. For them compelled pooling of scant resources requires compelled sharing of a household.

The "extended" form is especially familiar among black families. We may suppose that this reflects the truism that black citizens, like generations of white immigrants before them, have been victims of economic and other disadvantages that would worsen if they were compelled to abandon extended, for nuclear, living patterns. Even in husband and wife households, 13% of black families compared with 3% of white families include relatives under 18 years old, in addition to the couple's own children. In black households whose head is an elderly woman, as in this case, the contrast is even more striking: 48% of such black households, compared with 10% of counterpart white households, include related minor children not offspring of the head of the household. ...

MR. JUSTICE STEVENS, concurring in the judgment.

In my judgment the critical question presented ... is whether East Cleveland's housing ordinance is a permissible restriction on appellant's right to use her own property as she see fit.

... [Justice Stevens reviews the zoning decisions of the Supreme Court, especially *Belle Terre*.]

... The intrusion on that basic property right has not previously gone beyond the point where the ordinance defines family to include only persons related by blood, marriage, or adoption. ...

[Fn. 7 ... East Cleveland is a predominantly Negro community, with a Negro City Manager and

City Commission."]

... Since this ordinance has not been shown to have any "substantial relation to the public health, safety, morals or general welfare" of the city ..., and since it cuts so deeply into a fundamental right normally associated with the ownership of residential property ... it must fall ....

CHIEF JUSTICE BURGER, dissenting ... [stressed failure to seek variance; no exhaustion.]

MR. JUSTICE STEWART, with whom MR. JUSTICE RHENQUIST joins, dissenting.

* * *

To suggest that the biological fact of common ancestry necessarily gives related persons constitutional rights of association superior to those of unrelated persons is to misunderstand the nature of the associational freedoms that the Constitution has been understood to protect. ...

The appellant is considerably closer to the constitutional mark in asserting that the East Cleveland ordinance intrudes upon "the private realm of family life which the state cannot enter." ...

* * *

When the Court has found that the Fourteenth Amendment placed a substantive limitation on a State's power to regulate, it has been in those rare cases in which the personal interests at issue have been deemed "implicit in the concept of ordered liberty." ... *Palko v. Connecticut,* 302 U.S. 319, 325 [Harlan, J., dissenting]. The interest that the appellant may have in permanently sharing a single kitchen and a suite of contiguous rooms with some of her relatives simply does not rise to that level. ...

MR. JUSTICE WHITE, dissenting.

* * *

There are some "liberties," however, which require that infringing legislation be given closer judicial scrutiny .... It is this category of interest which, as I understand it, Mr. Justice Stewart refers to an "implicit in the concept of ordered liberty." ...

I cannot believe that the interest in residing with more than one set of grandchildren is one that calls for any kind of heightened protection under the Due Process Clause.

... [Justice White also rejects Justice Powell's "deeply rooted in the country's traditions" test as "far too expansive a charter for this Court and a far less meaningful and confining guiding principle than" Stewart suggests. He concludes:]

Mrs. Moore's interest in having the offspring of more than one dependent son live with her qualifies as a liberty protected by the Due Process Clause; but, because of the nature of that particular interest, the demands of the Clause are satisfied once the Court is assured that the challenged proscription is the product of a duly enacted or promulgated statute, ordinance or regulation and that it is not wholly lacking in purpose or utility. ...

c. Notes and Questions

1) *Meyer* Questions

Who was the author of the *Meyer* opinion? What other famous case did he write? What "test" for identifying unwritten fundamental rights did this Court use?

2) *Moore* Notes

In *Moore,* the Supreme Court justices spoke openly about the test by which some family relations may be deemed entitled to special constitutional protection under the substantive due process doctrine. Did any single approach to determining the content of substantive due process win the endorsement of a majority of the Court? How important are long-established traditions in the various opinions?

3) Subsequent Substantive Due Process Family Autonomy Decisions

In *Pierce v. Society of Sisters,* 268 U.S. 510 (1925), the Supreme Court held that an Oregon law requiring parents of children between ages 8–16 to send their children to public school was unconstitutional. A private military academy and a religious order that operated an orphanage and a private school filed suit. The Supreme Court again emphasized the rights of parents in vindicating the private schools.

> [W]e think it entirely plain that the Act of 1922 unreasonably interferes with the liberty of parents and guardians to direct the upbringing and education of children under their control. ... The fundamental theory of liberty upon which all governments in this Union repose excludes any general power of the State to standardize its children by forcing them to accept instruction from public teachers only. The child is not the mere creature of the State; those who nurture him and direct his destiny have the right, coupled with the high duty, to recognize and prepare him for additional obligations.

268 U.S. at 534—35.

In *Prince v. Massachusetts,* 321 U.S. 158 (1944), the Court extended great rhetorical respect for parental prerogatives in child rearing, but upheld the conviction of a woman under Massachusetts child labor laws who allowed her nine-year-old niece and legal ward to accompany her and join her in selling religious tracts on public sidewalks. The Court emphasized family privacy, stating:

> It is cardinal with us that the custody, care and nurture of the child reside first in the parents, whose primary function and freedom include preparation for obligations the state can neither supply nor hinder. ... And it is in recognition of this that [*Meyer* and *Pierce*] have respected the private realm of family life which the state cannot enter.

Id. at 166. "But," the Court further said, "the family itself is not beyond regulation in the public interest ... ." *Id.* Finding that there were substantial risks of physical and other harm to children from selling unpopular religious tracts on busy public streets, the Court upheld the conviction.

In *Wisconsin v. Yoder,* 406 U.S. 205 (1972), the Court affirmed overturning the compulsory education law convictions of three Amish parents who refused to send their 14- and 15-year-old eighth-grade graduated children to school. The Court found that the effect of two additional years of schooling would contravene the freedom of religion of both the Amish parents and their children by exposing Amish children to worldly influences that would interfere with the religious development of Amish children and their integration into the Amish way of life. The Court also reaffirmed parental autonomy: "The history and culture of Western civilization reflect a strong tradition of parental concern for the nurture and upbringing of their children. This primary role of the parents in the upbringing of their children is now established beyond debate as an enduring American tradition." *Id.*

In *Parham v. J.R.,* 442 U.S. 584 (1979), the Supreme Court reversed a federal district court ruling that parents could not commit their children to state mental health facilities for treatment without an adversarial hearing before a formal tribunal. The Court held that ordinary commitment procedures in which a doctor approves the parental decision to commit the child are constitutionally sufficient, and emphasized the importance of parental authority.

Our jurisprudence historically has reflected Western Civilization concepts of the family as a unit with broad parental authority over minor children. Our cases have consistently followed that course. ... Surely, this includes a "high duty" to recognize symptoms of illness and seek and follow medical advice. The law's concept of the family rests on a presumption that parents possess what a child lacks in maturity, experience, and capacity for judgment required for making life's difficult decisions. More important, historically it has recognized that natural bonds of affection lead parents to act in the best interests of their children.

... That some parents "may at times be acting against the interests of their child" ... creates a basis for caution, but is hardly a reason to discard wholesale those pages of human experience that teach that parents generally do act in the child's best interests. The statist notion that governmental power should supersede parental authority in *all* cases because *some* parents abuse and neglect children is repugnant to American tradition.

Id at 602. Justice Stewart, concurring, added: "For centuries it has been a canon of the common law that parents speak for their minor children. So deeply imbedded in our traditions is this principle of law that the Constitution itself may compel a State to respect it." *Id* at 621 . *See further* ¶2 of §II of *Moore* plurality.

4) Principles Underlying Family Autonomy

Family autonomy is clearly a well-established and powerful doctrine, imbedded by numerous Supreme Court decisions in constitutional law. What are the theoretical underpinnings of this doctrine?

5) The "Trilemma" Conflict Between Family Autonomy and Other Values

Family autonomy is not the only value cherished by our society. Family autonomy may conflict with other important social values, especially the values of equality and personal privacy. James Fishkin has described three fundamental principles of modern liberalism: (1) the principle of merit (the belief that limited goods and opportunities ought to be distributed on the basis of merit), (2) the principle of equality (the belief that a person's life opportunities—i.e., chances to compete successfully for goods and opportunities on the basis of merit—should not depend upon immutable characteristics such as race, sex, etc.), and (3) the principle of family autonomy (the belief that the state should not coercively intervene in private family relations, child rearing practices, etc.). Fishkin asserts the "trilemma" of the impossibility of achievement of all three goals simultaneously.

The linchpin of the trilemma ... is the connection between the autonomy of families and the unequal development of talents and other qualifications that takes place under background conditions of inequality. If qualifications tend to develop unequally [in different families], then we are faced with a hard choice between the principle of merit and equality of life chances. Those who have unequal opportunities to develop qualifications [because of family failures or family disadvantages] will have unequal life chances, if assignment to positions is governed by the principle of merit. Correspondingly, they can have equal life chances only if assignment to positions violates the principle of merit. ...

Fishkin, *infra,* at 67. Thus, he argues:

> If taken seriously, the liberal strategy of attempting to ration fairly opportunities for
> the achievement of unequal positions would require systematic intrusions into the
> family. Only then could the maintenance of background inequalities be rendered
> compatible with equal opportunities for the development of talents and other
> qualifications.

Id. at 3, 4.

6) Doctrine of Judicial Noninterference

The principle of family autonomy has two dimensions. The first respects the
autonomy of the family unit, recognizing it as a self-governing association with exclusive
jurisdiction over internal matters. The second protects the interests of the family as
against the rest of the world. The principle of judicial noninterference in family disputes
has its most practical manifestation as a restraint upon judicial resolution of intrafamily
disputes. As a general rule, courts will not attempt to settle intrafamily disputes regarding
the domestic rights and duties of family members *inter se* in an ongoing family. The
exceptions to this rule generally fall into three categories: courts will act to resolve
intrafamily disputes (1) if the family is breaking up or has broken up (e.g., upon death,
incapacity, divorce, separation, desertion, abandonment, emancipation), (2) if the family
has failed to function as a family (e.g., in cases of neglect, abuse, abandonment, etc.), or
(3) if the conduct complained of involves a violation of exceptionally strong public
policy (e.g., if the life of a child or incompetent adult is at risk, child labor, compulsory
education, polygamy, etc.). Courts protect the family as an institution against intrusion by
others — usually the state. Dean Roscoe Pound explained many decades ago:

> Individual interests in the domestic relations require to be secured in two aspects.
> On the one hand, they must be secured as between the parties thereto. On the other
> hand, they must be secured as against the rest of the world. The law has never attempted
> to deal fully with the first of these tasks. Religion, *boni mores* and the internal discipline
> of the household have largely sufficed to secure the interests of the members of the
> household, as among themselves, and little has been needed beyond legal recognition
> and limitation of domestic discipline. The other task, on the contrary, has called forth a
> great deal of law. Here, as elsewhere, individual interests have been developed from
> group interests. But a further development has been required, namely, a development of
> individual interests of dependent members of the household, not only as against the
> world at large but also as against the husband or parent.

Pound, *infra*, at 179.

3. Practical and Ethical Considerations

Should lawyers follow a "noninterference" standard as well as the courts? Many of
the problems that clients in family law cases bring to lawyers are largely non-legal

problems (financial problems, problems of maturity, interpersonal relationship skill problems, emotional development deficits, childrearing problems, etc.); would parties sometimes be better off if the lawyer sent the client to a family counselor, clergy, financial advisor, child psychologist? Do lawyers make some family problems worse by their involvement—by their filing or threat of filing legal proceedings or obtaining orders, or exacerbating feelings by coercive legal measures? Is it ethical for lawyers to fail to refer clients to other professionals when that might help the clients? What are the implications of the multi-disciplinary practice rules for such connections?

4. Bibliography

Contemporary Family Law, Vol. 1, Ch. 1 (Lynn D. Wardle, Christopher Blakesley & Jacqueline Y. Parker eds., 1988).

James S. Fishkin, Justice, Equal Opportunity and the Family (1998).

Bruce C. Hafen, *The Constitutional Status of Marriage, Kinship, and Sexual Privacy*, 81 Mich. L. Rev. 464 (1983).

Sanford N. Katz & Jeffrey A. Kuhn, Recommendations for A Model Family Court: A Report from the National Family Court Symposium 7 (1991).

Steven J. Messinger, *On Moving Toward a Family Court in Georgia Without the Need for Constitutional Revision*, 12 Ga. St. U. L. Rev. 667 (1996).

Roscoe Pound, *Individual Interests in the Domestic Relations*, 14 Mich. L. Rev. 177 (1916).

Carl E. Schneider, *Moral Discourse and the Transformation of American Family Law* 83 Mich. L. Rev. 1803 (1985).

Jana B. Singer, *The Privatization of Family Law*, 1992 Wisc. L. Rev. 1443 (1992).

Lee E. Teitelbaum, *Family History and Family Law*, 1985 Wisc. L.Rev. 1135 (1985).,

Lynn D. Wardle, *Liberty, Equality & the Quest for Family Justice in the United States* in Families & Justice 208–229 (Brussels: Bruylant, 1997).

PART II
THE CREATION OF SPOUSAL RELATIONS

CHAPTER 3

Marriage Regulation in General; Constitutional Right to Marry; Marriage Essentials; Monogamy

A. MARRIAGE REGULATIONS IN GENERAL

1. Background

a. Importance of Marriage Regulation

The regulation of marriage is one of the most important concerns in all legal systems. Over 2000 years ago, Aristotle wrote that regulating marriage age was the "first care" of prudent legislators. Aristotle, *Politica* in 10 the Works of Aristotle 1334–35 (W. Ross ed. 1921). Today the regulation of marriage is no less important. It is also ubiquitous; no matter how sophisticated or primitive the legal system, marriage is regulated in all nations. Why? Is the oft-celebrated importance of marriage to social order merely a widely-accepted myth or fable?

b. Marriage at Common Law

Blackstone summarized the law of England regarding marriage in his day as follows:

> Our law considers marriage in no other light than as a civil contract. The *holiness* of the matrimonial state is left entirely to the ecclesiastical law: the temporal courts not having jurisdiction to consider unlawful marriage as a sin, but merely as a civil inconvenience. The punishment, therefore, of annulling, of incestuous or other unscriptural marriages, is the province of the spiritual courts; which act *pro salute animae* (for the welfare of the soul). And, taking it in this civil light, the law treats it as it does all other contracts: allowing it to be good and valid in all cases, where the parties at the time of making it were, in the first place, *willing* to contract; secondly, *able* to contract; and lastly, actually *did* contract, in the proper forms and solemnities required by law.

Blackstone, *infra at* *434.

2. Statutes, Cases, and Doctrines

a. Marriage is Favored

American legal policy historically has strongly favored marriage, and nominally still does. This sentiment is reflected in legislation and judicial decisions that support and legitimate existing marriages, which (at least retrospectively) disfavor interpretation or application of marriage restrictions in a way that would invalidate intended (or even *de facto*) marriages, and, until recently, discouraging and even restricting divorce.

The importance of marriage to society and the favored status of marriage in law have been praised in numerous Supreme Court opinions. In the19th century, the Supreme Court described the importance of marriage in these terms: "Upon it society may be said to be built, and out of its fruits spring social relations and social obligations and duties, with which government is necessarily required to deal." *Reynolds v. United States,* 98 U.S. 145, 165 (1878). In *Murphy v. Ramsey,* 114 U.S. 15, 45 (1885), the Court observed that "no legislation can be supposed more ... necessary in the founding of a free, self-governing commonwealth ... than that which seeks to establish it on the basis of the idea of the family, as consisting in and springing from the union for life of one man and one woman in the holy estate of matrimony; the sure foundation of all that is stable and noble in our civilization; the best guaranty of that reverent morality which is the source of all beneficent progress in social and political movement." In *Maynard v. Hill,* 125 U.S. 190 (1888), Justice Field both glorified marriage and endorsed legislative restrictions of it when he declared:

> Marriage, as creating the most important relation in life, as having more to do with the morals and civilization of a people than any other institution, has always been subject to the control of the legislature. That body prescribes the age at which parties may contract to marry, the procedure or form essential to constitute marriage, the duties and obligations it creates, its effects upon the property rights of both, present and prospective, and the acts which may constitute grounds for its dissolution.

125 U.S. at 205. (In that case, the court also recognized the right of the legislature to establish rules regulating the creation and dissolution of marriage and upheld a private legislative bill of divorce granted a man *ex parte,* without notice to his wife, who lived in another state.) *See also Meyer v. Nebraska,* 262 U.S. 390, 393 (1923); *Skinner v. Oklahoma,* 316 U.S. 535 (1942); and *Griswold v. Connecticut,* 381 U.S. 479, 484 (1965). The court has reiterated and enhanced these statements about marriage's importance in many other cases since.

b. Notes and Questions

Why is marriage important? What would be the effect upon society if the law ceased to regulate marriage? Find the parallel case law in your homestate celebrating the importance of marriage. Do any provisions of your homestate constitution refer to or explicitly protect marriage as an institution? Both President Clinton and President Bush supported welfare reform legislation that would provide states with up to $350 million for programs that would encourage, strengthen and support marriage—such as marriage skill training. Should the government encourage marriage that way? Why/not?

3. Practical and Ethical Considerations

a. Mere Rhetoric?

If marriage is so important to society, why is it so unregulated? It is commonly (and accurately) said that it is harder to get a driver's license in America than a marriage license. When things are really important to Americans, they tend to protect them with laws, legal processes, and lawyers. Do the absence of significant legal requirements, the presence of only modest procedural requirements, and the universal American state policy that professional legal assistance is not mandated (or even encouraged) in getting married suggest anything about how we value marriage? By contrast, in Europe, marriage regulations are strict, formalities bureaucratic, waiting periods long, and the divorce rate much lower than in the USA. Is there any causal connection between such legal requirements and the relative rates of divorce?

b. Practice

Would greater involvement of lawyers before marriage likely have any effect upon marriage stability or success? If so, what effect? Under what conditions do you think persons considering marriage are likely to consult with an attorney?

c. Ethical Dilemmas

If a lawyer advises a couple regarding the legality of a proposed marriage, can he or she later represent one of them in a divorce action? If the attorney advises one of them about terms of a proposed ante-nuptial contract, may he or she represent the other in a divorce action? May a lawyer ethically advise parties to go to another jurisdiction to enter into a marriage that is forbidden in the state of their residence and where the lawyer practices?

4. Bibliography

See B.4., infra.

B. THE CONSTITUTIONAL RIGHT TO MARRY

1. Background

a. History of a Constitutional Right to Marry

Since 1790, the U.S. Supreme Court has decided more than 60 cases discussing the right to marry, marriage rights, etc. About fifteen of them (all decided since 1920) have some constitutional aspect. Wardle, 1998, *infra.* The first Supreme Court case to mention a constitutional right to marry was *Meyer v. Nebraska*, 290 U.S. 390 (1923). Prior to that decision, the Supreme Court cases that included phrases like "right to marry" or "marriage rights" were referring to the property or inheritance rights flowing from marital status, or to the legal capacity to marry under the marriage laws then in effect. A few cases decided before 1920 emphasized the power of the legislature to regulate the marital relationship, and the importance of legislative control of marriage—two important elements of the later-developed constitutional right to marry. *See id.*
Skinner v. Oklahoma, 316 U.S. 535 (1942). In *Skinner,* the Court overturned an order for involuntary sterilization of a prisoner, noting: "We are dealing here with legislation which involves one of the basic civil rights of man. Marriage and procreation are fundamental to the very existence and survival of the race." *Id.* at 541. In *Griswold v. Connecticut*, 381 U.S. 479 (1965), concerning distribution of contraceptives to married couples, the Court noted:

We deal with a right of privacy older than the Bill of Rights—older than our political parties, older than our school system. Marriage is a coming together for better or for worse, hopefully enduring, and intimate to the degree of being sacred. It is an association that promotes a way of life, not causes; a harmony in living, not political faiths; a bilateral loyalty, not commercial or social projects. Yet it is an association for as noble a purpose as any involved in our prior decisions.

Id. at 486. Thus, before 1966, the Supreme Court had never held that there was a constitutional right to marry, but had alluded to such a right in dicta in cases dealing with other (nonmarital) issues. Since 1967, the Supreme Court has continued to mention the constitutional right to marry in dicta in more than a dozen cases. The Court has made specific reference to a constitutional right to marry in at least five recent cases in which it reviewed direct or indirect marriage regulations. *Loving v. Virginia*, 388 U.S. 1 (1967) (antimiscegenation laws unconstitutional); *Boddie v. Connecticut*, 401 U.S. 371 (1971) (divorce filing fee for indigents unconstitutional); *Sosna v. Iowa*, 419 U.S. 393 (1975) (divorce residency requirement upheld); *Zablocki v. Redhail*, 434 U.S. 374 (1978) (law restricting marriage by "deadbeat dads" unconstitutional); *Turner v. Safley*, 482 U.S. 78 (1987) (near-ban on prisoner marriages invalid). These cases establish that the right to marry is a constitutionally protected right because it is deeply rooted in the history and traditions of our people; because it is one of the natural common denominators of all humanity and of all civilization; because it is essential to the ordered liberty of our society; because it is the principal foundation for home and family; and because it is closely linked with responsible procreation and childrearing. The cases also consistently indicate that the regulation of marriage is primarily a matter of legislation, and that because marriage is so important to society, some regulation of the right to marriage is both expected and appropriate. However, there are some limits beyond which the Constitution does not permit the government to restrict the right to marry; but the standard of judicial review of laws regulating the right to marry usually is more accommodating than the ordinary standard of strict scrutiny applicable to laws infringing upon fundamental rights. Wardle, 1998, *infra*.

2. Statutes, Cases, and Doctrines

a. *Loving v. Virginia*

Richard Perry Loving et ux., v. Virginia
388 U.S. 1 (1967)

MR. CHIEF JUSTICE WARREN delivered the opinion of the Court.

This case presents a constitutional question never addressed by this Court: whether a statutory scheme adopted by the State of Virginia to prevent marriages between persons solely on the basis of racial classifications violates the Equal Protection and Due Process Clauses of the Fourteenth Amendment. For reasons which seem to us to reflect the central meaning of those constitutional commands, we conclude that these statutes cannot stand consistently with the Fourteenth Amendment.

In June 1958, two residents of Virginia, Mildred Jeter, a Negro woman, and Richard Loving, a white man, were married in the District of Columbia pursuant to its laws. Shortly after their marriage, the Lovings returned to Virginia and established their marital abode in Caroline County. At the October

Term, 1958, of the Circuit Court of Caroline County, a grand jury issued an indictment charging the Lovings with violating Virginia's ban on interracial marriages. On January 6, 1959, the Lovings pleaded guilty to the charge and were sentenced to one year in jail; however, the trial judge suspended the sentence for a period of 25 years on the condition that the Lovings leave the State and not return to Virginia together for 25 years. He stated in an opinion that:

> Almighty God created the races white, black, yellow, malay and red, and he placed them on separate continents. And but for the interference with his arrangement there would be no cause for such marriages. The fact that he separated the races shows that he did not intend for the races to mix.

After their convictions, the Lovings took up residence in the District of Columbia. On November 6, 1963, they filed a motion in the state trial court to vacate the judgment and set aside the sentence on the ground that the statutes which they had violated were repugnant to the Fourteenth Amendment. The motion not having been decided by October 28, 1964, the Lovings instituted a class action in the United States District Court for the Eastern District of Virginia requesting that a three-judge court be convened to declare the Virginia antimiscegenation statutes unconstitutional and to enjoin state officials from enforcing their convictions. On January 22, 1965, the state trial judge denied the motion to vacate the sentences, and the Lovings perfected an appeal to the Supreme Court of Appeals of Virginia. On February 11, 1965, the three-judge District Court continued the case to allow the Lovings to present their constitutional claims to the highest state court.

The Supreme Court of Appeals upheld the constitutionality of the antimiscegenation statutes and, after modifying the sentence, affirmed the convictions. The Lovings appealed this decision, and we noted probable jurisdiction on December 12, 1966 ....

The two statutes under which appellants were convicted and sentenced are part of a comprehensive statutory scheme aimed at prohibiting and punishing interracial marriages. The Lovings were convicted of violating § 20-58 of the Virginia Code:

> Leaving State to evade law.–If any white person and colored person shall go out of this State, for the purpose of being married, and with the intention of returning, and be married out of it, and afterwards return to and reside in it, cohabiting as man and wife, they shall be punished as provided in § 20-59, and the marriage shall be governed by the same law as if it had been solemnized in this State. The fact of their cohabitation here as man and wife shall be evidence of their marriage.

Section 20-59, which defines the penalty for miscegenation, provides:

> Punishment for marriage.-If any white person intermarry with a colored person, or any colored person intermarry with a white person, he shall be guilty of a felony and shall be punished by confinement in the penitentiary for not less than one nor more than five years.

...The Lovings have never disputed in the course of this litigation that Mrs. Loving is a "colored person" or that Mr. Loving is a "white person" within the meanings given those terms by the Virginia statutes.

Virginia is now one of 16 States which prohibit and punish marriages on the basis of racial classifications. Penalties for miscegenation arose as an incident to slavery and have been common in Virginia since the colonial period. The present statutory scheme dates from the adoption of the Racial Integrity Act of 1924, passed during the period of extreme nativism which followed the end of the First World War. The central features of this Act, and current Virginia law, are the absolute prohibition of a "white person" marrying other than another "white person," a prohibition against issuing marriage licenses until the issuing official is satisfied that the applicants' statements as to their race are correct, certificates of "racial composition" to be kept by both local and state registrars, and the carrying forward of earlier prohibitions against racial intermarriage.

I.

* * *

While the state court is no doubt correct in asserting that marriage is a social relation subject to the State's police power, *Maynard v. Hill* ... (1888), the State does not contend in its argument before this Court that its powers to regulate marriage are unlimited notwithstanding the commands of the Fourteenth Amendment. Nor could it do so in light of *Meyer v. State of Nebraska* ... and *Skinner v. State of Oklahoma* .... Instead, the State argues that the meaning of the Equal Protection Clause, as illuminated by the statements of the Framers, is only that state penal laws containing an interracial element as part of the definition of the offense must apply equally to whites and Negroes in the sense that members of each race are punished to the same degree. Thus, the State contends that, because its miscegenation statutes punish equally both the white and the Negro participants in an interracial marriage, these statutes, despite their reliance on racial classifications do not constitute an invidious discrimination based upon race. The second argument advanced by the State assumes the validity of its equal application theory. The argument is that, if the Equal Protection Clause does not outlaw miscegenation statutes because of their reliance on racial classifications, the question of constitutionality would thus become whether there was any rational basis for a State to treat interracial marriages differently from other marriages. On this question, the State argues, the scientific evidence is substantially in doubt and, consequently, this Court should defer to the wisdom of the state legislature in adopting its policy of discouraging interracial marriages. Because we reject the notion that the mere "equal application" of a statute containing racial classifications is enough to remove the classifications from the Fourteenth Amendment's proscription of all invidious racial discriminations, we do not accept the State's contention that these statutes should be upheld if there is any possible basis for concluding that they serve a rational purpose. The mere fact of equal application does not mean that our analysis of these statutes should follow the approach we have taken in cases involving no racial discrimination where the Equal Protection Clause has been arrayed against a statute discriminating between the kinds of advertising which may be displayed on trucks in New York City..., or an exemption in Ohio's ad valorem tax for merchandise owned by a non-resident in a storage warehouse.... In these cases, involving distinctions not drawn according to race, the Court has merely asked whether there is any rational foundation for the discriminations, and has deferred to the wisdom of the state legislatures. In the case at bar, however, we deal with statutes containing racial classifications, and the fact of equal application does not immunize the statute from the very heavy burden of justification which the Fourteenth Amendment has traditionally required of state statutes drawn according to race.

The State argues that statements in the Thirty-ninth Congress about the time of the passage of the Fourteenth Amendment indicate that the Framers did not intend the Amendment to make unconstitutional state miscegenation laws. Many of the statements alluded to by the State concern the debates over the Freedmen's Bureau Bill, which President Johnson vetoed, and the Civil Rights Act of 1866, 14 Stat. 27, enacted over his veto. While these statements have some relevance to the intention of Congress in submitting the Fourteenth Amendment, it must be understood that they pertained to the passage of specific statutes and not to the broader, organic purpose of a constitutional amendment. As for the various statements directly concerning the Fourteenth Amendment, we have said in connection with a related problem, that although these historical sources "cast some light" they are not sufficient to resolve the problem; "(a)t best, they are inconclusive. The most avid proponents of the post-War Amendments undoubtedly intended them to remove all legal distinctions among 'all persons born or naturalized in the United States.' Their opponents, just as certainly, were antagonistic to both the letter and the spirit of the Amendments and wished them to have the most limited effect." *Brown v. Board of*

Education of Topeka ...(1954). ... We have rejected the proposition that the debates in the Thirty-ninth Congress or in the state legislatures which ratified the Fourteenth Amendment supported the theory advanced by the State, that the requirement of equal protection of the laws is satisfied by penal laws defining offenses based on racial classifications so long as white and Negro participants in the offense were similarly punished. *McLaughlin v. State of Florida* ....

The State finds support for its "equal application" theory in the decision of the Court in *Pace v. State of Alabama* .... In that case, the Court upheld a conviction under an Alabama statute forbidding adultery or fornication between a white person and a Negro which imposed a greater penalty than that of a statute proscribing similar conduct by members of the same race. The Court reasoned that the statute could not be said to discriminate against Negroes because the punishment for each participant in the offense was the same. However, as recently as the 1964 Term, in rejecting the reasoning of that case, we stated "*Pace* represents a limited view of the Equal Protection Clause which has not withstood analysis in the subsequent decisions of this Court." *McLaughlin v. Florida* .... As we there demonstrated, the Equal Protection Clause requires the consideration of whether the classifications drawn by any statute constitute an arbitrary and invidious discrimination. The clear and central purpose of the Fourteenth Amendment was to eliminate all official state sources of invidious racial discrimination in the States. *Slaughter-House Cases* ... (1873); *Strauder v. State of West Virginia* ... (1880); *Ex parte Virginia* ... (1880); *Shelley v. Kraemer* ... (1948); *Burton v. Wilmington Parking Authority* ... (1961).

There can be no question but that Virginia's miscegenation statutes rest solely upon distinctions drawn according to race. The statutes proscribe generally accepted conduct if engaged in by members of different races. Over the years, this Court has consistently repudiated "(d)istinctions between citizens solely because of their ancestry" as being "odious to a free people whose institutions are founded upon the doctrine of equality." *Hirabayashi v. United States* ... (1943). At the very least, the Equal Protection Clause demands that racial classifications, especially suspect in criminal statutes, be subjected to the "most rigid scrutiny," *Korematsu v. United States* ... (1944), and, if they are ever to be upheld, they must be shown to be necessary to the accomplishment of some permissible state objective, independent of the racial discrimination which it was the object of the Fourteenth Amendment to eliminate. Indeed, two members of this Court have already stated that they "cannot conceive of a valid legislative purpose ... which makes the color of a person's skin the test of whether his conduct is a criminal offense." *McLaughlin v. Florida* ... (Stewart, J., joined by Douglas, J., concurring).

There is patently no legitimate overriding purpose independent of invidious racial discrimination which justifies this classification. The fact that Virginia prohibits only interracial marriages involving white persons demonstrates that the racial classifications must stand on their own justification, as measures designed to maintain White Supremacy. We have consistently denied the constitutionality of measures which restrict the rights of citizens on account of race. There can be no doubt that restricting the freedom to marry solely because of racial classifications violates the central meaning of the Equal Protection Clause.

II.

These statutes also deprive the Lovings of liberty without due process of law in violation of the Due Process Clause of the Fourteenth Amendment. The freedom to marry has long been recognized as one of the vital personal rights essential to the orderly pursuit of happiness by free men.

Marriage is one of the "basic civil rights of man," fundamental to our very existence and survival. *Skinner v. State of Oklahoma* ... (1942). See also *Maynard v. Hill* ... (1888). To deny this fundamental freedom on so unsupportable a basis as the racial classifications embodied in these statutes, classifications so directly subversive of the principle of equality at the heart of the Fourteenth Amendment, is surely to deprive all the State's citizens of liberty without due process of law. The Fourteenth Amendment requires that the freedom of choice to marry not be restricted by invidious racial discriminations. Under our Constitution, the freedom to marry or not marry, a person of another race resides with the individual and cannot be infringed by the State.

These convictions must be reversed. It is so ordered.

Reversed.

MR. JUSTICE STEWART, concurring.

I have previously expressed the belief that "it is simply not possible for a state law to be valid under our Constitution which makes the criminality of an act depend upon the race of the actor." *McLaughlin v. State of Florida* .... Because I adhere to that belief, I concur in the judgment of the Court.

b. *Zablocki v. Redhail*

Zablocki v. Redhail
434 U.S. 374 (1978)

MR. JUSTICE MARSHALL delivered the opinion of the Court.

At issue in this case is the constitutionality of a Wisconsin statute, Wis.Stat. §§ 245.10(1), (4), (5) (1973), which provides that members of a certain class of Wisconsin residents may not marry, within the State or elsewhere, without first obtaining a court order granting permission to marry. The class is defined by the statute to include any "Wisconsin resident having minor issue not in his custody and which he is under obligation to support by any court order or judgment." The statute specifies that court permission cannot be granted unless the marriage applicant submits proof of compliance with the support obligation and, in addition, demonstrates that the children covered by the support order "are not then and are not likely thereafter to become public charges." ...

I.

Appellee Redhail is a Wisconsin resident who, under the terms of § 245.10, is unable to enter into a lawful marriage in Wisconsin or elsewhere so long as he maintains his Wisconsin residency. The facts, according to the stipulation filed by the parties in the District Court, are as follows. In January 1972, when appellee was a minor and a high school student, a paternity action was instituted against him in Milwaukee County Court, alleging that he was the father of a baby girl born out of wedlock on July 5, 1971. After he appeared and admitted that he was the child's father, the court entered an order on May 12, 1972, adjudging appellee the father and ordering him to pay $109 per month as support for the child until she reached 18 years of age. From May 1972 until August 1974, appellee was unemployed and indigent, and consequently was unable to make any support payments.

On September 27, 1974, appellee filed an application for a marriage license with appellant Zablocki, the County Clerk of Milwaukee County, and a few days later the application was denied on the sole ground that appellee had not obtained a court order granting him permission to marry, as required by § 245.10. Although appellee did not petition a state court thereafter, it is stipulated that he would not have been able to satisfy either of the statutory prerequisites for an order granting permission to marry. First, he had not satisfied his support obligations to his illegitimate child, and as of December 1974 there was an arrearage in excess of $3,700. Second, the child had been a public charge since her birth, receiving benefits under the Aid to Families with Dependent Children program. It is stipulated that the child's benefit payments were such that she would have been a public charge even if appellee had been current in his support payments.

On December 24, 1974, appellee filed his complaint in the District Court, on behalf of himself and the class of all Wisconsin residents who had been refused a marriage license pursuant to § 245.10(1) ....The statute was attacked on the grounds that it deprived appellee, and the class he sought to represent of equal protection and due process rights secured by the First, Fifth, Ninth, and Fourteenth Amendments to the United States Constitution.

... [A three-judge district court ruled that the law infringed upon the fundamental right to marry, strict scrutiny was required for Equal Protection analysis; the law was not necessary, and was enjoined.]

II.

In evaluating §§ 245.10(1), (4), (5) under the Equal Protection Clause, "we must first determine what burden of justification the classification created thereby must meet, by looking to the nature of the classification and the individual interests affected." Since our past decisions make clear that the right to marry is of fundamental importance, and since the classification at issue here significantly interferes with the exercise of that right, we believe that "critical examination" of the state interests advanced in support of the classification is required. ...

The leading decision of this Court on the right to marry is *Loving v. Virginia* .... The Court's opinion could have rested solely on the ground that the statutes discriminated on the basis of race in violation of the Equal Protection Clause. ...But the Court went on to hold that the laws arbitrarily deprived the couple of a fundamental liberty protected by the Due Process Clause, the freedom to marry. ...

Although *Loving* arose in the context of racial discrimination, prior and subsequent decisions of this Court confirm that the right to marry is of fundamental importance for all individuals. Long ago, in *Maynard v. Hill* ..., the Court characterized marriage as "the most important relation in life" ... and as "the foundation of the family and of society, without which there would be neither civilization nor progress" ... . In *Meyer v. Nebraska*, ... the Court recognized that the right "to marry, establish a home and bring up children" is a central part of the liberty protected by the Due Process Clause..., and in *Skinner v. Oklahoma ex rel. Williamson* ..., marriage was described as "fundamental to the very existence and survival of the race" ....

More recent decisions have established that the right to marry is part of the fundamental "right of privacy" implicit in the Fourteenth Amendment's Due Process Clause. In *Griswold v. Connecticut* ..., the Court observed:

> We deal with a right of privacy older than the Bill of Rights—older than our political parties, older than our school system. Marriage is a coming together for better or for worse, hopefully enduring, and intimate to the degree of being sacred. It is an association that promotes a way of life, not causes; a harmony in living, not political faiths; a bilateral loyalty, not commercial or social projects. Yet it is an association for as noble a purpose as any involved in our prior decisions. ...

Cases subsequent to *Griswold* and *Loving* have routinely categorized the decision to marry as among the personal decisions protected by the right of privacy. ... For example, last Term in *Carey v. Population Services International* ..., we declared:

> While the outer limits ... have not been marked by the Court, it is clear that among the decisions that an individual may make without unjustified government interference are personal decisions "relating to marriage, *Loving v. Virginia* ...; procreation, *Skinner v. Oklahoma ex rel. Williamson* ...; contraception, *Eisenstadt v. Baird* ...; family relationships, *Prince v. Massachusetts* ...; and child rearing and education, *Pierce v. Society of Sisters* ...; *Meyer v. Nebraska* ....

See also Cleveland Board of Education v. LaFleur ... (1974) ("This Court has long recognized that freedom of personal choice in matters of marriage and family life is one of the liberties protected by the Due Process Clause of the Fourteenth Amendment") ....

It is not surprising that the decision to marry has been placed on the same level of importance as decisions relating to procreation, childbirth, child rearing, and family relationships. As the facts of this case illustrate, it would make little sense to recognize a right of privacy with respect to other matters of family life and not with respect to the decision to enter the relationship that is the foundation of the family in our society. The woman whom appellee desired to marry had a fundamental right to seek an abortion of their expected child, *see Roe v. Wade, supra,* or to bring the child into life to suffer the myriad social, if not economic, disabilities that the status of illegitimacy brings .... Surely, a decision to marry and raise the child in a traditional family setting must receive equivalent protection. And, if appellee's right to procreate means anything at all, it must imply some right to enter the only relationship in which the State of Wisconsin allows sexual relations legally to take place. [Fn11-

Wisconsin punishes fornication as a criminal offense: "Whoever has sexual intercourse with a person not his spouse may be fined not more than $200 or imprisoned not more than 6 months or both." Wis.Stat. § 944.15 (1973).]

By reaffirming the fundamental character of the right to marry, we do not mean to suggest that every state regulation which relates in any way to the incidents of or prerequisites for marriage must be subjected to rigorous scrutiny. To the contrary, reasonable regulations that do not significantly interfere with decisions to enter into the marital relationship may legitimately be imposed. See *Califano v. Jobst* .... The statutory classification at issue here, however, clearly does interfere directly and substantially with the right to marry.

... Some of those in the affected class, like appellee, will never be able to obtain the necessary court order, because they either lack the financial means to meet their support obligations or cannot prove that their children will not become public charges. These persons are absolutely prevented from getting married. Many others, able in theory to satisfy the statute's requirements, will be sufficiently burdened by having to do so that they will in effect be coerced into forgoing their right to marry. And even those who can be persuaded to meet the statute's requirements suffer a serious intrusion into their freedom of choice in an area in which we have held such freedom to be fundamental. [Fn12 - The directness and substantiality of the interference with the freedom to marry distinguish the instant case from *Califano v. Jobst*, ...]

III.

When a statutory classification significantly interferes with the exercise of a fundamental right, it cannot be upheld unless it is supported by sufficiently important state interests and is closely tailored to effectuate only those interests. ... Appellant asserts that two interests are served by the challenged statute: the [statute] furnishes an opportunity to counsel the applicant as to the necessity of fulfilling his prior support obligations: and the welfare of the out-of-custody children is protected. We may accept for present purposes that these are legitimate and substantial interests, but, since the means selected by the State for achieving these interests unnecessarily impinge on the right to marry, the statute cannot be sustained.

* * *

The statute actually enacted, however, does not expressly require or provide for any counseling whatsoever, nor for any automatic granting of permission to marry by the court, and thus it can hardly be justified as a means for ensuring counseling of the persons within its coverage. ...

Th[e] "collection device" rationale cannot justify the statute's broad infringement on the right to marry [either].

First, with respect to individuals who are unable to meet the statutory requirements, the statute merely prevents the applicant from getting married, without delivering any money at all into the hands of the applicant's prior children. More importantly, regardless of the applicant's ability or willingness to meet the statutory requirements, the State already has numerous other means for exacting compliance with support obligations, means that are at least as effective as the instant statute's and yet do not impinge upon the right to marry. ...

There is also some suggestion that § 245.10 protects the ability of marriage applicants to meet support obligations to prior children by preventing the applicants from incurring new support obligations. But the challenged provisions ... are grossly underinclusive with respect to this purpose, since they do not limit in any way new financial commitments by the applicant other than those arising out of the contemplated marriage. The statutory classification is substantially overinclusive as well: Given the possibility that the new spouse will actually better the applicant's financial situation, by contributing income from a job or otherwise, the statute in many cases may prevent affected individuals from improving their ability to satisfy their prior support obligations. ... Since the support obligation is the same whether the child is born in or out of wedlock, the net result of preventing the marriage is simply more illegitimate children.

The statutory classification created by §§ 245.10(1), (4), (5) thus cannot be justified by the interests advanced in support of it. The judgment of the District Court is, accordingly,

Affirmed.

MR. CHIEF JUSTICE BURGER, concurring.

I join Mr. Justice MARSHALL's opinion for the Court. With all deference, Mr. Justice STEVENS' opinion does not persuade me that the analysis in the Court's opinion is in any significant way inconsistent with the Court's unanimous holding in *Califano v. Jobst* .... Unlike the intentional and substantial interference with the right to marry effected by the Wisconsin statute at issue here, the Social Security Act provisions challenged in *Jobst* did not constitute an "attempt to interfere with the individual's freedom to make a decision as important as marriage" ..., and, at most, had an indirect impact on that decision. It is with this understanding that I join the Court's opinion today.

MR. JUSTICE STEWART, concurring in the judgment.

I cannot join the opinion of the Court. To hold, as the Court does, that the Wisconsin statute violates the Equal Protection Clause seems to me to misconceive the meaning of that constitutional guarantee.

...

The problem in this case is not one of discriminatory classifications, but of unwarranted encroachment upon a constitutionally protected freedom. I think that the Wisconsin statute is unconstitutional because it exceeds the bounds of permissible state regulation of marriage, and invades the sphere of liberty protected by the Due Process Clause of the Fourteenth Amendment.

I.

I do not agree with the Court that there is a "right to marry" in the constitutional sense. That right, or more accurately that privilege, is under our federal system peculiarly one to be defined and limited by state law. *Sosna v. Iowa*.... A State may not only "significantly interfere with decisions to enter into marital relationship," but may in many circumstances absolutely prohibit it. Surely, for example, a State may legitimately say that no one can marry his or her sibling, that no one can marry who is not at least 14 years old, that no one can marry without first passing an examination for venereal disease, or that no one can marry who has a living husband or wife. But, just as surely, in regulating the intimate human relationship of marriage, there is a limit beyond which a State may not constitutionally go.

The Constitution does not specifically mention freedom to marry, but it is settled that the "liberty" protected by the Due Process Clause of the Fourteenth Amendment embraces more than those freedoms expressly enumerated in the Bill of Rights. ...

It is evident that the Wisconsin law now before us directly abridges that freedom. The question is whether the state interests that support the abridgment can overcome the substantive protections of the Constitution.

* * *

[T]he law may be seen as simply a collection device ... for enforcing parental support obligations. But since it operates by denying permission to marry, it also clearly reflects a legislative judgment that a person should not be permitted to incur new family financial obligations until he has fulfilled those he already has. ... These interests are legitimate concerns of the State. But it does not follow that they justify the absolute deprivation of the benefits of a legal marriage.

On several occasions this Court has held that a person's inability to pay money demanded by the State does not justify the total deprivation of a constitutionally protected liberty. In *Boddie v. Connecticut* ..., the Court held that the State's legitimate purposes in collecting filing fees for divorce actions were insufficient under the Due Process Clause to deprive the indigent of access to the courts where that access was necessary to dissolve the marital relationship. ...

The principle of those cases applies here as well. The Wisconsin law makes no allowance for the truly indigent. The State flatly denies a marriage license to anyone who cannot afford to fulfill his support obligations and keep his children from becoming wards of the State. ...To deny these people permission to marry penalizes them for failing to do that which they cannot do. Insofar as it applies to indigents, the state law is an irrational means of achieving these objectives of the State.

...[T]he State's legitimate concern with the financial soundness of prospective marriages must stop short of telling people they may not marry because they are too poor or because they might persist in their financial irresponsibility. The invasion of constitutionally protected liberty and the chance of erroneous prediction are simply too great. A legislative judgment so alien to our traditions and so offensive to our shared notions of fairness offends the Due Process Clause of the Fourteenth Amendment.

II.

In an opinion of the Court half a century ago, Mr. Justice Holmes described an equal protection claim as "the usual last resort of constitutional arguments." *Buck v. Bell*, ... [In this case it] is no more than substantive due process by another name.

* * *

MR. JUSTICE POWELL, concurring in the judgment.

I concur in the judgment of the Court that Wisconsin's restrictions on the exclusive means of creating the marital bond ..., cannot meet applicable constitutional standards. I write separately because the majority's rationale sweeps too broadly in an area which traditionally has been subject to pervasive state regulation. The Court apparently would subject all state regulation which "directly and substantially" interferes with the decision to marry in a traditional family setting to "critical examination" or "compelling state interest" analysis. Presumably, "reasonable regulations that do not significantly interfere with decisions to enter into the marital relationship may legitimately be imposed." ... The Court does not present, however, any principled means for distinguishing between the two types of regulations. Since state regulation in this area typically takes the form of a prerequisite or barrier to marriage or divorce, the degree of "direct" interference with the decision to marry or to divorce is unlikely to provide either guidance for state legislatures or a basis for judicial oversight.

I.

On several occasions, the Court has acknowledged the importance of the marriage relationship to the maintenance of values essential to organized society. "This Court has long recognized that freedom of personal choice in matters of marriage and family life is one of the liberties protected by the Due Process Clause of the Fourteenth Amendment." *Cleveland Board of Education v. LaFleur* .... Our decisions indicate that the guarantee of personal privacy or autonomy secured against unjustifiable governmental interference by the Due Process Clause "has some extension to activities relating to marriage ...

Thus, it is fair to say that there is a right of marital and familial privacy which places some substantive limits on the regulatory power of government. But the Court has yet to hold that all regulation touching upon marriage implicates a "fundamental right" triggering the most exacting judicial scrutiny. [Fn1-Although the cases cited in the text indicate that there is a sphere of privacy or autonomy surrounding an existing marital relationship into which the State may not lightly intrude, they do not necessarily suggest that the same barrier of justification blocks regulation of the conditions of entry into or the dissolution of the marital bond. See generally Henkin, Privacy and Autonomy, 74 Colum.L.Rev. 1410, 1429–1432 (1974).]

The principal authority cited by the majority is *Loving v. Virginia*, ... Although *Loving* speaks of the "freedom to marry" as "one of the vital personal rights essential to the orderly pursuit of happiness by free men," the Court focused on the miscegenation statute before it. ...

In my view, analysis must start from the recognition of domestic relations as "an area that has long been regarded as a virtually exclusive province of the States." *Sosna v. Iowa* .... The marriage relation traditionally has been subject to regulation, initially by the ecclesiastical authorities, and later by the secular state. As early as in *Pennoyer v. Neff* ... (1878), this Court noted that a State "has absolute right to prescribe the conditions upon which the marriage relation between its own citizens shall be created, and the causes for which it may be dissolved." The State, representing the collective expression of moral aspirations, has an undeniable interest in ensuring that its rules of domestic relations reflect the widely held values of its people. "Marriage, as creating the most important relation in life, as having more to do with the morals and civilization of a people than any other institution, has always been subject to the control of the legislature. That body prescribes the age at which parties may contract to marry, the procedure or form essential to constitute marriage, the duties and obligations it creates, its effects upon the property rights of both, present and prospective, and the acts which may constitute grounds for its dissolution." *Maynard v. Hill* ... (1888). State regulation has included bans on incest, bigamy, and homosexuality, as well as various preconditions to marriage, such as blood tests. Likewise, a showing of fault on the part of one of the partners traditionally has been a prerequisite to the dissolution of an unsuccessful union. A "compelling state purpose" inquiry would cast doubt on the network of restrictions that the States have fashioned to govern marriage and divorce.

II.

State power over domestic relations is not without constitutional limits. ...

The Wisconsin measure in this case does not pass muster under either due process or equal protection standards. Appellant identifies three objectives which are supposedly furthered by the statute in question: (i) a counseling function; (ii) an incentive to satisfy outstanding support obligations; and (iii) a deterrent against incurring further obligations. The opinion of the Court amply demonstrates that the asserted counseling objective bears no relation to this statute. ... No further discussion is required here.

The so-called "collection device" rationale presents a somewhat more difficult question. I do not agree with the suggestion in the Court's opinion that a State may never condition the right to marry on satisfaction of existing support obligations simply because the State has alternative methods of compelling such payments. ... The vice inheres, not in the collection concept, but in the failure to make provision for those without the means to comply with child-support obligations. ... [In *Boddie v. Connecticut*] the Court struck down filing fees for divorce actions as applied to those wholly unable to pay, holding "that a State may not, consistent with the obligations imposed on it by the Due Process Clause of the Fourteenth Amendment, pre-empt the right to dissolve this legal relationship without affording all citizens access to the means it has prescribed for doing so." ... The monopolization present in this case is total, for Wisconsin will not recognize foreign marriages that fail to conform to the requirements of § 245.10.

The third justification, only obliquely advanced by appellant, is that the statute preserves the ability of marriage applicants to support their prior issue by preventing them from incurring new obligations. The challenged provisions ... are so grossly underinclusive with respect to this objective, given the many ways that additional financial obligations may be incurred ... quite apart from a contemplated marriage, that the classification "does not bear a fair and substantial relation to the object of the legislation."

* * *

Apparently, no other jurisdiction has embraced this approach as a method of reducing the number of children on public assistance. ...

MR. JUSTICE STEVENS, concurring in the judgment.

Because of the tension between some of the language in Mr. Justice MARSHALL's opinion for the Court and the Court's unanimous holding in *Califano v. Jobst*, 434 U.S. 47 (1977), a further exposition of the reasons why the Wisconsin statute offends the Equal Protection Clause of the Fourteenth Amendment is necessary.

* * *

A classification based on marital status is fundamentally different from a classification which determines who may lawfully enter into the marriage relationship. The individual's interest in making the marriage decision independently is sufficiently important to merit special constitutional protection. ... It is not, however, an interest which is constitutionally immune from evenhanded regulation. Thus, laws prohibiting marriage to a child, a close relative, or a person afflicted with venereal disease, are unchallenged even though they "interfere directly and substantially with the right to marry." ... This Wisconsin statute has a different character.

Under this statute, a person's economic status may determine his eligibility to enter into a lawful marriage. A noncustodial parent whose children are "public charges" may not marry even if he has met his court-ordered obligations. Thus, within the class of parents who have fulfilled their court-ordered obligations, the rich may marry and the poor may not. This type of statutory discrimination is, I believe, totally unprecedented, as well as inconsistent with our tradition of administering justice equally to the rich and to the poor.

* * *

In sum, the public-charge provision is either futile or perverse insofar as it applies to childless couples, couples who will have illegitimate children if they are forbidden to marry, couples whose economic status will be improved by marriage, and couples who are so poor that the marriage will have no impact on the welfare status of their children in any event. ... [T]his clumsy and deliberate legislative discrimination between the rich and the poor is irrational in so many ways that it cannot withstand scrutiny under the Equal Protection Clause of the Fourteenth Amendment.
MR. JUSTICE REHNQUIST, dissenting.

I substantially agree with my Brother POWELL's reasons for rejecting the Court's conclusion that marriage is the sort of "fundamental right" which must invariably trigger the strictest judicial scrutiny. I disagree with his imposition of an "intermediate" standard of review, which leads him to conclude that the statute, though generally valid as an "additional collection mechanism" offends the Constitution by its "failure to make provision for those without the means to comply with child-support obligations." ... I think that under the Equal Protection Clause the statute need pass only the "rational basis test," *Dandridge v. Williams* ..., and that under the Due Process Clause it need only be shown that it bears a rational relation to a constitutionally permissible objective. ... The statute so viewed is a permissible exercise of the State's power to regulate family life and to assure the support of minor children, despite its possible imprecision in the extreme cases envisioned in the concurring opinions.

[In *Califano v. Jobst*, the Court upheld a Social Security regulation that discriminated on the basis of marital classification, holding:] "The broad legislative classification must be judged by reference to characteristics typical of the affected classes rather than by focusing on selected, atypical examples."
...

The analysis applied in *Jobst* is equally applicable here too. The Wisconsin Legislature has "adopted this rule in the course of constructing a complex social welfare system that necessarily deals with the intimacies of family life." ... Because of the limited amount of funds available for the support of needy children, the State has an exceptionally strong interest in securing as much support as their parents are able to pay. Nor does the extent of the burden imposed by this statute so differentiate it from that considered in *Jobst* as to warrant a different result. In the case of some applicants, this statute makes the proposed marriage legally impossible for financial reasons; in a similar number of extreme cases, the Social Security Act makes the proposed marriage practically impossible for the same reasons. I cannot conclude that such a difference justifies the application of a heightened standard of review to the statute in question here. In short, I conclude that the statute, despite its imperfections, is sufficiently rational to satisfy the demands of the Fourteenth Amendment.

c. Notes and Questions

1) *Loving* Notes

For a fascinating report of the Loving couple, their courtship, marriage, family, and case, written by a scholar who personally knew the family, *see* Pratt, *infra*. For an analysis of the equal protection significance of *Loving see* Nolan, *infra*. Was *Loving* primarily a case about eliminating racism or protecting marriage? If the case had involved a state law prohibiting interracial private associations, would the result have been the same? If the case had involved a prohibition against intra-family marriage, would the result have been the same? Why or why not?

Advocates of same-sex marriage often use the "*Loving* analogy" to support their claim for legalization of same-sex marriage. *See* Eskridge, *infra;* Koppelman, *infra;* Strasser, *infra.* Opponents of same-sex marriage generally reject the *Loving* analogy. *See* Wardle, *infra;* Coolidge, *infra.* What are the strengths and weaknesses of the *Loving* analogy argument for same-sex marriage? *Loving* involved laws passed by a once-popular political movement (White Supremacy) to capture and redefine a powerful social institution (marriage) for purposes irrelevant to that institution but intended to promote the ideology of the movement. Are current efforts to redefine marriage comparable? Why or why not?

2) *Zablocki* Notes

How did the majority in *Zablocki* respond to Justice Powell's observation that the Court lacked any "principled means for distinguishing between" regulations that substantially and directly interfere with marriage and require heightened scrutiny, and those that reasonably regulate it and do not? Should age, incest, and licensing restrictions on marriage be subject to strict scrutiny? Why/why not? Did the Court find marriage to be a "fundamental right" or a "fundamental interest"? What, if any, difference does that make? Was the "tradition-and-history" test for discerning unwritten "fundament rights" important in the majority opinion in *Zablocki*? Note that while the judgment in *Zablocki* was 8–1, six separate opinions were filed, and only three justices joined the majority opinion without also joining another opinion. How did the Court's assessment of the social significance of marriage affect its legal analysis? Is the reliance on the state prohibition of non-marital sexual relations valid after *Lawrence*?

3) *" Turner v. Safley*, 482 U.S. 78 (1987),

In *Turner*, the Court unanimously struck down Missouri prison regulations severely limiting marriage by inmates to "compelling" cases (in practice limited to pregnancy or birth of a child out of wedlock). Justice O'Connor, for the Court, noted that even incarcerated prisoners could enjoy some "important attributes of marriage," including the public expression of emotional support, spiritual significance, expectation of later consummation of the marital relationship, and certain government benefits. While legitimate interests in security and prisoner rehabilitation could justify some regulations, Missouri's near-total ban on inmate marriage was necessary for neither interest. Does the Court's mention of functional benefits of marriage support arguments that alternative relationships that are deemed "functional equivalents" of marriage in some respects must be given marital status and benefits in law? Is there a difference between whether a state must not deny the right to enjoy important functional attributes of a relationship that is deemed "fundamental" for constitutional law, and whether another relationship should be deemed "fundamental" because it shares some of those attributes?

4) Right to Marry and Marital Status Distinguished

The cases and materials discussed above deal with the right to marry. That is separate from the status of marriage. The Supreme Court has explicitly held that governments may give preferred status to marriage. *Califano v. Jobst, supra.* Apart from that (perhaps because of that), the restriction of access to enter marriage is scrutinized carefully. Government restrictions on persons entering into a marriage relationship raise different questions from government preference of the status of marriage created by entering into lawful marriage.

5) Does Right to Marry Protect Private or Public Interests?

Former law school Dean, Bruce C. Hafen has written:

> Litigants ... see privacy as an individual right which is independent of the relationships it may protect. The use of individual rights analysis, as typically understood, can be inappropriate and even harmful in the context of family relationships. For example, contemporary legal writers take for granted that "the right to marry" is grounded "in respect for freedom of choice in intimate personal relationships," since "choice of domestic companionship constitutes the kind of intimate personal decision" that is at the heart of the Court's evolving privacy doctrines. Thus, the right to marry cases are seen by these writers as part of constitutional doctrine based essentially on individual autonomy. With that premise firmly in place, any legal restraint on freely entering or leaving marital relationships is suspect in their eyes. With the scales between individual and social interests thereby tipped heavily toward the individual side, few, if any, attempts at the state regulation would withstand scrutiny.

Hafen, *infra* at 466–67. Does individual-rights analysis "fit" joint-mutual relationships like marriage? Do individuals have a private right to conferral of a public status on any relationship they choose? Is the essence of the constitutional right to marry the private choice of one's life partner? *Goodridge v. Dep't. Pub. H.*, 798 N.E.2d 941, 953 (Mass. 2003) ("right to marry their chosen partner"); Meyer, *infra*, at 454 ("the [*Lawrence*] Court ultimately appeared to link constitutional protection to contemporary society's acceptance of the legitimacy of the family bonds constructed . . . ."); Ball, *infra* at 1231 (*Lawrence*'s "expansive approach to the liberty interests protected by the Due Process Clause ... bode[s] well for future constitutional claims that lesbians and gay men have the right to marry individuals of their choice."). Is this sound? Why/why not? What implications does this have for consanguinity, polygamy, and marital age restrictions?

3. Practical and Ethical Considerations

a. Lawyer's Role

Clients seldom consult their lawyers before they marry. If they did, would more professional responsibility conflicts arise? To what extent may a lawyer, consistent with standards of legal ethics, urge a position that marriage regulations are unconstitutional as written or applied when there is little precedential support for the position but for which some general theoretical arguments may exist? Is the assertion of "novel" theoretical arguments justifiable on a "shotgun" approach to practice? Does this raise any "Rule 11" issues?

4. Bibliography

Carlos A. Ball, *The Positive in the Fundamental Right to Marry: Same-Sex Marriage in the Aftermath of* Lawrence v. Texas, 88 Minn. L. Rev. 1184 (2004).

William Blackstone, Commentaries on the Laws of England *434.

Margaret F. Brinig, *The Supreme Court's Impact on Marriage,* 41 How. L.J. 271 (1998).

David Orgon Coolidge, *Playing the* Loving *Card: Same-Sex Marriage and the Politics of Analogy*, 12 J. Pub. L. 201 (1998)

William Eskridge, Jr., *A History of Same-Sex Marriage*, 79 Va. L. Rev. 1419 (1993).

Bruce C. Hafen, *The Constitutional Status of Marriage, Kinship, and Sexual Privacy—Balancing the Individual and Social Interests*, 81 Mich. L. Rev. 463 (1983).

Lynne Marie Kohm, *Liberty and Marriage—*Baehr *and Beyond: Due Process in 1998,* 12 BYU J. Pub. L. 253 (1998).

Andrew Koppelman, Note, *The Miscegenation Analogy: Sodomy Law as Sex Discrimination*, 98 Yale L.J. 145 (1988).

David D. Meyer, *Domesticating* Lawrence, 2004 U. Chi. L. Forum 453.

Laurence C. Nolan, *The Meaning of* Loving*: Marriage, Due Process and Equal Protection As Equality and Marriage, From* Loving *to* Zablocki, 41 How. L.J. 245 (1998).

Robert A. Pratt, *Crossing the Color Line: A Historical Assessment and Personal Narrative of* Loving v. Virginia, 41 How. L.J. 229 (1998).

Mark Strasser, *Family, Definitions, and the Constitution: On the Antimiscegenation Analogy*, 25 Suffolk U.L.Rev. 981 (1991).

Lynn D. Wardle, Loving v. Virginia *and the Constitutional Right to Marry*, 41 How. L.J. 289 (1998).

C. MARRIAGE ESSENTIALS - IN GENERAL

1. Background

a. Essentials and Formalities

Marriage regulations may be divided into *essentials* (called variously capacity, mandatory requirement, prohibitions, and substantive mandates) and *formalities*. *Essentials* are necessary for a valid marriage; violation of those requirements or prohibitions will (or may) render the marriage invalid. Some nations distinguish *essentials'* defects that render a marriage *void ab initio* and those which render the marriage merely *voidable* (or similar categories—as absolute and relative impediments in Argentina). *Formalities* are deemed directory and violation of them may be punished, but generally will not affect the validity of the marriage.

A survey of contemporary marriage laws around the world reveals that certain *essentials* for valid marriage are widespread. The prevailing general rule may be summarized by the statement: *A man and a woman of due age and competence, unmarried and unrelated within prohibited degree, by exercising their voluntary consent, may marry.* This identifies six essentials for valid marriage. (1) Historically, all nations permitted only heterosexual marriage until 2002; now The Netherlands, Belgium, Spain, Canada, and possibly South Africa, and several sub-jurisdictions (like Massachusetts) allow same-sex marriage while dozens of nations (now 32 explicitly) and numerous sub-jurisdictions constitutionally define marriage as male-female. (2) Most nations prohibit polygamous marriage and in those few nations where polygamy is permitted, it is restricted and generally disfavored. (3) All nations prohibit marriage between some close relatives, including close ascendant-descendant relatives and between siblings, and many extend consanguinity prohibitions even further. (4) Minimum age requirements also are ubiquitous in modern legal systems. (5) The parties to the marriage must be both mentally and physically competent to marry. (6) Personal consent is required everywhere for a valid marriage, though the details of what kind and evidence of consent is required vary. Wardle, 1995, *infra*. Additionally, in many legal systems there are unique marriage restrictions. For example, in several states one that attempted to or did kill a married person may not marry the (surviving) spouse.

b. Void and Voidable Defects

The effect of violation of a marriage prohibition depends upon the type of prohibition. The void-voidable distinction developed at common law. Blackstone noted:

> [The parties to a marriage] must be *able* to contract. In general, all persons are able to contract themselves in marriage, unless they labor under some particular disabilities, and incapacities. What those are, it will here be our business to inquire.
>
> Now, these disabilities are of two sorts: first, such as are canonical, and therefore sufficient by the ecclesiastical laws to avoid the marriage in the spiritual court; but these in our law only make the marriage voidable, and not *ipso facto* void, until sentence of nullity be obtained. Of this nature are pre-contract; consanguinity, or relation by blood; and affinity, or relation by marriage; and some particular corporal infirmities. And these canonical disabilities are either grounded upon the express words of the divine law, or are consequences plainly deducible from thence: it therefore being sinful in the persons, who labor under them, to attempt to contract matrimony together, they are properly the object of the ecclesiastical magistrate's coercion; in order to separate the offenders, and inflict penance for the offence, *pro salute animarum* (for the welfare of their souls). But such marriages not being void *ab initio* (from the beginning), but voidable only be sentence of separation, they are esteemed valid to all civil purposes, unless such separation is actually made during the life of the parties. For, after the death of either of them, the courts of common law will not suffer the spiritual court to declare such marriages to have been void; because such declaration cannot now tend to the reformation of the parties. And therefore when a man had married his first wife's sister, and after her death the bishop's court was proceeding to annul the marriage and bastardize the issue, the court of king's bench granted a prohibition *quoad hoc* (as to this); but permitted them to proceed to punish the husband for incest. These canonical disabilities being entirely the province of the ecclesiastical courts, our books are perfectly silent concerning them. But there are a few statutes, which serve as directories to those courts, of which it will be proper to take notice. ...
>
> The other sort of disabilities are those which are created, or at least enforced, by the municipal laws. And, though some of them may be grounded on natural law, yet they are regarded by the laws of the land, not so much in the light of any moral offense, as on account of the civil inconveniences they draw after them. These civil disabilities make the contract void *ab initio* (from the beginning), and not merely voidable; not that they dissolve a contract already formed, but they render the parties incapable of forming any contract at all: they do not put asunder those who are joined together, but they previously hinder the junction. And, if any persons under these legal incapacities come together, it is a meretricious, and not a matrimonial, union.
>
> The first of these legal disabilities is a prior marriage, or having another husband or wife living; in which case, besides the penalties consequent upon it as a felony, the second marriage is to all intents and purposes void: polygamy being condemned both by the law of the New Testament, and the policy of all prudent states, especially in these northern climates. And Justinian, even in the climate of modern Turkey, is express, that "*duas uxores eodem tempore habere non licet* (it is not lawful to have two wives at one

time)."

The next legal disability is want of age. This is sufficient to avoid all other contracts, on account of the imbecility of judgment in the parties contracting; *a fortiori*, therefore, it ought to avoid this, the most important contract of any. Therefore, if a boy under fourteen, or a girl under twelve years of age, marries, this marriage is only inchoate and imperfect; and, when either of them comes to the age of consent aforesaid, they may disagree and declare the marriage void, without any divorce or sentence in the spiritual court. This is founded on the civil law. But the canon law pays a greater regard to the constitution than the age of the parties: for if they are *habiles ad matrimonium* (fit for marriage), it is a good marriage, whatever their age may be. And in our law it is so far a marriage, that, if at the age of consent they agree to continue together, they need not be married again. If the husband be of years of discretion, and the wife under twelve, when she comes to years of discretion he may disagree as well as she may: for in contracts the obligation must be mutual; both must be bound, or neither: and so it is, *vice versa*, when the wife is of years of discretion and the husband under.

Another incapacity arises from want of consent of parents or guardians. ...

A fourth incapacity is want of reason; without a competent share of which, as no other, so neither can the matrimonial contract, be valid. ...

William Blackstone, Commentaries on the Laws of England *434–437.

For purposes of modern marriage law, there are three major differences between void and voidable marriages. First, attacks on voidable marriages may be brought only by the parties themselves and only while both are still alive and married to each other; greater latitude regarding standing and timing exists for void marriages. Second, voidable marriages may be ratified when the defect is eliminated, whereas generally void marriages are not ratifiable. Third, the scope of relief available when a marriage is declared void sometimes may not be as extensive as when the marriage is voidable.

2. Statutes, Cases and Doctrines2. Statutes, Cases and Doctrines

a. Uniform Marriage and Divorce Act, § 207

(1) The following marriages are prohibited:

> (a) a marriage entered into prior to the dissolution of an earlier marriage of one of the parties;

> (b) a marriage between an ancestor and a descendant, or between a brother and a sister, whether the relationship is by the half or the whole blood, or by adoption;

> (c) a marriage between an uncle and a niece or between an aunt and a nephew, whether the relationship is by the half or the whole blood, except as to marriages permitted by the established customs of aboriginal cultures.

(2) Parties to a marriage prohibited under this section who cohabit after removal of the impediment are lawfully married as of the date of the removal of the impediment.

(3) Children born of a prohibited marriage are legitimate.

Compare this model marriage prohibition law with your homestate marriage prohibitions.

3. Practical and Ethical Considerations

See §D.3., *infra.*

4. Bibliography

See §D.4., *infra.*

D. MONOGAMY

1. Background

a. History

The history of the monogamous marriage rule is reviewed in *Reynolds, infra.*

b. Sequential v. Simultaneous Polygamy

Historically the monogamy ideal prohibited both sequential and simultaneous serial marriages while former spouses were living. Thus, divorce and remarriage was practically impossible, and polygamous marriage was prohibited. Divorce and remarriage (sequential polygamy) is no longer prohibited or socially stigmatized (it is almost the norm); a man may have three or five (or more) wives, as long as he takes care to divorce before he remarries. *But see* the Tom Green case, *infra* § 2.b.3. Simultaneous multiple spouses (polygamy) are still prohibited in all states. Is that reasonable? Why/why not?

c. Policy against Polygamy

In *Mormon Church v. United States*, 136 U.S. 1 (1889), echoing a theme set earlier in *Reynolds,* § D.2.a., *infra*, the Supreme Court related form of marriage with form of politics. "The organization of a community for the spread and practice of polygamy is, in a measure, a return to barbarism. It is contrary to the spirit of Christianity and of the civilization which Christianity has produced in the Western world." *Id.* at 49. Later, Justice Douglas, who practiced serial polygamy, moralized about the evils of polygamy: "The establishment or maintenance of polygamous households is a notorious example of promiscuity. The permanent advertisement of their existence is an example of the sharp repercussions which they have in the community. ... [P]olygamous practices have long been branded as immoral in the law. Though they have different ramifications, they are in the same genus as [prostitution and debauchery]." *Cleveland v. United States*, 329 U.S. 14, 19 (1946). Justice Murphy dissented, noting:

> [W]e are dealing here with polygyny, one of the basic forms of marriage. Historically, its use has far exceeded that of any other form. It was quite common among ancient civilizations and was referred to many times by the writers of the Old Testament; even today it is to be found frequently among certain pagan and non-Christian peoples of the world. We must recognize then, that polygyny, like other forms of marriage, is basically a cultural institution rooted deeply in the religious beliefs and social mores of those societies in which it appears. It is equally true that the belief and mores of the dominant culture of the contemporary world condemn the practice as immoral and substitute monogamy in its place. To those beliefs and mores I subscribe, but that does not alter the fact that polygyny is a form of marriage built upon a set of social and moral principles. It must be recognized and treated as such.

The Court states that polygamy is "a notorious example of promiscuity." The important fact, however, is that, despite the differences that may exist between polygamy and monogamy, such differences do not place polygamy in the same category as prostitution or debauchery. ... It takes no elaboration here to point out that marriage, even when it occurs in a form of which we disapprove, is not to be compared with prostitution or debauchery or other immoralities of that character.

Id. at 26 (Murphy, J., dissenting). Was Douglas or Murphy closer to the truth? Does it matter for marriage policy? Why/why not?

2. Statutes, Cases and Doctrines

a. *Reynolds v. United States*

Reynolds v. United States
98 U.S. 145

ERROR to the Supreme Court of the Territory of Utah.

This is an indictment found in the District Court for the third judicial district of the Territory of Utah, charging George Reynolds with bigamy, in violation of sect. 5352 of the Revised Statutes, which, omitting its exceptions, is as follows:

"Every person having a husband or wife living, who marries another, whether married or single, in a Territory, or other place over which the United States have exclusive jurisdiction, is guilty of bigamy, and shall be punished by a fine of not more than $500, and by imprisonment for a term of not more than five years."

* * *

The court, in summing up to the jury, declined to instruct them, as requested by the prisoner, that if they found that he had married in pursuance of and conformity with what he believed at the time to be a religious duty, their verdict should be "not guilty," but instructed them that if he, under the influence of a religious belief that it was right, had "deliberately married a second time, having a first wife living, the want of consciousness of evil intent—the want of understanding on his part that he was committing crime—did not excuse him, but the law inexorably, in such cases, implies criminal intent." The court also said: "I think it not improper, in the discharge of your duties in this case, that you should consider what are to be the consequences to the innocent victims of this delusion. As this contest goes on, they multiply, and there are pure-minded women and there are innocent children—innocent in a sense even beyond the degree of the innocence of childhood itself. These are to be the sufferers; and as jurors fail to do their duty, and as these cases come up in the Territory, just so do these victims multiply and spread themselves over the land."

To the refusal of the court to charge as requested, and to the charge as given, the prisoner excepted. The jury found him guilty, as charged in the indictment; and the judgment that he be imprisoned at hard labor for a term of two years, and pay a fine of $500, rendered by the District Court, having been affirmed by the Supreme Court of the Territory, he sued out this writ of error.

The assignments of error are set out in the opinion of the court.

MR. CHIEF JUSTICE WAITE delivered the opinion of the court.

* * *

5. As to the defence of religious belief or duty.

On the trial, the plaintiff in error, the accused, proved that at the time of his alleged second marriage he was, and for many years before had been, a member of the Church of Jesus Christ of Latter-Day Saints, commonly called the Mormon Church, and a believer in its doctrines; that it was an accepted doctrine of that church "that it was the duty of male members of said church, circumstances permitting, to practise polygamy ....

Upon this proof he asked the court to instruct the jury that if they found from the evidence that he "was married as charged—if he was married—in pursuance of and in conformity with what he believed at the time to be a religious duty, that the verdict must be 'not guilty.'" This request was refused, and the court did charge "that there must have been a criminal intent, but that if the defendant, under the influence of a religious belief that it was right—under an inspiration, if you please, that it was right—deliberately married a second time, having a first wife living, the want of consciousness of evil intent—the want of understanding on his part that he was committing a crime—did not excuse him; but the law inexorably in such case implies the criminal intent."

Upon this charge and refusal to charge the question is raised, whether religious belief can be accepted as a justification of an overt act made criminal by the law of the land. The inquiry is not as to the power of Congress to prescribe criminal laws for the Territories, but as to the guilt of one who knowingly violates a law which has been properly enacted, if he entertains a religious belief that the law is wrong.

Congress cannot pass a law for the government of the Territories which shall prohibit the free exercise of religion. The first amendment to the Constitution expressly forbids such legislation. Religious freedom is guaranteed everywhere throughout the United States, so far as congressional interference is concerned. The question to be determined is, whether the law now under consideration comes within this prohibition.

The word "religion" is not defined in the Constitution. ... The precise point of the inquiry is, what is the religious freedom which has been guaranteed.

... [The Court briefly reviews Jefferson's and Madison's views about religious freedom, and concludes:] Congress was deprived of all legislative power over mere opinion, but was left free to reach actions which were in violation of social duties or subversive of good order.

Polygamy has always been odious among the northern and western nations of Europe, and, until the establishment of the Mormon Church, was almost exclusively a feature of the life of Asiatic and of African people. At common law, the second marriage was always void (2 Kent, Com. 79), and from the earliest history of England polygamy has been treated as an offence against society. After the establishment of the ecclesiastical courts, and until the time of James I, it was punished through the instrumentality of those tribunals, not merely because ecclesiastical rights had been violated, but because upon the separation of the ecclesiastical courts from the civil the ecclesiastical were supposed to be the most appropriate for the trial of matrimonial causes and offences against the rights of marriage, just as they were for testamentary causes and the settlement of the estates of deceased persons.

By the statute of 1 James I (c. 11), the offence, if committed in England or Wales, was made punishable in the civil courts, and the penalty was death. As this statute was limited in its operation to England and Wales, it was at a very early period re-enacted, generally with some modifications, in all the colonies. In connection with the case we are now considering, it is a significant fact that on the 8th of December, 1788, after the passage of the act establishing religious freedom, and after the convention of Virginia had recommended as an amendment to the Constitution of the United States the declaration in a bill of rights that 'all men have an equal, natural, and unalienable right to the free exercise of religion, according to the dictates of conscience,' the legislature of that State substantially enacted the statute of James I, death penalty included, because, as recited in the preamble, "it hath been doubted whether bigamy or polygamy be punishable by the laws of this Commonwealth." 12 Hening's Stat. 691. From that day to this we think it may safely be said there never has been a time in any State of the Union when polygamy has not been an offence against society, cognizable by the civil courts and punishable with more or less severity. In the face of all this evidence, it is impossible to believe that the constitutional guaranty of religious freedom was intended to prohibit legislation in respect to this most important feature of social life. Marriage, while from its very nature a sacred obligation, is nevertheless, in most civilized nations, a civil contract, and usually regulated by law. Upon it society may be said to be built, and out of its fruits spring social relations and social obligations and duties, with which government is necessarily required to deal. In fact, according as monogamous or polygamous marriages are allowed, do we find the principles on which the government of the people, to a greater or less extent, rests. Professor Lieber says, polygamy leads to the patriarchal principle, and which, when applied to large communities, fetters the people in stationary despotism, while that principle cannot long exist in connection with monogamy. Chancellor Kent observes that this remark is equally striking and profound. ... An exceptional colony of polygamists under an exceptional leadership may sometimes exist for a time without appearing to disturb the social condition of the people who surround it; but there cannot be a doubt that, unless restricted by some form of constitution, it is within the legitimate scope of the power of every civil government to determine whether polygamy or monogamy shall be the law of social life under its dominion.

In our opinion, the statute immediately under consideration is within the legislative power of Congress. It is constitutional and valid as prescribing a rule of action for all those residing in the Territories, and in places over which the United States have exclusive control. This being so, the only question which remains is, whether those who make polygamy a part of their religion are excepted from the operation of the statute. If they are, then those who do not make polygamy a part of their religious belief may be found guilty and punished, while those who do, must be acquitted and go free. This would be introducing a new element into criminal law. Laws are made for the government of actions, and while they cannot interfere with mere religious belief and opinions, they may with practices. Suppose one believed that human sacrifices were a necessary part of religious worship, would it be seriously contended that the civil government under which he lived could not interfere to prevent a sacrifice? Or if a wife religiously believed it was her duty to burn herself upon the funeral pile of her dead husband, would it be beyond the power of the civil government to prevent her carrying her belief into practice?

So here, as a law of the organization of society under the exclusive dominion of the United States, it is provided that plural marriages shall not be allowed. Can a man excuse his practices to the contrary because of his religious belief? To permit this would be to make the professed doctrines of religious belief superior to the law of the land, and in effect to permit every citizen to become a law unto himself. Government could exist only in name under such circumstances.

A criminal intent is generally an element of crime, but every man is presumed to intend the necessary and legitimate consequences of what he knowingly does. Here the accused knew he had been once married, and that his first wife was living. He also knew that his second marriage was forbidden by law. When, therefore, he married the second time, he is presumed to have intended to break the law. And the breaking of the law is the crime. Every act necessary to constitute the crime was knowingly done, and the crime was therefore knowingly committed. Ignorance of a fact may sometimes be taken as evidence of a want of criminal intent, but not ignorance of the law. The only defence of the accused in this case is his belief that the law ought not to have been enacted. It matters not that his belief was a part of his professed religion: it was still belief, and belief only.

In *Regina v. Wagstaff* (10 Cox Crim. Cases, 531), the parents of a sick child, who omitted to call in medical attendance because of their religious belief that what they did for its cure would be effective, were held not to be guilty of manslaughter, while it was said the contrary would have been the result if the child had actually been starved to death by the parents, under the notion that it was their religious duty to abstain from giving it food. But when the offence consists of a positive act which is knowingly done, it would be dangerous to hold that the offender might escape punishment because he religiously believed the law which he had broken ought never to have been made. No case, we believe, can be found that has gone so far.

* * *

Judgment affirmed.

MR. JUSTICE FIELD [concurred except as to admissibility of wife's testimony in former trial].

b. Notes and Questions

1) Reynolds Subsequent History

Reynolds was eventually resentenced to two years' imprisonment and a $5000 fine. He served 18 months in prison (one month in the Nebraska State Penitentiary and the rest in the Utah State Penitentiary), and was viewed by all members of the (Mormon) Church of Jesus Christ of Latter-day Saints as a "living martyr to the cause of Zion." Van Orden, *infra*, at 93–99. His sentence was reduced by 6 months by an act of Congress lobbied for by George Q. Cannon, for whose sake Reynolds had agreed to stand as a test case. His fine was paid by Sunday School children who made donations. While he was in prison, two of his own children died (he was allowed to attend both funerals). *Id.*

2) Nineteenth Century "Mormon" Polygamy

Historical and legal discussion of polygamous marriage in the United States often focuses on four or five decades of nineteenth-century Mormon polygamy. Starting about 1850, leaders of The Church of Jesus Christ of Latter-day Saints in the Utah Territory openly taught and many members faithfully practiced the principle of "plural marriage." They believed that it was the Lord's will that worthy men, able to support multiple wives, should do so, and eventually thousands of "plural marriage" families were formed in the isolated religious communities they settled in the West. The "plural marriage" practiced by the Mormon pioneers in the West has been described as "Puritan polygamy" because it was moral, religiously regulated, and motivated by community faith values rather than self-gratification. (Indeed, many early converts to the Church were from "Puritan" New England, and brought their strait-laced moral views with them.) Several explanations for the practice have been suggested relating to the rugged wilderness conditions, economic situation, the welfare of widows, absence of husbands on missions, and the generation of posterity within the faith, but for most of those who practiced plural marriage, it was primarily a matter of religious faith—that God commanded it at that specific time to build Zion. Ironically, Mormon women were more independent and liberated than other American women; women in the Utah Territory were the first to vote and had that privilege for decades before women in most other states (until Congress repealed female suffrage in the campaign against polygamy).

When Mormon pioneers led by Brigham Young arrived in the territory west of the Rocky Mountains (now Utah) in 1847, polygamy was not illegal there. However, even before the Civil War began, some politicians were calling for public measures to be taken against the unconventional "Mormon" church. The 1856 Republican Party Platform called for elimination of the "twin relics of barbarism"—slavery and polygamy. In 1862, Congress adopted the Morrill Act, making plural marriage a criminal offense in federal territory, including Utah. As non-Mormons began to discover the rich natural resources of the western territory settled by the Mormons, conflict developed, and federal prosecution of polygamy was one of the tools in the conflict. In 1882, the Edmunds Act punished "unlawful cohabitation" and precluded polygamists from voting. And in 1887, the Edmunds-Tucker Act disinherited children born of polygamous unions, annulled the corporation of the Mormon Church and confiscated most of its property, including the Salt Lake City temple. Many Mormon polygamists were willing to cease living as husband and wife, to cease sleeping in the same room, and to reside in separate houses. Federal anti-polygamy prosecutors, however, demanded that the women who had practiced polygamy be treated as illicit paramours, their children as illegitimate offspring, and that the men stop giving them support, food, housing, clothing, respect, and medical care. The Mormon polygamists refused to stop supporting their families, and during the 1880s (a decade of anti-Mormon polygamy prosecution), 1,000 Mormon men went to prison convicted of polygamy or unlawful cohabitation, and thousands of others went into hiding.

When their appeals to courts and lawmakers were exhausted without remedy, and Church leaders were satisfied that God had accepted their sacrifice in obedience, the prophet-leader of the Church issued an Official Declaration in 1890 prohibiting further plural marriages. Eventually persons continuing to enter into polygamous marriages were excommunicated from The Church of Jesus Christ of Latter-day Saints. Some dissenters declined to abandon plural marriage and formed various "fundamentalist" break-off churches, usually with very small membership (hundreds); they can still be found, usually in the west.

3) Policy against Polygamy

In *Reynolds*, the Court emphasized the theory that the practice of polygamy had political effects for society. The Court was persuaded by the scholarship of "Professor Leiber" that the type of social relations and government of a society directly reflect the type of family relations and government of the family, and that polygamy leads to patriarchialism and despotism. *Id.* at 165. Is that true? Reasonable? A proper concern of marriage regulation? Note that Chief Justice Waite hinted that exceptions to the polygamy-despotism rule might exist; if *Reynolds* had shown that Mormon plural marriage was such an exceptional community, would the marriage law have to accommodate an exception for them just as education law had to accommodate the Amish in *Wisconsin v. Yoder, supra* Ch. 2?

Some socio-biologists theorize that mate attraction is deeply rooted in the need for men to find women with reproductive and childrearing potential and for women to find men who are able to provide protection, security, resources, and social status for themselves and their offspring. Cere, *infra* at 10–12. Taken to its logical conclusion, this seems to support polygamy. "Men in position of power tend to practice polygyny; legitimate polygyny where it is allowed; functional polygyny where it is not." Townsend, *infra* at 236. (Would Townsend have been more accurate if he had said "insecure men" or "carnal men"?) However, Townsend himself argues that socio-biological theory supports monogamy.

4) Native American Polygamy, Muslim Polygamy, and Interjurisdictional Recognition

Some Native American Indian tribes historically practiced polygamy. While plural marriage among the Mormons was uniformly rejected, polygamous Indian marriages were generally recognized as valid in American courts. *See e.g. Hallowell v. Commons*, 210 F. 793 (8th Cir. 1914); *Ortley v. Ross*, 110 N.W. 982 (Neb. 1907). Would they still be recognized as valid today? There is an effort on the part of some tribal courts today to use marriage law to recover traditional marriage customs and cultural heritage, but there appears to be no effort to revive polygamy. Lopez, *infra*, at 292–293.

Today polygamous marriage is still accepted in many leading schools of Islam and in many countries with significant Muslim population polygamy is valid, at least among Muslims. (For example, in India, "polygamy remains to this day a legal option for Muslim men, although it is exercised relatively rarely (about 5 percent of marriages), and largely by wealthier men." Nusbaum, *infra*, at 44.) Would/should an American court recognize as valid for any (or all) purposes polygamous marriages validly entered into in such countries among citizens of those countries? If entered into in a Muslim ceremony in a Muslim community in an American state?

Some American courts have recognized such marriages as valid for purpose of some incidents of marriage. The most renowned case is *In re Dalip Singh Bir's Estate,* 188 P.2d 499 (Cal. Dist. Ct. App. 1948), which involved a man from India who entered into legal plural marriage there, then later died intestate in California where both wives (still living in India) filed claims to share his estate. Reversing the trial court ruling that rejected the inheritance claims of the second wife, the California appellate court held that California public policy would not be violated by dividing the estate between both surviving wives, particularly since the polygamous marriage was valid where contracted, and the only interested parties were the two wives, neither of whom contested the right of the other to share in the estate. *See also Gibson v. Hughes*, 192 F.Supp. 564 (D.C.N.Y. 1961) (recognizing second wife, from France, as valid worker's compensation claimant even though she married worker in French Morocco before his interlocutory divorce was final).

However, other incidents of marriage that are identified with the essence of marriage or of public policy may be denied recognition. For example, in *People v. Ezeonu,* 588 N.Y.S.2d 116 (N.Y. Sup. Ct. 1992), a New York court rejected as "repugnant to public policy" an alleged polygamous marriage validly entered into in Nigeria between a defendant, charged with rape, and the thirteen year-old victim. The defendant's previous marriage to another woman in New York rendered the subsequent Nigerian polygamous marriage void. U.S. immigration law bars persons who practice polygamy from immigrating. 8 U.S.C. § 1101(f) (2000); 8 C.F.R. § 316.10 (2001).

5) Current Polygamy Restrictions and Enforcement

All fifty states have criminal statutes prohibiting bigamy or polygamy and most states have civil statutes prohibiting or declaring these marriages void. In only about one fourth of the states is it clear that bigamous marriages are void without judicial proceedings. Federal law prohibits immigration of persons who practice polygamy or advocate it and prohibits polygamists from voting in federal elections.

In the western United States, especially where various fundamentalist break-off religious groups have congregated, the practice of polygamous marriage still exists, though it is usually covert. However, because prosecutors have other priorities, there is seldom any criminal investigation or prosecution of persons practicing polygamy unless some incident occurs that raises public concern. (Those incidents, however, occur with some regularity.) In 1999, for example, two high-profile prosecutions of Utah polygamists grabbed headlines. A polygamist father, John Daniel Kingston, "gave" his teen-age daughter, Mary Ann, to his brother (her uncle), David Orrin Kingston, to be his polygamous (allegedly his fifteenth) wife. After cooperating for a while, Mary Ann ran away from the marriage, when she was sixteen years old—she reportedly wanted to finish high school. Her father, John, found her, took her to a remote location in rural Utah, and belt whipped her at least 28 times, until she passed out. Then he left her there, unconscious in a barn. When she revived, she walked six or seven miles to a pay phone and dialed 911. The father was prosecuted for child abuse, and the uncle was prosecuted for incest and sexual abuse of a minor. Both men were convicted and the uncle was sentenced to two consecutive five-year prison terms.

In 2000, Thomas Green, a publicity-gathering polygamist who flaunted his polygamous practices in interviews on national and international television, was prosecuted for bigamy, sex with a minor, and criminal nonsupport. Mr. Green married his wives sequentially, legally divorcing each one before marrying the next one, but continuing to live as husband and wife with all of them and hold them all out as wives. However, under Utah's common law marriage statute, Green was found to still be married to his "former" wives. Mr. Green was convicted of four counts of bigamy, one count of criminal nonsupport of his children (his 30th child was born during his trial), and sentenced to five years and a repayment of welfare fine; he was also convicted of sex with a child based on his consummation of a marriage with his thirteen-year-old step-daughter (by polygamous marriage). His constitutional challenge to the bigamy law was rejected and his convictions were affirmed by the Utah Supreme Court. *State v. Green*, 99 P.3d 820 (2004); *State v. Green*, 108 P.3d 790 (2005). Are there any differences between Tom Green's style of polygamy and the nineteenth-century Mormon practice of plural marriage?

Sympathizers of polygamists, including some civil rights groups, argue that there is no need to prohibit or prosecute polygamy, that consenting adults should be able to define marriage as they choose, that polygamy is a "victimless crime," and that if polygamy leads to abuses, those abuses can be prosecuted independently. However, many women and children "refugees" of polygamy, such as the members of Tapestry Against Polygamy, maintain that abuse, incest, child sexual exploitation, medical neglect, forced child labor, evasion of education laws, and welfare fraud are inherent in twenty-first century polygamous marriages, that the isolated, communal culture of polygamy makes it very difficult for wives to resist or to escape. Because of the closed nature of polygamous families and communities, the "code of silence," etc., prosecution is difficult.

6) Presumption of Validity of Last Marriage

One of the most important rules courts apply in cases in which there has been more than one marriage is the presumption of the validity of the last marriage. No matter how many prior marriages there were, the last-in-time is entitled to the presumption of validity. But that is a rebuttable presumption. To rebut the presumption, a person claiming to be a former spouse need only show (1) proof of a valid marriage (generally a marriage certificate or other official record), and (2) evidence that no divorce or annulment was recorded in any state in which either spouse was domiciled (not merely residing) since the marriage. *See Spearman v. Spearman*, 482 F.2d 1203 (5th Cir. 1973), Chapter 6A, *infra*.

3. Practical and Ethical Considerations

a. Different Kinds of Polygamists

There are four types of violators of the laws against polygamy: (1) innocent victims of bigamists or unintentional bigamists; (2) persons who carelessly remarry before a former marriage is finally dissolved; (3) polygamists who openly practice plural marriage with the consent of all involved; and (4) philanderers who secretly marry persons their current spouses do not know about, and whose subsequent "spouses" are unaware that they have existing spouses. All violators are categorized together as polygamists, and all multiple simultaneous marriages are void. Should the punishment and prosecution of all violators be the same?

b. Liabilities and Responsibilities?

If a client wants to enter into a marriage that is prohibited by local law (involving polygamy, incest, or an underage person), what are the attorney's ethical obligations to the client, to the bar, and to the state? Is the answer different if the client wants to marry a relative, same-sex partner, or plural wife than if the client wants to marry a 13-year-old? If the attorney facilitates a valid marriage in another jurisdiction, might he/she be liable to third parties (such as parents, spouses), or criminally, or for violating professional ethics?

4. Bibliography

William Blackstone, Commentaries on the Laws of England, vol. 1, *422–434.

The Book of Mormon, Jacob 2:*passim.*

W. Buckland, A Textbook of Roman Law from Augustus to Justinian (1921).

Dan Cere, The Experts' Story of Courtship (Institute for American Values Council on Families, 2000).

P. Corbett, The Roman Law of Marriage (1930).

Edwin Brown Firmage & Richard Collin Mangrum, Zion in the Courts: A Legal History of the Church of Jesus Christ of Latter-Day-Saints, 1830–1900 (1988).

Orma Linford, *The Mormons and the Law: The Polygamy Cases*, 9 Utah L. Rev. 308 (1964).

Martha C. Nussbaum, *India: Implementing Sex Equality Through Law*, 2 Chi. J. Int'l L. 35 (2001).

Antoinette Sedillo Lopez, *Evolving Indigenous Law: Navajo Marriage-Cultural Traditions and Modern Challenges*, 17 Ariz. J. Int'l & Comp. L. 283 (2000).

John Marshall Townsend, What Women Want—What Men Want: Why the Sexes Still See Love and Commitment So Differently (1998).

Bruce A. Van Orden, Prisoner for Conscience Sake, The Life of George Reynolds (1992).

Lynn D. Wardle, *International Marriage and Divorce Regulation and Recognition: A Survey*, 29 Family Law Q. 497 (Fall 1995).

CHAPTER 4

Physical Requirements for Marriage— Consanguinity; Physical Capacity; Same-Sex Marriage

A. PHYSICAL REQUIREMENTS: CONSANGUINITY AND AFFINITY

1. Background

a. Consanguinity and Affinity Distinguished

Consanguinity refers to the genealogical relationship between persons who are descended from a common ancestor. Affinity refers to the relationship between persons who are married and the relatives of their spouses. Both affinity and consanguinity are measured in terms of "degrees of kinship." The prevailing method of determining degrees of kinship is to count the generations between the first person and the common ancestor, and then add to that the number of generations between the common ancestor and the second person.

b. History of Consanguinity and Affinity Restrictions

Restrictions concerning intra-family marriage have existed in virtually all human societies. Anglo-American consanguinity and affinity marriage restrictions can be found in Leviticus, chapter 18, which prohibits a man to marry, *inter alia*, his mother, stepmother, daughter, daughter-in-law, sister, half-sister, sister-in-law, granddaughter, aunt, and aunt-in-law. In medieval England, the prohibitions against consanguinity and affinity were expanded even further, until marriages which seemed secure could be easily terminated if a disaffected spouse could find some relationship of blood or marriage in their genealogy. As one noted British authority explained:

> Elaborate and highly artificial rules [grew] up around the table of prohibited degrees set out in Leviticus, and they were extended to include blood relationships and relationships by marriage to the seventh degree, and also around the doctrine of spiritual affinity invented by Justinian. Indeed, it was said by Coke that a marriage could be annulled because the husband had stood godfather to his wife's cousin. The marriage of Roger Donnington was declared null and void because before its celebration he had had sexual intercourse with a third cousin of his future wife ... .

Rayden's, *infra*, at 3. In 1540, a statute of Henry VIII of England declared that no marriage could be impeached on ground of consanguinity and affinity except those within the "levitical degrees," and this rule was firmly imbedded in the common law that came to America. Wardle, 1988, *infra* § 5:14.

2. Statutes, Cases, and Doctrines

a. *In re May's Estate*

In re May's Estate

305 N.Y. 486, 114 N.E.2d 4 (1953)

LEWIS, Chief Judge

In this proceeding, involving the administration of the estate of Fannie May, deceased, we are to determine whether the marriage in 1913 between the respondent Sam May and the decedent, who was his niece by the half blood which marriage was celebrated in Rhode Island, where concededly such marriage is valid is to be given legal effect in New York where statute law declares incestuous and void a marriage between uncle and niece. Domestic Relations Law, s 5, subd. 3, McK.Consol. Laws.

The question thus presented arises from proof of the following facts: The petitioner Alice May Greenberg, one of six children born of the Rhode Island marriage of Sam and Fannie May, petitioned in 1951 for letters of administration of the estate of her mother Fannie May, who had died in 1945. Thereupon, the respondent Sam May, who asserts the validity of his marriage to the decedent, filed an objection to the issuance to petitioner of such letters of administration upon the ground that he is the surviving husband of the decedent and accordingly, under section 118 of the Surrogate's Court Act, he has the paramount right to administer her estate. Contemporaneously with, and in support of the objection filed by Sam May, his daughter Sirel Lenrow and his sons Harry May and Morris B. May who are children of the challenged marriage filed objections to the issuance of letters of administration to their sister, the petitioner, and by such objections consented that letters of administration be issued to their father Sam May.

The petitioner, supported by her sisters Ruth Weisbrout and Evelyn May, contended throughout this proceeding that her father is not the surviving spouse of her mother because, although their marriage was valid in Rhode Island, the marriage never had validity in New York where they were then resident and where they retained their residence until the decedent's death.

The record shows that for a period of more than five years prior to his marriage to decedent the respondent Sam May had resided in Portage, Wisconsin; that he came to New York in December, 1912, and within a month thereafter he and the decedent both of whom were adherents of the Jewish faith went to Providence, Rhode Island, where, on January 21, 1913, they entered into a ceremonial marriage performed by and at the home of a Jewish rabbi. The certificate issued upon that marriage gave the age of each party as twenty-six years and the residence of each as "New York, N. Y." Two weeks after their marriage in Rhode Island the respondent May and the decedent returned to Ulster County New York, where they lived as man and wife for thirty-two years until the decedent's death in 1945. Meantime the six children were born who are parties to this proceeding.

A further significant item of proof to which more particular reference will be made was the fact that in Rhode Island on January 21, 1913, the date of the marriage here involved, there were effective statutes which prohibited, the marriage of an uncle and a niece, excluding, however, those instances of which the present case is one where the marriage solemnized is between persons of the Jewish faith within the degrees of affinity and consanguinity allowed by their religion.

In Surrogate's Court, where letters of administration were granted to the petitioner, the Surrogate ruled that although the marriage of Sam May and the decedent in Rhode Island in 1913 was valid in that State, such marriage was not only void in New York as opposed to natural law but is contrary to the provisions of subdivision 3 of section 5 of the Domestic Relations Law. Accordingly the Surrogate concluded that Sam May did not qualify in this jurisdiction for letters of administration as the surviving spouse of the decedent.

At the Appellate Division the order of the Surrogate was reversed on the law and the proceeding was remitted to Surrogate's Court with direction that letters of administration upon decedent's estate be granted to Sam May who was held to be the surviving spouse of the decedent. In reaching that decision the Appellate Division concluded that the 1913 marriage of Sam May and the decedent in Rhode Island, being concededly valid in that State, is valid in New York where the degree of consanguinity of uncle and niece is not so close as to be repugnant to our concept of natural law, and that of the statute.

Domestic Relations Law, s 5, subd. 3 which declares such a marriage to be incestuous and void lacks express language which gives it extraterritorial force. The case comes to us upon appeal as of right by the petitioner and her two sisters Ruth Weisbrout and Evelyn May.

We regard the law as settled that, subject to two exceptions presently to be considered, and in the absence of a statute expressly regulating within the domiciliary State marriages solemnized abroad, the legality of a marriage between persons sui juris is to be determined by the law of the place where it is celebrated. ...

In *Van Voorhis v. Brintnall, supra,* the decision turned upon the civil status in this State of a divorced husband and his second wife whom he had married in Connecticut to evade the prohibition of a judgment of divorce which, pursuant to New York law then prevailing, forbade his remarriage until the death of his former wife. In reaching its decision, which held valid the Connecticut marriage there involved, this court noted the fact that in the much earlier case of Decouche v. Savetier, 1817, 3 Johns.Ch. 190, 211, Chancellor Kent had recognized the general principle ... "that the rights dependent upon nuptial contracts, are to be determined by the lex loci." Incidental to the decision in *Van Voorhis v. Brintnall, supra,* which followed the general rule that ... "recognizes as valid a marriage considered valid in the place where celebrated," *Id.,* 86 N.Y. at page 25, this court gave careful consideration to, and held against the application of two exceptions to that rule viz., cases within the prohibition of positive law; and cases involving polygamy or incest in a degree regarded generally as within the prohibition of natural law.

We think the Appellate Division in the case at bar rightly held that the principle of law which ruled *Van Voorhis v. Brintnall* and kindred cases cited, *supra,* was decisive of the present case and that neither of the two exceptions to that general rule is here applicable.

The statute of New York upon which the appellants rely is subdivision 3 of section 5 of the Domestic Relations Law which, insofar as relevant to our problem, provides:

"§ 5. Incestuous and void marriages

"A marriage is incestuous and void whether the relatives are legitimate or illegitimate between either: ...

"3. An uncle and niece or an aunt and nephew.

"If a marriage prohibited by the foregoing provisions of this section be solemnized it shall be void, and the parties thereto shall each be fined not less than fifty nor more than one hundred dollars and may, in the discretion of the court in addition to said fine, be imprisoned for a term not exceeding six months. Any person who shall knowingly and willfully solemnize such marriage, or procure or aid in the solemnization of the same, shall be deemed guilty of a misdemeanor and shall be fined or imprisoned in like manner."

Although the New York statute quoted above declares to be incestuous and void a marriage between an uncle and a niece and imposes penal measures upon the parties thereto, it is important to note that the statute does not by express terms regulate a marriage solemnized in another State whereas in our present case, the marriage was concededly legal. In the case at hand, as we have seen, the parties to the challenged marriage were adherents of the Jewish faith which, according to Biblical law and Jewish tradition made the subject of proof in this case permits a marriage between an uncle and a niece; they were married by a Jewish rabbi in the State of Rhode Island where, on the date of such marriage in 1913 and ever since, a statute forbidding the marriage of an uncle and a niece was expressly qualified by the following statutory exceptions appearing in 1913 in Rhode Island General Laws, tit. XXIV, ch. 243, §§ 4, 9; now tit. XXXVI, ch. 415, §§ 4, 9:

"§ 4. The provisions of the preceding sections shall not extend to, or in any way affect, any marriage which shall be solemnized among the Jews, within the degrees of affinity or consanguinity allowed by their religion."

"§ 9. Any marriage which may be had and solemnized among the people called Quakers, or Friends, in the manner and form used or practiced in their societies, or among persons professing the

Jewish religion, according to their rites and ceremonies, shall be good and valid in law; and wherever the words "minister" and "elder" are used in this chapter, they shall be held to include all of the persons connected with the society of Friends, or Quakers, and with the Jewish religion, who perform or have charge of the marriage ceremony according to their rites and ceremonies."

As section 5 of the New York Domestic Relations Law (quoted *supra)* does not expressly declare void a marriage of its domiciliaries solemnized in a foreign State where such marriage is valid, the statute's scope should not be extended by judicial construction. *Van Voorhis v. Brintnall, supra,* 86 N.Y. at page 33. Indeed, had the Legislature been so disposed it could have declared by appropriate enactment that marriages contracted in another State which if entered into here would be void shall have no force in this State. *Putnam v. Putnam,* 8 Pick. 433, 435, 25 Mass. 433, 435. Although examples of such legislation are not wanting, we find none in New York which serve to give subdivision 3 of section 5 of the Domestic Relations Law extraterritorial effectiveness. *Van Voorhis v. Brintnall, supra,* 86 N.Y. at pages 25–37. Accordingly, as to the first exception to the general rule that a marriage valid where performed is valid everywhere, we conclude that, absent any New York statute expressing clearly the Legislature's intent to regulate within this State marriages of its domiciliaries solemnized abroad, there is no "positive law" in this jurisdiction which serves to interdict the 1913 marriage in Rhode Island of the respondent Sam May and the decedent.

As to the application of the second exception to the marriage here involved between persons of the Jewish faith whose kinship was not in the direct ascending or descending line of consanguinity and who were not brother and sister we conclude that such marriage, solemnized, as it was, in accord with the ritual of the Jewish faith in a State whose legislative body has declared such a marriage to be "good and valid in law," was not offensive to the public sense of morality to a degree regarded generally with abhorrence and thus was not within the inhibitions of natural law.

A remaining point relates to an assertion by the petitioner-appellant that it was an abuse of discretion for the Appellate Division to have awarded costs against her personally. The award of costs in the Appellate Division was a matter of statutory discretion, Surrogate's Court Act, s 283, subd. 2, with which we will not interfere.

The decree of the Surrogate's Court should be affirmed, with one bill of costs to respondents, payable out of the estate.

DESMOND, Judge (dissenting).

It is fundamental that every State has the right to determine the marital status of its own citizens, *Maynard v. Hill* … . Exercising that right, New York has declared in section 5 of the Domestic Relations Law that a marriage between uncle and niece is incestuous, void and criminal. Such marriages, while not within the Levitical forbidden degrees of the Old Testament, have been condemned by public opinion for centuries (*see* 1 Bishop on Marriage, Divorce and Separation, s 738), and are void, by statute in (it would seem) forty-seven of the States of the Union (all except Georgia, *see* Martindale-Hubbell, Law Digests, and except, also, that Rhode Island, one of the forty-seven, exempts from its local statute "any marriage which shall be solemnized among the Jews, within the degrees of affinity or consanguinity allowed by their religion," Gen.L. of R.I., ch. 415, § 4). It is undisputed here that this uncle and niece were both domiciled in New York in 1913, when they left New York for the sole purpose of going to Rhode Island to be married there, and that they were married in that State conformably to its laws (*see* above) and immediately returned to New York and ever afterwards resided in this State. That Rhode Island marriage, between two New York residents, was, in New York, absolutely void for any and all purposes, by positive New York law which declares a strong public policy of this State. *See* Penal Law, § 1110.

The general rule that "a marriage valid where solemnized is valid everywhere" (*see* Restatement, Conflict of Laws, § 121) does not apply. To that rule there is a proviso or exception, recognized, it would seem, by all the States, as follows: "unless contrary to the prohibitions of natural law or the express prohibitions of a statute." *See Thorp v. Thorp,* 90 N.Y. 602, 605. Section 132 of the Restatement of

Conflict of Laws states the rule apparently followed throughout America: "A marriage which is against the law of the state of domicile of either party, though the requirements of the law of the state of celebration have been complied with, will be invalid everywhere in the following cases: ... (b) incestuous marriage between persons so closely related that their marriage is contrary to a strong public policy of the domicile." ... The old and famous New York case of *Wightman v. Wightman*, 4 Johns.Ch. 343, 349, 350, decided in 1820 when there were no marriage statutes in our State, says that marriages may be declared by "appropriate legislation," to be incestuous. New York, as a sovereign State with absolute powers over the marital status of its citizens, has enacted such legislation, but we, by this decision, are denying it efficacy.

Van Voorhis v. Brintnall, 86 N.Y. 18, does not save this marriage. That case dealt not with a marriage void under section 5 of the Domestic Relations Law, but one forbidden by section 8 thereof. Section 8 forbids the guilty party, in a New York divorce judgment, to marry again within a certain time, and the Van Voorhis ruling was that, by section 8, the Legislature did not intend to make such marriages contracted outside this State absolutely void, but merely stated an in personam prohibition against the adjudged adulterer marrying, for a period of time. ... This court's opinion in the *Van Voorhis* case, while stating the general rule that the validity of a marriage depends on the law of the place of marriage, noted that there are exceptions thereto in cases of incest, within the prohibition of natural law, and "prohibition by positive law." 86 N.Y. at page 26. Section 5 of the Domestic Relations Law, the one we are concerned with here, lists the marriages which are "incestuous and void" in New York, as being those between parent and child, brother and sister, uncle and niece, and aunt and nephew. All such misalliances are incestuous, and all, equally, are void. The policy, language, meaning and validity of the statute are beyond dispute. It should be enforced by the courts.

The order should be reversed and the proceeding remitted to the Surrogate for appropriate proceedings, with costs to abide the event.

CONWAY, DYE, FULD and FROESSEL, JJ., concur with LEWIS, C. J. ...

VAN VOORHIS, J., taking no part.

Decree affirmed.

b. Notes and Question

1) Contemporary Restrictions of Consanguinity and Affinity

All states except Alabama have explicit civil statutes prohibiting certain marriages of consanguinity. All states except Ohio and Vermont have explicit criminal incest statutes outlawing incestuous relations. (The civil and criminal proscriptions are similar but not always identical.) In thirty states (including Utah, and most of the West) marriages within the fourth degree (including first cousins) are prohibited. In twenty states (mostly Eastern) first-cousin marriages are allowed. Rhode Island still has an exception for marriages by Jewish couples. Colorado and Minnesota allow consanguineous marriages "if permitted by aboriginal cultures." Nevada also has a similar provision. Some states except from their general prohibition of first-cousin marriages persons over 65 or incapable of producing children. Marriages in violation of consanguinity restrictions generally have been invalidated, and often denied interjurisdictional recognition. For example, in *Catalano v. Catalano,* 170 A.2d 726 (Conn. 1961), a marriage between an uncle and niece that was valid (by legal dispensation) in Italy where it was contracted was declared invalid and the surviving wife denied a widow's allowance even though the parties had been married for seven years, lived together in Connecticut for two years, and had a child.

Generally, the law recognizes no distinction between relationships of the half and the whole blood for purposes of consanguinity and affinity restrictions, as *May's Estate* illustrates. In *Singh v. Singh,* 569 A.2d 1112 (Conn. 1990), the Connecticut Supreme Court ruled that marriage of an uncle and niece related by the half blood (the wife's mother was the husband's half-sister) was prohibited and void in Connecticut even though they had been lawfully married later in another state, and even though it meant the wife would be expelled by the INS and not permitted to immigrate for at least two years. In some states the statutes (especially criminal statutes) defining prohibited degrees expressly mention half-blood relations in the prohibition of relations between brother and sister but are silent about half-blood in other relations; some of these statutes have been construed under the *inclusio unios* axiom to limit the half-blood restriction to the brother-sister relations. Calif. Penal Code § 285; *State v. Bartley,* 263 S.W. 95 (Mo. 1924). But the general common law presumption is that the prohibited relations in consanguinity and incest statutes include both whole and half-blood, as well as both legitimate and illegitimate. *People v. Baker,* 69 Cal.2d 44, 47, 442 P.2d 675, 69 Cal.Rptr. 595 (1968)

Whether persons related by adoption within the prohibited degrees of consanguinity may intermarry has produced inconsistent results. Many statutes are unclear. Some early cases held that sexual intercourse with adopted relations within the prohibited degrees did not constitute criminal incest. *See e.g. State v. Lee,* 17 So. 2d 277, 196 Miss. 311 (1944); *People v. Kaiser,* 51 P. 702 (Cal. 1897). Many recent cases hold that if the parties are related closely by adoption, the consanguinity marriage restrictions will prohibit their marriage, *see In re Marriage of M.E.W. and M.L.B.,* 4 Pa. D. & C. 3d 51 (Allegheny Cnty Orph. Ct. 1977), but if they are on the fringes of the prohibition (first cousins) and related only by adoption, the marriage may be permitted or recognized. *In re Enderle Marriage License,* 1 Pa. D. & C. 2d 114 (Phila. Orphans Ct. 1954). Likewise, if parties are related by blood within the prohibited degrees, the adoption of one of them by another family does not appear to take them out of the consanguinity marriage prohibition. *See e.g. State v. Sharon H.,* 429 A.2d 1321 (Del. Super. 1981). In 1978, a Colorado court ruled, on rather conclusory analysis, that a prohibition against the marriage of adoptive brother-sister did not rationally further the state interest in family harmony and was unconstitutional. *Israel v. Allen,* 577 P.2d 762 (Colo. 1978).

Sixteen states prohibit marriages between persons related by affinity (none of the states are in the west). Lineal kin of a spouse or spouses of lineal kin are the relationships in which marriage is prohibited. Collateral affinity, however, is not prohibited. *See* Lynn D. Wardle, *Marriage Prohibitions, infra.*

Much of the legal commentary addressing consanguinity since 2001 has been in the context of discussing same-sex family relationships (marriage, parenting, or domestic violence), *see* Grossman, *infra;* and Zgonjanin, *infra;* or assisted reproduction, *see* Mabry. *infra.* Many recent cases mentioning consanguinity have involved domestic abuse or violence, *see State v. Rodgers,* 827 N.E.2d 872 (Ohio Com. Pl., 2005); incest, *see State v. Johnson,* 695 N.W.2d 165 (Neb., 2005); or potential bias or nepotism, *Wilmore v. State,* 602 S.E.2d 343 (Ga. App., 2004).

2) Social Interests in Restricting Consanguinity and Affinity

Four principal justifications have been offered for consanguinity and affinity marriage restrictions. One that was popular in the early part of the twentieth century period of scientific racism was eugenics. This justification emphasizes the increased risk of defective offspring of couples who are closely related genetically. The second justification is sociological, and emphasizes the need for a zone of harmonious family relations that is free from mating competition and potential sexual exploitation. The importance of a "safe haven" for children and vulnerable dependents remains a sociologically important consideration. The third justification is moral. Both the Old and New Testaments contain explicit condemnation of incestuous behavior, which clearly influenced the early common law prohibitions of consanguineous marriages. The repugnance of incest is not limited to the Judeo-Christian religious tradition, but some form of incest taboo appears to be a nearly ubiquitous moral rule in nearly all cultures. The fourth justification for laws forbidding consanguinity and affinity is historical or traditional. Since all societies have had such restrictions, and many modern restrictions have existed for many centuries in Anglo-American law, there is reluctance to abandon or change them.

The Supreme Court has occasionally alluded to the social interest in discouraging or preventing incest. *See Zablocki v. Redhail*, 434 U.S. 374, 386 (1978). Justice Powell, concurring, explained, "[t]he State, representing the collective expression of moral aspirations, has an undeniable interest in ensuring that its rules of domestic relations reflect the widely held values of its people. ... State regulation has included bans on incest, bigamy, and homosexuality, as well as various preconditions to marriage, such as blood tests." *Zablocki*, 434 U.S. at 398 (1978) (Powell, J., concurring); *Griswold v. Connecticut,* 381 U.S. 479, 505 (1965) (White, J., concurring) ("[T]he state's policy against all forms of promiscuous or illicit sexual relationships, be they premarital or extramarital, [is] concededly a permissible and legitimate legislative goal."); *id.* at 498 (Goldberg, J., concurring) ("[T]he Court's holding today that it in no way interferes with a State's proper regulation of sexual promiscuity or misconduct."); *Poe v. Ullman*, 367 U.S. 497, 546–47 (1961) (Harlan, J., dissenting). However, some western nations have relaxed their incest prohibitions. *See e.g.* Mary Ann Glendon, *infra*, at 55–58; Peter F.G. Rook & Robert Ward, *infra* § 3.38 at 104 (citing Criminal Law Revision Committee, Fifteenth report on *Sexual Offences*, Cmnd. 9213, Part VIII, pp. 63–73, English law reform proposes decriminalize incest between brother and sister if twenty-one years old). *See also* Greenberg, *infra*.

3) Valid Policies?

Are these justifications still valid? In days of prenatal screening, DNA testing, in utero treatment, genetic engineering, high-tech contraception, sterilization, abortion-on-demand, "mixed" families (half-siblings, step-relations, etc.), moral relativitism, and strict separation of church and state, should the marriage of close relatives still be forbidden? Why or why not?

3. Practical and Ethical Considerations

In an initial consultation interview, Brother Bill and Sister Sue tell Lawyer Linda that they are in love with each other and want to marry. They are biological half-siblings, having the same father but different mothers, and were raised in separate families. Bill is 25 and Sue is 26. They want Linda to find a jurisdiction in which they could lawfully marry or, alternatively, to file suit for them against the local law that forbids half-blood siblings reared in separate homes from marrying. They are cohabiting non-maritally and Sue is pregnant with Bill's child. Sexual relations between half-blood siblings is criminal incest in the local jurisdiction. Lawyer Linda personally favors the existing law, and has personal moral objections to marriage between siblings of the whole or half-blood. Please explain whether, as a matter of professional ethics, Linda is—(a) required to represent them in seeking all the legal relief they want? (b) required to look for a jurisdiction in which they might marry, but not to bring suit challenging the local law? (c) not required to assist them in finding a jurisdiction where they might marry or to represent them in challenging the local law? (d) permitted but not required to report their incest to law enforcement authorities? (e) required to report their incest to law enforcement authorities? As a general rule, (f) is a family lawyer professionally obligated to represent a party seeking a legal remedy that he or she personally considers inappropriate or immoral?

4. Bibliography

American Law Institute, Model Penal Code § 2.30 (1985).

Ralph C. Brashier, *Consanguinity, Sibling Relationships, and the Default Rules of Inheritance Law: Reshaping Half-Blood Statutes to Reflect the Evolving Family*, 58 SMU L. Rev. 137 (2005).

Carolyn S. Bratt, *Incest Statutes and the Fundamental Right of Marriage: Is Oedipus Free to Marry*, 18 Fam. L.Q. 257 (1984).

Contemporary Family Law, vol. I, Ch. 2 (Lynn D. Wardle, Christopher L. Blakesley & Jacqueline Y. Parker, eds., 1988).

Mary Ann Glendon, Abortion and Divorce in Western Law (1988).

Julie A. Greenberg, *Defining Male and Female Intersexuality and the Collusion Between Law and Biology*, 41 Ariz. L. Rev. 265 (1999).

Joanna L. Grossman, *Fear and Loathing in Massachusetts: Same-Sex Marriage and Some Lessons from the History of Marriage and Divorce*, 14 B.U. Pub. Int. L.J. 87 (2004).

Katherine L. Hann, *Inbreeding and Fertility in a South Indian Population*, 12 Annals of Human Biology 267 (No. 3 1985).

Cynthia R. Mabry, *"Who Is My Real Father:"—The Delicate Task of Identifying A Father and Parenting Children Created from An In Vitro Mix-Up*, 18 Nat'l Black L.J. 1 (2004–2005).

Sheldon C. Reed, Counseling in Medical Genetics 34-41 (2d ed. 1963).

Claude Levi-Strauss, The Elementary Structures of Kinship (James Harle Bell, John Richard von Sturmer & Rodney Needham, trans., 1969).

Sanja Zgonjanin, *What Does It Take to be A (Lesbian) Parent? On Intent and Genetics*, 16 Hastings Wo.'s L.J. 251 (2005).

Lynn D. Wardle, *Marriage Prohibitions* in 1 Family Law in the United States (L. Wardle, C. Blakesley & J. Parker, eds. 1980).

B. PHYSICAL CAPACITY TO MARRY

1. Background

a. Impotence

Physical capacity to marry refers to the fact that at common law, it was expected that both parties would be able to engage in marital (sexual) relations with each other. Sexual consummation was the test for physical capacity. Impotence, meaning the inability to engage in *vera copula*, "ordinary and complete" sexual intercourse, was a marriage defect but only rendered the marriage voidable. Thus, inability to sexually consummate a marriage does not make the marriage void *ab initio*, but gives the spouse of the disabled person a basis for seeking annulment. Cohabitation after discovery of the defect presumably would ratify the marriage. *Impotence* must be distinguished from *infertility*. Ability to procreate was *not* an essential requirement for marriage. Infertility or sterility, the inability to produce offspring, did not and does not affect marriage validity. Rather, only impotence was the basis for a finding of want of physical capacity to marry. *See* Contemporary Family Law *infra, §* 2.46.

b. Disease

Early in this century, a eugenic movement resulted in many states enacting laws prohibiting the marriage of persons infected with certain diseases. Epileptics, persons infected with tuberculosis, and some persons with serious (then incurable) sexually transmitted diseases were barred from marrying in many states. However, disease was not a ground for invalidating or prohibiting marriage at common law, and in the absence of such statutes, infection does not render a marriage invalid. Today, such statutes are rare. Directory physical examination requirements to detect and notify of diseases before marriage do not render void a marriage in violation of them. *See* Contemporary Family Law *infra, §* 2.47.

2. Statutes, Cases, and Doctrines

a. Current Statutes

Today, statutes in one-third of the states identify impotence as a defect rending a marriage voidable. In a few other states, impotence is grounds for divorce (indicating that in those states it is not a voidable defect that nullifies the marriage, but grounds for terminating the marriage).

b. Definition of "Male" and "Female"

What is the gender of a post-operative transsexual (a man who has undergone surgery to look/be more like a woman, or a woman who has undergone surgery to look/be more like a man)? What is the legal test for determining a person's sex? Is this essentially the same question as whether same-sex marriage is permitted?

In a leading English case, *Corbett v. Corbett*, 2 WLR 1306, 2 All Eng Rptr 33 (PDA 1970), the court applied a chromosomal test for gender and declared null the marriage of a male-to-female postoperative who went by the name "April," worked as a female model, and had married a man. In the absence of legislation otherwise, that appears to be the predominant American approach as well. *See e.g. Kantaras v. Kantaras*, 884 So.2d 155 (Fl. Dist. Ct. App. 2004); *In re Estate of Gardiner,* 42 P.3d 120 (Kan. 2002); *Littleton v. Prange*, 9 S.W.3d 223 (Tex.Civ.App.1999); *In re Ladrach*, 32 Ohio Misc.2d 6, 513 N.E.2d 828 (1987); *Anonymous v. Mellon*, 91 Misc.2d 375, 380, 398 N.Y.S.2d 99 (1977); *B v. B.*, 355 N.Y.S.2d 712 (1974); *Hartin v. Dir. of Bur. of Recs.*, 75 Misc.2d 229, 232, 347 N.Y.S.2d 515 (1973); *Anonymous v. Anonymous*, 325 N.Y.S.2d 499 (1971); *Anonymous v. Weiner*, 50 Misc.2d 380, 270 N.Y.S.2d 319 (1966); *but see MT v. JT*, 355 A.2d 204 (N.J. Super. 1976).

In a proceeding to administer the estate of a wealthy man, Marshall, who died intestate in Kansas, this question arose when his son, Joe, claimed to be the sole heir because his estranged father's marriage to a post-operative male-to-female, J'Noel, was invalid. J'Noel was born male in Wisconsin, and had been married as a man for five years. He underwent sex-change surgeries and therapies, after which his/her birth certificate was reissued to indicate that J'Noel was a female. J'Noel met the wealthy, aged, Marshall (a donor to and benefactor of the college where J'Noel taught) in the spring of 1998, allegedly had sex with him that July and married him in Kansas in September, 1998; eleven months later Marshall died intestate and J'Noel claimed to be the surviving spouse entitled to an inheritance along with Joe, the administrator of the estate. Joe challenged the validity of the marriage. How should that issue have been decided? There also was a potential "full faith and credit" issue arising from the Wisconsin revised birth certificate. *See In re Estate of Gardiner,* 22 P.3d 1086 (Kan.App. 2001), rev'd, *In re Estate of Gardiner,* 42 P.3d 120 (Kan. 2002). *See also* Kogan, *infra;* Zakaria, *infra.*

3. Practical and Ethical Considerations

See A.3., *supra.*

4. Bibliography

Contemporary Family Law, vol. I, Ch. 2 (Lynn D. Wardle, Christopher L. Blakesley & Jacqueline Y. Parker, eds., 1988).
Terry S. Kogan, *Transsexuals, Intersexuals, and Same-Sex Marriage,* 18 BYU J. Pub. L. 371 (2004).
Teresa A. Zakaria, Note, *By Any Other Name: Defining Male & Female in Marriage Statutes,* Ave Maria L. Rev. 349 (2005).

C. SAME-SEX MARRIAGE

1. Background

a. The Movement to Legalize Same-Sex Marriage in the United States

Until 2004, same-sex marriage was not permitted in any American state, but there has been a litigation campaign to legalize same-sex marriage by judicial decree since the early 1970s. The first effort was in the 1970s and early 1980s. Then, in a series of cases, nearly a dozen courts unanimously rejected all claims that states are obliged to allow same-sex marriage. *Baker v. Belson.* 191 N.W.2d 185 (Minn. 1971), *app. dism'd for want of subst'l federal question,* 409 U.S. 810 (1972) (Minnesota law prohibiting same sex marriage does not offend the First, Eighth, Ninth, or Fourteenth Amendments to the Constitution);.*Burkett v. Zablocki,* 54 F.R.D. 626 (E.D. Wis. 1972) (dismissing claim of same-sex couple seeking marriage license after plaintiffs fail to file memoranda); *Jones v. Hallahan,* 501 S.W.2d 588 (Ky. 1973) (affirming judgment that two females were not entitled to a marriage license; "the relationship proposed by the appellants does not authorize the issuance of a marriage license because what they propose is not a marriage." *Id.* at 590); *Frances B. v. Mark B.,* 78 Misc. 2d 112, N.Y. (Sup. Ct. 1974) (holding marriage ceremony between woman and another female who fraudulently held herself out as a man a "nullity"; "marriage has always been considered as the union of a man and a woman." *Id*. at 716; "defendant cannot function as a husband by assuming male duties and obligations inherent in the marriage relationship." *Id*. at 717); *Singer v. Hara*, 522 P.2d 1187 (Wash. App. 1974) (affirming denial of marriage license to persons of the same sex; "marriage, as a legal relationship, may exist only between one man and one woman," *id*. at 1190; rejecting claims based on state Equal Rights Amendment, and other constitutional claims); *McConnell v. Nooner*, 547 F.2d 54 (8th Cir. 1976) (rejecting claims to increased veteran's benefits based on same-sex marriage; there is no "right to marry [someone of the same sex] under Minnesota law [or] under the United States Constitution." *Id*. at 56); *Adams v. Howerton*, 486 F. Supp. 1119 (C.D. Cal. 1980), *aff'd on the basis of federal law*, 673 F.2d 1036 (9th Cir.), *cert. denied* 458 U.S. 1111 (1982) (upholding denial of petition for "immediate relative" status of Australian male who claimed to have married an American male in Colorado; under Colorado law, marriage "necessarily and exclusively involves a contract, a status, and a relationship between persons of different sexes," *id*. at 1122, and "Congress, as a matter of federal law, did not intend that a person of one sex could be a 'spouse' to a person of the same sex for immigration law purposes." *Id*. at 1123); *De Santo v. Barnsley*, 476 A.2d 952 (Pa. Super Ct. 1984) (refusing to recognize attempted common law marriage between two men in divorce action; "common law marriage is limited to two persons of the opposite sex." *Id*. at 954); *In re Ladrach*, 513 N.E.2d 828 (Ohio 1987) (rejecting marriage license claim of transsexual male and another male; finding sex change operation did not change sex for purpose of marriage; "there is not authority in Ohio for the issuance of a marriage license to consummate a marriage between a post-operative male to female transsexual person and a male person." *Id*. at 832); *see also Jennings v. Jennings*, 315 A.2d 816 (Md. Spec. Ct. App. 1974) (in dispute over administration of decedent's estate, court declares in dicta that "Maryland does not recognize a marriage between persons of the same sex." *Id*. at 820 n.7); *Slayton v. Texas*, 633 S.W.2d 934 (Tex. Ct. App. 1982) (affirming conviction for indecency with a child even though the prosecution did not allege the male defendant had a "non-spousal" relationship with the male victim; "neither participant can be the other's spouse any more than a person can simultaneously be man and fish." *Id*. at 937).

The second litigation wave began in the 1990s and still continues. Again, most courts have rejected the claims for same-sex marriage. *See e.g. Callender v. Corbett*, No. 296666 (Ariz. Super. Ct., Pima County, Apr. 13, 1994) (rejecting claims of homosexual couples to same-sex marriage; marriage license law allowing only heterosexual couples to marry does not discriminate against homosexuals, but "merely codifies what has traditionally been defined as marriage." *Id*. at 3.); *Dean v. District of Columbia*, 653 A.2d 307 (D.C. 1995), (exhaustive opinion upholding denial of marriage license to two men, rejecting multiple statutory and constitutional arguments for same-sex marriage); *In re Estate of Cooper*, 564 N.Y.S.2d 684 (N.Y. Sup. Ct. 1990) (survivor of a homosexual relationship may not claim spousal rights against decedent's will; the court declined to "elevate[] homosexual unions to the same level achieved by the marriage of two people of the opposite sex." *Id*. at 687); *Storrs v. Holcomb*, 645 N.Y.S.2d (Sup. Ct. 1996) (holding that New York does not recognize or authorize same-sex marriage).

However, between 1993 and 1999, state courts in three states rendered decisions based on interpretation of state constitutions that favored or ordered legalization of same-sex marriages or unions. In *Baehr v. Lewin*, 852 P.2d 44 (1993), the Hawaii Supreme

Court held that claims that denial of marriage licenses to same-sex couples violated the equality provisions of the Hawaii Constitution presented could not be dismissed on the pleadings. Later, in *Baehr v. Miike,* 1996 WL 694235 (November 1996) a Hawaii trial court ruled that the state had failed to show that denial of same-sex marriage was justified by a compelling state interest, and the court ordered the state to issue marriage licenses to same-sex couples. However, that order was stayed pending appeal to the state supreme court, and while the appeal was pending, the Hawaii legislature proposed and in 1998, the citizens ratified (by 69 percent to 29 percent) an amendment to the state constitution validating the marriage statute barring same-sex marriage.

Likewise, a trial court opinion in Alaska rejecting the state's motion for summary judgment in a similar suit by a same-sex couple seeking a marriage license opined that denial of marriage for same-sex couples violated both the equality provisions and the privacy provision of the Alaska Constitution. *Brause v. Bureau of Vital Statistics,* 1998 WL 88743 (Anchorage Superior Ct, 1997). While the case was still pending, the Alaska legislature proposed and in 1998, the citizens ratified (by 69 percent to 31 percent) an amendment to the state constitution defining marriage as the union of a man and a woman. The third decision in 1999, by the Vermont Supreme Court, held that denial of marriage or an equivalent status for same-sex couples violated the Common Benefits Clause of the state constitution. *Baker v. State,* 744 A.2d 864 (Vt. 1999). The court invited the legislature to fashion an appropriate remedy, and four months later the legislature passed "Civil Union" legislation conferring virtually all of the legal benefits and rights of marriage upon same-sex couples who register. *See infra, Chapter* 8.

In an October 2003 judgment, effective six months later, the Massachusetts Supreme Court ruled (by a 4-3 vote) that the state constitution compelled the state to offer equal status and benefits to same-sex couples as provided to married heterosexual couples. *Goodridge v. Dep't. of Health,* 798 N.E.2d. 941 (Mass. 2003). *Goodridge* has re-ignited the litigation campaign for same-sex marriage.

2. Statutes, Cases, and Doctrines

a. *Goodridge v. Dep't Pub. H.*
Goodridge v. Department of Public Health
798 N.E.2d 941 (Mass. 2003)

MARSHALL, C.J.

Marriage is a vital social institution. The exclusive commitment of two individuals to each other nurtures love and mutual support; it brings stability to our society. For those who choose to marry, and for their children, marriage provides an abundance of legal, financial, and social benefits. In return it imposes weighty legal, financial, and social obligations. The question before us is whether, consistent with the Massachusetts Constitution, the Commonwealth may deny the protections, benefits, and obligations conferred by civil marriage to two individuals of the same sex who wish to marry. We conclude that it may not. The Massachusetts Constitution affirms the dignity and equality of all individuals. It forbids the creation of second-class citizens. In reaching our conclusion we have given full deference to the arguments made by the Commonwealth. But it has failed to identify any constitutionally adequate reason for denying civil marriage to same-sex couples.

We are mindful that our decision marks a change in the history of our marriage law. Many people hold deep-seated religious, moral, and ethical convictions that marriage should be limited to the union of one man and one woman, and that homosexual conduct is immoral. Many hold equally strong religious, moral, and ethical convictions that same-sex couples are entitled to be married, and that homosexual persons should be treated no differently than their heterosexual neighbors. Neither view answers the question before us. Our concern is with the Massachusetts Constitution as a charter of governance for every person properly within its reach. "Our obligation is to define the liberty of all, not to mandate our own moral code." *Lawrence v. Texas*, 539 U.S. 558, (2003) (*Lawrence*), quoting *Planned Parenthood of Southeastern Pa. v. Casey*, 505 U.S. 833, 850 (1992).

Whether the Commonwealth may use its formidable regulatory authority to bar same-sex couples from civil marriage is a question not previously addressed by a Massachusetts appellate court. It is a question the United States Supreme Court left open as a matter of Federal law in *Lawrence, supra* at 2484, where it was not an issue. There, the Court affirmed that the core concept of common human dignity protected by the Fourteenth Amendment to the United States Constitution precludes government intrusion into the deeply personal realms of consensual adult expressions of intimacy and one's choice of an intimate partner. The Court also reaffirmed the central role that decisions whether to marry or have children bear in shaping one's identity. *Id.* at 2481. The Massachusetts Constitution is, if anything, more protective of individual liberty and equality than the Federal Constitution; it may demand broader protection for fundamental rights; and it is less tolerant of government intrusion into the protected spheres of private life.

Barred access to the protections, benefits, and obligations of civil marriage, a person who enters into an intimate, exclusive union with another of the same sex is arbitrarily deprived of membership in one of our community's most rewarding and cherished institutions. That exclusion is incompatible with the constitutional principles of respect for individual autonomy and equality under law.

I

The plaintiffs are fourteen individuals from five Massachusetts counties.

. . . In March and April, 2001, each of the plaintiff couples attempted to obtain a marriage license from a city or town clerk's office. As required under G.L. c. 207, they completed notices of intention to marry on forms provided by the registry, *see* G.L. c. 207, § 20, and presented these forms to a Massachusetts town or city clerk, together with the required health forms and marriage license fees. *See* G.L. c. 207, § 19. In each case, the clerk either refused to accept the notice of intention to marry or denied a marriage license to the couple on the ground that Massachusetts does not recognize same-sex marriage. Because obtaining a marriage license is a necessary prerequisite to civil marriage in Massachusetts, denying marriage licenses to the plaintiffs was tantamount to denying them access to civil marriage itself, with its appurtenant social and legal protections, benefits, and obligations.

On April 11, 2001, the plaintiffs filed suit in the Superior Court against the department and the commissioner seeking a judgment that "the exclusion of the [p]laintiff couples and other qualified same-sex couples from access to marriage licenses, and the legal and social status of civil marriage, as well as the protections, benefits and obligations of marriage, violates Massachusetts law." *See* G.L. c. 231A. The plaintiffs alleged violation of the laws of the Commonwealth, including but not limited to their rights under arts. 1, 6, 7, 10, 12, and 16, and Part II, c. 1, § 1, art. 4, of the Massachusetts Constitution. The department, represented by the Attorney General, admitted to a policy and practice of denying marriage licenses to same-sex couples. It denied that its actions violated any law or that the plaintiffs were entitled to relief. The parties filed cross motions for summary judgment.

A Superior Court judge ruled for the department. ... After the complaint was dismissed and summary judgment entered for the defendants, the plaintiffs appealed. Both parties requested direct appellate review, which we granted.

II

... [F]or all the joy and solemnity that normally attend a marriage, G.L. c. 207, governing entrance to marriage is a licensing law. The plaintiffs argue that because nothing in that licensing law specifically prohibits marriages between persons of the same sex, we may interpret the statute to permit "qualified same sex couples" to obtain marriage licenses, thereby avoiding the question whether the law is constitutional. *See School Comm. of Greenfield v. Greenfield Educ. Ass'n,* 385 Mass. 70, 79 (1982) and cases cited. This claim lacks merit.

We interpret statutes to carry out the Legislature's intent, determined by the words of a statute interpreted according to "the ordinary and approved usage of the language." *Hanlon v. Rollins,* 286 Mass. 444, 447 (1934). The everyday meaning of "marriage" is "[t]he legal union of a man and woman as husband and wife," Black's Law Dictionary 986 (7th ed.1999), and the plaintiffs do not argue that the term "marriage" has ever had a different meaning under Massachusetts law. *See e.g. Milford v. Worcester,* 7 Mass. 48, 52 (1810) (marriage "is an engagement, by which a single man and a single woman, of sufficient discretion, take each other for husband and wife"). This definition of marriage, as both the department and the Superior Court judge point out, derives from the common law. ... Far from being ambiguous, the undefined word "marriage," as used in G.L. c. 207, confirms the General Court's intent to hew to the term's common-law and quotidian meaning concerning the genders of the marriage partners.

The intended scope of G.L. c. 207 is also evident in its consanguinity provisions. ... Sections 1 and 2 of G.L. c. 207 prohibit marriages between a man and certain female relatives and a woman and certain male relatives, but are silent as to the consanguinity of male-male or female-female marriage applicants. *See* G.L. c. 207, §§ 1–2. The only reasonable explanation is that the Legislature did not intend that same-sex couples be licensed to marry. We conclude, as did the judge, that G.L. c. 207 may not be construed to permit same-sex couples to marry.

III

A

The larger question is whether, as the department claims, government action that bars same-sex couples from civil marriage constitutes a legitimate exercise of the State's authority to regulate conduct, or whether, as the plaintiffs claim, this categorical marriage exclusion violates the Massachusetts Constitution. ... The plaintiffs' claim that the marriage restriction violates the Massachusetts Constitution can be analyzed in two ways. Does it offend the Constitution's guarantees of equality before the law? Or do the liberty and due process provisions of the Massachusetts Constitution secure the plaintiffs' right to marry their chosen partner? In matters implicating marriage, family life, and the upbringing of children, the two constitutional concepts frequently overlap, as they do here. *See e.g. M.L.B. v. S.L.J.,* 519 U.S. 102, 120 (1996) (noting convergence of due process and equal protection principles in cases concerning parent-child relationships); *Perez v. Sharp,* 32 Cal.2d 711, 728 (1948) (analyzing statutory ban on interracial marriage as equal protection violation concerning regulation of fundamental right). *See also Lawrence, supra* at 2482 ("Equality of treatment and the due process right to demand respect for conduct protected by the substantive guarantee of liberty are linked in important respects, and a decision on the latter point advances both interests") .... We begin by considering the nature of civil marriage itself. Simply put, the government creates civil marriage. In Massachusetts, civil marriage is, and since pre-Colonial days has been, precisely what its name implies: a wholly secular institution. ...

In a real sense, there are three partners to every civil marriage: two willing spouses and an approving State. ... Civil marriage is created and regulated through exercise of the police power. ... In broad terms, it is the Legislature's power to enact rules to regulate conduct, to the extent that such laws are "necessary to secure the health, safety, good order, comfort, or general welfare of the community" (citations omitted). *Opinion of the Justices,* 341 Mass. 760, 785 (1960). ...

Without question, civil marriage enhances the "welfare of the community." It is a "social institution of the highest importance." *French v. McAnarney, supra.* Civil marriage anchors an ordered society by encouraging stable relationships over transient ones. It is central to the way the Commonwealth identifies individuals, provides for the orderly distribution of property, ensures that children and adults are cared for and supported whenever possible from private rather than public funds, and tracks important epidemiological and demographic data.

Marriage also bestows enormous private and social advantages on those who choose to marry. Civil marriage is at once a deeply personal commitment to another human being and a highly public celebration of the ideals of mutuality, companionship, intimacy, fidelity, and family. "It is an association that promotes a way of life, not causes; a harmony in living, not political faiths; a bilateral loyalty, not commercial or social projects." *Griswold v. Connecticut*, 381 U.S. 479, 486 (1965). Because it fulfils yearnings for security, safe haven, and connection that express our common humanity, civil marriage is an esteemed institution, and the decision whether and whom to marry is among life's momentous acts of self-definition.

Tangible as well as intangible benefits flow from marriage. The marriage license grants valuable property rights to those who meet the entry requirements, and who agree to what might otherwise be a burdensome degree of government regulation of their activities. ...

The benefits accessible only by way of a marriage license are enormous, touching nearly every aspect of life and death. The department states that "hundreds of statutes" are related to marriage and to marital benefits. With no attempt to be comprehensive, we note that some of the statutory benefits conferred by the Legislature on those who enter into civil marriage include, as to property: joint Massachusetts income tax filing (G.L. c. 62C, § 6); tenancy by the entirety (a form of ownership that provides certain protections against creditors and allows for the automatic descent of property to the surviving spouse without probate) (G.L. c. 184, § 7); extension of the benefit of the homestead protection (securing up to $300,000 in equity from creditors) to one's spouse and children (G.L. c. 188, § 1); automatic rights to inherit the property of a deceased spouse who does not leave a will (G.L. c. 190, § 1); the rights of elective share and of dower (which allow surviving spouses certain property rights where the decedent spouse has not made adequate provision for the survivor in a will) (G.L. c. 191, § 15, and G.L. c. 189); entitlement to wages owed to a deceased employee (G.L. c. 149, § 178A [general] and G.L. c. 149, § 178C [public employees]); eligibility to continue certain businesses of a deceased spouse (e.g., G.L. c. 112, § 53 [dentist]); the right to share the medical policy of one's spouse (e.g., G.L. c. 175, § 108, Second [*a*] [3] [defining insured's "dependent" to include one's spouse]), (*see Connors v. Boston*, 430 Mass. 31, 43 (1999) [domestic partners of city employees not included within term "dependent" as used in G.L. c. 32B, § 2]); thirty-nine week continuation of health coverage for the spouse of a person who is laid off or dies (e.g., G.L. c. 175, § 110G); preferential options under the Commonwealth's pension system (*see* G.L. c. 32, § 12[2] ["Joint and Last Survivor Allowance"]); preferential benefits in the Commonwealth's medical program, MassHealth (e.g., 130 Code Mass. Regs. § 515.012[A], prohibiting placing lien on long-term care patient's former home if spouse still lives there); access to veterans' spousal benefits and preferences (e.g., G.L. c. 115, § 1 [defining "dependents"] and G.L. c. 31, § 26 [State employment] and § 28 [municipal employees]); financial protections for spouses of certain Commonwealth employees (fire fighters, police officers, and prosecutors, among others) killed in the performance of duty (e.g., G.L. c. 32, §§ 100-103); the equitable division of marital property on divorce (G.L. c. 208, § 34); temporary and permanent alimony rights (G.L. c. 208, §§ 17 and 34); the right to separate support on separation of the parties that does not result in divorce (G.L. c. 209, § 32); and the right to bring claims for wrongful death and loss of consortium, and for funeral and burial expenses and punitive damages resulting from tort actions (G.L. c. 229, §§ 1 and 2; G.L. c. 228, § 1. *See Feliciano v. Rosemar Silver Co., supra*).

* * *

Where a married couple has children, their children are also directly or indirectly, but no less auspiciously, the recipients of the special legal and economic protections obtained by civil marriage ... . It is undoubtedly for these concrete reasons, as well as for its intimately personal significance, that civil marriage has long been termed a "civil right." *See e.g. Loving v. Virginia*, 388 U.S. 1, 12 (1967) ("Marriage is one of the 'basic civil rights of man,' fundamental to our very existence and survival"), quoting *Skinner v. Oklahoma*, 316 U.S. 535, 541 (1942); *Milford v. Worcester*, 7 Mass. 48, 56 (1810) (referring to "civil rights incident to marriages"). ...

Without the right to marry—or more properly, the right to choose to marry—one is excluded from the full range of human experience and denied full protection of the laws for one's "avowed commitment to an intimate and lasting human relationship." *Baker v. State, supra* at 229. Because civil marriage is central to the lives of individuals and the welfare of the community, our laws assiduously protect the individual's right to marry against undue government incursion. Laws may not "interfere directly and substantially with the right to marry." *Zablocki v. Redhail, supra* at 387. *See Perez v. Sharp*, 32 Cal.2d 711, 714 (1948) ("There can be no prohibition of marriage except for an important social objective and reasonable means"). ...

B

For decades, indeed centuries, in much of this country (including Massachusetts) no lawful marriage was possible between white and black Americans. That long history availed not when the Supreme Court of California held in 1948 that a legislative prohibition against interracial marriage violated the due process and equality guarantees of the Fourteenth Amendment, *Perez v. Sharp*, 32 Cal.2d 711, 728 (1948), or when, nineteen years later, the United States Supreme Court also held that a statutory bar to interracial marriage violated the Fourteenth Amendment, *Loving v. Virginia*, 388 U.S. 1 (1967). As both *Perez* and *Loving* make clear, the right to marry means little if it does not include the right to marry the person of one's choice, subject to appropriate government restrictions in the interests of public health, safety, and welfare. *See Perez v. Sharp, supra* at 717 ("the essence of the right to marry is freedom to join in marriage with the person of one's choice"). *See also Loving v. Virginia, supra* at 12. In this case, as in *Perez* and *Loving*, a statute deprives individuals of access to an institution of fundamental legal, personal, and social significance—the institution of marriage—because of a single trait: skin color in *Perez* and *Loving*, sexual orientation here. As it did in *Perez* and *Loving*, history must yield to a more fully developed understanding of the invidious quality of the discrimination.

The Massachusetts Constitution protects matters of personal liberty against government incursion as zealously, and often more so, than does the Federal Constitution, even where both Constitutions employ essentially the same language. ... Fundamental to the vigor of our Federal system of government is that "state courts are absolutely free to interpret state constitutional provisions to accord greater protection to individual rights than do similar provisions of the United States Constitution." *Arizona v. Evans*, 514 U.S. 1, 8 (1995).

The individual liberty and equality safeguards of the Massachusetts Constitution protect both "freedom from" unwarranted government intrusion into protected spheres of life and "freedom to" partake in benefits created by the State for the common good. ... The liberty interest in choosing whether and whom to marry would be hollow if the Commonwealth could, without sufficient justification, foreclose an individual from freely choosing the person with whom to share an exclusive commitment in the unique institution of civil marriage.

The Massachusetts Constitution requires, at a minimum, that the exercise of the State's regulatory authority not be "arbitrary or capricious." ...

The plaintiffs challenge the marriage statute on both equal protection and due process grounds. With respect to each such claim, we must first determine the appropriate standard of review. Where a statute implicates a fundamental right or uses a suspect classification, we employ "strict judicial scrutiny." *Lowell v. Kowalski*, 380 Mass. 663 (1980). For all other statutes, we employ the "'rational basis' test" *English v. New England Med. Ctr.*, 405 Mass. 423, 428 (1989). For due process claims, rational basis analysis requires that statutes "bear[ ] a real and substantial relation to the public health, safety, morals, or some other phase of the general welfare." *Coffee-Rich, Inc. v. Commissioner of Pub. Health, supra*, quoting *Sperry & Hutchinson Co. v. Director of the Div. on the Necessaries of Life*, 307 Mass. 408 (1940). For equal protection challenges, the rational basis test requires that "an impartial lawmaker could logically believe that the classification would serve a legitimate public purpose that transcends the harm to the members of the disadvantaged class." *English v. New England Med. Ctr.*, *supra* at 429 quoting *Cleburne v. Cleburne Living Ctr., Inc.*, 473 U.S. 432, 452 (1985) (Stevens, J., concurring). ...

For the reasons we explain below, we conclude that the marriage ban does not meet the rational basis test for either due process or equal protection. Because the statute does not survive rational basis review, we do not consider the plaintiffs' arguments that this case merits strict judicial scrutiny.

The department posits three legislative rationales for prohibiting same-sex couples from marrying: (1) providing a "favorable setting for procreation"; (2) ensuring the optimal setting for child rearing, which the department defines as "a two-parent family with one parent of each sex"; and (3) preserving scarce State and private financial resources. We consider each in turn.

The judge in the Superior Court endorsed the first rationale, holding that "the state's interest in regulating marriage is based on the traditional concept that marriage's primary purpose is procreation." This is incorrect. Our laws of civil marriage do not privilege procreative heterosexual intercourse between married people above every other form of adult intimacy and every other means of creating a family. General Laws c. 207 contains no requirement that the applicants for a marriage license attest to their ability or intention to conceive children by coitus. Fertility is not a condition of marriage, nor is it grounds for divorce. People who have never consummated their marriage, and never plan to, may be and stay married. *See Franklin v. Franklin,* 154 Mass. 515, 516 (1891) ("The consummation of a marriage by coition is not necessary to its validity"). People who cannot stir from their deathbed may marry. *See* G.L. c. 207, § 28A. While it is certainly true that many, perhaps most, married couples have children together (assisted or unassisted), it is the exclusive and permanent commitment of the marriage partners to one another, not the begetting of children, that is the sine qua non of civil marriage.

Moreover, the Commonwealth affirmatively facilitates bringing children into a family regardless of whether the intended parent is married or unmarried, whether the child is adopted or born into a family, whether assistive technology was used to conceive the child, and whether the parent or her partner is heterosexual, homosexual, or bisexual. If procreation were a necessary component of civil marriage, our statutes would draw a tighter circle around the permissible bounds of nonmarital child bearing and the creation of families by noncoital means. The attempt to isolate procreation as "the source of a fundamental right to marry," 440 Mass. at 370 (Cordy, J., dissenting), overlooks the integrated way in which courts have examined the complex and overlapping realms of personal autonomy, marriage, family life, and child rearing. Our jurisprudence recognizes that, in these nuanced and fundamentally private areas of life, such a narrow focus is inappropriate.

The "marriage is procreation" argument singles out the one unbridgeable difference between same-sex and opposite-sex couples, and transforms that difference into the essence of legal marriage. Like "Amendment 2" to the Constitution of Colorado, which effectively denied homosexual persons equality under the law and full access to the political process, the marriage restriction impermissibly "identifies persons by a single trait and then denies them protection across the board." *Romer v. Evans,* 517 U.S. 620, 633 (1996). In so doing, the State's action confers an official stamp of approval on the destructive stereotype that same-sex relationships are inherently unstable and inferior to opposite-sex relationships and are not worthy of respect.

The department's first stated rationale, equating marriage with unassisted heterosexual procreation, shades imperceptibly into its second: that confining marriage to opposite-sex couples ensures that children are raised in the "optimal" setting. ...

The department has offered no evidence that forbidding marriage to people of the same sex will increase the number of couples choosing to enter into opposite-sex marriages in order to have and raise children. There is thus no rational relationship between the marriage statute and the Commonwealth's proffered goal of protecting the "optimal" child rearing unit. Moreover, the department readily concedes that people in same-sex couples may be "excellent" parents. These couples (including four of the plaintiff couples) have children for the reasons others do—to love them, to care for them, to nurture them. But the task of child rearing for same-sex couples is made infinitely harder by their status as outliers to the marriage laws. ... Excluding same-sex couples from civil marriage will not make children of opposite-sex marriages more secure, but it does prevent children of same-sex couples from enjoying the immeasurable advantages that flow from the assurance of "a stable family structure in which children will be reared, educated, and socialized." 440 Mass. at 381 (Cordy, J., dissenting). ...

In this case, we are confronted with an entire, sizeable class of parents raising children who have absolutely no access to civil marriage and its protections because they are forbidden from procuring a marriage license. It cannot be rational under our laws, and indeed it is not permitted, to penalize children by depriving them of State benefits because the State disapproves of their parents' sexual orientation.

The third rationale advanced by the department is that limiting marriage to opposite-sex couples furthers the Legislature's interest in conserving scarce State and private financial resources. The marriage restriction is rational, it argues, because the General Court logically could assume that same-sex couples are more financially independent than married couples and thus less needy of public marital benefits, such as tax advantages, or private marital benefits, such as employer-financed health plans that include spouses in their coverage.

An absolute statutory ban on same-sex marriage bears no rational relationship to the goal of economy.

... Here, the plaintiffs seek only to be married, not to undermine the institution of civil marriage. They do not want marriage abolished. They do not attack the binary nature of marriage, the consanguinity provisions, or any of the other gate-keeping provisions of the marriage licensing law. Recognizing the right of an individual to marry a person of the same sex will not diminish the validity or dignity of opposite-sex marriage, any more than recognizing the right of an individual to marry a person of a different race devalues the marriage of a person who marries someone of her own race. If anything, extending civil marriage to same-sex couples reinforces the importance of marriage to individuals and communities. That same-sex couples are willing to embrace marriage's solemn obligations of exclusivity, mutual support, and commitment to one another is a testament to the enduring place of marriage in our laws and in the human spirit. [We are concerned only with the withholding of the benefits, protections, and obligations of civil marriage from a certain class of persons for invalid reasons. Our decision in no way limits the rights of individuals to refuse to marry persons of the same sex for religious or any other reasons. It in no way limits the personal freedom to disapprove of, or to encourage others to disapprove of, same-sex marriage. Our concern, rather, is whether historical, cultural, religious, or other reasons permit the State to impose limits on personal beliefs concerning whom a person should marry.]

It has been argued that, due to the State's strong interest in the institution of marriage as a stabilizing social structure, only the Legislature can control and define its boundaries. ... It is the function of courts to determine whether these criteria are met and whether these limits are exceeded. ... To label the court's role as usurping that of the Legislature, see e.g. post at 394–395 (Cordy, J., dissenting), is to misunderstand the nature and purpose of judicial review. We owe great deference to the Legislature to decide social and policy issues, but it is the traditional and settled role of courts to decide constitutional issues.

... As a public institution and a right of fundamental importance, civil marriage is an evolving paradigm. The common law was exceptionally harsh toward women who became wives: a woman's legal identity all but evaporated into that of her husband. ... Alarms about the imminent erosion of the "natural" order of marriage were sounded over the demise of antimiscegenation laws, the expansion of the rights of married women, and the introduction of "no-fault" divorce. Marriage has survived all of these transformations, and we have no doubt that marriage will continue to be a vibrant and revered institution.

We also reject the argument suggested by the department, and elaborated by some amici, that expanding the institution of civil marriage in Massachusetts to include same-sex couples will lead to interstate conflict. We would not presume to dictate how another State should respond to today's decision. But neither should considerations of comity prevent us from according Massachusetts residents the full measure of protection available under the Massachusetts Constitution. The genius of our Federal system is that each State's Constitution has vitality specific to its own traditions, and that, subject to the minimum requirements of the Fourteenth Amendment, each State is free to address difficult issues of individual liberty in the manner its own Constitution demands.

The marriage ban works a deep and scarring hardship on a very real segment of the community for no rational reason. The absence of any reasonable relationship between, on the one hand, an absolute disqualification of same-sex couples who wish to enter into civil marriage and, on the other, protection of public health, safety, or general welfare, suggests that the marriage restriction is rooted in persistent prejudices against persons who are (or who are believed to be) homosexual. "The Constitution cannot control such prejudices but neither can it tolerate them. Private biases may be outside the reach of the law, but the law cannot, directly or indirectly, give them effect." *Palmore v. Sidoti*, 466 U.S. 429, 433 (1984) (construing Fourteenth Amendment). Limiting the protections, benefits, and obligations of civil marriage to opposite-sex couples violates the basic premises of individual liberty and equality under law protected by the Massachusetts Constitution.

IV

We consider next the plaintiffs' request for relief. We preserve as much of the statute as may be preserved in the face of the successful constitutional challenge. See *Mayor of Boston v. Treasurer & Receiver Gen.*, 384 Mass. 718, 725 (1981); *Dalli v. Board of Educ.*, 358 Mass. 753, 759 (1971). See also G.L. c. 4, § 6, Eleventh.

Here, no one argues that striking down the marriage laws is an appropriate form of relief. Eliminating civil marriage would be wholly inconsistent with the Legislature's deep commitment to fostering stable families and would dismantle a vital organizing principle of our society. We face a problem similar to one that recently confronted the Court of Appeal for Ontario, the highest court of that Canadian province, when it considered the constitutionality of the same-sex marriage ban under Canada's Federal Constitution, the Charter of Rights and Freedoms (Charter). See *Halpern v. Toronto (City)*, 172 O.A.C. 276 (2003). . . .

We construe civil marriage to mean the voluntary union of two persons as spouses, to the exclusion of all others. ...

In their complaint the plaintiffs request only a declaration that their exclusion and the exclusion of other qualified same-sex couples from access to civil marriage violates Massachusetts law. We declare that barring an individual from the protections, benefits, and obligations of civil marriage solely because that person would marry a person of the same sex violates the Massachusetts Constitution. We vacate the summary judgment for the department. We remand this case to the Superior Court for entry of judgment consistent with this opinion. Entry of judgment shall be stayed for 180 days to permit the Legislature to take such action as it may deem appropriate in light of this opinion.

So ordered.

GREANEY, J. (concurring).

I agree with the result reached by the court, the remedy ordered, and much of the reasoning in the court's opinion. In my view, however, the case is more directly resolved using traditional equal protection analysis.

* * *

A classification may be gender based whether or not the challenged government action apportions benefits or burdens uniformly along gender lines. This is so because constitutional protections extend to individuals and not to categories of people. Thus, when an individual desires to marry, but cannot marry his or her chosen partner because of the traditional opposite-sex restriction, a violation of art. 1 has occurred. *See Commonwealth v. Chou,* 433 Mass. 229, 237–238, 741 N.E.2d 17 (2001) (assuming statute enforceable only across gender lines may offend Massachusetts equal rights amendment). I find it disingenuous, at best, to suggest that such an individual's right to marry has not been burdened at all, because he or she remains free to choose another partner, who is of the opposite sex.

The equal protection infirmity at work here is strikingly similar to (although, perhaps, more subtle than) the invidious discrimination perpetuated by Virginia's antimiscegenation laws and unveiled in the decision of *Loving v. Virginia, supra.* ... and concluded that "restricting the freedom to marry solely because of racial classifications violates the central meaning of the Equal Protection Clause." *Id.* at 12, That our marriage laws, unlike antimiscegenation laws, were not enacted purposely to discriminate in no way neutralizes their present discriminatory character.

* * *

(b) I am hopeful that our decision will be accepted by those thoughtful citizens who believe that same-sex unions should not be approved by the State. I am not referring here to acceptance in the sense of grudging acknowledgment of the court's authority to adjudicate the matter. My hope is more liberating. The plaintiffs are members of our community, our neighbors, our coworkers, our friends. As pointed out by the court, their professions include investment advisor, computer engineer, teacher, therapist, and lawyer. The plaintiffs volunteer in our schools, worship beside us in our religious houses, and have children who play with our children, to mention just a few ordinary daily contacts. We share a common humanity and participate together in the social contract that is the foundation of our Commonwealth. Simple principles of decency dictate that we extend to the plaintiffs, and to their new status, full acceptance, tolerance, and respect. We should do so because it is the right thing to do. The union of two people contemplated by G.L. c. 207 "is a coming together for better or for worse, hopefully enduring, and intimate to the degree of being sacred. It is an association that promotes a way of life, not causes; a harmony in living, not political faiths; a bilateral loyalty, not commercial or social projects. Yet it is an association for as noble a purpose as any involved in our prior decisions." *Griswold v. Connecticut,* 381 U.S. 479, 486, (1965). Because of the terms of art. 1, the plaintiffs will no longer be excluded from that association.

SPINA, J. (dissenting, with whom Sosman and Cordy, JJ., join).

What is at stake in this case is not the unequal treatment of individuals or whether individual rights have been impermissibly burdened, but the power of the Legislature to effectuate social change without interference from the courts, pursuant to art. 30 of the Massachusetts Declaration of Rights. The power to regulate marriage lies with the Legislature, not with the judiciary. ... Today, the court has transformed its role as protector of individual rights into the role of creator of rights, and I respectfully dissent.

1. *Equal protection.* Although the court did not address the plaintiffs' gender discrimination claim, G.L. c. 207 does not unconstitutionally discriminate on the basis of gender. A claim of gender discrimination will lie where it is shown that differential treatment disadvantages one sex over the other. ... General Laws c. 207 enumerates certain qualifications for obtaining a marriage license. It creates no distinction between the sexes, but applies to men and women in precisely the same way. It does not create any disadvantage identified with gender, as both men and women are similarly limited to marrying a person of the opposite sex. ...

Similarly, the marriage statutes do not discriminate on the basis of sexual orientation. As the court correctly recognizes, constitutional protections are extended to individuals, not couples. *Ante* at 326 n. 15, 798 N.E.2d at 957. The marriage statutes do not disqualify individuals on the basis of sexual orientation from entering into marriage. All individuals, with certain exceptions not relevant here, are free to marry. Whether an individual chooses not to marry because of sexual orientation or any other reason should be of no concern to the court.

The court concludes, however, that G.L. c. 207 unconstitutionally discriminates against the individual plaintiffs because it denies them the "right to marry the person of one's choice" where that person is of the same sex. *Ante* at 328, 798 N.E.2d at 958. To reach this result the court relies on *Loving v. Virginia,* 388 U.S. 1, 12 (1967) and transforms "choice" into the essential element of the institution of marriage. The *Loving* case did not use the word "choice" in this manner, and it did not point to the result that the court reaches today. ...

2. *Due process.* The marriage statutes do not impermissibly burden a right protected by our constitutional guarantee of due process implicit in art. 10 of our Declaration of Rights. There is no restriction on the right of any plaintiff to enter into marriage. Each is free to marry a willing person of the opposite sex ... .

* * *

Although this court did not state that same-sex marriage is a fundamental right worthy of strict scrutiny protection, it nonetheless deemed it a constitutionally protected right by applying rational basis review. ... In this Commonwealth and in this country, the roots of the institution of marriage are deeply set in history as a civil union between a single man and a single woman. There is no basis for the court to recognize same-sex marriage as a constitutionally protected right.

3. *Remedy.* The remedy that the court has fashioned both in the name of equal protection and due process exceeds the bounds of judicial restraint mandated by art. 30. ... Here, the alteration of the gender-specific language alters precisely what the Legislature unambiguously intended to preserve, the marital rights of single men and women. Such a dramatic change in social institutions must remain at the behest of the people through the democratic process.

Where the application of equal protection principles does not permit rewriting a statute in a manner that preserves the intent of the Legislature, we do not rewrite the statute. In *Dalli v. Board of Educ.,* 358 Mass. 753, (1971), the court refused to rewrite a statute in a manner that would include unintended individuals. "To attempt to interpret this [statute] as including those in the category of the plaintiff would be to engage in a judicial enlargement of the clear statutory language beyond the limit of our judicial function. We have traditionally and consistently declined to trespass on legislative territory in deference to the time tested wisdom of the separation of powers as expressed in art. [30] of the Declaration of Rights of the Constitution of Massachusetts even when it appeared that a highly desirable and just result might thus be achieved." *Id.* at 759, Recently, in *Connors v. Boston,* 430 Mass. 31, (1999), we refused to expand health insurance coverage to include domestic partners because such an expansion was within the province of the Legislature, where policy affecting family relationships is most appropriate and frequently considered. *Id.* at 42–43. Principles of equal protection do not permit the marriage statutes to be changed in the manner that we have seen today.

* * *

The court has extruded a new right from principles of substantive due process, and in doing so it has distorted the meaning and purpose of due process. The purpose of substantive due process is to protect existing rights, not to create new rights. Its aim is to thwart government intrusion, not invite it. ...

SOSMAN, J. (dissenting, with whom Spina and Cordy, JJ., join).

In applying the rational basis test to any challenged statutory scheme, the issue is not whether the Legislature's rationale behind that scheme is persuasive to us, but only whether it satisfies a minimal threshold of rationality. Today, rather than apply that test, the court announces that, because it is persuaded that there are no differences between same-sex and opposite-sex couples, the Legislature has no rational basis for treating them differently with respect to the granting of marriage licenses. Reduced to its essence, the court's opinion concludes that, because same-sex couples are now raising children, and withholding the benefits of civil marriage from their union makes it harder for them to raise those children, the State must therefore provide the benefits of civil marriage to same-sex couples just as it does to opposite-sex couples. Of course, many people are raising children outside the confines of traditional marriage, and, by definition, those children are being deprived of the various benefits that would flow if they were being raised in a household with married parents. That does not mean that the Legislature must accord the full benefits of marital status on every household raising children. Rather, the Legislature need only have some rational basis for concluding that, at present, those alternate family structures have not yet been conclusively shown to be the equivalent of the marital family structure that has established itself as a successful one over a period of centuries. People are of course at liberty to raise their children in various family structures, as long as they are not literally harming their children by doing so. ... That does not mean that the State is required to provide identical forms of encouragement, endorsement, and support to all of the infinite variety of household structures that a free society permits.

* * *

It is not, however, our assessment that matters. Conspicuously absent from the court's opinion today is any acknowledgment that the attempts at scientific study of the ramifications of raising children in same-sex couple households are themselves in their infancy and have so far produced inconclusive and conflicting results. Notwithstanding our belief that gender and sexual orientation of parents should not matter to the success of the child rearing venture, studies to date reveal that there are still some observable differences between children raised by opposite-sex couples and children raised by same-sex couples. See post at 386-387, 798 N.E.2d at 998-999 (Cordy, J., dissenting). Interpretation of the data gathered by those studies then becomes clouded by the personal and political beliefs of the investigators, both as to whether the differences identified are positive or negative, and as to the untested explanations of what might account for those differences. (This is hardly the first time in history that the ostensible steel of the scientific method has melted and buckled under the intense heat of political and religious passions.) Even in the absence of bias or political agenda behind the various studies of children raised by same-sex couples, the most neutral and strict application of scientific principles to this field would be constrained by the limited period of observation that has been available. Gay and lesbian couples living together openly, and official recognition of them as their children's sole parents, comprise a very recent phenomenon, and the recency of that phenomenon has not yet permitted any study of how those children fare as adults and at best minimal study of how they fare during their adolescent years. The Legislature can rationally view the state of the scientific evidence as unsettled on the critical question it now faces: are families headed by same-sex parents equally successful in rearing children from infancy to adulthood as families headed by parents of opposite sexes? Our belief that children raised by same-sex couples *should* fare the same as children raised in traditional families is just that: a passionately held but utterly untested belief. The Legislature is not required to share that belief but may, as the creator of the institution of civil marriage, wish to see the proof before making a fundamental alteration to that institution.

* * *

Shorn of these emotion-laden invocations, the opinion ultimately opines that the Legislature is acting irrationally when it grants benefits to a proven successful family structure while denying the same benefits to a recent, perhaps promising, but essentially untested alternate family structure. Placed in a more neutral context, the court would never find any irrationality in such an approach. ...

Or, to the extent that the court is going to invoke such emotion-laden and value-laden rhetoric as a means of heightening the degree of scrutiny to be applied, the same form of rhetoric can be employed to justify the Legislature's proceeding with extreme caution in this area. ... Before making a fundamental alteration to that cornerstone, it is eminently rational for the Legislature to require a high degree of certainty as to the precise consequences of that alteration, to make sure that it can be done safely, without either temporary or lasting damage to the structural integrity of the entire edifice. The court today blithely assumes that there are no such dangers and that it is safe to proceed (see ante at

340, 798 N.E.2d at 967), an assumption that is not supported by anything more than the court's blind faith that it is so.

... Absent consensus on the issue (which obviously does not exist), or unanimity amongst scientists studying the issue (which also does not exist), or a more prolonged period of observation of this new family structure (which has not yet been possible), it is rational for the Legislature to postpone any redefinition of marriage that would include same-sex couples until such time as it is certain that that redefinition will not have unintended and undesirable social consequences. Through the political process, the people may decide when the benefits of extending civil marriage to same-sex couples have been shown to outweigh whatever risks—be they palpable or ephemeral—are involved. However minimal the risks of that redefinition of marriage may seem to us from our vantage point, it is not up to us to decide what risks society must run, and it is inappropriate for us to arrogate that power to ourselves merely because we are confident that "it is the right thing to do." *Ante* at 350, 798 N.E.2d at 973 (Greaney, J., concurring).

As a matter of social history, today's opinion may represent a great turning point that many will hail as a tremendous step toward a more just society. As a matter of constitutional jurisprudence, however, the case stands as an aberration. To reach the result it does, the court has tortured the rational basis test beyond recognition. ... I respectfully dissent.

CORDY, J. (dissenting, with whom Spina and Sosman, JJ., join).

The court's opinion concludes that the Department of Public Health has failed to identify any "constitutionally adequate reason" for limiting civil marriage to opposite-sex unions, and that there is no "reasonable relationship" between a disqualification of same-sex couples who wish to enter into a civil marriage and the protection of public health, safety, or general welfare. Consequently, it holds that the marriage statute cannot withstand scrutiny under the Massachusetts Constitution. Because I find these conclusions to be unsupportable in light of the nature of the rights and regulations at issue, the presumption of constitutional validity and significant deference afforded to legislative enactments, and the "undesirability of the judiciary substituting its notions of correct policy for that of a popularly elected Legislature" responsible for making such policy, ... I respectfully dissent. Although it may be desirable for many reasons to extend to same-sex couples the benefits and burdens of civil marriage (and the plaintiffs have made a powerfully reasoned case for that extension), that decision must be made by the Legislature, not the court.

* * *

The plaintiffs contend that because the right to choose to marry is a "fundamental" right, the right to marry the person of one's choice, including a member of the same sex, must also be a "fundamental" right.

* * *

While the institution of marriage is deeply rooted in the history and traditions of our country and our State, the right to marry someone of the same sex is not. No matter how personal or intimate a decision to marry someone of the same sex might be, the right to make it is not guaranteed by the right of personal autonomy.

* * *

"[T]o rein in" the otherwise potentially unlimited scope of substantive due process rights, *id.* at 722, both Federal and Massachusetts courts have recognized as "fundamental" only those "rights and liberties which are, objectively, 'deeply rooted in this Nation's history and tradition,' *Moore v. East Cleveland, supra* at 503, ... and 'implicit in the concept of ordered liberty.' " *Id.* at 720–721, quoting *Palko v. Connecticut*, 302 U.S. 319, 325 (1937). ... In the area of family-related rights in particular, the Supreme Court has emphasized that the "Constitution protects the sanctity of the family precisely because the institution of the family is deeply rooted." *Moore v. East Cleveland, supra.*

* * *

Similarly, Massachusetts courts have declined to recognize rights that are not so deeply rooted. As this court noted in considering whether to recognize a right of terminally ill patients to refuse life-prolonging treatment, "the law always lags behind the most advanced thinking in every area," and must await "some common ground, some consensus."

* * *

Given this history and the current state of public opinion, as reflected in the actions of the people's elected representatives, it cannot be said that "a right to same-sex marriage is so rooted in the traditions and collective conscience of our people that failure to recognize it would violate the fundamental principles of liberty and justice that lie at the base of all our civil and political institutions. Neither ... [is] a right to same-sex marriage ... implicit in the concept of ordered liberty, such that neither liberty nor justice would exist if it were sacrificed." ... In such circumstances, the law with respect to same-sex marriages must be left to develop through legislative processes, subject to the constraints of rationality, lest the court be viewed as using the liberty and due process clauses as vehicles merely to enforce its own views regarding better social policies, a role that the strongly worded separation of powers principles in art. 30 of the Declaration of Rights of our Constitution forbids, and for which the court is particularly ill suited.

. . . .

The central purpose of the ERA was to eradicate discrimination against women and in favor of men or vice versa. ... The Massachusetts marriage statute does not subject men to different treatment from women; each is equally prohibited from precisely the same conduct. *See Baker v. State,* 170 Vt. 194, 215 n. 13 (1999) ("there is no discrete class subject to differential treatment solely on the basis of sex"). *Compare Commonwealth v. King,* 374 Mass. 5, 16, (1977) (law prohibiting prostitution applied to both male and female prostitutes and therefore did not discriminate), and *Personnel Adm'r of Mass. v. Feeney,* 442 U.S. 256, 274–275 (1979) (declining to characterize veterans' preference as sex discrimination because it applied to both male and female veterans), with *Attorney Gen. v. Massachusetts Interscholastic Athletic Ass'n, supra,* and *Lowell v. Kowalski,* 380 Mass. 663 (1980) (where statutes and rules at issue advantaged one sex over another).

By contrast, here there is no evidence that limiting marriage to opposite-sex couples was motivated by sexism in general or a desire to disadvantage men or women in particular. Moreover, no one has identified any harm, burden, disadvantage, or advantage accruing to either gender as a consequence of the Massachusetts marriage statute. In the absence of such effect, the statute limiting marriage to couples of the opposite sex does not violate the ERA's prohibition of sex discrimination.

* * *

Civil marriage is the institutional mechanism by which societies have sanctioned and recognized particular family structures, and the institution of marriage has existed as one of the fundamental organizing principles of human society. *See* C. N. Degler, *The Emergence of the Modern American Family,* in The American Family in Social-Historical Perspective 61 (3d ed.1983); A. J. Hawkins, *Introduction,* in Revitalizing the Institution of Marriage for the Twenty-First Century: An Agenda for Strengthening Marriage xiv (2002); C. Lasch, *Social Pathologists and the Socialization of Reproduction,* in The American Family in Social-Historical Perspective, *supra* at 80; W. J. O'Donnell & D. A. Jones, Marriage and Marital Alternatives 1 (1982); L. Saxton, The Individual, Marriage, and the Family 229–230, 260 (1968); M. A. Schwartz & B. M. Scott, Marriages and Families: Diversity and Change 4 (1994); Wardle, *"Multiply and Replenish": Considering Same-Sex Marriage in Light of State Interests in Marital Procreation,* 24 Harv. J.L. & Pub. Pol'y 771, 777–780 (2001); J. Q. Wilson, The Marriage Problem: How Our Culture Has Weakened Families 28, 40, 66–67 (2002). Marriage has not been merely a contractual arrangement for legally defining the private relationship between two individuals (although that is certainly part of any marriage). Rather, on an institutional level, marriage is the "very basis of the whole fabric of civilized society," J. P. Bishop, Commentaries on the Law of Marriage and

Divorce, and Evidence in Matrimonial Suits § 32 (1852), and it serves many important political, economic, social, educational, procreational, and personal functions.

Paramount among its many important functions, the institution of marriage has systematically provided for the regulation of heterosexual behavior, brought order to the resulting procreation, and ensured a stable family structure in which children will be reared, educated, and socialized. ... *See Milford v. Worcester,* 7 Mass. 48, 52 (1810) (civil marriage "intended to regulate, chasten, and refine, the intercourse between the sexes; and to multiply, preserve, and improve the species"). *See also* P. Blumstein & P. Schwartz, American Couples: Money, Work, Sex 29 (1983); C. N. Degler, *supra* at 61; G. Douglas, *Marriage, Cohabitation, and Parenthood—From Contract to Status?,* in Cross Currents: Family Law and Policy in the United States and England 223 (2000); S. L. Nock, *The Social Costs of De-Institutionalizing Marriage,* in Revitalizing the Institution of Marriage for the Twenty-First Century: An Agenda for Strengthening Marriage, *supra* at 7; L. Saxton, *supra* at 239–240, 242; M. A. Schwartz & B. M. Scott, *supra* at 4–6; Wardle, *supra* at 781–796; J. Q. Wilson, *supra* at 23–32. Admittedly, heterosexual intercourse, procreation, and child care are not necessarily conjoined (particularly in the modern age of widespread effective contraception and supportive social welfare programs), but an orderly society requires some mechanism for coping with the fact that sexual intercourse commonly results in pregnancy and childbirth. The institution of marriage is that mechanism.

The institution of marriage provides the important legal and normative link between heterosexual intercourse and procreation on the one hand and family responsibilities on the other. The partners in a marriage are expected to engage in exclusive sexual relations, with children the probable result and paternity presumed. ... Whereas the relationship between mother and child is demonstratively and predictably created and recognizable through the biological process of pregnancy and childbirth, there is no corresponding process for creating a relationship between father and child. Similarly, aside from an act of heterosexual intercourse nine months prior to childbirth, there is no process for creating a relationship between a man and a woman as the parents of a particular child. The institution of marriage fills this void by formally binding the husband-father to his wife and child, and imposing on him the responsibilities of fatherhood. *See* J. Q. Wilson, *supra* at 23–32. *See also* P. Blumstein & P. Schwartz, *supra* at 29; C. N. Degler, *supra* at 61; G. Douglas, *supra* at 223; S. L. Nock, *supra* at 7; L. Saxton, *supra* at 239–240, 242; M. A. Schwartz & B. M. Scott, *supra* at 4–6; Wardle, *supra* at 781–796. The alternative, a society without the institution of marriage, in which heterosexual intercourse, procreation, and child care are largely disconnected processes, would be chaotic.

The marital family is also the foremost setting for the education and socialization of children. Children learn about the world and their place in it primarily from those who raise them, and those children eventually grow up to exert some influence, great or small, positive or negative, on society. The institution of marriage encourages parents to remain committed to each other and to their children as they grow, thereby encouraging a stable venue for the education and socialization of children. More macroscopically, construction of a family through marriage also formalizes the bonds between people in an ordered and institutional manner, thereby facilitating a foundation of interconnectedness and interdependency on which more intricate stabilizing social structures might be built.

*   *   *

It is difficult to imagine a State purpose more important and legitimate than ensuring, promoting, and supporting an optimal social structure within which to bear and raise children. At the very least, the marriage statute continues to serve this important State purpose.

*   *   *

In considering whether such a rational basis exists, we defer to the decision-making process of the Legislature, and must make deferential assumptions about the information that it might consider and on which it may rely. ...

We must assume that the Legislature (1) might conclude that the institution of civil marriage has successfully and continually provided this structure over several centuries; (2) might consider and credit studies that document negative consequences that too often follow children either born outside of marriage or raised in households lacking either a father or a mother figure, and scholarly commentary contending that children and families develop best when mothers and fathers are partners in their parenting; and (3) would be familiar with many recent studies that variously support the proposition that children raised in intact families headed by same-sex couples fare as well on many measures as children raised in similar families headed by opposite-sex couples; support the proposition that children of same-sex couples fare worse on some measures; or reveal notable differences between the two groups of children that warrant further study.

* * *

We must also assume that the Legislature would be aware of the critiques of the methodologies used in virtually all of the comparative studies of children raised in these different environments, cautioning that the sampling populations are not representative, that the observation periods are too limited in time, that the empirical data are unreliable, and that the hypotheses are too infused with political or agenda driven bias. *See e.g.* R. Lerner & A. K. Nagai, No Basis: What the Studies Don't Tell Us About Same-Sex Parenting, Marriage Law Project (Jan.2001) (criticizing forty-nine studies on same-sex parenting—at least twenty-six of which were cited by amici in this case—as suffering from flaws in formulation of hypotheses, use of experimental controls, use of measurements, sampling and statistical testing, and finding false negatives); Stacey, (How) Does the Sexual Orientation of Parents Matter, 66 Am. Soc. Rev. 159, 159–166 (2001) (highlighting problems with sampling pools, lack of longitudinal studies, and political hypotheses).

Taking all of this available information into account, the Legislature could rationally conclude that a family environment with married opposite-sex parents remains the optimal social structure in which to bear children, and that the raising of children by same-sex couples, who by definition cannot be the two sole biological parents of a child and cannot provide children with a parental authority figure of each gender, presents an alternative structure for child rearing that has not yet proved itself beyond reasonable scientific dispute to be as optimal as the biologically based marriage norm. *See Baker v. State*, 170 Vt. 194, 222, 744 A.2d 864 (1999) ("conceivable that the Legislature could conclude that opposite-sex partners offer advantages in th[e] area [of child rearing], although ... experts disagree and the answer is decidedly uncertain"). Cf. *Marcoux v. Attorney Gen.*, 375 Mass. 63, 65, 375 N.E.2d 688 (1978). Working from the assumption that a recognition of same-sex marriages will increase the number of children experiencing this alternative, the Legislature could conceivably conclude that declining to recognize same-sex marriages remains prudent until empirical questions about its impact on the upbringing of children are resolved.

The fact that the Commonwealth currently allows same-sex couples to adopt, *see Adoption of Tammy*, 619 N.E.2d 315 (Mass. 1993), does not affect the rationality of this conclusion. The eligibility of a child for adoption presupposes that at least one of the child's biological parents is unable or unwilling, for some reason, to participate in raising the child. In that sense, society has "lost" the optimal setting in which to raise that child—it is simply not available. In these circumstances, the principal and overriding consideration is the "best interests of the child," considering his or her unique circumstances and the options that are available for that child. The objective is an individualized determination of the best environment for a particular child, where the normative social structure—a home with both the child's biological father and mother—is not an option. That such a focused determination may lead to the approval of a same-sex couple's adoption of a child does not mean that it would be irrational for a legislator, in fashioning statutory laws that cannot make such individualized determinations, to conclude generally that being raised by a same-sex couple has not yet been shown to be the absolute equivalent of being raised by one's married biological parents.

... The Legislature may rationally permit adoption by same-sex couples yet harbor reservations as to whether parenthood by same-sex couples should be affirmatively encouraged to the same extent as parenthood by the heterosexual couple whose union produced the child.

As long as marriage is limited to opposite-sex couples who can at least theoretically procreate, society is able to communicate a consistent message to its citizens that marriage is a (normatively) necessary part of their procreative endeavor; that if they are to procreate, then society has endorsed the institution of marriage as the environment for it and for the subsequent rearing of their children; and that benefits are available explicitly to create a supportive and conducive atmosphere for those purposes. If society proceeds similarly to recognize marriages between same-sex couples who cannot procreate, it could be perceived as an abandonment of this claim, and might result in the mistaken view that civil marriage has little to do with procreation ... [T]he Legislature could conclude that the consequence of such a policy shift would be a diminution in society's ability to steer the acts of procreation and child rearing into their most optimal setting.

* * *

There is no reason to believe that legislative processes are inadequate to effectuate legal changes in response to evolving evidence, social values, and views of fairness on the subject of same-sex relationships. ... Deliberate consideration of, and incremental responses to rapidly evolving scientific and social understanding is the norm of the political process—that it may seem painfully slow to those who are already persuaded by the arguments in favor of change is not a sufficient basis to conclude that the processes are constitutionally infirm. ...

b. *Standhardt v. Superior Court*

Standhardt v. Superior Court
77 P.3d 451 (Ariz. Ct. App. 2003)
(rev. denied, May 26, 2004)

TIMMER, Presiding Judge.

* * *

In the wake of *Lawrence [v. Texas,* 539 U.S. 558 (2003)], we are asked to declare that Arizona's prohibition of same-sex marriages, Arizona Revised Statutes ("A.R.S.") sections 25-101(C) and -125(A) (2003), similarly violates the federal and state constitutions. For the reasons that follow, we hold that Arizona's prohibition of such state-licensed unions does not violate Petitioners' rights under either constitution. ... **BACKGROUND**

Days after the Supreme Court issued *Lawrence,* Harold Donald Standhardt and Tod Alan Keltner, homosexual men in a committed relationship, applied to the Clerk of the Superior Court of Arizona, Maricopa County, for a marriage license. The Clerk denied the application in light of A.R.S. §§ 25-101(C) and -125(A), which, respectively, prohibit marriages between persons of the same sex and define a valid marriage as one between a man and a woman. [FN1 Section 25-101(C) provides as follows: "Marriage between persons of the same sex is void and prohibited." Section 25-125(A) defines a "valid marriage," in pertinent part, as one "contracted by a male person and a female person with a proper marriage license."]

After being turned away by the Clerk, Standhardt and Keltner petitioned this court to both compel the Clerk to issue them a marriage license and declare §§ 25-101(C) and -125(A) unconstitutional under the federal and state constitutions.

* * *

I. Fundamental right

Petitioners first argue that Arizona's prohibition of same-sex marriages impermissibly infringes on their right to marry each other, which, they contend, is guaranteed as a fundamental liberty interest by the due process provisions of both the Fourteenth Amendment to the United States Constitution and Article 2, Section 4, of the Arizona Constitution, and assured as a fundamental privacy right explicitly granted by Article 2, Section 8, of the Arizona Constitution. The State responds that while Petitioners possess a fundamental right to enter opposite-sex marriages, they do not have an equivalent right to enter same-sex marriages.

A. Due process

We begin with the well-accepted premise that the substantive due process guarantee "provides heightened protection against government interference with certain fundamental rights and liberty interests." *[Washington v.] Glucksberg*, 521 U.S. [702] at 720 [(1997)]. In addition to the freedoms protected in the Bill of Rights, such rights and interests are those "'deeply rooted in this Nation's history and tradition,' ... and 'implicit in the concept of ordered liberty,' such that 'neither liberty nor justice would exist if they were sacrificed.'" *Id.* at 720-21 (citations omitted); ... Thus, using our Nation's history, legal traditions, and practices as a guidepost, the Supreme Court has conferred fundamental-right status on the right to marry, *Loving v. Virginia*, 388 U.S. 1, 12 (1967), and the right to marital privacy, *Griswold v. Connecticut*, 381 U.S. 479, 485 (1965).

Arizona courts have similarly construed Arizona's Due Process Clause. ... It therefore follows that fundamental rights protected by the due process provision of our state constitution are those firmly entrenched in our state's history and tradition and implicit in the concept of ordered liberty that may be, or may not be, shared with the rest of the country.

Neither the United States Supreme Court nor any Arizona court has explicitly recognized that the fundamental right to marry includes the freedom to choose a same-sex spouse. Petitioners argue, however, that the Court in *Lawrence* implicitly recognized such a right. We therefore turn to that case before considering whether such a right otherwise exists.

In *Lawrence*, the Court held that a Texas statute that prohibited certain same-gender sexual activity violated homosexuals' liberty interests protected by the Due Process Clause. 539 U.S. at __. To reach this decision, the Court overruled *Bowers v. Hardwick*, 478 U.S. 186 (1986), which had upheld a Georgia sodomy law as applied to homosexual individuals. *Lawrence*, 539 U.S. at __, __

                                              * * *

Significantly, during a discussion of cases casting doubt on the ongoing viability of *Bowers*, the Court reflected on the attributes of liberty as follows:

> In *Planned Parenthood of Southeastern Pa. v. Casey*, 505 U.S. 833 (1992), the Court reaffirmed the substantive force of the liberty protected by the Due Process Clause. The *Casey* decision again confirmed that *our laws and tradition afford constitutional protection to personal decisions relating to marriage, procreation, contraception, family relationships, child rearing, and education. Id.*, at 851, 112 S.Ct. 2791. In explaining the respect the Constitution demands for the autonomy of the person in making these choices, we stated as follows:
> "These matters, involving the most intimate and personal choices a person may make in a lifetime, choices central to personal dignity and autonomy, are central to the liberty protected by the Fourteenth Amendment. At the heart of liberty is the right to define one's own concept of existence, of meaning, of the universe, and of the mystery of human life. Beliefs about these matters could not define the attributes of personhood were they formed under compulsion of the State." *Ibid.*
> ...*Persons in a homosexual relationship may seek autonomy for these purposes, just as heterosexual persons do.* The decision in *Bowers* would deny them this right.

Id. at 2481–82 (emphasis added). Petitioners seize on the italicized language as expressing the Court's view that persons have a fundamental liberty interest to enter same-sex marriages. We disagree with Petitioners' interpretation for three reasons.

First, as the State points out, elsewhere in its decision the Court explicitly stated that the case before it "[did] not involve whether the government must give formal recognition to any relationship that homosexual persons seek to enter." *Id.* at 2484; *see also id.* at 2478 (stating liberty of persons to choose personal relationship "whether or not entitled to formal recognition in the law" should counsel against attempts to define meaning of relationship or set its boundaries "absent injury to a person or abuse of an institution the law protects"). It therefore follows that the Court did not intend by its comments to address same-sex marriages.

Second, Petitioners mistakenly equate the "purposes" for which persons in a homosexual relationship may seek autonomy with the personal choices described in *Casey,* including the choice to marry. ... Because the Court's citation to "these purposes" appears immediately after the *Casey* quote, we understand the Court to refer to the reasons given in that case for affording constitutional protection to certain personal choices. In other words, "[p]ersons in a homosexual relationship may seek autonomy" to make "intimate and personal choices" that reflect "one's own concept of existence, of meaning, of the universe, and of the mystery of human life" free from government compulsion. *Id.* at 2481–82. In light of the context of the quoted discussion, the issue whether *Bowers* remained viable, and the Court's eventual holding, striking the Texas law, we view the language in question as acknowledging a homosexual person's right to define his or her own existence, and achieve the type of individual fulfillment that is a hallmark of a free society, by entering a homosexual relationship. We do not view the language as stating that such a right includes the choice to enter a state-sanctioned, same-sex marriage.

Third, and finally, because other language in *Lawrence* indicates that the Court did not consider sexual conduct between same-sex partners a fundamental right, it would be illogical to interpret the quoted language as recognizing a fundamental right to enter a same-sex marriage. Specifically, the Court applied without explanation the rational basis test, rather than the strict scrutiny review utilized when fundamental rights are impinged, to hold the Texas statute unconstitutional. ... Although the Court spoke of a person's liberty interest to engage in same-gender sexual relations, and described such conduct as "one element in a personal bond that is more enduring," *id.* at 2478, 2484, the Court did not declare that participation in such conduct is a fundamental right. ... If the Court did not view such an intimate expression of the bond securing a homosexual relationship to be a fundamental right, we must reject any notion that the Court intended to confer such status on the right to secure state-sanctioned recognition of such a union.

* * *

Petitioners assert that because the "freedom of choice to marry" recognized in *Loving* is unrestricted, it encompasses the right to marry anyone, including a same-sex partner, even in the face of traditional, societal disapproval of such unions. We disagree. Implicit in *Loving* and predecessor opinions is the notion that marriage, often linked to procreation, is a union forged between one man and one woman. 388 U.S. at 12 ("Marriage is one of the 'basic civil rights of man,' fundamental to our very existence and survival.") (citation omitted); *Baehr,* 74 Haw. at 552–55 (discussing Supreme Court opinions construing fundamental right to marry and concluding right "presently contemplates unions between men and women"). Thus, while *Loving* expanded the traditional scope of the fundamental right to marry by granting interracial couples unrestricted access to the state-sanctioned marriage institution, that decision was anchored to the concept of marriage as a union involving persons of the opposite sex. In contrast, recognizing a right to marry someone of the same sex would not expand the established right to marry, but would redefine the legal meaning of "marriage." We therefore conclude that *Loving* does not mandate a conclusion that the fundamental right to choose one's spouse necessarily includes the choice to enter a same-sex marriage. [FN1 Petitioners' citation to other examples of traditional marital principles that have collapsed over time similarly do not persuade us that the fundamental right to marry includes the freedom to choose a same-sex spouse. ... These shifts in principles governing marriage have involved aspects of the marital relationship that are extrinsic to its core meaning: the legal union between one man and one woman.]

* * *

Although same-sex relationships are more open and have garnered greater societal acceptance in recent years, same-sex marriages are neither deeply rooted in the legal and social history of our Nation or state nor are they implicit in the concept of ordered liberty. *Glucksberg,* 521 U.S. at 720–21.

Despite changing attitudes about both homosexuality and the attributes of "family," no state in this Nation has enacted legislation allowing same-sex marriages. To the contrary, Congress and the majority of states, including Arizona, have enacted legislation in recent years explicitly limiting marriage to opposite-sex unions.

This court does not dispute that a homosexual person's choice of life partner is an intimate and important decision. However, not all important decisions sounding in personal autonomy are protected fundamental rights. *Id.* at 727–28 ("That many of the rights and liberties protected by the Due Process Clause sound in personal autonomy does not warrant the sweeping conclusion that any and all important, intimate, and personal decisions are so protected"). The history of the law's treatment of marriage as an institution involving one man and one woman, together with recent, explicit reaffirmations of that view, lead invariably to the conclusion that the right to enter a same-sex marriage is not a fundamental liberty interest protected by due process.

B. Arizona's explicit privacy provision

Petitioners next argue that the explicit privacy provision in our constitution, Ariz. Const. art. 2, § 8, confers a fundamental right to enter a same-sex marriage. They rely on cases holding that Arizona's privacy provision bestows greater rights than the federal constitution in the areas of medical treatment and search and seizure. ...

First, although the records of Arizona's 1910 constitutional convention do not reflect the framers' intent in adopting the privacy provision ... it is unlikely the framers intended to confer a right to enter a same-sex marriage. ... "Marriage" at that time was commonly defined as a civil status existing between one man and one woman. *Dean*, 653 A.2d at 315 (citing Black's Law Dictionary 762 (2d ed.1910)).

Second, the existence of greater privacy rights under the state constitution in the areas of individual health care and home searches does not compel a conclusion that the privacy provision also imparts greater rights in the choice of marriage partner. Affording greater privacy rights in the propriety of an individual's medical decisions and in home searches militates against government intrusions. Neither situation involves requiring the state to affirmatively involve itself in a relationship, as is the case with marriage . ...

For these reasons, we decide that the privacy provision in the Arizona Constitution does not afford greater rights in marriage than those conferred by the federal and state due process provisions. ...

C. Rational basis review

. ... Petitioners bear the burden of proving that Arizona's prohibition of same-sex marriages is not rationally related to any conceivable legitimate state interest. ...

The State contends it has a legitimate interest in encouraging procreation and child-rearing within the stable environment traditionally associated with marriage, and that limiting marriage to opposite-sex couples is rationally related to that interest. Essentially, the State asserts that by legally sanctioning a heterosexual relationship through marriage, thereby imposing both obligations and benefits on the couple and inserting the State in the relationship, the State communicates to parents and prospective parents that their long-term, committed relationships are uniquely important as a public concern. ... Because the State's interest in committed sexual relationships is limited to those capable of producing children, it contends it reasonably restricts marriage to opposite-sex couples. [FN15 This position has support among courts and commentators. *See Adams v. Howerton*, 486 F.Supp. 1119, 1124–25 (C.D.Cal.1980) (rejecting contention that same-sex couples can marry and holding state has "interest in encouraging and fostering procreation of the race and providing status and stability to the environment in which children are raised"), *aff'd*, 673 F.2d 1036 (9th Cir.1982); *Singer v. Hara*, 11 Wash.App. 247, 259–60, 522 P.2d 1187, 1195 (1974) ("[M]arriage exists as a protected legal institution primarily because of societal values associated with the propagation of the human race."); H.R.Rep. No. 104-664, at 14 (1996), *reprinted in* 1996 U.S.C.C.A.N. 2905, 2918 ("Were it not for the possibility of begetting children inherent in heterosexual unions, society would have no particular interest in encouraging citizens to come together in a committed relationship."); Maggie Gallagher, *What Is*

Marriage For? The Public Purposes of Marriage Law, 62 La. L.Rev. 773, 782 (2002) ("The public legal union of a man and woman is designed first and foremost to protect the children that their sexual union (and that type of sexual union alone) regularly produces"); Lynn D. Wardle, *"Multiply and Replenish": Considering Same-Sex Marriage in Light of State Interests in Marital Procreation*, 24 Harv. J.L. & Pub. Pol'y 771, 792 (2001) ("Traditional marriage facilitates procreation by increasing the relational commitment, complementarity, and stability needed for the long term responsibilities that result from procreation").]

. ... Although *Griswold* and *Loving* described marriage as a personal right, neither case suggested that a state cannot infringe upon that right for social purposes, such as encouraging procreation and protecting children. Indeed, the Court recognized in *Loving* that "marriage is a social relation subject to the State's police power." 388 U.S. at 7. We therefore reject Petitioners' contention.

Petitioners more persuasively argue that the State's attempt to link marriage to procreation and child-rearing is not reasonable because (1) opposite-sex couples are not required to procreate in order to marry, and (2) same-sex couples also raise children, who would benefit from the stability provided by marriage within the family. However, as the State notes, "[a] perfect fit is not required" under the rational basis test, and we will not overturn a statute "merely because it is not made with 'mathematical nicety, or because in practice it results in some inequality.'" *Big D Constr. Corp.*, 163 Ariz. at 566.

Allowing all opposite-sex couples to enter marriage under Arizona law, regardless of their willingness or ability to procreate, does not defeat the reasonableness of the link between opposite-sex marriage, procreation, and child-rearing. First, if the State excluded opposite-sex couples from marriage based on their intention or ability to procreate, the State would have to inquire about that subject before issuing a license, thereby implicating constitutionally rooted privacy concerns. ... Second, in light of medical advances affecting sterility, the ability to adopt, and the fact that intentionally childless couples may eventually choose to have a child or have an unplanned pregnancy, the State would have a difficult, if not impossible, task in identifying couples who will never bear and/or raise children. Third, because opposite-sex couples have a fundamental right to marry, *Loving*, 388 U.S. at 12, excluding such couples from marriage could only be justified by a compelling state interest, narrowly tailored to achieve that interest, *Glucksberg*, 521 U.S. at 721, which is not readily apparent.

* * *

Likewise, although some same-sex couples also raise children, exclusion of these couples from the marriage relationship does not defeat the reasonableness of the link between opposite-sex marriage, procreation, and child-rearing. Indisputably, the only sexual relationship capable of producing children is one between a man and a woman. The State could reasonably decide that by encouraging opposite-sex couples to marry, thereby assuming legal and financial obligations, the children born from such relationships will have better opportunities to be nurtured and raised by two parents within long-term, committed relationships, which society has traditionally viewed as advantageous for children. Because same-sex couples cannot by themselves procreate, the State could also reasonably decide that sanctioning same-sex marriages would do little to advance the State's interest in ensuring responsible procreation within committed, long-term relationships.

... [C]hildren in same-sex families could benefit from the stability offered by same-sex marriage, particularly if such children do not have ties with both biological parents. But although the line drawn between couples who may marry (opposite-sex) and those who may not (same-sex) may result in some inequity for children raised by same-sex couples, such inequity is insufficient to negate the State's link between opposite-sex marriage, procreation, and child-rearing. ...

Petitioners lastly argue that the State's limitation of marriage to opposite-sex unions is not reasonably related to its interests in procreation, because excluding same-sex couples from the marriage relationship does not impact procreation. We agree with Petitioners that allowing same-sex couples to marry would not inhibit opposite-sex couples from procreating. But the reasonableness of the State's position is not dependent on the contrary conclusion. Rather, as previously explained, *supra*, the State does not have the same interest in sanctioning marriages between couples who are incapable of procreating as it does with opposite-sex couples. We therefore reject Petitioners' argument.

In summary, Petitioners have failed to prove that the State's prohibition of same-sex marriage is not rationally related to a legitimate state interest. We hold that the State has a legitimate interest in encouraging procreation and child-rearing within the marital relationship, and that limiting marriage to opposite-sex couples is rationally related to that interest. Even assuming that the State's reasoning for prohibiting same-sex marriages is debatable, see ..., or arguably unwise ..., it is not "arbitrary or irrational" ... . Consequently, A.R.S. §§ 25-101© and -125(A) do not violate Petitioners' substantive due process or explicit privacy rights and must be upheld.

II. Equal protection

* * *

Petitioners contend that the State's purpose in prohibiting same-sex marriages is to "single out gay persons to impose a particular disability on them," which cannot serve a legitimate state objective for the reasons explained in *Romer v. Evans*. In *Romer*, the Court addressed an equal protection challenge to Colorado's "Amendment 2" to its constitution, which prohibited all legislative, executive, or judicial action designed to protect homosexual persons from discrimination. 517 U.S. at 624. The Court held that Amendment 2 did not bear a rational relation to a legitimate end due to its "peculiar property of imposing a broad and undifferentiated disability on a single named group," with a breadth "so discontinuous with the reasons offered for it that the amendment seems inexplicable by anything but animus toward the class it affects." *Id.* at 632.

In contrast to Amendment 2, A.R.S. §§ 25-101(C) and -125(A) are not so exceptional and unduly broad as to render the State's reasons for their enactment "inexplicable by anything but animus" towards Arizona's homosexual residents. Arizona's prohibition of same-sex marriages furthers a proper legislative end and was not enacted simply to make same-sex couples unequal to everyone else ... Consequently, we reject Petitioners' equal protection challenge ... .

CONCLUSION

For the foregoing reasons, we hold that the fundamental right to marry protected by our federal and state constitutions does not encompass the right to marry a same-sex partner. ... Because Arizona's prohibition against same-sex marriage rationally furthers a legitimate state interest, we further decide that the prohibition does not deprive Petitioners of their constitutional rights to substantive due process, privacy, or equal protection of the laws. Consequently, it is for the people of Arizona, through their elected representatives or by using the initiative process, rather than this court, to decide whether to permit same-sex marriages. ... [W]e deny relief.

CONCURRING: JOHN C. GEMMILL and MAURICE PORTLEY, JJ. ... .

c. Notes and Questions

1) *Goodridge* Notes.

After the *Goodridge* decision, the Massachusetts Senate leadership proposed a bill to create Vermont-style "civil unions" with all of the legal status, rights, and benefits of marriage for same-sex couples, but without the label of "marriage," and then filed a special proceeding with the Supreme Judicial Court seeking an advisory opinion (allowed under a unique provision of the Massachusetts Constitution) whether that "civil union" scheme would satisfy the requirements of the *Goodridge* ruling. In *Opinions of the Justices to the Senate*, 802 N.E.2d 565 (Mass., 2004), again by 4-3 vote, the Justices ruled that creating civil unions for same-sex couples, but forbidding them to marry, "violates the equal protection and due process requirements of the Constitution of the

Commonwealth and the Massachusetts Declaration of Rights. ... The bill maintains an unconstitutional, inferior, and discriminatory status for same-sex couples." *Id.* at 572. The legislature then proposed a state constitutional amendment, House 3190, as amended, providing that "only the union of one man and one woman shall be valid or recognized as a marriage in the commonwealth," but also that "[t]wo persons of the same sex shall have the right to form a civil union." Before the next legislature met to vote on the possible amendment (which gay activists disliked because of the first part, and marriage defenders opposed because of the second part), petitions were being circulated for another state constitutional amendment defining marriage as the union of a man and a woman.

Is there a difference in the method of analysis of the statutory question and the method of analysis of the constitutional question in the main opinion? If so, is it proper? What are the roles of the judiciary and the legislature in re-defining basic social institutions? Is there a difference between legal (judicial) analysis and political or policy analysis? Between good writing and good analysis?

2) *Standhardt* Notes.

The Arizona Supreme Court denied review in *Standhardt*. Apart from the outcome, is the analysis in *Standhardt* or in the *Goodridge* majority opinion more disciplined? Legal? Consistent with precedent? Bold? Which of the six opinions in the two cases is most persuasive? Why? *Standhardt* was followed by similarly analytical opinions by intermediate appellate courts in *Morrison v. Sadler*, 821 N.E. 2d. 15 (Ind. App. 2005), *Lewis v. Harris*, 875 A.2d 259 (N.J. App. Div. 2005), and *Hernandez v. Robles*, 805 N.Y.S.2d 354 (N.Y. App. Div. 2005).

3) Arguments For and Against Same-Sex Marriage

Pro: Claims for same-sex marriage assert variations of primarily four types of arguments. The first argument is the basic human right argument. There are many versions of this argument, but all of them assert that marriage is a basic human right, and that laws denying homosexuals the right to marry therefore deny gay and lesbian couples a basic human right. A second claim often made by same-sex marriage advocates is that the principle or value of tolerance requires legalization of same-sex marriage. Third, the most successful argument recently asserts that allowing heterosexual couples to marry while denying marriage to same-sex couples violates the principle of equality under law. In support of equality claims, some have argued that homosexual behavior is biologically determined. Advocates of same-sex marriage also compare their cause to the struggle for racial equality and argue that it violates the principle of equality to forbid same-sex marriage just as it does to forbid interracial marriage. Supporters of same-sex marriage also claim that denial of same-sex marriage is improper gender discrimination. Finally, a variety of arguments are made by same-sex marriage advocates that could be called "invidious discrimination" arguments. Today, many decent, open-minded people are wary of legal classifications that deny benefits to or impose special burdens upon minorities simply because of their nonconformist or unpopular lifestyles. History is filled with many examples of religious groups, ethnic minorities, and unpopular political movements that have suffered significant social persecution and legal discrimination because of prejudice against their nonconforming beliefs or behaviors. There is special concern when the group that is disfavored is demonized with the taint of immorality, for discrimination against some alleged "immoral" classes has often been used to justify or exacerbate self-righteous persecution and oppression. Gays and lesbians claim to be just another class of persons persecuted because of their minority sexual preferences, and that they are merely the latest victims of excessive and intolerant moral zeal.

Con: It is undoubtedly true that the right to marriage is a basic human right. The key term is marriage, and the fundamental question is: What is marriage? If marriage refers specifically to a heterosexual relationship between two consenting adults, then it is not a violation of the basic human right to marry for a state not to confer the legal status of marriage upon same-sex couples. The "tolerance" claim confuses tolerance with preference. As Bruce Hafen has very cogently explained, relations and conduct may be legally categorized in three ways—as "protected," "tolerated," and "prohibited." Marriage is the classic example of a preferred relationship. It is one of the most highly preferred, historically favored relations in the law. Thus, the claim for same-sex marriage is not a claim for mere tolerance, but for special preference. Tolerance is not the same as preference, and marriage is preferred, not merely tolerated.

The evidence for the biological determinism equality claim is very tenuous. There are significant methodological flaws in many of the studies, and at most, they suggest biological factors may be among the influences associated with homosexual behavior, not necessarily a determinant. Moreover, even if a biological cause could be shown (like the biological basis for alcoholism, drug addiction, and aggressive behavior), that would not mean that laws prohibiting same-sex marriage would be impermissible any more than laws prohibiting drunk driving, drug abuse, violence, or rape are impermissible. Likewise, the analogy to racial discrimination is strained. Race is unrelated to almost any legitimate purpose the law could have for distinguishing between two persons, especially irrelevant to the purposes of marriage; but homosexual behavior is directly related to the fundamental purposes of marriage laws—that is, the regulation of sexual behavior and protection of the mores that define the core identity, boundaries, and basic structure for the moral order of a society. As General Colin Powell put it: "Skin color is a benign non-behavioral characteristic. Sexual orientation is perhaps the most profound of human behavioral characteristics. Comparison of the two is a convenient but invalid argument." Heterosexual marriage is the oldest gender-equality institution in the law; the requirement that marriage consist of both a man and a woman emphasizes the absolute equality and equal necessity of both sexes for the most fundamental unit of society, and the indispensable and equal contribution of both genders to the basic institution of our society. Redefining marriage to include same-sex couples does not just impact gay and lesbian couples, for transmutation of the basic social unit will directly affect all families, all children, and numerous institutions (e.g., schools, faith communities, etc.) throughout society, and will deprive the rising generation of the benefits of the institution of exclusively conjugal marriage. Gays and lesbians are not a powerless, discrete, and insular minority. History, morality, public health, and social interest justify disparate treatment of same-sex unions, concubinage, polygamy, and other forms of domestic relationships.

4) Social Interests re: Same-Sex Marriage

There are many social interests in and public purposes for legal marriage for which heterosexual marriages today still provide tremendous benefits to society that are distinct from those associated with homosexual unions. Opponents of same-sex marriage argue that heterosexual marriages provide tremendous benefits to society that are unequaled by homosexual unions. Thus, they claim that committed conjugal marriage provides (1) the environment for the safest and most beneficial expression of sexual intimacy; (2) the best environment into which children can be born; (3) the optimal childrearing environment linking procreation and childrearing and providing the benefits of dual-gender parenting to model intergender relations and show children how to relate to persons of their own and the opposite gender; (4) the best security for the status of those who take the greatest risks and invest the greatest personal effort in maintaining families; (5) the strongest and most stable companionate unit of society, and the most secure setting for gender integrationist and intergenerational transmission of social knowledge and skills; (6) protection for the basic unit of society; a fundamental institution of such profound importance to society that there is great danger if its meaning and definition become ambiguous; (7) the best seed-ground for democracy and the most important schoolroom for self-government; and (8) interjurisdictional comity and consistency. Conjugal marriages arguably contribute much more to the social interests in and public policy reasons for legalized marriage than do same-sex unions, and overall the benefits and value of heterosexual marriages to society far exceed those of same-sex unions.

On the other hand, doesn't the institution of marriage contribute to stability of unions? Wouldn't legalizing same-sex marriage result in "domesticizing" homosexual relations? If marriage is so important, wouldn't expanding the notion of marriage increase the social good? Hasn't the definition of marriage evolved over time and across cultures? Isn't inclusiveness valuable in itself? Are male-female unions really unique and different in socially significant ways from male-male and female-female relationships? Are there different purposes for marriage and other relationships?

5) State Court Rulings for Same-Sex Marriage or Unions

Courts in at least eight states have ruled in favor of same-sex marriage or marriage-equivalent unions. *See Baehr v. Lewin*, 852 P.2d 44, 67 (Haw. 1993); *Baehr v. Miicke*, 196 WL 694235 (Haw. Cir. Ct. 1996) (overturned by state constitutional amendment); *Brause v. Bureau of Vital Statistics*, No. 3AN-95-6562, 1998 WL 88743 at 6 (Alaska. Super. Ct., Feb. 27, 1998) (overturned by state constitutional amendment); *Baker v. State*, 744 A.2d 864 (Vt. 1999) (resulting Civil Unions); *Goodridge v. Department of Public Health*, 798 N.E.2d 941, 943, 959 (Mass. 2003); *In re Opinion of the Justices to the Senate*, 802 N.E.2d 565, 569-71 (Mass. 2004); *Li v. State*, 2004 WL 1258167 (Or. Cir. April 20, 2004), *rev'd*, 110 P.3d 91 (Ore. 2005) (because of state constitutional amendment); *Andersen v. King County*, 2004 WL 1738447 *3,4,11 (Wash. Super. 2004); *Castle v. State*, 2004 WL 1985215, *11 (Wash.Super. Sep 07, 2004) (both pending on appeal); *Hernandez v. Robles*, 794 N.Y.S.2d 579 (N.Y.Sup., Feb. 4, 2005) *rev'd, Hernandez v. Robles*, 26 A.D.3d 98, 805 N.Y.S.2d 354 (N.Y.App. Div., 2005); *see also Samuels v. New York State Dept. Of Health*, 811 N.Y.S.2d 136, (N.Y.App. Div.,2006); *In re Coordination Proceeding, Special Title* [Rule 1550(c)] *Marriage Cases*, No. 4365, 2005 WL 583129 (Cal. Super. Crt. San. Fran., Mar. 14, 2005).

6) Federal and State Defense of Marriage Acts

In response to the decisions in Hawaii and to the vigorous effort to get courts to legalize same-sex marriage, Congress was so concerned about the effort to legalize same-sex marriage through the back door and to force states to recognize same-sex marriages from other states that in 1996 it overwhelmingly passed, and President Clinton signed, the Defense of Marriage Act (or DOMA). DOMA contains two operative provisions. The first provides that for purposes of federal law and federal programs, the term "marriage" and related marital terms refer only to unions of a man and a woman. This bars administrative or judicial "interpretation" of federal law to recognize same-sex couples as married. The other main provision of DOMA clarifies that federal full faith and credit principles do not *compel* any state to recognize same-sex marriage. Nor does federal law *forbid* any state from recognizing same-sex marriages performed where such are valid. DOMA simply protects the right of each state to decide that issue for itself—that is, whether to recognize same-sex marriages. Defense of Marriage Act, Pub. L. 104-199, 110 Stat. 2419 (Sep. 21, 1996) (codified at 28 U.S.C. § 1738C). More than 40 states have enacted state DOMAs, laws generally clarifying that same-sex marriage is not permitted in the state, and also providing that same-sex marriages that may be legally performed in other jurisdictions will not be recognized as valid marriages in the state. *See generally* Coolidge and Duncan, *infra*. Additionally, in nineteen states, constitutional amendments defining marriage as the union of man and woman, and (in most of them) barring the extension of status or benefits equivalent to marriage (e.g., broad "civil unions" or domestic partnerships) have been passed. Similar state marriage amendment proposals will be on the ballots in seven states in 2006.

In the summer after *Goodridge* was decided, a proposed Federal Marriage Amendment defining marriage as the union of a man and a woman received affirmative vote of 55 percent of the members of the House of Representatives, and 48-50 on a procedureal vote in the Senate – far short of the required 2/3 of each House for proposing an amendment, but an impressive early showing nonetheless. In June 2006, the Senate cloture vote on the proposed amendment was 49-48, a slight majority but 18 votes short.

The Constitutions of at least 78 sovereign nations (of 191 in the United Nations) protect marriage and/or family; at least 32 national constitutions contain provisions that define marriage like the proposed Federal Marriage Protection Amendment. Should marriage be protected in the Constitution of the United States? Why/ why not?

7) International Developments in the Movement for Same-Sex Marriage

Until 2001, same-sex marriage had never had been permitted in any nation in history. Since then, same-sex marriage has been legalized in the Netherlands (2001), Belgium (2003), Canada (2005), and Spain (2005), possibly South Africa (2005), and in a few sub-jurisdictions in other countries (such as Massachusetts in the U.S.). Since 1989, many European nations (and European-settled nations like New Zealand) have enacted legislation authorizing the formal registration of same-sex "domestic partnerships" and extending to such relationships essentially all of the economic and many of the noneconomic legal consequences of marriage. Less extensive forms of domestic partnership are allowed in other nations. (*See infra* Ch. 8.)

The right to marry is still identified in numerous international documents as one of the fundamental rights of humanity. The Universal Declaration of Human Rights, for instance, declares that "[m]en and women of full age, without any limitation due to race, nationality or religion, have the right to marry and to found a family." Universal Declaration of Human Rights, Article 16. Likewise, many other multilateral international conventions and documents list "the right to marry and to found a family" as basic human rights. The national constitutions or fundamental charters of more than 130 nations make specific reference to and guarantee special constitutional protections for "the right to marry" and/or the "fundamental" importance of marriage and the family, and some imply a definition. At least 32 nations have constitutional provisions that define marriage as the union of a man and a woman. Why does the United States Constitution not have such a provision?

3. Practical and Ethical Considerations

What considerations go into the decision of an attorney to accept or reject a same-sex marriage or under-age marriage case? Do they differ? *See* Parley, *infra,* at 3–9, 100–116.

4. Bibliography

Contemporary Family Law, vol. I, Ch. 2 (Lynn D. Wardle, Christopher L. Blakesley & Jacqueline Y. Parker, eds., 1988).

David Orgon Coolidge, *Same-Sex Marriage?* Baehr v. Miike *and the Meaning of Marriage,* 38 S. Tex. L. Rev. 1 (1997).

David Orgon Coolidge & William C. Duncan, *Definition or Discrimination? State Marriage Recognition Statutes in the "Same-Sex Marriage" Debate,* 32 Creighton L. Rev. 3 (1998).

David Orgon Coolidge & William C. Duncan, *Reaffirming Marriage: A Presidential Priority,* 24 Harv. J. L. & Pub. Pol'y 623 (2001).

Peter Lubin & Dwight Duncan, *Follow the Footnote or the Advocate as Historian of Same-Sex Marriage,* 47 Cath. U. L. Rev. 1271 (1998).

William Eskridge, The Case for Same-Sex Marriage (1996).

William Eskridge, Gaylaw (1999).

Carey Goldberg, *Vermont Town Meeting Turns Into Same-Sex Unions Forum,* N.Y. Times, March 8, 2000.

Richard D. Mohr, *The Case for Gay Marriage,* 9 Notre Dame J.L. Ethics & Pub. Pol'y 215 (1995).

Louis Parley, The Ethical Family Lawyer, A Practical Guide to Avoiding Professional Dilemmas (A.B.A., Fam. L. Section 1995).

Rayden's Practice and Law of Divorce (9th ed., Joseph Jackson, C. F. Turner, & D. R. Ellison eds. 1964).

Mark Strasser, *Family, Definitions, and the Constitution: On the Antimiscegenation Analogy,* 25 Suffolk U. L. Rev. 981 (1991).

Mark Strasser, Legally Wed: Same-Sex Marriage and the Constitution (1997).

Contemporary Family Law, vol. I, Ch. 5, §5.14 (Lynn D. Wardle, Christopher L. Blakesley & Jacqueline Y. Parker, eds., 1988).

Lynn D. Wardle, *A Critical Analysis of Constitutional Claims for Same-Sex Marriage,* 1996 B.Y.U.L.Rev. 1–101.

Lynn D. Wardle, *Legal Claims for Same-Sex Marriage: Efforts to Legitimate a Retreat from Marriage by Redefining Marriage,* 39 So. Tex. L. Rev. 735-768 (1998)

Lynn D. Wardle, *Is Marriage Obsolete?* 10 Mich. J. Gender & L. 189–235 (2003).

Lynn D. Wardle, *State Marriage Amendments: Developments, Precedents, and Significance,* 7 Fla. Coastal L. Rev. 403 (2005).

Mary Ann Glendon, The Transformation of Family Law: State, Law, and Family in the United States and Western Europe (University of Chicago Press 1989).

Peter F.G. Rook & Robert Ward, Sexual Offenses (1990).

CHAPTER 5
Marital Age; Mental Requirements; Agreement

A. AGE OF MARRIAGE REQUIREMENTS

1. Background

a. History of Marital Age Restrictions

The common law imposed few but clear restrictions upon the marriage of minors.

Whether an individual was old enough to enter into marriage was not, in English common law, a question of contract, but one of capacity to marry. At common law there were three age groups of individuals with differing legal capacities to marry. Under seven years of age, a child was entirely incapable of contracting marriage. If either party to the marriage was under seven, the marriage was completely void. From age seven until the "age of discretion," which was fourteen years old for boys and twelve years old for girls, individuals could enter into lawful but "imperfect" marriages. The marriages were valid but could be voided at will, apparently by either party to the marriage, until both had reached the age of discretion. Marriages after the age of discretion were valid.
***

Parental approval for a marriage generally was not required at common law. However, in 1753, Parliament enacted Lord Hardwicke's Act, which provided that all marriages of persons under twenty-one years of age solemnized by license (thus excluding marriage by banns) were void if entered into without the consent of the party's guardian or mother was required.
***

The English common law marital age restrictions passed into American common law and were applied until superseded by statutory authority. However, the requirement of parental consent enacted by Parliament just a few years before the colonies declared their independence apparently did not work its way into the general common law in the American states.

Wardle, *infra*, at 5-7.

b. Overview of American Statutes Restricting Marriage by Minors

Today all American states have statutes in effect that can be characterized as age restrictions on marriage. Actually, age is a criterion in four distinct types of marriage regulations:
***

1. Age of Consent Statutes
***

Today, in all American jurisdictions except [two,] men and women are free to marry of their own volition--without parental or judicial consent--at age eighteen. In Nebraska [Neb. Rev. Stats. §§ 42-105 & 43-2101] . . . the age of consent is nineteen; in Mississippi [Miss. Code Ann. § 93-1-5] it is twenty-one. This may be called the age of marriage by individual consent, or simply, the age of consent.

***

2. Marriage With Parental or Judicial Permission

All states require the consent of a parent or parent substitute for the marriage of at least some persons under the age of individual consent. Although the details of parental consent requirements vary enormously among the states, the most common legislative approach consists of two parts: a requirement of parental consent for older minors, and a requirement of both parental and judicial consent in the case of younger minors or in other exceptional cases.

Twenty-five states follow the basic pattern that sixteen and seventeen year-olds can marry only with parental consent. Additionally, nine other states follow the same approach with different age parameters. In seven of these thirty-four states, judges have clear statutory discretion to override the refusal of parents to consent to the marriage of their minors, and in one other, Utah, the court has explicit discretion to decline to annul a marriage despite the age deficiency if it is in the best interests of the child.

***

In ten other states, all persons under the age of individual consent can marry only with parental approval. In seven other states both parental and judicial consent are required for all marriages of persons under eighteen. In one of the latter states, Iowa, the judge can override the refusal of the parents to consent and authorize the marriage.

3. Exceptional Circumstances

Twenty-nine states provide specific statutory exceptions authorizing marriage of persons younger than an express or implied minimum age of marriage when extraordinary circumstances exist. The most common scheme, adopted in fifteen states, requires parental and judicial approval for such marriages. In five other states judicial approval alone is needed. ***

Usually the statute refers to some vague condition such as "extraordinary circumstances" or "in the best interest of the parties." However, in fifteen states proof that the bride-to-be is pregnant or has borne a child of the prospective groom out of wedlock is specifically mentioned in the statute as being sufficient, or a required, exceptional condition. On the other hand, statutes in four states explicitly provide that proof of pregnancy alone is not sufficient cause to authorize a marriage under the "extraordinary circumstances" provision.

4. Minimum Age of Capacity

Most American jurisdictions have some statutory provision that at least appears to suggest a minimum age of marriageability. The age varies from New Hampshire's and North Carolina's age thirteen for females to Ohio's age eighteen for men. However, the appearance is illusory. Very few of these statutes can be said to establish a genuine minimum age of *capacity* to marry--i.e., the age under which no one can enter a valid marriage under any circumstances.

In the broadest sense, almost all states have a minimum age of marriageability inasmuch as they have statutes authorizing marriage with parental or judicial consent only in a specified age range. Approximately forty states have statutes mentioning a minimum age at which minors can marry with parental or judicial consent. But [the parental consent part of] these statutes have generally been construed to be "directory," thus, having no effect on the validity of a marriage. ***

5. Non-Compliance and Nullity

In English common law, the marriage of an individual under seven was a complete nullity. The marriage of a male between ages seven and fourteen, or a female between ages seven and twelve was a valid but "imperfect" marriage. Apparently, either party could nullify the marriage until both had reached the age of discretion, and the marriage could be disaffirmed privately as well as publicly, i.e., with or without a judicial decree. After the parties reached the age of discretion, the marriage became perfect and the former defect expired.

Today, it is commonly said that "non-age" is only a voidable defect, even if the statute uses the term "void." But this is an overbroad generalization***

First, marriage by one who has reached the age of individual consent to marry is valid. The marriage cannot be avoided on the ground of lack of general (age) capacity to marry.

Second, at the other end of the spectrum, marriage by one who has not reached the minimum age of capacity to marry is void. The marriage is a complete nullity and cannot ripen into a valid marriage by the mere passage of time or even by ratification after reaching the age of majority.

Third, the absence of parental consent generally does not render a marriage invalid unless there is express statutory authority to that effect. Parental consent is deemed to be a mere "directory" requirement in most states and explicit legislation usually is required before courts will abandon this well-established rule. However, some parental consent statutes appear mandatory.

The general rule regarding who may attack the defect of non-age or lack of parental consent appears to be that only the under-age party can seek an annulment on these grounds. At one time it was apparently the rule in some jurisdictions that the under-age party's spouse also could raise the defect, yet no modern statute or case supporting that position can be found. It is generally said that there must be express statutory authority for a parent to bring suit to annul a child's marriage for non-age or for want of parental consent.

Wardle, *infra,* at 7-17 (1983).

c. Choice of Law

If parties go to another state to marry for the purpose of evading local age restrictions, and return to their homestate to live, it is unlikely that the homestate will invalidate the marriage absent an explicit marriage evasion statute. The Restatement, Second, Conflict of Laws § 283(2) (1971), appears to endorse the general rule that "migratory" marriages which would be void in the state of domicile of the parties are valid everywhere if valid under the law of the state where the marriage was performed. Wardle, *infra,* at 46. However, if the out-of-state marriage that circumvents local marriage age rules is deemed to violate "the strong public policy" of the homestate, it would not be recognized as valid in that state. Wardle, *supra* at 47, citing Restatement, Second, § 283, comment *k.*

2. Statutes, Cases and Doctrines

a. *Medlin v. Medlin*
In Re the Marriage of: Michael Joe Medlin v. Michelle Ann Medlin
981 P.2d 1087 (Ariz. App. 1999)

KLEINSCHMIDT, Judge.

The Husband, Michael Joe Medlin, the petitioner in this dissolution proceeding, argues that the trial judge erred by awarding the Wife spousal maintenance because he and his Wife were never legally married under Arizona law. He also argues that the trial court abused its discretion in awarding attorneys' fees to the Wife. He requests that the order be vacated and the matter remanded with directions to annul the marriage.

The parties, who were both Arizona residents, married in Nevada in 1987. At the time, the Wife was twenty-two years old and the Husband was sixteen. The Husband was under the legal custody of his mother, who refused to consent to the marriage. The parties were nonetheless able to have the marriage solemnized because the Husband had a note from his stepfather which described the Husband as his son and gave consent to the marriage.

The Husband and Wife lived together until October 1996 when the Husband, acting without a lawyer, filed a petition for dissolution. By mutual agreement, most of the property was divided, but the parties had not decided the issue of spousal maintenance. Following trial, the court awarded the Wife spousal maintenance of three hundred dollars per month for six years or until she remarried or either party died.

The Husband then hired an attorney and filed a motion to amend the petition to request an annulment, arguing that the marriage was void under the laws of Arizona because he never had consent to marry from his custodial parent, as required under Arizona Revised Statutes Annotated ("A.R.S.") sections 25-102 and 122.

The trial judge denied the motion, relying on A.R.S. section 25-112(A) which provides that all out-of-state marriages that are valid under the laws of the state of solemnization are valid in Arizona. The judge found that since the laws of Nevada allow a stepfather to consent to the marriage of a minor, the marriage was valid. Although A.R.S. section 25-112(C) provides that the parties cannot evade the laws of Arizona by getting married out-of-state, the trial judge, employing a rationale that is not clear to us, found this provision only applied to the act of solemnization and not to the parties' capacity to contract. He also found that any dispute the Husband had concerning the validity of the marriage was waived once he filed the petition for dissolution of marriage.

The Husband waived his objection to the validity of the marriage. He filed a petition for dissolution of his marriage that indicated he had been married to the Wife since 1987. The Husband did not object to the validity of the marriage during the settlement conference or during the trial. It was only after the trial, and after the Wife was awarded spousal maintenance, that the Husband decided to hire an attorney and contest the validity of the marriage. An issue raised for the first time after trial is deemed to have been waived. *.

In any event, the request to annul the marriage has no merit. Section 25-112, A.R.S., provides:

A. Marriages valid by the laws of the place where contracted are valid in this state, except marriages that are void and prohibited by § 25-101.

B. Marriages solemnized in another state or country by parties intending at the time to reside in this state shall have the same legal consequences and effect as if solemnized in this state, except marriages that are void and prohibited by § 25-101.

C. Parties residing in this state may not evade the laws of this state relating to marriage by going to another state or country for solemnization of the marriage.

(Emphasis added.)

The statute specifically states that the parties cannot evade the laws of the state relating to marriage. We interpret that to mean all marriage laws and not just those relating to the act of solemnization. *See In re Mortenson's Estate,* * (1957) (first cousins could not evade the laws of Arizona by marrying in another state). By marrying in Nevada without proper consent, the parties evaded the laws of Arizona. Therefore, we must look to the law of Arizona to determine the validity of the marriage. *

Section 25-101, A.R.S., declares certain marriages, like those between close relatives, prohibited and void. The marriage of a minor without consent of a parent is not listed as one of these. Instead the proscription against a minor marrying without consent is found in A.R.S. section 25-102, which provides that a minor "shall not" marry without the consent of a custodial parent or guardian, and in section 25-122, which provides that a marriage license cannot issue without the consent of a custodial parent. Neither statute declares that a marriage obtained in violation thereof is void.

This case is like Horton, in which the court found that a marriage in New Mexico between two Arizona residents was valid in Arizona despite the parties' evasion of the laws of Arizona by marrying sooner than one year after the wife had obtained a divorce. The court reasoned that the Arizona law did not expressly declare such marriages void. Horton, 22 Ariz. at 492, 198 P. at 1106. Although Horton declared the marriage in that case valid, it left open the possibility for a different result if the law which was evaded concerned a party's incapacity to contract. Id. at 493-94, 198 P. at 1107.

In Arizona, only marriages that are void or voidable may be annulled. * Generally, marriages are considered a civil contract and can be annulled by a party incapable of contracting. * Since marriages in which one or both of the parties are incapable of contracting are not void under A.R.S. section 25-101, they are voidable.

This conclusion is in accord with the law of other states that hold marriages voidable when a minor marries before reaching the age a minor is allowed to marry by law. *See Taylor v. Taylor,* * (1947) (where statute declared that minors were incapable of contracting marriage, marriage found voidable); *Kibler v. Kibler,* * (1930) (marriage of minors, although declared void under the statute, found voidable); *Hunt v. Hunt,* * (1909) (marriage of minors, although forbidden and prohibited under the statute, found voidable); *State ex rel. Scott v. Lowell,* * (1899) (although statute declared males over eighteen and females over fifteen capable of contracting for marriage and another statute placed restrictions on public officers and clergyman from solemnizing a marriage of minors below those ages, marriages of minors found voidable); *Smith v. Smith,* * (1890) (where marriage of minors declared void under the statute, the court ruled marriage could be ratified).

When a marriage is voidable, it can be ratified by the minor once he or she reaches the age of majority. *

Ratification of an underage marriage is normally accomplished by the parties merely continuing to live together as husband and wife after the age of majority is attained. *

The parties in this case cohabited for approximately seven years after the Husband reached his eighteenth birthday, thereby ratifying the marriage. The trial judge's decree of dissolution and award of spousal maintenance is affirmed.
        ***
The decision of the trial court is affirmed.

CONCURRING: WILLIAM F. GARBARINO, Presiding Judge, and EDWARD C. VOSS, Judge.

b. Notes and Questions

1) Constitutionality of Minimum Marriage Age Laws

"[A]ll states impose minimum marriage age requirements, and we assume that these laws are constitutional." *Chen v. Ashcroft*, 281 F.3d 221, 229 (3rd Cir. 2004) (Judge Alito denying asylum commenting on China's rule that men must be 25 to marry, and women at least 23). In *Moe v. Dinkins*, 533 F. Supp. 623 (S.D.N.Y. 1981), *aff'd* 669 F.2d 67 (2d Cir. 1982), 15-year-old Maria was pregnant by 18-year-old Raoul, with whom she was living, and they wanted to marry, but Maria's mother refused to give her permission allegedly because she wanted to continue to receive welfare payments for Maria. Maria, Raoul and [apparently later] their one-year old son, Ricardo, sought declaratory and injunctive relief against the parental consent requirement of New York Domestic Relations Law §§ 15.2 and 15.3 (Section 15). The former provided that all male applicants for a marriage license between ages 16 and 18 and all female applicants between ages 14 and 18 must obtain "written consent to the marriage from both parents of the minor or minors or such as shall then be living," and the latter required that a woman between ages 14 and 16 obtain judicial approval of the marriage, as well as the parental consent required by Section 15.2. The federal court rejected their claims noting that it was well-established that "[t]he power of the State to control the conduct of children reaches beyond the scope of authority over adults." *Prince v. Massachusetts*, 321 U.S. 158, 163 (1944). The federal district court in *Moe* explained:

This power to adjust minors' constitutional rights flows from the State's concern with the unique position of minors. In *Bellotti v. Baird*, 443 U.S. 622, (1979), the Court noted "three reasons justifying the conclusion that the constitutional rights of children cannot be equated with those of adults: the peculiar vulnerability of children; their inability to make critical decisions in an informed and mature manner; and the importance of the parental role in child- rearing." Id. at 634.

While it is evident that the New York law before this court directly abridges the right of minors to marry, in the absence of parental consent, the question is whether the State interests that support the abridgement can overcome the substantive protection of the Constitution. The unique position of minors and marriage under the law leads this court to conclude that Section 15 should not be subjected to strict scrutiny, *** It is this court's view that Section 15 should be looked at solely to determine whether there exists a rational relation between the means chosen by the New York legislature and the legitimate state interests advanced by the State. ***

The State interests advanced to justify the parental consent requirement of Section 15 include the protection of minors from immature decision-making and preventing unstable marriages. *** The State interests in mature decision-making and in preventing unstable marriages are legitimate under its parens patriae power.

*** The requirement of parental consent ensures that at least one mature person will participate in the decision of a minor to marry.

*** Although the possibility for parents to act in other than the best interest of their child exists, the law presumes that the parents "possess what the child lacks in maturity" and that "the natural bonds of affection lead parents to act in the best interest of their children." *Parham v. J. R.*, 442 U.S. 584, 610 (1979) (procedure for voluntary commitment of children under eighteen to state hospitals by their parents held constitutional). *******

*** New York's Section 15 merely delays plaintiffs' access to the institution of marriage. Cf. *Sosna v. Iowa*, 419 U.S. at 406, 95 S.Ct. at 560 (durational residency requirement of one year for divorce proceedings held constitutional). ******* The rights or benefits flowing from the marriage of minors are only temporarily suspended by Section 15. *******

The fact that the State has elected to use a simple criterion, age, to determine probable maturity in the absence of parental consent, instead of requiring proof of maturity on a case by case basis, is reasonable, even if the rule produces seemingly arbitrary results in individual cases.

*** Plaintiffs' reliance on the abortion and contraception cases is misplaced. ***** *Planned Parenthood v. Danforth*, 428 U.S. 52 (1976) (state may not impose a blanket prohibition requiring consent of parent as a condition for abortion of an unmarried minor during the first twelve weeks of pregnancy). These cases can be distinguished from the instant case in that a pregnant minor's options are much different than those facing a minor in other situations, such as deciding whether to marry. A minor not permitted to marry before the age of maturity is required simply to postpone her decision. She and her intended spouse may preserve the opportunity for a later marriage should they continue to desire it. ***** Giving birth to an unwanted child involves an irretrievable change in position for a minor as well as for an adult, whereas the temporary denial of the right to marry does not. Plaintiffs are not irretrievably foreclosed from marrying. The gravamen of the complaint, in the instant case, is not total deprivation but only delay.

This court concludes that Section 15's requirement of parental consent is rationally related to the State's legitimate interests in mature decision-making with respect to marriage by minors and preventing unstable marriages. It is also rationally related to the State's legitimate interest in supporting the fundamental privacy right of a parent to act in what the parent perceives to be the best interest of the child free from state court scrutiny. *******

533 F. Supp. at 629-31.

2) Constitutionality of Gender Differences in Minimum Marriage Age Laws

The marriage age statute in *Moe* provided a different marriage age for men and women. Is such discrimination constitutionally permissible? Why or why not? *Stanton v. Stanton*, 421 U.S. 7, (1975) (gender-difference in age at which girls (18) and boys (21) attained majority could not, under any test, survive an attack based on equal protection).

In *Berger v. Adornato*, 76 Misc.2d 122 (Sup.Ct. Onondaga County 1973), a New York state court held that Section15.2, discussed in *Moe*, violated the Equal Protection Clause of the Fourteenth Amendment because it established a different age standard for marriage for males than for females. *See generally* Nelson, *infra*, at 98 n. 491 (citing *Berger* and another New York state case ruling that differential marital age restrictions are unconstitutional).

In *Phelps v. Bing*, 58 Ill.2d 32, 316 N.E.2d 775 (1974), the Illinois Supreme Court ruled that the state's marital age requirement under which males had to be 21 to obtain a license to marry without parental consent, 18 to marry with consent and 16 to marry by court order, but females only had to be 18 to marry without parental consent, 16 to marry with consent and 15 to marry by court order, violated the equal protection provision of the state constitution, and upheld an order to compel a clerk to issue a marriage license to the 20-year-old male plaintiff. The court noted that the state had not asserted that there was any compelling justification for the age differential, and it could think of none itself. If you were charged to zealously defend that marital age law, what arguments or evidence might you present in support of the gender-based age difference? (Do boys/men and girls/women mature in the same ways at the same speed?)

3) Social Policy Underlying Marital Age Restrictions

Restrictions on the age of marriage exist in all American states, and they existed for hundreds of years at common law. The movement toward "children's liberation" which has resulted in dramatic judicial or legislative law reform in such areas as the right of minors to have abortions without parental consent, and with only token (if any) parental notice, the right of minors to have access to contraceptives without parental approval or notice, etc., has had virtually no noticeable impact on the traditional policy of parental supervision of the rights of minors to marry. The policy behind the practice of parental control of marital decisions of minors was reviewed in one law review article as follows:

> Perhaps the fundamental reason why age restrictions have survived in all states, with remarkable conceptual uniformity, is because the public generally supports them. Age restrictions are widely considered necessary to prevent immature persons from entering marriages that are likely to fail. Marriage restrictions are believed to protect the individuals involved from the traumas of divorce and to protect society from the burdens of broken families. These prevailing beliefs can be stated in terms of the following simple argument:
>
> 1. Marriages involving teenagers are more unstable than other marriages and are more likely to end in divorce than other marriages.
>
> 2. Unstable marriages and divorce are very undesirable because they are traumatic for the persons involved and burdensome for society in general.
>
> 3. Therefore, it is in the best interests of teenagers who want to marry, and of society, to restrict or prohibit teenage marriages.
> ***
>
> A. The First Premise: The Risks of Marital Failure
>
> There is no question that teenage marriages are high-risk undertakings. For more than fifty years empirical studies have repeatedly confirmed the existence of a clear, inverse relationship between age at marriage and marital failure.
> ***
>
> Another very important report, published in 1953, confirmed the findings of the earlier researchers: "Couples who marry while young are over-represented in divorce actions, and tend to break up sooner than other marriages." The divorce rate for couples who married very young was found to be four times greater than that of those who married in their late 20's.
>
> One of the most thorough studies of marriage and divorce, published in 1970, found that "[t]he 'worst' age for men to marry [in terms of the rate of dissolution] was between fourteen and nineteen years of age***" Among women the highest rates of divorce were for those who married between ages of fourteen and seventeen, and the second highest rate of divorce was for women who married at age eighteen or nineteen.

The following year a study of persons married twenty years or more revealed that the divorce rate of persons who had married young was twice the rate for those who married at an older age, and for men who married as teenagers the divorce rate was three times as high.

Another study, published in 1972, utilized multivariate analysis of a large sample of white women under forty-five who had married young. Controlling for such other potentially significant factors as education, religious affiliation, pregnancy, and residence, the researchers found "there is a difference of about ten points between the rates [of marital disruption] for women marrying at ages fourteen to seventeen and eighteen to nineteen, [and] a five point difference between twenty to twenty-one and twenty-two to twenty-four." These scholars concluded "[a]ge of marriage is *predominant* in affecting stability [of marriage]."

Wardle, *supra* at 25-26.

Another policy is to protect and support parental authority. Parental authority is nothing if it is not the power to say "no." While an adult child does not need parental approval to marry, a minor child is still subject to the authority of his or her parents, and the State is willing to support that authority by giving the parents a veto power over the marriage decision.

4) Options

Ironically, a pregnant teenager has only four options: (1) to marry the father, (2) to not marry the father and bear and raise the child out of wedlock, (3) to not marry the father and to give the child up for adoption, and (4) to have an abortion. The abortion cases appear to have judicially created the right (*de facto* if not *de jure*) of pregnant minors to have an abortion without parental consent. Historically, the pregnant teen has been able to choose to bear the child out of wedlock without parental consent. She also may give the child up for adoption without parental consent. The only option that she may not choose without parental consent is to marry. Does that make sense?

3. Practical and Ethical Considerations

Hal (17) and Wanda (16) consult Lawyer Luke in an effort to find a state in which they might marry without parental consent. Is Lawyer Luke ethically or morally obliged to notify their parents? May he do so? Will he violate his professional responsibility if he does so? May he ethically counsel them about where they might marry without parental consent? Why do you think China's age of marriage requirements are so high (25 for men, 23 for women)?

4. Bibliography

Contemporary Family Law, vol. I, Ch. 2 (Lynn D. Wardle, Christopher L. Blakesley & Jacqueline Y. Parker, eds., 1988).

William E. Nelson, *The Changing Meaning of Equality in Twentieth-Century Constitutional Law*, 52 Wash & Lee L. Rev. 3 (1995).

Lynn D. Wardle, *Rethinking Marital Age Restrictions*, 22 J. Fam. L. 1, 5-7 (1983).

B. MENTAL COMPETENCY

1.Background

a. Blackstone

Capacity to contract marriage was required for a valid marriage at common law. Blackstone explained: "[S]ince consent is absolutely requisite to matrimony *** neither idiots not lunatics are capable of consenting to anything *** and modern resolutions have adhered to the reason of the civil law, by determining that the marriage of a lunatic, not being in a lucid interval, was absolutely void." Blackstone at *438-439.

b. *Buck v. Bell*

In *Buck v. Bell*, 274 US 200, 207 (1927), the Supreme Court upheld a Virginia law providing involuntary sterilization of persons deemed mentally defective. Justice Oliver Wendell Holmes' tragic and erroneous dicta about "three generations of imbeciles is enough" (the victim of his prejudice had been an honor student), and that "society can prevent those who are manifestly unfit from continuing their kind" reflected then-popular eugenic notions.

2. Statutes, Cases and Doctrines

a. *Hendrickson*

In the Matter of the Estate of Delbert P. Hendrickson, Deceased
248 Kan. 72, 805 P.2d 20 (1991)

McFARLAND, Justice: Ruby M. Hendrickson filed proceedings to probate the estate of her deceased common-law husband, Delbert P. Hendrickson. Decedent's children, Gene R. Hendrickson and Judy L. Martin, contested Ruby's status as the widow of the decedent. The magistrate court held in favor of Ruby. The district court, on appeal, held Ruby had failed to carry her burden of proof to establish the existence of the common-law marriage. The Court of Appeals affirmed the district court ***.   *** In the case before us, the only issue is whether or not the decedent had sufficient mental capacity to enter into a common-law marriage.   The facts may be summarized as follows. Delbert Hendrickson was born in 1915. In 1939 he married his first wife, Irene. In 1944, he was discharged from the United States Army with a 50% disability rating. The reason for the resultant disability pension was either a "nervous breakdown" or "back problems." The son, Gene, testified he believed the former version; Ruby testified Delbert told her the latter version. No official records were introduced into evidence. Three children were born to the marriage, Gene, Judy, and Rodney. Delbert was a poor provider, and the family had many financial problems. Delbert had various hospitalizations. Gene testified he understood the cause was mental illness. In 1968, Delbert's disability pension was increased to reflect 100% disability. Irene was, during her married life, the stabilizing spouse and manager of the family. She had to perform this role quietly and indirectly, or Delbert would become angry. In December 1987, Irene died.   About 1981, the younger son, Rodney, was killed in a truck accident. His parents received about $100,000 from litigation over the loss of Rodney. During the period of time at issue herein (1988), about $50,000 and a small farm near Neodesha remained. The two remaining children were married adults and lived some distance from Delbert, who stayed on the farm. Delbert would have problems from time to time managing his finances and Gene would straighten out the problems.   In March of 1988, Ruby and Delbert met through Ruby's son. This son had an interest in horses and would go to Delbert's farm to ride. Ruby started accompanying the son to the farm and began helping Delbert. Ruby was 55 years old and Delbert was 73. Commencing in July 1988, Ruby would spend some nights on the farm. There was considerable testimony that the two discussed marriage, and that Delbert wanted to marry Ruby. During this summer, heart disease became a problem for Delbert and this required treatment at the Veterans Administration (V.A.) hospital in Wichita. He was hospitalized various times during that summer and fall. Ruby was involved in making the arrangements and providing the transportation. In November 1988, Delbert returned to the Wichita V.A. hospital. His condition was poor and he was transferred to the V.A. hospital in Oklahoma City where more specialized treatment was available.   A staff member of the V.A. hospital telephoned Ruby, in late November 1988, requesting that she come and see Delbert. She was advised Delbert was going to die. Ruby had no private transportation and arrived by bus late at night on November 23, 1988. The V.A. hospital had quarters ready for her at its "Hospitality House." The following morning, Thanksgiving, Ruby went to the hospital. Delbert's physician and a nurse accompanied her to Delbert's room. Ruby testified that, in the presence of these staff members, Delbert asked her to marry him yet that day and she agreed. Delbert looked quite ill and was wearing an oxygen mask. Shortly thereafter, the hospital chaplain arrived and asked if the wedding was on. Hospital staff advised the media and at 1:00 p.m. that day the chaplain performed the ceremony--designated as a common-law marriage at the time as there was no marriage license. Local newspapers and a television station granted coverage due to the human interest angle of the story. Introduced into evidence was a copy of the brief film clip used by the television station on its evening news show. The couple is portrayed sitting on the edge of Delbert's bed. Delbert is smiling and holding Ruby's hand. He then removes his oxygen mask and kisses Ruby. Later that day, Ruby telephoned Delbert's children to tell them of the marriage (Delbert did not have a telephone in his room).

　　　Ruby moved into Delbert's hospital room. On December 3, 1988, Delbert was discharged and the V.A. hospital staff took the couple back to Ruby's home in Fredonia. Delbert's son, Gene, and his son-in-law, Lornell Martin, testified that Delbert telephoned them shortly after his arrival in Fredonia. He told them things happened so fast he did not realize what was going on. This testimony is rather unclear as to whether Delbert was referring to the wedding or the theft of money from Ruby in a purse snatch at the hospital.   Delbert's condition deteriorated and he was rehospitalized in Wichita where he died on December 12, 1988. He had resided in Fredonia approximately one week.   *** The marriage occurred in Oklahoma. The validity of the marriage should be determined under that state's law. Oklahoma recognizes common-law marriage. *** See In re Sanders Estate, 67 Okla. 3, 168 Pac. 197 (1917). The parties have presented no research to us on the requirements for a valid common-law marriage in Oklahoma. Apparently, they are satisfied that Kansas and Oklahoma have identical applicable law in this area. *** We will, under these circumstances, decide the matter as though the marriage had occurred in Kansas.   *** The facts herein preclude any possibility that Ruby pressured Delbert into marrying her. If anybody took advantage of Delbert's condition, it was Delbert. Ruby was requested by a hospital staff member (either Delbert's physician or a social worker) to journey to Oklahoma to visit Delbert, as the hospital believed Delbert was dying. She arrived by bus in the middle of the night and, the following morning, was taken by Delbert's physician to see him. Delbert asked her to marry him, the ceremony to be later that day. Inferentially, the wedding machinery was already in gear when Ruby arrived in Delbert's room. This may well have been perceived by Ruby as a dying man's last request. Ruby was certainly under pressure to agree.   "The test of mental capacity to contract is whether the person possesses sufficient mind to understand in a reasonable manner the nature and effect of the act in which he is engaged." *DeBauge Bros., Inc. v. Whitsitt*, 212 Kan. 758, 762, 512 P.2d 487 (1973). As related to the degree of mental capacity required to contract a marriage, there is a split of authority on whether the same degree of mental capacity necessary for entering into an ordinary contract is required or whether a lesser degree will suffice. * The test for mental capacity previously cited herein from *Baughman v. Baughman* is so archaic in language that it should be modernized. We adopt the test quoted in the above A.L.R.2d citation at 1044, which itself was taken from *Johnson v. Johnson*, 104 N.W.2d 8 (N.D.1960), as follows:" '[T]he best accepted test as to whether there is a mental capacity sufficient to contract a valid marriage is whether there is a capacity to understand the nature of the contract and the duties and responsibilities which it creates.' "   As noted by the trial court, it is unfortunate that in this unusual case where medical professionals were involved in the whole scenario, including attendance at the ceremony, that these people gave no testimony. Likewise, the testimony of the chaplain and the media people present would have been very pertinent. For whatever reason, the facts known by these people and the relevant medical opinions were not available to the trial court and are not before us. The only testimony as to what transpired in Oklahoma City on the crucial day is that of Ruby. Plus, we have the brief television film clip. The film contains no audio of the couple's words.   The matter of who has the burden of proof is determinative herein. The trial court and the Court of Appeals placed the burden of proving mental capacity upon Ruby, in reliance upon *Driscoll v. Driscoll*, 220 Kan. 225, 227, 552 P.2d 629 (1976), wherein we said: "The burden of proving a common-law or consensual marriage rests upon the party asserting it."   *Driscoll* was a divorce action. There was no issue of mental capacity in *Driscoll*. As a general statement of law, the citation from *Driscoll* is sound. However, on the issue of mental capacity another element comes into play. In Kansas there is a presumption of sanity and competency which cuts a path through many areas of the law. *** Also, PIK Civ.2d 15.61, dealing with adjudication of an incapacitated person, provides in part: "A person is presumed to be competent, but that presumption is overcome if the evidence establishes that the person is incapacitated."   We adopt the following statement from Annot., Mental Capacity to Marry, 82 A.L.R.2d § 9, p. 1053: "The general presumption is that a person who has contracted a marriage was mentally capable of contracting it, and the burden is on the party alleging mental incapacity to prove it."

Certainly, there are sound practical reasons for the presumption of sanity, competency, and capacity. A high percentage of all litigation involves attempts to hold persons accountable for alleged wrongful acts or omissions. If the party seeking such accountability had to prove in his or her case in chief that the other party was sane, competent, or had capacity (depending on the type of litigation involved), the burden would be insurmountable.   ***   In the case before us, the trial court clearly stated in its conclusion that neither party had satisfactorily proved their respective claims as to capacity. Under these circumstances, whoever had the burden of proof necessarily loses. We conclude the trial court erred in not applying the presumption of capacity and not placing the burden of proof on those claiming incapacity to rebut that presumption. This presumption, plus Ruby's evidence in support of capacity and the trial court's comments, requires reversal of the judgment herein and an entry of judgment holding that a valid common-law marriage existed between Delbert and Ruby.   The judgment of the Court of Appeals is reversed. The judgment of the district court is reversed. Judgment is entered in favor of appellant, and the case is remanded to the district court for further proceedings consistent with this opinion. ABBOTT, J., not participating.

b. Notes and Questions

1) Overview of Current Law

Marriage is a legal contract. One must have mental capacity to enter into a contract. Thirty-eight states prohibit marriage by persons lacking mental capacity; some use language like "imbeciles," "idiots," and "lunatics." Four states allow marriage by such women if over age 45 or if they have been sterilized. Such provisions raise serious constitutional, moral, and policy issues. It is estimated that six million Americans are mentally retarded, and such laws create impediments to their marriages.

2) Test for Capacity

The old test for mental capacity to enter marriage was "sufficient understanding to deal in the common transactions of life." Recent courts have adopted a test more sympathetic to disabled persons wishing to marry. The new test is "sufficient understanding to enter marriage." The idea is that marriage is a matter more of the heart than of the head. A person might be found to have capacity to enter marriage, even though he or she lacks capacity to own a credit card or manage his or her financial affairs.

One of the most frequently quoted description of the kind of mental condition that is sufficient to sustain the validity of a marriage comes from *Fischer v. Adams*, 151 Neb. 512, 515, 38 N.W.2d 337, 339 (1949). There the court opined:

> It is the general rule in this state that a marriage contract will not be voided on the grounds of mental incapacity unless there existed at the time of the marriage such a want of understanding as to render the party incapable of assenting to the contract. Whatever may have been the mental condition at other times, the condition at the time of the marriage itself must govern the question of capacity. If the afflicted person is cognizant of the nature and obligations of the marriage contract, a decree avoiding the contract is not authorized.
> ***
> Every variation from a normal mental condition is not sufficient to avoid a marriage contract. The mental derangement relied upon must have a direct bearing upon the contract. If the party has sufficient capacity to understand the nature of the contract and the obligations and responsibilities it creates, the marriage is valid. Mere weakness or imbecility of mind is not sufficient, nor eccentricity or partial dementia, but it must be such a derangement as prevents the party from comprehending the nature of the contract and from giving to it his free and intelligent consent in order to warrant a decree nullifying the purported marriage.*

In *Fischer,* the court rejected an attack on the validity of the secret marriage of a relatively wealthy 80-year-old widower who had been hospitalized for a stroke and senile dementia to his 55-year-old nurse. His children by his first wife charged that the nurse was a gold-digger, and they presented evidence that she had deprived their father of his mail, that she concealed their approaching marriage from his children, and that she attempted unsuccessfully to obtain control of his property after her marriage to him, which was thwarted by the children obtaining the appointment of a guardian of their father's property. The court noted that the appointment of a property guardian did not establish that at the time of the marriage the man lacked requisite mental capacity to contract a valid marriage.

3) Temporary Incapacity

Temporary lack of capacity is ground for invalidating marriage. It usually arises in cases of severe intoxication by alcohol or drug use. As one court put it: "Intoxication at the time of entering into a marriage, where such intoxication will render one *non compos mentis* and incapable of knowing the nature of the contact and its consequences, voids or invalidates the marriage or renders it voidable. *** Intoxication to a lesser degree, however, has no such effect on the marriage." *Mahan v. Mahan*, 88 So.2d 545, 547 (Fla. 1956). Seven states have specific statutes, and there are cases decided under the common law in another dozen states providing that marriage by one temporarily lacking capacity are invalid. However, such marriage may be ratified during a "lucid interval." What do you think is the most common evidence of ratification? (Would cohabitation in the condition and repute of marriage after regaining capacity suffice?)

3. Practical and Ethical Considerations

What must/should/may a lawyer do if he suspects that the man his client is trying to marry lacks mental capacity to marry? Must/should/may he provide legal assistance to facilitate the marriage? Must/should/may he contact the man's family or some public official with authority to protect the mentally incapacitated?

4. Bibliography

William Blackstone, Commentaries on the Law of England * 438-439.
Contemporary Family Law, vol. I, Ch. 2 (Lynn D. Wardle, Christopher L. Blakesley & Jacqueline Y. Parker, eds., 1988).
Brian J. Linn & Lesly A. Bowers, *The Historical Fallacies Behind Legal Prohibitions of Marriages Involving Mentally Retarded Persons* – *The Eternal Child Grows Up*, Gonzaga L. Rev. 625 (1978).

C. AGREEMENT TO MARRY

1. Background

a. Blackstone

At common law, capacity and consent were distinguished and both were required for marriage validity. Blackstone summarized English law as follows: "Our law considers marriage in no other light than as a civil contract. *** [T]he law treats it as it does all other contacts: allowing it to be good and valid in all cases, where the parties at the time of making it were, in the first place, *willing* to contact; second, *able* to contract; and lastly, actually *did* contract in the proper forms and solemnities required by law." Blackstone at *433.

b. Overview of Law of Consent in general

Consent must be given by both parties to have a valid marriage. If the marriage was a formal, ceremonial marriage, and the parties said "I do," a strong presumption arises that they gave consent. But the law allows the presumption to be challenged and rebutted. In cases of informal marriage (cl marriage) proof of consent by words in the present tense is generally required before a marriage will be found.

Lack of consent may result in four settings. First, fraud – nondisclosure or misrepresentation of material information at the time of the marriage – will render the marriage void or voidable. Traditionally, the law required that the misrepresentation or nondisclosure go "to the essentials of the marriage" itself – a very narrow ground meaning "exclusive procreation." Most often that meant if a woman were pregnant by another man and she concealed that fact from her husband, their marriage was invalid. (Theoretically, if the man secretly intended to engage in extramarital relations after marriage, the marriage also could be annulled for fraud - though I have never seen such a case.)

Second, *force or duress* may undermine consent and invalidate a marriage. Generally, courts require great duress so that either there will be a wedding or a funeral. Three elements usually are identified: (1) the duress was at the time of the marriage, (2) constituted a grave threat, and (3) was against the law. (Thus, mere threat to file a complaint with the police that defendant engaged in sex with an underage girl usually is inadequate.)

Third, *marriage for a limited purpose* often arises because of immigration. It is important to distinguish the family law question from the immigration law question. That is, a marriage may satisfy the requirements of state law for a valid marriage, yet fail to satisfy the requirements of federal law for immigration, or vice versa. When a statute uses a term of domestic relations like "parent," "child," or "spouse," it is presumed that the term refers to the relationship defined by local family law. But that is not always true, and the question inevitably turns on legislative intent. For example, when Congress wrote "spouse" they may have meant "lawful spouse" or they may have meant "either lawful spouse or any person in a spouse-like relationship."

As a general rule, if the parties intended to obtain the status of marriage or an exclusive incident of marriage (e.g., legitimation by marriage) the courts will find that the marriage is valid, even if the parties did not desire all of the incidents of marriage.

Finally, *marriage in jest* is uncommon today (leading cases date to the roaring 20's), but there are rare precedents annulling a marriage for want of consent because the parties only were playing a game, making a mock marriage for amusement of the party, without any intent to marry. *See* Contemporary Family Law, vol. 1, §§ 2.27-2.36.

2. Statutes, Cases and Doctrines

a. *Fattibene v. Fattibene*

Mary V. Fattibene v. Arthur T. Fattibene
183 Conn. 433, 441 A.2d 3 (Conn. 1981)

ARMENTANO, Associate Justice.

The plaintiff married the defendant in Washington, D. C. on May 30, 1953, and commenced this dissolution action in April, 1976, alleging that irreconcilable differences between them had irretrievably broken down their marriage. The defendant alleged by way of an affirmative defense that the marriage was invalid because the plaintiff was not legally divorced from her prior living husband at the time of her marriage to him. In addition to this defense, the defendant counterclaimed alleging intolerable habitual intemperance, fraud in the inducement of the marriage, and irretrievable breakdown of the marriage.

After a contested hearing before a state referee, the court found that the marriage was a valid one, and that it had broken down irretrievably; it rendered a decree dissolving the marriage. ***

The defendant has appealed claiming that the court erred (1) in finding that the parties' marriage was valid; ***.   VALIDITY OF THE MARRIAGE   Prior to her marriage to the defendant, the plaintiff had previously married James T. Williams. In a decree dated June 6, 1952, the United States District Court for the District of Columbia awarded the plaintiff an absolute divorce from Williams. On appeal, the defendant claims the decree dissolving the marriage was invalid, therefore making his marriage to the plaintiff void. The first issue is not whether the marriage between the parties is void because of an invalid divorce decree, but rather, whether the divorce decree can be collaterally attacked by the defendant. The rule is the same in both Connecticut and the District of Columbia; the defendant has no standing to attack collaterally an earlier divorce decree to which he was a stranger and in which he had no legally protected interest which would have been affected by the decree itself at the time it was rendered. *   ***   In the counterclaim to the complaint, the defendant sought an annulment of the marriage based on the plaintiff's fraudulent nondisclosure at the time of the marriage of her prior marital status and of the previous birth of a child. Although there is evidence in the record to the contrary, the defendant alleges that he did not learn of the nondisclosed facts until the commencement of this action, over twenty-five years after the wedding ceremony, and never condoned the plaintiff's fraud or cohabitated with her after discovering it. The trial court decided that a valid marriage existed between the parties and dissolved it, rather than declare it null and void. The defendant claims on appeal that the trial court erred.   The Superior Court has authority to annul a marriage performed in another state if the marriage would have been invalid in that state or violates a strong public policy of this state. Since the parties married in Washington, D. C., we must look to the law of that jurisdiction. *   *** Section 30-103 [of the District of Columbia Code] provides in part: "The following marriages in said District shall be illegal, and shall be void from the time when their nullity shall be declared by decree, namely: *** Second. Any marriage the consent to which of either party has been procured by force or fraud." A marriage falling within § 30-103 is not void ab initia but voidable. * The burden is on the one claiming the fraud to prove its existence by clear and convincing proof. *

"(F)raud in its procurement will vitiate the contract upon which marriage is based as well as any other contract, and will justify its annulment by the courts." * The rule to determine whether fraud in a case is sufficient to justify an annulment is set out in *Reynolds v. Reynolds*, 85 Mass. (3 Allen) 605 (1862). See * Clark, Domestic Relations § 2.17, pp. 103-106. The *Reynolds* case established the doctrine of essentials which requires the misrepresentations claimed by the party seeking an annulment to be related to the sexual obligations of the marriage, that is, the ability or willingness to have sexual relations and the ability to bear children. *   This rule is followed in the reported decisions of the District of Columbia. In the following cases the court granted an annulment based on fraud: *Stone v. Stone*, 136 F.2d 761 (U.S.App.D.C.1943) (husband concealed fact he suffered from venereal disease); *Zoglio v. Zoglio, supra* (wife failed to keep promise to have normal and natural sexual relations); *Kaufman v. Kaufman*, 164 F.2d 519 (U.S.App.D.C.1947) (husband unable to have sexual relations). On the other hand, the claimed fraud did not justify an annulment in the following cases: *Williamson v. Williamson, supra* (misconception by husband of wife's personality traits); *Burroughs v. Burroughs*, 4 F.2d 936 (U.S.App.D.C.1925) (despite sexual relations, wife barren).

There is no evidence in the appeal before us that the nondisclosures by the plaintiff interfered with the sexual relations of the parties or prevented the birth of children. On the contrary, two children were born of this marriage. The nondisclosures were more similar to a "misconception as to the character, fortune, health, or temper, (which) however brought about, will (not) support an allegation of fraud ***. These are accidental qualities which do not constitute the essential and material elements on which the marriage relation exists." *Williamson v. Williamson, supra*, 539; Clark, op. cit., pp. 113-14.

Although we are unable to find any District of Columbia case in point, two Connecticut cases are factually similar. In *Gordon v. Gordon*, 11 Conn.Sup. 302 (1942), the husband had failed to disclose to his wife his prior criminal record and the existence of four minor children whom he was boarding out. In *Fournier v. Fournier*, 14 Conn.Sup. 171 (1946), the claimed fraud rested on the wife's nondisclosure of a prior marriage to a man whom she never divorced but as to whom she had a good faith belief, never proven false, that he was dead. In both cases " 'the existence or nonexistence of the fact thus concealed or misrepresented (did not) operate, as between the parties to the marriage, to prevent some essential purpose of marriage and work a practical destruction of that relation.' * In the absence of a contrary decision, it will be presumed that the law of the District of Columbia is the same as the law of this state. *   The trial court did not err when it failed to grant the defendant's claim for an annulment based on the plaintiff's nondisclosures or the alleged invalid divorce decree.   ***

There is no error.   In this opinion the other Judges concurred.

b. *Kober v. Kober*

Jacqueline Kober v. Josef Kober
16 N.Y.2d 191, 211 N.E.2d 817, 264 N.Y.S.2d 364 (1965)

VAN VOORHIS, Judge.

This is an annulment suit. The question is one of pleading. The appeal presents solely whether the second cause of action in the wife's amended complaint is sufficient in law. Special Term denied the defendant husband's motion to dismiss for insufficiency, stating: 'Whether the issue herein refers to matters vital to the marriage relationship must be determined at the trial.' The Appellate Division reversed, holding that the fraud alleged in the second cause of action was not vital to the marriage relationship. *** The material portions of this cause of action allege that the parties were married at New York City on June 28, 1963 (this annulment action was begun April 22, 1964) and that at and before the marriage the defendant husband falsely and fraudulently concealed from the plaintiff that he had been an officer in the German Army and a member of the Nazi party during World War II, and 'was fanatically anti-Semitic; that he believed in, advocated, approved and even applauded Hitler's 'Final Solution' of the Jewish question, namely the extermination of the Jewish people; and that he would require plaintiff to 'weed out' all of her Jewish friends and to cease socializing with them.' The next paragraph alleges that plaintiff married defendant believing him to be without fanatic anti-Semitism and without the belief that the Jewish people should be exterminated, 'all of which he had at the date thereof, and during the marriage and all of which he expressed after and during the marriage so as to make the marital relationship unworkable.' The next paragraph further alleges: 'That plaintiff relied on defendant's apparent normal character, high moral beliefs and absence of fanatic anti-Semitism and would not have married him had she known prior to the aforementioned marriage that the defendant had been a member of the Nazi Party, was fanatically anti-Semitic, believed that all Jews should be exterminated, and that he would require plaintiff to cease socializing with all her Jewish friends, and had the defendant not been guilty of said fraudulent concealment.'***

[W]e hold that this portion of the amended complaint states a cause of action. In *Shonfeld v. Shonfeld* * an annulment was granted * husband against wife, where the former had stated that he was in no position to marry because he was not able to make a living, in response to which the defendant had stated fraudulently that, if it was merely a matter of sufficient money to establish him in a business of his own, she had enough, if such an opportunity presented itself. The opportunity did arise, but she refused to advance the money before marriage, and the trial court had found as facts that the representations thus made were false, were believed and relied upon, and induced the plaintiff's consent to the marriage, and that if they had not been made he would not have consented. The case reached this court in the posture that a decree of annulment had been refused upon the ground that these representations did not go 'to the essence of the marriage contract.' The decree was granted in this court upon the ground that, if the true facts had been known to the husband, he would not have entered into the marriage. 'The obligation of a husband to support a wife is no less lightly to be entered into than the other obligations of the marital relation. The ability to support is correspondingly important. * * * The business which defendant's mythical money was to establish was plaintiff's only prospect of supporting her. The misrepresentation was not a mere exaggeration or misstatement of her means or prospects, which might or might not be an incentive to marriage. It was a definite statement of an existing fact without which, as defendant clearly understood, no marriage was presently practicable' (supra, p. 482, 184 N.E. p. 62). The development of the law of annulment was reviewed, the court pointing out * that the fraud need no longer 'necessarily concern what is commonly called the essentials of the marriage relation the rights and duties connected with cohabitation and consortium attached by law to the marital status. * Any fraud is adequate which is 'material, to that degree that, had it not been practiced, the party deceived would not have consented to the marriage' *, and is 'of such a nature as to deceive an ordinarily prudent person.' * (See *Woronzoff-Daschkoff v. Woronzoff-Daschkoff,* *). Although it is not enough to show merely that one partner married for money and was disappointed *, and the decisions upon the subject of annulment of marriage have not always been uniform, there have been circumstances where misrepresentation of love and affection, with intention to make a home, were held sufficient (*Schinker v. Schinker, ***), likewise in case of fraudulent misrepresentations concerning the legitimacy of children of the wife by a supposedly prior marriage (*Domschke v. Domschke, ***), or concerning prior marital status (*Smith v. Smith, ***). Concealment of prior marital status was held to be sufficient in *Costello v. Costello* (*), concealment of affliction with tuberculosis in *Yelin v. Yelin* (*) and *Sobol v. Sobol* (*); failure to reveal treatment of a mental disorder (schizophrenia, catatonic type) was held to be enough in *Schaeffer v. Schaeffer* (*); material misrepresentation of age in *Tacchi v. Tacchi* (*); fraudulent promise to become a United States citizen in *Siecht v. Siecht*, Sup. (*), where after years of married life the husband learned that his wife was a member of the Deutsche Bund and that her failure to become a citizen had been deliberate because of disloyalty to the United States. In *Laage v. Laage* (*), an annulment was granted to a wife by reason of the husband's false representation that he was a naturalized American citizen, after she had stated to him that she would not marry a German-born alien. In *Brillis v. Brillis* (*), a marriage was annulled where the evidence established that the defendant did not intend, at the time when he induced plaintiff's consent to the marriage, to establish a home for his wife and to support her, and that his purpose in entering into the marriage, unknown to plaintiff, was to facilitate his re-entry into the United States from Greece as a nonquota immigrant. In *Harris v. Harris* (*), an annulment was granted on account of the concealment by the husband of previous criminal activities. A recent annulment suit in this court was *Sophian v. Von Linde* (*). Although a third cause of action was sustained that the defendant misrepresented his intentions to have normal sexual relations with his wife, the first cause of action was also sustained * based on misrepresentation by the defendant of his age, origin and ancestry. We affirmed, notwithstanding the dissent of two Justices at the Appellate Division based on *Lapides v. Lapides* * and other decisions holding or purporting to hold that misrepresentations of the nature alleged in the *Sophian* first cause of action were not vital to the marriage relationship. ***   Plaintiff alleges that she *** would not have married him had she known his true nature, in these respects, which he manifested 'after and during the marriage so as to make the marital relationship unworkable.'

These allegations go beyond merely requiring 'a wife, in order to preserve marital harmony, to give up friendships which she had made in the past', or asking the courts to 'lay down a viable line of separation between political and philosophical views too extreme to be concealed during the courting relationship from those not so extreme which may be concealed intentionally or inadvertently without impairing the agreement to marry' as said by the Appellate Division majority *. A fanatical conviction, to be effectuated where possible through the mobilization of superior force, that a race or group of people living in the same community should be put to death as at Auschwitz, Belsen, Dachau or Buchenwald, evinces a diseased mind and makeup which parallels the ground for annulment stated in subdivision (c) of section 140 of the Domestic Relations Law, where a party to the marriage is an idiot or lunatic.

The continuation of defendant's addiction to this anti-social and fanatical objective after and during marriage, which had been concealed and inferentially misrepresented during courtship, would so plainly make the marital relationship unworkable in this jurisdiction, where the marriage was contracted, that it would depart from the realities to conclude that it was not essential to this married relationship, or that, to defendant's knowledge, plaintiff would have consented to the marriage without its concealment. At least the trier of the fact could so find if evidence is adduced to sustain the allegations of the second cause of action in this pleading. ***   The order appealed from should be reversed and that of Special Term reinstated, without costs.DYE, FULD and BERGAN, JJ., concur with VAN VOORHIS, J.DESMOND, C. J., and BURKE and SCILEPPI, JJ., dissent and vote to affirm upon the majority opinion at the Appellate Division.   Order reversed, etc.

c. *Lutwak*

Lutwak et al. v. United States

344 U.S. 604 (1953)

MR. JUSTICE MINTON delivered the opinion of the Court.

The petitioners, Marcel Max Lutwak, Munio Knoll, and Regina Treitler, together with Leopold Knoll and Grace Klemtner, were indicted on six counts in the Northern District of Illinois, Eastern Division. The first count charged conspiracy to commit substantive offenses set forth in the remaining five counts and conspiracy 'to defraud the United States of and concerning its governmental function and right of administering' the immigration laws and the Immigration and Naturalization Service, by obtaining the illegal entry into this country of three aliens as spouses of honorably discharged veterans. Grace Klemtner was dismissed from the indictment ***. The jury acquitted Leopold Knoll and convicted the three petitioners on the conspiracy count. The Court of Appeals affirmed, *, and we granted certiorari,*.

We are concerned here only with the conviction of the petitioners of the alleged conspiracy. Petitioner Regina Treitler is the sister of Munio Knoll and Leopold Knoll, and the petitioner Lutwak is their nephew. Munio Knoll had been married in Poland in 1932 to one Maria Knoll. There is some evidence that Munio and Maria were divorced in 1942, but the existence and validity of this divorce are not determinable from the record. At the time of the inception of the conspiracy, it the summer of 1947, Munio, Maria and Leopold were refugees from Poland, living in Paris, France, while Regina Treitler and Lutwak lived in Chicago, Illinois. Petitioner Treitler desired to get her brothers into the United States.

Alien spouses of honorably discharged veterans of World War II were permitted to enter this country under the provisions of the so-called War Brides Act ***.

The first count of the indictment charged that the petitioners conspired to have three honorably discharged veterans journey to Paris and go through marriage ceremonies with Munio, Leopold and Maria. The brothers and Maria would then accompany their new spouses to the United States and secure entry into this country by representing themselves as alien spouses of World War II veterans. It was further a part of the plan that the marriages were to be in form only, solely for the purpose of enabling Munio, Leopold and Maria to enter the United States. The parties to the marriages were not to live together as husband and wife, and thereafter would take whatever legal steps were necessary to sever the legal ties. It was finally alleged that the petitioners conspired to conceal these acts in order to prevent disclosure of the conspiracy to the immigration authorities.

The conspiracy to commit substantive offenses consisted in that part of the plan by which each of the aliens was to make a false statement to the immigration authorities by representing in his application for admission that he was married to his purported spouse, and to conceal from the immigration authorities that he had gone through a marriage ceremony solely for the purpose of gaining entry into this country with the understanding that he and his purported spouse would not live together as man and wife, but would sever the formal bonds of the ostensible marriage when the marriage had served its fraudulent purpose.

***

From the evidence favorable to the Government, the jury could reasonably have believed that the following acts and transactions took place, and that the petitioners conspired to bring them about. Lutwak, a World War II veteran, was selected to marry Maria Knoll, his aunt by marriage. He went to Paris where he went through a marriage ceremony with Maria. They traveled to the United States, entering the port of New York on September 9, 1947. They represented to the immigration authorities that Maria was the wife of Lutwak, and upon that representation Maria was admitted. They never lived together as man and wife, and within a few months Munio and Maria commenced living together in this country as man and wife, holding themselves out as such. Lutwak, in the meantime, represented himself to friends as an unmarried man. Lutwak and Maria were divorced on March 31, 1950.

Lutwak and Mrs. Treitler also found two women--Bessie Benjamin Osborne and Grace Klemtner-- who were honorably discharged veterans of World War II, and who were willing to marry Munio and Leopold so that the brothers could come to the United States. Bessie Osborne was introduced to

Treitler by Lutwak, and went to Paris accompanied by Treitler. There she went through a pretended marriage ceremony with Munio Knoll, and on their arrival at New York City, Munio was admitted on November 13, 1947, on the representation that he was married to Bessie Osborne. The marriage was never consummated and was never intended to be. The parties separated after entering the United States, and they never lived together as husband and wife at any time. Bessie Osborne's suit for divorce from Munio was pending at the time of the trial.

Still later, Grace Klemtner, who was also a World War II veteran and an acquaintance of Regina Treitler, went to Paris and went through a pretended marriage ceremony with Leopold. They then traveled to the United States, where Leopold was admitted on December 5, 1947, upon the representation that he was the husband of Grace Klemtner. They immediately separated after their entry into this country, and they never lived together as husband and wife at any time until about the time Grace Klemtner appeared before the grand jury which returned the indictment. This was approximately April 1, 1950, more than two years after the marriage ceremony in Paris. Bessie Osborne and Grace Klemtner received a substantial fee for participating in these marriage ceremonies.
***

Petitioners present three principal contentions: (1) Their conspiracy was not unlawful because the marriages involved were valid marriages; (2) The trial court erred in permitting the ostensible wives of these marriages to testify against their so-called husbands; ***.

At the trial, it was undisputed that Maria, Munio and Leopold had gone through formal marriage ceremonies with Lutwak, Bess Osborne and Grace Klemtner, respectively. Petitioners contended that, regardless of the intentions of the parties at the time of the ceremonies, the fact that the ceremonies were performed was sufficient to establish the validity of the marriages, at least until the Government proved their invalidity under French law. They relied on the general American rule of conflict of laws that a marriage valid where celebrated is valid everywhere unless it is incestuous, polygamous, or otherwise declared void by statute. * Neither side presented any evidence of the French law, and the trial court ruled that in the absence of such evidence, the French law would be presumed to be the same as American law. The court later instructed the jury that 'if the subjects agree to a marriage only for the sake of representing it as such to the outside world and with the understanding that they will put an end to it as soon as it has served its purpose to deceive, they have never really agreed to be married at all.' The petitioners claim that the trial court erred in presuming that the French law relating to the validity of marriages is the same as American law, and they further contend that even under American law these marriages are valid.

We do not believe that the validity of the marriages is material. No one is being prosecuted for an offense against the marital relation. We consider the marriage ceremonies only as a part of the conspiracy to defraud the United States and to commit offenses against the United States. In the circumstances of this case, the ceremonies were only a step in the fraudulent scheme and actions taken by the parties to the conspiracy. By directing in the War Brides Act that 'alien spouses' of citizen war veterans should be admitted into this country, Congress intended to make it possible for veterans who had married aliens to have their families join them in this country without the long delay involved in qualifying under the proper immigration quota. Congress did not intend to provide aliens with an easy means of circumventing the quota system by fake marriages in which neither of the parties ever intended to enter into the marital relationship; that petitioners so believed is evidenced by their care in concealing from the immigration authorities that the ostensible husbands and wives were to separate immediately after their entry into this country and were never to live together as husband and wife. The common understanding of a marriage, which Congress must have had in mind when it made provision for 'alien spouses' in the War Brides Act, is that the two parties have undertaken to establish a life together and assume certain duties and obligations. Such was not the case here, or so the jury might reasonably have found. Thus, when one of the aliens stated that he was married, and omitted to explain the true nature of his marital relationship, his statement did, and was intended to, carry with it implications of a state of facts which were not in fact true.

Because the validity of the marriages is not material, the cases involving so- called limited purpose marriages, cited by petitioners to support their contention that the marriages in the instant case are valid, are inapplicable. All of those cases are suits for annulment in which the court was requested to grant relief to one of the parties to a marriage on the basis of his own admission that the marriage had been a sham. Where the annulment was denied, one or more of the following factors influenced the court: (1) A reluctance to permit the parties to use the annulment procedure as a quick and painless substitute for divorce, particularly because this might encourage people to marry hastily and inconsiderately; (2) A belief that the parties should not be permitted to use the courts as the means of carrying out their own secret schemes; and (3) A desire to prevent injury to innocent third parties, particularly children of the marriage. These factors have no application in the circumstances of the instant case. Similarly inapplicable are the cases where a marriage was entered into in order to render the wife incompetent to testify against her husband in a pending trial because in none of those cases was it proved that the parties to the marriage did not intend to enter into the marital relationship in good faith. Much more cosely related is the case of *United States v. Rubenstein*, 2 Cir., 151 F.2d 915, 918-- 919, in which the court held that where two persons entered into a marriage solely for the purpose of facilitating the woman's entry into this country, and with no intention by either party to enter into the marriage relationship as it is commonly understood, for the purposes of that case they were never married at all. In the instant case, as in the *Rubenstein* case, there was no good faith--no intention to marry and consummate the marriages even for a day. With the legal consequences of such ceremonies under other circumstances, either in the United States or France, we are not concerned.

II.

Much of the evidence of the conspiracy comes from the lips of the so-called wives of these spurious marriages. The next question with which we are confronted is whether these so-called wives are competent to testify against their purported husbands in this criminal prosecution and thus incriminate the so-called husbands.

Civil marriage ceremonies were entered into by the parties in Paris as above indicated. Must these ostensible marriages be recognized as creating spouses in order that the marital relationship may be claimed to prevent the wives from testifying against the husbands? At common law the wife could testify neither for nor against her husband in a criminal case, but since Funk v. United States, *, the wife may testify in favor of the husband.
***

Under [Fed. R. Crim. Pro. 26], the competency of witnesses is to be governed by the principles of the common law as they may be interpreted by the courts in the light of reason and experience. *** Therefore, it is open to us to say whether we shall go further and abrogate this common-law rule disqualifying one spouse from testifying in criminal cases against the other spouse.

When the good faith of the marital relation is pertinent and it is made to appear to the trial court, as it was here, that the relationship was entered into with no intention of the parties to live together as husband and wife but only for the purpose of using the marriage ceremony in a scheme to defraud, the ostensible spouses are competent to testify against each other. Here again, we are not concerned with the validity or invalidity of these so- called marriages. We are concerned only with the application of a common-law principle of evidence to the circumstances of this case. *** The reason for the rule at common law disqualifying the wife is to protect the sanctity and tranquility of the marital relationship. It is hollow mockery for the petitioners in arguing for the policy of the rule to invoke the reason for the rule and to say to us 'the husband and wife have grown closer together as an emotional, social, and cultural unit' and to speak of 'the close emotional ties between husband and wife' and of 'the special protection society affords to the marriage relationship.' In a sham, phony, empty ceremony such as the parties went through in this case, the reason for the rule disqualifying a spouse from giving testimony disappears, and with it the rule.

***

*** We therefore hold that in the circumstances of this case, the common-law rule prohibiting antispousal testimony has no application. These ostensible wives were competent to testify.

***

Finding no reversible error in this record, the judgment is affirmed.

MR. JUSTICE JACKSON, whom MR. JUSTICE BLACK and MR. JUSTICE FRANKFURTER join, dissenting.

***

1. We are not convinced that any crime has been proved, even on the assumption that all evidence in the record was admissible. These marriages were formally contracted in France, and there is no contention that they were forbidden or illegal there for any reason. It is admitted that some judicial procedure is necessary if the parties wish to be relieved of their obligations. Whether by reason of the reservations with which the parties entered into the marriages they could be annulled may be a nice question of French law, in view of the fact that no one of them deceived the other. We should expect it to be an even nicer question whether a third party, such as the state in a criminal process, could simply ignore the ceremony and its consequences, as the Government does here.

We start with marriages that either are valid or at least have not been proved to be invalid in their inception. The Court brushes this question aside as immaterial, but we think it goes to the very existence of an offense. If the parties are validly married, even though the marriage is a sordid one, we should suppose that would end the case. On the other hand, if the marriage ceremonies were for some reason utterly void and held for naught, as if they never had happened, the Government could well claim that entry into the United States as married persons was fraud. But between these two extremes is the more likely case--marriages that are not void but perhaps voidable. In one of these cases, the parties (on the trial) expressed their desire to stay married, and they were acquitted; and no one contends that their marriage is void. Certainly if these marriages were merely voidable and had not been adjudged void at the time of the entry into this country, it was not a fraud a represent them as subsisting. We should think that the parties to them might have been prosecuted with as much reason if they had represented themselves to be single. Marriages of convenience are not uncommon and it cannot be that we would hold it a fraud for one who has contracted a marriage not forbidden by law to represent himself as wedded, even if there were grounds for annulment or divorce and proceedings to that end were contemplated.

The effect of any reservations of the parties in contracting the marriages would seem to be governed by the law of France. It does not seem justifiable to assume what we all know is not true--that French law and our law are the same. Such a view ignores some of the most elementary facts of legal history-- the French reception of Roman law, the consequences of the Revolution, and the Napoleonic codifications. If the Government contends that these marriages were ineffectual from the beginning, it would seem to require proof of particular rules of the French law of domestic relations.

2. 'The federal courts have held that one spouse cannot testify against the other unless the defendant spouse waives the privilege. * * *' Griffin v. United States, 336 U.S. 704, 714, 69 S.Ct. 814, 819, 93 L.Ed. 993, and cases cited. The Court condones a departure from this rule here because, it says, the relationship was not genuine. We need not decide what effect it would have on the privilege if independent testimony established that the matrimonial relationship was only nominal. Even then, we would think the formal relationship would be respected unless the trial court, on the question of privilege, wanted to try a collateral issue. However, in this case, the trial court could only conclude that the marriage was a sham from the very testimony whose admissibility is in question. The Court's position seems to be that privileged testimony may be received to destroy its own privilege. We think this is not allowable, for the same reason that one cannot lift himself by his own bootstraps.

***

For these reasons we are impelled to dissent.

d. Notes and Questions

1. Fraud Going to the Essentials of the Marriage

To support a claim for annulment based on fraud, the fraudulent representation must be related to "the essential" of the marriage. There are two competing views of what kind of fraud is necessary. The broad view is subjective and looks to what particular parties may deem essential to the marriage relationship. The strict (and traditional) view is objective and requires that the fraud must go to the essentials of the marriage, meaning the known-but-concealed ability or intent to have sexual relations or to bear children of the marriage (including pregnancy by another). *See generally* Contemporary Family Law, *infra*, at vol. 1, §§ 2.33-2.35.

2. New York Fraud

The liberal or sympathetic view of what constitutes fraud developed in New York because of its unique laws. By the 1960s, the divorce law in New York was very strict, allowing divorce for only reason of adultery. (It was essentially the same divorce law that had been drafted by Alexander Hamilton when he was in the state legislature nearly 200 years earlier.) The courts of New York applied that law very strictly. However, to accommodate the need for an "escape valve," the New York courts granted annulments very generously, and interpreted their grounds for divorce, particularly the fraud ground, very liberally. In most other states, where the divorce laws were both much more liberal in text and in application, the traditional, strict common law requirement that only fraud going to the essentials of the marriage would vitiate a marriage was followed. Thus, one writer commented:

> When true divorce was unavailable, the ecclesiastical courts of Medieval Europe found themselves under increasing pressure to grant annulments. Much the same thing occurred in New York where the unhappily married faced with the unpleasant options of intra-state divorce based on faked evidence, or out-of-state divorce based on fictitious residence, were eager to find some more respectable road to freedom. Where medieval lawyers conjured up marvels with the concepts of consanguinity, affinity and pre-contract, their New York successors demonstrated equal ingenuity with the word 'fraud.'

Blake, *infra,* at 194.

3. Immigration Law

In 1986 Congress enacted the Immigration Marriage Fraud Amendments (IMFA), 8 U.S.C. §§1154(g), 1255(e) which provided that aliens married to a U.S. citizen for less than two years would be granted only conditional entry, subject to mandatory joint spouses petition for removal of the conditional status (and investigation into the genuineness of the marriage) two years later, and that if the marriage occured during deportation or exclusion proceedings, the alien would have to leave the United States for two years before obtaining that conditional status. These amendments were based, in part, on since-challenged data provided by the Immigration and Naturalization Service suggesting that 30% of all marriage-based visa petitions involved sham marriages. In 1990, Congress fine-tuned the IMFA providing a few more exceptions (for battered women, eliminating some evidentiary requirements), but retaining the general structure of the 1986 amendments. *See Pritchett v. I.N.S.*, 993 F.2d 80, (5th Cir. 1993); *Salas-Velazquez v. I.N.S.*, 34 F.3d 705 (8th Cir. 1994); *Ghaly v. I.N.S.*, 48 F.3d 1426 (7th Cir. 1995); *Ramilo v. Department of Justice*, 13 F.Supp.2d 1055 (D. Ha. 1998); James A. Jones, *infra;* Redmond, *infra.* The *Lutwak* case has been cited hundreds of time and is still good law. *See e.g. In re Marriage of Kunz,* __ P.3d __, 2006 WL 1171876 (Utah App., 2006).

3. Practical and Ethical Considerations

Omitted.

4. Bibliography

William Blackstone, Commentaries on the Law of England * 429-439.

Contemporary Family Law, vol. 1, Ch. 2 (Lynn D. Wardle, Christopher L. Blakesley & Jacqueline Y. Parker, eds., 1988).

Nelson Manfred Blake, The Road to Reno 194 (1962).

J. Jackson, The Law Relating to the Formation and Annulment of Marriage (1951).

James A Jones, Comment, *The Immigration Marriage Fraud Amendments: Sham Marriages of Sham Legislation?* 24 Fla. St. U. L. Rev. 679 (1997).

Mary L. Fasciotti & Luanne Bethke Redmond, *Marriage, Divorce and the Immigration Laws*, 81 Ill. B.J. 644 (1993).

CHAPTER 6

Common Law Marriage; Marriage Formalities; Covenant Marriage

A. COMMON LAW MARRIAGE

1. Background

a. History of Common Law Marriages

From the earliest times, the common law left the regulation of marriage to the Church; canon law was marriage law until superseded by statute. In pre-medieval and medieval times, the Church was in many different territories and cultures, often with a precarious influence; it did not attempt to regulate marriage too closely but generally accommodated existing local marriage customs.

Under early church doctrine, becoming "one flesh" (consummation) was the essence of marriage. As Cretney writes: "This caused problems with regard to the marriage of Joseph and the Virgin Mary (who, according to one interpretation, had exchanged vows of life-long chastity)." Stephen Cretney, Principles of Family Law 6 (3d ed. 1979). By the twelfth century, however, it became accepted in canon law that a valid marriage could be formed by mere exchange of consents, so long as the words were in the present tense (*sponsalia per verba de praesenti*). No formal ceremony was needed. If the words were in the future tense ("I will marry you" instead of "I do marry you") those words alone were not sufficient to create a valid marriage. However, if sexual intercourse took place after the exchange of consent in future tense, a marriage was created. Thus, *sponsalia per verba de futuro* plus consummation created a valid, informal marriage. "Thus, the church reconciled the two views: that of the early church that consummation was necessary to form a marriage; [and] that, derived from Roman law, that consent was the vital factor." *Id.*

> It is thus that [Pope] Alexander III writes to the Bishop of Norwich: – 'We understand from your letter that a certain man and woman at the command of their lord mutually received each other, no priest being present, and no such ceremony being performed as the English church is wont to employ, and then that before any physical union, another man solemnly married the said woman and knew her. We answer that if the first man and the woman received each other by mutual consent directed to time present, saying the one to the other, 'I receive you as mine (*meum*),' and 'I receive you as mine (*meam*),' then, albeit there was no such ceremony as aforesaid, and albeit there was no carnal knowledge, the woman ought to be restored to the first man, for after such consent she could not and ought not to marry another. If however there was no such consent but such words as aforesaid, and no sexual union preceded by a consent *de futuro*, then the woman must be left to the second man who subsequently received her and knew her, and she must be absolved from the suit of the first man ....

Pollock & Maitland, *infra,* at 371.

In 1215, at the Lateran Council, Church authorities prescribed certain forms of marriage to be observed by practicing Christians (e.g., publishing banns, formal celebration in a church, etc.). Failure to observe these requirements could subject the party to spiritual discipline (penance, etc.), but did not
impair the validity of the marriage. Informal marriages, though unblessed, were still valid under Canon and civil law.

The canon law of the Catholic Church changed in 1563 when the Council of Trent decreed the presence of a priest and witnesses, but this came too late to enter English law, as Henry VIII had already broken from the Church. The English Church adopted similar requirements in the Ecclesiastical Canons of 1603-04, but they were deemed merely directory, affecting spiritual standing not marriage validity. Thus, informal marriages of the two types aforementioned were recognized by common law courts well into the eighteenth century (and, hence, called "common law" marriages).

The laws of England changed in 1753 when Parliament passed Lord Hardwicke's Act, which mandated, *inter alia,* that banns be published before all marriages, unless a "license" to marry was obtained from the Bishop; required all marriages to be solemnized by a priest "in holy orders" (which included only the "high churches" with professional "orders," Roman Catholic and Church of England); required Anglican liturgy be observed; and mandated parental consent for minors under 21, etc. Lord Hardwicke's Act was adopted in part in response to the practice of so-called "Fleet marriages." You must understand that the cost of getting a proper Anglican marriage was quite expensive, especially for the impoverished workers in England. But there was an alternative.

> There was a prison located in "Fleet Street" in the City of London. "There was in the Fleet present a colony of degraded ecclesiastics who derived their livelihood from celebrating clandestine marriages for fees smaller than those legally taken at the parish church. Already incarcerated for debts or delinquencies, the reverend functionaries were beyond the reach of episcopal correction. In some instances, their profits were very great. Thus we are told, by one of them, 6,000 couples were married in a single year; whilst at the neighboring parish church at St. Andrews Holborn, the number of marriages solemnized in the same period was but fifty-three. These clandestine connections were also celebrated at Mayfair in Tyburn, and in other parts of London; and through the instrumentality of the hedge parsons, they were common all over the kingdom -- in fact, more so than marriages in the face of the church.

J. Bishop, *infra,* at vol. 1, § 293, n. 3.

One Fleet minister, "John Gainhem, solemnized thirty-six thousand marriages between 1709-1740." Stein, *Common Law Marriage: Its History and Certain Contemporary Problems*, 9 J. Fam. L. 271, 275 (1969). Lord Hardwicke's Act, which cut off the "hedge parsons," took effect on March 26, 1754. "In one Fleet marriage register, there were two hundred-seventeen marriages performed on March 25, 1754.

Thus, after 1753, "common law" marriages were no longer permitted in England. However, under the Treaty of Union, Acts of Parliament (including Lord Hardwicke's Act, of course) were not binding in Scotland, so common law marriages and marriages by minors continued to be allowed in Scotland, and the Scottish border town of Gretna Green became legendary over the next two centuries as a haven for English lovers who wished to marry but could not, or feared they could not, satisfy the requirements of proper marriage under English law.

Lord Hardwicke's Act was not accepted in America as part of the common law received from England. "Common law" marriages continued to be accepted, unless superseded by statute. A few statutes in colonial America required banns (Connecticut, New Hampshire, and Maryland) or ministerial solemnization (Virginia, Georgia & NC and the three states aforementioned), but most states followed the famous ruling of Chancellor Kent in *Fenton v. Reed*, 4 Johns 52 (1809), and recognized *sponsalia per verba de praesenti* common law marriages.

b. Current Status of Common Law Marriage

Common law marriage is permitted in only a minority in American jurisdictions today; only 12 states and the District of Columbia have permitted common law marriage (in addition to the District of Columbia, the states that permit common law marriage are: Alabama, Colorado, Iowa, Kansas, Montana, Ohio, Oklahoma, Pennsylvania, Rhode Island, South Carolina, Texas and Utah). Not only has common law marriage been specifically rejected by most American jurisdictions, but also the modern trend even in jurisdictions that permit common law marriage is one of reluctant acceptance, tolerance, and disfavor.

2. Statutes, Cases and Doctrines

a. *Krug v. Krug*

Krug v. Krug
292 Ala. 498, 296 So.2d 715 (1974)

MERRILL, JUSTICE.

This appeal is from a decree which held that the marriage between appellant, Clara Ann Capps Krug, and Raymond H. Krug, Jr., a soldier now deceased, on December 31, 1969 was 'void and of no legal force and effect' and that there was 'no common law marriage, in compliance with the law, between these parties.'

The complainants-appellees, the father and mother of Raymond H. Krug, Jr., filed the bill of complaint against Raymond Jr.'s wife, Clara Ann, and the bill, as last amended, sought to declare their marriage invalid, to acquire Raymond Jr.'s personal property, to remove his body from its burial place in Enterprise to the State of Wisconsin, to declare his will invalid and to annul its probate and to secure a declaration of rights as to the service insurance policy.

The cause was presented by stipulation and exhibits. The undisputed facts are that on June 8, 1967, Clara Ann, who had always lived in Coffee County, Alabama, was married to Gordon A. Cook and that marriage was terminated by divorce on December 23, 1969, in Coffee County. The divorce decree contained the statutory language required in Alabama, that 'neither party to this suit shall again marry, except to each other until 60 days after the rendition of this decree,' which is required by Tit. 34, s 38, Code 1940.

Nevertheless, Raymond Jr. and Clara Ann, both 19 years of age, went to Georgia and were married on December 31, 1969. Raymond Jr. was stationed at Ft. Rucker. They returned to Coffee County after the marriage and on January 2, 1970, he designated 'Clara Ann Krug' as beneficiary under his Servicemens' Life Insurance Policy, and on January 7, he executed a will devising all his property to 'my wife, Clara Ann Krug,' and also executed a power of attorney to his wife. A joint checking account was opened at a bank in Enterprise with personalized checks showing both of their names.

They visited Raymond Jr.'s parents in Wisconsin. He introduced Clara Ann as his wife and his parents had a reception for them and introduced Clara Ann as his wife. They received some gifts, at least some money, at the reception. They lived together in Wisconsin as they had in Alabama and held each other out to the people as husband and wife.

They returned to Alabama and Raymond Jr. secured a credit card for Clara Ann, secured an identification card for her as his wife entitling her to the privileges of a military dependent, including the Officer's Club at Ft. Rucker, all of which Clara Ann used. On January 24, he executed an allotment authorization whereby the Army was authorized to allot to 'Mrs. Clara A. Krug, wife, the sum of $300.00 per month as support,' showing her address to be New Brockton, Alabama.

On January 19, 1970, Raymond Jr. left Ft. Rucker under military orders to serve in Viet Nam. The 60-day prohibition in Clara Ann's divorce decree expired on February 21, 1970.

While in Viet Nam, Raymond Jr. sent Clara Ann additional money, they exchanged letters almost daily, and tapes frequently, he addressed her mail to Mrs. Raymond H. Krug, Jr. He wrote of his desires to start a family and he started a Series E bond allotment to her and the bonds were made payable to her and to him.

Raymond H. Krug, Jr. was killed in action on May 14, 1970.

The trial court's opinion is full and comprehensive. ** The trial court held that (1) the marriage was void because of the prohibition in Tit. 34, s 38; (2) there was no common-law marriage; (3) the will was not properly proved and the property of Raymond Jr. held by Clara Ann should be delivered to his parents; (4) the prayer to remove the body of Raymond H. Krug, Jr. from its burial place in Enterprise to the State of Wisconsin was denied; and the proceeds of the service insurance policy which had been paid into court was the property of Clara Ann.

It appears that the trial court was somewhat reluctant to hold that the marriage was void and that there was no common law marriage, but felt 'compelled' to do so under our decisions which the court was trying to follow.

We agree with the court's statement in its opinion that: 'The court is impressed that the case at bar may be of first impression on the particular facts and circumstances indicated.'

It is our opinion that the particular facts and circumstances of this case place it without the application of our cases which support the result reached by the trial court.

Except for instances not here pertinent, a marriage valid where celebrated is valid everywhere. *

A statutory post-divorce restriction has no extraterritorial effect and does not invalidate a subsequent marriage solemnized in another state. *

The validity of the marriage in Georgia in the instant case is not questioned and it is conceded that it was valid in Georgia. *** The ceremonial marriage in Georgia was valid.

But Clara Ann was under the 60-day restriction of s 38, and she and Raymond Jr. returned to Alabama after their Georgia marriage. We have cases which hold that she possibly could have been subject to prosecution for bigamy if she remarried during that 60-day period of limitation. * Under these authorities, the Georgia marriage, though valid there, could be questioned in Alabama during the 60-day period.

It is established in this jurisdiction that where parties who are incompetent to marry enter an illicit relation, with a manifest desire and intention to live in a matrimonial union, rather than in a state of concubinage, and the obstacle to their marriage is subsequently removed, their continued cohabitation raises a presumption of an actual marriage immediately after the removal of the obstacle, and warrants a finding to that effect. *

It is the well-settled rule that if parties in good faith marry when in fact a legal impediment exists to their marriage, and they continue to cohabit as man and wife after the removal of the impediment to their lawful union, the law presumes a common-law marriage. *

The only obstacle or impediment to this marriage in Alabama was the 60-day waiting period, and once that passed, a common-law marriage would be presumed.

That brings us to the real issue in the case--whether a common-law marriage could be presumed in the instant case.

To constitute a common-law marriage in this state, there must first have been a mutual understanding to presently enter into the marriage relationship, permanent and exclusive of all others, after which there is a public recognition of the existence of a common law marriage. *

There is no question but that every stated requirement was met in this marriage so that it could be presumed to be a common-law marriage. The trial court stated: 'This court is firmly of the opinion from the evidence that the parties fully meant to be husband and wife; they held themselves out to be such and all the evidence indicates that they considered themselves married.' But the trial court quoted the following from *Beck, supra*: '* * * that in order to constitute a valid common-law marriage, the man and woman, following their mutual consent to live as man and wife, must so live as to gain the recognition of the public that they are living as man and wife rather than in a state of concubinage. * * *' Also quoted is another excerpt from *Beck* where this court, in discussing the word 'cohabitation' stated that cohabitation may or may not include sexual activity, but it does include '* * * such things as eating together, sharing household duties, payment of household expenses, holding themselves out to the public as man and wife, and all of the numerous aspects of day-to-day mutual existence of married persons.* **

Since the 60-day prohibitory period extended to February 21, 1970, and Raymond Jr. left for Viet Nam on January 19, the trial court concluded that he and Clara Ann did not live together for any time after the obstacle or impediment to their marriage had been removed. The trial court's opinion on this point concludes:

> Certainly these parties were not eating together, sharing household duties, and doing the numerous aspects of day to day mutual existence for the reason that he was at war and she was at home. In an attempt to go no further than our courts have gone, this court feels that it must hold that these parties were not married under the common law, and so determines.***

Here, the only single reason for not holding this marriage a valid common-law marriage is that the parties did not live together after the statutory impediment was removed. While the couple did not live together after the statutory impediment was removed in the sense that they were in the same house or in the same locality, nevertheless, they did live as husband and wife and the facts come sufficiently under this court's holding in *Beck v. Beck,* * to clearly show that there was a sufficient living together to gain the recognition of the public that they were living as husband and wife rather than in a state of concubinage. The wife was the daily beneficiary of her husband's planning and love. He supported her. He provided marriage fringe benefits, including a club membership. He wrote her almost daily. What more could be expected of an absent husband. She, likewise, wrote him almost daily and sent him tapes frequently. Plans for the future were being jointly made.

We have set forth just a few instances which support the premise that they were living as husband and wife, though thousands of miles apart, and their activities were such to gain the recognition of the public of marital status. One could hardly say that absence from the same house or the same locality is such that their activities can not gain public recognition of their marital status.

Here, the only reason they did not live together was that the husband had been ordered to combat duty in Viet Nam where his wife could not accompany him and live with him. There is ample evidence that after the statutory impediment had been removed that the parties still considered themselves man and wife and held each other out as such. Their separation was not voluntary, but *** by Army orders.

In weighing the particular undisputed facts of this case and having regard to the peculiar circumstances of these parties, we hold that this marriage was entitled to the protection accorded a common-law marriage.

It results that the decree of the trial court is reversed i[n] holding that the marriage is void and of no legal effect **.

Affirmed in part, reversed in part and remanded.

b. *Etienne v. DKM*

Etienne v. DKM Enterprises, Inc
136 Cal. App. 3d 487; 186 Cal. Rptr. 321 (1982)

PUGLIA, J.

Raphel and Bobby Etienne commenced this action after Raphel injured his arm while attempting to cut down a tree with a chainsaw supplied by defendant. The first four causes of action of the complaint involve only Raphel and relate to the injuries he received in the accident. The fifth and sixth causes of action involve only plaintiff Bobby, Raphel's alleged common law wife, who seeks damages for negligent infliction of emotional distress and for loss of consortium. Defendant moved for summary judgment as to the fifth and sixth causes of action. The motion was supported by competent proof that Bobby and Raphel were not legally married. Under the circumstances of this case, and as tacitly assumed by the parties, lawful marriage to Raphel is an essential element of Bobby's cause of action both for negligent infliction of emotional distress (*Drew v. Drake* (1980) 110 Cal.App.3d 555, 557-558) and for loss of consortium (*Tong v. Jocson* (1977) 76 Cal.App.3d 603, 605).

The trial court granted defendant's summary judgment motion, ruling that plaintiffs' counter declarations were insufficient as a matter of law to establish a common law marriage under the laws of the State of Texas. The first four causes of action contained in the complaint relating to Raphel are not affected by the order granting summary judgment. Bobby appeals. We shall affirm.

. . . .

II.

We must determine whether the trial court correctly ruled the counter declarations submitted by Bobby and Raphel, the sole evidence in support of their claim of a common law marriage, are insufficient as a matter of law to raise an issue of fact.

In California, only ceremonial marriages may be contracted. (Civ. Code, sec. 4100.) However, California does recognize common law marriages validly created in states which allow such marriages. (Civ. Code, sec. 4104; *Colbert v. Colbert* (1946) 28 Cal.2d 276, 280.) Texas is one of those states.

Texas Family Code Annotated (Vernon 1975) title 1, section 1.91, provides in pertinent part: "(a) In any judicial, administrative, or other proceeding, the marriage of a man and woman may be proved by evidence that: . . . [para.] (2) they agreed to be married, and after the agreement they lived together in this state as husband and wife and there represented to others that they were married . . . ."

Bobby and Raphel are California domiciliaries. In their counter-declarations, Bobby and Raphel declare they have lived together (in California) for more than eight years and have on more than one occasion vacationed in the State of Texas where they remained for as long as seven to eight days. While in Texas they agreed and understood they were married and there told family members they were married.

The trial court ruled this evidence insufficient as a matter of law to satisfy the Texas requirements of a valid common law marriage. We agree. The evidence fails to establish cohabitation or holding out in the State of Texas.

In *Kelly v. Consolidated Underwriters* (Tex.Civ.App. 1927) 300 S.W. 981, affirmed in *Consolidated Underwriters v. Kelly* (Tex.Com.App. 1929) 15 S.W.2d 229, the appellant sought to collect death benefits as the wife of a deceased worker killed in an industrial accident. Appellant and deceased had lived together, holding themselves out as husband and wife continuously for 18 years in Louisiana, a state in which common law marriages could not be consummated. During four years of this period the deceased had been temporarily employed in several nearby states, including Texas, in which common law marriages could be consummated. Appellant had visited him in all of these states for periods of one to three months during which she and the deceased cohabited and held themselves out as husband and wife. On the facts shown, the Texas Court of Civil Appeals denied legal effect to the relationship, characterizing as a "temporary sojourn" the habitation of the deceased and appellant in the states providing for common law marriages which "did not convert their illegal relations into a lawful marriage." (300 S.W. at p. 982.)

The weight of authority elsewhere also holds that a brief sojourn in a state in which common law marriage can be consummated does not satisfy the requirement of cohabitation necessary to validate such a marriage.

In re Estate of Stahl (1973) 13 Ill.App.3d 680 is a case in point. Plaintiff sought to assert her right to the intestate share of decedent's estate based on the claim that she and decedent lived together in Illinois. At one point during their relationship the parties traveled to Texas for a period of three days for the purpose of vacation and consideration of Texas as a future retirement site. The evidence suggested the parties held themselves out as husband and wife during their stay in Texas and privately exchanged marital vows in their hotel room. In denying plaintiff's claim, the court held: "Assuming that the agreement between the parties and the representations made to others while in Texas sufficiently meets two requirements of the statute, it is questionable whether the brief visit satisfies the third requirement of cohabitation within that state. Such provision could easily be construed as a self-imposed jurisdictional limitation to prevent mere transients from declaring themselves legally married under Texas law." (*In re Estate of Stahl, supra,* 301 N.E.2d at p. 84; accord, *Grant v. Superior Ct. in and for County of Pima* (1976) 27 Ariz.App. 427.

Wharton and Wharton (1982) 55 Ore.App. 564, is also instructive. In *Wharton,* the parties were Oregon domiciliaries. Plaintiff contended that she and defendant established a common law marriage pursuant to Idaho law. Oregon, like California, recognizes a common law marriage if the marriage was valid where consummated. (*Walker v. Hildenbrand* (1966) 243 Ore. 117, 119.) The evidence indicated that over a 10-year period the couple spent an average of 10 days each year in Idaho, and at all times while in Idaho conducted themselves as a married couple and were considered to be married by their relatives and by business and social contacts in both Idaho and Oregon. Notwithstanding that the Idaho common law marriage statute does not expressly require cohabitation "in the State of Idaho," the court held a common law marriage pursuant to Idaho law had not been established. "In this case, the parties' contacts with Idaho were that of mere visitors. Although there were a great number of trips by the parties to Idaho, each visit was a temporary sojourn for business or pleasure. . . . . We conclude that the parties' contacts with Idaho were insufficient to constitute the basis of a common law marriage under Idaho law." (*Wharton and Wharton, supra,* 639 P.2d at p. 654; accord *.)

We are persuaded by our review of the cases in which the issue has been considered that a brief sojourn whether for business or social purposes by a nondomiciliary couple in a state which provides for the creation of a common law marriage is insufficient to consummate such a marriage. Here over the span of eight years plaintiffs, California domiciliaries, were in Texas for two separate periods of seven to eight days with no intention of establishing either a Texas domicile or residence.

Bobby relies on *Estate of McKanna* (1951) 106 Cal.App.2d 126, for the proposition that the cohabitation and holding out necessary to sustain the claim of a common law marriage in Texas need not occur exclusively in that state. The authority cited for that proposition (*McKanna, supra,* at pp. 130-131) antedates enactment by the Texas Legislature in 1969 of the Family Code which expressly requires cohabitation and holding out in the State of Texas to effectuate a valid common law marriage. (See Tex. Gen. Laws (1969) ch. 888, pp. 2707, 2717.) Clearly, *McKanna* is not authority for the present requirements of Texas law.

The trial court correctly ruled the evidence presented was insufficient as a matter of law to demonstrate a valid common law marriage under the laws of Texas. Summary judgment was properly granted.

The order is affirmed.

c. *Spearman v. Spearman*

Mary Spearman v. Viva Spearman
482 F.2d 1203 (5th Cir. 1973)

RONEY, CIRCUIT JUDGE:

This case requires us to decide which of two claimants qualifies as the "widow" under a policy of life insurance issued pursuant to the Federal Employees' Group Life Insurance Act, 5 U.S.C.A. § 8701 et seq. The District Court found that, although both claimants had married the insured, the second wife did not qualify as the insured's "lawful widow" because she did not establish that insured's first marriage had been terminated by either divorce or annulment. We affirm.

At the time of his death, on October 1, 1969, Edward Spearman was insured by Metropolitan Life Insurance Company under Group Policy No. 17000-G in the amount of $10,000. The policy provided that, if no beneficiary were designated, the proceeds were to be paid to the "widow" of the insured. The parties stipulated that the policy designated no beneficiary.

After Spearman's death, both defendants claimed to be his "widow" and claimed the proceeds of his life insurance policy. The first wife, Mary Spearman, is a resident of Alabama and was married to insured on October 2, 1946, in Russell County, Alabama. Two children, twin girls, were born of this marriage, and both carry the surname of Spearman. The second wife, Viva Spearman, a resident of California, married insured on June 7, 1962, in Monterey County, California. This marriage produced no offspring.

Metropolitan filed this interpleader action and paid the proceeds of the policy into the registry of the District Court.

The Applicable Law

A. The Definition of "Widow"

The decision in this case turns on the definition of the term "widow" as used in the life insurance policy. The policy itself does not define "widow," nor does the Federal Employees' Group Life Insurance Act, *supra*, provide any guidance. This question is not however, one of first impression. In *Tatum v. Tatum*, *, the Ninth Circuit, by looking to judicial interpretations of an analogous federal statute, the National Service Life Insurance Act, *, determined that the term "widow" meant "lawful widow." The *Tatum* court then turned to state law to provide a definition of the term "lawful widow." Other courts look to state law for a definition of "widow," apparently following the lead of *De Sylva v. Ballentine*, 351 U.S. 570 (1956), which held that federal courts should look to state law in defining terms describing familial relations. "[T]here is no federal law of domestic relations, which is primarily a matter of state concern." 351 U.S. at 580. *

This case is complicated by the fact that the widows each married Spearman, and now live, in different states. For the validity of each marriage viewed separately, the law of the state where the marriage occurred controls. For the law to determine which of two conflicting marriages is the valid one, and therefore to determine which spouse is the "widow," we hold that California law should apply, following the *Brinson* case, *supra*, which held that the law of an insured's domicile at the time of his death should govern. * This holding is appropriate here since California was not only Spearman's domicile, but also he accepted Government employment in California and entered into the insurance contract while there.

California law is in accord with the general rule which provides that a second marriage cannot be validly contracted if either spouse is then married. E. g., *People v. Coronado*, * (1943); cf. *Sohnlein v. Winchell*,* (1964).

In a contest between conflicting marriages under California law, once the first wife presents evidence that her marriage has not been dissolved, then the burden of persuasion shifts to the second wife to establish that her spouse's marriage to his first wife had been dissolved. Otherwise, the first wife is deemed to have established her status as the lawful wife.

According to the California rule, as in most states, the process of establishing which wife enjoys the status of lawful wife involves these shifting presumptions and burdens of persuasion:

1. Initially, when a person has contracted two successive marriages, a presumption arises in favor of the validity of the second marriage. Cal. Evid. Code § 663; *Tatum v. Tatum,* *,. Absent any contrary evidence, the second wife is deemed to be the lawful wife.

2. The presumption of validity accorded the second marriage is, however, merely a rule of evidence. It is a rebuttable presumption, the effect of which is to cast upon the first wife the burden of establishing the continuing validity of her marriage by demonstrating that it had not been dissolved by death, divorce, or annulment at the time of the second marriage. Cal. Evid. Code §§ 604, 606; *Tatum v. Tatum,* * .

3. California formerly required the first wife to prove that her husband had not dissolved their marriage by showing that no record of either divorce or annulment existed in any jurisdiction in which the husband may have resided. *See Nidever Estate,* * (1960). This strict burden has now been somewhat relaxed. The current rule is that, to rebut the presumption of validity inuring to the second or subsequent marriage, the first spouse need examine the records of only those jurisdictions in which either she or her husband have been in fact domiciled. *See Goldberg Estate,* * (1962).

4. If the first wife shows that an examination of the pertinent records of such jurisdictions and all of the available evidence demonstrate that her marriage remains undissolved, the burden of demonstrating the invalidity of the first marriage then shifts to the party asserting its invalidity, the second wife in this case. *In re Smith's Estate, supra.* Unless the second wife then can establish that her husband's first marriage has been dissolved, the first wife qualifies as the "lawful widow."

B. The Putative Spouse Doctrine

Even if the second wife cannot qualify as the insured's "widow," she may nevertheless be entitled to one-half of the proceeds of the life insurance policy as insured's "putative spouse." *,

A putative spouse is one whose marriage is legally invalid but who has engaged in (1) a marriage ceremony or a solemnization, on the (2) good faith belief in the validity of the marriage. According to *Estate of Foy,* 109 Cal. App.2d 329, 240 P.2d 685 (1952),

> [t]he term "putative marriage" is applied to a matrimonial union which has been solemnized in due form and good faith on the part of one or of both of the parties but which by reason of some legal infirmity is either void or voidable. The essential basis of such marriage is the belief that it is valid. *

The theory under which the "putative spouse" is entitled to recover a share of the insurance proceeds is that, as the insured's "putative spouse," she is entitled to share in the property accumulated by the family unit during its existence. The general rule, therefore, is that the "putative spouse" is entitled to the same share in this property as would have been accorded a de jure spouse under the community property laws. *

> In effect, the innocent putative spouse was in partnership or a joint enterprise with her spouse, contributing her [earnings and services] to the common enterprise. Thus, their accumulated property was held in effect in tenancy-in-common in equal shares.

Sousa v. Freitas, *

The California courts have uniformly held that, when the premiums on an insurance policy have been paid with community funds, the chose in action represented by the policy constitutes community property. * Thus, where premiums on an insurance policy are paid during the existence of a "putative marriage," the proceeds should be treated according to the community property laws.

Since the proportionate contribution of each spouse is immaterial in California, *Vallera v. Vallera, supra,* and assuming that all of the insurance premiums were paid during the time when the "putative spouse" believed in good faith that she had a valid marriage, then it is presumed that she contributed one-half of the premiums and is therefore entitled to one-half of the proceeds.

The Decision

Applying these rules to the facts before it, the District Court first looked to the law of Alabama and concluded that Mary, the first wife, was validly married in Alabama in 1946. The subsequent marriage to Viva in 1962 in California was valid under California law, unless there was a preexisting marriage. At this point, the presumption in favor of the most recent marriage to Viva required Mary to show that her marriage had not been dissolved or annulled at the time of the insured's marriage to Viva. This showing she successfully made by establishing that no petition for annulment or divorce had been filed, by either herself or the insured, in any of their known domiciles since 1946, including Columbus, Georgia, Phenix City, Alabama, and Monterey, California. *See Tatum v. Tatum, supra; Hunter v. Hunter, supra; Vargas v. Superior Court, supra; Berg Estate, supra; Goldberg Estate, supra.*

After Mary had rebutted the presumption of validity initially attaching to Viva's marriage, the burden of persuasion shifted to Viva. *See In re Smith's Estate, supra.* This burden failed for want of proof: Viva introduced no credible evidence that either Mary or the insured had ever been a party to any legal proceeding that had annulled or dissolved their marriage. The District Court then correctly ruled that Mary had established the continuing validity of her marriage to the insured and that Viva had failed to establish otherwise.

Having failed to prove her claim as insured's "widow" under the policy of life insurance, Viva then pursued the theory that, as the insured's "putative spouse," she was entitled to one-half of the proceeds of the life insurance policy. The District Court found that Viva could not qualify as the insured's "putative spouse" because she could not meet the requirement of a good faith belief in the existence of a valid marriage. This finding is not clearly erroneous, and must remain undisturbed under Rule 52(a), Fed. R. Civ. P. The evidence before the District Court showed that Viva knew (1) that the insured had fathered two children by Mary Spearman, (2) that Mary and both children carried the Spearman name, (3) that Mary had secured a support decree against the insured, (4) that the insured returned to Alabama each year on his vacation, and (5) that while on these vacations the insured lived in the same house with Mary and his two children. On these facts, the District Court's finding of an absence of good faith was amply supported. As the District Court stated in its thorough opinion, "Viva admits that she was aware of the possibility, if not the likelihood, of [insured's] prior marriage to Mary, and, yet, she took no steps to perfect her marital status."

Viva contends that the District Court's view of the "bona fide belief" requirement rests upon an erroneous interpretation of the California decisions. She argues that these decisions require only that the "putative spouse" have neither actual knowledge of invalidity nor a belief that the marriage was invalid. Under Viva's view, then, so long as she did not actually know of her marriage's invalidity and maintained a belief in its validity, no matter how unreasonable that belief may have been, she qualified as the insured's "putative spouse." We decline to adopt such a test of good faith. Rather, we think that the District Court correctly held that a good faith belief in the validity of the marriage must be posited on a view of the facts known to the spouse in question.

Such an objective test is perfectly consonant with the California decisions that have developed and applied the "putative spouse" doctrine. Viva argues that, since the decisions applying the good faith standard have always involved spouses who either knew or believed that their marriage was actually invalid, ***, the test of good faith is satisfied by a spouse who has no actual knowledge of the marriage's invalidity and who believes in its validity. We disagree. Although no California case has been cited to us that tests good faith by examining its reasonability, the cases that have discussed good faith do not preclude such an approach. Two cases,***, specifically advert to the fact that the "putative spouses" involved in each had received no information about the invalidity of their marriages. The language in all of these California "putative spouse" cases indicates that a broad approach to good faith is proper. Nowhere do these cases explicitly reject an objective test of good faith.

Costs will be taxed to appellant.

Affirmed.

d. Notes and Questions

1) *Krug* and "Safety Net" Common Law Marriage

As *Krug* illustrates, common law marriage is often used as a "safety net" to validate a marriage that was not valid when celebrated. Cohabitation after removal of the impediment to marriage is presumed to create a valid common law marriage. Thus, if parties living in a common law marriage state celebrate a ceremonial marriage before a divorce of one of them is final, their cohabitation after the divorce becomes final, or after the prior spouse dies, presumptively creates a valid common law marriage. Likewise, if underage parties celebrate a marriage, but continue to cohabit as husband and wife after the age-impediment expires, a common law marriage usually is presumed. *Krug* appears to be good law still in Alabama, though the burden of proof on the party claiming a common law marriage has been emphasized. *Gibson v. Gibson,* 486 So.2d 1111 (Ala. Civ. App. 1986).

The common law marriage doctrine also functions as an equitable "escape" valve to allow courts to give legal consequences to relationships that looked like marriages and functioned like marriages but which the parties (usually by the deliberate decision of at least one of them) failed or refused to formalize as a legal marriage. For example, common law marriage has been used to justify awarding benefits (such as social security benefits, insurance benefits, inheritance benefits, etc.) to the surviving partner after the death of a partner with whom the survivor lived for many years as a spouse. For a list of hundreds of American cases discussing common law marriage, *see* R.H.S., *Validity of common-law marriage, infra.*

2) *Etienne* and Common Law Marriage of Non-residents

Since only a minority of American jurisdictions recognize common law marriage, the question frequently arises whether residents of other states can enter into common law marriages while temporarily visiting a common law marriage jurisdiction. It appears that residency is not determinative; that is, actual legal residency in a jurisdiction permitting common law marriage is not required for a couple to enter into a valid common law marriage. Nevertheless, under prevailing principles of choice of law, some substantial residential connection between the couple and the common law marriage jurisdiction will be required.

3) *Spearman* and the "Putative Spouse" Doctrine

The authority on putative marriage in American law describes it this way: "The classic putative marriage doctrine is substantive, ameliorative or corrective; it is designed to allow all the civil effects--rights, privileges, and benefits--which obtain in a legal marriage to flow to parties to a null marriage who had a good faith belief that their 'marriage' was legal and valid. Most jurisdictions in the United States have developed equitable analogues to the putative spouse doctrine that provide all or part of the relief afforded by the classic doctrine." Blakesley, *infra,* at 2. Professor Blakesley notes that California and Texas apply this doctrine most purely; Arizona and Washington apply variations of the doctrine; and about a half-dozen other states use similar equitable doctrines to achieve similar results. Blakesley, *infra,* at 37-52.

The requirements of the putative spouse doctrine described in *Spearman* are usually strictly applied, as *Spearman* illustrates. *See Allen v. Allen*, 703 A.2d 1115 (R.I. 1997) (man's failure to acknowledge his prior marriage on the marriage license, his failure to identify the date his "divorce" became final, and his admission that he was married at the time of the second marriage prevent finding of good faith necessary for invocation of the putative spouse doctrine). The putative marriage doctrine has been codified in Alaska. AS § 25.05.051 provides in part:

> If, during the lifetime of a husband or wife with whom a marriage is still in force, a person remarries and the parties to the subsequent marriage live together as husband and wife, and one of the parties to the subsequent marriage believes in good faith that the former husband or wife is dead or that the former marriage has been annulled or dissolved by a divorce or is without knowledge of the former marriage, then after the death or divorce of the other party to the former marriage, if they continue to live together as husband and wife in good faith on the part of one of them, they are legally married from the time of removal of the impediment....

In *Batey v. Batey*, 933 P.2d 551 (Alaska 1997), the Alaska Supreme Court read AS §25.05.051 to require good faith to exist at the time of the putative marriage, and ruled that a couple who knew when they went through a marriage ceremony that the man's former marriage to another woman was still valid, did not acquire a putative marriage after the man's former wife got a divorce, even though they mistakenly believed that the divorce had legitimated their marriage. *See* Blakesley, *infra*.

A looser equitable doctrine is "marriage by estoppel," rarely but potentially invoked in cases to prevent a party from denying the validity of a marriage even though the legal requirements for it (or for putative spouse status) may not be fully satisfied. *See In re Marriage of Recknor*, 138 Cal. App. 3d 539 (Cal. Ct. App. 1982) (equitable marriage); *Madewell v. United States*, 84 F.Supp. 329 (E.D.Tenn. 1949) (similar); *Torres v. Torres*, 366 A.2d 716 (N.J. Super. 1976), *infra* Ch. 6.B.2.a.; *see also Watts v. Watts*, 137 Wis. 2d 506, 405 N.W.2d 303 (Wis. 1987) (rejecting equitable marriage but endorsing contract, unjust enrichment, constructive trust, etc.); Bowman, *infra*, at 770 ("American courts and legislatures have attempted to deal with the problems arising from the abolition of common law marriage by a variety of doctrines: variants on common law marriage, as in New Hampshire; theories of marriage by estoppel , as in Tennessee; theories of implied contract, quasi contract, and equitable remedies such as unjust enrichment, as in California and a number of other states; and piecemeal approaches to the different legal areas in which problems arise, undertaken either by the legislature or the judiciary."); Note, *infra* at 614-615 (tracing Tennessee cases).

Spearman also demonstrates the "borrowing" of state family law in federal law. The federal Defense of Marriage Act, 1 U.S.C. §7 (1996) represents one notable statutory exception to that doctrine.

4) Utah Statutory Common Law Marriages

In 1987, the Utah Legislature enacted Utah Code Ann. § 30-1-4.5 (1998) authorizing judicial and administrative recognition of common law marriages in Utah. The purpose of the law "was ... to prevent the exclusion of an alleged 'common law' spouse's income when an applicant for government benefits was made, thus preventing welfare fraud." *In re Marriage of Gonzalez,* 1 P.3d 1074, ¶ 21 (Utah 2000). Thus, to solve a welfare problem the legislature amended the general marriage laws. The statute has been invoked in a fair number of cases and has had some interesting applications, including use in the prosecution of Tom Green, an outspoken polygamist, for bigamy. In that case, Green had married a number of women in sequence, divorcing each former wife before marrying a subsequent (usually very young) wife, but continuing to live as husband and wife with a number of his former divorced wives as well as his latest legal wife (and flaunting his polygamous lifestyle in national and international media). The prosecution relied in part on the common law marriage statute, arguing that those common law marriages made some subsequent formal marriages bigamous.

5) Native America Common Law Marriages

Common law marriage is also permitted by Navajo Tribal Code Tit. 9, § 3E because "Navajo people who live in isolated and remote areas of the reservation and who may not be able to afford the costs of a traditional ceremony may choose to live as married without formalizing their union. *Lopez, infra* at 300-301. Interestingly, the Navajo Supreme Court has held that Navajo tradition and marriage custom did not permit common law marriage. *Id.* at 299, citing *In re Validation of Marriage of Francisco*, 16 Indian L. Rep. 6113 (Navajo Nation S.Ct. 1989).

6) Choice of Law

Evasion of local marriage formalities by marriage during a temporary visit out-of-state usually is successful. The Restatement, Second, Conflict of Laws (1971) indicates that if the marriage formalities of the state of celebration are observed, the marriage will be respected even if it was in violation of homestate marriage formality laws.

Common law marriage appears to be the exception - perhaps because (ironically) it is not deemed a mere matter of formality. Residents of states where common law marriage is not allowed generally may not contract a valid common law marriage by a brief, transient visit to a state in which common law marriage is allocated. Why? Is this distinction sound? In unusual circumstances, courts may declare a valid common law marriage to exist based on a brief cohabitation in a common law marriage state in order to avoid an inequitable result in a particular case. If a valid common law marriage has been contracted in a jurisdiction where it is lawful by parties residing there, and they later move to a state that does not allow common law marriage, the prevailing rule is that the validity of that marriage will be recognized in other states.

3. Practical and Ethical Considerations

a. Hard Swearing

Often common law marriage cases boil down to his word against her word - hard swearing. Does that dilemma have anything to do with why common law marriages have long been disfavored, and formal marriages long been favored in legal policy? What is a lawyer required/permitted/prohibited to do if he suspects that a client is going to give false testimony on a common law marriage claim under oath because the client believes (perhaps correctly) that such evidence is necessary to obtain the legal remedies he seeks?

4. Bibliography

J. Bishop, Commentaries on the Law of Marriage and Divorce, vol. 1(6th ed. 1881).

Christopher L. Blakesley, *The Putative Marriage Doctrine* 60 Tul. L. Rev. 1 (1985).

Cynthia Grant Bowman, *A Feminist Proposal to Bring Back Common Law Marriage,* 75 Or. L. Rev. 709 (1996).

Contemporary Family Law, vol. 1, Ch. 3 (Lynn D. Wardle, Christopher L. Blakesley, & Jacqueline Y. Parker, 1988).

John B. Crawley, *Is the Honeymoon Over for Common-Law Marriage? The Continued Viability of Common Law Marriage Doctrine,* 39 Cumb. L. Rev. 399 (1998-99).

Stephen M Cretney & J.M. Masson, Principles of Family Law (5th ed. 1990).

Note, *Informal Marriages in Tennessee--Marriage by Estoppel, by Prescription and by Ratification,* 3 Vand. L. Rev. 610 (1950).

F. Pollock & F. Maitland, The History of English Law, vol. 2 (2d ed. 1923).

R.H.S., *Validity of common-law marriages in American jurisdictions,* 133 A.L.R. 758 (1941 & Supps.)

Antoinette Sedillo Lopez, *Evolving Indigenous Law: Navajo Marriage-Cultural Traditions and Modern Challenges,* 17 Ariz. J. Int'l & Comp. L. 283 (2000).

B. Marriage Formalities

1. Background

a. Distinguishing Formalities from Marriage Prohibitions

The marriage prohibitions discussed in the previous sections embody substantial public policies regarding the nature of the marriage relationship. Behind them are profound assumptions which are fundamentally moral: i.e., the belief that marriage between a brother and sister, between one already married to another and a plural partner, between persons too young to make informed and mature decision, etc., offend strongly held community values about the nature and importance of marriage.

Not all marriage laws embody such profound social policies. Many marriage regulations exist to further valid, but less intense, state policies such as administrative convenience, certainty in the public records, dignity of the ordinance, certainty of compliance with other requirements, etc. These requirements may be called marriage formalities. There is no "bright line" distinguishing marriage prohibition from marriage formalities, but there is a significant difference in the result of noncompliance: violation of the former renders a marriage voidable or void, whereas in most cases marriage formalities are deemed directory only, rendering the violators subject to personal liability but not affecting the validity of their marriage. However, there are exceptions to this rule of thumb, most notably common law marriages and marriages by minors.

b. Licensure

Licensing requirements insure that other marriage requirements and prohibitions are properly observed, and provide a degree of pre-marriage publication of the marriage. Historically, requirements of the publication of *banns* existed long before the Church adopted them in 1215 at the Lateran Council. The Council of Trent in 1563 declared void marriages performed without proper banns, and that became the law of Catholic kingdoms. But the Decree of the Council of Trent came after King Henry VIII's break with Rome and was not enforced in English ecclesiastical courts. In 1753, however, Parliament adopted Lord Hardwicke's Act which mandated the publication of banns in the parish chapel on three consecutive Sundays prior to the marriage unless a formal license was obtained from a bishop dispensing with the requirement. Today in England, the vast majority of marriages still are preceded by the publication of banns.

The custom of publishing banns came to America with the colonists, and became part of the statutory law of many American colonies and early states. But today only one state, Georgia, statutorily authorizes the publication of banns. Marriage licensing today insures public notice of prospective marriages. Licensed marriage is authorized by statute in all states, and mandated in most of them. Marriage license statutes require the couple intending to marry to file an application for a marriage license (open to public inspection by statute in at least 22 states). Most (at least 30) states also require that the couple wait a certain period before receiving or using the license. Licensing encourages compliance with other requirements (e.g., age, parental permission, physical examination, etc.), insures that information the state wants the couple to have will be provided to them prior to marriage (e.g., whether either has a venereal disease, rh compatibility, birth control information, etc.), and insures accurate public records of marriages. In most states, the license expires if not used within a specified period of time. Violation of licensing requirements generally do not effect the validity of the marriage. But violators may be subject to fines and imprisonment. *See generally* Wardle, *infra.*

c. Solemnization

As early as 1215, the Christian church encouraged formal solemnization of marriage, and persons who married informally could be compelled by threat of excommunication to celebrate a formal marriage "in the face of the church," i.e., before a priest and two witnesses. But it was not until the Council of Trent in 1563 that marriages not properly solemnized were declared null and void by the Catholic Church. The ecclesiastical courts of protestant England did not follow the Decrees of the Council of Trent, and it was not until 1753, when Parliament passed Lord Hardwicke's Act, that marriage solemnization in a specific form became necessary for a valid marriage in England.

In America, the formalities imposed by Lord Hardwicke's Act were not received into the common law. In fact, no formal solemnization was necessary until state legislatures began to impose solemnization requirements. Some solemnization is necessary for a valid marriage in all but 13 American jurisdictions. However, in the absence of a statute specifically providing otherwise, failure to comply with the solemnization requirements will not affect the validity of the marriage.

Solemnization requirements of most contemporary interest fall into three categories: those regulating who may perform a marriage ceremony, those regulating the form of the marriage ceremony, and those concerning physical presence of the parties at the marriage ceremony.

Traditionally the Christian church has considered marriage to be a sacred rite (though this became a point of dispute between Martin Luther and the Pope). Marriages solemnized by a priest have been valid since the earliest days of the common law. Lord Hardwicke's Act required all marriages to be solemnized by someone "in holy orders"-- meaning, apparently, only priests of the Anglican or Catholic church. Thus, in *Regina v. Millis*, 10 C & F 536, 8 Eng Rep 844 (1844), the House of Lords overturned the bigamy conviction of the defendant because the evidence showed that his first marriage was performed by "a regular minister of the congregation of protestant dissenters commonly called Presbyterians . . . ."

The strong tradition of separation of church and state begun by the Puritans who settled this country led to a different tradition in America. In some colonies, ministers were not allowed to perform marriages. Today, the authority to marry is regulated entirely by statute. In all states, clergymen, some judges and others are authorized to perform marriages, although in nearly half the states a clergyman must register or be licensed by the state in some manner before performing marriages. Persons with only "mail order" ministerial credentials, however, generally are not considered bona fide ministers. Ordinarily a defect in the authority of the person performing the marriage will not effect the validity of the marriage, but if the parties marrying lack a reasonable and good faith belief that the person marrying them is properly authorized to do so, the marriage may not be valid.

Lord Hardwicke's Act required all marriages to be performed according to the rubric of the Church of England. In the United States, the form of marriage ceremonies in general is not established in any state. However, in West Virginia, the form of civil marriage ceremony is specified, and in another state or two the courts are authorized to specify the form. Failure to comply does not affect the validity of the marriage.
Proxy marriage occurs when one of the parties is not physically present at the marriage ceremony. Proxy marriage was well-accepted historically, Queen Mary I, Christopher Columbus, and many others being married while physically absent. Today, proxy marriage is most common during wartime and among immigrants from nations where it is practiced. Statutes in about one-third of the states explicitly approve of proxy marriage. Five states explicitly disapprove of it, and about a dozen other state statutes seem to require physical presence of both parties for a valid marriage. *See* Contemporary Family Law, *infra*.

2. Statutes, Cases and Doctrines

a. *Torres v. Torres*

Juan Torres v. Diamelba Torres a/k/a Rodriguez
366 A.2d 713 (N.J. Super. Ch. Div., 1976)

HECKMAN, J.S.C.

The matter comes before the court on plaintiff's motion for summary judgment to annul a marriage contracted by proxy in Cuba. The material facts are not in dispute and lend themselves to resolution by summary judgment. *. Plaintiff, a Cuban national at the time of the marriage, had known defendant in Cuba for sometime before escaping to the United States on May 8, 1967. Defendant, also a Cuban national, remained domiciled in Cuba, and plaintiff took up residence in New Jersey. Plaintiff states by way of affidavit that he sent his proxy to Cuba on October 28, 1967, where a ceremony of marriage took place. A copy of the Cuban certificate of marriage was produced by defendant. The authenticity of the certificate is not in issue. Some months after the marriage defendant came to the United States to live with plaintiff. A child was born to the couple on April 7, 1969. The parties resided together in New Jersey until January 1975.

The sole issue presented is whether a proxy marriage will be recognized by the State of New Jersey. Research has failed to disclose any precedent in this State, although the issue has been raised in other trial courts of this State.

Plaintiff in his trial brief relies upon *Lopez v. Lopez*, 102 N.J.Super. 253, 245 A.2d 771 (Ch.Div.1968), which involved a plaintiff husband who was a resident of New Jersey and a defendant-wife who was a resident of Cuba. These people were purportedly married by proxy on or about May 4, 1966. The entire problem arose as a result of defendant's repeated refusal to join her husband in New Jersey. The court found as a fact that the wife fraudulently induced plaintiff to enter into the proxy marriage never intending to reside in New Jersey with her husband. *Lopez*, *. The court therein, by way of obiter dictum, declared all proxy marriages subject to annulment on the ground that they failed to comply with the statutory requirement of solemnization, N.J.S.A. 37:1--10. The court utilized the definition of 'solemnization' as found in *Respole v. Respole*, 34 Ohio Ops. 1, 70 N.E.2d 465, 170 A.L.R. 942 (C.P.1946):

> Solemnization of marriage, or the celebration of the marriage ceremony or rites comprehends a personal appearance together by the contracting parties before one authorized by law to celebrate marriage ceremonies, and that the marriage ceremonies or rites be entered into and performed by the parties to such marriage together with the minister or other person authorized to perform such in the presence of each other and one or more witnesses, in order that the fact of the marriage contract may have due publication for the sake of notoriety and the certainty of its being made.

This interpretation of the word 'solemnization' need not be accepted by the State of New Jersey. Justice Pashman, in *Parkinson v. J & S Tool Co.*,64 N.J. 159, 313 A.2d 609 (1974), dealing with a de facto spouse claiming under workmen's compensation dependent status, spoke of the intent of N.J.S.A. 37:1--10. The purpose of the statute was to invalidate common-law marriages and any other marriage in which there was a lack of legal process and lack of commitment. (At 163, 313 A.2d 609). The intent of the statute is to prevent illegitimate common-law unions which are marked by this lack of commitment and which union may dissolve at any moment. The uncertainty as to economic support and dependency are the primary concerns of the State.

The interest of the State, as evidenced by this statute, is not diminished by recognizing a proxy marriage. The marriage in this case occurred on October 28, 1967 in a country recognizing such ceremonies of marriage. Plaintiff husband complied with the necessary legal processes of the Cuban statute in that he specifically named a person to stand in his stead in Cuba, by executing a special power of attorney. The marriage was recorded by the proper authorities in Havana, Cuba, and a certificate of marriage was issued by the Register of Vi[t]al Statistics of Havana, Cuba. The requirement of New Jersey that there be a recognition of legal process has thus been met by the parties.

The only other requirement of the statute is that there be a showing of commitment. This requirement is evidenced by the facts in this case. Plaintiff husband went to great lengths to become married, a certificate of marriage was issued, defendant came to the United States, the couple used the same surname, they lived together as man and wife in the same house for seven years, and a child was born to them. In the eyes of the public, these people constituted a family unit.

The requirement of solemnization can thus be met by both a showing of legal process and a showing of commitment. I find no reason in the law to justify the conclusion that all proxy marriages are void. Lopez, supra, by obiter dictum declared proxy marriages to be void, but the decision is based on an alternative ground--fraud.

There is nothing in the facts at bar nor in New Jersey law so strongly indicative of an inflexible and unyielding conviction as to warrant setting aside this marriage.

In addition, I find plaintiff husband barred by the doctrines of collateral estoppel and unclean hands from attacking the marriage of which he was the prime beneficiary and primarily responsible for its creation. * Thus, to effect equity and justice and in good conscience, I must deny plaintiff's motion.

b. Notes and Questions

1) *Torres* Notes

Following *Torres*, would New Jersey recognize a proxy marriage contracted in that state? Did the court convincingly distinguish *Lopez*? If the *Torres* court had followed the general rule of marriage recognition, how would it have ruled and why? Is not equitable estoppel the applicable doctrine, not collateral estoppel. What are the two elements essential for solemnization in New Jersey law?

2) Marriage Formalities around the World

Marriage formalities required by law differ dramatically among nations, but two of the most common formal requirements are some form of notice to society before marriage, and some form of registration upon marriage. Many states require licensing, some require solemnization, most require witnesses. (Italy seems to have more regulations than most nations, and a lower rate of divorce.) Some exceptions to the marriage formality requirements are allowed for cultural sub-groups, such as religious communities. Customary marriages among indigenous peoples are often permitted and deemed legal even if they deviate from the normal marriage formality requirements. In many countries, such as Russia, Switzerland, the Netherlands, Austria, and Argentina, religious officials may not perform legal marriages, though religious celebration after the civil marriage is not forbidden. In many nations, however, either out of respect for the free exercise of religion or as a matter of basic human rights, religious officials may perform weddings which have legal effect. *See,* Wardle, *infra.*

3) Authority to Solemnize

Since clergy are permitted to solemnize marriages in most states, questions arise regarding which clergy and whether any registration or certification is needed. In *Ranieri v. Ranieri*, 146 A.D.2d 34, 539 N.Y.S.2d 382, (N.Y.A.D. 2 Dept., Mar., 1989) an appellate court ruled that a marriage solemnized in New York by a Universal Life Church minister was void because that person was not authorized by law to perform marriages. The couple that was married believed in good faith that the minister was authorized to perform marriage ceremonies. However, when the marriage fell apart, both parties requested the court to declare the marriage void. New York Domestic Relations Law § 11 provides, in pertinent part, that "No marriage shall be valid unless solemnized by . . . 1. A clergyman or minister of any religion . . . ." However, the Universal Life Church provides mail order ministerial certificates for $3.00 and reportedly had over a million mail order ministers, and because of the lack of control by an ecclesiastical governing board, and the absence of a definite congregation and meeting place, several New York cases had held that Universal Life Church ministers were not authorized to solemnize marriages. *See also Ravenal v. Ravenal*, 72 Misc.2d 100, 338 N.Y.S.2d 324 (N.Y. Supreme Ct., N.Y. Cnty, 1972); *Matter of Rubino v. City of New York*, 125 Misc.2d 936, 480 N.Y.S.2d 971 (Supr. Ct. N.Y. Cnty. 1984). *See also State v. Lynch* , 301 N.C. 479, 272 S.E.2d 349 (N.C. 1980); *Cramer v. Commonwealth*, 214 Va. 561, 202 S.E.2d 911 (1974). *But see Cramer v. Commonwealth*, 214 Va. 561, 202 S.E.2d 911 (1988). However, the court skirted the question why the marriage should be declared void. *See generally* Contemporary Family Law, vol. 1, §§ 3:01-3:30

3. Practical and Ethical Considerations

a. Retroactive Recharacterization

Most legal issues about informal marriage arise long after the parties entered into the relationship; parties who enter into nonmarital or informal relationships seldom consult attorneys about what they need to do in order to obtain the protection of the law or legal status (marriage) they seem to be deliberately avoiding. So the cases often involve an attempted after-the-fact, retroactive transformation or recharacterization of the legal nature of the relationship in an effort to achieve what at least one party and her lawyer consider a fairer economic consequence of the dissolution of the relationship than would result if the relationship is not characterized as marital or an equitable equivalent. What is the effect of such retroactive recharacterizations on the institution and integrity of marriage, and on social attitudes about formal marriage? How does that social cost compare with the personal cost the party who belatedly wishes he had a more formal relationship? How should the fact that he/she made a choice earlier to disregard the legal forms required affect the policy analysis? If children are involved, should that affect the policy analysis? If so, how?

b. Mere Formalities

Are there any cases in which clients might have good reason to evade the formalities required? Are there real church-state conflicts regarding marriage formalities. Would a lawyer be justified in advising a client to avoid a formal marriage requirement in order to satisfy the client's personal religious beliefs? If the effect would not render the marriage void or voidable but might subject the client to misdemeanor criminal liability?

4. Bibliography

Contemporary Family Law, vol. 1, Ch. 3 (Lynn D. Wardle, Christopher L. Blakesley, & Jacqueline Y. Parker, 1988).

Lynn D. Wardle, *International Marriage and Divorce Regulation and Recognition: A Survey*, 29 Family Law Q. 497-517 (Fall 1995).

C. COVENANT MARRIAGE AND THE MARRIAGE REFORM MOVEMENT

1. Background

a. Movement to Strengthen Marriage and Marriage Preparation in the U.S.

A movement to improve marriage and marriage preparation began as a reaction to the high divorce rates and tremendous stress (especially for children) associated with no-fault divorce-on-demand. In the decade of the 1990s, every state and Congress adopted at least one new law or program designed to strengthen marriages. In 1997, Louisiana enacted a "Covenant Marriage" law that contained requirements for counseling to get married and additional counseling to get divorced for couples who opted for that form of marriage. The following year, Arizona passed a similar law; in 2001, Arkansas also enacted a covenant marriage law. By 1999 similar covenant marriage proposals were introduced in at least 20 state legislatures, and bills to make divorce more difficult to obtain had been introduced in more than half of the state legislatures. Clearly, there is a "widespread dissatisfaction with the current social and legal landscape of marriage and divorce, and a sense that marriage itself is threatened under no-fault divorce." Scott & Scott, *infra.*

The marriage revitalization movement continues. In 2001, Minnesota passed legislation to strengthen marriage by offering a fifty dollar waiver of marriage license fees to couples who complete a twelve hour premarital education course involving a premarital inventory, and material about communication and conflict management skills. *See* Minn. Stat. §§ 517.18 et seq. A similar bill reducing marriage license costs for couple who take marriage counseling also was enacted in Maryland. *See* Peterson, *infra.* In South Carolina, the Attorney General set up a Commission to study how to strengthen marriage. *See* South Carolina Marriage Commission, *infra,*. Oklahoma has been a leader in adopting marriage-strengthening and encouraging laws. McLaughlin, *infra*; Sollee, *infra.* The Princeton Principles link marriage and public good. *See* Witherspoon, *infra.*

The Louisiana covenant marriage law requires couples who agree to enter a covenant marriage to undergo premarital counseling and to file a declaration of intent to enter into a covenant marriage with their application for a marriage license. They also must agree to obtain marriage counseling before seeking a divorce. The grounds upon which divorce may be granted are restricted to serious fault (adultery, felony conviction and severe sentence, abandonment for a year, physical or sexual abuse of a spouse or child) or for separation for two years (or separation for one year if there are no minor children of the marriage or in cases of abuse). The Arizona law contains similar provisions.

2. Statutes, Cases and Doctrines

a. Ariz. Rev. Stats. §§ 25-901, et seq,

§ 25-901. Covenant marriage; declaration of intent; filing requirements
A. Persons who have the legal capacity to marry pursuant to this title may enter into a covenant marriage by declaring their intent to do so on their application for a license obtained pursuant to § 25-121 and by complying with the requirements of this chapter. The marriage license shall be recorded as provided by § 25-123 with an indication that the marriage is a covenant marriage.
B. A declaration of intent to enter into a covenant marriage shall contain all of the following:
1. The following written statement:
A COVENANT MARRIAGE
We solemnly declare that marriage is a covenant between a man and a woman who agree to live together as husband and wife for as long as they both live. We have chosen each other carefully and have received premarital counseling on the nature, purposes and responsibilities of marriage. We understand that a covenant marriage is for life. If we experience marital difficulties, we commit ourselves to take all reasonable efforts to preserve our marriage, including marital counseling. With full knowledge of what this commitment means, we do declare that our marriage will be bound by Arizona law on covenant marriages and we promise to love, honor and care for one another as husband and wife for the rest of our lives.
2. An affidavit by the parties that they have received premarital counseling from a member of the clergy or from a marriage counselor. Premarital counseling shall include a discussion of the seriousness of covenant marriage, communication of the fact that a covenant marriage is a commitment for life, a discussion of the obligation to seek marital counseling in times of marital

difficulties and a discussion of the exclusive grounds for legally terminating a covenant marriage by dissolution of marriage or legal separation.

3. The signatures of both parties witnessed by a court clerk.

C. A notarized attestation that is signed by the clergy or counselor must be submitted with the application for a license and confirm that the parties were counseled as to the nature and purpose of the marriage and the grounds for its termination and that the counselor provided to the parties the informational pamphlet developed by the supreme court pursuant to this chapter.

§ 25-902. Existing marriages; conversion to covenant marriage; recording requirements

A husband and wife may enter into a covenant marriage by recording the declaration prescribed in § 25-901, subsection B and a certified copy of their original marriage certificate with the clerk of the superior court and paying the marriage license fee as prescribed in § 12-284, subsection A. A husband and wife applying for a covenant marriage license under this section need not receive premarital counseling required by § 25-901.

§ 25-903. Dissolution of a covenant marriage; grounds

Notwithstanding any law to the contrary, if a husband and wife have entered into a covenant marriage pursuant to this chapter the court shall not enter a decree of dissolution of marriage pursuant to chapter 3, article 2 of this title unless it finds any of the following:

1. The respondent spouse has committed adultery.

2. The respondent spouse has committed a felony and has been sentenced to death or imprisonment in any federal, state, county or municipal correctional facility.

3. The respondent spouse has abandoned the matrimonial domicile for at least one year before the petitioner filed for dissolution of marriage and refuses to return. A party may file a petition based on this ground by alleging that the respondent spouse has left the matrimonial domicile and is expected to remain absent for the required period. If the respondent spouse has not abandoned the matrimonial domicile for the required period at the time of the filing of the petition, the action shall not be dismissed for failure to state sufficient grounds and the action shall be stayed for the period of time remaining to meet the grounds based on abandonment, except that the court may enter and enforce temporary orders pursuant to § 25-315 during the time that the action is pending.

4. The respondent spouse has physically or sexually abused the spouse seeking the dissolution of marriage, a child, a relative of either spouse permanently living in the matrimonial domicile or has committed domestic violence as defined in § 13-3601 or emotional abuse.

5. The spouses have been living separate and apart continuously without reconciliation for at least two years before the petitioner filed for dissolution of marriage. A party may file a petition based on this ground by alleging that it is expected that the parties will be living separate and apart for the required period. If the parties have not been separated for the required period at the time of the filing of the petition, the action shall not be dismissed for failure to state sufficient grounds and the action shall be stayed for the period of time remaining to meet the grounds based on separation, except that the court may enter and enforce temporary orders pursuant to § 25-315 during the time that the action is pending.

6. The spouses have been living separate and apart continuously without reconciliation for at least one year from the date the decree of legal separation was entered.

7. The respondent spouse has habitually abused drugs or alcohol.

8. The husband and wife both agree to a dissolution of marriage.

§ 25-904. Decree of legal separation; grounds [same grounds plus]:

9. The respondent spouse's habitual intemperance or ill treatment of the other spouse is of such a nature as to render their living together insupportable.

b. Notes and Questions

1) ALI

The drafters of the ALI's proposed Principles of the Law of Family Dissolution are so opposed to the principles of covenant marriage that in Chapter 7 on Agreements, they propose to disallow those conditions to be enforced, even as a matter of private, consensual contract.

2. Recommendations

If you were approached by a state legislator who wanted your advice regarding whether he should introduce a covenant marriage bill in your state legislature, what would you advise him? Why? If you were approached by a couple belonging to a church that strongly supports marriages and strongly discourages divorce and they asked for your advice regarding whether they should select covenant marriage or traditional marriage before they get married in their temple (or synagogue or house of worship) in Arizona, what would you advise them, and why?

See generally Americans for Divorce Reform, *infra*; Hawkins, *infra;* Spaht, *infra;*, Symeonides, *infra;* Nichols, *infra;* Scott & Scott, *infra;* Wardle, *infra.*

3. Practical and Ethical Considerations

a. Practical Issues re: Covenant Marriage

What do you think are the most practical issues regarding covenant marriage? What is the likelihood of interjurisdictional recognition in a sister state with a strong no-fault divorce policy? Can angry spouses be forced into pre-divorce counseling? Will/can/should such requirements be enforced by denial of divorce? What "smaller" incentives to encourage pre-divorce marriage-saving counseling might be recommended? What policies underlie covenant marriage law reforms? Are those policies good? Wise? Is the method of implementation good/wise?

4. Bibliography

Americans for Divorce Reform, Review of Current Events in the Marriage Movement: January through August, 1999 < http://www.divorcereform.org> (searched August, 1999).

Contemporary Family Law, vol. 1, Chs. 2 & 3 (Lynn D. Wardle, Christopher L Blakesley & Jacqueline Y. Parker, eds. 1988).

Alan J. Hawkins, *Perspectives on Covenant Marriage*, The Family in America, Nov. 1998, 1-8.

Abraham McLaughlin, *Bush's controversial bid to promote marriage*, in The Christian Science Monitor (June 4, 2001) in SmartMarriages Archive <http://archives.his.com/smartmarriages/msg01462.html>.

Gary H. Nichols, Note, *Covenant Marriage: Should Tennessee Join the Noble Experiment*, 28 U. Memphis. Rev. 397 (1999).

Karen S. Peterson, *More states adopting covenant marriages*, USA Today, April 10, 2001.

Elizabeth Scott and Robert E. Scott, *Marriage As A Relational Contract*, 84 Va. L. Rev. 1225 (1998).

Diane Sollee, *Marriage: What's the Buzz*, SmartMarriages newsletter cmfce, in SmartMarriages Archives <http://archives.his.com/smartmarriages/msg01458.html>.

South Carolina Marriage Commission: Condon creates panel on family, marriage, faith-based programs, Associated Press (June 19, 2001) in SmartMarriages Archive <http://archives.his.com/smartmarriages/msg01495.html>.

Katherine Shaw Spaht, *Louisiana's Covenant Marriage: Social Analysis and Legal Implications*, 59 La. L. Rev. 64 (1998).

Katherine Shaw Spaht and Symeon Symeonides, *Covenant Marriage and the Conflict of Laws,* 32 Creighton

Rev. 1085 (1999).

Amy L. Stewart, *Covenant Marriage: Legislating Family Values*, 32 Ind. L. Rev. 509, 514 (1999).

Lynn D. Wardle, *Divorce Reform at the Turn of the Millennium: Certainties and Possibilities*, 33 Fam. L. Q. 783 (1999).

The Witherspoon Institute, Princeton Principles on Marriage and the Public Interest (2006).

CHAPTER 7

Antenuptial Contracts and Failure of Marriage Expectations

A. ANTENUPTIAL CONTRACTS

1. Background

a. Introduction

An antenuptial agreement (or premarital contract) is a contract made before marriage by the prospective parties to the marriage. Specifically it refers to a contract for which marriage is an express or implied condition and the reason for drafting the contract. Antenuptial contracts may be operative on death, divorce, separation or annulment, address property issues, address some support issues, address noneconomic relations, govern economic relations during marriage, and govern rights and economic relations after marriage.

Antenuptial contracts operative on death have a long and honorable history in Anglo-American law. English law for centuries has facilitated the efforts of parties to circumvent some of the economic effects and disability of marriage, especially for women. The legal control of the husband of the property of his wife and the legal restrictions of dower and curtsey have been avoided by premarital conveyances, trusts, uses, and contracts. The history of antenuptial contracts is the history of the wealthy seeking to maintain control of their (or their family's) property after marriage.

As more and more of our society have become wealthy (by historical standards), it is only logical that antenuptial contracts have increased in use. Also, as marriage at older ages (after more wealth has been acquired) has increased, particularly as remarriage after divorce or after death of a spouse has increased, and especially if there were children of the former marriage for whom the remarrying parent wants to provide, the use of antenuptial agreements has increased.

b. Common Law

Because of the property system at common law, there was great incentive on the part of the bride-to-be and her family to make contractual and other legal arrangements to protect the property that the bride owned or might inherit. As explained in Chapter 16, in the absence of such prenuptial arrangements, upon marriage the husband acquired an estate in (including temporary control over) most of the property of his wife. He could alienate his interest in her property. If the marriage was unsuccessful, that could leave her in a grim financial situation, and even if the marriage was a happy marriage, the loss of control of the property, for the duration of the marriage or the life of the partner or forever, was not always a desirable consequence of the marriage and provided incentive for evasion. On the other hand, the wife acquired an interest (dower) in some of the property of the husband, including a life-estate in one-third of the land owned by the husband during marriage. That made it potentially difficult for the husband to alienate or encumber his property, and gave the husband an incentive to evade this rule by premarital agreement.

These incidents of marriage resulted in part from the dominant concern of the common law from feudal times that ownership or control of property be consolidated in the hands of a single individual, to whom the king/state could look for the performance of critical duties (such as payment of taxes, and duties of fealty). Thus, the search for an effective mechanism to evade the husband's control and potential consumption or disposal of his wife's property and to evade the wife's dower interest in the husband's property appears to have been a major concern of wealthy families during much of the common law era. In 1536, Parliament enacted the Statute of Uses, and by the seventeenth century, courts of equity had come to recognize "trusts" whereby the conveyance of property for "the use" of a woman to be married limited the husband's control over the property and preserved the beneficial use to the wife. The right of a woman to waive her dower interest by premarital agreement also came to be recognized. The use of antenuptial contracts by wealthy individuals and families became so common that the Statute of Frauds in 1677 required that such contracts be in writing.

Not all terms or provisions in antenuptial contracts were enforceable. Historically there have been two general restrictions on antenuptial contracts: the agreement may not alter "the essentials" of the marriage relation (dealing with sexual relations and childbearing), and the contract could not provide incentive for divorce. The latter condition became a significant doctrinal impediment to enforcement of antenuptial contracts potentially operative upon divorce during the nineteenth and first-half of the twentieth centuries. If the terms of an antenuptial agreement provided significant financial benefits to either party (different from those otherwise flowing from the termination of the marriage), the agreement could be seen as giving that party an incentive to divorce, and that was contrary to public policy and could make the agreement void and unenforceable. Since the main purpose of the agreement was to alter the financial consequences of marriage, and were thought to give an incentive for divorce, antenuptial contracts were generally disfavored, presumed against public policy.

With the dramatic explosion of divorces associated with the shift to no-fault divorce at the beginning of the 1970s, courts began to favor party autonomy and to see advantages (fewer demands upon the courts) if the parties were allowed to negotiate and decide between themselves what the economic consequences of divorce would be. Thus, public policy changed from disfavoring antenuptial contracts to favoring them, and the presumption shifted from presumed invalidity to presumed validity.

One of the early leading cases to enforce premarital agreements after the death of a spouse was Del *Vechio v. Del Vechio*, 143 So.1d 17 (Fla. 1962), in which the Supreme Court of Florida summarized their rule as follows:

> A valid antenuptial agreement contemplates a fair and reasonable provision therein for the wife, or, absent such a provision, a full and frank disclosure to the wife, before the signing of the agreement, of the husband's worth, or, absent such disclosure, a general and approximate knowledge by her of the prospective husband's property. The term "approximate" is, for this purpose, held synonymous with "near," "close to," or "approaching."

143 So.2d at 20. Eight years later the same court applied the same test in the context of the enforcement of an antenuptial agreement upon divorce. *Posner v. Posner*, 233 So. 2d 381 (Fla. 1970), became one of the seminal cases for the enforcement of premarital

agreements upon divorce. Thus, the standard under which antenuptial agreements became enforceable upon divorce was essentially the same as the standard for enforcement of such agreements upon death of a spouse.

The *Del Vechio* ruling about enforcement of prenuptial agreements upon death made economic sense as Florida attracts older (retired) persons, many of whom have remarried or wished to remarry, but who also wish to preserve most of their fortune for the benefit of the children of their former marriage. (Thus, in *Del Vechio*, where a wealthy 68-year-old man widower asked his 35-year-old mistress/bride-to-be to sign an antenuptial agreement, the court noted that "[i]t appears the son [of the father's prior marriage] was the moving party in promoting the antenuptial agreement, the reason being his desire to protect his interest in the hardware business [i.e., the father's chain of hardware stores]." 143 So. 2d at 19.

In recent years, however, some writers have encouraged courts to return to a more skeptical policy because of concern that most women who make such agreements lack equal bargaining power when they sign premarital contracts, and that the agreements may be the result of undue influence, duress, coercion, fraud, or ignorance. Other writers argue that equality of bargaining power is not the test for contract validity, that invalidation of antenuptial contracts itself works a species of fraud upon the party who in good faith relies upon an antenuptial contract to protect his or his children's financial security, and that it encourages the less-wealthy party to engage in the questionable tactic of signing an agreement one day to get an economic advantage and attacking it the next to get greater profit. There seems to be no disagreement that antenuptial contracts signed under duress, coercion, or fraud will be unenforceable; the debate is over how low or high the standard will be. Because the agreement is signed by parties planning to marry who are not dealing with each other entirely at arm's length, the ordinary commercial contract standard applied to transactions among persons whose only or overwhelming motive is financial self-interest (highly deferential to party autonomy) is seldom applied by courts in reviewing the validity of antenuptial contracts. However, one group of courts applies something close to the standard applied in a commercial context; while another group of courts applies a significantly more searching standard of substantive and procedural fairness.

2. Statutes, Cases, and Doctrines

a. Uniform Premarital Agreement Act

Most states have enacted the Uniform Premarital Agreement Act. Utah's version below substitutes "fraudulent" for "unconscionable," but may be more protective of children. Where it differs, the uniform language is shown in [brackets] and Utah's different language in <angle-brackets>. Section numbers (-1, -2, etc.) are the same.

Utah Code § 30-8-1 Title.

This act shall be known as the "Uniform Premarital Agreement Act."

Utah Code § 30-8-2 Definitions.

As used in this chapter:

(1) "Premarital agreement" means an agreement between prospective spouses made in contemplation of marriage and to be effective upon marriage.

(2) "Property" means an interest, present or future, legal or equitable, vested or contingent, in real or personal property, including income and earnings.

Utah Code § 30-8-3 Writing -- Signature requires.

A premarital agreement must be in writing and signed by both parties. It is enforceable without consideration.

Utah Code § 30-8-4 Content.

(1) Parties to a premarital agreement may contract with respect to:

(a) the rights and obligations of each of the parties in any of the property of either or both of them whenever and wherever acquired or located;

(b) the right to buy, sell, use, transfer, exchange, abandon, lease, consume, expend, assign, create a security interest in, mortgage, encumber, dispose of, or otherwise manage and control property;

(c) the disposition of property upon separation, marital dissolution, death, or the occurrence or nonoccurrence of any other event;

(d) the modification or elimination of spousal support; ["the making of a will, trust or other arrangement to carry out the terms of the agreement;"]

(e) the ownership rights in and disposition of the death benefit from a life insurance policy;

(f) the choice of law governing the construction of the agreement, <except that a court of competent jurisdiction may apply the law of the legal domicile of either party, if it is fair and equitable>; and

(g) any other matter, including their personal rights and obligations, not in violation of public policy or a statute imposing a criminal penalty.

(2) The right of a child to support, <health and medical provider expenses, medical insurance, and child care coverage> may not be affected by a premarital agreement.

30-8-5 Effect of marriage --Amendment --Revocation.

(1) A premarital agreement becomes effective upon marriage.

(2) After marriage, a premarital agreement may be amended or revoked only by a written agreement signed by the parties. The amended agreement or the revocation is enforceable without consideration.

Utah Code § 30-8-6 Enforcement.

(1) A premarital agreement is not enforceable if the party against whom enforcement is sought proves that:

(a) that party did not execute the agreement voluntarily; or

(b) the agreement was [unconscionable] <fraudulent> when it was executed and, before execution of the agreement, that party:

(i) was not provided a reasonable disclosure of the property or financial obligations of the other party insofar as was possible;

(ii) did not voluntarily and expressly waive, in writing, any right to disclosure of the property or financial obligations of the other party beyond the disclosure provided; and

(iii) did not have, or reasonably could not have had, an adequate knowledge of the property or financial obligations of the other party.

(2) If a provision of a premarital agreement modifies or eliminates spousal support and that modification or elimination causes one party to the agreement to be eligible for support under a program of public assistance at the time of separation or marital dissolution, a court, notwithstanding the terms of the agreement, may require the other party to provide support to the extent necessary to avoid that eligibility.

(3) An issue of [unconscionability] <fraud> of a premarital agreement shall be decided by the court as a matter of law.

Utah Code § 30-8-7 Enforcement --Void marriage.

If a marriage is determined to be void, an agreement that would otherwise have been a premarital agreement is enforceable only to the extent necessary to avoid an inequitable result.

Utah Code § 30-8-8 Limitations of actions.

Any statute of limitations applicable to an action asserting a claim for relief under a premarital agreement is tolled during the marriage of the parties to the agreement.

[Sections 9-13 omitted]

b. *Button v. Button*

In re the marriage of Florence S. Button v. Charles H. Button
131 Wis.2d 84, 388 N.W.2d 546 (1986)

SHIRLEY S. ABRAHAMSON, Justice.

This is an appeal from a judgment of the circuit court for Walworth county, Circuit Judge Robert D. Read, dividing property upon divorce in accordance with the terms of a written property agreement which the circuit court found binding under sec. 767.255(11), Stats. 1983-84. This court took jurisdiction of the appeal upon certification by the court of appeals. Secs. 808.05 (2), 809.61, Stats. 1983-84.

Sec. 767.255 provides for division of property upon divorce. The statute requires the court to presume that certain property shall be divided equally between the parties but authorizes the court to alter this distribution after considering certain factors, including any written agreement between the parties. The statute provides that a written agreement for property distribution shall be binding upon the court and the court shall presume any agreement to be equitable as to both parties. No written agreement shall be binding, however, where the terms of the agreement are inequitable as to either party. Sec. 767.255 provides, inter alia, as follows:

> Upon every judgment of annulment, divorce or legal separation ... the court shall divide the property of the parties and divest and transfer the title of any such property accordingly ... Any property shown to have been acquired by either party prior to or during the course of the marriage as a gift, bequest, devise or inheritance ... shall remain the property of such party.... The court shall presume that all other property is to be divided equally between the parties, but may alter this distribution without regard to marital misconduct after considering:
>
> ...
>
> (11) Any written agreement made by the parties before or during the marriage concerning any arrangement for property distribution; such agreements shall be binding upon the court except that no such agreement shall be binding where the terms of the agreement are inequitable as to either party. The court shall presume any such agreement to be equitable as to both parties.

The circuit court concluded that the provisions in the parties' 1974 postnuptial written agreement dividing the property in the event of a divorce were binding under sec. 767.255 (11), Stats. 1983-84, but that the provisions waiving support and alimony were "not enforceable as being against public policy and contrary to the laws of the State of Wisconsin." Florence S. Button appeals only from that part of the judgment directing a division of property pursuant to the 1974 written agreement; neither party appeals from that part of the judgment awarding limited maintenance.

As a result of dividing the property at the dissolution of this 14-year marriage according to the 1974 agreement, the circuit court awarded Mrs. Button assets valued at $7,882.10 and awarded Mr. Button assets valued at $255,103.99. The circuit court's entire finding relating to the division of property in the event of divorce is as follows:

> The Court notes that Mrs. Button was 54 years of age when she signed the June 19, 1974 agreement, some five years after the initial agreement and the marriage of the parties. The court also notes that she had already given her daughter $12,000 from funds brought to the marriage by her from funds she received at the time of the death of her first husband. She clearly wanted to

be able to dispose of her own property as she saw fit and it is reasonable to assume she understood that Mr. Button would be able to do the same thing as a result of this agreement. In light of the entire record, the Court is convinced that Mrs. Button was well aware of the consequences of the June 19, 1974 agreement and it is enforceable as written with regard to the distribution of the property.

The court of appeals certified the following issue: "When is equitableness of an antenuptial or postnuptial agreement [under sec. 767.255 (11)] to be determined--as of the time of execution of the agreement or as of the time of divorce?" Although the circuit court found the agreement equitable, it did not state whether it examined the agreement as of the date of execution or as of the divorce.

The parties present a second issue, namely, what constitutes an equitable agreement? The circuit court apparently considered four factors: Mrs. Button's age, Mrs. Button's transfer to her child of property which she brought into the marriage, Mrs. Button's desire to retain the power to dispose of her separate property, and Mrs. Button's awareness of the consequences of the postnuptial agreement.

This court is addressing both of these issues for the first time. We conclude that an agreement is inequitable under sec. 767.255 (11) if it fails to satisfy any one of the following requirements: each spouse has made fair and reasonable disclosure to the other of his or her financial status; each spouse has entered into the agreement voluntarily and freely; and the substantive provisions of the agreement dividing the property upon divorce are fair to each spouse. The first two requirements must be assessed as of the time of the execution of the agreement. As we shall explain, the third requirement is also assessed as of the time of the execution of the agreement and, if circumstances significantly changed since the agreement, then also at the divorce.

Because the circuit court did not consider and apply the three requirements discussed herein, we reverse that part of the judgment ordering property division on the basis of the written agreement and remand the cause to the circuit court to consider whether the terms of the written agreement are inequitable and not binding under sec. 767.255 (11) under the test set forth herein.

The relevant facts are as follows. The parties married on September 12, 1969, having known each other for approximately five years prior to their marriage. Both parties had been married previously; Mrs. Button had one adult child from her prior marriage and Mr. Button had three adult children. When they were married, Mrs. Button was 50 years old, and Mr. Button 61 years old. Mrs. Button began the divorce action in 1983.

Prior to the marriage, Mrs. Button had acquired some personal property and other assets with a total worth of no more than $3,000 and a life insurance policy on the life of her former husband in the amount of $12,000. Mr. Button had an upholstery business, a stock portfolio, personal property and real estate upon which a duplex residence and the business were located. He had inherited a substantial part of this property and, under sec. 767.255, inherited property is considered separate property not generally subject to division upon divorce.

The parties entered into a written prenuptial agreement on August 15, 1969. While this prenuptial agreement is not the agreement in issue here, the facts relating to the execution of the 1969 agreement are stated because they may bear on the determination of whether the 1974 agreement is inequitable.

Mrs. Button testified that there was no discussion of Mr. Button's finances prior to their marriage, although she was aware that he owned a duplex house, an upholstery business, a car, and a snowmobile. Mrs. Button also testified that Mr. Button's attorney told her that "if [you] wanted to take it to another attorney [you] could, but if [you] did that then you would say that you didn't trust Charles and Charlie said that's right and [the attorney] said the same thing." Mrs. Button also stated that she did not read the agreement before signing it. Mr. Button's attorney testified that he believed that both parties understood the agreement, although he has no record of any financial disclosures being made between the parties. Mr. Button testified that he did not make any financial disclosures to Mrs. Button. Neither Mrs. Button nor Mr. Button's attorney had any recollection of Mrs. Button's being advised of the rights she was surrendering by signing the agreement.

Mrs. Button testified that soon after their marriage, Mr. Button instructed her to stop working outside the home because her contribution to the marriage would be greater if she devoted all her time to being a homemaker. Mrs. Button had been employed as a produce worker at a supermarket. Mr. Button denied that he made this demand. Mrs. Button did cease to work outside the home within 6 months after the marriage. She testified that she worked hard in the house. After the marriage, Mr. Button continued working outside the home as an upholsterer.

In 1970 Mrs. Button received $12,000 from the life insurance policy on the death of her first husband. These funds were held in her own name until 1974, when she placed the funds in a joint account with her daughter. In 1982, apparently after the parties separated, Mrs. Button transferred $12,000 to her daughter. Mrs. Button's daughter testified that she used these funds for Mrs. Button.

In June 1974, after Mr. Button sold his upholstery business to his son for $85,000, the parties signed a postnuptial agreement which expressly rescinded and terminated the 1969 prenuptial agreement. Mr. Button's assets had appreciated in value during the marriage to approximately $110,000. Mrs. Button's assets were essentially the same as before marriage, except that sometime during the marriage Mr. Button gave her a joint interest in shares of stock having a value of $3,000. During the marriage Mr. Button paid for the household expenses and vacation trips from his income and property.

The 1974 agreement--which is the agreement to be tested under sec. 767.255 (11)--was drafted by Mr. Button's attorney. Mrs. Button did not have independent counsel. She testified that the agreement was never explained to her and that no financial disclosures were made. Mrs. Button also testified, however, that she was generally aware of Mr. Button's property, that they filed joint tax returns and that she had access to copies of the returns. She also testified that she was unfamiliar with tax returns, having never prepared one herself. Furthermore, Mr. Button acknowledged that the full extent of his financial holdings could not be discerned from his tax returns.

The 1974 postnuptial agreement provided that in the event of a divorce all property owned by either party prior to marriage would remain the separate property of that party and that all property acquired after the marriage would be deemed the separate property of the party acquiring the property. In the event of divorce, Mrs. Button was to accept as full property settlement her own articles of personal property, her own separate property and one-half of all properties acquired jointly by the parties.

At the time of divorce Mrs. Button was in ill health, confined to a skilled care nursing home receiving public assistance. In addition to receiving $255,103 in property, Mr. Button was working parttime after the divorce.

We now turn to the question of what is an inequitable agreement for purposes of sec. 767.255 (11). The statute does not define inequitable. We must interpret inequitableness in light of the language and purpose of sec. 767.255 (11).

Sec. 767.255 (11) permits marital partners to reach their own agreements about financial arrangements. Sec. 767.255 (11) states that the court is to presume the agreement dividing property is equitable. We read this provision, which puts the burden of production of evidence and the burden of persuasion on the spouse challenging the agreement, as demonstrating the legislature's interest in giving effect to the parties' agreement to the extent possible.

The legislature has recognized that prenuptial and postnuptial agreements dividing property serve a useful function. They allow parties to structure their financial affairs to suit their needs and values and to achieve certainty. This certainty may encourage marriage and may be conducive to marital tranquility by protecting the financial expectations of the parties. The right to enter into an agreement regulating financial affairs in a marriage is important to a large number of citizens.

Sec. 767.255 (11), however, sets forth a competing public policy. While sec. 767.255 (11) embodies the public policy of freedom of contract, it also empowers a divorce court to override the parties' agreement if the agreement is inequitable. This latter policy reflects the unique role of the marriage contract in society. Marriage is not simply a contract between two parties. Marriage is a legal status in which the state has a special interest. Certain rights and obligations dictated by the state flow from marriage, and the legislature requires a divorce court to scrutinize an agreement between the spouses carefully. The parties are free to contract, but they contract in the shadow of the court's obligation to review the agreement on divorce to protect the spouses' financial interests on divorce.

After studying the language and purpose of sec. 767.255 (11), we conclude that an agreement is inequitable under 767.255(11) if it is unfair either in its procurement or in its substantive provisions.

Fairness in procurement depends on two factors: whether each spouse makes fair and reasonable disclosure to the other spouse of his or her financial status, and whether each spouse enters into the agreement voluntarily and freely. Obviously these two factors are determined as of the date of the execution of the contract. If the parties fail to satisfy either of these factors, the agreement is inequitable under sec. 767.255(11).

An agreement is inequitable if either spouse has not made fair and reasonable disclosure to the other of his or her assets, liabilities and debts. A party might not have entered into the agreement had she or he known the facts. Where it can be shown that a spouse had independent knowledge of the opposing spouse's financial status, this independent knowledge serves as a substitute for disclosure. This case does not raise the question of whether a spouse may waive disclosure and we do not decide that issue.

The public interest requires that a financial agreement between spouses or prospective spouses be executed under conditions of candor and fairness. Married persons and persons about to marry stand in a confidential relationship and must deal fairly with each other. Fair and reasonable disclosure of financial status is a significant aspect of the duty of fair dealing.

An agreement is also inequitable if it is not entered into voluntarily and freely. In determining whether the agreement was entered into voluntarily and freely, the relevant inquiry is whether each spouse had a meaningful choice. Some factors a circuit court should consider are whether each party was represented by independent counsel, whether each party had adequate time to review the agreement, whether the parties understood the terms of the agreement and their effect, and whether the parties understood their financial rights in the absence of an agreement. If the agreement was not entered into voluntarily and freely, the agreement is inequitable under sec. 767.255 (11).

The first two requirements are issues of "procedural fairness." The third requirement is an issue of "substantive fairness." Substantive fairness is an amorphous concept. We can set forth general principles, but the courts must determine substantive fairness on a case by case basis. In determining substantive fairness a court must be mindful of the two principal legislative concerns reflected in sec. 767.255 (11)--the protection of the parties' freedom to contract and the protection of the parties' financial interests at divorce. Sec. 767.255 (11) allows parties freedom to contract but does not allow them to ignore the state's interest in protecting the financial interests of the parties at divorce.

An agreement need not approximate a division a circuit court might make under sec. 767.255 to meet the requirement of substantive fairness. If the parties are permitted to do only that which a circuit court would do under sec. 767.255, the parties would not have a meaningful right to contract or to divide their property as they wish. A party should be able to enter into an agreement, for example, which preserves property acquired before marriage for persons other than the spouse. To meet the requirement of substantive fairness an agreement need not divide the property in conformity with how a divorce court would divide the property, but it should in some manner appropriate to the circumstances of the parties take into account that each spouse contributes to the prosperity of the marriage by his or her efforts.

In framing the agreement the parties should consider the circumstances existing at the execution of the agreement and those reasonably foreseeable. The parties should consider that the duration of the marriage is unknown and that they wish the agreement to govern their financial arrangements whether the marriage lasts a short time or for many years. The parties should consider such factors as the objectives of the parties in executing an agreement, the economic circumstances of the parties, the property brought to the marriage by each party, each spouse's family relationships and obligations to persons other than to the spouse, the earning capacity of each person, the anticipated contribution by one party to the education, training or increased earning power of the other, the future needs of the respective spouses, the age and physical and emotional health of the parties, and the expected contribution of each party to the marriage, giving appropriate economic value to each party's contribution in homemaking and child care services.

In assessing the fairness of the substantive terms of the agreement, a circuit court considers these factors and evaluates the terms of the agreement from the perspective of the parties at the execution of the agreement. We conclude that the court should look at the substantive fairness of the agreement as of the time it was made if the court is to give effect to the parties' freedom to contract. At execution the parties know their property and other relevant circumstances and are able to make reasonable predictions about the future; they should then be able to draft a fair agreement considering these factors.

Clearly an agreement fair at execution is not unfair at divorce just because the application of the agreement at divorce results in a property division which is not equal between the parties or which a court might not order under sec. 767.255. If, however, there are significantly changed circumstances after the execution of an agreement and the agreement as applied at divorce no longer comports with the reasonable expectations of the parties, an agreement which is fair at execution may be unfair to the parties at divorce.

Using this approach to assess substantive fairness, a circuit court would look at the fairness of the substantive terms of the agreement as of the execution of the agreement and, if there have been significantly changed circumstances after the execution of the agreement, at divorce. This approach protects the parties' freedom to contract and the parties' financial interests at divorce.

To summarize, an agreement is inequitable under sec. 767.255 (11) if it fails to satisfy any one of the three requirements: each spouse has made fair and reasonable disclosure to the other about his or her financial status; each spouse enters into the agreement voluntarily and freely; the substantive terms of the agreement dividing the property upon divorce are fair to each spouse.

The circuit court's determination of inequitableness under sec. 767.255 (11), as does the circuit court's determination of a property division under 767.255, requires the circuit court to exercise its discretion. A discretionary determination must be made on the basis of the facts and the applicable law. A discretionary determination must be the product of a rational mental process by which the facts of record and the law relied upon are stated and considered together for the purpose of achieving a reasoned and reasonable determination. The decision will be upheld by an appellate court if the circuit court considered the relevant law and facts and set forth a process of logical reasoning.

Because the circuit court has not considered this agreement in this case under the three-part test we have set forth, we remand the cause to the circuit court to exercise its discretion under the test set forth herein.

Accordingly, we reverse the judgment dividing the property on the basis of the agreement and remand the cause for further proceedings not inconsistent with this decision. In reaching its decision the circuit court should consider the entire record in this matter and may reopen the proceedings for further testimony or briefing if it so elects.

The judgment is reversed and the cause is remanded to the circuit court.

c. Notes and Questions

1) Statutes

In 1935, only 18 states had any kind of statutes addressing antenuptial contracts (apart from the Statute of Uses and Statute of Frauds). Today, most states have adopted some statute regulating antenuptial contracts. In fact, the Commissioners of Uniform State Laws are so enthusiastic about them that they have adopted *two* model or uniform laws regarding premarital agreements. The Uniform Premarital Agreement Act (UPAA), 9C ULA 35 (2001), was adopted by the Commissioners in 1983. The Uniform Marital Property Act, 9A ULA 103 (2001), is a statutory community property act (which only one state, Wisconsin, has adopted) was proposed the same year and contains essentially the same core provisions regarding marital property agreements. The UPAA has been adopted by more than half of the states (27 states as of 2005). One of the most comprehensive and controversial discussions of the UPAA is *In re Marriage of Bonds v. Bonds*, 24 Cal. 4th 1, 5 P.3d 815, 99 Cal. Rptr. 2d 252 (2000) (enforcing agreement with highly paid baseball player signed by unrepresented, young Swedish-born woman with no higher education who spoke English as a second language).

2) Time of Evaluation

One of the leading points of disagreement is whether conscionability of a premarital agreement should be adjudged as of the time of agreement only, the time of enforcement only, or both. One of the leading decisions to address this point is *Gross v. Gross*, 11 Ohio St.3d 99, 464 N.E.2d 500 (1984), where the Ohio Supreme Court opted in favor of dual-time examination. *But see Pendleton v. Fireman,* 24 Cal.4th 39, 5 P.3d 839, 99 Cal.Rptr.2d 278 (2000); Goldberg, *infra.* What position does the UPAA take on this issue?

3) UPAA Trigger Points

Despite the unusually clear and concise Uniform Premarital Agreement Act, and the aspiration expressed in the ninth section of it, there is little uniformity among the states regarding when premarital agreements will or will not be enforced. The cases are usually very fact-specific and reflect the courts' desire to do equity in each given case. There appear to be several common issues as to which there are a variety of different state positions. A number of particular factors seem to be trigger points for philosophical disagreement among the courts regarding enforcement of premarital agreements. Can you identify or suggest some of these points of doctrinal divergence (in addition to the timing issue noted in the previous note)? The use of unconscionability as a standard for enforcement of agreements (as in *Button*) has been criticized as benefiting "[o]nly those who are not prepared to accept responsibility for a poor decision . . . ." Marrow, *infra*, at 223. Do you agree? Why/why not?

Under the UPAA: a) Are verbal antenuptial agreements enforceable? b) May the parties contract for the elimination of alimony in the event of divorce? c) May the parties contract regarding the religion in which the children of the marriage will be raised? d) May the parties contract to eliminate child care expense obligations? e) If the parties sign an antenuptial agreement and then live together for eight years without ever getting married, is the agreement enforceable upon separation? f) Is an agreement enforceable if there was not reasonable disclosure but there was adequate knowledge of the financial condition of the party seeking enforcement? g) Is an agreement waiving alimony enforceable if the party against whom enforcement is sought would be left on public welfare? h) Is an agreement generally enforceable if the marriage is annulled?

4) The ALI Proposal

In May 2000, the American Law Institute approved a proposed set of standards for antenuptial contracts that is very paternalistic and deviates substantially from existing law. Principles of the Law of Family Dissolution, Chapter 7, Agreements (2002). For example, it provides that an antenuptial agreement is not presumed to be proper unless executed "at least 30 days before the parties' marriage" and it is "unenforceable if either party rescinds it . . . within 30 days of its execution . . . ." *Id.* at § 7.05. Additionally, a court has power to refuse to enforce a valid agreement if the court believes that "it would work a substantial injustice" including, *inter alia*, if a child was born to or adopted by the parties after the agreement was signed, or a certain number of years has passed since the signing; again, the party relying on the agreement has the burden of proof. *Id.* at § 7.07. Enforcement of "covenant marriage" agreements and other marriage-reinforcement commitments is barred. *Id.* § 7.12. Agreements to limit modification of alimony are not enforceable if the court opines that they would cause "a substantial injustice." *Id.* at § 7.18. *See* Wardle, *Deconstructing Family, infra.* Would this be a drastic change from the UPAA? From your homestate law? Is it an improvement? Why/why not?

3. Practical and Ethical Considerations

Drafting and reviewing antenuptial agreements is one area in which lawyers do get involved not infrequently in advising individuals and couples before marriage. May a lawyer represent both parties in drafting an antenuptial agreement? If she does not represent them both, may she advise generally both and later represent one or the other? What if you represent one of the parties but the other party is unrepresented? What are a lawyer's professional responsibilities to his client if he believes that the agreement is not in her best interests but she intends to sign it anyway?

4. Bibliography

Brian Bix, *Bargaining in the Shadow of Love: The Enforcement of Premarital Agreements and How We Think About Marriage*, 40 Wm. & Mary L. Rev. 145 (1998).

Contemporary Family Law, vol. 1, Ch.. 5 (Lynn D. Wardle, Christopher L. Blakesley & Jacqueline Y. Parker, 1988).

Charlotte K. Goldberg, *"If It Ain't Broke, Don't Fix It": Premarital Agreements and Spousal Support Waivers in California*, 33 Loy. L.A. L. Rev. 1245 (2000).

Paul Bennett Marrow, *Squeezing Subjectivity from the Doctrine of Unconscionability*, 53 Cleve. St. L. Rev. 187 (2005-06).

Lynn D. Wardle, *Deconstructing Family: A Critique of the American Law Institute's "Domestic Partners" Proposal,* 2001 B.Y.U. L. Rev. 1189.

B. FAILURE OF MARRIAGE EXPECTATIONS

1. Background

a. History of Heart Balm Actions

An agreement to marry is a contract and its breach historically was the basis for a contract claim. In common law England, where marriage had significant economic ramifications, and marriages for political, economic, and social-advancement purposes were not uncommon, ecclesiastical courts had jurisdiction to enforce promises to marry. "Unwilling parties were subject to admonition and censure and, at a time when one's standing in the church was all important, the threat was sufficient to bring about the proposed marriage." R. Brockelbank, *The Nature of the Promise to Marry -- A Study in Comparative Law*, 41 Ill. L. Rev. 1, 3 (1946).

After Lord Hardwicke's Act abolished ecclesiastical jurisdiction over such suits, actions were brought in the common law courts for damages from breach of contract to marry. Such actions for damages to repair a broken heart (called "heart balm" actions) were not uncommon during the nineteenth and early part of the twentieth century. But they were generally deemed disreputable claims, sometimes involving little more than a species of extortion or seduction-and-blackmail, and sometimes large sums were paid in settlement of such claims to avoid damage to the defendant's reputation. During the progressive reform era of the twentieth century, especially beginning in the 1930s, many states abolished "heart balm" actions, including actions for breach of promise to marry. "Reformers, who argued that trying to measure lost love with money was ridiculous, impossible, and wrongful, successfully persuaded many state legislatures and high courts to abandon the earlier law of broken engagements." Rebecca Tushnet, Note, *Rules of Engagement*, 107 Yale L.J. 2583, 2585 (1998). The historical justification for the breach of promise to marry claim was economic; later, "jurists who rewrote the justification for breach of promise [from economic harm to emotional harm] thought that they were saving it, because a focus on the economic benefits of marriage seemed unenlightened and outdated. But the switch to an emotional justification eventually doomed the action, as courts and legislatures became uncomfortable with awarding money for emotional harms." *Id.* at 2586.

Nearly half of the states have now legislatively abolished actions for breach of promise to marry. Before 1990, no state had abolished such actions by judicial decree. But such claims are unpopular with judges, and courts now are generally very strict in interpreting heart balm claims, and statutes abolishing such claims have been liberally construed in some cases to abolish not only the traditional heart balm claims (breach of promise to marry, alienation of affections, criminal conversation), but even to eliminate claims similar to them or arising out of the same factual elements. Six states have adopted very short statutes of limitation for heart balm claims. Ten states make it illegal to even threaten a suit for breach of promise to marry.

b. History of Recovery of Gifts

Often gifts are given in contemplation of marriage to one or both parties to be married. When an agreement to marry is rescinded, and if the gift is especially valuable, questions may arise regarding whether the gift must be returned. Historically the rule has been that if the donor intended the gift to be *unconditional*, it need not be returned. If the donor intended the gift to be *conditional* (conditioned upon the marriage of the parties), the gift generally must be returned. However, if the *donor* was the party who broke the engagement, the gift need not be returned, even if the gift was conditional, unless the termination of agreement to marry was *justified*.

The nature of the gift, the circumstances of transfer, and the cause of the breach of promise to marry are all factors under the historical test. Some courts assume that gifts given at the time of or after engagement are conditional upon the marriage or the willingness to marry. An engagement ring, for example, symbolizes the parties' agreement to marry, and is the classic example of a conditional-upon-marriage gift. On the other hand, a gift given to the fiancé on her or his birthday would not likely be presumed to be conditioned upon marriage. Gifts of family heirlooms are generally deemed to be conditional (it is assumed that the donor intended them to stay within the family).

If the donee broke the engagement, or if both parties mutually agreed to end the engagement, the donor could recover his or her conditional gifts. However, if the donor unjustifiably and unilaterally broke the engagement, he or she could not recover even conditional gifts. Thus, a determination of whether there was "fault," and, if so, who was "at fault," were legally significant. That was not always easy for the courts to determine. With the abolition of "fault" in divorce, this is not a popular kind of action today. Several courts have moved from a "fault-based" rule of recovery to a no-fault rule. As the New York Court of Appeals put it in *Gaden v. Gaden*, 272 N.E.1d 471, 476 (N.Y. 1971):

> The purpose of the initial heart balm legislation was to rid the courts of these actions where the "wounded" party appears in court to unfold his or her sorrows before a sympathetic jury. To require a determination of fault in order to recover engagement gifts would simply condone this same type of actions in yet another form. The result would be to encourage every disappointed donee to resist the return of engagement gifts by blaming the donor for the breakup of the contemplated marriage, thereby promoting dramatic courtroom accusations and counter- accusations of fault.

2. Statutes, Cases and Doctrines

a. *Lindh v. Surman*

Rodger Lindh v. Janis Surman
742 A.2d 643 (Pa. 1999)

Before FLAHERTY, C.J., and ZAPPALA, CAPPY, CASTILLE, NIGRO, NEWMAN and SAYLOR, JJ.
NEWMAN, Justice.

In this appeal, we are asked to decide whether a donee of an engagement ring must return the ring or its equivalent value when the donor breaks the engagement.

The facts of this case depict a tumultuous engagement between Rodger Lindh (Rodger), a divorced, middle-aged man, and Janis Surman (Janis), the object of Rodger's inconstant affections. In August of 1993, Rodger proposed marriage to Janis. To that purpose, he presented her with a diamond engagement ring that he purchased for $17,400. Rodger testified that the price was less than the ring's market value because he was a "good customer" of the jeweler's, having previously purchased a $4,000 ring for his ex-wife and other expensive jewelry for his children. Janis, who had never been married, accepted his marriage proposal and the ring. Discord developed in the relationship between Rodger and Janis, and in October of 1993 Rodger broke the engagement and asked for the return of the ring. At that time, Janis obliged and gave Rodger the ring. Rodger and Janis attempted to reconcile. They succeeded, and Rodger again proposed marriage, and offered the ring, to Janis. For a second time, Janis accepted. In March of 1994, however, Rodger called off the engagement. He asked for the return of the ring, which Janis refused, and this litigation ensued.

Rodger filed a two-count complaint against Janis, seeking recovery of the ring or a judgment for its equivalent value. The case proceeded to arbitration, where a panel of arbitrators awarded judgment for Janis. Rodger appealed to the Court of Common Pleas of Allegheny County, where a brief non-jury trial resulted in a judgment in favor of Rodger in the amount of $21,200. Janis appealed to the Superior Court, which affirmed the trial court in a 2-1 panel decision. Judge Ford Elliott, writing for the majority, held that no-fault principles should control, and that the ring must be returned regardless of who broke the engagement, and irrespective of the reasons. In a Dissenting Opinion, Judge Schiller criticized the Majority Opinion for creating what he termed a "romantic bailment" because of its refusal to examine the actions of the donor in breaking the engagement, thereby creating a *per se* rule requiring the return of an engagement ring in all circumstances. We granted allocatur to answer this novel question of Pennsylvania law.

We begin our analysis with the only principle on which all parties agree: that Pennsylvania law treats the giving of an engagement ring as a conditional gift. *See Pavlicic v. Vogtsberger*, 390 Pa. 502, 136 A.2d 127 (1957). In *Pavlicic*, the plaintiff supplied his ostensible fiancee with numerous gifts, including money for the purchase of engagement and wedding rings, with the understanding that they were given on the condition that she marry him. When the defendant left him for another man, the plaintiff sued her for recovery of these gifts. Justice Musmanno explained the conditional gift principle:

> A gift given by a man to a woman on condition that she embark on the sea of matrimony with him is no different from a gift based on the condition that the donee sail on any other sea. If, after receiving the provisional gift, the donee refuses to leave the harbor,--if the anchor of contractual performance sticks in the sands of irresolution and procrastination--the gift must be restored to the donor.

Id. at 507, 136 A.2d at 130.

Where the parties disagree, however, is: (1) what is the condition of the gift (i.e., acceptance of the engagement or the marriage itself), and (2) whether fault is relevant to determining return of the ring. Janis argues that the condition of the gift is acceptance of the marriage proposal, not the performance of the marriage ceremony. She also contends that Pennsylvania law, which treats engagement gifts as implied-in-law conditional gifts, has never recognized a right of recovery in a donor who severs the engagement. In her view, we should not recognize such a right where the donor breaks off the engagement, because, if the condition of the gift is performance of the marriage ceremony, that would reward a donor who prevents the occurrence of the condition, which the donee was ready, willing, and eagerly waiting to perform.

Janis first argues that the condition of the gift is acceptance of the proposal of marriage, such that acceptance of the proposal vests absolute title in the donee. This theory is contrary to Pennsylvania's view of the engagement ring situation. In *Ruehling v. Hornung*, 98 Pa.Super. 535 (1930), the Superior Court provided what is still the most thorough Pennsylvania appellate court analysis of the problem:

> It does not appear whether the engagement was broken by plaintiff or whether it was dissolved by mutual consent. It follows that in order to permit a recovery by plaintiff, it would be necessary to hold that the gifts were subject to the implied condition that they would be returned by the donee to the donor whenever the engagement was dissolved. Under such a rule *the marriage would be a necessary prerequisite* to the passing of an absolute title to a Christmas gift made in such circumstances. We are unwilling to go that far, *except as to the engagement ring*.

Id. at 540 (emphasis added). This Court later affirmed that "[t]he promise to return an antenuptial gift made in contemplation of marriage *if the marriage does not take place* is a fictitious promise implied in law." *Semenza v. Alfano*, 443 Pa. 201, 204, 279 A.2d 29, 31 (1971) (emphasis added). Our caselaw clearly recognizes the giving of an engagement gift as having an implied condition that the marriage must occur in order to vest title in the donee; mere acceptance of the marriage proposal is not the implied condition for the gift.

Janis' argument that Pennsylvania law does not permit the donor to recover the ring where the donor terminates the engagement has some basis in the few Pennsylvania authorities that have addressed the matter. The following language from *Ruehling* implies that Janis' position is correct:
We think that it [the engagement ring] is always given subject to the implied condition that if the marriage does not take place either because of the death, or a disability recognized by the law on the part of, either party, or by breach of the contract by the donee, or its dissolution by mutual consent, the gift shall be returned.

Ruehling, 98 Pa.Super. at 540. Noticeably absent from the recital by the court of the situations where the ring must be returned is when the donor breaks the engagement. Other Pennsylvania authorities also suggest that the donor cannot recover the ring when the donor breaks the engagement. *See* 7 Summary of Pennsylvania Jurisprudence 2d § 15:29, p. 111 ("upon breach of the marriage engagement by the donee, the property may be recovered by the donor"); 17 Pennsylvania Law Encyclopedia, "Gifts," § 9, p. 118 (citing to a 1953 common pleas court decision, "[i]f, on the other hand, the donor wrongfully terminates the engagement, he is not entitled to return of the ring").

This Court, however, has not decided the question of whether the donor is entitled to return of the ring where the donor admittedly ended the engagement. In the context of our conditional gift approach to engagement rings, the issue we must resolve is whether we will follow the fault-based theory, argued by Janis, or the no-fault rule advocated by Rodger. Under a fault-based analysis, return of the ring depends on an assessment of who broke the engagement, which necessarily entails a determination of why that person broke the engagement. A no-fault approach, however, involves no investigation into the motives or reasons for the cessation of the engagement and requires the return of the engagement ring simply upon the nonoccurrence of the marriage.

The rule concerning the return of a ring founded on fault principles has superficial appeal because, in the most outrageous instances of unfair behavior, it appeals to our sense of equity. Where one fiancee has truly "wronged" the other, depending on whether that person was the donor of the ring or the donee, justice appears to dictate that the wronged individual should be allowed to keep, or have the ring returned. However, the process of determining who is "wrong" and who is "right," when most modern relationships are complex circumstances, makes the fault-based approach less desirable. A thorough fault-based inquiry would not only end with the question of who terminated the engagement, but would also examine that person's reasons. In some instances the person who terminated the engagement may have been entirely justified in his or her actions. This kind of inquiry would invite the parties to stage the most bitter and unpleasant accusations against those whom they nearly made their spouse, and a court would have no clear guidance with regard to how to ascertain who was "at fault." The Supreme Court of Kansas recited the difficulties with the fault-based system:

What is fault or the unjustifiable calling off of an engagement? By way of illustration, should courts be asked to determine which of the following grounds for breaking an engagement is fault or justified? (1) The parties have nothing in common; (2) one party cannot stand prospective in-laws; (3) a minor child of one of the parties is hostile to and will not accept the other party; (4) an adult child of one of the parties will not accept the other party; (5) the parties' pets do not get along; (6) a party was too hasty in proposing or accepting the proposal; (7) the engagement was a rebound situation which is now regretted; (8) one party has untidy habits that irritate the other; or (9) the parties have religious differences. The list could be endless.

Heiman v. Parrish, 262 Kan. 926, 942 P.2d 631, 637 (1997).
A ring-return rule based on fault principles will inevitably invite acrimony and encourage parties to

portray their ex-fiancees in the worst possible light, hoping to drag out the most favorable arguments to justify, or to attack, the termination of an engagement. Furthermore, it is unlikely that trial courts would be presented with situations where fault was clear and easily ascertained and, as noted earlier, determining what constitutes fault would result in a rule that would defy universal application.

The approach that has been described as the modern trend is to apply a no- fault rule to engagement ring cases. *See Vigil v. Haber*, 888 P.2d at 455 (N.M.1994). Courts that have applied no-fault principles to engagement ring cases have borrowed from the policies of their respective legislatures that have moved away from the notion of fault in their divorce statutes. *See, e.g., Vigil, supra* (relying on the New Mexico legislature's enactment of the first no-fault divorce statute); *Aronow v. Silver*, 223 N.J.Super. 344, 538 A.2d 851 (1987) (noting New Jersey's approval of no-fault divorce). As described by the court in *Vigil*, this trend represents a move "towards a policy that removes fault-finding from the personal-relationship dynamics of marriage and divorce." *Vigil*, 888 P.2d at 457. Indeed, by 1986, with the passage by the South Dakota legislature of no-fault divorce provisions, all fifty states had adopted some form of no-fault divorce. Doris Jonas Freed & Timothy B. Walker, *Family Law in the Fifty States: An Overview*, 19 Fam. L. Q. 331, 335 (1986). Pennsylvania, no exception to this trend, recognizes no-fault divorces. *See* 23 Pa.C.S. § 3301 (c), (d). We agree with those jurisdictions that have looked towards the development of no-fault divorce law for a principle to decide engagement ring cases, and the inherent weaknesses in any fault-based system lead us to adopt a no-fault approach to resolution of engagement ring disputes.

Having adopted this no-fault principle, we still must address the original argument that the donor should not get return of the ring when the donor terminates the engagement. Such a rule would be consonant with a no- fault approach, it is argued, because it need not look at the reasons for termination of the engagement; if there is proof that the donor ended the relationship, then he has frustrated the occurrence of the condition and cannot benefit from that. In other words, we are asked to adopt a no- fault approach that would always deny the donor return of the ring where the donor breaks the engagement.

We decline to adopt this modified no-fault position, and hold that the donor is entitled to return of the ring even if the donor broke the engagement. We believe that the benefits from the certainty of our rule outweigh its negatives, and that a strict no-fault approach is less flawed than a fault-based theory or modified no-fault position.

We affirm the Order of the Superior Court.

CAPPY, Justice, dissenting.

***

An engagement ring is a traditional token of the pledge to marry. It is a symbol of nuptial intent dating back to AD 860. The engagement ring was to be of a valued metal representing a financial sacrifice for the husband to be. Two other customs regarding the engagement ring were established in that same century: forfeiture of the ring by a man who reneged on a marriage pledge; surrender of the ring by the woman who broke off an engagement. *See* Charles Panati, *Extraordinary Origins of Everyday Things (copyright 1987)*. This concept is consistent with conditional gift law, which has always been followed in Pennsylvania. *Stanger v. Epler*, 382 Pa. 411, 115 A.2d 197 (1955); *Ruehling v. Hornung*, 98 Pa.Super. 535 (1930); C.J.S. Gifts § 61. When the marriage does not take place the agreement is void and the party who prevented the marriage agreement from being fulfilled must forfeit the engagement ring. *Pavlicic v. Vogtsberger*, *.

The majority urges adoption of its position to relieve trial courts from having the onerous task of sifting through the debris of the broken engagement in order to ascertain who is truly at fault and if there lies a valid justification excusing fault. *** Are broken engagements truly more disturbing than cases where we ask judges and juries to discern possible abuses in nursing homes, day care centers, dependency proceedings involving abused children, and criminal cases involving horrific, irrational injuries to innocent victims? The subject matter our able trial courts address on a daily basis is certainly of equal sordidness as any fact pattern they may need to address in a simple case of who broke the engagement and why.

I can envision a scenario whereby the prospective bride and her family have expended thousands of dollars in preparation for the culminating event of matrimony and she is, through no fault of her own, left standing at the altar holding the caterer's bill. To add insult to injury, the majority would also strip her of her engagement ring. ***

Accordingly, as I see no valid reason to forgo the established precedent in Pennsylvania for determining possession of the engagement ring under the simple concept of conditional gift law, I cannot endorse the modern trend advocated by the majority. Respectfully, I dissent.

CASTILLE, Justice, dissenting.

I dissent from the majority's opinion because I do not believe that a no-fault policy should be applied to broken engagements and the issue of which party retains the engagement ring. The Restatement of Restitution, § 58 comment c, discusses the return of engagement rings and states that:

> Gifts made in the hope that a marriage or contract of marriage will result are not recoverable, in the absence of fraud. Gifts made in anticipation of marriage are not ordinarily expressed to be conditional and, although there is an engagement to marry, if the marriage fails to occur without the fault of the donee, normally the gift cannot be recovered. If, however, the donee obtained the gift fraudulently or if the gift was made for a purpose which could be obtained only by the marriage, a donor who is not himself at fault is entitled to restitution if the marriage does not take place, even if the gift was money. If there is an engagement to marry and the donee, having received the gift without fraud, later wrongfully breaks the promise of marriage, the donor is entitled to restitution if the gift is an engagement ring, a family heirloom or other similar thing intimately connected with the marriage, but not if the gift is one of money intended to be used by the donee before the marriage.

I believe that the Restatement approach is superior to the no-fault policy espoused by the majority because it allows equity its proper place in the outcome. Here, it is undisputed that appellee twice broke his engagement with appellant. Clearly, appellant was not at fault in the breaking off of the couple's engagement, and there is no allegation that she fraudulently induced appellee to propose marriage to her twice. Fairness dictates that appellant, who is the innocent party in this couple's ill-fated romantic connection, retain the engagement ring, which was given to her by appellee as an unconditional gift. I would therefore reverse the order of the Superior Court.

Justices CAPPY and SAYLOR join this dissenting opinion.

b. Notes and Questions

1) How Far to Extend Anti-Heart Balm Statutes

In *Miller v. Ratner*, 688 A.2d 976 (Md.App. 1997) the Maryland Court of Special Appeals distinguished between breach of promise to marry, and the tort of deceit arising out of false representation that one is free to marry when, in fact, one is already married. In *Miller*, the plaintiff asserted claims of breach of contract, tortious interference with prospective advantage, intentional infliction of emotional distress, and civil conspiracy to inflict severe emotional distress, but the court construed all of the plaintiff's claims to be of or arising out of the breach-of-promise-to-marry claim, which the Maryland legislature had abolished. The court noted: "In the case sub judice, there was neither evidence, nor averments, that there was any legal impediment to a marriage between Lonnie Miller and Warren Ratner. Nor was there any allegation that when the initial promises in respect to marriage were made, they were not sincere. The case at bar is a pure "change of mind" case. It is exactly that type of case that heart balm statutes are intended to prohibit." 688 A.2d at 991.

2) Why the Hostility to Heart Balm Actions

Are the objections to heart balm actions unique to heart balm actions? Don't most tort actions and many contract actions involve similar concerns about who is "at fault" for a disagreement or a breach? Don't parties come to court to air their grievances, to make accusations and cross-accusations, and to put blame on their opposing parties in *most* civil cases? So why single out marriage-related causes of action for restriction or abolition? Couldn't the same things be said of "palimony" suits among nonmarital cohabitants? Of custody litigation? Of claims for interference with visitation? Of child support enforcement claims? Of suits to invalidate antenuptial contracts? Of claims of dissipation of assets in property division disputes? Does hostility to heart balm actions suggest a hostility to protecting marital relations? Do anti-heart balm actions simply reflect the devaluation of marriage and distaste for using law to protect, defend and vindicate marriage relations? Why/ why not?

3) *Lindh* and engagement rings

Did the court correctly apply the "conditional gift" doctrine? What is the "condition" upon which the gift of an engagement ring is given? Is it a one-way condition (that donee be willing to marry) or a two-way condition (that each party be willing to marry) or a no-way condition (if either party backs out both will be restored to the status quo ante). By accepting and wearing the ring has the donee lost anything for which some remuneration (like the ring) should be given (or kept) as compensation? Is the majority's concern about difficulties for the courts uniquely applicable in engagement ring cases? Is this evidence of a flood of civil cases?

In *Albinger v. Harris*, 310 P.3d 27 (Mont. 2002), a case involving a domestic violence aggressor seeking to recover an engagement ring, the Montana Supreme Court held that an engagement ring was an irrevocable inter vivos gift, relying in part on the abolition of heartbalm actions, and noting:

> Only in engagement ring cases does precedent from other jurisdictions weigh heavily for conditional gift theory in the absence of an expressed condition. * Considering it "unduly harsh and unnecessary" to require a hopeful suitor to express any condition upon which a ring might be premised, many courts stepped in to impute the condition of marriage. * In practice, courts presume the existence of the implied condition of marriage attaching to an engagement ring in the absence of an expressed intent to the contrary. * A party meets the burden of establishing the conditional nature of the gift by proving by a preponderance of the evidence that the ring was given in contemplation of marriage.* "Not only does this rule of law establish a 'bright line' for situations where the parties involved are unlikely to have considered the necessity of making an 'agreement to the contrary,' but the rule also eliminates the need for a trial court to attempt the often impossible task of determining which, if either, party is at fault." *McIntire v. Raukhorst* (1989), 65 Ohio App.3d 728, 585 N.E.2d 456, 458.

Id. at 34-35.

4) Etiquette

Dear Abby's advice: "Easy rule: the ring belongs to the person who paid for it, until the marriage has taken place." See Dear Abby, Prince Georges Maryland Journal, April 16, 1996, at B4. This is simple. Is it fair? Why/why not?

3. Practical and Ethical Considerations

If the prospective bridegroom had consulted you in this case, what would you have advised him? Can you see the importance of being familiar with the particular law of a local jurisdiction (state) when it comes to advising clients about questions such as those concerning the return of gifts upon breakup of an engagement? Since marriage really is a contract, why don't more couples consult lawyers about marriages they are considering?

4. Bibliography

Contemporary Family Law, vol. 1, Chs. 4 & 7 (Lynn D. Wardle, Christopher L. Blakesley & JacquelPard&f, 1988).

Rebecca Tushnet, Note. *Rules of Engagement*, 107 Yale L. J. 2583 (1998).

CHAPTER 8

Quasi-Marriage; Choice of Law; International and Comparative

A. QUASI-MARRIAGE

1. Background

Not all marriage-like relationships are marriages. For a variety of reasons, some people intentionally live together in sexual relationships but do not want the legal status of marriage. Other couples want to have the legal status of marriage but are legally unable to do so because they are related within prohibited degrees, are of the same sex, are unable (or unwilling) to get divorced from a previous spouse, or for other reasons. Other couples celebrate marriage and believe they are married but discover (often after the death of one of the parties) that their marriage was not valid so they cannot claim the status and benefits of a surviving spouse.

Marriage validity and marriage benefit claims usually arise in a context in which one party urges the court to give priority to achieving an equitable economic result rather than to give strict application to the law. Family law generally has more than its fair share of cases to which the old maxim "hard cases make bad law" applies. Courts have created equitable doctrines to give judges the leeway to reach results they consider fair where strict application of the law might not allow such results. The most notable examples of such equitable doctrines are the *putative spouse* and *estoppel* doctrines, described in Chapter 6. Other doctrines are described below.

2. Statutes, Cases and Doctrines

a. *Bacot*

Succession of Samuel Wilds Bacot, Jr.
502 So. 2d 1118 (La. Ct. App., 4th Cir. 1987)

Before GULOTTA, CIACCIO and LOBRANO, JJ.

LOBRANO, JUDGE

This appeal involves the validity, vel non, of a document purported to be the last will and testament of the deceased, Samuel Wilds Bacot, Jr. (Bacot). Collateral to the issue of the validity of the document in question is the issue of whether a man can be the concubine of another man.

Bacot, an admitted homosexual, never married and had no natural children. Throughout his lifetime, Bacot was also known as Samuel W. Bacot, Wilds Bacot and Pat Bacot.

On January 5, 1982, Bacot executed an authentic act wherein he adopted Elmo Orgeron, Jr. (Orgeron), an adult male, as his son and heir. On that same day, Bacot executed a last will and testament in statutory form, naming Orgeron as executor and sole legatee.

In September of 1984, Bacot was admitted to Charity Hospital in New Orleans (CHNO) suffering with acute chronic virulent type B herpes simplex. This disease caused a buildup of toxic ammonia on Bacot's brain, which increased as his hospitalization progressed. Several weeks later on October 4, 1984, at approximately 2:00 a.m., Bacot asked Carolyn McLain (McLain), a CHNO nurse to bring him a

189

pen and paper so that he could write a will. McLain honored Bacot's request. That night, Bacot wrote the document in question. It is short, is written on a single sheet of stenographic paper and reads, "I leave all to Danny". The document is signed "Wilds Bacot" and contains a series of marks resembling a slash--date of either "10/4/84 or 4/10/84." McLain later retrieved the document from Bacot. She signed, dated it, placed Bacot's CHNO patient number on the document and placed it in his medical file.

Shortly thereafter, Bacot slipped into a coma and died on October 14, 1984. He never regained consciousness and never indicated to anyone the identity of the "Danny" named in the document.

On October 19, 1984, Orgeron petitioned the Civil District Court of Orleans Parish to probate the statutory testament of January 5, 1982. Several homosexual lovers of Bacot, Danny Washington, Danny Poirier and Danny Butler, intervened in the probate proceedings. Each attempted to probate the document in question asserting it to be Bacot's olographic last will and testament and each claiming to be the "Danny" named as legatee. In addition, Bacot's cousins, H. William Jolly, III, Mary Etta Jolly, and Bob Conway Jolly, intervened asserting the statutory testament to be deficient in form and claiming to be the true owners of the succession assets. The Jolly's later amended their original petition to allege the document in question to be the valid olographic testament of Bacot which supersedes the statutory testament.

Following a two day trial, the trial Judge decreed the document in question to be the valid olographic will of Bacot executed on October 4, 1984 and that, as such, it revoked the prior statutory will. The Court found Danny Washington to be the "Danny" referred to as Bacot's intended sole legatee but limited his legacy to one-tenth (1/10) of the movable property of the succession under Civil Code Article 1481 finding Washington lived in open concubinage with Bacot. The Court based its decision on Washington and Bacot's longtime homosexual love affair and cohabitation wherein they assumed duties and obligations usually manifested by married people. The Court decreed the remainder of the estate to Orgeron as Bacot's adopted son.

All parties appealed the judgment of the trial court ***.

*** [The appellate court upheld the ruling of trial court that the "olographic will was valid.]
CONCUBINAGE:

The same argument on the concubinage issue is urged. Since the trial court only had the issue of the validity of the wills before it, it should not have concluded that Danny Washington was a concubine, and therefore was only entitled to 1/10th of decedent's movables. Theoretically, that argument has merit; however, because the issue is a legal one, that is, whether a man can live in concubinage with another man, we shall address that issue since no amount of evidence will change the result we reach.

Using the mandate of Civil Code Article 1714 and Washington's long term relationship with Bacot, the trial judge concluded that Washington is the "Danny" referred to in the will but not "without its own problems". Referring to Civil Code Article 1481, the court determined that Washington was Bacot's "concubine" and therefore was prohibited from receiving more than 1/10 of the value of the movables of the estate. Civil Code Article 1481 reads in pertinent part:

"Those who have lived together in open concubinage are respectively incapable of making to each other, whether inter vivosor mortis causa, any donation of immovables; and if they make a donation of movables, it can not exceed one- tenth part of the whole value of their estate. Those who afterwards marry are excepted from this rule."

Neither the 1808, 1825, nor our present day civil code defines "concubinage" or "open concubinage". In Purvis v. Purvis, 162 So. 239 (La.App. 2nd Cir.1935), the court defined a concubine as follows:

A concubine should be distinguished from a courtesan or mistress. She is one who occupies the position, performs the duties, and assumes the responsibilities of a wife, without the title and privileges flowing from a legal marriage.

Id. at 240.

It is clear, however, that in referring to concubinage, our civil code has always used language which relates only to relationships between men and women. *******

3. When the mother of the child was known as living in a state of concubinage with the father, and resided as such in his house at the time when the child was conceived.

That article was subsequently amended to include the phrase "... mother and alleged father were known as living in a state of concubinage." See, Art. 209(4) prior to Act 702, 1981.

Article 160, as amended by Act 229 of 1986, dealing with permanent alimony, provides, in part:

"Permanent periodic alimony shall be revoked if it becomes unnecessary and terminates if the spouse to whom it has been awarded remarries or enters into open concubinage."

We therefore are presented with the issue of whether there was ever an intent for the concept of concubinage to apply to homosexual relationships.

Concubinage, in some form, has existed since early recorded history as far back as the Book of Genesis. "Pilegesh (Biblical date): A concubine recognized among the ancient Hebrews. She enjoyed the same rights in the house as the legitimate wife. Since it was regarded as the highest blessing to have many children, while the greatest curse was childlessness, legitimate wives themselves gave their maids to their husbands to atone, at least in part for their own barrenness...." Succession of Lannes, 187 La. 17, 174 So. 94, 97 (1937), citing Gen. XXXV:22, xlix, 4.

During the Roman Empire, concubinage was widely recognized but only existed as an inferior or secondary status to marriage and was afforded only certain types of legal recognition. Badillo v. Tio, 6 La.Ann. 129 (La.1851). The Roman concubine was a female cohabitor who never acquired the social or legal status of her male partner nor did the children of such a union. *[FN5 Kathryn Venturators Lorio, "Concubinage and Its' Alternatives: A proposal For a More Perfect Union", 26 Loy.Law Rev. 1 (1980) (hereinafter, Lorio).]*

Concubinage was acceptable even for married men but was distinguished from casual love affairs because of its more permanent nature. It continued as a recognized institution in Rome until Emperor Constantine forbade it; subsequent Christian emperors condemned the practice and it fell into disuse.

Concubinage, in our law, as in ancient times, has traditionally been viewed as a union between a man and a woman, living together as husband and wife but outside of marriage. Unlike marriage, it is not a civil contract and lacks the formalities required by our civil code. See, La.C.C. Arts. 86 and 88. It differs from putative marriage in that the parties have no reasonable belief that they are married. See, La.C.C. Art. 117. Common law marriages have been recognized as states of concubinage in Louisiana. See, Succession of Marinoni, 177 La. 592, 148 So. 888 (1933), at 894.

The Louisiana prohibition against donations between concubines has its origin in the French law which existed prior to the Code Napoleon. The French expression, "don de concubin a' concubine ne baut", prohibiting donations between concubines, was affirmed by Article 132 of the Royal Ordinance of 1629. *   Although the Projet of the Code Napoleon recommended the prohibition of donations between concubines, the redactors deleted this provision because of the public scandals which attended succession proceedings under the old law. Succession of Jahraus, supra. However, the redactors of the civil code of 1808 followed the recommendation of the Projet of the Code Napoleon and again prohibited those living together in open "concubinage" from making universal donations or donations of universal title to each other. La.C.C. 1808, Art. 10. Planiol suggests that society has a supreme interest in the duration of unions which create families. Concubinage was frowned upon as a means of avoiding the responsibilities of family associated with marriage, especially the obligations associated with the birth of children. See, Planiol, Civil Law Treatise, Vol. 1, Sec. 697 (La.Law Institute, English Translation, 1959). Those same considerations were carried over into Article 1468 of the 1825 Civil Code which narrowed the prohibition by limiting a donation to only a percentage of the movables, and excepting those who later married. The emphasis was again placed on marriage. Present day article 1481 is nearly identical to article 1468 of the 1825 code.

The jurisprudence interpreting article 1481 indicates that several factors are necessary for the restriction to apply, with the necessary element being the maintenance of a status resembling marriage. Succession of Jahraus, supra.

First, there must be an absence of good faith as to the existence of a legal marriage. * The parties must be "reciprocally guilty; otherwise no disability attaches to the donor."* A stable relationship is required and mere acts of sexual intercourse even if frequent and habitual will not constitute a state of concubinage.*

Second, Article 1481 requires that concubinage be "open", that is aboveboard. If the parties attempt to conceal the relationship by referring to it as anything other than concubinage, it is not "open". * Thus, parties who disguise the relationship are not living in open concubinage. Even disguising the relationship as a marriage is sufficient to render it closed concubinage. ***

Third, an exception to the prohibition exists for those who later marry each other. The fact that the relationship ceases is not sufficient to lift the prohibition. Thus, persons who discontinue living together are still prohibited from donating to each other absent a subsequent legal marriage between them. *

In the recent decision of Thomas v. Thomas, 440 So.2d 879 (La.App. 2nd Cir.1983), writ den., the court had occasion to consider a recent amendment to Louisiana Civil Code Article 160, involving permanent alimony. Article 160 was amended to read in pertinent part as follows: [FN8 As previously noted Article 160 was again amended by the 1986 legislature. However, concubinage still terminates alimony. ***]

"This alimony shall be revoked if it becomes unnecessary and terminates if the spouse to whom it has been awarded remarries or enters into open concubinage."

The Thomas Court was called upon to reconsider the law on concubinage and stated as follows:

"In defining and applying the term open concubinage, the courts have historically insisted that a definite meaning be ascribed to both the words 'open' and 'concubinage,' before finding that the legal requisites of open concubinage have been proven. 'Concubinage' is derived from the Latin term concubinatus. This term signified, in Roman civilization, a relationship or cohabitation in which the man and woman generally resided together as husband and wife without the benefit of the formalities, civil effects and legal consequences of a formal marriage. (citations omitted) Thus to this day, concubinage has retained the signification of a relationship in which a man and woman live together as husband and wife without being legally married." Thomas, supra at 881.

Other courts have used varying descriptions to convey the significance of the concubinage relationship. Concubinage has been described as depicting a "state of affairs in which the man and woman exercise, with respect to each other, the rights and privileges of marriage." Succession of Lannes, supra. It has also been called a relationship of sexual content in which man and woman live together as husband and wife in a state approximating marriage. Succession of Filhiol, 119 La. 998, 44 So. 843 (1907).

It is a familiar rule of statutory construction that the words of a legislative act should not be extended beyond their proper and natural meaning in order to meet particular cases. When our legislature amended Article 160 to provide for termination of permanent alimony upon proof that the spouse receiving alimony was living in "open concubinage" the phrase "open concubinage" had been in our law for some 174 years. Our legislature did not see fit to extend the concept of concubinage to any other type of sexual relationship. In addressing this very issue, the court in Thomas v. Thomas, supra, noted:

The term open concubinage has a well-established legal significance, and we believe that in employing this term, the legislature intended that it be accorded its traditional and firmly established meaning; had they intended otherwise, they could have employed a different precept which emphasized habitual sexual acts, rather than quasi-marital status.

Thomas, *supra*; at p. 884.

Thus, concubinage has traditionally been described and held to be a relationship in which a man and a woman, that is, two people capable of contracting marriage, are involved in an open, illicit sexual relationship approximating marriage. As has often been observed, the word concubinage describes "a status, and not mere acts of fornication or adultery, however frequent or habitual." *** The last sentence of article 1481, which removes the prohibition for those who later marry was designed to effect that end.

There is not now, nor has there ever been in our law a legal mechanism for recognizing marriage between persons of the same sex. See, La.C.C. Art. 88. Homosexuals living together, no matter what the duration, can never marry, and therefore such individuals can never be concubines to one another. A concubine is as essential to a state of concubinage as a ghost is to Hamlet. Thus, a man cannot live in open concubinage with another man. The trial court erred in finding that Civil Code Article 1481 applies to the instant case.

We need not address the issue of the validity of the statutory will as we have found the olographic will valid which revokes all prior wills.

For the foregoing reasons, the judgment of the trial court decreeing Danny Washington to be the concubine of Samuel Wilds Bacot, Jr. is reversed.

AFFIRMED IN PART, REVERSED IN PART AND REMANDED.

b. *Baker v. State of Vermont*
Stan Baker, et al. v. State of Vermont, et al.
744 A.2d 864 (Vt. 1999)
Present AMESTOY, C.J., and DOOLEY, MORSE, JOHNSON and SKOGLUND, JJ.
AMESTOY, C.J.

May the State of Vermont exclude same-sex couples from the benefits and protections that its laws provide to opposite-sex married couples? ***

We conclude that under the Common Benefits Clause of the Vermont Constitution, which, in pertinent part, reads,

> That government is, or ought to be, instituted for the common benefit, protection, and security of the people, nation, or community, and not for the particular emolument or advantage of any single person, family, or set of persons, who are a part only of that community ....

Vt. Const., ch. I, art 7., plaintiffs may not be deprived of the statutory benefits and protections afforded persons of the opposite sex who choose to marry. We hold that the State is constitutionally required to extend to same- sex couples the common benefits and protections that flow from marriage under Vermont law. Whether this ultimately takes the form of inclusion within the marriage laws themselves or a parallel "domestic partnership" system or some equivalent statutory alternative, rests with the Legislature. Whatever system is chosen, however, must conform with the constitutional imperative to afford all Vermonters the common benefit, protection, and security of the law.

Plaintiffs are three same-sex couples who have lived together in committed relationships for periods ranging from four to twenty-five years. Two of the couples have raised children together. Each couple applied for a marriage license from their respective town clerk, and each was refused a license as ineligible under the applicable state marriage laws. Plaintiffs thereupon filed this lawsuit against defendants – the State of Vermont, the Towns of Milton and Shelburne, and the City of South Burlington--seeking a declaratory judgment that the refusal to issue them a license violated the marriage statutes and the Vermont Constitution.

The State, joined by Shelburne and South Burlington, moved to dismiss the action on the ground that plaintiffs had failed to state a claim for which relief could be granted. *** The trial court granted the

State's and Town's motions, denied plaintiffs' motion, and dismissed the complaint. The court ruled that the marriage statutes could not be construed to permit the issuance of a license to same-sex couples. The court further ruled that the marriage statutes were constitutional because they rationally furthered the State's interest in promoting "the link between procreation and child rearing." This appeal followed.

*** [Relying on "the plain meaning of the words" the Vermont Supreme Court affirmed the lower court's interpretation of the Vermont marriage law to bar issuance of marriage licenses to same-sex couples.]

*** [Plaintiffs argue] that the underlying purpose of marriage is to protect and encourage the union of committed couples and that, absent an explicit legislative prohibition, the statutes should be interpreted broadly to include committed same-sex couples. Plaintiffs rely principally on our decision in In re B.L.V.B., 160 Vt. 368, 369, 628 A.2d 1271, 1272 (1993). There, we held that a woman who was co- parenting the two children of her same-sex partner could adopt the children without terminating the natural mother's parental rights. Although the statute provided generally that an adoption deprived the natural parents of their legal rights, it contained an exception where the adoption was by the "spouse" of the natural parent. * Technically, therefore, the exception was inapplicable. We concluded, however, that the purpose of the law was not to restrict the exception to legally married couples, but to safeguard the child, and that to apply the literal language of the statute in these circumstances would defeat the statutory purpose and "reach an absurd result." ***

Contrary to plaintiffs' claim, B.L.V.B. does not control our conclusion here. *** Unlike B.L.V.B., it is far from clear that limiting marriage to opposite-sex couples violates the Legislature's "intent and spirit." Rather, the evidence demonstrates a clear legislative assumption that marriage under our statutory scheme consists of a union between a man and a woman. Accordingly, we reject plaintiffs' claim that they were entitled to a license under the statutory scheme governing marriage.

II. The Constitutional Claim   ***

*** [T]he Common Benefits Clause of the Vermont Constitution differs markedly from the federal Equal Protection Clause in its language, historical origins, purpose, and development. While the federal amendment may thus supplement the protections afforded by the Common Benefits Clause, it does not supplant it as the first and primary safeguard of the rights and liberties of all Vermonters. See id. at 449, 450 A.2d at 347 (Court is free to "provide more generous protection to rights under the Vermont Constitution than afforded by the federal charter"); ***.   ***

"[L]abels aside," Vermont case law has consistently demanded in practice that statutory exclusions from publicly-conferred benefits and protections must be "premised on an appropriate and overriding public interest." * The rigid categories utilized by the federal courts under the Fourteenth Amendment find no support in our early case law and, while routinely cited, are often effectively ignored in our more recent decisions. As discussed more fully below, these decisions are consistent with the text and history of the Common Benefits Clause which, similarly, yield no rigid categories or formulas of analysis. ***

*** When a statute is challenged under Article 7, we first define that "part of the community" disadvantaged by the law. We examine the statutory basis that distinguishes those protected by the law from those excluded from the state's protection. ***

We look next to the government's purpose in drawing a classification that includes some members of the community within the scope of the challenged law but excludes others. ***

We must ultimately ascertain whether the omission of a part of the community from the benefit, protection and security of the challenged law bears a reasonable and just relation to the governmental purpose. Consistent with the core presumption of inclusion, factors to be considered in this determination may include: (1) the significance of the benefits and protections of the challenged law; (2) whether the omission of members of the community from the benefits and protections of the challenged law promotes the government's stated goals; and (3) whether the classification is significantly underinclusive or overinclusive. ***

Ultimately, the answers to these questions, however useful, cannot substitute for " '[t]he inescapable fact ... that adjudication of ... claims may call upon the Court in interpreting the Constitution to exercise that same capacity which by tradition courts always have exercised: reasoned judgment.' " Id. (quoting Planned Parenthood of Southeastern Pa. v. Casey, 505 U.S. 833, 849 (1992)). *****

E. The Standard Applied

* The first step in our analysis is to identify the nature of the statutory classification. As noted, the marriage statutes apply expressly to opposite- sex couples. Thus, the statutes exclude anyone who wishes to marry someone of the same sex.

Next, we must identify the governmental purpose or purposes to be served by the statutory classification. The principal purpose the State advances in support of the excluding same-sex couples from the legal benefits of marriage is the government's interest in "furthering the link between procreation and child rearing." The State has a strong interest, it argues, in promoting a permanent commitment between couples who have children to ensure that their offspring are considered legitimate and receive ongoing parental support. The State contends, further, that the Legislature could reasonably believe that sanctioning same-sex unions "would diminish society's perception of the link between procreation and child rearing ... [and] advance the notion that fathers or mothers ... are mere surplusage to the functions of procreation and child rearing." The State argues that since same-sex couples cannot conceive a child on their own, state-sanctioned same-sex unions "could be seen by the Legislature to separate further the connection between procreation and parental responsibilities for raising children." Hence, the Legislature is justified, the State concludes, "in using the marriage statutes to send a public message that procreation and child rearing are intertwined."

* It is beyond dispute that the State has a legitimate and long-standing interest in promoting a permanent commitment between couples for the security of their children. It is equally undeniable that the State's interest has been advanced by extending formal public sanction and protection to the union, or marriage, of those couples considered capable of having children, i.e., men and women. And there is no doubt that the overwhelming majority of births today continue to result from natural conception between one man and one woman. *****

It is equally undisputed that many opposite-sex couples marry for reasons unrelated to procreation, that some of these couples never intend to have children, and that others are incapable of having children. Therefore, if the purpose of the statutory exclusion of same-sex couples is to "further [ ] the link between procreation and child rearing," it is significantly underinclusive. *****

Furthermore, while accurate statistics are difficult to obtain, there is no dispute that a significant number of children today are actually being raised by same-sex parents, and that increasing numbers of children are being conceived by such parents through a variety of assisted-reproductive techniques. *****

Thus, with or without the marriage sanction, the reality today is that increasing numbers of same-sex couples are employing increasingly efficient assisted-reproductive techniques to conceive and raise children. * The Vermont Legislature has not only recognized this reality, but has acted affirmatively to remove legal barriers so that same-sex couples may legally adopt and rear the children conceived through such efforts. See 15A V.S.A. § 1-102(b) (allowing partner of biological parent to adopt if in child's best interest without reference to sex). The state has also acted to expand the domestic relations laws to safeguard the interests of same-sex parents and their children when such couples terminate their domestic relationship. See 15A V.S.A. § 1-112 (vesting family court with jurisdiction over parental rights and responsibilities, parent-child contact, and child support when unmarried persons who have adopted minor child "terminate their domestic relationship").

Therefore, to the extent that the state's purpose in licensing civil marriage was, and is, to legitimize children and provide for their security, the statutes plainly exclude many same-sex couples who are no different from opposite-sex couples with respect to these objectives. If anything, the exclusion of same-sex couples from the legal protections incident to marriage exposes their children to the precise risks that the State argues the marriage laws are designed to secure against. ***

The State also argues that because same-sex couples cannot conceive a child on their own, their exclusion promotes a "perception of the link between procreation and child rearing," and that to discard it would "advance the notion that mothers and fathers ... are mere surplusage to the functions of procreation and child rearing" *** [But the] State does not suggest that the use of [assisted reproductive by male-female couples] technologies undermines a married couple's sense of parental responsibility, or fosters the perception that they are "mere surplusage" to the conception and parenting of the child so conceived. *** [T]here is no reasonable basis to conclude that a same-sex couple's use of the same technologies would undermine the bonds of parenthood, or society's perception of parenthood.

The question thus becomes whether the exclusion of a relatively small but significant number of otherwise qualified same-sex couples from the same legal benefits and protections afforded their opposite-sex counterparts contravenes the mandates of Article 7. ***

*** In Loving v. Virginia, *, the United States Supreme Court, striking down Virginia's anti-miscegenation law, observed that "[t]he freedom to marry has long been recognized as one of the vital personal rights." The Court's point was clear; access to a civil marriage license and the multitude of legal benefits, protections, and obligations that flow from it significantly enhance the quality of life in our society.

*** [T]he benefits and protections incident to a marriage license under Vermont law have never been greater. They include, for example, the right to receive a portion of the estate of a spouse who dies intestate and protection against disinheritance through elective share provisions, under 14 V.S.A. §§ 401-404, 551; preference in being appointed as the personal representative of a spouse who dies intestate, under 14 V.S.A. § 903; the right to bring a lawsuit for the wrongful death of a spouse, under 14 V.S.A. § 1492; the right to bring an action for loss of consortium, under 12 V.S.A.§ 5431; the right to workers' compensation survivor benefits under 21 V.S.A. § 632; the right to spousal benefits statutorily guaranteed to public employees, including health, life, disability, and accident insurance, under 3 V.S.A. § 631; the opportunity to be covered as a spouse under group life insurance policies issued to an employee, under 8 V.S.A. § 3811; the opportunity to be covered as the insured's spouse under an individual health insurance policy, under 8 V.S.A. § 4063; the right to claim an evidentiary privilege for marital communications, under V.R.E. 504; homestead rights and protections, under 27 V.S.A. §§ 105-108, 141-142; the presumption of joint ownership of property and the concomitant right of survivorship, under 27 V.S.A. § 2; hospital visitation and other rights incident to the medical treatment of a family member, under 18 V.S.A. § 1852; and the right to receive, and the obligation to provide, spousal support, maintenance, and property division in the event of separation or divorce, under 15 V.S.A. §§ 751-752. ***

*** Considered in light of the extreme logical disjunction between the classification and the stated purposes of the law--protecting children and "furthering the link between procreation and child rearing"--the exclusion [of same-sex couples from marriage] falls substantially short ***. The laudable governmental goal of promoting a commitment between married couples to promote the security of their children and the community as a whole provides no reasonable basis for denying the legal benefits and protections of marriage to same-sex couples, who are no differently situated with respect to this goal than their opposite-sex counterparts. ***

*** [The opinion summarily rejects other asserted state justifications for restricting marriage to male-female couples.] Among these are the State's purported interests in "promoting child rearing in a setting that provides both male and female role models," minimizing the legal complications of surrogacy contracts and sperm donors, "bridging differences" between the sexes, discouraging marriages of convenience for tax, housing or other benefits, maintaining uniformity with marriage laws in other states, and generally protecting marriage from "destabilizing changes." The most substantive of the State's remaining claims relates to the issue of childrearing. It is conceivable that the Legislature could conclude that opposite-sex partners offer advantages in this area, although we note that child-development experts disagree and the answer is decidedly uncertain. The argument, however, contains a more fundamental flaw, and that is the Legislature's endorsement of a policy diametrically at odds with the State's claim. In 1996, the Vermont General Assembly enacted, and the Governor signed, a law removing all prior legal barriers to the adoption of children by same-sex couples. See 15A V.S.A. § 1-102. At the same time, the Legislature provided additional legal protections in the form of court-ordered child support and parent-child contact in the event that same-sex parents dissolved their "domestic relationship." Id. § 1-112. In light of these express policy choices, the State's arguments that Vermont public policy favors opposite-sex over same-sex parents or disfavors the use of artificial reproductive technologies are patently without substance.

Similarly, the State's argument that Vermont's marriage laws serve a substantial governmental interest in maintaining uniformity with other jurisdictions cannot be reconciled with Vermont's recognition of unions, such as first-cousin marriages, not uniformly sanctioned in other states. *** Vermont has sanctioned adoptions by same-sex partners,* notwithstanding the fact that many states have not. *** Thus, the State's claim that Vermont's marriage laws were adopted because the Legislature sought to conform to those of the other forty- nine states is not only speculative, but refuted by two relevant legislative choices which demonstrate that uniformity with other jurisdictions has not been a governmental purpose. ***

Thus, viewed in the light of history, logic, and experience, we conclude that none of the interests asserted by the State provides a reasonable and just basis for the continued exclusion of same-sex couples from the benefits incident to a civil marriage license under Vermont law. *** It remains only to determine the appropriate means and scope of relief compelled by this constitutional mandate.   ***

We hold only that plaintiffs are entitled under Chapter I, Article 7, of the Vermont Constitution to obtain the same benefits and protections afforded by Vermont law to married opposite-sex couples. We do not purport to infringe upon the prerogatives of the Legislature to craft an appropriate means of addressing this constitutional mandate, other than to note that the record here refers to a number of potentially constitutional statutory schemes from other jurisdictions. These include what are typically referred to as "domestic partnership" or "registered partnership" acts, which generally establish an alternative legal status to marriage for same-sex couples, impose similar formal requirements and limitations, create a parallel licensing or registration scheme, and extend all or most of the same rights and obligations provided by the law to married partners. *

*** Absent legislative guidelines defining the status and rights of same-sex couples, consistent with constitutional requirements, uncertainty and confusion could result. Therefore, we hold that the current statutory scheme shall remain in effect for a reasonable period of time to enable the Legislature to consider and enact implementing legislation in an orderly and expeditious fashion. *** In the event that the benefits and protections in question are not statutorily granted, plaintiffs may petition this Court to order the remedy they originally sought.   ***

The concurring and dissenting opinion confuses decisiveness with wisdom and judicial authority with finality. Our mandate is predicated upon a fundamental respect for the ultimate source of constitutional authority, not a fear of decisiveness. ***

The State's interest in extending official recognition and legal protection to the professed commitment of two individuals to a lasting relationship of mutual affection is predicated on the belief that legal support of a couple's commitment provides stability for the individuals, their family, and the broader community. ***

The past provides many instances where the law refused to see a human being when it should have. See e.g. Dred Scott, 60 U.S. at 407 .... *** The challenge for future generations will be to define what is most essentially human. The extension of the Common Benefits Clause to acknowledge plaintiffs as Vermonters who seek nothing more, nor less, than legal protection and security for their avowed commitment to an intimate and lasting human relationship is simply, when all is said and done, a recognition of our common humanity.

The judgment of the superior court upholding the constitutionality of the Vermont marriage statutes*** is reversed. The effect of the Court's decision is suspended, and jurisdiction is retained in this Court, to permit the Legislature to consider and enact legislation consistent with the constitutional mandate described herein.

DOOLEY, J., concurring.

I concur in Part I of the majority opinion, the holding of Part II, and the mandate. I do not, however, concur in the reasoning of Part II. ***

The marriage statutes do not facially discriminate on the basis of sexual orientation. There is, however, no doubt that the requirement that civil marriage be a union of one man and one woman has the effect of discriminating against lesbian and gay couples, like the plaintiffs in this case, who are unable to marry the life partners of their choice. The majority proclaims that most decisions have concluded that lesbians and gay men are not a suspect classification,***

Vermont's legal climate differs considerably from that in other jurisdictions where courts have held that lesbians and gay men are not a suspect classification. ***

The majority errs *** [in relying on federal caselaw and concluding that sexual orientation is not a suspect classification in Vermont] because the *Bowers* [v. *Hardwicke*] rationale *** is not applicable in Vermont today. Although Vermont, like all states, once criminalized sodomy *** it repealed this law in 1977 and does not now prohibit, or otherwise restrict, homosexual conduct between adults, except on the same terms that it restricts heterosexual conduct. ***

Since 1992, it has generally been the policy of Vermont to prohibit discrimination based on sexual orientation. See 1991, No. 135 (Adj.Sess.). This includes discrimination based on "female or male homosexuality." 1 V.S.A. § 143. Thus, I believe our "legal climate" is vastly different from that in Bowers, where, after considering that twenty- four states had criminalized sodomy between consenting adults, the United States Supreme Court concluded that there was no fundamental right, deeply rooted in the Nation's history, to engage in such conduct. ***

*** [Justice Dooley cites with favor decisions of Oregon courts finding that sexual orientation is a suspect classification as a matter of state constitutional law.]

*** I will briefly explain my disagreement with the majority's rationale for reaching the same result.

The majority's analysis under Chapter I, Article 7 proceeds in three steps: (1) there is one equality standard imposed by Article 7, and it applies to claims of civil rights discrimination and economic discrimination alike; (2) the equality standard is higher, that is, more active, than the standard imposed by the Equal Protection Clause of the Fourteenth Amendment for analyzing claims of economic discrimination; and (3) under the new standard, the denial of the benefits of marriage to lesbians and gay men violates Chapter I, Article 7. In the first two steps, the majority makes statements entirely contrary to our existing Article 7 jurisprudence. As to the third step, I find no standard in the Court's decision--it is entirely a matter of "judgment."

The first step in the Court's analysis requires overruling a long series of precedents holding that where a statutory scheme affects fundamental constitutional rights or involves suspect classifications, Article 7 requires "a more searching scrutiny." *** It is ironic that in a civil rights case we overrule our precedent requiring the State to meet a higher burden in civil rights cases, but still conclude, under the lower standard, that the State has not met its burden. [In omitted footnotes Justice Dooely criticizes the majority's description of precedents as "neither fair nor accurate" and "inaccurate."]

which the majority bases it.

The second step is also at variance with our Article 7 law, even as it seeks to rely upon it. ***
Again, I find great irony in the fact that we are doing this unnecessarily in a case where the main theme

of the State and many amici is that we must defer to the Legislature on the issue before us.
***

*** Most of these decisions [cited by the majority] reflect judicial attitudes prevalent in the era of Lochner v. New York,***

*** Finally, concerning the third step of the majority's analysis, I question whether the majority's new standard is ascertainable, is consistent with our limited role in constitutional review, and contains appropriate judicial discretion. ***The majority calls the federal approach "rigid" at one point, 744 A.2d at 878, but then describes it, as applied in Tanner, as an invitation to subjective judicial decision-making. 744 A.2d at 878 n.10. The two criticisms are as inconsistent as any criticisms could be.***

I cannot endorse, in this vitally important area of constitutional review, a standard that relies wholly on factors and balancing, with no mooring in any criteria or guidelines, however imperfect they may be. *** In the end, the approach the majority has developed relies too much on the identities and personal philosophies of the men and women who fill the chairs at the Supreme Court, too little on ascertainable standards that judges of different backgrounds and philosophies can apply equally, and very little, if any, on deference to the legislative branch.

The final irony in this decision for me is that the balancing and weighing process set forth in the Court's opinion describes exactly the process we would expect legislators to go through if they were facing the question before us free from the political pressures necessarily created by deeply held moral convictions, in both directions, of substantial members of their constituents. We are judges, not legislators. ***

JOHNSON, J., concurring in part and dissenting in part.

*** I concur with the majority's holding, but I respectfully dissent from its novel and truncated remedy, which in my view abdicates this Court's constitutional duty to redress violations of constitutional rights. I would grant the requested relief and enjoin defendants from denying plaintiffs a marriage license based solely on the sex of the applicants.

*** Passing this case on to the Legislature will not alleviate the instability and uncertainty that the majority seeks to avoid, and will unnecessarily entangle this Court in the Legislature's efforts to accommodate the majority's mandate within a "reasonable period of time." 744 A.2d at 887.

This case concerns the secular licensing of marriage. *** In granting a marriage license, the State is not espousing certain morals, lifestyles, or relationships, but only identifying those persons entitled to the benefits of the marital status. ***

*** [W]ithin a few pages of rejecting the State's doomsday speculations as a basis for upholding the unconstitutionally discriminatory classification, the majority relies upon those same speculations to deny plaintiffs the relief to which they are entitled as the result of the discrimination. * ***

*** In our system of government, civil rights violations are remedied by courts, not because we issue "Holy Writ" or because we are "the only repository of wisdom." 744 A.2d at 888. It is because the courts "must ultimately define and defend individual rights against government in terms independent of consensus or majority will." L. Tribe, American Constitutional Law § 15.3, at 896 (1978).***

. . . I write separately to state my belief that this is a straightforward case of sex discrimination.

[T]he marriage statutes establish a classification based on sex. *** Not only do the rationalizations advanced by the State fail to pass constitutional muster under this or any other form of heightened scrutiny, they fail to satisfy the rational-basis test as articulated under the Common Benefits Clause.
***

[Under Vermont's marriage statute a] woman is denied the right to marry another woman because her would-be partner is a woman, not because one or both are lesbians. Similarly, a man is denied the right to marry another man because his would-be partner is a man, not because one or both are gay. Thus, an individual's right to marry a person of the same sex is prohibited solely on the basis of sex, not on the basis of sexual orientation. Indeed, sexual orientation does not appear as a qualification for marriage under the marriage statutes. ***

*** The State first contends that the marriage statutes merely acknowledge that marriage, by its very nature, cannot be comprised of two persons of the same sex. Thus, in the State's view, it is the definition of marriage, not the statutes, that restricts marriage to two people of the opposite sex. This argument is circular. *** This question is not resolved by resorting to a historical definition of marriage; it is that very definition that is being challenged in this case.

The State's second argument, also propounded by the majority, see 744 A.2d at 880 n.13, is that the marriage statutes do not discriminate on the basis of sex because they treat similarly situated males the same as similarly situated females. Under this argument, there can be no sex discrimination here because "[i]f a man wants to marry a man, he is barred; a woman seeking to marry a woman is barred in precisely the same way. For this reason, women and men are not treated differently." C. Sunstein, Homosexuality and the Constitution, 70 Ind. L.J. 1, 19 (1994). But consider the following example. Dr. A and Dr. B both want to marry Ms. C, an X-ray technician. Dr. A may do so because Dr. A is a man. Dr. B may not because Dr. B is a woman. Dr. A and Dr. B are people of opposite sexes who are similarly situated in the sense that they both want to marry a person of their choice. The statute disqualifies Dr. B from marriage solely on the basis of her sex and treats her differently from Dr. A, a man. This is sex discrimination.***

Before applying the rational-basis standard to the State's justifications, it is helpful to examine the history of the marriage laws in Vermont. There is no doubt that, historically, the marriage laws imposed sex-based roles for the partners to a marriage--male provider and female dependent--that bore no relation to their inherent abilities to contribute to society. Under the common law, husband and wife were one person. * The legal existence of a woman was suspended by marriage; she merged with her husband and held no separate rights to enter into a contract or execute a deed. * She could not sue without her husband's consent or be sued without joining her husband as a defendant. * Moreover, if a woman did not hold property for her "sole and separate use" prior to marriage, the husband received a freehold interest in all her property, entitling him to all the rents and profits from the property. *
***

[T]he State asserts public purposes--uniting men and women to celebrate the "complementarity" (sic) of the sexes and providing male and female role models for children--based on broad and vague generalizations about the roles of men and women that reflect outdated sex-role stereotyping. The State contends that (1) marriage unites the rich physical and psychological differences between the sexes; (2) sex differences strengthen and stabilize a marriage; (3) each sex contributes differently to a family unit and to society; and (4) uniting the different male and female qualities and contributions in the same institution instructs the young of the value of such a union. The State relies on social science literature, such as Carol Gilligan's In a Different Voice: Psychological Theory and Women's Development (1982), to support its contention that there are sex differences that justify the State requiring two people to be of opposite sex to marry.   ***

To begin with, carried to its logical conclusion, the State's rationale could require all marriages to be between people, not just of the opposite sex, but of different races, religions, national origins, and so forth, to promote diversity. Moreover, while it may be true that the female voice or point of view is sometimes different from the male, such differences are not necessarily found in comparing any given man and any given woman. *** In short, the "diversity" argument is based on illogical conclusions from stereotypical imaginings that would be condemned by the very case cited for its support. *

*** [T]he State claims an interest in "preserving the existing marital structure" [and] in "instructing the young of the value of uniting male and female qualities." *** [These also are circuitous stereotypes.]

Many of the State's remaining justifications, which I place into a third category, assume highly questionable public purposes. [N]one of these justifications are even remotely, much less reasonably, related to the challenged classification ***.

*** [T]he State argues that increased use of technologically assisted reproduction "may lead men who conceive children by sexual union to perceive themselves as sperm donors, without any responsibility for their offspring." *** If the state purpose is to discourage technologically assisted reproduction, I agree with the majority that the classification is significantly underinclusive. The State does nothing to discourage technologically assisted reproduction by individuals or opposite-sex couples. Moreover, opposite-sex couples may obtain marriage licenses without regard to whether or not they will use technologically assisted reproduction. The public purpose provides no rationale for the different treatment.

The State also asserts that it has an interest in furthering the link between procreation and child rearing "to ensure that couples who engage in sexual intercourse accept[ ] responsibility for the potential children they might create." But the State cannot explain how the failure of opposite-sex couples to accept responsibility for the children they create relates at all to the exclusion of same-sex couples from the benefits of marriage. ***

The State further contends that prohibiting individuals from marrying same-sex partners will deter marriages of convenience entered into solely to obtain tax benefits or government assistance. Two persons of the opposite sex are completely free to enter into a marriage of convenience, however, without the State examining their motives. ***

    ***

*** None of the State's justifications meets the rational-basis test under the Common Benefits Clause. Finding no legally valid justification for the sex-based classification, I conclude that the classification is a vestige of the historical unequal marriage relationship that more recent legislative enactments and our own jurisprudence have unequivocally rejected. The protections conferred on Vermonters by the Common Benefits Clause cannot be restricted by the outmoded conception that marriage requires one man and one woman, creating one person--the husband.

c. Vermont Civil Union Statute

15 Vermont Statutes Annot. § 1202 Requisites of a valid civil union
For a civil union to be established in Vermont, it shall be necessary that the parties to a civil union satisfy all of the following criteria:
(1) Not be a party to another civil union or a marriage.
(2) Be of the same sex and therefore excluded from the marriage laws of this state.
(3) Meet the criteria and obligations set forth in 18 V.S.A. chapter 106.
15 Vermont Statutes Annot. § 1203 Person shall not enter a civil union with a relative
(a) A woman shall not enter a civil union with her mother, grandmother, daughter, granddaughter, sister, brother's daughter, sister's daughter, father's sister or mother's sister.
(b) A man shall not enter a civil union with his father, grandfather, son, grandson, brother, brother's son, sister's son, father's brother or mother's brother.
(c) A civil union between persons prohibited from entering a civil union in subsection (a) or (b) of this section is void.
15 Vermont Statutes Annot. § 1204 Benefits, protections and responsibilities of parties to a civil union
(a) Parties to a civil union shall have all the same benefits, protections and responsibilities under law, whether they derive from statute, administrative or court rule, policy, common law or any other source of civil law, as are granted to spouses in a marriage.
(b) A party to a civil union shall be included in any definition or use of the terms "spouse," "family," "immediate family," "dependent," "next of kin," and other terms that denote the spousal relationship, as those terms are used throughout the law.
(c) Parties to a civil union shall be responsible for the support of one another to the same degree and in the same manner as prescribed under law for married persons.

(d) The law of domestic relations, including annulment, separation and divorce, child custody and support, and property division and maintenance shall apply to parties to a civil union .

(e) The following is a nonexclusive list of legal benefits, protections and responsibilities of spouses, which shall apply in like manner to parties to a civil union :

(1) laws relating to title, tenure, descent and distribution, intestate succession, waiver of will, survivorship, or other incidents of the acquisition, ownership, or transfer, inter vivos or at death, of real or personal property, including eligibility to hold real and personal property as tenants by the entirety (parties to a civil union meet the common law unity of person qualification for purposes of a tenancy by the entirety);

(2) causes of action related to or dependent upon spousal status, including an action for wrongful death, emotional distress, loss of consortium, dramshop, or other torts or actions under contracts reciting, related to, or dependent upon spousal status;

(3) probate law and procedure, including nonprobate transfer;

(4) adoption law and procedure;

(5) group insurance for state employees, and continuing care contracts;

(6) spouse abuse programs under 3 V.S.A. § 18;

(7) prohibitions against discrimination based upon marital status;

(8) victim's compensation rights under 13 V.S.A. § 5351;

(9) workers' compensation benefits;

(10) laws relating to emergency and nonemergency medical care and treatment, hospital visitation and notification, including the Patient's Bill of Rights under 18 V.S.A. chapter 42 and the Nursing Home Residents' Bill of Rights under 33 V.S.A. chapter 73;

(11) terminal care documents under 18 V.S.A. chapter 111, and durable power of attorney for health care execution and revocation under 14 V.S.A. chapter 121;

(12) family leave benefits under 21 V.S.A. chapter 5, subchapter 4A;

(13) public assistance benefits under state law;

(14) laws relating to taxes imposed by the state or a municipality other than estate taxes;

(15) laws relating to immunity from compelled testimony and the marital communication privilege;

(16) the homestead rights of a surviving spouse and homestead property tax allowance;

(17) laws relating to loans to veterans under 8 V.S.A. § 1849;

(18) the definition of family farmer under 10 V.S.A. § 272;

(19) laws relating to the making, revoking and objecting to anatomical gifts by others;

(20) state pay for military service under 20 V.S.A. § 1544;

(21) application for absentee ballot under 17 V.S.A. § 2532;

(22) family landowner rights to fish and hunt under 10 V.S.A. § 4253;

(23) legal requirements for assignment of wages under 8 V.S.A. § 2235; and

(24) affirmance of relationship under 15 V.S.A. § 7.

(f) The rights of parties to a civil union, with respect to a child of whom either becomes the natural parent during the term of the civil union , shall be the same as those of a married couple, with respect to a child of whom either spouse becomes the natural parent during the marriage.

d. Notes and Questions

1) *Bacot* Questions

If you were a judge in the *Bacot* case, how would you have ruled, and why? Should there be a similar status or doctrine to "concubinage" for same-sex couples? Don't they contribute at least as much, and do no more harm to the public policy underlying marriage status as nonmarital heterosexual concubinage relations? What are some of the concerns about concubinage that have persuaded lawmakers in most American states not to adopt the concubinage doctrine or status?

2) *Baker* Questions

Which opinion contains the most credible legal analysis? Did the majority grasp or address the states' core state interest in keeping marriage male-female? What standard of review did the majority apply? How did it differ from comparable federal equality review?

Several months after the *Baker* decision, traditional "town meetings" held in 50 towns around Vermont voted unanimously (50 of 50) to reject same-sex marriage, and voted overwhelmingly against "Civil Unions" (in 46 of 50 towns). *See* Vermont, *infra*. Goldberg, *infra*. A few months later, however, the Vermont legislature passed a law creating a broad form of domestic partnership for same-sex couples, called "Civil Unions," in lieu of legalizing same-sex marriage.

Baker was the first court of last resort to rule that a state must give marriage or marriage-equivalent legal status and benefits to same-sex couples. It led to creation of marriage-equivalent Civil Unions in Vermont, and later in California and Connecticut, and paved the way for *Goodridge* and same-sex marriage four years later in Massachusetts (*see supra*, Chapter 4).

3) Unintended Marriage

The general question of intentional non-marital quasi-marriage in general, and the Utah common law statute in particular, raise the question whether courts could confer marital status on a relationship even if there was no evidence of both parties' intent to marry, or even in the face of evidence of one party's (or both parties') clear and consistent intent not to marry? Apart from the putative marriage doctrine (in which the intent to marry of the claiming spouse is an essential prerequisite), could marital status properly be conferred as a result of the parties having assumed and enjoyed the general reputation and social or legal benefits of marital status, even though the parties secretly (between themselves) but very clearly intended not to be legally married? For example, if a child or survivor of the union were to be denied some significant benefits because the parties were not married, which he or she would get if the parties were married, could a court properly determine that the parties were married in spite of clear evidence that they intended not to be married?

4) Nonmarital Cohabitation

The definition of marriage also defines the contours of nonmarital relationships. All intimate interpersonal adult relationships that are not marriages are, by definition, nonmarital relationships. In contemporary times, *nonmarital cohabitation* is the most noteworthy kind of nonmarital relationship because in a relatively short span of time nonmarital cohabitation changed from being socially condemned and relatively rare to being socially accepted and relatively common. Nonmarital cohabitation increased about 800 percent between 1960 and 1997, and that year nearly half of unmarried women between ages 25 and 39 reported that they had cohabited nonmaritally with a partner, and about one-fourth were still living with a nonmarital partner. David Popenoe & Barbara

Dafoe Whitehead, Should We Live Together? What Young Adults Need to Know about Cohabitation before Marriage, A Comprehensive Review of Recent Research at 3 (The National Marriage Project: The Next Generation Series, 1999).

The reasons why individuals enter nonmarital relationships are probably as many and varied as the individuals themselves, but five categories of reasons are noteworthy. First, historically, inability to marry probably was a major reason why persons entered into nonmarital liaisons. For example, in times or places when divorce was very restricted, expensive, or simply not permitted, persons who married imprudently and then separated from their spouses not infrequently later entered into marriage-like relationships that were socially accepted as de facto marriages, but which were not valid marriages. Today, in the United States, where unilateral no-fault divorce is neither difficult nor expensive, one might think that this is not a credible cause for nonmarital cohabitation. Second, some spouses simply leave a marriage without divorce (perhaps hoping to escape divorce costs, hassle, alimony, property division, etc.), and begin to cohabit with another (nonmarital) partner. Third, a common related concern is that not infrequently parties who are wary of divorce simply refuse to marry; one partner wants to marry but because the other (or a relative or friend of the other) previously was treated unfairly in a divorce, that party refuses to marry--thinking (perhaps mistakenly, *see* Chapter 31, *infra*) that by not marrying they will avoid the heartache and financial obligations of divorce if the relationship breaks up. Fourth, fear of or repudiation of the social institution of marriage is another reason some persons enter nonmarital liaisons. This may be of particular concern to casualties (mostly children) of a generation of unilateral no-fault divorce whose memories of parental marital dissatisfaction, or painful recollection of the bitterness of their parents' divorce, or whose bitter disappointments in a former marriage, or whose rejection of the formalism and social expectations of marriage propel them into alternative nonmarital liaisons. Fifth, nonmarital cohabitation may be viewed by some to be a "trial" marriage, in essence, a warm-up or preparation for marriage (though, in practice, cohabitation seems to impair subsequent marital integrity).

Nonmarital cohabitation was discouraged (at times prohibited) throughout most of American legal history. However, when the "baby boom" generation hit the young adult age, most states abandoned or restricted the doctrines that had denied legal recognition to nonmarital cohabitation. In the landmark case of *Marvin v. Marvin*, 557 P.2d 106 (Cal. 1976) (printed and discussed in Chapter 31, *infra*), the California Supreme Court reversed the judgment of lower courts that had rejected the palimony claim of a woman who had cohabited for seven years with actor Lee Marvin (initially, while he was still married to another woman), and rejected the defendant's contention that any contract involving an illicit relationship is unenforceable. Rather, the court held that only "if sexual acts form an inseparable part of the consideration" would a cohabitation agreement (express or implied) be against public policy. *Id.* at 114. Other states, such as Illinois--in *Hewitt v. Hewitt*, 394 N.E.2d 1204 (Ill. 1979) (printed and discussed in Chapter 31, *infra*)--have adhered to a somewhat traditional, stricter policy (*Hewitt* also noted the strong prohibition of common law marriage).

Nonmarital cohabitation is now permitted, *de jure* in most, and *de facto* in all American jurisdictions (even if they vary in the recognition of palimony claims and other incidents). Most states recognize the possibility of certain legally enforceable marriage-like economic incidents arising out of nonmarital cohabitation. Legally permitted but not legally regulated nonmarital cohabitation forces us to ask the question, "why marriage?" It is possible to regulate economic relations of dependent or interdependent adult cohabitants (including property control, support, division of property upon breakup, and transmission of property upon death, etc.) without the institution of legal marriage. Criteria like "economic dependency" or "economic interrelatedness" or "marriage-like relationship" or other functionally equivalent-to-marriage factors arguably could replace all references to "marriage" or "married" or "spouses" in our laws. Would that be practical or desirable? Alternatively, the state could define marriage or the benefits of marriage so broadly that virtually all cohabitational relationships would be deemed "marriages" for legal purposes. Either one obscures the boundary between marriage and nonmarital liaisons.

A long line of constitutional cases recognizes a "right" to marry, and it could be argued that a right to enter into certain alternative nonmarital liaisons, likewise, must be recognized. But the right recognized in the marriage cases seems, by definition, not to include nonmarital liaisons. On the other hand, some informal relations have existed throughout history; could some nonmarital relationships be found to be deeply rooted in the traditions and history of our nation? Does marriage promote important social interests that nonmarital liaisons do not serve as well? Would that be a constitutional distinction?

5) The Risks of Nonmarital Cohabitation

Whether recognizing nonmarital liaisons would harm conventional marriage and family institutions is a hotly contested question today. Nonmarital cohabitation has been extensively examined by social scientists and has been found to entail significant risks with respect to most of the important reasons for and goals of nonmarital cohabitation. For example, one study reportedly found that children of cohabiting unmarried couples are economically disadvantaged compared to children of married parents; they have a mean household income per adult one-third lower than married couples; and white children living with cohabiting couples are four times more likely to live below poverty level than children living with married couples. Manning & Lichter, *infra*. A reported Canadian study showed that 10 percent of couples living together are unmarried, fewer than one-third of all cohabitation relationships survive five years, "premarital cohabitation actually leads to less stable marriages," "cohabiting unions are less stable than marital unions," and "they weaken the institution of marriage by undermining 'its central foundation of permanence.'" Wu & Balakrishnan, *infra*. Likewise, cohabitation is more likely among persons less committed to marriage, persons who agree strongly with divorce, including children of divorced parents, and daughters of women who view marriage as unhappy; cohabitation before marriage leads to higher rates of divorce; cohabitation increases acceptance of divorce; and both divorce and cohabitation may have a feedback effect increasing acceptance of dissolution. Axinn & Thornton, *infra*. Similarly another study revealed that one-fourth of all unions of Americans age nineteen and over in the late 1980s began non-maritally; however, unions that began with marriage were more stable than those that begin with nonmarital cohabitation; in any six-month period, unions that began as marriages were 45–55 percent less likely to be dissolved than those that began with cohabitation; and the odds of dissolution in any six-month interval are 63–71 percent lower if the couple is married. Teachman et al., *infra*. Busby noted that "Yllo and Straus (1981) . . . found that 'cohabiting couples had higher rates of violence than married couples. Severe violence was almost five times as likely in cohabitating relationships [than in marriages].'" Similarly, a 1993 British study by the Family Education Trust, using data on documented cases of child abuse and neglect between 1982 and 1988 found high correlations between child abuse and the marital status of the parents. "Specifically, the British study found that--compared with a stable nuclear family--the incidence of abuse was 33 times higher when the mother was living with a boyfriend not related to the child. And even when the live-in boyfriend was the biological father of the children, the chances of abuse were still 20 times more likely." Abbott, *infra.*

One of the most complete compilations of data on outcomes of nonmarital cohabitation in the United States is contained in David Popenoe and Barbara Dafoe Whitehead, Should We Live Together? What Young Adults Need to Know about Cohabitation before Marriage, A Comprehensive Review of Recent Research, *infra.* "[V]irtually all research on the topic has determined that the chances of divorce ending a marriage preceded by cohabitation are significantly greater than for a marriage not preceded by cohabitation." *Id.* at 4. Likewise, "[a]ccording to recent studies cohabitants tend not to be as committed as married couples in their dedication to the continuation of the relationship . . . . and they are more oriented toward their own personal autonomy." *Id.* at 5. "Most cohabiting relationships are relatively short lived and an estimated 60 percent end in marriage. . . . In general, cohabiting relationships tend to be less satisfactory than marriage relationships." *Id.* at 6. "Annual rates of depression among cohabiting couples are more than three times what they are among married couples. And women in cohabiting relationships are more likely than married women to suffer physical and sexual abuse. Some research has shown that aggression is at least twice as common among cohabitors as it is among married persons." *Id.* at 7. "[T]hree quarters of children born to cohabiting parents will see their parents split up before they reach age sixteen, whereas only about a third of children born to married parents face a similar fate." *Id.* at 7. Studies also indicate that in cohabiting couples there are "far higher levels of child abuse than is found in intact families." *Id.* at 8. Likewise, "[w]hile the 1996 poverty rate for children living in married couple households was about 6 percent, it was 31 percent for children living in cohabiting households . . . ." *Id.* at 8. The authors conclude: "Despite its widespread acceptance by the young, the remarkable growth of unmarried cohabitation in recent years does not appear to be in children's or the society's best interest. The evidence suggests that it has weakened marriage and the intact, two-parent family and thereby damaged our social well-being, especially that of women and children." *Id.* at 16. Do you agree? Why/why not?

Nonmarital cohabitation might be compared to the Roman relationship of *concubinatus* (concubinage), a legal, nonmarital union distinct from marriage and from legal prostitution. Concubinage was once recognized in several French- and Spanish-history states, and remnants of the status survive, prominently in Louisiana. Is "domestic partnership" just another form of "concubinage"?

6) The Vermont Civil Union Statute

The Vermont Civil Union law, 15 V.S.A. § 1201, took effect in 2000. It provides a legal status for same-sex couples with rights and obligations similar to marriage obtainable by licensure similar to marriage licensing. To date, the overwhelming majority of persons registering civil unions have come from outside of Vermont. Goldberg, *infra*. What are the major benefits to same-sex couples who register in civil unions? What are the major obligations incurred? In what ways do the requirements for marriage differ from those for civil unions? What is the theory behind the creation of the Vermont "civil union" status? What are some possible criticisms or challenges to that theory? *See generally* Johnson, *infra;* Coolidge & Duncan, *infra*.

The Vermont legislature also created another status of "reciprocal beneficiary," granting rights such as hospital visitation and medical decision-making, durable power of attorney, anatomical gifts, disposition of remains, and abuse protection to reciprocal beneficiaries. 15 V.S.A. § 1301. What is the difference between "Civil union" or "domestic partnership" and simple nonmarital cohabitation? What about such relationships makes them valuable to society? Why should special protections be extended to persons in such relationships? Marriage clearly contributes tremendous benefits to society; do nonmarital unions such as domestic partnerships or civil unions make similar contributions? Why/why not? Are those contributions comparable so that comparable legal status is merited? Should they receive comparable legal status and benefits? Why/why not?

7) Domestic Partnership

A number of private companies and a few (but increasing number of) government agencies and entities have extended employment benefits traditionally provided to the spouses and children of employees to the "domestic partners" of employees as well. The underlying policy seems to be that, from the perspective of the employer, it doesn't matter what the relationship between the employee and his or her benefit sharers is, and that extending benefits will make some employees happier and, presumably, better employees. Opponents view these developments as "baby steps" to recognition of same-sex marriage and other homosexual family relations as functional equivalents of traditional marriages and families, and as threats to the unique legal status and public valuation of the traditional family. To date, few courts have addressed whether domestic partnership is constitutionally required though several have ruled on statutory grounds that the government entities and agencies providing benefits to domestic partners lacked legal authority to do so. However, an extremely broad ruling by an Oregon Appeals court in *Tanner v. Oregon Health Sciences University*, 971 P.2d 435 (Or. Ct. App. 1998), found that provision of "domestic partnership" benefits was mandated by equality and fundamental rights principles of state and federal constitutional law. Several nations in Europe have most of the economic and many of the noneconomic (usually excluding general co-parenting) rights of marriage to same-sex couples living in registered "domestic partnerships." *See* § 6.2., *infra*.

There are many different kinds of legal regimes that are called "domestic partnerships." *See* Wardle, *Counting, infra*. Most types of "domestic partnership" that have been adopted in the United States are very limited compared to the broad registered "domestic partnerships" of Vermont, Denmark, Norway, etc. For example, initially the California domestic partnership act allowed same-sex couples to register domestic partnership, but the only general consequences of that registration is to allow those couples hospital visitation privileges and to extend state employees' domestic partners certain employee dependents' benefits, and allow municipalities to do likewise. Cal. Gov. Code. tit.2 D.5, pt. 5, ch. 1, art. 9 (1999). (A few years later, however, California passed a marriage-equivalent form of domestic partnership.) Domestic partnership seems to have more general appeal and less popular opposition than same-sex marriage. Thus, most jurisdictions also have been reluctant to extend marriage-like status to same-sex couples, and only a few countries have allowed more than limited, often token, domestic partnership status. Nonetheless, in the last decade the movement to legalize same-sex domestic partnership (as an alternative to or step toward same-sex marriage) has achieved some notable successes in a small but growing number of affluent jurisdictions. One student writer claims that: "Today, 13 percent of all United States employers offer benefits to the domestic partners of their employees. For larger companies, those with more than 5,000 employees, the figure is 25 percent." Zielinski, *infra* at 281. Those percentages are growing. "Of the companies that offer benefits for unmarried employees' partners, about half exclude heterosexual couples." *Id.* at 283.

8) The ALI Domestic Partnership Proposal
    In 2000, the American Law Institute approved a significant new proposal for family law reform called the *Principles of the Law of Family Dissolution.* They propose to expand of the types of relationships that enjoy privileged "family" status and benefits in law to include many "alternative" relationships, and "deconstruct" and "level" family relations. In Chapter 6 (Domestic Partners) the ALI proposes to expand the types of relationships that may claim the full economic protections and privileges of marital status upon dissolution. It includes same-sex and heterosexual cohabitants who "for a significant period of time share a primary residence and a life together as a couple . . . ." Principles, § 6.01. Although contracting is possible, there is no prior registration, and the status of "domestic partner" is a retroactive determination made, like "palimony" determinations among nonmarital cohabitants today, upon breakup, by a court. In addition to proving the status by a normal civil proof standard, two strong presumptions aid the establishment of domestic partnership claims. *Id.* § 6.03 (1)–(5). The fact that one or both parties is (or are) married to another, or they could not marry without violating consanguinity, incest or similar "moral" laws, is no bar to finding that they are also domestic partners. § 6.03(7)(k), *id.* cmnt. d, § 6.01(5), *id.*, cmnt. c & d. Section 6.05 provides that "[d]omestic-partnership property should be divided according to the principles set forth for the division of marital property," and § 6.06 provides that "a domestic partner is entitled to compensatory payments [alimony] on the same basis as a spouse . . . ." In other words, nonmarital domestic partners would enjoy the same property division and alimony rights as married couples. Is this good policy? Why/why not? What benefits flow to the public from this policy? What costs are there to society? Should nonmarital cohabitation be encouraged or rewarded? Should the economic consequences be the same for domestic partners as for spouses? Why not half? Are the expectations of cohabitants the same as those of spouses? Is their investment in the relationship, or their economic interdependence the same as it is for spouses?

3. Practical and Ethical Concerns

If a lawyer has strong (or even moderate) personal or moral objections to nonmarital cohabitation, should he or she represent clients or couples seeking such benefits? Why/why not? If he or she has a strong ideological or personal preference for such relationships, should she or he represent a party seeking to deny or oppose such a claim? Why/why not?

4. Bibliography

American Law Institute, Principles of the Law Family Dissolution: Analysis and Recommendations. Tentative Draft No. 4 § 6.01(1) (April 10, 2000).

Faith Abbot, *No Bomb, No Book*, The Human Life Rev., Winter 1998, at 31, 43.

William G. Axinn & Arland Thornton, *The Relationship Between Cohabitation and Divorce: Selectivity or Causal Influence*, 29 Demography 357 (1992)

Dean M. Busby, *Violence in the Family* in Family Research, a 60-Year Review, 1930–1990 at 361 (Steven G. Bahr, ed., 1991).

David Orgon Coolidge & William C. Duncan, *Beyond Baker: The Case for a Vermont Marriage Amendment*, 25 Vt. L. Rev. 61 (2000).

Development in the Law, Statutory Protection for Gays and Lesbians in Private Employment, 109 Harv. L. Rev. 1625 (1996).

Kris Franklin, *"A Family Like Any Other Family:" Alternative Methods of Defining Family Law*, 18 N.Y.U. Rev. L. & Soc. Change 1027 (1990/1991).

Carey Goldberg, *Vermont Town Meeting Turns Into Same-Sex Unions Forum*, N.Y. Times, March 8, 2000.

Greg Johnson, *Vermont Civil Unions: The New Language of Marriage*, 25 Vt. L. Rev. 15 (2000).

W.D. Manning & D.T. Lichter, *Parental Cohabitation and Children's Economic Well-Being*, 58 J. Marr. & Fam. 998 (1996) as described in 29 Fam. Plng. Persp. 143 (1997).

Raymond C. O'Brien, *Domestic Partnership: Recognition and Responsibility*, 32 San Diego L. Rev. 163 (1995).

David Popenoe & Barbara Dafoe Whitehead, Should We Live Together? What Young Adults Need to Know about Cohabitation before Marriage, A Comprehensive Review of Recent Research, The National Marriage Project: The Next Generation Series <http://www.smartmarriages.com/cohabit.html>

Mark Strasser, *Equal Protection at the Crossroads: On Baker, Common Benefits, and Facial Neutrality*, 42 Ariz. L. Rev. 935 (2000).

Jay D. Teachman, Jeffrey Thomas, & Kathleen Paasch, *Legal Status and the Stability of Coresidential Unions*, 28 Demography 571, 579 (1991)

Vermont House Passes 'Civil Unions' Bill, Church and State Update, May 20, 2000 (Office of Government Information, The Lutheran Church--Missouri Synod), http://WWW.OGI.LCMS.ORG.

Lynn D. Wardle, *Counting the Costs of Civil Unions: Some Potential Detrimental Effects on Family Law*, 11 Widener J. Pub. L. 401 (2002).

Lynn D. Wardle, *Legal Claims to Legitimate Same-Sex Marriage: Efforts to Legitimate a Retreat from Marriage by Redefining Marriage*, 39 So. Tex. L. Rev. 735 (1998).

Lynn D. Wardle, *Deconstructing Family: A Critique of the American Law Institute's "Domestic Partners" Proposal*, 2001 B.Y.U. L. Rev. 1189.

Zheng Wu & T.R. Balakrishnan, *Dissolution of Premarital Cohabitation in Canada*, 32 Demography 521, 526, 529 (1995).

Debbie Zielinski, Note, *Domestic Partnership Benefits: Why Not Offer Them to Same-Sex Partners and Unmarried Opposite Sex Partners*, 13 J.L. & Health 281 (1999).

B. CHOICE OF LAW

1. Background

a. Marriage Recognition in General

"If there is one thing that the people are entitled to expect from their lawmakers, it is rules of law that will enable individuals to tell whether they are married, and, if so, to whom." *Estin v. Estin*, 334 U.S. 541, 553 (1948) (Justice Jackson, dissenting). Rules concerning recognition of marriages contracted in other jurisdicions are not unimportant, given the tremendous mobility of people today. Choice of law problems regarding marriage validity arise in large part because it is not uncommon for Americans to get married in a different state than that in which one or both of the parties reside. It is not uncommon for people to meet, fall in love with, and eventually marry someone who is from a different state or nation (for instance, while attending college, while on vacation, while visiting relatives, or while working temporarily in a different state). Also, with many families spread over many states, it is not uncommon for couples to get married in a state in which neither of them is residing.

Specific marriage recognition legislation is of two types. One type may be called general marriage validity rules and the other type may be called marriage evasion rules. The latter generally refuse to recognize some marriages of residents of the state who are forbidden to marry by the law of that state, who "evade" the marriage prohibitions by going to another state where their marriage is permitted, get married there, then return to the state of former residence to live as a married couple. The other type of marriage recognition laws state principles for recognition of marriages performed in other states regardless of the residence of the parties. Most state marriage recognition statutes reflect the historic American common law rule that a marriage valid where performed is presumed to be valid everywhere, unless it violates the strong public policy of another state where the issue of marriage validity arises.

b. Marriage Recognition in The Restatement, Second, Conflict of Laws

In the absence of a statute addressing the marriage validity issue, courts turn to general principles of conflicts of laws. The Restatement, Second, Conflict of Laws (1971) generally endorses an approach that is harmonious with or incorporates the traditional common law marriage recognition approach, though its expression of it contains the Restatement Second's typical "most significant relationship" shibboleth. The Restatement, Second, contains three choice of law provisions of particular significance to determining the validity of marriages performed out of the state (s) in which an issue of marriage validity arises in court. First, Section Six describes the general principles applicable when no choice of law statute exists.

§6. Choice-of Law Principles
(1) A court, subject to constitutional restrictions, will follow a statutory directive of its own state on choice of law.

The second significant provision of the Restatement, Second, is the "most significant relationship" principle described in Section 283.

§283. Validity of Marriage
(1) The validity of marriage will be determined by the local law of the state which, with respect to the particular issue, has the most significant relationship to the spouses and the marriage under the principles stated in §6.
(2) A marriage which satisfies the requirements of the state where the marriage was

contracted will everywhere be recognized as valid unless it violates the strong public policy of another state which had the most significant relationship to the spouses and the marriage at the time of the marriage.

Commenting upon Section 283(2), the drafters noted:

[T]he general rules [is] that a marriage which meets the requirement of the state where the marriage is contracted will be held valid everywhere. So, for example, a marriage will usually be valid everywhere if it complies with the requirements of the state where it was contracted as to such matters as:
1. the capacity of either party to marry;
2. whether the consent of a parent or guardian is necessary;
3. whether the parties are within one of the forbidden degrees of relationships;
4. physical examination before marriage.

The drafters of this section also suggested that marriage out-of-state to evade local rules prohibiting "the marriage of minors below a certain age" (i.e., minimum age of capacity to marry provisions) may be deemed to violate "the strong public policy" of the homestate, and may not be valid under choice of law principles. *Id.* at § 283, comment *k*. Thus, under the Restatement, Second, if parties go to another state to marry for the purpose of evading local age restrictions, and return to their homestate to live, it is unlikely that even a court in the homestate would invalidate the marriage absent an explicit marriage evasion statute, unless their marriage violates a historically and contemporaneously deeply held, strong public policy.

Finally, when the issue concerns marriage "incidents" rather than marriage validity, the rule is straightforward. Section 284. Incidents of Foreign Marriage provides: "A state usually gives the same incidents to a foreign marriage, which is valid under the principle stated in §283, that it gives to a marriage contracted within its territory."

2. Statutes, Cases and Doctrines

a. *American Airlines v. Mejia*
American Airlines, Inc. v. Libardo Abraham Mejia
766 So.2d 305 (Fla.App. 2000)
FARMER, Judge.

We have in hand a probate order determining that appellee was the spouse of the deceased. This determination arises in the midst of a wrongful death action in federal court in which his claim to be the spouse is being contested by appellant, the defendant in the federal court action. We reverse.

Carmen Cabrejo was a flight attendant for American Airlines (American). In December 1995, American Flight 965 crashed en route from Miami to Cali, Colombia. Carmen, a native of Colombia, died in the crash. At the time of her death she had five living siblings. She also had a "permanent companion," appellee Libardo Mejia. Claiming that he was Cabrejo's "common-law" husband, Libardo filed the wrongful death action in the United States District Court for the Southern District of Florida against American. He alleged that, as Carmen's common-law husband, he was her "surviving spouse" under the Florida Wrongful Death Act (WDA). American filed a motion for partial summary judgment on all of Libardo's claims, arguing that he was not Carmen's spouse under Colombian law and also within the meaning of WDA. The federal court stayed the action. Meanwhile Libardo filed the present probate proceeding, seeking a determination that he is Carmen's surviving spouse.

Libardo acknowledged that he and Carmen never participated in a formal, civil or religious ceremony of marriage. He argued, however, that they were entitled under Colombian law to claim the status of "Union Marital de Hecho " (union). This status, he contends, equates with a common law marriage in the United States and thus makes him Carmen's surviving spouse under Florida law. Libardo adduced evidence that he and Carmen lived together, owned seven properties together, and had reciprocal wills--all in Colombia.

American argued that an union should be distinguished from formal and common law marriages. It pointed out that Colombia itself treats a formal marriage under its law differently from the informal union enjoyed by Carmen and Libardo, and that under its law an union is not considered a marriage at all, and its partners are not considered spouses. Alternatively, American argued that even if the union could be recognized as a marriage under Florida law, Carmen and Libardo's union would then be bigamous because she was still formally married to another man under Colombian law. [FN3. Carmen went through a marriage ceremony with Elias Gomez in Panama in 1978. But nine years earlier Gomez had been married to a woman still living, from whom he had not been divorced. Carmen and Gomez ultimately separated, and she then married Humberto Gonzalez, who died in 1985. Her union with Libardo came still later.] The trial judge found as a matter of law that an union "is a marriage which a Florida Court must recognize as a valid marriage." We disagree. [FN4. The trial judge also found as a factual matter that Carmen's earlier marriage to Gomez was null and void because Gomez was still married when they celebrated their marriage. We have no basis to disturb his finding in this regard, which rests on competent substantial evidence. Our disagreement with the trial court is only with his determination that an union is a marriage.]

We begin with the proposition that the meaning and effect of the law of a foreign nation is a question of law as to which our review is de novo. [FN5. We also recognize the basic principle that a valid marriage according to the law of a foreign nation will be recognized as such in the United States. See generally Montano v. Montano, 520 So.2d 52, 52-53 (Fla. 3d DCA 1988). Moreover, although Florida no longer recognizes the validity of common law marriages contracted in this state after 1968, it will respect a common law marriage validly created in a jurisdiction recognizing such marriages. See § 741.211, Fla. Stat. (1999); and Anderson v. Anderson, 577 So.2d 658, 660 (Fla. 1st DCA 1991).] *** We also follow the definitions in the controlling Florida statute as to what constitutes a marriage and who will be considered a spouse. Section 741.212 provides as follows:

For purposes of interpreting any state statute or rule, the term 'marriage' means only a legal union between one man and one woman as husband and wife, and the term 'spouse' applies only to a member of such a union.

§ 741.212(3), Fla. Stat. (1999). By its clear text this definition controls determinations of marriage and the related question of who is a spouse when the question arises under the Florida Probate Code and WDA. It applies to "any state statute." [e.s.] Under the plain meaning of this text, the union of Carmen and Libardo will be considered a marriage in Florida if it constitutes "a legal union between one man and one woman as husband and wife " [e.s.] under Colombian law; and conversely Libardo will be deemed a spouse of Carmen only if their union is a marriage.

Both sides offered the relevant Colombian law, along with translations and exegeses by experts in its jurisprudence. We have examined these materials de novo. It is apparent upon such a study that the explanation of Libardo's expert does not materially contradict the explanation offered by American's on the essential issue--i.e., whether an union is a marriage under Colombian law and thus whether Libardo is therefore a spouse.

The law of Columbia distinguishes between marriage and union marital de hecho. Under its positive law, marriage is "a solemn contract by which a man and a woman join for the purpose of living together...." Colombian Civil Code (CCC), Art. 113. A marriage is created "by the free and mutual consent of the contracting parties, declared before a legally competent official, in the manner and with the solemnities and requirements established by this Code...." CCC Art. 115. A contract is solemn when it "is subject to adherence with certain special formalities, so that without them there would be no resulting civil effect." CCC Art. 1.500. A civil marriage is terminated by the death of a spouse or by a legally decreed divorce. CCC Art. 152. Children born of a marriage are considered legitimate, while a child born to permanent companions is considered extramarital, and the father must formally and voluntarily recognize the child as his. Affidavit of Juan Luis Moreno Quijano, at 19.

The partners to a marriage acquire the civil status of "spouse," which entails certain rights and obligations. Decree No. 1260 of 1970. Spouses are obligated to be faithful and assist one another, are entitled to joint control of their household, and must live together in a residence established for their home. CCC Art. 176, 177, 178, 179. Significantly for our purposes, a married spouse may not marry another person. CCC Art. 260. Spouses have the right of support. CCC Art. 411. Through their marriage, they create an estate known as a "conjugal society," which itself may be dissolved only by death, dissolution of marriage, a legal separation decreed by law, a separation of assets by legal decree, or by a public document executed before a notary. CCC Art. 180. Each spouse has the right of inheritance from the other. CCC Art. 1.046 and 1.047. A needy surviving spouse has a right to a "conjugal share" from the separate estate of the deceased spouse.*   Under Colombian law, an union is "the union between a man and a woman, who although unmarried [e.s.] create a permanent and singular life in common ..." Art. 1, Law 54 of 1990. The partners who create an union become "permanent companions to each other." Id. No formalities are necessary to establish an union, the fact of which may be demonstrated by the ordinary rules of evidence. Art. 4, Law 54 of 1990. An union is dissolved by, among other things, the simple fact of one of the permanent companions marrying another person. Art. 5(b), Law 54 of 1990. The effect of establishing an union is to create a presumptive "patrimonial society" between the companions upon the condition that the union has existed for not less than 2 years. Art. 2, Law 54 of 1990. Unlike a surviving spouse of a marriage, a surviving permanent companion has no right of inheritance in the personal estate of the deceased companion. Arts. 5-6, Law 54 of 1990.

As we have seen, the union marital de hecho was codified by Law 54 of 1990. The Colombian Constitutional Court has explained the historical background of Law 54 of 1990 as follows:

The Civil Code provides for the establishment of conjugal society solely by the mere fact of matrimony.... This is a society of community property.... Contrary to above, the [Civil] Code and the laws prior to Law 54 of 1990 did not have any similar provisions with respect to concubinage. [FN7. The Colombian court defined concubinage as "the result of ostensible and permanent sexual relations between a man and a woman who are not married to each other and, as such, it is a de facto situation." Judgment C-239 of May 1994.] This is logical if one takes into account the prevailing moral climate at the time that the [Civil] Code of Colombia was adopted, and those circumstances explain the unjust legal regulations that were especially damaging to women and to biological or extra-matrimonial children.

By the middle of this century, the jurisprudence of the Supreme Court of Justice was entrusted with beginning the process of establishing justice in the case of free unions and on behalf of women, who are generally the weaker half of the relationship, due to financial, cultural or social factors in general....

In a country where approximately half of the unions are de facto unions, it was natural that the laws that elevated the status of married women and biological children would motivate the courts to come to the defense of the concubine.

...

[C]oncubinage does not generate, as does matrimony, a society of assets that the law hastens to recognize and regulate. However, based on equity, it is [submitted] that a conjunction of interests by the lovers, whether deliberate or not, and a lengthy common work endeavor could constitute a de facto society, which is almost always a product of circumstance more than of reasoned and voluntary activity....

...

[I]t is evident that the provisions intended to prevent the coexistence of two societies of community property pursuant to general title, one resulting from matrimony and the other from de facto marital union, are based on the rule established by ... Article 2082 of the Civil Code [stating] 'Likewise, all societies of community property pursuant to general title are prohibited except between spouses. [e.s.]

Judgment C-239 of May 1994.
        Our explication of these differences between a marriage and an union under Colombian law and this historical background surely demonstrate of their own force why the Colombian union under Law 54 of 1990 cannot be considered a marriage for purposes of Florida law, especially under section 741.212(3). The principal difference for our purposes is that marriage is a solemn contract dissoluble only by death or divorce, while an union is an informal circumstance that may be ended simply by one of the permanent companions marrying someone else. The children born of marriage need no recognition to be deemed legitimate, while the children born during an union are deemed extramarital and must be formally recognized by their father.
        As the Colombian Constitutional Court itself explained about the union under Law 54 of 1990:

There is an immense gap between this and the establishment of the same rights and obligations that exist between spouses. Suffice it to bear in mind that the mere decision of one of its members is sufficient to put an end to a de facto marital union, something that does not occur in matrimony.
        In summary, to maintain that between permanent companions there exists a relationship identical to that which binds spouses is an assertion that would not hold up to the slightest scrutiny, as it is tantamount to claiming that a true matrimony could be celebrated outside the jurisdiction of the State, and that, at the same time, [the State] could impose regulations that would go against [the de facto union's] essential nature, which is nothing more than that of being a free union." [emphasis supplied]

Judgment C-239 (May 1994).
        Just two years after that opinion, the Constitutional Court again addressed the subject and reaffirmed the same conclusion:

The petitioner has requested that the Constitutional Court reform a series of [laws] relative to spouses, the conjugal society, the conjugal portion, etc., and that [these laws] should also include permanent companions.
        [The petitioner] bases his [contentions] on [the argument] that, in his opinion, the Constitution established equality between matrimony and free union. Thereby, attributing rights or obligations to spouses that are not established for permanent companions, implies discrimination due to family origin, prohibited under [the Constitution].
        It is true that Article 42 of the Constitution recognized that the family is formed 'by natural or legal ties, by the free determination of a man and a woman to contract matrimony or by the responsible decision to form it.' However, to maintain based on the above that the Constitution established equality between matrimony and free union is a major leap. Matrimony is different from free union and, therefore, the legal status of spouses and permanent companions is also different." [emphasis supplied]

Judgment No. C-174/95.
        Accordingly, we hold that the union between Carmen and Libardo was not "a legal union between

one man and one woman as husband and wife " within the meaning of Florida law, and therefore they were not the spouses of one another.

REVERSED.

KLEIN and STEVENSON, JJ., concur.

b. Review *In re May's Estate* in Chapter 4

c. Notes and Questions

1) *Mejia* and *May's Estate* Questions

What choice of law rule was applied in *Mejia*? Did the public policy exception even come into play in that case? Is the choice of law rule regarding recognition of nonmarital domestic relationships the same as the rule for marriage recognition? Why/why not? Is it possible for a state with a law forbidding recognition of same-sex marriage to recognize a same-sex domestic partnership from another state? If S-2 does not authorize domestic partnership, is it likely to recognize a domestic partnership created in S-1? Why/why not? What rule for proof of foreign law was applied in *Mejia*?

How does marriage recognition in the rule applied by the majority in *May's Estate* compare with the rule proposed by the Restatement, Second? Is there a difference between the marriage recognition rule applied by the majority in *May's Estate* and that suggested by the dissent?

2) *Catalono v. Catalono* hypothetical

After Fred's first wife died in Connecticut where they had lived together and raised their children, Fred went to Italy to visit some of his relatives. While there, he married his niece, Maria. The marriage was valid under Italian law (under special dispensation), but uncle-niece marriages are prohibited under Connecticut law. Fred returned to Connecticut, where Maria later joined him, they lived together, and had a child. Then Fred died, and Maria petitioned for a widow's allowance out of Fred's pending estate. Her petition was opposed by the children from Fred's first marriage who argued that Maria was not their father's widow because her marriage to Fred violated Connecticut's consanguinity restriction and the Marriage Evasion Act, which validates foreign marriages of Connecticut citizens "provided each party would have legal capacity to contract such marriage in this state." How should the court rule on Maria's petition, and why? *See* State Nonrecognition (of Same-Sex Marriage) Statutes (DOMAs), *infra*.

3) Favor Validitatis

An underlying policy value that can be seen in many marriage recognition cases is the premise or presumption *favor validitatis* -- that is, the law favors marriage validity. Thus, when other factors are balanced, the benefit of the doubt usually falls to upholding the validity of the marriage. Even when the other factors are not in equipoise, courts tend to start with the presumption that the marriage should be upheld as valid unless the law or public policy compell the invalidation of the marriage. Why didn't the court in Mejia apply the *favor validitatis* presumption?

4) State Nonrecognition (of Same-Sex Marriage) Statutes (DOMAs)

Shortly after the Hawaii Supreme Court ruled that the state might be required by its interpretation of the Hawaii Constitution to legalize same-sex marriage there was an explosion of law review articles and notes arguing that if any state legalized same-sex marriage all states would have to recognize as valid marriages of same-sex couples that had been solemnized in the state that allowed same-sex marriage, either as a matter of existing conflicts rules or as required by the Full Faith and Credit Clause (art. IV., cl. 1) of the U.S. Constitution. In response, lawmakers in several states enacted laws clarifying that same-sex marriages would not be recognized in the state, even if performed in another jurisdiction where same-sex marriage was valid. In 1996 Congress enacted the Defense of Marriage Act providing that for purposes of federal law, "marriage" and marital terms do not include same-sex unions, 1 U.S.C. §7, and further providing that as a matter of Congress' power to regulate full faith and credit, no state is required to recognize same-sex marriage as valid unless it chooses to do so (any state may choose to do so, but no state is compelled to do so as a matter of federal full faith and credit law). 28 U.S. C. § 1638 C. Advocates of same-sex marriage who had envisioned using the Full Faith and Credit Clause (U.S. Constitution, Article IV) to compel all states to recognize same-sex marriages if any state allowed them, criticized DOMA unconstitutional, intolerant, and unnecessary. Nonetheless, by June 2006 at least than forty-three states had enacted state DOMA laws, and twenty had constitutional provisions, or both, effectively barring domestic and interjurisdictional recognition of same-sex marriages in the state. See Marriage Law Project Homepage <http://marriagelaw.cua.edu>.

5) Domestic Partnership Recognition

About two-thirds of the couples registering "Civil Unions" in Vermont in the first year were from out of state. Are other states constitutionally required to recognize Vermont Civil Unions? Why/why not? If not, as a matter of policy should they do so? Why/why not? How might these statutes be relevant to questions about recognition of domestic partnership from other jurisdictions? The Nebraska law explicitly forbids recognition of same-sex marriages, domestic partnerships, and civil unions. Is that constitutional? Good policy? Why/why not? See Goldberg, infra. Suppose a Georgia court custody decree prohibited Mother from having overnight visitation as long as her lesbian partner was in her home. Mother and lesbian partner go to Vermont and register a "civil union." Mother returns to Georgia and files a motion asking the court to rescind the visitation restriction arguing that the Vermont civil union registration should be given full faith and credit. How should the court rule, and why? See Burns v. Burns, 560 S.E.2d 47 (Ga. App. 2002) (ex-wife who allowed lesbian partner to sleep over when child was visiting violated visitation order because Georgia does not recognize their civil union). If a gay couple from New York register a civil union in Vermont, and return to New York where one of them thereafter dies, allegedly as the result of medical mistakes, may the other bring a wrongful death action in New York under the law allowing surviving spouses to bring such actions because Vermont treats civil unions the same as spouses? See Langan v. St. Vincent's Hosp., 802 N.Y.S.2d 476 (App. Div. 2005), (discussed in Chapter 1, supra), (rejecting the claim because the New York wrongful death law controlled, reversing lower court which allowed the claim under interstate recognition principles).

3. Practical and Ethical Concerns

a. Public policy

The key to the interjurisdictional recognition of same-sex domestic partnerships is the "public policy" or *ordre public* exception to the general presumption of validity of the foreign relationship. Should there be such an exception? Should it be construed broadly or narrowly? Should it matter whether the legal status or rights in question are created by registration or adjudication?

b. Counseling Clients

If an attorney in Nebraska, which has a strong policy against recognizing same-sex marriages, domestic partnerships, or civil unions, is consulted by two men who express their desire to marry or enter into a marriage-like union and she tells them about the Civil Unions available in Vermont, and the couple go to Vermont, register a Civil Union, then return to Nebraska expecting to enjoy the same benefits in Nebraska they would enjoy if they had remained in Vermont, and they are surprised and disappointed to learn that Nebraska will not recognize their status or extend those benefits, has the attorney committed malpractice or violated any ethical obligation? Does the couple have any claim against the attorney? Why/why not?

4. Bibliography

Patrick J. Borchers, Baker v. General Moters: *Implications for Interjurisdictional Recognition of Non-Traditonal Marriages,* 32 Creighton L. Rev. 147 (1998).

Clive, Eric M., "Marriage: An unnecessary Legal Concept?" In *Marriage and Cohabitation in Contemporary Societies, Areas of Legal, Social and Ethical Change,* edited by John M. Eekelaar & Sanford N. Katz, 71–81. Toronto: Butterworths, 1980 (hereinafter "Cohabitation").

David Orgon Coolidge & William C. Duncan, *Definition or Discrimination? State Marriage Recognition Statues in the "Same-Sex Marriage" Debate,* 32 Creighton L. Rev. 3 (1998).

Barbara J. Cox, *Same-Sex Marriage and Choice of Law: If We Marry in Hawaii, Are We Still Married When We Return Home?,* 1994 Wis. L. Rev. 1033, 1062–1118 (1994).

Ruth Deech, "The Case Against Legal Recognition of Cohabitation." *Id.* at 300–312.

Mary Ann Glendon, *The New Marriage and the New Property.* Toronto: Butterworths, 1981.

Carey Goldberg, *Gays and Lesbians Head for Vermont to Make It Legal, but How Legal Is It?,* N.Y.Times, June 23, 2000.

L. Lynn Hogue, *State Common-Law Choice of Law Doctrine and Same-Sex Marriage: How Will States Enforce the Public Policy Exception,* 32 Creighton L. Rev. 29 (1998).

William N., Eksridge, Jr., "A History of Same-Sex Marriage." *Virginia Law Review* 79 (1993) 1419.

Robert P. George and Gerard V. Bradley, "Marriage and the Liberal Imagination." *Georgetown Law Journal* 84 (1996): 301–320.

Bruce C. Hafen, "The Constitutional Status of Marriage, Kinship, and Sexual Privacy--Balancing the Individual and Social Interests." *Michigan Law Review* 81 (1983) 463–574.

Richard S. Myers, *Same-Sex "Marriage" and the Public Policy Exception,* 32 Creighton L. Rev. 45 (1998).

Linda J. Silberman, *Can the Island of Hawaii Bind the World? A Comment on Same-Sex Marriage and Federalism Values,* 16 Quinnipiac L. Rev. 191, 192–203 (1996).

Mark Strasser, *DOMA and the Two Faces of Federalism,* 32 Creighton L. Rev. 457 (1998).

Lynn D. Wardle, *Rethinking Marital Age Restrictions,* 22 J. Fam. L. 1 (1983).

Lynn D. Wardle, Williams v. North Carolina, *Divorce Recognition, and Same-Sex Marriage Recogniton,* 32 Creighton L. Rev. 187 (1998).

Walter Otto Weyrauch, "Metamorphoses of Marriage: Formal and Informal Marriage in the United States," in Cohabitation at 265–281.

C. INTERNATIONAL AND COMPARATIVE MARRIAGE REGULATION

1. Background

a. International Developments re: Domestic Partnership

In 1989, Denmark became the first nation to give legal status to same-sex couples by creating domestic partnerships, extending to such relationships essentially all of the economic and many of the noneconomic legal incidents of marriage. Since then approximately two dozen other nations (of the 191 independent nations in the U.N.) have also recognized domestic partnerships, under a variety of labels. *See* Blumberg, *infra* (listing at least 18 nations with some form of domestic partnership in 2004). The extent of legal recognition and benefits provided varies tremendously, from protection of an interest in realty acquired during the relationship, to protection of health care decision-making, to provision of a few selected economic benefits, to marriage-equivalent benefits. However, with the exception of Scandinavia and a few other nations, most of these "domestic partnership" laws are quite modest. Many of the domestic partnership laws grant only nominal status and few real marital benefits to same-sex couples. In 2006, a report prepared by a committee of the French Assembly emphasized the differences between such relationships and marriage and strongly recommended against equivalent legal benefits and status.

2. Statutes, Cases and Doctrines

a. International Marriage Recognition Rules

Outside the United States, most countries distinguish between marriage *formalities* and marriage *essentials* (often called *capacity* in choice of law literature) for purposes of marriage recognition. The predominant rule regarding marriage formalities is to apply the law of the place where the marriage was celebrated. "[T]here is no rule more firmly established in private international law than that which applies the maxim *locus regit actum* to the formalities of a marriage." P.M. North and J.J. Fawcett, Cheshire and North, Private International Law 558 (London: Butterworths, 11th ed. 1987). Exceptions to this *lex loci celebrationis* rule regarding marriage formalities include consular marriages and marriages by members of the military serving abroad in some circumstances, and to validate marriages that would be invalid under the formalities law of the place of celebration, reference sometimes is made either to personal law, or *renvoi* (that is, the forum applies the law referred to by the choice of law rules of the place of celebration).

There are two dominant choice of law systems widely used for international marriage recognition regarding marriage essentials. One is the rule of *personal law* (the law that defines the personal status of the parties). The other is the rule of *lex loci celebrationis* (the law of the place of celebration).

The *personal law* system includes two different rules for determining personal law: *lex patriae* (the law of one's nationality) and *lex domicilii* (the law of one's domicile). *Lex patriae*, which applies the law of the nationality of the couple, is the traditional choice of law rule for marriage recognition in most of Continental Europe, as well as in most Arab countries with western legal systems. The other personal law regime looks to the law of the domicile (*lex domicilii*). This is the choice of law rule for marriage recognition in the

United Kingdom, many commonwealth countries, and some Latin American countries. When the marriage involved parties of different nationalities or domiciles, the courts traditionally gave preference to the husband's personal law on the notion that the husband is the head of the family. Today, it is likely that the law of both parties might be consulted or if one of the parties is a resident of the forum state, forum law would be given priority. *Favor validitatis* may also influence the choice of law when the parties are from different jurisdictions.

The other major system for deciding marriage validity with reference to *essentials* is the *lex loci celebrationis* rule. States that follow that regime apply the law of the place of celebration to essentials as well as to formalities in determining marriage validity. Countries that follow *lex loci celebrationis* today include the United States, several Latin American countries, and Scandinavian countries *inter se*. In those states, a marriage that is valid under the law of the place of celebration is generally valid in the forum also. Evasive marriages can be a significant problem in *lex loci celebrationis* states, because the restrictive policies of the state with greatest interest in regulating marriage (usually the state of domicile or nationality) may be evaded by the simple expedient of crossing a border to celebrate the marriage, and then returning to the restrictive state to live. Thus, *lex loci celebrationis* countries generally assert the right to refuse to apply the law of the place of celebration to evasive marriages of their own citizens. States in the United States, however, generally are very tolerant of evasive marriages today. The *lex loci celebrationis* rule (like the personal law rule) is subject to the *ordre public* exception in choice of law. That is, if a strong public policy of the forum state is violated, a marriage valid where performed will not be recognized even in a state that generally follows the *lex loci celebrationis* rule.

b. Recognition Treaties and International Agreements

There have been numerous bilateral treaties, conventions, and regional agreements addressing various aspects of international marriage recognition. Lennart Pålsson, *Marriage in Comparative Conflict of Laws: Substantive Conditions* (1972). Several *multilateral* documents and agreements dealing with marriage recognition or regulation purport to be worldwide in scope. For example, the Universal Declaration of Human Rights declares that all "men and women of full age, without any limitation due to race, nationality or religion, have the right to marry . . . ." The Convention on Consent to Marriage, Minimum Age for Marriage and Registration of Marriages, provides that "no marriage shall be legally entered into without the full and free consent of both parties," and strives to eliminate child marriages. The International Convention on the Elimination of All Forms of Racial Discrimination, promulgated by the United Nations in 1966, requires signers to guarantee all persons, regardless of race, color, national origin, and ethnicity "the right to marriage and choice of spouse." The International Covenant on Civil and Political Rights, establishes the right to marry and the prohibition of discrimination set out in the Universal Declaration.

Several notable *multilateral* conventions provide *regional* marriage recognition rules, such as the 1889 and 1940 Montevideo Treaties on International Civil Law, which are influential in Latin America, which reportedly adopt the general principle of *lex loci celebrationis* to determine marriage validity. The 1928 Code of Private International Law (Bustamante Code), approved by at least fifteen Latin American nations, provides that all substantive marriage issues are governed by the personal law of the parties, and each state is free to determine whether domicile or nationality (or other criteria) provides the personal law. The American Convention on Human Rights appears to reinforce the choice of law rule generally prevailing in Latin America that the law of the place of celebration governs all questions concerning marriage celebration and validity. The Scandinavian Convention Containing Provisions in the Field of Private International Law Relating to Marriage, Adoption and Guardianship (Denmark, Finland, Iceland, Norway, and Sweden), provides generally that *lex loci celebrationis* governs capacity to marry when at least one of the parties to a marriage is a habitual resident of that place, unless the party requests application of the *lex patriae*. The European Convention for the Protection of Human Rights and Fundamental Freedoms obligates member states to guarantee the right to marry without religious obstacle. The Paris Convention to Facilitate the Celebration of Marriages Abroad authorizes the state of celebration to grant a dispensation from marriage impediments based on the personal law of a habitual resident of the state of celebration. The Luxembourg (C.I.E.C.) Convention on the Recognition of Decisions Concerning Marital Relations provides that when a divorce or annulment has been recognized in a contracting state, it may not refuse to allow a party to remarry on the ground that some other state (presumably the state of nationality or domicile of the applicant) would not recognize the divorce or annulment. The 1976 Hague Convention on Celebration and Recognition of the Validity of Marriages provides, generally, a *lex loci celebrationis* rule for both the formal requirements as well as the substantive validity of the marriage, but only six states ratified it.

3. Practical and Ethical Concerns

Are the risks of nonrecognition greater in the international context or in the interstate context? Why? Would the answer to the question in B.3., *supra* be any different if the attorney had referred the couple to the Netherlands to get married, or to Denmark to register a domestic partnership? Why/why not? If a jurisdiction allows same-sex couples to register as domestic partners, must it also permit heterosexual couples to register as domestic partners? *See Irizarry v. Board of Education of the City of Chicago*, 251 F.3d 0604 (7th Cir. 2001)

4. Bibliography

Grace Ganz Blumberg, *Legal Recognition of Same-Sex Conjugal Relationships: The 2003 California Domestic Partners Rights and Responsibilities Act in Comparative Civil Rights and Family Law Perspective,* 51 U.C.L.A. L. Rev. 1555 (2004).

Carey Goldberg, *Gays and Lesbians Head for Vermont to Make It Legal, but How Legal Is It?*, N.Y. Times, June 23, 2000.

D. Marianne Blair & Merle H. Weiner, Family Law in the World Community (2003).

Barbara Stark, International Family Law: An Introduction (2005).

Lynn D. Wardle, *International Marriage and Divorce Regulation and Recognition,* 29 Fam. L. Q. 497 (1995).

Lynn D. Wardle, *International Marriage Recognition: A World Dilemma,* in Families Across Frontiers 75–88 (Nigel Lowe & Gillian Douglas, eds., 1996).

PART III
THE CREATION OF PARENT-CHILD RELATIONS

CHAPTER 9

Constitutional Rights Concerning Procreation and Parentage

A. CONSTITUTIONAL RIGHTS CONCERNING PROCREATION AND PARENTAGE

1. Background

a. Constitutional Rights Concerning Procreation

The Constitution says nothing about procreation, nor does any amendment. In the absence of textual protection, extraordinary protection as a fundamental right generally must be deeply rooted in the traditions and history of our people, or essential to the concept of ordered liberty. The Supreme Court has interpreted various provisions and penumbras of the Constitution as protecting certain facets of parental procreation as fundamental constitutional rights. (Interestingly, however, most of the cases have dealt with protecting the right of potential parents *to avoid* becoming parents, rather than the right to become parents. Most of those cases are reviewed in Chapter 15, *infra*.)

However, there have been a few significant cases in which the Court has protected the right to procreate. For instance, *Skinner v. Oklahoma*, 316 U.S. 535 (1942), involved an Oklahoma law which provided for the involuntary sterilization of any person convicted for a third time of a felony involving moral turpitude. After Mr. Skinner had been convicted of three felonies (including one conviction for stealing chickens) an Oklahoma court ordered that a vasectomy be performed on Mr. Skinner. The United States Supreme Court reversed that order, holding that it violated the equal protection clause of the Constitution. Justice Douglas, writing for the Court, noted that if the case had involved mere classifications and no important federal right, the Court would let the law and order stand. However, the case implicated fundamental rights. "We are dealing here with legislation which involves one of the basic civil rights of man. Marriage and procreation are fundamental to the very existence and survival of the race." 316 U.S. at 541. Thus, *Skinner* directly linked the constitutional right of procreation to marriage.

Similarly, in *Zablocki v. Redhail*, 434 U.S. 374 (1978), the Court declared a Wisconsin law unconstitutional that required noncustodial parents under child support orders to get a court order before they could obtain a marriage license, and the court order could only be given upon proof that the children were not and were unlikely to become welfare charges. Mr. Redhail had fathered a child out of wedlock and a paternity order imposing a child support obligation had been entered against him, but he had been unemployed and paid no child support. When he sought a marriage license in order to marry another woman (who was pregnant with his child), the Milwaukee County Clerk (Zablocki) denied the marriage license because Mr. Redhail had not obtained the necessary judicial order. Mr. Redhail then filed a class action suit in federal court alleging that the law denied him due process and equal protection of the law. A three-judge district court agreed that the statute infringed upon a fundamental right to marry and did not involve any compelling state interest, and therefore violated equal protection. The U.S. Supreme Court affirmed. The majority opinion noted that marriage is closely linked with traditional family relations such as "procreation, childbirth, child rearing, and family relationships." 434 U.S. at 386. [Indeed, the Court acknowledged that sexual intercourse outside of marriage was forbidden, and marriage was "the only relationship in which the State . . . allows sexual relations legally to take place." *Id.*]

b. Constitutional Rights Concerning Parentage

The Supreme Court has decided many cases concerning or mentioning certain aspects of parenting that are constitutionally protected. Most of those cases deal with intrusions upon parental child rearing decisions, and they are discussed in Chapter 21, *infra*. However, the Court has also decided a few cases dealing with either the creation of or termination of paternity or parental status. In several cases, the Court has held that states may not deprive parents of their parental rights in judicial proceedings without observing substantial procedural protections. For instance, in *Santosky v. Kramer*, 455 U.S. 745 (1982), the court held that parental rights could not be terminated without adherence to the "clear and convincing" standard of proof. Likewise, in *Stanley v. Illinois*, 405 U.S. 645 (1972), printed below, the Court held that an unwed father of children whose mother had died could not be deprived of custody of the children by simply relying on a presumption that unwed fathers were unfit. In *Caban v. Mohammed*, 441 U.S. 380 (1978), the Court held that the Constitution provides fathers as well as mothers with the same type of hearing and adoption veto rights over an illegitimate child, when the father had lived with and raised the child before terminating his rights. *See further Quillion v. Walcott*, 434 U.S. 246 (1978); and *Lehr v. Robertson*, 463 U.S. 248 (1983); all three cases are discussed in Ch. 12 (concerning termination of parental rights in connection with adoption). These cases are clearly connected to the parents' rights' cases discussed in Chapters 2 and 21. Strong deference to parental rights is one principle distinguishing American law from European family law, which is more paternalistic.

The Court also has decided at least two significant cases concerning a law restricting the assertion of a claim for parentage. *Michael H. v. Gerald D.*, 491 U.S. 110 (1989), printed below, upheld a California statute that barred the adulterous father of a child born of an extramarital liaison with a married woman the right to assert a parentage claim over the objection of the mother and her husband. The Court in *Little v. Streater*, 452 U.S. 1 (1981), ruled that in at least some cases, it is a denial of due process for the state asserting a paternity claim against an indigent man to refuse to provide him with scientific blood tests usable as evidence of paternity for free.

2. Statutes, Cases, Doctrines

a. *Stanley v. Illinois*

Peter Stanley, Sr. v. State of Illinois
405 U.S. 645 (1972)

Mr. JUSTICE WHITE delivered the opinion of the Court.

Joan Stanley lived with Peter Stanley intermittently for 18 years, during which time they had three children. [FN1 Uncontradicted testimony of Peter Stanley, App. 22] When Joan Stanley died, Peter Stanley lost not only her but also his children. Under Illinois law, the children of unwed fathers become wards of the State upon the death of the mother. Accordingly, upon Joan Stanley's death, in a dependency proceeding instituted by the State of Illinois, Stanley's children [FN2 Only two children are involved in this litigation.] were declared wards of the State and placed with court-appointed guardians. Stanley appealed, claiming that he had never been shown to be an unfit parent and that since married fathers and unwed mothers could not be deprived of their children without such a showing, he had been deprived of the equal protection of the laws guaranteed him by the Fourteenth Amendment. The Illinois Supreme Court accepted the fact that Stanley's own unfitness had not been established but rejected the equal protection claim, holding that Stanley could properly be separated from his children upon proof of the single fact that he and the dead mother had not been married. Stanley's actual fitness as a father was irrelevant. *

Stanley presses his equal protection claim here. The State continues to respond that unwed fathers are presumed unfit to raise their children and that it is unnecessary to hold individualized hearings to determine whether particular fathers are in fact unfit parents before they are separated from their children. We granted certiorari * to determine whether this method of procedure by presumption could be allowed to stand in light of the fact that Illinois allows married fathers--whether divorced, widowed, or separated--and mothers--even if unwed--the benefit of the presumption that they are fit to raise their children.

I

At the outset we reject any suggestion that we need not consider the propriety of the dependency proceeding that separated the Stanleys because Stanley might be able to regain custody of his children as a guardian or through adoption proceedings. The suggestion is that if Stanley has been treated differently from other parents, the difference is immaterial and not legally cognizable for the purposes of the Fourteenth Amendment. This Court has not, however, embraced the general proposition that a wrong may be done if it can be undone. * Surely, in the case before us, if there is delay between the doing and the undoing petitioner suffers from the deprivation of his children, and the children suffer from uncertainty and dislocation.

It is clear, moreover, that Stanley does not have the means at hand promptly to erase the adverse consequences of the proceeding in the course of which his children were declared wards of the State. It is first urged that Stanley could act to adopt his children. But under Illinois law, Stanley is treated not as a parent but as a stranger to his children, and the dependency proceeding has gone forward on the presumption that he is unfit to exercise parental rights. Insofar as we are informed, Illinois law affords him no priority in adoption proceedings. It would be his burden to establish not only that he would be a suitable parent but also that he would be the most suitable of all who might want custody of the children. Neither can we ignore that in the proceedings from which this action developed, the 'probation officer,' see App. 17, the assistant state's attorney, *see id.*, at 29--30, and the judge charged with the case, see *id.*, at 16--18, 23, made it apparent that Stanley, unmarried and impecunious as he is, could not now expect to profit from adoption proceedings. The Illinois Supreme Court apparently recognized some or all of these considerations, because it did not suggest that Stanley's case was undercut by his failure to petition for adoption.

Before us, the State focuses on Stanley's failure to petition for 'custody and control'--the second route by which, it is urged, he might regain authority for his children. Passing the obvious issue whether it would be futile or burdensome for an unmarried father--without funds and already once presumed unfit--to petition for custody, this suggestion overlooks the fact that legal custody is not parenthood or adoption. A person appointed guardian in an aciion for custody and control is subject to removal at any time without such cause as must be shown in a neglect proceeding against a parent. Ill.Rev.Stat., c. 37, s 705--8. He may not take the children out of the jurisdiction without the court's approval. He may be required to report to the court as to his disposition of the children's affairs. * Obviously then, even if Stanley were a mere step away from 'custody and control,' to give an unwed father only 'custody and control' would still be to leave him seriously prejudiced by reason of his status.

We must therefore examine the question that Illinois would have us avoid: Is a presumption that distinguishes and burdens all unwed fathers constitutionally repugnant? We conclude that, as a matter of due process of law, Stanley was entitled to a hearing on his fitness as a parent before his children were taken from him and that, by denying him a hearing and extending it to all other parents whose custody of their children is challenged, the State denied Stanley the equal protection of the laws guaranteed by the Fourteenth Amendment.

II

Illinois has two principal methods of removing nondelinquent children from the homes of their parents. In a dependency proceeding it may demonstrate that the children are wards of the State because they have no surviving parent or guardian. * In a neglect proceeding it may show that children should be wards of the State because the present parent(s) or guardian does not provide suitable care.
*

The State's right--indeed, duty--to protect minor children through a judicial determination of their interests in a neglect proceeding is not challenged here. Rather, we are faced with a dependency statute that empowers state officials to circumvent neglect proceedings on the theory that an unwed father is not a 'parent' whose existing relationship with his children must be considered. [FN4 Even while refusing to label him a 'legal parent,' the State does not deny that Stanley has a special interest in the outcome of these proceedings. It is undisputed that he is the father of these children, that he lived with the two children whose custody is challenged all their lives, and that he has supported them.] 'Parents,' says the State, 'means the father and mother of a legitimate child, or the survivor of them, or the natural mother of an illegitimate child, and includes any adoptive parent, * but the term does not include unwed fathers.

Under Illinois law, therefore, while the children of all parents can be taken from them in neglect proceedings, that is only after notice, hearing, and proof of such unfitness as a parent as amounts to neglect, an unwed father is uniquely subject to the more simplistic dependency proceeding. By use of this proceeding, the State, on showing that the father was not married to the mother, need not prove unfitness in fact, because it is presumed at law. Thus, the unwed father's claim of parental qualification is avoided as 'irrelevant.'

In considering this procedure under the Due Process Clause, we recognize, as we have in other cases, that due process of law does not require a hearing 'in every conceivable case of government impairment of private interest.' Cafeteria and Restaurant Workers Union etc. v. McElroy* That case explained that '(t)he very nature of due process negates any concept of inflexible procedures universally applicable to every imaginable situation' and firmly established that 'what procedures due process may require under any given set of circumstances must begin with a determination of the precise nature of the government function involved as well as of the private interest that has been affected by governmental action.' Id., at *; Goldberg v. Kelly *.

The private interest here, that of a man in the children he has sired and raised, undeniably warrants deference and, absent a powerful countervailing interest, protection. It is plain that the interest of a parent in the companionship, care, custody, and management of his or her children 'come(s) to this Court with a momentum for respect lacking when appeal is made to liberties which derive merely from shifting economic arrangements.' *

The Court has frequently emphasized the importance of the family. The rights to conceive and to raise one's children have been deemed 'essential,' *Meyer v. Nebraska*, *, 'basic civil rights of man,' *Skinner v. Oklahoma*, *, and '(r)ights far more precious . . . than property rights,' *May v. Anderson*, *. 'It is cardinal with us that the custody, care and nurture of the child reside first in the parents, whose primary function and freedom include preparation for obligations the state can neither supply nor hinder.' *Prince v. Massachusetts*, *. The integrity of the family unit has found protection in the Due Process Clause of the Fourteenth Amendment, *Meyer v. Nebraska*, *, the Equal Protection Clause of the Fourteenth Amendment, *Skinner v. Oklahoma*, *, and the Ninth Amendment, *Griswold v. Connecticut*, *.

Nor has the law refused to recognize those family relationships unlegitimized by a marriage ceremony. The Court has declared unconstitutional a state statute denying natural, but illegitimate, children a wrongful-death action for the death of their mother, emphasizing that such children cannot be denied the right of other children because familial bonds in such cases were often as warm, enduring, and important as those arising within a more formally organized family unit. *Levy v. Louisiana*, *. 'To say that the test of equal protection should be the 'legal' rather than the biological relationship is to avoid the issue. For the Equal Protection Clause necessarily limits the authority of a State to draw such 'legal' lines as it chooses.' *

These authorities make it clear that, at the least, Stanley's interest in retaining custody of his children is cognizable and substantial.

For its part, the State has made its interest quite plain: Illinois has declared that the aim of the Juvenile Court Act is to protect 'the moral, emotional, mental, and physical welfare of the minor and the best interests of the community' and to 'strengthen the minor's family ties whenever possible, removing him from the custody of his parents only when his welfare or safety or the protection of the public cannot be adequately safeguarded without removal . . .' * These are legitimate interests, well within the power of the State to implement. We do not question the assertion that neglectful parents may be separated from their children.

But we are here not asked to evaluate the legitimacy of the state ends, rather, to determine whether the means used to achieve these ends are constitutionally defensible. What is the state interest in separating children from fathers without a hearing designed to determine whether the father is unfit in a particular disputed case? We observe that the State registers no gain towards its declared goals when it separates children from the custody of fit parents. Indeed, if Stanley is a fit father, the State spites its own articulated goals when it needlessly separates him from his family. ***

It may be, as the State insists, that most unmarried fathers are unsuitable and neglectful parents. It may also be that Stanley is such a parent and that his children should be placed in other hands. But all unmarried fathers are not in this category; some are wholly suited to have custody of their children. This much the State readily concedes, and nothing in this record indicates that Stanley is or has been a neglectful father who has not cared for his children. Given the opportunity to make his case, Stanley may have been seen to be deserving of custody of his offspring. Had this been so, the State's statutory policy would have been furthered by leaving custody in him.

***

***[I]t may be argued that unmarried fathers are so seldom fit that Illinois need not undergo the administrative inconvenience of inquiry in any case, including Stanley's. The establishment of prompt efficacious procedures to achieve legitimate state ends is a proper state interest worthy of cognizance in constitutional adjudication. But the Constitution recognizes higher values than speed and efficiency. Indeed, one might fairly say of the Bill of Rights in general, and the Due Process Clause in particular, that they were designed to protect the fragile values of a vulnerable citizenry from the overbearing concern for efficiency and efficacy that may characterize praiseworthy government officials no less, and perhaps more, than mediocre ones.

Procedure by presumption is always cheaper and easier than individualized determination. But when, as here, the procedure forecloses the determinative issues of competence and care, when it explicitly disdains present realities in deference to past formalities, it needlessly risks running roughshod over the important interests of both parent and child. It therefore cannot stand. *[FN9 We note in passing that the incremental cost of offering unwed fathers an opportunity for individualized hearings on fitness appears to be minimal. If unwed fathers, in the main, do not care about the disposition of their children, they will not appear to demand hearings.]*

Bell v. Burson held that the State could not, while purporting to be concerned with fault in suspending a driver's license, deprive a citizen of his license without a hearing that would assess fault. Absent fault, the State's declared interest was so attenuated that administrative convenience was insufficient to excuse a hearing where evidence of fault could be considered. That drivers involved in accidents, as a statistical matter, might be very likely to have been wholly or partially at fault did not foreclose hearing and proof in specific cases before licenses were suspended.

We think the Due Process Clause mandates a similar result here. The State's interest in caring for Stanley's children is de minimis if Stanley is shown to be a fit father. It insists on presuming rather than proving Stanley's unfitness solely because it is more convenient to presume than to prove. Under the Due Process Clause, that advantage is insufficient to justify refusing a father a hearing when the issue at stake is the dismemberment of his family.

III

The State of Illinois assumes custody of the children of married parents, divorced parents, and unmarried mothers only after a hearing and proof of neglect. The children of unmarried fathers, however, are declared dependent children without a hearing on parental fitness and without proof of neglect. Stanley's claim in the state courts and here is that failure to afford him a hearing on his parental qualifications while extending it to other parents denied him equal protection of the laws. We have concluded that all Illinois parents are constitutionally entitled to a hearing on their fitness before their children are removed from their custody. It follows that denying such a hearing to Stanley and those like him while granting it to other Illinois parents is inescapably contrary to the Equal Protection Clause. *[FN10 **]*

The judgment of the Supreme Court of Illinois is reversed and the case is remanded to that court for proceedings not inconsistent with this opinion. It is so ordered. Reversed and remanded.

Mr. JUSTICE POWELL and Mr. JUSTICE REHNQUIST took no part in the consideration or decision of this case. Mr. JUSTICE DOUGLAS joins in Parts I and II of this opinion.
Mr. CHIEF JUSTICE BURGER, with whom Mr. JUSTICE BLACKMUN concurs, dissenting.

The only constitutional issue raised and decided in the courts of Illinois in this case was whether the Illinois statute that omits unwed fathers from the definition of 'parents' violates the Equal Protection Clause. ***

No due process issue was raised in the state courts; and no due process issue was decided by any state court.

***

In regard to the only issue that I consider properly before the Court, I agree with the State's argument that the Equal Protection Clause is not violated when Illinois gives full recognition only to those father-child relationships that arise in the context of family units bound together by legal obligations arising from marriage or from adoption proceedings. Quite apart from the religious or quasi-religious connotations that marriage has--and has historically enjoyed--for a large proportion of this Nation's citizens, it is in law an essentially contractual relationship, the parties to which have legally enforceable rights and duties, with respect both to each other and to any children born to them. Stanley and the mother of these children never entered such a relationship. The record is silent as to whether they ever privately exchanged such promises as would have bound them in marriage under the common law. * In any event, Illinois has not recognized common-law marriages since 1905. * Stanley did not seek the burdens when he could have freely assumed them.

Where there is a valid contract of marriage, the law of Illinois presumes that the husband is the father of any child born to the wife during the marriage; as the father, he has legally enforceable rights and duties with respect to that child. When a child is born to an unmarried woman, Illinois recognizes the readily identifiable mother, but makes no presumption as to the identity of the biological father. It does, however, provide two ways, one voluntary and one involuntary, in which that father may be identified. First, he may marry the mother and acknowledge the child as his own; this has the legal effect of legitimating the child and gaining for the father full recognition as a parent. Ill. Rev. Stat., c. 3, s 12, subd. 8. Second, a man may be found to be the biological father of the child pursuant to a paternity suit initiated by the mother; in this case, the child remains illegitimate, but the adjudicated father is made liable for the support of the child until the latter attains age 18 or is legally adopted by another. * Stanley argued before the Supreme Court of Illinois that the definition of 'parents,' set out in Ill. Rev. Stat., c. 37, s 701--14, as including 'the father and mother of a legitimate child, or the survivor of them, or the natural mother of an illegitimate child, (or) . . . any adoptive parent,' violates the Equal Protection Clause in that it treats unwed mothers and unwed fathers differently. Stanley then enlarged upon his equal protection argument when he brought the case here; he argued before this Court that Illinois is not permitted by the Equal Protection Clause to distinguish between unwed fathers and any of the other biological parents included in the statutory definition of legal 'parents.'

The Illinois Supreme Court correctly held that the State may constitutionally distinguish between unwed fathers and unwed mothers. Here, Illinois' different treatment of the two is part of that State's statutory scheme for protecting the welfare of illegitimate children. In almost all cases, the unwed mother is readily identifiable, generally from hospital records, and alternatively by physicians or others attending the child's birth. Unwed fathers, as a class, are not traditionally quite so easy to identify and locate. Many of them either deny all responsibility or exhibit no interest in the child or its welfare; and, of course, many unwed fathers are simply not aware of their parenthood.

Furthermore, I believe that a State is fully justified in concluding, on the basis of common human experience, that the biological role of the mother in carrying and nursing an infant creates stronger bonds between her and the child than the bonds resulting from the male's often casual encounter. This view is reinforced by the observable fact that most unwed mothers exhibit a concern for their offspring either permanently or at least until they are safely placed for adoption, while unwed fathers rarely burden either the mother or the child with their attentions or loyalties. Centuries of human experience buttress this view of the realities of human conditions and suggest that unwed mothers of illegitimate children are generally more dependable protectors of their children than are unwed fathers. While these, like most generalizations, are not without exceptions, they nevertheless provide a sufficient basis to sustain a statutory classification whose objective is not to penalize unwed parents but to further the welfare of illegitimate children in fulfillment of the State's obligations as parens patriae.

Stanley depicts himself as a somewhat unusual unwed father, namely, as one who has always acknowledged and never doubted his fatherhood of these children. He alleges that he loved, cared for, and supported these children from the time of their birth until the death of their mother. He contends that he consequently must be treated the same as a married father of legitimate children. Even assuming the truth of Stanley's allegations, I am unable to construe the Equal Protection Clause as requiring Illinois to tailor its statutory definition of 'parents' so meticulously as to include such unusual unwed fathers, while at the same time excluding those unwed, and generally unidentified, biological fathers who in no way share Stanley's professed desires.

*** Shortly after the death of the mother, Stanley turned these two children over to the care of a Mr. and Mrs. Ness; he took no action to gain recognition of himself as a father, through adoption, or as a legal custodian, through a guardianship proceeding. Eventually it came to the attention of the State that there was no living adult who had any legally enforceable obligation for the care and support of the children; it was only then that the dependency proceeding here under review took place and that Stanley made himself known to the juvenile court in connection with these two children. *[FN5 As the* *majority notes, *, Joan Stanley gave birth to three children during the 18 years Peter Stanley was living 'intermittently' with her. At oral argument, we were told by Stanley's counsel that the oldest of these three children had previously been declared a ward of the court pursuant to a neglect proceeding that was 'proven against' Stanley at a time, apparently, when the juvenile court officials were under the erroneous impression that Peter and Joan Stanley had been married.]* Even then, however, Stanley did not ask to be charged with the legal responsibility for the children. He asked only that such legal responsibility be given to no one else. He seemed, in particular, to be concerned with the loss of the welfare payments he would suffer as a result of the designation of others as guardians of the children. Not only, then, do I see no ground for holding that Illinois' statutory definition of 'parents' on its face violates the Equal Protection Clause; I see no ground for holding that any constitutional right of Stanley has been denied in the application of that statutory definition in the case at bar.***

b. *Michael H. and Victoria D. v. Gerald D.*

Michael H. and Victoria D. v. Gerald D.
491 U.S. 110 (1989)

JUSTICE SCALIA announced the judgment of the Court and delivered an opinion, in which THE CHIEF JUSTICE joins, and in all but footnote 6 of which Justice O'CONNOR and Justice KENNEDY join.

Under California law, a child born to a married woman living with her husband is presumed to be a child of the marriage. Cal. Evid. Code Ann. § 621 (West Supp.1989). The presumption of legitimacy may be rebutted only by the husband or wife, and then only in limited circumstances. *Ibid.* The instant appeal presents the claim that this presumption infringes upon the due process rights of a man who wishes to establish his paternity of a child born to the wife of another man, and the claim that it infringes upon the constitutional right of the child to maintain a relationship with her natural father.

I

The facts of this case are, we must hope, extraordinary. On May 9, 1976, in Las Vegas, Nevada, Carole D., an international model, and Gerald D., a top executive in a French oil company, were married. The couple established a home in Playa del Rey, California, in which they resided as husband and wife when one or the other was not out of the country on business. In the summer of 1978, Carole became involved in an adulterous affair with a neighbor, Michael H. In September 1980, she conceived a child, Victoria D., who was born on May 11, 1981. Gerald was listed as father on the birth certificate and has always held Victoria out to the world as his daughter. Soon after delivery of the child, however, Carole informed Michael that she believed he might be the father.

In the first three years of her life, Victoria remained always with Carole, but found herself within a variety of quasi-family units. In October 1981, Gerald moved to New York City to pursue his business interests, but Carole chose to remain in California. At the end of that month, Carole and Michael had blood tests of themselves and Victoria, which showed a 98.07% probability that Michael was Victoria's father. In January 1982, Carole visited Michael in St. Thomas, where his primary business interests were based. There Michael held Victoria out as his child. In March, however, Carole left Michael and returned to California, where she took up residence with yet another man, Scott K. Later that spring, and again in the summer, Carole and Victoria spent time with Gerald in New York City, as well as on vacation in Europe. In the fall, they returned to Scott in California.

In November 1982, rebuffed in his attempts to visit Victoria, Michael filed a filiation action in California Superior Court to establish his paternity and right to visitation. In March 1983, the court appointed an attorney and guardian ad litem to represent Victoria's interests. Victoria then filed a cross-complaint asserting that if she had more than one psychological or de facto father, she was entitled to maintain her filial relationship, with all of the attendant rights, duties, and obligations, with both. In May 1983, Carole filed a motion for summary judgment. During this period, from March through July 1983, Carole was again living with Gerald in New York. In August, however, she returned to California, became involved once again with Michael, and instructed her attorneys to remove the summary judgment motion from the calendar.

For the ensuing eight months, when Michael was not in St. Thomas he lived with Carole and Victoria in Carole's apartment in Los Angeles and held Victoria out as his daughter. In April 1984, Carole and Michael signed a stipulation that Michael was Victoria's natural father. Carole left Michael the next month, however, and instructed her attorneys not to file the stipulation. In June 1984, Carole reconciled with Gerald and joined him in New York, where they now live with Victoria and two other children since born into the marriage.

In May 1984, Michael and Victoria, through her guardian ad litem, sought visitation rights for Michael pendente lite. To assist in determining whether visitation would be in Victoria's best interests, the Superior Court appointed a psychologist to evaluate Victoria, Gerald, Michael, and Carole. The psychologist recommended that Carole retain sole custody, but that Michael be allowed continued contact with Victoria pursuant to a restricted visitation schedule. The court concurred and ordered that Michael be provided with limited visitation privileges pendente lite.

On October 19, 1984, Gerald, who had intervened in the action, moved for summary judgment on the ground that under Cal. Evid. Code § 621 there were no triable issues of fact as to Victoria's paternity. This law provides that "the issue of a wife cohabiting with her husband, who is not impotent or sterile, is conclusively presumed to be a child of the marriage." Cal. Evid. Code Ann. § 621(a) (West Supp.1989). The presumption may be rebutted by blood tests, but only if a motion for such tests is made, within two years from the date of the child's birth, either by the husband or, if the natural father has filed an affidavit acknowledging paternity, by the wife. §§ 621(c) and (d).

On January 28, 1985, having found that affidavits submitted by Carole and Gerald sufficed to demonstrate that the two were cohabiting at conception and birth and that Gerald was neither sterile nor impotent, the Superior Court granted Gerald's motion for summary judgment, rejecting Michael's and Victoria's challenges to the constitutionality of § 621. The court also denied their motions for continued visitation pending the appeal under Cal. Civ. Code § 4601, which provides that a court may, in its discretion, grant "reasonable visitation rights ... to any ... person having an interest in the welfare of the child." Cal. Civ. Code Ann. § 4601 (West Supp.1989). It found that allowing such visitation would "violat[e] the intention of the Legislature by impugning the integrity of the family unit." *

On appeal, Michael asserted, inter alia, that the Superior Court's application of § 621 had violated his procedural and substantive due process rights. Victoria also raised a due process challenge to the statute, seeking to preserve her de facto relationship with Michael as well as with Gerald. She contended, in addition, that as § 621 allows the husband and, at least to a limited extent, the mother, but not the child, to rebut the presumption of legitimacy, it violates the child's right to equal protection. Finally, she asserted a right to continued visitation with Michael under § 4601. After submission of briefs and a hearing, the California Court of Appeal affirmed the judgment of the Superior Court and upheld the constitutionality of the statute. *. It interpreted that judgment, moreover, as having denied permanent visitation rights under § 4601, regarding that as the implication of the Superior Court's reliance upon § 621 and upon an earlier California case, Vincent B. * (1982), which had held that once an assertion of biological paternity is "determined to be legally impossible" under § 621, visitation against the wishes of the mother should be denied under § 4601. *

The Court of Appeal denied Michael's and Victoria's petitions for rehearing, and, on July 30, 1987, the California Supreme Court denied discretionary review. On February 29, 1988, we noted probable jurisdiction of the present appeal. * Before us, Michael and Victoria both raise equal protection and due process challenges. We do not reach Michael's equal protection claim, however, as it was neither raised nor passed upon below. *

II

The California statute that is the subject of this litigation is, in substance, more than a century old. *** In their present form, the substantive provisions of the statute are as follows:

"§ 621. Child of the marriage; notice of motion for blood tests

"(a) Except as provided in subdivision (b), the issue of a wife cohabiting with her husband, who is not impotent or sterile, is conclusively presumed to be a child of the marriage.

"(b) Notwithstanding the provisions of subdivision (a), if the court finds that the conclusions of all the experts, as disclosed by the evidence based upon blood tests performed pursuant to Chapter 2 (commencing with Section 890) of Division 7 are that the husband is not the father of the child, the question of paternity of the husband shall be resolved accordingly.

"(c) The notice of motion for blood tests under subdivision (b) may be raised by the husband not later than two years from the child's date of birth.

"(d) The notice of motion for blood tests under subdivision (b) may be raised by the mother of the child not later than two years from the child's date of birth if the child's biological father has filed an affidavit with the court acknowledging paternity of the child.

"(e) The provisions of subdivision (b) shall not apply to any case coming within the provisions of Section 7005 of the Civil Code [dealing with artificial insemination] or to any case in which the wife, with the consent of the husband, conceived by means of a surgical procedure."

III

We address first the claims of Michael. At the outset, it is necessary to clarify what he sought and what he was denied. California law, like nature itself, makes no provision for dual fatherhood. Michael was seeking to be declared the father of Victoria. The immediate benefit he evidently sought to obtain from that status was visitation rights. See Cal. Civ. Code Ann. § 4601 (West 1983) (parent has statutory right to visitation "unless it is shown that such visitation would be detrimental to the best interests of the child"). But if Michael were successful in being declared the father, other rights would follow--most importantly, the right to be considered as the parent who should have custody, *, a status which "embrace[s] the sum of parental rights with respect to the rearing of a child, including the child's care; the right to the child's services and earnings; the right to direct the child's activities; the right to make decisions regarding the control, education, and health of the child; and the right, as well as the duty, to prepare the child for additional obligations, which includes the teaching of moral standards, religious beliefs, and elements of good citizenship." *. All parental rights, including visitation, were automatically denied by denying Michael status as the father. While Cal. Civ. Code Ann. § 4601 places it within the discretionary power of a court to award visitation rights to a nonparent, the Superior Court here, affirmed by the Court of Appeal, held that California law denies visitation, against the wishes of the mother, to a putative father who has been prevented by § 621 from establishing his paternity. *.

Michael raises two related challenges to the constitutionality of § 621. First, he asserts that requirements of procedural due process prevent the State from terminating his liberty interest in his relationship with his child without affording him an opportunity to demonstrate his paternity in an evidentiary hearing. We believe this claim derives from a fundamental misconception of the nature of the California statute. While § 621 is phrased in terms of a presumption, that rule of evidence is the implementation of a substantive rule of law. California declares it to be, except in limited circumstances, irrelevant for paternity purposes whether a child conceived during, and born into, an existing marriage was begotten by someone other than the husband and had a prior relationship with him. As the Court of Appeal phrased it: "'The conclusive presumption is actually a substantive rule of law based upon a determination by the Legislature as a matter of overriding social policy, that given a certain relationship between the husband and wife, the husband is to be held responsible for the child, and that the integrity of the family unit should not be impugned.' " * Of course the conclusive presumption not only expresses the State's substantive policy but also furthers it, excluding inquiries into the child's paternity that would be destructive of family integrity and privacy.

This Court has struck down as illegitimate certain "irrebuttable presumptions." See, e.g., *Stanley v. Illinois,* * (1972); *Vlandis v. Kline,* * (1973); *Cleveland Board of Education v. LaFleur,* * (1974). Those holdings did not, however, rest upon procedural due process. A conclusive presumption does, of course, foreclose the person against whom it is invoked from demonstrating, in a particularized proceeding, that applying the presumption to him will in fact not further the lawful governmental policy the presumption is designed to effectuate. But the same can be said of any legal rule that establishes general classifications, whether framed in terms of a presumption or not. In this respect there is no difference between a rule which says that the marital husband shall be irrebuttably presumed to be the father, and a rule which says that the adulterous natural father shall not be recognized as the legal father. Both rules deny someone in Michael's situation a hearing on whether, in the particular circumstances of his case, California's policies would best be served by giving him parental rights. Thus, as many commentators have observed, *, our "irrebuttable presumption" cases must ultimately be analyzed as calling into question not the adequacy of procedures but--like our cases involving classifications framed in other terms, * --the adequacy of the "fit" between the classification and the policy that the classification serves. * We therefore reject Michael's procedural due process challenge and proceed to his substantive claim.

Michael contends as a matter of substantive due process that, because he has established a parental relationship with Victoria, protection of Gerald's and Carole's marital union is an insufficient state interest to support termination of that relationship. This argument is, of course, predicated on the assertion that Michael has a constitutionally protected liberty interest in his relationship with Victoria. It is an established part of our constitutional jurisprudence that the term "liberty" in the Due Process Clause extends beyond freedom from physical restraint. See, e.g., *Pierce v. Society of Sisters*, * (1925); *Meyer v. Nebraska*, * (1923). Without that core textual meaning as a limitation, defining the scope of the Due Process Clause "has at times been a treacherous field for this Court," giving "reason for concern lest the only limits to ... judicial intervention become the predilections of those who happen at the time to be Members of this Court." *Moore v. East Cleveland*, * (1977). The need for restraint has been cogently expressed by Justice WHITE:

That the Court has ample precedent for the creation of new constitutional rights should not lead it to repeat the process at will. The Judiciary, including this Court, is the most vulnerable and comes nearest to illegitimacy when it deals with judge-made constitutional law having little or no cognizable roots in the language or even the design of the Constitution. Realizing that the present construction of the Due Process Clause represents a major judicial gloss on its terms, as well as on the anticipation of the Framers ..., the Court should be extremely reluctant to breathe still further substantive content into the Due Process Clause so as to strike down legislation adopted by a State or city to promote its welfare. Whenever the Judiciary does so, it unavoidably pre-empts for itself another part of the governance of the country without express constitutional authority. *Moore*, * (dissenting opinion).

In an attempt to limit and guide interpretation of the Clause, we have insisted not merely that the interest denominated as a "liberty" be "fundamental" (a concept that, in isolation, is hard to objectify), but also that it be an interest traditionally protected by our society. As we have put it, the Due Process Clause affords only those protections "so rooted in the traditions and conscience of our people as to be ranked as fundamental." *Snyder v. Massachusetts*, * (1934) (Cardozo, J.). Our cases reflect "continual insistence upon respect for the teachings of history [and] solid recognition of the basic values that underlie our society...." *Griswold v. Connecticut*, * (1965) (Harlan, J., concurring in judgment).

This insistence that the asserted liberty interest be rooted in history and tradition is evident, as elsewhere, in our cases according constitutional protection to certain parental rights. Michael reads the landmark case of *Stanley v. Illinois*, * (1972), and the subsequent cases of *Quilloin v. Walcott*, * (1978), *Caban v. Mohammed*, * (1979), and *Lehr v. Robertson*, * (1983), as establishing that a liberty interest is created by biological fatherhood plus an established parental relationship--factors that exist in the present case as well. We think that distorts the rationale of those cases. As we view them, they rest not upon such isolated factors but upon the historic respect--indeed, sanctity would not be too strong a term-- traditionally accorded to the relationships that develop within the unitary family. *[FN3. Justice BRENNAN asserts that only a "pinched conception of 'the family' " would exclude Michael, Carole, and Victoria from protection. Post, at 2353. We disagree. The family unit accorded traditional respect in our society, which we have referred to as the "unitary family," is typified, of course, by the marital family, but also includes the household of unmarried parents and their children. Perhaps the concept can be expanded even beyond this, but it will bear no resemblance to traditionally respected relationships--and will thus cease to have any constitutional significance--if it is stretched so far as to include the relationship established between a married woman, her lover, and their child, during a 3-month sojourn in St. Thomas, or during a subsequent 8-month period when, if he happened to be in Los Angeles, he stayed with her and the child.]* In Stanley, for example, we forbade the destruction of such a family when, upon the death of the mother, the State had sought to remove children from the custody of a father who had lived with and supported them and their mother for 18 years. As Justice Powell stated for the plurality in Moore v. East Cleveland, supra,*: "Our decisions establish that the Constitution protects the sanctity of the family precisely because the institution of the family is deeply rooted in this Nation's history and tradition."

Thus, the legal issue in the present case reduces to whether the relationship between persons in the situation of Michael and Victoria has been treated as a protected family unit under the historic practices of our society, or whether on any other basis it has been accorded special protection. We think it impossible to find that it has. In fact, quite to the contrary, our traditions have protected the marital family (Gerald, Carole, and the child they acknowledge to be theirs) against the sort of claim Michael asserts.

The presumption of legitimacy was a fundamental principle of the common law. H. Nicholas, Adulturine Bastardy 1 (1836). Traditionally, that presumption could be rebutted only by proof that a husband was incapable of procreation or had had no access to his wife during the relevant period. Id., at 9-10 (citing Bracton, De Legibus et Consuetudinibus Angliae, * (1569)). As explained by Blackstone, nonaccess could only be proved "if the husband be out of the kingdom of England (or, as the law somewhat loosely phrases it, extra quatuor maria [beyond the four seas]) for above nine months...." 1 Blackstone's Commentaries 456 (J. Chitty ed. 1826). And, under the common law both in England and here, "neither husband nor wife [could] be a witness to prove access or nonaccess." J. Schouler, Law of the Domestic Relations § 225, p. 306 (3d ed. 1882); *. The primary policy rationale underlying the common law's severe restrictions on rebuttal of the presumption appears to have been an aversion to declaring children illegitimate, *, thereby depriving them of rights of inheritance and succession, 2 J. Kent, Commentaries on American Law* 175, and likely making them wards of the state. A secondary policy concern was the interest in promoting the "peace and tranquillity of States and families," Schouler, supra, § 225, at 304, *, a goal that is obviously impaired by facilitating suits against husband and wife asserting that their children are illegitimate. Even though, as bastardy laws became less harsh, "[j]udges in both [England and the United States] gradually widened the acceptable range of evidence that could be offered by spouses, and placed restraints on the 'four seas rule' ... [,] the law retained a strong bias against ruling the children of married women illegitimate." *

We have found nothing in the older sources, nor in the older cases, addressing specifically the power of the natural father to assert parental rights over a child born into a woman's existing marriage with another man. Since it is Michael's burden to establish that such a power (at least where the natural father has established a relationship with the child) is so deeply embedded within our traditions as to be a fundamental right, the lack of evidence alone might defeat his case. But the evidence shows that even in modern times--when, as we have noted, the rigid protection of the marital family has in other respects been relaxed--the ability of a person in Michael's position to claim paternity has not been generally acknowledged. ***

Moreover, even if it were clear that one in Michael's position generally possesses, and has generally always possessed, standing to challenge the marital child's legitimacy, that would still not establish Michael's case. As noted earlier, what is at issue here is not entitlement to a state pronouncement that Victoria was begotten by Michael. It is no conceivable denial of constitutional right for a State to decline to declare facts unless some legal consequence hinges upon the requested declaration. What Michael asserts here is a right to have himself declared the natural father and thereby to obtain parental prerogatives. What he must establish, therefore, is not that our society has traditionally allowed a natural father in his circumstances to establish paternity, but that it has traditionally accorded such a father parental rights, or at least has not traditionally denied them. Even if the law in all States had always been that the entire world could challenge the marital presumption and obtain a declaration as to who was the natural father, that would not advance Michael's claim. Thus, it is ultimately irrelevant, even for purposes of determining current social attitudes towards the alleged substantive right Michael asserts, that the present law in a number of States appears to allow the natural father-- including the natural father who has not established a relationship with the child--the theoretical power to rebut the marital presumption, *. What counts is whether the States in fact award substantive parental rights to the natural father of a child conceived within, and born into, an extant marital union that wishes to embrace the child. We are not aware of a single case, old or new, that has done so. This is not the stuff of which fundamental rights qualifying as liberty interests are made. *[FN6 - Justice BRENNAN criticizes our methodology in using historical traditions specifically relating to the rights of an adulterous natural father, rather than inquiring more generally "whether parenthood is an interest that historically has received our attention and protection." Post, at 2350. There seems to us no basis for the contention that this methodology is "nove[l]," post, at 2351. For example, in Bowers v. Hardwick, * (1986), we noted that at the time the Fourteenth Amendment was ratified all but 5 of the 37 States had criminal sodomy laws, that all 50 of the States had such laws prior to 1961, and that 24 States and the District of Columbia continued to have them; and we concluded from that record, regarding that very specific aspect of sexual conduct, that "to claim that a right to engage in such conduct is 'deeply rooted in this Nation's history and tradition' or 'implicit in the concept of ordered liberty' is, at best, facetious." * In Roe v. Wade, *, we spent about a fifth of our opinion negating the proposition that there was a longstanding tradition of laws proscribing abortion. ***

We do not understand why, having rejected our focus upon the societal tradition regarding the natural father's rights vis-a-vis a child whose mother is married to another man, Justice BRENNAN would choose to focus instead upon "parenthood." Why should the relevant category not be even more general--perhaps "family relationships"; or "personal relationships"; or even "emotional attachments in general"? Though the dissent has no basis for the level of generality it would select, we do: We refer to the most specific level at which a relevant tradition protecting, or denying protection to, the asserted right can be identified. ****

One would think that Justice BRENNAN would appreciate the value of consulting the most specific tradition available, since he acknowledges that "[e]ven if we can agree ... that 'family' and 'parenthood' are part of the good life, it is absurd to assume that we can agree on the content of those terms and destructive to pretend that we do." Post, at 2351. Because such general traditions provide such imprecise guidance, they permit judges to dictate rather than discern the society's views. The need, if arbitrary decisionmaking is to be avoided, to adopt the most specific tradition as the point of reference--or at least to announce, as Justice BRENNAN declines to do, some other criterion for selecting among the innumerable relevant traditions that could be consulted--is well enough exemplified by the fact that in the present case Justice BRENNAN's opinion and Justice O'CONNOR's opinion, post, p. 2346, which disapproves this footnote, both appeal to tradition, but on the basis of the tradition they select reach opposite results. Although assuredly having the virtue (if it be that) of leaving judges free to decide as they think best when the unanticipated occurs, a rule of law that binds neither by text nor by any particular, identifiable tradition is no rule of law at all.

*** In this case, the existence of such a tradition [repudiating the claimed right], continuing to the *present day, refutes any possible contention that the alleged right is "so rooted in the traditions and conscience of our people as to be ranked as fundamental,"* Snyder, *, or *"implicit in the concept of ordered liberty,"* Palko v. Connecticut, * (1937).]

In *Lehr v. Robertson*, a case involving a natural father's attempt to block his child's adoption by the unwed mother's new husband, we observed that "[t]he significance of the biological connection is that it offers the natural father an opportunity that no other male possesses to develop a relationship with his offspring," *, and we assumed that the Constitution might require some protection of that opportunity, *id.*, * . Where, however, the child is born into an extant marital family, the natural father's unique opportunity conflicts with the similarly unique opportunity of the husband of the marriage; and it is not unconstitutional for the State to give categorical preference to the latter. In *Lehr* we quoted approvingly from Justice Stewart's dissent in *Caban v. Mohammed*, *, to the effect that although " '[i]n some circumstances the actual relationship between father and child may suffice to create in the unwed father parental interests comparable to those of the married father,' " " 'the absence of a legal tie with the mother may in such circumstances appropriately place a limit on whatever substantive constitutional claims might otherwise exist.' " * In accord with our traditions, a limit is also imposed by the circumstance that the mother is, at the time of the child's conception and birth, married to, and cohabitating with, another man, both of whom wish to raise the child as the offspring of their union. It is a question of legislative policy and not constitutional law whether California will allow the presumed parenthood of a couple desiring to retain a child conceived within and born into their marriage to be rebutted.

We do not accept Justice BRENNAN's criticism that this result "squashes" the liberty that consists of "the freedom not to conform." *. It seems to us that reflects the erroneous view that there is only one side to this controversy--that one disposition can expand a "liberty" of sorts without contracting an equivalent "liberty" on the other side. Such a happy choice is rarely available. Here, to provide protection to an adulterous natural father is to deny protection to a marital father, and vice versa. If Michael has a "freedom not to conform" (whatever that means), Gerald must equivalently have a "freedom to conform." One of them will pay a price for asserting that "freedom"--Michael by being unable to act as father of the child he has adulterously begotten, or Gerald by being unable to preserve the integrity of the traditional family unit he and Victoria have established. Our disposition does not choose between these two "freedoms," but leaves that to the people of California. Justice BRENNAN's approach chooses one of them as the constitutional imperative, on no apparent basis except that the unconventional is to be preferred.

IV

We have never had occasion to decide whether a child has a liberty interest, symmetrical with that of her parent, in maintaining her filial relationship. We need not do so here because, even assuming that such a right exists, Victoria's claim must fail. Victoria's due process challenge is, if anything, weaker than Michael's. Her basic claim is not that California has erred in preventing her from establishing that Michael, not Gerald, should stand as her legal father. Rather, she claims a due process right to maintain filial relationships with both Michael and Gerald. This assertion merits little discussion, for, whatever the merits of the guardian ad litem's belief that such an arrangement can be of great psychological benefit to a child, the claim that a State must recognize multiple fatherhood has no support in the history or traditions of this country. Moreover, even if we were to construe Victoria's argument as forwarding the lesser proposition that, whatever her status vis-a-vis Gerald, she has a liberty interest in maintaining a filial relationship with her natural father, Michael, we find that, at best, her claim is the obverse of Michael's and fails for the same reasons.

Victoria claims in addition that her equal protection rights have been violated because, unlike her mother and presumed father, she had no opportunity to rebut the presumption of her legitimacy. We find this argument wholly without merit. We reject, at the outset, Victoria's suggestion that her equal protection challenge must be assessed under a standard of strict scrutiny because, in denying her the right to maintain a filial relationship with Michael, the State is discriminating against her on the basis of her illegitimacy. * Under California law, Victoria is not illegitimate, and she is treated in the same manner as all other legitimate children: she is entitled to maintain a filial relationship with her legal parents.

We apply, therefore, the ordinary "rational relationship" test to Victoria's equal protection challenge. The primary rationale underlying § 621's limitation on those who may rebut the presumption of legitimacy is a concern that allowing persons other than the husband or wife to do so may undermine the integrity of the marital union. When the husband or wife contests the legitimacy of their child, the stability of the marriage has already been shaken. In contrast, allowing a claim of illegitimacy to be pressed by the child--or, more accurately, by a court-appointed guardian ad litem--may well disrupt an otherwise peaceful union. Since it pursues a legitimate end by rational means, California's decision to treat Victoria differently from her parents is not a denial of equal protection.

The judgment of the California Court of Appeal is Affirmed.

JUSTICE O'CONNOR, with whom JUSTICE KENNEDY joins, concurring in part.

I concur in all but footnote 6 of Justice SCALIA's opinion. This footnote sketches a mode of historical analysis to be used when identifying liberty interests protected by the Due Process Clause of the Fourteenth Amendment that may be somewhat inconsistent with our past decisions in this area. * I would not foreclose the unanticipated by the prior imposition of a single mode of historical analysis. *Poe v. Ullman*, * (1961) (Harlan, J., dissenting).

JUSTICE STEVENS, concurring in the judgment.

As I understand this case, it raises two different questions about the validity of California's statutory scheme. First, is Cal. Evid. Code Ann. § 621 (West Supp.1989) unconstitutional because it prevents Michael and Victoria from obtaining a judicial determination that he is her biological father-- even if no legal rights would be affected by that determination? Second, does the California statute deny appellants a fair opportunity to prove that Victoria's best interests would be served by granting Michael visitation rights?

On the first issue I agree with Justice SCALIA that the Federal Constitution imposes no obligation upon a State to "declare facts unless some legal consequence hinges upon the requested declaration." Ante, at 2343. "The actions of judges neither create nor sever genetic bonds." *Lehr v. Robertson,* * (1983).

On the second issue I do not agree with Justice SCALIA's analysis. He seems to reject the possibility that a natural father might ever have a constitutionally protected interest in his relationship with a child whose mother was married, to and cohabiting with, another man at the time of the child's conception and birth. I think cases like *Stanley v. Illinois*, *, and *Caban v. Mohammed*, *, demonstrate that enduring "family" relationships may develop in unconventional settings. I therefore would not foreclose the possibility that a constitutionally protected relationship between a natural father and his child might exist in a case like this. Indeed, I am willing to assume for the purpose of deciding this case that Michael's relationship with Victoria is strong enough to give him a constitutional right to try to convince a trial judge that Victoria's best interest would be served by granting him visitation rights. I am satisfied, however, that the California statute, as applied in this case, gave him that opportunity.

*** The presumption established by § 621 denied Michael the benefit of the first sentence of § 4601 because, as a matter of law, he is not a "parent." It does not, however, prevent him from proving that he is an "other person having an interest in the welfare of the child." On its face, therefore, the statute plainly gave the trial judge the authority to grant Michael "reasonable visitation rights."
***

Under the circumstances of the case before us, Michael was given a fair opportunity to show that he is Victoria's natural father, that he had developed a relationship with her, and that her interests would be served by granting him visitation rights. On the other hand, the record also shows that after its rather shaky start, the marriage between Carole and Gerald developed a stability that now provides

Victoria with a loving and harmonious family home. In the circumstances of this case, I find nothing fundamentally unfair about the exercise of a judge's discretion that, in the end, allows the mother to decide whether her child's best interests would be served by allowing the natural father visitation privileges. Because I am convinced that the trial judge had the authority under state law both to hear Michael's plea for visitation rights and to grant him such rights if Victoria's best interests so warranted, I am satisfied that the California statutory scheme is consistent with the Due Process Clause of the Fourteenth Amendment.

I therefore concur in the Court's judgment of affirmance.

JUSTICE BRENNAN, with whom JUSTICE MARSHALL and JUSTICE BLACKMUN join, dissenting.

In a case that has yielded so many opinions as has this one, it is fruitful to begin by emphasizing the common ground shared by a majority of this Court. Five Members of the Court refuse to foreclose "the possibility that a natural father might ever have a constitutionally protected interest in his relationship with a child whose mother was married to, and cohabiting with, another man at the time of the child's conception and birth." Ante, at 2347 (STEVENS, J., concurring in judgment), see infra, at 2352-2355, post, at 2360 (WHITE, J., dissenting). Five Justices agree that the flaw inhering in a conclusive presumption that terminates a constitutionally protected interest without any hearing whatsoever is a procedural one. See infra, at 2358; post, at 2360 (WHITE, J., dissenting); ante, at 2347 (STEVENS, J., concurring in judgment). Four Members of the Court agree that Michael H. has a liberty interest in his relationship with Victoria, see infra, at 2353; post, at 2360 (WHITE, J., dissenting), and one assumes for purposes of this case that he does, see ante, at 2347 (STEVENS, J., concurring in judgment).

In contrast, only one other Member of the Court fully endorses Justice SCALIA's view of the proper method of analyzing questions arising under the Due Process Clause. ***

I

Once we recognized that the "liberty" protected by the Due Process Clause of the Fourteenth Amendment encompasses more than freedom from bodily restraint, today's plurality opinion emphasizes, the concept was cut loose from one natural limitation on its meaning. This innovation paved the way, so the plurality hints, for judges to substitute their own preferences for those of elected officials. Dissatisfied with this supposedly unbridled and uncertain state of affairs, the plurality casts about for another limitation on the concept of liberty.

It finds this limitation in "tradition." Apparently oblivious to the fact that this concept can be as malleable and as elusive as "liberty" itself, the plurality pretends that tradition places a discernible border around the Constitution. The pretense is seductive; it would be comforting to believe that a search for "tradition" involves nothing more idiosyncratic or complicated than poring through dusty volumes on American history. Yet, as Justice WHITE observed in his dissent in Moore v. East Cleveland, *: "What the deeply rooted traditions of the country are is arguable." Indeed, wherever I would begin to look for an interest "deeply rooted in the country's traditions," one thing is certain: I would not stop (as does the plurality) at Bracton, or Blackstone, or Kent, or even the American Law Reports in conducting my search. Because reasonable people can disagree about the content of particular traditions, and because they can disagree even about which traditions are relevant to the definition of "liberty," the plurality has not found the objective boundary that it seeks.

Even if we could agree, moreover, on the content and significance of particular traditions, we still would be forced to identify the point at which a tradition becomes firm enough to be relevant to our definition of liberty and the moment at which it becomes too obsolete to be relevant any longer. The plurality supplies no objective means by which we might make these determinations. Indeed, as soon as the plurality sees signs that the tradition upon which it bases its decision (the laws denying putative fathers like Michael standing to assert paternity) is crumbling, it shifts ground and says that the case has nothing to do with that tradition, after all. "[W]hat is at issue here," the plurality asserts after canvassing the law on paternity suits, "is not entitlement to a state pronouncement that Victoria was begotten by Michael." Ante, at 2343. But that is precisely what is at issue here, and the plurality's last-minute denial of this fact dramatically illustrates the subjectivity of its own analysis.

It is ironic that an approach so utterly dependent on tradition is so indifferent to our precedents. Citing barely a handful of this Court's numerous decisions defining the scope of the liberty protected by the Due Process Clause to support its reliance on tradition, the plurality acts as though English legal treatises and the American Law Reports always have provided the sole source for our constitutional principles. They have not. ***
***

If we had looked to tradition with such specificity in past cases, many a decision would have reached a different result. Surely the use of contraceptives by unmarried couples, *Eisenstadt v. Baird,* *, or even by married couples, *Griswold v. Connecticut,*;* the freedom from corporal punishment in schools, *Ingraham v. Wright,* *; the freedom from an arbitrary transfer from a prison to a psychiatric institution, *Vitek v. Jones,** ; and even the right to raise one's natural but illegitimate children, *Stanley v. Illinois,* *, were not "interest[s] traditionally protected by our society," ante, at 2341, at the time of their consideration by this Court. If we had asked, therefore, in *Eisenstadt, Griswold,Ingraham, Vitek,* or *Stanley* itself whether the specific interest under consideration had been traditionally protected, the answer would have been a resounding "no." That we did not ask this question in those cases highlights the novelty of the interpretive method that the plurality opinion employs today.

The plurality's interpretive method is more than novel; it is misguided. It ignores the good reasons for limiting the role of "tradition" in interpreting the Constitution's deliberately capacious language. *** Moreover, *** the plurality acts as if the only purpose of the Due Process Clause is to confirm the importance of interests already protected by a majority of the States. Transforming the protection afforded by the Due Process Clause into a redundancy mocks those who, with care and purpose, wrote the Fourteenth Amendment.

In construing the Fourteenth Amendment to offer shelter only to those interests specifically protected by historical practice, moreover, the plurality ignores the kind of society in which our Constitution exists. We are not an assimilative, homogeneous society, but a facilitative, pluralistic one, in which we must be willing to abide someone else's unfamiliar or even repellent practice because the same tolerant impulse protects our own idiosyncracies. Even if we can agree, therefore, that "family" and "parenthood" are part of the good life, it is absurd to assume that we can agree on the content of those terms and destructive to pretend that we do. In a community such as ours, "liberty" must include the freedom not to conform. The plurality today squashes this freedom by requiring specific approval from history before protecting anything in the name of liberty.

The document that the plurality construes today is unfamiliar to me. It is not the living charter that I have taken to be our Constitution; it is instead a stagnant, archaic, hidebound document steeped in the prejudices and superstitions of a time long past. This Constitution does not recognize that times change, does not see that sometimes a practice or rule outlives its foundations. I cannot accept an interpretive method that does such violence to the charter that I am bound by oath to uphold.

II

***

[T]o describe the issue in this case as whether the relationship existing between Michael and Victoria "has been treated as a protected family unit under the historic practices of our society, or whether on any other basis it has been accorded special protection," *, is to reinvent the wheel. The better approach--indeed, the one commanded by our prior cases and by common sense--is to ask whether the specific parent-child relationship under consideration is close enough to the interests that we already have protected to be deemed an aspect of "liberty" as well. *** [T]he question is not what "level of generality" should be used to describe the relationship between Michael and Victoria, *, but whether the relationship under consideration is sufficiently substantial to qualify as a liberty interest under our prior cases.

On four prior occasions, we have considered whether unwed fathers have a constitutionally protected interest in their relationships witi ι their children. * Though different in factual and legal circumstances, these cases have produced a unifying theme: although an unwed father's biological link to his child does not, in and of itself, guarantee him a constitutional stake in his relationship with that child, such a link combined with a substantial parent-child relationship will do so. "When an unwed father demonstrates a full commitment to the responsibilities of parenthood by 'com [ing] forward to participate in the rearing of his child,' ... his interest in personal contact with his child acquires substantial protection under the Due Process Clause. At that point it may be said that he 'act[s] as a father toward his children.'" *Lehr **. This commitment is why Mr. Stanley and Mr. Caban won; why Mr. Quilloin and Mr. Lehr lost; and why Michael H. should prevail today. Michael H. is almost certainly Victoria D.'s natural father, has lived with her as her father, has contributed to her support, and has from the beginning sought to strengthen and maintain his relationship with her.
***

The evidence is undisputed that Michael, Victoria, and Carole did live together as a family; that is, they shared the same household, Victoria called Michael "Daddy," Michael contributed to Victoria's support, and he is eager to continue his relationship with her. Yet they are not, in the plurality's view, a "unitary family," whereas Gerald, Carole, and Victoria do compose such a family. The only difference between these two sets of relationships, however, is the fact of marriage. The plurality, indeed, expressly recognizes that marriage is the critical fact in denying Michael a constitutionally protected stake in his relationship with Victoria: no fewer than six times, the plurality refers to Michael as the "adulterous natural father" (emphasis added) or the like. * See also* (referring to the "marital family" of Gerald, Carole, and Victoria) (emphasis added); ante, at 2345 (plurality's holding limited to those situations in which there is "an extant marital family"). *** Significantly, our decisions in those cases in no way relied on the need to protect the marital family. Hence the plurality's claim that Stanley, Quilloin, Caban, and Lehr were about the "unitary family," as that family is defined by today's plurality, is surprising indeed.

The plurality's exclusive rather than inclusive definition of the "unitary family" is out of step with other decisions as well. This pinched conception of "the family," crucial as it is in rejecting Michael's and Victoria's claims of a liberty interest, is jarring in light of our many cases preventing the States from denying important interests or statuses to those whose situations do not fit the government's narrow view of the family. From *Loving v. Virginia,* * to *Levy v. Louisiana,* * to *Moore v. East Cleveland,* *, we have declined to respect a State's notion, as manifested in its allocation of privileges and burdens, of what the family should be. Today's rhapsody on the "unitary family" is out of tune with such decisions.

III
***

A

We must first understand the nature of the challenged statute: it is a law that stubbornly insists that Gerald is Victoria's father, in the face of evidence showing a 98 percent probability that her father is Michael. What Michael wants is a chance to show that he is Victoria's father. By depriving him of this opportunity, California prevents Michael from taking advantage of the best-interest standard embodied in § 4601 of California's Civil Code, which directs that parents be given visitation rights unless "the visitation would be detrimental to the best interests of the child." Cal. Civ. Code Ann. § 4601 (West Supp.1989). ·
***
***

B

The question before us, therefore, is whether California has an interest so powerful that it justifies granting Michael no hearing before terminating his parental rights.

"Many controversies have raged about the cryptic and abstract words of the Due Process Clause but there can be no doubt that at a minimum they require that deprivation of life, liberty or property by adjudication be preceded by notice and opportunity for hearing appropriate to the nature of the case." *Mullane v. Central Hanover Bank & Trust Co.,* * (1950). When a State seeks to limit the procedures that will attend the deprivation of a constitutionally protected interest, it is only the State's interest in streamlining procedures that is relevant. ***

The purported state interests here, however, stem primarily from the State's antagonism to Michael's and Victoria's constitutionally protected interest in their relationship with each other and not from any desire to streamline procedures. Gerald D. explains that § 621 promotes marriage, maintains the relationship between the child and presumed father, and protects the integrity and privacy of the matrimonial family. * It is not, however, § 621, but the best-interest principle, that protects a stable marital relationship and maintains the relationship between the child and presumed father. *** *** The State's purported interest in protecting matrimonial privacy thus does not measure up to Michael's and Victoria's interest in maintaining their relationship with each other.

Make no mistake: to say that the State must provide Michael with a hearing to prove his paternity is not to express any opinion of the ultimate state of affairs between Michael and Victoria and Carole and Gerald. ***
***

IV

The atmosphere surrounding today's decision is one of make-believe. Beginning with the suggestion that the situation confronting us here does not repeat itself every day in every corner of the country, *, moving on to the claim that it is tradition alone that supplies the details of the liberty that the Constitution protects, and passing finally to the notion that the Court always has recognized a cramped vision of "the family," today's decision lets stand California's pronouncement that Michael--whom blood tests show to a 98 percent probability to be Victoria's father--is not Victoria's father. When and if the Court awakes to reality, it will find a world very different from the one it expects.
JUSTICE WHITE, with whom JUSTICE BRENNAN joins, dissenting.

California law, as the plurality describes it, *, tells us that, except in limited circumstances, California declares it to be "irrelevant for paternity purposes whether a child conceived during, and born into, an existing marriage was begotten by someone other than the husband"*. This I do not accept, for the fact that Michael H. is the biological father of Victoria is to me highly relevant to whether he has rights, as a father or otherwise, with respect to the child. Because I believe that Michael H. has a liberty interest that cannot be denied without due process of the law, I must dissent.

I

Like JUSTICES BRENNAN, MARSHALL, BLACKMUN, and STEVENS, I do not agree with the plurality opinion's conclusion that a natural father can never "have a constitutionally protected interest in his relationship with a child whose mother was married to, and cohabiting with, another man at the time of the child's conception and birth." *. Prior cases here have recognized the liberty interest of a father in his relationship with his child. In none of these cases did we indicate that the father's rights were dependent on the marital status of the mother or biological father. The basic principle enunciated in the Court's unwed father cases is that an unwed father who has demonstrated a sufficient commitment to his paternity by way of personal, financial, or custodial responsibilities has a protected liberty interest in a relationship with his child.

We have not before faced the question of a biological father's relationship with his child when the child was born while the mother was married to another man. On several occasions however, we have considered whether a biological father has a constitutionally cognizable interest in an opportunity to establish paternity. ***
***

In the case now before us, Michael H. is not a father unwilling to assume his responsibilities as a parent. To the contrary, he is a father who has asserted his interests in raising and providing for his child since the very time of the child's birth. In contrast to the father in *Lehr*, Michael had begun to develop a relationship with his daughter. There is no dispute on this point. Michael contributed to the child's support. Michael and Victoria lived together (albeit intermittently, given Carole's itinerant lifestyle). There is a personal and emotional relationship between Michael and Victoria, who grew up calling him "Daddy." Michael held Victoria out as his daughter and contributed to the child's financial support. (Even appellee concedes that Michael has "made greater efforts and had more success in establishing a father-child relationship" than did Mr. Lehr. *.) The mother has never denied, and indeed has admitted, that Michael is Victoria's father. *Lehr* was predicated on the absence of a substantial relationship between the man and the child and emphasized the "difference between the developed parent-child relationship that was implicated in *Stanley* and *Caban*, and the potential relationship involved in *Quilloin* and [*Lehr*]." * "When an unwed father demonstrates a full commitment to the responsibilities of parenthood by 'com[ing] forward to participate in the rearing of his child,' *Caban*, *, his interest in personal contact with his child acquires substantial protection under the Due Process Clause." *Lehr*, *. The facts in this case satisfy the *Lehr* criteria, which focused on the relationship between father and child, not on the relationship between father and mother. Under *Lehr* a "mere biological relationship" is not enough, but in light of Carole's vicissitudes, what more could Michael have done? It is clear enough that Michael more than meets the mark in establishing the constitutionally protected liberty interest discussed in Lehr and recognized in *Stanley v. Illinois*, supra, and *Caban v. Mohammed*, supra. He therefore has a liberty interest entitled to protection under the Due Process Clause of the Fourteenth Amendment.

II

California plainly denies Michael this protection, by refusing him the opportunity to rebut the State's presumption that the mother's husband is the father of the child. California law not only deprives Michael of a legal parent-child relationship with his daughter Victoria but even denies him the opportunity to introduce blood-test evidence to rebut the demonstrable fiction that Gerald is Victoria's father. ***

The interest in protecting a child from the social stigma of illegitimacy lacks any real connection to the facts of a case where a father is seeking to establish, rather than repudiate, paternity. *** It is hardly rare in this world of divorce and remarriage for a child to live with the "father" to whom her mother is married, and still have a relationship with her biological father.

The State's professed interest in the preservation of the existing marital unit is a more significant concern. *** On the facts of this case, however, Gerald was well aware of the liaison between Carole and Michael. *** [T]he argument that the conclusive presumption preserved the sanctity of the marital unit had more sway in a time when the husband was similarly prevented from challenging paternity. ***

As the Court has said: "The significance of the biological connection is that it offers the natural father an opportunity that no other male possesses to develop a relationship with his offspring. If he grasps that opportunity and accepts some measure of responsibility for the child's future, he may enjoy the blessings of the parent-child relationship and make uniquely valuable contributions to the child's development." *Lehr*, *. It is as if this passage was addressed to Michael. Yet the plurality today recants. Michael eagerly grasped the opportunity to have a relationship with his daughter (he lived with her; he declared her to be his child; he provided financial support for her) and still, with today's opinion, his opportunity has vanished. He has been rendered a stranger to his child.

Because Cal. Evid. Code Ann. § 621, as applied, should be held unconstitutional under the Due Process Clause of the Fourteenth Amendment, I respectfully dissent.

c. Notes and Questions

1) Informality and Significance of Establishing Parentage

In many civil law jurisdictions, official registration of birth and civil status is very important, and recording birth information is highly and formally regulated and has significant legal ramifications. In the United States, however, the establishment of parentage historically has been and largely still is relatively informal. For most parents and children, parentage is established by two presumptions -- the presumption of the maternity of the woman who gave birth to a child, and the presumption of the paternity of her husband, if she is married. In addition, most states have enacted statutory presumptions for use in paternity cases that assume paternity by open acknowledgment and/or cohabitation with the mother of a child born out of wedlock, thus covering many children born out of wedlock. Parentage is important in American law primarily for two reasons: to establish and enforce the parental obligation to provide child support (which otherwise the state would have to provide), and to establish and enforce the parent's right to associate with the child (control custody or exercise visitation). In both cases, the establishment of parentage usually has direct benefits for children, but most parentage actions are brought by adults for their own adult purposes and interests.

2) Biological Parentage

The legal concept of parentage has long been tied to biological parentage. That is, the strong presumption in the law has been that the biological parents of a child are also the legal parents of the child, charged with all of the legal responsibilities, duties, and burdens of parentage, and also entitled to claim all of the legal rights and privileges of parentage. Thus, the search for the legal parent has usually been a search for the biological parent. As later chapters will show, the development of modern procreative technologies often creates situations in which the assumption that biological parentage constitutes legal parentage is challenged. Even before modern procreative technologies, some cases arose in which the biological assumption was challenged or rejected in the law. Lord Mansfield's rule that a married man could not, except in rare cases, challenge the presumption that he was the legal father of the children born to his wife is one well-known exception.

Why have biological parentage and legal parentage been, and to a great extent still are, so strongly linked? Why should biological parents be preferred over social parents (the person(s) who have socialized the child)? Would it make more sense to assign parentage to those adults who test highest on parental skill tests, or to those who are willing to pay the most for the privilege of raising a child, or to those who most earnestly desire to raise a child? Would not an agency of experts do a better job of choosing legal parents for a child than the present system which leaves it to the whims and hormones of any two persons old enough to engage in procreative sex? If the biological connection is deemed significant, why not choose among the relatives of the child (parents, grandparents, aunts, uncles, etc.) and select the most promising parents? (Is this like the King's decree that the sun rise in the east and set in the west -- a rule that merely recognizes a situation over which the law has no control?)

3) Stanley Questions

The majority opinion discusses both the due process and equal protection clauses in connection with Mr. Stanley's constitutional rights. Does the opinion recognize substantive rights for Mr. Stanley? If so, what are they? Why would Justice Scalia refer to this case as a landmark case in Michael H.? Would *Stanley's* footnote 9 extend to other proceedings involving parents? Three other cases following *Stanley* addressed claims of nonmarital fathers. In *Michael H. v. Gerald D.*, how does Michael H. want the court to read these cases?

Following the Supreme Court decision, the Illinois Juvenile Court held a hearing, found Peter Stanley unfit, and placed the children in state custody.

4) *Michael H.* Questions

In *Michael H. v. Gerald D.*, 491 U.S. 110 (1989), the Supreme Court ruled that the Constitution did not require states to grant the paramour of a married woman a paternity claim. (1) Do you agree that biological parentage in such circumstances should be entitled to no constitutional protection? Why (or why not)? (2) Of course, nothing in *Michael H.* suggests that the states are constitutionally unable to grant such a claim to the adulterous stranger. Does that mean that if a state allows an adulterous stranger to the marriage to assert a paternity claim ten years (or five years, or even just two years) after the child has been born, the husband (and/or wife) has no constitutional claim for impermissible interference with parental relations? (3) What constitutional difference, if any, does (or should) the fact of marriage (and who was married to whom) make in determining what paternity claim the biological father may assert, or what protection will be afforded the paternity claim of the husband who undertakes parental responsibilities for a child he knows or believes is not his own? (4) Are these questions *really* answered (substantively) by the Constitution? Does not the Constitution establish a procedure for answering these questions, rather than giving the answers directly, and that procedure is the republican form of self-government, whereby the elected representatives of the people determine, state-by-state, how these substantive questions should be answered? Under the Constitution, is it not the responsibility of the legislature, not the judiciary, to weigh and balance such competing interests? (5) *Michael H.* might be viewed as an adoption case, construing the California statutes as allowing the husband (with his wife's approval) to adopt the biological child of his wife that is born during marriage by not challenging the paternity of the child within two years of the birth of the child. What, if anything, does the dissent in *Michael H.* suggest about scrutiny of adoption statutes which do not provide the biological father of the child some time (arguably at least four years) in which to assert a paternity claim? What, if anything, does the plurality opinion suggest about the same subject? (6) What about Victoria D.? When she lived with Michael H., she called him "Daddy". Has she not already experienced having two daddies?

While the Supreme Court in *Michael H.* rejected the claim that the Constitution mandates that a state allow a man claiming to be the father of a child born to a married woman not his wife to assert a claim and present evidence to establish his paternity; it did not suggest that the Constitution prohibits states from allowing such claims and evidence. Many states have enacted laws so providing. In fact, shortly after the Supreme Court decided *Michael H.*, the California legislature amended its evidence code to permit a "presumed father" to seek blood testing to establish paternity of a child born to a married women if he does so within two years of the birth of the child. Additionally, several state courts have concluded that their state constitutions or state statutes confer on the putative fathers of children born to other men's wives the kinds of claims and procedural opportunities that Michael H. claimed unsuccessfully as a matter of federal constitutional law in *Michael H. See e.g. McDaniels v. Carlson*, 738 P.2d 254 (Wash. 1987); *Ross v. Ross*, 783 P.2d 331 (Kan. 1990); *In re J.W.T.*, 872 S.W.2d 189 (Tex. 1994); *Ban v.*

Quigley, 812 P.2d 1014 (Ariz. App. 1990). Other courts have reached the same conclusion the Supreme Court did in *Michael H. See e.g. G.F.C. v. S.G. and D.G.*, 686 So.2d 1382 (Fla. App. 1997); and others have allowed such claims only in limited (established relationship) circumstances. *See Weidenbacher v. Duclos*, 661 A.2d 988 (Conn. 1995); *Allen v. Stone*, 474 S.E.2d 554 (W.Va. 1996); *C.C. v. A.B.*, 550 N.E.2d 365 (Mass. 1990).

5) Nonpaternity

Unlike Gerald D., some husbands in his situation want to prove nonpaternity when they learn the child of the marriage is a nonbiological child. Suppose there is no statute of limitation as it was in the California statute, should the court allow the husband to prove nonpaternity and allow the child to lose her status of a marital child even if the mother stipulates to his nonpaternity? Read *Cleo A.E. v. Rickie Gene E.,* 438 S.E.2d 886 (W. Va. Ct. of App. 1993). Whose interests were served by the court's decision? Does the liberty interest to be a parent include the right not to be a parent? If so, would the California statute be unconstitutional for husbands like Gerald D.?

6) Maternity in General

Before the days of egg donation, embryo transfer, in vitro fertilization, and surrogate motherhood, few questions arose concerning maternity because the visible physical condition of pregnancy and third-party assisted childbirth made the identity of the biological mother of a child easily known in most cases. Even today, there are comparatively few cases involving disputes over maternity. *See* Chapter 11, *infra.*

3. Practical and Ethical Considerations

a. Stereotypes and Discrimination

On what evidence did *Stanley's* dissenting justices base their opinion that mothers have stronger bonds with their children than fathers and that unwed mothers were generally more dependable protectors of their children than unwed fathers? Is there more persuasive evidence? If so, how would such evidence affect the majority opinion? Should courts be more vigilant, as an ethical consideration, when admitting evidence that may lead to stereotyping, and in turn may lead to discrimination?

4. Bibliography

Contemporary Family Law vol. 2, Ch. 9 (Lynn D. Wardle, Christopher L. Blakesley & Jacqueline Y. Parker, eds. 1988).

Lynn D. Wardle, *Parenting in American Law -- Today and Tomorrow* in the Legal Relationship between Parents and Children 111-147 (Choo Soo Kim ed. 1997).

CHAPTER 10

Conventional Paternity and Legitimacy

A. PATERNITY

1. Background

a. Methods of Establishing Paternity

Today there are three principal ways to establish paternity: 1) conclusive legal presumption of paternity, 2) admission or acknowledgment of paternity by the father, usually by administrative process (typically a voluntary filing by the father), or 3) by adjudication of paternity in a judicial proceeding.

b. Scientific Tests of Paternity and Maternity

Although no scientific evidence proves maternity or paternity, the development of genetic scientific tests of blood and tissue has created a more reliable method to prove biological parenthood to a greater degree of certainty. The three testing systems are the human blood and tissue typing system (the oldest, including the ABO system of antigens), the human leukocyte antigen (HLA) system, and the DNA system (all states now use and prefer DNA testing). Results of these scientific tests, including statistical analysis, are admissible in paternity litigation in every state under certain conditions.

2. Statutes, Cases and Doctrines

a. Uniform Acts

The National Conference of Commissioners on Uniform State Laws (NCCUSL) and the American Bar Association (ABA) have promulgated four separate acts dealing with paternity.

The *Uniform Act on Paternity* (UAP), 9B Uniform Laws Annot. 347 (1987), is the oldest uniform law on paternity; it was approved by the NCCUSL and the ABA in 1960. It has been adopted by six states (including Utah). The UAP was drafted "to replace the antiquated 'bastardy' proceeding with its preliminary examination and other quasi-criminal features." UAP Prefatory Note, 9B ULA 347 (1987). (It replaced the 1922 Uniform Illegitimacy Act, which, like the 1952 Blood Tests to Determine Paternity Act of 1952, was an earlier effort to address the same problem.). The UAP provides that the father of a child born out of wedlock "is liable to the same extent as the father of a child born in wedlock ... for the reasonable expenses of the mother's pregnancy and confinement and for the education, necessary support and funeral expenses of the child." § 1.

The *Uniform Parentage Act* (UPA), 9B Uniform. Laws Annot. 287 (1987), was approved by the NCCUSL in 1973. The UPA was intended to provide "substantive legal equality for all children regardless of the marital status of their parents ... ." UPA Prefatory Note, 9B ULA at 289 (1987). The UPA was revised in 2000 and in 2002. The UPA of 1973 is still important because it was adopted in nineteen states as of 2000 and in part by other states. Under the UPA (as amended 2002), "a child born to parents who are not married to each other has the same rights under the law as a child born to parents who are married to each other." *Id.* § 202. The parental status of the natural mother is established by the woman having given birth to the child (except as modified by its provisions regulating surrogacy), or adjudication of the woman's maternity, or adoption by the woman, or under certain circumstances when there is a gestational mother. *Id.* § 201 (1)(a).

The parental status for the "natural father" is established by an irrebuttable presumption under *Id.* § 204, or an effective acknowledgment, or an adjudication of paternity, or adoption, or consent to assisted reproduction, or an adjudication confirming the man as parent of a child born to a gestational mother if the agreement was validated under Article 8 or is enforceable under other law. § 201 (b). A man (under § 204) is presumed to be the natural father of a child if (1) born to his wife, or within 300 days after termination of the marriage, (2) born to a woman with whom he had an invalid solemnized marriage before birth, (3) born to a woman he formally married or tried to marry after birth, if he acknowledged the child, agreed to be named on a birth certificate, or signed a support agreement, and if (4) for the first two years of the child's life, he resided in the same household with the child and openly held out the child as his own. *Id.* § 204.

Article 3 provides nonjudicial procedures for the acknowledgment of paternity by the mother and a man claiming to be the genetic father. Article 6 sets forth the civil proceedings to adjudicate parentage. The natural mother and the man whose paternity is to be adjudicated must always be joined as parties. *Id.* § 603. Personal jurisdiction over the defendant is required, including the use of the long-arm provision for establishing personal jurisdiction under Uniform Interstate Family Support Act, which is enacted in every state. *Id.* § 604. A paternity action against one who is not a presumed, acknowledged, or adjudicated father may be brought at any time, except that after the child becomes an adult only the child may initiate the action. *Id.* § 606. If there is a presumed father, the adjudication of parentage must be commenced within two years of the child's birth by a presumed father, the mother, or another individual; otherwise, a proceeding to disprove paternity between a child and the presumed father may be maintained at any time if a court determines that the presumed father and the child's mother neither cohabited nor engaged in sexual intercourse with each other during the probable time of conception and the presumed father never openly held out the child as his own. *Id.* § 607.

The *Uniform Putative and Unknown Fathers Act* (UPUFA), 9B Uniform Laws Annot. 51 (1994 Cum. Supp.), also was approved by the NCCUSL in 1988. No state has yet adopted it. The UPUFA was designed to provide for the rights of "an expanding population of unwed men who wish to play a role in the upbringing of their children," 9B ULA 52 (1994 Cum. Supp.), and goes further than any of the other Acts to give a putative father standing and procedural protections in actions regarding a child. This may be why no state has yet to adopt the UPUFA.

Additionally, the *Uniform Act on Blood Tests to Determine Paternity* has been adopted by four states. Perhaps the greater use and power of DNA testing which can use but does not require blood testing has rendered this Act less useful than some other uniform laws. The existence of four separate uniform acts, none of which has been adopted by even half of the states, belies the notion of "uniform" law in this area.

Larry K. Butcher v. Commonwealth of Kentucky
96 S.W. 3d 3 (KY. 2002)

II. ADMISSION OF PATERNITY TEST

Appellant next claims that the trial court erred in admitting into evidence the results of a DNA paternity test indicating a 99.74 percent likelihood that Appellant was the father of H.B.'s child.
* * *

A brief explanation of the paternity test employed is necessary for our analysis. The test at issue, like similar paternity tests used throughout the nation, involves three separate tiers or determinations: probability of exclusion, paternity index, and probability of paternity. *** See generally D.H. Kaye, *"The Probability of an Ultimate Issue: The Strange Cases of Paternity Testing,"* 75 Iowa L. Rev. 75 (1989). The first tier, probability of exclusion, seeks to "exclude" Appellant as a possible father of H.B.'s child. As explained by the expert who conducted the testing in this case, Mr. DeGuglielmo, exclusionary testing looks for inconsistencies between the genetic make-up of the child and the alleged father that would necessarily indicate a lack of relation.

An exclusion analysis is premised on the basic notion that half of the child's DNA comes from each parent. It requires a comparison of the DNA of the mother with that of the child, excluding the DNA that matches between them. Since the remaining DNA of the child necessarily comes from the biological father, it can then be isolated and compared with the DNA of the alleged father. *** If the alleged father's DNA does not "match" the child's DNA at all, he can be excluded as a possible parent.

With respect to Appellant's DNA testing, Mr. DeGuglielmo testified that his team analyzed "a panel of eight different genetic markers...eight different tests that we use to try to find something that would say that Appellant could not be the father of [the child]." He concluded, however, "Each test showed that Mr. Butcher was included in the group of people who could potentially be the father of the child."

Once it is established that an alleged father cannot be excluded as a possible parent, as in Appellant's case, the second part of the paternity test takes effect. As Mr. DeGuglielmo explained at trial, "When we don't find any exclusion, we then have to make some relevance to the information that we have there....So we do a statistical evaluation to say how likely that match that we see is." Applying a formula that factors the frequency of "matches" between the alleged father and the child results in an assessment expressed numerically as a paternity index. As explained in [*Griffith v. State*, 976 S.W.2d 241, 243 (Tex. Ct. App. 1998)]: The paternity index is a value reflecting the likelihood that a tested man is the father of the child as opposed to an untested man of the same race. It is expressed as a number. If a paternity index can be assigned to a man, it means that he is that many more times likely to be the father than any other randomly selected male of his race.

Mr. DeGuglielmo testified that tests performed on the eight genetic markers previously discussed yielded a paternity index of 388/1, meaning Appellant was 388 times more likely to be the father of the child than a randomly selected male of the same race.

The third and final part of the paternity test translates the paternity index into a percentage that is more understandable. This percentage constitutes the end test result-the probability of paternity. It is calculated using Bayes' Theorem, a formula that takes into account actual events and circumstances, as opposed to random sequences of events. *Id.*; *see also Davis v. State*, 476 N.E.2d 127, 137-138

(Ind.Ct.App.1985). In paternity tests generally, this formula combines the paternity index and another value representing the prior probability that an event occurred, including such factors as access to the mother, fertility, and date of conception. The result is a percentage that can be used to assess the overall probability of paternity. The formula is as follows:

Probability of Paternity = $\dfrac{\text{Paternity Index}}{\text{Paternity Index} + 1}$

* * * * * * * *

The resulting quotient [ed. note: using a .5 (fifty percent) as the prior probability] indicates the percentage of random men that would be excluded as possible fathers of a child because they lack the necessary genetic material. In other words, as the percentage reflecting the probability of paternity increases, the alleged father becomes increasingly outnumbered by men who could not be the child's father. Because this concept is not easily conveyed or understood, the probability of paternity is accepted as simply representing the percent likelihood that the tested male is actually the father of the child. *Griffith*, 976 S.W.2d at 243.

Appellant's paternity test resulted in a probability of paternity of 99.74 percent. That is, there was a 99.74 percent likelihood that Appellant was the father of H.B.'s child. Although Mr. DeGuglielmo did not testify that he had used a prior probability value of .5 in reaching his expert conclusions, the mathematical results of the test suggest that he did. Appellant centers his appeal on this issue of prior probability.

* * * * * * * *

c. *Plemel v. Walter*

Plemel v. Walter
303 Or. 262, 735 P.2d 1209 (1987)

[Ed. Note: The paternity tests that were used this case were based on the ABO system, which classifies the ABO antigens in the blood, and 18 other blood systems. The ABO system was the first system to provide a scientific basis for evidence to exclude falsely accused fathers. This system calculates the same determinations as the DNA tests did in *Butcher v. Commonwealth*: the probability of exclusion, paternity index and probability of paternity. This case provides a more detailed discussion of these determinations. This case emphasizes the importance that these determinations must not be presented in such a manner that might confuse the jury.]
* * * * * * *

With respect to the disposition of this case, we conclude that it is necessary to remand for a new trial. Lovrien [the expert witness] testified that Walter's paternity index of 178 meant that he was 178 times more likely to be the father of Plemel's child than "an average man." While that testimony was accurate, other statements made by him, as we noted above, could have led the jury to infer that the paternity index was the probability that Walter was the father. Lovrien also testified that the paternity index was based on the assumption that "the most logical person" had been identified and accused of being the father and that if there was a zero prior probability that Walter was the father, the paternity index would be meaningless. From these statements the jury could have inferred that the significance of the paternity index would depend to some extent on the other evidence presented in the case, but this relationship was not made clear by Lovrien. Perhaps particularly confusing to the jury was the following statement made by Lovrien near the close of his testimony: "[A]ssuming that the right man has been accused or investigated, then the laboratory is used as a means of investigating, if he denies fatherhood, then you want a good laboratory test to say well if he is not the father, let's show that he is not. And that is what we did. We used a good laboratory test here. And if he is not the father, he should have been excluded, but he wasn't." On the record before us, we cannot say that the result would have been the same if Lovrien's testimony had been presented under the conditions set forth above.

The decision of the Court of Appeals is reversed. The judgment of the trial court is reversed, and the case is remanded to the trial court for a new trial.

d. Notes and Questions

1) Jurisdiction Over the Person in Paternity Actions and the Uniform Interstate Family Support Act

Paternity actions require in personam jurisdiction over the defendant because such actions involve the determination of paternity as well as an order for support. For nonresident defendants, the forum state must rely on its long-arm statute to satisfy due process if jurisdiction is not based on the defendant's physical presence in the state or on his consent. In the past, most long-arm statutes did not explicitly authorize the assertion of jurisdiction over nonresidents in paternity cases. However, states are now required under the Uniform Interstate Family Support Act (UIFSA) (discussed more fully in Chapter 36) to enact its Section 201, in order for states to be eligible to receive federal funds for welfare benefits. Section 201 is its long-arm provision, which allows states to take jurisdiction in paternity and support cases against a defendant who has engaged in sexual intercourse in the forum state when the child may have been conceived in that act of intercourse.

2) Statutes of Limitations

Fathers of children born out of wedlock, like fathers of legitimate children, are liable for the support of their children throughout their minority. However, a determination of paternity is necessary before the father of an unacknowledged child born out of wedlock is liable for support of the child. Accordingly, the imposition of any limitation period on paternity actions that is shorter than the period of minority will cause the child born out of wedlock to be disadvantaged vis-a-vis the legitimate child who can bring an action for support throughout the period of minority. In 1982, the United States Supreme Court held that a Texas one-year statute of limitations on paternity actions violated the Equal Protection Clause of the Fourteenth Amendment. *Mills v. Habluetzel*, 456 U.S. 91 (1982). A year later the Court invalidated on the same grounds a Tennessee statute providing a two-year limitations period for paternity actions. *Pickett v. Brown*, 426 U.S. 1 (1983). The Court unanimously invalidated on Equal Protection grounds a six-year statute of limitations on paternity actions by or for children born out of wedlock since, *inter alia*, the state allowed the fathers and some children to assert paternity claims after six years. Short statutes of limitations on paternity actions are no longer problematic. In 1984, Congress enacted the Child Support Enforcement Amendments of 1984, which required every state receiving particular federal funds "to have procedures which permit the establishment of paternity of any child at any time prior to the child's 18th birthday" 42 U.S.C.A. § 66 6(A) (1985)(Supp). In the days of shorter statutes of limitations, some courts avoided the limitations bar by reading into the statutes an exception: statutes of limitations upon actions in favor of minors toll until the minor comes of age.

3) Standing to Sue for Paternity

One of the most interesting and complicated issues in paternity actions is who has standing to sue to establish or disestablish paternity. Since paternity actions are permitted by statute in all states, the first source of authority to answer that question should be statutory. But most limit who may file to the mother, her husband, the child or his or her guardian, and a putative father (usually for a limited time). Some courts have ruled that it violates Equal Protection to deny the child himself or herself a claim for paternity. *Spada v. Pauley*, 385 N.W.2d 746 (Mich Ct App 1986) (mother's paternity claim was barred by statute of limitations; paternity claim in divorce action brought by the putative father who had married her several years after the birth of the child was precluded; denial of paternity claim asserted later by her son, then a teenager, unconstitutional). *See R. McG v. J.W.*, 615 P.2d 666 (Colo. 1981).

4) Finality of Paternity Determination

In a growing number of cases, DNA testing has shown that a man previously adjudicated the father in a paternity action is not the biological father of the child. Several states have allowed such evidence to disestablish paternity. *See Langston v. Riffe*, 754 A.2d 389 (Md. 2000). Others have barred such evidence by res judicata or rules for reopening judgments. *See e.g. Paternity of Cheryl*, 746 N.E.2d 488 (Mass 2001). If paternity is disestablished, courts generally will terminate future support payments, but the courts are divided on whether to collect arrearages. No state currently allows the recoupment of support already paid. *See* Roberts, *infra*.

5) Standard of Proof of Paternity

"In jurisdictions where paternity proceedings are regarded [as] civil in nature, as they are in Pennsylvania, the general rule is that the burden of proof of paternity is by a preponderance of the evidence." In *Rivera v. Minnich*, 483 U.S. 574 (1987), the Supreme Court held that due process was satisfied by use of the preponderance of evidence standard in paternity proceedings.

6) Access to Scientific Tests re: Paternity

DNA and sophisticated blood and antigen testing (like HLA testing) can be very expensive. Not infrequently, the defendants in paternity cases cannot afford them. Would it ever (or always) deny due process for a state to refuse to pay for the costs of such tests if the state is bringing the action? In *Little v. Streater*, 452 U.S. 1 (1981), the Court held that a Connecticut statute, which provided that in paternity actions the cost of blood grouping tests is to be borne by the party requesting them, denied due process when the statute was applied to indigent defendants. The Court emphasized that the Connecticut statute required a defendant to respond to a prima facie case with evidence other than his own denial. The blood grouping test would be such evidence, but for the cost.

7) Assistance of Counsel

In *Lassiter v. Department of Social Services of Durham County, North Carolina*, 453 U.S. 927 (1981), the Court held that in some cases the failure to appoint counsel for an indigent parent in a proceeding for termination of parental status could deprive the parent of due process, but in the case at bar where the petition contained no allegations upon which criminal charges could be based, no expert witnesses testified, no specially troublesome points of law were raised, and the presence of counsel could not have made a determinative difference it was not unconstitutional for the state to refuse to provide legal assistance to the defendant. Constitutionally, is appointment of counsel ever (or always) constitutionally required in paternity cases?

8) Economic Fairness

When does indigency so deprive a defendant of due process that the state must provide the defendant with the service or material that could strengthen his defense and possibly affect the outcome of the proceeding? But what does that have to do with paternity actions? If they are private—the mother suing the putative father for a declaration of paternity and for private support payments and reimbursement of (half of) the costs of prenatal care, delivery, etc., why should the state have to provide counsel, access to scientific testing for evidence, etc.? In other private lawsuits, does the state have a duty to see that the defendant is fairly represented and able to put on a fair defense? Why might or should paternity suits be treated differently?

9) Presumption of Paternity of Child Born to a Married Woman

Historically, one of the strongest presumptions known in law was the presumption that "every child born to a married woman is in law the legitimate child of her husband," a presumption founded on the "strong repugnance [of the common law] to any inquiry into the paternity of such child" which "absolve[d] the court from difficult inquiries." 2 F. Pollock & F. Maitland, *infra* at 398–99. The presumption was most notably manifest in the rule of evidence that barred married persons from giving any evidence that would tend to bastardize a child born during coverture. The most famous expression of this rule was made by Lord Mansfield who declared in *Goodright v. Moss*, 2 Cowp. 591, 98 Eng. Rep. 1257 (1777), that "the law of England is clear, that the declarations of a father or mother, cannot be admitted to bastardize the issue born after marriage. ... It is a rule, founded in decency, morality, and policy, that they (the parents) shall not be permitted to say after marriage, that they have had no connection, and therefore that the offspring is spurious." *Id.* Lord Mansfield also noted an exception (that made sense in an island-nation dependent upon its shipping)—"if the husband was within the four seas at the time the child was born," then he might be permitted to prove nonaccess to bastardize the child born to his unfaithful wife. Lord Mansfield's Rule came to America with the common law. But the application of the Rule has varied remarkably from state to state. Some jurisdictions have abolished the rule.

The presumption of marital paternity is generally applied only in civil cases. If paternity is disputed in a criminal case, could the presumption of paternity be made to put on the husband the burden of proving that he is not the father of the unsupported child? Would it make a difference if the presumption were irrebuttable or rebuttable? Criminal statutes should be strictly construed; would either presumption undermine the constitutional presumption of innocence?

The Supreme Court has upheld tougher standards and procedures for obtaining U.S. citizenship for children of U.S. fathers born out of wedlock abroad than for children of U.S. mothers born out of wedlock abroad. *Tuan Anh Nguyen v. I.N.S.*, 533 U.S. 53 (2001), and *Miller v. Albright*, 523 U.S. 420 (1998). In both cases, in addition to noting Congress' plenary power over immigration, the Court relied upon the substantial difference between the situation and parental relationship of a mother and of a father.

From the child's point of view is there a difference? From the state's view? Why or why not? Is this related to the difference in the presumption of paternity?

10) Scientific Paternity Testing

DNA testing, blood testing and tissue typing, including HLA tissue testing, are important sources of influential evidence in paternity suits. The early blood testing system (ABO system) was useful because it produced statistically reliable evidence to exclude paternity. HLA and DNA testing systems, however, produced statistically reliable evidence to establish paternity. In fact, the potentially unjustified influence that such "scientific evidence" may have in paternity cases is the source of some concern today. *See* Blakesley, *infra*, Ellman & Kaye, *infra*; Jensen, *infra*. For example, there has been wide acceptance by courts of HLA blood (tissue) testing results to establish (not disprove) paternity. But the reliance on HLA testing is not without its criticism. There are serious conceptual problems with admitting statistical estimates of the "probability of paternity."

> An example helps to illustrate the difference between the probability of exclusion and the probability of paternity. Suppose it is known only that the mother lived in Los Angeles at the time of the child's conception, and that mother and child are Caucasian. One might assume that the actual father must also have lived in Los Angeles, but of course that is far from certain. He might have been visiting from elsewhere, or the mother might have become impregnated on a weekend trip to San Diego. But if we ignore those possibilities and limit our universe of possible fathers to Caucasian males past the age of puberty who resided in the Los Angeles area at the time of conception, we have a suspect list of about two million. A test which eliminates even 95% of the suspects would still leave 100,000 possible fathers. The fact that the defendant was one of the remaining 100,000 is hardly overwhelming evidence. Although the test has a probability of exclusion of 95%, the probability of paternity in this example is only one in 100,000.

Ellman & Kaye, *infra* at 1141. Moreover, the calculation of probability of paternity using HLA test results requires a quantification of the "prior probability of paternity" based on all other evidence (nonmathematical). It appears that the experts who calculate probability of paternity based on HLA test results routinely assume a 50 percent "prior probability of paternity." While this percentage may be exceptionally generous to the defendant in many cases, "[t]here seems to be no basis for the blanket assumption that the prior probability is one-half" on either a case-by-case basis or as a matter of statistical analysis. *Id.* at 1149–51.

> One can imagine a case in which the defendant has produced credible evidence that the mother had had intercourse with other men, but not with him, during the conception period. Indeed, even had the defendant in *Cramer* shown that he was imprisoned in another state during the critical period, the expert's calculation of a 98.3% chance of paternity would not have been affected.

Id. at 1150–51. Professors Ellman and Kaye conclude:

In short, even the use of a well-founded prior probability derived from general experience in other paternity litigation yields a "probability of paternity" figure that excludes consideration of all the non-statistical evidence in that particular case. To label such a figure the "probability of paternity" is surely misleading, especially when the jury is not informed that the expert's calculation is based on such background statistics.

Id. at 1150.

What standard should the court use to allow the admission of this scientific evidence? Until recently, most states and the federal courts follow the *Frye* test or a version of it: whether the evidence was "sufficiently established to have gained general acceptance in the particular field in which it belongs." Read *Frye v. United States*, 293 F. 1013, 1014 (1923). In 1993, the United States Supreme Court in *Daubert v. Merrell Dow Pharmaceuticals, Inc.*, 509 U.S. 579, and its progeny held that the *Frye* test had been superseded by the adoption of the Federal Rules of Evidence and they provided a multiple-factor test. As a result, states that have patterned their rules of evidence after the Federal Rules of Evidence are likely to follow *Daubert* and its progeny; the others continue to follow the *Frye* test.

11) DNA Testing

DNA identity testing has become popular and has the potential for higher levels of statistical analysis. DNA testing compares the placement of genes along the chromosome (genetic loci) of a sample with those taken from a subject to try to exclude the subject as the source of a biological specimen. As one expert explains, "There are only three legitimate conclusions from DNA identity testing: 1) exclusion—the individual cannot be the source of the evidentiary sample; 2) nonexclusion—the individual cannot be excluded from being the source; and 3) no results—the analysis cannot be performed." Charles M. Strom, *infra.* DNA testing is evolving rapidly.

No DNA test is fool-proof. Today there are five common DNA technologies; all of them have their limits. For example, while DNA fingerprinting can produce statistically strong results, this test only works when the DNA is in very good condition and available in reasonably large quantities. DNA fingerprinting also is difficult to perform in the laboratory. "In practice, even in the best hands, fewer than half of all evidentiary samples can be successfully fingerprinted." *Id. at* 20. RFLP testing has been the subject of tremendous debates in the scientific community about how to properly perform the statistical calculations; one method of calculation commonly used for a while has been discredited and replaced. Statement of the results of DNA testing may be misleading. For example, the director of one DNA lab in Chicago reported that in a case he knew of a "lab quoted odds of more than 10 billion to 1 (i.e., more than the number of people living on earth) against this genotype existing elsewhere, but in fact the genotype had been observed once in the lab's database of 500 individuals (and once in the accused individual)." *Id. at* 23. PCR testing may be subject to the issues of contamination if the evidentiary sample is small or degraded. PCR Using Dot Blotting measure loci that have only two or three alleles per locus and are much less powerful statistically than other tests. Mitochondrial Sequencing tests mitochondria that are inherited only from one's mother and so is inappropriate in paternity testing. Contamination is a potential problem for several DNA tests, and even if the test is done in the best laboratory, the complex testing and calculation might be done incorrectly. *Id. at* 24.

12) The Biological Presumption of Legal Paternity

Debate is growing over the use and legal significance for examining legal parentage through scientific tests that may identify biological parentage with a high level of potential accuracy. New procreative technologies are eroding the old biological presumptions of legal parentage. For example, DNA and other tests may disprove the biological assumption that underlies the historic legal presumption of the husband's paternity of a child born to an unfaithful wife. This has given rise to some hotly debated decisions regarding traditional presumptions of paternity, rules of standing, evidence, estoppel, etc. *See e.g. Michael H. v. Gerald D.* If a man can prove with DNA testing that he is the biological father of the child born to a married woman, should he instead of (or in addition to) her husband be given paternity rights, including custody, visitation, or inheritance? If a man can prove (in or after a divorce proceeding) that he is not the biological father of a child born to his wife before or during their marriage, should he be obligated to support the child, despite his wife's deception? (*See generally* Morgan, *infra,* Parness, *infra,* and Anderlik, Ch. 9, *supra.*) What if he is a rapist? Some cases suggest a strict liability theory of biological paternity—a male is strictly held to the financial liabilities of paternity if his sperm conceived the child—even if the mother represented (falsely) that she was using birth control, or promised (deceitfully) to abort if she became pregnant, or expressly agreed (falsely) not to pursue paternity or child support, or feigned fidelity, or even if she obtained his sperm while he was unconscious, or otherwise without his consent. Most courts have held that the nonbiological father who assumed the responsibilities of parentage is estopped from denying paternity, or is liable for child support, or cannot recover damages from the deceitful mother. Several states have passed legislation providing statutory relief in cases of "paternity fraud."

3. Practical and Ethical Considerations

a. Contingent Fee Contracts in Paternity Cases

Contingency fee contracts in domestic relations cases generally are deemed to violate public policy and be unenforceable. The Model Rules of Professional Responsibility, Rule 1.5(d), expresses the essence of this long-recognized rule:

(D) A Lawyer shall not enter into an arrangement for, charge or collect:

(1) Any fee in a domestic relations matter, the payment or amount of which is contingent upon the securing of a divorce or upon the amount of alimony or support, or property settlement in lieu thereof.

Contingent fee contracts in paternity (support) actions are included in this ban in some jurisdictions. *See e.g., Davis v. Taylor,* 344 S.E.2d 19 (N.C. App. 1986). On the other hand, an ethics opinion in Alabama suggests that the prohibition on contingency fees in "domestic relations" cases does not apply to a paternity suit between unmarried persons because their relations are not formal domestic relations. Alabama Op. 87–96. Many cases have held that after the child support/paternity order has been entered, a contingency fee to collect arrearages owing is not barred. Louis Parley, *infra.* Fixed fee agreements that include a "result" factor have sometimes been distinguished from contingency fees and upheld. *Eckell v. Wilson,* 597 A.2d 696 (Pa. Super. Ct. 1991) (equitable distribution case). *But see State ex rel Oklahoma Bar Ass'n v. Fagin*, 848 P.2d 11 (Okla 1992).

The basic concern behind the ban on contingency fees in domestic relations litigation is that the contingent fee may give the attorney an inducement to prevent reconciliation (especially in divorce cases), to protect distraught clients in difficult personal circumstances from the possible overreaching of greedy attorneys, to protect the funds that are needed by the client to live on, to avoid the appearance that the attorney has a direct pecuniary interest in promoting the divisive domestic controversy, and because court awards of attorneys fees are potentially available (in some cases). Louis Parley, *infra*. (1) Do these or similar concerns apply to suits to establish paternity and recover support for the child, and if so, how much weight do or should those concerns have? (The policies underlying the rule against contingent fee contracts in paternity and support cases are undoubtedly worthy ones, especially the concern that they allow attorneys to take some of the award intended to be used directly for the support of the child. Does this policy presume a degree of segregation between the assets of the custodial parent and the child support award? Is that unrealistic? If a mother must ultimately pay for the attorney out of her own funds, which she is using to support the child, is not the child just as much affected economically as if the attorney's fee came out of the child support award?

4. Bibliography

William Blackstone, Commentaries on the Laws of England (1756).
> Contemporary Family Law, vol. 2, Chs. 8 & 9 (1988).
Christopher L. Blakesley, *Scientific Testing and Proof of Paternity: Some Controversy and Key Issues for Family Law Counsel*, 57 La. L. Rev. 379 (1997).
Stephen Cretney, Principles of Family Law (3d ed. 1979).
Ira Ellman & Kaye, *Probabilities and Proof: Can HLA and Blood Group Testing Prove Paternity?* 54 N.Y.U.L.Rev. 1131 (1979).
Brent Jensen, Comment, *Artificial Insemination and the Law*, 1982 B.Y.U. L. Rev. 935.
Allan Z. Litovsky & Kirsten Schultz, *Scientific Evidence of Paternity: A Survey of State Statutes*, 39 Jurimetrics J. 79 (Fall 1998).
Laura W. Morgan, *It's Ten O'Clock: Do You Know Where Your Sperms Are? Toward a Strict Liability Theory of Parentage*, 11 Divorce Litig. 1 (Jan. 1999).
Louis Parley, The Ethical Family Lawyer 47 n. 53; 47-52 (American Bar Association, Family Law Section, 1995).
2 F. Pollock & F. Maitland, The History of English Law (2d ed. 1898 reprinted 1968).
Paula Roberts, *Truth and Consequences: Part III. Who Pays When Paternity is Disestablished?*, 37 Fam. L. Q. 69 (2003).
Charles M. Strom, *Genetic Justice: A Lawyer's Guide to the Science of DNA Testing*, 87 Ill. B.J. 18, 19 (1999).
Jeffrey A. Parness, *Old-Fashioned Pregnancy, Newly-Fashioned Paternity*, 53 Syracuse L. Rev. 57 (2003).

B. LEGITIMACY

1. Background

a. History of Legal Discrimination Against Illegitimates

At common law, a person born out of wedlock was denied significant legal rights. Blackstone summarized the status of disabilities of illegitimacy as follows:

1. Who are bastards. A bastard, by our English laws, is one that is not only begotten, but born, out of lawful matrimony. The civil and canon laws do not allow a child to remain a bastard, if the parents afterward intermarry; and herein they differ most materially from our law, which, though not so strict as to require that the child shall be *begotten*, yet makes it an indispensable condition, to make it legitimate, that it shall be *born* after lawful wedlock. ... The main end and design of marriage, therefore, being to ascertain and fix upon some certain person to whom the care, the protection, the maintenance, and the education of the children should belong, this end is undoubtedly better answered by legitimating all issue born after wedlock, than by legitimating all issue of the same parties, even born before wedlock, so as wedlock afterward ensues; 1. Because of the very great uncertainty there will generally be in the proof that the issue was generally begotten by the same man; whereas, by confining the proof to the birth, and not to the begetting, our law has rendered it perfectly certain what child is legitimate, and who is to take care of the child. 2. Because, by the Roman law, a child may be continued a bastard or made legitimate, at the option of the father and mother, by a marriage *ex post facto*; thereby opening a door to many frauds and partialities which, by our law, are prevented. 3. Because, by those laws, a man may remain a bastard till forty years of age, and then become legitimate by the subsequent marriage of his parents; whereby the main end of marriage, the protection of infants, is totally frustrated. 4. Because this rule of the Roman law admits of no limitations as to the time or number of bastards so to be legitimated; but a dozen of them may, twenty years after their birth, by the subsequent marriage of their parents, be admitted to all the privileges of legitimate children. This is plainly a great discouragement to the matrimonial state; to which one main inducement is usually not only the desire of having *children*, but also the desire of procreating lawful heirs. ....

* * *

As bastards may be born before the coverture or marriage state is begun, or after it is determined, so, also, children born during wedlock may, in some circumstances, be bastards. As if the husband be out of the kingdom of England (or, as the law somewhat loosely phrases it, *extra quatuor maria*) for above nine months, so that no access to his wife can be presumed, her issue during that period shall be bastards. But, generally, during the coverture access of the husband shall be presumed, unless the contrary can be shown; which is such a negative as can only be proved by showing him to be elsewhere; for the general rule is *praesumitur pro legitimatione*. In a *divorce a mensa et thoro*, if the wife breeds children, they are bastards; for the law will presume the husband and wife are conformable to the sentence of separation, unless access be proved; but in a voluntary separation by agreement, the law will suppose access, unless the negative be shown. So, also, if there is an apparent impossibility of procreation on the part of the husband, as if he be only eight years old, or the like, there the issue of the wife shall be bastards. Likewise, in case of divorce in the spiritual court a vinculo matrimonii, all the issue born during the coverture are bastards; because such divorce is always upon some cause that rendered the marriage unlawful and null from the beginning.

2. Let us next see the duty of parents to their bastard children by our law, which is principally that of maintenance; for though bastards are not looked upon as children to any civil purposes, yet the ties of nature, of which maintenance is one, are not so easily dissolved; and they hold, indeed, as to many other intentions, as, particularly, that a man shall not marry his bastard sister or daughter. The civil law, therefore, when it denied maintenance to bastards begotten under certain atrocious circumstances, was neither

consonant to nature nor reason, however profligate and wicked the parents might justly be esteemed.

The method in which the English law provides maintenance for them is as follows: when a woman is delivered, or declares herself with child, of a bastard, and will by oath before a justice of peace charge any person as having got her with child, the justice shall cause such person to be apprehended, and commit him till he gives security, either to maintain the child, or appear at the next Quarter Sessions to dispute and try the fact. . . . Yet such is the humanity of our laws, that no woman can be compulsively questioned concerning the father of her child till one month after her delivery; which indulgence is, however, very frequently a hardship upon parishes, by giving the parents opportunity to escape.

3. I proceed next to the rights and incapacities which appertain to a bastard. The rights are very few, being only such as he can *acquire*; for he can *inherit* nothing, being looked upon as the son of nobody, and sometimes called *filius nullius,* sometimes *filius populi.* Yet he may gain a surname by reputation, though he has none by inheritance. All other children have their primary settlement in their father's parish; but a bastard in the parish where born, for he hath no father. . . . The incapacity of a bastard consists principally in this, that he can not be heir to any one, neither can he have heirs, but of his own body; for, being *nullius filius,* he is therefore of kin to nobody, and has no ancestor from whom any inheritable blood can be derived. A bastard was also, in strictness, incapable of holy orders; and, though that were dispensed with, yet he was utterly disqualified from holding any dignity in the Church; but this doctrine seems now obsolete, and in all other respects there is no distinction between a bastard and another man. And really any other distinction but that of not inheriting, which civil policy renders necessary, would, with regard to the innocent offspring of his parent's crimes, be odious, unjust, and cruel to the last degree; and yet the civil law, so boasted of for its equitable decisions, made bastards, in some cases, incapable even of a gift from their parents. A bastard may, lastly, be made legitimate, and capable of inheriting, by the transcendent power of an act of Parliament, and not otherwise; as was done in the case of John of Gant's bastard children, by a statute of Richard the Second.

1 W. Blackstone, *infra* at *455-59.

The common law was not alone in its harsh treatment of children born out of wedlock. In ancient Israel, children born out of wedlock suffered significant limitations also. "A bastard shall not enter into the congregation of the Lord; even to his tenth generation he shall not enter into the congregation of the Lord." Deuteronomy 23:2 (KJV).

At common law an illegitimate child could not become legitimate. "The child who is born of an unmarried woman is a bastard and nothing can make him legitimate."2 F. Pollock & F. Maitland, *infra* at 397. This rule was laid down in the days of King Henry II and never retreated from until statutes enacted in the twentieth century began to soften the harshness of the common law doctrine of illegitimacy. *See* S. Cretney, *infra*, at 574. In civil law countries, post-birth marriage of the parents of a child born out of wedlock caused the child to become legitimate. But the common law rejected this position.

Today, virtually all American jurisdictions provide that a child born out of wedlock is legitimated by the subsequent marriage of his or her parents. *See* Blakesley, *infra*. Additionally, paternity can be acknowledged without marriage in most states if the father evidences paternity in a statutorily approved manner, such as by agreeing to be named on the birth certificate, receiving the child into one's home, holding oneself out to be the father of the child, providing support for the child, etc.

b. Historical Policies Behind Discrimination Against Illegitimates

The distinction between legitimacy and illegitimacy historically has been of great importance in the law. English common law treated the illegitimate person harshly, denying numerous property and civil rights and generally imposing second-class legal status. Literature suggests that social opprobrium and discrimination of the time was at least as great. Blackstone mentioned five justifications for the severe discrimination of the common law against illegitimacy: 1) to provide for the stable care, protection and education of all children (by encouraging the marriage of their parents), 2) to reinforce the preference of the law for the marital state, 3) to provide certainty in law of paternity, 4) to avoid fraudulent claims of paternity, and 5) to simplify administration of distributions based upon paternity. Given the circumstances of his day, discrimination on the basis of legitimacy made practical, if unjust, sense. Then wealth was in rudimentary forms of property (principally realty and its income). Preservation and stability of property was the primary object of the law. Intrafamily intergenerational transfer of wealth was critical. Disposition of property from parent to child, particularly father to eldest son, was the essential scheme. Likewise, support was a family (fundamentally a paternal) responsibility. The only proof of paternity was testimonial and circumstantial evidence; reliable scientific evidence had not been developed. Thus, the property system (indeed the basic legal system) needed some generally reliable, socially acceptable, if arbitrary, basis for establishing legal paternity.

Marriage of the parents was probably as reliable a characteristic of parentage as any other factor at that time. The church (ecclesiastical courts) exercised primary control (and virtually exclusive jurisdiction) over marriage. By making marriage the basis for legal paternity, the powerful institutional support of the church was assured, and the moral appeal of virtue was enlisted. To the extent that marriage of parents was an underinclusive classification, and it was, it must be remembered that any other classification would have been at least equally underinclusive, and proof of paternity in cases that fell outside the classification would depend upon proofs that were not inherently reliable and which could be easily fabricated. Thus, adoption of marriage of the parents as the litmus test for paternity of a child clearly served the last four purposes noted by Blackstone (albeit the harsh peripheral doctrines which developed did not). The injustice of the requirement of legitimacy was no greater than the injustice of any other categorical approach that could have been taken at that time, and both the social demand for certainty and predictability as well as the unreliability of proof of paternity made individualized inquiry unacceptable.

2. Statutes, Cases and Doctrines

a. Summary of Selected Supreme Court Decisions Regarding Discrimination on the Basis of Illegitimacy

In the twentieth century the Supreme Court began to ask "why" (perhaps echoing Shakespeare's eloquent lament, "Why bastard, wherefore base? When my dimensions are as well compact, my mind as generous, and my shape as true, as honest madam's issue?

Why brand they us with base? With baseness? bastardy? base, base?" William Shakespeare, *King Lear,* Act 1, scene 2), and the results were revolutionary.

While the Supreme Court decisions on illegitimacy date to 1820, *see Stevenson's Heirs v. Sullivant,* 18 U.S. (5 Wheat.) 207 (1820), the most significant development in constitutional analysis came from 1968–1988. During this period the Court decided more than twenty such cases.

In 1968 the Supreme Court decided *Levy v. Louisiana,* 391 U.S. 68 (1968) and *Glona v. American Guarantee & Liability Ins. Co.,* 391 U.S. 73 (1968). Both cases involved a Louisiana wrongful death statute which provided that wrongful death actions could be brought by children for the death of their parents, and by parents for the death of their children. However, the statute did not include illegitimate children within the definition of "children." In *Levy,* five illegitimate children sought to recover for the wrongful death of their mother, and in *Glona,* the mother of an illegitimate child sought to recover for the wrongful death of her child. In both cases, Louisiana courts upheld the statute and denied recovery. The Supreme Court reversed in both cases. Justice Douglas wrote the opinion for the majority. *In Levy,* he began by emphasizing the personhood of illegitimate children: "We start from the premise that illegitimate children are not single 'nonpersons.' They are humans, live, and have their being. They are clearly single 'persons' within the meaning of the Equal Protection Clause of the 14th Amendment." 391 U.S. at 70. Applying a rational basis test, he concluded that "it is invidious to discriminate against [illegitimate children] when no action, conduct, or demeanor of theirs is possibly relevant to the harm that was done the mother." *Id* at 71. In *Glona,* Justice Douglas observed that denying wrongful death recovery to mothers of illegitimate children was equally irrational because it would be "far fetched to assume that women have illegitimate children so that they can be compensated in damages for their death." *Glona,* at 75.

Three years later the Supreme Court reached an apparently inconsistent conclusion in *Labine v. Vincent,* 401 U.S. 532 (1971), upholding a Louisiana law providing that all legitimate children could inherit from their parents or by will, while some naturalized or acknowledged illegitimate children could only inherit under a will, but other illegitimate children could not inherit by will or by intestate succession.

A year later, in *Weber v. Aetna Casualty Insurance Co.,* 406 U.S. 164 (1972), the Court distinguished *Labine. Weber* involved a Louisiana Worker's Compensation scheme which gave preference in recovery of worker's compensation benefits to legitimate and statutorial acknowledged illegitimate children. Unacknowledged children were entitled to recover only to the extent that the claims of the preferred claimants did not exhaust the fund. Louisiana law did not permit a married man to acknowledge his children born to another woman. The decedent in *Weber* was married, but was not living with his wife (who was committed to a mental hospital). Living in his home were his four legitimate children and one unacknowledged illegitimate child of the woman he was living with (who bore another illegitimate child of his after he died). When the man died in an industrial accident, the unacknowledged children received nothing because the four legitimate children exhausted the worker's compensation benefits. On appeal, the Supreme Court held the Louisiana statute unconstitutional. Justice Powell, writing for the majority, distinguished *Labine* because in that case the deceased father could have simply insured that his illegitimate children would receive some of his estate by making a will or marrying their mother. In this case, the deceased could neither marry the mother of the illegitimate children nor legally acknowledge them under the Louisiana statute. He further declared:

> The status of illegitimacy has expressed through the ages society's condemnation of irresponsible liaisons beyond the bonds of marriage. But visiting this condemnation on the head of the infant is illogical and unjust. Moreover, imposing disability on the illegitimate child is contrary to the basic concept of our system. The legal burdens should bear some relationship to individual responsibility or wrongdoing. Obviously, no child is responsible for his birth and penalizing the illegitimate child is an ineffectual—as well as an unjust—way of deterring the parent.

Id. at 175. Justice Rehnquist dissented, emphasizing federalism, i.e., that the Supreme Court should not scrutinize too rigorously state legislation dealing with such matters as the recover of the death of injured workers, intestate succession, etc. *Id.* at 184.

Gomez v. Perez, 409 U.S. 535 (1973), involved a Texas law extending the right of paternal support to legitimate children but denied the right to paternal support to illegitimate children. In a Per Curiam opinion, the Supreme Court held that discrimination violated the Equal Protection Clause of the Fourteenth Amendment: "[A] State may not invidiously discriminate against illegitimate children by denying them substantial benefits accorded to children generally." *Id.* at 538.

In *Parham v. Hughes*, 421 U.S. 347 (1979), the Court upheld a Georgia statute that denied the father of an illegitimate child a wrongful death claim. Justice Stewart authored a plurality opinion for himself, Chief Justice Burger, Rehnquist, and Stevens. The Georgia statute did not discriminate against illegitimate children, but penalized fathers who refused to legitimate their offspring. The difference in statutory treatment between unwed mothers and unwed fathers was justified by the difference in their circumstances: unwed mothers are easily identifiable, but there is always a question of proof to establish the paternity of an illegitimate child. See Nolan, *infra*, for a comprehensive analysis of these and the remaining cases involving both state and federal law. The latest two cases were heard in 1998 and in 2001, where the Supreme Court upheld on a strong deference-to-Congress grounds an immigration law that made illegitimate children born to U.S. mothers abroad citizens upon birth, but required illegitimate children born to U.S. fathers to apply for citizenship before majority. See *Miller v. Albright*, 523 U.S. 420 (1998); *Nguyen and Boulais v. Immigration and Naturalization Service*, 533 U.S. 53(2001).

b. *Lalli v. Lalli*

Lalli v. Lalli
439 U.S. 259 (1978)

Mr. JUSTICE POWELL announced the judgment of the Court and delivered an opinion, in which THE CHIEF JUSTICE and Mr. Justice STEWART join.

This case presents a challenge to the constitutionality of § 4-1.2 of New York's Estates, Powers, and Trusts Law, which requires illegitimate children who would inherit from their fathers by intestate succession to provide a particular form of proof of paternity. Legitimate children are not subject to the same requirement.

I

Appellant Robert Lalli claims to be the illegitimate son of Mario Lalli who died intestate on January 7, 1973, in the State of New York. Appellant's mother, who died in 1968, never was married to Mario. After Mario's widow, Rosamond Lalli, was appointed administratrix of her husband's estate, appellant petitioned the Surrogate's Court for Westchester Count y for a compulsory accounting, claiming that he and his sister Maureen Lalli were entitled to inherit from Mario as his children. Rosamond Lalli opposed the petition. She argued that even if Robert and Maureen were Mario's children, they were not lawful distributees of the state because they had failed to comply with § 4- 1.2, which provides in part:

"An illegitimate child is the legitimate child of his father so that he and his issue inherit from his father if a court of competent jurisdiction has, during the lifetime of the father, made an order of filiation declaring paternity in a proceeding instituted during the pregnancy of the mother or within two years from the birth of the child."

Appellant conceded that he had not obtained an order of filiation during his putative father's lifetime. He contended, however, that § 4-1.2, by imposing this requirement, discriminated against him on the basis of his illegitimate birth in violation of the Equal Protection Clause of the Fourteenth Amendment. Appellant tendered certain evidence of his relationship with Mario Lalli, including a notarized document in which Lalli, in consenting to appellant's marriage, referred to him as "my son," and several affidavits by persons who stated that Lalli had acknowledged openly and often that Robert and Maureen were his children.

The Surrogate's Court noted that § 4-1.2 had previously, and unsuccessfully, been attacked under the Equal Protection Clause. After reviewing recent decisions of this Court concerning discrimination against illegitimate children, * the court ruled that appellant was properly excluded as a distributee of Lalli's estate and therefore lacked status to petition for a compulsory accounting.

On direct appeal the New York Court of Appeals affirmed. ... It understood *Labine* to require the State to show no more than that "there is a rational basis for the means chosen by the Legislature for the accomplishment of a permissible State objective." ... After discussing the problems of proof peculiar to establishing paternity, as opposed to maternity, the court concluded that the State was constitutionally entitled to require a judicial decree during the father's lifetime as the exclusive form of proof of paternity.

On remand [for reconsideration in light of *Trimble*], the New York Court of Appeals, with two judges dissenting, adhered to its former disposition. ... It acknowledged that Trimble contemplated a standard of judicial review demanding more than "a mere finding of some remote rational relationship between the statute and a legitimate State purpose" ..., though less than strictest scrutiny. Finding § 4-1.2 to be "significantly and determinatively different" from the statute overturned in Trimble, the court ruled that the New York law was sufficiently related to the State's interest in " 'the orderly settlement of estates and the dependability of titles to property passing under intestacy laws,' " ... to meet the requirements of equal protection.

... We now affirm.

II

We begin our analysis with *Trimble*. At issue in that case was the constitutionality of an Illinois statute providing that a child born out of wedlock could inherit from his intestate father only if the father had "acknowledged" the child and the child had been legitimated by the intermarriage of the parents. The appellant in *Trimble* was a child born out of wedlock whose father had neither acknowledged her nor married her mother. He had, however, been found to be her father in a judicial decree ordering him to contribute to her support. When the father died intestate, the child was excluded as a distributee because the statutory requirements for inheritance had not been met.

We concluded that the Illinois statute discriminated against illegitimate children in a manner prohibited by the Equal Protection Clause. Although, as decided in *Mathews v. Lucas* ..., and reaffirmed in Trimble ..., classifications based on illegitimacy are not subject to "strict scrutiny," they nevertheless are invalid under the Fourteenth Amendment if they are not substantially related to permissible state interests. Upon examination, we found that the Illinois law failed that test.

* * *

The Illinois statute, however, was constitutionally flawed because, by insisting upon not only an acknowledgment by the father, but also the marriage of the parents, it excluded "at least some significant categories of illegitimate children of intestate men [whose] inheritance rights can be recognized without jeopardizing the orderly settlement of estates or the dependability of titles to property passing under intestacy laws" .... We concluded that the Equal Protection Clause required that a statute placing exceptional burdens on illegitimate children in the furtherance of proper state objectives must be more " 'carefully tuned to alternative considerations' " ..., than was true of the broad disqualification in the Illinois law.

III

The New York statute, enacted in 1965, was intended to soften the rigors of previous law which permitted illegitimate children to inherit only from their mothers. ... By lifting the absolute bar to paternal inheritance, § 4-1.2 tended to achieve its desired effect. As in *Trimble*, however, the question before us is whether the remaining statutory obstacles to inheritance by illegitimate children can be squared with the Equal Protection Clause.

A

At the outset we observe that § 4-1.2 is different in important respects from the statutory provision overturned in *Trimble*. The Illinois statute required, in addition to the father's acknowledgment of paternity, the legitimation of the child through the intermarriage of the parents as an absolute precondition to inheritance. ...

Under § 4-1.2, by contrast, the marital status of the parents is irrelevant. The single requirement at issue here is an evidentiary one—that the paternity of the father be declared in a judicial proceeding sometime before his death. The child need not have been legitimated in order to inherit from his father. ...

A related difference between the two provisions pertains to the state interests said to be served by them. The Illinois law was defended, in part, as a means of encouraging legitimate family relationships. No such justification has been offered in support of § 4-1.2. The Court of Appeals disclaimed that the purpose of the statute, "even in small part, was to discourage illegitimacy, to mold human conduct or to set societal norms" .... The absence in § 4-1.2 of any requirement that the parents intermarry or otherwise legitimate a child born out of wedlock and our review of the legislative history of the statute, ..., confirm this view.

* * *

B

The primary state goal underlying the challenged aspects of § 4-1.2 is to provide for the just and orderly disposition of property at death. We long have recognized that this is an area with which the States have an interest of considerable magnitude. ...

This interest is directly implicated in paternal inheritance by illegitimate children because of the peculiar problems of proof that are involved. Establishing maternity is seldom difficult. As one New York Surrogate's Court has observed: "[T]he birth of the child is a recorded or registered event usually taking place in the presence of others. In most cases the child remains with the mother and for a time is necessarily reared by her. That the child is the child of a particular woman is rarely difficult to prove." *In re Ortiz*, ...(1969). Proof of paternity, by contrast, frequently is difficult when the father is not part of a formal family unit. "The putative father often goes his way unconscious of the birth of a child. Even if conscious, he is very often totally unconcerned because of the absence of any ties to the mother. Indeed the mother may not know who is responsible for her pregnancy" ....

Thus, a number of problems arise that counsel against treating illegitimate children identically to all other heirs of an intestate father. These were the subject of a comprehensive study by the Temporary State Commission on the Modernization, Revision and Simplification of the Law of Estates. ... The Commission issued its report and recommendations to the legislature in 1965. ... The statute now codified as § 4-1.2 was included.

Although the overarching purpose of the proposed statute was "to alleviate the plight of the illegitimate child" ..., the Bennett Commission considered it necessary to impose the strictures of § 4-1.2 in order to mitigate serious difficulties in the administration of the estates of both testate and intestate decedents. The Commission's perception of some of these difficulties was described by Surrogate Sobel, a member of "the busiest [surrogate's] court in the State ...."

> An illegitimate, if made an unconditional distributee in intestacy, must be served with process in the estate of his parent or if he is a distributee in the estate of the kindred of a parent. ... And, in probating the will of his parent (though not named a beneficiary) or in probating the will of any person who makes a class disposition to "issue" of such parent, the illegitimate must be served with process. ... How does one cite and serve an illegitimate of whose existence neither family nor personal representative may be aware? And of greatest concern, how achieve finality of decree in any estate when there always exists the possibility however remote of a secret illegitimate lurking in the buried past of a parent or an ancestor of a class of beneficiaries? Finality in decree is essential in the Surrogates' Courts since title to real property passes under such decree. Our procedural statutes and the Due Process Clause mandate notice and opportunity to be heard to all necessary parties. Given the right to intestate succession, all illegitimates must be served with process. This would be no real problem with respect to those few estates where there are "known" illegitimates. But it presents an almost insuperable burden as regards "unknown" illegitimates. The point made in the [Bennett] commission discussions was that instead of affecting only a few estates, procedural problems would be created for many—some members suggested a majority—of estates. ...

Even where an individual claiming to be the illegitimate child of a deceased man makes himself known, the difficulties facing an estate are likely to persist. Because of the particular problems of proof, spurious claims may be difficult to expose. The Bennett Commission therefore sought to protect "innocent adults and those rightfully interested in their estates from fraudulent claims of heirship and harassing litigation instituted by those seeking to establish themselves as illegitimate heirs." Commission Report 265.

C

As the State's interests are substantial, we now consider the means adopted by New York to further these interests. In order to avoid the problems described above, the Commission recommended a requirement designed to ensure the accurate resolution of claims of paternity and to minimize the potential for disruption of estate administration. Accuracy is enhanced by placing paternity disputes in a judicial forum during the lifetime of the father. As the New York Court of Appeals observed in its first opinion in this case, the "availability [of the putative father] should be a substantial factor contributing to the reliability of the fact-finding process." ... In addition, requiring that the order be issued during the father's lifetime permits a man to defend his reputation against "unjust accusations in paternity claims," which was a secondary purpose of § 4-1.2. Commission Report 266.

The administration of an estate will be facilitated, and the possibility of delay and uncertainty minimized, where the entitlement of an illegitimate child to notice and participation is a matter of judicial record before the administration commences. Fraudulent assertions of paternity will be much less likely to succeed, or even to arise, where the proof is put before a court of law at a time when the putative father is available to respond, rather than first brought to light when the distribution of the assets of an estate is in the offing.

Appellant contends that § 4-1.2, like the statute at issue in *Trimble*, excludes "significant categories of illegitimate children" who could be allowed to inherit "without jeopardizing the orderly settlement" of their intestate fathers' estates. ... He urges that those in his position—"known" illegitimate children who, despite the absence of an order of filiation obtained during their fathers' lifetimes, can present convincing proof of paternity—cannot rationally be denied inheritance as they pose none of the risks § 4-1.2 was intended to minimize.

We do not question that there will be some illegitimate children who would be able to establish their relationship to their deceased fathers without serious disruption of the administration of estates and that, as applied to such individuals, § 4-1.2 appears to operate unfairly. But few statutory classifications are entirely free from the criticism that they sometimes produce inequitable results. Our inquiry under the Equal Protection Clause does not focus on the abstract "fairness" of a state law, but on whether the statute's relation to the state interests it is intended to promote is so tenuous that it lacks the rationality contemplated by the Fourteenth Amendment.

The Illinois statute in Trimble was constitutionally unacceptable because it effected a total statutory disinheritance of children born out of wedlock who were not legitimated by the subsequent marriage of their parents. The reach of the statute was far in excess of its justifiable purposes. Section 4-1.2 does not share this defect. Inheritance is barred only where there has been a failure to secure evidence of paternity during the father's lifetime in the manner prescribed by the State. This is not a requirement that inevitably disqualifies an unnecessarily large number of children born out of wedlock.

The New York courts have interpreted § 4-1.2 liberally and in such a way as to enhance its utility to both father and child without sacrificing its strength as a procedural prophylactic. For example, a father of illegitimate children who is willing to acknowledge paternity can waive his defenses in a paternity proceeding ..., or even institute such a proceeding himself. ... In addition, the courts have excused "technical" failures by illegitimate children to comply with the statute in order to prevent unnecessary injustice.

* * *

Even if, as Mr. JUSTICE BRENNAN believes, § 4-1.2 could have been written somewhat more equitably, it is not the function of a court "to hypothesize independently on the desirability or feasibility of any possible alternative[s]" to the statutory scheme formulated by New York. ... "These matters of practical judgment and empirical calculation are for [the State]. ... In the end, the precise accuracy of [the State's] calculations is not a matter of specialized judicial competence; and we have no basis to question their detail beyond the evident consistency and substantiality." ... [FN11 - The dissent of Mr. JUSTICE BRENNAN would reduce the opinion in Trimble v. Gordon, supra, to a simplistic holding that the Constitution requires a State, in a case of this kind, to recognize as sufficient any "formal acknowledgment of paternity." This reading of Trimble is based on a single phrase lifted from a footnote. ... It ignores both the broad rationale of the Court's opinion and the context in which the note and the phrase relied upon appear. ...]

The important state interests of safeguarding the accurate and orderly disposition of property at death, emphasized in Trimble and reiterated in our opinion today, could be frustrated easily if there were a constitutional rule that any notarized but unsworn statement identifying an individual as a "child" must be accepted as adequate proof of paternity regardless of the context in which the statement was made.

We conclude that the requirement imposed by § 4-1.2 on illegitimate children who would inherit from their fathers is substantially related to the important state interests the statute is intended to promote. We therefore find no violation of the Equal Protection Clause.

The judgment of the New York Court of Appeals is Affirmed.

For the reasons stated in his dissent in Trimble v. Gordon, ..., (1977), Mr. JUSTICE REHNQUIST concurs in the judgment of affirmance.

Mr. JUSTICE STEWART, concurring.

It seems to me that Mr. JUSTICE POWELL's opinion convincingly demonstrates the significant differences between the New York law at issue here and the Illinois law at issue in Trimble v. Gordon ... . Therefore, I cannot agree with the view expressed in Mr. Justice BLACKMUN's opinion concurring in the judgment that Trimble v. Gordon is now "a derelict" ....

Mr. JUSTICE BLACKMUN, concurring in the judgment.

I agree with the result the Court has reached and concur in its judgment. ... My point of departure, of course, is at the plurality's valiant struggle to distinguish, rather than overrule, *Trimble v. Gordon* .... Four Members of the Court, like the Supreme Court of Illinois, found the case "constitutionally indistinguishable from *Labine v. Vincent*, ... (1971)" and were in dissent.

* * *

I would overrule *Trimble*, but the Court refrains from doing so on the theory that the result in Trimble is justified because of the peculiarities of the Illinois Probate Act there under consideration. This, of course, is an explanation, but, for me, it is an unconvincing one. I therefore must regard Trimble as a derelict, explainable only because of the overtones of its appealing facts and offering little precedent for constitutional analysis of State intestate succession laws. If *Trimble* is not a derelict, the corresponding statutes of other States will be of questionable validity until this Court passes on them, one by one, as being on the *Trimble* side of the line or the *Labine-Lalli* side.

Mr. JUSTICE BRENNAN, with whom Mr. JUSTICE WHITE, Mr. JUSTICE MARSHALL, and Mr. JUSTICE STEVENS join, dissenting.

* * *

The present case illustrates the injustice of the departure from *Trimble* worked by today's decision sustaining the New York rule. All interested parties concede that Robert Lalli is the son of Mario Lalli. Mario Lalli supported Robert during his son's youth. Mario Lalli formally acknowledged Robert Lalli as his son. ... Yet, for want of a judicial order of filiation entered during Mario's lifetime, Robert Lalli is denied his intestate share of his father's estate.

* * *

I see no reason to retreat from our decision in *Trimble v. Gordon.* ...

c. Notes and Questions

1) Modern Policy Regarding Illegitimacy

Today, illegitimacy has largely been abolished as an operative legal classification. It is neither necessary nor desirable to achieve valid child-protective or administrative management policies to categorize on the basis of legitimacy. Usually classification on the basis of paternity will achieve the same goals and purposes historically given to justify classification on the basis of illegitimacy. However, statutes that penalize parents for not legitimating their children generally are not subject to the same degree of rigorous judicial scrutiny. Is that fair?

2) Legitimation

All states allow children born out of wedlock, under conditions prescribed by the particular state, to be legitimated by the father. Legitimating a child creates the full parent-child relationship. All states have now enacted statutes that provide that children born into marriages that are invalid retain their status of legitimacy, and that the child is legitimated if the child's parents later intermarry and the father acknowledges the child. Some states provide a judicial process for legitimation. Under the Uniform Parentage Act (UPA), all children are on equal status with their parents. The act provides a procedure for identifying the father, beginning with the presumption of children born to a married woman. Therefore, determining paternity is not necessarily equivalent to legitimation.

3) "Softening" the Label

The term *bastard* has evolved over the years to "softer" terms: *illegitimate children, children born out of wedlock, nonmarital children.*

3. Practical and Ethical Considerations

a. Settlement Agreements

It was common among states in the past to allow the mother and the putative father to agree to settle paternity cases with the putative father paying a lump sum to settle all support obligations (without acknowledging paternity) because of the difficulty of proving paternity. Settlement agreements supported the policy that some support for children was better than none if paternity was not proved. Is this still good policy? Should a child be bound by such agreements? Might such agreements be unconstitutional? See *Dones v. Dones-Carter*, 534 N.W.2d 221 (Mich. App. Ct. 1995), appeal denied 552 N.W.2d 170 (Mich. 1996). Is this akin to "buying" freedom from paternity obligations?

4. Bibliography

William Blackstone, Commentaries on the Laws of England (1756).
Christopher C. Blakesley & J. Parker eds. (1988).
Stephen Cretney, Principles of Family Law (3d ed. 1979).
Harry D. Krause, Illegitimacy: Law and Social Policy (1971).
Laurence C. Nolan, *"Unwed Children" and Their Parents Before the United States Supreme Court from Levy to Michael H.: Unlikely Participants in Constitutional Jurisprudence*, 28 Cap. U. L. Rev. 1 (1999).
Louis Parley, The Ethical Family Lawyer (American Bar Association, Family Law Section, 1995).
Jeffrey A. Parness, *Old-Fashioned Pregnancy, Newly-Fashioned Paternity*, 53 Syracuse L. Rev. 57 (2003).
F. Pollock & F. Maitland, The History of English Law (2d ed. 1898 reprinted 1968).
Alan Watson, The Law of Persons in the Later Roman Republic (1967).

CHAPTER 11

New Reproductive Techniques and New Parentage Issues

A. NEW REPRODUCTIVE TECHNIQUES IN GENERAL

1. Background

a. Overview

Throughout most of human history, human reproduction could occur only by means of human sexual intercourse. Laws regulating family relations were based upon that factual assumption. New reproductive technologies, however, have dramatically changed the possibilities. It is now not only possible to have sex without pregnancy but to have pregnancy without sexual intercourse, pregnancy without parentage, and parentage by procreation without sex or pregnancy. Of course, it has long been possible (by adoption and similar legal procedures) to have parentage without having any biological relations but those legal rules always involved an after-the-birth legal procedure that adjusted the legal consequences of what were deemed immutable facts of procreation-through-sexual-intercourse. Those facts are no longer immutable, and assisted reproduction technologies are creating parenting possibilities that defy the assumptions of the traditional parentage rules and create dilemmas that call into question the rules that govern the establishment of legal parentage.

b. Techniques

The techniques facilitating human procreation by means other than normal sexual intercourse (usually called "assisted reproduction technology," or ART) are noted below.

1) Artificial Insemination (AI)

AI is the simplest method of artificial (or assisted) procreation, and is largely unregulated. It may be performed successfully without the involvement of any medical professional (as the *Robin Y* case illustrates *infra*), and for those who prefer professional assistance, it is available at thousands of doctors' offices and clinics throughout the country. In its simplest form, it simply requires the donation of sperm from a man (usually obtained by his masturbation into a container) and the mechanical injection of it into the vagina of the woman (a simple turkey baster will suffice). It is estimated that more 30,000 children are born each year in the United States through artificial insemination. Artificial insemination is largely unregulated. It raises legal issues when the donor (AID) is not the husband (AIH) of the recipient. The Uniform Parentage Act (UPA) provides that if sperm is given to a physician for use in AI, the donor is not the legal father, but the husband of the recipient who in writing agrees to the artificial insemination of his wife is the legal father (about thirty states follow this approach). In this unregulated environment, possibilities for ethical dilemmas abound; insemination using the sperm of a brother or father apparently is not illegal.

2) In Vitro Fertilization (IVF)

IVF involves the removal of an egg or eggs from a woman, the donation of sperm from a man, and the combination of them ex utero (usually in a petri dish or similar container) producing one or (usually) more multi-cell human zygotes or embryos which may be immediately implanted into the uterus of the woman who wants to bear a child, or frozen for later implantation. IVF procedures are becoming increasingly precise and sophisticated. For example, gamete intrafallopian transfer (GIFT) collects the eggs, combines them with sperm outside the body, then transfers them back into the fallopian tube(s); zygote intrafallopian transfer (ZIFT) collects the eggs, fertilizes and monitors them outside the body, then transfers them back into the fallopian tube; and intercytoplasmic sperm injection (ICSI) in which an egg is fertilized by injecting a single sperm cell past both the outer and inner membrane of the egg cell. President's Commission, *infra*, at Chapter 2. IVF is expensive; yet, it is common. *Id*. The Centers for Disease Control (CDC) reported in 2005 that 399 responding IFV clinics (of 437 known clinics) performed 122,872 ART cycles resulting in 35,785 life-birth deliveries of 48,756 infants in 2003. CDC, *infra*. The pregnancy rate ranged from 18 to 43 percent (depending on age), and live birth resulted in 11 to 37 percent of the cycles; multiple births occurred in 17 to 34 percent of the deliveries. *Id*. Egg donation is a growth industry; egg donors, typically, are paid several thousand dollars. Because the IVF embryos may be frozen, dilemmas arise when the parties divorce or change their minds before implantation. *See Davis v. Davis*, 842 SW2d 588 (Tenn. 1992) (divorcing couple had used IVF to create frozen embryos; the woman wanted to donate the zygotes to another woman, but the man did not want to become a father; the Tennessee Supreme Court held for the father, finding that his right not to become an unwilling parent was paramount); *Kass v. Kass*, 696 N.E.2d 174 (1998) (divorcing 40-year-old woman argued that frozen zygotes were her best hope of having children; her estranged husband did not want to become the father of her children; parties had signed agreement providing that the IVF clinic could donate the zygotes for research if they did not both agree to the disposition of the zygotes; New York Court of Appeals unanimously enforced the agreement and rejected the woman's claim of a constitutional right of procreation).

Given the highly controversial issues and potential public consequences raised by IVF, the paucity of legal regulation is notable. Indirect regulation of IVF and other forms of ART - such as regulations of the practice of medicine, licensing of hospitals and fertility laboratories, informed consent laws, laws applicable to sexually transmitted infection screening, medical privacy laws, and insurance laws - is not uncommon. However, direct legal regulation is sparse. The President's Council on Bioethics, *infra*, reported in 2004 that: "There is only one federal statute that aims at the regulation of assisted reproduction: the Fertility Clinic Success Rate and Certification Act of 1992," and it merely requires annual reporting of clinic-specific success rates, and authorizes promulgation of model standards for certifying embryology laboratories. While thirty-eight states have enacted laws regulating some aspect of ART, only five states (New Hampshire, Pennsylvania, Louisiana, New Mexico and South Dakota) have anything resembling a comprehensive scheme of regulation, and only the latter three states address specifically the context of ART (as distinct from abortion).

3) Surrogacy

Traditional surrogacy involves a woman (surrogate) conceiving by means of artificial insemination and bearing the child for another person or couple. Typically, the surrogate is acting for a married couple in which the wife is infertile and the sperm used in the insemination usually comes from the husband of the woman for whom she is bearing the child. With the development of in vitro fertilization, the surrogate could be genetically unrelated to the child and be used only to gestate the child (gestational surrogacy). Surrogacy is being used to bear children for single men, single women, and for same-sex lesbian and gay couples. As the possibilities have become public (mostly through high-profile litigation such as that in the cases reported below), some state legislatures have enacted statutes specifically regulating surrogacy contracts. Several states legislatures have proscribed the arrangement where money is exchanged, others have strictly regulated the procedure (although the effectiveness of such regulation remains unclear), while others have done nothing.

4) Posthumous Conception

Posthumous conception is possible because sperm and eggs may be frozen and used for conception purposes after the donor's death. In some cases sperm can be taken from a dead man. In *Hecht v. Superior Court*, 20 Cal.Rptr.2d 275 (Cal. App. 1993), a man by contract and will expressly donated and bequeathed vials of his frozen sperm to his girlfriend before he committed suicide. His adult children by a former marriage sought to enjoin the girlfriend from receiving the vials. The California Court of Appeals awarded the frozen sperm to the girlfriend because the sperm was not subject to the property division with the former wife, and the dead man had clearly expressed his intent to give the sperm to his girlfriend. No state has enacted legislation pertaining to the issues raised in *Hecht*. The Uniform Anatomical Gift Act, which is law in all fifty states, may apply.

5) Cloning

In February 1998, when Dr. Ian Wilmut announced that a lamb named Dolly had been produced by cloning an adult sheep, it immediately raised the specter of human cloning. While there has been much controversy and debate about experimentation to develop human cloning, and several bills have been introduced in Congress, no regulatory legislation has been adopted. Congress did ban all federal funding of life-threatening (rather than life-enhancing) research involving human embryos but that law has been effectively circumvented by agencies sympathetic to research. State legislation to restrict human cloning was adopted in several states.

2. Statutes, Cases and Doctrines

a. Uniform Laws

At least four separate "uniform laws" dealing with parentage have been proposed in the United States that could apply to artificial procreation. These acts are not binding when drafted, but are promulgated as model laws by the National Conference of

Commissioners of Uniform State Laws, a group of state-appointed legal experts. Generally, the American Bar Association also recommends them to the various state legislatures for adoption. However, until a legislature of a particular state enacts them, they are of no legal effect in that state. Three of these uniform laws are described in Chapter 10. The Uniform Status of Children of Assisted Conception Act (USCACA) was promulgated in 1988 to deal specifically with assisted conception. It was repealed in 2000, and became Article 7 of the revised UPA (2000). UPA (2002) §702 provides that "[a] donor is not a parent of a child conceived by means of assisted reproduction." It also defines donor to include donors of sperm and eggs. §703 also provides: "A man who provides sperm for, or, consents to, assisted reproduction by a woman . . . with the intent to be the parent of her child, is a parent of the resulting child." The state legislatures, except for five, have largely ignored the efforts to create uniformity by model legislation.

b. *In the Matter of Baby M*

In the Matter of Baby M, a pseudonym for an actual person
537 A.2d 1227 (N.J. 1988)

WILENTZ, C.J.

***

I.   FACTS

In February 1985, William Stern and Mary Beth Whitehead entered into a surrogacy contract. It recited that Stern's wife, Elizabeth, was infertile, that they wanted a child, and that Mrs. Whitehead was willing to provide that child as the mother with Mr. Stern as the father.

The contract provided that through artificial insemination using Mr. Stern's sperm, Mrs. Whitehead would become pregnant, carry the child to term, bear it, deliver it to the Sterns, and thereafter do whatever was necessary to terminate her maternal rights so that Mrs. Stern could thereafter adopt the child. Mrs. Whitehead's husband, Richard, was also a party to the contract; Mrs. Stern was not. Mr. Whitehead promised to do all acts necessary to rebut the presumption of paternity under the Parentage Act. * Although Mrs. Stern was not a party to the surrogacy agreement, the contract gave her sole custody of the child in the event of Mr. Stern's death. Mrs. Stern's status as a nonparty to the surrogate parenting agreement presumably was to avoid the application of the baby-selling statute to this arrangement. *

Mr. Stern, on his part, agreed to attempt the artificial insemination and to pay Mrs. Whitehead $10,000 after the child's birth, on its delivery to him. In a separate contract, Mr. Stern agreed to pay $7,500 to the Infertility Center of New York ("ICNY"). The Center's advertising campaigns solicit surrogate mothers and encourage infertile couples to consider surrogacy. ICNY arranged for the surrogacy contract by bringing the parties together, explaining the process to them, furnishing the contractual form, and providing legal counsel.

The history of the parties' involvement in this arrangement suggests their good faith. William and Elizabeth Stern were married in July 1974, having met at the University of Michigan, where both were Ph.D. candidates. Due to financial considerations and Mrs. Stern's pursuit of a medical degree and residency, they decided to defer starting a family until 1981. Before then, however, Mrs. Stern learned that she might have multiple sclerosis and that the disease in some cases renders pregnancy a serious health risk. Her anxiety appears to have exceeded the actual risk, which current medical authorities assess as minimal. Nonetheless that anxiety was evidently quite real, Mrs. Stern fearing that pregnancy might precipitate blindness, paraplegia, or other forms of debilitation. Based on the perceived risk, the Sterns decided to forego having their own children. The decision had special significance for Mr. Stern. Most of his family had been destroyed in the Holocaust. As the family's only survivor, he very much wanted to continue his bloodline.

Initially the Sterns considered adoption, but were discouraged by the substantial delay apparently involved and by the potential problem they saw arising from their age and their differing religious backgrounds. They were most eager for some other means to start a family.

The paths of Mrs. Whitehead and the Sterns to surrogacy were similar. Both responded to advertising by ICNY. The Sterns' response, following their inquiries into adoption, was the result of their long-standing decision to have a child. Mrs. Whitehead's response apparently resulted from her sympathy with family members and others who could have no children (she stated that she wanted to give another couple the "gift of life"); she also wanted the $10,000 to help her family.

***

Mrs. Whitehead had reached her decision concerning surrogacy before the Sterns, and had actually been involved as a potential surrogate mother with another couple. After numerous unsuccessful artificial inseminations, that effort was abandoned. Thereafter, the Sterns learned of the Infertility Center, the possibilities of surrogacy, and of Mary Beth Whitehead. The two couples met to discuss the surrogacy arrangement and decided to go forward. On February 6, 1985, Mr. Stern and Mr. and Mrs. Whitehead executed the surrogate parenting agreement. After several artificial inseminations over a period of months, Mrs. Whitehead became pregnant. The pregnancy was uneventful and on March 27, 1986, Baby M was born.

Not wishing anyone at the hospital to be aware of the surrogacy arrangement, Mr. and Mrs. Whitehead appeared to all as the proud parents of a healthy female child. Her birth certificate indicated her name to be Sara Elizabeth Whitehead and her father to be Richard Whitehead. In accordance with Mrs. Whitehead's request, the Sterns visited the hospital unobtrusively to see the newborn child.

Mrs. Whitehead realized, almost from the moment of birth, that she could not part with this child. She had felt a bond with it even during pregnancy. Some indication of the attachment was conveyed to the Sterns at the hospital when they told Mrs. Whitehead what they were going to name the baby. She apparently broke into tears and indicated that she did not know if she could give up the child. She talked about how the baby looked like her other daughter, and made it clear that she was experiencing great difficulty with the decision.

Nonetheless, Mrs. Whitehead was, for the moment, true to her word. Despite powerful inclinations to the contrary, she turned her child over to the Sterns on March 30 at the Whiteheads' home.

The Sterns were thrilled with their new child. They had planned extensively for its arrival, far beyond the practical furnishing of a room for her. It was a time of joyful celebration--not just for them but for their friends as well. The Sterns looked forward to raising their daughter, whom they named Melissa. While aware by then that Mrs. Whitehead was undergoing an emotional crisis, they were as yet not cognizant of the depth of that crisis and its implications for their newly enlarged family.

Later in the evening of March 30, Mrs. Whitehead became deeply disturbed, disconsolate, stricken with unbearable sadness. She had to have her child. She could not eat, sleep, or concentrate on anything other than her need for her baby. The next day she went to the Sterns' home and told them how much she was suffering.

The depth of Mrs. Whitehead's despair surprised and frightened the Sterns. She told them that she could not live without her baby, that she must have her, even if only for one week, that thereafter she would surrender her child. The Sterns, concerned that Mrs. Whitehead might indeed commit suicide, not wanting under any circumstances to risk that, and in any event believing that Mrs. Whitehead would keep her word, turned the child over to her. It was not until four months later, after a series of attempts to regain possession of the child, that Melissa was returned to the Sterns, having been forcibly removed from the home where she was then living with Mr. and Mrs. Whitehead, the home in Florida owned by Mary Beth Whitehead's parents.

The struggle over Baby M began when it became apparent that Mrs. Whitehead could not return the child to Mr. Stern. Due to Mrs. Whitehead's refusal to relinquish the baby, Mr. Stern filed a complaint seeking enforcement of the surrogacy contract. He alleged, accurately, that Mrs. Whitehead had not only refused to comply with the surrogacy contract but had threatened to flee from New Jersey with the child in order to avoid even the possibility of his obtaining custody. The court papers asserted that if Mrs. Whitehead were to be given notice of the application for an order requiring her to relinquish custody, she would, prior to the hearing, leave the state with the baby. And that is precisely what she did. After the order was entered, ex parte, the process server, aided by the police, in the presence of the Sterns, entered Mrs. Whitehead's home to execute the order. Mr. Whitehead fled with the child, who had been handed to him through a window while those who came to enforce the order were thrown off balance by a dispute over the child's current name.

The Whiteheads immediately fled to Florida with Baby M. They stayed initially with Mrs. Whitehead's parents, where one of Mrs. Whitehead's children had been living. For the next three months, the Whiteheads and Melissa lived at roughly twenty different hotels, motels, and homes in order to avoid apprehension. From time to time Mrs. Whitehead would call Mr. Stern to discuss the matter; the conversations, recorded by Mr. Stern on advice of counsel, show an escalating dispute about rights, morality, and power, accompanied by threats of Mrs. Whitehead to kill herself, to kill the child, and falsely to accuse Mr. Stern of sexually molesting Mrs. Whitehead's other daughter.

Eventually the Sterns discovered where the Whiteheads were staying, commenced supplementary proceedings in Florida, and obtained an order requiring the Whiteheads to turn over the child. Police in Florida enforced the order, forcibly removing the child from her grandparents' home. She was soon thereafter brought to New Jersey and turned over to the Sterns. The prior order of the court, issued ex parte, awarding custody of the child to the Sterns pendente lite, was reaffirmed by the trial court after consideration of the certified representations of the parties (both represented by counsel) concerning the unusual sequence of events that had unfolded. Pending final judgment, Mrs. Whitehead was awarded limited visitation with Baby M.

The Sterns' complaint, in addition to seeking possession and ultimately custody of the child, sought enforcement of the surrogacy contract. Pursuant to the contract, it asked that the child be permanently placed in their custody, that Mrs. Whitehead's parental rights be terminated, and that Mrs. Stern be allowed to adopt the child, i.e., that, for all purposes, Melissa become the Sterns' child.

The trial took thirty-two days over a period of more than two months. It included numerous interlocutory appeals and attempted interlocutory appeals. There were twenty-three witnesses to the facts recited above and fifteen expert witnesses, eleven testifying on the issue of custody and four on the subject of Mrs. Stern's multiple sclerosis; the bulk of the testimony was devoted to determining the parenting arrangement most compatible with the child's best interests. Soon after the conclusion of the trial, the trial court announced its opinion from the bench. 525 A.2d 1128 (1987). It held that the surrogacy contract was valid; ordered that Mrs. Whitehead's parental rights be terminated and that sole custody of the child be granted to Mr. Stern; and, after hearing brief testimony from Mrs. Stern, immediately entered an order allowing the adoption of Melissa by Mrs. Stern, all in accordance with the surrogacy contract. Pending the outcome of the appeal, we granted a continuation of visitation to Mrs. Whitehead, although slightly more limited than the visitation allowed during the trial.
***

Mrs. Whitehead appealed. This Court granted direct certification. * The briefs of the parties on appeal were joined by numerous briefs filed by amici ***.
***

II. INVALIDITY AND UNENFORCEABILITY OF SURROGACY CONTRACT

We have concluded that this surrogacy contract is invalid. Our conclusion has two bases: direct conflict with existing statutes and conflict with the public policies of this State, as expressed in its statutory and decisional law.

One of the surrogacy contract's basic purposes, to achieve the adoption of a child through private placement, though permitted in New Jersey "is very much disfavored." * Its use of money for this purpose--and we have no doubt whatsoever that the money is being paid to obtain an adoption and not, as the Sterns argue, for the personal services of Mary Beth Whitehead--is illegal and perhaps criminal. * In addition to the inducement of money, there is the coercion of contract: the natural mother's irrevocable agreement, prior to birth, even prior to conception, to surrender the child to the adoptive couple. Such an agreement is totally unenforceable in private placement adoption. * * *

A. Conflict with Statutory Provisions

The surrogacy contract conflicts with: (1) laws prohibiting the use of money in connection with adoptions; (2) laws requiring proof of parental unfitness or abandonment before termination of parental rights is ordered or an adoption is granted; and (3) laws that make surrender of custody and consent to adoption revocable in private placement adoptions.

(1) Our law prohibits paying or accepting money in connection with any placement of a child for adoption. * Violation is a high misdemeanor. * Excepted are fees of an approved agency (which must be a non-profit entity, *) and certain expenses in connection with childbirth.

Considerable care was taken in this case to structure the surrogacy arrangement so as not to violate this prohibition. The arrangement was structured as follows: the adopting parent, Mrs. Stern, was not a party to the surrogacy contract; the money paid to Mrs. Whitehead was stated to be for her services--not for the adoption; the sole purpose of the contract was stated as being that "of giving a child to William Stern, its natural and biological father"; the money was purported to be "compensation for services and expenses and in no way ... a fee for termination of parental rights or a payment in exchange for consent to surrender a child for adoption"; the fee to the Infertility Center ($7,500) was stated to be for legal representation, advice, administrative work, and other "services." Nevertheless, it seems clear that the money was paid and accepted in connection with an adoption.

The Infertility Center's major role was first as a "finder" of the surrogate mother whose child was to be adopted, and second as the arranger of all proceedings that led to the adoption. Its role as adoption finder is demonstrated by the provision requiring Mr. Stern to pay another $7,500 if he uses Mary Beth Whitehead again as a surrogate, and by ICNY's agreement to "coordinate arrangements for the adoption of the child by the wife." The surrogacy agreement requires Mrs. Whitehead to surrender Baby M for the purposes of adoption. The agreement notes that Mr. and Mrs. Stern wanted to have a child, and provides that the child be "placed" with Mrs. Stern in the event Mr. Stern dies before the child is born. The payment of the $10,000 occurs only on surrender of custody of the child and "completion of the duties and obligations" of Mrs. Whitehead, including termination of her parental rights to facilitate adoption by Mrs. Stern. As for the contention that the Sterns are paying only for services and not for an adoption, we need note only that they would pay nothing in the event the child died before the fourth month of pregnancy, and only $1,000 if the child were stillborn, even though the "services" had been fully rendered. Additionally, one of Mrs. Whitehead's estimated costs, to be assumed by Mr. Stern, was an "Adoption Fee," presumably for Mrs. Whitehead's incidental costs in connection with the adoption.

Mr. Stern knew he was paying for the adoption of a child; Mrs. Whitehead knew she was accepting money so that a child might be adopted; the Infertility Center knew that it was being paid for assisting in the adoption of a child. The actions of all three worked to frustrate the goals of the statute. It strains credulity to claim that these arrangements, touted by those in the surrogacy business as an attractive alternative to the usual route leading to an adoption, really amount to something other than a private placement adoption for money.

The prohibition of our statute is strong. Violation constitutes a high misdemeanor,*, a third-degree crime, *, carrying a penalty of three to five years imprisonment. * The evils inherent in baby-bartering are loathsome for a myriad of reasons. The child is sold without regard for whether the purchasers will be suitable parents. * The natural mother does not receive the benefit of counseling and guidance to assist her in making a decision that may affect her for a lifetime. In fact, the monetary incentive to sell her child may, depending on her financial circumstances, make her decision less voluntary. * Furthermore, the adoptive parents * may not be fully informed of the natural parents' medical history.

(2) The termination of Mrs. Whitehead's parental rights, called for by the surrogacy contract and

actually ordered by the court, *, fails to comply with the stringent requirements of New Jersey law. Our law, recognizing the finality of any termination of parental rights, provides for such termination only where there has been a voluntary surrender of a child to an approved agency or to the Division of Youth and Family Services ("DYFS"), accompanied by a formal document acknowledging termination of parental rights,*, or where there has been a showing of parental abandonment or unfitness. A termination may ordinarily take one of three forms: an action by an approved agency, an action by DYFS, or an action in connection with a private placement adoption. The three are governed by separate statutes, but the standards for termination are substantially the same, except that whereas a written surrender is effective when made to an approved agency or to DYFS, there is no provision for it in the private placement context. *

***

Since the termination was invalid, it follows, as noted above, that adoption of Melissa by Mrs. Stern could not properly be granted.

(3) The provision in the surrogacy contract stating that Mary Beth Whitehead agrees to "surrender custody ... and terminate all parental rights" contains no clause giving her a right to rescind. ***

*** The trial court's award of specific performance therefore reflects its view that the consent to surrender the child was irrevocable. *** Such a provision, however, making irrevocable the natural mother's consent to surrender custody of her child in a private placement adoption, clearly conflicts with New Jersey law.

***

B. Public Policy Considerations

The surrogacy contract's invalidity, resulting from its direct conflict with the above statutory provisions, is further underlined when its goals and means are measured against New Jersey's public policy. The contract's basic premise, that the natural parents can decide in advance of birth which one is to have custody of the child, bears no relationship to the settled law that the child's best interests shall determine custody. * The fact that the trial court remedied that aspect of the contract through the "best interests" phase does not make the contractual provision any less offensive to the public policy of this State.

The surrogacy contract guarantees permanent separation of the child from one of its natural parents. Our policy, however, has long been that to the extent possible, children should remain with and be brought up by both of their natural parents. * That was the first stated purpose of the previous adoption act, *, "it is necessary and desirable (a) to protect the child from unnecessary separation from his natural parents...." While not so stated in the present adoption law, this purpose remains part of the public policy of this State. * This is not simply some theoretical ideal that in practice has no meaning. The impact of failure to follow that policy is nowhere better shown than in the results of this surrogacy contract. A child, instead of starting off its life with as much peace and security as possible, finds itself immediately in a tug-of-war between contending mother and father.

***

The policies expressed in our comprehensive laws governing consent to the surrender of a child, discussed *supra* *, stand in stark contrast to the surrogacy contract and what it implies. Here there is no counseling, independent or otherwise, of the natural mother, no evaluation, no warning.

***

Under the contract, the natural mother is irrevocably committed before she knows the strength of her bond with her child. ***

***

Worst of all, however, is the contract's total disregard of the best interests of the child. There is not the slightest suggestion that any inquiry will be made at any time to determine the fitness of the Sterns as custodial parents, of Mrs. Stern as an adoptive parent, their superiority to Mrs. Whitehead, or the effect on the child of not living with her natural mother.

This is the sale of a child, or, at the very least, the sale of a mother's right to her child, the only mitigating factor being that one of the purchasers is the father. Almost every evil that prompted the prohibition on the payment of money in connection with adoptions exists here.

The differences between an adoption and a surrogacy contract should be noted, since it is asserted that the use of money in connection with surrogacy does not pose the risks found where money buys an adoption. *

First, and perhaps most important, all parties concede that it is unlikely that surrogacy will survive without money. ***

Second, the use of money in adoptions does not produce the problem--conception occurs, and usually the birth itself, before illicit funds are offered. With surrogacy, the "problem," if one views it as such, consisting of the purchase of a woman's procreative capacity, at the risk of her life, is caused by and originates with the offer of money.

Third, with the law prohibiting the use of money in connection with adoptions, the built-in financial pressure of the unwanted pregnancy and the consequent support obligation do not lead the mother to the highest paying, ill-suited, adoptive parents. She is just as well-off surrendering the child to an approved agency. In surrogacy, the highest bidders will presumably become the adoptive parents regardless of suitability, so long as payment of money is permitted.

Fourth, the mother's consent to surrender her child in adoptions is revocable, even after surrender of the child, unless it be to an approved agency, where by regulation there are protections against an ill-advised surrender. In surrogacy, consent occurs so early that no amount of advice would satisfy the potential mother's need, yet the consent is irrevocable.
***

The long-term effects of surrogacy contracts are not known, but feared--the impact on the child who learns her life was bought, that she is the offspring of someone who gave birth to her only to obtain money; the impact on the natural mother as the full weight of her isolation is felt along with the full reality of the sale of her body and her child; the impact on the natural father and adoptive mother once they realize the consequences of their conduct. Literature in related areas suggests these are substantial considerations, although, given the newness of surrogacy, there is little information. *.
***

Beyond that is the potential degradation of some women that may result from this arrangement. In many cases, of course, surrogacy may bring satisfaction, not only to the infertile couple, but to the surrogate mother herself. The fact, however, that many women may not perceive surrogacy negatively but rather see it as an opportunity does not diminish its potential for devastation to other women.

In sum, the harmful consequences of this surrogacy arrangement appear to us all too palpable. In New Jersey the surrogate mother's agreement to sell her child is void. Its irrevocability infects the entire contract, as does the money that purports to buy it.

III. TERMINATION
***

Although the question of best interests of the child is dispositive of the custody issue in a dispute between natural parents, it does not govern the question of termination. It has long been decided that the mere fact that a child would be better off with one set of parents than with another is an insufficient basis for terminating the natural parent's rights. * Furthermore, it is equally well settled that surrender of a child and a consent to adoption through private placement do not alone warrant termination. *. It must be noted, despite some language to the contrary, that the interests of the child are not the only interests involved when termination issues are raised. The parent's rights, both constitutional and statutory, have their own independent vitality. *.
***

IV.CONSTITUTIONAL ISSUES

Both parties argue that the Constitutions--state and federal--mandate approval of their basic claims. The source of their constitutional arguments is essentially the same: the right of privacy, the right to procreate, the right to the companionship of one's child, those rights flowing either directly from the fourteenth amendment or by its incorporation of the Bill of Rights, or from the ninth amendment, or through the penumbra surrounding all of the Bill of Rights. They are the rights of personal intimacy, of marriage, of sex, of family, of procreation. Whatever their source, it is clear that they are fundamental rights protected by both the federal and state Constitutions. *Lehr v. Robertson,* *; *Santosky v. Kramer,* *:; *Zablocki v. Redhail,* *; *Quilloin v. Walcott,* *; *Carey v. Population Servs. Int'l,* *; *Roe v. Wade,* *; *Stanley v. Illinois,* *; *Griswold v. Connecticut,* *; *Skinner v. Oklahoma,* *; *Meyer v. Nebraska,* *. The right asserted by the Sterns is the right of procreation; that asserted by Mary Beth Whitehead is the right to the companionship of her child. We find that the right of procreation does not extend as far as claimed by the Sterns. As for the right asserted by Mrs. Whitehead, since we uphold it on other grounds (i.e., we have restored her as mother and recognized her right, limited by the child's best interests, to her companionship), we need not decide that constitutional issue, and for reasons set forth below, we should not.

***

V. CUSTODY

Having decided that the surrogacy contract is illegal and unenforceable, we now must decide the custody question without regard to the provisions of the surrogacy contract that would give Mr. Stern sole and permanent custody. *** With the surrogacy contract disposed of, the legal framework becomes a dispute between two couples over the custody of a child produced by the artificial insemination of one couple's wife by the other's husband. Under the Parentage Act the claims of the natural father and the natural mother are entitled to equal weight, i.e., one is not preferred over the other solely because he or she is the father or the mother. * The applicable rule given these circumstances is clear: the child's best interests determine custody.

***

The Whiteheads also contend that the award of custody to the Sterns pendente lite was erroneous and that the error should not be allowed to affect the final custody decision. .

***

There were eleven experts who testified concerning the child's best interests, either directly or in connection with matters related to that issue. Our reading of the record persuades us that the trial court's decision awarding custody to the Sterns (technically to Mr. Stern) should be affirmed since "its findings ... could reasonably have been reached on sufficient credible evidence present in the record." * More than that, on this record we find little room for any different conclusion. The trial court's treatment of this issue, *, is both comprehensive and, in most respects, perceptive. We agree substantially with its analysis with but few exceptions that, although important, do not change our ultimate views.

Our custody conclusion is based on strongly persuasive testimony contrasting both the family life of the Whiteheads and the Sterns and the personalities and characters of the individuals. The stability of the Whitehead family life was doubtful at the time of trial. Their finances were in serious trouble (foreclosure by Mrs. Whitehead's sister on a second mortgage was in process). Mr. Whitehead's employment, though relatively steady, was always at risk because of his alcoholism, a condition that he seems not to have been able to confront effectively. Mrs. Whitehead had not worked for quite some time, her last two employments having been part-time. One of the Whiteheads' positive attributes was their ability to bring up two children, and apparently well, even in so vulnerable a household. Yet substantial question was raised even about that aspect of their home life. The expert testimony contained criticism of Mrs. Whitehead's handling of her son's educational difficulties. Certain of the experts noted that Mrs. Whitehead perceived herself as omnipotent and omniscient concerning her children. She knew what they were thinking, what they wanted, and she spoke for them. As to Melissa, Mrs. Whitehead expressed the view that she alone knew what that child's cries and sounds meant. Her inconsistent stories about various things engendered grave doubts about her ability to explain honestly and sensitively to Baby M--and at the right time--the nature of her origin. Although faith in professional counseling is not a sine qua non of parenting, several experts believed that Mrs. Whitehead's contempt for professional help, especially professional psychological help, coincided with her feelings of omnipotence in a way that could be devastating to a child who most likely will need such help. In short, while love and affection there would be, Baby M's life with the Whiteheads promised to be too closely controlled by Mrs. Whitehead. The prospects for wholesome, independent psychological growth and development would be at serious risk.

The Sterns have no other children, but all indications are that their household and their personalities promise a much more likely foundation for Melissa to grow and thrive. There is a track record of sorts--during the one- and-a-half years of custody Baby M has done very well, and the relationship between both Mr. and Mrs. Stern and the baby has become very strong. The household is stable, and likely to remain so. Their finances are more than adequate, their circle of friends supportive, and their marriage happy. Most important, they are loving, giving, nurturing, and open-minded people. They have demonstrated the wish and ability to nurture and protect Melissa, yet at the same time to encourage her independence. Their lack of experience is more than made up for by a willingness to learn and to listen, a willingness that is enhanced by their professional training, especially Mrs. Stern's experience as a pediatrician. They are honest; they can recognize error, deal with it, and learn from it. They will try to determine rationally the best way to cope with problems in their relationship with Melissa. When the time comes to tell her about her origins, they will probably have found a means of doing so that accords with the best interests of Baby M. All in all, Melissa's future appears solid, happy, and promising with them.

Based on all of this we have concluded, independent of the trial court's identical conclusion, that Melissa's best interests call for custody in the Sterns. ***
***

VI. VISITATION

The trial court's decision to terminate Mrs. Whitehead's parental rights precluded it from making any determination on visitation. 525 A.2d 1128. Our reversal of the trial court's order, however, requires delineation of Mrs. Whitehead's rights to visitation. It is apparent to us that this factually sensitive issue, which was never addressed below, should not be determined de novo by this Court. We therefore remand the visitation issue to the trial court for an abbreviated hearing and determination as set forth below.
***

We have decided that Mrs. Whitehead is entitled to visitation at some point, and that question is not open to the trial court on this remand. The trial court will determine what kind of visitation shall be granted to her, with or without conditions, and when and under what circumstances it should commence. It also should be noted that the guardian's recommendation of a five-year delay is most unusual--one might argue that it begins to border on termination. Nevertheless, if the circumstances as further developed by appropriate proofs or as reconsidered on remand clearly call for that suspension under applicable legal principles of visitation, it should be so ordered.
***

CONCLUSION

We have found that our present laws do not permit the surrogacy contract used in this case. Nowhere, however, do we find any legal prohibition against surrogacy when the surrogate mother volunteers, without any payment, to act as a surrogate and is given the right to change her mind and to assert her parental rights. Moreover, the Legislature remains free to deal with this most sensitive issue as it sees fit, subject only to constitutional constraints.
***

The judgment is affirmed in part, reversed in part, and remanded for further proceedings consistent with this opinion.

c. *Johnson v. Calvert*

Anna Johnson, v. Mark Calvert et al.
851 P.2d 776, (Cal. 1993)

PANELLI, Justice.

In this case we address several of the legal questions raised by recent advances in reproductive technology. When, pursuant to a surrogacy agreement, a zygote formed of the gametes of a husband and wife is implanted in the uterus of another woman, who carries the resulting fetus to term and gives birth to a child not genetically related to her, who is the child's "natural mother" under California law? Does a determination that the wife is the child's natural mother work a deprivation of the gestating woman's constitutional rights? And is such an agreement barred by any public policy of this state?

FACTS

[On January 15, 1990, Mark and Crispina Calvert, a married couple who desired to have a child, and Anna Johnson signed a contract providing that an embryo created by the sperm of Mark and the egg of Crispina would be implanted in Anna and the child born would be taken into Mark and Crispina's home "as their child." Anna agreed she would relinquish "all parental rights" to the child in favor of Mark and Crispina. In return, Mark and Crispina would pay Anna $10,000 in a series of installments, the last to be paid six weeks after the child's birth. Mark and Crispina were also to pay for a $200,000 life insurance policy on Anna's life. *[FN4 - At the time of the agreement, Anna already had a daughter, Erica, born in 1987.]* Prior to the birth of the child, relations broke down. As a result lawsuits were filed by each party.]

DISCUSSION

Determining Maternity Under the Uniform Parentage Act

[The court concluded that under the Uniform Parentage Act (the Act), adopted by California, both could prove maternity under the Act.]

***Disregarding the presumptions of paternity that have no application to this case, then, we are left with the undisputed evidence that Anna, not Crispina, gave birth to the child and that Crispina, not Anna, is genetically related to him. Both women thus have adduced evidence of a mother and child relationship as contemplated by the Act. * Yet for any child California law recognizes only one natural mother, despite advances in reproductive technology rendering a different outcome biologically possible. *[FN8 - We decline to accept the contention of amicus curiae the American Civil Liberties Union (ACLU) that we should find the child has two mothers. Even though rising divorce rates have made multiple parent arrangements common in our society, we see no compelling reason to recognize such a situation here. The Calverts are the genetic and intending parents of their son and have provided him, by all accounts, with a stable, intact, and nurturing home. To recognize parental rights in a third party with whom the Calvert family has had little contact since shortly after the child's birth would diminish Crispina's role as mother.]*

We see no clear legislative preference in Civil Code section 7003 as between blood testing evidence and proof of having given birth. "May" indicates that proof of having given birth is a permitted method of establishing a mother and child relationship, although perhaps not the exclusive one. The disjunctive "or" indicates that blood test evidence, as prescribed in the Act, constitutes an alternative to proof of having given birth. It may be that the language of the Act merely reflects "the ancient dictum mater est quam [gestation] demonstrate (by gestation the mother is demonstrated). This phrase, by its use of the word 'demonstrated,' has always reflected an ambiguity in the meaning of the presumption. It is arguable that, while gestation may demonstrate maternal status, it is not the sine qua non of motherhood. Rather, it is possible that the common law viewed genetic consanguinity as the basis for maternal rights. Under this latter interpretation, gestation simply would be irrefutable evidence of the more fundamental genetic relationship." * This ambiguity, highlighted by the problems arising from the use of artificial reproductive techniques, is nowhere explicitly resolved in the Act.

Because two women each have presented acceptable proof of maternity, we do not believe this case can be decided without enquiring into the parties' intentions as manifested in the surrogacy agreement. Mark and Crispina are a couple who desired to have a child of their own genetic stock but are physically unable to do so without the help of reproductive technology. They affirmatively intended the birth of the child, and took the steps necessary to effect in vitro fertilization. But for their acted-on intention, the child would not exist. Anna agreed to facilitate the procreation of Mark's and Crispina's child. The parties' aim was to bring Mark's and Crispina's child into the world, not for Mark and Crispina to donate a zygote to Anna. Crispina from the outset intended to be the child's mother. Although the gestative function Anna performed was necessary to bring about the child's birth, it is safe to say that Anna would not have been given the opportunity to gestate or deliver the child had she, prior to implantation of the zygote, manifested her own intent to be the child's mother. No reason appears why Anna's later change of heart should vitiate the determination that Crispina is the child's natural mother.

We conclude that although the Act recognizes both genetic consanguinity and giving birth as means of establishing a mother and child relationship, when the two means do not coincide in one woman, she who intended to procreate the child--that is, she who intended to bring about the birth of a child that she intended to raise as her own--is the natural mother under California law. *[FN10 - *** The dissent would decide parentage based on the best interests of the child. Such an approach raises the repugnant specter of governmental interference in matters implicating our most fundamental notions of privacy, and confuses concepts of parentage and custody. Logically, the determination of parentage must precede, and should not be dictated by, eventual custody decisions. ***]*

Our conclusion finds support in the writings of several legal commentators. ***

In deciding the issue of maternity under the Act we have felt free to take into account the parties' intentions, as expressed in the surrogacy contract, because in our view the agreement is not, on its face, inconsistent with public policy.
***

Anna urges that surrogacy contracts violate several social policies. Relying on her contention that she is the child's legal, natural mother, she cites the public policy embodied in Penal Code section 273, prohibiting the payment for consent to adoption of a child. She argues further that the policies underlying the adoption laws of this state are violated by the surrogacy contract because it in effect constitutes a prebirth waiver of her parental rights.

We disagree. Gestational surrogacy differs in crucial respects from adoption and so is not subject to the adoption statutes. The parties voluntarily agreed to participate in in vitro fertilization and related medical procedures before the child was conceived; at the time when Anna entered into the contract, therefore, she was not vulnerable to financial inducements to part with her own expected offspring. As discussed above, Anna was not the genetic mother of the child. The payments to Anna under the contract were meant to compensate her for her services in gestating the fetus and undergoing labor, rather than for giving up "parental" rights to the child. Payments were due both during the pregnancy and after the child's birth. We are, accordingly, unpersuaded that the contract used in this case violates the public policies embodied in Penal Code section 273 and the adoption statutes. For the same reasons, we conclude these contracts do not implicate the policies underlying the statutes governing termination of parental rights. (*See* Welf. & Inst.Code, § 202.)

It has been suggested that gestational surrogacy may run afoul of prohibitions on involuntary servitude. (*See* U.S. Const., Amend. XIII; Cal. Const., art. I, § 6; Pen.Code, § 181.) Involuntary servitude has been recognized in cases of criminal punishment for refusal to work. * We see no potential for that evil in the contract at issue here, and extrinsic evidence of coercion or duress is utterly lacking. We note that although at one point the contract purports to give Mark and Crispina the sole right to determine whether to abort the pregnancy, at another point it acknowledges: "All parties understand that a pregnant woman has the absolute right to abort or not abort any fetus she is carrying.

Any promise to the contrary is unenforceable." We therefore need not determine the validity of a surrogacy contract purporting to deprive the gestator of her freedom to terminate the pregnancy.

Finally, Anna and some commentators have expressed concern that surrogacy contracts tend to exploit or dehumanize women, especially women of lower economic status. Anna's objections center around the psychological harm she asserts may result from the gestator's relinquishing the child to whom she has given birth. Some have also cautioned that the practice of surrogacy may encourage society to view children as commodities, subject to trade at their parents' will.

We are all too aware that the proper forum for resolution of this issue is the Legislature, where empirical data, largely lacking from this record, can be studied and rules of general applicability developed. However, in light of our responsibility to decide this case, we have considered as best we can its possible consequences.

We are unpersuaded that gestational surrogacy arrangements are so likely to cause the untoward results Anna cites as to demand their invalidation on public policy grounds. Although common sense suggests that women of lesser means serve as surrogate mothers more often than do wealthy women, there has been no proof that surrogacy contracts exploit poor women to any greater degree than economic necessity in general exploits them by inducing them to accept lower- paid or otherwise undesirable employment. We are likewise unpersuaded by the claim that surrogacy will foster the attitude that children are mere commodities; no evidence is offered to support it. The limited data available seem to reflect an absence of significant adverse effects of surrogacy on all participants.

The argument that a woman cannot knowingly and intelligently agree to gestate and deliver a baby for intending parents carries overtones of the reasoning that for centuries prevented women from attaining equal economic rights and professional status under the law. *** Certainly in the present case it cannot seriously be argued that Anna, a licensed vocational nurse who had done well in school and who had previously borne a child, lacked the intellectual wherewithal or life experience necessary to make an informed decision to enter into the surrogacy contract.

Constitutionality of the Determination That Anna Johnson Is Not the Natural Mother

Anna argues at length that her right to the continued companionship of the child is protected under the federal Constitution.
***

Anna relies mainly on theories of substantive due process, privacy, and procreative freedom, citing a number of decisions recognizing the fundamental liberty interest of natural parents in the custody and care of their children. (*See e.g. Santosky v. Kramer* (1982) *; *Lassiter v. Department of Social Services* (1981) *; *Smith v. Organization of Foster Families* (1977) *; *Stanley v. Illinois* (1972) *.) Most of the cases Anna cites deal with the rights of unwed fathers in the face of attempts to terminate their parental relationship to their children. (*See e.g. Stanley v. Illinois*, *; *Quilloin v. Walcott* (1978) *; *Caban v. Mohammed* (1979) *; *Lehr v. Robertson* (1983) *.) These cases do not support recognition of parental rights for a gestational surrogate. Although Anna quotes language stressing the primacy of a developed parent-child relationship in assessing unwed fathers' rights (*see Lehr v. Robertson*, *), certain language in the cases reinforces the importance of genetic parents' rights. (*Lehr v. Robertson*, * ["The significance of the biological connection is that it offers the natural father an opportunity that no other male possesses to develop a relationship with his offspring. If he grasps that opportunity and accepts some measure of responsibility for the child's future, he may enjoy the blessings of the parent-child relationship and make uniquely valuable contributions to the child's development."] *.)

Anna's argument depends on a prior determination that she is indeed the child's mother. Since Crispina is the child's mother under California law because she, not Anna, provided the ovum for the in vitro fertilization procedure, intending to raise the child as her own, it follows that any constitutional interests Anna possesses in this situation are something less than those of a mother. As counsel for the minor points out, the issue in this case is not whether Anna's asserted rights as a natural mother were unconstitutionally violated, but rather whether the determination that she is not the legal natural mother at all is constitutional.

Anna relies principally on the decision of the United States Supreme Court in *Michael H. v. Gerald D.* (1989) *, to support her claim to a constitutionally protected liberty interest in the companionship of the child, based on her status as "birth mother." In that case, a plurality of the court held that a state may constitutionally deny a man parental rights with respect to a child he fathered during a liaison with the wife of another man, since it is the marital family that traditionally has been accorded a protected liberty interest, as reflected in the historic presumption of legitimacy of a child born into such a family. * The reasoning of the plurality in *Michael H.* does not assist Anna. Society has not traditionally protected the right of a woman who gestates and delivers a baby pursuant to an agreement with a couple who supply the zygote from which the baby develops and who intend to raise the child as their own; such arrangements are of too recent an origin to claim the protection of tradition. To the extent that tradition has a bearing on the present case, we believe it supports the claim of the couple who exercise their right to procreate in order to form a family of their own, albeit through novel medical procedures.

Moreover, if we were to conclude that Anna enjoys some sort of liberty interest in the companionship of the child, then the liberty interests of Mark and Crispina, the child's natural parents, in their procreative choices and their relationship with the child would perforce be infringed. Any parental rights Anna might successfully assert could come only at Crispina's expense. As we have seen, Anna has no parental rights to the child under California law, and she fails to persuade us that sufficiently strong policy reasons exist to accord her a protected liberty interest in the companionship of the child when such an interest would necessarily detract from or impair the parental bond enjoyed by Mark and Crispina.

Amicus curiae ACLU urges that Anna's right of privacy, embodied in the California Constitution (Cal. Const., art. I, § 1), requires recognition and protection of her status as "birth mother." We cannot agree. Certainly it is true that our state Constitution has been construed to provide California citizens with privacy protections encompassing procreative decisionmaking--broader, indeed, than those recognized by the federal Constitution. * However, amicus curiae fails to articulate persuasively how Anna's claim falls within even the broad parameters of the state right of privacy. *** A woman who enters into a gestational surrogacy arrangement is not exercising her own right to make procreative choices; she is agreeing to provide a necessary and profoundly important service without (by definition) any expectation that she will raise the resulting child as her own.

Drawing an analogy to artificial insemination, Anna argues that Mark and Crispina were mere genetic donors who are entitled to no constitutional protection. That characterization of the facts is, however, inaccurate. Mark and Crispina never intended to "donate" genetic material to anyone. Rather, they intended to procreate a child genetically related to them by the only available means. Civil Code section 7005, governing artificial insemination, has no application here.

Finally, Anna argues that the Act's failure to address novel reproductive techniques such as in vitro fertilization indicates legislative disapproval of such practices. Given that the Act was drafted long before such techniques were developed, we cannot agree. Moreover, we may not arrogate to ourselves the power to disapprove them. It is not the role of the judiciary to inhibit the use of reproductive technology when the Legislature has not seen fit to do so; any such effort would raise serious questions in light of the fundamental nature of the rights of procreation and privacy. Rather, our task has been to resolve the dispute before us, interpreting the Act's use of the term "natural mother" (Civ.Code, § 7003, subd. (1)) when the biological functions essential to bringing a child into the world have been allocated between two women.

DISPOSITION

The judgment of the Court of Appeal is affirmed.

ARABIAN, Justice, concurring to opinion by PANELLI, Justice.

I concur in the decision to find under the Uniform Parentage Act that Crispina Calvert is the natural mother of the child, she at all times intended to parent and raise as her own with her husband Mark, the child's natural father. That determination answers the question on which this court granted review, and in my view sufficiently resolves the controversy between the parties to warrant no further analysis. I therefore decline to subscribe to the dictum in which the majority find surrogacy contracts "not ..inconsistent with public policy."*

***

*** I do not think it wise for this court to venture unnecessarily into terrain more appropriately cleared by the Legislature in the first instance. ***

KENNARD, Justice, dissenting.

When a woman who wants to have a child provides her fertilized ovum to another woman who carries it through pregnancy and gives birth to a child, who is the child's legal mother? Unlike the majority, I do not agree that the determinative consideration should be the intent to have the child that originated with the woman who contributed the ovum. In my view, the woman who provided the fertilized ovum and the woman who gave birth to the child both have substantial claims to legal motherhood. Pregnancy entails a unique commitment, both psychological and emotional, to an unborn child. No less substantial, however, is the contribution of the woman from whose egg the child developed and without whose desire the child would not exist.

For each child, California law accords the legal rights and responsibilities of parenthood to only one "natural mother." When, as here, the female reproductive role is divided between two women, California law requires courts to make a decision as to which woman is the child's natural mother, but provides no standards by which to make that decision. The majority's resort to "intent" to break the "tie" between the genetic and gestational mothers is unsupported by statute, and, in the absence of appropriate protections in the law to guard against abuse of surrogacy arrangements, it is ill-advised. To determine who is the legal mother of a child born of a gestational surrogacy arrangement, I would apply the standard most protective of child welfare--the best interests of the child.

***

VI. THE UNIFORM PARENTAGE ACT

The only California statute defining parental rights is the Uniform Parentage Act (hereafter also UPA). *** The UPA was never intended by the Legislature to govern the issues arising from new reproductive technologies *such as gestational surrogacy. ***

***

When a child is born by gestational surrogacy, as happened here, the two women who played biological roles in creating the child will both have statutory claims under the UPA to being the child's natural mother. ***

By its use of the phrase "the natural mother," however, the UPA contemplates that a child will have only one natural mother. (§ 7003, subd. (1), italics added.) But the UPA provides no standards for determining who that natural mother should be when, as here, two different women can offer biological proof of being the natural mother of the same child under its provisions. Thus, the UPA by its terms cannot resolve the conflict in this case.

VII. ANALYSIS OF THE MAJORITY'S "INTENT" TEST

***

*** Ultimately, however, I cannot agree that "intent" is the appropriate test for resolving this case.

***

The first argument that the majority uses in support of its conclusion that the intent of the genetic mother to bear a child should be dispositive of the question of motherhood is "but-for" causation. *** Neither the "but for" nor the "substantial factor" test of causation provides any basis for preferring the genetic mother's intent as the determinative factor in gestational surrogacy cases: Both the genetic and the gestational mothers are indispensable to the birth of a child ***.

*** The majority draws its second rationale from a student note: " 'The mental concept of the child is a controlling factor of its creation, and the originators of that concept merit full credit as conceivers.' "
*

***

The problem with this argument, of course, is that children are not property. Unlike songs or inventions, rights in children cannot be sold for consideration, or made freely available to the general public. Our most fundamental notions of personhood tell us it is inappropriate to treat children as property. Although the law may justly recognize that the originator of a concept has certain property rights in that concept, the originator of the concept of a child can have no such rights, because children cannot be owned as property. Accordingly, I cannot endorse the majority's "originators of the concept" or intellectual property rationale for employing intent to break the "tie" between the genetic mother and the gestational mother of the child.

Next, the majority offers as its third rationale the notion that bargained-for expectations support its conclusion regarding the dispositive significance of the genetic mother's intent. ***

*** But the courts will not compel performance of all contract obligations. *** Just as children are not the intellectual property of their parents, neither are they the personal property of anyone ***.

***

*** [I]n making the intent of the genetic mother who wants to have a child the dispositive factor, the majority renders a certain result preordained and inflexible in every such case: as between an intending genetic mother and a gestational mother, the genetic mother will, under the majority's analysis, always prevail. The majority recognizes no meaningful contribution by a woman who agrees to carry a fetus to term for the genetic mother beyond that of mere employment to perform a specified biological function.

***

To summarize, the woman who carried the fetus to term and brought a child into the world has, like the genetic mother, a substantial claim to be the natural mother of the child. The gestational mother has made an indispensable and unique biological contribution, and has also gone beyond biology in an intangible respect that, though difficult to label, cannot be denied. Accordingly, I cannot agree with the majority's devaluation of the role of the gestational mother.

***

The majority's final argument in support of using the intent of the genetic mother as the exclusive determinant of the outcome in gestational surrogacy cases is that preferring the intending mother serves the child's interests ***.

I agree with the majority that the best interests of the child is an important goal ***. The problem with the majority's rule of intent is that application of this inflexible rule will not serve the child's best interests in every case.

***

VIII. THE BEST INTERESTS OF THE CHILD
***

*** In the absence of legislation that is designed to address the unique problems of gestational surrogacy, this court should look not to tort, property or contract law, but to family law, as the governing paradigm and source of a rule of decision.

The allocation of parental rights and responsibilities necessarily impacts the welfare of a minor child. And in issues of child welfare, the standard that courts frequently apply is the best interests of the child. (*See* §§ 222.20, 222.36, 224.64 [* adoption and temporary placement], 4600 [child custody], 4601 [visitation].) Indeed, it is highly significant that the UPA itself looks to a child's best interests in deciding another question of parental rights. (§ 7017,*.) This "best interests" standard serves to assure that in the judicial resolution of disputes affecting a child's well-being, protection of the minor child is the foremost consideration. Consequently, I would apply "the best interests of the child" standard to determine who can best assume the social and legal responsibilities of motherhood for a child born of a gestational surrogacy arrangement.

***

Here, the child born of the gestational surrogacy arrangement between Anna Johnson and Mark and Crispina Calvert has lived continuously with Mark and Crispina since his birth in September 1990. The trial court awarded parental rights to Mark and Crispina, concluding that as a matter of law they were the child's "genetic, biological and natural" parents. In reaching that conclusion, the trial court did not treat Anna's statutory claim to be the child's legal mother as equal to Crispina's, nor did the trial court consider the child's best interests in deciding between those two equal statutory claims. Accordingly, I would remand the matter to the trial court to undertake that evaluation. ***

d. Notes and Comments

1) Civil Liability?

If the semen or egg were genetically defective and the child was born with some genetic impairment, could the contracting parents bring a products liability or implied warranty lawsuit? In the case of artificial insemination of animals, that appears to be permitted. *See Reimschiissel v. Russell,* 649 P.2d 26 (Utah, 1982) (claim for breach of implied warranty because cow had disease possibly due to tainted artificial insemination fails for insufficient evidence). If the disappointed owner of a defective cow can sue, why not the disappointed parent of a longed-for child born through assisted procreation technology? If a suit could be brought, who would be the defendant(s)? The egg or sperm donor? The clinic? The lawyer setting up the transaction? Could a disappointed husband sue his wife if genetic testing revealed that a genetic defect afflicting their child came through her genes? Could a disappointed wife sue her husband if genetic testing revealed that a genetic defect afflicting their child came through his gene?

2) *Baby M.*

Baby M was the first major decision to address surrogacy, and the case attracted a great deal of attention. The exhaustive New Jersey Supreme Court opinion in the case was 35 pages long, plus a lengthy appendix containing the terms of the surrogacy agreement signed by the parties. Upon remand, the superior court held further proceedings for the purpose of defining visitation. The court ruled that Baby M's best interests would best be served by unsupervised, liberal visitation with the mother; the court directed the parties to participate in counseling with a court-appointed mental health professional to the extent that the counselor deemed advisable. To protect the privacy of Baby M, the court ordered the parties to refrain from publicly discussing their relationship with child, or her personal activities, or from selling "movie rights" in fictional portrayal of their activities without prior approval of court.

3) *Johnson v. Calvert* Notes

In *In re Marriage of Buzzanca* , 72 Cal. Rptr. 2d 280 (Cal.App. 4 Dist., 1998) the court applied the intent-to-parent test of *Johnson v. Calvert* in an unusual setting, summarized by the appellate court in its introduction:

> Jaycee was born because Luanne and John Buzzanca agreed to have an embryo genetically unrelated to either of them implanted in a woman--a surrogate--who would

carry and give birth to the child for them. After the fertilization, implantation and pregnancy, Luanne and John split up, and the question of who are Jaycee's lawful parents came before the trial court.

Luanne claimed that she and her erstwhile husband were the lawful parents, but John disclaimed any responsibility, financial or otherwise. The woman who gave birth also appeared in the case to make it clear that she made no claim to the child.

The trial court then reached an extraordinary conclusion: Jaycee had no lawful parents. First, the woman who gave birth to Jaycee was not the mother; the court had--astonishingly--already accepted a stipulation that neither she nor her husband were the "biological" parents. Second, Luanne was not the mother. According to the trial court, she could not be the mother because she had neither contributed the egg nor given birth. And John could not be the father, because, not having contributed the sperm, he had no biological relationship with the child. [therefore, the trial court ruled, John had no support obligation.]

We disagree. Let us get right to the point: Jaycee never would have been born had not Luanne and John both agreed to have a fertilized egg implanted in a surrogate.

The trial judge erred because he assumed that legal motherhood, under the relevant California statutes, could only be established in one of two ways, either by giving birth or by contributing an egg. He failed to consider the substantial and well-settled body of law holding that there are times when fatherhood can be established by conduct apart from giving birth or being genetically related to a child. The typical example is when an infertile husband consents to allowing his wife to be artificially inseminated. As our Supreme Court noted in such a situation over 30 years ago, the husband is the "lawful father" because he consented to the procreation of the child. (*See People v. Sorensen* (1968) 68 Cal.2d 280, 284-286, 66 Cal.Rptr. 7, 437 P.2d 495.)

The same rule which makes a husband the lawful father of a child born because of his consent to artificial insemination should be applied here--by the same parity of reasoning that guided our Supreme Court in the first surrogacy case, *Johnson v. Calvert* *--to both husband and wife. Just as a husband is deemed to be the lawful father of a child unrelated to him when his wife gives birth after artificial insemination, so should a husband and wife be deemed the lawful parents of a child after a surrogate bears a biologically unrelated child on their behalf. In each instance, a child is procreated because a medical procedure was initiated and consented to by intended parents. The only difference is that in this case--unlike artificial insemination--there is no reason to distinguish between husband and wife. We therefore must reverse the trial court's judgment and direct that a new judgment be entered, declaring that both Luanne and John are the lawful parents of Jaycee.

72 Cal.Rptr.2d at 282. Would this court's "symmetry" ("just as . . . so should") argument be convincing in every case? Aren't there some very real, practical differences between the relationship that men and women actually have with an unborn child that might justify a deviation in some cases from the "just as ... so should" symmetry argument for strict gender equality in parentage claims?

In *Belsito v. Clark*, 644 N.E.2d 760 (Ohio Com.Pl., 1994) the court declined to follow the *Johnson* approach and held that in Ohio "the law requires that [the man and woman who] provided the child with its genetics . . . must be designated as the legal and natural parents." 644 N.E.2d at 762. ." *Id.:*

The court in *Johnson [v. Calvert]* looked for the intent to procreate and to raise the child, in order to identify the natural mother. Since the genetic mother in Johnson intended to procreate, she was the natural parent. The Johnson court discarded both genetics and birth as the primary means of identifying the natural maternal parent, and replaced both with a test that involves intent of the parties.

In a somewhat similar case, a New York court of appeals determined the gestational surrogate to be the natural mother based on the *Johnson* precedent of intent to procreate. *McDonald v. McDonald* (1994), 608 N.Y.S.2d 477. (In *McDonald*, the gestational surrogate received the egg from an anonymous donor; her husband provided the sperm.) Under the *Johnson* test, either the gestational surrogate or the genetic parents could be recognized as the natural and legal parents, depending on which party intended to procreate and raise the child.

Since both cases emanate from outside the appellate jurisdiction that binds this court, they can only be considered as persuasive and not binding. In light of Ohio law, this court finds neither case to be persuasive, for the following three important reasons: (1) the difficulty in applying the *Johnson* intent test; (2) public policy; and (3) *Johnson*'s failure to recognize and emphasize the genetic provider's right to consent to procreation and to surrender potential parental rights.

644 N.E.2d at 764.

As a matter of statutory interpretation, does the majority or dissent in *Johnson* make the better case? Why? As a matter of social policy analysis, which do you prefer? Why?

4) Insemination Possibilities in the Absence of Regulation

In *Jhordan C. v. Mary K.*, 224 Cal. Rptr. 530 (Cal. App. 1986), a single woman decided to have a child by artificial insemination and raise the child with her friend, Victoria. After interviewing prospective semen donors, Mary chose Jhordan who agreed to donate sperm without any expectation of paternity, though he was promised the chance to have limited contact (how limited was disputed) with the child. Mary, a nurse, self-inseminated using Jhordan's sperm, and Devin was born. When Mary cut off Jhordan's meetings with Devin, Jhordan filed a suit for filiation and visitation, and agreed to pay child support (including past welfare support Mary had received from the state). From a trial court order establishing Jhordan's paternity and awarding him liberal visitation, Mary appealed, arguing that, as a mere semen donor for AI, Jhordan had no claim to paternity asking the court to interpret liberally the UPA provision in effect in California (Calif. Civil Code § 7005) that provides:

(A) If, under the supervision of a licensed physician and with the consent of her husband, a wife is inseminated artificially with semen donated by a man not her husband, the husband is treated in law as if he were the natural father of a child thereby conceived . . . .

(B) The donor of semen provided to a licensed physician for use in artificial insemination of a woman other than the donor's wife is treated in law as if he were not the natural father of a child conceived thereby.

The court of appeals, however, applied the statute literally, and since the semen had been provided directly to Mary, and not provided to a physician, the statutory denial of paternity to the semen donor did not apply. The trial court's order was affirmed.

A celebrated similar case in New York involved a lesbian couple. Each had artificially inseminated herself with sperm from a different gay man, and each had given birth to a daughter. One of the men wanted more contact with his offspring than the mother approved, leading him to file suit for filiation and visitation. He had agreed that Robin Y. and Sandra R. would raise, as co-parents, a child born of the insemination of Sandra R. with his sperm; that he would have no parental rights or obligations; and that he would make himself known to the child if the child ever made inquiry about her biological origin. *Thomas S. v. Robin Y.*, 599 N.Y.S.2d 377 (Fam. Ct. N.Y. City, 1993). The Family Court found by clear and convincing evidence, based upon the blood tests, that petitioner was the biological father of Ry. Nevertheless, citing the doctrine of equitable estoppel, the court refused to enter an order of filiation and dismissed the proceeding. The court characterized petitioner as an "outsider attacking her [Ry's] family [and] refusing to give it respect," concluding that "a declaration of paternity would be a statement that her family is other than what she knows it to be and needs it to be" and, therefore, "would not be in her best interests." * The court added, "Even were there an adjudication of paternity, I would deny [petitioner's] application for visitation." * On appeal, the trial court order was reversed. *Thomas S. v. Robin Y.*, 618 N.Y.S.2d 356 (1994), and an appeal to the New York Court of Appeals was dismissed. *Thomas S. v. Robin Y.*, 655 N.E.2d 708, (N.Y. 1995). The appellate court ruled that "a sperm donor who is known to his child as her father and who, despite residing in California, has had considerable contact with her at the instance of her mother, is entitled to an order of filiation" under New York law.

5) Fundamental Concerns

The new procreative technologies open up the possibility of parenthood for thousands of couples who, because of infertility, would never have been able to have biological children. They also provide a means whereby persons unable or unwilling to make the commitments or enter into the kind of union in which procreative behavior is sanctioned might have offspring. The troubling dimension of these new possibilities is that "[t]hey create a class of 'mothers' who must not care for the children they have borne and of 'fathers' who need not support and may not raise the offspring they have sired. They ask us, in some of their incarnations, to separate procreation from parental obligation. It is this aspect of the new techniques which may ultimately pose the greatest challenge to American family law." Carl E. Schneider & Lynn D. Wardle, *infra.*

In its landmark 2004 report, the President's Commission on Bioethics, Procreation and Responsibility noted that "[t]here are *no* nationally uniform laws or policies relating to access to assisted reproduction," "[t]here is no comprehensive mechanism for regulation of commerce in human gametes, embryos, and assisted reproductive technology services," "[t]he current regulatory landscape is a patchwork," there is "relatively little oversight or deliberation" restraining the movement of experimental procedures to clinical practice, and "[t]here is no uniform system for public review and deliberation regarding the larger human or social significance of new reproductive biotechnologies." *President's Commission, infra* at 5-6.

6) Paternity Issues

AI usually involves anonymous semen donation; surrogacy may involve an egg from an anonymous donor. Should that be permitted? Should/does a child have a right to know or discover his or her biological/genetic heritage? Many children of ART yearn to know who their "other parent" is. For children raised by same-sex couples, this may be especially poignant. In Europe, some decisions and commentary on the European Convention on Human Rights suggest that the desire to connect with or know of one's actual biological ancestry and origins has a foundation in human rights' law. When Britain banned anonymous semen donation in 2005, the immediate effect was a significant drop in semen donation for AI.

In *C.C.A. v. J.M.A.*, 744 So.2d 515, ((Fla App. 2 Dist. 1999) the court held that it was abuse of discretion for the trial court to rule that the husband was not estopped from disavowing paternity when a married couple initially agreed not to have children and the husband had a vasectomy; later they changed their minds but recruited a surrogate to father a child by ordinary sexual intercourse because the husband did not want to undergo vasectomy reversal surgery; when that resulted in miscarriage, the wife, without husband's knowledge and, according to him, over his express objection to further attempts to have children, conceived a child with another man; the husband knew he was not the father but held himself out as child's father for two years before the separation.

7) Constitutional Right to Use Artificial Insemination?

In *Gerber v. Hickman*, 264 F.3d 882 (9th Cir. 2001), a prisoner sentenced to life imprisonment without possibility of parole (Mr. Gerber) sought to send semen from prison via overnight delivery to a clinic where his wife could be artificially inseminated. Because he was ineligible for conjugal visits, and because of his wife's age, he believed that long-distance artificial insemination provided him with the only means of procreating. California prison officials denied his request because the procedure was not medically necessary. Mr. Gerber filed a federal civil rights complaint claiming violation of an alleged constitutional right to procreation. After a federal district court dismissed his complaint for failure to state a claim upon which relief could be granted, a split panel of the Ninth Circuit Court of Appeals reversed, vacated and remanded. Judge Bright, for the majority, concluded, first, that "a general [constitutionally-protected] right to procreate exists during periods of imprisonment," analogizing the case at bar to *Turner v. Safley*, 482 U.S. 78 (1987), and *Skinner v. Oklahoma*, 316 U.S. 535 (1942). The panel majority next held that the California Department of Corrections had failed to prove that legitimate penological interests justified restricting Mr. Gerber's right to send semen for artificial insemination. The panel rejected the state's argument that equal treatment of men and women required the ban because the record on the Rule 12 (b)(6) motion was inadequate to show any problem, noting that men and women are not equally situated with regard to artificial insemination, and rejecting safety concerns as speculative. Judge Silverman dissented, noting that protection against forced sterilization in *Skinner* and of the right to marry in *Turner* are "a far cry from holding that inmates retain a constitutional right to procreate from prison via FedEx." 264 F.3d at 893. (He also noted that the case was "a seminal case in more ways than one." *Id.*) A year later, the 9th Circuit *en banc* reversed, 6-5. "A holding that the state of California must accommodate Gerber's request to artificially inseminate his wife as a matter of constitutional right would be a radical and unprecedented interpretation of the Constitution," Judge Silverman concluded in the majority opinion. Do you think that there is a general constitutional right to engage in procreative activity? Using ART? Why/why not? For an interesting critique of the initial Ninth Circuit panel decision, *see Recent Case*, 115 Harv.

L. Rev. 1541 (2002) (arguing that state interests underlying incarceration ought to be considered in the first step, deciding whether there is a constitutional right, not just the second step as the majority opined).

8) Posthumous Conception Cases

The state supreme courts of New Jersey and Massachusetts held that children conceived posthumously from their father's frozen sperm and their living mother's eggs through the procedure of artificial insemination were the legitimate children of their deceased fathers under the respective state law. In each case, their parents were married at the time the sperm was frozen, the fathers were undergoing treatment for cancer which would likely cause them to become sterile, and the sperm was frozen for the purpose of each father being able to have children after the treatment terminated. Both fathers died shortly after the sperm was frozen. *See In the Matter of Kolacy*, 753 A.2d (N.J. Super. Ch. 2000) and *Woodward v. Commissioner of Social Security*, 760 N.E.2d 257 (Mass. 2002).

9) Use of Artificial Reproduction by Gay and Lesbian Couples

Artificial reproduction technology has enabled gay and lesbian partners to plan and have children who are biologically related to one of the partners. Beginning in the 1960s and 1970s, lesbian couples, in growing numbers, began using artificial insemination to create families. Today, lesbian couples use all available reproductive technology, and have generated a "gay-by boom." In some cases, one partner may be the genetic mother and the other partner the gestational mother. *See generally,* Amy Agigian, *infra.* Gay couples are increasingly using artificial reproduction to have children. Unlike lesbian couples, where the donor of the semen can remain unknown, the surrogate is usually known to the gay couple. Should polygamous families (in places where polygamy is illegal) be allowed to use ART? Incestuous couples? Why/why not?

3. Practical and Ethical Considerations

a. ART for Child-raisers

It is not impossible to use surrogacy to produce children for groups of prospective child-raisers (for example, for a commune, for a retirement community, for a society that has taken vows of celibacy, for a brother and sister who are legally barred from marrying or having sex with each other, for same-sex couples in states that prohibit same-sex marriage or unions, etc.). What considerations might underlie the law's response?

Use of ART by same-sex couples to acquire children to raise is highly restricted (in most nations, absolutely prohibited) in Europe and in most of the rest of the world. Why do you think it is otherwise in the United States of America? Which policy is best for children? Why?

4. Bibliography

Amy Agigian, Baby Steps: How Lesbian Alternative Insemination is Changing the World (2000).
Centers for Disease Control and Prevention (CDC), 2003 Assisted Reproduction Technology (ART) Report, available at http://www.cdc.gov/ART/ART2003/nation.htm .

Marsha Garrison, *Law Making for Baby Making: An Interpretive Approach to the Determination of Legal Parentage*, 113 Harv. L. Rev. 835 (2000).

Laurence C. Nolan, *Posthumous Conception: A Private or Public Matter?*, 11 BYU J. Pub. L. 1 (1997).

Carl E. Schneider & Lynn D. Wardle, *Genetics and Artificial Procreation in the U.S.A.*, in Biomedicine, the Family and Human Rights 55 (2002)

The President's Council of Bioethics, Procreation and Responsibility: The Regulation of New Biotechnologies, (March 2004) available at http://bioethicsprint.bioethics.gov/reports/reproductionandresponsibility/index.html (seen April 5, 2006).

Lynn D. Wardle, *Parenting in American Law -- Today and Tomorrow* in The Legal Relationship between Parents and Children 111-147 (Choo Soo Kim ed. 1997).

CHAPTER 12

Adoption: History; First-Step: Terminating the Existing Parent-Child Relationship

A. ADOPTION: HISTORY AND GENERAL REQUIREMENTS

1. Background

a. History of Adoption

"Adoption as a practice is certainly as old as the human race. . . . Hammurabi's Babylonian code, the oldest set of written laws, spelled out guidelines for the adoption practice." Silverman, *infra,* at 85. The Old Testament, in Exodus, describes how Pharaoh's daughter took Moses and raised him "and he became her son," but Moses never forgot that he was an Hebrew. Exodus 2:1-12. Greek mythology tells that Hercules was the adopted son of Hera, and that Oedipus was taken in and raised by King Polybus and Queen Merope of Corinth after he was abandoned by his father who had been warned by the Oracle at Delphi that he would be killed by his son.

Adoption for the sake of the child, however, is a relatively modern and thoroughly American legal device. Adoption in Roman law existed for the benefit of the adopter, not for the welfare of children. The were two forms of adoption in Roman law. *Adrogatio* had the affect of extinguishing one family line (merging it into another) for the purpose of saving another. Originally, only a *paterfamilias* (clan or family head) could be adrogated. When one was adopted, he lost his patria potestas, and he and all of his family became subject to the patria potestas of the adrogator. Generally, the adrogator had to be at least 60 years old, have no descendants of his own, and be at least 18 years older than the one to be adrogated. During most of the Roman era *adrogation* had to be approved by the legislative body (comitia curita). The second form of Roman adoption, *adoptio,* affected only an individual, and not his family. The adoptee first had to be released from the potestas of his prior paterfamilias. This was affected through a fictitious sale. The Twelve Tables provided that if a father sold his son three times, the son was free. So the paterfamilias would sell his son to a straw man twice (who would transfer him back) and the third time he would be sold to the adopter. Adoption terminated all inheritance rights in the old paterfamilias. Though in later Roman times, this was modified. After Justinian, the adoptee did not pass into the potestas of the new family, and adoption could not be compelled. If the adopting paterfamilias emancipated the adoptee, the adoption was automatically dissolved and the child reverted to the paterfamilias of his original family. W. Buckland, infra. For many centuries the civil law of European nations, following the Roman law, recognized adoption, but only in the Roman fashion – i.e., for the benefit of the persons adopting and not to provide families for children without parents. Thus, generally the adopted person had to be an adult.

Adoption was unknown at common law . In fact, adoption was not permitted in Britain until 1926 when Parliament enacted the Adoption Act. Adoption Act, 1926, 16 & 17 Geo. 5, c. 29. Before then, the legal status of children born out of wedlock was illegitimate, not favored nor protected by the law.

> [I]n Victorian times, pregnant unmarried women would arrange for their child to be delivered in a private lying-in house, the owner of which would receive a lump sum of money in exchange for arranging the baby's "adoption." The child was removed to "the worst class of these baby-farming house" the owners of which received either a small lump sum or an inadequate weekly allowance. There the children were "so culpably neglected, so ill-treated, and so badly nurtured" (e.g., on a diet consisting of a mixture of laudanum, lime, cornflour, water, milk and washing powder) "that with rare exceptions they all of them die in a very short time.

Stephen Cretney, *infra* at 532.

In America, apprenticeship fulfilled some of the need for adoptions in colonial days. By the middle of the nineteenth century there was a strong movement to create a legal device whereby children who had been orphaned or abandoned could be fully and formally taken into the families of those who cared for them. Some of the earliest legislation provided for the transfer of children by deed. In fact, transfer of custody by deed or similar legal instrument is still used in some states. The 1973 Uniform Probate Code authorizes the use of power of attorney, will, and deed. Uniform Probate Code §§ 5-104 & 5-202.

In 1851, Massachusetts made adoption a matter of judicial jurisdiction. Since that time, adoption in American law has operated to protect the interests of children as well as to accommodate the interests of the adopting parents and to protect the interests of the biological parents. This primary focus on the welfare of children without families distinguished American adoption from the classic Roman, civilian, and common law approaches, and set the standard which the world now follows. Thus, the heart of this child-centered model of adoption was the creation of family relationships that imitated and were intended to replicate the relationship that exists between parents and child(ren) in a birth (natural) family. *See generally* Kawashima, *infra*, at 443; Huard, *infra* at 743; Phillips, *infra* at § 12:01

b. Two Discrete Steps in the Adoption Process

Adoption involves two discrete legal processes. First, the legal relationship between the child and his or her legal parent or parents must be terminated. Second, the permanent placement of the child into a new family (placement) must be approved, and a new parental relationship must be established in law. Historically, the law focused upon the second step. The forms and procedures for creating the new parent-child relationship were strictly observed, as adoption was in derogation of the common law. The adopting parents had to see that all the "i's" were dotted and all the "t's" were crossed or the court would not grant the adoption petition. Requirements for adoption are still strictly construed and rigorously examined in most states.

However, the focus of concern in recent years has shifted to the first step, the termination of the parent-child relationship. Because parental rights are now deemed fundamental constitutional liberties, state action depriving individuals of those rights, as by terminating parental rights upon adoption, will be upheld only if necessary to achieve compelling state interests. Moreover, full and adequate procedural protections must be provided to the parents in termination proceedings. The modern emphasis upon the parental rights of fathers of children born out of wedlock has also renewed attention on this step in the adoption process.

Although distinct steps, termination and placement are intertwined. The creation of the new parent-child relationship cannot occur under present legal doctrine, which assumes exclusive parenting by one mother and one father, until the parental rights of the prior legal parent(s) have been terminated. Termination of parental rights alone does not give the adoptive parents any legal rights of parenthood although temporary placement may occur. There are several different procedures for terminating parental rights, but they all fall into one of two categories: voluntary termination or involuntary termination.

c. Conflicting Policies Underlying Termination of Parental Rights

Two powerful conflicting sets of policies underlie the termination of parental rights in connection with adoption. First, parental rights are among the fundamental liberties protected by the Fourteenth Amendment. Courts and legislatures are required to give special protection to these rights. It is generally believed among child care professionals that if the biological parents can be made adequate in parenting skills, their children usually will be better off being raised by them rather than by loving strangers. On the other hand, however, experience teaches that some parents are not able to provide adequately for a child, or have little commitment to their children, and that perpetuating the "limbo" of foster care when the child might be raised by loving adoptive parents severely and unnecessarily harms the child.

The other set of conflicting policies involves timing. The child's time-perspective is very immediate; there is need to establish a stable, continuous parent-child bond. On the other hand, however, hasty or premature termination of parental rights may irreparably and unnecessarily deprive potentially fit parents of the opportunity to raise their own offspring and deprive the child of the chance to be raised by his or her biological parents. As a backlash to some arguably over-active intervention by state agencies in the 1960s and 1970s, a trend developed in the late 1970s and 1980s toward protecting parental rights and preventing their premature termination. Recently, however, as the numbers of children in "limbo" in state foster care has climbed and efforts to terminate parental rights have stalled as the parents fail to make changes adequate to allow the children to be safely returned to them, the pendulum has swung back, and now the trend is to limit the time in which parents who have lost custody of their children due to abuse or neglect may invoke ongoing but incomplete rehabilitation to thwart the termination of their parental rights and the placement of their children for adoption. *See e.g.* the Adoption and Safe Families Act of 1997, Pub.L. 105-89.

d. Voluntary Termination of Parental Rights

The first and preferred method of freeing a child for adoption is by voluntary termination of parental rights by the parents of the child to be adopted. There are several different ways in which voluntary termination of parental rights may occur. First, all states allow parents to voluntarily terminate their parental rights by *relinquishing* a child for adoption. Adoption is one of the few contexts in which the law allows persons who are responsible for the care and custody of minor children to abandon obligations of parenthood. Because the legal consequences of relinquishing parental rights are so final, and the rights relinquished are so important, and because so often the decision to relinquish a child for adoption is made at a time when the parents (especially the mother) are in an emotional turmoil, all states have statutes which precisely specify how the parental rights are to be voluntarily terminated or relinquished. Most states require

significant formalities to underscore to the person relinquishing the child the importance
and finality of the action. Written relinquishment is required in all states. Requirements
that the relinquishment form be signed before a judge, or trusted agency officials, or be
notarized, or be signed in the presence of witnesses are not uncommon. In most states the
relinquishment may not be signed before the child has been born, and many states do not
allow a mother to sign a voluntary relinquishment form for a certain period of time after
the child has been born. The payment of money to induce the signing of the
relinquishment is prohibited in all states (although most states specifically permit
reimbursement of medical and related expenses). These statutes have been designed
primarily to protect vulnerable parents against hasty or coerced relinquishment of
parental rights. Accordingly, the statutes generally are strictly construed; total
compliance is required. The statutes are also intended to provide the persons who must
rely upon them with a rock-solid basis for making or taking a permanent adoption
placement. Accordingly, if the requirements of the relinquishment of parental rights
statutes are fully satisfied, the courts historically have been very reluctant to revoke the
voluntary relinquishment despite a later change of mind and the most sincere personal
appeals. In some states (and under federal law, in cases involving the adoption of Indian
children) the parent has a right to rescind the relinquishment within a certain amount of
time. Barring such a statute, however, the prevailing rule is that a voluntary
relinquishment may not be set aside or rescinded unless extreme duress, coercion, fraud
or similar grounds exist. The design of the adoption statues is to ensure prior care and
deliberation, because after the parent has consented to adoption, other profound interests
are created, including the need for finality and reliability for the sake of the child, the
adoptive family unit, and the integrity of the adoption system. Thus, the law strongly
disfavors the disruption which recision of termination of parental rights would create.
However, the details concerning the requirements for a valid voluntary termination of
parental rights and the conditions in which it may be withdrawn vary significantly from
state to state.

    Parents may also voluntarily terminate parental rights by *giving up their parental
rights to a state child welfare agency.* While this is deemed "voluntary," often it occurs
as a result of a process of bargaining in which the parents pit the threat of criminal
prosecution for child abuse or neglect against the offer of leniency if the parents agree to
voluntarily terminate their parental rights. The voluntary termination of parental rights
to the agency makes possible a later adoption, though not all children whose parents give
up parental rights are placed for adoption (especially older or seriously troubled children
and children of color).

    Parents may also voluntarily terminate parental rights by expressly or implicitly
waiving their parental rights. Thus, as *Lehr v. Robertson*, 463 U.S. 248 (1983), *infra*,
shows, the failure of the father of a child born out of wedlock properly and timely to
assert his claim of paternity is deemed a "waiver" of his parental rights.

e. Involuntary Termination of Parental Rights

    Probably the most frequently litigated element of modern adoptions concerns
involuntary termination of parental rights. Such litigation occurs when one or both of the
biological parents refuse voluntarily to relinquish parental rights and consent to the
adoption. In some cases the parent does not oppose the adoption but (perhaps for reasons
pertaining to psychology or self-perception, or family pressure) is unwilling to

"abandon" the child formally. In recent years, the adoption may be vigorously opposed by some biological parent(s) who vehemently want to retain, at least formally, their parental rights. In such cases, the child may only be adopted if the parental rights are terminated involuntarily. This issue may arise in a variety of contexts, but probably the three most common today involve: (1) contested adoptions of children born out of wedlock, where the mother has relinquished the child for adoption but the biological father refuses to consent (sometimes motivated by pressure from his parents who want to raise the grandchild, or motivated by his desire to manipulate the mother of the child into continuing a relationship), (2) stepparent adoptions, where the husband (usually) of the custodial parent seeks to adopt his wife's children of a former marriage, and the inactive noncustodial father objects, and (3) where an abused or neglected child has been in foster care for some time, and the biological parents have not been rehabilitated by developing adequate parenting skills, but they still will not voluntarily relinquish the children for adoption.

Because the right of parents to raise and nurture their children is one of the Fourteenth Amendment "liberties" recognized by the Supreme Court, the standard of proof required to terminate parental rights is substantial; the Constitution requires "clear and convincing" evidence. *Santosky v. Kramer*, 455 U.S. 745 (1982). When the termination of parental rights proceeding is initiated by the state, rather than arising in a private civil action for adoption, the procedures (and the court) may differ somewhat. Courts pay particular attention and generally resolve doubts in favor of the parent opposing the termination of parental rights.

In recent years there has been a great deal of litigation concerning what "process" is due the biological father who opposes adoption. It is now clear that if the father has established an actual (albeit de facto) parental relationship with the child, he is entitled to substantial procedural protections, i.e., notice, an opportunity to intervene and to be heard, etc., even if he has not formalized (i.e., legitimated) the relationship. *Stanley v. Illinois*, 405 U.S. 645 (1972); *Caban v. Mohammed*, 442 U.S. 380 (1979). When a father has ceased to maintain a parental relationship for a substantial period of time, less procedural protection is required. *Quilloin v. Walcott*, 434 U.S. 246 (1978). If the biological father has failed to establish a parental relationship with a child born out of wedlock, he is entitled to no more procedural protection than a fair legal opportunity to assert his parental claim. Failing to establish this relationship, his rights may be cut off without further procedural protections for him. *Lehr v. Robertson*, 463 U.S. 248 (1983).

f. Required Notice and Joinder in Adoption Proceedings

By statute, certain persons must be made parties in adoption proceedings in every state. Others must be notified and given a chance to join or intervene. Failure to join or notify the necessary parties may render the adoption decree voidable. The persons who must be notified or made parties to adoption proceedings vary from state to state. Different states require joinder of some or all of the following potential parties: the biological mother of the child, the biological father, the presumed father, the stepparents, the person being adopted, any legal custodian or guardian, the interested private or public adoption agency, the adoptive parent or parents, and possibly his or her spouse. *See generally* Annot., 48 A.L.R. 4th 860 (1986). Generally, a person whose parental rights have been actually or constructively terminated before the adoption proceeding begins need not be notified or made a party to the adoption proceeding.

2. Statutes, Cases and Doctrines

a. *Quilloin v. Walcott*
Leon Webster Quilloin v. Ardell Williams Walcott et al.
434 U.S. 246, 98 S.Ct. 549 (1978)

Mr. JUSTICE MARSHALL delivered the opinion of the Court.

The issue in this case is the constitutionality of Georgia's adoption laws as applied to deny an unwed father authority to prevent adoption of his illegitimate child. The child was born in December 1964 and has been in the custody and control of his mother, appellee Ardell Williams Walcott, for his entire life. The mother and the child's natural father, appellant Leon Webster Quilloin, never married each other or established a home together, and in September 1967 the mother married appellee Randall Walcott. In March 1976, she consented to adoption of the child by her husband, who immediately filed a petition for adoption. Appellant attempted to block the adoption and to secure visitation rights, but he did not seek custody or object to the child's continuing to live with appellees. Although appellant was not found to be an unfit parent, the adoption was granted over his objection.

***   I

Generally speaking, under Georgia law a child born in wedlock cannot be adopted without the consent of each living parent who has not voluntarily surrendered rights in the child or been adjudicated an unfit parent. Even where the child's parents are divorced or separated at the time of the adoption proceedings, either parent may veto the adoption. In contrast, only the consent of the mother is required for adoption of an illegitimate child. Ga.Code § 74-403(3) (1975). To acquire the same veto authority possessed by other parents, the father of a child born out of wedlock must legitimate his offspring, either by marrying the mother and acknowledging the child as his own, § 74-101, or by obtaining a court order declaring the child legitimate and capable of inheriting from the father, § 74-103. But unless and until the child is legitimated, the mother is the only recognized parent and is given exclusive authority to exercise all parental prerogatives, § 74-203, including the power to veto adoption of the child.

Appellant did not petition for legitimation of his child at any time during the 11 years between the child's birth and the filing of Randall Walcott's adoption petition. However, in response to Walcott's petition, appellant filed an application for a writ of habeas corpus seeking visitation rights, a petition for legitimation, and an objection to the adoption. *[FN7- It does appear that appellant consented to entry of his name on the child's birth certificate. ***]* Shortly thereafter, appellant amended his pleadings by adding the claim that §§ 74-203 and 74-403(3) were unconstitutional as applied to his case, insofar as they denied him the rights granted to married parents, and presumed unwed fathers to be unfit as a matter of law.

The petitions for adoption, legitimation and writ of habeas corpus were consolidated for trial in the Superior Court of Fulton County, Ga. The court expressly stated that these matters were being tried on the basis of a consolidated record to allow "the biological father . . . a right to be heard with respect to any issue or other thing upon which he desire[s] to be heard, including his fitness as a parent . . . ." After receiving extensive testimony from the parties and other witnesses, the trial court found that, although the child had never been abandoned or deprived, appellant had provided support only on an irregular basis. Moreover, while the child previously had visited with appellant on "many occasions," and had been given toys and gifts by appellant "from time to time," the mother had recently concluded that these contacts were having a disruptive effect on the child and on appellees' entire family. The child himself expressed a desire to be adopted by Randall Walcott and to take on Walcott's name, and the court found Walcott to be a fit and proper person to adopt the child.

On the basis of these findings, as well as findings relating to appellees' marriage and the mother's custody of the child for all of the child's life, the trial court determined that the proposed adoption was in the "best interests of [the] child." The court concluded, further, that granting either the legitimation or the visitation rights requested by appellant would not be in the "best interests of the child," and that both should consequently be denied. The court then applied §§ 74-203 and 74-403(3) to the situation at hand, and, since appellant had failed to obtain a court order granting legitimation, he was found to lack standing to object to the adoption. Ruling that appellant's constitutional claims were without merit, the court granted the adoption petition and denied the legitimation and visitation petitions.

Appellant took an appeal to the Supreme Court of Georgia, claiming that §§ 74-203 and 74-403(3), as applied by the trial court to his case, violated the Equal Protection and Due Process Clauses of the Fourteenth Amendment. In particular, appellant contended that he was entitled to the same power to veto an adoption as is provided under Georgia law to married or divorced parents and to unwed mothers, and, since the trial court did not make a finding of abandonment or other unfitness on the part of appellant, *see* n. 2, *supra*, the adoption of his child should not have been allowed.

Over a dissent which urged that § 74-403(3) was invalid under *Stanley v. Illinois*, the Georgia Supreme Court affirmed the decision of the trial court. *. The majority relied generally on the strong state policy of rearing children in a family setting, a policy which in the court's view might be thwarted if unwed fathers were required to consent to adoptions. The court also emphasized the special force of this policy under the facts of this case, pointing out that the adoption was sought by the child's stepfather, who was part of the family unit in which the child was in fact living, and that the child's natural father had not taken steps to support or legitimate the child over a period of more than 11 years. The court noted in addition that, unlike the father in Stanley, appellant had never been a de facto member of the child's family unit.

Appellant brought this appeal pursuant to 28 U.S.C. § 1257(2), continuing to challenge the constitutionality of §§ 74-203 and 74-403(3) as applied to his case, and claiming that he was entitled as a matter of due process and equal protection to an absolute veto over adoption of his child, absent a finding of his unfitness as a parent. In contrast to appellant's somewhat broader statement of the issue in the Georgia Supreme Court, on this appeal he focused his equal protection claim solely on the disparate statutory treatment of his case and that of a married father. We*** now affirm.

II

At the outset, we observe that appellant does not challenge the sufficiency of the notice he received with respect to the adoption proceeding, *, nor can he claim that he was deprived of a right to a hearing on his individualized interests in his child, prior to entry of the order of adoption. Although the trial court's ultimate conclusion was that appellant lacked standing to object to the adoption, this conclusion was reached only after appellant had been afforded a full hearing on his legitimation petition, at which he was given the opportunity to offer evidence on any matter he thought relevant, including his fitness as a parent. Had the trial court granted legitimation, appellant would have acquired the veto authority he is now seeking.

The fact that appellant was provided with a hearing on his legitimation petition is not, however, a complete answer to his attack on the constitutionality of §§ 74-203 and 74-403(3). The trial court denied appellant's petition, and thereby precluded him from gaining veto authority, on the ground that legitimation was not in the "best interests of the child"; appellant contends that he was entitled to recognition and preservation of his parental rights absent a showing of his "unfitness." Thus, the underlying issue is whether, in the circumstances of this case and in light of the authority granted by Georgia law to married fathers, appellant's interests were adequately protected by a "best interests of the child" standard. We examine this issue first under the Due Process Clause and then under the Equal Protection Clause.

A

Appellees suggest that due process was not violated, regardless of the standard applied by the trial court, since any constitutionally protected interest appellant might have had was lost by his failure to petition for legitimation during the 11 years prior to filing of Randall Walcott's adoption petition. We would hesitate to rest decision on this ground, in light of the evidence in the record that appellant was not aware of the legitimation procedure until after the adoption petition was filed. But in any event we need not go that far, since under the circumstances of this case appellant's substantive rights were not violated by application of a "best interests of the child" standard.

We have recognized on numerous occasions that the relationship between parent and child is constitutionally protected. *See e.g. Wisconsin v. Yoder,* * (1972); *Stanley v. Illinois, supra* ; *Meyer v. Nebraska,* * (1923). "It is cardinal with us that the custody, care and nurture of the child reside first in the parents, whose primary function and freedom include preparation for obligations the state can neither supply nor hinder." *Prince v. Massachusetts,* * (1944). And it is now firmly established that "freedom of personal choice in matters of . . . family life is one of the liberties protected by the Due Process Clause of the Fourteenth Amendment." *Cleveland Board of Education v. LaFleur,* * (1974).

We have little doubt that the Due Process Clause would be offended "[i]f a State were to attempt to force the breakup of a natural family, over the objections of the parents and their children, without some showing of unfitness and for the sole reason that to do so was thought to be in the children's best interest." *Smith v. Organization of Foster Families,* * (1977) (Stewart, J., concurring in judgment). But this is not a case in which the unwed father at any time had, or sought, actual or legal custody of his child. Nor is this a case in which the proposed adoption would place the child with a new set of parents with whom the child had never before lived. Rather, the result of the adoption in this case is to give full recognition to a family unit already in existence, a result desired by all concerned, except appellant. Whatever might be required in other situations, we cannot say that the State was required in this situation to find anything more than that the adoption, and denial of legitimation, were in the "best interests of the child."

B

Appellant contends that even if he is not entitled to prevail as a matter of due process, principles of equal protection require that his authority to veto an adoption be measured by the same standard that would have been applied to a married father. In particular, appellant asserts that his interests are indistinguishable from those of a married father who is separated or divorced from the mother and is no longer living with his child, and therefore the State acted impermissibly in treating his case differently. We think appellant's interests are readily distinguishable from those of a separated or divorced father, and accordingly believe that the State could permissibly give appellant less veto authority than it provides to a married father.

Although appellant was subject, for the years prior to these proceedings, to essentially the same child-support obligation as a married father would have had, compare § 74-202 with § 74-105 and § 30-301, he has never exercised actual or legal custody over his child, and thus has never shouldered any significant responsibility with respect to the daily supervision, education, protection, or care of the child. Appellant does not complain of his exemption from these responsibilities and, indeed, he does not even now seek custody of his child. In contrast, legal custody of children is, of course, a central aspect of the marital relationship, and even a father whose marriage has broken apart will have borne full responsibility for the rearing of his children during the period of the marriage. Under any standard of review, the State was not foreclosed from recognizing this difference in the extent of commitment to the welfare of the child.

For these reasons, we conclude that §§ 74-203 and 74-403(3), as applied in this case, did not deprive appellant of his asserted rights under the Due Process and Equal Protection Clauses. The judgment of the Supreme Court of Georgia is accordingly,

Affirmed.

b. *Caban v. Mohammed*
Abdiel Caban v. Kazim Mohammed and Maria Mohammed
441 U.S. 380 (1979)

Mr. JUSTICE POWELL delivered the opinion of the Court.

The appellant, Abdiel Caban, challenges the constitutionality of § 111 of the New York Domestic Relations Law (McKinney 1977), under which two of his natural children were adopted by their natural mother and stepfather without his consent. We find the statute to be unconstitutional, as the distinction it invariably makes between the rights of unmarried mothers and the rights of unmarried fathers has not been shown to be substantially related to an important state interest.

I

Abdiel Caban and appellee Maria Mohammed lived together in New York City from September 1968 until the end of 1973. During this time Caban and Mohammed represented themselves as being husband and wife, although they never legally married. Indeed, until 1974 Caban was married to another woman, from whom he was separated. While living with the appellant, Mohammed gave birth to two children: David Andrew Caban, born July 16, 1969, and Denise Caban, born March 12, 1971. Abdiel Caban was identified as the father on each child's birth certificate, and lived with the children as their father until the end of 1973. Together with Mohammed, he contributed to the support of the family.

In December 1973, Mohammed took the two children and left the appellant to take up residence with appellee Kazim Mohammed, whom she married on January 30, 1974. For the next nine months, she took David and Denise each weekend to visit her mother, Delores Gonzales, who lived one floor above Caban. Because of his friendship with Gonzales, Caban was able to see the children each week when they came to visit their grandmother.

In September 1974, Gonzales left New York to take up residence in her native Puerto Rico. At the Mohammeds' request, the grandmother took David and Denise with her. According to appellees, they planned to join the children in Puerto Rico as soon as they had saved enough money to start a business there. During the children's stay with their grandmother, Mrs. Mohammed kept in touch with David and Denise by mail; Caban communicated with the children through his parents, who also resided in Puerto Rico. In November 1975, he went to Puerto Rico, where Gonzales willingly surrendered the children to Caban with the understanding that they would be returned after a few days. Caban, however, returned to New York with the children. When Mrs. Mohammed learned that the children were in Caban's custody, she attempted to retrieve them with the aid of a police officer. After this attempt failed, the appellees instituted custody proceedings in the New York Family Court, which placed the children in the temporary custody of the Mohammeds and gave Caban and his new wife, Nina, visiting rights.

In January 1976, appellees filed a petition under § 110 of the New York Domestic Relations Law to adopt David and Denise. In March, the Cabans cross-petitioned for adoption. After the Family Court stayed the custody suit pending the outcome of the adoption proceedings, a hearing was held on the petition and cross petition before a Law Assistant to a New York Surrogate in Kings County, N.Y. At this hearing, both the Mohammeds and the Cabans were represented by counsel and were permitted to present and cross-examine witnesses.

The Surrogate granted the Mohammeds' petition to adopt the children, thereby cutting off all of appellant's parental rights and obligations. In his opinion, the Surrogate noted the limited right under New York law of unwed fathers in adoption proceedings: "Although a putative father's consent to such an adoption is not a legal necessity, he is entitled to an opportunity to be heard in opposition to the proposed stepfather adoption." Moreover, the court stated that the appellant was foreclosed from adopting David and Denise, as the natural mother had withheld her consent. Thus, the court considered the evidence presented by the Cabans only insofar as it reflected upon the Mohammeds' qualifications as prospective parents. The Surrogate found them well qualified and granted their adoption petition.

The New York Supreme Court, Appellate Division, affirmed. It stated that appellant's constitutional challenge to § 111 was foreclosed by the New York Court of Appeals' decision in In re Malpica-Orsini, * (1975), appeal dism'd for want of substantial federal question sub nom. *Orsini v. Blasi,*

* (1976). * The New York Court of Appeals dismissed the appeal in a memorandum decision based on *In re Malpica-Orsini, supra.*

On appeal to this Court, appellant presses two claims. First, he argues that the distinction drawn under New York law between the adoption rights of an unwed father and those of other parents violates the Equal Protection Clause of the Fourteenth Amendment. Second, appellant contends that this Court's decision in *Quilloin v. Walcott,* * (1978), recognized the due process right of natural fathers to maintain a parental relationship with their children absent a finding that they are unfit as parents.

II

*** Absent one of these circumstances [e.g., abandonment], an unwed mother has the authority under New York law to block the adoption of her child simply by withholding consent. The unwed father has no similar control over the fate of his child, even when his parental relationship is substantial--as in this case. He may prevent the termination of his parental rights only by showing that the best interests of the child would not permit the child's adoption by the petitioning couple.
***

*** Accordingly, it is clear that § 111 treats unmarried parents differently according to their sex.

III

*** The question before us, therefore, is whether the distinction in § 111 between unmarried mothers and unmarried fathers bears a substantial relation to some important state interest. Appellees assert that the distinction is justified by a fundamental difference between maternal and paternal relations--that "a natural mother, absent special circumstances, bears a closer relationship with her child . . . than a father does." Tr. of Oral Arg. 41.

Contrary to appellees' argument and to the apparent presumption underlying § 111, maternal and paternal roles are not invariably different in importance. Even if unwed mothers as a class were closer than unwed fathers to their newborn infants, this generalization concerning parent- child relations would become less acceptable as a basis for legislative distinctions as the age of the child increased. The present case demonstrates that an unwed father may have a relationship with his children fully comparable to that of the mother. Appellant Caban, appellee Maria Mohammed, and their two children lived together as a natural family for several years. *** There is no reason to believe that the Caban children-- aged 4 and 6 at the time of the adoption proceedings--had a relationship with their mother unrivaled by the affection and concern of their father. We reject, therefore, the claim that the broad, gender-based distinction of § 111 is required by any universal difference between maternal and paternal relations at every phase of a child's development.
***

We find that the distinction in § 111 between unmarried mothers and unmarried fathers, as illustrated by this case, does not bear a substantial relation to the State's interest in providing adoptive homes for its illegitimate children. It may be that, given the opportunity, some unwed fathers would prevent the adoption of their illegitimate children. This impediment to adoption usually is the result of a natural parental interest shared by both genders alike; it is not a manifestation of any profound difference between the affection and concern of mothers and fathers for their children. Neither the State nor the appellees have argued that unwed fathers are more likely to object to the adoption of their children than are unwed mothers; nor is there any self-evident reason why as a class they would be.

The New York Court of Appeals in *In re Malpica-Orsini, supra,* suggested that the requiring of unmarried fathers' consent for adoption would pose a strong impediment for adoption because often it is impossible to locate unwed fathers when adoption proceedings are brought, whereas mothers are more likely to remain with their children. *** But in cases such as this, where the father has established a substantial relationship with the child and has admitted his paternity, a State should have no difficulty in identifying the father even of children born out of wedlock. Thus, no showing has been made that the different treatment afforded unmarried fathers and unmarried mothers under § 111 bears a substantial relationship to the proclaimed interest of the State in promoting the adoption of illegitimate children.

In sum, we believe that § 111 is another example of "overbroad generalizations" in gender-based classifications. *** The effect of New York's classification is to discriminate against unwed fathers even when their identity is known and they have manifested a significant paternal interest in the child. The facts of this case illustrate the harshness of classifying unwed fathers as being invariably less qualified and entitled than mothers to exercise a concerned judgment as to the fate of their children. Section 111 both excludes some loving fathers from full participation in the decision whether their children will be adopted and, at the same time, enables some alienated mothers arbitrarily to cut off the paternal rights of fathers. We conclude that this undifferentiated distinction between unwed mothers and unwed fathers, applicable in all circumstances where adoption of a child of theirs is at issue, does not bear a substantial relationship to the State's asserted interests.

*** Because we have ruled that the New York statute is unconstitutional under the Equal Protection Clause, we similarly express no view as to whether a State is constitutionally barred from ordering adoption in the absence of a determination that the parent whose rights are being terminated is unfit.

The judgment of the New York Court of Appeals is
Reversed.
Mr. JUSTICE STEWART, dissenting.
***

The Constitution does not require that an unmarried father's substantive parental rights must always be coextensive with those afforded to the fathers of legitimate children. In this setting, it is plain that the absence of a legal tie with the mother provides a constitutionally valid ground for distinction. The decision to withhold from the unwed father the power to veto an adoption by the natural mother and her husband may well reflect a judgment that the putative father should not be able arbitrarily to withhold the benefit of legitimacy from his children.

Even if it be assumed that each married parent after divorce has some substantive due process right to maintain his or her parental relationship, cf. *Smith v. Organization of Foster Families*, *, it by no means follows that each unwed parent has any such right. Parental rights do not spring full-blown from the biological connection between parent and child. They require relationships more enduring. The mother carries and bears the child, and in this sense her parental relationship is clear. The validity of the father's parental claims must be gauged by other measures. By tradition, the primary measure has been the legitimate familial relationship he creates with the child by marriage with the mother. *** It seems to me that the absence of a legal tie with the mother may in such circumstances appropriately place a limit on whatever substantive constitutional claims might otherwise exist by virtue of the father's actual relationship with the children.
***

In my view, the gender-based distinction drawn by New York falls in this latter category. With respect to a large group of adoptions--those of newborn children and infants--unwed mothers and unwed fathers are simply not similarly situated, as my Brother STEVENS has demonstrated. Our law has given the unwed mother the custody of her illegitimate children precisely because it is she who bears the child and because the vast majority of unwed fathers have been unknown, unavailable, or simply uninterested. ***

The majority of the States have incorporated these basic common-law rules in their statutes identifying the persons whose participation or consent is requisite to a valid adoption. *See generally* Note, 59 Va.L.Rev. 517 (1973); Comment, 70 Mich.L.Rev. 1581 (1972). These common-law and statutory rules of law reflect the physical reality that only the mother carries and gives birth to the child, as well as the undeniable social reality that the unwed mother is always an identifiable parent and the custodian of the child--until or unless the State intervenes. The biological father, unless he has established a familial tie with the child by marrying the mother, is often a total stranger from the State's point of view. I do not understand the Court to question these pragmatic differences. * An unwed father

who has not come forward and who has established no relationship with the child is plainly not in a situation similar to the mother's. New York's consent distinctions have clearly been made on this basis, and in my view they do not violate the Equal Protection Clause of the Fourteenth Amendment. *
***

I agree that retroactive application of the Court's decision today would work untold harm, and I fully subscribe to Part III of Mr. Justice STEVENS' dissent.

Mr. JUSTICE STEVENS, with whom THE CHIEF JUSTICE and Mr. JUSTICE REHNQUIST join, dissenting.
***

I

This case concerns the validity of rules affecting the status of the thousands of children who are born out of wedlock every day. All of these children have an interest in acquiring the status of legitimacy; a great many of them have an interest in being adopted by parents who can give them opportunities that would otherwise be denied; for some the basic necessities of life are at stake. The state interest in facilitating adoption in appropriate cases is strong--perhaps even "compelling."
***

Men and women are different, and the difference is relevant to the question whether the mother may be given the exclusive right to consent to the adoption of a child born out of wedlock. Because most adoptions involve newborn infants or very young children, it is appropriate at the outset to focus on the significance of the difference in such cases.

Both parents are equally responsible for the conception of the child out of wedlock. But from that point on through pregnancy and infancy, the differences between the male and the female have an important impact on the child's destiny. Only the mother carries the child;*[FN10 - In fact, there is some sociological and anthropological research indicating that by virtue of the symbiotic relationship between mother and child during pregnancy and the initial contact between mother and child directly after birth a physical and psychological bond immediately develops between the two that is not then present between the infant and the father or any other person. E. g., 1 & 2 J. Bowlby, Attachment and Loss (1969, 1973); M. Mahler, The Psychological Birth of the Human Infant (1975).]* it is she who has the constitutional right to decide whether to bear it or not. ***

*** [A]s a matter of equal protection analysis, it is perfectly obvious that at the time and immediately after a child is born out of wedlock, differences between men and women justify some differential treatment of the mother and father in the adoption process.
***

Most particularly, these differences justify a rule that gives the mother of the new born infant the exclusive right to consent to its adoption. Such a rule gives the mother, in whose sole charge the infant is often placed anyway, the maximum flexibility in deciding how best to care for the child. It also gives the loving father an incentive to marry the mother, and has no adverse impact on the disinterested father. Finally, it facilitates the interests of the adoptive parents, the child, and the public at large by streamlining the often traumatic adoption process and allowing the prompt, complete, and reliable integration of the child into a satisfactory new home at as young an age as is feasible. *[FN15- These are not idle interests. A survey of adoptive parents registered on the New York State Adoption Exchange as of January 1975 showed that over 75% preferred to adopt children under 3 years old; over half preferred children under 1 year old. New York Department of Social Services, Adoption in New York State 20 (Program Analysis Report No. 59, July 1975). Moreover, adoption proceedings, even when judicial in nature, have traditionally been expeditious in order to accommodate the needs of all concerned. Thus, 61% of all Family Court adoption proceedings in New York during the fiscal year 1972-1973 were disposed of within 90 days. Nineteenth Annual Report of the Judicial Conference to the Governor of the State of New York and the Legislature 352 (Legislative Doc. No. 90, 1974).]* Put most simply, it permits the maximum participation of interested natural parents without so burdening the adoption process that its attractiveness to potential adoptive parents is destroyed.

***

The mere fact that an otherwise valid general classification appears arbitrary in an isolated case is not a sufficient reason for invalidating the entire rule. Nor, indeed, is it a sufficient reason for concluding that the application of a valid rule in a hard case constitutes a violation of equal protection principles. We cannot test the conformance of rules to the principle of equality simply by reference to exceptional cases.

***

I respectfully dissent.

c. *Lehr v. Robertson*

Jonathan Lehr v.Lorraine Robertson et al.
463 U.S. 248 (1983)

STEVENS, Justice.

The question presented is whether New York has sufficiently protected an unmarried father's inchoate relationship with a child whom he has never supported and rarely seen in the two years since her birth. The appellant, Jonathan Lehr, claims that the Due Process and Equal Protection Clauses of the Fourteenth Amendment, as interpreted in *Stanley v. Illinois,* * (1972), and *Caban v. Mohammed,* * (1979) give him an absolute right to notice and an opportunity to be heard before the child may be adopted. We disagree.

Jessica M. was born out of wedlock on November 9, 1976. Her mother, Lorraine Robertson, married Richard Robertson eight months after Jessica's birth. On December 21, 1978, when Jessica was over two years old, the Robertsons filed an adoption petition in the Family Court of Ulster County, New York. The court heard their testimony and received a favorable report from the Ulster County Department of Social Services. On March 7, 1979, the court entered an order of adoption. In this proceeding, appellant contends that the adoption order is invalid because he, Jessica's putative father, was not given advance notice of the adoption proceeding.

The State of New York maintains a "putative father registry." A man who files with that registry demonstrates his intent to claim paternity of a child born out of wedlock and is therefore entitled to receive notice of any proceeding to adopt that child. Before entering Jessica's adoption order, the Ulster County Family Court had the putative father registry examined. Although appellant claims to be Jessica's natural father, he had not entered his name in the registry.

In addition to the persons whose names are listed on the putative father registry, New York law requires that notice of an adoption proceeding be given to several other classes of possible fathers of children born out of wedlock-- those who have been adjudicated to be the father, those who have been identified as the father on the child's birth certificate, those who live openly with the child and the child's mother and who hold themselves out to be the father, those who have been identified as the father by the mother in a sworn written statement, and those who were married to the child's mother before the child was six months old. Appellant admittedly was not a member of any of those classes. He had lived with appellee prior to Jessica's birth and visited her in the hospital when Jessica was born, but his name does not appear on Jessica's birth certificate. He did not live with appellee or Jessica after Jessica's birth, he has never provided them with any financial support, and he has never offered to marry appellee. Nevertheless, he contends that the following special circumstances gave him a constitutional right to notice and a hearing before Jessica was adopted.

On January 30, 1979, one month after the adoption proceeding was commenced in Ulster County, appellant filed a "visitation and paternity petition" in the Westchester County Family Court. In that petition, he asked for a determination of paternity, an order of support, and reasonable visitation privileges with Jessica. Notice of that proceeding was served on appellee on February 22, 1979. Four days later appellee's attorney informed the Ulster County Court that appellant had commenced a paternity proceeding in Westchester County; the Ulster County judge then entered an order staying appellant's paternity proceeding until he could rule on a motion to change the venue of that proceeding to Ulster County. On March 3, 1979, appellant received notice of the change of venue motion and, for the first time, learned that an adoption proceeding was pending in Ulster County.

On March 7, 1979, appellant's attorney telephoned the Ulster County judge to inform him that he planned to seek a stay of the adoption proceeding pending the determination of the paternity petition. In that telephone conversation, the judge advised the lawyer that he had already signed the adoption order earlier that day. According to appellant's attorney, the judge stated that he was aware of the pending paternity petition but did not believe he was required to give notice to appellant prior to the entry of the order of adoption.

Thereafter, the Family Court in Westchester County granted appellee's motion to dismiss the paternity petition, holding that the putative father's right to seek paternity "... must be deemed severed so long as an order of adoption exists." App. 228. Appellant did not appeal from that dismissal. [FN6] On June 22, 1979, appellant filed a petition to vacate the order of adoption on the ground that it was obtained by fraud and in violation of his constitutional rights. The Ulster County Family Court received written and oral argument on the question whether it had "dropped the ball" by approving the adoption without giving appellant advance notice. Tr. 53. After deliberating for several months, it denied the petition, explaining its decision in a thorough written opinion. *

The Appellate Division of the Supreme Court affirmed. * The majority held that appellant's commencement of a paternity action did not give him any right to receive notice of the adoption proceeding, that the notice provisions of the statute were constitutional, and that *Caban v. Mohammed,* * , was not retroactive. *[FN7 -Caban was decided on April 24, 1979, about two months after the entry of the order of adoption. ***]* Parenthetically, the majority observed that appellant "could have insured his right to notice by signing the putative father registry." * One justice dissented on the ground that the filing of the paternity proceeding should have been viewed as the statutory equivalent of filing a notice of intent to claim paternity with the putative father registry.

The New York Court of Appeals also affirmed by a divided vote. ***

Appellant has now invoked our appellate jurisdiction. He offers two alternative grounds for holding the New York statutory scheme unconstitutional. First, he contends that a putative father's actual or potential relationship with a child born out of wedlock is an interest in liberty which may not be destroyed without due process of law; he argues therefore that he had a constitutional right to prior notice and an opportunity to be heard before he was deprived of that interest. Second, he contends that the gender-based classification in the statute, which both denied him the right to consent to Jessica's adoption and accorded her fewer procedural rights than her mother, violated the Equal Protection Clause.

The Due Process Claim.
***

In the vast majority of cases, state law determines the final outcome.* Rules governing the inheritance of property, adoption, and child custody are generally specified in statutory enactments that vary from State to State. Moreover, equally varied state laws governing marriage and divorce affect a multitude of parent-child relationships. The institution of marriage has played a critical role both in defining the legal entitlements of family members and in developing the decentralized structure of our democratic society. In recognition of that role, and as part of their general overarching concern for serving the best interests of children, state laws almost universally express an appropriate preference for the formal family.

In some cases, however, this Court has held that the Federal Constitution supersedes state law and provides even greater protection for certain formal family relationships. In those cases, as in the state cases, the Court has emphasized the paramount interest in the welfare of children and has noted that the rights of the parents are a counterpart of the responsibilities they have assumed. Thus, the "liberty" of parents to control the education of their children that was vindicated in *Meyer v. Nebraska*, * (1923), and *Pierce v. Society of Sisters*,* (1925), was described as a "right, coupled with the high duty, to recognize and prepare [the child] for additional obligations." * The linkage between parental duty and parental right was stressed again in *Prince v. Massachusetts*, * (1944), when the Court declared it a cardinal principal "that the custody, care and nurture of the child reside first in the parents, whose primary function and freedom include preparation for obligations the state can neither supply nor hinder." *. In these cases the Court has found that the relationship of love and duty in a recognized family unit is an interest in liberty entitled to constitutional protection. *See also Moore v. City of East Cleveland*, * (1977) (plurality opinion). "[S]tate intervention to terminate [such a] relationship ... must be accomplished by procedures meeting the requisites of the Due Process Clause." *Santosky v. Kramer*, * (1982).

***

Stanley [v. Illinois] involved the constitutionality of an Illinois statute that conclusively presumed every father of a child born out of wedlock to be an unfit person to have custody of his children. The father in that case had lived with his children all their lives and had lived with their mother for eighteen years. There was nothing in the record to indicate that Stanley had been a neglectful father who had not cared for his children. * Under the statute, however, the nature of the actual relationship between parent and child was completely irrelevant. Once the mother died, the children were automatically made wards of the state. Relying in part on a Michigan case recognizing that the preservation of "a subsisting relationship with the child's father" may better serve the child's best interest than "uprooting him from the family which he knew from birth," *, the Court held that the Due Process Clause was violated by the automatic destruction of the custodial relationship without giving the father any opportunity to present evidence regarding his fitness as a parent.

*** [JUSTICE POWELL reviews *Quilloin* and *Caban*.]

The difference between the developed parent-child relationship that was implicated in Stanley and Caban, and the potential relationship involved in Quilloin and this case, is both clear and significant. When an unwed father demonstrates a full commitment to the responsibilities of parenthood by "com[ing] forward to participate in the rearing of his child," Caban, * , his interest in personal contact with his child acquires substantial protection under the due process clause. At that point it may be said that he "act[s] as a father toward his children." *. But the mere existence of a biological link does not merit equivalent constitutional protection. The actions of judges neither create nor sever genetic bonds. "[T]he importance of the familial relationship, to the individuals involved and to the society, stems from the emotional attachments that derive from the intimacy of daily association, and from the role it plays in 'promot[ing] a way of life' through the instruction of children as well as from the fact of blood relationship." *Smith v. Organization of Foster Families for Equality and Reform*, * (1977) (quoting *Wisconsin v. Yoder*, * (1972)).

The significance of the biological connection is that it offers the natural father an opportunity that no other male possesses to develop a relationship with his offspring. If he grasps that opportunity and accepts some measure of responsibility for the child's future, he may enjoy the blessings of the parent-child relationship and make uniquely valuable contributions to the child's development. If he fails to do so, the Federal Constitution will not automatically compel a state to listen to his opinion of where the child's best interests lie.

In this case, we are not assessing the constitutional adequacy of New York's procedures for terminating a developed relationship. Appellant has never had any significant custodial, personal, or financial relationship with Jessica, and he did not seek to establish a legal tie until after she was two years old. We are concerned only with whether New York has adequately protected his opportunity to form such a relationship.

II

The most effective protection of the putative father's opportunity to develop a relationship with his child is provided by the laws that authorize formal marriage and govern its consequences. ***

*** By mailing a postcard to the putative father registry, [Lehr] could have guaranteed that he would receive notice of any proceedings to adopt Jessica. The possibility that he may have failed to do so because of his ignorance of the law cannot be a sufficient reason for criticizing the law itself. The New York legislature concluded that a more open-ended notice requirement would merely complicate the adoption process, threaten the privacy interests of unwed mothers, create the risk of unnecessary controversy, and impair the desired finality of adoption decrees. Regardless of whether we would have done likewise if we were legislators instead of judges, we surely cannot characterize the state's conclusion as arbitrary.

*** The Constitution does not require either a trial judge or a litigant to give special notice to nonparties who are presumptively capable of asserting and protecting their own rights. Since the New York statutes adequately protected appellant's inchoate interest in establishing a relationship with Jessica, we find no merit in the claim that his constitutional rights were offended because the family court strictly complied with the notice provisions of the statute.

The Equal Protection Claim.

***

The legislation at issue in this case, sections 111 and 111a of the New York Domestic Relations Law, is intended to establish procedures for adoptions. Those procedures are designed to promote the best interests of the child, protect the rights of interested third parties, and ensure promptness and finality. To serve those ends, the legislation guarantees to certain people the right to veto an adoption and the right to prior notice of any adoption proceeding. The mother of an illegitimate child is always within that favored class, but only certain putative fathers are included. Appellant contends that the gender-based distinction is invidious.

As we noted above, the existence or nonexistence of a substantial relationship between parent and child is a relevant criterion in evaluating both the rights of the parent and the best interests of the child. In *Quilloin v. Walcott, supra,* we noted that the putative father, like appellant, "ha[d] never shouldered any significant responsibility with respect to the daily supervision, education, protection, or care of the child. Appellant does not complain of his exemption from these responsibilities...." *. We therefore found that a Georgia statute that always required a mother's consent to the adoption of a child born out of wedlock, but required the father's consent only if he had legitimated the child, did not violate the Equal Protection Clause. Because, like the father in Quilloin, appellant has never established a substantial relationship with his daughter, *see* p. 2994, *supra,* the New York statutes at issue in this case did not operate to deny appellant equal protection.

We have held that these statutes may not constitutionally be applied in that class of cases where the mother and father are in fact similarly situated with regard to their relationship with the child. In *Caban v. Mohammed,** (1979), the Court held that it violated the Equal Protection Clause to grant the mother a veto over the adoption of a four- year-old girl and a six-year-old boy, but not to grant a veto to their father, who had admitted paternity and had participated in the rearing of the children. The Court made it clear, however, that if the father had not "come forward to participate in the rearing of his child, nothing in the Equal Protection Clause [would] preclude[ ] the State from withholding from him the privilege of vetoing the adoption of that child." *.

Jessica's parents are not like the parents involved in Caban. Whereas appellee had a continuous custodial responsibility for Jessica, appellant never established any custodial, personal, or financial relationship with her. If one parent has an established custodial relationship with the child and the other parent has either abandoned or never established a relationship, the Equal Protection Clause does not prevent a state from according the two parents different legal rights.

The judgment of the New York Court of Appeals is Affirmed.

JUSTICE WHITE, with whom JUSTICE MARSHALL and JUSTICE BLACKMUN join, dissenting.

***

According to Lehr, he and Jessica's mother met in 1971 and began living together in 1974. The couple cohabited for approximately 2 years, until Jessica's birth in 1976. Throughout the pregnancy and after the birth, Lorraine acknowledged to friends and relatives that Lehr was Jessica's father; Lorraine told Lehr that she had reported to the New York State Department of Social Services that he was the father. Lehr visited Lorraine and Jessica in the hospital every day during Lorraine's confinement. According to Lehr, from the time Lorraine was discharged from the hospital until August, 1978, she concealed her whereabouts from him. During this time Lehr never ceased his efforts to locate Lorraine and Jessica and achieved sporadic success until August, 1977, after which time he was unable to locate them at all. On those occasions when he did determine Lorraine's location, he visited with her and her children to the extent she was willing to permit it. When Lehr, with the aid of a detective agency, located Lorraine and Jessica in August, 1978, Lorraine was already married to Mr. Robertson. Lehr asserts that at this time he offered to provide financial assistance and to set up a trust fund for Jessica, but that Lorraine refused. Lorraine threatened Lehr with arrest unless he stayed away and refused to permit him to see Jessica. Thereafter Lehr retained counsel who wrote to Lorraine in early December, 1978, requesting that she permit Lehr to visit Jessica and threatening legal action on Lehr's behalf. On December 21, 1978, perhaps as a response to Lehr's threatened legal action, appellees commenced the adoption action at issue here.

***

The "nature of the interest" at stake here is the interest that a natural parent has in his or her child, one that has long been recognized and accorded constitutional protection. We have frequently "stressed the importance of familial bonds, whether or not legitimized by marriage, and accorded them constitutional protection." *Little v. Streater*, * (1981). *** It is beyond dispute that a formal order of adoption, no less than a formal termination proceeding, operates to permanently terminate parental rights.

Lehr's version of the "facts" paints a far different picture than that portrayed by the majority. The majority's recitation, that "[a]ppellant has never had any significant custodial, personal, or financial relationship with Jessica, and he did not seek to establish a legal tie until after she was two years old," *, obviously does not tell the whole story. *** This case requires us to assume that Lehr's allegations are true--that but for the actions of the child's mother there would have been the kind of significant relationship that the majority concedes is entitled to the full panoply of procedural due process protections.

***

*** [T]the "nature" of the interest is the parent-child relationship; how well-developed that relationship has become goes to its "weight," not its "nature." ***

*** The procedures adopted by the State, however, must at least represent a reasonable effort to determine the identity of the putative father and to give him adequate notice.

II

In this case, of course, there was no question about either the identity or the location of the putative father. The mother knew exactly who he was and both she and the court entering the order of adoption knew precisely where he was and how to give him actual notice that his parental rights were about to be terminated by an adoption order. Lehr was entitled to due process, and the right to be heard is one of the fundamentals of that right, which "has little reality or worth unless one is informed that the matter is pending and can choose for himself whether to appear or default, acquiesce or contest." *

***

No state interest is substantially served by denying Lehr adequate notice and a hearing. The State no doubt has an interest in expediting adoption proceedings to prevent a child from remaining unduly long in the custody of the State or foster parents. But this is not an adoption involving a child in the custody of an authorized state agency. Here the child is in the custody of the mother and will remain in her custody. Moreover, had Lehr utilized the putative father register, he would have been granted a prompt hearing, and there was no justifiable reason, in terms of delay, to refuse him a hearing in the circumstances of this case.

***

Because in my view the failure to provide Lehr with notice and an opportunity to be heard violated rights guaranteed him by the Due Process Clause, I need not address the question whether § 111-a violates the Equal Protection Clause by discriminating between categories of unwed fathers or by discriminating on the basis of gender.

Respectfully, I dissent.

d. *Galison v. District of Columbia*

Edward Galison v. District of Columbia
402 A.2d 1263 (D.C. 1979)

See Chapter 13, *infra*.

e. Notes and Questions

1) Liberal Construction of Grounds for Terminating Parental Rights

When an action for adoption is filed by stepparents, the courts sometimes interpret the grounds for terminating parental rights more liberally than when a bare action to terminate parental rights is brought by the state (e.g., in an abuse, neglect, or dependency proceeding). The effect of the termination of parental rights in adoption does not just sever a child from a family relation but also integrates the child more completely into an ongoing family.

For example, in *In re J.J.J.*, 718 P.2d 948 (Alaska 1986), the Alaska Supreme Court applied a statutory provision whereby failure to pay support or communicate with a child for twelve months constitutes an abandonment of parental rights and estops the parent from objecting to the adoption of the child by another. The court held that the twelve month period did not have to precede the filing of the adoption petition immediately, i.e., that even if the defaulting parent had subsequently contributed to the support of or communicated with the child, that did not preclude application of the statute. Moreover, the court stated: "We take this opportunity to clarify that, in order for a noncustodial parent to block a stepparent adoption, he or she must have maintained *meaningful contact* with a child, and must have provided *regular payments of child support*, unless prevented from doing so by circumstances beyond the noncustodial parent's control." *Id.* at 953 (emphasis added).

2) Paid Adoption vs. "Baby Selling"

In all states it is a crime to sell a child. *See e.g.* Ala. Code Ann. § 26-10A-34. Laws forbidding "baby-selling" were enacted in many states in response to the congressional hearings in the 1950s (called the "Kefauver" hearings because they were chaired by Senator Kefauver) which revealed sensational information about black market adoptions. However, nearly half of the states have no specific restriction on the payment of fees in connection with adoption, and the laws in many of the states that do have such restrictions are ambiguous. W. Meezan, infra at 182-85. *But see* Me. Rev. St. Ann. title 18-A § 9-306 (listing permissible fees).

In a controversial 1978 article, Elizabeth Landes and Richard Posner applied economic analysis to adoptions, advocating steps to "a free baby market" in adoptions. Landes & Posner, *infra* at 347.

> Just as a buyers' queue is a symptom of a shortage, a sellers' queue is a symptom of a glut. The thousands of children in foster care. . .are comparable to an unsold inventory stored in a warehouse. . . . We believe that the large number of children in foster care is, in part, a manifestation of a regulatory pattern that (1) combines restrictions on the sell of babies with the effective of monopolization of the adoption market by adoption agencies, and (2) fails to provide effectively for the termination of the natural parents' rights.

Id. at 326-27.

> . . . [T]he constraints placed on independent adoption are sufficiently stringent to prevent it from approximating a free market. Women have little or no incentive to put a child up for adoption rather than retain or abort it (since abortions are relatively inexpensive, and public assistance is ordinarily available to cover their medical expenses and maintenance costs regardless of whether they keep or give up the child). At this same time, the constraints on payment discourage the emergence of an effective middle man function to match up the prospective sellers and buyers--the middle man activity *per se* cannot be compensated. . . .
>
> . . . .
>
> The foregoing analysis suggests that the baby shortage in black-market are the result of legal restrictions that prevent the market from operating freely in the sell of babies as other goods. . . .

Id. at 337-39.

In a later article, Judge Posner defended his baby-selling thesis by arguing that we already have, even apart from the black market, a relatively free market in babies.

> [M]any babies are lawfully 'sold' by adoption agencies, many of which charge thousands of dollars, and in independent adoption, often by the mother herself--for it is not considered unlawful to use part of the fee paid by the adoption parents to defray the medical and other maintenance costs of the mother during pregnancy. It seems that to obtain lawfully a healthy white infant (rather available through adoption agencies), a couple must be prepared to lay out at least $5,000. Black-market prices of $25,000, and even $50,000, have been rumors. But the equilibrium baby price in a free market. . . might not exceed $5,000. . . . No doubt many lawful and semi-lawful "baby sells" are taking place today at approximately free-market prices.
>
> There is a lawful market in babies, only a severely regulated one. . . .

Posner, *infra*.

3) The Federal Adoption and Safe Families Act

In 1997, Congress enacted the Adoption and Safe Families Act of 1997, Pub.L. 105-89, which provided financial incentives for states that increased the rate of adoption by, *inter alia*, reducing the time children are in foster care, reducing the time parents of such children have to "rehabilitate themselves" before their parental rights are terminated, expediting adoption procedures for children in foster care, etc. Two years later it appeared that the Act had increased adoptions significantly, even faster than lawmakers expected. The law was passed to encourage states to facilitate adoptions for the estimated 520,000 children in the foster care system, who, reportedly, spend between two and six years in the system, often living in multiple foster homes. In September 1999, the U.S. Department of Health and Human Services announced that 35 states had qualified for awards totaling $20 million as rewards for increasing adoptions under the Adoption and Safe Families Act of 1997. Illinois increased its adoption rate by 112 percent and received $6.869 million in incentive rewards; Texas increased adoptions by 55 percent for $1.35 million; [and California increased by 20 percent for $1.8 million. Associated Press Newswires, State to receive share of federal adoption money, Sep. 29, 1999 (Westlaw search Oct. 4, 1999)]. *See generally* American Bar Association, Center on Children and the Law, Congress Passes Major New Adoption/Foster Care Reform Law <http://www.abanet.org/child/adofost.html> (searched Oct. 4, 1999); The Adoption and Safe Families Act of 1997 <http://www.frontiernet.net/~jmb184/emancipated/>(searched Oct. 4, 1999); National Conference of State [Legislators, Federal-State Relations, Bill Analysis of P.L. 105-89, Adoption and Safe Families Act of 1997<http://www.ncsl.org/statefed/hr867.htm>].

Professor Cynthia Mabry argues that the time lines set forth in the Act and the states' failure to provide access to timely and appropriate services ensures that poor parents' parental rights will be terminated needlessly. She discusses ways in which state representatives, including family court judges, and private individuals may assist poor parents in satisfying conditions that will allow the parents to avoid a termination decree. Mabry, *infra*.

4) Effect of Voluntary Termination of Parental Rights If Adoption is Not Completed

It is usually said that adoption completely extinguishes the parent-child relationship between the adopted child and the biological parent(s) whose parental rights are relinquished or terminated. Conceptually, however, completion of the entire adoption process (including the establishment in law of a new parent-child relationship) is not necessary for the termination of parental rights to be effective. However, the termination of parental rights may be conditional -- predicated upon completion of the adoption. There may be good policy reasons why lawmakers may insist that a private, voluntary termination of parental rights in connection with adoption should not be effective unless the adoption is completed.

For instance, what if the child is born out of wedlock? Mother (M) agrees to termination of parental rights (TPR) on assumption that child will be adopted by adoptive parents (AP). The father of the child (F) intervenes to object, and successfully blocks the adoption. F wants custody; M wants custody (she would rather the child be adopted, but if that is not possible, she would rather raise the child herself than "doom the child" -- in her view -- to being raised by (F)). May she claim custody, or is her voluntary TPR still effective and binding to bar her claim for custody? This issue also arises when a parent (F) agrees to relinquish parental rights and duties (including the duty to support the child) in order to allow the new spouse (S) of the other parent (M) to adopt the child, but the new spouse (S) of the other parent (M) never completes the adoption of the child, and the other parent (M) is unable to support the child alone. In *Kimble v. Kimble*, 341 S.E.2d

420 (W. Va. 1986), F & M were divorced. F was ordered to pay child support. M married another man, S. F agreed to relinquish his parental rights so that S could adopt his child. However, S never adopted the child, and a year later M brought an action against F to recover delinquent support and to increase the amount of support. The trial court held that the agreement to terminate parental rights signed by F effectively barred M from subsequently seeking to enforce the prior support order. The appellate court vacated that judgment, noting that the agreement relinquishing parental rights and agreeing to the adoption was predicated upon court approval; that by statute parental support obligations are terminated upon the entry of an adoption order (which never occurred in this case); and that public policy is to protect the child's right to support. The court noted that the prevailing rule appears to be that judicially-imposed support obligations may not be terminated by private agreement between the parents (citing, *inter alia,* relatively recent cases from Florida, Hawaii, Indiana, Kansas, Louisiana, Maryland, Michigan, Missouri and Texas). *See* Annot., 100 A.L.R. 1129 (1980). However, the court observed that courts also have uniformly held, that consent for adoption may release a noncustodial parent of a decretal obligation to make child support payments "under theories of either release or equitable estoppel." Thus, the court ruled that "where the welfare of the child has not been adversely affected, a custodial parent may be barred by the doctrine of equitable estoppel from seeking enforcement of the decretal obligation" against a noncustodial parent who formally consented to adoption in exchange for the release of the child support obligation. However, if the welfare of the child would be impaired, the equitable doctrine may not be applied. The parent will then be liable for support arrearage from the time when the welfare of the child became adversely affected.

5) Controversial Cases Revoking Adoptions For Failure to Obtain Biological Father's Consent

There have been some highly controversial decisions in the 1990s upsetting adoptions because an unknown biological father did not consent to the adoption. In the "Baby Jessica" case, Clara and Daniel, both unmarried, had sex, resulting in Clara's pregnancy. Daniel saw that Clara was pregnant, but made no inquiries and took no action. By then she was dating Scott. Out of embarrassment, Clara named Scott as the father of her "Baby Jessica," and she and Scott signed papers relinquishing parental rights and consenting to adoption. The DeBoers came from Michigan to Iowa, and the child was placed with them for adoption on February 25, 1991. A few days later, Clara informed Daniel that he was the real father. Daniel asked her to get the baby back, but she was unable to do so. Daniel immediately hired an attorney and, within fifteen days of the placing of Baby Jessica for adoption, filed an affidavit of paternity and petition for adoption, which an Iowa court rejected. Two weeks later, he intervened in the adoption proceeding, and subsequently the Iowa court denied the adoption and ordered Baby Jessica be returned to her biological parents in Iowa, finding that the failure to obtain the consent of the real biological father rendered the adoption defective. The DeBoers appealed and were allowed to keep custody of the child in Michigan pending the disposition of the appeal. Eventually they lost in the Iowa state courts, Michigan state courts, and the U.S. Supreme Court declined to hear their appeal. Two and a half years after she was placed with the DeBoers, a frightened and crying Baby Jessica was taken from the DeBoers arms and returned to Iowa to live with Clara and Daniel (who, a dissenting judge noted, had two other children whom he had failed to support, one of whom he has never seen or supported). *Scarnecchia, infra; In re B.G.C., A Child, C.C. Natural Mother,* 496 N.W.2d 239 (Iowa 1992); *In re Baby Girl Clausen,* 502 N.W.2d 649 (Mich. 1993).

In the "Baby Richard" case another single woman, Daniella, consented to the adoption of her "Baby Richard," but refused to reveal the identity of the father, Otakar, from whom she was estranged. The baby was placed for adoption four days after birth. Daniella told Otakar that the baby had died, but he began to make inquiries. Nearly two months after Baby Richard was placed for adoption, he learned of the adoption. Otakar immediately tried to stop the adoption, but the trial court ruled that his consent was unnecessary because he was unfit and had failed to show sufficient interest in the welfare of the child. Otakar appealed, and after the Illinois intermediate court of appeals affirmed, the Illinois Supreme Court reversed and ordered the three-year-old child be returned to his biological parents. *Petition of Does,* 638 N.E.2d 181 (Ill. 1994). Public outcry against the decision was heightened when, two years after he succeeded in overturning the adoption and getting the child back, Otakar reportedly "again took off, leaving the woman to take care of Richard and another child," and Daniella and her two children were left "living in a hotel." Editorial, *How to Know Real Fathers,* Omaha World-Herald, Jan. 27, 1999.

6) Paternity Registries

Paternity registries evolved as the states were attempting to interpret what notice was due an unwed father to satisfy the due process requirements of the Fourteenth Amendment after *Stanley v. Illinois.* The concept of the paternity registry, as illustrated in *Lehr,* was a convenient means for the state to use to identify unwed fathers in order to give them notice if adoption/termination proceedings were filed in the state. If the unwed father had registered with the state, he would receive notice of such filing. If he had not registered, then he was not due notice. After the *Baby Jessie* and *the Baby Richard* cases, more states enacted paternity registries, attempting to alleviate the issue of the unwed father arguing he had not received notice. About 32 states have paternity registries. The Uniform Paternity Act of 2002 provides procedures for the paternity registry. Notwithstanding these registries, notice problems still remain. For example, registries are intrastate and not interstate Signing in one state, thus, does not assure notice and opportunity to be heard if the adoption proceeding is filed in another state. Many unwed fathers are also unaware of the state registry. Some registries have short time periods for registering. Court decisions are mixed in interpreting the application of these registry statutes to fathers who have not registered because they are unaware of child's birth, deceived about the birth, or thwarted in their attempts to locate the child. *See* Beck, *infra. See also* Parness, *infra* (criticizes treatment of unwed biological fathers during adoption of newborns and under paternity laws).

7) Revocation of Relinquishment by Biological Mother.

Because the birth mother has carried the child for nine months and usually has developed some prenatal (and often a postnatal) bond with the child, giving a child up for adoption is usually a wrenching experience for most mothers. Some (especially those acting without the support of a caring adoption agency to help them cope with the loss issues) attempt to revoke their relinquishment of parental rights, leading to no little litigation. *See e.g. In re L.M.I & J.A.I.,* 119 S.W.3d 707, 709 (Tex. 2003) (denying revocation relinquishment of parental rights of the unwed Spanish-speaking 15-year-old mother); *In re Baby Boy L,* 534 N.Y.S.2d 706 (N.Y. App. Div. 1998) (overturning lower court decision setting aside relinquishment signed by 17-year-old mother pressured by her mother to sign); *Gunderman v. Helms (In re Adoption of B.T.D.),* 68 P.3d 1021 (Utah 2003) (reversing and remanding lower court order allowing revocation of consent because of duress) .State laws vary regarding revocation of consents. *See* Adamec & Pierce, *infra* at 35-39. Historically revocation was strongly disfavored, but a few states now provide limited revocation periods. The Uniform Adoption Act, proposed in 1994, requires that consents be executed only after the child is born, but limits the time period of revocation to "192 hours" (eight days) after the birth of the child. Unif. Adoption Act § 2-404, 9 U.L.A. 53 (1999); *id.* (revocation also is allowed if the adoption agency agrees). To reduce revocation crises, most states now regulate when the biological mother may sign a relinquishment of parental rights.

8) Non-Parental Consent

Most states require children, varying from ten to fourteen years, to give their consent. If the child has a guardian, the guardian must give consent. An adoption agency must consent if it is involved.

3. Practical and Ethical Considerations

a. Classified Ads

Many local newspapers accept classified ads from prospective adoptive parents, advertising their desire to adopt. Might such ads encourage "baby selling"? Conversely, parents have used such ads to offer their child for adoption. (A Pennsylvania couple, through an advertisement in a Baltimore newspaper, offered to place their child for adoption upon payment of compensation.) What public policy and ethical issues do these situations raise? And for whom?

b. Adoption Expenses vs. Babyselling

In re Adoption No. 9979, 591 A.2d 468 (Md. 1991) (Maryland Court of Appeals ruled that payment of $488 for maternity clothing for the pregnant biological mother - maternity blouses, slacks, dresses, bras, winter coat, etc.- was prohibited under the anti-babyselling statute that prohibited "any compensation for the placement" except for "reasonable and customary charges or fees for hospital or medical or legal services."). How does this interpretation of the statute serve the policies against babyselling?

c. How Well Does Adoption Work?

Adoption has been described as "the 'perfect solution' to the dilemma of parentless children and childless want-to-be parents . . . ." Hollinger, *infra,* at 345. It is "perfect" for the child because it affords the parentless child a parent-led family environment which generally provides the child with the optimal, individualized, love-driven parenting. The imitative parenting model of adoption provides best for children because it is grounded in powerful realities of human nature. It understands that what motivates successful parenting is found in the nature of the unifying relationship between mother-and-father and child, not in any legalism or government incentive of coercion. No other model for the relationship, from friendship to partnership, from commercial to fiduciary, comes close to working as well to motivate the level of commitment to children that is needed for adults to make the sacrifices necessary to provide for the tangible and intangible needs of children.

A wealth of social science research supports imitative adoption. Numerous studies report that children adopted at birth are at least as likely to live with two parents in a middle-class family, to do as well or better in both school and in social competency tests, are generally less depressed, more optimistic, appear to have higher self-esteem, self-confidence, and feelings of security. They are more willing to give voluntary service, are less involved in alcohol or drug use, theft, weapons or police trouble, enjoy similar or better health, achieve higher educational attainments, and have fewer mental health problems as children living with their birth parents. Fagan, *infra*, at 3. Studies have even shown that adoption has been extraordinarily successful in enabling even children who have suffered extremely severe forms of deprivation and abuse in their early lives, that could be expected to cause difficulties in development, to recover and flourish. For example, one major study of children of the Vietnamese War who arrived in Norway for adoption at ages ranging from two to five, reported that when those children arrived, "'[m]any could not walk. They were passive, apathetic, retarded and malnourished.' [Fifteen-plus years later], those children were found to be in remarkably good shape: they were basically well-adjusted and strongly attached to their families." Tizzard, *infra*, at 748. Imitative adoption provides maximum life-development benefits for parentless children.

d. How Many Prospective Adopters Are There?

It has long been estimated that every year between 1 million and 2 million Americans are able, willing and want to adopt an unrelated child or children. *Garrison, infra* at 891 n. 260 (2000) (estimates of more than a million); Gates, *infra* at 369 (estimated two million American families wanted to adopt in 1998); Pierce, *infra* (National Council For Adoption estimates about 2 million). More recent government statistics indicate that an even greater number of Americans desire to adopt. A study published by the Centers for Disease Control in 1999 reported that in 1995, 9.9 million ever-married women had ever considered adoption (more than one-fourth of all ever-married women); that 5.6 million of those women "are still seeking or planning to adopt or would consider adoption in the future;" and that 1.6 million of them had taken steps to adopt. Chandra, *infra*, at 83-85. However, less than one-third of those who had made an effort to adopt succeed in adopting one or more children.

4. Bibliography

Christine Adamec & William L. Pierce, The Encyclopedia of Adoption (1991).

Mary Beck, *Toward A National Putative Registry Database*, 25 Harv. J. L. & Pub. Pol'y 1031 (2002)

W. Buckland, A Textbook of Roman Law from Augustus to Justinian (1921).

Naomi Cahn, *Perfect Substitutes or the Real Thing?*, 52 Duke L.J. 1077 (2003).

Anjani Chandra, et al, *Adoption, Adoption Seeking, and Relinquishment for Adoption in the United States*, in Centers for Disease Control and Prevention/ National Center for Health Statistics, Advance Data, No. 306, May 11, 1999, in Adoption Factbook III, *supra*, at 78.

Stephen Cretney, Principles of Family Law (3d ed. 1979).

Janet Dolgin, *Just a Gene: Judicial Assumptions about Parenthood*, 40 UCLA L. Rev. 637 (1993), p.673-694.

Patrick F. Fagan, *Adoption: The Best Option*, in Adoption Factbook III, at 2 (National Council for Adoption,1999).

Marsha Garrison, *Law Making for Baby Making: An Interpretive Approach to the Determination of Legal Parentage,*113 Harv. L. Rev. 835 (2000).

Crystal J. Gates, 1999 Immigration Project, *China's Newly Enacted Intercountry Adoption Law: Friend or Foe?*, 7 Ind. J. Global Legal Stud. 369 (1999).

Mark Hansen, *Fears of the Heart*, ABA Journal, Nov. 1994, p.58-63.

Henshaw, *Trends in Abortion*, 1982-84 18 Fam. Plan. Prospectives 34 (1986).

Henshaw, Forrest, Sullivan & Tietze, *Abortion in the United States, 1979-80*, 14 Fam. Plan. Prospectives 1 (1982).

Joan Heifetz Hollinger, *The Uniform Adoption Act: A Reporter's Ruminations*, 30 Fam. L.Q. 345 (1996).

Huard, *The Law of Adoption: Ancient and Modern*, 9 Vand. L. Rev. 743 (1956).

Kawashima, *Adoption in Early America*, 20 J. Fam. L. 677 (1982).

Landes & Posner, *The Economics of the Baby Shortage*. 7 J. Legal stud. 323 (1978).

Alexandra Dylan Lowe, *Parents & Strangers: The Uniform Adoption Act Revisits the Parental Rights Doctrine*, 30 Fam. L. Q. 379 (1996).

Cynthia R. Mabry, *Second Chances-Insuring that Poor Families Remain Intact by Minimizing Socioeconomic Ramifications of Poverty*, 103 W. Va. L. Rev. 559 (2000).

W. Meezan, S. Cats, & E. Russo, Adoptions Without Agencies: A Study of Independent Adoption. (1978).

National Council for Adoption, Adoption Fact Book III (National Committee For Adoption 1999).

Note, *Will* Palmore v. Sidotti *Preclude the Use of Race As A Factor In Denying An Adoption?* 24 J. Fam. L. 497 (1985).

Note, *Developing a Concept of the Modern Single "Family": A Proposed Uniform Surrogate Parenthood Act*, 73 Geo. L. J. 1283 (1985).

Contemporary Family Law , vol. 2, Ch. 10 (L. Wardle, C. Blakesley, & J. Parker, eds. 1988)

Jeffrey A. Parness, *Participation of Unwed Biological Fathers in Newborn Adoptions: Achieving Substantive and Procedural Fairness*, 5 J. L. & Fam. Pol'y 223 (2003).

William L. Pierce, *Adoption, Adoption Seeking, and Relinquishment for Adoption in the US*, in National Council for Adoption's Adoption Factbook III (1999) at p. 72.

Richard Posner, *The Regulation of the Market in Adoptions*, 67 B.U.L. Rev. 59 (1987).

Scarnecchia, *A Child's Right to Protection from Transfer Trauma in a Contested Adoption Case*, 2 Duke J. Gender L. & Pol'y 41 (1995).

Mary Shanley, *Unwed Father's Rights, Adoption, and Sex Equality: Gender Neutrality and the Perpetuation of Patriarchy*, 95 Colum. L. Rev. 60 (1995).

Brett S. Silverman, *The Winds of Change in Adoption Laws: Should Adoptees Have Access to Adoption Records?*, 39 Fam. & Conciliation Courts Rev. 85, 85 (2000).

Barbara Tizard, *Intercountry Adoption: A Review of the Evidence*, 32 J. Child Psychol. and Psychiatry 743 (1991).

Barbara Bennett Woodhouse, *Hatching the Egg: A Child Centered Perspective on Parents' Rights*, 14 Cardozo Law Journal 1748 (1993).

Wall Street J., Feb. 27, 1987, at 1, col. 1.

CHAPTER 13

Adoption: Creation of New Parent-Child Relationship; Placement; Effects

A. PLACEMENT

1. Background

a. Adoption Standard and Adoption Placement Policies

Once parental rights have been terminated, the primary public concern is for the welfare of the child. Today, it is generally accepted that adoption of a child into a family with a mother and a father is the best means of securing the paramount interests of the child, superior to foster care placement, placement in a child-care institution, or placement into some other environment, even though those alternative placements may be supervised by professionals and must operate under state-established standards, while after an adoption is completed, the family is beyond the supervision of the state and its experts.

The "best interests of the child" standard invites (if not requires) reliance upon child welfare professionals such as social workers, child psychologists, child development specialists, medical doctors, etc. Because ascertaining what is in the "best interests of the child" often involves evaluation and prediction that professionals in therapeutic disciplines are believed to be able to perform better than most others, courts generally defer heavily to the decisions of child welfare and adoption agencies whose professional staff have experience and presumably special expertise in adoption placement matters. In ascertaining the "best interests of the child," adoption courts and agencies have considered a number of criteria, which vary from state to state. Some criteria are controversial. They may include such criteria as race, religion, marital status (giving preference to married couples over unmarried couples and over single individuals), age (of prospective adoptive parents), income (of prospective adoptive parents), and family relationship (sometimes giving preference to relatives of the child).

b. Types of Adoption Placements or Processes

Several categories and distinctions are commonly used in adoption cases. "Private" (or "direct" or "independent") placements and "Private" (or "direct" or "independent") adoptions are distinguished from "agency" placements and adoptions. Private placements are those arranged privately (usually by a family relation or friend of the mother of the child, or by her doctor or attorney) without the assistance of a state-run or state-approved adoption placement agency. Agency placements are those in which the adoptive parents have been screened and selected by a state-run or state-approved adoption agency. The adoption agency may be a public agency or a private agency. Generally, agency placements are preferred. Private adoptions have been outlawed in some states in the belief that there are fewer opportunities for abuse (such as "baby-selling"), and more competent child-placement decisions when an agency is involved, and more support for the parent(s) relinquishing the child for adoption (who often are pregnant unmarried teenagers who need counseling and support services to deal with the kind of sexual abuse or exploitation that may have resulted in the premature pregnancy as well as to cope with the loss - relinquishment - of a child). However, some persons who would relinquish their children for adoption are reluctant to deal with adoption agencies, and some persons who wish to adopt find agency bureaucracies and policies restrictive or daunting, thus, many states still allow private adoptions. "[C]ommentators report that, in California and other states that allow private adoption, up to eighty percent of all newborn adoptions are handled privately." Jana B. Singer, *The Privatizaton of Family Law*, 1992 Wis. L. Rev. 1443, 1483 [n.177] "Data gathered in 1987 showed that between 1980 and 1987, 28% of the adoptions of unrelated children were arranged without the benefit of an agency, compared to 23% in the 1970s." *Id.* at 1567, n. 176.

Another adoption classification dyad is "anonymous" and "nonanonymous" adoptions. An anonymous adoption occurs when neither the adopting parents nor the biological parents know the identities of each other; the placement is arranged by an agency or private intermediary who conceals the identities of each. Anonymous adoptions traditionally have been favored (in some states almost required) because they protect the privacy of the biological parents, are thought to make the adoption relinquishment a little less traumatic, are thought to remove a disincentive for the biological parent(s) to relinquish a child for adoption, and they eliminate the possibility of post-adoption interference by the natural parents with the integrity of the adoptive family.

Historically, statutes in virtually all American jurisdictions sealed adoption records and prohibited (usually with criminal penalties) the unauthorized disclosure of such records, underscoring the strength of the policy of preserving the anonymity of the identities of the parties to adoption. These sealing and nondisclosure statutes usually allowed for release of identifying information about the parties to the adoption only upon a showing of "good cause," which was liberally construed regarding medical reasons, but generally narrowly construed regarding other reasons (such as psychological reasons, yearning to know one's biological family or ancestry, etc.). An "open records" movement is now changing much of the policy and law in this area, as noted *infra*. Nonanonymous adoptions occur when the relinquishing and adopting parents, and usually the child, know the identities of each other. The most common type of nonanonymous adoptions are "stepparent" adoptions, i.e., when the custodial parent of a child remarries and the new spouse adopts the children formally to legitimate his or her parental relationship with the children. With divorce and remarriage common today, stepparent adoptions are very common.

Another classification focuses on the place of origin of the child. "International" adoptions involve children from abroad who are adopted by American couples, or vice versa (extremely rare). "Domestic" adoptions include "intrastate adoptions" in which the child was born and is domiciled in the same state in which the adopting parents live, and "interstate" adoptions in which the child is domiciled in a different state from where the adopting parents are domiciled.

Another classification looks to the age of the child being adopted, and distinguishes "newborn" adoptions -- which take place within days or weeks of the birth of the child --- from "adoptions of older children" which involve children who are not placed immediately with the adoptive parents. Older children as well as children with medical problems and often multi-racial children are often labeled "hard-to-place-children" or "children-with-special-needs" whom fewer couples care to adopt because most want the opportunity to raise a child from infancy who does not have serious known medical or other limitations and who visibly/racially blends into the adopting family. Some newborn children are considered both "special needs" and "hard to place" children because they are born with birth defects, or other handicaps (such as prenatal AIDS, or fetal alcohol or drug abuse syndrome) and because they are mixed race and thus look different than most of the pool of prospective adoptive parents.

2. Statutes, Cases and Doctrines

a. *Scott v. Family Ministries*
Richard S. Scott, M.D., v. Family Ministries
135 Cal.Rptr. 430 (Cal. App. 1976)
THOMPSON, Associate Justice.

The appeal at bench tests the right of a private state licensed adoption agency to impose religious restrictions upon prospective adoptive parents over and above the religious matching requirements of California Administrative Code, Title 22, section 30643. It raises incidental insubstantial issues of the sufficiency of pleadings, standing, and a claim of prejudice of the trial judge.

We determine that by reason of the significance of private licensed adoption agencies in the California statutory scheme and the extent to which the California law delegates to those agencies the governmental function of performing the steps leading to judicially authorized adoption, the activity of the agencies is state action. Accordingly, we conclude that if section 30643 of Title 22 of the Administrative Code is to be given a constitutional construction it must be interpreted as precluding the imposition of religious requirements upon prospective adoptive parents beyond the religious matching provisions of the section.

Facts

World Vision is an evangelical Christian relief organization operating in 30 countries. One of its principal functions is the operation of orphanages and child care centers. World Vision began relief work in Cambodia in 1970 with the consent of the Cambodian government. In 1974, it established the Tuol Kauk Nutrition Center in Phnom Penh. The center cared for needy children, as many as 120 at one time. Generally, the center admitted seriously ill children coming from refugee camps. Children who recovered and who had family or friends to care for them were discharged. Others remained in the care of the center. The Cambodian government authorized the center to find homes for children within its care, and seven were placed for adoption. If a child was brought to the center by a relative, a 'relinquishment' was obtained. If the child was brought to the center by a nonrelative, no 'relinquishment' was required. Persons bringing children to the center were told that the child could be placed for adoption in a Christian home, possibly in another country.

92 percent of the population of Cambodia is Buddhist.

In April, 1975, when the Cambodian tragedy escalated to disaster, World Vision decided to evacuate the children in its care as the capture of Phnom Penh by the Khmer Rouge became imminent. Twenty Cambodian children were evacuated on a World Vision chartered airplane from Phnom Penh to Thailand with the consent of the Cambodian government. Nineteen of the children reached the United States on a United States government flight and the twentieth was brought to the United States by the director of World Vision.

To comply with the immigration law, the 20 children were paroled into the United States by the Attorney General for the purpose of adoption. World Vision is not a California licensed adoption agency. World Vision transferred custody of the 20 children to Family Ministries with instructions that they be placed in Christian homes.

Family Ministries serves the evangelical Protestant religious community and places children for adoption only in evangelical Protestant homes. It requires adherence to a prescribed statement of faith and active membership in an evangelical Protestant church by all potential adoptive parents of children placed for adoption by it. Among other adherents of religious faith, Catholics, Episcopalians, Jews, Mormons, Seventh Day Adventists, and Buddhists are not members of an evangelical Protestant church.

Richard Scott, a medical doctor by profession and Episcopalian by religious persuasion, was among a group of physicians present at Los Angeles airport to attend the 20 Cambodian children when they arrived in the United States. He examined Toup Ven, one of the children, and found him physically sound. As Toup Ven was carried aboard a bus, he was struck by the bus door so that he required hospitalization for a scalp laceration. Dr. Scott attended Toup Ven in the hospital.

Dr. Scott telephoned Family Ministries to inquire concerning Toup Ven's status and the procedure for adopting the child. Family Ministries sent Scott a written statement of its requirements for adoptive parents. Scott signed the 'statement of faith' required by Family Ministries. He was informed by Family Ministries, however, that as an Episcopalian he was not a member of an evangelical Protestant church and hence was not qualified to adopt Toup Ven. Scott did not pursue further effort to secure the adoptive placement of Toup Ven from Family Ministries.

On April 25, 1975, Dr. and Mrs. Scott, suing for themselves and on behalf of Toup Ven, filed a complaint seeking to enjoin Family Ministries from enforcing its religious eligibility requirement and from taking any steps leading to the adoption of Toup Ven. The same day, Dr. and Mrs. Scott filed their petition to adopt Toup Ven.

On May 15, the Scotts, on their own account and on behalf of Toup Ven, filed an amended complaint alleging that the Episcopalian faith pursued by the Scotts rendered them ineligible for adoptive placement of children in the custody of Family Ministries and facts respecting the unknown religious affiliation of 'Asian' refugee children in the care of Family Ministries. The amended complaint seeks injunctive relief restraining Family Ministries from taking steps leading to the adoption of Toup Ven, the relinquishment of custody by Family Ministries of Toup Ven and other Asian children in its care to 'either a county, state or private non-sectarian adoption agency,' and ordering that the children 'be subject to only non-sectarian adoption to be handled by either county, state or private non-sectarian adoption agencies.' On May 16, the court granted a preliminary injunction against Family Ministries restraining it for 60 days from taking steps to place Toup Ven for adoption.
***

On June 16, 1975, Family Ministries moved to strike the complaint and filed a general demurrer to it on the ground that the Scotts lacked capacity to sue on behalf of Toup Ven and the other children and that the amended complaint failed to state a cause of action. The Scotts responded with Dr. Scott's petition to be appointed guardian ad litem of Toup Ven and the other 'Asian children.'

*** On July 7, the court granted Dr. Scott's petition and appointed him guardian ad litem of Toup Ven and the other children. *** The court concluded that someone was needed to represent the children, thus explaining its approval of Dr. Scott as their guardian ad litem. ***

The formal order of July 8 denies Family Ministries' motion to strike and overrules its demurrer.

Trial proceeded on the action for injunctive relief but not on the petition for adoption. On December 2, 1975, the trial court determined the matter. Its judgment: (1) restrains Family Ministries from exercising custody or control over the children and from placing them for adoption without further order of court; (2) orders Family Ministries to transfer custody of the children to the Los Angeles County Department of Adoptions; (3) vacates adoptive placements and placements for temporary or foster care of the children previously made by Family Ministries; (4) transfers custody of the children to the Los Angeles County Department of Adoptions; (5) orders that, until further order of court or administrative action by the Department of Adoptions, the children may remain in the homes in which they had been placed for adoption or foster care; (6) orders the Department of Adoptions to select 'parents who are best able to meet each child's needs, without regard to the religion of the prospective parents'; (7) authorizes the Department of Adoptions to treat the children as if they had been relinquished to the department pursuant to Civil Code section 224m; (8) expressly provides that the judgment shall be construed not to exclude as potential adoptive parents persons with whom the children had previously been placed for adoption or temporary care or to prohibit the department from engaging in cooperative placement with listed adoption agencies outside Los Angeles County; and (9) continues the jurisdiction of the court over the matter.

> The judgment does not rule upon the Scotts' petition to adopt Toup Ven.
> Family Ministries appealed from the entire judgment. ***
> Pleadings, Standing, Asserted Bias of Trial Judge [omitted] ***
> ***

No petition may be filed to adopt a child relinquished to a licensed adoption agency or a child declared free from the custody and control of either or both of his parents and referred to a licensed adoption agency for adoptive placement, except by the prospective adoptive parents with whom the child has been placed for adoption by the adoption agency.

(Civ.Code, s 224n.)

When a petition for adoption is filed, adoptive placements of licensed agencies are treated differently than private adoptions.
***

The process culminates in state court action entering a decree of adoption when the court is satisfied that 'the interest of the child will be promoted.' (Civ.Code, s 227.)

Religious Matching in Adoption

Virtually all states embody religious considerations, albeit with different degrees of conclusiveness, in their adoption laws. (Note, Infants: Adoption: Religion as a Criterion in Adoption Proceedings, 6 UCLA L.Rev. 459.) California's religious requirement is contained in California Administrative Code, Title 22, section 30643. That section states: 'In choosing adoptive parents for a child the (licensed adoption) agency shall select from its approved applicants the family which is best able to meet his needs. ( ) The child shall be placed with adoptive parents whose religious faith is the same as his own or that of his parents. Exception can be made in accordance with the expressed wishes of the parent(s).'

When religion is a factor in the adoption process, there is an inevitable tension between the state action involved in the procedure by which the state creates the incidents of parent and child (Estate of Pierce (1948) 32 Cal.2d 265, 268--269, 196 P.2d 1) and the Establishment of Religion clauses of the United States (First Amendment) and California (art. I, s 4) Constitutions (tenBroek, California's Adoption Law and Programs, 6 Hastings L.J., 261, 315--317; Comment, Religion, Adoption and the First Amendment, 7 Stan.L.Rev. 394, 402).

Many states resolve the tension and avoid unconstitutionality of religious considerations by 'religious matching' provisions similar to those contained in the California Administrative Code. (Note, Infants--Custody, Property and Maintenance--Children's Religion Held Sole Criterion in Proceedings against Welfare Agency for Change of Custody, 65 Harv.L.Rev. 694; note, Religion as a Factor in Adoption, Guardianship and Custody, 54 Col.L.Rev. 376.) Religious matching to one degree or another requires or gives preference to adoption by parents of the same faith as that of the natural parents of the child or of a religion for which the natural parents express a preference. (See e.g. Dickens v. Ernesto (1972) 30 N.Y.2d 61, 330 N.Y.S.2d 346, 281 N.E.2d 153.) The process preserves constitutionality by placing the state in a neutral position in which parentage or parents and not the state determines the religion of the home into which the child is to be adopted. (Petitions of Goldman (1954) 331 Mass. 647, 121 N.E.2d 843, cert. den. 348 U.S. 942, 75 S.Ct. 363, 99 L.Ed.2d 1295.) It recognizes the common law right of a natural parent to control the religious upbringing of his child. (Friedman, The Parental Right to Control the Religious Education of a Child, 29 Harv.L.Rev. 485.)

If, however, the state is permitted to specify the religious affiliation of the adoptive home without reference to natural parentage or parental preference, the state is no longer in the position of neutrality nor can the religious requirement be sustained upon the common law right of the natural parent. Then the state invades the area proscribed to it by the Establishment Clauses of the United States and California Constitutions. (Petitions of Goldman, supra, 121 N.E.2d at p. 846.)

A religious requirement imposed upon adoptive parents by the state is thus unconstitutional unless it is limited to religious matching. If Title 22, California Administrative Code, section 30643 is to be constitutional, it must be construed to provide for state action placing a child for adoption on the basis of religion only where the religion is that of the child or of his natural parent or is the parent's express preference. Because we are obligated to construe the section as constitutional rather than unconstitutional if possible, we adopt that construction.

The California statutory scheme is framed in a fashion which makes action of private licensed adoption agencies state action in the context of the establishment clauses.

'(T)he three main evils against which the Establishment Clause was intended to afford protection (are): 'sponsorship, financial support, and active involvement of the sovereign in religious activity.' . . . ( ) Every analysis in this area must begin with consideration of the cumulative criteria (of constitutionality) developed by (The Supreme) Court over many years. . . . First, the statute must have a secular legislative purpose; second, its principal or primary effect must be one that neither advances nor inhibits religion (citation); finally, the statute must not foster 'an excessive government entanglement with religion.' (Citation.)' (*Lemon v. Kurtzman* (1971) 403 U.S. 602, 612--613; *see also Committee for Public Education v. Nyquist* (1973) 413 U.S. 756, 770--773.)

Here the California statutory and regulatory scheme of adoption does not further a secular purpose unless it is construed to require the licensed adoption agency to maintain a position of neutrality by enforcing a religious requirement upon prospective adoptive parents only to achieve religious matching. Here the effect of the scheme advances particular religions if the agencies are permitted to impose a religious requirement beyond matching. Here the state government is inextricably entangled with the activity of licensed adoption agencies so as also to be entangled with any religious restriction beyond matching imposed by them upon prospective adoptive parents.

The agencies are delegated the governmental case work function in the adoption process. The state delegates to them the process of investigation and reporting to the court than in non-agency adoptions must be performed by the State Department of Health. The state delegates to the private licensed agencies the state's power and obligation to select adoptive parents and to bar all others from the right to adopt the particular child. The state delegates to the agencies the power to exercise discretion to institute a termination of a placement for adoption. In essence if a private licensed adoption agency imposes a religious restriction in exercising its delegated power and responsibility it is acting for and on behalf of the state when it does so.

We thus conclude that Family Ministries is bound by our construction of California Administrative Code, Title 22, section 30643 to the same extent as the state itself is bound.

Family Ministries seeks to avoid the impact of that conclusion by arguing that World Vision as custodian of the Cambodian children stands in the relationship of Loco parentis so as to be entitled to express a parent's religious preference pursuant to section 30643. The argument lacks merit.

In Adoption of McDonald (1954) *, an adoption agency argued that because a child had been released to it for adoption it had acquired the statutory right of a parent to consent to or refuse adoption. Our Supreme Court held that the statutory reference to parents meant only natural parents and not an agency standing in their stead. Adoption of McDonald compels rejection of Family Ministries' reliance upon religious preference expressed by World Vision.   **Trial Court's Judgment Removing Children from Custody of Family Ministries**

The construction of California Administrative Code, Title 22, section 30643 which we here adopt validates the trial court's decision removing the children from the custody of Family Ministries and placing their custody in the Los Angeles County Department of Adoptions. The section precludes Family Ministries from imposing a religious requirement upon prospective adoptive parents of children of unknown religion and unknown parentage. Family Ministries places children for adoption only with families who are active members of an evangelical Protestant church. It is thus incapable of complying with section 30643 in placing the 'Asian children.'

Significantly, the trial court order does not exclude as prospective adoptive parents persons with whom Family Ministries has placed the children, either pursuant to the vacated adoptive placements or as foster parents. The Los Angeles County Department of Adoptions is thus free, and presumably required, in the best interests of the children, to consider the potential emotional trauma of removing any one of them from his current environment for the purposes of adoption and the advantage to each child of continuity through adoption in the home where he is now placed.
***

The judgment is affirmed. Each party to bear their own costs.

WOOD, P.J., and HANSON, J., concur.

d. *Galison v. District of Columbia*

Edward Galison v. District of Columbia
402 A.2d 1263 (D.C. 1979)

NEBEKER, Associate Judge:

Appellant Galison was convicted, after trial to the court, of one count of arranging for the placement of a child under sixteen years of age without having been licensed as a "child-placing agency." D.C.Code 1973, §§ 32-785, -788. Appellant Goldstein was convicted of three counts under the same code provisions. Each argued that Congress, in enacting the provisions of title 32, chapter 7B (hereinafter the Baby Broker Act, or Act), did not intend to reach the conduct proved in these cases. Galison also contended that the government failed to prove that he was not licensed at the time of the alleged activities. We are of the opinion that the activities performed by Galison are within the reach of the Act and that his claim of insufficient evidence (proof of no license) is unpersuasive. On the other hand, we agree with appellant Goldstein that his conduct was not of the type intended to be prohibited by the Act, and therefore reverse his conviction. ***

I. Edward Galison

Appellant Galison is an attorney licensed to practice law in the State of New York. Prior to August 31, 1976, his associate, Spiegelman, was contacted in New York by a Florida attorney. The Florida attorney explained that he had been unable to arrange for an adoption in Florida of the expected child of a Florida resident. Upon locating a New York family that would agree to adopt the child, Spiegelman suggested to his Florida contact that the mother come to New York for the child's delivery. The expectant mother, however, indicated that she would be willing to travel only as far as the District of Columbia. The Florida attorney and Spiegelman arranged for the woman and her mother (the grandmother), to stay in the District of Columbia beginning on August 31, 1976.

Upon arrival in the District, the woman had a change of heart and decided that she would keep the child. She so advised Galison, who thereupon came to the District of Columbia and persuaded her that adoption was "the right thing to do." After he informed her that her medical and living expenses in the District would be paid for and that she would receive $2,000 in addition to her medical and living expenses, she executed documents by which she consented to the proposed adoption and authorized the hospital to release her yet-unborn child to appellant.

Later, in September, the expectant mother again desired to abandon the adoption plans and contacted Galison to inform him that she wanted to return to Florida. Galison explained that the prospective parents were waiting for the baby to be delivered and reminded her of the money that they had provided for her. Because of the money involved, the woman decided to remain in the District.

In October, one week before the baby was born, the grandmother telephoned Galison regarding a Washington newspaper article which stated that it was illegal to arrange an adoption without going through an agency. Galison assured the grandmother that his actions were legitimate. Galison then spoke with the woman and played on her sensitivities by telling her that the prospective parents had not contributed any of the money for her expenses, that he had taken the money from his own pocket and that she should consider all the money invested in her thus far. The woman relented.

Subsequent to the October 19th birth of the baby, the mother once again decided that she wanted to keep the baby, but she was "afraid of the money I owed and the money that he had invested in me. I was afraid to back out. I didn't know what to do." The grandmother contacted a social worker, and, as a result, the police were advised of the circumstances of the proposed child placement. Galison, meanwhile, once again attempted to persuade the mother to continue with the planned placement by arguing that it was in everyone's best interest and by reminding her that there was already $6,000 "invested" in her. The grandmother then obtained the release of the baby from the hospital, received approximately $2,200 from Galison, and gave the baby to Galison. Upon leaving the hospital with the baby, Galison was arrested.

We are asked to decide whether Congress intended the Baby Broker Act to prohibit Galison's activities. We resolve the issue in the affirmative. The purpose of the District's Baby Broker Act is expressed in D.C.Code 1973, § 32-781:

> The purpose of this chapter is to secure for each child under sixteen years of age who is placed in a family home, other than his own or that of a relative within the third degree, such care and guidance as will serve the child's welfare and the best interests of the District of Columbia; and to secure for him custody and care as near as possible to that which should have been given him by his parents.

To fulfill the purposes of the Act, I. e., to assure the care and guidance necessary for the welfare of the child and to protect the interests of the District, Congress required registration and licensing of individuals placing children. This requirement is evident in the specific provision of the Act with which appellant Galison is charged as having violated:

> No person other than the parent, guardian, or relative within the third degree, and no firm, corporation, association, or agency, other than a licensed child-placing agency, may place or arrange or assist in placing or arranging for the placement of a child under sixteen years of age in a family home or for adoption. . . . (D.C.Code 1973, § 32-785.)
>
> ***

On its face, § 32-785 proscribes all placement activities regardless of where they occur and regardless of the relationship of the individuals involved to the District. As § 32-781 states, however, the act was intended to apply only to situations in which the District has an interest (including the interest in serving the child's welfare). Therefore, some contact affecting a District of Columbia governmental interest, which is protected by the Act, must be shown before § 32-785 becomes applicable.

   ***

*** These provisions indicate some of the substantial District interests intended to be protected by the Act. These provisions also suggest that Congress intended these sections, at least, to be applied only when the District has a significant interest in the placement activity.

On the basis of this discussion and after analysis of the statute, we find that § 32-785 requires a substantial nexus similar to those required by the other sections of the statute mentioned above. The test to be used in determining the applicability of § 32-785 in this case, then, is whether the District has a significant interest in Galison's attempted placement.

We are of the opinion that the attempted placement by Galison offended two substantial interests of the District. The first interest is to protect the parental rights of natural mothers residing in the District. This is accomplished by regulating placement activity carried on within the District. Here, the natural mother resided in the District for a period of approximately two months. The woman's stay was not due to medical reasons alone, but was attributable primarily to an adoption plan developed by Galison. The plan provided that the woman remain in the District until the birth of the baby, at which time she would be required to surrender her child to Galison. After arriving in the District, she became an uncooperative if not an unwilling partner in the plan. Her discontent prompted Galison to undertake activities which were designed to persuade her to change her mind. Since the woman was residing in the District, the District had an interest in protecting her parental rights over her child, which were threatened by Galison's conduct. Inasmuch as Galison was not licensed to engage in such activity, he became subject to the sanctions of the Baby Broker Act.

A closely-related District interest is to protect mothers within the District from being coerced, compelled, forced or pressured to feel constrained or obliged to yield up their infants whether by threats of violence, financial withdrawal, or derision, regardless of how oblique or veiled the pressure may be. There is no requirement that the mother reside in the District to receive this protection. If pressure is exerted upon a mother while in the District to make a decision to surrender her child, the guardianship of the District is invoked. Here, on four separate occasions following her arrival in the District, the natural mother indicated to Galison that she had changed her mind and did not want to give up her child. [FN7] In each instance, discussions or negotiations ensued in which Galison attempted to persuade the woman to place the child. He reminded her of the expenses which he had incurred in anticipation of the child's adoption, of her personal gain of $2,000 for surrendering the child, and of the expectation of the family waiting to adopt the newborn child. On two of these occasions, Galison visited the District. The first time was for the purpose of pressuring the mother into going through with the placement. The second visit was with the intent of taking the child to New York, which Galison would have done, after overcoming the mother's express desire to keep the child, had he not been arrested. The mother's conduct after arrival in the District and her testimony at trial leaves no doubt that her compliance with Galison's plan was simply submission resulting from her fear of being unable to repay the "investment" which Galison claimed to have made in her. We, therefore, conclude that the District's interest in protecting the mother from any pressure to relinquish her child was offended by Galison's activities, and the provisions of the Act, as a consequence, became applicable.

Galison argues that the government failed to prove that he was not licensed at the time of the alleged offense. We disagree. The record shows that during the months of September and October of 1976, when appellant engaged in action that violated the Act, he was a New York State practicing attorney, but not a licensed child-placing agency in the District of Columbia. At trial, the government called the acting chief of Licensing and Certification as a witness. While his testimony was not a model of conciseness, it was sufficient to permit the court to find that Galison was unlicensed. ***

Galison also claims that the government failed to prove beyond a reasonable doubt that he was not a relative within the third degree of the child. (See supra note 3.) We endorse the trial court's determination that Galison had the burden of proving, as an affirmative defense, his relationship to the child. Absent that proof, this claim is dismissed as lacking merit. *

Accordingly, there is in fact evidence sufficient to support the court's judgment of conviction.

II. Leonard Goldstein

Appellant Goldstein is an attorney licensed to practice law in the State of Maryland and the District of Columbia. His primary business office is in Maryland, and the events recited herein occurred in Maryland except as otherwise noted. The events leading to his three convictions occurred in late

1975 and early 1976, and involved the placement of three infants, referred to at trial as Baby Doe, Baby Roe and Baby Poe, with three married couples, referred to, respectively, as the Norths, the Wests, and the Souths. The natural mothers, as well as the Norths and the Wests, were all residents of Maryland. The Souths resided in Virginia.

Each of the natural mothers was a patient of Dr. Stave or Dr. Rose, associates in the practice of obstetrics and gynecology in Maryland and private attending physicians at the Washington Hospital Center in the District of Columbia. Goldstein and Dr. Stave, although once acquainted, had had no contact for several years when Dr. Stave called Goldstein in late 1975. Dr. Stave advised Goldstein that one of his patients, Miss Doe, was expecting a child and wished to privately place the child for adoption. Goldstein responded to Dr. Stave's inquiries that private placements were legal in Maryland and that he, Goldstein, would be willing to assist in such a placement. Subsequently, Dr. Stave contacted Mr. and Mrs. North, who had been his patients for infertility. In response to his inquiry, they indicated that they would like to adopt Baby Doe. After unsuccessful attempts to obtain a satisfactory recommendation of an attorney to assist them in the adoption, the Norths obtained Dr. Stave's recommendation of Goldstein. The Norths thereafter retained Goldstein to assist in the proposed adoption. *[FN9 - Drs. Stave and Rose were codefendants of Goldstein in this case. Dr. Rose was acquitted of all charges. Dr. Stave was convicted of two counts of violating § 32-785 but did not appeal.]*

Upon the recommendation of Dr. Stave, Miss Doe went to the Washington Hospital Center for delivery of her baby. Goldstein arranged with the staff neonatologist to assure confidentiality of the identity of Baby Doe's mother by covering the baby's crib identification with the name "Goldstein." Similarly, all hospital billing accounts were maintained in Goldstein's name and paid out of an escrow fund established through him by the Norths. On the day of Baby Doe's birth, Goldstein secured from a Maryland court a temporary custody decree authorizing the Norths to take custody of the child. (Goldstein had visited Miss Doe and her parents at the hospital for the purpose of obtaining their signatures on various documents related to the Maryland adoption proceedings.) When the child was able to be released from the hospital, the staff instructed the Norths on the care of the child and released the child to them. Thereafter the Norths adopted the child in accordance with Maryland procedures.

The second placement also was initiated through Dr. Stave, who advised Goldstein that his patient, Miss Roe, wished to place her expected child for adoption. Miss Roe had indicated to Dr. Stave that each of the adoption agencies she had spoken with wanted her to be sent away from home during her pregnancy but that she wanted to remain at home. Dr. Stave asked Goldstein whether he knew of anyone interested in adopting the expected child. Goldstein advised a rabbi of the situation and the rabbi, in turn, advised the Wests, who retained Goldstein to assist in the placement.

When Goldstein was advised by Dr. Stave that Baby Roe had been born at Washington Hospital Center, he arranged to meet Miss Roe and her mother at the hospital to obtain their signatures on various legal documents. He then obtained an order of temporary custody for the Wests. When Baby Roe was able to be released from the hospital, Goldstein was unavailable and therefore sent an associate to the hospital. The hospital bills were paid from an escrow fund established by Goldstein for the Wests. A hospital nurse released the baby to Miss Roe's mother who, in turn, gave the baby to Mrs. West. [FN10] Thereafter the Wests adopted the child in accordance with Maryland procedures.

The third placement was initiated by Dr. Rose, whose patient, Miss Poe, desired to privately place her expected child. When Miss Poe began with unanticipated suddenness to deliver her child at home, Dr. Rose directed that she be taken to the Washington Hospital Center, where Baby Poe was born. The next day Dr. Rose contacted the Souths, whom he knew to be interested in adopting a child. They asked Dr. Rose to recommend an attorney; he recommended Goldstein but indicated that they need not use his services. Contacted by the Souths, Goldstein advised them to retain a Virginia attorney (since their proposed adoption would have to be processed in Virginia) but finally agreed to assist them. (This was the first time Goldstein had heard of Miss Poe or Baby Poe.) Goldstein arranged for the hospital bill to be transferred to his name and paid the bill from an escrow account established by him for the Souths. He met the Souths at the hospital, where they were instructed in the care of the child by the hospital staff. The child was released to its maternal grandfather, Mr. Poe, [FN11] who gave the child to Goldstein. Goldstein, in turn, gave the child to the Souths. The Souths returned to Virginia with the child and petitioned a Virginia court for adoption. At the time of trial, the Virginia court had entered an interlocutory decree of adoption.

At the outset it is acknowledged that the facts of this case appear, at least in their broadest outlines, to have some similarity to those of Galison's case. Both Goldstein and Galison attempted to place the children of unmarried expectant mothers, domiciled outside the District, who gave birth to their children in the District. In each case, a non-resident attorney participated in dealings between the natural and the adopting families and the hospital. Additionally, both cases present evidence of some child-placement activity being conducted by the defendants within the District.

The dissimilarities distinguishing the two cases, however, are stark. With reference to Goldstein's placements, the mothers' presence in the District was due to medical reasons to enter the hospital for delivery. In Galison's case, the mother did not come to the District solely for medical reasons nor, in fact, when she changed her mind about giving away her child, did she desire to remain in the District. Far from having made up her mind to give away her child, the mother in Galison's case consistently expressed to Galison her desire not to go through with the adoption plan. Furthermore, there exists no indication that Goldstein, like Galison, negotiated with the mothers in an attempt to persuade them to relinquish their parental rights over the children. On the contrary, Goldstein's contacts with the natural mothers and with the hospital personnel in the District were limited to carrying into effect the unchanged decisions arrived at by the natural mothers previous to entering the District and subsequent to consulting with their physicians in Maryland.

In short, these cases involve lawful Virginia or Maryland adoptions of children born to Maryland residents while in a District of Columbia hospital solely for medical reasons. The decision to place the child was made by each of the natural mothers before entering the District. The mothers evidenced no reluctance to follow their predetermined course after entering the District. Since the mothers were not residing in the District and no coercive activity was employed in an attempt to persuade them to relinquish their children, the District interests which were offended by Galison are not threatened here. Finding no other District interest threatened by Goldstein's conduct, we hold that the Baby Broker Act is inapplicable in his case.

The government argues, however, that the District has an interest in regulating Goldstein's conduct in order to protect children (and their mothers) whose presence in the District is merely for medical care. In the circumstances proved in this case, we disagree. The government's asserted nexus, mere presence within the geographical bounds of the District, arose solely by reason of the mothers' or the doctors' decisions to utilize the medical facilities of the Washington Hospital Center. Such presence, without more, is a fortuity in which the District's interests under the Act are not affected. We think that whatever the District's interest may be in these mothers giving birth to children in D.C. hospitals, it could not have been intended by Congress to override the interests of expectant mothers and their physicians in assuring that both the mothers and their children receive the best medical care available to them in this multi-jurisdictional metropolitan area. *

***

We hold, therefore, that Goldstein's conduct did not violate § 32-785. No district interest sought to be protected by the Act was threatened by Goldstein's placement activities.

No. 12196 is affirmed.

No. 12439 is reversed and remanded with instructions to enter a judgment of acquittal.

KERN, Associate Justice, concurring in part and dissenting in part:

I agree with the majority's conclusion that appellant Galison's conviction should stand, but I cannot agree that appellant Goldstein's "conduct was not of the type intended to be prohibited by the

Act." (at 1265). Therefore, I disagree with its conclusion that his conviction should be reversed.
***

What the appellant did is very clear. He "arranged" and "assisted" in placing and personally consummated the placement of the child. He was the intermediary who produced the prospective adopters and arranged contact (indirect though it was) with the mother. He it was who presented to the mother the document for release of her child and obtained her signature. He it was who arranged for the presence of the adopting parents at the hospital. And he it was who performed the final act of placement by accepting the child from the arms of its mother and physically handing it over to the adopting father. It would be difficult to imagine a more clear-cut infraction of the letter as well as the spirit of the law. ***

c. Notes and Questions

1) *Scott* and Religious Matching and Preferences in Adoption

Long before the common law countries ever created adoption for the sake of children, churches provided places to leave "foundling" children, and provided orphanages where abandoned and orphaned children were cared-for, educated, and provided vocational training, and from the earliest days of adoption, churches have been heavily involved in arranging for the adoption of children. Historically, the offering of such services by religious organizations provided a practical and moral antidote to the ever-present temptation to practice infanticide (or its modern counterpart, abortion). Many churches still consider the performance of child care services, including adoption services, as essential to their charitable purposes and ministerial duties to serve the needs of both the distressed parents (usually the neglected pregnant young woman) and of the needy child.

Now states through their government agencies have caught up, and both provide and regulate the provision by others of adoption services. May the state command a monopoly in providing such services? May it compel all other providers of such services to conform to all of its secular policies and values? May it forbid church-affiliated providers of adoption services from applying their own religious policies and values? Does the First Amendment compel church-run adoption agencies to abandon their religious-based policies and preferences in adoption placements? May a state-licensed adoption agency run by a church place children only with members of its own religion? May a state agency or state-licensed private adoption agency enforce "religious matching" policies that match the religion of the child (or his/her parent(s)) with the religion of the prospective adoptive parents? (Does the answer depend upon the age and degree of religious commitment of the child?) May state agencies or state-licensed private agencies enforce "parental preference" rules that enforce the religious-matching wishes of the parent(s) who relinquished parental rights? If a pregnant unwed mother (whose boyfriend does not want to claim paternity) insists that, for whatever reasons, she will release the child for adoption only if the agency will absolutely guarantee that the child will be placed with parents who have the same race or religion as she does, may a state agency (or state licensed private agency) give her that assurance? If prospective adoptive parents say they will only take a child of a certain race or birth-religion, should or must the agency refuse to consider them for adoption of any child? (If it places a child of that race or religion with such parents, would it be guilty of discrimination?) If a religious organization whose creed included the belief that races should not "mix" applied for a license to place children for adoption, and they admitted that they would only place children for adoption with parents of the same race, would it violate the fourteenth amendment of the Constitution for the state to grant that group a license? (Would it violate another amendment for the state to deny them a license?)

2) *Galison*

What did Galison do wrong? Was it "so" wrong that it deserved criminal conviction? Why/why not? Attorneys practicing adoption law must be careful to observe strictly the rules regarding payment lest they run into zealous protectionist prosecutors and courts.

3) **Racial Matching and Preferences in Adoption**

In *Palmore v. Sidoti*, 466 U.S. 429 (1984), *infra* Chapter 34, the Supreme Court held that a Florida court erred when it granted a white father's motion to modify a custody decree so as to divest a white mother of custody of their white child because the mother had been cohabiting with (and recently had married) a black man. The trial court noted that a child raised by parents of different races would be more vulnerable to peer pressures, and would suffer from the social stigmatization that was sure to follow the mixed-race family. The Supreme Court acknowledged that "[i]t would ignore reality to suggest that racial and ethnic prejudices do not exist .... There is risk that a child living with a step-parent of a different race may be subject to a variety of pressures and stresses not present if the child were living with parents of the same racial or ethnic origin." *Id.* at 433 . Nevertheless, the Court held that "[t]he effects of racial prejudice, however real, cannot justify a racial classification removing an infant child from the custody of its natural mother found to be an appropriate person to have such custody." *Id.* at 434.

Does *Palmore* mean that adoption agencies may not take race into consideration in making placement decisions? Racial matching historically has been a factor in adoption placement. Before the anti-discrimination era of the 1960's, race matching may have been an absolute, decisive, if unwritten, practice of most adoption agencies. Today, race generally is a nondecisive consideration, but is one of the significant factors taken into account by adoption agencies in making placement decisions.

Actually, while the Supreme Court had to correct the error of the Florida courts in *Palmore*, that decision did not change the prevailing legal doctrine regarding use of race as a factor in custody or adoption, but only endorsed recent lower courts' expressions of it. As early as 1955, a federal circuit court of appeals had indicated that the use of race as an absolute bar to adoption was impermissible. *In re Adoption of a Minor*, 228 F.2d 446 (D.C. Cir. 1955) (private adoption by black stepfather of his white wife's white child). In 1972, a federal district court enjoined enforcement of a Louisiana statute that permitted *only* same-race adoptions. *McKeither*, 341 F. Supp. 264 (E.D. La. 1972) (disapproving statutory denial of adoption by white couple of black child and mixed-race couple of any child). And in 1977, another federal court of appeals reiterated that while use of race as a mandatory dispositive consideration was impermissible, it was constitutionally permissible to use race in adoption placements in a "nondiscriminatory fashion" and "without discriminatory intent." *Drummond v. Fulton County Department of Family and Children Services*, 563 F.2d 1200 (5th Cir. 1977) (debatable denial of claim of unconstitutional violation when state agency rejected white foster parents' attempt to adopt black child who had lived with them for over two years). The U.S. Supreme Court has approved the noninvidious use by state agencies of race as a consideration in situations in which it is necessary to achieve a compelling state interest. *Palmore* makes it clear that social disapproval of mixed-race families (social racism) alone probably would not be sufficient basis for denial of adoption. However, if race is not an exclusive or solely-dispositive consideration, if consideration of race furthers the state's concern for the welfare of children, and if race is not used in a generalized manner to achieve discriminatory purposes or with discriminatory intent, "the state can justify its compelling interest in the 'best interests' of the child when it considers race as a factor in adoption proceedings." Note, *infra* at 513.

Since 1972, the most vocal proponents of racial matching in placement and adoption cases (with the exception of tribal Native Americans) have been from groups within the African-American community, especially the National Association of Black Social Workers. The group charges that transracial adoption robs black children of their racial identity and their ability to deal with racism, leading to psychological problems in adolescence and adulthood. They have been successful in reducing the number of transracial adoptions of black children (although international transracial adoption continues to grow). But many adoption specialists argue otherwise. *See. e.g.* Rita J. Simon et al., *infra*, (20-year study of 83 families, concluding transracial adoption is mostly a positive alternative to long-term foster care).

Opponents of racial matching in adoption argue that all of the legitimate concerns that underlie race-matching preferences can be achieved by the use of other factors (such as preference for placement with relatives, for cultural awareness of adoptive parents, etc.). Also, that "race" is a very ambiguous and dangerous concept (what is the "race" a child born to woman of Irish and Cherokee descent, and a man of African and Korean ancestry? Or, if a child has equal portions of Caucasian, Negro, Native American and Asian blood, what is her race?). They argue that the state should not prefer placement by race at all. However, a number of other writers, especially several black law professors, suggest that to ignore race in adoption placement is itself a racist policy, operating to effect the out-placement of minority children into the homes of majority-race childless couples, and they note that the Indian Child Welfare Act mandates racial (tribal, then Native American) preference. *See generally* Ruth-Arlene W. Howe, *Transracial Adoption: Old Prejudices and Discrimination Float Under a New Halo*, 6 B.U. Pub. Int. L.J. 409, 459 (1997); Twila L. Perry, *The Transracial Adoption Controversy: An Analysis of Discourse and Subordination*, 21 N.Y.U. Rev. L. & Soc. Change 33 (1993-1994); Twila L. Perry, *Race and Child Placement: The Best Interests Test and the Cost of Discretion*, 29 J. Fam. L. 51 (1990-1991). Professor David Rosettenstein has shown that anti-trans-racial adoption policies have not reduced trans-racial adoptions, but shifted them abroad. Parents who want to adopt children and would adopt children of different race cannot have such children placed with them for adoption in the United States. So they go abroad where orphaned children of different races are placed with them, and they adopt Korean, Chinese, and other Asian children, Indian and mixed race children from South and Central America, etc. *See* David S. Rosettenstein, *Transracial Adoption and the Statutory Preference Schemes: Before the"Best Interests" and After the "Melting Pot,"* 68 St. John's L. Rev. 137 (1994).

In 1994, Congress enacted the Howard Metzenbaum Multiethnic Placement Act of 1994 ("MEPA"), which was designed to achieve three purposes: 1) to reduce the time children in foster care must wait before becoming available for adoption, 2) to prevent racial discrimination in the placement of children in foster care and adoption, and 3) to facilitate and encourage recruitment of prospective foster and adoptive parents. (However, MEPA did not apply to those children covered by the Indian Child Welfare Act). In regard to racial matching, MEPA provided that,

> [a]n agency, or entity, that receives Federal Assistance and is involved in adoption or foster care placements may not
> (A) *categorically* deny to any person the opportunity to become an adoptive or parent, *solely* on the basis of race, color, or national origin of the adoptive or foster parent, or the child, involved, or
> (B) delay or deny the placement of a child for adoption or into foster care, or otherwise discriminate in making a placement decision, *solely* on the basis of the race, color, or national origin of the adoptive parent or foster parent, or the child involved.

42 U.S.C.A. § 5115a(b) (1995) (emphasis added). The Department of Health and Human Services federal guidelines regarding its implementation. 60 Fed. Reg. 20,272. Noncompliance could result in the loss of federal funds, law suits brought by individuals seeking injunctive relief or money damages in actions under Title VI of the Civil Rights Act.

Critics of race-matching in adoption were not satisfied because the terms "categorically" and "solely" allowed race to continue to be considered as a non-exclusive, non-dispositive factor in adoption placements. Two years later, in 1996, Congress repealed MEPA but strengthened its policy against race-matching in adoption with the "Removal of Barriers to Interethnic Adoption" (sometimes called "MEPA-II"), part of the Small Business Job Protection Act of 1996. The relevant provisions of MEPA-II provide:

> (1) Prohibited conduct
> A person or government that is involved in adoption or foster care placements may not--
> (A) deny to any individual the opportunity to become an adoptive or a foster parent, on the basis of the race, color, or national origin of the individual, or of the child, involved; or
> (B) delay or deny the placement of a child for adoption or into foster care, on the basis of the race, color, or national origin of the adoptive or foster parent, or the child, involved.
> (2) Enforcement
> Noncompliance with paragraph (1) is deemed a violation of title VI of the Civil Rights Act of 1964.
> (3) No effect on the Indian Child Welfare Act of 1978
> This section shall not be construed to affect the application of the Indian Child Welfare Act of 1978.

42 U.S.C. § 1996b. Interethnic adoption (Pub.L. 104-188, Title I, § 1808(c), Aug. 20, 1996, 110 Stat. 1904.).

Under MEPA-II, a delay or denial in placement of the child on the basis of race, color or national origin, does not have to be "categorical," nor does the delay or denial have to result from race, color or national origin being used as the sole consideration in the placement decision. Moreover, an individual may bring a civil rights action against any person or government violating MEPA-II. Under MEPA, a civil rights action could only be brought against an agency or entity that received federal funding. MEPA-II also sets out a [sic] specific percentages by which federal funding will be cut for noncompliance.

Hunter, *infra*, at 119-123. In 2003, the U.S. Department of Health and Human Services imposed a $1.8 million fine on Hamilton County, Ohio, for violating MEPA by race-matching in adoption. Bartholet, *infra*, at 224.

The debate over consideration of race in adoption still continues, though, as the MEPA provisions indicate, opponents of any consideration of race presently have the upper hand, at least in Congress. Ironically, some of those (liberals) who most vigorously oppose elimination of race as a consideration in education and employment are among the proponents of total elimination of race in adoption, while among those who most vigorously oppose "affirmative action" programs in education and employment (conservatives) are among the most supportive of allowing consideration of race in adoption. *See e.g.* R. Richard Banks, The Color of Desire: Fulfilling Adoptive Parents' Racial Preferences Through Discriminatory State Action, 107 Yale L.J. 875 (1998) (criticizing the policy of "facilitative accommodations" of the racial preference of prospective adoptive parents and calling for complete elimination of race as a consideration in adoption); Elizabeth Bartholet, Correspondence, *Private Race Preferences in Family Formation*, 107 Yale L.J. 2351, 2354 (1998) ("there is enormous resistance to [the Interethnic Adoption Act], and it appears so far to have had little impact. . . . Private foundations and nonprofit child welfare groups have joined forces with public agencies to promote "kinship care," in part to help ensure that children in need of homes remain within their racial group. "Cultural competence" is one of the code phrases in the post-MEPA era . . . ."); Jennifer L. Rosato, *"A Color of Their Own": Multiracial Children and the Family,* 36 Brandeis J. Fam. L. 41 (1997-98) (criticizing the Interethnic Adoption Act for "giving no preference to black parents unless they are as qualified as the white parents being considered," for appearing to "require placing a child with available white parents, even those unable or unwilling to develop the child's black identity." The author concludes: "Although this statute is well-meaning, it reflects a naive attitude of color-blindness. Sometimes race should matter in adoption and child custody decisions, and sometimes it should not. A more principled basis must be developed for determining when race is an appropriate consideration (such as when it furthers the child's best interests), and when it is inappropriate (such as when it simply perpetuates bipolarism)." *Id.* at 46.)

4) Sexual Orientation

Adoption of children by homosexual partners, couples, and individuals is very controversial. Historically, as homosexual relations were criminally prohibited, such adoptions were also prohibited (usually for "criminal" or "moral" disqualification). With growing social acceptance of homosexual relations, and particularly after the Supreme Court decision in *Lawrence v. Texas,* 539 U.S. 558 (2003), holding that sodomy laws are unconstitutional, support for "lesbigay" adoption (of children by adult gays and lesbians) has grown; so, also, has the opposition. By mid-2006, statutes or appellate decisions in twenty-one states and the District of Columbia had addressed the issue; thirteen states and the District allow lesbigay adoption; eight states prohibit it. *Compare* Fla. St. Ann. § 63.042(3) (disallowing same sex adoptions) *with* 15A Vt. St. Ann. § 1-102 (b)(allowing same sex adoptions).

In some states where lesbigay adoption is permitted, rules have been enacted to require all adoption agencies, including religiously-affiliated agencies, to place children for adoption with lesbigay couples and prospective adopters, regardless of rights of free exercise or rights of conscience. In Massachusetts, such a rule forced the Roman Catholic church in 2006 to close its adoption work, ending over a century of adoption service to Catholic families in that state; in California the ACLU successfully sued a Protestant church-affiliated adoption agency to change its policy of placing children for adoption only with nuclear (traditional) families. *ACLU, infra.* Are such rules constitutional? In the interests of children? Why/why not?

In stepparent adoption, the parental rights of the child's parent who is married to the child's stepparent are not terminated when the stepparent adopts the child. Prospective adopters in homosexual or unmarried heterosexual relationships compare themselves to stepparents, and seek what some call "second-parent" adoptions. As noted above, states have split on whether stepparent adoption provisions can be extended to same-sex partners' "second-parent" adoptions.

5) Adult Adoption

Modern American adoption law focuses on the best interests of children. But sometimes adults wish to be adopted. Usually this occurs when the person was raised by foster parents who never formally adopted him or her. Apart from the emotional significance of formally recognizing the familial bonding that has occurred, adoption provides the legal benefits without which intestate succession, eligibility for certain benefits (e.g., social security, insurance, etc.), and the right to maintain certain actions (e.g., wrongful death, workers compensation, etc.) would not be possible. In recent times, homosexuals have attempted to adopt each other in an attempt to gain legal recognition of their relationship. In 1984, it was estimated that between 60 and 120 adult adoptions occur in California every year between homosexual partners. Fowler, *infra* at 702. But most courts have been as unwilling to permit the adoption laws to be used for this purpose as they have been unwilling to permit marriage laws to be used for a similar purpose. For instance, in *In re Robert Paul P.*, 63 NY2d 652, 471 N.E.2d 424, 481 N.Y.S.2d 627 (1984) the Court of Appeals held that an adoption by one homosexual adult of another was improper. In that case a 57 year old man wished to adopt his 50 year old homosexual partner. The two had lived together in a homosexual relationship for 25 years and wished to obtain post-death protection of art work, prevent estate interference by family members, and have the personal satisfaction of legalizing the relationship. The Family Court denied the adoption petition, and the Appellate Division affirmed, reasoning that adoption laws were designed with the parent-child relationship in mind, that the parties' intent was to evade the New York laws proscribing homosexual marriage, and that the adoption laws should not be used for that purpose. The New York Court of Appeals agreed noting that: "If adoption laws are to be changed so as to permit sexual lovers, homosexual or heterosexual, to adopt one another for the purpose of giving a nonmatrimonial legal status to their relationship, or if a separate institution is to be established for the same purpose, it is for the Legislature, as a matter of State public policy, to do so. [T]he courts ought not to create the same under the rubric of adoption." *Id.* at 439.

3. Practical and Ethical Consideration

a. Race and Multi-racial Adoptees

The issue of racial identity continues. The 2000 Census allowed persons to select more than one racial category. For mutli-racial adoptees, should they be placed in multi-racial families?

4. Bibliography

ACLU Halts Legal Action after Promise from California Adoption Agency that It Won't Discriminate Based on Sexual Orientation, website of ACLU of So. Cal., Oct. 6, 2005, at http://www.aclu-sc.org/News/Releases/2005/101361/ (last seen May 18, 2006).

Elizabeth Bartholet, *The Challenge of Children's Advocacy: Problems and Progress in the Area of Child Abuse and Neglect*, 3 Whittier J. Ch. & Fam. Advocacy 215 (2004).

Fowler, *Adult Adoption: A "New" Legal Tool For Lesbians and Gay Men*, 14 Golden Gate U.L. Rev. 667 (1984).

Mary Jo Brooks Hunter, Special Report, *Minnesota Supreme Court Foster Care and Adoption Task Force*, 19 Hamline J. Pub. L. & Pol'y 1, 119 (1997).

Landes & Posner, *The Economics of the Baby Shortage*, 7 J. Legal stud. 323 (1978).

W. Meezan, S. Cats, & E. Russo, Adoptions Without Agencies: A Study of Independent Adoption. (1978).

Note, *Will* Palmore v. Sidoti *Preclude the Use of Race As A Factor In Denying An Adoption?* 24 J. Fam. L. 497 (1985).

Contemporary Family Law, vol. 2, Ch. 9 (1988).

Posner, *The Regulation of the Market in Adoptions,* 67 B.U.L. Rev. 59 (1987).

Rita J. Simon et al., The Case for Transracial Adoption (1994).

Lynn D. Wardle, *The "Inner Lives" of Children in Lesbigay Adoption: Narratives and Other Concerns*, 7 St. Thomas. U. L. Rev. 501 (2006).

Lynn D. Wardle, *Preference for Married Couple Adoptions – Constitutional and Policy Reflections*, 5 J. L. & Fam. Studs. 345-391 (2003).

B. LEGAL CONSEQUENCES OF ADOPTION

1. Background

a. Consequences of Adoption in General

The general effect of an adoption is to terminate completely the legal recognition of the parent-child relationship between the biological parents and to establish in law the same relationship between the adoptive parents and children that exists between biological parents and children. The purpose of adoption laws is that the child enjoy so far as is legally possible the same relationship that biological children of the adoptive parents would enjoy -- the same legal rights and duties. Thus, sexual exploitation by the adoptive parents of the child would ordinarily be proscribed under incest laws; if the adoptive parents die intestate, the adoptive children ordinarily would share in the estate as if they were the biological offspring of the decedents; the adoptive parents would have the same duty to support and be subject to the same penalties for nonsupport as if the children were the biological fruit of the marriage; etc. But there are some anomalies. Since adoption is a relatively recent development in legal history, some long-established doctrines that were designed to protect only the biological parent-child relationship have resisted reform. Also, incest/consanguinity restrictions generally apply to prohibit sexual contact or marriage between biological parents and their adopted offspring; but those proscriptions apply because of the biological nature of the relationship of the parties, not because of the legal relationship that once existed between them. *See* Zablotsky, *infra*, at 3,4.

b. Adoption Finality and Conflicting Policies

Historically, the stability of the adoption has been a compelling state concern, surpassed only by the concern that the biological parents' rights have not been terminated without due process of law. Adoption decrees have been deemed more final and irrevocable than any other type of civil judgment. The welfare of the minor has been considered to require no less. "Finality of an adoption decree is necessary so that the established rules of intestate succession may apply with certainty to adopted children. Furthermore, finality of such decrees is desirable in order to prevent the emotional strain which would otherwise be imposed upon both the adoptive child and parents, making it difficult for a normal parent-child relationship to develop." *Ratliff v. Meltzer*, 487 N.E.2d 836 (Ind. Ct. App. 1986). But even the powerful doctrine of finality of judgments, enhanced by additional policies favoring stability in families and protection for families who adopt children, is not absolute. If fraud on the court is shown, the adoption might be revoked. Also, if the adoption resulted from fraud and misrepresentation by the placing agency or person, they may be liable for damages under a theory of "wrongful adoption."

The same child-protective policy considerations also discourage invalidation of adoption on direct attack (on appeal). If a child has been living with adoptive parents for a substantial period of time (i.e., pending a lengthy appeal), the disruptive effects of ordering the child to be returned to biological parents could be extremely traumatic and detrimental. Nevertheless, since direct attack involves the pursuit of a timely pre-adoption challenge, overturning an adoption decree on direct appeal is justifiable conceptually. Expedited trial and appellate procedures can reduce the practical harm which protracted litigation challenges to the integrity of the adoption might cause.

c. Interstate Recognition of Adoption.

As a general rule, judgments from one state must be given full faith and credit in all other states. Adoptions are judgments. On the other hand, some prospective relationship judgments, especially those involving children, have been denied interstate recognition. For instance, for many years, when adoptions of adults were controversial, some states where adult adoptions were prohibited declined to give effect to adult adoption judgments from states where they were legal. Will states be required to recognize and give prospective domestic effect to judgments creating lesbigay adoptions, even if such are prohibited in the second state? *See* Wardle, *A Critical Analysis, infra*.

d. Access to Information About Biological Relatives

The movement by adopted children to have access to identifying information about their biological parents led to attempts to reform law through judicial as well as legislative means. However, reformers achieved only marginal success in the courts. *See Alma Society v. Mellon*, 601 F.2d 1225 (2d Cir. 1979). Courts were reluctant to create new fundamental rights, create new suspect categories, and because of countervailing privacy interests. The fact that adoption has historically been legislatively-controlled may also have contributed to the marginal success.

The open records movement redirected its energy to legislative reform and achieved far more favorable results. Over half of the states have liberalized their "sealed records" provisions in recent years by legislative amendment. At least six states now allow adult adoptees unrestricted access to adoption records. This approach has been criticized because it may disregard the interests of sensitive biological and adoptive parents, but advocates of open adoption argue that the search of biological "roots" outweighs others' interests in privacy. At least a dozen states provide for the release of nonidentifying information about biological parents (i.e., age, race, education, appearance, interests, other children, medical history, etc.). This approach has been criticized as not responding to the powerful emotional desire of some adopted persons for personal contact with biological parents. About the same number of states have petition and waiver release provisions: the adopted child can file a petition and the natural parents can file a waiver (either at the time of adoption or after being contacted by the state agency when the petition is filed). If both parties agree, then the information is disclosed. All states that do not provide for unrestricted access to the records have "good cause" exceptions; the adoptive child or any other person may obtain the identities of the parties involved in the adoption on good cause shown. Typically the requirement of good cause is strictly construed, but some cases recognize "psychological need" as "good cause."

There are four policies behind sealed records laws: 1) protect adoptive parents and family from interference by biological parent, 2) protect adopted child from stigma of illegitimacy and/or unwantedness, 3) protect privacy of biological parents who relinquish the child for adoption, and 4) to protect the integrity of the adoption process against black market competition. How should they be prioritized, and why?

e. Grandparent Visitation

All states have enacted "Grandparent Visitation" statutes which provide some grandparents (and sometimes other relatives) with a qualified right to visitation with grandchildren. A number of courts have addressed the question whether such statutes authorize courts to enter an order for grandparents to visit grandchildren after their adoption by strangers or by a stepparent, over the objection of the adoptive parents. The question is one of statutory interpretation when the statutes do not explicitly provide for visitation after adoption; not surprisingly, different courts interpreting different statutes have reached different conclusions. Many legislatures have positively addressed the issue of grandparent visitation in stepparent adoption.

f. Inheritance

The adopted child is often said to become in all respects the same as a biological child of the parents. While this policy holds true in most cases, it may not hold true in every case. For instance, adoption actually does not make the child the "heir of the body" of the adoptive parents; accordingly, a trust devise to the "heirs of the bodies" of the adoptive parents will not pass to the adoptive children of the trust beneficiaries. *Tootle v. Tootle*, 22 Ohio St. 3d 244 (1986). Pennsylvania courts have held that only persons adopted while children, not adult adoptees, have been permitted to inherit as "children." *See e.g. In re Estate of Ketcham*, 495 A.2d 594 (Pa. Super. 1985); *In re Estate of Kauffman*, A.2d (Pa. Super. Ct. 1986). One writer summarized the effect-of-adoption-on-inheritance provisions of American adoption laws as follows:

Forty-one state effect-of-adoption provisions ... address inheritance and succession matters, either directly or by cross-reference to state probate codes. Typically, these provisions effect one or more of the following: invest the child and the adopting parents with the right to inherit from one another [39 states]; divest the natural parents of the right to inherit from the child [28 states]; continue, under a variety of circumstances, the right of the child to inherit from the natural parents [seven states]; provide that when adoption is by a spouse of a natural parent (i.e., a stepparent), the inheritance rights between that natural parent and the child remain unchanged by an adoption decree [21 states].

Zablotsky, *infra*, at 5-6.

g. Informal Adoption

Because adoption was unknown at common law and is entirely a statutory action, and because the consequences of adoption are so profound, (i.e., to terminate all parental rights, privileges and duties of the biological parent(s) and to create a new parent-child relationship), adoption statutes are construed strictly. Every requirement must be satisfied in all respects before a court will enter an adoption decree. Fulfilling all details of the statutory requirements for adoption may discourage some persons. Occasionally, cases arise in which it appears that a couple agreed to adopt a child, or intended to adopt a child, or took a child into their home and treated the child in all respects as if they had adopted the child, without ever obtaining a judicial decree of adoption. In some cases, courts have recognized the claim of the person in the de facto parent-child relationship despite the absence of a de jure relationship as a matter of equity. Some courts and commentators have spoken of "equitable adoption" or "adoption by estoppel" to justify those decisions. However, it would be seriously erroneous to read the cases to suggest that an adoption will be recognized absent compliance with statutory requirements. The ultimate issue the courts have faced in those cases is whether or not a particular claimant who was not a biological or adoptive child of the deceased or injured parent is entitled to a particular benefit which by statute, will, or private contract can be claimed by a "child" (or similar term of familial relationship term). Thus, the holding of the court that the claimant is entitled to recover rests on interpretation of that term, not on interpretation or manipulation of the law of adoption. *See Reynolds v. City of Los Angeles*, 222 Cal. Rptr. 517 (Cal. App. 1986) (rejecting wrongful death action for unadopted child); *but see Holt v. Burlington Northern Railroad Co.*, 685 S.W.2d 851 (Mo. Ct. App. 1984) (allowing wrongful death action in similar situation because wrongful death statute was a remedial statute, not in derogation of the common law).

h. Wrongful Adoption

Because adoption judgments are usually final and non-revocable unless there is a defect in the adoption process or by statute, *supra*, a few courts have provided relief by recognizing the tort of wrongful adoption in cases when an agency or other placing person engages in unreasonable conduct, especially for negligent or intentional misrepresentation or concealment regarding the health of the child in order to induce adoption. See *Burr v. Board of County Commissioners of Stark County*, 491 N.E.2d 1101 (Ohio 1986) (affirming $125,000 verdict against a public adoption agency that told prospective parents that 17-month-old infant was "a nice, big, healthy baby boy," when the agency knew that the mother was a 31-year-old mental patient, that the child was born in the state mental institution in which the mother was living, that the father was unknown but was presumed to be another mental patient, that the child had previously been placed in two foster homes, and test records indicated that the child "may have low intelligence and was at risk of disease.").

2. Cases, Statutes and Doctrines

a. *Doe v. Sundquist*

Promise Doe v. Donald Sundquist, et al.
2 S.W.3d 919 (Tenn. 1999)

ANDERSON, CHIEF JUSTICE.

We granted this appeal to decide whether legislation allowing disclosure of sealed adoption records to adopted persons over the age of 21 impairs the vested rights of birth parents who surrendered children under the prior law and thus constitutes retrospective legislation in violation of article I, section 20 of the Tennessee Constitution. We also have considered whether the legislation violates the right to privacy under the Tennessee Constitution.

The trial court dismissed the plaintiffs' action for injunctive and declaratory relief, holding that the legislation did not impair the plaintiffs' vested rights or their rights to privacy under the Tennessee Constitution. The Court of Appeals reversed the trial court's judgment, concluding that the retrospective application of the legislation impaired the vested rights of birth parents who surrendered children under former law with an expectation that records of the adoption would not be released.

We agree with the trial court that retrospective application of legislation allowing disclosure of adoption records to adopted persons over the age of 21 does not impair the vested rights of birth parents in violation of article I, section 20 of the Tennessee Constitution, nor does it violate the right to privacy embraced in the Tennessee Constitution. We therefore reverse the Court of Appeals' judgment and reinstate the judgment of the trial court.

BACKGROUND

In 1995, the Tennessee Legislature enacted several new statutory provisions and amendments regarding the law of adoption. * Section 36-1-127(c) of the new law, which became effective July 1, 1996, provides in relevant part:

> (1)(A) All adoption records ... shall be made available to the following eligible persons: (i)[a]n adopted person ... who is twenty-one (21) years of age or older ...; (ii)[t]he legal representative of [such] a person ...;
> (B) Information ... shall be released ... only to the parents, siblings, lineal descendants, or lineal ancestors, of the adopted person ..., and only with the express written consent ... [of] the adopted person....

Id. The new law also provides for a "contact veto," under which a parent, sibling, spouse, lineal ancestor, or lineal descendant may register to prevent contact by the adopted person. Tenn. Code Ann. § 36-1-128 (1996 & Supp.1998).

In March of 1997, a group of plaintiffs filed an action in Davidson County for declaratory and injunctive relief, challenging the constitutionality of the disclosure portion of the new law. Plaintiff Promise Doe alleged that she was a birth parent who surrendered a child for adoption in 1990 with the assurance that the information she provided would remain confidential and sealed and could not be accessed by the child or the child's father. Plaintiff Jane Roe, a birth parent who surrendered a child for adoption in 1956, alleged that she had signed some papers after giving birth but was advised that the child had died. Roe also alleged that she was contacted by the Tennessee Department of Human Services in 1988 regarding her biological child's requests for identifying information. *[FN3 - Plaintiffs also included Kimberly C. and Russ C., adoptive parents, and Small World Ministries, Inc., a non-profit child-placing agency. These plaintiffs have not challenged the Court of Appeals' ruling, which was specifically limited to the plaintiffs who were birth parents.]*

The plaintiffs argued that they had a vested right in the confidentiality of their identity under the law in effect at the time they surrendered children for adoption and that retrospective application of the 1995 statute violates article I, section 20 of the Tennessee Constitution. The plaintiffs also argued that the legislation interfered with their right to privacy, specifically, familial and procreational privacy and the non- disclosure of personal information.

After initially granting a temporary restraining order that prevented disclosure of the records, the trial court denied the plaintiffs' request for a temporary injunction. The trial court concluded (a) that the plaintiffs failed to establish they had a vested right to confidential records under prior law that would invalidate the new law as retrospective legislation under article I, section 20 of the Tennessee Constitution, and (b) that the plaintiffs failed to establish that disclosure violated the right to privacy under the Tennessee Constitution. For these same reasons, the trial court later granted the State's motion to dismiss the action.

The Court of Appeals issued a stay pending disposition of the appeal. The court then concluded that the statute in question violated article I, section 20 for the following reasons:

[W]e find that the retrospective application of Section 36-1-127(c) does impair the vested rights of birth parents who surrendered their children for adoption under former law. Under the prior law, these birth parents had a reasonable expectation that any identifying information would remain confidential if they so desired.... [T]he DHS regulation mandating that birth parents be assured of the confidential aspects of the adoption-related services ... adopted in 1988 ... is indicative of the expectation of confidentiality prevalent under the prior law. The birth mother plaintiffs all proclaim that they were assured confidentiality and expected the same under that law. We find that this interest in the confidentiality of identifying information is a proper interest for the state to recognize and protect. Life- changing decisions were made based upon this expectation and to now deprive those who relied upon their legitimate expectation under the law would be to deprive them of a vested right.

The Court of Appeals specifically limited its holding to the plaintiffs who were birth parents. We granted review to consider this important issue of first impression.

ANALYSIS

Standard of Review

This case is on appeal from the trial court's dismissal of the plaintiffs' suit for failure to state a claim upon which relief can be granted. Tenn. R. Civ. P. 12.02(6). A Rule 12.02(6) motion tests the legal sufficiency of the plaintiff's complaint and not the strength of the plaintiff's evidence. *Riggs v. Burson,* * (Tenn.1997). In ruling on such a motion, courts must construe the complaint in favor of the plaintiff, accept the allegations of fact as true, and deny the motion unless it appears that the plaintiff can establish no facts supporting the claim that would warrant relief. *Id.* When the trial court's grant of a Rule 12.02(6) motion to dismiss is appealed, we must take the factual allegations contained in the complaint as true and review the lower courts' legal conclusions de novo without a presumption of correctness. *Stein v. Davidson Hotel Co.,* * (Tenn. 1997).

History of Adoption Statutes in Tennessee

We begin by reviewing the history of adoption laws in Tennessee. In 1852, the General Assembly granted jurisdiction to circuit and county courts authorizing the adoption of children; the function of the court was to record the names of the parties and the terms of the adoption. * In 1917, the legislature determined that in cases involving children whose parentage was unknown, and who had not been assigned by court order to a child-caring organization, a trial judge had the discretion to "require that all papers relating to the personal history of such child or family history if any is of record, be sealed and filed in the county archives, to be unsealed only by judicial order." *

Later amendments provided that records were to be sealed but could be disclosed in the discretion of the court. In 1949, for instance, legislation provided that an adopted person over the age of 21 could petition the trial judge to review the records and to release any information the judge determined was in the best interest of the adopted person and the State of Tennessee. * Similarly, the statute was amended in 1951 to require an adopted individual seeking information to file a court order; disclosure required the court to find that releasing the records was in the best interest of the adopted person and the public. *.

Other amendments created more inroads into the confidentiality provisions of the adoption statutes. In 1982, an amendment allowed an adopted person to file a written request and to receive non-identifying information from the Department of Human Services about the adopted person's biological family. * In 1985, an amendment provided for further disclosure of records if DHS received consent from the biological parents. * In 1989, an amendment provided that upon a written request of an adopted person over age 21, DHS was to search its records for information concerning the location of the birth parent(s) and, if found, request consent for disclosure of the information. If the birth parent consented, DHS was to provide the adopted person with the name, address, and identifying information of the birth parent. *

As previously noted, the 1995 amendments mandate disclosure of records upon the request of an adopted person over the age of 21 without requiring a court order or consent of the biological parents. Tenn.Code Ann. § 36-1-127(c)(1). Other portions of the legislation, however, establish a procedure by which a birth parent or related individual can "veto" any contact with the adopted party who has received the records. Tenn.Code Ann. § 36-1-128 (1996 & Supp.1998). We will now address the constitutionality of these disclosure provisions.

Retrospective Legislation

Article I, section 20 of the Tennessee Constitution provides that "no retrospective law, or law impairing the obligations of contracts, shall be made." We have construed this provision as prohibiting laws "which take away or impair vested rights acquired under existing laws or create a new obligation, impose a new duty, or attach a new disability in respect of transactions or considerations already passed." *Morris v. Gross,* * (Tenn.1978). A "vested right," although difficult to define with precision, is one "which it is proper for the state to recognize and protect and of which [an] individual could not be deprived arbitrarily without injustice." Id. at 905 (citation omitted).

In considering whether a statute impairs a vested right under article I, section 20, we frequently have observed that statutes which are procedural or remedial in nature may be applied retrospectively. *Saylors v. Riggsbee,* * (Tenn.1976). In general, a statute is procedural "if it defines the ... proceeding by which a legal right is enforced, as distinguished from the law which gives or defines the right." *Kuykendall v. Wheeler,* * (Tenn.1994) (citation omitted). A statute is remedial if it provides the means by which a cause of action may be effectuated, wrongs addressed, and relief obtained. *Dowlen v. Fitch,* * (1954). We have clarified, however, that even a procedural or remedial statute may not be applied retrospectively if it impairs a vested right or contractual obligation in violation of article I, section 20. *Kee v. Shelter Ins.,* * (Tenn.1993).

Our case law indicates that deciding whether a "vested right" exists and has been impaired by retrospective application of a statute entails consideration of many factors, none of which is dispositive. *E.g., Morris,* 572 S.W.2d at 907 (focusing on plaintiff's "vested right" to maintain an already filed cause of action despite new law that effectively dismissed the suit and prevented its refiling due to a shorter statute of limitations); *Saylors,* 544 S.W.2d at 610 (analyzing the substantive/procedural distinction in determining whether a statute impaired a vested right or contractual obligation); *Ford Motor Co. v. Moulton,* * (Tenn.1974) (analyzing whether legislation deprived a person of his reasonable expectations under the prior law). In short, there is no precise formula to apply in making this determination.

We therefore agree with the trial court that it is useful to employ a multi- factor analysis, such as that enunciated in *Ficarra v. Department of Regulatory Agencies,* 849 P.2d 6 (Colo.1993):

> [I]n determining whether a retroactive statute impairs or destroys vested rights, the most important inquiries are (1) whether the public interest is advanced or retarded, (2) whether the retroactive provision gives effect to or defeats the bona fide intentions or reasonable expectations of affected persons, and (3) whether the statute surprises persons who have long relied on a contrary state of the law.

Id. at 16 (alteration in original) (citation omitted). We add to these factors, which encompass the principles discussed in our case law, an additional factor discussed above: the extent to which a statute appears to be procedural or remedial. *E.g., Kuykendall,* 890 S.W.2d at 787.

In considering the first factor, we observe that the stated primary purpose of the new law reflects consideration of the public interest:

> [t]he primary purpose of this part is to provide means and procedures for the adoption of children and adults that recognize and effectuate to the greatest extent possible the rights and interests of persons affected by adoption, especially those of the adopted persons, which are specifically protected by the constitutions of the United States and the state of Tennessee....

Tenn.Code Ann. § 36-1-101(a) (1996 & Supp.1998). Moreover, with regard to the disclosure of records, the statute expressly provides:

> [t]he purpose of this part shall also be to favor the rights of adopted persons or other persons for whom any closed records are maintained and their families to obtain information concerning the lives of those persons and to permit them to obtain information about themselves from the adoption records, sealed records, sealed adoption records, or post-adoption records to which they are entitled, but also to recognize the rights of parents and adopted persons not to be contacted by the persons who obtain such information, except in compliance with this part.

Tenn.Code Ann. § 36-1-101(c) (emphasis added). The legislation in question is obviously related to achieving these legitimate goals, which the General Assembly has found to be in the public interest.

The second and third factors--the intentions or reasonable expectations of affected persons, and the surprise to persons who had relied on a contrary state of the law--are obviously related to some degree. The Court of Appeals' decision largely focused on its conclusion that the birth parents had a reasonable expectation of confidentiality based on the law as it existed when they surrendered their children for adoption. In our view, the Court of Appeals' analysis is flawed because it does not fully take into account the history of adoption laws in this State.

Early adoption statutes did not require either that records be sealed or that the identity of the parties remain confidential. Later amendments to the statutes provided that even if sealed, records could be disclosed upon a request by an adopted person and a judicial finding that disclosure was in the best interest of the adopted person and the public. Still other amendments enacted in 1982 and 1985 permitted disclosure of information under certain circumstances even without a judicial finding. There simply has never been an absolute guarantee or even a reasonable expectation by the birth parent or any other party that adoption records were permanently sealed. In fact, reviewing the history of adoption statutes in this state reveals just the opposite. Accordingly, we disagree with the Court of

Appeals' conclusion that the plaintiffs had a vested right in the confidentiality of records concerning their cases with no possibility of disclosure. *[FN5. Similarly, given this statutory history, we also disagree with the Court of Appeals' conclusion that the plaintiffs could reasonably rely on an alleged assurance of confidentiality from either a state agency or state regulation.]* Cf. Moulton, 511 S.W.2d at 695-97 (finding that reasonable expectation under prior law was impaired by retroactive application of statute reviving an otherwise barred cause of action).

Finally, we conclude that the 1995 amendments are both procedural and remedial. Under former statutes, disclosure of records required a judicial determination that disclosure was in the best interest of the adopted person and the public. Upon such a determination, there was no requirement that the birth parents or other individuals be notified or have the option to register a "veto" preventing contact. The new law, on the other hand, reflects the legislature's view that the disclosure of records is in the best interest of the adopted person and the public. It mandates disclosure of records if requested by an adopted person 21 years of age or older, yet, unlike prior law, balances disclosure by allowing a "veto" that prevents contact with the adopted person. Tenn.Code Ann. § 36-1-130 (1996). It does not create new rights or allow access to any records that previously were not to be released. In sum, we believe that these new methods and standards for disclosure are procedural in nature and reflect the legislature's effort to create legislation that advances the best interest of adopted persons and the public.

Accordingly, we have considered the public interest advanced by the 1995 legislation, the reasonable expectations of persons affected by the legislation, the surprise to persons relying on the statutory provisions in effect prior to the effective date of this legislation, and the extent to which the new law is procedural or remedial in nature. We conclude that retrospective application of the legislation now codified in Tenn.Code Ann. § 36-1-127(c) does not impair the vested rights of the plaintiffs in violation of article I, section 20 of the Tennessee Constitution.

Right to Privacy

The plaintiffs assert that disclosure pursuant to Tenn.Code Ann. § 36-1- 127(c) violates their right to privacy under article I, sections 1, 3, and 20, and article XI, section 8 of the Tennessee Constitution. They allege that the statute invades the rights of familial and procreational privacy, as well as the right to non-disclosure of personal information.

In *Davis v. Davis*, 842 S.W.2d 588 (Tenn.1992), we recognized that, although a right to privacy is not mentioned in either the federal or Tennessee Constitutions, "there can be little doubt about its grounding in the concept of liberty reflected in those two documents." *Id.* at 598. We observed that "the notion of individual liberty is ... deeply embedded in the Tennessee Constitution" and concluded "that there is a right of individual privacy guaranteed under and protected by the liberty clauses of the Tennessee Declaration of Rights." Id. at 599, 600. Although Tennessee's right of privacy incorporates some of the features of the right to privacy under the federal constitution, we are free to extend greater protection in applying our own state constitution. Id. at 600.

As the plaintiffs argue, and the State concedes, the right to privacy under the Tennessee Constitution includes the right of procreation. Id. The right to privacy also encompasses "the right of parents to care for their children without unwarranted state intervention." *Hawk v. Hawk,* * (Tenn.1993). These rights under our state constitution are likewise reflected in the United States Constitution. *E.g. Bellotti v. Baird*, 443 U.S. 622, 634 (1979); *Roe v. Wade*, 410 U.S. 113, 152 (1973).

The plaintiffs argue that disclosure of adoption records invades the rights to familial privacy by impeding a birth parent's freedom to determine whether to raise a family and disrupting both biological and adoptive families by releasing identifying information previously sealed. We disagree.

The disclosure provisions reflect the legislature's determination that allowing limited access to adoption records is in the best interest of both adopted persons and the public. The provisions do not, however, allow unfettered access in disregard of the sensitivities and privacy interests involved. To the contrary, disclosure is limited to an adopted individual or that individual's legal representative, 21 years of age or older. Moreover, extensive provisions are included to allow a birth parent or other related individual to register a "contact veto" and eliminate or reduce the risk that disclosure of identifying information will have a disruptive effect upon the lives of the biological and adoptive families. Similarly, the plaintiffs' disruption argument is dubious in that it is predicated upon a speculative risk of disruption that may or may not occur a minimum of 21 years after the adoption occurs. In short, the statute does not impede traditional familial privacy rights such as marrying, having children, or raising children.

The plaintiffs also argue that disclosure impedes the right to procreational privacy by impeding the birth parents' decision of whether to carry a child to term. We again disagree.

The decision of whether to carry a pregnancy to term implicates privacy rights under the federal and state constitutions. Davis, 842 S.W.2d at 601. This decision differs fundamentally from the decision of whether to surrender a child for adoption. The right of adoption is statutory. It was created to protect the interests of children whose parents are unable or unwilling to provide for their care, *Young v. Smith*, * (1950), and not to advance a procreational right to privacy of the biological parent. Although the prospect of having the records of the adoption released to the child 21 years later may have some bearing on the decision, it is far too speculative to conclude that it interferes with the right to procreational privacy. Moreover, the prospect of disclosure under the legislation at issue in this case is nothing new; as already discussed, disclosure has long been permitted in some form under Tennessee statutory law.

Finally, the plaintiffs contend that disclosure violates a privacy right to non-disclosure of personal information. We have held, however, that the confidentiality of records is a statutory matter left to the legislature. *E.g., Tennessean v. Electric Power Bd. of Nashville*, *(Tenn.1998); see also Thompson v. Reynolds*, * (Tenn.Ct.App.1993). Absent a fundamental right or other compelling reason, we reject the invitation to extend constitutional protection to the non-disclosure of personal information. *[FN7. The Sixth Circuit has likewise concluded on several occasions that there is no constitutional right to the non-disclosure of personal information. Jarvis v. Wellman, 52 F.3d 125, 126 (6th Cir.1995); Doe v. Wigginton, 21 F.3d 733, 740 (6th Cir.1994); J.P. v. DeSanti, 653 F.2d 1080, 1090 (6th Cir.1981).]*

CONCLUSION

We conclude that the disclosure of adoption records as provided in 1995 Tenn. Pub. Acts, ch. 523, codified at Tenn.Code Ann. § 36-1-127(c), does not impair the plaintiffs' vested rights in violation of article I, section 20 of the Tennessee Constitution and does not violate the plaintiffs' right to privacy under the Tennessee Constitution. Accordingly, we reverse the judgment of the Court of Appeals and reinstate the judgment of the trial court. The stay granted by the Court of Appeals prohibiting the release of adoption records under the provisions of Tenn.Code Ann. § 36-1-127(c) is lifted.

Costs of appeal are taxed to the appellees, for which execution shall issue if necessary.

DROWOTA, BIRCH, HOLDER, and BARKER, JJ., concur.

b. Notes and Questions

1) Sundquist and Opening Access to Sealed Adoption Records

A few months after the Tennessee Supreme Court decision, an Oregon Court of Appeals reached a similar conclusion in *Does 1, 2, 3, 4, 5, 6, and 7 v. State*, 993 P.2d 822 (Or.App. 1999), rev. denied 6 P.3d 1098 (Or. 2000). That case involved a challenge to the constitutionality of Oregon Measure 58, a voter-approved initiative adopted in 1998, which provided that previously sealed adoption information including the identity of biological parents who relinquished children for adoption would be available to adopted children when they become 21 years old. The law was challenged by seven mothers who had placed children for adoption between 1960 and 1994 when the law guaranteed confidentiality. In an editorial opinion published after the court had rejected their claim, the lawyer who represented the mothers, wrote:

> Neither the six anonymous birth mothers who filed suit nor other birth mothers are fictitious or faceless persons. They made difficult and intimate life-changing decisions to surrender newborn infants for adoption, based not only on promises and assurances of privacy and confidentiality, but also with the assurance of Oregon laws in existence since 1957 that their identities would be shielded from public disclosure except upon order of court – a rare event.
> Unfortunately, in Oregon a promise by the state is no longer worth much . . . .
> ***
> The birth mothers opposed to Measure 58 are not against open adoptions where all parties to the adoption [agree]*** .
> The birth mothers believe that they have the right to be let alone and to maintain the confidentiality of their identity.
> By destroying the birth mother's confidentiality, Measure 58 effectively deprives her of the choice for a permanently closed adoption. However, if she elects to have an abortion, she can do so without ever letting anyone but her doctor know ***.

I. Frank Hunsaker, *Respect, please don't confront, birth mothers*, The Oregonian, June 12, 2000. *See further* Samuels, *infra*.

2) Open Adoption

Open adoption allows both biological and adoptive parents cooperatively to agree to some level of openness among them and the child. This movement has arisen in the wake of the movement to unseal records. It is too soon to determine whether the law will embrace this concept. A few courts have enforced these agreements. Several states have enacted statutes. Some courts have specifically rejected such agreements as being in conflict with their adoption statutes.

3) Adoption Statistics

The U.S. government does not keep records on adoption. The most comprehensive information about adoption in the United States is compiled by the National Council for Adoption. The Adoption Factbook III, *infra* at 25-50, reports the following: In 1992 there were 115,689 domestic adoptions in the US; in 1996 there were 108,463 domestic adoptions in the US. Domestic adoptions were split almost evenly between related adoptions and unrelated adoptions. The unrelated adoptions were handled by public agencies (40%), private agencies (29%) and private individuals (31%) (in 1996).

The ratio of abortions per 1,000 live births was 334.4 in 1992. The ratio of infant adoptions per 1,000 abortions was 19.6 in 1992, and 19.4 in 1996. The ratio of infant adoptions per 1,000 nonmarital live births was 21.8 in 1992 and 18.7 in 1996 indicating that less than 2% of unmarried mothers choose adoption. Utah and Idaho are in the "top five" states with the highest ratios of adoptions per live nonmarital births, and Idaho, Utah, and Wyoming are in the top four best "adoption option" states (adoptions per 1,000 nonmarital births plus abortions), with ratios of 42-83 (compared to a U.S. average of 9.5) per 1,000. The number of unrelated adoptions rose steadily from 1951 to 1973, and has dropped steadily since then (with one slight blip). (What happened in 1973 that may have caused this change?) The numbers of related adoptions rose fairly steadily from

1951 to 1982 and then dropped dramatically (from 91,000 to 53,000) between 1982 and 1986. What happened in the 1980s to explain that drop?

There is a tremendous "demand" for children for adoption. For example, in 1984, "more than 2 million couples were in contention for the 58,000 children placed [for adoption], a ratio of 35 to 1." Wilson and Hitchings, *infra* at 112. *See* Chapter 12.

3. Practical and Ethical Considerations

a. The Law and Public Trust

Does the retroactive unsealing of adoption records to identify biological parents undermine the public's trust in adoption? Birth parents were promised confidentiality. What about the child's right to know? Should confidentiality be promised in the future?

4. Bibliography

Adoption Fact Book (National Committee For Adoption 1985).

Adoption Fact Book III (National Committee For Adoption 1999).

Carol Amandio and Stuart L. Deutsch, *Open Adoption: Allowing Adopted Children to "Stay in Touch" With Blood Relatives*, 22 J. Fam. L. 59 (1983-84).

Fowler, Adult Adoption: *A "New" Legal Tool For Lesbians and Gay Men*, 14 Golden Gate U.L. Rev. 667 (1984).

Henshaw, Trends in Abortion, 1982-84 18 Fam. Plan. Prospectives 34 (1986).

Henshaw, Forrest, Sullivan & Tietze, *Abortion in the United States*, 1979-80, 14 Fam. Plan. Prospectives 1 (1982).

Gilbert Holmes, *The Extended Family System in the Black Community: A Child Centered Model for Adoption Policy*, 68 Temple L. Rev. 1649 (1995).

Landes & Posner, *The Economics of the Baby Shortage*, 7 J. Legal Stud. 323 (1978).

W. Meezan, S. Cats, & E. Russo, Adoptions Without Agencies: A Study of Independent Adoption. (1978).

Note, *Developing a Concept of the Modern Single "Family": A Proposed Uniform Surrogate Parenthood Act*, 73 Geo.L.J. 1283 (1985).

Contemporary Family Law, vol. 2, Ch. 10 (1988).

Posner, *The Regulation of the Market in Adoptions*, 67 B.U.L. Rev. 59 (1987).

Elizabeth J. Samuels, *The Idea of Adoption: An Inquiry Into the History of Adult Adoptee Access to Birth Records*, 53 Rutgers L. Rev. 367 (2001).

Lynn D. Wardle, *A Critical Analysis of Interstate Adoption Recognition of Lesbigay Adoptions*, 3 Ave Maria L. Rev. 561-616 (2005).

Zablotsky, *To Grandmother's House We go: Grandparent Visitation After Step- Parent Adoption*, 32 Wayne L. Rev. 1 (1985).

CHAPTER 14

Adoption: International and Interstate Adoptions; Indian Child Welfare Act; Jurisdiction

A. INTERNATIONAL AND INTERSTATE ADOPTIONS

1. Background

a. Context of International Adoptions

Millions of parentless children around the world live severely deprived lives, often in gangs of "street children" where (like Dicken's Oliver) they resort to crime to support themselves. Tens of thousands are dumped into orphanage warehouses where they live lives of abject deprivation and neglect (as in 1990 Romania). A 1993 study of adoptions from Latin American countries found that the typical birth mothers were 14-18 years old, were functionally illiterate, lived below the poverty level, were unemployed, beggars or prostitutes, came from broken homes, and had histories of abuse, neglect and abandonment. *Intercountry Adoption, infra* at 10. One solution to the problem of parentless children whom the state and other institutions are unable to protect is international adoption.

Historically, intercountry adoption generally flourished after a war, when the international humanitarian concerns temporarily overrode nationalism. International adoption became a significant practice primarily after World War II, when American military and governmental officers stationed abroad opened their hearts and homes to the war orphans. However, intercountry adoption must overcome accusations of economic exploitation of developing cultures by childless couples from affluent nations. Periodically, (actually rare) incidents involving international babyselling and similar financial exploitation, have reportedly led to practices such as abduction, falsely telling mothers that children died in childbirth, etc., in order to get children to sell in adoption. Likewise, the notion that a child will always be better off in a more affluent country is under attack. *Intercountry Adoption, infra* at 6-7.

Additionally, international adoption is potentially complex, involving multiple bodies of law. For example, if a couple from the United States is adopting there are several preliminary steps between finding a child and legally adopting that child. First, the law of the child's country of domicile or habitual residence governs the termination of parental rights (usually the law of the parents' domicile), and that jurisdiction must also approve placement of the child with the prospective adoptive parents and grant them guardianship, custody, or adoption. Second, the child's home country must also approve the exit of the child for emigration. Third, the United States must provide an entrance visa for the child's immigration. Fourth, the state of the adoptive parents' domicile generally must decree an adoption or recognize the foreign adoption.

b. Interstate Adoption

Historically, along with the requirements of the state statute, subject matter jurisdiction for adoption was based on domicile. Some states held that it was the child's domicile; others held that it was the adoptive parents' domicile. See Homer J. Clark, *infra*. Some courts have recently held that the Uniform Child Custody Jurisdictional Act (see chapter 32) and the Parental Kidnapping Prevention Act (see chapter37) are the basis for jurisdiction. The Uniform Child Custody Jurisdictional and Enforcement Act, promulgated to replace the Uniform Child Custody Jurisdictional Act, does not apply to adoption jurisdiction, anticipating states will adopt the Uniform Adoption Act. Due process also requires proper notice to all the parties. Adoption may, however, involve two states. When adoption is interstate, the Interstate Compact on the Placement of Children also governs. This compact is a cooperative effort among states to assist in interstate adoption in order to promote the best interests of the child. The compact provides procedures for transferring the child from another state for placement, notifying the state that is receiving the child, and imposing penalties for noncompliance.

2. Statutes, Cases and Doctrines

a. The Hague Convention on Intercountry Adoption

The most significant instrument of international law to facilitate and promote international adoption was promulgated in 1993 by the Hague Conference on Private International Law, called the Hague Convention on Protection of Children and Co-Operation in Respect of Intercountry Adoption, 32 I.L.M. 1134 (in force May 1, 1995), generally known as the Hague Convention on Intercountry Adoption. The Preamble to the Hague Intercountry Adoption Convention "[r]ecognize[s] that the child, for the full and harmonious development of his or her personality, should grow up in a family environment, in an atmosphere of happiness, love and understanding," and that international "adoption may offer the advantage of a permanent family to a child" who is parentless, and provide for "the best interests of the child . . . with respect for his or her fundamental rights . . . .". The Convention is designed to facilitate and regulate international adoption in order to offer parentless children the opportunity of family life, to be raised in a parent-led home environment. Contracting nations are obligated to seek this objective first by "appropriate measures to enable the child to remain in the care of his or her family of origin." If preservation of the family of origin is not possible or appropriate, and "a suitable family cannot be found in his or her State of origin," then intercountry adoption "may offer the advantage of a permanent family" for the child. Carlson, *infra*, at 262. The Hague Convention gives preference to intercountry adoption over any form of impermanent care available within the child's country of origin, including foster or institutional care, Carlson, *infra*, at 255-265, and gives that placement priority over less permanent or institutional options (such as orphanages or foster care), even if the adopting couple does not share the child's cultural background. Hague Convention, *supra*, 32 I.L.M. at 1139. The bulk of the Hague Convention provisions provide basic procedural protections for facilitating and regulating Intercountry adoptions. "The overarching importance of the Convention lies in its endorsement of intercountry adoption when there is compliance with its internationally agreed minimum standards. . . . These standards, and the procedural framework for ensuring that they are complied with, are designed to safeguard the interests of the child . . . ." Pfund, *infra*, at

54. As of May, 2006, sixty-eight nations had signed, ratified, or acceded to the Hague Convention on Intercountry Adoption. Hague Conference, Full Status Report Convention # 33, *infra*.

The Hague Convention on Protection of Children and Co-operation in Respect of Intercountry Adoption, May 29, 1993, S. Treaty Doc. No. 105-51 (1998), was signed by the President in 1994 and approved by Congress with passage of the Intercountry Adoption Act of 2000, Public Law 106-279, on October 6, 2000. Codified at 42 U.S.C. § 14901, et seq. and in the Immigration and Nationality Act in Title 8 of the U.S. Code, the IAA provides for a Central Authority, the U.S. State Department, to accredit adoption agencies to provide intercountry adoption services. When a foreign decree of adoption is certified by the State Department, it "shall be treated by Federal and State agencies, courts . . . as conclusive evidence of the facts certified, 106 Pub. L. 279, § 301(a)(2), and "shall be recognized as a final adoption for purposes of all Federal, State and local laws . . . ." *Id.* §301(b). Congress also passed the Child Citizenship Act of 2000, Pub. L. No. 106-395 (2000), allowing foreign-born. children, under 18 years old, who are adopted by U.S. citizens, to become American citizens automatically when they enter the country as lawful permanent citizens. Those children, who enter the country to be adopted, acquire American citizenship when the adoption is full and final in the United States. However, the Hague Convention on Intercountry Adoption will not be fully ratified by the United States nor the IAA fully effective until the State Department and the U.S. Citizenship and Immigration Services (formerly INS, now a bureau of Homeland Security Department) establish regulations implementing it. On February 15, 2006, the State Department published the relevant rules (22 CFR Parts 96 & 98) and is now moving ahead to accredit American adoption providers.

b. Interstate Compact on the Placement of Children (ICPC)

The Interstate Compact on the Placement of Children is hereby enacted and entered into with all other jurisdictions that legally join in the compact which is, in form, substantially as follows:

INTERSTATE COMPACT ON PLACEMENT OF CHILDREN
ARTICLE I Purpose and Policy
It is the purpose and policy of the party states to cooperate with each other in the interstate placement of children so that:
(1) Each child requiring placement shall receive the maximum opportunity to be placed in a suitable environment and with persons or institutions having appropriate qualifications and facilities to provide necessary and desirable care.
(2) The appropriate authorities in a state where a child is to be placed may have full opportunity to ascertain the circumstances of the proposed placement, thereby promoting full compliance with applicable requirements for the protection of the child.
(3) The proper authorities of the state from which the placement is made may obtain the most complete information on the basis of which to evaluate a projected placement before it is made.
(4) Appropriate jurisdictional arrangements for the care of the children will be promoted.
ARTICLE II Definitions
As used in this compact:
(1) "Child" means a person who, by reason of minority, is legally subject to parental, guardianship, or similar control.

(2) "Sending agency" means a party state, officer, or employee thereof; a subdivision of a party state, or officer or employee thereof; a court of a party state; a person, corporation, association, Indian tribe, charitable agency, or other entity which sends, brings, or causes to be sent or brought any child to another party state.

(3) "Receiving state" means the state to which a child is sent, brought or caused to be sent or brought, whether by public authorities or private persons or agencies, and whether for placement with state or local public authorities or for placement with private agencies or persons.

(4) "Placement" means the arrangement for the care of a child in a family free, adoptive, or boarding home, or in a child-caring agency or institution but does not include any institution caring for the mentally ill, mentally defective or epileptic or any institution, primarily educational in character, and any hospital or other medical facility. ARTICLE III Conditions for Placement

(1) No sending agency shall send, bring, or cause to be sent or brought into any other party state any child for placement in foster care or as a preliminary to a possible adoption unless the sending agency shall comply with each and every requirement set forth in this article and with the applicable laws of the receiving state governing the placement of children therein. (2) Prior to sending, bringing, or causing any child to be sent or brought into a receiving state for placement in foster care or as a preliminary to a possible adoption, the sending agency shall furnish the appropriate public authorities in the receiving state written notice of the intention to send, bring, or place the child in the receiving state. The notice shall contain:

(a) The name, date, and place of birth of the child.

(b) The identity and address or addresses of the parents or legal guardian.

(c) The name and address of the person, agency, or institution to or with which the sending agency proposes to send, bring, or place the child.

(d) A full statement of the reasons for such proposed action and evidence of the authority pursuant to which the placement is proposed to be made.

(e) Any public officer or agency in a receiving agency state which is in receipt of a notice pursuant to Paragraph (2) of this article may request of the sending agency, or any other appropriate officer or agency of or in the sending agency's state, and shall be entitled to receive therefrom, such supporting or additional information as it may deem necessary under the circumstances to carry out the purpose and policy of this compact.

(f) The child shall not be sent, brought, or caused to be sent or brought into the receiving state until the appropriate public authorities in the receiving state shall notify the sending agency, in writing, to the effect that the proposed placement does not appear to be contrary to the interests of the child.

ARTICLE IV Penalty for Illegal Placement

The sending, bringing, or causing to be sent or brought into any receiving state of a child in violation of the terms of this compact shall constitute a violation of the laws respecting the placement of children of both the state in which the sending agency is located or from which it sends or brings the child and of the receiving state. Such violation may be punished or subjected to penalty in either jurisdiction in accordance with its laws. In addition to liability for any such punishment or penalty, any violation shall constitute full and sufficient grounds for the suspension or revocation of any license, permit, or other legal authorization held by the sending agency which empowers or allows it to place, or care for children.

ARTICLE V Retention of Jurisdiction

(1) The sending agency shall retain jurisdiction over the child sufficient to determine all matters in relation to the custody, supervision, care, treatment, and disposition of the child which it would have had if the child had remained in the sending agency's state, until the child is adopted, reaches majority, becomes self-supporting, or is discharged with the concurrence of the appropriate authority in the receiving state. Such jurisdiction shall also include the power to effect

or cause the return of the child or its transfer to another location and custody pursuant to law. The sending agency shall continue to have financial responsibility for support and maintenance of the child during the period of the placement. Nothing contained herein shall defeat a claim of jurisdiction by a receiving state sufficient to deal with an act of delinquency or crime committed therein.

(2) When the sending agency is a public agency, it may enter into an agreement with an authorized public or private agency in the receiving state providing for the performance of one or more services in respect of such case by the latter as agent for the sending agency.

(3) Nothing in this compact shall be construed to prevent any agency authorized to place children in the receiving agency from performing services or acting as agent in the receiving agency jurisdiction for a private charitable agency of the sending agency; nor to prevent the receiving agency from discharging financial responsibility for the support and maintenance of a child who has been placed on behalf of the sending agency without relieving the responsibility set forth in Paragraph (1) above.

***

ARTICLE VIII Limitations

This compact shall not apply to:

(1) The sending or bringing of a child into a receiving state by his parent, step-parent, grandparent, adult brother or sister, adult uncle or aunt, or his guardian and leaving the child with any such relative or nonagency guardian in the receiving state.

(2) Any placement, sending or bringing of a child into a receiving state pursuant to any other interstate compact to which both the state from which the child is sent or brought and the receiving state are party or to any other agreement between said states which has the force of law.

ARTICLE IX Enactment and Withdrawal

***

c. *Adoption of A.M.M. and A.N.M*
In the Matter of the Adoption OF A.M.M. and A.N.M.
949 P.2d 1155 (Kan. Ct. App. 1997)

ROGG, JUDGE:

C.P. and J.P., the prospective adoptive parents, appeal the district court's order granting the natural mother's motion to revoke her consent and dismiss the adoption petition based on failure to comply with the Interstate Compact on the Placement of Children (ICPC), K.S.A. 38-1201 et seq.

Factual background

On May 20, 1996, E.P. gave birth to twins, A.M.M. and A.N.M. At the time of their births, E.P. resided in Kansas City, Kansas. On May 24, 1996, E.P. moved to Kansas City, Missouri. Prior to the birth of the twins, E.P. had asked appellants, her former foster parents, if they would consider adopting the twins.

On December 15, 1996, E.P. moved to a different location in Kansas City, Missouri; she moved there with the twins and her two older children. She lived at this second location until February 12, 1997, at which time she moved to Lawrence.

While E.P. lived in Missouri, her two older children attended Missouri schools. She acquired Missouri telephone service and a Missouri bank account. She applied for and received Missouri public assistance. E.P. testified that at the time she moved to Missouri in May 1996, she intended to stay in Missouri, and during the period she was there, she considered herself a Missouri resident.

E.P. had several conversations with appellants about adopting the twins, and on January 17, 1997, E.P. attended a meeting with her former foster father, C.P., and his attorney to get some general adoption information. E.P.'s residence was discussed and it was noted that if she were a resident of

Missouri and if she proceeded with the adoption, the issue of the ICPC would have to be addressed, but if she were a Kansas resident, the ICPC would not apply.

C.P. testified that the parties discussed what steps could be taken in order for E.P. to establish residency in Kansas because the Kansas adoption procedure was less complicated. C.P. claimed that E.P. was going to move into a trailer he owned in Kansas and get a job in Lawrence.

E.P. testified that on January 19, 1997, she called appellants in Kansas and asked whether they would take care of the twins because she was under a lot of stress. They agreed and picked up the twins in Missouri and brought them back to their home in Kansas. The parties agreed that on that date, the placement with appellants was not for the purpose of an adoption.

On January 21, 1997, E.P. went to appellants' attorney's office in Kansas and signed consents to adoption for A.M.M. and A.N.M. On the forms, she listed her residence as Missouri, and she returned to Missouri after signing the forms. Then on January 22, 1997, E.P. went back to Kansas to sign power of attorney documents to allow appellants to give medical care to the twins.

On February 12, 1997, E.P. entered into a lease agreement with her former foster father to rent a trailer home in Kansas. She enrolled her children in school and applied for Kansas welfare benefits. By February 20, 1997, R.W., a potential father of the twins, had indicated his willingness to sign a consent for A.M.M.'s and A.N.M.'s adoption. The actual consent was not signed until February 28, 1997, however, because R.W. was involved in an accident. P.S., another potential father, signed a consent on February 25, 1997.

Between February 23 and February 25, E.P. communicated to appellants that she did not want to go through with the adoption. Appellants, however, proceeded to file a petition for adoption on February 26, 1997.

On February 27, 1997, E.P. filed a written revocation of consent and a petition for declaratory judgment seeking a declaration that her consent be revoked. On March 25, 1997, E.P. filed a motion to dismiss, claiming that the ICPC had not been complied with and, therefore, the petition should be dismissed.

On April 10, 1997, the district court held a hearing on the limited issue of noncompliance with the ICPC. After the hearing, the district court granted E.P.'s motion to dismiss. The court found that, at the time the twins were transferred to appellants, E.P. was a resident of Missouri and, therefore, the ICPC applied. The court further found the parties did not comply with the ICPC, and it revoked E.P.'s consent and dismissed the petition for adoption.

Placement for adoption

A pivotal issue concerns which date should be used to determine the natural mother's residency at the "time of placement for adoption" and, thus, whether the ICPC applies. The district court made the following finding regarding E.P.'s residency: "On January 21, 1997, [E.P.], still a resident of Missouri, came to Kansas and signed consents to the adoptions." The district court used January 21, 1997, as the date to determine residency under the ICPC.

Appellants claim that the district court looked at the wrong date to determine E.P.'s residency. They claim that the consent date was not the proper date to consider but, rather, February 25, 1997, should have been used because that was the date the "conditional" consent was satisfied, and on that date E.P. was a resident of Kansas. Appellants claim that until the conditions for the use of E.P.'s consents were satisfied, those being the date when both fathers indicated their support of the adoption and the uncertainty about E.P.'s residency had been resolved, it was not possible to determine the relationship of the parties or properly determine the residence of the birth mother.

K.S.A. 38-1202, art. III(a) states:

No sending agency shall send, bring, or cause to be sent or brought into any other party state any child for placement in foster care or as a preliminary to a possible adoption unless the sending agency shall comply with each and every requirement set forth in this article and with the applicable laws of the receiving state governing the placement of children therein. (Emphasis added.)

On January 19, 1997, appellants took physical custody of A.M.M. and A.N.M. At that point, all parties conceded and the district court found that the placement of the twins with appellants was not for the purpose of adoption. On January 21, 1997, E.P. signed consents to adoption in which she relinquished custody of A.M.M. and A.N.M. The consents specifically stated that she consented and agreed to the adoption of A.M.M. and A.N.M. by appellants. The consents further waived notice of any future hearings concerning the adoption. There is nothing in the ICPC requiring that a placement be unconditional before the ICPC comes into effect, and appellants cite no authority for such proposition. Courts in other jurisdictions have found the ICPC came into effect prior to the adoption petition being filed. See In re Adoption No. 10087, 324 Md. 394, 597 A.2d 456 (1991) (ICPC came into effect, when the child was transported across state lines for the purpose of adoption); In the Matter of T.M.M., 186 Mont. 460, 461-62, 608 P.2d 130 (1980).

The purpose of the ICPC is to protect the interests of children who fall within its parameters. K.S.A. 38-1202, art. I.

K.S.A. 38-1202, art. III(b) provides:

Prior to sending, bringing or causing any child to be sent or brought into a receiving state for placement in foster care or as a preliminary to a possible adoption, the sending agency shall furnish the appropriate public authorities in the receiving state written notice of the intention to send, bring, or place the child in the receiving state. The notice shall contain:

(1) The name, date and place of birth of the child.

(2) The identity and address or addresses of the parents or legal guardian.

(3) The name and address of the person, agency or institution to or with which the sending agency proposes to send, bring, or place the child.

(4) A full statement of the reasons for such proposed action and evidence of the authority pursuant to which the placement is proposed to be made.

The purpose of the statutory prior notice provision was discussed in *T.M.M.*, 186 Mont. at 464, 608 P.2d 130:

The prior written notice requirement is designed to provide the proper state authorities in both states with knowledge of, and background information concerning the proposed relocation of a minor child. Prior written notice provides the proper authorities in both states with an opportunity to investigate the facts surrounding the proposed placement in order to determine whether the proposed placement is in the best interests of the child.

Once E.P. signed consents for adoption of the twins, the status of appellants changed from that of providing respite care to that of placement preliminary to a possible adoption, and the ICPC came into effect.

If the date which appellants argue was used rather than the date the children were considered placed preliminary to an adoption, article III(a) would be rendered meaningless because a child could be placed with a party preliminary to an adoption prior to all the conditions being fulfilled.

It is the placement of a child as preliminary to a possible adoption which triggers the ICPC. The district court properly considered January 21, 1997, as the date on which to determine E.P.'s state of residency because that is the date the purpose of the placement of A.M.M. and A.N.M. became clear.

Appellants argue that even if the January 21, 1997, date was proper, E.P. lacked the requisite intent to remain in Missouri on that date. The district court made a finding that on that date, E.P. was a resident of Missouri.

"Where the trial court has made findings of fact and conclusions of law, the function of an appellate court is to determine whether the findings are supported by substantial competent evidence and whether the findings are sufficient to support the trial court's conclusions of law. Substantial evidence is evidence which possesses both relevance and substance and which furnishes a substantial basis of fact from which the issues can reasonably be resolved. Stated in another way, 'substantial evidence' is such legal and relevant evidence as a reasonable person might accept as being sufficient to support a conclusion. [Citation omitted.]" *Tucker v. Hugoton Energy Corp.*, 253 Kan. 373, 377, 855 P.2d 929 (1993).

"'[R]esidence' requires two elements: (1) bodily presence at the location, and (2) intent to remain there either permanently or for an indefinite period." *Teter v. Corley*, 2 Kan.App.2d 540, 543, 584 P.2d 651 (1978).

At the hearing before the district court, E.P. testified that on May 26, 1996, she moved to Kansas City, Missouri, and lived there until February 12, 1997. She claimed that when she moved there, she intended to stay there. She enrolled her two older children in Missouri schools. She had telephone service at her Missouri residence and had a Missouri bank account. She also applied for and received public assistance from the State of Missouri. She used her Missouri address as her residence on the consent forms and returned to Missouri after signing the forms.

"An appellate court does not reweigh the testimony or pass on the credibility of witnesses but accepts as true the evidence and all inferences to be drawn therefrom to support the findings of the trial court and disregards any conflicting evidence or other inferences that might be drawn therefrom." *State v. Orr*, 262 Kan. 312, Syl. ¶ 5, 940 P.2d 42 (1997).

Thus, there was substantial evidence supporting the district court's finding that E.P. was a resident of Missouri on the date the consents were signed.

Remedy under the ICPC

The district court allowed E.P. to revoke her consent and dismissed the adoption petition based on the parties' noncompliance with the ICPC. Appellants contend that if the ICPC applied, the district court imposed an improper remedy.

The ICPC does not define the penalties that should apply when a person, rather than an agency, fails to comply with the ICPC's notice requirements. K.S.A. 38-1202, art. IV. The issue of the proper remedy for failure to comply with the ICPC is an issue of first impression in Kansas. For guidance on how to handle this issue, it is helpful to review how other states have handled such an issue and their rationale.

In *T.M.M.*, 186 Mont. 460, 608 P.2d 130, the natural mother, a resident of Mississippi, executed a parent's consent relinquishing her rights in her child and allowing for adoption by the prospective adoptive parents, residents of Montana. The prospective adoptive parents picked up the child in Mississippi and, after a brief stay, returned to Montana. The prospective adoptive parents then filed a petition for adoption in Montana. The district court in Montana entered an order terminating the natural mother's rights.

The natural mother filed an action in Montana to withdraw her consent. The district court dismissed her challenge for lack of standing. The natural mother appealed, contending that the prospective adoptive parents did not follow the provisions of the ICPC.

The Montana Supreme Court found that pursuant to the ICPC, the prospective adoptive parents were required to furnish SRS with written notice of their intention to bring the child to Montana. The court stated: "By virtue of the failure of the prospective adoptive parents to comply with the Compact, the placement of the child with the prospective adoptive parents in Montana constituted an illegal placement under the provisions of the Compact." 608 P.2d 130. It went on to find that the "parent's consent" was the "legal authorization" held by the prospective adoptive parents and, therefore, their failure to comply with the terms and provisions of the Compact constituted sufficient grounds for revocation of the "parent's consent."

In *In re Adoption/Guardianship No. 3598*, 109 Md.App., 675 A.2d 170, cert. granted 678 A.2d 1047 (Md. 1996), the court was faced with the issue of how to remedy a situation in which the adoptive parents removed a child from the state in violation of the ICPC and held the child for a sufficient period of time that the best interests of the child appeared to dictate adoption, but a natural parent had contested the adoption. It held:

"Allowing violations to continue under the best interests of the child exception is problematic; the exception swallows up the rule. Every time there is a violation of the ICPC, the adoptive parents will have bonded with the child, making adoption the most attractive course. Permitting the adoption will send a message to other adoptive parents that it is not only permissible but advantageous to violate the ICPC, thus eroding the credibility of the ICPC. Eventually, all that will remain of the ICPC is a gutted shell. Ironically, a Compact created and adopted to protect the best interests of the child will be trivialized into non-existence. In this case, unlike other cases that have ignored the violations of the ICPC for the sake of the child's best interests, there is a willing and able natural father who wants custody of the child. We cannot conclude that such placement is contrary to the child's best interests. In cases in which a child can be returned to a natural parent, a circuit court should enforce the spirit of the [ICPC]." 109 Md.App. at 510, 675 A.2d 170.

In *Matter of Jon K.*, 141 Misc.2d 949, 950, 535 N.Y.S.2d 660 (1988), petitioners sought to adopt an infant who had been brought into New York in violation of the ICPC. The court held that the best interests of the child test did not preclude dismissing a petition for adoption where the ICPC was violated.

Other courts have used a best interests of the child test to nullify the failure to comply with the ICPC and allowed the child to remain with the adoptive parent. In *Mtr. of Baby E.*, 104 Misc.2d 185, 189, 427 N.Y.S.2d 705 (1980), the question before the court was what remedy was appropriate where an adoption petition was filed, but the ICPC had not been complied with. The court held that regardless of the violation of the ICPC, the adoption would be granted because it was in the child's best interests. * In these cases, it is important to note that a natural parent was not objecting to the adoption. Thus, the present case can be distinguished.

In *In re C.M.A.*, 557 N.W.2d 353, 358 (Minn.App.1996),*, the court held that a violation of the ICPC did not warrant vacation of the adoption decree where the violation was not knowingly done.

In *In re Baby Girl* 64, 850 S.W.2d 64 (Mo.1993), the natural mother signed a consent to adoption shortly after the birth of the child. The child was then taken from Missouri to Arkansas, and the adoptive parents filed a petition for adoption in Arkansas. The natural mother then sought to revoke her consent. Although the court spoke favorably of the holding in *T.M.M.*, it went on to hold:

"[T]he statute provides that 'any such violation shall constitute full and sufficient grounds for the suspension or revocation of any license, or permit, or other legal authorization held by the sending agency which empowers or allows it to place, or care for children.' We believe this language allows the trial court discretion to enter an order as to the continuing validity of a consent and the custody of the child that it finds just in light of the facts and circumstances of the case before it. Again, at the pinnacle of the court's decision must be the child's best interests, not the interests of the other parties or even 'public policy.' These matters must be determined on a case-by-case basis. Revocation of consent based merely on Compact noncompliance could produce a potentially harsh result that may be contrary to the child's best interests." 850 S.W.2d at 71.

In *In re Adoption of C.L.W.*, 467 So.2d 1106, 1111 (Fla.Dist.App.1985), where the natural mother sought to revoke her consent based on the adoptive parents' noncompliance with the ICPC, the court held:

"[T]he compact is not available to nullify the adoption proceedings below because no harm was suffered by the failure to comply with its requirement of notification to [Health and Rehabilitative Services]. That agency is not complaining and has now made the same determination concerning the best interests of the child as it would have been required to make if notified under the compact. Further, appellant, as well as appellees, had a duty as a 'sending agency' under the compact to notify HRS and she should not now be allowed to complain of such failure by the [adoptive parents] to do so. The requirement for notification is only in order that the receiving state ... can notify the 'sending agency' (either appellant or appellee) that the proposed placement with appellees would not be contrary to the best interests of the child."

In the present case, the district court expressly found E.P. to be a "sending agency," but it went on to find that both parties violated the ICPC's provisions. Appellants argue that because E.P. was the "sending agency" and because she violated the ICPC, the district court wrongfully rewarded her by allowing her to withdraw her consent.

E.P. counters by arguing that appellants should also be considered a "sending agency" because they "brought or caused the children to be brought into the state for purposes of adoption." She argues that appellants also had a duty to comply with the ICPC but failed to do so. In their brief, appellants claimed they "did not knowingly or intentionally violate the provisions of the ICPC."

" 'Sending agency' means a party state, officer or employee thereof; a subdivision of a party state, or officer or employee thereof; a court of a party state, a person, corporation, association, charitable agency or other entity which sends, brings, or causes to be sent or brought any child to another party state." (Emphasis added.) K.S.A. 38-1202, art. II(b).

Appellant C.P. knew that on January 17, 1997, when he and E.P. went to meet with his attorney, E.P. was a Missouri resident. C.P. testified that the parties discussed what steps would need to be taken in order for E.P. to establish residency in Kansas because the Kansas adoption procedure was less complicated, and they could avoid the requirements of the ICPC by doing so. C.P. claimed that they discussed that E.P. could move into a trailer he owned in Kansas in order to establish her residency in Kansas. Appellants were aware of the ICPC, and it appears that they were trying to avoid its application by having E.P. become a Kansas resident prior to the adoption.

Appellants erred in believing that the ICPC would not go into effect until an adoption petition was filed on the theory that the consents were conditional until that date. To allow appellants to claim that they had no duty to comply with the ICPC, when they knew of its existence at the time they were holding the twins preliminary to a prospective adoption, would go against the purpose of the ICPC. Their mistaken belief as to its application date is no excuse when they knew that it would apply in an interstate adoption. Based on the unique fact situation, appellants also violated the ICPC.

Appellants urge us to adopt a best interests of the child exception to counter any noncompliance with the ICPC. We decline to do so. As the Maryland Court of Appeals stated:

[I]t needs to be asked whether it is really good to make 'an exception' of each case on the plea of the 'best interests of the child.' It would not take many dismissals of adoption petitions and removal of children from homes in violation of placement laws to stop these efforts at evasion. They continue because failure to enforce the law encourages others to do likewise. *In re Adoption/Guardianship No. 3598*, 109 Md.App. at 506, 675 A.2d 170 (quoting American Public Welfare Association, The Interstate Compact on the Placement of Children: Compact Administrator's Manual, 3.157-3.158 [1993]).

Such rationale is persuasive and should be followed by this court. Strict compliance with the ICPC should be enforced. Furthermore, Kansas recognizes a parental preference in custody disputes between a parent not found to be unfit and a third-party nonparent. *Guardianship of Williams*, 254 Kan.

814, 826 (1994).

Therefore, based on the specific factual situation in this case, the district court did not err in revoking the consent of E.P. based on a violation of the ICPC.

Child in need of care case

The appellants ask us to consider the effect of a child in need of care case, 97 JC 183, concerning the children. Appellants do not provide any citations to the record to support their claim that the order of placement defeats the goal of the ICPC. The claim seems to be that the revoking of the consent gave the Kansas court jurisdiction over the children which it would otherwise not have. We generally decline to consider this claim as the appellants do not provide any citations to the record to support it. See Kansas Supreme Court Rule 6.02(d) (1996 Kan. Ct. R. Annot. 30). In any event, it appears the district court's order in the child in need of care case was based on a situation existing between the appellants and E.P. at the time of the dismissal of the adoption and would not require a reversal of the dismissal order in any event. Affirmed.

d. Notes and Questions

1) *A.M.M.* and Violation of the ICPC

Violations of the ICPC do not always result in invalidating the adoption. *See Adoption/Guardianship No. 3598*, 701 A.2d 110 (Md. 1997) (decision to allow application filed by third parties residing in Maryland to adopt child that was born in New York was not abuse of discretion, despite violations of the Interstate Compact on the Placement of Children). Should a strict *per se* invalidation rule for violation of the ICPC be adopted? Why/why not?

2) The Hague Convention on Intercountry Adoption

Most commentators are enthusiastic about the Hague Convention on Intercountry Adoption. *See* Bartholet, *infra*; Carlson, *infra*. But not all. Some see dangers to federalism in U.S. ratification of the Hague Convention, and additional costs and delays of a new, federal level of bureaucracy. *See* Croft, *infra; see also* Van Leeuwen, *infra*.

3. Practical and Ethical Considerations

a. Statistics on International Adoptions in the USA

The United States is, by far, the leading country of destination for intercountry adoptions. In 2004, 22,884 foreign-born children were adopted by American families. *See* U.S. State Dept., Office of Children's Issues, *infra*. Top countries of origin were China (mainland) with 7,044 children, Russia with 5,865 children, and Guatemala with 3,264 children. These were also the top three countries for 2003 and 2002. In 2001, the Child Welfare League of America reported that there were 19,237 intercountry adoptions by American families while there were 50,000 adopted from our public welfare system. No statistics were available for private adoptions. *See* Child Welfare League of America (CWLA), *International Adoption: Trends and Issues,* website http://ndas.cwla.org. Sixty-three percent of children of international adoption were girls in 2001. This high number is due primarily to mainland China's continued one-child policy, where girls are more often abandoned. Of the 4,649 children adopted from China in 2001, 96% were girls. *Id.* Romania, in June 2001, issued a moratorium on international adoption until new procedures are in effect. *Id*. Their numbers dropped from a high of 1,122 adoptions in 2000 to 57 adoptions in 2004. *See* U.S. State Dept., Office of Children's Issues, *infra*.

4. Bibliography

Elizabeth Bartholet, *International Adoptions: Propriety, Prospects and Pragmatics,* 13 J. Am. Acad. Matrim. Law. 181 (1996).

Richard R. Carlson, *The Emerging Law of Intercountry Adoption: An Analysis of the Hague Conference on Intercountry Adoption,* 30 Tulsa L.J. 243 (1994).

Richard R. Carlson, *The Emerging Law of Intercountry Adoption,* 30 Tulsa L. J. 244 (1994).

Child Welfare League of America (CWLA), *International Adoption: Trends and Issues,* website http://ndas.cwla.org.

Homer J. Clark, Jr., Domestic Relations §18.2 (1968).

Defense of Children International, The Hague Convention on Protection of Children in Respect of Intercountry Adoption <http://childhouse.uio.no/childrens_rights/dci_hagu.html>.

Gina M. Croft, Note, *The Ill Effects of A United States Ratification of the Hague Convention on Protection of Children and Cooperation in Respect of Intercountry Adoption,* 33 Ga. J. Int'l & Compar. L 621 (2005).

Bernadette W. Hartfield, *The Role of the Interstate Compact on the Placement of Children in Interstate Adoption,* 68 Neb. L. Rev. 292 (1989).

Hague Conference on Private International Law, Full Status Report # 33, Convention of 29 May 1993 on Protection of Children and Co-Operation in respect of Intercountry Adoption, available at http://hcch.e-vision.nl/index_en.php?act=conventions.status&cid=69 (last seen May 18, 2006). Peter H. Pfund, *Intercountry Adoption: The 1993 Hague Convention: Its Purpose, Implementation and Promise,* 28 Fam. L. Q. 53, 54 (1994).

Protection of Children and Co-Operation in Respect of Intercountry Adoption, <http://www.hcch.net/e/status/stat33e.html> (August 17, 2001); Status Sheet, *id.* at <http://www.hcch.net/e/status/adoshte.html>.

Intercountry Adoption, innocinti digest, December 1998, at 6-7.

U.S. Dept. of Justice, Immigration and Naturalization Service, 1998 Statistical Yearbook of the Immigration and Naturalization Service (November 2000) <http://www.ins.usdoj.gov/graphics/aboutins/statistics/1998yb.pdf> (seen Aug. 1, 2001).

U.S. State Dept., Office of Children's Issues, *Immigrant Visas Issued to Orphans Coming to the U.S.,* http://www.travel.state.gov/family/adoption/stats/stats (last seen May 18, 2006).

U.S. State Dept., Intercountry Adoption, *How Will the United States Implement the Hague Convention,* available at http://travel.state.gov/family/adoption/convention/convention_2313.html# (last seen May 18, 2006).

Michelle Van Leeuwen, Comments, *The Politics of Adoptions Across Borders: Whose Interests Are Served? (A Look At the Emerging Market of Infants from China),* 8 Pac. Rim L. & Pol'y J. 189, 189-199 (1999).

J.H.A. van Loon, Report on Intercountry Adoption, The Hague Conference on Private International Law, Prel. Doc. No. 1 (Apr. 1990).

B. INDIAN CHILD WELFARE ACT

1. Background

a. Indian Child Welfare Act

In 1978, Congress enacted the Indian Child Welfare Act (ICWA) based on findings that "an alarmingly high percentage of Indian families are broken up by the removal, often unwarranted, of their children from them by nontribal public and private agencies and that an alarmingly high percentage of such children are placed in non-Indian foster and adoptive homes and institutions" and that "the States . . . have often failed to recognize the essential tribal relations of Indian people and the cultural and social standards prevailing in Indian communities and families." Pub. L. 95-608, §2, 92 Stat. 3069 (Nov. 8, 1978), codified in 25 U.S.C. § 1901(4) & (5). The ICWA established a new federal policy "to promote the stability and security of Indian tribes and families by the establishment of minimum Federal standards for the removal of Indian children from their families and the placement of such children in foster or adoptive homes which will reflect the unique values of Indian culture . . . ."

2. Statutes, Cases and Doctrines

a. Indian Child Welfare Act

ICWA applies to both voluntary and involuntary "child placement proceedings" (defined to mean foster care placement, TPR (Termination of Parental Rights), preadoptive or adoptive placement, 25 U.S. C. § 1903 (1)) in state courts involving an Indian child. ICWA grants the Indian tribe exclusive jurisdiction if the Indian child resides on or is domiciled within the reservation. 25 U.S.C. § 1911(a). It also provides that for a child not so domiciled or residing, a state court must transfer jurisdiction to the Indian tribe if a parent, Indian custodian, or the child's tribe request that, unless a parent objects or there is "good cause to the contrary." 25 U.S.C. § 1911(b). The child's tribe has the right to intervene in any state court proceeding for foster care placement or TPR. Notice must be given to the Indian child's tribe of any involuntary proceeding for TPR or foster care placement, and special procedural protections apply. 25 U.S.C. §§ 1912, 1913. In voluntary cases where a parent consents to adoption, the consent must be in writing, executed before a judge, accompanied by the presiding judge's certificate of compliance with procedural protections, language comprehension, and the consent may not be taken before or within 10 days after birth of the child, and the consent may be withdrawn for any reason any time prior to entry to the final adoption decree; after entry of the decree the consent may be withdrawn for at least two years after the adoption upon grounds of fraud or duress. 25 U.S.C. § 1913. In state court adoption cases involving Indian children, "a preference shall be given, in the absence of good cause to the contrary, to a placement with (1) a member of the child's extended family; (2) other members of the Indian child's tribe; or (3) other Indian families." 25 U.S.C. § 1915(a).

b. *Mississippi Band of Choctaw Indians v. Holyfield*
Mississippi Band of Choctaw Indians v. Holyfield
490 U.S. 20 (1989)

Case Summary: *Mississippi Band of Choctaw Indians v. Holyfield*, 490 U.S. 20 (1989) illustrates the breadth of the tribal court preemption of state court jurisdiction in child placement (custody, guardianship, adoption) cases. The ICWA reserves exclusive jurisdiction to tribal courts of Indian children "domiciled" on a reservation. In *Mississippi Band*, an Indian mother and father, domiciled on the Choctaw reservation, decided to relinquish the twins the mother was carrying to non-Indians (the Holyfields) for adoption. The mother traveled off-reservation to give birth, turned the children over to the prospective adoptive parents, and she and the father signed consents to adoption. The Holyfields petitioned for adoption in state court and the adoption decree was signed. Two months later, the tribe petitioned to set aside the adoption on grounds that the children were "domiciled" on the reservation at birth and the ICWA gave the tribal court exclusive jurisdiction. The Mississippi state court rejected the claim, finding that the children born off the reservation by deliberate choice of the parents were not "domiciled" on the reservation under Mississippi law. The U.S. Supreme Court reversed concluding that

Congress intended a uniform national definition of domicile, emphasizing the congressional policy to protect Indian families and tribal court jurisdiction, and concluded that the common law rule that a child acquires the domicile of his or her parents applied in this case, giving the newborns the domicile of the reservation. Three dissenters (led by Stevens, J.) argued to protect the decision of the parents by allowing them to choose the domicile of their children off the reservation.

c. Notes and Questions

1) The "Existing Indian Family" Doctrine

Today, some controversy about the ICWA involves the "existing Indian family" doctrine that holds that the ICWA only applies to children in an existing Indian family. *See In re Bridget R.*, 41 Cal. App. 4th 1483 (1996); *Hampton v. J.A.L.*, 658 So.2d 331 (La. App. 1995), *aff'd*, 662 So.2d 478 (1995). However, the trend seems to be toward rejection of the "existing Indian child" doctrine in recognition of Congress' intent to protect tribal as well as familial interests in Indian children. *See In re Elliott*, 554 N.W.2d 32 (Mich. App. 1996); *Adoption of Riffle*, 922 P.2d 510 (Mont. 1996); In re Baby Boy Doe, 849 P.2d 925 (Idaho 1993), *cert. den. Sub. Nom Swenson v. Oglala Sioux Tribe*, 510 U.S. 860 (1993).

3. Practical and Ethical Considerations

a. Different Treatment

Are the ICWA and the MEPA-II (chapter 13) reconcilable?

4. Bibliography

Lupe Funaki, Kimberly Kennedy Bitner, & Gary Bryner, *Comment on the Indian Child Welfare Act*, Utah Juvenile Court Guidebook 207 (Lynn D. Wardle, Gen. Ed. 1998) (Appendix).
Michael C. Snyder, *An Overview of the Indian Child Welfare Act*, 7 St. Thomas L. Rev. 815 (1995).

CHAPTER 15

Preventing Procreation: Contraception and Abortion

A. CONTRACEPTION

1. Background

a. Birth Control Generally

Just as there have been efforts made throughout history to find technologies and socially acceptable ways to overcome childlessness, throughout history there also have been efforts made to prevent unwanted childbearing – that is, to allow persons to engage in sexual relations without risk of procreating. For example, the ancient book of Genesis describes (with disapproval) the contraceptive practice of Onan, the son of Judah (Genesis 38: 8-10). Modern medical technologies, particularly those developed since the 1950s, have given humanity unprecedented control of fecundity, though not without some notable risks and costs. Today, a variety of contraceptives make it possible for humans to engage in sexual relations with little risk of procreating. Because it is medically possible, does not necessarily mean, however, it is socially acceptable, morally justifiable, or legally permissible. The cases in this section examine the struggle to define where the line should be drawn (what practices to prevent childbearing should be legally permissible), who should draw that line, and the relevance of marriage and families to the issue of contraception and the scope of any relevant constitutional rights.

2. Statutes, Cases and Doctrines

a. *Griswold v. Connecticut*
Estelle T. Griswold et al., v. State of Connecticut
381 U.S. 479 (1965)
Mr. JUSTICE DOUGLAS delivered the opinion of the Court.
***

[Appellants, workers at the Planned Parenthood League's Center in New Haven, Connecticut] gave information, instruction, and medical advice to married persons as to the means of preventing conception. They examined the wife and prescribed the best contraceptive device or material for her use. Fees were usually charged, although some couples were serviced free of charge.

The statutes whose constitutionality is involved in this appeal are ss 53-- 32 and 54--196 of the General Statutes of Connecticut (1958 rev.). The former provides:

Any person who uses any drug, medicinal article or instrument for the purpose of preventing conception shall be fined not less than fifty dollars or imprisoned not less than sixty days nor more than one year or be both fined and imprisoned.

Section 54--196 provides:

Any person who assists, abets, counsels, causes, hires or commands another to commit any offense may be prosecuted and punished as if he were the principal offender.

The appellants were found guilty as accessories and fined $100 each, against the claim that the accessory statute as so applied violated the Fourteenth Amendment. The Appellate Division of the Circuit Court affirmed. The Supreme Court of Errors affirmed that judgment. ***
***

*** We do not sit as a super-legislature to determine the wisdom, need, and propriety of laws that touch economic problems, business affairs, or social conditions. This law, however, operates directly on an intimate relation of husband and wife and their physician's role in one aspect of that relation.
***

By *Pierce v. Society of Sisters, supra,* the right to educate one's children as one chooses is made applicable to the States by the force of the First and Fourteenth Amendments. By *Meyer v. State of Nebraska, supra,* the same dignity is given the right to study the German language in a private school. In other words, the State may not, consistently with the spirit of the First Amendment, contract the spectrum of available knowledge. ***
***

The foregoing cases suggest that specific guarantees in the Bill of Rights have penumbras, formed by emanations from those guarantees that help give them life and substance. *See Poe v. Ullman,* 367 U.S. 497, 516-- 522 (dissenting opinion). Various guarantees create zones of privacy. *** [First, Third, Fourth, Fifth, and Ninth Amendment cases discussed.]
***

The present case, then, concerns a relationship lying within the zone of privacy created by several fundamental constitutional guarantees. And it concerns a law which, in forbidding the use of contraceptives rather than regulating their manufacture or sale, seeks to achieve its goals by means having a maximum destructive impact upon that relationship. Such a law cannot stand in light of the familiar principle, so often applied by this Court, that a 'governmental purpose to control or prevent activities constitutionally subject to state regulation may not be achieved by means which sweep unnecessarily broadly and thereby invade the area of protected freedoms.' *NAACP v. Alabama,* 377 U.S. 288, 307. Would we allow the police to search the sacred precincts of marital bedrooms for telltale signs of the use of contraceptives? The very idea is repulsive to the notions of privacy surrounding the marriage relationship.

We deal with a right of privacy older than the Bill of Rights--older than our political parties, older than our school system. Marriage is a coming together for better or for worse, hopefully enduring, and intimate to the degree of being sacred. It is an association that promotes a way of life, not causes; a harmony in living, not political faiths; a bilateral loyalty, not commercial or social projects. Yet it is an association for as noble a purpose as any involved in our prior decisions.

Reversed.

Mr. JUSTICE GOLDBERG, whom THE CHIEF JUSTICE and Mr. JUSTICE BRENNAN join, concurring.

I agree with the Court that Connecticut's birth-control law unconstitutionally intrudes upon the right of marital privacy, and I join in its opinion and judgment. *** My conclusion that the concept of liberty *** embraces the right of marital privacy though that right is not mentioned explicitly in the Constitution is supported both by numerous decisions of this Court, referred to in the Court's opinion, and by the language and history of the Ninth Amendment. *** I add these words to emphasize the relevance of that Amendment to the Court's holding.
***

In determining which rights are fundamental, judges are not left at large to decide cases in light of their personal and private notions. Rather, they must look to the 'traditions and (collective) conscience of our people' to determine whether a principle is 'so rooted (there) * * * as to be ranked as fundamental.' *Snyder v. Com. of Massachusetts*, 291 U.S. 97, 105. The inquiry is whether a right involved 'is of such a character that it cannot be denied without violating those 'fundamental principles of liberty and justice which lie at the base of all our civil and political institutions' * * *.' *Powell v. State of Alabama*, 287 U.S. 45, 67. *** ***

I agree with Mr. Justice Harlan's statement in his dissenting opinion in *Poe v. Ullman*, 367 U.S. 497, 551--552: 'Certainly the safeguarding of the home does not follow merely from the sanctity of property rights. The home derives its pre-eminence as the seat of family life. And the integrity of that life is something so fundamental that it has been found to draw to its protection the principles of more than one explicitly granted Constitutional right. * * * Of this whole 'private realm of family life' it is difficult to imagine what is more private or more intimate than a husband and wife's marital relations.'

The entire fabric of the Constitution and the purposes that clearly underlie its specific guarantees demonstrate that the rights to marital privacy and to marry and raise a family are of similar order and magnitude as the fundamental rights specifically protected.

Although the Constitution does not speak in so many words of the right of privacy in marriage, I cannot believe that it offers these fundamental rights no protection. The fact that no particular provision of the Constitution explicitly forbids the State from disrupting the traditional relation of the family--a relation as old and as fundamental as our entire civilization--surely does not show that the Government was meant to have the power to do so. Rather, as the Ninth Amendment expressly recognizes, there are fundamental personal rights such as this one, which are protected from abridgment by the Government though not specifically mentioned in the Constitution.
***

Finally, it should be said of the Court's holding today that it in no way interferes with a State's proper regulation of sexual promiscuity or misconduct. As my Brother Harlan so well stated in his dissenting opinion in *Poe v. Ullman, supra*, 367 U.S. at 553.

Adultery, homosexuality and the like are sexual intimacies which the State forbids * * * but the intimacy of husband and wife is necessarily an essential and accepted feature of the institution of marriage, an institution which the State not only must allow, but which always and in every age it has fostered and protected. It is one thing when the State exerts its power either to forbid extra-marital sexuality * * * or to say who may marry, but it is quite another when, having acknowledged a marriage and the intimacies inherent in it, it undertakes to regulate by means of the criminal law the details of that intimacy.

In sum, I believe that the right of privacy in the marital relation is fundamental and basic--a personal right 'retained by the people' within the meaning of the Ninth Amendment. Connecticut cannot constitutionally abridge this fundamental right, which is protected by the Fourteenth Amendment from infringement by the States. I agree with the Court that petitioners' convictions must therefore be reversed.

Mr. JUSTICE HARLAN, concurring in the judgment.

I fully agree with the judgment of reversal, but find myself unable to join the Court's opinion. The reason is that it seems to me to evince an approach to this case very much like that taken by my Brothers BLACK and STEWART in dissent, namely: the Due Process Clause of the Fourteenth Amendment does not touch this Connecticut statute unless the enactment is found to violate some right assured by the letter or penumbra of the Bill of Rights.
***

In my view this Connecticut law as applied to married couples deprives them of 'liberty' without due process of law, as that concept is used in the Fourteenth Amendment. I therefore concur in the judgment of the Court reversing these convictions under Connecticut's aiding and abetting statute.

*** Suffice it to say that this is not the first time this Court has had occasion to articulate that the liberty entitled to protection under the Fourteenth Amendment includes the right 'to marry, establish a home and bring up children,' *Meyer v. State of Nebraska*, 262 U.S. 390, 399 ***. Surely the right invoked in this case, to be free of regulation of the intimacies of the marriage relationship, 'come(s) to this Court with a momentum for respect lacking when appeal is made to liberties which derive merely from shifting economic arrangements.' *

The Connecticut anti-contraceptive statute deals rather substantially with this relationship. For it forbids all married persons the right to use birth-control devices, regardless of whether their use is dictated by considerations of family planning, * health, or indeed even of life itself. * The anti-use statute *** prohibits doctors from affording advice to married persons on proper and effective methods of birth control. ***

***

*** I wholly fail to see how the ban on the use of contraceptives by married couples in any way reinforces the State's ban on illicit sexual relationships. ***

In these circumstances one is rather hard pressed to explain how the ban on use by married persons in any way prevents use of such devices by persons engaging in illicit sexual relations and thereby contributes to the State's policy against such relationships. ***

Mr. JUSTICE BLACK, with whom Mr. JUSTICE STEWART joins, dissenting.

*** In order that there may be no room at all to doubt why I vote as I do, I feel constrained to add that the law is every bit as offensive to me as it is my Brethren of the majority and my Brothers HARLAN, WHITE and GOLDBERG ***. There is no single one of the graphic and eloquent strictures and criticisms fired at the policy of this Connecticut law either by the Court's opinion or by those of my concurring Brethren to which I cannot subscribe--except their conclusion that the evil qualities they see in the law make it unconstitutional.

***

*** I like my privacy as well as the next one, but I am nevertheless compelled to admit that government has a right to invade it unless prohibited by some specific constitutional provision. For these reasons I cannot agree with the Court's judgment and the reasons it gives for holding this Connecticut law unconstitutional.

***

The due process argument which my Brothers HARLAN and WHITE adopt here is based, as their opinions indicate, on the premise that this Court is vested with power to invalidate all state laws that it consider to be arbitrary, capricious, unreasonable, or oppressive, or this Court's belief that a particular state law under scrutiny has no 'rational or justifying' purpose, or is offensive to a 'sense of fairness and justice.' If these formulas based on 'natural justice,' or others which mean the same thing, are to prevail, they require judges to determine what is or is not constitutional on the basis of their own appraisal of what laws are unwise or unnecessary. The power to make such decisions is of course that of a legislative body. ***

***

*** I merely point out that the reasoning stated in Meyer and Pierce was the same natural law due process philosophy which many later opinions repudiated, and which I cannot accept. ***

My Brother GOLDBERG has adopted the recent discovery that the Ninth Amendment as well as the Due Process Clause can be used by this Court as authority to strike down all state legislation which this Court thinks violates 'fundamental principles of liberty and justice,' or is contrary to the 'traditions and (collective) conscience of our people.' He also states, without proof satisfactory to me, that in making decisions on this basis judges will not consider 'their personal and private notions.' One may ask how they can avoid considering them. Our Court certainly has no machinery with which to take a Gallup Poll. And the scientific miracles of this age have not yet produced a gadget which the Court can use to determine what traditions are rooted in the '(collective) conscience of our people.' ***

***

So far as I am concerned, Connecticut's law as applied here is not forbidden by any provision of the Federal Constitution as that Constitution was written, and I would therefore affirm.

Mr. JUSTICE STEWART, whom Mr. JUSTICE BLACK joins, dissenting.

*** I think this is an uncommonly silly law. As a practical matter, the law is obviously unenforceable, except in the oblique context of the present case. As a philosophical matter, I believe the use of contraceptives in the relationship of marriage should be left to personal and private choice, based upon each individual's moral, ethical, and religious beliefs. As a matter of social policy, I think professional counsel about methods of birth control should be available to all, so that each individual's choice can be meaningfully made. But we are not asked in this case to say whether we think this law is unwise, or even asinine. We are asked to hold that it violates the United States Constitution. And that I cannot do.

***

*** We are here to decide cases 'agreeably to the Constitution and laws of the United States.' It is the essence of judicial duty to subordinate our own personal views, our own ideas of what legislation is wise and what is not. *** [T]he people of Connecticut can freely exercise their true Ninth and Tenth Amendment rights to persuade their elected representatives to repeal it. That is the constitutional way to take this law off the books.

b. Notes and Questions

1) *Griswold* Questions

How important was the marital context for the decision in *Griswold*? What does that suggest, if anything, about the scope of the constitutionally-protected right to engage in sexual or procreative activities? Note the different theories proffered in justification of the result, and the different constitutional amendments cited. What is the main doctrinal difference between Goldberg and Douglas and Harlan?

2) *Eisenstadt* and *Carey*

Seven years after *Griswold*, in *Eisenstadt v. Baird*, 405 U.S. 438 (1972), the Court invalidated a Massachusetts law that made it a felony for anyone other than a registered doctor or pharmacist to dispense contraceptives and allowed doctors and pharmacists to distribute contraceptives only to married persons except when necessary to prevent the spread of disease. A doctor who was convicted of violating the law when he gave a contraceptive to a young unmarried woman following an address at a college successfully challenged the law. Without stating that single persons have any fundamental right to engage in nonmarital sexual activity or use contraceptives, the Court held that the Massachusetts law violated the equal protection clause of the Fourteenth Amendment. Writing for the four-member majority, Justice Brennan rejected the state's claim that the law deterred premarital or illicit sex and furthered public health interests of the state as unfounded and unproven. He also declared that:

> [W]hatever the right of the individual to access to contraceptives may be, the rights must be the same for the unmarried and the married alike. . . . If the right of privacy means anything, it is the right of the individual, married or single, to be free of unwarranted governmental intrusion into matters so fundamentally affecting a person as the decision whether to bear or beget a child.

Id. at 453.

In 1977, the Supreme Court invalidated a New York statute making it a crime for anyone but a pharmacist to distribute contraceptives to persons sixteen or over, for anyone to advertise or display contraceptives, or for anyone to distribute contraceptives to minors under age sixteen. In *Carey v. Population Services International*, 431 U.S. 684 (1977), Justice Brennan, writing for a majority, found the prohibition against advertising and the restriction that only pharmacists distribute contraceptives to adults was unconstitutional under the plain principles of *Griswold* and *Eisenstadt. Id.* at 689-91. *See* Note 4, *infra*.

3) Constitutional Right of Adults to Use Contraceptives

In *Skinner v. Oklahoma*, 316 U.S. 535 (1942) the Supreme Court invalidated an Oklahoma law providing sterilization for any persons convicted three times of crimes of moral turpitude. The Court uttered it's now-famous declaration: "We are dealing here with legislation which involves one of the basic civil rights of man. Marriage and procreation are fundamental to the very existence and survival of the race." *Id.* at 541. The Oklahoma statute violated the Equal Protection guarantee, the Court reasoned, in imposing such a severe penalty on such a basic right upon the grounds of "conspicuously artificial" categories of crime. *Id.* at 542. While the *Skinner* holding is very specific, and the Court has not taken the opportunity to give much more guidance regarding the scope of the "basic civil right" involving procreation, some commentators argue for giving *Skinner* a broad reading as establishing a fundamental individual right to procreate.

As *Griswold* shows, clearly some dimensions of sexual intimacy are protected in at least some contexts by a substantive due process doctrine of liberty or privacy (e.g., consensual marital intercourse between husband and wife). It also is clear that some sexual practices in at least some contexts are not protected as fundamental constitutional rights (e.g., homosexual practices, sexual relations between adult males and minor females, the use for sexual stimulation of "kiddie porn," nonconsensual sex - such as rape, etc.). The question is how to distinguish the protected-as-a-fundamental-right from the unprotected. What standard does the Court suggest in the various *Griswold* opinions? If choice is an element, what are the boundaries of the choice? Why does the "right to procreate" include the right to use products designed to *prevent* conception and procreation? What is the scope of constitutionally-protected procreative rights? Is there any traditional indicia of constitutional super-consensus (e.g., the kind of broad consensus needed to bring the Constitution into being or to enact an amendment to it) about this issue or about who should decide the issue? Should legislators or judges draw the lines between permissible and impermissible? Why? Are there any relevant differences between the social consequences of procreative (sexual) behavior within marriage and outside of marriage? Does it matter to the children born as a result of the behavior?

Despite the broad *Eisenstadt* dicta, the extent to which unmarried adults have a constitutionally protected right of privacy to put contraceptives to their intended use, i.e., to engage in consensual, extramarital sexual relations, was arguably somewhat unclear until the Court decided *Lawrence v. Texas*, 539 U.S. 558 (2003). *Eisenstadt* was decided on equal protection doctrine, not on substantive due process. Prior to the Supreme Court's decision in *Bowers v. Hardwick,* 478 U.S. 186 (1986), rejecting the claim that the Constitution (right of privacy) bars states from criminally prohibiting private homosexual acts done by consenting adults, several lower courts held that consensual sexual intercourse between unmarried persons was protected by the constitutional right of privacy. However, in *Bowers* the Supreme Court rejected an expansive reading of its substantive due process (privacy) precedents, and emphasized that those cases involved protection of basic relationships of family ("family, marriage or procreation") by means of social regulations having "ancient roots." *Bowers* suggests that the contraceptive cases discussed above might not encompass private sexual intercourse between consenting unmarried persons. Likewise, in *Zablocki v. Redhail,* 434 U.S. 374, 386 (1977), the majority justified its holding that a Wisconsin law restricting marriage by persons with unpaid child support obligations was unconstitutional because *inter alia* the state allowed sexual relations legally to take place only within marriage; Wisconsin's fornication statute was quoted with approval. *Id.* at n. 11. *Bowers*, however, was overruled by *Lawrence v. Texas*, 539 U.S. 558 (2003). Judge Kennedy, writing for the majority, held that petitioners were free as adults to engage in private conduct [consensual homosexual sex] in the exercise of their liberty under the Due Process Clause of the Fourteenth Amendment:

> ...the Due Process Clause gives them the full right to engage in their conduct without intervention of the government. It is a promise of the Constitution that there is a realm of personal liberty which the government may not enter. The Texas statute furthers no legitimate state interest which can justify its intrusion into the personal and private life of the individual.

Id.

Lawrence v. Texas is discussed more fully in Chapter 19.

4) Constitutional Right of Minors to Use Contraceptives

The Supreme Court has only once discussed a statute restricting the use of or access to contraceptives by minors. In *Carey v. Population Services International*, 431 U.S. 684 (1977), Justice Brennan, who authored the opinion for the majority regarding contraceptive advertising and dispensing to adults, could not muster a majority for his analysis invalidating another provision of the New York law that prohibited the sale of contraceptives to minors under sixteen years. Writing for only four members of the Court, Justice Brennan reasoned that "the right of privacy in connection with decisions relating to procreation extends to minors as well as adults." *Id.* at 693. Since the state may not restrict access to contraceptives by adults, he reasoned, it may not restrict minors' access to contraceptives. *Id.* at 694. The state could adopt a policy imposing unwanted teenage pregnancy as a punishment for fornication, he declared. And since the state had conceded that "there is no evidence that teenage extramarital sexual activity increases in proportion to the availability of contraceptives," he rejected the argument "that juvenile sexual activity will be deterred by making contraceptives more difficult to obtain." *Id.* (Brennan, J.).

However, a majority of the Supreme Court refused to endorse Justice Brennan's analysis generally, or his declaration that the constitutional rights of procreative privacy recognized by the Court in cases involving adults extend to minors also. Justices White and Stevens separately agreed that the prohibition against distribution of contraceptives was unconstitutional, emphasizing (with apparent reference to the state's concession) that the state had failed to prove that the prohibition against distribution of contraceptives to minors deterred any minors from engaging in sexual relations. But they explicitly rejected as "frivolous" the idea that minors had a constitutional right "to put contraceptives to their intended use." *Id.* at 703 (White, J., concurring); *id.* at 713 (Stevens, J., concurring). Justice Stevens also emphatically distinguished the abortion cases. *Id.* at 703 (Stevens, J. concurring). Justice Powell likewise separately agreed that the law restricting sale of contraceptives to minors under 16 was unconstitutional. He, like Justice Stevens, found the law to be defective because, *inter alia*, it would even prevent parents from distributing contraceptives to their own children. *Id.* at 707-08 (Powell, J., concurring); *id.* at 713 (Stevens, J., concurring). But Justice Powell strongly endorsed other state regulations including parental consultation requirements. Chief Justice Burger and Justice Rehnquist dissented, the latter filing an opinion unequivocally endorsing the propriety of state legislation designed to "discourage unmarried minors under sixteen from having promiscuous sexual intercourse with one another." *Id.* at 719 (Rehnquist, J., dissenting).

The multiple opinions in *Carey* have spawned a kaleidoscope of theories and approaches, but no clear constitutional doctrine regarding the rights of minors to use contraceptives. In the decades since *Carey* was decided, the Supreme Court has not considered further the question of minors' rights regarding the use of contraceptives. In 1981, however, the Court decided a related case that has some bearing upon the issue. In *Michael M. v. Superior Court*, 450 U.S. 458 (1981), the Court upheld a California "statutory rape" criminal law against an equal protection (gender discrimination) challenge. The California law, like laws in many states, provided a criminal penalty for males, but not females, who violated the prohibition against sexual intercourse by males with underage girls. While there was no single opinion for the Court, a clear majority of the justices explicitly expressed their belief that states constitutionally have the authority to criminally prohibit sexual intercourse among teenagers. 450 U.S. at 473 n. 8 (Rehnquist, J., plurality opinion for four justices); *id.* at 497 (Stevens, J., dissenting opinion expressing "no doubt about the validity of a state law prohibiting all unmarried teenagers from engaging in sexual intercourse . . . ."). A dissenting opinion of Justice Brennan, however, joined by Justices Marshall and White, noted that the prior decisions of the Court would not foreclose a challenge to such a statute. *Id.* at 491 n. 5. Even though Justice White joined Brennan's dissent, the carefully-phrased Brennan footnote left room to accommodate his opinion in *Carey* that constitutional precedent does not bar the states from prohibiting sexual activity by teenagers. 431 U.S. at 702, 703.

3. Practical and Ethical Considerations

a. *Wisconsin v. Oakley*

David Oakley, a father of nine children, agreed to plea no contest to three counts of intentionally refusing to support his children. As a condition of probation, Mr. Oakley could not father anymore children unless he showed the court that he could provide for them and the ones he already had. In *Wisconsin v. Oakley*, 629 N.W.2d 200 (Wis. 2001), cert. denied 537 U.S. 813 (2002), the Supreme Court of Wisconsin upheld the condition of probation, finding no constitutional violation since the condition did not eliminate Mr. Oakley's ability to exercise his constitutional right to procreate. Do you agree with the court? As a practical matter, is this a realistic approach to enforcing the duty of support? What happens if he fathers another child? *But see Trammell v. State*, 751 N.E.2d 283 (Ind. App. Jun 18, 2001) (probation condition that woman convicted of felony neglect not get pregnant overbroad and unconstitutional.)

4. Bibliography

Janet Dolgin, *The Family in Transition: From* Griswold *to* Eisenstadt *and Beyond*, 82 Geo. L. J. 1519 (1994).
Bruce Hafen, *The Constitutional Status of Marriage, Kinship and Privacy–Balancing the Individual and Social Interests*, 81 Mich. L. Rev. 463 (1983).
Kenneth Karst, *The Freedom of Intimate Association*, 89 Yale L. J. 624 (1980).
Lynn D. Wardle, *Parents' Rights v. Minors' Rights Regarding the Provision of Contraceptives to Minors*, 68 Neb. L. Rev. 216-260 (1989).

B. ABORTION

1. Background

a. Basic Policy Issues

No subject of state regulation affecting family interests has been the focus of greater or more heated controversy during the past quarter of a century than the subject of abortion. The propriety of laws prohibiting, restricting, or regulating abortion was debated with growing intensity for more than a decade before the landmark 1973 Supreme Court ruling in *Roe v. Wade*, 410 U.S. 113 (1973). Since that decision, much litigation, and social and political controversy over abortion has swollen to even greater proportions. Between 1973 and 2000, abortion regulations were the subject of more than thirty *major* decisions of the United State Supreme Court, and of hundreds of decisions by lower federal courts and state courts. Obviously, abortion is more than a family law issue. It implicates important questions about medicine (i.e., medical procedures, professional autonomy, medical ethics), constitutional law (the constitutional doctrine of privacy, the balance of powers, federalism, judicial activism, substantive due process), individual rights (the rights of pregnant women, of husbands and unwed fathers, of minors, of parents, of "the unborn"), religion and morality (the morality of abortion, the role of religion in resolving public controversies), public policy (relating law and moral order in a democracy, population policy, private killing, health policy), welfare (access of indigents to medical procedures), etc. But the questions of family law are fundamental because abortion and the abortion decisions affect family interests, family relationships, other family laws, and basic family policies. Indeed the controversy over abortion goes to the very definition and composition of the family: Is a fetus a member of the family - a child? Is abortion a form of child abuse? What distinguishes the so-called "fundamental right" of abortion from the "fundamental wrong" of infanticide? Abortion also directly affects mother-father relations and interests; the legal interests of the husband-father may conflict with those of the wife-mother; and abortion restrictions raise fundamental issues of state regulation of private decisions of husbands and wives regarding childbearing; and if the pregnant female seeking an abortion is a minor, the abortion may raise questions regarding the rights of minors to obtain abortion without parental consent, or the rights of parents to participate in the most profound moral-medical dilemmas of their daughter, or the rights of minors to refuse medical treatment selected by their parents.

These questions are fundamentally policy questions, and the abortion cases are basically political decisions. That makes it very difficult to measure and predict the development of the doctrine of these cases. *Roe v. Wade* and its progeny are based upon controversial policy assumptions (about the status of the fetus, the "privacy" of the abortion decision, the validity of state interests in preventing abortion, the role of the judiciary, etc.). Persons who agree with those assumptions are likely to give the abortion decisions broad interpretation and application; persons who disagree with those assumptions are likely to give those decisions more restrictive interpretation and narrow application. The federal courts, by and large, have tended to be very defensive about the abortion cases, and to give them very broad reading.

b. Brief History of Abortion Regulation

The history of abortion law in Anglo-American law can be divided into three general areas: common law, statutory, and constitutional. According to Blackstone, abortion was prohibited at common law, from the thirteenth century, after the quickening of the fetus.

> Life is the immediate gift of God, a right inherent by nature in every individual; and it begins in contemplation of law as soon as an infant is able to stir in the mother's womb. For if a woman is quick with child, and by a potion or otherwise, killeth it in her womb; or if anyone beat her, whereby the child dieth in her body, and she is delivered of a dead child; this, though not murder, was by the ancient law homicide or manslaughter. But the modern law doth not look upon this offense in quite so atrocious a light, but merely as a heinous misdemeanor.

W. Blackstone, *infra,* at 129, 130.

The nineteenth century movement to codify and clarify the law coincided with the emergence of medicine as a science, rather than an art, and one of the defining issues in that emergence was the acceptance of the facts of human reproduction, and the belief that each individual human life *in utero* begins at conception. Influenced by the emerging medical profession, abortion law in all states stabilized upon the principle that abortion was illegal throughout gestation (from conception), except when necessary to save the life (or health in some states) of the mother. However, behind the written law was a different reality. Some doctors were willing to perform abortions surreptitiously, so the wealthy usually could obtain medically-assisted abortions, and dangerous back alley abortionists offered their services to desperate, poorer (mostly single) women.

With the development of safer abortion technology in the 1950s, the modern movement to liberalize abortion laws in America began. In 1959, the American Law Institute's proposed Model Penal Code (MPC) recommending expanding the exception to laws prohibiting abortion to permit abortion "when childbirth posed a grave danger to the physical or mental health of a woman, when there was a high likelihood of fetal abnormality, or when the pregnancy had resulted from rape or incest." By 1970, fourteen states had adopted the MPC abortion proposal. Thus, by 1973, when the Supreme Court entered the picture, there was a clear trend among the states to moderately liberalize the nineteenth century criminal abortion statutes to permit abortion in these three categories of "hard cases." In addition, four states repealed their nineteenth century abortion laws and replaced them with statutes that allowed any pregnant woman to receive an abortion with medical approval during early pregnancy.

Advocates of liberal abortion were dissatisfied with the Model Penal Code (it retained the general prohibition of abortion and only expanded the exceptions moderately), and frustrated with the reluctance of legislatures to enact significant reforms. By the late 1960s, a litigation campaign was underway to change abortion laws by judicial decree, fueled by the Supreme Court's new constitutional "privacy" decisions.

2. Statutes, Cases and Doctrines

a. *Roe v. Wade* and Constitutionalization of Abortion-on-Demand

In 1973, the United States Supreme Court announced its landmark decision in *Roe v. Wade*, 410 U.S. 113 (1973), establishing a woman's right to obtain an abortion as part of a constitutionally protected fundamental right of privacy. The case involved a challenge, brought by an indigent, pregnant single woman, to the Texas abortion laws which prohibited abortions except when necessary to save the life of the mother. A federal district court concluded that the Texas law was unconstitutional, and the Supreme Court affirmed.

Justice Blackmun began his opinion for the Court with the highly debatable declaration that: "It perhaps is not generally appreciated that the restrictive criminal abortion laws in effect in a majority of States today are of relatively recent vintage." 410 U.S. at 129. To support this introduction Justice Blackmun expounded for approximately twenty pages his perception of the world history of abortion laws. (One of the many interesting observations was the suggestion that the Hippocratic Oath prohibiting abortion could be discounted because Hippocrates was a Pythagorean and Pythagoreans were a minority in Greece.) Three possible reasons for Texas' restrictive abortion law were considered and rejected. The first was to discourage extramarital sex, and neither the State of Texas, nor the Court took this argument seriously. The second state interest, i.e., maternal health, received much more serious attention by the Court because it was argued that abortion was a risky medical procedure. The Court curiously concluded that the major motivation behind the restrictive laws was to protect a pregnant woman from "a procedure that placed her life in serious jeopardy." 410 U.S. at 149. But the Court held that this interest was not compelling because it found that mortality rates appeared to be lower for women undergoing early, legal abortions than for childbirth. The third reason advanced for laws prohibiting abortion was the protection of prenatal life. The Court suggested that the major purpose of abortion laws was to protect the pregnant woman, and the Court opined that since philosophers and theologians were still debating about when life begins, the protection of prenatal life did not justify laws prohibiting abortion. 410 U.S. at 159. Consequently, the Court held:

> This right of privacy, whether it be founded in the Fourteenth Amendment's concept of personal liberty and restrictions upon state action, as we feel it is, or, as the District Court determined, in the Ninth Amendment's reservation of rights to the people, is broad enough to encompass a woman's decision whether or not to terminate her pregnancy.

410 U.S. at 153.

The Court did not hold that the woman's right to terminate her pregnancy was absolute. Instead, the Court said that the state has a valid interest in regulating medical procedures in order to safeguard the pregnant woman's health. Another significant qualification on the woman's privacy right is the state's interest in protecting potential life: "At some point in pregnancy, these respective interests become sufficiently compelling to sustain regulation of the factors that govern the abortion decision." 410 U.S. at 154. The Court concluded that the point at which the State's important and legitimate interest in the health of the mother became sufficiently compelling was the end of the first trimester because until then mortality rates for abortion may be lower than for childbirth. After the first trimester, the abortion procedure may by reasonably regulated for the purpose of protecting the woman's health. "With respect to the State's important and legitimate interest in potential life," the Court held that the "compelling point is at viability." 410 U.S. at 163. The Court ruled that the State may prohibit abortions that are not necessary to save the mother's life "or health" after the fetus has become viable, i.e., biologically developed to the point that it is capable of sustaining meaningful life outside the mother's uterus. Thus, the Court divided pregnancy into three periods. During the last period only (after viability) the states may prohibit abortions, but even then states must permit all abortions that are recommended by a doctor to preserve a woman's life or health. Before viability the states may not prohibit abortion, but after the first trimester they may regulate the medical aspects of how abortions are performed if such regulations are necessary to protect the health of women seeking abortions. During the first trimester no regulation of abortions performed by doctors are permitted whatever.

Justices White and Rehnquist dissented arguing that "nothing in the language or history of the Constitution" supported the creation of a sweeping constitutional right to abortion, and that the legality of abortion is more appropriately left to legislative, than to judicial, judgment. 410 U.S. at 222 (White and Rehnquist, JJ., dissenting). Justice Rehnquist feared that confusion would result from the Court's utilization of a compelling state interest test because "the asserted right to an abortion is not 'so rooted in the traditions and conscience of our people as to be ranked as fundamental.'" 410 US at 221, 173-74 (Rehnquist J., dissenting). He characterized the majority decision as "judicial legislation." *Id.* Justice White saw the decisions as "an exercise of raw judicial power." 410 U.S. at 221 (White, J. dissenting with Rehnquist, J., joining). He characterized the issue as whether there is a right to an abortion for "pregnancies that pose no danger whatsoever to the life or health of the mother but are, nevertheless, unwanted for anyone or more of a variety of reasons--convenience, family planning, economics, dislike of children, the embarrassment of illegitimacy, etc." *Id.* In his view it did not violate the Constitution for states to prohibit abortions that were sought for reasons of convenience rather than to protect maternal life or health." The Court noted but reserved for later decision questions about the effect of the decision upon paternal and parental rights. 410 U.S. at 165 n. 67.

In the companion case, *Doe v. Bolton*, 410 U.S. 179 (1973), the Court struck down three Georgia procedural requirements for abortion that were based on the Model Penal Code. The requirement that the abortion be performed in an accredited hospital (only 54 of Georgia's 159 counties had accredited hospitals) was stricken because the performance of non-abortion surgery in unaccredited hospitals was permitted. Similarly, the Court invalidated the requirement that a hospital committee approve each abortion because it interfered with the woman's right to receive the medical care that was in her physician's best medical judgment. A provision requiring the concurrence of two doctors besides the woman's own physician was also invalidated because no other medical procedure required a similar consultation. However, the Court upheld a requirement that only abortions found by doctors to be "necessary" for health because the Court had interpreted the term "health" in an earlier case to include "psychological as well as physical well being," and the Georgia law was interpreted to allow medical judgment to "be exercised in the light of all factors – physical, emotional, psychological, familial, and the woman's age – relevant to the well-being of the patient. All these factors may relate to health. " 410 U.S. at 192.

As a result of the sweeping decisions of the United States Supreme Court in *Roe v. Wade* and *Doe v. Bolton,* all existing abortion laws in all the states were effectively invalidated, at least in part. Most states attempted to conform their statutes to the standards set out in *Roe,* but they had to face a host of follow-up policy decisions, including some relating to parental and spousal participation in abortion.

b. Supreme Court Abortion Decision 1973 -1992

Following *Roe* and *Doe* the Supreme Court quickly and significantly expanded its abortion privacy doctrine. The only regulations of abortion that were generally upheld related to abortion funding and (limited) parental participation. A few of the major Supreme Court abortion decisions during this period are summarized below.

In *Planned Parenthood v. Danforth*, 428 U.S. 52 (1976), *infra* Chapters 18 and 22, a spousal consent requirement for married women and a requirement of parental consent before an abortion could be performed upon an unmarried minor were declared unconstitutional, and a prohibition of amniocentesis abortions was also invalidated. However, the court upheld a simple informed consent requirement. In *Maher v. Roe*, 432 U.S. 464 (1977), the Supreme Court held that funding restrictions do not violate the right of privacy and they are rationally related to legitimate state interests in preserving prenatal life. In a companion case, *Beal v. Doe*, 432 U.S. 438 (1977), the Court upheld a Pennsylvania regulation providing state funds only for therapeutic abortions. In the third abortion-funding case decided that day, *Poelker v. Doe*, 432 U.S. 519 (1977), the Court upheld the policy of a city-funded hospital restricting the performance of elective abortions on the grounds that the public entity could opt to use its scarce resources to encourage childbirth rather than abortions. In *Colautti v. Franklin*, 439 U.S. 379 (1979), a Pennsylvania standard-of-care requirement designed to ensure adequate medical attention for babies whose mothers had undergone abortion after the point of fetal viability was declared unconstitutional as interpreted. In *Harris v. McRae*, 448 U.S. 297 (1980) and *Williams v. Zbaraz*, 448 U.S. 358 (1980), the Court upheld the congressional Hyde Amendments, and state counterparts, which prohibited the expenditure of funds to pay for abortions except when necessary to preserve the life of the mother (and in some years, to preserve her health, or in case of rape or incest). In *H. L. v. Matheson*, 450 U.S. 398 (1981), the Supreme Court upheld a Utah law that required doctors performing an abortion upon an unmarried minor to notify her parents "if possible" prior to the performance of an abortion. In *City of Akron v. Akron Center for Reproductive Health, Inc.*, 462 U.S. 416 (1983), the Court invalidated Akron, Ohio ordinances requiring that all abortions after the end of first trimester be performed in a hospital, requiring all minors under the age of 15 to obtain parental or judicial consent for abortion, requiring detailed "informed consent" requirement, and requiring that fetal remains be disposed of in a humane and sanitary manner. In *Planned Parenthood Association of Kansas, Missouri, Inc. v. Ashcroft*, 462 U.S. 476 (1983), statutes requiring second and third trimester abortions to be done in hospitals were ruled unconstitutional, but requirements that a second physician be present during the performance of post-viability abortions, that pathology reports be submitted in all abortions, and that minors secure parental consent or judicial consent before obtaining abortions were upheld. In *Thornburgh v. American College of Obstetricians and Gynecologists,* 476 U.S.747 (1986), the requirement of disclosure of facts of fetal development was also invalidated. The majority invalidated requirements that the physician performing post viability abortions exercise the degree of care required to preserve the life and health of an unborn child intended to be born alive and to use the abortion technique that would provide the best opportunity for the unborn child to be born alive unless it would present a significantly greater medical risk to the woman's life or health, and that a second physician be present during the performance of an abortion when the fetus was possibly viable.

A significant shift in the abortion doctrine occurred in *Webster v. Reproductive Health Center, Inc.*, 492 U.S. 490 (1989), when the Court upheld four Missouri statutes, including a preamble declaring legislative policy that "the life of each human being begins at conception," prohibiting the use of public funds, facilities, or employees to perform or encourage abortions not necessary to save the life of the mother, provisions requiring certain medical tests to determine if a fetus of twenty weeks gestation or more is viable, and four justices opined that the *Roe* trimester doctrine should be overruled, while one other justice (O'Connor) upheld the provisions without deciding whether to revise the *Roe* trimester doctrine. In *Hodgson v. Minnesota*, 497 U.S. 417 (1990),the Court struck down a two-parent notification requirement without a judicial bypass provision, but upheld the same requirement with a judicial bypass provision. In *Ohio v. Akron Center for Reproductive Health, Inc.*, 497 U.S. 502 (1990) ("*Akron II*") the Court upheld an Ohio law generally requiring that a parent be notified 24-hours before an abortion is performed on a minor child, unless a court order (judicial bypass) was obtained. And in *Rust v. Sullivan*, 500 U.S. 173 (1991), the Court upheld federal funding regulations which prohibited recipients of federal family planning funds from counseling, referring for, encouraging or promoting abortion, and required family planning fund recipients to be financially and physically separate from abortion providers.

In *Planned Parenthood v. Casey*, 505 U.S. 833 (1992), *infra*, the Court reached another milestone in its saga of confusing abortion jurisprudence when it reaffirmed (5-4), but tried to renovate, the *Roe* abortion privacy doctrine, and upheld four of five challenged abortion regulations.

c. *Planned Parenthood v. Casey*
Planned Parenthood of Southeastern Pennsylvania v. Robert P. Casey, et al
505 U.S. 833 (1992)

JUSTICE O'CONNOR, JUSTICE KENNEDY, and JUSTICE SOUTER announced the judgment of the Court and delivered the opinion of the Court with respect to Parts I, II, III, V-A, V-C, and VI, an opinion with respect to Part V-E, in which Justice STEVENS joins, and an opinion with respect to Parts IV, V-B, and -D.

I

Liberty finds no refuge in a jurisprudence of doubt. Yet 19 years after our holding that the Constitution protects a woman's right to terminate her pregnancy in its early stages, *Roe v. Wade*, 410

U.S. 113 (1973), that definition of liberty is still questioned. Joining the respondents as amicus curiae, the United States, as it has done in five other cases in the last decade, again asks us to overrule *Roe*. *

At issue in these cases are five provisions of the Pennsylvania Abortion Control Act of 1982, as amended in 1988 and 1989. 18 Pa. Cons.Stat. §§ 3203-3220 (1990). Relevant portions of the Act are set forth in the Appendix. *Infra*, at 2833. The Act requires that a woman seeking an abortion give her informed consent prior to the abortion procedure, and specifies that she be provided with certain information at least 24 hours before the abortion is performed. § 3205. For a minor to obtain an abortion, the Act requires the informed consent of one of her parents, but provides for a judicial bypass option if the minor does not wish to or cannot obtain a parent's consent. § 3206. Another provision of the Act requires that, unless certain exceptions apply, a married woman seeking an abortion must sign a statement indicating that she has notified her husband of her intended abortion. § 3209. The Act exempts compliance with these three requirements in the event of a "medical emergency," which is defined in § 3203 of the Act. *See* §§ 3203, 3205(a), 3206(a), 3209(c). In addition to the above provisions regulating the performance of abortions, the Act imposes certain reporting requirements on facilities that provide abortion services. §§ 3207(b), 3214(a), 3214(f).

*** The District Court entered a preliminary injunction against the enforcement of the regulations, and, after a 3-day bench trial, held all the provisions at issue here unconstitutional, entering a permanent injunction against Pennsylvania's enforcement of them. 744 F.Supp. 1323 (ED Pa.1990). The Court of Appeals for the Third Circuit affirmed in part and reversed in part, upholding all of the regulations except for the husband notification requirement. 947 F.2d 682 (1991). *** [The Supreme Court upheld all of the requirements except the spousal notification requirement.]
***

Our law affords constitutional protection to personal decisions relating to marriage, procreation, contraception, family relationships, child rearing, and education. *Carey v. Population Services International*, *. Our cases recognize "the right of the individual, married or single, to be free from unwarranted governmental intrusion into matters so fundamentally affecting a person as the decision whether to bear or beget a child." *Eisenstadt v. Baird*, *. Our precedents "have respected the private realm of family life which the state cannot enter." *Prince v. Massachusetts*, *. These matters, involving the most intimate and personal choices a person may make in a lifetime, choices central to personal dignity and autonomy, are central to the liberty protected by the Fourteenth Amendment. At the heart of liberty is the right to define one's own concept of existence, of meaning, of the universe, and of the mystery of human life. Beliefs about these matters could not define the attributes of personhood were they formed under compulsion of the State.
***

*** The ability of women to participate equally in the economic and social life of the Nation has been facilitated by their ability to control their reproductive lives. * The Constitution serves human values, and while the effect of reliance on Roe cannot be exactly measured, neither can the certain cost of overruling Roe for people who have ordered their thinking and living around that case be dismissed.
***

A finding of an undue burden is a shorthand for the conclusion that a state regulation has the purpose or effect of placing a substantial obstacle in the path of a woman seeking an abortion of a nonviable fetus. A statute with this purpose is invalid because the means chosen by the State to further the interest in potential life must be calculated to inform the woman's free choice, not hinder it. ***
***

Chief JUSTICE REHNQUIST, with whom JUSTICE WHITE, JUSTICE SCALIA, and JUSTICE THOMAS join, concurring in the judgment in part and dissenting in part.

The joint opinion, following ints newly-minted variations on *stare decisis*, retains the outer shell of *Roe* *, but beats a wholesale retreat from the substance of that case. We believe that *Roe* was wrongly decided, and that it can and should be overruled consistently with our traditional approach to *stare* *decisis* in constitutional cases. We would adopt the approach of the plurality in *Webster v. Reproductive Health Services*, *, and uphold the challenged provisions of the Pennsylvania statute in their entirety.

*** [The dissenters emphasize, *inter alia*, the inconsistencies of the abortion cases.]

We believe that the sort of constitutionally imposed abortion code of the type illustrated by our decisions following *Roe* is inconsistent "with the notion of a Constitution cast in general terms, as ours is, and usually speaking in general principles, as ours does." *Webster* *.

***

JUSTICE SCALIA, with whom THE CHIEF JUSTICE, JUSTICE WHITE, and JUSTICE THOMAS join, concurring in the judgment in part and dissenting in part.

*** A State's choice between two positions on which reasonable people can disagree is constitutional even when (as is often the case) it intrudes upon a "liberty" in the absolute sense. Laws against bigamy, for example--with which entire societies of reasonable people disagree--intrude upon men and women's liberty to marry and live with one another. But bigamy happens not to be a liberty specially "protected" by the Constitution.

*** The issue is whether [abortion] is a liberty protected by the Constitution of the United States. I am sure it is not. I reach that conclusion not because of anything so exalted as my views concerning the "concept of existence, of meaning, of the universe, and of the mystery of human life." * Rather, I reach it for the same reason I reach the conclusion that bigamy is not constitutionally protected-- because of two simple facts: (1) the Constitution says absolutely nothing about it, and (2) the longstanding traditions of American society have permitted it to be legally proscribed.

***

We should get out of this area, where we have no right to be, and where we do neither ourselves nor the country any good by remaining.

d. Supreme Court Abortion Doctrine Since Casey (1992)

Since *Casey,* the Court seems to have tried to avoid most abortion doctrine cases, but has decided several free speech cases curtailing the rights of abortion protestors to demonstrate in opposition to abortion, and has protected partial-birth abortion from state restriction. The major cases of this era are described below.

In *Bray v. Alexandria Women's Health Clinic,* 508 U.S. 263 (1993), by just one vote the Court held that opposition to abortion does not constitute animus against women in general, and also held that women seeking abortion do not constitute a "class" protected by § 42 U.S.C. 1985. In *National Organization for Women, Inc. v. Scheidler,* 510 U.S. 249 (1994), the Court held that an abortion clinic could assert RICO claims against peaceful, nonviolent anti-abortion protestors who illegally picketed to shut down the clinic. In *Madsen v. Women's Health Center, Inc.,* 512 U.S. 753 (1994), the Court significantly curtailed a broad injunction that had been issued against abortion clinic protesters, but upheld several strong anti-protest provisions, including a 36-feet buffer zone applied to clinic driveways and entrances. In *Lambert v. Wicklund,* 520 U.S. 292 (1997), the Court Per Curiam reversed the Ninth Circuit and a U.S. district court which had invalidated a Montana parental notice law. In *Mazurek v. Armstrong,* 520 U.S. 968 (1997), the Court Per Curiam also upheld a Montana law restricting the performance of abortion to licensed physicians. In *Hill v. Colorado,* 530 U.S. 703 (2000), the Court upheld a Colorado statute that forbids anyone within 100 feet of an abortion clinic from knowingly approaching within eight feet of another person with that person's consent "for the purpose of passing a leaflet or handbill to, displaying a sign to, or engaging in oral protest, education, or counseling with such other person." In *Stenberg v. Carhart,*

530 U.S. 914 (2000), by one vote, the Court held unconstitutional a Nebraska statute banning the highly controversial late-term "partial birth abortion"procedure (in which the doctor delivers the nearly-full-term baby breech – feet first – until the body has emerged but the head of the baby is still in the birth canal; then he plunges scissors into the base of the skull of the baby, sucks out the brains, crushes the head, and removes the dead infant). In *Scheidler v. National Organization for Women*, 537 U.S. 393 (2003), the Court held the federal Hobbs Act and Racketeer Influenced and Corrupt Organizations Act (RICO) did not apply to abortion clinic protestors. In *Ayotte v. Planned Parenthood*, 126 S.Ct. 961 (2006), the Supreme Court held that the Court of Appeals erred in holding New Hampshire's Parental Notification Prior to Abortion Act unconstitutional for lacking an exception for the preservation of a pregnant minor's health when a narrower remedy might be available.

e. Notes and Questions

1) Privacy or Isolation; Pro-Woman or Pro-Sexploitation?

By declaring that the right to abortion is constitutionally ordained to be exclusively a woman's private decision, has not the Supreme Court in *Roe* endorsed the sexist notion that reproductive matters are really only women's "private" concerns, that such things do not really matter to "real men?" Has the Court merely raised to constitutional status the age-old response of predatory men to the women whom they have exploited for sexual gratification: "Oh, it is your problem. You take care of it!" Has the Court abandoned women to their "privacy" and told them: "It is your private problem, you deal with it privately, and do not bother the public. You cannot look to the state for support in requiring the father to assume procreative responsibility by forbidding him the option of pressuring you into a cheap, morally shabby, quick-fix for which you alone will bear sole responsibility?" Just when women were finally getting some political clout, did the Supreme Court slam shut the door to the statehouse in their faces by unilaterally decreeing in *Roe* that states could not support pregnant women in resisting the pressure of their male partners to "get rid of it."

Does *Roe* really empower women, or does it liberate sexually irresponsible men from the unglamourous responsibilities of mutuality, connectedness, procreative responsibility, child support, and child-rearing? Among the most common reasons given by women for having an abortion is lack of support, or opposition from (essentially fear of losing or impairing a relationship with), the sexual partner who fathered the unborn child. During pregnancy, when mutuality may be needed more than ever before, when joint procreative responsibility is most important, should the Court have mandated that all states' laws conform to a judicially-created model of procreative relationships that is centrifugally individualistic?

Why cannot States protect the interest of husbands to be notified of what may be the most important decision concerning their hope for posterity? Is it true that the Supreme Court's abortion privacy doctrine "kills human relationships as efficiently as [abortion] kills unborn children"? Camille S. Williams, *What Abortion Has Cost Women: Twenty-Five Years Post-Roe*, AUL Legislators Educational Conference, Chicago, Ill., Aug. 22, 1998, at 1.

2) *Roe* and *Casey*

What remains of *Roe* after *Casey*? Is Justice O'Connor's undue burden test in *Casey* different from the strict scrutiny test? How does *Casey* affect the privacy doctrine? *See* Linda C. McClain, *infra*. Why should the free speech rights of citizens protesting abortion be given less protection than other demonstrators? Does the fact that the doctrine they are protesting was created by the Court influence the Court's willingness to protect their rights to protest? Why should partial-birth abortion procedures be given constitutionally-protected status? If a doctor used partial-birth procedures after the child was completely delivered, could the state prohibit that? Should ten minutes or ten inches in the delivery process make such a huge difference to the state's ability to prevent such an attack? What is the status of the child in the process of being delivered?

3. Practical and Ethical Considerations

a. Bar Associations

Should bar associations take a position of neutrality on controversial public issues? In 1990, the House of Delegates of the American Bar Association voted to take a pro abortion position, but voted to change its position and take a position of neutrality following mass resignation. The ABA's present position is to take a pro abortion position before viability and after viability, a proposition only to protect the woman's life or heath.

4. Bibliography

William Blackstone, Commentaries on the Laws of England 129, 130.*

Robert Destro, *Abortion and the Constitution: The Need for Life-Protective Amendment*, 63 Calif. L. Rev. 1250 (1975).

Ira Ellman, *Survey of Abortion Law*, 1980 Ariz. St. L.J., 67 (1980).

Cyrus Means, *The Phoenix of Abortional Freedom*, 17 N.Y.L.F. 335 (1971).

Linda C. McCain, *The Poverty of Privacy*, 3 Colum. J. Gender & L. 119 (1992).

Mohr, *Abortion in America, The Origins and Evolution of Policy*, 1800-1900 (1978).

John Noonan, An Almost Absolute Value of History, in The Morality of Abortion: Legal and Historical Perspectives (Noonan ed 1970).

Quay, *Justifiable Abortion--Medical and Legal Foundations*, 49 Geo. L.J. 395 (1961).

Nebinger, Criminal Abortion: Its Extent and Prevention, in Abortion in 19th Century America (1974).

Mark Strasser, *Misconceptions and Wrongful Births: A Call for Principled Jurisprudence*, 31 Ariz. St. L.J. 161, 185 (1999).

Lynn D. Wardle, The Abortion Privacy Doctrine (1980).

Lynn D. Wardle & Mary Anne Q. Wood, A Lawyer Looks at Abortion (1982).

Lynn D. Wardle, *The Quandary of Pro-life Free Speech: A Lesson from the Abolitionists*, 62 Albany L. Rev. 853-966 (1999).

Lynn D. Wardle, *Crying Stones: A Comparison of Abortion in Japan and the United States*, 14 N.Y.L. Sch. J. Int'l & Compar. L. 183-259 (1994).

Lynn D. Wardle, *"Time Enough":* Webster v. Reproductive Health Services *and the Prudent Pace of Justice*, 41 Fla. L. Rev. 881-986 (1989).

Lynn D. Wardle, *Rethinking* Roe v. Wade, 1985 B.Y.U. L. Rev. 231-64.

PART IV
ONGOING SPOUSAL RELATIONS

CHAPTER 16

Spousal Status and Economic Consequences of Marriage in General; Marital Property Regimes

A. SPOUSAL STATUS AND ECONOMIC CONSEQUENCES OF MARRIAGE IN GENERAL

1. Background

a. Marital Status - Individual or Joint?

Marriage creates a new individual status for both of the parties and to some extent a new unit or entity in law. Hafen (1989), *infra.* The law, like society and the rest of culture, treats individuals who are married differently in some important respects than individuals who are not married, because of powerful assumptions (deeply rooted in human experience and history) about the mutual and joint nature of the marriage relationship. For many purposes, they are treated as an economic partnership. But not for all purposes. And that inconsistency creates some confusion because the law still treats wives and husbands as individuals, with individual legal status, rights, and duties in many respects, while treating them as partners or co-directors of a marital entity with derivative joint or equal liability and rights for other purposes.

In this Part IV, the incidents of marriage are separated into "economic" and "non-economic." Economic relations include such things as ownership, control and management of property, responsibility for debt, liability for misconduct of the other, duty to and right to receive support, to doctrine of necessaries, etc. Non-economic dimensions include consortium, names, evidentiary privileges, and the basis for claims to recover for losses suffered by or to the other, etc. The categories overlap, as often non-economic rights are vindicated by claims for economic recovery. Similar questions about separateness or jointness, independence or mutuality/partnership arise in both categories.

In this Chapter we focus on property rights and duties, benefits and burdens during marriage. On one hand, husband and wife in all states are treated in many respects as separate owners with individual control and management of their own property, and individual liability for their debts – while at the same time the laws in all states also treat them in other regards as joint partners in a mutual marital economic "unit." Thus, there is some schizophrenia in the law of marital property. Of course, if marriages break up, there also is often disagreement and "hard swearing" by both parties objecting to the legal presumption of joint ownership of assets or joint liability for debts.

The question at the heart of most of the legal issues that arise concerning spousal property interests is: to what extent are married persons treated as separate individuals for purposes of ownership, control, and management or assets, and liability and responsibility for debts and obligations, and to what extent are they treated as mutual, joint, partners or co-responsible owners or obligors? In other words, to what extent is the marriage an economic unit or entity from which the spouses derive communal benefits and burdens (as partners, co-directors, or some similar derivative institutional theory), or to what extent is marriage a mere social "veil" covering the separate property interests of the separate individuals (who happen to be also husband and wife)? Are the assumptions underlying the mutuality/joint/partnership view of marriage still valid? Should they apply only to married couples? Why not cohabiting heterosexual couples? Why not same-sex couples? Why not other associations?

In recent years, a number of high-profile public officials and private individuals have been snared in controversy over spousal economic dilemmas. In 1984, Geraldine Ferraro, the Democratic nominee for Vice-President, was embarrassed about questions concerning her alleged nondisclosure of income or assets of her husband (Zacarro). Earlier, powerful Senator Jacob Javits was embarassed by questions about his wife's employment by a public relations firm doing business for Iran Airlines. As increasing numbers of married women seek to maintain (or at some point resume) careers after or in lieu of homemaking, questions about conflict of interest with spouses arise with increasing frequency. Both Bob and Elizabeth Dole were power-players in Washington, who worked diligently to avoid conflicts, while Hillary Clinton has been dogged by questions regarding her husband Bill's financial actions (and, of course, vice versa). The concerns are real; one spouse may "hide" assets in the name of the other, or benefit from income or gifts received by the other for the purpose of influencing the other spouse. On the other hand, how far should the law go in presuming that spouses are acting in concert with regard to separate careers, financial ventures, and investments?

2. Statutes, Cases and Doctrines

a. Supreme Court Cases Manifesting Spousal Property Assumptions

In recent years, the U.S. Supreme Court has decided a number of cases affecting the property rights of persons during marriage. The assumption of joint ownership and mutual responsibility underlies most decisions, even in the post-modern era.

Bennis v. Michigan, 516 U.S. 442 (1996), involved forfeiture of property owned jointly by husband and wife. Tina and John Bennis, husband and wife, were joint owners of two cars. John was convicted of "gross indecency" after he was arrested for engaging in a sex act with a prostitute in one of the cars. Michigan then sued John and Tina to have the car (worth $600) declared a public nuisance and abated under a state nuisance abatement law. Tina objected, asserting that "when she entrusted her husband to use the car, she did not know that he would use it to violate [the law]." *Id.* at 444. The trial court rejected Tina's "innocent owner" defense, acknowledged judicial discretion to award Tina half of the proceeds after costs, but declined to do so because the value of the car was so small. The state court of appeals reversed on grounds, *inter alia*, that the statute did not apply to an owner who was without knowledge of the illegal use of the vehicle, but the Michigan Supreme Court reversed and reinstated the total abatement, rejecting the innocent owner defense. The Supreme Court of the United States affirmed, 6-3. The Court (per Chief Justice Rehnquist) cited a long line of admiralty, alcohol, and other forfeiture cases (dating to 1827) upholding forfeiture notwithstanding the owners' lack of knowledge of criminal activity, and accepted the punitive and deterrent purpose of the abatement law. "'The law thus builds a secondary defense against a forbidden use and precludes evasions by dispensing with the necessity of judicial inquiry as to collusion between the wrongdoer and the alleged innocent owner.'" *Id.* at 452 citing *Van Oster v. Kansas*, 272 U.S. 465, 467-468 (1926). The majority concluded:

At bottom, petitioner's claims depend on an argument that the Michigan forfeiture statute is unfair because it relieves prosecutors from the burden of separating co-owners who are complicit in the wrongful use of property from innocent co-owners. This argument, in the abstract, has considerable appeal, as we acknowledged in *Goldsmith-Grant*, 254 U.S., at 510. Its force is reduced in the instant case, however, by the Michigan Supreme Court's confirmation of the trial court's remedial discretion*, and petitioner's recognition that Michigan may forfeit her and her husband's car whether or not she is entitled to an offset for her interest in it, *.

We conclude today, as we concluded 75 years ago, that the cases authorizing actions of the kind at issue are "too firmly fixed in the punitive and remedial jurisprudence of the country to be now displaced." * The State here sought to deter illegal activity that contributes to neighborhood deterioration and unsafe streets. The Bennis automobile, it is conceded, facilitated and was used in criminal activity. Both the trial court and the Michigan Supreme Court followed our longstanding practice, and the judgment of the Supreme Court of Michigan is therefore *Affirmed.*

Id. at 453. Justice Thomas joining and concurring, cited precedents allowing such forfeiture "both before and after the adoption of the Fifth and Fourteenth Amendments," and noting that "[t]his case is ultimately a reminder that the Federal Constitution does not prohibit everything that is intensely undesirable." *Id.* at 454. Justice Ginsberg, also joining and separately concurring, added that "it bears emphasis that the car in question belonged to John Bennis as much as it did to Tina Bennis. At all times he had her consent to use the car, just as she had his." *Id.* at 457. Justice Stevens, dissenting, argued:

> Some airline passengers have marijuana cigarettes in their luggage; some hotel guests are thieves; some spectators at professional sports events carry concealed weapons; and some hitchhikers are prostitutes. The State surely may impose strict obligations on the owners of airlines, hotels, stadiums, and vehicles to exercise a high degree of care to prevent others from making illegal use of their property, but neither logic nor history supports the Court's apparent assumption that their complete innocence imposes no constitutional impediment to the seizure of their property simply because it provided the locus for a criminal transaction.

Id. at 458-459. "It is conceded that petitioner was in no way negligent in her use or entrustment of the family car. Thus, no forfeiture should have been permitted." *Id.* at 466. Justice Kennedy came the closest to the family law concern when, dissenting, he noted: "Nothing in the rationale of the Michigan Supreme Court indicates that the forfeiture turned on the negligence or complicity of petitioner, or a presumption thereof, *and nothing supports the suggestion that the value of her co-ownership is so insignificant as to be beneath the law's protection.*" *Id.* at 473 (emphasis added). Should the fact that the co-owner was a wife (ironically, a principal private "victim" of the criminal activity for which the punishment of abatement was being imposed) have been considered? Changed the analysis? Why/why not? What assumption of mutuality and joint control underlies *Bennis?* What common characteristics are there between marriage and business partnerships? What differences? Are they analytically relevant? Was the enterprise in which Tina was presumably involved in good faith (maintaining a marriage, establishing a family) less socially important than the activity of the owner of a large hotel, cruise ship, or stadium, which so concerned the main dissenters (and which the majority saved for a later day)?

In *Egelhoff v. Egelhoff*, 532 U.S. 141 (2001), ERISA (the Employee Retirement Income Security Act of 1974) was interpreted by the Supreme Court to overturn a Washington statute providing that: "If a marriage is dissolved . . . a provision made prior to that event that relates to the payment or transfer at death of the decedent's interest in a nonprobate asset in favor of . . . the decedent's former spouse is revoked . . . ." (Wash. Rev. Code § 11.07.010(2)(a). David, a divorced man with two children from a prior marriage, married another woman, Donna, and designated her as his beneficiary of a life insurance policy and pension plan provided by his employer (Boeing Co.) and governed by ERISA. In April 1994, David and Donna divorced in Washington. Donna got certain property and David was awarded his pension and insurance, but he had not gotten around to formally removing Donna's name as his insurance and pension beneficiary when he died, two months after the divorce. His children by his former marriage (his heirs) sued Donna in state court to get the insurance and pension proceeds. The trial court ruled for Donna, ruling that the Washington statute was preempted by ERISA rules requiring pension plan administrators to comply with designation of beneficiaries. The state court of appeals reversed and the Washington Supreme Court agreed that ERISA did not clearly preempt the Washington statute. However, the U.S. Supreme Court reversed (7-2), holding that the state revocation-of-beneficiary-designation-by-divorce statute "directly conflicts by ERISA's requirements that plans be administered, and benefits be paid, in accordance with plan documents," *id.* at 1150, and was therefore preempted by ERISA because of the burden upon plan administrators who otherwise would have to comply with varying state rules. The majority opinion (per Thomas) noted:

> [R]espondents emphasize that the Washington statute involves both family law and probate law, areas of traditional state regulation. There is indeed a presumption against pre-emption in areas of traditional state regulation such as family law. See *e.g. Hisquierdo v. Hisquierdo*, 439 U.S. 572, 581(1979). But that presumption can be overcome where, as here, Congress has made clear its desire for pre-emption. Accordingly, we have not hesitated to find state family law pre-empted when it conflicts with ERISA or relates to ERISA plans. *See e.g. Boggs v. Boggs*, 520 U.S. 833 (1997) (holding that ERISA pre-empts a state community property law permitting the testamentary transfer of an interest in a spouse's pension plan benefits).

Id. at 151-152. Justice Breyer, dissenting, emphasized:

> [W]e must remember that petitioner has to overcome a strong presumption *against* pre-emption. That is because the Washington statute governs family property law--a "field of traditional state regulation," where courts will not find federal pre-emption unless such was the " 'clear and manifest purpose of Congress,' " *, or the state statute does " 'major damage' to 'clear and substantial' federal interests," *Hisquierdo v. Hisquierdo*, 439 U.S. 572, 581 (1979) *. No one can seriously argue that Congress has *clearly* resolved the question before us. And the only damage to federal interests that the Court identifies consists of the added administrative burden the state statute imposes upon ERISA plan administrators.
>
> The Court claims that the Washington statute "interferes with nationally uniform plan administration" by requiring administrators to "familiarize themselves with state

statutes." * But administrators have to familiarize themselves with state law in any event when they answer such routine legal questions as whether amounts due are subject to garnishment, *Mackey v. Lanier Collection Agency & Service, Inc.*, 486 U.S. 825, 838 (1988), who is a "spouse," who qualifies as a "child," or when an employee is legally dead. And were that "familiarizing burden" somehow overwhelming, the plan could easily avoid it by resolving the divorce revocation issue in the plan documents themselves, stating expressly that state law does not apply. The "burden" thus reduces to a one-time requirement that would fall primarily upon the few who draft model ERISA documents, not upon the many who administer them. So meager a burden cannot justify pre-empting a state law that enjoys a presumption against pre-emption.

Id. at 157.

Boggs v. Boggs, 520 U.S. 833 (1997) telegraphed the *Egelhoff* decision four years earlier. There, the surviving second wife of deceased pension plan participant brought action against the decedents's sons of a former marriage seeking declaratory judgment that ERISA preempted application of Louisiana's community property laws which would have allowed first wife to transfer to sons, by testamentary instrument, her interest in undistributed pension plan benefits. The federal district court ruled for the sons and the Fifth Circuit affirmed. However, The U.S. Supreme Court, per Justice Kennedy, reversed, holding that ERISA preempted application of Louisiana's community property laws which would have allowed first wife to make testamentary transfer of her interest in survivor's annuity, and her interest in participant's retirement benefits consisting of monthly annuity payments made to participant during his retirement, his individual retirement account (IRA), and his shares of stock pursuant to employee stock ownership plan (ESOP). The majority opinion noted, in part:

> Community property laws have, in the past, been pre-empted in order to ensure the implementation of a federal statutory scheme. *See e.g. McCune v. Essig*, 199 U.S. 382 (1905); *Wissner v. Wissner*, 338 U.S. 655 (1950); *Free v. Bland*, 369 U.S. 663 (1962); *Hisquierdo v. Hisquierdo*, 439 U.S. 572 (1979); *McCarty v. McCarty*, 453 U.S. 210 (1981); *Mansell v. Mansell*, 490 U.S. 581 (1989); cf. *Ridgway v. Ridgway*, 454 U.S. 46 (1981). *Free v. Bland, supra*, is of particular relevance here. A husband had purchased United States savings bonds with community funds in the name of both spouses. Under Treasury regulations then in effect, when a co-owner of the bonds died, the surviving co-owner received the entire interest in the bonds. After the wife died, her son--the principal beneficiary of her will--demanded either one-half of the bonds or reimbursement for loss of the community property interest. The Court held that the regulations pre-empted the community property claim . . . .
>
> *** The obligation to provide an accounting, moreover, as with the probate proceedings referred to in Free, is itself a burden of significant proportions. Under respondents' view, a pension plan participant could be forced to make an accounting of a deceased spouse's community property interest years after the date of death. If the couple had lived in several States, the accounting could entail complex, expensive, and time-consuming litigation. Congress could not have intended that pension benefits from pension plans would be given to accountants and attorneys for this purpose.

Id. at 853. *See also United States v. Williams*, 514 U.S. 527 (1995) (after government placed tax lien on all of Jerrold's property, including his jointly-owned home, he transferred his interest in the house to Lori, his wife as part of a division of assets in contemplation of divorce; she paid the lien under protest, but her suit for refund was dismissed because she personally did not owe the tax; Court affirms Ninth Circuit judgment that she could sue for a refund).

What assumptions about marital economic relations underlie these decisions? Are they reality-based? How much deference should courts (and Congress) give to state policies governing family economic relationships? Why? Congress appears to claim authority to regulate and does govern most aspects of pension and other beneficiary programs under the Commerce Clause; while the states control the regulation of other forms of marital property under the doctrine of reserved state sovereignty over family law. Is this division of regulatory authority defensible? Reasonable? Wise? Why/why not? *See also United States v. Craft, infra*, in Chapter 16.B.1.b.

b. Notes and Questions re: Forfeiture

21 U.S.C. § 853 provides for forfeiture of (1) property obtained through drug trafficking and other criminal activity, or purchased with the proceeds thereof, and (2) of substitute property when the criminal profits or purchases have been transferred or placed out of reach. However an "innocent party" including a bona fide purchaser or one who has vested separate or superior legal title at the time of commission of the criminal acts giving rise to forfeiture can override forfeiture as to his or her interest in (1), and illegally obtained property (1) that is subsequently transferred anyone except a bona fide purchaser is subject to forfeiture, but a noncriminal spouse's community property interest in (2) is not subject to forfeiture. (a) If H purchases a family home with proceeds of illegal drug sales and the home is held in the name of "H and W jointly" and H and W occupy the home in a community property state for two years and then the government prosecutes and convicts the husband for the illegal drug sales and traces the proceeds to the home purchase payment, is wife's interest in the home protected from forfeiture?

(b) If H & W purchase a jointly-held family home in a community property state with other money, and H is later convicted of illegally selling drugs, and $50,000 of his ill-gotten drug gains have been consumed (travel and high life) and is irretrievable, and the government seeks forfeiture of the family home, is W's interest protected from forfeiture? (c) If H uses the family car titled to H and W in a drug sale, would W's interest in the car be protected from forfeiture?

3. Practical and Ethical Considerations

To what extent, if any, may lawyers treat married persons as co-partners in a joint enterprise, discuss confidences disclosed by one with the other, etc? If Attorney Ann learns from client Hal that during the past 10 years of marriage he secretly has been siphoning funds out of the joint account into which he and his wife, Wendy, deposit equal amounts of money, and he wants legal advice on how to best to protect the $120,000 he has thereby secretly accumulated, what are the obligations, duties, and prerogatives of Ann regarding disclosure that information to Wendy?

Lawyers who are married to each other but who work in different offices have long faced one variation of the potential conflict-of-interest dilemma that Ferraro-Zacarro and Rodham-Clinton faced. What special professional responsibility are imposed on lawyers who are married to each other? Are the duties the same for lawyers who are cohabiting but not married? Should they be the same? Why/why not?

4. Bibliography

Bruce C. Hafen, The Family as an Entity , 22 U.C. Davis L. Rev. 865 (1989).
Bruce C. Hafen, The Constitutional Status of Marriage, Kinship, and Sexual Privacy Balancing the Individual and Social Interests, 81 Mich. L. Rev. 463, 509 (1983).
Alicia Brokars Kelly, *The Marital Partnership Pretense and Career Assets: The Ascendance of Self Over the Marital Community*, 81 B.U. L. Rev. 59 (2001).

B. MARITAL PROPERTY REGIMES IN GENERAL

1. Background

a. The Common Law Disabilities of Married Women

At common law, married women were largely denied the rights to own and control property that their husbands and unmarried brothers and sisters enjoyed. Blackstone summarized the disabilities and gave his opinion of the justification for them as follows:

> By marriage, the husband and wife are one person in law; that is, the very being or legal existence of the woman is suspended during the marriage, or at least is incorporated and consolidated into that of the husband, under whose wing, protection, and *cover* she performs every thing; and is, therefore, called in our law-French a *feme-covert, faemina viro co-operta*; is said to be *covert-baron,* or under the protection and influence of her husband, her *baron,* her lord; and her condition, during her marriage, is called her *coverture.* Upon this principle of a union of person in husband and wife depend almost all the legal rights, duties, and disabilities that either of them acquire by the marriage.
> ***
> But, though our law in general considers the man and wife as one person, yet there are some instances in which she is separately considered, as inferior to him, and acting by his compulsion; and, therefore, all deeds executive, and acts done by her, during her coverture, are void; except it be a fine, or the like matter of record, in which case she must be solely and secretly examined, to learn if her act be voluntary. She can not, but will, devise lands to her husband, unless under special circumstances; for at the time of making it she [is] supposed to be under his coercion. And in some felonies and other inferior crimes, committed by her, through constraint of her husband, the law excuses her; but this extends not to treason or murder.
> ***
> These are the child legal effects of marriage during coverture; upon which we may observe, that even the disabilities which the wife lies under are, for the most part, intended for her protection and benefit. So great a favorite is the female sex of the laws of England.

1 W. Blackstone, *infra* at *442-44.

Later legal scholars have questioned the validity Blackstone's "one flesh" justification. Pollock and Maitland, offered a different explanation for the legal disabilities of married women.

If we look for any one thought which governs the whole of this province of law, we shall hardly find it. In particular we must be on our guard against the common belief that the ruling principle is that which sees an "unity of person' between husband and wife. This is a principle which suggests itself from time to time; it has the warrant of holy writ; it will serve to round a paragraph, and may now and again lead us out of or into a difficulty; but a consistently operative principle it can not be. We do not treat the wife as a thing or as somewhat that is neither thing nor person; we treat her as a person. . . . The husband is the wife's guardian:--that we believe to be the fundamental principle; and it explains a great deal, when we remember that guardianship is a profitable right. As we shall see below, the husband's rights in the wife's lands can be regarded as an exaggerated guardianship. The wife's subjection to her husband is often insisted on; she is 'wholly within his power,' she is bound to obey him in all that is not contrary to the law of God; she and all her property ought to be at his disposal; she is 'under the rod.' . . .

2 F. Pollock & F. Maitland, *infra* at 405-06.

b. Property Ownership – Common Law

Common law property ownership has historically been a separate property regime, i.e., based upon (and giving strong preference to) the concept of individual, not family, ownership of property. The common law also historically has shown great preference for the oldest males (especially husbands, sons) who were the primary instruments of feudal duties (including military and quasi-military duties) owed to the king and his sub-Lords. The objective of the common law during feudal times was to consolidate in one person all the rights, privileges and duties that accompanied ownership of land. The English system seems to have been "consciously devised to simplify the law by concentrating the power of alienation in the hands of the living holder of the seisin and then passing his estate to a single male heir." Donahue, *infra*, at 81.

These and other influences combined in England to produce a system of property ownership in which the property rights of married women were suspended during marriage. With a few complex exceptions, married women were legally incapable of independently owning property at common law. Any real property a woman owned at the time of marriage (and most of her personal property, except possibly her "paraphernalia") became subject to her husband's possession and control. In return, the married woman obtained a "dower" interest in all real property owned outright by her husband during their marriage. The strictness of the common law disability of married women stimulated the practice of making antenuptial contracts between women of means (and their families) and the men they wished to marry (and their families). It also stimulated the development of "trusts," "uses," and other equitable devices to circumvent the legal disabilities.

The common law system of ownership of property during marriage came with English settlers to America, and became thoroughly imbedded in the law of the colonies that became the original states of the United States of America. (In Louisiana, and later in western states, the historical influence of French and Spanish law left a legacy of property ownership that varied significantly from the common law system.) The common law property ownership system spread into most of the later-created American states, as well.

During the nineteenth century, "Married Women's [Property] Acts" were adopted throughout America. These statutes repealed many of the common law disabilities of married women, particularly the property-ownership and contract-making restrictions. This meant that married women, like all men and single women, could own and convey property. That meant that the individual, married or single, was the unit of ownership, and reinforced the general common law principle of separate (title) property ownership: property belongs to the person (married or single) who acquires (the title to) it. The non-title spouse had no legal interest in the property (except dower and curtesy, which remained), though he or she had whatever equitable interest the legislature or courts may choose to give them in case of divorce or death of the title-owning spouse.

While this scheme of ownership works well enough in the case of unmarried persons, or when both spouses are employed, and it works quite well in the case of married persons who remain married, but in the case of a married couple who acquire significant property while the wife has been a full-time, nonearning homemaker-wife-mother and the husband has worked full-time, the separate (title) system creates a significant disparity in property ownership if there is a divorce (and possibly if there is a death). The problem is that all the property legally belongs to the spouse who acquired title to it – typically the husband -- and the other spouse, whose contributions to the marriage (and thereby to the acquisition of the property) may have been as great or even greater than those of the spouse with title had no legal interest in the property. As Lord Simon of Glaisdale put it: "The cockbird can feather his nest because he is not required to spend most of his time sitting in it." Fisher, *infra* at 8. The problem was particularly noticeable before the "gender equality" revolution of the 1970s, when the opportunities for women to earn significant income were relatively limited. To compensate for this great inequity, all common law states now authorize the "equitable division" (or its equivalent) of property upon divorce. *See infra* Chapter 28. To the extent that the separate (title) property system vests unequal management, control, administration, disposition, or testamentary powers to the earning spouse, they remain subject to some continuing criticism.

Equitable distribution has come under attack because it seems to be backward-looking, addressed to conditions that have largely been remedied by social changes of the past thirty years. Now "marital property" concepts are widespread in common law property states. "Marital property" is an equitable concept, a retrospective designation of property acquired during marriage by married persons. It is presumed to belong to both of them, or at least both of them have an equitable stake in the property. (Thus, "marital property" seems to be a limited common law imitation of "community property.") Marital property is a retrospective concept because it only arises and is used when a marriage fails and there is a divorce or annulment; courts *then* consider the property that was acquired during the marriage to be "marital property." But so long as the marriage is intact, the historical separate property title rules apply.

Recently, the Supreme Court reviewed the three ways by which married persons could co-own property in common law property systems. In *United States v. Craft*, 535 U.S. 274 (2002) the Supreme Court held that a tax lien incurred by a husband for failure to file income tax returns for eight years attached to his interest in a piece of land he and his wife owned by tenancy by the entireties. Writing for the six-person majority, Justice O'Connor explained:

A common idiom describes property as a 'bundle of sticks'--a collection of individual rights which, in certain combinations, constitute property. . . . State law determines only which sticks are in a person's bundle. Whether those sticks qualify as 'property' for purposes of the federal tax lien statute is a question of federal law.

. . . .

English common law provided three legal structures for the concurrent ownership of property that have survived into modern times: tenancy in common, joint tenancy, and tenancy by the entirety. 1 G. Thompson, Real Property §4.06(g) (D. Thomas ed. 1994) (hereinafter Thompson). The tenancy in common is now the most common form of concurrent ownership. 7 R. Powell & P. Rohan, Real Property §51.01[3] (M. Wolf ed. 2001) (hereinafter Powell). The common law characterized tenants in common as each owning a separate fractional share in undivided property. *Id.*, §50.01[1]. Tenants in common may each unilaterally alienate their shares through sale or gift or place encumbrances upon these shares. They also have the power to pass these shares to their heirs upon death. Tenants in common have many other rights in the property, including the right to use the property, to exclude from third parties from it, and to receive a portion of any income produced from it. *Id.*, §§50.03-50.06.

Joint tenancies were the predominant form of concurrent ownership at common law, and still persist in some States today. 4 Thompson §31.05. The common law characterized each joint tenant as possessing the entire estate, rather than a fractional share: '[J]oint-tenants have one and the same interest ... held by one and the same undivided possession.' 2 W. Blackstone, Commentaries on the Laws of England 180 (1766). Joint tenants possess many of the rights enjoyed by tenants in common: the right to use, to exclude, and to enjoy a share of the property's income. The main difference between a joint tenancy and a tenancy in common is that a joint tenant also has a right of automatic inheritance known as 'survivorship.' Upon the death of one joint tenant, that tenant's share in the property does not pass through will or the rules of intestate succession; rather, the remaining tenant or tenants automatically inherit it. *Id.* at 183; 7 Powell §51.01[3]. Joint tenants' right to alienate their individual shares is also somewhat different. In order for one tenant to alienate his or her individual interest in the tenancy, the estate must first be severed--that is, converted to a tenancy in common with each tenant possessing an equal fractional share. *Id.*, §51.04[1]. Most States allowing joint tenancies facilitate alienation, however, by allowing severance to automatically accompany a conveyance of that interest or any other overt act indicating an intent to sever. *Ibid.*

A tenancy by the entirety is a unique sort of concurrent ownership that can only exist between married persons. 4 Thompson §33.02. Because of the common- law fiction that the husband and wife were one person at law (that person, practically speaking, was the husband, *see* J. Cribbet et al., Cases and Materials on Property 329 (6th ed. 1990)), Blackstone did not characterize the tenancy by the entirety as a form of concurrent ownership at all. Instead, he thought that entireties property was a form of single ownership by the marital unity. Orth, Tenancy by the Entirety: The Strange Career of the Common-Law Marital Estate, 1997 B. Y. U. L. Rev. 35, 38-39. Neither spouse was considered to own any individual interest in the estate; rather, it belonged to the couple.

Like joint tenants, tenants by the entirety enjoy the right of survivorship. Also like a joint tenancy, unilateral alienation of a spouse's interest in entireties property is typically not possible without severance. Unlike joint tenancies, however, tenancies by the entirety cannot easily be severed unilaterally. 4 Thompson §33.08(b). Typically, severance requires the consent of both spouses, *id.*, §33.08(a), or the ending of the marriage in divorce, *id.*, §33.08(d). At common law, all of the other rights associated with the entireties property belonged to the husband: as the head of the household, he could control the use of the property and the exclusion of others from it and enjoy all of the income produced from it. *Id.*, §33.05. The husband's control of the property was so extensive that, despite the rules on alienation, the common law eventually provided that he could unilaterally alienate entireties property without severance subject only to the wife's survivorship interest. Orth, *supra*, at 40-41.

With the passage of the Married Women's Property Acts in the late 19th century granting women distinct rights with respect to marital property, most States either abolished the tenancy by the entirety or altered it significantly. 7 Powell §52.01[2]. Michigan's version of the estate is typical of the modern tenancy by the entirety. Following Blackstone, Michigan characterizes its tenancy by the entirety as creating no individual rights whatsoever: 'It is well settled under the law of this state that one tenant by the entirety has no interest separable from that of the other ... . Each is vested with an entire title.' * And yet, in Michigan, each tenant by the entirety possesses the right of survivorship. * Each spouse--the wife as well as the husband--may also use the property, exclude third parties from it, and receive an equal share of the income produced by it. * Neither spouse may unilaterally alienate or encumber the property, **, although this may be accomplished with mutual consent, *. Divorce ends the tenancy by the entirety, generally giving each spouse an equal interest in the property as a tenant in common, unless the divorce decree specifies otherwise. *

Because the husband enjoyed valuable individual rights ("sticks") in the property held by the entireties with his wife, including

> the right to use the property, the right to exclude third parties from it, the right to a share of income produced from it, the right of survivorship, the right to become a tenant in common with equal shares upon divorce, the right to sell the property with the respondent's consent and to receive half the proceeds from such a sale, the right to place an encumbrance on the property with the respondent's consent, and the right to block respondent from selling or encumbering the property unilaterally,

the majority held that the entireties property was subject to the tax lien.

Dissenting, Justice Thomas for three justices noted that every federal court to pass on the question previously had held that property held by the entireties was not subject to an individual's personal tax lien because "property held as a tenancy by the entirety does not belong to either spouse, but to a single entity composed of the married persons." Additionally, Justice Scalia noted the disparate impact of the ruling on homemaker-wives, noting:

> the Court nullifies (insofar as federal taxes are concerned, at least) a form of property ownership that was of particular benefit to the stay-at-home spouse or mother. She is overwhelmingly likely to be the survivor that obtains title to the unencumbered property; and she (as opposed to her business-world husband) is overwhelmingly unlikely to be the source of the individual indebtedness against which a tenancy by the entirety protects. It is regrettable that the Court has eliminated a large part of this traditional protection retained by many States.

c. Property Ownership – Community Property

Ten states (mostly in the west where Spanish Civil Law once prevailed) follow the "community property" system of property ownership during marriage. The states are California, Nevada, Arizona, New Mexico, Texas, Louisiana, Idaho, Washington, Wisconsin (Wisconsin has no Spanish or Civil Law tradition, but the Wisconsin legislature adopted the Uniform Marital Property Act which embodies a form of community property; it is the only state to have adopted the UMA.), and Alaska (which has enacted a voluntary community property regime, where the couple can choose by agreement to opt into this system. Ak. Stat. 34.77.060.). The theory of community property is that both spouses contribute equally to the marriage, and they should enjoy equally the fruits of the marriage, as equal partners. The main doctrinal principle of community property is that all property acquired during marriage is community property and belongs equally to both spouses, except property acquired by gift, devise, bequest or inheritance (which, like property acquired before marriage, is the separate property of the spouse acquiring it). Community property recognizes two kinds of property during marriage -- separate property and community property. The presumption and default assumption of the law is that property acquired during marriage is community property, unless it is shown to be separate property.

Community property developed as a result of different historical influences; mainly, the historical fact that the aristocratic families of France and Spain had more political power (vis-a-vis the king) than the nobility of England, and were able to establish and maintain legal principles that recognized and protected their family property interests, including separate property interests of their daughters who married. In other words, community property developed not so much to protect the interests of married women as to protect the property interests of the great property-owning families in which they were raised. "[W]hat looks at first blush like a system more favorable to the woman was in fact a system more favorable to the woman's family." Donahue, *infra* at 80.

Upon death or divorce in a community property state, each spouse receives one-half of the community property (technically each is entitled to one-half of each item of community property, but generally the courts try not to divide property, but award each item to the spouse most interested in it until both spouses have half of the total property). During marriage, control and management may be problematic, because dual control could create inconsistent or inequitable dealings. *See Kirschberg v. Feenstra,* 450 U.S. 455 (1981) (Louisiana statute allowing husband to encumber family home without notice to wife, but not vice versa, violates equal protection). But most states provide for a presumption of control and management in one spouse upon a gender-neutral basis (e.g., the spouse who earned the income is presumptively entitled to manage it, etc.). Courts in community property generally have power to make unequal divisions of community property when necessary to do equity. Thus, the result "equitable distribution" seems to be the same in community and common law property states. But in both theory and actual practice, community property states seem to come closer to spousal equality in property ownership that do common law separate (title) property jurisdictions.

2. Statutes, Cases and Doctrines

a. *Kirchberg v. Feenstra*

Karl J. Kirchberg v. Joan Paillot Feenstra
450 U.S. 455 (1981)

Justice MARSHALL delivered the opinion of the Court.

In this appeal we consider the constitutionality of a now superseded Louisiana statute that gave a husband, as "head and master" of property jointly owned with his wife, the unilateral right to dispose of such property without his spouse's consent. Concluding that the provision violates the Equal Protection Clause of the Fourteenth Amendment, we affirm the judgment of the Court of Appeals for the Fifth Circuit invalidating the statute.

I.

In 1974, appellee Joan Feenstra filed a criminal complaint against her husband, Harold Feenstra, charging him with molesting their minor daughter. While incarcerated on that charge, Mr. Feenstra retained appellant Karl Kirchberg, an attorney, to represent him. Mr. Feenstra signed a $3,000 promissory note in prepayment for legal services to be performed by appellant Kirchberg. As security on this note, Mr. Feenstra executed a mortgage in favor of appellant on the home he jointly owned with his wife. Mrs. Feenstra was not informed of the mortgage, and her consent was not required because a state statute, former Art. 2404 of the Louisiana Civil Code Ann. (West 1971), gave her husband exclusive control over the disposition of community property. *[FN1-Article 2404, in effect at the time Mr. Feenstra executed the mortgage in favor of appellant, provided in pertinent part: "The husband is the head and master of the partnership or community of gains; he administers its effects, disposes of the revenues which they produce, and may alienate them by an onerous title, without the consent and permission of his wife." This provision has been repealed. See infra, at 1197-1198, and nn. 3 and 4.]*

Mrs. Feenstra eventually dropped the charge against her husband. He did not return home, but instead obtained a legal separation from his wife and moved out of the State. Mrs. Feenstra first learned of the existence of the mortgage in 1976, when appellant Kirchberg threatened to foreclose on her home unless she paid him the amount outstanding on the promissory note executed by her husband. After Mrs. Feenstra refused to pay the obligation, Kirchberg obtained an order of executory process directing the local sheriff to seize and sell the Feenstra home.

Anticipating Mrs. Feenstra's defense to the foreclosure action, Kirchberg in March 1976 filed this action in the United States District Court for the Eastern District of Louisiana, seeking a declaratory judgment against Mrs. Feenstra that he was not liable under the Truth in Lending Act, 15 U.S.C. § 1601 et seq., for any nondisclosures concerning the mortgage he held on the Feenstra home. In her answer to Kirchberg's complaint, Mrs. Feenstra alleged as a counterclaim that Kirchberg has violated the Act, but also included a second counterclaim challenging the constitutionality of the statutory scheme that empowered her husband unilaterally to execute a mortgage on their jointly owned home. The State of Louisiana and its Governor were joined as third-party defendants on the constitutional counterclaim. The governmental parties, joined by appellant, moved for summary judgment on this claim. The District Court, characterizing Mrs. Feenstra's counterclaim as an attack on "the bedrock of Louisiana's community property system," granted the State's motion for summary judgment. 430 F.Supp. 642, 644 (1977).

While Mrs. Feenstra's appeal from the District Court's order was pending before the Court of Appeals for the Fifth Circuit, the Louisiana Legislature completely revised its code provisions relating to community property. In so doing, the State abandoned the "head and master" concept embodied in Art. 2404, and instead granted spouses equal control over the disposition of community property. La.Civ.Code Ann., Art. 2346 (West Supp.1981). *[FN3-Article 2346 provides that "[e]ach spouse acting alone may manage, control, or dispose of community property unless otherwise provided by law."]* The new code also provided that community immovables could not be alienated, leased, or otherwise encumbered without the concurrence of both spouses. La.Civ.Code Ann., Art. 2347 (West Supp.1981). These provisions, however, did not take effect until January 1, 1980, and the Court of Appeals was therefore required to consider whether Art. 2404, the Civil Code provision which had authorized Mr.

Feenstra to mortgage his home in 1974 without his wife's knowledge or consent, violated the Equal Protection Clause of the Fourteenth Amendment.

Because this provision explicitly discriminated on the basis of gender, the Court of Appeals properly inquired whether the statutory grant to the husband of exclusive control over disposition of community property was substantially related to the achievement of an important governmental objective. *See e. g. Wengler v. Druggist Mutual Insurance Co.*, 446 U.S. 142 (1980); *Craig v. Boren*, 429 U.S. 190 (1976). The court noted that the State had advanced only one justification for the provision--that "[o]ne of the two spouses has to be designated as the manager of the community." The court agreed that the State had an interest in defining the manner in which community property was to be managed, but found that the State had failed to show why the mandatory designation of the husband as manager of the property was necessary to further that interest. The court therefore concluded that Art. 2404 violated the Equal Protection Clause. However, because the court believed that a retroactive application of its decision "would create a substantial hardship with respect to property rights and obligations within the State of Louisiana," the decision was limited to prospective application. 609 F.2d 727, 735-736 (1979). Only Kirchberg appealed the judgment of the Court of Appeals to this Court. We noted probable jurisdiction. *

II.

By granting the husband exclusive control over the disposition of community property, Art. 2404 clearly embodies the type of express gender-based discrimination that we have found unconstitutional absent a showing that the classification is tailored to further an important governmental interest. In defending the constitutionality of Art. 2404, appellant Kirchberg does not claim that the provision serves any such interest. *[FN7-Nor will this Court speculate about the existence of such a justification. "The burden ... is on those defending the discrimination to make out the claimed justification...." Wengler v. Druggist Mutual Ins. Co., 446 U.S. 142, 151, 100 S.Ct. 1540, 1546, 64 L.Ed.2d 107 (1980). We note, however, that the failure of the State to appeal from the decision of the Court of Appeals and the decision of the Louisiana Legislature to replace Art. 2404 with a gender-neutral statute, suggest that appellant would be hard pressed to show that the challenged provision substantially furthered an important governmental interest.]* Instead, appellant attempts to distinguish this Court's decisions in cases such as *Craig v. Boren, supra*, and *Orr v. Orr*, 440 U.S. 268 (1979), which struck down similar gender-based statutory classifications, by arguing that appellee Feenstra, as opposed to the disadvantaged individuals in those cases, could have taken steps to avoid the discriminatory impact of Art. 2404. Appellant notes that under Art. 2334 of the Louisiana Civil Code, in effect at the time Mr. Feenstra executed the mortgage, Mrs. Feenstra could have made a "declaration by authentic act" prohibiting her husband from executing a mortgage on her home without her consent. *[FN8 - Article 2334, as it existed in 1974, provided: "Where the title to immovable property stands in the names of both the husband and the wife, it may not be leased, mortgaged or sold by the husband without the wife's consent where she has made a declaration by authentic act that her authority and consent are required for such lease, sale or mortgage and has filed such a declaration in the mortgage and conveyance records of the parish in which the property is situated." This Article has been replaced with a new code provision prohibiting either spouse from alienating or encumbering community immovables without the consent of the other spouse. See n. 3, supra.]* By failing to take advantage of this procedure, Mrs. Feenstra, in appellant's view, became the "architect of her own predicament" and therefore should not be heard to complain of the discriminatory impact of Art. 2404..

By focusing on steps that Mrs. Feenstra could have taken to preclude her husband from mortgaging their home without her consent, however, appellant overlooks the critical question: Whether Art. 2404 substantially furthers an important government interest. As we have previously noted, the "absence of an insurmountable barrier" will not redeem an otherwise unconstitutionally discriminatory law. *Trimble v. Gordon, *. See Frontiero v. Richardson*, 411 U.S. 677 (1973). Cf. *Taylor v. Louisiana*, 419 U.S. 522 (1975); *Reed v. Reed*, 404 U.S. 71 (1971). Instead the burden remains on the party seeking to uphold a statute that expressly discriminates on the basis of sex to advance an "exceedingly persuasive justification" for the challenged classification. *Personnel Administrator of Mass. v. Feeney*, 442 U.S. 256, 273 (1979). *See also Wengler v. Druggist Mutual Ins. Co., supra*, 446 U.S., at 151. Because appellant has failed to offer such a justification, and because the State, by declining to appeal from the decision below, has apparently abandoned any claim that an important government objective was served by the statute, we affirm the judgment of the Court of Appeals invalidating Art. 2404.

III.

Appellant's final contention is that even if Art. 2404 violates the Equal Protection Clause of the Fourteenth Amendment, the mortgage he holds on the Feenstra home is nonetheless valid because the Court of Appeals limited its ruling to prospective application. Appellant asserts that the opinion of the Court of Appeals is ambiguous on whether the court intended to apply its prospective ruling to his mortgage, which was executed in 1974, or only to those dispositions of community property made pursuant to Art. 2404 between December 12, 1979, the date of the court's decision, and January 1, 1980, the effective date of Louisiana's new community property law. Appellant urges this Court to adopt the latter interpretation on the ground that a contrary decision would create grave uncertainties concerning the validity of mortgages executed unilaterally by husbands between 1974 and the date of the Court of Appeals' decision.

We decline to address appellant's concerns about the potential impact of the Court of Appeals' decision on other mortgages executed pursuant to Art. 2404. The only question properly before us is whether the decision of the Court of Appeals applies to the mortgage in this case, and on that issue we find no ambiguity. This case arose not from any abstract disagreement between the parties over the constitutionality of Art. 2404, but from appellant's attempt to foreclose on the mortgage he held on the Feenstra home. Appellant brought this declaratory judgment action to further that end, and the counterclaim asserted by Mrs. Feenstra specifically sought as relief "a declaratory judgment that the mortgage executed on [her] home by her husband ... is void as having been executed and recorded without her consent pursuant to an unconstitutional state statute." Thus, the dispute between the parties at its core involves the validity of a single mortgage, and in passing on the constitutionality of Art. 2404, the Court of Appeals clearly intended to resolve that controversy adversely to appellant.

Accordingly, the judgment of the Court of Appeals is affirmed.

So ordered.

Justice STEWART, with whom Justice REHNQUIST joins, concurring in the result.

Since men and women were similarly situated for all relevant purposes with respect to the management and disposition of community property, I agree that Art. 2404 of the Louisiana Civil Code Ann. (West 1971), which allowed husbands but not wives to execute mortgages on jointly owned real estate without spousal consent, violated the Equal Protection Clause of the Fourteenth Amendment. *See Michael M. v. Sonoma County Superior Court*, 450 U.S. 464, 477-479, 101 S.Ct. 1200, 1208-1209 (STEWART, J., concurring).

While it is clear that the Court is correct in holding that the judgment of the Court of Appeals applied to the particular mortgage executed by Mr. Feenstra, it is equally clear that that court's explicit announcement that its holding was to apply only prospectively means that no other mortgage executed before the date of the decision of the Court of Appeals is invalid by reason of its decision.

b. Notes and Questions

1) Conceptual Challenge

Our system of property ownership during marriage is largely the legacy of ancient practices. The establishment of a system of property ownership during marriage is intellectually a significant challenge. What could and should be some of the guiding principles for such a system? Is the community (marital) property system the wisest?

Why/ why not? If both husband and wife are legal owners of all property acquired during marriage, does that mean that the grocer or furniture store salesperson must call the husband to be sure that the wife has his permission to buy groceries or a new lamp, or the electronic store must call the wife to see that husband has her permission to buy the big-screen television? Why/ why not? Since today many married women work and have their own income, are the presumptions that underlie the community (marital) property system still valid? In fact, are there not many different family economic arrangements in any state today? How can any one system do justice to all of the different marital expectations regarding property ownership and control?

2) Private vs. Public Property

The foregoing discussion of the property rights of married persons concerns the *private* property -- that is, traditional forms of wealth, including capital, income, wages, earnings, land, money, investments, savings, gifts, private pensions, etc.) All citizens have some private property, and most citizens depend primarily upon private property to support themselves and their families. Most of the clients that most of you will represent most of the time will depend upon mostly private property. Additionally, however, publicly-funded programs (including social security, various public welfare programs, public subsidies for persons with disabilities, medicaid, medicare, etc.) provide some form of property (support) for most persons, and most of the property for a minority of the population. These public benefits have been called *public* property, or the *new property*.

The term "new property" comes from a famous 1964 Yale Law Journal article by Professor Charles Reich, in which he suggested that employment income, benefits, and pensions were their primary form of wealth for most people, and that government benefits were the primary form of wealth for the poor. Charles Reich, "The New Property," 73 *Yale L.J.* 733, 738-739 (1964). Professor Reich proposed that both forms of wealth should be treated like new forms of property and that they "must be surrounded with the kinds of safeguards once reserved for personality." *Ibid.* In 1981, Professor Mary Ann Glendon explored the implications of "the new property" for family law in a very influential book, *The New Family and the New Property.* She argued that while legal ties between employee and employer are becoming stronger and more permanent, legal relations among family members are becoming looser and more transient, and that employment and government are replacing family as the primary providers of protection for the individual's economic and health security. Glendon at 2. Reich's recommendation has been adopted, at least in part because once the government has decided to provide benefits persons entitled to those benefits under law have a reasonable expectation or entitlement (property interest) that they may obtain the benefits according to the law, and deprivation of their benefit or entitlement without due process is prohibited. *Goldberg v. Kelly*, 397 U.S. 254 (1970).

With respect to both private and public property, a key question concerns what is the "unit" of ownership. That is, should control of private property and entitlement to public property be vested in the individual (single or married), or in some other economic unit? The answer to that question for private property is discussed in the beginning of this chapter (separate title approach, community property, married women's acts, equitable distribution, marital property, etc.).

The issue of the appropriate "unit" of ownership of property is especially complicated in the area of *public property.* That is, the government has established programs designed to prevent the tragedy of the needy going without necessary food, medical care, and shelter. Should those benefits be provided to individuals or to "families"? The easiest method of ownership to administer, as the English kings figured out a thousand or more years ago, is the individual. On the other hand, that is economically unrealistic in most cases. For most persons, "families" function as the operative "economic units." That is, family members pool their resources to provide for the needs of each other. Parents pay for the living expenses of children. Even after the children are legally emancipated and legally independent (usually at age 18), many parents continue to provide economically for their children by "helping" them get through college (by paying part or all of tuition, books, dorm or apartment rent, etc.), or "helping" them get started on their own (by paying for part or all of a car, an apartment, utility bills, etc.). Higher-earning spouses (usually husbands) pay for their spouse's living expenses, or a disproportionate share of the lesser-earning spouse's housing, transportation, food, fuel, and clothing expenses, etc. Often adults within families will support their aged parents, nieces, nephews, and grandchildren. A system of government benefits that looked only at the individual would probably fail to achieve the poverty-fighting purposes of the benefit program because it would only see a small part of the whole picture of economic reality. Thus, the "family" seems like the most realistic "economic unit" in our society.

If the "family" is to be the unit of ownership (eligibility for) public property, how should "family" be defined? The first reference may be to the "legal family," namely, persons related by blood, marriage or adoption. If this definition is chosen, one must ask "how closely related" - should we include the income of well-to-do uncles or grandparents in determining eligibility for public property (welfare) programs? What if a child's (Bobby's) biological father has abandoned him, his mother is an alcoholic in a treatment program, he (8-year-old Bobby) is living with his maternal grandmother, his aunt (his mother's sister) and his aunt's boyfriend? Should the welfare program look to the legal nuclear family (Bobby, mother, and father) to determine eligibility? It has been suggested that a disproportionate share of the persons who most need public assistance do not have functional legal families, or live in non-traditional (non-legal-family) relationships. (That is, living in nonmarital cohabitation arrangements, single-parent childrearing, and other non-traditional-legal arrangements is significantly associated with poverty.) Thus, using the traditional-legal-family as the unit of ownership or eligibility for public welfare benefits might fail to reach many of the very class of persons the public welfare benefit program is designed to cover.

Using the same (Bobby) hypothetical, should the law look to the residential relatives (Bobby, grandmother, aunt) instead of to the legal family? Or to the co-residents (Bobby, grandmother, aunt, and aunt's boyfriend)? Legally, however, the aunt and her boyfriend (and perhaps even the grandmother) have no legal obligation or duty to support Bobby.

Some writers have suggested that the "new family" should be mother and child, or co-residents, or inter-dependents (residential or otherwise).

If the law determines that some other unit than the individual or the legal family should be the unit of ownership for some property (usually public property), the effect of that decision upon family formation and stability must be considered. For example, the

"Great Society" welfare programs of the 1960s have been blamed by some scholars (including, famously, Senator Patrick Moynihan) for the disintegration of the Black American family, by *inter alia* giving young pregnant black women and single mothers powerful economic incentives *not* to marry (by offering them greater economic benefits if they did not marry than they could expect to get if they married the father(s) of their children, who typically either had low-paying jobs, or were on welfare themselves). While causation and precise effects are still widely debated, it is clear that welfare programs alter the economic situation (that is what they are designed to do) in ways that may have profound, unintended effects upon the family. Nevertheless, it is common today for public assistance programs to define eligibility for (define the economic unit for the program) as including something other than the traditional legal family.

3) Local Statutes and Cases

What is the regime of property ownership during marriage in your homestate? Does it differ depending on whether it is real or personal property? Where are the governing statutes found? What are the leading cases in your homestate concerning ownership, control and responsibility for property during (especially acquired during) marriage? To what extent is the system joint and mutual control and ownership? To what extent is it separate and independent ownership?

3. Practical and Ethical Considerations

In what ways might a lawyer's knowledge of the property law governing married parties be of value in helping his or her clients with financial planning during the marriage, and planning for transfer of wealth upon death?

4. Bibliography

1 W. Blackstone, Commentaries on the Laws of England * (1765-69).
Contemporary Family Law, vol. 2, Ch. 12 (1988).
Fisher on Matrimonial Property (2d ed., London: 1984).
1 F. Pollock & F. Maitland, The History of English Law (1898 ed. reprinted 1968).
Charles Donahue, Jr., *What Causes Fundamental Legal Ideas? Marital Property in England and France in the Thirteenth Century*, 78 Mich. L. Rev. 59 (1979).

C. MARITAL DISCRIMINATION

1. Background

a. Discrimination in General

Discrimination on the basis of marital status is an issue that arises in a number of different settings. For instance, many employers (including states and state entities) have policies forbidding "nepotism" - defined generally as: "Bestowal of patronage by public officers in appointing others to positions by reason of blood or marital relationship to appointing authority." Black's Law Dictionary 1191 (Rev. 4th ed. 1968). While preferential treatment in granting of public benefits on the basis of marriage surely is a form of discrimination that most would find offensive (discrimination against applicants who are not in the favored family), in an apparent effort to eliminate the temptation entirely some anti-nepotism laws having married persons work in the same unit, or forbid hiring relatives of current employees, which itself constitutes a form of discrimination against married persons (if the couple divorced and thereafter merely cohabited, they would not be under some anti-nepotism proscriptions). Is that kind of discrimination justified? What about rules of professional responsibility that bar married persons from handling certain cases (arguably even joining certain firms, departments or offices) when their spouse has been involved with on the other side of the case?

Many states have added "marital status" to the list of categories as to which discrimination is forbidden. What does that mean? Does that forbid only discrimination against married persons because of their status as married, or does that also forbid discrimination against persons who are not married (whose "marital status," in a sense, could be said to be "none" or "single") ? Is marital status, like race or religion, a matter which should be given general "suspect classification" status? For all purposes?

2. Statutes, Cases and Doctrines

a. *Prince George's County v. Greenbelt Homes*
Prince George's County v. Greenbelt Homes, Inc.,
431 A.2d 745 (Md. App., 1981).

LOWE, Judge.

Reluctant to plunge into the sea of matrimony, John Hemphill and Lynn Bradley were nonetheless eager to settle upon its shores. They had jointly contracted to purchase the right of "perpetual use and enjoyment" of a dwelling unit in a cooperative housing development known as Greenbelt Homes, Inc., situate in Prince George's County. Because the contract was "subject to an acceptance of the purchaser by Greenbelt Homes, Inc. as members," each applied for membership indicating on his application that they resided together and by the joint contract to purchase, inferentially intended to continue to do so in the dwelling unit described.

To their chagrin, they were denied membership "because (they) were not married." According to their precipitous complaint to the Human Relations Commission of Prince George's County, the spokesman for Greenbelt Homes, Inc., "said that in the past the Board (of Directors) has made exceptions to its policy of not selling to unmarried persons but never for an unmarried couple. He stated that not being married was the only reason for our rejection, that everything else was alright."

Anxious to fulfill its destiny as destroyer of discrimination, the Commission made ready to do battle, apparently to provide surcease for the sensitivities of those whom they clept "Complainants."

. . . .

. . . Greenbelt's Mutual Ownership Contract contained a covenant that "The member shall occupy the dwelling unit covered by this contract as a private dwelling from the date of occupancy ... for himself and his immediate family...."

Focusing on the word "family" (while ignoring its immediately preceding restrictive adjective), the Commission rejected the "generally accepted" interpretation of "family" applied by Greenbelt Homes, and took "notice" that Webster's Seventh New Collegiate Dictionary (1967 edition) listed a series of definitions for "family" broad enough to cover not only "(a) group of persons of common ancestry," but also "a group of individuals living under one roof...," a "group of things related by common characteristics," "fellowship" and more pointedly, "A basic unit in society having as its nucleus two or more adults living together, and cooperating in the care and rearing of their own or adopted children."

The Commission also took "notice" that s 10.0 of the Prince George's County Zoning Ordinance defines a family for housing occupancy purposes as, "An individual, or two or more persons related by blood or marriage, or a group of not more than five persons (excluding servants) not related by blood or marriage, living together as a single housekeeping group in a dwelling unit...."

The Commission further concluded that "Greenbelt Homes, Inc.'s claim (The Board of Directors acting as Greenbelt Homes, Inc.) that their verbally expressed, only, interpretation of 'family' being 'commonly accepted' is not valid."

It then held that Greenbelt's covenant, so interpreted, contravened a local ordinance against discrimination which proscribed "acting, or failing to act, or unduly delaying any action regarding any person because of ... marital status ... in such a way that such person is adversely affected in the area(s) of housing...." Prince George's County Code, § 2-186(3).

Caught up in the cause which by now seemingly surpassed its "complainants" (who we empirically note have since married and become ensconced elsewhere), the Commission ordered (among other things): "That Greenbelt Homes, Inc. revise their (sic) Membership Agreement and their (sic) Mutual Ownership Contract to eliminate any provisions which are contrary to federal, state and/or local laws and/or ordinances."

... [T]he Commission did not find that a covenant restricting membership to one's immediate "family" as that term is "COMMONLY ACCEPTED" would have been discriminating because of marital status. It found only that the definition applied by Greenbelt to its covenant was invalid and implicitly should be defined as broadly as any of Webster's alternatives, and at least as broadly as the Zoning Ordinance of which the Commission took "notice."

... Prince George's County filed suit for declaratory judgment and mandatory injunction in the Circuit Court for Prince George's County in equity to enforce the order of the Commission. . . .

The case was submitted on motions for summary judgment by both parties; that of the County was denied and that of Greenbelt granted. In its opinion . . . the judge did not define "family" as requested. In defining "marital status," however, he held that "People who are not married to one another do not have a marital status and for that reason it is clear that the legislative body did not intend for such to apply. If the County Council of Prince George's County wants that intent, the ordinance should be amended to prohibit marital status 'or lack thereof.' "

The issue raised on appeal by Prince George's County is "whether the appellee's practice of refusing to approve or enter into perpetual use agreements with unmarried heterosexual couples constitutes marital status discrimination within the meaning of § 2-186(3), Prince George's County Code?"

... Significantly, Maryland's statute with regard to "Discrimination in Housing" also makes it an unlawful practice to discriminate in regard to housing "because of ... marital status" (Md.Ann.Code Art. 49B, s 20). A declaration regarding that term in context takes on added interpretative importance. It is noteworthy that the term "marital status" appears 100 times in the Annotated Code of Maryland scattered in some 31 different, although often related, sections. Since Judge Ross' proclamation that "People who are not married to one another do not have a marital status..." is somewhat misleading, we will attempt to clarify the meaning of that term as used in the context of the housing discrimination law before addressing the Commission's erroneous definition of "family" in its even more restrictive context in the covenant. . . .

-marital status-

Under the facts presented, we point out that neither complainant (each of whom was "single," "unmarried") was denied membership individually because of his or her individual marital status. While each separately had a marital status, collectively they did not. Only marriage as prescribed by law can change the marital status of an individual to a new legal entity of husband and wife. The law of Maryland does not recognize common law marriages (*Henderson v. Henderson*, 199 Md. 449, 454, 87 A.2d 403 (1952), or other unions of two or more persons such as concubinage, *320 syneisaktism, relationships of homosexuals or lesbians as legally bestowing upon two people a legally cognizable marital status. Such relationships are simple illegitimate unions unrecognized, or in some instances condemned, by the law. That public policy message rings out from the procedural prerequisites for legitimating "marriages," Md.Ann. Code Art. 62, and the statutory condemnation of other relationships, *see e.g.* Md.Ann. Code Art. 27, s 18 (Bigamy) and ss 390 et seq. The obvious intent of our legislature is to encourage the proverbial concept that more belongs to a marriage than four bare legs in a bed. Even contemporary discrimination laws are not intended to promulgate promiscuity by favoring relationships unrecognized by statute or case law as having legal status.

Neither Mr. Hemphill nor Ms. Bradley was denied membership in Greenbelt Homes, Inc. because he or she was single. They were denied joint membership because neither Greenbelt nor the law of Maryland recognized their union as cloaking them with a "marital status." Greenbelt simply refused to acknowledge that the naked emperor was wearing clothes. The complainants who were not then married may not compel treatment as an entity * any more than a married couple may be treated as single for preferential tax treatment,*. We are what we are, and it is in that capacity which we must be judged even when we seek the judgment.

-family-

The crux of the Commission's order, however, was its finding that Greenbelt's "commonly accepted" definition of the term "family" is invalid. The Commission held that the term "family" as used in the contractual covenant included as a matter of law at the very least the two complainants, but interpretatively as many as "five persons ... not related by blood or marriage, living together as a single housekeeping group in a dwelling unit," which it gleaned from the local zoning ordinance.

The Court of Appeals has noted that the statutory use and definition of the word "family" may be (and often is) limited to the purposes of a specific act. * In that case the Court of Appeals was interpreting the use of the term "family" in the household exclusion provision of insurance contract, just as we are here concerned with an exclusionary provision in a contract. There the Court agreed with Greenbelt's observation of the "commonly accepted" interpretation of terms: "It would thus appear that in common parlance and usage the word 'family' more frequently connotes the existence of a marital or blood relationship, or a legal status approximating such relationship." *

Noting that common law marriages are not recognized in Maryland as a "legal status," the Court held that an unmarried woman living without consanguinal ties within an insured's household did not "in this State" possess a legal status which was the equivalent of being a "family" member. It would seem to follow that the Greenbelt covenant meant what Greenbelt intended it to mean, rather than what the Commission wanted it to mean. From at least as early as 1833, we are told that in construing covenants they must be viewed in context and in accordance with the intention of the covenantors. *

But even without a clear contextual intent, words express whatever meaning convention has attached to them. * In "The Theory of Legal Interpretation," 12 Harv.L.R. 417 (1899), Oliver Wendell Holmes pointed out that: "A word generally has several meanings, even in the dictionary. You have to consider the sentence in which it stands to decide which of those meanings it bears in the particular case, and very likely will see that it there has a shade of significance more refined than any given in the word-book."

It is apparent that the Commission's declaration of invalidity of Greenbelt's definitional application of the term "family" was an error of law affecting its decision *; or, if found as a fact, it was unsupported by competent material, and substantial evidence in view of the entire record as submitted. * It follows that without regard to the judge's rather broad definitional reasoning regarding the meaning of "marital status," he did not err in refusing to enforce the defective order of the Commission at the insistence of the County.

***

JUDGMENT AFFIRMED. ***

b. Notes and Questions

1) *Greenbelt* Questions

Did the court reach the correct decision? For the correct reasons? Are laws that prohibit discrimination on the basis of "marital status," without explanation or definition, ambiguous on their face? Do they clearly indicate whether discrimination only against persons who have the marital status (are marriage) is prohibited, or that discrimination on the basis of any category of domestic status of which marriage is an example (including single, divorced, separated, widowed, cohabiting, etc.) is barred? Did the court make a convincing effort to ascertain the legislative intent?

The cases interpreting the meaning of "marital status" in nondiscrimination statutes are split. *See* Skees, *infra;* Muller, *infra.* For instance, in *Smith v. Fair Employment and Housing Commission,* 913 P.2d 909 (Cal. 1996), the California Supreme Court upheld an order of the Commission compelling a devout Protestant woman who owned and rented out two duplexes (four apartments) to allow unmarried couples to rent her units; her refusal to rent to unmarried couples was found to violate the prohibition against marital status discrimination in the state civil rights law. In *County of Dane v. Norman,* (Wisc. 1993), however, the Wisconsin Supreme Court ruled, over a strong dissent, that a landlord's refusal to rent to a same-sex couple did not constitute "marital status" discrimination even though the count defined "marital status" as "being married, divorced, widowed, single, separated, or being a cohabitant." The court emphasized that cohabitation is conduct, not status, and that the ordinance giving status to cohabitants violated the state policy to favor and protect marriage. Some commentators suggest that the cases follow either a "narrow" interpretation of the "marital status" nondiscrimination rules, barring only discrimination against an individual on the sole basis of his or her status as married, single, divorced, etc., and those following a "broad" interpretation which includes a partner and bars any reliance on marital status. Beattie, *infra*; Muller, *infra.* However, that distinction seems to miss the core issue; *i.e.*, whether the law prohibiting "marital status" discrimination protects one specific, preferred category only (married couples), or does it ban using any domestic relations status (including single, divorced, etc.)?

Does *Lawrence v. Texas,* 539 U.S. 558 (2003) effectively prohibit discrimination on the basis of domestic status generally as a matter of constitutional law? Does it prohibit preference for marriage (such as law barring discrimination against married persons but not protecting unmarried couples)?

Religious defenses have been raised unsuccessfully in most prominent "marital status" discrimination cases. For instance, in *Smith*, the devout woman's free exercise claim was summarily rejected by the California court under *Employment Division v. Smith,* 494 U.S. 872 (1990). *See also Thomas v. v. Anchorage Equal Rights Comm'n,,* 230 F.3d. (9ᵗʰ Cir. 2000) (en banc), *cert denied* 531 U.S. 1143 (2001); *Swanner v. Anchorage Equal Rights Comm'n,* 874 P.2d 274 (Alaska 1994); Skees, *infra.*

2) Does our Law Really Favor Marriage?

While undoubtedly there is emotional and (some) symbolic preference for and favoring of marriage in our laws, that policy is not consistent or complete. For example, Professor Sonne found that:

one place where direct support is largely absent (or, at least, marginal) is at work. Although it may shock some, especially those waging the current "marriage wars," the law offers few workplace rights and benefits to marriage in itself. To be sure, there is some legal treatment, but it is largely limited to indirect public benefits (e.g., tax, Social Security) that are rooted more in presumptions of economic dependency, and corresponding child-rearing, than any objective value of marriage, and, as such, are not even useful to most modern couples to the degree both partners prefer to work--and would also be of little use to most unmarried pairs, if so offered, for the same reason.

Sonne, *infra*, at 868-69.

3. Practical and Ethical Concerns

What limitations do the Model Rules of Professional Conduct impose upon lawyers who are married to each other but work in separate offices, firms, or for different clients?

4. Bibliography

John C. Beattie, Note, Prohibiting Marital Status Discrimination: A Proposal for the Protection of Unmarried Couples, 42 Hastings L.J. 1415 (1991).

1 W. Blackstone, Commentaries on the Laws of England *(1765-69).

Comment, 16 New Eng. L. Rev. 573 (1981).

Contemporary Family Law, vol. 2, Ch.13 (1988).

Kevin Layton, Interspousal Tort Immunity in Utah (December, 1985).

McCurty, *Torts Between Persons in Domestic Relations*, 43 Harv. L. Rev. 1030, 1055 (1930).

Robert C. Muller, Case Comment, Donahue v. Fair Employment and Housing Commission: *A Free Exercise Defense to Marital Status Discrimination,* 74 B.U. L. Rev. 145 (1994).

F. Pollock & F. Maitland, The History of English Law (2d ed 1898, reissued 1968).

William Prosser, The Law of Torts 861 (4th ed. 1971).

James A. Sonne, *Love Doesn't Pay: The Fiction of Marriage Rights in the Workplace*, 40 U. Rich. L. Rev. 867 (2006).

W. Edward Skees, Case Note, *Marital Status Discrimination*, 36 Brandeis L.J. 328 (1997-98).

Robert G. Spector, *Marital Torts: The Current Legal Landscape*, 33 Fam. L.Q. 745 (1999).

CHAPTER 17

Economic Consequences: Necessaries, Family Support; Benefits and Tax Considerations

A. NECESSARIES, FAMILY SUPPORT, CONTRACT AND AGENCY

1. Background

a. Spousal Support at Common Law

Consistent with the suspension of most property-ownership rights of women during marriage, the common law imposed a duty upon husbands to support their wives. Conversely, the wife had the duty to render services to the husband in the home. Blackstone put it this way:

> [A] man cannot grant anything to his wife, or enter into covenant with her: for the grant would be to suppose her separate existence . . . . A woman, indeed, may be attorney for her husband; for that implies no separation from, but is rather a representation of, her Lord. . . . .
>
> The husband is bound to provide his wife with necessaries by law, as much as himself: and if she contracts debts for them, he is obliged to pay them; but, for anything besides necessaries, he is not chargeable. Also, if a wife elopes, and lives with another man, the husband is not chargeable even for necessaries; at least if the person who furnishes them is sufficiently apprized of her elopement. If the wife be indebted before marriage, the husband is bound afterwards to pay the debt; for he has adopted her and her circumstances together.

William Blackstone, Commentaries on the Laws of England *442-443. Full divorce was virtually unknown at common law, but the equivalent of legal separation might include an order to the husband to continue to support his wife, even though she was living separate and apart from him.

> In case of divorce *a mensa et thoro* [what would today be called legal separation], the law allows alimony to the wife: which is that allowance which is made to a woman for her support out of the husband's estate; being settled at the discretion of the ecclesiastical judge, on consideration of all the circumstances of the case. This is sometimes called her *estovers*; for which, if he refuses payment, there is (besides the ordinary process of excommunication) a writ a common law *de estoveriis habendis* (of recovering estovers), in order to recover it. It is generally proportioned to the rank and quality of the parties. But in the case of elopement, and living with an adulterer, the law allows her no alimony.

Id. at *442.

The equal protection revolution of the 1970s abolished the one-sided, gender-stereotyped duties of support-service. *See generally Orr v. Orr*, 440 U.S. 268 (1979) (alimony statute which provided that only husbands could be liable for and only wives could receive alimony violates equal protection). Now, state "Family Expense Acts" or "Support" laws provide that each spouse (regardless of gender) is liable for the support of his or her marriage partner. Since many wives do not work outside the home for significant periods during marriage, and since women still typically earn less than men when they are employed, these laws still primarily provide needed protection for married women; but men, too, may now claim the benefit of them.

The equalization of the duty of support does not mean that an economically wealthier spouse may selfishly impose upon the resources of the economically poorer spouse, or refuse to support a marriage partner above the mere subsistence level. The degree or amount of support required and right to draw upon it still depends upon the situation and circumstances of the parties, their status and conditions. At one time marital fault (desertion, adultery, etc.) would bar a spouse from recovery spousal support; but the extent to which such factors today are valid defenses to support claims is changing. *See* Homer Clark, The Law of Domestic Relations in the United States § 6.1 (1988).

b. Doctrine of Necessaries

The doctrine of necessary (described by Blackstone) still survives and provides that if a spouse (or parent) fails to provide "necessaries" for a dependent family member (spouse or child), that dependant person may purchase them on credit, charging the responsible spouse or parent, who will legally be liable to the supplier for the goods or services purchased. "Necessaries" included all goods and services which are "reasonably necessary," (or "suited," or "fit") for the condition and station of the family. Thus, necessaries are determined by subjective considerations (e.g., wealth, social status, past practices, etc.), not just those things necessary to sustain biological life. The common law doctrine of necessaries has been codified in some states (usually in "Family Expense Acts").

The equalization of the duty to provide necessaries to one's spouse is now widely accepted. Regardless of gender, one spouse is now generally held liable for the support and provision of necessaries to the other. Under the doctrine of necessaries a merchant, grocer, or medical service provider, for example, may sue a woman for necessaries provided to her husband. But it appears that a right to reimbursement may exist under some circumstances if a woman is forced to pay for necessaries furnished to the family for which the husband could have paid. *See* H. Clark, *supra* at 258.

2. Statutes, Cases and Doctrines

a. *Sharpe Furniture v. Buckstaff*

Sharpe Furniture, Inc. v. John D. Buckstaff, Jr., and Karen Buckstaff
299 N.W.2d 219 (Wis. 1980).

BEILFUSS, Chief Justice.

This is a review of a decision of the court of appeals which affirmed the judgment of the circuit court for Winnebago county. The judgment was entered against the defendants John D. Buckstaff, Jr., and his wife, Karen Buckstaff, requiring payment of sums due on the purchase of goods from the plaintiff, Sharpe Furniture, Inc., a Wisconsin corporation engaged in the business of retail furniture sales.

This controversy centers around the purchase of a sofa from Sharpe Furniture, Inc. (Sharpe). The purchase was made by Karen Buckstaff on August 15, 1973. On that date, Mrs. Buckstaff signed in her own name a special order for a "Henredon 6800 Sofa." Under the terms of the order she was to pay $621.50 within 60 days after the item was received from the factory. Interest at a rate of 1.5 percent per month was charged on the unpaid balance after that 60-day period. No representations were made to Sharpe at the time of the purchase that Mrs. Buckstaff was acting on behalf of her husband in purchasing the furniture. Indeed, John Buckstaff had previously written to the local credit bureau service to advise that office that he would not be responsible for any credit extended to his wife.

The Henredon sofa was received from the factory and delivered to the residence of the defendants on February 8, 1974. This piece of furniture has been a part of the Buckstaff home ever since its delivery. Despite this fact, neither John Buckstaff nor his wife have tendered payment for the sofa.

On November 20, 1975, Sharpe commenced this action against both Buckstaffs. The parties agreed to allow the trial court to decide the dispute on the basis of the undisputed facts as they appeared in the trial memoranda submitted by counsel. In addition to the facts already stated above, the informal stipulation of the parties reveals that John Buckstaff, Jr., is the president of Buckstaff Company of Oshkosh, Wisconsin. Mrs. Buckstaff is a housewife. Mr. Buckstaff earns a substantial income and the Buckstaff family is one of social and economic prominence in the Oshkosh area. It was further set forth that Mr. Buckstaff has always provided his wife with the necessaries of life and has never failed or refused to provide his wife with items which could be considered necessaries.

On the basis of these facts, the trial court found that Karen Buckstaff was liable on her contract and that John Buckstaff was also liable for the amount due on the sofa under the common law doctrine of necessaries. Judgment was entered accordingly. The court of appeals affirmed. John Buckstaff now seeks review of the decision of the court of appeals. Karen Buckstaff has not sought appellate relief from the entry of the judgment against her.

There are two issues which we must consider in reviewing the decision of the court of appeals:

1. Whether, under the common law doctrine of necessaries and in the absence of any contractual obligation on his part, a husband may be held liable for sums due as payment for necessary items purchased on credit by his wife.

2. Whether, in an action for recovery of the value of necessaries supplied on credit to a wife, it is essential for the plaintiff-creditor to prove either that the husband has failed, refused or neglected to provide the items which have been supplied by the plaintiff-creditor or that the items supplied were reasonably needed by the wife or the family.

Before proceeding to a discussion of the merits of this case, we examine the substance of the doctrine of necessaries.

The Wisconsin Supreme Court restated the common law rule of necessaries early on in the history of the jurisprudence of this state. In 1871, in the case of *Warner and Ryan v. Heiden*, 28 Wis. 517, 519 (1871), the court wrote:

> The husband is under legal obligations to support his wife, and nothing but wrongful conduct on her part can free him from such obligation. If he fails to provide her with suitable and proper necessaries, any third person who does provide her therewith, may maintain an action against him for the same. 1 Bishop on Mar. and Div., sec. 553. The same learned author, in the next section (sec. 554), thus defines what are necessaries which the husband is bound to furnish to his wife: "And, in general, we may say, that necessaries are such articles of food, or apparel, or medicine, or such medical attendance and nursing, or such provided means of locomotion, or provided habitation and furniture, or such provision for her protection in society, and the like, as the husband, considering his ability and standing, ought to furnish to his wife for her sustenance, and the preservation of her health and comfort."

This doctrine traditionally required the creditor to show that he supplied to the wife an item that was, in fact, a necessary and that the defendant had previously failed or refused to provide his wife with this item. *. When such a showing was made, the creditor was entitled to recovery as against the husband despite the fact that the husband had not contractually bound himself by his own act or by the act of an agent. The doctrine of necessaries is not imposed by the law of agency. This duty is placed upon a husband by virtue of the legal relationship of marriage. It arises as an obligation placed on him as a matter of public policy.

The appellant challenges the continued vitality of this common law rule. Mr. Buckstaff charges that the necessaries doctrine conflicts with contemporary trends toward equality of the sexes and a sex neutral society. He further argues that the doctrine is an outdated and inefficient means of compelling support. It is argued that various social welfare agencies and governmental institutions have replaced the doctrine of necessaries as a mechanism for the maintenance of the members of a household.

It is true that the necessaries rule has been justified in the past on the basis of a social view of the married woman as a person without legal capacity. However, the nature of the woman's obligations under the necessary rule in relation to the obligation of her husband is not at issue here. That question has been treated in our decision in Estate of Stromsted, --- Wis.2d ---, 299 N.W.2d 226 (1980), wherein we concluded the husband was primarily liable for necessities and the wife secondarily liable. The question presented in this case involves a consideration of the nature of the husband's obligation. We must decide whether such a liability imposed upon the husband furthers a proper purpose in contemporary society.

We are of the opinion that the doctrine of necessaries serves a legitimate and proper purpose in our system of common law. The heart of this common law rule is a concern for the support and the sustenance of the family and the individual members thereof. The sustenance of the family unit is accorded a high order of importance in the scheme of Wisconsin law. It has been codified as a part of our statutes, see e. g., sec. 767.08, Stats., and it has been recognized as a part of our case law.*. The necessaries rule encourages the extension of credit to those who in an individual capacity may not have the ability to make these basic purchases. In this manner it facilitates the support of the family unit and its function is in harmony with the purposes behind the support laws of this state. The rule retains a viable role in modern society.

We view the nature of the husband's liability as a contractual duty implied in law, i. e., a quasi-contractual obligation. In *Seegers v. Sprague*, 70 Wis.2d 997, 1004, 236 N.W.2d 227 (1975), the nature of the quasi-contract liability was discussed:

> (T)his court (has) recognized that subcontractors may have a basis for recovery in the quasi-contract action of unjust enrichment. In *Don Ganser* *, the elements of such action were listed as:
> " ... (1) a benefit conferred upon the defendant by the plaintiff, (2) appreciation by the defendant of the fact of such benefit, and (3) acceptance and retention by the defendant of the benefit, under circumstances such that it would be inequitable to retain the benefit without payment of the value thereof. "

We conclude that when an item or service is obtained for the benefit of the family which is necessary and no payment for that item or service has been made, the elements of an action for an implied-in-law contract exist and the husband is primarily liable.

In light of the proper function of the necessaries rule in relation to the support of the family, in the absence of an express contract to the contrary, we hold that a husband incurs the primary obligation, implied as a matter of law, to assume liability for the necessaries which have been procured for the sustenance of his family.

Mr. Buckstaff's second argument is that, as a matter of law, he is not liable for the necessaries purchased by his wife because Sharpe did not plead or prove that he as a husband failed, refused or neglected to provide a sofa for his wife. It is also argued that liability cannot be found in the face of the parties' stipulation which states that Mr. Buckstaff has always provided his wife with the necessaries of life and has never failed or refused to provide her with items which would constitute necessaries.

There are three leading cases in Wisconsin concerning the nature of a creditor's action under the law of necessaries. The most recent of these cases was decided in 1924.

The law of necessaries was first recognized in the case of *Warner and Ryan v. Heiden*, 28 Wis. 517 (1871). In that case the court ruled that a husband could be held liable for attorney's fees incurred by his wife in the course of defending against a criminal charge. Id. at 521. Such legal fees were viewed as necessaries for which the husband was responsible.

In the case of *Eder v. Grifka*, 149 Wis. 606, 136 N.W. 154 (1912), it was held that, besides demonstrating that necessaries were furnished by the creditor to the defendant's spouse, a plaintiff-creditor must also plead and prove that the defendant wilfully refused to provide the necessaries for his wife. The court wrote:

> A husband is not ipso facto liable for all necessaries that may be furnished his wife. It is only under circumstances and conditions showing a necessity that they be furnished her by others, such as his misconduct compelling her to leave him and their home, his wilful refusal to provide for her, or his deserting her, that the husband is liable for them.

* In the absence of these special circumstances, the rule of Eder allowed no recovery for the creditor. The merchant sold to the wife at his own risk.

The merchant's burden of proof was modified by the decision in *Simpson Garment Co. v. Schultz*, 182 Wis. 506, 196 N.W. 783 (1924). The *Simpson Garment Company* decision involved a defendant whose wife purchased a coat, a dress and a slip for her daughter. The daughter was about to graduate from high school and lacked the proper attire for the commencement exercises. The wife pledged the defendant's credit in order to purchase the items and when her husband refused to pay, a lawsuit was commenced. The defendant was found liable for the cost of the garments. In discussing the plaintiff's prima facie burden, the court said:

> When a merchant sues a husband for necessaries sold to his wife or some member of his family, it is incumbent upon him to show, among other things, (1) that the articles purchased were such as are suitable for the wife or member of the family in view of the family's social position in the community in which they live and in view of the defendant's financial ability to pay for them; and (2) that the articles sold were reasonably needed by the wife or member of the family to whom they were sold at the time of the sale.*

The *Simpson Garment Company* rule required only that the creditor show that the item was "reasonably needed" by the wife or family, and not that the husband wilfully refused to provide his wife with the necessary item as suggested by *Eder v. Grifka, supra.*

In applying the rule of the *Simpson Garment Company* decision to the case at bar, the creditor Sharpe must prevail over Mr. Buckstaff's two-pronged attack on the judgment. The latter's arguments are directed at the second element of the necessaries doctrine, i. e., reasonable need of the family. Buckstaff's first argument, that the court's judgment of liability is invalid in the absence of a finding of refusal or neglect by a husband, must be rejected. Under *Simpson Garment Company*, the refusal or neglect of the husband is not an element essential to recovery by the creditor. Mr. Buckstaff's second contention is that the sofa should not be considered a necessary in view of the stipulation that he as a husband provided his wife with all necessaries. Whether or not, as a general matter, a man provides his wife with necessaries is irrelevant to a determination of whether a particular item is reasonably needed under the *Simpson Garment Company rule.* * This stipulation, which is phrased in terms of the conclusion which it seeks to establish, is not probative of whether the sofa in issue was reasonably needed.

We have reviewed the stipulation of the parties in this matter and we are satisfied that ample evidence supported the trial court's conclusion that the Henredon sofa was a legally necessary item. The Buckstaffs are a prominent family and their socio-economic standing justifies a finding that the sofa at issue here was a suitable and proper item for their household. With reference to the element of reasonable need, we note that the sofa has been in use in the Buckstaff home since its delivery. Such continued use gives rise to an inference of reasonable need. This inference is not rebutted by the stipulation stating that Mr. Buckstaff provided his wife with "all necessaries."

Several spousal agency theories have been advanced as a ground for liability by both the respondent and by the Wisconsin Merchants Federation as amicus curiae. Having found that Mr. Buckstaff is liable on the independent ground provided by the necessaries rule, we need not reach these questions.

The decision of the court of appeals is affirmed.

ABRAHAMSON, Justice (concurring).

I join the court in retaining the doctrine of necessaries and imposing liability on Mr. Buckstaff for the cost of the sofa. I do not agree, however, with that portion of the opinion in which the court adopts a rule placing primary liability on the husband to the creditor for necessaries supplied to the family. *[FN1 - The court formulates the rule of necessaries as follows: "In light of the proper function of the necessaries rule in relation to the support of the family, in the absence of an express contract to the contrary, we hold that a husband incurs the primary obligation, implied as a matter of law, to assume liability for the necessaries which have been procured for the sustenance of his family." The court's view that the husband is primarily liable for necessaries is reiterated by the court in In the Matter of the Estate of Stromsted, 99 Wis.2d 136, 299 N.W.2d 226 (1980). ¶ I interpret the phrase "in the absence of an express contract to the contrary" as retaining the rule that had Mrs. Buckstaff expressly promised that she would pay for the sofa, or had Sharpe Furniture expressly agreed not to seek reimbursement from Mr. Buckstaff, the husband would not be liable to the creditor under the doctrine of necessaries. 1 Schouler, Marriage, Divorce, Separation and Domestic Relations sec. 97 (Sixth Ed. 1921). I assume the majority's use of the phrase "express contract" in this sentence includes both an express agreement and an agreement evidenced by circumstances which show a mutual intention to contract (contract implied in fact). See In the Matter of the Estate of Stromsted, *.]*

This case presents neither a novel fact situation nor a novel question of law. I believe that resolution of this case requires the court to do no more than apply the common law doctrine of necessaries to the facts. Mrs. Buckstaff is a full-time homemaker; her contribution to the support of the family is her domestic labor. Apparently she has no earnings or property in her own name. *[FN2 - Had Mrs. Buckstaff earnings or property, Sharpe Furniture, which had obtained a default judgment in the sum of $715.00 plus interest against her, would have collected its judgment from her assets, released Mr. Buckstaff from any liability, and saved itself the expense of fighting Mr. Buckstaff's appeal to the court of appeals and to this court.]* Mr. Buckstaff is employed outside the home. He has income and property in his own name. Mrs. Buckstaff ordered the sofa for the family home, but she did not personally promise to pay for the sofa. On these facts the law in Wisconsin imposes the duty to support on the husband. The common law doctrine of necessaries which arises from and is ancillary to the duty to support allows a merchant to collect the cost of the necessary goods from the husband after extending credit to the wife. As the majority points out, the elements of the common law doctrine of necessaries have been proved in this case. Imposing liability for the sofa on Mr. Buckstaff comports not only with the common law doctrine of necessaries but also with the Wisconsin law of support which follows the contemporary trend toward equality of the sexes.

I recognize, as does the majority, that if the common law doctrine of necessaries is to survive as a rule of law it must be modified in accordance with the developing laws recognizing equal rights and responsibilities of both marital partners and the changes in the economic and social conditions of society. The common law doctrine of necessaries was premised on the legal disability of the married woman and on the husband's duty to support. Today, the married woman is free to contract, *, and the duty of support rests not on the husband alone but on both the husband and wife. Sec. 767.08, Stats. While these changes in the law will require an alteration of the doctrine of necessaries, I would leave that alteration to a case in which the application of the common law doctrine conflicts with the married women statutes and the support statutes. This is not the case.

I believe the court has erred in adopting a flat, general rule which places primary liability on the husband to the creditor who supplies necessaries to the family. In my opinion, the rule suffers from two infirmities: First, the rule is not in harmony with the legislatively established public policy of this state which is to impose the obligation to support on both the husband and wife on the basis of their respective economic resources and not on one spouse or the other on the basis of gender. *. Second, the rule discriminates against men and thus contravenes the state and federal constitutional guarantees of equal protection of law. These constitutional provisions apply to the decisions of the courts, just as they do to the acts of the state legislature.*

I am persuaded that the majority rule which effects an unequal distribution of economic benefits and burdens on the basis of gender cannot pass muster under the federal and Wisconsin constitutions. *See e. g. Wengler v. Druggists Mutual Ins. Co.*, 446 U.S. 142 (1980); *Califano v. Westcott*, 443 U.S. 76, 99 S.Ct. 2655 (1979); *Orr v. Orr*, 440 U.S. 268 (1979); *Califano v. Webster*, 430 U.S. 313 (1977); *Califano v. Goldfarb*, 430 U.S. 199 (1977); *Craig v. Boren*, 429 U.S. 190 (1977); *Weinberger v. Wiesenfeld*, 420 U.S. 636 (1975); *Schlesinger v. Ballard*, 419 U.S. 498 (1975); *Kahn v. Shevin*, 416 U.S. 351 (1975); *Frontiero v. Richardson*, 411 U.S. 677 (1973); *Reed v. Reed*, 404 U.S. 71 (1971).

The New Jersey Supreme Court similarly concluded that a rule imposing liability for necessaries solely on the husband was unconstitutional under the federal and state constitutions, reasoning as follows:

> Under the (common law) rule, even a husband who is economically dependent on his wife would be liable for the necessary expenses of both spouses, while the wife would not be liable for either. In perpetuating additional benefits for a wife when the benefits may not be needed, the rule runs afoul of the equal protection clause. *Orr, supra*, 440 U.S. at 282-283.
>
> We recognize that in many instances the present rule correctly operates to favor a needy wife. Even wives who have entered the work force generally earn substantially less than their husbands.... However, that is an insufficient reason to retain a gender based classification that denigrates the efforts of women who contribute to the finances of their families and denies equal protection to husbands. *Weinberger v. Weisenfield, supra*, 420 U.S. at 645.
>
> Although the New Jersey Constitution does not contain an equal protection clause, the same result follows as under the United States Constitution. The relevant section of the New Jersey Constitution provides 'All persons are by nature free and independent, and have certain natural and unalienable rights, among which are those of enjoying and defending life and liberty, of acquiring, possessing, and protecting property, and of pursuing and obtaining safety and happiness.' Art. 1, sec. 1, par. 1. In interpreting that section, this Court stated that it provides comparable or superior protection against unequal protection of the law. *Peper v. Princeton University Board of Trustees*, 77 N.J. 55, 79 (389 A.2d 465) (1978) (discrimination on the basis of gender in private employment may deny equal protection of the laws under Art. 1, sec. 1, par. 1 of the New Jersey Constitution). For reasons previously set forth, we conclude that the rule concerning necessaries with its inherent discrimination against husbands constitutes a denial of equal protection of the laws under the New Jersey Constitution.

Jersey Shore Medical Center-Fitkin Hospital v. Estate of Sidney Baum, 417 A.2d 1003, 1008-09 (NJ

1980).

I believe the reasoning of the New Jersey Supreme Court is applicable to the rule adopted by the majority.

For the reasons I have set forth, I concur in the disposition of the case but not in the rule adopted by the court imposing primary liability for necessaries on the husband. *[FN4 - In In the Matter of the Estate of Stromsted, 299 N.W.2d 226 (1980), the court imposes secondary liability for necessaries on the wife.]*

b. *Marriage of Hirsch*
In re the Marriage OF Clement L. and Claudia H. Hirsch
211 Cal.App.3d 104, 259 Cal.Rptr. 39 (Cal. App. 4th Dist. 1989)
WALLIN, Acting Presiding Justice.

Husband appeals from an order denying his motion to classify certain debts satisfied with his post-dissolution separate property as community obligations.

* * *

Claudia Mirken and Clement Hirsch were married in 1963 and separated in 1970. Prior to and during the marriage, Clement owned shares of stock in the Bank of Los Angeles and served on its board of directors. In 1966, the bank merged with United States National Bank (USNB) and Clement's shares were converted into USNB stock. Clement sat on the new board of directors from January 1966 until March 1971, six months after the parties had separated.

In November 1973, the trial court entered an interlocutory decree dividing the community property. The decree contained an express reservation of jurisdiction to divide community property or pay community debts not then known or established.

Shortly thereafter, USNB collapsed and Clement learned he had been named as a defendant in two federal court actions alleging various statutory and contractual causes of action, plus negligence and intentional misconduct as a director of USNB. Clement promptly moved to establish a community reserve from which any ultimate liability arising out of the actions could be satisfied. The court denied the motion on the basis that Clement's liability, if any, was too uncertain at that time. It stated Clement could seek reimbursement from Claudia for her contributive share at a later date.

Thereafter, a third lawsuit was filed against Clement arising out of his tenure on the USNB board. Clement then sent an accounting to Claudia's counsel of the funds expended by him in defense of the USNB litigation and requested reimbursement for one-half that amount. The letter also stated, "[s]ettlement negotiations are on-going, and if a reasonable settlement of the law suits [sic] and claims are made, Mr. Hirsch will look to [Claudia] for a contribution of one-half of any amounts payable pursuant to such settlement." Claudia responded by disclaiming any financial responsibility for the USNB lawsuits and making clear she did not wish to participate in any settlement negotiations.

Upon the advice of counsel, Clement settled all three lawsuits and moved for a postjudgment order declaring the settlement amounts and expenses of defense community debts. He sought reimbursement for $423,130.19, one-half the amount he expended in settling the lawsuits, including attorney's fees and costs.

Believing Civil Code section 5122 to be the applicable statute *[FN1 - Civil Code section 5122 provides, "(a) A married person is not liable for any injury or damage caused by the other spouse except in cases where he or she would be liable therefor if the marriage did not exist. ¶] (b) The liability of a married person for death or injury to person or property shall be satisfied as follows: ¶] (1) If the liability of the married person is based upon an act or omission which occurred while the married person was performing an activity for the benefit of the community, the liability shall first be satisfied from the community property and second from the separate property of the married person. ¶] (2) If the liability of the married person is not based upon an act or omission which occurred while the married person was performing an activity for the benefit of the community, the liability shall first be*

satisfied from the separate property of the married person and second from the community property....]
for determining the character of the settlement obligations, Clement presented testimony that his
reason for serving on the board of USNB was to benefit the community. He said he agreed to sit on the
USNB board and various other boards because the positions were prestigious, challenging and offered
the potential to develop contacts in the business community. The parties stipulated Clement's USNB
director's salary constituted community income.

Jacob Shearer, the attorney who represented Clement in the USNB lawsuits, testified he believed
Clement's exposure to liability was limited to the negligence causes of action. Apparently there had
been an article in the Wall Street Journal which Shearer believed should have put the board on notice
of the problems which eventually led to USNB's collapse. In Shearer's opinion, Clement's failure to
heed the warnings constituted "gross negligence." However, he did not feel Clement was exposed to
any liability for the alleged intentional torts. At the most, he felt Clement's exposure amounted to
continued malfeasance in ignoring instances of self-dealing by C. Arnholt Smith, the owner of USNB,
and ignoring the Journal article. Shearer testified one of the lawsuits was nothing more than a "strike
suit" and that he recommended settlement of all three lawsuits because defense costs alone would
exceed $1 million.

Claudia presented little evidence in support of her contention the settlement obligations should be
characterized as Clement's separate debt. Her attorney testified the causes of action in the USNB
lawsuits were based primarily on intentional conduct by Clement. In addition, the court had before it
Claudia's earlier declaration stating she urged Clement to resign from the board but he refused.

After the hearing, the court made the following findings in its memorandum of intended decision:
"[T]he liabilities incurred by [Clement] in the settlement of the three lawsuits and the attendant attorneys
fees arising out of his service as a member of the board of directors of the United States National Bank
during and after the marriage of the parties are not community obligations. [Clement's] motion to have
these liabilities declared to be community obligations and requesting reimbursement from the
community is denied. [¶] The basis for this intended decision is that the settlement obligations and the
attorneys fees in connection therewith were incurred by [Clement] as a result of his tortious conduct and
pursuant to the holding of *In re Marriage of Stitt* should therefore not be charged against the
community."

The proposed order submitted by Claudia's counsel and ultimately signed by the court was in
substantial conformity with the memorandum of intended decision except it deleted any reference to the
Stitt decision. Clement appeals, contending the trial court erred in failing to apply the "benefit of the
community" test of Civil Code section 5122 to the allegedly tortious conduct which formed the basis of
the lawsuits against him. Had the court properly applied this test, Clement argues, it would have found
the amounts paid to settle those lawsuits were community obligations.

* * *

Since the passage of the Family Law Act in 1970 there has been a surprising absence of
guidelines for classifying debts arising out of allegedly tortious conduct. Although the trial court's role is
obvious once a debt has been properly characterized as a community obligation, the appropriate
method for reaching that determination has not been made clear.

We begin with the fundamental principle applicable to the division of property in a dissolution
proceeding: " 'In dividing the community property equally under the mandate of Civil Code section 4800,
subdivision (a), the court must distribute both the assets and the obligations of the community so that
the residual assets awarded to each party after the deduction of the obligations are equal.' (*In re
Marriage of Fonstein* (1976) *.)" (*In re Marriage of Schultz* (1980) *.) "[T]ransactions of the spouses inter
se are subject to review and the separate debts of one spouse may be excluded from the shared
community obligations. [Citation.] 'Between the spouses, certain obligations which are properly
characterized as separate may be assigned to the responsible person if unpaid, or reimbursement may
be ordered in favor of the community if the debt was paid from community assets.' [Citation.]" (*In re

Marriage of Lister (1984) *.) Although a creditor may be able to reach a community asset to satisfy a debt incurred by one spouse alone, in a dissolution action the court may properly require the debtor spouse to bear the entire burden of the obligation if it finds that debt to be a separate obligation.

Relying on *In re Marriage of Stitt, supra*, 147 Cal.App.3d 579, 195 Cal.Rptr. 172 [1983], the court below found the settlement obligations incurred by Clement to be his separate debt because the underlying lawsuits alleged tortious conduct committed by him. In *Stitt*, wife incurred attorney's fees in defending against civil and criminal charges of embezzlement from her employer. Wife settled the civil action and was convicted in the criminal action. In a subsequent dissolution proceeding, wife argued the attorney's fees should be regarded as a community obligation because they were incurred during marriage. Husband conceded the community was responsible to the attorneys for the obligation, but contended that as part of the dissolution action, the court could properly assign that obligation to wife as her separate debt. Husband relied on section 5122, which states that a married person is generally not liable for damages caused by a tortfeasor spouse. The trial court agreed with husband, finding wife was required to satisfy the attorney's fee obligation from her share of the community assets.

On appeal, the court was similarly persuaded that section 5122 was applicable and operated to shield the community from liability for the tortious acts of wife: "We use the term 'community obligation' for convenience. It has been said that there are no separate debts as distinguished from community debts. [Citations.] However, for practical purposes the spousal obligations are to be viewed first from the creditor's standpoint, which may encompass both community and separate property, then from the standpoint of the spouses who are interested not only in the equal division of the community property and liabilities but also in preventing a 'separate debt' of one spouse from being included in the shared community obligations. [Citation.]

" ....

"Because husband did not participate in wife's embezzlement and no benefit to the community was shown, ... [¶] ... in the settlement of marital rights the court could seek an equitable result because of the separate nature of the obligation. In this instance the court found it appropriate to assign the full financial responsibility for the wife's embezzlement to the wife, preventing her assertion of 'community debt' from diminishing the husband's share of the community property. This was consistent with the general principle found in section 1714 that the actor is solely responsible for wilful and negligent acts unless shared, mitigated or excused because of other principles of law." *

In a remarkable leap, the court then states, "[r]eturning to section 5122, we find a legislative direction that between the spouses the mere fact of marriage should not change the usual rules of personal responsibility for the consequences of criminal or tortious activity. Although the section spells out the order in which creditors may satisfy tort claims from the property of the spouses, it does not forbid one spouse from later disclaiming responsibility for the tort liability of the other in a dissolution proceeding."*

We are mystified as to where the *Stitt* court found this so-called legislative direction to apply section 5122 in a dissolution proceeding and effect an "equitable" division of property where any tortious conduct is involved, be it negligent or intentional. The proper statutory focus in the assignment of spousal obligations is section 4800. And although the "benefit of the community" language of subdivision (b) of section 5122 is useful in characterizing an obligation as separate or community in nature, the section itself is a creditors' statute, designed for their protection; it is not a legislative return to the pre-1970 "fault" concept of division of marital property.

Confined to its facts, *Stitt* is correct. An innocent spouse is not required to share in losses incurred by the intentionally tortious or criminal conduct of a spouse where there is no benefit to the community. But the holding in *Stitt* is overbroad because it includes negligent as well as intentional torts. Thus, to the extent *Stitt* holds the negligent conduct of a spouse engaged in an activity benefiting the community provides sufficient justification to characterize a debt as a separate obligation, it is incorrect.

A few examples illustrate the point. Assume a spouse who is an attorney commits malpractice and is held liable for a substantial judgment. Since the law practice was an activity intended to produce income for the community, the malpractice judgment would be a shared community debt, even though it results from one spouse's negligence. But the same result should also follow when the negligence occurs while driving the family car on a personal errand. Neither spouse should bear the entire financial burden of such a loss. Finally even criminal or intentionally tortious conduct which results in obtaining substantial ill-gotten assets for the community creates a shared community debt. A spouse who temporarily doubles the value of the community through a fraudulent scheme should not forfeit all of his or her rights to the honestly obtained assets when restitution is made.

Turning to the facts before us, it is impossible to know whether the tortious conduct which gave rise to the resulting obligation was negligent or intentional since Clement settled those lawsuits before trial. However, as stated ante, the characterization of the conduct alone does not resolve the question. Even if Clement's conduct was intentionally tortious, he presented evidence his activities benefited the community. Clement's exposure to liability arose out of his actions while serving on the board of USNB, which took place for the most part during his marriage to Claudia. The remuneration he received for serving on the board was undisputedly community property.

Claudia presented no evidence that Clement's service on the board was to protect his separate property stock or further any of his separate property businesses. There was therefore no legitimate basis to characterize the settlement obligations as Clement's separate debt.

The order is reversed and the matter remanded to the trial court to determine the reasonableness of the attorney's fees incurred by Clement in defending the lawsuits.

SMALLWOOD, J., concur[s].

CROSBY, J., concurs in the result.

c. *State of Washington v. Clark*
The State of Washington v. M'Lissa Clark, also known as Daling, Petitioner
563 P.2d 1253 (Wash. 1977)

HICKS, Associate Justice.

In January 1976, following a jury trial, M'Lissa Clark Daling was convicted of one count of possession of a controlled substance (a felony) and one count of possession of marijuana (a misdemeanor). She wishes an appellate review of her trial at public expense. From a finding of nonindigency by the trial court, she petitions this court. The sole issue on appeal is the indigency of petitioner. If she is indigent, she is entitled to an appeal at public expense. *

The record upon which we are asked to act is sketchy in the extreme. However, it appears that M'Lissa Clark was arrested June 12, 1975, and a trial took place in September. A mistrial resulted and the matter was reset for trial in January 1976. In November 1975, after the mistrial but prior to her new trial, M'Lissa Clark married Jay Daling.

Following the marriage, the couple moved to the Waterville area where Jay Daling owned 250 acres of wheat land. This land had been inherited by him some years preceding the marriage.

In January 1976, M'Lissa Daling was tried and convicted. After the conviction, she requested appellate review at public expense for the reason that she was an indigent. The burden of proof establishing her indigency is on petitioner. RAP 15.2(a); *State v. Rutherford*, 63 Wash.2d 949, 954, 389 P.2d 895 (1964).

Upon considering petitioner's request and in examining the resources available to her, the trial court found that, while petitioner's separate assets and the marital community assets were insufficient, her husband had ample assets to finance an appeal. There was no indication in the record whether Jay Daling was willing or unwilling to finance an appeal and, consequently, the trial court made no finding in that regard. The trial court concluded that petitioner, M'Lissa Clark Daling, was not an indigent person entitled to an appeal at public expense. An order was entered accordingly. This court has been petitioned to review that order, and to find it erroneous.

At the time of petitioner's marriage in November, her husband was aware that the trial of his bride was scheduled for January. Marriage, under the circumstances, carried the risk that his spouse might be found guilty and be required to spend some time in confinement, absent an appeal. In point of fact, petitioner's sentence was deferred except for 25 days in the county jail.

Assuming, as we must, that petitioner's desired appeal has probable merit and that it is not frivolous, should petitioner's spouse in this instance be obliged to finance any appeal that may be taken? According to the findings of the trial court, Jay Daling can finance his wife's appeal without any financial hardship. In determining that M'Lissa Daling was not an indigent person, the trial court necessarily found her spouse's separate property to be a resource available to her.

Amicus curiae has favored us with a brief on this matter. Amicus frames the issue thusly:

May the separate (non-community) property of a criminal defendant's spouse be considered to defeat the defendant's claim of 'indigency' for purposes of receiving state-provided counsel and trial transcript on appeal?

After analyzing a number of cases, amicus concludes that the husband should not be responsible for the wife's appeal in this case. We do not agree.

RCW 26.16.200 provides:

Neither husband or wife is liable for the debts or liabilities of the other incurred before marriage, nor for the separate debts of each other, nor is the rent or income of the separate property of either liable for the separate debts of the other: Provided, That the earnings and accumulations of the husband shall be available to the legal process of creditors for the satisfaction of debts incurred by him prior to marriage, and the earnings and accumulations of the wife shall be available to the legal process of creditors for the satisfaction of debts incurred by her prior to marriage. For the purpose of this section neither the husband nor the wife shall be construed to have any interest in the earnings of the other: Provided Further, That no separate debt may be the basis of a claim against the earnings and accumulations of either a husband or wife unless the same is reduced to judgment within three years of the marriage of the parties.

RCW 26.16.205 provides:

The expenses of the family and the education of the children, including stepchildren, are chargeable upon the property of both husband and wife, or either of them, and in relation thereto they may be sued jointly or separately: Provided, That with regard to stepchildren, the obligation shall cease upon the termination of the relationship of husband and wife.

While the act of M'Lissa Clark for which she was tried occurred before she became Mrs. Daling, the trial in which she was convicted occurred after her marriage. Following her trial, she decided she wanted an appeal. There was no obligation for appeal costs before that time. The expense of this appeal, while related to an antenuptial act, is not an antenuptial debt. Thus, RCW 26.16.200 and cases decided thereunder regarding antenuptial debts are not apposite in this instance. Would the expense of an appeal in this case be a separate debt of the wife, collectible solely from her assets, or is the family-support statute (RCW 26.16.205) applicable?

RCW 26.16.205 has been the law of this state since 1881. Family-expense statutes, such as this, are generally considered to be at least as broad as the common-law duty to provide 'necessaries' for the family. * Should liability extend to providing a criminal appeal for a wife from a husband's separate property? This is a question of first impression in this state.

The Supreme Court of Colorado had such a case before it in *Read v. Read*, 119 Colo. 278, 202

P.2d 953 (1949). There the wife had been convicted of murder in the second degree, a divorce action was in progress, she was destitute, and the question of the expenses of an appeal in the criminal matter was before the court. The trial court's order provided that the husband should finance the appeal. On review the Supreme Court of Colorado, after determining that the husband was liable for necessaries, said *:

> The question then posed is whether court costs, attorney fees and incidental expenses incurred in the defense of the criminal case by the wife, and a review of the judgment therein, are necessaries for which the husband is liable. Such necessaries include food, wearing apparel, medicines and medical attention, a habitation and necessary furniture and other articles for the wife's protection in society, consistent with the husband's ability to pay, and such articles and things as are necessary for her sustenance as well as preservation of her health and comfort. The term 'necessaries' is incapable of exact definition; its meaning is variable, depending upon the circumstances, financial and otherwise, of the parties. We have said that plaintiff is entitled to have the judgment of conviction reviewed by this court and the necessity for expenses incurred therewith is as apparent and as vital as would be medical expenses incurred in case of her illness. Suffering and anguish resulting from her conviction may be as serious and disastrous as bodily ailments. The trial court found that plaintiff is destitute and that her husband is financially able to bear the expenses incurred in reviewing her conviction. The court further found that such allowed expenses were 'necessaries.' If they are such, defendant is liable therefor. . . . Under the attendant circumstances the expenses in presenting her case in this court for review are 'necessaries' for which defendant is liable, and the allowances thereof by the trial court were, under the circumstances here presented, right and proper.

(Citation omitted.)

To the same effect is *Elder v. Rosenwasser*, 238 N.Y. 427, 144 N.E. 669 (1924). There the wife's attorney, whom she had employed, had defended her in a civil action for libel and in a criminal action for assault and grand larceny. The defense terminated successfully for the wife. The husband failed to pay and the attorney brought suit. In discussing the case, the court said at pages 429--30, 144 N.E. at page 670:

> Where a wife living with her husband whom he is obliged to support is arrested on a criminal charge or prosecuted in a civil action which may result in her incarceration, the necessity for a lawyer may be as urgent and as important as the necessity for a doctor when she is sick. . . . In this case we think there was evidence which justified the Municipal Court in determining that the services were necessaries and that the amounts allowed were reasonable.

Minnesota finds legal services for a wife to be a 'necessary' under proper circumstances. In an action against the husband for legal services and expenses incurred in procuring the legal restoration of the wife's competency, the plaintiff's attorney prevailed. The husband had not wanted the services and he had said he would not pay for them. The court found that under the circumstances attorney fees and expenses were 'necessaries,' and the obligation to provide them was enforced against the husband. *Carr v. Anderson*, 154 Minn. 162, 191 N.W. 407 (1923).

We are persuaded that legal expenses, including a review of trial court proceedings, falls within the purview of RCW 26.16.205 as a family expense when a criminal action is involved and a spouse's liberty is at stake. It would follow that the separate assets of Jay Daling, petitioner's husband, may be considered in determining whether M'Lissa Clark Daling is an indigent person. The trial court did consider Jay Daling's separate assets when it found that petitioner was not an indigent person. The trial court was correct.

We find the above dispositive of the matter before us, however, we find it necessary to consider one more case. *Christiansen v. Dept. of Social Security*, 15 Wash.2d 465, 131 P.2d 189 (1942), a departmental 3-judge opinion with two judges concurring in the result, holding that a wife's separate property is not a 'resource' of the husband's such as to preclude him from eligibility for a senior-citizen grant, was not cited by petitioner or amicus curiae, nor did either discuss the family-expense statute. In *Christiansen*, the Department of Social Security, through its acting director, denied respondent's application for a senior-citizen grant solely on the ground that his wife had assets readily convertible into cash in the amount of $1454. The Department contended this was a resource of the husband even though it was conceded to be the separate property of the wife. The husband was 87 years old and the wife was 67. She had not made application for a grant.

In its contention that the wife's separate property was a 'resource' of the husband when he applied for a senior-citizen grant, the Department relied on RCW 26.16.205 (Rem.Rev.Stat. s 6906) as construed and applied in *In re DeNisson*, 197 Wash. 265, 84 P.2d 1024 (1938). In that case, the wife had been adjudged mentally incompetent and a guardian had been appointed for her estate. This court held that necessary living expenses of her destitute husband were part of the 'expenses of the family,' and in the guardianship proceedings, gave him an allowance for his support from the wife's separate estate. *DeNisson* was found to be inapplicable in *Christiansen* because 'no court has assumed jurisdiction of her (Mrs. Christiansen's) person or of her property.' Nor could any form of action be brought by the husband or in his behalf to compel his wife to make him an allowance in anticipation of the accrual of debts to be incurred for his support.

In addition to finding *DeNisson* not controlling, the court stated the following facts as reasons for finding no resource in the wife's separate property: the wife's failure to support the husband would not be grounds for divorce; she would not be liable to criminal prosecution for failure to support her husband even though financially able to do so, though the reverse would not be true; and if the wife sues for divorce, she could not be compelled to pay temporary support during the pendency of the action.

We find that, with the passage of time and changes in statutes, the above reasons are today questionable. A wife now may be criminally liable for failure to support her husband under such circumstances as her husband would be liable for failure to support her. RCW 26.20.030. In marriage dissolution proceedings, the obligations of the wife and husband are the same. RCW 26.09.050, .090. We do not find *Christiansen* persuasive in the case at bench and we confine it to its facts.

The order of the trial court denying petitioner's motion for order of indigency is affirmed. The time for perfecting her appeal shall run from the date of the remittitur herein.

WRIGHT, C.J., and ROSELLINI, HAMILTON, STAFFORD, UTTER, BRACHTENBACH, HOROWITZ and DOLLIVER, JJ., concur.

d. Family Expense Laws

Today most states have enacted "Family Expense" statutes that codify in large part, and generally expand, the common law doctrine of necessaries. What is the family expense doctrine found in your homestate statutes? Does your homestate have also (or instead) a common law "necessaries" doctrine? If so, what is the leading (or most recent) reported case from your homestate describing that doctrine or applying it? *See* Chapter 17 in the Supplement.

e. Notes and Questions

1) Family Expense/ Necessaries

In *Landmark Medical Center v. Gauthier*, 635 A.2d 1145 (R.I. 1994) the Rhode Island Supreme Court reviewed the response of various states to the equal protection dilemma of the gender-based duties in the common law doctrine of necessaries:

> In response to that [equality problem] states have fashioned various legislative schemes to create a modern approach to the necessaries doctrine. Maryland abrogated the doctrine entirely, concluding that the doctrine should no longer be part of Maryland's common law and that any expansion of the doctrine to include liability of married women should be left to the Legislature. *Condore v. Prince George's County*, 289 Md. 516, 425 A.2d 1011 (1981). In contrast, the Supreme Court of Arkansas decided to uphold the necessaries doctrine "unless altered or repealed by the General Assembly." *Davis v. Baxter County Regional Hospital*, 313 Ark. 388, 392, 855 S.W.2d 303, 305 (1993). The Florida court elected to leave the common law doctrine intact pending legislative review. *Shands Teaching Hospital and Clinics, Inc. v. Smith*, 497 So.2d 644 (Fla.1986). The Supreme Court of Virginia concluded that the doctrine was unconstitutional and should be completely abolished. *Schilling v. Bedford County Memorial Hospital*, 225 Va. 539, 303 S.E.2d 905 (1983). Following that decision, the Virginia General Assembly amended Virginia Code § 55-37 to expressly provide that "[t]he doctrine of necessaries as it existed at common law shall apply equally to both spouses." Va.Code Ann. § 55-37 (Michie 1986). The Connecticut and Illinois Legislatures have reacted by enacting statutes that make both spouses jointly liable for family expenses including reasonable and necessary medical care. *See* Conn.Gen.Stat. § 46b-37 (rev.1989) and Illinois, 750 ILCS 65/15 (Michie 1993).
>
> Most of the jurisdictions that have considered the modern application of the necessaries doctrine have generally held that judicial expansion of the doctrine to include both spouses is the appropriate measure. We follow the pattern of these jurisdictions. *******

635 A.2d at 1150.

The common law doctrine of "necessaries" and "family expense statutes" are very important to businesses, and business creditors. For example, in *Landmark Medical Center, supra*, the Rhode Island Supreme Court retroactively expanded the common-law doctrine of necessaries to impose a mutual burden on both spouses (not just men) to pay necessary expenses incurred by the other spouse, and applied it to hold a wife with a history of mental illness liable for medically necessary expenses incurred by husband prior to his death. In *Borgess Medical Center v. Smith*, 386 N.W.2d 684 (Mich Ct. App. 1986) a woman was held liable for medical expenses of last illness incurred by her husband when his estate was inadequate to pay for them, even though statute provided that married woman's estate is not liable for debts of her husband. Is there some irony in allowing a doctrine created to provide for needy family members to be used routinely to provide recovery for corporate entities from surviving, sometimes economically struggling, widows or widowers. Why/why not?

Are psychological counseling services "necessaries" sometimes, always, never? Why/why not? If sought by a disgruntled, separated or divorcing spouse, are they "necessaries"? Why/why not? *See Allen v. Keating*, 517 N.W.2d 830 (Mich.App.1994).

2) Domestic Services

The common law counterpart of the husband's duty to provide necessaries was the duty of wives to provide "domestic services which pertain to the comfort, care, and well-being of her family and consortium to her husband." *North Carolina Baptist Hospitals, Inc. v. Harris,* 354 S.E.2d 471, 473 (N.C. 1987) (holding wife liable for medical expenses of deceased husband). Both spouses' duties arose "from the fact of the marriage, not from any express undertaking" by the parties. *Id.* The wife's duty of domestic service had economic value to the husband, but was it enforceable? Has the duty to provide domestic service also been equalized today? Is it enforceable today? Could working wife Wanda sue husband Hal for failing to pick up and wash his dirty socks, or failing to do "his share" of the housework? What is his proper amount of housework? Do men and women generally have the same opinion about how much house cleaning is "necessary"? When there is a disagreement, whose view legally is entitled to prevail and on what basis? If husband hires a housekeeper to do the work his working wife doesn't have time to do, may he or the housekeeper sue the wife to pay for the service? Could wife sue messy, slovenly husband to provide or pay for a housekeeper? How does that compare to the legal resolution of disagreements about whether certain items of furniture or certain quality or quantity of clothing are "necessaries." If stingy, tight-fisted husband refuses to buy a heater for his vehicle, refuses to buy homemaker wife (who has a modest amount of separate income) any clothing except a cheap coat, refuses to buy new appliances and moderate conveniences for the bare-bones home, and refuses to give her money to pay for her visits to her married daughters does she have a valid legal claim against him for such funds? *See McGuire v. McGuire,* 59 N.W.2d 336 (Neb. 1953). Should some (or all) of these disputes be resolved by other means than lawsuits and other decision-makers than judges? Why/why not? Do we not get close to the heart of the policy behind the "family autonomy" or "noninterference" doctrine when we address such issues?

3) Married Women Employment, Marital Satisfaction, and Marriage Stability

Demographer William J. Goode reports that research in both Russia and the United States indicates that husbands are more satisfied in marriages in which wives work. Goode, *infra.* (That is not surprising because the working women contribute additional income to the family but still carry the lion's share of the homemaking responsibilities. Women generally have higher standards of home cleanliness, tidiness, food preparation, etc., than men, and tend to spend more time in such chores; men generally care less about such matters, or have lower standards, and are less willing to engage in "extra" work to maintain higher standards.) Thus, working wives seem to be associated with higher levels of husband satisfaction in marriage.

Other data suggests that working out of the home is associated with higher levels of satisfaction for married women. For example:

> In an interesting study, Keith and Schafer (1983) interviewed 135 dual-earner husbands and wives, and they found that work orientation, feelings of being a provider, and financial stress were associated with lower depression. On the other hand, the number of hours the married women worked was directly related to depression. The more hours she worked per week, the higher her depression. The two effects cancelled each other out so that the overall relationship between employment and mental health was minimal. Gray (1983) found that 77 percent of the 300 professional women she

surveyed experienced strain between work and family demands. But they also reported that this stress did not significantly decrease their sense of well-being.

Garrett & Chadwick, *infra* at 73. Thus, paid employment may be associated with more marital satisfaction for *both* husbands and wives.

Ironically, the rate and risk of divorce is *higher* in couples where the wife works. "[T]he steady increase of women in the work force in western nations correlates with the rise of divorce, "seem[ing] to prove, in the view of many analysts, that when women work the divorce rate climbs; presumably, they are no longer as tolerant of their lot when they have an alternative." Goode, *supra*, at 111. Goode hypothesizes that "the temptations of individual opportunity in a successful economy . . . can move family members to consider their own interests above those of the family as a unit," and also that "a corrupt polity, which teaches its citizens to adjust to whatever its demands may be, since family ties cannot help enough against them, cannot guarantee an adequate reward for selflessly giving to each other over many years" and can also lead family members to put their own interests above those of the family as a unit.' Goode, *supra* at 328 .

Goode also explains that historically there is a negative correlation between economic class and divorce -- the more educated, more wealthy, more prestigious have less divorce. As there has been less difference between the income of lower- and upper-class women and their husbands, they have had less to lose from divorce and less to gain from staying married. Middle and upper class women historically have had more to gain from staying married and more to lose from divorce. Now that middle and upper class women are working, their economic position vis-a-vis their husbands is more like lower class women (they are less dependant financially upon their husbands), and that may explain why divorce by middle-class women now appears to imitate the higher divorce rate of lower class women. Thus, Goode reports: "When we look at the relationships between divorce and income we find that the negative association between class or income and divorce rate holds for men, but the relationship seems to be *reversed* for women: the higher their income, the higher the divorce rate. Since most of these women are married to these men [people generally marry within the same class], obviously some statistical tensions exist between these two opposing relationships." Goode, *supra* at 332.

3. Practical and Ethical Considerations

How may the necessaries doctrine affect counsel you might give to a client contemplating divorce? Should legal services be necessaries? All legal services? Why/why not? *See* Zielinski, *infra*.

4. Bibliography

Sallie L. Rubenzer, *Necessaries and Family Purpose Debts*, Wis. Law. October,1996, at 15.
John Witte, Jr., *The Goods and Goals of Marriage*, 76 Notre Dame L. Rev. 1019 (2001).
Angela Zielinski, Comment, *Attorneys' Fees as Necessaries of Life: Expanding A Domestic Violence Victim's Access to Safety and Justice*, 60 Mont. L. Rev. 201 (1999).

B. PUBLIC AND PRIVATE BENEFITS AND TAX CONSIDERATIONS

1. Background

a. Status and Benefits

Marriage is not only a legal status. It is a status that is used as a qualification for many public and private benefits. For example, Professor David Cruz has written:

> Marriage is *** an economic institution, to which attach significant financial rewards. As Professors Patricia Cain, David Chambers, William Eskridge, and numerous others have noted, statutes typically guarantee government employees payment of benefits including health and life insurance and disability payments for civil spouses, and many private sector employees contractually receive similar benefits for civil spouses. The dollar value of these benefits can be large, and they are triggered by civil marriage.
>
> In addition to such purely economic bonuses for which civil marriage makes a (mixed-sex) couple eligible, the law has adopted numerous default rules that are keyed to civil marriage , providing further benefits for those who marry at law--"off-the-rack rules" in Professor Eskridge's catchy phrasing. As Tom Gallanis has pointed out, in many contexts laws set default rules authorizing actions to be taken by, or inheritances to be awarded to, individuals in a specified order, usually giving priority to one's civil spouse, so that unmarried couples must incur time and expense to designate a partner as the appropriate decisionmaker or suffer the consequences of important decisions being vested elsewhere or legacies being directed to someone else. These default rules spare civilly married couples the costs in money and time of hiring attorneys, drafting documents, and taking whatever other steps are necessary to overcome statutory presumptions, and they protect even those civilly married couples who--as many people do--fail to adopt health-care directives or draft wills due perhaps to the entailed discomfiture of facing one's own mortality.

Cruz, *infra* at 931-32. The number, importance and extent of such benefits have increased over the years. Today, "[t]he word 'marriage' appears in more than 800 sections of federal statutes and regulations, and the word 'spouse' appears more than 3,100 times." H.R. Rep. No. 104-664, *infra,* at 10. Thus, marriage is a powerful trigger of rights, benefits, privileges (as well as duties, responsibilities and obligations) in federal law. The relative impact of the status of marriage under state law is even more profound. A Hawaii Report, for example, identified over 300 Hawaiian statutory provisions containing references to marriage, husband, wife, spouse, and similar familial terms used in a widely disparate variety of statutes and programs in state law in Hawaii. See Report, *infra*, at 105-126, App. B.

Why over the centuries (and through the millennia) has marriage been used as a categorical qualification or test for so many legal and economic (public and private) benefits? Are there some benefits that are linked to the unique circumstances of or designed to be supportive of marriage? Are all of the benefits triggered or conferred by marital status really "marital" benefits? Is marriage just used as a category of convenience sometimes? Always? Never?

2. Statutes, Cases and Doctrines.

a. The "Marriage Penalty" and "Marriage Bonus"

The current U.S. income tax structure creates what have been called a "marriage penalty" and a "marriage bonus" for married couples. That is, a married couple will pay either more tax (the "marriage penalty") or less tax (the "marriage bonus") than they would pay if they were taxed as single individuals. As one monograph put it: "Marriage is rarely a tax-neutral event. When a couple marries, they are treated as one tax unit that must pay on the couple's combined taxable income. The couple's income is subject to progressive tax rates that impose higher taxes as the couple's combined income rises. . . ." 2001 Tax Legislation, *infra* at 56, ¶220. The tax brackets can exacerbate the combined-income discrepancy in a "progressive" tax structure. Another source of the discrepancy is that the standard deduction and tax bracket breakpoint for individuals is roughly 60% but for married couples it is roughly one-half. For example, in 2000, the standard deduction for two single individuals was $8,800 ($4,400 per individual) while the standard deduction for a married couple was $7,350. *Id.* at 57. On the other hand, if a couple is living on the income of one of them (the other does not earn income), and they are taxed as a "couple," they will pay less tax than the one income earner would pay if taxed as an individual. Thus, mathematically, married couples whose incomes are split more evenly than 70-30 generally suffer a marriage penalty, and those with a larger dual-income disparity generally benefit from a marriage bonus. *Id.*

Whether a married couple has a "penalty" or a "bonus" depends upon the tax brackets they are in and the amount they earn. Married couples in which both spouses earn moderate-to-high incomes, or who have roughly equal or similar incomes, incur a "marriage penalty," while one-earner married couples or couples with one high-earner and one low-earner receive a "marriage bonus"). Some critics say the "marriage penalty" is really a penalty on earning, not a tax on marriage, and the "marriage bonus" really a bonus for unemployed or underemployed married persons.

For example, in 1997 it was computed that "marriage penalty" taxes on a two-equal-earner couple would be:

EXAMPLE #1	Husband	Wife	Couple
Adjusted Gross Income	*$30,500*	*$30,500*	*$61,000*
Minus pers. exemp & ded	$ 6,550	$ 6,550	$11,800
Taxable Income	$23,950	$23,950	$49,200
Tax Liability	*$ 3,592*	*$3,592($7,184)*	*$8,563*
Marriage Penalty $ 1,378			

On the other hand, one-earner couples usually have a "marriage bonus"; for example:

EXAMPLE #2	Husband	Wife	Couple
Adjusted Gross Income	$48,000	-0-	$48,000
Tax Liability	*$8,332*	*$8,332*	*$5,370*
Marriage Bonus $2,962			

The Congressional Budget Office found that the highest proportion of marriage penalties occur when the higher earning spouse made between $20,000 and $75,000. The highest proportion of marriage bonuses occur when the higher earning spouse earns less than $20,000 or more than $75,000. In other words, the marriage penalty hurts two-earning middle-class couples most, while single-earner and dual-earner poor and more-wealthy couples get marriage bonuses. Similar penalties arise from or are exacerbated by the earned income credit, social security benefits taxation, dependent care credit, limitation on itemized deductions, the phaseout of personal exemptions and child credit, etc.

Three mutually inconsistent concepts of "tax equity" conflict to create marriage penalty and bonus dilemmas: the notion that tax should be "marriage neutral," the equal taxation of equal income, and progressive taxation. *Id.* at 59-59.

Three remedies to the "marriage penalty" have been proposed. One bill was introduced to allow married couples to *choose* whether to be taxed as married couples or as single individuals. Another proposal would allow married couples to *split* the total income of the couple and be *taxed individually* at the rate of single persons earning that income. A third alternative is to adopt a *flat(ter) tax* system. In the summer of 2000 Congress passed but the President vetoed, a bill to reduce or eliminate the IRS "marriage penalty." *See* House Bill No. 2488, *infra*.

Early in 2001, Congress passed and the new President signed a bill to ameliorate some of the "marriage penalty." *See* 2001 Tax Legislation, *infra,* at 3. The Economic Growth and Tax Relief Reconciliation Act of 2001 increased the standard deduction for married couples (it will become equal to that for two individual filers in 2009); increases the size of the 15-percent bracket for married couples (beginning in 2005; it will become equal to that for two individual filers in 2008); increasing the phaseout point for earned income credit and education IRA contributions. *Id.* at 59-61.

b. Notes and Questions

1) Tax policy dilemmas
Before 1948, all persons, married or single, were taxed as individuals. That gave incentive to "income splitting" by couples in community property states (but not in separate property states); in 1948, the tax law was amended to permit all married couples to split their income regardless of whether they lived in community or separate property states. That made the married couple the basic unit of taxation. Separate rate schedules for married and single adults were introduced in 1969. 2001 Tax Legislation, *infra*, at 59. Should we "turn the clock back" to 1968? To 1947? Why/why not?

Why should married couples be taxed differently than individuals? If it is true that married couples enjoy economic benefits, economies of scale, and benefits of the altruism (love) that enhance the "value" of their dollar, why should married couples complain about paying more tax; don't they get more real economic benefits? Do some nonmarital cohabitants enjoy the best of both worlds - they get the economies of scale and are taxed as individuals. Should tax policies promote or encourage behavior (marriage, or nonmarital cohabitation)? Do the social benefits of marriage justify some tax benefits? Or should government "stay out" of lifestyle choices and not use the tax laws to promote or discourage any particular lifestyles? Is it possible or desirable to eliminate all discrepancy between married and unmarried filers? Does the outcry in recent years over the tax penalty indicate that the gender-income gap is abating? Why/why not? It was suggested (before the latest tax reforms) that the "marriage penalty" disproportionately disadvantaged minority families. *See* Brown, *infra*, at 287 ("African-American households are more likely to pay a marriage penalty and White households are more likely to receive a marriage bonus").

Professor Sonne recently has challenged the idea that tax policy penalizes or prefers marriage.

The tax system "treats a married couple as a single economic unit [wherein] [s]pouses report their combined income on a joint return, and calculate their tax liability based on that combined income." This "income" is then subject to a tax structure that, at least as it has developed under the current progressive rate approach (i.e., where higher income is taxed at higher rates), can be supported by a theory that "a [married] couple acts as an economic unit by pooling its resources, and should be taxed accordingly." By taking a resource-based approach, the system, intentionally or not, does not reflect all marriages, but only those fitting the "economic unit" mold. Thus, there are "marriage bonuses in some situations and marriage penalties in others," with the difference based primarily not on marriage itself, but on the choices of individuals and couples. In the end, it is more these choices than marital status as such that create a difference, if any, between married and unmarried (like Social Security). To be sure, such choices can be influenced by the tax system, but this influence should not be overemphasized.

Sonne, *infra*, at 907. Does ignoring marriage indicate a policy (non-favoritism) toward the institution?

3. Practical and Ethical Considerations

If parties seek to marry solely for the purpose of obtaining some legal benefit extended only to married couples, and they do not otherwise live as husband and wife, is that "marriage for a limited purpose" a valid marriage? Why/why not? (See *supra* Chapter 5.) Is it ethical for lawyers to assist clients to escape tax liabilities by marriage or divorce? Is it ethical for lawyers to advise clients to minimize or eliminate tax liability by other associations, transfers or arrangements? Why/why not? If there is a difference in the answers to the last two questions, please justify it.

4. Bibliography

2001 Tax Legislation, Law, Explanation and Analysis, Economic Growth and Tax Relief Reconciliation Act of 2001 (CCH Inc. 2001).

William Blackstone, Commentaries on the Laws of England *442-443.

Dorothy A. Brown, The Marriage Penalty/Bonus Debate: Legislative Issues in Black and White, 16 N.Y.L. Sch. J. Hum. Rts. 287 (1999).

Homer Clark, The Law of Domestic Relations in the United States § 6.1 (1988).

David B. Cruz, *"Just Don't Call It Marriage": The First Amendment and Marriage As An Expressive Resource*, 74 S. Cal. L. Rev. 925 (2001).

H. Dean Garrett & Bruce A. Chadwick, *Women's Religiosity, Employment, and Mental Illness* in Religion, Mental Health and the Latter-day Saints at 71 (Daniel K. Judd ed., 1999).

William J. Goode, World Changes in Divorce Patterns 95 (1993).

H.R. Rep. No. 104-664, Defense of Marriage Act, Committee on the Judiciary, House of Representatives, 104th Cong., 2d Sess. (1996).

House Resolution 1836, 107thCong., 1st Sess. (2001).

House Bill No. 2488, 106th Cong., 1st Sess., (1999), passed House of Representatives July 22, 2000, passed Senate July 30, 2000, enrolled August 15, 2000, vetoed September 23, 2000.

Report of the (Hawaii) Commission on Sexual Orientation and the Law (Dec. 8, 1995).

James A. Sonne, *Love Doesn't Pay: The Fiction of Marriage Rights in the Workplace*, 40 U. Rich. L. Rev. 867 (2006).

CHAPTER 18

Non-Economic Consequences of Marriage in General; Consortium and Heartbalm Actions; Privileges and Immunities

A. NON-ECONOMIC CONSEQUENCES OF MARRIAGE IN GENERAL

1. Background

a. The Policy Behind the Common Law Disabilities of Married Women

At common law, married women were denied many substantive and procedural legal rights which their husbands and unmarried sisters enjoyed. Blackstone summarized these disabilities and gave his opinion of the justification for them as follows:

> By marriage, the husband and wife are one person in law; that is, the very being or legal existence of the woman is suspended during the marriage, or at least is incorporated and consolidated into that of the husband, under whose wing, protection, and *cover* she performs every thing; and is, therefore, called in our law-French a *feme-covert, faemina viro co-operta*; is said to be *covert-baron*, or under the protection and influence of her husband, her *baron* , her lord; and her condition, during her marriage, is called her *coverture*. Upon this principle of a union of person in husband and wife depend almost all the legal rights, duties, and disabilities that either of them acquire by the marriage. I speak not at present of the rights of property, but of such as are merely *personal*. For this reason, a man can not grant any thing to his wife, or enter into covenant with her, for the grant would be to suppose her separate existence; and to covenant with her would be only to covenant with himself; and, therefore, it is also generally true that all compacts made between husband and wife, when single, are voided by the intermarriage. A woman, indeed, may be attorney for her husband, for that implies no separation from, but is rather a representation of, her lord. And a husband may also bequeath any thing to his wife by will; for that can not take effect till the coverture is determined by his death.
>
> . . . In criminal prosecutions, it is true, the wife may be indicted and punished separately; for the union is only a civil union. But, in trials of any sort, they are not allowed to be evidence for or against each other; partly because it is impossible their testimony should be indifferent, but principally because of the union of person; and, therefore, if they were admitted to be witnesses *for* each other, they would contradict one maxim of law, *"nemo propria causa testis esse debet;"* and if *against* each other, they would contradict another maxim, *"nemo tenetur seipsum accusare."* But where the offense is directly against the person of the wife, this rule has been usually dispensed with; . . . .
>
> . . . .

In the civil law the husband and the wife are considered as two distinct persons, and may have separate estates, contracts, debts, and injuries; and, therefore, in our ecclesiastical courts, a woman may sue and be sued without her husband.

But, though our law in general considers man and wife as one person, yet there are some instances in which she is separately considered, as inferior to him, and acting by his compulsion; and, therefore, all deeds executed, and acts done by her, during her coverture, are void; except it be a fine, or the like matter of record, in which case she must be solely and secretly examined, to learn if her act be voluntary. She cannot by will, devise lands to her husband, unless under special circumstances; for at the time of making it she supposed to be under his coercion. And in some felonies and other inferior crimes, committed by her, through constraint of her husband, the law excuses her; but this extends not to treason or murder.

The husband, also (by the old law), might give his wife moderate correction; for, as he is to answer for her misbehavior, the law thought it reasonable to intrust him with this power of restraining her, by domestic chastisement, in the same moderation that a man is allowed to correct his apprentices or children . . . . But this power of correction was confined within reasonable bounds .... The civil law gave the husband the same, or a larger authority, over his wife . . . . But with us, in the politer reign of Charles the Second, this power of correction began to be doubted; and a wife may now have security of the peace against her husband . . . . Yet the lower rank of people, who were always fond of the old common law, still claim, and exert their ancient privilege; and the courts of law will still permit a husband to restrain a wife of her liberty, in case of any gross misbehavior.

These are the chief legal effects of marriage during coverture; upon which we may observe, that even the disabilities which the wife lies under are, for the most part, intended for her protection and benefit. So great a favorite is the female sex of the laws of England.

1 W. Blackstone, *infra* at *442-45.

2. Statutes, Cases and Doctrines

a. The "Name" Game
In the 1970s and 1980s, the right of married women to keep and use their birth family surname, or a hyphenated surname, or some other name was a *huge* issue. However, it was much ado about nothing. With rare (and usually uninformed) exception, the caselaw consistently (and historically for centuries) has protected the right of all adults, married or single, male or female, to choose the name by which they will be known. Social custom may "dictate" some form of preferred name, but legally the married (or single) woman (or man) is not required to bow to the convention.

b. Contracts Between Spouses
At common law a woman was incapable of entering into most legal contracts. Throughout the nineteenth century, the right of a married woman to repudiate her contract (or, more precisely, her defense of marital incapacity against any effort to enforce her contracts), waned as the Married Women's Property Acts grew in popularity and scope. Today it is absolutely clear that a married woman has full, individual legal capacity to contract. In contract law her position is no different from that of a married

man. Of course, in some property systems, the fact of marriage may entail some limitations (mutual agreement) upon alienating or encumbering some forms of property (such as the family home). But the limitations are gender-neutral.

c. Medical Decision-making

It has long been an accepted practice in medicine to allow the family of an incapacitated patient to make medical decisions for the patient under a theory of agency or tacit authorization or as the-best-situated-to-exercise-substitute-judgment. Should spouses generally be given priority among family members as surrogate decision-makers for the incompetent patient? The Conference of Commissioners on Uniform State Laws has given inconsistent answers to this question.

The drafters of the Model Health-Care Consent Act did not think so. That proposed legislation (adopted only in Indiana) provides that if a patient becomes incompetent without appointing a medical decision-making agent and lacking a general guardian, "consent to health care may be given . . . (2) by a spouse, parent, adult, child, or adult sibling unless disqualified . . . ." *Id.* § 4, 9 U.L.A. 461 (Supp. 2001).

The drafters explained that "[w]ithin this class [the family], the spouse, parents, adult children and adult siblings are ranked equally. Any member of the class is authorized to act. *Any decision establishing priority among family members would be largely arbitrary.* The objective is to have someone who has a close personal relationship with the patient and who will consider his best interests acting for him." *Id.* at 462, Cmnt. (emphasis added). (This proposed Act was withdrawn by the Commissioners in 1997. 9(Part 1B) U.L.A. 81 (2005).

However, The drafters of the Uniform Health-Care Decisions Act (1993) ("UH-CDA"), enacted in eight states, decided that spouses should be given priority. Section 5 of the Act provides that if a patient becomes incapacitated and has not appointed an available decision-making agent or guardian, the following persons may (in order listed) act as the decision-making surrogate for the patient: "(1) the spouse, unless legally separated; (2) an adult child; (3) a parent; or (4) an adult brother or sister." UH-CDA § 5(b), 9 (Part IB) U.L.A. 83 (2005).

Drafters of the Uniform Rights of the Terminally Ill Act (1989), enacted in five states and the Virgin Islands, agreed that the spouse should be given priority. 9C U.L.A. 311 (2001), & *id.* 17 (Supp. 2006). Section 7 of that Act provides that in the absence of a "living will" or other appointment or designation by the incompetent patient of a substitute decision-maker, the authority to make the decision to withhold or withdraw treatment for an incompetent "may be exercised by the following individuals, in order of priority: (1) the spouse of the individual; (2) an adult child of the individual or, if there is more than one adult child, a majority of the adult children who are reasonably available for consultation; (3) the parents of the individual; (4) an adult sibling of the individual or, if there are more than one adult sibling, a majority of the adults siblings who are reasonably available for consultation; or (5) the nearest other adult relative of the individual by blood or adoption who is reasonably available for consultation." 9C U.L.A. 339 at § 7(b). What do you think? Why?

Should a husband have the right to order the withdrawal of food and hydration from his incapacitated wife who signed no power of attorney or "living will," but whom a court found would not want to have her life prolonged in a persistent vegetative condition from which there was no rational hope of recovery? Even if her parents who have been close to her want to continue the care and are willing to help provide it? Even if the husband has, since the disabling of his wife, started living with another woman and had two children by her? Why/why not? In 2004, food and hydration was removed from a woman, Terri Schiavo, at her husband's request (backed by numerous controversial court orders). She lingered and slowly died of starvation and dehydration over 13 days, galvanizing public attention, igniting political fireworks, and provoking enormous debate. *See* Clark, *infra*; Colby, *infra*; Campo-Flores, *infra* (history of legal battle over Terri Schiavo); Mayo, *infra*; Miller, *infra*.

d. Reproduction - Mutual or Individual Decision

At common law, procreative decisions were presumed to be mutual, and in recent times those presumptions became codified. The requirement of mutual consent to sex, without and within marriage, perpetuates one dimension of that rule. Individual access to contraceptives also insures procreation by mutual agreement in another dimension. The abolition of most significant remnants of the "spousal rape" exemption further underscores this principle. The common requirement that husband and wife both agree to adopt before a child may be adopted by a married couple also manifests the mutuality in procreation requirement.

The sole exception is for abortion, which exploded forcefully and grew quickly in the 1970s and 1980s. In several abortions cases, the U.S. Supreme Court created the rule that a married woman does not need the consent of her husband to abort a child conceived by the mutual decision and mutual act of both of them. The Court even invalidated a requirement that a wife merely *notify* her husband of her decision to abort their child. A strong minority of justices have protested that the interests of a husband in his unborn child are very important, deserving of equal legal protection. But the majority of the Court was unwilling to defy advocates of absolute female autonomy in reproductive decision-making.

e. *Planned Parenthood v. Danforth*
Planned Parenthood of Central Missouri v. Danforth
428 U.S. 52 (1976)

Mr. Justice BLACKMUN delivered the opinion of the Court.
***

C. The Spouse's Consent.

Section 3(3) requires the prior written consent of the spouse of the woman seeking an abortion during the first 12 weeks of pregnancy, unless "the abortion is certified by a licensed physician to be necessary in order to preserve the life of the mother."

The appellees defend § 3(3) on the ground that it was enacted in the light of the General Assembly's "perception of marriage as an institution," Brief for Appellee Danforth 34, and that any major change in family status is a decision to be made jointly by the marriage partners. Reference is made to an abortion's possible effect on the woman's childbearing potential. It is said that marriage always has entailed some legislatively imposed limitations: Reference is made to adultery and bigamy as criminal offenses; to Missouri's general requirement, Mo.Rev.Stat. § 453.030.3 (1969), that for an adoption of a child born in wedlock the consent of both parents is necessary; to similar joint-consent requirements imposed by a number of States with respect to artificial insemination and the legitimacy of children so conceived; to the laws of two States requiring spousal consent for voluntary sterilization; and to the long-established requirement of spousal consent for the effective disposition of an interest in real property. It is argued that "(r)ecognizing that the consent of both parties is generally necessary . . . to begin a family, the legislature has determined that a change in the family structure set in motion by mutual consent should be terminated only by mutual consent," Brief for Appellee Danforth 38, and that what the legislature did was to exercise its inherent policymaking power "for what was believed to be in the best interests of all the people of Missouri." *Id.*, at 40.

The appellants on the other hand, contend that § 3(3) obviously is designed to afford the husband the right unilaterally to prevent or veto an abortion, whether or not he is the father of the fetus, and that this not only violates *Roe v. Doe* but is also in conflict with other decided cases. *** They also refer to the situation where the husband's consent cannot be obtained because he cannot be located. And they assert that § 3(3) is vague and overbroad.

*** We now hold that the State may not constitutionally require the consent of the spouse, as is specified under § 3(3) of the Missouri Act, as a condition for abortion during the first 12 weeks of pregnancy. We thus agree with the dissenting judge in the present case, and with the courts whose decisions are cited above, that the State cannot "delegate to a spouse a veto power which the state itself is absolutely and totally prohibited from exercising during the first trimester of pregnancy." 392 F.Supp., at 1375. Clearly, since the State cannot regulate or proscribe abortion during the first stage, when the physician and his patient make that decision, the State cannot delegate authority to any particular person, even the spouse, to prevent abortion during that same period.

We are not unaware of the deep and proper concern and interest that a devoted and protective husband has in his wife's pregnancy and in the growth and development of the fetus she is carrying. Neither has this Court failed to appreciate the importance of the marital relationship in our society. *See* e. g. *Griswold v. Connecticut,* *; *Maynard v. Hill,**. Moreover, we recognize that the decision whether to undergo or to forego an abortion may have profound effects on the future of any marriage, effects that are both physical and mental, and possibly deleterious. Notwithstanding these factors, we cannot hold that the State has the constitutional authority to give the spouse unilaterally the ability to prohibit the wife from terminating her pregnancy, when the State itself lacks that right. *See Eisenstadt v. Baird,**. It seems manifest that, ideally, the decision to terminate a pregnancy should be one concurred in by both the wife and her husband. No marriage may be viewed as harmonious or successful if the marriage partners are fundamentally divided on so important and vital an issue. But it is difficult to believe that the goal of fostering mutuality and trust in a marriage, and of strengthening the marital relationship and the marriage institution, will be achieved by giving the husband a veto power exercisable for any reason whatsoever or for no reason at all. Even if the State had the ability to delegate to the husband a power it itself could not exercise, it is not at all likely that such action would further, as the District Court majority phrased it, the "interest of the state in protecting the mutuality of decisions vital to the marriage relationship." 392 F.Supp., at 1370.

We recognize, of course, that when a woman, with the approval of her physician but without the approval of her husband, decides to terminate her pregnancy, it could be said that she is acting unilaterally. The obvious fact is that when the wife and the husband disagree on this decision, the view of only one of the two marriage partners can prevail. Inasmuch as it is the woman who physically bears the child and who is the more directly and immediately affected by the pregnancy, as between the two, the balance weighs in her favor. Cf. *Roe v. Wade*, 410 U.S., at 153, 93 S.Ct., at 726.

We conclude that § 3(3) of the Missouri Act is inconsistent with the standards enunciated in *Roe v. Wade*, 410 U.S., at 164-165, and is unconstitutional. ***
***

Mr. Justice STEWART, with whom Mr. Justice POWELL joins, concurring.

While joining the Court's opinion, I write separately to indicate my understanding of some of the constitutional issues raised by this litigation.
***

As to the provision of the law that requires a husband's consent to an abortion, § 3(3), the primary issue that it raises is whether the State may constitutionally recognize and give effect to a right on his part to participate in the decision to abort a jointly conceived child. This seems to me a rather more difficult problem than the Court acknowledges. Previous decisions have recognized that a man's right to father children and enjoy the association of his offspring is a constitutionally protected freedom. *See Stanley v. Illinois,* *; *Skinner v. Oklahoma ex rel. Williamson,* *. But the Court has recognized as well that the Constitution protects "a Woman's decision whether or not to terminate her pregnancy." *Roe v. Wade, supra,* 410 U.S., at 153, 93 S.Ct., at 727 (emphasis added). In assessing the constitutional validity of § 3(3) we are called upon to choose between these competing rights. I agree with the Court that since "it is the woman who physically bears the child and who is the more directly and immediately affected by the pregnancy . . . the balance weighs in her favor." Ante, at 2842.

***

Mr. Justice WHITE, with whom The CHIEF JUSTICE and Mr. Justice REHNQUIST join, concurring in the judgment in part and dissenting in part.

***

Section 3(3) of the Act provides that a married woman may not obtain an abortion without her husband's consent. The Court strikes down this statute in one sentence. It says that "since the State cannot . . . proscribe abortion . . . the State cannot delegate authority to any particular person, even the spouse, to prevent abortion . . . ." Ante at 2841. But the State is not under § 3(3) delegating to the husband the power to vindicate the State's interest in the future life of the fetus. It is instead recognizing that the husband has an interest of his own in the life of the fetus which should not be extinguished by the unilateral decision of the wife. It by no means follows, from the fact that the mother's interest in deciding "whether or not to terminate her pregnancy" outweighs the State's interest in the potential life of the fetus, that the husband's interest is also outweighed and may not be protected by the State. A father's interest in having a child perhaps his only child may be unmatched by any other interest in his life. *See Stanley v. Illinois,* *. It is truly surprising that the majority finds in the United States Constitution, as it must in order to justify the result it reaches, a rule that the State must assign a greater value to a mother's decision to cut off a potential human life by abortion than to a father's decision to let it mature into a live child. Such a rule cannot be found there, nor can it be found in *Roe v. Wade, supra.* These are matters which a State should be able to decide free from the suffocating power of the federal judge, purporting to act in the name of the Constitution.

***

Missouri has a law which prevents a woman from putting a child up for adoption over her husband's objection, Mo.Rev.Stat. § 453.030 (1969). This law represents a judgment by the State that the mother's interest in avoiding the burdens of child rearing do not outweigh or snuff out the father's interest in participating in bringing up his own child. That law is plainly valid, but no more so than § 3(3) of the Act now before us, resting as it does on precisely the same judgment.

***

f. *Planned Parenthood v. Casey*
Planned Parenthood of Southeastern Pennsylvania v. Casey
505 U.S. 833 (1992)

Justice O'CONNOR, Justice KENNEDY, and Justice SOUTER announced the judgment of the Court and delivered the opinion of the Court with respect to Parts I, II, III, V-A, V-C, and VI, an opinion with respect to Part V-E, in which Justice STEVENS joins, and an opinion with respect to Parts IV, V-B, and -D.

***

C.

Section 3209 of Pennsylvania's abortion law provides, except in cases of medical emergency, that no physician shall perform an abortion on a married woman without receiving a signed statement from the woman that she has notified her spouse that she is about to undergo an abortion. The woman has the option of providing an alternative signed statement certifying that her husband is not the man who impregnated her; that her husband could not be located; that the pregnancy is the result of spousal sexual assault which she has reported; or that the woman believes that notifying her husband will cause him or someone else to inflict bodily injury upon her. A physician who performs an abortion on a married woman without receiving the appropriate signed statement will have his or her license revoked, and is liable to the husband for damages.

*** [The majority reviews the district court's findings and studies about the evils of domestic violence introduced to support to claim that the Pennsylvania law could result in wife-beating.]

*** In well-functioning marriages, spouses discuss important intimate decisions such as whether to bear a child. But there are millions of women in this country who are the victims of regular physical and psychological abuse at the hands of their husbands. Should these women become pregnant, they may have very good reasons for not wishing to inform their husbands of their decision to obtain an abortion. Many may have justifiable fears of physical abuse, but may be no less fearful of the consequences of reporting prior abuse to the Commonwealth of Pennsylvania. Many may have a reasonable fear that notifying their husbands will provoke further instances of child abuse; these women are not exempt from § 3209's notification requirement. Many may fear devastating forms of psychological abuse from their husbands, including verbal harassment, threats of future violence, the destruction of possessions, physical confinement to the home, the withdrawal of financial support, or the disclosure of the abortion to family and friends. These methods of psychological abuse may act as even more of a deterrent to notification than the possibility of physical violence, but women who are the victims of the abuse are not exempt from § 3209's notification requirement. And many women who are pregnant as a result of sexual assaults by their husbands will be unable to avail themselves of the exception for spousal sexual assault, § 3209(b)(3), because the exception requires that the woman have notified law enforcement authorities within 90 days of the assault, and her husband will be notified of her report once an investigation begins, § 3128(c). If anything in this field is certain, it is that victims of spousal sexual assault are extremely reluctant to report the abuse to the government; hence, a great many spousal rape victims will not be exempt from the notification requirement imposed by § 3209.

The spousal notification requirement is thus likely to prevent a significant number of women from obtaining an abortion. It does not merely make abortions a little more difficult or expensive to obtain; for many women, it will impose a substantial obstacle. We must not blind ourselves to the fact that the significant number of women who fear for their safety and the safety of their children are likely to be deterred from procuring an abortion as surely as if the Commonwealth had outlawed abortion in all cases.

Respondents attempt to avoid the conclusion that § 3209 is invalid by pointing out that it imposes almost no burden at all for the vast majority of women seeking abortions. They begin by noting that only about 20 percent of the women who obtain abortions are married. They then note that of these women about 95 percent notify their husbands of their own volition. *** [But the number of violations is irrelevant, says the Court.]
***

We recognize that a husband has a "deep and proper concern and interest ... in his wife's pregnancy and in the growth and development of the fetus she is carrying." * With regard to the children he has fathered and raised, the Court has recognized his "cognizable and substantial" interest in their custody. *Stanley v. Illinois,* *; *see also Quilloin v. Walcott,* *; *Caban v. Mohammed,* *; *Lehr v. Robertson,* *. If these cases concerned a State's ability to require the mother to notify the father before taking some action with respect to a living child raised by both, therefore, it would be reasonable to conclude as a general matter that the father's interest in the welfare of the child and the mother's interest are equal.

Before birth, however, the issue takes on a very different cast. It is an inescapable biological fact that state regulation with respect to the child a woman is carrying will have a far greater impact on the mother's liberty than on the father's. The effect of state regulation on a woman's protected liberty is doubly deserving of scrutiny in such a case, as the State has touched not only upon the private sphere of the family but upon the very bodily integrity of the pregnant woman. * The Court has held that "when the wife and the husband disagree on this decision, the view of only one of the two marriage partners can prevail. Inasmuch as it is the woman who physically bears the child and who is the more directly and immediately affected by the pregnancy, as between the two, the balance weighs in her favor." *Danforth*, *. This conclusion rests upon the basic nature of marriage and the nature of our Constitution: "[T]he marital couple is not an independent entity with a mind and heart of its own, but an association of two individuals each with a separate intellectual and emotional makeup. If the right of privacy means anything, it is the right of the individual, married or single, to be free from unwarranted governmental intrusion into matters so fundamentally affecting a person as the decision whether to bear or beget a child." *Eisenstadt v. Baird*, *. The Constitution protects individuals, men and women alike, from unjustified state interference, even when that interference is enacted into law for the benefit of their spouses.

There was a time, not so long ago, when a different understanding of the family and of the Constitution prevailed. In *Bradwell v. State*, *, three Members of this Court reaffirmed the common-law principle that "a woman had no legal existence separate from her husband, who was regarded as her head and representative in the social state; and, notwithstanding some recent modifications of this civil status, many of the special rules of law flowing from and dependent upon this cardinal principle still exist in full force in most States." * Only one generation has passed since this Court observed that "woman is still regarded as the center of home and family life," with attendant "special responsibilities" that precluded full and independent legal status under the Constitution. *Hoyt v. Florida*, *. These views, of course, are no longer consistent with our understanding of the family, the individual, or the Constitution.

In keeping with our rejection of the common-law understanding of a woman's role within the family, the Court held in Danforth that the Constitution does not permit a State to require a married woman to obtain her husband's consent before undergoing an abortion. * The principles that guided the Court in Danforth should be our guides today. For the great many women who are victims of abuse inflicted by their husbands, or whose children are the victims of such abuse, a spousal notice requirement enables the husband to wield an effective veto over his wife's decision. Whether the prospect of notification itself deters such women from seeking abortions, or whether the husband, through physical force or psychological pressure or economic coercion, prevents his wife from obtaining an abortion until it is too late, the notice requirement will often be tantamount to the veto found unconstitutional in Danforth. The women most affected by this law--those who most reasonably fear the consequences of notifying their husbands that they are pregnant--are in the gravest danger.

The husband's interest in the life of the child his wife is carrying does not permit the State to empower him with this troubling degree of authority over his wife. The contrary view leads to consequences reminiscent of the common law. A husband has no enforceable right to require a wife to advise him before she exercises her personal choices. If a husband's interest in the potential life of the child outweighs a wife's liberty, the State could require a married woman to notify her husband before she uses a postfertilization contraceptive. Perhaps next in line would be a statute requiring pregnant married women to notify their husbands before engaging in conduct causing risks to the fetus. After all, if the husband's interest in the fetus' safety is a sufficient predicate for state regulation, the State could reasonably conclude that pregnant wives should notify their husbands before drinking alcohol or smoking. Perhaps married women should notify their husbands before using contraceptives or before undergoing any type of surgery that may have complications affecting the husband's interest in his wife's reproductive organs. And if a husband's interest justifies notice in any of these cases, one might reasonably argue that it justifies exactly what the Danforth Court held it did not justify--a requirement of the husband's consent as well. A State may not give to a man the kind of dominion over his wife that parents exercise over their children.

Section 3209 embodies a view of marriage consonant with the common- law status of married women but repugnant to our present understanding of marriage and of the nature of the rights secured by the Constitution. Women do not lose their constitutionally protected liberty when they marry. The Constitution protects all individuals, male or female, married or unmarried, from the abuse of governmental power, even where that power is employed for the supposed benefit of a member of the individual's family. These considerations confirm our conclusion that § 3209 is invalid.

***

Chief Justice REHNQUIST, with whom Justice WHITE, Justice SCALIA, and Justice THOMAS join, concurring in the judgment in part and dissenting in part.

*** We believe that *Roe* was wrongly decided, and that it can and should be overruled consistently with our traditional approach to stare decisis in constitutional cases. We would adopt the approach of the plurality in *Webster v. Reproductive Health Services*, *, and uphold the challenged provisions of the Pennsylvania statute in their entirety.

*** [The dissenters emphasize, *inter alia*, the inconsistencies of the abortion cases.]

In *Roe*, the Court observed that certain States recognized the right of the father to participate in the abortion decision in certain circumstances. Because neither *Roe* nor *Doe* involved the assertion of any paternal right, the Court expressly stated that the case did not disturb the validity of regulations that protected such a right. *Roe v. Wade, supra*, 410 U.S., at 165, n. 67. But three years later, in *Danforth*, the Court extended its abortion jurisprudence and held that a State could not require that a woman obtain the consent of her spouse before proceeding with an abortion. *.

We believe that the sort of constitutionally imposed abortion code of the type illustrated by our decisions following *Roe* is inconsistent "with the notion of a Constitution cast in general terms, as ours is, and usually speaking in general principles, as ours does." *Webster* *.

***

C.

Section 3209 of the Act contains the spousal notification provision. ***

We first emphasize that Pennsylvania has not imposed a spousal consent requirement of the type the Court struck down in *Planned Parenthood of Central Mo. v. Danforth*, *. Missouri's spousal consent provision was invalidated in that case because of the Court's view that it unconstitutionally granted to the husband "a veto power exercisable for any reason whatsoever or for no reason at all." *. But the provision here involves a much less intrusive requirement of spousal notification, not consent. Such a law requiring only notice to the husband "does not give any third party the legal right to make the [woman's] decision for her, or to prevent her from obtaining an abortion should she choose to have one performed." *Hodgson*, *. *Danforth* thus does not control our analysis. Petitioners contend that it should, however; they argue that the real effect of such a notice requirement is to give the power to husbands to veto a woman's abortion choice. The District Court indeed found that the notification provision created a risk that some woman who would otherwise have an abortion will be prevented from having one. 947 F.2d, at 712. For example, petitioners argue, many notified husbands will prevent abortions through physical force, psychological coercion, and other types of threats But Pennsylvania has incorporated exceptions in the notice provision in an attempt to deal with these problems. For instance, a woman need not notify her husband if the pregnancy is the result of a reported sexual assault, or if she has reason to believe that she would suffer bodily injury as a result of the notification. 18 Pa.Cons.Stat. § 3209(b) (1990). Furthermore, because this is a facial challenge to the Act, it is insufficient for petitioners to show that the notification provision "might operate unconstitutionally under some conceivable set of circumstances." *United States v. Salerno*, 481 U.S. 739, 745 (1987). Thus, it is not enough for petitioners to show that, in some "worst case" circumstances, the notice provision will operate as a grant of veto power to husbands. *. Because they are making a facial challenge to the provision, they must "show that no set of circumstances exists under which the [provision] would be valid." *Ibid*. (internal quotation marks omitted). This they have failed to do.

[FN2. *** In most instances the notification requirement operates without difficulty. As the District

Court found, the vast majority of wives seeking abortions notify and consult with their husbands, and thus suffer no burden as a result of the provision. * In other instances where a woman does not want to notify her husband, the Act provides exceptions. For example, notification is not required if the husband is not the father, if the pregnancy is the result of a reported spousal sexual assault, or if the woman fears bodily injury as a result of notifying her husband. Thus, in these instances as well, the notification provision imposes no obstacle to the abortion decision.

*** The joint opinion concentrates on the situations involving battered women and unreported spousal assault, and assumes, without any support in the record, that these instances constitute a "large fraction" of those cases in which women prefer not to notify their husbands (and do not qualify for an exception). * This assumption is not based on any hard evidence, however. ***] The question before us is therefore whether the spousal notification requirement rationally furthers any legitimate state interests. We conclude that it does. First, a husband's interests in procreation within marriage and in the potential life of his unborn child are certainly substantial ones. See * Danforth, 428 U.S., at 69 ("We are not unaware of the deep and proper concern and interest that a devoted and protective husband has in his wife's pregnancy and in the growth and development of the fetus she is carrying"); *; Skinner , *. The State itself has legitimate interests both in protecting these interests of the father and in protecting the potential life of the fetus, and the spousal notification requirement is reasonably related to advancing those state interests. By providing that a husband will usually know of his spouse's intent to have an abortion, the provision makes it more likely that the husband will participate in deciding the fate of his unborn child, a possibility that might otherwise have been denied him. This participation might in some cases result in a decision to proceed with the pregnancy. As Judge Alito observed in his dissent below, "[t]he Pennsylvania legislature could have rationally believed that some married women are initially inclined to obtain an abortion without their husbands' knowledge because of perceived problems--such as economic constraints, future plans, or the husbands' previously expressed opposition-that may be obviated by discussion prior to the abortion."*

The State also has a legitimate interest in promoting "the integrity of the marital relationship." *. This Court has previously recognized "the importance of the marital relationship in our society." Danforth, *. In our view, the spousal notice requirement is a rational attempt by the State to improve truthful communication between spouses and encourage collaborative decisionmaking, and thereby fosters marital integrity. See Labine, * ("[T]he power to make rules to establish, protect, and strengthen family life" is committed to the state legislatures). *** [P]etitioners see the law as a totally irrational means of furthering whatever legitimate interest the State might have. But, in our view, it is unrealistic to assume that every husband-wife relationship is either (1) so perfect that this type of truthful and important communication will take place as a matter of course, or (2) so imperfect that, upon notice, the husband will react selfishly, violently, or contrary to the best interests of his wife. See Danforth, at 103-104 (STEVENS, J., concurring in part and dissenting in part) (making a similar point in the context of a parental consent statute). The spousal notice provision will admittedly be unnecessary in some circumstances, and possibly harmful in others, but "the existence of particular cases in which a feature of a statute performs no function (or is even counterproductive) ordinarily does not render the statute unconstitutional or even constitutionally suspect." *. The Pennsylvania Legislature was in a position to weigh the likely benefits of the provision against its likely adverse effects, and presumably concluded, on balance, that the provision would be beneficial. Whether this was a wise decision or not, we cannot say that it was irrational. We therefore conclude that the spousal notice provision comports with the Constitution. See Harris v. McRae, 448 U.S., at 325-326 ("It is not the mission of this Court or any other to decide whether the balance of competing interests ... is wise social policy").
***

g. Notes and Questions

1) *Danforth, Casey* and Spousal/Paternal Participation

Is the use of "delegation" analysis in *Danforth* and *Casey* to invalidate the spousal consent law persuasive? the issue boils down to a matter of state delegation, why can the state "delegate" to a married woman the power to kill the living-but-unborn child of a child-wanting married man (a power the state clearly does not possess on its own)?

Both *Danforth* and *Casey* emphasize that if the husband and wife disagree about having an abortion, the views of only one of them can prevail, and since the woman bears the greater risk and burden it is not illogical to defer to her in tie-breaker situations. What raises that logic to constitutional command? Isn't that kind of gender-based tie-breaker exactly the kind of gender discrimination that other Supreme Court decisions have repudiated for being sexist and stereotypical? Would a similar tie-breaker rule (absolute maternal preference) be constitutionally valid in custody or other child-welfare disputes? The historic standard for making decisions regarding disputed parental decisions affecting children (e.g., custody decisions, medical treatment disagreements, etc.) has been and still is "best interests of the child." Why didn't the Court adopt that standard instead of the "mother-always-wins" rule? Is it possible that a father might sometimes be acting more in the interests of a living-but-unborn child than the mother? If the mother's life or health is not seriously jeopardized, isn't a father seeking to save the life of their child from a procedure designed to kill the child acting in the best interests of the child?

Is it *really*, as the majority says in *Casey*, "an inescapable biological fact that state regulation with respect to the child a woman is carrying will have a far greater impact on the mother's liberty than on the father's"? From what perspective? In the short-run or in the long-run? (Constitutionally, must the *immediate* always prevail over the *ultimate*?) If the woman can have other children but the man cannot (e.g., he has testicular cancer) why should her wishes receive mandatory priority? What if her reason for getting an abortion are totally irrational, and selfish? Isn't a father's relationship with each of his offspring individually of inestimable value of deserving of constitutional protection? If the woman's right to make the abortion decision entirely by herself derives from the fact that it is a unique relationship decision (mother-child) why must other relationship interests be constitutionally excluded, including the interest of the "child" *in utero*? Is it artificial for the Court to insist that the fetus or unborn child is just a "potential" something, rather than a reality, an existing human being in utero? If the child is really just a "potentiality," then isn't the pregnancy just a "potential" problem, and abortion just a "potential" solution?

Children impose disproportionate and different burdens at different times in the process of childrearing, from conception to majority (and beyond). Mutual consent is the usual standard for both assuming and eliminating those burdens. Is it unconstitutional to require mutual consent for parents to release a child for adoption (i.e., to give one parent the "veto power" to force the financial and other obligations of parenthood on both of them)? Pregnancy follows sexual relations (or artificial procreation); if that was mutually consensual, why should not mutual consent be required to end pregnancy by abortion?

Given the extensive and broad exceptions to the Pennsylvania spousal notification provision, was there any real risk of spousal abuse resulting from the notification law, or was that just convenient rhetoric? While the *Casey* case was pending, a lawsuit was also pending in Utah in which parties sought to invalidate, *inter alia*, a Utah spousal notification provision that had been in effect since 1974 (for 18 years). The plaintiffs' lawyers tried earnestly to find some evidence that some woman, sometime during that 18 year period in which spousal notice had been required, had been the victim of spouse abuse because she had been required to inform her husband of her desire to have an abortion. They put newspaper advertisements in papers in at least three states pleading for anyone with knowledge of such incidents to come forward. However, they did not find a single witness that any woman had been abused in 18 years as a result of Utah's spousal notification statute. However, in a deposition of an employee of the leading abortion clinic in Utah, the lawyer defending the Utah law (former BYU law professor Mary Anne Wood) discovered that the clinic had one case in which a husband had abused (threatened) his wife in connection with an abortion. In that case, however, the husband had tried to force his wife to have an abortion; when she told the clinic counselor that she didn't want an abortion and the counselor advised that it would be best for her not to have an abortion at that time, the husband became very angry and threatening.

Among the most common reasons given by women for having an abortion is lack of support, or opposition from (essentially fear of losing or impairing a relationship with), the sexual partner who fathered the unborn child. During pregnancy, when mutuality may be needed more than ever before, when joint procreative responsibility is most important, should the Court have mandated that all states' laws conform to a judicially-created model of procreative relationships that is rigidly individualistic? Thus, one feminist argues that the Supreme Court's abortion privacy doctrine "kills human relationships as efficiently as [abortion] kills unborn children." Williams, *infra*. Do you agree? Why/why not?

2) Father's Autonomy and Interest in Prenatal Children

After *Carey*, what (if any) recognizable parental interests do husbands have in the lives of the unborn offspring that their wives are carrying, and how can they protect those interests? *See* Chapter 22, *infra*. In many cases courts have rejected pleas by the biological fathers of unborn children to give them protection for or legal custody of their prenatal offspring or to enjoin their estranged wives or girlfriends from having abortions. *See e.g. Jones v. Smith*, 278 So. 2d 339 (Fla. Dist. Ct. App. 1973), cert. denied, 415 U.S. 958 (1974); Rothenberger v. Doe, 374 A.2d 57 (N.J.Super.Ch. 1977); *Coleman v. Coleman*, 471 A.2d 1115 (Md.App.,1984); *Doe v. Smith*, 530 N.E.2d 331 (Ind. Ct. App. 1988); *John Doe v. Jane Smith*, 527 N.E.2d 177 (Ind. 1988), denying separate application for injunction, 108 S. Ct. 2136 (Stevens, Circuit Justice 1988); and *Conn v. Conn*, 525 N.E.2d 612 (Ind. Ct. App.), aff'd, 526 N.E.2d 958 (Ind.), cert. denied, 109 S. Ct. 391 (1988); *Steinhoff v. Steinhoff*, 140 Misc. 2d 397, 531 N.Y.S.2d 78 (Sup. Ct. Nassau County June 30, 1988). That creates an interesting dilemma. As one law review writer puts it:

> When a female determines she is pregnant, she has the freedom to decide if she has the maturity level to undertake the responsibilities of motherhood, if she is financially able to support a child, if she is at a place in her career to take the time to have a child, or if she has other concerns precluding her from carrying the child to term. After weighing her options, the female may choose abortion. Once she aborts the fetus, the female's interests in and obligations to the child are terminated.
>
> In stark contrast, the unwed father has no options. His responsibilities to the child begin at conception and can only be terminated with the female's decision to abort the fetus or with the mother's decision to give the child up for adoption. Thus, he must rely on the decisions of the female to determine his future. The putative father does not have

the luxury, after the fact of conception, to decide that he is not ready for fatherhood. Unlike the female, he has no escape route.

McCulley, *infra. See also* Sharrin, *infra.* Why cannot States protect the interest of husbands to be notified of what may be the most important decision concerning their hope for posterity - a decision to destroy their living offspring *in utero*?

If a man offers to pay for an abortion and his girlfriend rejects his offer, should that be a defense to a later claim for child support for the child he offered to abort? *See S.P.B.* in Chapter 20, *infra.*

3. Practical and Ethical Considerations

To what extent may an attorney treat husband and wife as partners and agents of each other? If an attorney has strong moral objections to unilateralism within marriage, or to abortion, and a married woman asks him to help her get an abortion without her husband's consent or knowledge because they already have two children and she wants to return to market employment and thinks having another child will ruin her plans, what should the attorney do? If a man whose wife has informed him that she is going to have an abortion despite his objection approaches the same attorney and asks his help in stopping the abortion - he will do anything to protect the unborn child, what, if anything, could or should the attorney do within the bounds of professional ethics?

It has long been said, that "'[w]omen and children first!' [is] the 'moral result' of the civilizational imperative that 'men are expendable and women and children are not.'" McKenzie, *infra.* What does that mean? What does it connote for public policy and family law? Is that true? Why/why not?

4. Bibliography

Annette E. Clark, *The Right to Die: The Broken Road from* Quinlan *to* Schiavo, 37 Loyola U. Chi. L.J. 279 (2006).

William H. Colby, *From* Quinlan *to* Cruzan *to* Schiavo: *What Have We Learned?* 37 Loyola U. Chi. L.J. 279 (2006).

Campo-Flores, *The Legacy of Terri Schiavo,* Newsweek, April 4, 2005, at 22.

Contemporary Family Law, vol. 2, Ch. 13 (1988).

Thomas William Mayo, *Living and Dying in a Post*-Schiavo World, 38 J. Health L. 587 (2005).

Eric C. Miller, Note, *Listening to the Disabled: End of Life Medical Decision Making and the Never Competent,* 74 Fordham L. Rev. 2889 (2006).

Melanie G. McCulley, *The Male Abortion: The Putative Father's Right to Terminate His Interests in and Obligation to the Unborn Child,* 7 J.L. & Pol'y 1, 1-2 (1998).

Ross McKenzie, *'This is how a man dies. This is how a man lives,'* Townhall.com (May 23, 2002) <http://www.townhall.com/columnists/rossmackenzie/rm20020523.shtml>.

Andrea M. Sharrin, Note, *Potential Fathers and Abortion: A Woman's Womb Is Not a Man's Castle,* 55 Brook. L. Rev. 1359 (1990).

Lynn D. Wardle & Mary Anne Wood, A Lawyer Looks At Abortion (1982).

Lynn D. Wardle, *The Quandary of Pro-life Free Speech: A Lesson from the Abolitionists,* 62 Albany L. Rev. 853 (1999).

Camille S. Williams, *What Abortion Has Cost Women: Twenty-Five Years Post*-Roe, AUL Legislators Educational Conference, Chicago, Ill., Aug. 22, 1998, at 1.

B. CONSORTIUM AND "HEARTBALM" ACTIONS

1. Background

a. History and Policy of Consortium

The term consortium literally translated means "fellowship." In law it refers to the "conjugal fellowship of husband and wife, and the right of each to the company, cooperation, affection, and aid of the other in every conjugal relation." Black's Law Dictionary 382 (4th rev. ed. 1968). Thus, it refers to the legally protected relational interests between spouses; although recently it also has been used to describe the legally protectible relationship between parents and children. Originally, the primary element of consortium for which recovery was permitted was the service of the wife to her husband.

> At early common law, a husband's right to consortium developed through analogy to a master-servant relationship: a man could bring an action for intentional injury to or enticement away of a servant. As the wife owed certain services to the husband ... her status was not unlike that of a servant. Accordingly, the early English courts held that a cause of action was presented when the husband sued for damages as a result of an intentional tort against his wife ....
>
> Conversely, the wife had no parallel cause of action for injury to her husband .... Because a woman's legal identity was merged into her husband's upon marriage .... In addition, the husband was the master and owed no services to his wife; should she recover, the proceeds would be considered his property.

Note, *Consortium, infra* at 707-09. Early in the twentieth century, Dean Roscoe Pound summarized the concept:

> As against the world at large, the claims which the husband may assert with respect to the marital relation are four. (1) He has an interest in the society of his wife which may be infringed by abducting her, by enticing her away or by so injuring her as to deprive the husband of her companionship. . . . (2) He has an interest in the affection of the wife which may be infringed by persuasion or pressure addressed to her mind and will. . . . (3) He has an interest in the chastity of the wife, which is so related to his feelings of self-respect and to his honor as to be in effect an interest in personality. (4) He has an interest in the services of the wife in the household.
> ***
> A wife may assert four claims growing out of the marital relations against the world at large. (1) She has an interest in the society of her husband, quite apart from any economic advantage, as something so related to her spiritual existence as to be in effect an interest of personality. (2) She has an interest in the affection of the husband, in all respects analogous to the interest of the husband in the affection of the wife, which is clearly an interest of personality. (3) She has an interest in the chastity and constancy of the husband, involving her self-respect and honor, and hence obviously an interest of personality. (4) She has an interest in the relation as an economically advantageous [one], providing her with support and shelter . . . .

Roscoe Pound, *infra*, at 188, 193. Consortium consists of the first three claims on each list.

b. "Heartbalm" Actions in General

Actions to protect the interest that one spouse has in the marital relationship he or she has with the other are called "heartbalm" actions because the plaintiff seeks a remedy (usually monetary damages) to give "balm" to soothe a broken "heart." Derived from the common law writ of ravishment, they have long been unpopular for many reasons, in part because of fear or suspicion of abuse of potential for abuse, blackmail, and extortion, in part because the injury or loss is so intangible, in part because it requires judges to admit evidence of "dirty laundry" behavior, and in part because it involves a moral judgment (that many judges today are reluctant to make) about "fault" causing injury to or breakup of the marriage. Some courts have cited the enactment of "no-fault" divorce laws to justify judicial repeal or curtailing of "heartbalm" actions.

"Heartbalm" actions have a significant common law history.

Early English common law recognized two tort causes of action against third parties who interfered with the marriage relation: enticement and seduction. Enticement, which evolved into the tort of alienation of affections, punished the inducement of a wife to leave her husband. Unlike enticement, seduction, which evolved into the tort of criminal conversation, required an adulterous relationship between the plaintiff's wife and the defendant. Some commentators assert that alienation of affections did not really evolve from enticement, which was grounded squarely in property rights, but arose as a separate tort in America and one that was never formally recognized in England. It is true that the term "alienation of affections" first appeared in a New York suit in 1866. Many jurisdictions, however, use the terms alienation of affections and enticement interchangeably.

Quickly after its introduction, every U.S. state, except Louisiana, recognized the tort of alienation of affections. A majority of U.S. jurisdictions also recognized the tort of criminal conversation. While the elements of the two torts varied slightly from jurisdiction to jurisdiction, the fundamental elements were virtually the same in every state adopting them.

. . . .

Beginning in the 1930s, criticism of alienation of affections and criminal conversation torts reached a fevered pitch. In 1935, Indiana became the first state to enact a "heartbalm statute," abolishing the jurisdiction's heartbalm torts, including alienation of affections and criminal conversation. . . .

Jones, *infra*, at 67-68, 70; *see also* Tushnet, *infra*, at 2587 (1998) ("From the 1930s through the 1950s, a wave of antiheartbalm proposals swept the United States. Responding to charges that heartbalm actions enabled designing women to blackmail worthy men, legislators in many states passed statutes eliminating breach-of-promise and related actions.")

2. Statutes, Cases and Doctrines

a. Consortium Statutes or Cases

Find the statute or a leading case describing the consortium doctrine in your homestate.

b. Notes and Questions

1) Consortium--In General

There appear to be three different doctrines in American jurisdictions regarding the recovery of damages for injury or destruction of consortium. First, most states appear to grant to both husband and wife the right to recover for loss of consortium. *Hitaffer v. Argonne Co.*, 183 F.2d 811 (D.C. Cir. 1950) initiated this trend. In that case a woman brought suit seeking recovery for loss of spousal aid, assistance, enjoyment, and sexual relations against the company that employed her husband who had been injured on the job and had recovered worker's compensation benefits. The trial court granted summary judgment for the employer finding that the common law did not allow women to recover for loss of consortium, and no statute extended such a cause of action to women either. The federal court of appeals reversed emphasizing that the fact that men could recover for loss of consortium refuted most of the policy arguments relied on by the employer against extension of the cause of action to wives. The cause of action for consortium is essentially for non-economic losses. The primary reason for the common law prohibition of consortium action by wives was the common law disability of married women, which was abolished long ago in the United States. The fact that wives are permitted to recover for alienation of affections, criminal conversation, and for selling drugs to their husbands shows that the law recognizes the consortium rights in other contexts. The recovery by the man of benefits compensating for economic loss would not overlap and bar recovery by his wife for her non-economic injuries; she had an independent right to enjoy the society and companionship of her husband, which worker's compensation did not cover. Nor would the Worker Compensation statute's prohibition of suits by covered employees of persons asserting the rights of employees bar a suit by the wife to recover for injuries to her own consortium interests. Since the 1970s, the development of the equal protection doctrine provides even stronger support for the *Hitaffer* result. Courts in nearly forty states appear to take this position. Note, *Consortium, infra* at 707.

Second, some jurisdictions deny the right to recover to both the husband and wife. Apparently this approach is based on the historical fact that the wife could not bring an action for injury to consortium at common law, and deference to the principle of gender equality. This position manifests an underlying dislike for allowing recovery for injury to intangible, profoundly emotional relationships, and perhaps some fear of or reaction to cases where an exorbitant consortium award is made by an inflamed jury. This position is taken in Kansas, and was taken in Utah in 1997, when Utah Code Annot. § 30-2-11 was enacted.

The third position is to allow recovery for loss of consortium by the husband only; the wife may not recover for loss of consortium. The reason for this discriminatory treatment is primarily historical (that is the way it was at common law, when the wife owed her domestic service to her husband and the husband owed a duty of support to his wife). This was the prevailing rule in American jurisdictions a couple of decades ago; recent case law for this position, however, is scarce. *See Bates v. Donnafiedl*, 481 P.2d 347 (Wyo 1971); *Roseberry v. Starkovich*, 387 P.2d 321 (1963). Courts which take this position defer to the legislature to change the rule; thus, the old rule survives primarily because of legislative inertia. Obviously, this approach raises some equal protection questions, and it is questionable whether the rule would survive constitutional scrutiny if it were applied to deny a woman recovery for loss of consortium in a situation in which a man could recover if the injury had been to the wife. However, a credible argument can be made that some limitation on "double recovery" is necessary to prevent both spouses from recovering for the same elements of damage to their economic and marital unit. However, adoption of a gender-based rule to limit recovery is difficult to justify. Does this violate the constitutional guarantee of equal protection?

2) Consortium: Independent or Derivative?

In states that recognize a cause of action for loss of consortium, the question follows: is it independent or derivative? In *Hitaffer,* the D.C. Court of Appeals noted that it was independent (thus getting around Workers' Compensation Act bar to recovery in that case where husband had accepted WCA award). The principal questions are whether the loss of consortium claim must fail if the claim by the injured spouse fails (presumable yes if derivative, no if independent); whether contributory negligence of the injured spouse is imputed to bar or reduce recovery in action for loss of consortium (presumably yes if derivative, no if independent); whether the claim for loss of consortium must be joined with the personal injury claim by injured spouse (presumably yes if derivative, no if independent); and whether the statute of limitations running on the claim of the injured spouse bars the consortium claim (usually yes if derivative, no if independent).

The primary argument for derivative treatment is that the basis for recovery is interference with the mutual relationship, so if one party cannot recover or was negligent, the other party should not be allowed to recover. This approach considers the personal injury claim of the injured party and the consortium claim of the spouse to be so interrelated that together they represent two parts of one legal remedy providing complete recovery for damages flowing from the injury to a married person. The leading argument for independent treatment is that the noninjured spouse's claim is for her own physical and psychological pain and injury. Prosser, Harper & James favor treatment as independent claims because different interests are invaded. One who sells drugs to a husband cannot set up consent of the husband as a defense to action by the wife, and consent of a child is no bar to an action by his parents for such injuries.

3) Alienation of Affections

In *Gorman v. McMahon,* 792 So.2d 307 (Miss. Ct. App. 2001), the Mississippi Court of Appeals upheld the recovery by a husband for alienation of affections against a doctor who had an adulterous affair with the plaintiff's wife (who was then in her sixth marriage). The court affirmed a jury verdict for $50,000 based on evidence of loss of consortium including the cost of lost services in cooking meals, cleaning the home, taking care of his needs, paying half of the household bills; additional compensation for the costs of hiring a private investigator to confirm that the affair was occurring, legal fees incurred by him in connection with the divorce, medical expenses for depression and for physical problems resulting from his wife's affair. Utah courts have repeatedly upheld the cause of action for alienation of affections in the context of seduced spouses. *See Sharp v. Roskelly,* 818 P.2d 4 (Utah 1991) (married doctor seduced married assistant); *Norton v. MacFarlane,* 818 P.2d 8 (doctor may be sued for alienation of affections by husband of seduced wife); *Nelson v. Jacobsen,* 669 P.2d 1207 (Utah 1983) (husband may maintain alienation action against seducer of wife whose acts caused domestic violence). Alienation of affections claims have been abolished by legislation in over 30 states, and by judicial action in about a half-dozen other states. *See generally* 2 Contemporary Family Law, *infra,* § 13:02 .

3. Practical and Ethical Considerations

Omitted.

4. Bibliography

Jill Jones, Comment: *Fanning an Old Flame: Alienation of Affections and Criminal Conversation Revisited*, 26 Pepperdine L. Rev. 61 (1999).
Rebecca Tushnet, Note, *Rules of Engagement*, 107 Yale L.J. 2583, 2587 (1998).
Contemporary Family Law, vol. 2, Ch. 13 (1988).

C. Spousal Privileges and Immunities

1. Background

a. History of Interspousal Immunity

The doctrine of interspousal tort immunity was a natural consequence of two common law ideas about the nature of the marital relationship: the concept of the legal unity of the husband and the wife and the notion that the husband was the "profitable guardian" of all the possessions of the wife.

The idea that the husband and wife were one had ancient roots far beyond those of the common law. Biblical text was literally read to support this notion. Genesis 2:24. Likewise, the ancient Roman law recognized the unity of the man and the wife in the marital relationship. Regardless of its roots, the unity of the husband and wife was well recognized at common law. Blackstone deftly summarized the idea when he wrote:

> By marriage, the husband and wife are one person in the law: that is, the very being or legal existence of the woman is suspended during the marriage, or at least is incorporated and consolidated into that of the husband under whose wing, protection and cover she performs everything . . . upon this principle of a union of person in husband and wife depend almost all the legal rights, duties and disabilities that either of them acquire by marriage.

Blackstone, *infra* at 442.

Since the husband and wife were recognized as "one" it was not possible for either spouse to commit a tort against the other spouse, because allowing such would be tantamount to admitting that the husband could commit a tort against himself.

Another concept which lent support to the interspousal tort immunity doctrine, was the nature of the marital relationship at common law. Marriage was not a partnership as it is today, rather it was a guardianship, profitable to the husband. This concept had the effect of vesting in the husband complete control over the property of his wife. Since a grant of damages to the wife on a tort claim immediately accrued to her husband under the guardianship principle, to allow a tort claim by the wife would have had the paradoxical result of a husband compensating himself for his own misconduct. Layton *infra*.

b. The Trend Toward Abolition of Interspousal Immunity

Most states have abolished the doctrine of interspousal immunity. First, the doctrine was abolished in contract actions. Next, it was repudiated in actions based on intentional tort. For instance, in *Townsend v. Townsend,* S.W.2d (Mo. 1986), the Missouri Supreme Court held that the doctrine of interspousal immunity did not bar the assertion of a claim by a woman against her husband for damages for injuries she suffered when he intentionally and maliciously shot her in the back with a shotgun. Next, interspousal tort immunity was rejected in suits arising out of automobile accidents when the defending spouse is insured. The prevalence of automobile insurance and no-fault auto accident principles has encouraged this development. And in recent years, the doctrine of interspousal immunity has been held not to bar suits by one spouse against another for ordinary torts which do not involve "the 'give and take' of married life." For instance, in *S.A.V. v. K.G.V.,* 708 S.W.2d 651 (Mo. 1986), the Missouri Supreme Court abrogated the doctrine of interspousal immunity and ruled that a woman could maintain an action against her husband for "willfully, recklessly and *negligently* transmitt[ing] herpes disease to her without informing her of his infection. ... We hold that the archaic doctrine of spousal immunity is no longer available as a bar to negligence actions." 708 S.W.2d at 652. The Massachusetts Supreme Judicial Council went even further. While insisting that suits arising out of ordinary marital relations would not be actionable, it held that ordinary accidents in which one spouse was negligent in a manner that would render him or her liable to a third party were actionable between them.

Some commentators would justify retention of interspousal tort immunity on the basis of concepts of implied consent or assumption of the risk. This notion was endorsed more than 50 years ago. McCurty, *infra* at 1055. While marital torts are now generally cognizable, "[c]ourts usually articulate the notion that every act that is tortious between strangers should not necessarily be tortious between spouses. They have noted that there are 'mutual concessions implied in the marital relationship,' and that courts must respect the 'ebb and flow of married life.' [G]enerally courts have limited liability to situations where there has been a clear abuse of any possible marital privilege, ..." Spector, *infra*, at 747-748.

c. Marital Testimonial Privilege

The history and recent status of this evidentiary rule is discussed in *Trammel v. United States, infra.*

2. Statutes, Cases and Doctrines

a. *Trammel v. United States*

Otis Trammel v. United States
445 U.S. 40 (1980)

Mr. Chief Justice BURGER delivered the opinion of the Court.

We granted certiorari to consider whether an accused may invoke the privilege against adverse spousal testimony so as to exclude the voluntary testimony of his wife. 440 U.S. 934, 99 S.Ct. 1277, 59 L.Ed.2d 492 (1979). This calls for a re-examination of *Hawkins v. United States*, 358 U.S. 74, 79 S.Ct. 136, 3 L.Ed.2d 125 (1958).

I

On March 10, 1976, petitioner Otis Trammel was indicted with two others, Edwin Lee Roberts and Joseph Freeman, for importing heroin into the United States from Thailand and the Philippine Islands and for conspiracy to import heroin in violation of 21 U.S.C. §§ 952(a), 962(a), and 963. The indictment also named six unindicted co-conspirators, including petitioner's wife Elizabeth Ann Trammel.

According to the indictment, petitioner and his wife flew from the Philippines to California in August 1975, carrying with them a quantity of heroin. Freeman and Roberts assisted them in its distribution. Elizabeth Trammel then traveled to Thailand where she purchased another supply of the drug. On November 3, 1975, with four ounces of heroin on her person, she boarded a plane for the United States. During a routine customs search in Hawaii, she was searched, the heroin was discovered, and she was arrested. After discussions with Drug Enforcement Administration agents, she agreed to cooperate with the Government.

Prior to trial on this indictment, petitioner moved to sever his case from that of Roberts and Freeman. He advised the court that the Government intended to call his wife as an adverse witness and asserted his claim to a privilege to prevent her from testifying against him. At a hearing on the motion, Mrs. Trammel was called as a Government witness under a grant of use immunity. She testified that she and petitioner were married in May 1975 and that they remained married. She explained that her cooperation with the Government was based on assurances that she would be given lenient treatment. She then described, in considerable detail, her role and that of her husband in the heroin distribution conspiracy.

After hearing this testimony, the District Court ruled that Mrs. Trammel could testify in support of the Government's case to any act she observed during the marriage and to any communication "made in the presence of a third person"; however, confidential communications between petitioner and his wife were held to be privileged and inadmissible. The motion to sever was denied.

At trial, Elizabeth Trammel testified within the limits of the court's pretrial ruling; her testimony, as the Government concedes, constituted virtually its entire case against petitioner. He was found guilty on both the substantive and conspiracy charges and sentenced to an indeterminate term of years pursuant to the Federal Youth Corrections Act, 18 U.S.C. § 5010(b).

In the Court of Appeals petitioner's only claim of error was that the admission of the adverse testimony of his wife, over his objection, contravened this Court's teaching in *Hawkins v. United States*, supra, and therefore constituted reversible error. The Court of Appeals rejected this contention. It concluded that *Hawkins* did not prohibit "the voluntary testimony of a spouse who appears as an unindicted co-conspirator under grant of immunity from the Government in return for her testimony." 583 F.2d 1166, 1168 (CA10 1978).

II.

The privilege claimed by petitioner has ancient roots. Writing in 1628, Lord Coke observed that "it hath beene resolved by the Justices that a wife cannot be produced either against or for her husband." 1 E. Coke, A Commentarie upon Littleton 6b (1628). *See generally* 8 J. Wigmore, Evidence § 2227 (McNaughton rev. 1961). This spousal disqualification sprang from two canons of medieval jurisprudence: first, the rule that an accused was not permitted to testify in his own behalf because of his interest in the proceeding; second, the concept that husband and wife were one, and that since the woman had no recognized separate legal existence, the husband was that one. From those two now long-abandoned doctrines, it followed that what was inadmissible from the lips of the defendant-husband was also inadmissible from his wife.

Despite its medieval origins, this rule of spousal disqualification remained intact in most common-law jurisdictions well into the 19th century. *See id.,* § 2333. It was applied by this Court in *Stein v. Bowman*, 13 Pet. 209, 220-223 (1839), in *Graves v. United States*, 150 U.S. 118 (1893), and again in *Jin Fuey Moy v. United States*, 254 U.S. 189, 195 (1920), where it was deemed so well established a proposition as to "hardly requir[e] mention." Indeed, it was not until 1933, in *Funk v. United States*, 290 U.S. 371, that this Court abolished the testimonial disqualification in the federal courts, so as to permit the spouse of a defendant to testify in the defendant's behalf. *Funk*, however, left undisturbed the rule that either spouse could prevent the other from giving adverse testimony. *Id.,* at

373, 54 S.Ct., at 212. The rule thus evolved into one of privilege rather than one of absolute disqualification.*

The modern justification for this privilege against adverse spousal testimony is its perceived role in fostering the harmony and sanctity of the marriage relationship. Notwithstanding this benign purpose, the rule was sharply criticized. Professor Wigmore termed it "the merest anachronism in legal theory and an indefensible obstruction to truth in practice." 8 Wigmore § 2228, at 221. The Committee on Improvements in the Law of Evidence of the American Bar Association called for its abolition. 63 American Bar Association Reports 594-595 (1938). In its place, Wigmore and others suggested a privilege protecting only private marital communications, modeled on the privilege between priest and penitent, attorney and client, and physician and patient. *See* 8 Wigmore § 2332 et seq. *[Fn 5 - This Court recognized just such a confidential marital communications privilege in Wolfle v. United States, 291 U.S. 7, 54 S.Ct. 279, 78 L.Ed. 617 (1934), and in Blau v. United States, 340 U.S. 332, 71 S.Ct. 301, 95 L.Ed. 306 (1951). In neither case, however, did the Court adopt the Wigmore view that the communications privilege be substituted in place of the privilege against adverse spousal testimony. The privilege as to confidential marital communications is not at issue in the instant case; accordingly, our holding today does not disturb Wolfle and Blau.]*

These criticisms influenced the American Law Institute, which, in its 1942 Model Code of Evidence advocated a privilege for marital confidences, but expressly rejected a rule vesting in the defendant the right to exclude all adverse testimony of his spouse. *See* American Law Institute, Model Code of Evidence, Rule 215 (1942). In 1953 the Uniform Rules of Evidence, drafted by the National Conference of Commissioners on Uniform State Laws, followed a similar course; it limited the privilege to confidential communications and "abolishe[d] the rule, still existing in some states, and largely a sentimental relic, of not requiring one spouse to testify against the other in a criminal action." *See* Rule 23(2) and comments. Several state legislatures enacted similarly patterned provisions into law.

In *Hawkins v. United States*, 358 U.S. 74, 79 S.Ct. 136, 3 L.Ed.2d 125 (1958), this Court considered the continued vitality of the privilege against adverse spousal testimony in the federal courts. There the District Court had permitted petitioner's wife, over his objection, to testify against him. With one questioning concurring opinion, the Court held the wife's testimony inadmissible; it took note of the critical comments that the common- law rule had engendered, *id.*, at 76, and n. 4, 79 S.Ct., at 137, but chose not to abandon it. Also rejected was the Government's suggestion that the Court modify the privilege by vesting it in the witness-spouse, with freedom to testify or not independent of the defendant's control. The Court viewed this proposed modification as antithetical to the widespread belief, evidenced in the rules then in effect in a majority of the States and in England, "that the law should not force or encourage testimony which might alienate husband and wife, or further inflame existing domestic differences." *Id.*, at 79, 79 S.Ct., at 139.

Hawkins, then, left the federal privilege for adverse spousal testimony where it found it, continuing "a rule which bars the testimony of one spouse against the other unless both consent." *Id.*, at 78. Accord, *Wyatt v. United States*, 362 U.S. 525, 528 (1960). *[Fn 7 - The decision in Wyatt recognized an exception to Hawkins for cases in which one spouse commits a crime against the other. 362 US. at 526. This exception, placed on the ground of necessity, was a longstanding one at common law. See Lord Audley's Case, 123 Eng.Rep. 1140 (1631); 8 Wigmore § 2239. It has been expanded since then to include crimes against the spouse's property, see Herman v. United States, 220 F.2d 219, 226 (CA4 1955), and in recent years crimes against children of either spouse, United States v. Allery, 526 F.2d 1362 (CA8 1975). Similar exceptions have been found to the confidential marital communications privilege. See 8 Wigmore § 2338.]* However, in so doing, the Court made clear that its decision was not meant to "foreclose whatever changes in the rule may eventually be dictated by 'reason and experience.' " 358 U.S., at 79.

III.

A.

The Federal Rules of Evidence acknowledge the authority of the federal courts to continue the evolutionary development of testimonial privileges in federal criminal trials "governed by the principles of the common law as they may be interpreted . . . in the light of reason and experience." Fed.Rule Evid. 501. Cf. *Wolfle v. United States*, 291 U.S. 7, 12 (1934). The general mandate of Rule 501 was substituted by the Congress for a set of privilege rules drafted by the Judicial Conference Advisory Committee on Rules of Evidence and approved by the Judicial Conference of the United States and by this Court. That proposal defined nine specific privileges, including a husband-wife privilege which would have codified the Hawkins rule and eliminated the privilege for confidential marital communications. *See* proposed Fed.Rule Evid. 505. In rejecting the proposed Rules and enacting Rule 501, Congress manifested an affirmative intention not to freeze the law of privilege. Its purpose rather was to "provide the courts with the flexibility to develop rules of privilege on a case-by-case basis," 120 Cong.Rec. 40891 (1974) (statement of Rep. Hungate), and to leave the door open to change. *See also* S.Rep.No.93-1277, p. 11 (1974); H.R.Rep.No.93-650, p. 8 (1973), U.S.Code Cong. & Admin.News 1974, p. 7051.

Although Rule 501 confirms the authority of the federal courts to reconsider the continued validity of the Hawkins rule, the long history of the privilege suggests that it ought not to be casually cast aside. That the privilege is one affecting marriage, home, and family relationships-- already subject to much erosion in our day--also counsels caution. At the same time, we cannot escape the reality that the law on occasion adheres to doctrinal concepts long after the reasons which gave them birth have disappeared and after experience suggest the need for change. This was recognized in Funk where the Court "decline[d] to enforce . . . ancient rule[s] of the common law under conditions as they now exist." 290 U.S., at 382, 54 S.Ct., at 215. For, as Mr. Justice Black admonished in another setting, "[w]hen precedent and precedent alone is all the argument that can be made to support a court-fashioned rule, it is time for the rule's creator to destroy it." *Francis v. Southern Pacific Co.*, 333 U.S. 445, 471 (1948) (dissenting opinion).

B.

Since 1958, when *Hawkins* was decided, support for the privilege against adverse spousal testimony has been eroded further. Thirty-one jurisdictions, including Alaska and Hawaii, then allowed an accused a privilege to prevent adverse spousal testimony. 358 U.S., at 81, n. 3, 79 S.Ct., at 140 (STEWART, J., concurring). The number has now declined to 24. *[Fn 9 - Eight States provide that one spouse is incompetent to testify against the other in a criminal proceeding [HI, IO, MS, MC, OH, PA, TX, & WY; cit.] Sixteen States provide a privilege against adverse spousal testimony and vest the privilege in both spouses or in the defendant-spouse alone [AK, CO, ID, MI, MN, MO, MN, NV, NJ, NM, OR, UT, VA, WA, WV; cit.] Nine States entitle the witness-spouse alone to assert a privilege against adverse spousal testimony [AL, CA, CN, GA, KY, LA, MD, MA, RI, ; cit]. The remaining 17 States have abolished the privilege in criminal cases [AZ, AR, DE, FL, IL, IN, KS, ME, NH, NY, ND, OK, SC, SD, TN, VT, WI; cit.]. In 1901, Congress enacted a rule of evidence for the District of Columbia that made husband and wife "competent but not compellable to testify for or against each other," except as to confidential communications. This provision, which vests the privilege against adverse spousal testimony in the witness-spouse, remains in effect. See 31 Stat. 1358, §§ 1068, 1069, recodified as D.C.Code § 14-306 (1973).]* In 1974, the National Conference on Uniform State Laws revised its Uniform Rules of Evidence, but again rejected the Hawkins rule in favor of a limited privilege for confidential communications. *See* Uniform Rules of Evidence, Rule 504. That proposed rule has been enacted in Arkansas, North Dakota, and Oklahoma--each of which in 1958 permitted an accused to exclude adverse spousal testimony. *[Fn 10 - In 1965, California took the privilege from the defendant-spouse and vested it in the witness-spouse, accepting a study commission recommendation that the "latter [was] more likely than the former to determine whether or not to claim the privilege on the basis of the probable effect on the marital relationship." See Cal.Evid.Code Ann. §§ 970-973 (West 1966 and Supp.1979) and 1 California Law Revision Commission, Recommendation and Study relating* to *The Marital "For and Against" Testimonial Privilege at F-5 (1956). See also 6 California Law Revision Commission, Tentative Privileges Recommendation--Rule 27.5, pp. 243-244 (1964). ¶Support for the common-law rule has also diminished in England. In 1972, a study group there proposed giving the privilege to the witness-spouse, on the ground that "if [the wife] is willing to give evidence . . . the law would be showing excessive concern for the preservation of marital harmony if it were to say that she must not do so." Criminal Law Revision Committee, Eleventh Report, Evidence (General) 93.]* The trend in state law toward divesting the accused of the privilege to bar adverse spousal testimony has special relevance because the laws of marriage and domestic relations are concerns traditionally reserved to the states. *See Sosna v. Iowa,* 419 U.S. 393, 404, 95 S.Ct. 553, 559 (1975). Scholarly criticism of the *Hawkins* rule has also continued unabated.

C.

Testimonial exclusionary rules and privileges contravene the fundamental principle that " 'the public . . . has a right to every man's evidence.' " *United States v. Bryan,* 339 U.S. 323, 331 (1950). As such, they must be strictly construed and accepted "only to the very limited extent that permitting a refusal to testify or excluding relevant evidence has a public good transcending the normally predominant principle of utilizing all rational means for ascertaining truth." *Elkins v. United States,* 364 U.S. 206, 234 (1960) (Frankfurter, J., dissenting). Accord, *United States v. Nixon,* 418 U.S. 683, 709-710 (1974). Here we must decide whether the privilege against adverse spousal testimony promotes sufficiently important interests to outweigh the need for probative evidence in the administration of criminal justice.

It is essential to remember that the Hawkins privilege is not needed to protect information privately disclosed between husband and wife in the confidence of the marital relationship--once described by this Court as "the best solace of human existence." *Stein v. Bowman,* 13 Pet., at 223. Those confidences are privileged under the independent rule protecting confidential marital communications. *Blau v. United States,* 340 U.S. 332 (1951); *. The *Hawkins* privilege is invoked, not to exclude private marital communications, but rather to exclude evidence of criminal acts and of communications made in the presence of third persons.

No other testimonial privilege sweeps so broadly. The privileges between priest and penitent, attorney and client, and physician and patient limit protection to private communications. These privileges are rooted in the imperative need for confidence and trust. The priest-penitent privilege recognizes the human need to disclose to a spiritual counselor, in total and absolute confidence, what are believed to be flawed acts or thoughts and to receive priestly consolation and guidance in return. The lawyer-client privilege rests on the need for the advocate and counselor to know all that relates to the client's reasons for seeking representation if the professional mission is to be carried out. Similarly, the physician must know all that a patient can articulate in order to identify and to treat disease; barriers to full disclosure would impair diagnosis and treatment.

The Hawkins rule stands in marked contrast to these three privileges. Its protection is not limited to confidential communications; rather it permits an accused to exclude all adverse spousal testimony. As Jeremy Bentham observed more than a century and a half ago, such a privilege goes far beyond making "every man's house his castle," and permits a person to convert his house into "a den of thieves." 5 Rationale of Judicial Evidence 340 (1827). It "secures, to every man, one safe and unquestionable and every ready accomplice for every imaginable crime." *Id.*, at 338.

The ancient foundations for so sweeping a privilege have long since disappeared. Nowhere in the common-law world--indeed in any modern society--is a woman regarded as chattel or demeaned by denial of a separate legal identity and the dignity associated with recognition as a whole human being. Chip by chip, over the years those archaic notions have been cast aside so that "[n]o longer is the female destined solely for the home and the rearing of the family, and only the male for the marketplace and the world of ideas." *Stanton v. Stanton,* 421 U.S. 7, 14-15 (1975).

The contemporary justification for affording an accused such a privilege is also unpersuasive.

When one spouse is willing to testify against the other in a criminal proceeding--whatever the motivation--their relationship is almost certainly in disrepair; there is probably little in the way of marital harmony for the privilege to preserve. In these circumstances, a rule of evidence that permits an accused to prevent adverse spousal testimony seems far more likely to frustrate justice than to foster family peace. *[Fn 12 - It is argued that abolishing the privilege will permit the Government to come between husband and wife, pitting one against the other. That, too, misses the mark. Neither Hawkins, nor any other privilege, prevents the Government from enlisting one spouse to give information concerning the other or to aid in the other's apprehension. It is only the spouse's testimony in the courtroom that is prohibited.]* Indeed, there is reason to believe that vesting the privilege in the accused could actually undermine the marital relationship. For example, in a case such as this the Government is unlikely to offer a wife immunity and lenient treatment if it knows that her husband can prevent her from giving adverse testimony. If the Government is dissuaded from making such an offer, the privilege can have the untoward effect of permitting one spouse to escape justice at the expense of the other. It hardly seems conducive to the preservation of the marital relation to place a wife in jeopardy solely by virtue of her husband's control over her testimony.

IV.

    Our consideration of the foundations for the privilege and its history satisfy us that "reason and experience" no longer justify so sweeping a rule as that found acceptable by the Court in Hawkins. Accordingly, we conclude that the existing rule should be modified so that the witness-spouse alone has a privilege to refuse to testify adversely; the witness may be neither compelled to testify nor foreclosed from testifying. This modification--vesting the privilege in the witness-spouse--furthers the important public interest in marital harmony without unduly burdening legitimate law enforcement needs.

    Here, petitioner's spouse chose to testify against him. That she did so after a grant of immunity and assurances of lenient treatment does not render her testimony involuntary. Cf. Bordenkircher v. Hayes, 434 U.S. 357 (1978). Accordingly, the District Court and the Court of Appeals were correct in rejecting petitioner's claim of privilege, and the judgment of the Court of Appeals is

    Affirmed.

    Mr. Justice STEWART, concurring in the judgment.

    [T]he Court in this case simply accepts the very same arguments that the Court rejected when the Government first made them in the Hawkins case in 1958. I thought those arguments were valid then, and I think so now.

    The Court is correct when it says that "[t]he ancient foundations for so sweeping a privilege have long since disappeared." * But those foundations had disappeared well before 1958; their disappearance certainly did not occur in the few years that have elapsed between the Hawkins decision and this one.

b. Notes and Questions

1) Modern Policies for Interspousal Immunity

    The historic reasons for interspousal tort immunity (primarily related to the civil disabilities of married women) have long ago ceased to be persuasive in the United States. Nevertheless, the doctrine of interspousal immunity continues to find substantial (if waning) support for several reasons. The primary justifications for interspousal immunity asserted today (and, in parenthesis, common responses to them) are listed below:

    1) Interspousal tort actions will destroy harmony in the marital relationship. (Response--no more than contract actions, etc.)

2) The doctrine helps preserve the unity of the husband and the wife. (Concept long abandoned.)

3) The doctrine helps to prevent collusive and fraudulent claims. (Courts can do so without altogether prohibiting action).

4) Retention of the doctrine helps to prevent trivial and numerous claims. (Courts can do so without altogether prohibiting action.)

5) Other types of actions such as divorce or criminal proceedings provide adequate redress to the injured spouse. (Not if injury is economic; "no-fault" movement.)

6) If the doctrine is to be abrogated then it is the duty of the legislature and not the courts to effect the change. (It is a common law doctrine created by courts.) Layton, *infra*.

By 1992, it was reported that 38 states had repealed the spousal immunity rule either by judicial opinion or statute; nine other states had limited it with exceptions for intentional acts or automobile accidents, and only three states still had full common law interspousal immunity in tort.

2) Spousal Immunity for Parenting

(1) Sadly, many children have died while riding in a car driven by their father because their father was negligent in some way (including failing to put the children in car seats, infant restraints, or have the children wear seat belts). Could a wife sue her husband for such negligence that resulted in the death of her (their) only child? If they had insurance and she was suing because they were poor and needed the insurance money to pay for the hospital and funeral expenses, would that affect your analysis? If she was seeking a divorce, would that affect your analysis? If the father/husband had been drinking and that caused the accident, would that affect your analysis?

(2) On a hot day in August, 1998, five little girls, ages 2-6 (two pairs of sisters who were first cousins, and a friend) died after they locked themselves in the trunk of a car owned by the parents of two of the girls that was parked at their home in West Valley City, Utah. When the mother who was watching the children discovered that they were missing she frantically called police and instituted a massive search; police discovered the bodies of the little girls in the trunk that hot afternoon after it was too late. If the parents of the other three girls who died believe that the mother at whose home and in whose car the children died was negligent, could they sue her for negligence? If the other parents are poor and couldn't afford funeral costs, and the mother-defendant had home owners' insurance, would that make a difference in your analysis? Could the husband of the mother at whose home and in whose car the children died (the father of two of the dead children) sue his wife for negligence? If he was poor and couldn't afford funeral costs, and the mother-defendant had home owners' insurance, would that make a difference in your analysis? If the girls had gotten locked in the trunk before, and the husband had warned his wife specifically about that risk, would that affect your analysis?

3) Spouse's Authority to Consent to Searches

As noted elsewhere, the privacy of the spousal relationship is protected even to the extent that the testimony of one spouse against another may not be compelled. But, as a general rule, the testifying spouse may voluntarily choose to give testimony against the other spouse even over the objection of the other spouse. However, if the testimony relates to confidential communications made between husband and wife, either spouse may prevent the disclosure of the conversation; i.e., only if both spouses agree will the testimony be admitted. So, as to spousal communications, disclosure is only permitted with the consent of both spouses. One spouse may not disclose such information (in testimony) without the consent of the other.

But the confidentiality of the spousal relationship extends beyond words and conversations. May one spouse unilaterally consent to the search of the premises used by the other? In one case a court held that the common law wife of the criminal defendant could consent to a police search of the apartment she and her common law husband used to share, to which she had a key, even though the couple was separated and in the process of breaking up. Because she retained a key to the premises and intended to return later to remove her furniture, she was legally entitled to exercise common authority over the dwelling, the court reasoned. *Sullivan v. State*, 716 P.2d 684 (Okla. Crim. App. 1986).

4) Relationship of Spouses in Criminal Law Generally

At common law the wife was responsible for her criminal conduct. However, her status as a married woman provided some protection; if she acted in the presence of her husband, she was presumed to be acting at his direction and thus she could invoke a defense of coercion. Being "one" meant that the wife and husband could not be guilty of a criminal conspiracy with each other. Clark, *infra*, at § 7.1. The nineteenth century Married Women's Property Acts largely conferred upon married women independent legal capacity and undermined the above-noted common law rules. Married couples may now be convicted of criminal conspiracy, and the wife's defense of coercion for acting in the presence of her husband has been eliminated. *Id.*, at § 7.3.

There is some authority at common law that a husband could not be guilty of rape against his wife. The presumption might be that the "unity" theory prevented denial of the unity, or, more particularly, that the agreement to sex in marriage was irrevocable and constituted universal consent by each to the sexual demands of the other. However, the basis for the practice (which may not have been a doctrinal rule) may have been evidentiary, not normative - faced with a "he said vs. she said" dispute, in which the victim and perpetrator are parties to a sexual relationship, have had a history of voluntary sexual relations, and the law presumes consent, prosecutors may have had practical reasons for declining to prosecute. In the nineteenth and twentieth century, that rule (if it ever was a rule) was limited and distinguished in cases where the parties were separated or there was a legal order protecting the wife.

In 1980, the American Law Institute approved a marital rape exemption in the Model Penal Code. The reasoning behind the proposed exemption emphasizes the relatively minimal harm (in contrast to rape between persons who do not have a history of voluntary sexual relations with each other), other methods that the wife usually has to protect herself, and the undesirability and difficulty of using heavy criminal rape laws to police marital conduct. The "marital exemption" defense to rape claims has been uniformly unsuccessful in recent years. "By 1990, no state retained an absolute marital rape exemption, although thirty-five states placed limits on the prosecution of marital rapists. Such prosecutorial limitations include noncohabitation or aggravated force requirements, ceilings on punishment, ..." Note, *infra*, at 681. *See e.g. Warren v. State*, 355 S.E.2d 221 (Ga. 1985); *People v. Liberta*, 474 N.E.2d 567 (N.Y. 1984); *People v. M.D.*, 595 N.E.2d 702 (Ill. App. 1992). Should marital rape be treated any differently in criminal law than other relational rape? Why/why not? If so, how?

3. Practical and Ethical Considerations

In what kind of cases will spouses immunity and privilege issues arise most often? In cases where the parties are separated, is there any reason to preserve immunity or privilege? Why/why not? What potential conflict of interest issues does this raise for lawyers?

4. Bibliography

American Law Institute, Model penal Code and Commentary, Part II, Vol. 2, § 213.1, and cmnt. (1980).
Homer H. Clark, Jr., The Law of Domestic Relations in the United States (2d ed. 1988).
Contemporary Family Law, vol. 2, Ch. 13 (1988).
Kevin Layton, Interspousal Tort Immunity in Utah (December, 1985) (LDW student's paper).
Note, *Ultimate Weapon?: Demythologizing Spousal Rape and Reconceptualizing Its Prosecution*, 48 Stan. L. Rev. 677 (1996).

CHAPTER 19

Spouse Abuse; Consequences of Quasi-Marriage

A. SPOUSE ABUSE

1. Background

a. "Correction"at Common Law

At common law, the husband could "correct" his wife by "moderate" and "reasonable" correction without incurring legal liability. Blackstone wrote:

> The husband, also (by the old law), might give his wife moderate correction; for, as he is to answer for her misbehavior, the law thought it reasonable to intrust him with this power of restraining her, by domestic chastisement, in the same moderation that a man is allowed to correct his apprentices or children .... But this power of correction was confined within reasonable bounds, and the husband was prohibited from using any violence to his wife *aliter quam ad virum, ex causa regiminis et castigationis uxoris suoe, licte et rationabiliter pertinet* (otherwise than lawfully and reasonably belongs to the husband for the due government and correction of the wife." The civil law gave the husband the same, or a larger authority, over his wife; allowing him, for some misdemeanors, *flagellis et fustibus acriter verberare uxorem* (to beat his wife severely with scourges and sticks): for others, only *modicam castigationem adhibere* (to use moderate chastisement). But with us, in the politer reign of Charles the Second, this power of correction began to be doubted; and a wife may now have security of the peace against her husband, or, in return, a husband against his wife. Yet the lower rank of people, who were always fond of the old common law, still claim, and exert their ancient privilege; and the courts of law will still permit a husband to restrain a wife of her liberty, in case of any gross misbehavior.

1 W. Blackstone, *infra* at *445.

Until recently, many American states followed the English common law "rule of thumb" – that it was not unlawful for a husband to correct his wife with a rod or switch if it was no thicker than his thumb. For example, in the famous case of *State v. Rhodes*, 61 N.C. 453 (1868) a man was indicted for assault and battery upon his wife, upon evidence which the jury found to establish that he struck her "three licks with a switch about the size of one of his fingers (but not as large as a man's thumb) without any provocation except some words uttered by her and not recollected by the witnesses." The trial judge ruled that the husband had the right to whip his wife with a switch no larger than his thumb, and entered a judgment of "not guilty." The N.C. Supreme Court, noting that no permanent injury resulted, affirmed, but for a different reason –

> not that the husband has the *right* to whip his wife much or little; but that we will not interfere with family government in trifling cases. ... We will not inflict upon society the greater evil of raising the curtain upon domestic privacy, to punish the lesser evil of trifling violence. Two boys under fourteen years of age fight upon the play-ground, and

457

yet the courts will take no notice of it, not for the reason that boys have the *right* to fight, but because the interests of society require that they should be left to the more appropriate discipline of the school room and of the home.

61 N.C. at 459. Is the principle that courts should "not interfere with family government in trifling cases" flawed? Was its application here flawed? Why/why not? What is a "trifling" case of whipping? Was the problem the "thumb" rule? Would the "pinky finger" rule be OK? The "straw" rule? The "flat of the hand" rule? The "one slap" rule? The "no touching" rule? Should there be a public rule at all? Isn't the rule reflective of norms that vary over time and across cultures? Who should decide? Why?

Before the days of vigorous legal response to domestic violence, victims were not entirely without remedies. As the *Rhodes* case suggests, judges expected that the problem would be dealt with extrajudicially by an appropriate community. Before World War II, couples often lived in reasonable proximity to their families; the woman often had a father or brother (or in-laws) living nearby who might take it upon himself (with or without invitation) to intervene to teach an abusive husband (with a whip or board, if necessary) that wife-beating of their daughter/sister (in-law) would not be tolerated. Neighbors might intervene by the same means for the same purpose. Church leaders could exert tremendous moral (and social) influence upon an abusive husband (threatening to expel from church membership and thereby stigmatize) or fellow church members might "have a talk" (verbal or otherwise) with an abusive husband. Church "sisters" of the abused woman could exert tremendous pressure themselves upon the abuser or upon their husbands/fathers/brothers to do something. Do such communities still exist? Are such remedies still possible? Practical? Preferable to legal remedies such as prosecution?

b. The Reality of Domestic Violence

Physical violence by spouses towards each other, most dangerously by the husband toward the wife, historically has not been uncommon. It is especially common in couples that (sometimes as a result of filing for) divorce. *See infra*, Chapter 27.

A study based on the National Family Violence Survey reported that some domestic partner violence (including married and unmarried couples) occurred in about 16% of families surveyed. However, a study based on the National Crime Survey reported that the rate of criminal violence in families was less than 3% per year. The authors explained that the difference was probably due to the fact that the "NCS is presented to respondents as a study of crime, whereas the others are presented as studies of family problems. The difficulty with a 'crime survey' . . . is that most people think of being kicked by their spouses as a wrong, but not a 'crime' in the legal sense." Strauss & Gelles, *infra*. Another social scientist has written: "Substantial discrepancies among estimates of the prevalence, incidence, and correlates of family violence compromise the usefulness of the research results." Weis, *infra* at 117. Nonetheless, it is clear that domestic violence is a serious problem.

The causes of abuse are many. "[One study] found that, of the forty-two characteristics or "risk markers" studied in female victims, only one -- having witnessed violence between parents or care givers in childhood -- was consistently correlated with being the victim of a male partner's violence. . . . Conversely, for husbands who were violent toward their female partners three risk markers -- witnessing of parental violence while growing up, sexual aggression toward the wife, and use of violence toward the children were consistently found. Alcohol use, income level, occupational status, education level, and assertiveness were also consistent risk markers, although less strong." Hanson, *infra*.

The gender of assaulters is a subject of much dispute. The conventional wisdom among activists is that domestic abuse is something that men inflict upon women. To some extent the definition of abuse is critical; if abuse is defined as serious assault (causing death or serious injury) one set of statistics is produced; if minor physical assaults including slapping, scratching and throwing things, the ratio is different. If emotional abuse (however defined) is included in the definition, the picture changes again. According to a 1985 National Family Violence Survey, women commit slightly more minor assaults than men on their partners and men are slightly more guilty of severe assaults on their partners than women. Straus, *infra* at 210. On the other hand, it appears that men commit criminal assaults (that is serious enough to be reported to police) nearly ten times more often than women. Kurz, *infra*, at 90. In the summer of 1999, an extensive U.S. government study found that women assault men at least as often as men hit women. That is a very provocative subject. The study revealed that about 27 percent of women and 34 percent of men reported they had been physically abused by a partner, and about 37 percent of women and 22 percent of men admitted that they had engaged in such violence. When the partners were interviewed, about three-fourths agreed that physical violence took place and agreed on the extent of the abuse, the report says. (The study by University of Wisconsin Psychology Professor Terrie Moffitt for the U.S. Justice Department, covered research done with 1,037 young New Zealand adults, 52 percent male and 48 percent female and covered a 21-year period.) Richard Gelles, of the School of Social Work at the University of Pennsylvania, and co-author of two other government studies on domestic violence, said Moffitt's study was consistent with his own research. Gelles has criticized advocates of protection from domestic violence for "[trying] to ignore the fact women hit men." However, Gelles' findings have been contradicted by another government-funded study, which found in 1997 that women are three times more likely to be assaulted in some way by a male partner and 17 times more likely to be badly beaten over a lifetime than men are by women. All experts agree that men are much more likely to injure women than the other way around. A spokeswoman for the National Clearinghouse for the Defense of Battered Women suggested that the studies show that women tend to take more responsibility for their actions, and that when women strike men they do so in self-defense. *Study, infra*.

Domestic abuse is not just an "issue", but a complex, multifaceted set of public policy issues. A large part of the matter concerns setting public values about what kind of conduct is acceptable within marriage. What are the appropriate sources of such standards? To what extent should the instruments of the law and the institutions of the legal system be devoted to shaping and manipulating those standards? What are the best legal methods to reinforce those values? In a multi-cultural society should the law attempt to accommodate different standards reflecting different cultural and ethnic values? *See* Maugham, *infra*. There are definition issues, reporting issues, family (and individual) autonomy issues (including whether the victim of long-term abuse is really "free to choose" whether to report/prosecute/leave), state intervention issues, allocation of scarce resources issues, police, prosecutorial and judicial discretion issues, evidence issues, issues of due process of law, issues of proportionality in remedies, and a host of other issues.

A recent National Violence Against Women survey reports that the annual rate of physical assault reported among married and unmarried couples in the United States is 1.3% reported by women and 0.9% by men, with a lifetime rate of about 22.1 percent reported by women and 7.4% reported by men. Tjaden & Thoennes, *infra*, at 26. Thus, over three-fourths of women in all relationships are never victims of assault from their partners, and since violence in cohabitation is higher than in marriages, it is safe to state that an even higher percentages of wives never experience spousal violence. Rates of violence appear to be falling; according to the National Crime Victimization Survey, reported by the Department of Justice, the rate of violent crimes fell by 15% in just one year, 1999-2000. U.S. Department of Justice, *infra*. Does this data hold any significance for public policy regarding domestic violence?

Over 835,000 men are victims of violence by an intimate each year (and 1.3 million women). Tjaden & Thoennes, *infra*, at 6. Yet most government programs, studies, and laws (and, of course, state university classes) focus primarily on the problems of domestic violence against women, largely ignoring violence by women. Hoff, *infra*. Is that sound policy? Does that violate equal protection? Why/why not?

c. Domestic Violence in Nonmarital Cohabitation

The risks and rates of domestic violence among nonmarital cohabitants are much greater than among married couples. As one experienced commentator noted:

> Having treated more than 3,000 child abusers and domestic violence offenders, we at [X, a service providing organization] have found that the most potent predictor of both forms of family violence is an insecure individual with a fragile sense of self and need for attachment driven by fear of abandonment or fear of engulfment, in an insecure relationship. Almost by definition, cohabiting relationships are insecure, often driven by fear of abandonment and engulfment that prevent commitment, which is why you see more child abuse and domestic violence in cohabiting relationships. Even in gay and lesbian relationships, abuse is less likely to occur when both parties describe the relationship as a marriage.

Stosny, *infra*. See also § 15.C., *infra*.

2. Statutes, Cases and Doctrines

a. The Definition of Domestic Violence

Two terms, *domestic abuse* and *domestic violence* are often used interchangeably to describe the same problem. Literally, *abuse* is the broader term, as it connotes any kind of mistreatment, misuse, maltreatment, harmful practice, and historically had special reference to insulting, demeaning, and coarse language, whereas *violence* literally means physical force used to injure or cause damage (but secondarily it may connote great force or passion in language). In colloquial usage, *violence* generally refers to physical attacks while *abuse* has a broader connotation including emotional and verbal attacks as well. Because both are forceful terms and carry heavy moral and emotional stigma, they are often used for effect, which compounds the confusion. *Domestic abuse* is now generally defined as any kind of mistreatment including *emotional* as well as *physical* abuse. An American Bar Association Commission defines *domestic violence* as "a pattern of behavior that one intimate partner or spouse exerts over another as a means of control. Domestic violence may include physical violence, coercion, threats, intimidation, isolation, and emotional, sexual or economic abuse." American Bar Association, *infra* at 26. Thus, both terms are often used to mean the same thing. Of course, statutes define abuse in a variety of ways, (not necessarily the same in one state or code section as another) and the exact language of a particular statute must always be carefully consulted.

The reprehensible stigma associated with the terms *abuse* and *neglect* compounds the dilemma in defining the terms. On the one hand, it seems advantageous to define the terms broadly and inclusively to give parties and law enforcement officials maximum flexibility in obtaining desired legal protections and remedies. On the other hand, the inclusion under the same umbrella of minor infractions (swearing) with major assaults (killing, beating) can both over-stigmatize the minor offense (creating enforcement problems) and trivialize the major offense.

What kind of behavior is of primary concern to the law? What other behaviors are of legitimate public concern? What are the social interests to be protected? Should just one term, provision, procedure or remedy be used to deal with so many different behaviors of such different moral repugnance? Why/why not?

Find the statutes in your homestate that provide civil remedies for and criminal responses to domestic violence. Where are they located? How is domestic violence or abuse defined? Describe the procedures.

b. The Response to Domestic Violence

As reports of the incidence of domestic violence mushroomed in the 1980s and 1990s, as public concern about the issue increased, and as the influence of groups determined to do something about the problem grew, policy makers and public officials responded. A number of approaches were implemented, from establishing or increasing support for shelters where women who were victims or who were fearful of domestic abuse could flee for security and protection, to mandatory reporting requirements, to increasing police awareness of and response to (unpopular) domestic violence calls, to mandating arrest in cases of alleged domestic violence, to tough (sometimes mandatory) prosecution policies, to tough (sometimes mandatory) sentencing guidelines, to facilitating requests for civil remedies such as restraining orders, protective orders, and injunctions with low-fee or no-fee filing, prepared fill-in-the-blank forms, ex parte, immediate hearings, and almost guaranteed on-request protective orders. The swing in public policy has been phenomenal – from almost-automatic disregard of most domestic abuse claims (law enforcement brushing them aside, police, social workers, medical workers, prosecutors and judges treating them as trivial, giving them low priority, pro forma processing of such reports or claims, nominal, minimal penalties, if any) to almost-automatic treatment of most domestic abuse claims as very serious matters (mandatory reporting by medical, social worker, and law enforcement personnel, quick police response, mandatory or near-mandatory arrest policies, mandatory or near-mandatory prosecution policies, and the virtual "rubber stamping" of protective and restraining orders by judges fearful of the outcry from activists that would come if they failed to sign them). Swisher, *infra,* at Chapter 6.

c. Mandatory Reporting, Arresting and Prosecution

Now, a second generation is taking a new look at the public response to domestic violence and criticizing some of the tough/mandatory response policies for being over-reactive, for being almost a form of "domestic abuse" themselves. For example, Professor Linda G. Mills tells the story of a California woman, Laura, who, after four years of marriage to Tom, got into a fight with him one night. Tom had never been violent but that night the quarrel escalated into some shoving. When he pushed her, she stumbled into a lamp and suffered a bruise and a severe headache. To be safe, she went to an emergency room for evaluation and treatment, and responded truthfully to the doctor's question about what had happened. He immediately told Laura that he was required under California law to report the domestic violence to the police. Laura was horrified but her objections were irrelevant; the doctor had an absolute legal duty to report. When police arrived at their home, Laura pleaded with them not to arrest Tom, vouching that he was a good man and not violent. The officers told her that Los Angeles has a mandatory arrest policy and they had no choice. Over her protests, Tom was arrested and spent three days in jail. Because he was arrested and missed work they faced the possibility that Tom might lose his job and with it the crucial health benefits their daughter needs. Laura visited the prosecutor and pleaded with her not to prosecute, but she informed Laura that the City Attorney's office had a mandatory prosecution policy; that if Laura didn't agree to testify they would subpoena her, and that her statements to the doctor would be used as evidence against Tom. Mills, *infra*, at 552-553.

At least four states (California, Colorado, Kentucky and Rhode Island) mandate reporting spousal violence injuries to police. However, according to an article in the Journal of the American Medical Association, nearly half (44%) of abused women who visit emergency rooms are opposed to laws requiring doctors to report domestic-violence injuries to police, without the victim's consent. Among the concerns of these women are their loss of control to choose what is best for their circumstances, and the possibility that sudden police intervention could exacerbate the hostility. Advocates of mandatory reporting believe that giving the woman a choice leaves her vulnerable to coercion by the abuser and burdens her with another difficult decision. Some studies have reported that mandatory arrest and/or prosecution is the most effective way to prevent further domestic violence. Attorney General's Task Force, *infra* at 22-24. However, other studies have questioned that finding and suggest that recidivism in abuse cases is effected more by the abuser's perception that he or she was treated fairly by the legal system. Epstein, *infra*. In 1997, the American Medical Association recommended a moratorium on mandatory reporting. *See* Guido, *infra;* Rodriguez, *infra*.

To what extent should the state intervene in families when there is domestic abuse? Does the kind or extent of the abuse matter? Does the nature of the intervention (whether criminal or civil, whether sought by the parties or sought by third parties) matter? If so, how? Who should determine whether, when and how the state intervenes to protect against, recover recompense for, or punish domestic abuse?

d. *People v. Liberta*

The People of the State of New York v. Mario Liberta
64 N.Y.2d 152, 474 N.E.2d 567, 485 N.Y.S.2d 207 (1984)

WACHTLER, Judge.

The defendant, while living apart from his wife pursuant to a Family Court order, forcibly raped and sodomized her in the presence of their 2 1/2 year old son. Under the New York Penal Law a married man ordinarily cannot be prosecuted for raping or sodomizing his wife. The defendant, however, though married at the time of the incident, is treated as an unmarried man under the Penal Law because of the Family Court order. On this appeal, he contends that because of the exemption for married men, the statutes for rape in the first degree (Penal Law, § 130.35) and sodomy in the first degree (Penal Law, § 130.50) violate the equal protection clause of the Federal Constitution (U.S., Const., 14th Amdt.). The defendant also contends that the rape statute violates equal protection because only men, and not women, can be prosecuted under it.

I

Defendant Mario Liberta and Denise Liberta were married in 1978. Shortly after the birth of their son, in October of that year, Mario began to beat Denise. In early 1980 Denise brought a proceeding in the Family Court in Erie County seeking protection from the defendant. On April 30, 1980 a temporary order of protection was issued to her by the Family Court. Under this order, the defendant was to move out and remain away from the family home, and stay away from Denise. The order provided that the defendant could visit with his son once each weekend.

On the weekend of March 21, 1981, Mario, who was then living in a motel, did not visit his son. On Tuesday, March 24, 1981 he called Denise to ask if he could visit his son on that day. Denise would not allow the defendant to come to her house, but she did agree to allow him to pick up their son and her and take them both back to his motel after being assured that a friend of his would be with them at all times. The defendant and his friend picked up Denise and their son and the four of them drove to defendant's motel.

When they arrived at the motel the friend left. As soon as only Mario, Denise, and their son were alone in the motel room, Mario attacked Denise, threatened to kill her, and forced her to perform fellatio on him and to engage in sexual intercourse with him. The son was in the room during the entire episode, and the defendant forced Denise to tell their son to watch what the defendant was doing to her.

The defendant allowed Denise and their son to leave shortly after the incident. Denise, after going to her parents' home, went to a hospital to be treated for scratches on her neck and bruises on her head and back, all inflicted by her husband. She also went to the police station, and on the next day she swore out a felony complaint against the defendant. On July 15, 1981 the defendant was indicted for rape in the first degree and sodomy in the first degree.

II

Section 130.35 of the Penal Law provides in relevant part that "A male is guilty of rape in the first degree when he engages in sexual intercourse with a female * * * by forcible compulsion". "Female", for purposes of the rape statute, is defined as "any female person who is not married to the actor" * . Section 130.50 of the Penal Law provides in relevant part that "a person is guilty of sodomy in the first degree when he engages in deviate sexual intercourse with another person * * * by forcible compulsion". "Deviate sexual intercourse" is defined as "sexual conduct between persons not married to each other consisting of contact between the penis and the anus, the mouth and penis, or the mouth and the vulva" (Penal Law, § 130.00, subd. 2). Thus, due to the "not married" language in the definitions of "female" and "deviate sexual intercourse", there is a "marital exemption" for both forcible rape and forcible sodomy. The marital exemption itself, however, has certain exceptions. For purposes of the rape and sodomy statutes, a husband and wife are considered to be "not married" if at the time of the sexual assault they "are living apart * * * pursuant to a valid and effective: (i) order issued by a court of competent jurisdiction which by its terms or in its effect requires such living apart, or (ii) decree or judgment of separation, or (iii) written agreement of separation" (Penal Law, § 130.00, subd. 4).

Defendant moved to dismiss the indictment, asserting that because he and Denise were still married at the time of the incident he came within the "marital exemption" to both rape and sodomy.

The People opposed the motion, contending that the temporary order of protection required Mario and Denise to live apart, and they in fact were living apart, and thus were "not married" for purposes of the statutes. The trial court granted the defendant's motion and dismissed the indictment, concluding that the temporary order of protection did not require Mario and Denise to live apart from each other, but instead required only that he remain away from her, and that therefore the "marital exemption" applied.

On appeal by the People, the Appellate Division, *, reversed the trial court, reinstated the indictment, and remanded the case for trial. The Appellate Division held that a Family Court order of protection is within the scope of "[an] order * * * which by its terms or in its effect requires such living apart" even though it is directed only at a husband, and thus found that Mario and Denise were "not married" for purposes of the statute at the time of the incident.

The defendant was then convicted of rape in the first degree and sodomy in the first degree and the conviction was affirmed by the Appellate Division, *. Defendant asserts on this appeal that the temporary order of protection is not the type of order which enables a court to treat him and Denise as "not married" and that thus he is within the marital exemption. Defendant next asserts, assuming that because of the Family Court order he is treated just as any unmarried male would be, that he cannot be convicted of either rape in the first degree or sodomy in the first degree because both statutes are unconstitutional. Specifically, he contends that both statutes violate equal protection because they burden some, but not all males (all but those within the "marital exemption"), and that the rape statute also violates equal protection for burdening only men, and not women. The lower courts rejected the defendant's constitutional arguments, finding that neither statute violated the equal protection clause in the Fourteenth Amendment. Although we affirm the conviction of the defendant, we do not agree with the constitutional analysis of the lower courts and instead conclude that the marital and gender exemptions must be read out of the statutes prohibiting forcible rape and sodomy.

III

We first address the defendant's argument that, despite the order of protection, he was within the "marital exemption" to rape and sodomy and thus could not be prosecuted for either crime. Until 1978, the marital exemption applied as long as the marriage still legally existed. In 1978, the Legislature expanded the definition of "not married" to include those cases where the husband and wife were living apart pursuant to either a court order "which by its terms or in its effect requires such living apart" or a decree, judgment, or written agreement of separation *. We agree with the Appellate Division that the order of protection in the present case falls squarely within the first of these situations.

The legislative memorandum submitted with the original version of the 1978 amendment, after referring to the situations brought within the scope of "not married", stated: "In each of the alternatives set forth in this bill, there must be documentary evidence of a settled and mutual intention to dissolve the marital relationship, or a court determination that the spouses should, for the well-being of one or both, live apart" (N.Y.Legis.Ann., 1978, pp. 403-404). Although the language of the amendment was subsequently changed to the form in which it was enacted, this legislative memorandum was submitted with the final version of the bill. In addition to this clear statement of legislative intent, the plain language of the statute indicates that an order of protection is within the meaning of an order "which by its terms or in its effect requires [the spouses to live] apart". This language would be virtually meaningless if it did not encompass an order of protection, as the statute separately provides for the other obvious situation where a court order would require spouses to live apart, i.e., where there is a decree or judgment of separation

Accordingly, the defendant was properly found to have been statutorily "not married" to Denise at the time of the rape.

IV

The defendant's constitutional challenges to the rape and sodomy statutes are premised on his being considered "not married" to Denise and are the same challenges as could be made by any unmarried male convicted under these statutes. The defendant's claim is that both statutes violate equal protection because they are underinclusive classifications which burden him, but not others similarly situated (*see* Tribe, American Constitutional Law, p. 997). A litigant has standing to raise this claim even though he does not contend that under no circumstances could the burden of the statute be imposed upon him (*see Michael M. v. Sonoma County Superior Ct.*, 450 U.S. 464, 472, n. 8, 473. This rule of standing applies as well to a defendant in a criminal prosecution who, while conceding that it is within the power of a State to make criminal the behavior covered by a statute, asserts that the statute he is prosecuted under violates equal protection because it burdens him but not others. ** Thus, defendant's constitutional claims are properly before this court.

A. THE MARITAL EXEMPTION

As noted above, under the Penal Law a married man ordinarily cannot be convicted of forcibly raping or sodomizing his wife. This is the so-called marital exemption for rape. * Although a marital exemption was not explicit in earlier rape statutes (*), an 1852 treatise stated that a man could not be guilty of raping his wife (Barbour, Criminal Law of State of New York [2d ed.], p. 69). The assumption, even before the marital exemption was codified, that a man could not be guilty of raping his wife, is traceable to a statement made by the 17th century English jurist Lord Hale, who wrote: "[T]he husband cannot be guilty of a rape committed by himself upon his lawful wife, for by their mutual matrimonial consent and contract the wife hath given up herself in this kind unto her husband, which she cannot retract" (1 Hale, History of Pleas of the Crown, p. 629). Although Hale cited no authority for his statement it was relied on by State Legislatures which enacted rape statutes with a marital exemption and by courts which established a common-law exemption for husbands.

The first American case to recognize the marital exemption was decided in 1857 by the Supreme Judicial Court of Massachusetts, which stated in dictum that it would always be a defense to rape to show marriage to the victim (*Commonwealth v. Fogerty*, 74 Mass. 489). Decisions to the same effect by other courts followed, usually with no rationale or authority cited other than Hale's implied consent view. In New York, a 1922 decision noted the marital exemption in the Penal Law and stated that it existed "on account of the matrimonial consent which [the wife] has given, and which she cannot retract" (*People v. Meli*, 193 N.Y.S.365, 366 [Sup.Ct.]).

Presently, over 40 States still retain some form of marital exemption for rape. *[FN6. Statutes in nine States provide a complete exemption to rape as long as there is a valid marriage (Alabama, Arkansas, Kansas, Montana, South Dakota, Texas, Vermont, Washington, West Virginia). In 26 other States, statutes provide for a marital exemption but with certain exceptions, most typically where the spouses are living apart pursuant to either a court order or a separation agreement (Alaska, Arizona, Colorado, Idaho, Indiana, Kentucky, Louisiana, Maine, Maryland, Michigan, Minnesota, Missouri, Nevada, New Mexico, New York, North Carolina, North Dakota, Ohio, Oklahoma, Pennsylvania, Rhode Island, South Carolina, Tennessee, Utah, Wyoming, Wisconsin). In three other States (Georgia, Mississippi, Nebraska) and the District of Columbia the exemption appears to still exist as a common-law doctrine, and it may still have a limited application in Virginia (see Weishaupt v. Commonwealth, 227 Va. 389, 315 S.E.2d 847). Finally, in Connecticut, Delaware, Hawaii, and Iowa, there is a marital exemption for some, but not all degrees of forcible rape (see, generally, for statutory references, Schwartz, Spousal Exemption for Criminal Rape Prosecution, 7 Vt.L.Rev. 33, 38-41 [hereafter cited as "Rape Prosecution"]; Note, Clancy, Equal Protection Considerations of the Spousal Sexual Assault Exclusion, 16 N.Eng.L.Rev. 1, 2-3, n. 4 [hereafter cited as "Equal Protection Considerations"]; "Abolishing the Marital Exemption", supra, at n. 4, at pp. 203-205).]* While the marital exemption is subject to an equal protection challenge, because it classifies unmarried men differently than married men, the equal protection clause does not prohibit a State from making classifications, provided the statute does not arbitrarily burden a particular group of individuals (*Reed v. Reed*, 404 U.S. 71, 75-76). Where a statute draws a distinction based upon marital status, the classification must be reasonable and must be based upon "some ground of difference that rationally explains the different treatment" (*Eisenstadt v. Baird*, 405 U.S. 438, 447, cert. den. 451 U.S. 987.

We find that there is no rational basis for distinguishing between marital rape and nonmarital rape. The various rationales which have been asserted in defense of the exemption are either based upon archaic notions about the consent and property rights incident to marriage or are simply unable to withstand even the slightest scrutiny. We therefore declare the marital exemption for rape in the New York statute to be unconstitutional.

Lord Hale's notion of an irrevocable implied consent by a married woman to sexual intercourse has been cited most frequently in support of the marital exemption ("Equal Protection Considerations", supra, n. 6, 16 N.Eng.L.Rev., at p. 21). Any argument based on a supposed consent, however, is untenable. Rape is not simply a sexual act to which one party does not consent. Rather, it is a degrading, violent act which violates the bodily integrity of the victim and frequently causes severe, long-lasting physical and psychic harm (see Coker v. Georgia, 433 U.S. 584; Note, Rape Reform and a Statutory Consent Defense, 74 J. of Crim.L. & Criminology 1518, 1519, 1527-1528). To ever imply consent to such an act is irrational and absurd. Other than in the context of rape statutes, marriage has never been viewed as giving a husband the right to coerced intercourse on demand (**). Certainly, then, a marriage license should not be viewed as a license for a husband to forcibly rape his wife with impunity. A married woman has the same right to control her own body as does an unmarried woman (**) If a husband feels "aggrieved" by his wife's refusal to engage in sexual intercourse, he should seek relief in the courts governing domestic relations, not in "violent or forceful self-help" (*)

The other traditional justifications for the marital exemption were the common-law doctrines that a woman was the property of her husband and that the legal existence of the woman was "incorporated and consolidated into that of the husband" (1 Blackstone's Commentaries [1966 ed.], p. 430; see State v. Smith, supra, at pp. 204-205, 426 A.2d 38; "Marital Rape Exemption", supra, n. 5, 52 N.Y.U.L.Rev., at pp. 309-310). Both these doctrines, of course, have long been rejected in this State. Indeed, "[n]owhere in the common-law world--[or] in any modern society--is a woman regarded as chattel or demeaned by denial of a separate legal identity and the dignity associated with recognition as a whole human being" (Trammel v. United States, 445 U.S. 40, 52).

Because the traditional justifications for the marital exemption no longer have any validity, other arguments have been advanced in its defense. The first of these recent rationales, which is stressed by the People in this case, is that the marital exemption protects against governmental intrusion into marital privacy and promotes reconciliation of the spouses, and thus that elimination of the exemption would be disruptive to marriages. While protecting marital privacy and encouraging reconciliation are legitimate State interests, there is no rational relation between allowing a husband to forcibly rape his wife and these interests. The marital exemption simply does not further marital privacy because this right of privacy protects consensual acts, not violent sexual assaults (*). Just as a husband cannot invoke a right of marital privacy to escape liability for beating his wife, he cannot justifiably rape his wife under the guise of a right to privacy.

Similarly, it is not tenable to argue that elimination of the marital exemption would disrupt marriages because it would discourage reconciliation. Clearly, it is the violent act of rape and not the subsequent attempt of the wife to seek protection through the criminal justice system which "disrupts" a marriage (*) Moreover, if the marriage has already reached the point where intercourse is accomplished by violent assault it is doubtful that there is anything left to reconcile (**). This, of course, is particularly true if the wife is willing to bring criminal charges against her husband which could result in a lengthy jail sentence.

Another rationale sometimes advanced in support of the marital exemption is that marital rape would be a difficult crime to prove. A related argument is that allowing such prosecutions could lead to fabricated complaints by "vindictive" wives. The difficulty of proof argument is based on the problem of showing lack of consent. Proving lack of consent, however, is often the most difficult part of any rape prosecution, particularly where the rapist and the victim had a prior relationship (see "Spousal Exemption to Rape", supra, at n. 4, 65 Marq.L.Rev., at p. 125; "Marital Rape Exemption", supra, n. 5,

52 N.Y.U.L.Rev., at p. 314). Similarly, the possibility that married women will fabricate complaints would seem to be no greater than the possibility of unmarried women doing so (*) The criminal justice system, with all of its built-in safeguards, is presumed to be capable of handling any false complaints. Indeed, if the possibility of fabricated complaints were a basis for not criminalizing behavior which would otherwise be sanctioned, virtually all crimes other than homicides would go unpunished.

The final argument in defense of the marital exemption is that marital rape is not as serious an offense as other rape and is thus adequately dealt with by the possibility of prosecution under criminal statutes, such as assault statutes, which provide for less severe punishment. The fact that rape statutes exist, however, is a recognition that the harm caused by a forcible rape is different, and more severe, than the harm caused by an ordinary assault (*). "Short of homicide,[rape] is the 'ultimate violation of self' " (*Coker v. Georgia*, 433 U.S. 584, 597). Under the Penal Law, assault is generally a misdemeanor unless either the victim suffers "serious physical injury" or a deadly weapon or dangerous instrument is used (Penal Law, §§ 120.00, 120.05, 120.10). Thus, if the defendant had been living with Denise at the time he forcibly raped and sodomized her he probably could not have been charged with a felony, let alone a felony with punishment equal to that for rape in the first degree.

Moreover, there is no evidence to support the argument that marital rape has less severe consequences than other rape. On the contrary, numerous studies have shown that marital rape is frequently quite violent and generally has *more* severe, traumatic effects on the victim than other rape (*).

Among the recent decisions in this country addressing the marital exemption, only one court has concluded that there is a rational basis for it (see *People v. Brown*, 632 P.2d 1025 [Col.]). *** Justice Holmes wrote: "It is revolting to have no better reason for a rule of law than that so it was laid down in the time of Henry IV. It is still more revolting if the grounds upon which it was laid down have vanished long since, and the rule simply persists from blind imitation of the past" (Holmes, The Path of the Law, 10 Harv.L.Rev. 457, 469). This statement is an apt characterization of the marital exemption; it lacks a rational basis, and therefore violates the equal protection clauses of both the Federal and State Constitutions (U.S. Const., 14th Amdt., § 1; N.Y. Const., art. I, § 11).

B. THE EXEMPTION FOR FEMALES

Under the Penal Law only males can be convicted of rape in the first degree. Insofar as the rape statute applies to acts of "sexual intercourse", which, as defined in the Penal Law (*) can only occur between a male and a female, it is true that a female cannot physically rape a female and that therefore there is no denial of equal protection when punishing only males for forcibly engaging in sexual intercourse with females. The equal protection issue, however, stems from the fact that the statute applies to males who forcibly rape females but does not apply to females who forcibly rape males.

Rape statutes historically applied only to conduct by males against females, largely because the purpose behind the proscriptions was to protect the chastity of women and thus their property value to their fathers or husbands (*). ***

A statute which treats males and females differently violates equal protection unless the classification is substantially related to the achievement of an important governmental objective. *** The People bear the burden of showing both the existence of an important objective and the substantial relationship between the discrimination in the statute and that objective (*) This burden is not met in the present case, and therefore the gender exemption also renders the statute unconstitutional.

The first argument advanced by the People in support of the exemption for females is that because only females can become pregnant the State may constitutionally differentiate between forcible rapes of females and forcible rapes of males. This court and the United States Supreme Court have upheld statutes which subject males to criminal liability for engaging in sexual intercourse with underage females without the converse being true (**). The rationale behind these decisions was that the primary purpose of such "statutory rape" laws is to protect against the harm caused by teenage pregnancies, there being no need to provide the same protection to young males (*see Michael M. v. Sonoma County Superior Ct.*, 450 U.S. at pp. 470-473, *People v. Whidden*, 415 N.E.2d 927, *supra*).

There is no evidence, however, that preventing pregnancies is a primary purpose of the statute prohibiting forcible rape, nor does such a purpose seem likely. ***

The People also claim that the discrimination is justified because a female rape victim "faces the probability of medical, sociological, and psychological problems unique to her gender". This same argument, when advanced in support of the discrimination in the statutory rape laws, was rejected by this court in *People v. Whidden* ***
***

As to the "infrequency" argument, while forcible sexual assaults by females upon males are undoubtedly less common than those by males upon females this numerical disparity cannot by itself make the gender discrimination constitutional. ***

*** The fact that the act of a female forcibly raping a male may be a difficult or rare occurrence does not mean that the gender exemption satisfies the constitutional test. A gender-neutral law would indisputably better serve, even if only marginally, the objective of deterring and punishing forcible sexual assaults. ***

Accordingly, we find that section 130.35 of the Penal Law violates equal protection because it exempts females from criminal liability for forcible rape.

V

[Having found that the statutes for rape in the first degree and sodomy in the first degree unconstitutionally underinclusive, the Court of Appeals concluded that the Legislature would prefer to eliminate the exemptions and thereby preserve the statutes and struck the marital exemption from the statutes, making them gender-neutral.]
***

Accordingly, the order of the Appellate Division should be affirmed.
COOKE, C.J., and JASEN, JONES, MEYER and KAYE, JJ., concur. SIMONS, J., took no part.

e. Notes and Questions

1) *Liberta* and Spousal Rape Notes

In a fascinatingly ironic twist, Judge Wachtler, who wrote the highly-acclaimed *Liberta* opinion, had an adulterous affair with a woman, and after the breakup he stalked her with phone calls, unwanted mail, and threats. Eventually he was convicted of extortion and sentenced to prison. *See* Wachtler, *infra*.

2) No Constitutional Claim Against Non-Responsive Policy

A spouse protected by a restraining order does not have a procedural Due Process claim under the Fourteenth Amendment for loss of a property interest or legal entitlement to protection against police who failed to act quickly upon her report of violation of the order by her ex-husband. *Castle Rock v. Gonzalez*, ___ U.S. ___, 125 S.Ct. 2796 (2005). Ms. Gonzalez based her suit against local police on a Colorado state law that commands that police "shall use every reasonable means to enforce" restraining orders against domestic violence. When her ex-husband had abducted the parties' three daughters in violation of a TRO, Ms. Gonzalez, promptly notified the police. The police investigated, visiting the wife at her home shortly after 7:30 P.M. the day of the abduction, but they advised her to be patient and wait until 10:00 P.M. and then to wait until midnight before they acted, even though she knew at one point where her ex-husband was because he had telephoned her. The police did not act after another phone call she made at ten minutes after midnight, nor after Ms. Gonzalez personally visited the police station forty minutes later. Two and one-half hours later, the ex-husband took the bodies of the three little girls whom he had murdered to the police station, and he was killed by police when he started shooting at them. The Tenth Circuit Court of Appeals (en banc) held that wife had a valid 1983 claim against the City of Castle Rock because the statute had given her a protectable procedural due process interest in the enforcement of the TRO. The U.S. Supreme Court reversed, holding, *inter alia*, that under the Colorado statute, police still had discretion as to how to proceed, especially when the perpetrator was not actually present and his whereabouts were uncertain. The *Gonzalez* decision extended the ruling in *DeShaney v. Winnebago Cnty Dep't Soc. Servs.*, 489 U.S. 189 (1989) rejecting a similar claim based on neglect of child abuse by social workers. While a federal constitutional claim is barred, might state legislators impose civil liability on police for neglect in such circumstances? Should they? Why/why not?

3) Discretion in Responding to Domestic Violence

There are risks if police are reluctant to arrest alleged abusers in domestic violence cases, and if courts are cautious about issuing ex parte protective orders. Likewise, there are risks and costs if police are quick to arrest and courts are quick to issue protective orders. Considering the competing risks, should ex parte protective orders be automatically issued in every case of domestic physical violence, regardless of severity and mitigating circumstances? Should mandatory arrest laws (requiring arrest in every domestic physical violence case) be enacted?

Consider the following: Suppose you are moonlighting as a police officer while finishing law school. One quiet night, just after you have finished reading materials in your family law casebook about domestic violence, at 3:00 a.m., you get a domestic violence call. You and your partner respond immediately. A man came home very late and very drunk, and started speaking abusively to his wife. Her two little children were awakened by the row. Tired, angry, and fed up with his filthy language and drunkenness, she headed to the door with the kids in tow; he stepped toward the door; she thought (he says wrongly) that he was going to try to block her way, so she hit him in the mouth, hard, and his mouth started to bleed. He has had experience with domestic violence before (he was arrested), and he knows how the system works; so he called the police and reported his wife for domestic violence. When you arrive, he is still very drunk, very angry, now bloody, and he demands that you arrest his wife. She is much smaller than he is, but packs quite a wallop. Her two little daughters are clinging to her, frightened. (This hypothetical is based on an actual 1995 case.)

If you have discretion to arrest or not, would you arrest her? If so, what would you do with her little daughters? Would you arrest both husband and wife? If so, what would you do with the children then? What do you think would be in the best interests of the children in this case? Of the adults? Of the family? As a police officer, do you have the authority to accomplish that? As a police officer, what is/should be your role, authority and function in this kind of case? Do the courts have the authority to accomplish what would be in the best interests of the children, adults, or family? What is/should be the role, authority, and function of the courts?

3. Practical and Ethical Considerations

(a) If a lawyer working in a prosecutor's office believes that it would be detrimental to the individuals and family involved and would not accomplish any legitimate public benefit to pursue a domestic violence prosecution, but the office has a "mandatory prosecution" policy and allows no exceptions to the policy, what might/should she do?

(b) If a lawyer in private practice obtains a protective order at the request of a client, and a few days later his client asks him to terminate the order, and dismiss or withdraw the complaint, and the lawyer believes that this would not be in his client's best interests, and suspects that she is under some form of (probably psychological) duress, at least not thinking clearly, what can/should he do?

(c) What should be the lawyer's role if his client advises him or her that she is a victim of "mild" domestic violence? Is reporting always best? Prosecution? A civil protection order? Counseling? Divorce? Patience? Why?

4. Bibliography

American Bar Association, Commission on Domestic Violence , When Will They Ever Learn? Educating to End Domestic Violence: A Law School Report (1997).

Attorney General's Task Force on Family Violence (1984).

1 William Blackstone, Commentaries on the Laws of England * (1765-69).

Deborah Epstein, *Effective Intervention in Domestic Violence Cases: Rethinking the Roles of Prosecutors, Judges, and the Court System*,11 Yale J.L. & Feminism 3 (1999).

Bert H. Hoff, *The Risk of Serious Physical Injury from Assault by a Woman Intimate: A Re-Examination of National Violence Against Women Survey Data on Type of Assault by an Intimate* <http://www.vix.com/menmag/nvawrisk.htm>.

Demi Kurz, *Physical Assaults by Husbands: A Major Social Problem* in Current Controversies on Family Violence 89 (Richard J. Gelles & Donileen R. Loseke, eds. 1993).

Michelle Guido, *Mandatory reports of domestic abuse worry victims*, (San Jose) Mercury News, Aug. 1, 2001 <http://www0.mercurycenter.com/premium/nation/docs/dvstudy0801.htm>.

Amy B. Levin, Comment, *Chile Witnesses of Domestic Violence: How Should Judges Apply the Best Interests of the Child Standard in Custody and Visitation Cases Involving Domestic Violence?*, 47 UCLA L. Rev. 813 UCLA (2000).

W. Somerset Maugham, *The Moon and Sixpence* in Collected Short Stories (1965).

Linda G. Mills, Commentary, *Killing Her Softly: Intimate Abuse and the Violence of State Intervention*, 113 Harv. L. Rev. 550 (1999).

Michael A. Rodriguez, et al; Mandatory Reporting of Domestic Violence to the Police, 286 J.A.M.A. (Aug. 1, 2001) <http://jama.ama-assn.org/issues/v286n5/rfull/jbr10044.html>.

Lori L. Schick, Comment, *Breaking the "Rule of Thumb" and Opening the Curtains--Can the Violence Against Women Act Survive Constitutional Scrutiny?*, 28 U. Tol. L. Rev. 887, 887 (1997).

Steven Stosny, Compassion Workshops - Training Institute #905, quoted by Diane Solee, SmartMarriages Newlsetter, May 30, 2001.

Straus, *Physical Assaults by Women Partners: A Major Social Problem*, in Women, Men & Gender: Ongoing Debates (M.R. Walsh ec., 1997).

Straus and Gelles, *How Violent Are American Families: Estimates from the National Family Violence Resurvey and Other Studies* in Family Abuse and Its Consequences: New Directions in Research 20 (Hotaling, et al. eds. 1988).

Study Spotlights Abuse of Males by Females, USA Today in S.L. Tribune, July 14, 1999 <http://www.sltrib.com/07141999/nation_w/8047.htm> (searched 14 July 99).

Peter N. Swisher, Anthony Miller, and Jana B. Singer, Family Law: Cases, Materials and Problems (1998).

Patricia Tjaden & Nancy Thoennes, Full Report of Prevalence, Incidence and Consequences of Violence

Against Women: Findings from the National Violence Against Women Survey, U.S. Department of Justice, National Institute of Justice & Centers for Disease Control and Prevention Research Report, Nov. 2000. NCJ 183781 (2000)
    <http://www.ncjrs.org/pdffiles1/nij/183781.pdf>

James Martin Truss, Comment, *The Subjection of Women...Still: Unfulfilled Promises of Protection for Women Victims of Domestic Violence*, 26 St. Mary's L.J. 1149, 1157 (1995).

U.S. Department. of Justice, Bureau of Justice Statistics, Criminal Victimization 2000: Changes 1999-2000 with Trends, 1993-2000
    <http://www.ojp.usdoj.gov/bjs/abstract/cv00.htm> (seen 29 May 2002).

Sol Wachtler, After the Madness: A Judge's Own Prison Memoir (1997).

Joseph G. Weis, *Family Violence Research Methodology and Design* in Family Violence 117 (Lloyd Ohlin & Michael Tonry eds. 1989).

Iren Hanson, Frieze & Angela Browne, *Violence in Marriage* in Family Violence 181 (Lloyd Ohlin & Michael Tonry eds. 1989).

B. ECONOMIC CONSEQUENCES OF NONMARITAL COHABITATION

1. Background

The lack of marital status means that nonmarital couples and individuals in other nonmarital relationships are not eligible for the many economic benefits extended exclusively to married individuals. *See* Chapter 17, *supra*. The number, value, and significance in everyday life of those government benefits have increased dramatically in the last thirty years of the twentieth century.

2. Statutes, Cases and Doctrines

a. *Beaty v. Truck Insurance Exchange*
Larry Beaty v. Truck Insurance Exchange
6 Cal.App.4th 1455, 8 Cal.Rptr.2d 593 (1992), *rev. denied* (Aug. 27, 1992)
PUGLIA, Presiding Justice.

The issue presented is whether an insurer violates the Unruh Civil Rights Act (Civ.Code, § 51 et seq.; hereafter referred to as the Unruh Act) when it refuses to offer a couple cohabitating in a homosexual relationship the same insurance policy and at the same premium it regularly offers to married couples. Plaintiffs Larry Beaty and Boyce Hinman applied to defendant Truck Insurance Exchange for a joint umbrella liability insurance policy. Defendant denied the application because joint umbrella policies are issued only to married couples. Defendant offered instead to issue each plaintiff individual umbrella coverage. Plaintiffs refused because they wanted a joint policy at the same premium as would be charged a married couple.

Plaintiffs brought suit claiming, inter alia, defendant's refusal to issue them a joint umbrella policy under the same terms and conditions as defendant offers to married couples constitutes unlawful discrimination in violation of the Unruh Act. The trial court sustained defendant's demurrer without leave to amend and entered judgment of dismissal.

On appeal, plaintiffs reiterate their claim defendant violated the Unruh Act by unlawfully discriminating against them on the basis of (1) sexual orientation and (2) marital status. We shall reject plaintiffs' contentions and affirm the judgment.

For purposes of this appeal, we accept as true all facts properly alleged in the complaint. * Plaintiffs are a homosexual couple who have lived together and shared the common necessities of life for approximately 18 years. For the past eight years plaintiffs have owned a home as joint tenants. They maintain a joint credit card account and a joint bank account, and jointly own two cars and the furnishings in their home. Plaintiffs each have wills and life insurance policies naming the other as primary beneficiary. They have also been issued joint homeowners and automobile insurance policies by defendant.

In February 1986, plaintiffs applied to defendant for a joint umbrella liability insurance policy in the amount of one million dollars. [FN1 "[Umbrella liability policies] are policies of insurance sold at comparatively modest cost to pick up where primary coverages end, in order to provide an extended protection up to one million, five million, ten million, or more. ***] *** Defendant refused to issue plaintiffs a joint umbrella policy for a single premium because such policies are issued only to married couples. Instead, defendant offered plaintiffs separate umbrella policies, each with its own premium. Plaintiffs refused the offer.

In July 1988, plaintiffs requested a ruling from the California Department of Insurance (Department) whether defendant's refusal to issue them a joint umbrella policy violated sections 679.71 and 1852 of the Insurance Code. In March 1989, the Department informed plaintiffs no action would be taken on their request and plaintiffs were free to "to pursue any legal remedies available" to them.

In September 1989, plaintiffs filed their first amended complaint (complaint) in superior court seeking damages and injunctive and declaratory relief. Plaintiffs asserted the refusal to issue them a joint umbrella policy violated (1) section 51 et seq. of the Civil Code (the Unruh Act); (2) section 679.71 of the Insurance Code, which bars an insurer from discrimination in the issuance of policies; and (3) section 1861.05 of the Insurance Code, which bars discrimination in the setting of rates for insurance policies.
***

II

At the outset, we note this case bears a remarkable similarity to *Hinman v. Department of Personnel Admin.*, (1985) 167 Cal.App.3d 516, 213 Cal.Rptr. 410 (hereafter cited as *Hinman*). This similarity is hardly coincidental, as the plaintiffs in Hinman--Boyce Hinman and Larry Beaty--are the plaintiffs in the instant action.

At issue in Hinman was whether the denial to a cohabitant in a homosexual relationship with a state employee of dental insurance coverage under that employee's group policy unlawfully discriminated against such employee in violation of the equal protection clause of the state Constitution. Hinman, a state employee, applied for dental coverage for himself and for Beaty under the prepaid group plan offered through Hinman's employment. When coverage for Beaty was denied, Hinman and Beaty brought suit against the Department of Personnel Administration. They charged the refusal to provide coverage to Beaty constituted discrimination on the basis of sexual orientation and marital status.

We rejected these claims. * No evidence was presented showing the denial of coverage to Beaty was on the basis of his or Hinman's sexual orientation. Indeed, the record in that case revealed all unmarried employees received identical treatment. The distinction was simply "on the basis of married and unmarried employees ***" *

With regard to the claim the denial of coverage was based on marital status in violation of the equal protection clause, we noted statutory distinctions based upon marital status need only be rationally related to a legitimate state purpose. * Given the state's legitimate interest in promoting marriage, and noting that interest is furthered by conferring statutory rights upon married persons which are not afforded unmarried partners, we had no difficulty in upholding the decision of the Department of Personnel Administration denying benefits to Beaty. *
***

[The appellate court rejected appellants' claim of that the denial of the umbrella policy was discrimination on the basis of sexual orientation, forbidden by the Unrah Act, because "plaintiffs' complaint alleges that all unmarried individuals are treated the same with regard to the issuance of umbrella policies since plaintiffs are not and cannot be married. To the extent plaintiffs were treated differently than a 'married couple,' it is because they are not married and not because they are homosexuals."

[The court of appeals also rejected the appellants' claim that discrimination on the basis of marital status violates the Unruh Act because "the Unruh Act makes no mention of discrimination on the basis of 'marital status,' and no court had construed the Act to ban marital status discrimination.] Moreover,

[W]e decline plaintiffs' invitation to expand the Unruh Act to include "marital status" as an additional category of prohibited discrimination. There is a strong policy in this state in favor of marriage *, and in the context here presented that policy would not be furthered (and in the case of an unmarried heterosexual couple, would actually be thwarted) by including marital status among the prohibited categories. It is for the Legislature, not the courts, to determine whether nonmarital relationships such as that involved in this case "deserve the statutory protection afforded the sanctity of the marriage union." *

Moreover, the term "marital status" is hardly foreign to the Legislature. There are scores of statutes in which the Legislature has included "marital status" in anti-discrimination legislation. * Clearly the Legislature knows how to designate marital status as a prohibited category of discrimination when inclined to do so. Because it has not done so in the Unruh Act, we refuse to do so on our own accord.

    ***

Moreover, the Unruh Act prohibits "arbitrary" discrimination. * Thus, a court must consider whether the defendant possesses a legitimate business interest which justifies different treatment: " 'A business * establishment may, of course, promulgate reasonable deportment regulations that are rationally related to the services performed and the facilities provided.' " *

On its face there is nothing arbitrary about defendant's issuance of joint umbrella policies only to married persons. Given the legal unity of interest and the shared responsibilities attendant upon a marriage, an insurer could reasonably conclude there is no significant risk in covering both an insured and his or her spouse with a joint policy for a single premium. With regard to unmarried couples of whatever sexual orientation, an insurer could conclude the relationship lacks the assurance of permanence necessary to assess with confidence the risks insured against in a joint umbrella policy.

Equally important, the shared responsibilities and the legal unity of interest in a marital relationship--a status not conferred on unmarried couples whatever their sexual orientation--provide a fair and reasonable means of determining eligibility for services or benefits. *

In Hinman, the state employer extended dental insurance benefits to the employee's "family members," which included only the employee's spouse and, in some instances, unmarried children up to age 23. In upholding this scheme against an equal protection attack, we held "the use of the definition of 'family member' ... is a reasonable means of administering the dental benefit program.... '[R]ecognizing and favoring those with established marital and familial ties not only furthers the state's interest in promoting such relationships but assures a more readily verifiable method of proof.... [N]umerous problems of standards and difficulties of proof would arise if we imposed upon an administrative agency the function of deciding which relationships merited treatment equivalent to the treatment afforded those with formal marriages. The inevitable questions would include issues such as the factors deemed relevant, [i.e.] the length of the relationship.... The potential for administrative intrusions into rights of privacy and association would be severe if agencies bore the burden of ferreting out the "true depth" and intimacy of a relationship in order to determine whether the existence and nature of the relationship was the equivalent of marriage. [Citation.]'

"The same difficulties would attend a dental benefits scheme allowing enrollment of homosexual partners. The responsible agencies would have to establish standards which would reach the very foundations of the privacy rights of both homosexual partners in order to properly determine whether the relationship meets some arbitrary standard equating with marriage, and still exclude other unmarried nonspouses, such as roommates, acquaintances or companions.... The great potential for different opinions by the employer, insurers and unions as to who is an eligible homosexual partner could expose all parties to allegations of discriminatory treatment and the making public of any administrative examination of the sexual relationships involved." *

As in *Hinman*, the fact the parties are married provides a reasonable and relevant means whereby an insurer can predict the risk involved in offering umbrella coverage. In order to assess the risk with regard to unmarried individuals, the insurer would necessarily be required to undertake a "massive intrusion" * into the private lives of applicants--e.g., inquire into their sexual fidelity and emotional and economic ties. * We see no reason why an insurer, any more than an administrative agency, should be forced to engage in such inquiry, which could only lead to inconsistent results and predictably to allegations of discriminatory treatment by the insurer. *

Finally, *Harris* holds that before extending the categories set forth in the Unruh Act, the court must consider the consequences of allowing the type of claim sought by the plaintiffs: "When uncertainty arises in a question of statutory interpretation, consideration must be given to the consequences that will flow from a particular interpretation." (52 Cal.3d at p. 1165, 278 Cal.Rptr. 614, 805 P.2d 873.) What plaintiffs seek to achieve by this litigation is that both defendant and this court treat them as if they were in fact married. The result would be that all de facto couples would be treated as a married unit.

Any such holding would be contrary to the strong policy in this state favoring marriage (*See Marvin v. Marvin* (1976) * and would ignore the fact de facto couples are not generally entitled to the benefits afforded to married couples. Indeed, married couples receive special consideration in a number of areas not available to unmarried individuals, including the right to bring a wrongful death action if a third party kills the other spouse (Code Civ.Proc. 377; cf. *Nieto v. City of Los Angeles* (1982) 138 Cal.App.3d 464, 470-471, 188 Cal.Rptr. 31 [holding no unlawful discrimination in refusing to extend this right to unmarried cohabitants]), the right to sue for loss of consortium and negligent infliction of emotional distress (cf. *Elden v. Sheldon, supra*, 46 Cal.3d at pp. 274-275, 277-278, 250 Cal.Rptr. 254, 758 P.2d 582 [denying this right to unmarried cohabitants]), the marital communications privilege (cf. *People v. Delph, supra*, 94 Cal.App.3d at pp. 415-416, 156 Cal.Rptr. 422 [refusing to extend this privilege to non-marital partners]), and community property laws, including the right to divide community property and to seek spousal support on the termination of marriage (Civ.Code, §§ 4800, 4801; cf. *Marvin v. Marvin, supra*, 18 Cal.3d at p. 684, fn. 24, 134 Cal.Rptr. 815, 557 P.2d 106 [refusing to extend to unmarried cohabitants the rights the Family Law Act gives to valid or putative spouses]; *see also Elden v. Sheldon, supra*, 46 Cal.3d at p. 275, 250 Cal.Rptr. 254.)

Our refusal to grant plaintiffs the relief they seek reaffirms "our recognition of a strong public policy favoring marriage. [Citation.] No similar policy favors the maintenance of nonmarital relationships.... In the absence of legislation which grants to members of a nonmarital relationship the same benefits as those granted to spouses, no basis exists in this context for extending to nonmarital relations the preferential status afforded to marital relations." *

In light of the foregoing considerations, we must decline to extend the protection of the Unruh Act to plaintiffs even as we would to an unmarried, cohabitating heterosexual couple.

In the final analysis, plaintiffs' "real quarrel is with the California Legislature if they wish to legitimize the status of a homosexual partner. Plaintiffs may achieve the reform they seek here only by attacking Civil Code section 4100, which defines marriage to be a civil contract 'between a man and a woman.' We cannot change that law here." (Hinman, *.)

The judgment is affirmed.

b. Notes and Questions

1) None, Some or All?

Historically, eligibility for benefits extended by law to married couples was an all-or-nothing proposition. If you were married you were eligible for marital benefits, and if you were not married you were not eligible. Today, there are growing calls to revise that all-or-nothing system. At least three developments have contributed to the criticism of those traditional all-or-nothing marital benefit rules.

First, the significant "socialization" of economic life in America has dramatically increased the number of government benefits available to eligible individuals. A century ago, in a largely private economy, before significant federal (and state) income tax, welfare programs, social security, employee benefit and pension laws mandating protections for spouses, etc., the fact that the government did not recognize a couple's relationship as a marriage would have comparatively minimal economic consequences (though in the life of any particular individual, it could be very significant). Today, with so many economic dimensions of our lives controlled, regulated, and subject to government rules, the fact that the government does not recognize a couple's relationship as a marriage has potentially greater economic significance.

Second, the kinds and numbers of private as well as public benefits that now use "marriage" as an eligibility requirement seem to have expanded. When the marital benefits provided by government were few, they were well-considered and closely linked to marriage, reflecting, supporting and reinforcing essential incidents, characteristics and purposes of the marital relationship. Now, however, with so many benefits using "marriage" as a qualification or eligibility condition, it may be asked whether marital status has just become the bureaucrat's tool of conveniences, a simple and politically safe classification that may be selected as a requirement for eligibility even though the benefit offered is not closely or significantly related to the nature or purposes of marriage. Thus, some benefits that use marriage as an eligibility requirement might not be true "marital benefits." Critics argue that people ought to be able to get basic welfare benefits (subsistence food, clothing, shelter and medical assistance, for example) regardless of the morality of their lifestyles.

Third, as various forms of nonmarital relationship have increased in number and in social acceptance, persons in or supporting those in nonmarital relationships have begun to lobby for those benefits. For reasons ranging from a desire for the social validation that equal (or partial) economic treatment with married couples will entail to purely economic motives, they ask why they should not enjoy all of the same benefits that are enjoyed by married couples. If they cannot have the status of marriage, why not at least the benefits?

Reactions to these criticisms and reform calls have varied among jurisdictions. The two simplest responses have been to ignore the complaints and continue the all-or-nothing system, on one hand, and to add to the eligibility list for all of those important benefits the term describing such other relationships. The latter approach is recommended by the American Law Institute, Chapter 6 on Domestic Partners, *infra*. That "one-click" response has the advantage of being quick, simple, and all-encompassing. But it also has the disadvantage that it may repeat the mistake that is the subject of the second criticism noted above - of defining eligibility for benefits on the basis of bureaucratic convenience rather than on the basis of consideration of the purpose of providing the public benefits and the nature and qualities of the relationships that are chosen to be eligible for them.

Another response is to extend to some nonmarital relationships selected benefits. That approach can be coherent, consistent more carefully tailored in the public interest to reflect the policy behind the particular benefit and nature of the different relationships. The disadvantages are (1) that it takes a lot of effort (to review and evaluate each and every benefit and each kind of potential relationship) and (2) usually results in the throwing together of a "token" list of some benefits selected because they will satisfy the demands of one group without provoking serious opposition from another group. In an era of shaky marriages, what (if any) effect would extension to selected alternative relationships of specific valuable benefits previously enjoyed only by married couples likely have upon the institution of marriage? Why?

2) Freedom from Economic Obligations

One reason why some couples (or individuals) who could marry choose to live in nonmarital relationships is to avoid the economic obligations of marriage. There are some economic advantages to not being married. Unmarried persons do not have a legal obligation arising from marriage to support their partners, and their nonmarital partner has no noncontractual legal interest in their separate property. They do not incur the risk of the marriage penalty in income taxation. Should the law allow people who live together to do that? Even if during the relationship it results in a lack of fair support by the richer of the poorer cohabitant, and a disproportionate division of assets acquired directly as a result of mutual contributions but legally belonging to only one of the partners? Even if later, when the relationship fails, it leaves one party who contributed to the success of the nonlegal economic "unit" without any legal basis for claiming a share of the gain or profit?

3. Practical and Ethical Considerations

Cases in which unmarried couples seek economic benefits of marriage often are brought "after the fact." That is, the couple seeks legal advice after the incident occurs or conditions arise for which they seek the marital benefits, and it is too late to counsel them to avoid the controversy by getting married. But suppose a couple who could marry but wish to cohabit without marriage come to lawyer Leo and ask him to represent them in obtaining future benefits from some public (or private) agency that are offered only to married couples. Suppose Leo believes that it would be in the best interests of this couple to marry. Should he encourage them to marry? If so, how hard should he push? If not, why not?

4. Bibliography

David B. Cruz, *"Just Don't Call It Marriage": The First Amendment and Marriage As An Expressive Resource,* 74 S. Cal. L. Rev. 925 (2001).

C. NON-ECONOMIC CONSEQUENCES OF NONMARITAL COHABITATION

1. Background

a. Non-economic Benefits and Burdens in General

Parties who live together without marriage not only lose the economic benefits of marriage, *see* § 19.B., *supra,* but they also are ineligible for many of the non-economic benefits of marriage. Thus, they cannot claim the privilege against disclosure of marital communications, cannot claim spousal immunity, cannot recover for loss of consortium, may not enjoy certain hospital and post-mortem access rights, may not be able to make medical decisions for each other, etc. Many of these disadvantages may be overcome by private arrangement, contracts, wills, living wills, appointments, nominations, etc., but not all of them.

By the same token, unmarried couples may benefit from the lack of marital status. Anti-nepotism laws may not cover them. Their separate legal identities are unclouded. Anti-heartbalm provisions do not impede them (should they wish to sue each other for those kinds of losses). Also social expectations of support, loyalty, fidelity and mutuality are much lower.

b. Domestic Violence by Unmarried Partners

The widespread popular perception that marriage is a particularly violent institution has been enhanced because of sloppy definitions and fact-gathering. "Domestic violence is perhaps the only area in which social scientists use the term *husband* to mean any or all of the following: the man one is married to, the man one used to be married to, the man one lives with [outside of marriage], the man one is merely having sex with, and/or the man one used to have sex with." Waite at 151. However, the notion that there is a high risk of violence in marriage has been thoroughly discredited by research showing that "outside of hying thee to a nunnery, the safest place for a woman to be is inside marriage." *Id.* at 152. Nonmarital cohabitation has been very extensively examined by social scientists and has been found to entail significantly higher rates and risks of violence than marriage. For example, one study of national survey data found that cohabiting couples are more than three times more likely to report that their arguments have become physical than married couples (13% to 4%). *Id.,* at 155. About the same (3:1) ratio exists in reports of hitting, shoving, and throwing things. *Id.* Another study reported that "[s]evere violence was almost five times as likely in cohabiting relationships [than in marriages]." Busby, *infra* at 361. An extensive report on nonmarital cohabitation by sociologists Drs. Popenoe and Whitehead., agree that the studies convincingly show that among cohabiting couples there are "far higher levels of child abuse than is found in intact families." Popenoe & Whitehead, *infra.* at 8. Women in cohabiting relationships are much more likely than married women to suffer physical and sexual abuse. Some conservative research has shown that "aggression is at least twice as common among cohabitors as it is among married persons." *Id.* at 7. Other studies have documented that rates of domestic violence are higher and the type of violence more severe in nonmarital cohabitation than in marriage. *See* Stets & Straus, *infra.* Similarly,

A 1993 British study by the Family Education Trust, using data on documented cases of child abuse and neglect between 1982 and 1988 found a high degree of correlation between child abuse and the marital status of the parents. *** Specifically, the British study found that -- compared with a stable nuclear family -- the incidence of abuse was 33 times higher when the mother was living with a boyfriend not related to the child. And even when the live-in boyfriend was the biological father of the children, the chances of abuse were still 20 times more likely.

Abbot, *infra*, at 43. Another study notes that cohabiting men are four times more likely than husbands to cheat on their partners, and cohabiting women are eight times more likely than wives to be unfaithful to their partners. The Marriage Movement, *infra*. This data may at least partly explain the reports that "[a]nnual rates of depression among cohabiting couples are more than three times what they are among married couples." Popenoe & Whitehead, *infra*, at 7. It also may be one reason why cohabitation relationships are generally so short-lived. For example, a Canadian study that showed that 10% of couples living together are unmarried; fewer that one-third of all cohabitation relationships survive five years, "premarital cohabitation actually leads to less stable marriages," "cohabiting unions are less stable than marital unions," and "they weaken the institution of marriage by undermining 'its central foundation of permanence'." Wu, *infra,* at 526, 529. Likewise, that may partially explain why cohabitation before marriage leads to a higher rate of divorce. Popenoe & Whitehead, *infra*.

A study of relationship violence among a sample of 283 gays and lesbians revealed "that 47.5% of lesbians and 29.7% of gays have been victimized by a same-sex partner. Further, lesbians reported an overall perpetration [of domestic violence] rate of 38% compared to 21.8% for gay men." Waldner-Halgrud, *Victimization, infra.* at 173. The authors of this study noted that their findings were consistent with earlier studies of domestic violence in lesbian couples that had reported rates of abuse ranging from 30% to 75% depending on definition of violence, time-frame and sampling techniques. *Id.* citing Brand, *infra,* (30% report being abused in lesbian relationships); Bologna, *infra,* (50% of lesbians in relationships abused); Waterman, *infra,* (31% abuse rate); Schlit, *infra,* (38% lesbian partner abuse); Lie *infra,* (52% lesbian abuse), Renzetti, *infra,* (71% report severity and frequency of abuse increases over time); Lockhart, *infra,* (25% of current; 75% any instance). Sexual coercion seems to be a particular problem. One study reported that approximately 31% of lesbians had sex against their will compared to 18% of heterosexual women. Duncan, *infra.* Another study reported that approximately 12% of gay men were forced to have sex compared to 4% of heterosexual men. Baier, *infra.* However, another reported that "none of the 12 coercion items [ranging from plying with alcohol, or use of guilt, to holding down, use of weapons and physical force] revealed gender differences in methods used to coerce partners into unwanted sexual behavior," and also noted that when prior heterosexual experience is eliminated lesbian women do not show greater levels of sexual coercion than gay men. Waldner-Halgrud, *Sexualization, infra.* at 95. Another study found that a greater proportion of lesbians report being victimized by their past female partners than prior male partners. Lie, *infra.* "[W]hat this body of research collectively suggests is that gays and lesbians have higher rates of sexual coercion than what is experienced by their heterosexual counterparts." However, "woman-to-woman violence does not receive the attention that violence in heterosexual relationships does . . . ." Wise, *infra*. Thus, while rates of violence in lesbian and heterosexual relationships are at least comparable, heterosexual relations are commonly perceived as being more dangerous.

Thus, the risk and rate of domestic violence among nonmarital cohabitants (regardless of sexual orientation) are much higher than the risk and rate of domestic violence by married couples. The difference is so substantial that the old term "spouse abuse" should be replaced by the more accurate term of "partner abuse" or "relationship violence," "domestic violence," because "wife beating" usually consists of "nonmarital cohabitant beating."

2. Statutes, Cases and Doctrines

a. Regulation of Domestic Violence by Unmarried Partners

Find the Statutes in your homestate that provide civil remedies for victims of domestic violence. Find the Statutes in your homestate that provide civil remedies for victims of domestic violence.

b. Notes and Questions

1) Questions About Domestic Violence Statutes

Regarding the civil remedies for domestic violence: Who is protected by or subject to orders issued under the act? Is assistance of counsel necessary to get immediate protection? Is there a filing fee? If so, how much is it? How long do ex parte temporary or preliminary orders last? How soon are hearings scheduled? May parties against whom such orders are issued seek and obtain cross-orders? What provision is made for investigation of the facts? For enforcement of the orders?

Regarding the criminal provisions: How do these criminal remedies for domestic violence differ from remedies available for other kinds of violence and assault?

2) Non-Marital Cohabitants and Consortium

Whether unmarried cohabitants can bring an action for loss of consortium is an issue that has arisen in recent years. The courts are split, but the prevailing rule now appears to be that marriage is an essential element to recovery for loss or injury to consortium. For instance, in *Butcher v. Superior Court*, 188 Cal Rptr 503 (Ct. App. 1983), a California appellate court held that a woman could recover for loss of consortium resulting from injuries to her nonmarital cohabitant. The parties had lived together for more than ten years, had two children, and had a stable, marriage-like relationship which was injured just as directly and in the same manner, as if they had been married. However, other California appellate courts have declined to permit recovery of consortium because the relationship injured was not stable and substantial, *Lieding v. Commercial Diving Center*, 191 Cal. Rptr. 559 (Ct. App. 1983), or have insisted that marriage is a necessary element of the consortium cause of action, finding that it would impose an impossible burden on the courts to adopt a "functional equivalent" test. *See e.g. Elden v. Sheldon*, 210 Cal. Rptr. 755 (Ct. App. 1985); *Hendrix v. General Motors Corp.*, 193 Cal. Rptr. 922 (Ct. App. 1983). Most other courts also appear to agree that marriage is a necessary element of a consortium action. *See e.g. Weaver v. G.D. Searle & Co.*, 558 F. Supp. 720 (N.D. Ala. 1983) (dismissing man's action against manufacturer of IUD for loss of consortium due to massive reproductive tract damages sustained by his girlfriend with whom he was sexually active during period in question and whom he married after the injuries were suffered); *Childers v. Shannon*, 444 A.2d 1141 (N.J. Super. 1982) (recovery for loss of consortium denied to couple married after injuries); *Sostock v. Reiss*, 415 N.E.2d 1094 (Ill. 1980) (comparing suit for loss of consortium by engaged person to suit for alienation of affections; no legal right involved); *Sawyer v. Bailey*, 413 A.2d 165 (Maine 1980) (no cause of action for loss of consortium from injuries sustained during engagement period); *Tremblay v. Carter*, 390 So.2d 816 (Fla. 1980) (increased cohabitation does not justify extension of consortium claim to unmarried persons; marriage produces significant legal changes, even if couple previously cohabited). *But see Norman v. General Motors Corp.*, F. Supp. (D. Nev. 1985) (federal district court held that marriage is not required to sustain an action for loss of consortium in Nevada; if plaintiff and the injured nonspouse were "involved in a significant relationship" Nevada courts would not "arbitrarily deny a claim for loss of consortium" to the parties, the federal court predicted); *Bulloch v. United States*, 487 F. Supp. 1078 (D.N.J. 1980) (similar analysis and prediction which turned out to be wrong; *see Childers, supra*).

In January 2001, Diane Whipple was mauled to death by two large, dangerous dogs in the hallway outside the San Francisco apartment where she and her lesbian partner lived, in the presence of one of the dog's keepers, Marjorie Knoeller. In March, 2002, Ms. Knoeller was convicted of murder, and her husband, Robert Noel (both are attorneys), was convicted of involuntary manslaughter. After that sensational mauling incident, the California Legislature passed a law giving same-sex partners the same right to sue for wrongful death as spouses or family members. Whipple's partner filed a lawsuit against Knoller and Noel. Kravitz, *infra*. At least seven states (California, Connecticut, Hawaii, Maine, Massachusetts, New Jersey, and Vermont), as well as the District of Columbia, provide some sort of general protection for same-sex couples who register. Knauer, *infra*, at 1261; Ayoub & Wong, *infra* at 561 n.1. Should wrongful death claims be extended to same-sex partners? Should any different requirements (such as time together, degree of financial interdependency) apply than apply to married couples? Why/why not? Wrongful death statutes generally extend claims to those persons the legislature believes will most likely suffer economically from the untimely death. Most states identify spouses, children, and (sometimes) parents and siblings; a few extend the claim to some or all of those who can take under intestacy laws. Culhane, *infra*, at 175. *See also supra* Chapters 1 and 8.

3. Practical and Ethical Considerations

Traditionally, lawyers rarely got involved with cohabitation until after it ended and one disgruntled ex-partner wanted a share of the property held by the other. Today, however, cohabiting couples increasingly seek legal assistance to create or formalize specific legal incidents of their informal relationships.

4. Bibliography

Faith Abbot, *No Bomb, No Book*, The Human Life Rev., Winter 1998, at 31.

Lena Ayoub & Shina Ming-Wong, *Separated and Unequal*, 32 Wm. Mitchell L. Rev. 559 (2006).

J. L. Baier, M.G. Rosenzweig & E.G. Whipple, *Patterns of sexual behavior, coercioin, and victimization of university students*, 32 J. College Student Development 310 (1991).

M. J. Bologna, C.K. Waterman & L.J. Dawson, *Violence in Gay Male and Lesbian Relationships: Implications for Practitioner and Policy Makers*, presented at Third National Conference for Family Violence Researchers, Durham, NH (July 1987).

P.A. Brand & A.H. Kidd, *Frequency of Physical aggression in heterosexual and female homosexual dyads*, 59 Psychological Reports 1307 (1986).

Dean M. Busby, *Violence in the Family* in Family Research, a 60-Year Review, 1930-1990 at 361 (Steven G. Bahr, ed., 1991).

John G. Culhane, *Even More Wrongful Death: Statutes Divorced from Reality*, 32 Fordham Urban L.J. 171 (2005).

D. Duncan, *Prevalence of sexual assault victimization among heterosexual and gay/lesbian university students*, 66 Psychological Reps. 65 (1990).

Nancy J. Knauer, *A Marriage Skeptic Responds to Pro-Marriage Proposals to Abolish Civil Marriage*, 27 Cardozo L. Rev. 1261 (2006).

David Kravitz, *Dog attack case opens door to new legal rights for gays*, Associated Press Newswires, March 22, 2002.

G.W. Lie, R. Schilit, R.J. Bish, M. Montagne & L. Reyes, *Lesbians in currently aggressively relationships: How frequently do they report aggressive past relationships?* 6 Violence and Victims 121 (1991).

G. Lie & S. Gentlewarrior, *Intimate violence in lesbian relationships: Discussion of survey findings and practice implications*, 15 J. Social Serv. Res. 41 (1991).

L.L. Lockhart, B.A. White, V. Causby, & A. Isaaac, *Letting out the secret: Violence in lesbian relationships*, 9 J. Interpersonal Violence 469.

The Marriage Movement: A Statement of Principles, <www.marriagemovement.org>, (June 29, 2000).

David Popenoe & Barbara Dafoe Whitehead, Should We Live Together? What Young Adults Need to Know about Cohabitation before Marriage, A Comprehensive Review of Recent Research, <http://www.smartmarriages.com/cohabit.html>.

C. Renzetti, *Building a Second Closet: Third Party Responses to Victims of Lesbian Partner Abuse*, 38 Fam. Relations 157 (1989).

C. Renzetti, *Violent Betrayal: Partner Abuse in Lesbian Relationships* (Sage 1992).

R. Schlit, G. Lie & M. Montagne, *Substance Use as a Correlate of Violence in Intimate Lesbian Relationships*, 19 J. Homosexuality 51 (1990).

Ann E. Stets & Marray A. Straus, *The Marriage License as a Hitting License: A Comparison of Assaults in Dating, Cohabiting, and Married Couples*, 4 J. Fam. Viol. 161 (1989).

Linda J. Waite & Maggie Gallagher, The Case for Marriage, Why Married People Are Happier, Healthier, and Better Off Financially (2000).

Lisa K. Waldner-Haugrud & Linda Vaden Gratch, *Sexual Coercion in Gay/Lesbian Relationships: Descriptive and Gender Differences*, 12 Violence and Victims 87 (1997).

Lisa K. Waldner-Haugrud, Linda Vaden Gratch & Brian Magruder, *Victimization and Perpetration Rates of Violence in Gay and Lesbian Relationships: Gender Issues Explored*, 12 Violence & Victims 173 (1997).

C.K. Waterman, L.J. Dawson & M.J. Bologna, *Sexual Coercion in Gay Male and Lesbian Relationships: Predictors and Implications for Support Services*, 26 J. Sex Res. 118 (1989).

Amy J. Wise & Sharon L. Bowman, *Comparison of Beginning Counselors' Responses to Lesbian vs. Heterosexual Partner Abuse*, 12 Violence and Victims 127 (1997).

Zheng Wu & T.R. Balakrishnan, *Dissolution of Premarital Cohabitation in Canada*, 32 Demography 521, 526, 529 (1995).

PART V
ONGOING PARENT-CHILD RELATIONS

CHAPTER 20

Minority Status: Emancipation; Parental Liability and Immunity; Support of Parents and Children; Property Ownership and the UTMA (UGMA)

A. MINORITY AND EMANCIPATION

1. Background

a. The Dilemma of Minority

Because children are born into a state of total incapacity, and only slowly acquire the experience, knowledge and judgment to be accountable for their own acts (which the law calls "competency"), guardians must act for them until they are accountable individually. The "dilemma of minority" results from two factors. One is a biological fact: all persons are born totally dependent and incompetent. They are incapable of providing for themselves or of making responsible decisions for many years. However, over a period of time they gradually become independent and competent, and by the time they have reached legal "majority" (21 years after birth at common law, and 18 years in most states today), *see generally* H. Clark, Law of Domestic Relations 309 (1988), most persons have become adequately independent and rational. But the process of maturation is individualized --some persons have achieved general independence and judgmental maturity while they are young adolescents, while other persons remain dependent and show immature judgment long after they reach legal age. This undeniable "fact of life" has long been recognized by the Supreme Court. "We have recognized three reasons justifying the conclusion that the constitutional rights of children cannot be equated with those of adults: the peculiar vulnerability of children; their inability to make critical decisions in an informed, mature manner; and the importance of the parental role in child rearing." *Belotti v. Baird*, 443 U.S. 622, 634 (1979) (Powell, J., plurality opinion).

The other factor contributing to the dilemma of minority is that our legal system is predicated on individual independence and competence as the moral basis for personal liberty and accountability. The classic explanation of this premise was made by John Stuart Mill in his treatise, *On Liberty*. After describing his general principle of "Liberty" ("That the only purpose for which power can be rightfully exercised over any member of a civilized community, against his will, is to prevent harm to others." John Stuart Mill, On Liberty 9, 10 (1959)), Mill qualified his general principle by excluding minors:

> It is, perhaps, hardly necessary to say that this doctrine is meant to apply only to human beings in the maturity of their faculties. We are not speaking of children, or of young persons below the age which the law may fix as that of manhood or womanhood. Those who are still in a state to require being taken care of by others, must be protected against their own actions as well as against external injury. . . . Liberty, as a principle, has no application to any state of things anterior to the time

when mankind have become capable of being improved by free and equal
discussion.

Id. at 10. *See also* 1 Jeremy Benthan, Theory of Legislation 248 (Boston 1840)
quoted in Michael Wald, *Children's Rights: A Framework for Analysis,* 12 U.C.D.
L.Rev. 255, 256 (1979).

Thus, while children are "persons" in the eyes of the law from the moment of
birth, their parents are considered to be their natural legal guardians and Anglo-
American law traditionally has adhered to a nearly irrebuttable presumption that
parents have the legal right and duty to act for their children. The exceptions that have
generally been recognized were traditionally discrete and narrow--essentially
involving (1) "emergencies" when waiting for parental consent would cause
immediate and irreparable harm to the child; or (2) "emancipation" when the parent
and the child mutually agreed by their actions that the child was no longer in need of
parental support or direction; or (3) "extraordinary public policy" when the
requirement of parental consent might thwart a strong public policy (usually a health
policy) designed to foster the best interests of children. (In recent years, the number
of these "extraordinary public policies" has multiplied, and today there are numerous
statutes authorizing specific exceptions to the general rule of parental guardianship
(e.g., for drug treatment, pregnancy treatment, venereal disease treatment, abortion, or
contraceptive use`). *See generally* Dodson, *Legal Rights of Adolescents: Restrictions
on Liberty, Emancipation, and Status Offenses* in Legal Rights of Children 114 (R.
Horowitz & H. Davidson, eds. 1984).

Thus, the transition from dependence and incompetence to independence and
competence creates the dilemma of minority and minors' rights and the law. The
transition is a complex, highly individualized process; but the law has created only
two categories to deal with that transition: incompetence (minority) and competence
(majority). Of course, the law could deal with the highly variable and individualized
nature of the transition from incompetence to competence on an individual case-by-
case basis. But there are several practical problems with that. (For a discussion of the
problems of indeterminacy *see* Wald, *supra,* at 268 n. 55; Mnookin, *Child
Adjudication: Judicial Functions in the Face of Indeterminancy*, 39 L & Contemp.
Prob. 226 (1975).) First, there is no clear consensus establishing any standard or
definition for determining maturity or legal competence.

> [T]he problem of determining "maturity" makes clear why the State generally may
> resort to objective, though inevitably arbitrary, criteria such as age limits . . . for
> lifting some or all of the legal disabilities of minority. Not only is it difficult to
> define, let alone determine, maturity, but the fact that a minor may be very much of
> an adult in some respects does not mean that his or her need and opportunity for
> growth under parental guidance and discipline have ended.

Bellotti v. Baird, 443 U.S. 662, 644 n. 23 (1979) (Powell, J., plurality opinion).
Second, even if there were an accepted standard or definition of maturity, there is no
generally recognized test for measuring maturity. Third, there is no consensus about
who should decide the question. (Families are obviously in the best position, but it is
against families that the individual would be asserting the claim of maturity and

independence.) Finally, the expense and burden that would be involved if a public agency were to make such a determination would render such individualized process impractical, if not financially impossible, or at least guarantee that it would be merely a token bureaucratic exercise.

Historically, the law has taken a categorical approach--setting a specific age and following the general presumption that before that age all minors are incompetent, and after that age they are competent. Such age distinctions, however, are unavoidably arbitrary. Wald, *supra*, at 267; Dodson, *supra*, at 117. With respect to property rights, the role of the law has been largely conservative and largely uncontroversial. With respect to non-economic issues (education, religion, associations, speech, etc.), the law historically has protect the best interests of the child, traditionally by a rebuttable assumption of deference to the parents but more recently by carving out numerous exceptions in favor of alternative care-givers (medical professionals, counselors, etc.).

Thus, the legal role and status of children, the prerogatives of parents, and the interests of the state raise extremely perplexing questions. Not surprisingly, there is no consistent, coherent legal theory that provides any framework of understanding for the rights of minors in transition between dependent childhood and independent adulthood. When courts are forced to address questions involving claims of legal rights of minors, they respond by applying "largely *ad hoc* analysis."

b. Stair-step Legal Competence

The "bright line" age of competence was not quite as simple as all-or-none. While general legal competence was achieved at the age of majority, the common law recognized growing legal rights and responsibilities of minors as they matured. Blackstone summarizes it thus:

> A male at *twelve* years old may take the oath of allegiance; at *fourteen* is at years of discretion, and therefore may consent or disagree to marriage, may choose his guardian, and, if his discretion be actually proved, may make his testament of his personal estate; at *seventeen* may be an executor; and at *twenty-one* is at his own disposal, and may alienate his lands, goods, and chattels. A female also at *seven* years of age may be betrothed or given in marriage; at *nine* is entitled to dower; at *twelve* is at years of maturity, and therefore may consent or disagree to marriage, and, if proved to have sufficient discretion, may bequeath her personal estate; at *fourteen* is at years of legal discretion, and may choose a guardian; at *seventeen* may be an executrix; and at *twenty-one* may dispose herself or her lands. So that full age in male or female is twenty-one years, which age is completed on the day preceding the anniversary of the person's birth; who till that time is an infant and so styled in law.

William Blackstone, Commentaries on the Laws of England *464.

c. Emancipation in Anglo-American Law

The doctrine of emancipation is largely an invention of American law. In the nineteenth century, English law provided that a child of the age of discretion (age 14 for boys and age 16 for girls) did not have to submit entirely to parental control, and thus would decline to grant a writ of *habeas corpus* to force a child of the age of discretion to return to his or her parents' home. However, there was no general emancipation doctrine in England. In the United States, however, courts would terminate the legal rights and duties that arose from the parent-child relationship and the disabilities of minority upon a showing of sufficient maturity and economic independence of the minor. Historically, most cases in the eighteenth and nineteenth centuries involved protecting the earnings of an emancipated child against the claim of his father who had failed to support the child. Now it is most often an issue in connection with child support; often used by a parent as a defense against prosecution or civil claim for nonpayment of support.

A child is released from his or her legal disabilities at the age of majority and is no longer under the control and care of an adult. The child may be released from these disabilities prior to reaching the age of majority under the doctrine of emancipation. Emancipation relieves the parents of their responsibilities to the child depending on the extent of the emancipation. Emancipation may be total or partial. There are three methods by which a child may be emancipated. A child may be emancipated by operation of law, by judicial emancipation, or by judicial declaration. At common law, the prevailing methods by operation of law were marriage and military service. Many states have enacted statutes codifying the common law and have included other methods of emancipation. Marriage emancipates a child in all states, either totally or partially. Parental consent may be required. Military enlistment is not as important as it once was for emancipation purposes because most states have lowered the age of majority from 21 to 18. Statutory emancipation is often for a specific purpose, leaving the other disabilities undisturbed.

A child may be emancipated by judicial emancipation. At common law, there were certain factual circumstances that a court would recognize to emancipate the child, either absolutely or partially. The child is usually capable of living on his or her own, having the maturity and financial capability. Parental consent is necessary, unless the court implies parental consent or the child has been abandoned. A child may be judicially emancipated when the child voluntarily abandons the parent's reasonable discipline.

A child may be emancipated by judicial declaration. At least sixteen states have created a judicial proceeding for emancipation in order to clarify in that particular state the grounds for emancipation, who has standing to petition, and other procedural requirements. The standard for granting or denying a petition is usually the best interest of the child.

2. Statutes, Cases and Doctrines

a. *Wulff v. Wulff*

Wulff v. Wulff
500 N.W. 2d 845 (Neb. 1993)

HASTINGS, Chief JUSTICE.

The respondent, Steven J. Wulff, has appealed the March 5, 1991, order of the district court entered upon motion of the petitioner, Jean M. Wulff, also known as Jean M. Tierney, which order modified a dissolution decree as previously modified in earlier proceedings.

Although the original decree is not contained in the record, according to an affidavit filed by the respondent, a decree of dissolution was entered by the district court on December 30, 1988. That decree provided that the care and custody of the couple's two minor children be placed with the petitioner and ordered the respondent to pay child support.

On March 5, 1990, the respondent filed a motion to terminate child support. He asserted that since the entry of the decree the parties' elder daughter had become emancipated and no longer lived with the petitioner and that the younger daughter was currently residing with the respondent. It also appears in the record that the elder daughter had moved in with her boyfriend and later gave birth to a baby. A modification of decree was entered by the district court on April 11, which found that custody of the parties' younger minor child should be granted to the respondent and ordered the petitioner to pay child support of $250 per month for her benefit. It was further ordered that "the parties' oldest child, [name of child], has become emancipated by reason of her moving out of the home and living independently; that the child support obligation for that child shall cease as of April 1, 1990."

The petitioner filed an application to modify the decree on August 31, 1990, asserting that the elder child had moved back into the petitioner's home and that "it would be in the best interests of both minor children if neither party were to pay child support to the other as both parties currently have one child residing with them." A hearing was held on the application to modify on December 13. On March 5, 1991, the district court found that "as of the date of the Application for Modification, the [elder] minor child, [name of child], was not emancipated," and ordered the respondent to pay child support as of the first day of each month after the date of the application for modification, until and including December 1, 1990. The petitioner adduced evidence that since her daughter had moved back into the petitioner's home, the petitioner had been providing her with board and room and was also helping her daughter with some of the expenses of her baby. The petitioner also agrees that she has not been paying child support to the respondent for the benefit of her younger daughter since she filed the current application for modification and is $1,000 in arrears because of failure to make the September, October, November, and December payments. The evidence discloses that the elder daughter would reach the age of majority, 19 years, on December 24, 1990, the year in which the present hearing was held.

The order of the district court from which this appeal is taken decreed that as of the date of application for modification which was filed on August 31, 1990, the parties' minor child, who had been found emancipated by order of the court on April 11, 1990, was not now emancipated.

The respondent's assignments of error may be consolidated into claims that the court erred (1) in finding that the order which had declared the child emancipated was not res judicata, (2) in failing to find that once a child has become emancipated that status cannot be changed, (3) in failing to find that a minor's having a baby out of wedlock is a substantial act which emancipates that minor child, and (4) in modifying the decree as to child support retroactively to the date of filing the application rather than prospectively. We affirm.

The respondent also asserts that the district court erred in not sustaining his demurrer ore tenus at the commencement of trial, but does not discuss this assignment of error in his brief. This court will not consider assignments of error which are not discussed in the brief. *

Regarding the claim of res judicata, full and complete general jurisdiction over child custody and support is vested in the district court in which a petition for dissolution is properly filed. * A decree in a divorce case, insofar as minor children are concerned, is never final in the sense that it cannot be changed. *Bartlett v. Bartlett*, 193 Neb. 76, 225 N.W.2d 413 (1975).

Modification of an award of child support is not justified unless the applicant proves that a material change in circumstances has occurred since the entry of the decree or a previous modification. *

It is true that in the absence of proof of new facts and circumstances arising since the time of the original decree, an allowance of child support therein will be deemed res judicata. *Shipley v.*

Shipley, 175 Neb. 119, 120 N.W.2d 582 (1963).

While the respondent concedes that an order for custody or support is not res judicata where there has been a material change in circumstances, he contends that the district court erred in treating this case as a question of custody or support, rather than as a question of emancipation. He further asserts, in essence, that the district court lacked authority to find that the emancipation had been revoked or rescinded. However, under the above-cited authorities, it is clear that a district court has broad discretion in dealing with matters which affect the care and custody of a minor child. Where issues of child support and emancipation are integrated, a district court must have the authority to adjudicate both. **

As noted in Shipley, an allowance of child support is deemed res judicata in the absence of new facts and circumstances which would justify the modification of the award. However, a child's status as an emancipated or unemancipated minor is necessarily at issue where the district court finds a material change in circumstances which would justify modification of child support. Thus, in the context of an action for modification of child support, the determination of a child's status as an emancipated minor is not res judicata.

In *Wadoz v. United Nat. Indemnity Co.*, 274 Wis. 383, 80 N.W.2d 262 (1957), the Supreme Court of Wisconsin discussed the question of whether a minor's emancipation had been rescinded in the context of a negligence action brought by the parents against a daughter who had left the parental home to enter a convent but had later returned, noting that [t]o emancipate means to free or release a child from the parental power, making the person released sui juris....

"Emancipation," as the term is used in the law of parent and child, means the freeing of the child for the period of its minority from the care, custody, control, and service of its parents.... Emancipation of a minor may be partial or complete, express or implied.... Complete emancipation gives to the minor his time and earnings and does away with the parent's right of custody and control.... The child may be emancipated for the balance of its minority or for a shorter period, and conditionally or unconditionally.... Emancipation occurs where the parent renounces all the legal duties and voluntarily surrenders all the legal rights of his position to the child or to others. In determining whether a child has been emancipated, the intention of the parent governs.... Whether a child has been emancipated must be determined largely on the peculiar facts and circumstances of each case, and therefore is ordinarily a question for the jury.... Whether there has been an emancipation is a question of fact, but what is emancipation is a question of law. (Citations omitted.)

The Wisconsin court further noted that under the law of that state, there could be a mutual presumption of the filial relationship and a return to the status of an unemancipated minor. Although the plaintiffs' counsel in that case had cited authority to support the proposition that emancipation could not be revoked, the court found that in the cases cited by the plaintiffs, either the effort to rescind emancipation had been unilateral or the rights of the minors or third persons acquired during emancipation would have been prejudiced without their consent. The court concluded that "[n]o authorities are cited which indicate that mutual rescission of emancipation is forbidden." *

In *Vaupel v. Bellach*, 261 Iowa 376, 154 N.W.2d 149 (1967), in which the plaintiff brought an action for contribution against a child following judgment against the plaintiff for personal injuries received by that child's mother while she was riding in an automobile driven by her child, the Supreme Court of Iowa similarly found that "[e]mancipation is not necessarily a continuing status, even if once established, it may be terminated at anytime during the child's minority." *Id.* at 380, 154 N.W.2d at 151.

We agree with that proposition. Thus, it was appropriate under the circumstances of this case for the district court to determine as a question of fact whether the child's emancipation had been rescinded as a result of the change in circumstances.

The respondent next contends that a minor child's giving birth and becoming a parent results in emancipation of the minor child. While Neb.Rev.Stat. s 43-2101 (Reissue 1988) provides that "[a]ll persons under nineteen years of age are declared to be minors, but in case any person marries under the age of nineteen years, his or her minority ends," there is no provision which provides that a minor is irrevocably emancipated by the act of giving birth.

The respondent argues that *Nuckols v. Nuckols* * is analogous to the instant case. In *Nuckols*, the court found that a parent's responsibility for medical expenses, pursuant to a child support order which had been modified after the effective date of a statute lowering the age of majority to 18, extended until the children reached the age of 21 or became emancipated. The court concluded that upon consideration of the facts and circumstances disclosed in the record, "the trial court properly determined that the parties' daughter, having attained the age of eighteen, became emancipated upon giving birth to her child." *Id.** It is not evident from the opinion what other facts and circumstances in the record affected the determination that the daughter had become emancipated upon giving birth.

However, other jurisdictions have found that becoming a parent is not sufficient by itself to result in emancipation. *See e.g. Griffin v. Griffin*, 384 Pa.Super. 188, 558 A.2d 75 (1989) (in state whose child support statutes do not limit child support to minor children, college student who has had child should not, for that reason alone, be treated differently for purposes of child support for educational expenses from college student who has not had a child); *Doerrfeld v. Konz*, 524 So.2d 1115 (Fla.App.1988) (minor child's giving birth and becoming parent was not on its own sufficient to result in emancipation); In re Marriage of Clay, 670 P.2d 31 (Colo.App.1983) (daughter who was dependent upon mother for financial support, had not established own residence, and was not married to or receiving support from father of her child was not emancipated); *Hicks v. Fulton County Department of Family & Children Services*, 155 Ga.App. 1, 270 S.E.2d 254 (1980) (fact that minor abandoned her father's home and bore an illegitimate child did not establish that child had emancipated herself); *French v. French*, 599 S.W.2d 40 (Mo.App.1980) (daughter's receipt of payments from Aid to Families with dependent children following birth of her child did not emancipate her).

In French, the court noted that emancipation may be accomplished by express or implied agreement and it is never presumed.... A child becomes emancipated when he marries ... or when he enters the military.... Under those circumstances, the parent or parents are relieved of their duty to support their child because the child has entered into a new relationship, status, or position, which is inconsistent with control and support of the child by the parent. (Citations omitted.).

Thus, giving birth may be one factor to be considered in the determination of whether a minor has achieved a new status or position inconsistent with parental control, but should not alone be dispositive. The district court did not err in failing to find that a minor child becomes emancipated by giving birth to a child.

As his final assignment of error, the respondent asserts that the court erred in making the modified decree retroactive, rather than prospective. The general rule in Nebraska has been to allow a modification of a child support order prospectively from the time of the modification order itself. *

When a divorce decree provides for the payment of stipulated sums monthly for the support of a minor child or children, contingent only upon a subsequent order of the court, such payments become vested in the payee as they accrue. Generally, the courts are without authority to reduce the amounts of such accrued payments. *

Upon occasion, depending on the equities involved, this court has approved modification of a child support order retroactive to the filing date of the application for modification. *

Although the district court had found in its order of April 11, 1990, that the elder daughter had "become emancipated by reason of her moving out of her home and living independently," it is evident from the record that she was not self- supporting even at that time and that whatever support she had received from her boyfriend and his mother had since ceased. In its order of March 5, 1991, the district court found upon consideration of the evidence that as of the date of application for modification, August 31, 1990, the daughter was not emancipated. The testimony adduced at the hearing is consistent with a finding of the child's continuing dependence on the support of her parents. Quoting Annot., 98 A.L.R.3d 334 (1980), this court noted in *Accent Service Co., Inc. v. Ebsen,* * that "even in the absence of statute, parents are under a legal as well as a moral obligation to support, maintain, and care for their children, the basis of such a duty resting not only upon the fact of the parent-child relationship, but also upon the interest of the state as parens patriae of children and of the community at large in preventing them from becoming a public burden...."

While the change in circumstances supports the conclusion that the child was not emancipated and that petitioner would be entitled to child support, as noted above, the general rule in Nebraska is to allow modification of a child support order prospectively from the time of the modification order itself. However, the district court's order of March 5, 1991, ordered the respondent to pay child support beginning with the first day of each month following the date of application for modification up to and including December 1, 1990. Although the district court did not cancel or reduce accrued payments due to the respondent from the petitioner, it did order any child support arrearage on the part of the petitioner to be credited to the child support obligation of the respondent.

Modification of child support is an issue entrusted to the discretion of the trial court. Appellate review of such issues is de novo on the record, but absent an abuse of discretion by the trial court, its decision will be affirmed on appeal. *

A judicial abuse of discretion exists when a judge, within the effective limits of authorized judicial power, elects to act or refrain from action, but the selected option results in a decision which is untenable and unfairly deprives a litigant of a substantial right or a just result in matters submitted for disposition through a judicial system. *

The record reflects that the elder daughter was dependent on her parents for support as of the date of application for modification and that the petitioner was continuing to make payments for medical expenses both related to and unrelated to the birth of the daughter's child. As previously stated, the elder daughter attained the age of majority on December 24, 1990. Under these circumstances, the district court did not abuse its discretion in ordering child support payments retroactive to the filing date of the application for modification, until and including December 1, 1990. The judgment of the district court is correct and is affirmed.

b. Notes and Questions

In *Wulff,* the court states that giving birth is one of the factors for determining whether a minor is emancipated. What other factors should a court consider? Would it be better to codify the factors as some states have done? *Wulff* was a postdivorce child support case. How much do you think that fact may have influenced the court's decision as to the emancipation issue? Was the father more concerned about the termination of his duty to support than the daughter's welfare?

3. Practical and Ethical Considerations

a. The Incorrigible Child

In many cases, parents, schools, courts and social services are unable to deal effectively with defiant adolescents above the age of fifteen, who are still financially dependent upon their parents for the basics of life. Their parents may also be financially liable for their torts. (See next section below). Courts routinely will not grant an order for emancipation under these circumstances. One court's rationale follows: "The rights of parents to raise and to nurture their children are among the most fundamental and basic of human rights. From this premise flows the corollary that parental obligations and responsibilities cannot be lightly shed or abrogated by a child's parent or guardian. Although unfortunate, it is one of the realities of life that parents must shoulder burdensome responsibilities for children who misbehave, or become physically or emotionally ill. A decree legally excusing parents from the obligations and duties of parenthood should not be granted without a substantial reason." *In Re Thomas C.*, 691 A.2d 1140 (Conn. Super. Ct. 1996). Is this good public policy? Would it make a difference whether it is the parent or the child who is petitioning? Would it make a difference if the child refuses to live at home?

4. Bibliography

1 Jeremy Benthan, Theory of Legislation 248 (Boston 1840) quoted in Michael Wald, *Children's Rights: A Framework for Analysis*, 12 U.C.D. L.Rev. 255, 256 (1979).
William Blackstone, Commentaries on the Laws of England *461- *464.
Homer H. Clark, Jr., The Law of Domestic Relations in the United States §8.3 (2d ed. 1988).
John DeWitt Gregory, Peter N. Swisher & Sheryl L. Scheible, Understanding Family Law (1993).
Dodson, *Legal Rights of Adolescents: Restrictions on Liberty, Emancipation, and Status Offenses* in Legal Rights of Children 114 (R. Horowitz & H. Davidson, eds. 1984).
John Stewart Mill, On Liberty (1959).
Mnookin, *Child Adjudication: Judicial Functions in the Face of Indeterminancy*, 39 L & Contemp. Prob. 226 (1975).

B. PARENTAL LIABILITY

1. Background

a. Parental Liability at Common Law for the Acts of the Child

Blackstone did not discuss parental liability at common law but suggested the basis for our modern statutes that impose parental liability. He noted: "An infant cannot be sued but under the protection, and joining the name, of his guardian; for he is to defend him against all attacks as well by law as otherwise . . . ." William Blackstone, Commentaries on the Laws of England *464.

2. Statutes, Cases and Doctrines

a. *Bryan v. Kitanora*

Bryan v. Kitanora
529 F.Supp. 394 (D. Haw. 1982)

PENCE, District JUDGE.

I. INTRODUCTION

On the night of July 13, 1979, a group of juveniles allegedly stole a 1978 Ford van in Hilo and drove approximately 35 miles to Pohakuloa Training Area, where they attempted to steal guns and ammunition from a military ammunition depot. During the attempted theft, the juveniles shot and injured the plaintiffs, who were military personnel standing guard at the ammunition depot. At the time of the incident, the juveniles involved were between 14 and 16 years of age.

Plaintiffs brought this suit against both the juveniles and their parents. Plaintiffs assert that the parents are liable under section 577-3 of the Hawaii Revised Statutes (HRS), which provides that parents are jointly and severally liable for the tortious acts of their unmarried minor children.

Defendants challenge the constitutionality of this statute by way of motions to dismiss and motions for partial summary judgment. Defendants claim that the statute unconstitutionally burdens the family by imposing liability on parents without fault in a manner that violates the due process and equal protection clauses of the 14th amendment of the United States Constitution.

II. HAWAII'S PARENTAL LIABILITY STATUTE

Hawaii's parental liability statute finds its origin in the Acts of 1846 which were drafted by John Ricord, the first Attorney General of the Kingdom of Hawaii. The provision became codified as section 1288 of the Civil Code, and provided that the father "shall be the natural guardian of their (children's) persons and of their property; he shall be liable in damages for the tortious acts committed by them ...."

In 1931, the provisions of the Civil Code relating to parental responsibilities were revised to make both the mother and the father responsible for the acts of their children.

Hawaii's parental liability statute, HRS section 577-3, reads, in relevant part, as follows:

> The father and mother of unmarried minor children shall jointly and severally be liable in damages for tortious acts committed by their children, and shall be jointly and severally entitled to prosecute and defend all actions in which the children or their individual property may be concerned.

Although this section also provides that the guardianship of an unmarried minor may, under certain circumstances, devolve upon one parent, the parental liability portion of the statute specifically imposes liability on both the mother and father, without reference to custody, and does not apply to guardians who are not the mother or the father of the child.

Hawaii's parental liability statute has not been extensively interpreted by the Hawaii Supreme Court. In *Day v. Day*, 8 Haw. 715 (1891), that court held that the statute could not be interpreted to impose liability on a parent when the child, because of his young age, was not himself legally responsible for his torts.

In *Victoria v. Palama*, 15 Haw. 127 (1903), defendant's seven-year-old son accidentally shot another minor with a shotgun, destroying the vision of one eye. The Supreme Court upheld a directed verdict against the father stating that "the father can be held responsible in damages for the torts of his infant in every case where the infant itself would be liable at the common law." 15 Haw. at 129.

Finally, in *Rathburn v. Kaio*, 23 Haw. 541 (1916), the court held that the statute could not be used to impose liability on parents for acts which the court found to be an alleged breach of contract and not tortious in nature.

It does not appear that the Supreme Court of Hawaii has ever heard a challenge to the constitutionality of section 577-3.

III. THE PISCATAWAY CASE

In *Piscataway Township Bd. of Ed. v. Caffiero*, 86 N.J. 308, 431 A.2d 799 (1981), appeal dismissed for want of a sub. fed. ques., --- U.S. ----, 102 S.Ct. 560 (1981), the Board of Education brought suit against the parents of minors who had allegedly damaged school property. The basis for the action was a New Jersey statute which subjects the parents or guardians of minor public school children to liability for damage to school property caused by their children. A New Jersey

Superior Court held that the statute violated the 14th Amendment of the United States Constitution, but the appellate division reversed, holding that the statute violated neither the due process nor the equal protection clauses of the 14th Amendment. *Piscataway Township Bd. of Ed. v. Caffiero*, 173 N.J.Super. 204, 413 A.2d 981 (1980). The Supreme Court of New Jersey affirmed the appellate division and the parents filed an appeal to the United States Supreme Court.

On November 9, 1981, the Supreme Court dismissed the appeal for want of a substantial federal question. *Caffiero v. Piscataway Township Bd. of Ed.*, --- U.S. ----, 102 S.Ct. 560 (1981). This disposition is the equivalent to an affirmance on the merits. *Hicks v. Miranda*, 422 U.S. 332 (1975); *McCarthy v. Philadelphia Civil Serv. Comm'n.*, 424 U.S. 645 (1976). This court is therefore bound by the result in *Piscataway* to the extent that the two cases may involve the same legal issues. *Hicks, supra*, 422 U.S. at 343-44; *McCarthy, supra*, 424 U.S. at 646.

Defendants claim that this case is distinguishable from *Piscataway* because the Hawaii parental liability statute is much broader than the New Jersey statute which applied only to the parents and guardians of public school children who damage school property. Defendants also argue that HRS 577-3 contains constitutional obligations not found in the New Jersey statute.

Defendants' argument has merit. Although dismissal of an appeal is binding on subsequent cases involving similar facts, such a dismissal does not necessarily adopt the opinion or reasoning of the court below. Although the reasoning of the New Jersey Supreme Court in Piscataway is broad enough to control many of the issues involved here, this court finds that the Hawaii statute differs significantly from the New Jersey statute upheld in Piscataway and therefore requires detailed consideration of its alleged constitutional defects.

IV. SUBSTANTIVE DUE PROCESS AND EQUAL PROTECTION

Defendants' principal contention is that the Hawaii statute is violative of the due process and the equal protection clauses of the 14th Amendment because it unreasonably interferes with a right that is "fundamental", in this case the right of parents to raise a family without the state's imposing unreasonable financial burdens upon them. Although the due process and equal protection clauses of the 14th Amendment have in many instances been interpreted differently by the Supreme Court, both have been used similarly to protect fundamental substantive rights.

Under both substantive due process and fundamental rights equal protection analysis, a court must first identify a right that is affected by the challenged state action. Under equal protection analysis, if a statute interferes with the exercise of a fundamental right, it cannot be upheld unless it is "supported by sufficiently important state interests and is closely tailored to only those interests." If a fundamental right is not affected, it suffices that the statute have a rational relation to a legitimate government purpose.

Defendants argue that the Hawaii parental liability statute affects fundamental rights associated with the family. They base their argument on a series of Supreme Court decisions that recognize the importance of personal decisions affecting the family. These cases have held that some personal choices affecting the family are so important that they must be deemed fundamental rights for the purposes of constitutional analysis. For example, the Court has held that freedom of choice in marriage, child bearing, and child rearing, are within this category.

Defendants attempt to bring the Hawaii parental liability statute within the scope of these decisions by arguing that it discourages persons from having children and interferes with the raising of children by placing a severe economic burden on the parents. This court rejects defendants' conclusions.

Those rights found to be fundamental by the Court share the characteristic of involving freedom of choice. For example, in *Zablocki v. Redhail, supra*, the Court found unconstitutional a statute which interfered with a person's decision to marry by requiring an individual with child support obligations to seek court approval before marrying. Similarly, in the abortion and birth control cases, the Court expressed concern over regulation which interfered with a person's right to decide whether or not to have children.

The Hawaii statute places no real burden on either the decision to have a child or decisions concerning childrearing. This court could not reasonably conclude that the threat of potential tort liability plays any role in the decision of parents whether or not to have children. Likewise, the Hawaii statute does not prevent parents from making decisions concerning their children. In fact, it promotes the making of such decisions by providing parents with an incentive to play a greater role in the supervision of their children.

The only interest with which the statute may interfere is the parents' interest in raising a family without any economic limitations imposed by the state. This interest, however, is not one that rises to the level of a fundamental right. Unlike other interests held to be fundamental, it is not one that includes personal choice. This court finds the case at bar similar to *Dandridge v. Williams*, 397 U.S. 471 (1969), where the Court found that a ceiling on welfare payments to large families did not affect a fundamental interest and accordingly applied the rational basis test in upholding the challenged regulations. This court similarly finds that the defendants here have not shown that the Hawaii parental liability statute affects a right that is fundamental. Although some families may undergo financial strain as a result of the statute, this fact alone does not establish encroachment on a fundamental interest. Therefore, this court must give effect to HRS section 577-3 if it can be shown to have a rational basis.

HRS section 577-3 clearly has a rational relation to legitimate government interests. One justification for the statute is that it provides a remedy for tort victims who would otherwise receive no compensation for their injuries. Imposition of vicarious liability without fault is normally justified by the policy decision that the person held liable is in a position to shift the costs of an injury to the public at large through the purchase of liability insurance. This rationale certainly holds true in the case of the Hawaii parental liability statute. A minor is, in almost all cases, judgment proof and without personally acquired insurance. If fault is not imputed to the parent, the child's victim must bear the entire cost of the injury suffered. The child's parents, however, are in a position to spread the cost of the injury to the public at large through the purchase of liability insurance.

Another possible justification for the statute is that it deters juvenile delinquency by providing an incentive to parents to exercise greater supervision over the activities of their children. Defendants argue that the statute is not tailored to meet this goal because the statute imposes liability even where parents have exercised due care in supervising their children. The legislature, however, may have wished to impose an even greater duty on parents to affirmatively prevent tortious acts by their children. In any event, this court need not find that the statute is the best method for deterring juvenile delinquency, or that it deters juvenile delinquency at all, but only that it has a rational basis. This court cannot say that HRS section 577-3 is without a rational relation to a legitimate government purpose.

V. PROCEDURAL DUE PROCESS

Defendants claim that HRS section 577-3 violates the due process clause of the 14th Amendment because it creates an "irrebuttable presumption" that natural parents are responsible for the torts of their children, regardless of their due care or lack of custody over the children. The Court has held some legislative schemes unconstitutional because they denied important benefits on the basis of status through the use of "irrebuttable presumptions". These decisions, however, have come under considerable attack and the continuing validity of the "irrebuttable presumption" doctrine is much in doubt. Commentators have argued that the prohibition on irrebuttable presumptions is no more than equal protection analysis in disguise since the objectionable portion of each statute is the manner in which it classifies individuals. This view is supported by the fact that irrebuttable presumptions have been upheld by the Court where the presumption did not involve a suspect classification and did not affect the exercise of a fundamental right.

This court finds that HRS section 577-3 does not contain an unconstitutional "irrebuttable presumption". Parents are not automatically liable under the statute for all damages caused by their children. They have the opportunity at trial to present any defenses available to their children. The parents are only precluded from using the defense that they themselves are without fault. [Fn 28 Defendants rely on the case of Bell v. Burson, 402 U.S. 535 (1971). In that case, the Supreme Court considered the constitutionality of Georgia's Motor Vehicle Responsibility Act, which provides for the suspension of the license and motor vehicle registration of uninsured motorists involved in accidents who do not post security for the amount of damages claimed by injured parties. The Court held that the system was in violation of the due process clause because it confiscated a substantial benefit from uninsured motorists without any finding of fault or probable fault. The Court did not expressly mention the "irrebuttable presumption" doctrine. Bell is distinguishable from this case. The Court, in Bell, stated that "we are not dealing here with a no-fault scheme. Since the statutory scheme makes liability an important factor in the State's determination to deprive an individual of his licenses, the State may not, consistently with due process, eliminate consideration of that factor in its prior hearing." 402 U.S. at 541. Under HRS s 557-3, as in a no-fault scheme, the fault of the parents is not a relevant factor. Only the fault of the children is at issue, and the parents have an opportunity to litigate this question before liability is imposed. Moreover, Bell involved what was, in essence, a punitive scheme attempting to insure the compensation of tort victims by threatening uninsured defendants with the penalty of license revocation. HRS s 577-3 only requires that parents compensate the victims of their children's torts. It does not impose an unrelated penalty for failure to do so.]

This court has already held that imposition of liability without fault does not threaten the exercise of a fundamental right. The statute might be defective if it operated by means of an invidious classification, but for all intents and purposes, this presents an equal protection and not a due process claim. The only "process" which could alter the alleged irrebuttable presumption is an abolishment of the classification scheme adopted by the statute. This court addresses this problem under the more appropriate rubric of the Equal Protection Clause.

VI. EQUAL PROTECTION

(4) Defendants allege that HRS section 577-3 violates the Equal Protection Clause because it discriminates against natural parents. Unless a statutory classification infringes on fundamental personal rights or is made on the basis of an inherently suspect distinction such as race, religion, or alienage, it is valid so long as it is rationally related to a legitimate state interest. This court has already held that HRS section 577-3 does not affect the exercise of a fundamental personal right. Neither does it involve a suspect classification. A suspect class is one that is "saddled with such disabilities, or subjected to such a history of purposeful unequal treatment, or relegated to such a position of political powerlessness as to command extraordinary protection from the majoritarian political process." Natural parents are certainly not such a group. HRS section 577-3 is therefore valid so long as its singling out of natural parents is rationally related to a legitimate state interest.

Defendants argue that HRS section 577-3 is defective because it fails to impose liability on those other than natural parents who are equally responsible for a child's conduct. The statute's inclusion of only the mother and the father does not render it unconstitutional. It is within the discretion of the legislature to address only part of a problem or to select only one phase of a field for regulation. The legislature's refusal to extend the statute to appointed guardians is not without logic. The legislature may have wished to encourage persons to take on appointed guardianships by relieving them of an added financial burden of parenthood, or it may have decided that it would be unfair to make a newly appointed guardian liable for the torts of an already incorrigible child. In any event, this court cannot say that the distinction drawn by the statute between parents and others responsible for a child's behavior is not rationally related to a legitimate government purpose.

Defendants also argue that HRS section 577-3 is overinclusive because it can be interpreted to apply to natural parents who have never had custody over their offspring. Defendants maintain that this possibility renders the statute invalid on its face. This court declines to adopt such a position.

Ordinarily, a person to whom a statute may constitutionally be applied cannot challenge that statute on the grounds that it might conceivably be applied unconstitutionally to others. An exception to this rule is sometimes found where First Amendment freedoms are at stake. Even in the First Amendment area, however, the doctrine of facial overbreadth is not invoked where a limiting construction can be placed on the challenged statute.

This court finds that the application of HRS section 577-3 could easily be interpreted and narrowed to require a nexus between natural parentage and a significant period of custody of control of the child. In this case, this court need not address the statute's exact constitutional scope. All but one of the defendants in this case have custody of their children. The other parent, Doris Sasake, had custody of her son until eight months prior to the incident at Pohakuloa. On the facts before it, this court cannot say that application of the statute to any of the defendants would be unconstitutional. [Fn 37 This court cannot say that the legislature would be unreasonable to conclude that a parent, though losing custody of a child shortly before that child commits a tort, still exerts a strong influence over the child's behavior and should bear responsibility along with the custodial parent for that child's tortious acts. The only fact that this court has before it is that Ms. Sasake lacked custody over her son for eight months prior to the incident at Pohakuloa. This fact alone does not give this court a basis for concluding that the statute would be unconstitutional as applied to her.] This court therefore declines to reach the question of whether the statute might be unconstitutional as applied under some other factual circumstances.

For the reasons above set forth: Defendants' Motions to Dismiss and Motions for Partial Summary Judgment are HEREBY DENIED.

b. Notes and Questions

1) *Bryan* and Parental Liability Statutes

The purpose of parental liability statutes is to encourage parents to control the child from delinquent behavior. Most statutes are limited to property damage and with exposure to liability limited to a certain amount. Hawaii and other states have also enacted liquor liability laws to specifically impose liability on parents and others who provide alcohol to child drunk drivers who injure others. "This new liquor liability statute significantly expands their potential liability for the acts of unrelated minors based upon whether adults know of consumption on premises the adults own, occupy or control." Napier, *infra*, at 22.

2) Parental Immunity in Tort

At common law there apparently was no substantive immunity protecting parents from tort liability to children. However, there was no need for immunity. Procedurally children were held strictly to lack personal standing to bring suit. Their parents could not sue one another (on behalf of a child) because of the legal unity of husband and wife; furthermore, married women lacked general capacity to sue. As these procedural barriers began to break down in the nineteenth century, courts created the substantive doctrine of parental immunity. The basic policy reasons for the doctrine are disrupting family harmony, frustrating the parent-child relationship, and the possibility of fraud and collusion between parent and child when insurance is involved. The modern trend has been to abolish the doctrine partially or totally. States follow the same rules when parents sue their minor children. *See* H. Clark, Jr., Domestic Relations, § 9.2 (1968). Many states have abrogated the doctrine in connection with automobile accidents, where the state has required automobile liability insurance. Similarly, there has been a retreat from the doctrine in other areas where there is liability insurance. Some states have abrogated the rule in circumstances regarding the parent's negligent exercise of parental control and have adopted a "reasonable parent standard." The Restatement (Second), of Torts § 316 (1965) provides for parental liability for injuries caused by tortious acts of children when the parent knows or has reason to know of the need, ability, and opportunity to control the child's unreasonable or wilful injury-causing behavior. Since the Columbine High School shootings, and with the public perception that juvenile crime is increasing, there have been increased calls to repeal or curtail parental immunity, and to strengthen the principle of parental liability for the tortious acts of children in their custody or control. *See generally* Burton, *infra.*

3. Practical and Ethical Considerations

a. Parental Liability Statutes and the Noncustodial Parent

Is it fair to apply parental liability statutes to the noncustodial parent when the child is not in her physical custody at the time of the act? Or, as footnote 37 in *Bryan v. Kitamura, supra,* seems to suggest, that noncustodial parents should also be encouraged to exert influence to control the child from delinquent behavior.

4. Bibliography

William Blackstone, Commentaries on the Laws of England *461- *464.
Valerie D. Burton, Comment, *Reconciling the Burden: Parental Liability for the Tortious Acts of Minors*, 51 Emory L.J. 877 (2002).
Homer H. Clark, Jr., The Law of Domestic Relations in the United States §8.3 (2d ed. 1988).
John DeWitt Gregory, Peter N. Swisher & Sheryl L. Scheible, Understanding Family Law (1993).
Patricia Mathias Napier, *Liquor Liability Law Update*, 8 Haw. B.J. 22 (May 2004).

C. ECONOMIC RELATIONS - SUPPORT OF CHILDREN AND PARENTS

1. Background

a. Child Support at Common Law

In Blackstone's day the support duties of parents depended first on whether the child was legitimate or illegitimate. If the child was legitimate, Blackstone declared that:

> The duty of parents to provide for the *maintenance* of their children, is a principle of natural law; a voluntary obligation . . . laid on them not only by nature itself, but by their own proper act, in bringing them into the world. . . . By begetting them, therefore, they have entered into a voluntary obligation, to endeavor, as far as in them lies, that the life which they have bestowed shall be supported and preserved. And thus, the children will have a perfect *right* of receiving maintenance from their parents.
> * * * *

[In English law] there is an obligation on every man to provide for those descended from his loins . . . . The father, and mother, grandfather, and grandmother of poor impotent persons shall maintain them at their own charges, if of sufficient ability, according as the quarter sessions shall direct: and if a parent runs away, and leaves his children, the church-wardens and overseers of the parish shall seize his rents, goods, and chattels, and dispose of them toward their relief. . . .

[However,] [n]o person is bound to provide a maintenance for his issue, unless where the children are impotent and unable to work . . . and then is only obliged to fund them with necessaries, the penalty on refusal being no more than 20 s. *(shillings)* a month. For the policy of our laws, which are ever watchful to promote industry, did not mean to compel a father to maintain his idle and lazy children in ease and indolence . . . . [But by statute if a Catholic or Jewish parent refused to support a Protestant child, the court had authority to order him "to do what is just and reasonable."]

William Blackstone, Commentaries on the Laws of England *437.

Illegitimate children, "though . . . not looked upon as children to any civil purposes, yet the ties of nature, of which maintenance is one, are not so easily dissolved." *Id.* at 458. Thus, English law provided that:

> When a woman is delivered, or declares herself with child, of a bastard, and will by oath before a justice of peace charge any person having got her with child, the justice shall cause the person to be apprehended, and commit him till he gives security, either to maintain the child, or appear at the next quarter sessions to dispute and try the fact. . . . [The court] may take order for the keeping of the [child], by charging the mother or the reputed father with the payment of money or other sustentation for that purpose. And if such putative father, or lewd mother, run away from the parish, the overseers by direction of two justices may seize their rents, goods, and chattels, in order to bring up the said ... child. Yet such is the humanity of our laws, that no woman can be compulsively questioned concerning the father of her child, till one month after her delivery: which indulgence is, however, very frequently a hardship upon parishes, by giving the parents opportunity to escape.

William Blackstone, Commentaries on the Laws of England *458, 459. Thus, while English law imposed on the biological parents of the child born out of wedlock the duty to provide security to support the child, yet the duty was easily evaded by parents (mothers and fathers) willing to abandon the child. When abandoned, the care and maintenance of such children was the responsibility of the parish. The Elizabethan Poor Laws (1601), in theory at least, provided state support if the parents were unable to support the child. 2 Contemporary Family Laws 14:01 (Lynn D. Wardle, Christopher L. Blakesley & Jacqueline Y. Parker, eds. 1988).

b. Filial Support at Common Law

At common law, the child who was able had a duty to support his or her needy parents:

> The *duties* of children to their parents arise from a principle of natural justice and retribution. For to those, who gave us existence, we naturally owe subjection and

obedience during our minority, and honor and reverence ever after: they, who protected the weakness of our infancy, or entitled to our protection in the infirmity of their age; they who by sustenance and education have enable their offspring to prosper ought in return to be supported by that offspring, in case they stand in need of assistance. Upon this principle proceed all the duties of children to their parents which are enjoined by positive laws. . . .

. . . [T]he law does not hold the tie of nature to be dissolved by any misbehavior of the parent; and therefore a child is equally justifiable in defending the person, or maintaining the cause or suit, of a bad parent, as a good one; and is equally compellable, if of sufficient ability, to maintain and provide for a wicked and unnatural progenitor, as for one who has shown the greatest tenderness and parental piety.

William Blackstone, Commentaries on the Laws of England *453-454.

c. Stepparent's Support Obligations at Common Law

[I]f a mother or grandmother marries again, and was before such second marriage of sufficient ability to keep the child, the husband shall be charged to maintain it; for this being a debt of hers, when single, shall like others extend to charge the husband. But at her death the relation being dissolved, the husband is under no further obligation."

William Blackstone, Commentaries on the Laws of England *449.

A minority of American states have stepparent support statutes. Unless there is a statute, stepparents are not liable for the support of stepchildren unless the relationship of *in loco parentis* exists, or if contract or equitable estoppel principles apply. Contract and equitable principles do not usually arise until divorce of the parent and stepparent, and the parent wants to hold the stepparent liable for post divorce support of the stepchildren. The relationship of *in loco parentis* arises when a stepparent voluntarily and intentionally takes the child into his or her home and assumes the responsibility for the child. Since this relationship is based on the intention of the stepparent, it is terminated at will and in most cases when the marriage ends.

2. Statutes, Cases and Doctrines

a. People in the Interest of S.P.B.
People in the Interest of S. P. B.
651 P.2d 1213 (Colo. 1982)

DUBOFSKY, JUSTICE.

[P. D. G., the natural father of S. P. B., appeals a child support order of the El Paso County District Court. P. D. G. questions whether the constitutional rights to due process and equal protection of the laws under the state and federal constitutions are violated by the Uniform Parentage Act (UPA), section 19-6-101, et seq., C.R.S.1973 (1978 Repl. Vol. 8)].

The issue underlying this appeal arose in the course of a proceeding to determine the paternity of and support for S. P. B., a child. The respondent- appellant P. D. G. admitted to paternity of S. P. B. but denied any obligation to support the child. P. D. G. and the child's mother,

C. F. B., have never married and are not presently living together. P. D. G. asserts that when C. F. B. informed him that she was pregnant, he responded that he did not want her to have the baby and offered to pay for an abortion. P. D. G. claims that this exchange took place within the first trimester of C. F. B.'s pregnancy. C. F. B. did not agree to an abortion and subsequently gave birth to S. P. B. C. F. B. has had custody of S. P. B. since birth.

The appellant argues that the statutory imposition of the duty of child support upon both parents without granting the father the right to decide whether to terminate the pregnancy violates his right to equal protection of the laws under the federal constitution, U.S.Const. Amend. XIV, and under the state constitution, Colo.Const. Art. II, § 25. The appellant further argues that the statute creates a presumption which, consistent with due process, he should have an opportunity to rebut. Specifically, the appellant contends that the availability of legalized abortion, combined with C. F. B.'s decision to have the child against his wishes, serves as an "intervening factor" which breaks the nexus between himself and the child and which extinguishes his obligation to support it. The district court rejected these arguments and ordered P. D. G. to pay child support in the amount of $150 per month and one-half of the birth expenses of the child.

At the outset it is important to point out what is not at issue here. There is no question but that the duty to support a child falls upon both its parents. Section 19-6-102, C.R.S.1973 (1978 Repl. Vol. 8). It is equally clear that this obligation of support extends to all parents, regardless of their marital status. Section 19-6-103, C.R.S.1973 (1978 Repl. Vol. 8). Illegitimate children have the same judicially enforceable right to support as to legitimate children. *Gomez v. Perez*, 409 U.S. 535 (1973).

I

The crux of P. D. G.'s equal protection argument is that the UPA, while gender-neutral on its face, operates to deny him equal protection by implicitly accommodating the decision of C. F. B. to carry the fetus to term while ignoring his own express desire that the pregnancy be terminated.

Gender-based distinctions must serve important governmental objectives, and a discriminatory classification must be substantially related to the achievement of those objectives in order to withstand judicial scrutiny under the equal protection clause. *Mississippi University for Women v. Hogan*, 458 U.S. 718 (1982); *R. McG. v. J. W.*, 615 P.2d 666 (Colo.1980). The General Assembly articulated the state's objective in promulgating the UPA in section 19-1-102 of the Children's Code, of which the UPA is a part. The objective includes: (1)(a) To secure for each child subject to these provisions such care and guidance, preferably in his own home, as will best serve his welfare and the interests of society;....

We recognized the importance of the state's interest in promoting the welfare of the child in *R. McG. v. J. W., supra.* In this instance, the state's objective of protecting the best interests of the child is furthered by the statutory provision for child support orders in the course of proceedings to determine the existence of a parent-child relationship. Section 19-6-116, C.R.S.1973 (1978 Repl. Vol. 8). The appellant does not dispute the significance of the state's objective.

The state has little choice in the means employed to achieve its objective. The statute's tacit accommodation of the mother's decision not to terminate her pregnancy is the only constitutional course open to the state. A woman has a fundamental right to decide in conjunction with her physician whether to terminate her pregnancy. *Roe v. Wade*, 410 U.S. 113 (1973). Further, the United States Supreme Court declared in *Maher v. Roe*, 432 U.S. 464, 472, n. 7 (1977), "A woman has at least an equal right to choose to carry the fetus to term as to choose to abort it." In *Planned Parenthood of Missouri v. Danforth*, 428 U.S. 52 (1976), the United States Supreme Court ruled that the "state cannot delegate to a spouse a veto power which the state itself is absolutely and totally prohibited from exercising during the first trimester of pregnancy." Here, the equal treatment which appellant seeks could only be achieved by according a father the right to compel the mother of his child to procure an abortion. This result is clearly foreclosed by *Roe, Maher*, and *Danforth*.

As the Supreme Court noted in *Danforth*, 428 U.S. at 71, "The obvious fact is that when the wife and the husband disagree on this decision, the view of only one of the two partners can prevail. Inasmuch as it is the woman who bears the child and who is the more directly and immediately affected by the pregnancy, as between the two, the balance weighs in her favor."

Thus, at no stage does the appellant's right to be free from gender-based classifications outweigh the substantial and legitimate competing interest. The appellant's right is overridden prior to childbirth by the state's interest in protecting C. F. B.'s fundamental right to make decisions relating to her pregnancy, and thereafter by the state's interest in ensuring that children receive adequate support. We find no violation of equal protection in the statutory obligation of both parents to pay child support or in the denial to the appellant of the right to demand the termination of C. F. B.'s pregnancy.

II

The appellant claims that section 19-6-116 violates due process by creating an irrebuttable presumption that a father should share in the duty of child support. He submits that so long as there existed an unalterable nexus between conception and childbirth, the presumption was valid, but contends that the current availability of legalized abortion creates the possibility of demonstrating that the nexus has been broken. In support of his position that he should not shoulder any of the responsibility for support of S. P. B., the appellant made an offer of proof in district court that he had promised to pay for an abortion within the first trimester of C. F. B.'s pregnancy. The appellant argues that the statute must, consistent with due process considerations, provide him an opportunity to rebut the presumption.

Statutes creating permanent irrebuttable presumptions have long been disfavored under the due process clauses of the Fifth and Fourteenth Amendments to the United States Constitution. *Vlandis v. Kline*, 412 U.S. 441 (1973). The most common remedy applied is requiring the decision maker to permit rebuttal and thus to allow exceptions to general rules. As a threshold requirement for invocation of this remedy, a case must be appropriate for review under a heightened standard of scrutiny. *Weinberger v. Salfi*, 422 U.S. 749 (1975); Tribe, American Constitutional Law § 16-32 (1978). The presence of a gender- based classification makes irrebuttable presumption analysis relevant here.

A statutory presumption can be invalidated only when a two-pronged test is met: when the presumption is not necessarily or universally true and when the state has reasonable alternative means of making the crucial determination. *Vlandis*, 412 U.S. at 452. Because the appellant's challenge to the child support statute fails to satisfy the second element of the *Vlandis* test, we need not examine the first.

The statutory presumption of a shared parental obligation of child support protects three critical interests: the interest of the child in receiving adequate support, the interest of the state in ensuring that children not become its wards, and the interest of the parents in being free from governmental intrusion into the intimate sphere of family life. In view of these critical functions, the state has no "reasonable alternative means of making the crucial determination" that a nexus exists between conception and child birth. The alternative, which the appellant propounds, is a case-by-case determination of whether the presumed nexus was broken by the father's offer to pay for an abortion, by prior agreement between the parties, by a subsequent "release" of one party's obligation by another, or by any of a multitude of legal theories which ingenious litigants and their lawyers might advance. A judicial inquiry of this nature represents unconscionable governmental interference with privacy rights which the Supreme Court has deemed inviolate. *See e.g. Carey v. Population Services International*, 431 U.S. 678 (1977); *Eisenstadt v. Baird*, 405 U.S. 438 (1972); *Griswold v. Connecticut*, 381 U.S. 479 (1965).

There are additional untoward consequences which lurk behind the establishment of a rule of law that fathers could avoid the obligation to support their children in the manner suggested by appellant. Once the criteria for proving a firm offer of an abortion had been enunciated, any man could forever escape this duty simply by making the offer in the prescribed manner. Taking this theory to its logical extreme, a woman could similarly avoid her obligation of support by proving that she had made a firm offer to procure an abortion and that the father, by declining it, assumed all responsibility for their child. The statutory presumption that parents who have participated in the conception of a child assume a joint responsibility for that child reflects the well-considered judgment of the legislature as to the only feasible means of achieving legitimate societal goals. The presumption embodied in section 19-6-116 furthers the substantial interests which the state has in protecting the respective rights of children, of parents, and of itself. Therefore, we conclude that the presumption contained in section 19-6-116 does not deny due process to the appellant.

Further, we note that our decision accords with those of the three other appellate courts which have reached this issue, although each followed a somewhat different path to the same result. The Texas Court of Appeals held that the decision whether to bear children is a fundamental liberty, and that a woman's exercise of that liberty does not break the nexus between conception and child birth so as to deny equal protection or due process to the father. *D. W. L. v. M. J. B. C.*, 601 S.W.2d 475 (Tex.Civ.App.1980). Basing its decision on state law, the Alabama Supreme Court held in *Harris v. State*, 356 So.2d 623 (Ala.Sup.Ct.1978) that an unmarried father could no more escape his legal obligation to his child because its mother had refused to obtain an abortion than could his married counterpart. The Maryland Court of Appeals upheld the constitutionality of Maryland's paternity statute in *Dorsey v. English*, 283 Md. 522, 390 A.2d 1133 (1978). The father argued, as does the appellant in this case, that the mother's independent decision to bring the fetus to full term so attenuated his role in the birth of the child that the statute imposing support obligations on both treated him unequally. The court concluded that the statute treated the parties equally and rejected the father's contentions.

We have examined the appellant's other arguments and find them without merit.

Finally, we hold, based on our review of the record, that the trial court did not abuse its discretion in ordering appellant to pay one-half the birth expenses of S. P. B. and $150 per month in child support.

Judgment affirmed.

LEE, J., does not participate.

b. Notes and Questions

1) *S.P.B.*, Gender Equality, Abortion and Child Support

Some putative fathers also have employed the claim or defense of fraud and misrepresentation in paternity proceedings to avoid their duty to pay support or to recover from the mother damages for the amount of the support awarded. The putative father argues that the mother lied to him regarding her ability to conceive or her use of contraceptives. Thus, the putative father could not have agreed to become a father and should not be made to pay support or should be allowed to recover damages because his right to procreative choice or his right to privacy has been violated. Courts unanimously have held that such claims or defenses are against public policy. McCulley, *infra* (citing numerous cases); Evans, *infra*. Is this fair? Is this equal? Is it good public policy? Why/why not? *See generally and contrast* Evans, *infra;* McCulley, *infra*; Sharrin, *infra*; and Heister, *infra*.

The Alabama Supreme Court also rejected an equal protection claim against the paternity obligation of a man who had offered to pay for an(other) abortion for his pregnant girlfriend when she declined and later sued him for child support.

Harris contends that Alabama's paternity determination proceeding statutes deny the father of an illegitimate child equal protection of the laws. In short, Harris says that because Mary did not consent to have an abortion when he requested her to do so, coupled with the fact that he agreed to pay for the abortion, he has been denied any decision as to the birth of the child; therefore, he is not liable for the child's maintenance, care and education.

*** [The Court reviews the holding in *Planned Parenthood v. Danforth* that the State cannot give a husband a "veto" over his wife's decision to have an abortion.]

We hold that the decision not to have an abortion was that of Mary Moore, and hers alone, and by not having one at the request of Harris, Harris cannot now shirk his obligations to the child as required by the statute. We find no constitutional infirmities in the paternity determination proceedings statutes.

Harris v. State, 356 So.2d 623, 624 (Ala. 1978). Is this analysis persuasive? Does it even address the critical issue(s)? How should the courts rule in such cases, and why? Is intent (to become a parent) relevant for child support obligations? Should it be? Is assumption of the risk the critical principle? Since the law now lets mothers eliminate the obligation (child) should the law provide fathers with an "equal way out?"

3. Practical and Ethical Considerations

a. Residential Stepparents

It is most likely that a residential stepparent, whether he or she intends it or not, contributes directly or indirectly to the support of minor stepchildren even without being *in loco parentis* with the stepchild. Would it be good public policy in cases where there are residential stepparents that when child support is ordered that the income of the stepparent also be considered?

4. Bibliography

William Blackstone, Commentaries on the Laws of England.

Jill E. Evans, *In Search of Paternal Equality: A Father's Right to Pursue a Claim of Paternal Misrepresentation*, 36 Loy. U. Chi. L.J. 1045 (2005).

Erika M. Heister, Note, *Child Support Statutes and the Father's Right Not to Procreate*, 2 Ave Maria L. Rev. 213 (2004).

Melanie G. McCulley, *The Male Abortion: The Putative Father's Right to Terminate His Interests in and Obligations to the Unborn Child*, 7 J.L. & Pol'y 1, 23 (1998.

Andrea M. Sharrin, Note, *Potential Fathers and Abortion: A Woman's Womb is Not a Man's Castle*, 55 Brook. L. Rev. 1359 (1990).

Contemporary Family Law, vol. 2, Ch. 12 (1988).

D. PROPERTY OWNERSHIP - THE UTMA / THE UGMA

1. Background

a. Property Ownership by Minors at Common Law

In matters of property, the incapacity of minority has not created exceptional controversy. Minors may own personal and real property, but they cannot effectively manage property. As minors, they have the right to disaffirm their own contracts, deeds, etc. Thus, parents (or some other adult) are the natural guardians or conservators of the property of their minor children, who "come into their own" property rights upon reaching the arbitrary but "bright line" age of majority (now 18 for most purposes in most states, but 21 for some purposes and under the Uniform Transfers to Minors Act). Blackstone wrote:

> Of the several species of guardians, the first are guardians *by nature:* viz., the father and (in some cases) the mother of the child. For if an estate be left to an infant, the father is by common law the guardian, and must account to his child for the profits. And, with regard to daughters, it seems by construction of the statute 4 & 5 Ph. & Mar., c. 8 (Abduction, 1558), that the father might by deed or will assign a guardianship to any woman child under the age of sixteen; and, if none be so assigned, the mother shall in this case the guardian. There are also guardians *for nurture*; which are, of course, the father or mother, till the infant attains the age of fourteen years: and in default of father or mother, the ordinary usually assigns some discrete person to take care of the infant's personal estate, and to provide for his maintenance and education.
> ***
> [T]he guardian, when the ward comes of age, is bound to give him an account of all that has been transacted on his behalf, and must answer for all losses by his willful default or negligence. In order, therefore, to prevent disagreeable contests with young gentlemen, it has become a practice for many guardians, of large estates especially, to indemnify themselves by applying to the court of chancery, acting under its direction, and accounting annually before the officers of that court. For the lord chancellor is, by right derived from the crown, the general and supreme guardians of all infants, as well as idiots and lunatics; that is, of all such persons as have not discretion enough to manage their own concerns. In case, therefore, any guardian abuses his trust, the court will check him and punish him; nay, sometimes will proceed to the removal of him and appoint another in his stead.

William Blackstone, Commentaries on the Laws of England *461- *464.

However, at common law, the father's control of the property of his children was a trust, and his children also owed him a reciprocal duty, as Blackstone explained: " A father has no other power over his son's estate, than as his trustee or guardian; for, though he may receive the profits during minority, yet he must account for them when he comes of age. He may indeed have the benefit of his children's labor while they live with him, and are maintained by him; but this is no more than he is entitled to from his apprentices or servants." Blackstone, *infra*, at *453.

2. Statutes, Cases and Doctrines

a. The Uniform Transfers to Minors Act and The Uniform Gifts to Minors Act

The Uniform Transfers to Minors Act (UTMA) was adopted by the National Conference of Commissioners on Uniform State Laws in 1983 to replace the Uniform

Gifts to Minors Act (UGMA) (which had been adopted in 1956 and revised in 1966). As of 2004, 48 states plus the District of Columbia had adopted the UTMA.

The UTMA uses the term "transfers" rather than gifts because, unlike the earlier versions, it applies not just to gifts but also to judgments and other property transferred to the minor. It also encompasses all types of property.

The key provisions of the UTMA provide that minority continues to age twenty-one for purposes of the Act (UTMA 1, 21), regardless of age of majority otherwise, that during minority all types of property may be transferred to and held by an adult (or trust company) as "custodian" for a minor (1), that a conveyance "to X [adult or trust company] as custodian for Y [the minor] under the Uniform Transfers to Minor Act" is generally sufficient to create a valid transfer to a minor and bring it under the UTMA (4-10), that the transfer irrevocably vests ownership of the property in the minor, but gives the custodian "all rights, powers, and duties" of a custodian (12), that the custodian, therefore, is not a trustee (because title is in the minor not custodian) but the custodian has all control over the property for the minor (13); the custodian may let the minor have the use of such property as he deems appropriate, but providing some to the minor is not in lieu of and does not satisfy a child support obligation (15); third persons may assert claims against the property by suing the custodian in his custodial capacity, so the minority bar or rescission rule does not apply (18); the custodian is not personally liable for the liability of the estate unless he failed to reveal he was acting as custodian (in contract) or would otherwise be personally liable (18); and the minor is not personally liable for claims against the estate arising before age 21 unless he otherwise would be personally liable (18).

b. *Sutliff v. Sutliff*

Carlene S. Sutliff v. Gregory L. Sutliff
528 A.2d 1318 (Pa. 1987)

HUTCHINSON, JUSTICE.
***

The father and his parents gave substantial assets to the children under the UGMA. The children's aggregate accounts contained cash, stocks and bonds worth over $466,000. These assets were divided equally among the children. Father is the custodian of those assets given by his parents; Fred K. Collins, the father's business associate, is custodian of those assets given by the father.

*** An interim support order providing $400 per week exclusively for the support of the minor children was entered against the father. Collins and he used the UGMA funds to fulfill up to 75% of the support obligation.
***

The [trial] court held that the custodians could use the children's UGMA funds to fulfill the father's support obligations to the children [relying on the statutory language of UMGA]

§5305 (b) The custodian shall pay over to the minor for expenditure by him or expend for the minor's benefit so much of all the custodial property as the custodian deems advisable for the support, maintenance, education and benefit of the minor, in the manner, at the time or times, and to the extent that the custodian, in his discretion, deems suitable and proper, with or without court order, with or without regard to the duty of himself or of any other person to support the minor, or his ability to do so, and with or without regard to any other income or property or the minor, which may be applicable or available for any such purpose.

***

Both parties appeal.

....Indeed parents have a duty to support their minor children even if it causes them some hardship.***

The purpose of the UGMA is to provide an inexpensive, easy mechanism for giving property to minors. Before the passage of the UGMA, a trust or guardianship was required. These methods were unwieldy, raised federal tax problems and were often prohibitively expensive for all but large gifts. The UGMA seeks to solve the problem of administrative expense and complexity while preserving certain federal tax benefits for the donor. Property transferred under the UGMA is owned by the donee-minor; the minor is vested with full and indefeasible title. A custodian holds, manages, invests and dispenses the property during the child's minority, but must deliver the property and proceeds, plus accumulated interest and profit, to the minor when he reaches the age of [majority]. Unlike a trust for support or education, the proceeds of which must be used for the stated purpose, the UGMA property and proceeds may generally be used by custodians for the child's support. It is, however, the custodian's duty to use the property for the child's benefit. We have stated that a custodian may not use UMGA property to benefit himself, and suggested that a custodian may not use it to fulfill an existing support obligation.

The minor-custodian relationship under UGMA involves at a minimum the fiduciary obligation of an agent. The custodian is expected to use the property for the minor's benefit and act in the minor's interest. An agency relationship is a fiduciary one, and the agent is subject to a duty of loyalty to act only for the principal's benefit. A custodian under UGMA should be held to a no less rigorous standard. Indeed, a custodian's duties may be more properly analogous to those of a trustee with the broadest possible discretionary powers. A trustee owes a fiduciary duty to the beneficiary. He violates that duty when he has a personal interest in trust dealings that might affect his judgment.

Were we to permit unrestrained credit against child support for these custodians' distributions, the father's action as custodian would be self-serving and Collin's would benefit the father, not the children. When he can "reasonably" do so, the father is obliged to provide support for his minor children regardless of the UGMA property. ***If however, the parent's assets are not adequate, the court should state, on the record, both the children's total needs and the parent's reasonable contribution. [The trial court's] failure to separate the issue of father's reasonable obligation from the children's needs has led to much of the confusion in this case.

On the record, it is plain that father and his business associate exercised their powers as custodians of the children's UGMA property to fulfill some part of the father's support obligation out of the children's assets. To the extent that this expenditure of the children's assets relieved the father from his "reasonable" support obligation, it is, we believe, a breach of loyalty by the father, discussed *supra*, and brings into question Collin's good faith in exercising his custodial discretion. We also believe that these facts present a conflict of interest which would require the custodians' removal. A support order must state the amount for which the father is personally responsible and must pay from his own funds.

Even if a parent lacks the resources to fully provide for his children's needs, no court should grant him or her the unbridled right to pay as much of the children's support from UGMA funds as he or she sees fit. This would be akin to removing the parent's support obligation to the extent the children have assets and is contrary to law. Child support is a parent's personal obligation and must be paid by him.

Under this analysis, UGMA property, like other assets, can be used for the children's needs if the father could not or would not fulfill his support obligation. The parent's obligation remains paramount.

Although a parent has an absolute duty to support his or her minor children, this support obligation does not always extend to financing a college education***

A parent-custodian who uses custodial funds to satisfy his own support obligation violates his duty of loyalty and hereafter is subject to surcharge and removal for such violation. It seems to us, however, that automatic removal and surcharge for past acts of the custodians which violate this fiduciary duty of loyalty are inappropriate because it has not heretofore been considered in the context of UGMA. Any custodian, however, who uses UGMA funds to satisfy a parent's support obligation is subject to surcharge and removal if his acts were in bad faith.

In this case, the question of bad faith was not considered by the lower courts. For this reason, the record is inadequate for a decision on the issue. ***

c. Notes and Questions

1) *Sutliff* note

The *Sutliff* rule has been widely cited by tax and trust attorneys, and many courts. *See Ricco v. Novitski*, 874 A.2d 75 (Pa. Super. 2005) (under *Sutliff* father cannot avoid child support even though Special Needs Disability Trust established in settlement of malpractice claim for severely disabled child will provide ample funds for child).

2) Children's Earnings

At common law, the child's earnings belonged to the parents. Many states continue to follow the common law rule.

3) Tax

The Internal Revenue Code allows certain deductions and credits for parents in preparation of their federal income. *See* chapter 37 for the treatment of these deductions and credits for parents who are separated or divorced.

It is estimated that 1.2 million children in the United States are being raised by approximately the same number of their grandparents; 40 percent of those arrangements last for five or more years. This may increase testamentary disposition and inter vivos gifts to the grandchildren. Gifts under the UTMA may be the simplest way for grandparents to provide financial security for their grandchildren. Knaplund, *infra*, at 2-3. As of January 1, 2006, the limit on donor gift-giving to any individual without incurring gift tax rose to $12,000 per year per donee; couples may combine their exclusions to give a joint $24,000 gift to an individual. Thus, each parent or grandparent may give up to $12,000 to each of their children or grandchildren per year; use of the UTMA is recommended. Special tax considerations (*e.g.*, tax rate for donee depending on age) may apply. Berek, *infra*, at 94.

3. Practical and Ethical Considerations

a. *Sutliff v. Sutliff*

In *Sutliff*, the court found there was a conflict of interest regarding both custodians. Why was there a conflict of interest regarding Fred K. Collins? What was the conflict?

4. Bibliography

Thomas E. Allison, *The Uniform Transfers to Minors Act -- New and Improved, But Shortcomings Still Exist*, 10 U. Ark. Little Rock L. J. 339 (1987/1988).

David A. Berek, *Higher Exclusion Limit Opens New Opportunities for Gifts to Minors*, 94 Ill. B.J. 94 (Feb. 2006).

William Blackstone, Commentaries on the Laws of England *449.

LexisNexis, The Economic Growth and Tax Relief Reconciliation Act of 2001: An Analysis.

Kristine S. Knaplund, *Grandparents Raising Grandchildren and the Implications for Inheritance*, 48 Ariz. L. Rev. 1 (2006)

CHAPTER 21

Non-Economic Relations Between Parent and Child: Childrearing in General

A. NON-ECONOMIC RELATIONS BETWEEN PARENT AND CHILD IN GENERAL

1. Background

a. Non-economic rights and duties of parents at common law

Blackstone identified three principal duties of parents to their children: "their maintenance, their protection, and their education." William Blackstone, Commentaries on the Laws of England *447. The maintenance duty (support) is discussed in Chapter 20, *supra*.

The parental duty to protect children at common law was "permitted" and the law worked more as "a check than a spur," according to Blackstone. William Blackstone, Commentaries on the Laws of England *450. It justified a parent's suit on behalf of children as well as a parent's "assault and battery in defense of the persons of his children . . . ." *Id.*

> The last duty of parents to their children is that of giving them an *education* suitable to their station in life: a duty pointed out by reason, and of far the greatest importance of any. *** Our laws, though their defects in this particular cannot be denied, have in one instance made a wise provision for breeding up the rising generation: since the poor and laborious part of the community, when past the age of nurture, are taken out of the hands of their parents, by the public in such a manner, as may render their abilities, in their several stations, of the greatest advantage to the commonwealth. The rich, indeed, are left to their own option, whether they will breed up their children to be ornaments or disgraces to their family. Yet in one case, that of religion, they are under peculiar restrictions: for it is provided, that if any person sends any child under his government beyond the seas, either to prevent its good education in England, or in order to enter into or reside in any popish college, or to be instructed, persuaded, strengthened in the popish religion; in such case, besides the disabilities incurred by the child so sent, the parent or person sending shall forfeit 100*l.*, which shall go to the sole use and benefit of him that shall discover the offense. And if any parent, or other, shall send or convey any person beyond sea, to enter into, or be resident in, or trained up in, any priority, abbey, nunnery, popish university, college, or school, or house of jesuits, or priests, or in any private popish family, in order to be instructed, persuaded, confirmed in the popish religion; or shall contribute anything towards their maintenance when abroad by any pretext whatever, the person both sending and sent shall be disabled to sue in law or equity, or to be executor or administrator to any person, or to enjoy any legacy or deed of gift, or to bear any office in the realm, and shall forfeit all his goods and chattels, and likewise all his real estate for life.

The *power* of parents over their children is derived from . . . their duty: this authority being given them, partly to enable the parent more effectually to perform his duty, and partly as a recompense for his care and trouble in the faithful discharge of it. *****

The power of a parent by our English laws is much more moderate [than under Roman law]; but still sufficient to keep the child in order and obedience. He may lawfully correct his child, being under age, in a reasonable manner; for this is for the benefit of his education. The consent or concurrence of the parent to the marriage of his child under age, was also *directed* by our ancient law to be obtained: but now it is absolutely *necessary*; for without it the contract is void. And this also is another means, which the law has put into the parent's hands, in order to better to discharge his duty; first, of protecting his children from the snared of artful and designing persons; and, next, of settling them properly in life, by preventing the ill consequences of too early and precipitate marriages. ***** The legal power of a father (for a mother, as such, is entitled to no power, put only to reverence and respect), ***** over the persons of his children ceases at the age of twenty-one: for they are then enfranchised by arriving at years of discretion *****. Yet, till that age arrives, this empire of the father continues even after his death; for he may by his will appoint a guardian to his children. He may also delegate part of his parental authority, during his life, to the tutor or schoolmaster, of his child; who is then *in loco parentis* (in the place of a parent), and has such a portion of the power of the parent committed to his charge, viz., that of restraint and correction, as may be necessary to answer the purposes for which he is employed.

William Blackstone, Commentaries on the Laws of England *452-453.

b. Non-economic rights and duties of children at common law

Children also had legal duties in the parent-child relationship at common law.

The *duties* of children to their parents arise from a principle of natural justice and retribution. For to those, who gave us existence, we naturally owe subjection and obedience during our minority, and honor and reverence ever after: they, who protected the weakness of our infancy, are entitled to our protection in the infirmity of their age; they who by sustenance and education have enabled their offspring to prosper, ought in return to be supported by that offspring, in case they stand in need of assistance. Upon this principle proceed all the duties of children to their parents which are enjoined by positive laws. *****

William Blackstone, Commentaries on the Laws of England *453

c. Dwindling Parental Rights

Generally, parents are deemed the lawful guardians of their children and are entitled to control, train, direct, and speak for their children. This guardianship relationship is grounded in the reality that children are born completely incompetent and dependent, and mature in a slow process over the course of many years. Historically, the law has taken a "bright line" approach to determining competency - adopting a fixed age at which the law confers competency and before which the law denies the competency of minor. But in recent years there has been no little controversy about this as minors, and organizations, anxious for minors to become liberated from the restraint of their parents, have urged that minors enjoy certain personal rights which they may exercise without parental permission, and even against outright parental opposition. In the past four decades "children's rights" have achieved unprecedented recognition, particularly in the courts. As the renown British jurist, Lord Denning, observed in a case nearly 40 years ago, a parent's right is "a dwindling right which the courts will hesitate to enforce against the wishes of the child, the older he is." *Hewer v. Bryant*, [1969] 3 All E.R. 578. Parental authority, he noted, "starts with a right of control and ends with little more than [a right to give] advice." *Id.*

2. Statutes, Cases and Doctrines.

a. Review *Meyer v. Nebraska*, 262 U.S. 390 (1923), in Chapter 2.D.2, *infra.*

b. *Pierce v. Society of the Sisters*
Pierce v. Society of Sisters
268 U.S. 510 (1925)
Mr. JUSTICE McREYNOLDS delivered the opinion of the Court.

These appeals are from decrees, based upon undenied allegations, which granted preliminary orders restraining appellants from threatening or attempting to enforce the Compulsory Education Act adopted November 7, 1922 (Laws Or. 1923, p. 9), under the initiative provision of her Constitution by the voters of Oregon. Judicial Code, § 266 (Comp. St. § 1243). They present the same points of law; there are no controverted questions of fact. Rights said to be guaranteed by the federal Constitution were specially set up, and appropriate prayers asked for their protection.

The challenged act, effective September 1, 1926, requires every parent, guardian, or other person having control or charge or custody of a child between 8 and 16 years to send him 'to a public school for the period of time a public school shall be held during the current year' in the district where the child resides; and failure so to do is declared a misdemeanor. There are exemptions--not specially important here--for children who are not normal, or who have completed the eighth grade, or whose parents or private teachers reside at considerable distances from any public school, or who hold special permits from the county superintendent. The manifest purpose is to compel general attendance at public schools by normal children, between 8 and 16, who have not completed the eighth grade. And without doubt enforcement of the statute would seriously impair, perhaps destroy, the profitable features of appellees' business and greatly diminish the value of their property.

Appellee the Society of Sisters is an Oregon corporation, organized in 1880, with power to care for orphans, educate and instruct the youth, establish and maintain academies or schools, and acquire necessary real and personal property. It has long devoted its property and effort to the secular and religious education and care of children, and has acquired the valuable good will of many parents and guardians. It conducts interdependent primary and high schools and junior colleges, and maintains orphanages for the custody and control of children between 8 and 16. In its primary schools many children between those ages are taught the subjects usually pursued in Oregon public schools during the first eight years. Systematic religious instruction and moral training according to the tenets of the Roman Catholic Church are also regularly provided. Il courses of study, both temporal and religious, contemplate continuity of training under appellee's charge; the primary schools are essential to the system and the most profitable. It owns valuable buildings, especially constructed and equipped for school purposes. The business is remunerative--

the annual income from primary schools exceeds $30,000--and the successful conduct of this requires long time contracts with teachers and parents. The Compulsory Education Act of 1922 has already caused the withdrawal from its schools of children who would otherwise continue, and their income has steadily declined. The appellants, public officers, have proclaimed their purpose strictly to enforce the statute.

After setting out the above facts, the Society's bill alleges that the enactment conflicts with the right of parents to choose schools where their children will receive appropriate mental and religious training, the right of the child to influence the parents' choice of a school, the right of schools and teachers therein to engage in a useful business or profession, and is accordingly repugnant to the Constitution and void. And, further, that unless enforcement of the measure is enjoined the corporation's business and property will suffer irreparable injury.

Appellee Hill Military Academy is a private corporation organized in 1908 under the laws of Oregon, engaged in owning, operating, and conducting for profit an elementary, college preparatory, and military training school for boys between the ages of 5 and 21 years. The average attendance is 100, and the annual fees received for each student amount to some $800. The elementary department is divided into eight grades, as in the public schools; the college preparatory department has four grades, similar to those of the public high schools; the courses of study conform to the requirements of the state board of education. Military instruction and training are also given, under the supervision of an army officer. It owns considerable real and personal property, some useful only for school purposes. The business and incident good will are very valuable. In order to conduct its affairs, long time contracts must be made for supplies, equipment, teachers, and pupils. Appellants, law officers of the state and county, have publicly announced that the Act of November 7, 1922, is valid and have declared their intention to enforce it. By reason of the statute and threat of enforcement appellee's business is being destroyed and its property depreciated; parents and guardians are refusing to make contracts for the future instruction of their sons, and some are being withdrawn.

The Academy's bill states the foregoing facts and then alleges that the challenged act contravenes the corporation's rights guaranteed by the Fourteenth Amendment and that unless appellants are restrained from proclaiming its validity and threatening to enforce it irreparable injury will result. The prayer is for an appropriate injunction.

[On motions for preliminary injunctions, a three-judge federal court] ruled that the Fourteenth Amendment guaranteed appellees against the deprivation of their property without due process of law consequent upon the unlawful interference by appellants with the free choice of patrons, present and prospective. It declared the right to conduct schools was property and that parents and guardians, as a part of their liberty, might direct the education of children by selecting reputable teachers and places. Also, that appellees' schools were not unfit or harmful to the public, and that enforcement of the challenged statute would unlawfully deprive them of patronage and thereby destroy appellees' business and property. Finally, that the threats to enforce the act would continue to cause irreparable injury; and the suits were not premature.

No question is raised concerning the power of the state reasonably to regulate all schools, to inspect, supervise and examine them, their teachers and pupils; to require that all children of proper age attend some school, that teachers shall be of good moral character and patriotic disposition, that certain studies plainly essential to good citizenship must be taught, and that nothing be taught which is manifestly inimical to the public welfare.

The inevitable practical result of enforcing the act under consideration would be destruction of appellees' primary schools, and perhaps all other private primary schools for normal children within the state of Oregon. Appellees are engaged in a kind of undertaking not inherently harmful, but long regarded as useful and meritorious. Certainly there is nothing in the present records to indicate that they have failed to discharge their obligations to patrons, students, or the state. And there are no peculiar circumstances or present emergencies which demand extraordinary measures relative to primary education.

Under the doctrine of *Meyer v. Nebraska*, 262 U. S. 390, we think it entirely plain that the Act of 1922 unreasonably interferes with the liberty of parents and guardians to direct the upbringing and education of children under their control. As often heretofore pointed out, rights guaranteed by the Constitution may not be abridged by legislation which has no reasonable relation to some purpose within the competency of the state. The fundamental theory of liberty upon which all governments in this Union repose excludes any general power of the state to standardize its children by forcing them to accept instruction from public teachers only. The child is not the mere creature of the state; those who nurture him and direct his destiny have the right, coupled with the high duty, to recognize and prepare him for additional obligations.

Appellees are corporations, and therefore, it is said, they cannot claim for themselves the liberty which the Fourteenth Amendment guarantees. Accepted in the proper sense, this is true. * But they have business and property for which they claim protection. These are threatened with destruction through the unwarranted compulsion which appellants are exercising over present and prospective patrons of their schools. And this court has gone very far to protect against loss threatened by such action. *

The courts of the state have not construed the act, and we must determine its meaning for ourselves. Evidently it was expected to have general application. ***

Generally, it is entirely true, as urged by counsel, that no person in any business has such an interest in possible customers as to enable him to restrain exercise of proper power of the state upon the ground that he will be deprived of patronage. But the injunctions here sought are not against the exercise of any proper power. Appellees asked protection against arbitrary, unreasonable, and unlawful interference with their patrons and the consequent destruction of their business and property. Their interest is clear and immediate, within the rule approved in *Truax v. Raich*, *Truax v. Corrigan*, and *Terrace v. Thompson*, *supra*, and many other cases where injunctions have issued to protect business enterprises against interference with the freedom of patrons or customers. [Case citations omitted.].

The suits were not premature. The injury to appellees was present and very real, not a mere possibility in the remote future. If no relief had been possible prior to the effective date of the act, the injury would have become irreparable. Prevention of impending injury by unlawful action is a well- recognized function of courts of equity.

The decrees below are affirmed.

c. *Prince v. Massachusetts*

Prince v. Commonwealth of Massachusetts
321 U.S. 158 (1944)

Mr. JUSTICE RUTLEDGE delivered the opinion of the Court.

The case brings for review another episode in the conflict between Jehovah's Witnesses and state authority. This time Sarah Prince appeals from convictions for violating Massachusetts' child labor laws, by acts said to be a rightful exercise of her religious convictions.

When the offenses were committed she was the aunt and custodian of Betty M. Simmons, a girl nine years of age. Originally there were three separate complaints. They were, shortly, for (1) refusal to disclose Betty's identity and age to a public officer whose duty was to enforce the statutes; (2) furnishing her with magazines, knowing she was to sell them unlawfully, that is, on the street; and (3) as Betty's custodian, permitting her to work contrary to law. The complaints were made, respectively, pursuant to Sections 79, 80 and 81 of Chapter 149, Gen.Laws of Mass. (Ter.Ed.). The Supreme Judicial Court reversed the conviction under the first complaint on state grounds; but sustained the judgments founded on the other two. 313 Mass. 223, 46 N.E.2d 755.

They present the only questions for our decision. These are whether Sections 80 and 81, as applied, contravene the Fourteenth Amendment by denying or abridging appellant's freedom of religion and by denying to her the equal protection of the laws.

Section 80 and 81, so far as pertinent, read:

'Whoever furnishes or sells to any minor any article of any description with the knowledge that the minor intends to sell such article in violation of any provision of sections sixty-nine to seventy-three, inclusive, or after having received written notice to this effect from any officer charged with the enforcement thereof, or knowingly procures or encourages any minor to violate any provisions of said sections, shall be punished by a fine of not less than ten nor more than two hundred dollars or by imprisonment for not more than two months, or both.' (Section 80)

'Any parent, guardian or custodian having a minor under his control who compels or permits such minor to work in violation of any provision of sections sixty to seventy-four, inclusive, * * * shall for a first offence be punished by a fine of not less than two nor more than ten dollars or by imprisonment for not more than five days, or both; * * *.' (Section 81)

The story told by the evidence has become familiar. It hardly needs repeating, except to give setting to the variations introduced through the part played by a child of tender years. Mrs. Prince, living in Brockton, is the mother of two young sons. She also has legal custody of Betty Simmons who lives with them. The children too are Jehovah's Witnesses and both Mrs. Prince and Betty testified they were ordained ministers. The former was accustomed to go each week on the streets of Brockton to distribute 'Watchtower' and 'Consolation,' according to the usual plan. She had permitted the children to engage in this activity previously, and had been warned against doing so by the school attendance officer, Mr. Perkins. But, until December 18, 1941, she generally did not take them with her at night.

That evening, as Mrs. Prince was preparing to leave her home, the children asked to go. She at first refused. Childlike, they resorted to tears and, motherlike, she yielded. Arriving downtown, Mrs. Prince permitted the children 'to engage in the preaching work with her upon the sidewalks.' That is, with specific reference to Betty, she and Mrs. Prince took positions about twenty feet apart near a street intersection. Betty held up in her hand, for passersby to see, copies of 'Watch Tower' and 'Consolation.' From her shoulder hung the usual canvas magazine bag, on which was printed 'Watchtower and Consolation 5 cents per copy.' No one accepted a copy from Betty that evening and she received no money. Nor did her aunt. But on other occasions, Betty had received funds and given out copies.

Mrs. Prince and Betty remained until 8:45 p.m. A few minutes before this Mr. Perkins approached Mrs. Prince. A discussion ensued. He inquired and she refused to give Betty's name. However, she stated the child attended the Shaw School. Mr. Perkins referred to his previous warnings and said he would allow five minutes for them to get off the street. Mrs. Prince admitted she supplied Betty with the magazines and said, '(N)either you nor anybody else can stop me * * *. This child is exercising her God-given right and her constitutional right to preach the gospel, and no creature has a right to interfere with God's commands.' However, Mrs. Prince and Betty departed. She remarked as she went, 'I'm not going through this any more. We've been through it time and time again. I'm going home and put the little girl to bed.' It may be added that testimony, by Betty, her aunt and others, was offered at the trials, and was excluded, to show that Betty believed it was her religious duty to perform this work and failure would bring condemnation 'to everlasting destruction at Armageddon.'

*** The only question remaining therefore is whether, as construed and applied, the statute is valid. Upon this the court said: 'We think that freedom of the press and of religion is subject to incidental regulation to the slight degree involved in the prohibition of the selling of religious literature in streets and public places by boys under twelve and girls under eighteen and in the further statutory provisions herein considered, which have been adopted as a means of enforcing that prohibition.' *

Appellant does not stand on freedom of the press. Regarding it as secular, she concedes it may be restricted as Massachusetts has done. Hence, she rests squarely on freedom of religion under the First Amendment, applied by the Fourteenth to the states. She buttresses this foundation, however, with a claim of parental right as secured by the due process clause of the latter Amendment. Cf. *Meyer v. Nebraska*, 262 U.S. 390. These guaranties, she thinks, guard alike herself and the child in what they have done. Thus, two claimed liberties are at stake. One is the parent's, to bring up the child in the way he should go, which for appellant means to teach him the tenets and the practices of their faith. The other freedom is the child's, to observe these; and among them is 'to preach the gospel * * * by public distribution' of 'Watchtower' and 'Consolation,' in conformity with the scripture: 'A little shall lead them.'

If by this position appellant seeks for freedom of conscience a broader protection than for freedom of the mind, it may be doubted that any of the great liberties insured by the First Article can be given higher place than the others. All have preferred position in our basic scheme. *. All are interwoven there together. Differences there are, in them and in the modes appropriate for their exercise. But they have unity in the charter's prime place because they have unity in their human sources and functionings. Heart and mind are not identical. Intuitive faith and reasoned judgment are not the same. Spirit is not always thought. But in the everyday business of living, secular or otherwise, these variant aspects of personality find inseparable expression in a thousand ways. They cannot be altogether parted in law more than in life.

To make accommodation between these freedoms and an exercise of state authority always is delicate. It hardly could be more so than in such a clash as this case presents. On one side is the obviously earnest claim for freedom of conscience and religious practice. With it is allied the ' parent's claim to authority in her own household and in the rearing of her children. The parent's conflict with the state over control of the child and his training is serious enough when only secular matters are concerned. It becomes the more so when an element of religious conviction enters. Against these sacred private interests, basic in a democracy, stand the interests of society to protect the welfare of children, and the state's assertion of authority to that end, made here in a manner conceded valid if only secular things were involved. The last is no mere corporate concern of official authority. It is the interest of youth itself, and of the whole community, that children be both safeguarded from abuses and given opportunities for growth into free and independent well-developed men and citizens. Between contrary pulls of such weight, the safest and most objective recourse is to the lines already marked out, not precisely but for guides, in narrowing the no man's land where this battle has gone on.

The rights of children to exercise their religion, and of parents to give them religious training and to encourage them in the practice of religious belief, as against preponderant sentiment and assertion of state power voicing it, have had recognition here, most recently in *West Virginia State Board of Education v. Barnette*, 319 U.S. 624. Previously in *Pierce v. Society of Sisters*, *, this Court had sustained the parent's authority to provide religious with secular schooling, and the child's right to receive it, as against the state's requirement of attendance at public schools. And in *Meyer v. Nebraska*, *, children's rights to receive teaching in languages other than the nation's common tongue were guarded against the state's encroachment. It is cardinal with us that the custody, care and nurture of the child reside first in the parents, whose primary function and freedom include preparation for obligations the state can neither supply nor hinder. *Pierce v. Society of Sisters, supra.* And it is in recognition of this that these decisions have respected the private realm of family life which the state cannot enter.

But the family itself is not beyond regulation in the public interest, as against a claim of religious liberty. *Reynolds v. United States*,*; *Davis v. Beason*, *. And neither rights of religion nor rights of parenthood are beyond limitation. Acting to guard the general interest in youth's well being, the state as parens patriae may restrict the parent's control by requiring school attendance, regulating or prohibiting the child's labor, and in many other ways. Its authority is not nullified merely because the parent grounds his claim to control the child's course of conduct on religion or conscience. Thus, he cannot claim freedom from compulsory vaccination for the child more than for himself on religious grounds. The right to practice religion freely does not include liberty to expose the community or the child to communicable disease or the latter to ill health or death. * The catalogue need not be lengthened. It is sufficient to show what indeed appellant hardly disputes, that the state has a wide range of power for limiting parental freedom and authority in things affecting the child's welfare; and that this includes, to some extent, matters of conscience and religious conviction.

But it is said the state cannot do so here. This, first, because when state action impinges upon a claimed religious freedom, it must fall unless shown to be necessary for or conducive to the child's protection against some clear and present danger, cf. *Schenck v. United States*, 249 U.S. 47; and, it is added, there was no such showing here. The child's presence on the street, with her guardian, distributing or offering to distribute the magazines, it is urged, was in no way harmful to her, nor in any event more so than the presence of many other children at the same time and place, engaged in shopping and other activities not prohibited. Accordingly, in view of the preferred position the freedoms of the First Article occupy, the statute in its present application must fall. It cannot be sustained by any presumption of validity. * And, finally, it is said, the statute is, as to children, an absolute prohibition, not merely a reasonable regulation, of the denounced activity.

Concededly a statute or ordinance identical in terms with Section 69, except that it is applicable to adults or all persons generally, would be invalid. *. But the mere fact a state could not wholly prohibit this form of adult activity, whether characterized locally as a 'sale' or otherwise, does not mean it cannot do so for children. Such a conclusion granted would mean that a state could impose no greater limitation upon child labor than upon adult labor. Or, if an adult were free to enter dance halls, saloons, and disreputable places generally, in order to discharge his conceived religious duty to admonish or dissuade persons from frequenting such places, so would be a child with similar convictions and objectives, if not alone then in the parent's company, against the state's command.

The state's authority over children's activities is broader than over like actions of adults. This is peculiarly true of public activities and matters of employment. A democratic society rests, for its continuance, upon the healthy, well-rounded growth of young people into full maturity as citizens, with all that implies. It may secure this against impeding restraints and dangers, within a broad range of selection. Among evils most appropriate for such action are the crippling effects of child employment, more especially in public places, and the possible harms arising from other activities subject to all the diverse influences of the street. It is too late now to doubt that legislation appropriately designed to reach such evils is within the state's police power, whether against the parents claim to control of the child or one that religious scruples dictate contrary action.

It is true children have rights, in common with older people, in the primary use of highways. But even in such use streets afford dangers for them not affecting adults. And in other uses, whether in work or in other things, this difference may be magnified. This is so not only when children are unaccompanied but certainly to some extent when they are with their parents. What may be wholly permissible for adults therefore may not be so for children, either with or without their parents' presence.

Street preaching, whether oral or by handing out literature, is not the primary use of the highway, even for adults. While for them it cannot be wholly prohibited, it can be regulated within reasonable limits in accommodation to the primary and other incidental uses. But, for obvious reasons, notwithstanding appellant's contrary view, the validity of such a prohibition applied to children not accompanied by an older person hardly would seem open to question. The case reduces itself therefore to the question whether the presence of the child's guardian puts a limit to the state's power. That fact may lessen the likelihood that some evils the legislation seeks to avert will occur. But it cannot forestall all of them. The zealous though lawful exercise of the right to engage in propagandizing the community, whether in religious, political or other matters, may and at times does create situations difficult enough for adults to cope with and wholly inappropriate for children, especially of tender years, to face. Other harmful possibilities could be stated, of emotional excitement and psychological or physical injury. Parents may be free to become martyrs themselves. But it does not follow they are free, in identical circumstances, to make martyrs of their children before they have reached the age of full and legal discretion when they can make that choice for themselves. Massachusetts has determined that an absolute prohibition, though one limited to streets and public places and to the incidental uses proscribed, is necessary to accomplish its legitimate objectives. Its power to attain them is broad enough to reach these peripheral instances in which the parent's supervision may reduce but cannot eliminate entirely the ill effects of the prohibited conduct. We think that with reference to the public proclaiming of religion, upon the streets and in other similar public places, the power of the state to control the conduct of children reaches beyond the scope of its authority over adults, as is true in the case of other freedoms, and the rightful boundary of its power has not been crossed in this case.

In so ruling we dispose also of appellant's argument founded upon denial of equal protection. It falls with that based on denial of religious freedom, since in this instance the one is but another phrasing of the other. Shortly, the contention is that the street, for Jehovah's Witnesses and their children, is their church, since their conviction makes it so; and to deny them access to it for religious purposes as was done here has the same effect as excluding altar boys, youthful choristers, and other children from the edifices in which they practice their religious beliefs and worship. The argument hardly needs more than statement, after what has been said, to refute it. However Jehovah's Witnesses may conceive them, the public highways have not become their religious property merely by their assertion. And there is no denial of equal protection in excluding their children from doing there what no other children may do.

Our ruling does not extend beyond the facts the case presents. We neither lay the foundation 'for any (that is, every) state intervention in the indoctrination and participation of children in religion' which may be done 'in the name of their health and welfare' nor give warrant for 'every limitation on their religious training and activities.' The religious training and indoctrination of children may be accomplished in many ways, some of which, as we have noted, have received constitutional protection through decisions of this Court. These and all others except the public proclaiming of religion on the streets, if this may be taken as either training or indoctrination of the proclaimer, remain unaffected by the decision.

The judgment is affirmed.

Affirmed.

Mr. JUSTICE JACKSON.

***

It is difficult for me to believe that going upon the streets to accost the public is the same thing for application of public law as withdrawing to a private structure for religious worship. But if worship in the churches and the activity of Jehovah's Witnesses on the streets 'occupy the same high estate' and have the 'same claim to protection' it would seem that child labor laws may be applied to both if to either. If the *Murdock* doctrine stands along with today's decision, a foundation is laid for any state intervention in the indoctrination and participation of children in religion, provided it is done in the name of their health or welfare.

This case brings to the surface the real basis of disagreement among members of this Court in previous Jehovah's Witness cases. * Our basic difference seems to be as to the method of establishing limitations which of necessity bound religious freedom.

My own view may be shortly put: I think the limits begin to operate whenever activities begin to affect or collide with liberties of others or of the public. *** They raise money, not merely by passing the plate to those who voluntarily attend services or by contributions by their own people, but by solicitations and drives addressed to the public by holding public dinners and entertainments, by various kinds of sales and Bingo games and lotteries. All such money-raising activities on a public scale are, I think, Caesar's affairs and may be regulated by the state so long as it does not discriminate against one because he is doing them for a religious purpose, and the regulation is not arbitrary and capricious, in violation of other provisions of the Constitution.

*** [T]he Court now draws a line based on age that cuts across both true exercise of religion and auxiliary secular activities. I think this is not a correct principle for defining the activities immune from regulation on grounds of religion, and *Murdock* overrules the grounds on which I think affirmance should rest. I have no alternative but to dissent from the grounds of affirmance of a judgment which I think was rightly decided, and upon right grounds, by the Supreme Judicial Court of Massachusetts. *

Mr. JUSTICE ROBERTS and Mr. JUSTICE FRANKFURTER join in this opinion.

Mr. JUSTICE MURPHY, dissenting.

This attempt by the state of Massachusetts to prohibit a child from exercising her constitutional right to practice her religion on the public streets cannot, in my opinion, be sustained.
***

Religious training and activity, whether performed by adult or child, are protected by the Fourteenth Amendment against interference by state action, except insofar as they violate reasonable regulations adopted for the protection of the public health, morals and welfare. Our problem here is whether a state, under the guise of enforcing its child labor laws, can lawfully prohibit girls under the age of eighteen and boys under the age of twelve from practicing their religious faith insofar as it involves the distribution or sale of religious tracts on the public streets.
***

As the opinion of the Court demonstrates, the power of the state lawfully to control the religious and other activities of children is greater than its power over similar activities of adults. But that fact is no more decisive of the issue posed by this case than is the obvious fact that the family itself is subject to reasonable regulation in the public interest. We are concerned solely with the reasonableness of this particular prohibition of religious activity by children.
***

The state, in my opinion, has completely failed to sustain its burden of proving the existence of any grave or immediate danger to any interest which it may lawfully protect. There is no proof that Betty Simmons' mode of worship constituted a serious menace to the public. It was carried on in an orderly, lawful manner at a public street corner. And 'one who is rightfully on a street which the state has left open to the public carries with him there as elsewhere the constitutional right to express his views in an orderly fashion. This right extends to the communication of ideas by handbills and literature as well as by the spoken word.' *Jamison v. Texas*, 318 U.S. 413, 416. The sidewalk, no less than the cathedral or the evangelist's tent, is a proper place, under the Constitution, for the orderly worship of God. Such use of the streets is as necessary to the Jehovah's Witnesses, the Salvation Army and others who practice religion without benefit of conventional shelters as is the use of the streets for purposes of passage.

It is claimed, however, that such activity was likely to affect adversely the health, morals and welfare of the child. Reference is made in the majority opinion to 'the crippling effects of child employment, more especially in public places, and the possible harms arising from other activities subject to all the diverse influences of the street.' To the extent that they flow from participation in ordinary commercial activities, these harms are irrelevant to this case. And the bare possibility that such harms might emanate from distribution of religious literature is not, standing alone, sufficient justification for restricting freedom of conscience and religion. Nor can parents or guardians be subjected to criminal liability because of vague possibilities that their religious teachings might cause injury to the child. The evils must be grave, immediate, substantial. * Yet there is not the slightest indication in this record, or in sources subject to judicial notice, that children engaged in distributing literature pursuant to their religious beliefs have been or are likely to be subject to any of the harmful 'diverse influences of the street.' Indeed, if probabilities are to be indulged in, the likelihood is that children engaged in serious religious endeavor are immune from such influences. Gambling, truancy, irregular eating and sleeping habits, and the more serious vices are not consistent with the high moral character ordinarily displayed by children fulfilling religious obligations. Moreover, Jehovah's Witness children invariably make their distributions in groups subject at all times to adult or parental control, as was done in this case. The dangers are thus exceedingly remote, to say the least. And the fact that the zealous exercise of the right to propagandize the community may result in violent or disorderly situations difficult for children to face is no excuse for prohibiting the exercise of that right.

No chapter in human history has been so largely written in terms of persecution and intolerance as the one dealing with religious freedom. From ancient times to the present day, the ingenuity of man has known no limits in its ability to forge weapons of oppression for use against those who dare to express or practice unorthodox religious beliefs. And the Jehovah's Witnesses are living proof of the fact that even in this nation, conceived as it was in the ideals of freedom, the right to practice religion in unconventional ways is still far from secure. Theirs is a militant and unpopular faith, pursued with a fanatical zeal. They have suffered brutal beatings; their property has been destroyed; they have been harassed at every turn by the resurrection and enforcement of little used ordinances and statutes. *See* Mulder and Comisky, 'Jehovah's Witnesses Mold Constitutional Law,' 2 Bill of Rights Review, No. 4, p. 262. To them, along with other present-day religious minorities, befalls the burden of testing our devotion to the ideals and constitutional guarantees of religious freedom. We should therefore hesitate before approving the application of a statute that might be used as another instrument of oppression. Religious freedom is too sacred a right to be restricted or prohibited in any degree without convincing proof that a legitimate interest of the state is in grave danger.

d. *Wisconsin v. Yoder*

State of Wisconsin v. Jonas Yoder et al.
406 U.S. 205 (1972)

Mr. Chief JUSTICE BURGER delivered the opinion of the Court.

On petition of the State of Wisconsin, we granted the writ of certiorari in this case to review a decision of the Wisconsin Supreme Court holding that respondents' convictions for violating the State's compulsory school-attendance law were invalid under the Free Exercise Clause of the First Amendment to the United States Constitution made applicable to the States by the Fourteenth Amendment. For the reasons hereafter stated we affirm the judgment of the Supreme Court of Wisconsin.

Respondents Jonas Yoder and Wallace Miller are members of the Old Order Amish religion, and respondent Adin Yutzy is a member of the Conservative Amish Mennonite Church. They and their families are residents of Green County, Wisconsin. Wisconsin's compulsory school-attendance law required them to cause their children to attend public or private school until reaching age 16 but the respondents declined to send their children, ages 14 and 15, to public school after they complete the eighth grade. *[Fn1. The children, Frieda Yoder, aged 15, Barbara Miller, aged 15, and Vernon Yutzy, aged 14, were all graduates of the eighth grade of public school.]* The children were not enrolled in any private school, or within any recognized exception to the compulsory- attendance law, and they are conceded to be subject to the Wisconsin statute.

On complaint of the school district administrator for the public schools, respondents were charged, tried, and convicted of violating the compulsory-attendance law in Green County Court and were fined the sum of $5 each. Respondents defended on the ground that the application of the compulsory-attendance law violated their rights under the First and Fourteenth Amendments. The trial testimony showed that respondents believed, in accordance with the tenets of Old Order Amish communities generally, that their children's attendance at high school, public or private, was contrary to the Amish religion and way of life. They believed that by sending their children to high school, they would not only expose themselves to the danger of the censure of the church community, but, as found by the county court, also endanger their own salvation and that of their children. The State stipulated that respondents' religious beliefs were sincere.

In support of their position, respondents presented as expert witnesses scholars on religion and education whose testimony is uncontradicted. They expressed their opinions on the relationship of the Amish belief concerning school attendance to the more general tenets of their religion, and described the impact that compulsory high school attendance could have on the continued survival of Amish communities as they exist in the United States today. The history of the Amish sect was given in some detail, beginning with the Swiss Anabaptists of the 16th century who rejected institutionalized churches and sought to return to the early, simple, Christian life de-emphasizing material success, rejecting the competitive spirit, and seeking to insulate themselves from the modern world. As a result of their common heritage, Old Order Amish communities today are characterized by a fundamental belief that salvation requires life in a church community separate and apart from the world and worldly influence. This concept of life aloof from the world and its values is central to their faith.

A related feature of Old Order Amish communities is their devotion to a life in harmony with nature and the soil, as exemplified by the simple life of the early Christian era that continued in America during much of our early national life. Amish beliefs require members of the community to make their living by farming or closely related activities. Broadly speaking, the Old Order Amish religion pervades and determines the entire mode of life of its adherents. Their conduct is regulated in great detail by the Ordnung, or rules, of the church community. Adult baptism, which occurs in late adolescence, is the time at which Amish young people voluntarily undertake heavy obligations, not unlike the Bar Mitzvah of the Jews, to abide by the rules of the church community.

Amish objection to formal education beyond the eighth grade is firmly grounded in these central religious concepts. They object to the high school, and higher education generally, because the values they teach are in marked variance with Amish values and the Amish way of life; they view secondary school education as an impermissible exposure of their children to a 'worldly' influence in conflict with their beliefs. The high school tends to emphasize intellectual and scientific accomplishments, self-distinction, competitiveness, worldly success, and social life with other students. Amish society emphasizes informal learning-through-doing; a life of 'goodness,' rather than a life of intellect; wisdom, rather than technical knowledge, community welfare, rather than competition; and separation from, rather than integration with, contemporary worldly society.

Formal high school education beyond the eighth grade is contrary to Amish beliefs, not only because it places Amish children in an environment hostile to Amish beliefs with increasing emphasis on competition in class work and sports and with pressure to conform to the styles, manners, and ways of the peer group, but also because it takes them away from their community, physically and emotionally, during the crucial and formative adolescent period of life. During this period, the children must acquire Amish attitudes favoring manual work and self-reliance and the specific skills needed to perform the adult role of an Amish farmer or housewife. They must learn to enjoy physical labor. Once a child has learned basic reading, writing, and elementary mathematics, these traits, skills, and attitudes admittedly fall within the category of those best learned through example and 'doing' rather than in a classroom. And, at this time in life, the Amish child must also grow in his faith and his relationship to the Amish community if he is to be prepared to accept the heavy obligations imposed by adult baptism. In short, high school attendance with teachers who are not of the Amish faith--and may even be hostile to it-- interposes a serious barrier to the integration of the Amish child into the Amish religious community. Dr. John Hostetler, one of the experts on Amish society, testified that the modern high school is not equipped, in curriculum or social environment, to impart the values promoted by Amish society.

The Amish do not object to elementary education through the first eight grades as a general proposition because they agree that their children must have basic skills in the 'three R's' in order to read the Bible, to be good farmers and citizens, and to be able to deal with non-Amish people when necessary in the course of daily affairs. They view such a basic education as acceptable because it does not significantly expose their children to worldly values or interfere with their development in the Amish community during the crucial adolescent period. While Amish accept compulsory elementary education generally, wherever possible they have established their own elementary schools in many respects like the small local schools of the past. In the Amish belief higher learning tends to develop values they reject as influences that alienate man from God.

On the basis of such considerations, Dr. Hostetler testified that compulsory high school attendance could not only result in great psychological harm to Amish children, because of the conflicts it would produce, but would also, in his opinion, ultimately result in the destruction of the Old Order Amish church community as it exists in the United States today. The testimony of Dr. Donald A. Erickson, an expert witness on education, also showed that the Amish succeed in preparing their high school age children to be productive members of the Amish community. He described their system of learning through doing the skills directly relevant to their adult roles in the Amish community as 'ideal' and perhaps superior to ordinary high school education. The evidence also showed that the Amish have an excellent record as law- abiding and generally self-sufficient members of society.

Although the trial court in its careful findings determined that the Wisconsin compulsory school-attendance law 'does interfere with the freedom of the Defendants to act in accordance with their sincere religious belief' it also concluded that the requirement of high school attendance until age 16 was a 'reasonable and constitutional' exercise of governmental power, and therefore denied the motion to dismiss the charges. The Wisconsin Circuit Court affirmed the convictions. The Wisconsin Supreme Court, however, sustained respondents' claim under the Free Exercise Clause of the First Amendment and reversed the convictions. A majority of the court was of the opinion that the State had failed to make an adequate showing that its interest in 'establishing and maintaining an educational system overrides the defendants' right to the free exercise of their religion.' 49 Wis.2d 430, 447, 182 N.W.2d 539, 547 (1971).

I

There is no doubt as to the power of a State, having a high responsibility for education of its citizens, to impose reasonable regulations for the control and duration of basic education. *See e.g. Pierce v. Society of Sisters*, 268 U.S. 510, 534, 45 S.Ct. 571, 573, 69 L.Ed. 1070 (1925). Providing public schools ranks at the very apex of the function of a State. Yet even this paramount responsibility was, in Pierce, made to yield to the right of parents to provide an equivalent education in a privately operated system. There the Court held that Oregon's statute compelling attendance in a public school from age eight to age 16 unreasonably interfered with the interest of parents in directing the rearing of their off-spring, including their education in church-operated schools. As that case suggests, the values of parental direction of the religious upbringing and education of their children in their early and formative years have a high place in our society. *See also Ginsberg v. New York*, *(1968); *Meyer v. Nebraska*, (1923); *. Thus, a State's interest in universal education, however highly we rank it, is not totally free from a balancing process when it impinges on fundamental rights and interests, such as those specifically protected by the Free

Exercise Clause of the First Amendment, and the traditional interest of parents with respect to the religious upbringing of their children so long as they, in the words of *Pierce*, 'prepare (them) for additional obligations.' 268 U.S., at 535, 45 S.Ct., at 573.

It follows that in order for Wisconsin to compel school attendance beyond the eighth grade against a claim that such attendance interferes with the practice of a legitimate religious belief, it must appear either that the State does not deny the free exercise of religious belief by its requirement, or that there is a state interest of sufficient magnitude to override the interest claiming protection under the Free Exercise Clause. Long before there was general acknowledgment of the need for universal formal education, the Religion Clauses had specifically and firmly fixed the right to free exercise of religious beliefs, and buttressing this fundamental right was an equally firm, even if less explicit, prohibition against the establishment of any religion by government. The values underlying these two provisions relating to religion have been zealously protected, sometimes even at the expense of other interests of admittedly high social importance. The invalidation of financial aid to parochial schools by government grants for a salary subsidy for teachers is but one example of the extent to which courts have gone in this regard, notwithstanding that such aid programs were legislatively determined to be in the public interest and the service of sound educational policy by States and by Congress. *

The essence of all that has been said and written on the subject is that only those interests of the highest order and those not otherwise served can overbalance legitimate claims to the free exercise of religion. We can accept it as settled, therefore, that, however strong the State's interest in universal compulsory education, it is by no means absolute to the exclusion or subordination of all other interests. E.g., *Sherbert v. Verner*, * (1963); *McGowan v. Maryland*, * (1961) (separate opinion of Frankfurter, J.); *Prince v. Massachusetts*, * (1944).

II

We come then to the quality of the claims of the respondents concerning the alleged encroachment of Wisconsin's compulsory school-attendance statute on their rights and the rights of their children to the free exercise of the religious beliefs they and their forbears have adhered to for almost three centuries. In evaluating those claims we must be careful to determine whether the Amish religious faith and their mode of life are, as they claim, inseparable and interdependent. A way of life, however virtuous and admirable, may not be interposed as a barrier to reasonable state regulation of education if it is based on purely secular considerations; to have the protection of the Religion Clauses, the claims must be rooted in religious belief. Although a determination of what is a 'religious' belief or practice entitled to constitutional protection may present a most delicate question, the very concept of ordered liberty precludes allowing every person to make his own standards on matters of conduct in which society as a whole has important interests. Thus, if the Amish asserted their claims because of their subjective evaluation and rejection of the contemporary secular values accepted by the majority, much as Thoreau rejected the social values of his time and isolated himself at Walden Pond, their claims would not rest on a religious basis. Thoreau's choice was philosophical and personal rather than religious, and such belief does not rise to the demands of the Religion Clauses.

Giving no weight to such secular considerations, however, we see that the record in this case abundantly supports the claim that the traditional way of life of the Amish is not merely a matter of personal preference, but one of deep religious conviction, shared by an organized group, and intimately related to daily living. That the Old Order Amish daily life and religious practice stem from their faith is shown by the fact that it is in response to their literal interpretation of the Biblical injunction from the Epistle of Paul to the Romans, 'be not conformed to this world . . . .' This command is fundamental to the Amish faith. Moreover, for the Old Order Amish, religion is not simply a matter of theocratic belief. As the expert witnesses explained, the Old Order Amish religion pervades and determines virtually their entire way of life, regulating it with the detail of the

Talmudic diet through the strictly enforced rules of the church community.

The record shows that the respondents' religious beliefs and attitude toward life, family, and home have remained constant--perhaps some would say static-- in a period of unparalleled progress in human knowledge generally and great changes in education. The respondents freely concede, and indeed assert as an article of faith, that their religious beliefs and what we would today call 'life style' have not altered in fundamentals for centuries. Their way of life in a church-oriented community, separated from the outside world and 'worldly' influences, their attachment to nature and the soil, is a way inherently simple and uncomplicated, albeit difficult to preserve against the pressure to conform. Their rejection of telephones, automobiles, radios, and television, their mode of dress, of speech, their habits of manual work do indeed set them apart from much of contemporary society; these customs are both symbolic and practical.

As the society around the Amish has become more populous, urban, industrialized, and complex, particularly in this century, government regulation of human affairs has correspondingly become more detailed and pervasive. The Amish mode of life has thus come into conflict increasingly with requirements of contemporary society exerting a hydraulic insistence on conformity to majoritarian standards. So long as compulsory education laws were confined to eight grades of elementary basic education imparted in a nearby rural schoolhouse, with a large proportion of students of the Amish faith, the Old Order Amish had little basis to fear that school attendance would expose their children to the worldly influence they reject. But modern compulsory secondary education in rural areas is now largely carried on in a consolidated school, often remote from the student's home and alien to his daily home life. As the record so strongly shows, the values and programs of the modern secondary school are in sharp conflict with the fundamental mode of life mandated by the Amish religion; modern laws requiring compulsory secondary education have accordingly engendered great concern and conflict. The conclusion is inescapable that secondary schooling, by exposing Amish children to worldly influences in terms of attitudes, goals, and values contrary to beliefs, and by substantially interfering with the religious development of the Amish child and his integration into the way of life of the Amish faith community at the crucial adolescent stage of development, contravenes the basic religious tenets and practice of the Amish faith, both as to the parent and the child.

The impact of the compulsory-attendance law on respondents' practice of the Amish religion is not only severe, but inescapable, for the Wisconsin law affirmatively compels them, under threat of criminal sanction, to perform acts undeniably at odds with fundamental tenets of their religious beliefs. See *Braunfeld v. Brown*, 366 U.S. 599, 605 (1961). Nor is the impact of the compulsory-attendance law confined to grave interference with important Amish religious tenets from a subjective point of view. It carries with it precisely the kind of objective danger to the free exercise of religion that the First Amendment was designed to prevent. As the record shows, compulsory school attendance to age 16 for Amish children carries with it a very real threat of undermining the Amish community and religious practice as they exist today; they must either abandon belief and be assimilated into society at large, or be forced to migrate to some other and more tolerant region.

In sum, the unchallenged testimony of acknowledged experts in education and religious history, almost 300 years of consistent practice, and strong evidence of a sustained faith pervading and regulating respondents' entire mode of life support the claim that enforcement of the State's requirement of compulsory formal education after the eighth grade would gravely endanger if not destroy the free exercise of respondents' religious beliefs.

III

Neither the findings of the trial court nor the Amish claims as to the nature of their faith are challenged in this Court by the State of Wisconsin. Its position is that the State's interest in universal compulsory formal secondary education to age 16 is so great that it is paramount to the undisputed claims of respondents that their mode of preparing their youth for Amish life, after the traditional elementary education, is an essential part of their religious belief and practice. Nor does the State undertake to meet the claim that the Amish mode of life and education is inseparable from and a part of the basic tenets of their religion--indeed, as much a part of their religious belief and practices as baptism, the confessional, or a sabbath may be for others.

Wisconsin concedes that under the Religion Clauses religious beliefs are absolutely free from the State's control, but it argues that 'actions,' even though religiously grounded, are outside the protection of the First Amendment. But our decisions have rejected the idea that religiously grounded conduct is always outside the protection of the Free Exercise Clause. It is true that activities of individuals, even when religiously based, are often subject to regulation by the States in the exercise of their undoubted power to promote the health, safety, and general welfare, or the Federal Government in the exercise of its delegated powers. See e.g. Gillette v. United States, * (1971); Braunfeld v. Brown, * (1961); Prince v. Massachusetts, * (1944); Reynolds v. United States, * (1879). But to agree that religiously grounded conduct must often be subject to the broad police power of the State is not to deny that there are areas of conduct protected by the Free Exercise Clause of the First Amendment and thus beyond the power of the State to control, even under regulations of general applicability. *. This case, therefore, does not become easier because respondents were convicted for their 'actions' in refusing to send their children to the public high school; in this context belief and action cannot be neatly confined in logic-tight compartments. *

Nor can this case be disposed of on the grounds that Wisconsin's requirement for school attendance to age 16 applies uniformly to all citizens of the State and does not, on its face, discriminate against religions or a particular religion, or that it is motivated by legitimate secular concerns. A regulation neutral on its face may, in its application, nonetheless offend the constitutional requirement for governmental neutrality if it unduly burdens the free exercise of religion. Sherbert v. Verner, supra; cf. Walz v. Tax Commission, 397 U.S. 664, 90 S.Ct. 1409, 25 L.Ed.2d 697 (1970). The Court must not ignore the danger that an exception from a general obligation of citizenship on religious grounds may run afoul of the Establishment Clause, but that danger cannot be allowed to prevent any exception no matter how vital it may be to the protection of values promoted by the right of free exercise. By preserving doctrinal flexibility and recognizing the need for a sensible and realistic application of the Religion Clauses 'we have been able to chart a course that preserved the autonomy and freedom of religious bodies while avoiding any semblance of established religion. This is a 'tight rope' and one we have successfully traversed.' Walz v. Tax Commission, supra, at 672, 90 S.Ct., at 1413.

We turn, then, to the State's broader contention that its interest in its system of compulsory education is so compelling that even the established religious practices of the Amish must give way. Where fundamental claims of religious freedom are at stake, however, we cannot accept such a sweeping claim; despite its admitted validity in the generality of cases, we must searchingly examine the interests that the State seeks to promote by its requirement for compulsory education to age 16, and the impediment to those objectives that would flow from recognizing the claimed Amish exemption. *

The State advances two primary arguments in support of its system of compulsory education. It notes, as Thomas Jefferson pointed out early in our history, that some degree of education is necessary to prepare citizens to participate effectively and intelligently in our open political system if we are to preserve freedom and independence. Further, education prepares individuals to be self-reliant and self-sufficient participants in society. We accept these propositions.

However, the evidence adduced by the Amish in this case is persuasively to the effect that an additional one or two years of formal high school for Amish children in place of their long-established program of informal vocational education would do little to serve those interests. Respondents' experts testified at trial, without challenge, that the value of all education must be assessed in terms of its capacity to prepare the child for life. It is one thing to say that compulsory education for a year or two beyond the eighth grade may be necessary when its goal is the preparation of the child for life in modern society as the majority live, but it is quite another if the goal of education be viewed as the preparation of the child for life in the separated agrarian community that is the keystone of the Amish faith. *See Meyer v. Nebraska,**.

The State attacks respondents' position as one fostering 'ignorance' from which the child must be protected by the State. No one can question the State's duty to protect children from ignorance but this argument does not square with the facts disclosed in the record. Whatever their idiosyncrasies as seen by the majority, this record strongly shows that the Amish community has been a highly successful social unit within our society, even if apart from the conventional 'mainstream.' Its members are productive and very law-abiding members of society; they reject public welfare in any of its usual modern forms. The Congress itself recognized their self-sufficiency by authorizing exemption of such groups as the Amish from the obligation to pay social security taxes.

It is neither fair nor correct to suggests that the Amish are opposed to education beyond the eighth grade level. What this record shows is that they are opposed to conventional formal education of the type provided by a certified high school because it comes at the child's crucial adolescent period of religious development. Dr. Donald Erickson, for example, testified that their system of learning-by-doing was an 'ideal system' of education in terms of preparing Amish children for life as adults in the Amish community, and that 'I would be inclined to say they do a better job in this than most of the rest of us do.' As he put it, 'These people aren't purporting to be learned people, and it seems to me the self-sufficiency of the community is the best evidence I can point to--whatever is being done seems to function well.'

We must not forget that in the Middle Ages important values of the civilization of the Western World were preserved by members of religious orders who isolated themselves from all worldly influences against great obstacles. There can be no assumption that today's majority is 'right' and the Amish and others like them are 'wrong.' A way of life that is odd or even erratic but interferes with no rights or interests of others is not to be condemned because it is different.

The State, however, supports its interest in providing an additional one or two years of compulsory high school education to Amish children because of the possibility that some such children will choose to leave the Amish community, and that if this occurs they will be ill-equipped for life. The State argues that if Amish children leave their church they should not be in the position of making their way in the world without the education available in the one or two additional years the State requires. However, on this record, that argument is highly speculative. There is no specific evidence of the loss of Amish adherents by attrition, nor is there any showing that upon leaving the Amish community Amish children, with their practical agricultural training and habits of industry and self-reliance, would become burdens on society because of educational shortcomings.
***

There is nothing in this record to suggest that the Amish qualities of reliability, self-reliance, and dedication to work would fail to find ready markets in today's society. Absent some contrary evidence supporting the State's position, we are unwilling to assume that persons possessing such valuable vocational skills and habits are doomed to become burdens on society should they determine to leave the Amish faith, nor is there any basis in the record to warrant afinding that an additional one or two years of formal school education beyond the eighth grade would serve to eliminate any such problem that might exist.

Insofar as the State's claim rests on the view that a brief additional period of formal education is imperative to enable the Amish to participate effectively and intelligently in our democratic process, it must fall. The Amish alternative to formal secondary school education has enabled them to function effectively in their day-to-day life under self-imposed limitations on relations with the world, and to survive and prosper in contemporary society as a separate, sharply identifiable and highly self-sufficient community for more than 200 years in this country. In itself this is strong evidence that they are capable of fulfilling the social and political responsibilities of citizenship without compelled attendance beyond the eighth grade at the price of jeopardizing their free exercise of religious belief. When Thomas Jefferson emphasized the need for education as a bulwark of a free people against tyranny, there is nothing to indicate he had in mind compulsory education through any fixed age beyond a basic education. Indeed, the Amish communities singularly parallel and reflect many of the virtues of Jefferson's ideal of the 'sturdy yeoman' who would form the basis of what he considered as the ideal of a democratic society. Even their idiosyncratic separateness exemplifies the diversity we profess to admire and encourage.

The requirement for compulsory education beyond the eighth grade is a relatively recent development in our history. Less than 60 years ago, the educational requirements of almost all of the States were satisfied by completion of the elementary grades, at least where the child was regularly and lawfully employed. The independence and successful social functioning of the Amish community for a period approaching almost three centuries and more than 200 years in this country are strong evidence that there is at best a speculative gain, in terms of meeting the duties of citizenship, from an additional one or two years of compulsory formal education. Against this background it would require a more particularized showing from the State on this point to justify the severe interference with religious freedom such additional compulsory attendance would entail.
***

The requirement of compulsory schooling to age 16 must therefore be viewed as aimed not merely at providing educational opportunities for children, but as an alternative to the equally undesirable consequence of unhealthful child labor displacing adult workers, or, on the other hand, forced idleness. The two kinds of statutes--compulsory school attendance and child labor laws--tend to keep children of certain ages off the labor market and in school; this regimen in turn provides opportunity to prepare for a livelihood of a higher order than that which children could pursue without education and protects their health in adolescence.

In these terms, Wisconsin's interest in compelling the school attendance of Amish children to age 16 emerges as somewhat less substantial than requiring such attendance for children generally. For, while agricultural employment is not totally outside the legitimate concerns of the child labor laws, employment of children under parental guidance and on the family farm from age 14 to age 16 is an ancient tradition that lies at the periphery of the objectives of such laws. There is no intimation that the Amish employment of their children on family farms is in any way deleterious to their health or that Amish parents exploit children at tender years. Any such inference would be contrary to the record before us. Moreover, employment of Amish children on the family farm does not present the undesirable economic aspects of eliminating jobs that might otherwise be held by adults.

IV

Finally, the State, on authority of *Prince v. Massachusetts*, argues that a decision exempting Amish children from the State's requirement fails to recognize the substantive right of the Amish child to a secondary education, and fails to give due regard to the power of the State as parens patriae to extend the benefit of secondary education to children regardless of the wishes of their parents. Taken at its broadest sweep, the Court's language in *Prince*, might be read to give support to the State's position. However, the Court was not confronted in *Prince* with a situation comparable to that of the Amish as revealed in this record; this is shown by the Court's severe characterization of the evils that it thought the legislature could legitimately associate with child labor, even when performed in the company of an adult. * The Court later took great care to confine *Prince* to a narrow scope in *Sherbert v. Verner*, when it stated:

'On the other hand, the Court has rejected challenges under the Free Exercise Clause to governmental regulation of certain overt acts prompted by religious beliefs or principles, for 'even when the action is in accord with one's religious convictions, (it) is not totally free from legislative restrictions.' *Braunfeld v. Brown*, *. The conduct or actions so regulated have invariably posed some substantial threat to public safety, peace or order. *See e.g. Reynolds v. United States*, *; *Jacobson v. Massachusetts*, *; *Prince v. Massachusetts*, *.

This case, of course, is not one in which any harm to the physical or mental health of the child or to the public safety, peace, order, or welfare has been demonstrated or may be properly inferred. The record is to the contrary, and any reliance on that theory would find no support in the evidence.

Contrary to the suggestion of the dissenting opinion of Mr. Justice DOUGLAS, our holding today in no degree depends on the assertion of the religious interest of the child as contrasted with that of the parents. It is the parents who are subject to prosecution here for failing to cause their children to attend school, and it is their right of free exercise, not that of their children, that must determine Wisconsin's power to impose criminal penalties on the parent. The dissent argues that a child who expresses a desire to attend public high school in conflict with the wishes of his parents should not be prevented from doing so. There is no reason for the Court to consider that point since it is not an issue in the case. The children are not parties to this litigation. The State has at no point tried this case on the theory that respondents were preventing their children from attending school against their expressed desires, and indeed the record is to the contrary. The State's position from the outset has been that it is empowered to apply its compulsory-attendance law to Amish parents in the same manner as to other parents--that is, without regard to the wishes of the child. That is the claim we reject today.

Our holding in no way determines the proper resolution of possible competing interests of parents, children, and the State in an appropriate state court proceeding in which the power of the State is asserted on the theory that Amish parents are preventing their minor children from attending high school despite their expressed desires to the contrary. Recognition of the claim of the State in such a proceeding would, of course, call into question traditional concepts of parental control over the religious upbringing and education of their minor children recognized in this Court's past decisions. It is clear that such an intrusion by a State into family decisions in the area of religious training would give rise to grave questions of religious freedom comparable to those raised here and *** in *Pierce* *. On this record we neither reach nor decide those issues.

The State's argument proceeds without reliance on any actual conflict between the wishes of parents and children. It appears to rest on the potential that exemption of Amish parents from the requirements of the compulsory-education law might allow some parents to act contrary to the best interests of their children by foreclosing their opportunity to make an intelligent choice between the Amish way of life and that of the outside world. The same argument could, of course, be made with respect to all church schools short of college. There is nothing in the record or in the ordinary course of human experience to suggest that non-Amish parents generally consult with children of ages 14--16 if they are placed in a church school of the parents' faith.

Indeed it seems clear that if the State is empowered, as parens patriae, to 'save' a child from himself or his Amish parents by requiring an additional two years of compulsory formal high school education, the State will in large measure influence, if not determine, the religious future of the child. Even more markedly than in Prince, therefore, this case involves the fundamental interest of parents, as contrasted with that of the State, to guide the religious future and education of their children. The history and culture of Western civilization reflect a strong tradition of parental concern for the nurture and upbringing of their children. This primary role of the parents in the upbringing of their children is now established beyond debate as an enduring American tradition. If not the first, perhaps the most significant statements of the Court in this area are found in *Pierce v. Society of*

Sisters, in which the Court observed:

> 'Under the doctrine of *Meyer v. Nebraska*, *, we think it entirely plain that the Act of 1922 unreasonably interferes with the liberty of parents and guardians to direct the upbringing and education of children under their control. As often heretofore pointed out, rights guaranteed by the Constitution may not be abridged by legislation which has no reasonable relation to some purpose within the competency of the State. The fundamental theory of liberty upon which all governments in this Union repose excludes any general power of the State to standardize its children by forcing them to accept instruction from public teachers only. The child is not the mere creature of the State; those who nurture him and direct his destiny have the right, coupled with the high duty, to recognize and prepare him for additional obligations.' 268 U.S., at 534--535.

The duty to prepare the child for 'additional obligations,' referred to by the Court, must be read to include the inculcation of moral standards, religious beliefs, and elements of good citizenship. ***

However read, the Court's holding in Pierce stands as a charter of the rights of parents to direct the religious upbringing of their children. And, when the interests of parenthood are combined with a free exercise claim of the nature revealed by this record, more than merely a 'reasonable relation to some purpose within the competency of the State' is required to sustain the validity of the State's requirement under the First Amendment. To be sure, the power of the parent, even when linked to a free exercise claim, may be subject to limitation under Prince if it appears that parental decisions will jeopardize the health or safety of the child, or have a potential for significant social burdens. But in this case, the Amish have introduced persuasive evidence undermining the arguments the State has advanced to support its claims in terms of the welfare of the child and society as a whole. The record strongly indicates that accommodating the religious objections of the Amish by forgoing one, or at most two, additional years of compulsory education will not impair the physical or mental health of the child, or result in an inability to be self-supporting or to discharge the duties and responsibilities of citizenship, or in any other way materially detract from the welfare of society.

In the fact of our consistent emphasis on the central values underlying the Religion Clauses in our constitutional scheme of government, we cannot accept a parens patriae claim of such all-encompassing scope and with such sweeping potential for broad and unforeseeable application as that urged by the State.

V

For the reasons stated we hold, with the Supreme Court of Wisconsin, that the First and Fourteenth Amendments prevent the State from compelling respondents to cause their children to attend formal high school to age 16. Our disposition of this case, however, in no way alters our recognition of the obvious fact that courts are not school boards or legislatures, and are ill-equipped to determine the 'necessity' of discrete aspects of a State's program of compulsory education. This should suggest that courts must move with great circumspection in performing the sensitive and delicate task of weighing a State's legitimate social concern when faced with religious claims for exemption from generally applicable education requirements. It cannot be overemphasized that we are not dealing with a way of life and mode of education by a group claiming to have recently discovered some 'progressive' or more enlightened process for rearing children for modern life.

Aided by a history of three centuries as an identifiable religious sect and a long history as a successful and self-sufficient segment of American society, the Amish in this case have convincingly demonstrated the sincerity of their religious beliefs, the interrelationship of belief with their mode of life, the vital role that belief and daily conduct play in the continued survival of Old Order Amish communities and their religious organization, and the hazards presented by the

State's enforcement of a statute generally valid as to others. Beyond this, they have carried the even more difficult burden of demonstrating the adequacy of their alternative mode of continuing informal vocational education in terms of precisely those overall interests that the State advances in support of its program of compulsory high school education. In light of this convincing showing, one that probably few other religious groups or sects could make, and weighing the minimal difference between what the State would require and what the Amish already accept, it was incumbent on the State to show with more particularity how its admittedly strong interest in compulsory education would be adversely affected by granting an exemption to the Amish. *

Nothing we hold is intended to undermine the general applicability of the State's compulsory school-attendance statutes or to limit the power of the State to promulgate reasonable standards that, while not impairing the free exercise of religion, provide for continuing agricultural vocational education under parental and church guidance by the Old Order Amish or others similarly situated. ***

Affirmed.

Mr. JUSTICE POWELL and Mr. JUSTICE REHNQUIST took no part in the consideration or decision of this case.

Mr. JUSTICE STEWART, with whom Mr. JUSTICE BRENNAN joins, concurring.
***

This case in no way involves any questions regarding the right of the children of Amish parents to attend public high schools, or any other institutions of learning, if they wish to do so. As the Court points out, there is no suggestion whatever in the record that the religious beliefs of the children here concerned differ in any way from those of their parents. ***

It is clear to me, therefore, that this record simply does not present the interesting and important issue discussed in Part II of the dissenting opinion of Mr. Justice DOUGLAS. With this observation, I join the opinion and the judgment of the Court.

Mr. JUSTICE WHITE, with whom Mr. JUSTICE BRENNAN and Mr. JUSTICE STEWART join, concurring.
***

This would be a very different case for me if respondents' claim were that their religion forbade their children from attending any school at any time and from complying in any way with the educational standards set by the State. Since the Amish children are permitted to acquire the basic tools of literacy to survive in modern society by attending grades one through eight and since the deviation from the State's compulsory-education law is relatively slight, I conclude that respondents' claim must prevail, largely because 'religious freedom--the freedom to believe and to practice strange and, it may be, foreign creeds--has classically been one of the highest values of our society.' *Braunfeld v. Brown*, 366 U.S. 599, 612 (1961) (Brennan, J., concurring and dissenting).
***

There is evidence in the record that many children desert the Amish faith when they come of age. *** In the circumstances of this case, although the question is close, I am unable to say that the State has demonstrated that Amish children who leave school in the eighth grade will be intellectually stultified or unable to acquire new academic skills later. The statutory minimum school attendance age set by the State is, after all, only 16.

*** I join the Court because the sincerity of the Amish religious policy here is uncontested, because the potentially adverse impact of the state requirement is great, and because the State's valid interest in education has already been largely satisfied by the eight years the children have already spent in school.

Mr. JUSTICE DOUGLAS, dissenting in part.

I agree with the Court that the religious scruples of the Amish are opposed to the education of their children beyond the grade schools, yet I disagree with the Court's conclusion that the matter is within the dispensation of parents alone. The Court's analysis assumes that the only interests at stake in the case are those of the Amish parents on the one hand, and those of the State on the other. The difficulty with this approach is that, despite the Court's claim, the parents are seeking to vindicate not only their own free exercise claims, but also those of their high-school-age children.

***

The views of the two children in question were not canvassed by the Wisconsin courts. The matter should be explicitly reserved so that new hearings can be held on remand of the case.

***

e. Notes and Questions

1) *Meyer, Pierce, Prince, Yoder* and Parent's Rights

The Constitution of the United States does not explicitly mention parents' rights. Nevertheless, American courts have long recognized that parents are entitled to very broad latitude in raising their children. The leading Supreme Court cases on parental rights include the four cases reviewed above. Give a synthesis of these four cases.

The latest major decision addressing parent's rights, *Troxel v. Granville*, 530 U.S. 57 (2000), is included in Chapter 23, *infra*. In *Troxel* the Court held unconstitutional as applied a Washington grandparent's visitation law that a court had applied to allow the parents of the unwed father of the children to obtain greater visitation with their grandchildren after their son died (by suicide) and the mother of the children limited the grandparents to one short visit per month. The plurality emphasized heavily the presumption that a parent will act in the best interests of his or her children in making child-visitation decisions, and the parent's "fundamental right to make decisions concerning the care, custody, and control of her [children]." *Id.* at 72. Does this decision have implications for disputes about custody between a biological parent and his or her former same-sex partner who seeks visitation? If so, what? Why?

2) Minor's Rights

Children are not without rights, even though they are under the tutelage and instruction of their parents. They are, after all, "persons," even if not in the full sense of being the subject of all the legal rights and duties of competent adults.

a) Children vs. State (Procedural Rights).

Children are entitled to essentially the same procedural protections against the state deprivations of their life, liberty and property. The Court has held that "there is nothing about juvenile or minority status ... that justifies a ... failure to provide the most basic protective safeguards inherent in procedural due process." Bruce Hafen, *Privacy and Protection: The Risks of Children's "Rights,"* 63 A.B.A.J. 1383, 85 (1977). Thus, in 1967 the Supreme Court held in *In re Gault*, 387 U.S. 1 (1967), that minors may not be deprived basic procedural protections in juvenile court proceedings. In *Goss v. Lopez*, 419 U.S. 565 (1975) the Court held that students facing suspension from a state-run school are entitled to certain procedural protections such as prior notice and an opportunity for a hearing. However, in *Ingraham v. Wright*, 430 U.S. 651 (1977), minors do not always enjoy the same procedural rights as parents. For instance, the Court held that common law restraints upon the infliction of "moderate correction" by means of corporal punishment are sufficient, and more formal procedural protections such as notice and prior hearing are not necessary. In *New Jersey v. T.C.O.*, 469 U.S. 325 (1985), the Court held that the probable cause requirements of the Fourth Amendment do not require exclusion of evidence taken by a school official from a students purse under less rigorous standards in juvenile court delinquency proceedings. *See generally* Bruce Hafen, *Children's Liberation and the New Egalitarianism: Some Reservations About Abandoning Youth to Their "Rights"*, 1976 B.Y.U. L.Rev. 605, 33-37, 44-48.

b) *Children vs. State (Substantive Rights).*

The Supreme Court also has held that children possess certain substantive constitutional rights which may not be infringed by the state. For instance, the Supreme Court has recognized the religious liberties of children against state-mandated intrusion. In *West Virginia State Board of Education v. Barnette*, 319 U.S. 624 (1943) the Court invalidated a state statute which required all school children to salute the flag including Jehovah's Witnesses who believed as a matter of church doctrine that flag saluting is idolatrous and violative of one of the Ten Commandments. The Court concluded: "We think the action of the local authorities in compelling the flag salute and pledge transcends constitutional limitations on their power and invades the sphere of intellect and spirit which is the purpose of the First Amendment of our Constitution to reserve from all official control." *Id.* Likewise, in *Tinker v. Des Moines School District*, 393 U.S. 503 (1969) the Court found that the First Amendment rights of three students had been violated when they were summarily suspended for wearing black armbands to school to protest the Vietnam war. The Court declared: "Students in school as well as out of school are 'persons' under our Constitution. They are possessed of fundamental rights which the State must respect .... In the absence of a specific showing of constitutionally valid reasons to regulate their speech, students are entitled to freedom of expression of their views." *Id.* at 511. In a series of cases decided during the past two decades the Supreme Court has clarified that minors enjoy the right to be free from invidious discrimination on the basis of illegitimate birth. But, the Court also has held that "[t]he state's authority over children's activities is broader than over like actions of adults." *Prince v. Massachusetts*, 321 U.S. at 168; in *Bethel School District No. 403 v. Fraser*, 478 U.S. Ct. 675 (1986), the Supreme Court held that minors do not enjoy the same latitude of expression under the first amendment as adults. *Id.* at 683-84.

c) *Child vs. Parents (Autonomy Rights).*

It is also clear that children enjoy some substantive rights which they may assert even against their parents and over parental objection. The first substantive right which children enjoy and which may be asserted against their parents is the right to be free of risk to their health caused by parental abuse or neglect. In *Prince v. Massachusetts*, while giving a ringing endorsement of parental rights, the Supreme Court upheld the conviction of a woman for violation of child labor laws in allowing her nine year old niece to sell unpopular religious tracts on public street corners. The Court explained: "It is in the interest of youth itself, and of the whole community, that children be both safeguarded from abuses and given opportunities for growth into free and independent well-developed men and citizens." 321 U.S. at 165. "Parents may be free to become martyrs themselves. But it does not follow they are free, in identical circumstances, to make martyrs of their children before they have reached the age of full and legal discretion when they can make that choice for themselves." *Id.* at 170. In *Wisconsin v. Yoder* the Court declared: "To be sure, the power of the parent, even when linked to a free exercise claim, may be subject to limitation under *Prince* if it appears that parental decisions will jeopardize the health or safety of the child, or have a potential for significant social burdens." 405 U.S. at 233-34.

3) Parent-Child Testimonial Privilege

Most courts in which a parent-child testimonial privilege has been asserted have rejected the claim giving at least one of three reasons: 1) because they reasoned it was beyond their authority to create such a privilege, 2) because the facts of the case did not merit the creation of the privilege, or 3) because the privilege would have prevented a just determination of a child-abuse or -neglect prosecution. In Kraft, *The Parent-Child Testimonial Privilege: Who's Minding the Kids,* 18 Fam. L. Q. 505, 36-42 (198), the author suggests that children who are required to testify against their parents are exploited twice, first by the parent who inappropriately confides in the child his criminal activities and, second, by the judicial system that requires the child's testimony versus his parent when the child is not old enough to appreciate the public policy considerations that necessitate his or her breach of parental confidence.

Nevertheless, some courts have recognized a qualified parent-child testimonial privilege. The importance of the inviolability of the parent-child relationship was articulated eloquently in *In re Agosto*, 553 F. Supp. 1298, 1302 (D.Nev 1983):

> [A] central aspect of the cohesiveness of the relationship between parent and child in the context of the family is the reciprocal communication between the two, inspired by both confidentiality and loyalty on which the relationship is based. . . . [I]n a cohesive family unit in which the members communicate openly with each other, children ... tend to be more well-adjusted, and delinquency is more infrequent. In the modern day, in which it is opined that the family, as a functional unit in society, is becoming obsolete, it is urged that society's interest in protecting the family unit is especially compelling. . . . [T]he family relationship cannot be protected in the absence of an expectation of privacy in intrafamily communications in light of the sanctity of the family unit and its component relationships ... [I]n the complexities of life in the modern world, the import of a cohesive family unit is inestimable... [T]he insularity of the family increases in response to the stresses of contemporary life in an ever-burgeoning population. Thus, the relationships within the family unit become more important."

4) Loss of Consortium

American courts historically refused to allow recovery for loss of consortium to either a parent or a child for injury to the other. Often courts ruled that the non-pecuniary or intangible harm to the parental relationship from a negligent tort was, for policy reasons, too speculative or too difficult to assess, and some emphasized that the law provided only recovery for purely economic loss. The majority of states do not recognize a loss of consortium claim by children for parents nor by parents for children. Scott Korzenowski, Note, *Valuable in Life, Valuable in Death, Why Not Valuable When Severely Injured? The Need to Recognize a Parent's Loss of a Child's Consortium in Minnesota*, 80 Minn. L. Rev. 677, 682-83 (1996).

5) Breastfeeding
In *Dike v. School Board*, 650 F.2d 783 (5th Cir. 1981), the U.S. Court of Appeals for the Fifth Circuit held that a mother's decision to breast-feed her child is encompassed within her constitutionally protected interest in nurturing and rearing her children. Five years later, the same court held that a female prisoner who gives birth while incarcerated is not entitled to an injunction against application to her of prison rules and regulations which would prevent her from breast-feeding her newly-born son. *Southerland v. Thigpen*, 784 F.2d 713 (5th Cir. 1986).

3. Practical and Ethical Considerations

a. Intrafamily Disputes Regarding Children
The major cases in this section deal with the rights of parents and the State. But, suppose husband and wife disagree as to the education of the children. Suppose both parents feel very strongly about their respective positions, leading one parent to petition the court. How and why should the court respond? *Kilgrow v. Kilgrow*, 107 S2d 885 (Ala. 1958). Suppose the child of these parents disagree with the parents' decision. How and why should the court respond?

4. Bibliography

William Blackstone, Commentaries on the Laws of England *447.

Bruce Hafen, *Children's Liberation and the New Egalitarianism: Some Reservations About Abandoning Youth to Their "Rights"*, 1976 B.Y.U.L.Rev. 605, 33-37, 44-48.

Bruce Hafen, *Privacy and Protection: The Risks of Children's "Rights*, 63 A.B.A.J. 1383, 85 (1977).

Scott Korzenowski, Note, *Valuable in Life, Valuable in Death, Why Not Valuable When Severely Injured? The Need to Recognize a Parent's Loss of a Child's Consortium in Minnesota*, 80 Minn. L. Rev. 677, 682-83 (1996).

Kraft, *The Parent-Child Testimonial Privilege: Who's Minding the Kids*, 18 Fam. L. Q. 505, 36-42 (198).

Lee E. Teitelbaum, *Foreword: The Meanings of Rights of Children*, 10 New Mex. L. Rev. 235 (1980).

CHAPTER 22

Non-Economic Relations: Medical Treatment; Discipline

A. MEDICAL TREATMENT

1. Background

Although the rights of parents are quite broad as decision makers for their child (see chapter 20), they may be limited by the state's intervention under the doctrine of *parens patriae*. This doctrine allows the state to intervene in family matters to protect children from being harmed by the parents' decisions or actions. Determining whether the child is being harmed is sometimes very challenging, especially in cases of medical treatment and disciplining the child.

The parent's right to decide the medical treatment for the child is restricted only to the extent to protect the child from harm. If there is a custody order, the custodian exercises that right. The corollary to this parental right of medical treatment decision-making is that medical treatment cannot be given to the child without the parents' consent. The child lacks the capacity to consent because of this child's minority status. The caregiver may be sued for battery if parental consent is not obtained. There are three general exceptions to the parental consent principle. The earliest exception that developed at common law was the emergency treatment exception. If parents were not available to give consent and a delay in treatment would endanger the child's "life, limb or mental well-being," the medical provider could proceed and treat the child. The emergency treatment exception is the law in all states.

The other two exceptions to the parental consent principle permit emancipated minors and certain unemancipated minors who are "mature minors" to consent to some non-emergency treatment. All states have statutes recognizing some form of emancipated minor and "mature minor" exceptions, but the laws vary from state to state.

If parents are available and do not give consent for medical treatment under circumstances that withholding the treatment would endanger the child's life, the state under its *parens patriae* power intervenes. But, intervening by the state may raise constitutional issues.

2. Statutes, Cases and Doctrines

a. *State v. McKown*

State v. McKown
475 N.W.2d 63 (Minn. 1991), cert. denied 112 S.Ct. 882 (1992)
TOMLJANOVICH, Justice.

On May 9, 1989, 11-year-old Ian Lundman died at his home in Independence, Minnesota. [FN1 *The facts upon which the appealed indictments are based and upon which the district court dismissed those indictments are drawn from testimony delivered before a Hennepin County Grand Jury.*] Ian's death was apparently caused by diabetic ketoacidosis, a complication of diabetes mellitus. Ian was occasionally ill in the weeks preceding his death and became seriously ill two or three days before he died.

Kathleen McKown, Ian's mother, and William McKown, Ian's step-father, are Christian Scientists. In accord with their religious beliefs, Ian was treated with Christian Science spiritual healing methods throughout his final illness. He did not receive conventional medical care at any time during that illness.

In late September and early October, 1989, the Hennepin County Attorney presented evidence related to Ian Lundman's illness and death to the Hennepin County Grand Jury. The grand jurors heard testimony from medical doctors indicating that Ian's diabetes was apparently treatable through conventional medicine and that his condition probably could have been stabilized as late as two hours before he died. The jurors also heard testimony regarding the nature and practice of Christian Science healing, and regarding the specific healing methods used in treating Ian Lundman.

Following this testimony, the county attorney instructed the grand jury as to the definition of second degree manslaughter. [FN2 *The county attorney relied primarily on the established jury instruction for second degree manslaughter, see 10 Minn.Dist. Judges Ass'n, Minnesota Practice, CRIMJIG 11.24 (3d ed.1990), including the instructions defining "culpable negligence," and "recklessness."*] Having heard this instruction, two of the jurors asked, "Can you explain child neglect at all. Is there any sort of * * * statute that would apply?" The county attorney replied, "Well, I can read you the statute. There's a criminal, it's Minnesota Statute 609.378 * * *." He then read the entire child neglect statute aloud to the jurors, and asked, "Did that answer your question, ma'am?" The juror who posed the question responded, "Mm-hmm." [FN3 *The child neglect provision read to the jurors is found at Minn.Stat. § 609.378 (1988):(a). Id. A parent, legal guardian, or caretaker who wilfully deprives a child of necessary food, clothing, shelter, health care, or supervision appropriate to the child's age, when the parent, guardian, or caretaker is reasonably able to make the necessary provisions and which deprivation substantially harms the child's physical or emotional health, * * * is guilty of neglect of a child and may be sentenced to imprisonment for not more than one year or to payment of a fine of not more than $3,000, or both. * * * * * *If a parent, guardian, or caretaker responsible for the child's care in good faith selects and depends upon spiritual means or prayer for treatment or care of disease or remedial care of the child, this treatment shall constitute "health care" as used in clause (a).Id.*]

After deliberating, the grand jury returned indictments charging both Kathleen and William McKown with second degree manslaughter. [FN4 *Minn.Stat. § 609.205 (1988) reads: [a] person who causes the death of another by any of the following means is guilty of manslaughter in the second degree and may be sentenced to imprisonment for not more than seven years or to payment of a fine of not more than $14,000, or both: (1) by the person's culpable negligence whereby the person creates an unreasonable risk, and consciously takes chances of causing death or great bodily harm to another * * *. Id.*]

The McKowns moved the District Court for the Fourth Judicial District, the Honorable Eugene J. Farrell presiding, to dismiss the indictments against them for lack of probable cause, because the indictments violated due process of law and their rights to freely exercise their religious beliefs, and because the grand jury was improperly instructed with respect to the McKowns' duty of care. The district court dismissed the indictments. It concluded that the child neglect statute and the second degree manslaughter statute were *in pari materia*, such that the spiritual treatment and prayer exception to the child neglect statute also operated as a defense to the charge of second degree manslaughter. The court determined that the McKown's rights had been prejudiced because the grand jury was not instructed as to the effect of the spiritual healing and prayer exception. It also concluded that the indictments violated due process of law in that the child neglect statute informed individuals that they might rely on spiritual healing and prayer without violating that statute, but did not state that doing so might expose them to other criminal charges if the treatment failed.

On appeal by the state, the court of appeals concluded that while the child neglect and second degree manslaughter statutes were not *in pari materia,* the trial court was correct to dismiss the indictments as violations of due process. 461 N.W.2d 720. The court reasoned that the child neglect statute did not provide fair notice of potential liability under other criminal statutes, that it permitted arbitrary enforcement, that the McKowns may well have relied on the spiritual treatment and prayer exception to the child neglect statute in determining the course of their son's treatment, and that the state had not clearly enough defined when reliance on spiritual healing became criminal conduct.

The state appealed to this court for reinstatement of the indictments charging respondents with second degree manslaughter. It contends that the court of appeals was correct in concluding that the spiritual healing and prayer exception to the child neglect statute does not apply to the second degree manslaughter statute because the two provisions are not *in pari materia.* It argues that both the trial court and the court of appeals were incorrect, however, in concluding that the indictments violate due process of law.

I.

The trial court concluded that the child neglect statute and the second degree manslaughter statute are *in pari materia,* requiring that they be interpreted in light of one another. We disagree.

"Statutes 'in pari materia' are those relating to the same person or thing or having a common purpose." * Such statutes should be construed in light of one another. *See id.; Doe v. State Bd. of Medical Examiners,* 435 N.W.2d 45, 49 (Minn.1989). In *Doe,* this court held that Minn.Stat. § 13.41, Subd. 4 (1986), governing all state licensing agencies, and Minn.Stat. § 147.01, Subd. 4 (1986), which applied specifically to the state Board of Medical Examiners, were indeed *in pari materia.* The court therefore concluded that a general phrase in section 147.01 could be read to incorporate a similar, but more specific phrase in section 13.41. *See id.* [FN5 **]

Unlike the statutes at issue in *Doe,* the child neglect and second degree manslaughter statutes are not *in pari materia* and thus, the spiritual treatment and prayer exception to the former cannot be imported into the latter. The child neglect provision applies specifically to individuals with legal responsibility for a child who wilfully neglect that responsibility and thereby cause the child substantial physical or emotional harm. The statute defining second degree manslaughter, however, permits the state to prosecute anyone who causes the death of another by exposing that person to an unreasonable risk of death or great bodily injury. The two statutes are therefore clearly based on separate and distinct purposes. Further, nothing in the language of either provision suggests they are so closely related as to require they be interpreted in light of one another, and neither contains an explicit mandate to construe them together. *See Apple Valley Red-E-Mix,* 352 N.W.2d at 406 (that two statutes have different purposes and that neither mentions the other is evidence that the two are not *in pari materia*).

In *State v. Bolsinger,* 221 Minn. 154, 21 N.W.2d 480 (1946), the appellant contended that a statute allowing the prosecution of an individual who took the life of another by operating a vehicle in a "reckless or grossly negligent manner," Minn.Stat. § 169.11 (1941), was unconstitutionally vague. This court disagreed, relying in part on the definitions assigned to "reckless" and "grossly negligent" in other contemporary homicide statutes. *See Bolsinger,* 221 Minn. at 156, 21 N.W.2d at 486. The court explained that this was appropriate because

[t]he statute in question and those relating to homicide in force at the time of its enactment relate to one common subject matter, that of homicide. As such, they should be construed as constituting one systematic body [of] law. Each statute should be construed in the light of, with reference to, and in connection with the others. So construed, the statute in question should be fitted to the statutes in force at the time of its enactment and carried into effect conformably to them.

Id. at 162, 21 N.W.2d at 486.

Thus, the words "reckless" and "grossly negligent" as used in section 169.11 carried the same meaning as they did in other, then-existing homicide statutes.

Respondents here suggest a significantly different application of the doctrine of *in pari materia.* First, they contend that "culpable negligence" as used in the second degree manslaughter statute, adopted in 1963, should be defined in light of "neglect of a child" as used in section 609.378, enacted by the legislature in 1983. The statutory language at issue in *Bolsinger,* however, was construed in light of identical language in existing homicide provisions--the question was whether "reckless" and "grossly negligent" meant the same thing in the one statute as in the others. Second, respondents argue for interpreting the earlier of two statutes in light of the later, while in *Bolsinger* the court adopted precisely the opposite approach. Finally, the court in *Bolsinger* noted several times that the statute at issue and those considered *in pari materia* with it were all homicide statutes, "relate[d] to one common subject matter * * *." *Id.* Here the statutes do not appear to bear the same sort of common purpose. Therefore, application of the doctrine of *in pari materia* in this case is neither necessary nor appropriate.

Respondent also contends that the legislative history underlying the spiritual treatment and prayer exception establishes that it was intended to exempt those who rely on such treatment methods from *all* criminal prosecution related to their reliance on spiritual treatment and prayer in caring for their children. Although legislative history may be useful in interpreting an ambiguous statute, this court generally does not consider it when faced with a clearly worded provision. *See Handle With Care, Inc. v. Dept. of Human Services,* 406 N.W.2d 518, 522 (Minn.1987); *Molberg v. Marsden,* 294 Minn. 493, 494, 200 N.W.2d 298, 299 (1972) (where language of statute is clear, it defines legislative intent leaving no room for further judicial interpretation). The language of the exception is not ambiguous; it expressly states that relying on spiritual treatment and prayer does not in itself constitute child neglect. *See* Minn.Stat. § 609.378(a) (1988). Thus, we need not consult the exception's legislative history in our interpretation of it. [FN6 *Respondent correctly indicates that the legislative history underlying the spiritual treatment and prayer exception contains at least one statement suggesting one representative's intention to protect those who rely on such treatment methods from all prosecution. However, this court has noted that the legislative intent underlying a particular statute is not necessarily reflected in the recorded statements of a particular member and that such statements must "be treated with caution." Handle With Care, 406 N.W.2d at 522, 522 n. 8.]*

We therefore conclude that the child neglect statute and the second degree manslaughter statute are not *in pari materia.* The doctrine of *in pari materia* is simply an interpretive tool this court relies on in certain instances to determine the meaning of ambiguous statutory language. Because neither statute is ambiguously worded, we have no need of the doctrine in this instance. Further, because the statutes at issue are not so closely related in either language or purpose as to suggest that they ought be interpreted together, application of the doctrine here would be inappropriate.

II.

Both the trial court and the court of appeals concluded the indictments issued against respondents violate the constitutional guarantee of due process of law. We agree.

The essence of respondents' argument is not that either the manslaughter statute or the child neglect statute is so vaguely worded as to make it unreasonably difficult to discern what conduct each prohibits. *See Kolender v. Lawson,* 461 U.S. 352, 357, 103 S.Ct. 1855, 1858, 75 L.Ed.2d 903 (1983) (due process requires criminal statutes to define offenses clearly enough that ordinary people can determine what they prohibit). Rather, respondents contend the child neglect statute misled them in that it unequivocally stated they could, in good faith, select and depend upon spiritual means or prayer without further advising them that, should their chosen treatment method fail, they might face criminal charges beyond those provided in the child neglect statute itself. In short, respondents argue that the child neglect statute does not go far enough to provide reasonable notice of the potentially serious consequences of actually relying on the alternative treatment methods the statute itself clearly permits. Neither the United States Supreme Court nor this court has directly addressed a similar due process claim. ** In *United States v. Colon-Ortiz,* 866 F.2d 6 (1st Cir.1989), *cert. denied,* 490 U.S. 1051, 109 S.Ct. 1966, 104 L.Ed.2d 434 (1989), however, the United States Court of Appeals for the First Circuit relied on a due process rationale much like that suggested here by respondents.

In *Colon-Ortiz,* the appellant challenged a federal statute prohibiting the distribution of cocaine. That statute, 21 U.S.C. § 841(b)(1)(B), provides that a person convicted of violating it "shall be sentenced to a term of imprisonment * * *, a fine * * *, or both." It goes on to state that "the court shall not place on probation or suspend the sentence of any person sentenced under this [provision]. No person sentenced under this [provision] shall be eligible for parole during the term of imprisonment imposed * * *." 21 U.S.C. § 841(b)(1)(B). Relying on this latter statement and on several remarks in the underlying legislative history clearly indicating the intention to impose mandatory prison sentences, the trial court concluded it was required to sentence the appellant to prison, despite the language in section 841 indicating that a court could choose to impose only a fine. *Colon-Ortiz,* 866 F.2d at 9-10.

The First Circuit agreed with the appellant's contention that the statute did not provide fair notice conviction would necessarily result in the imposition of a prison sentence. It reasoned that

> [t]he person of ordinary intelligence * * * should not have to guess at the meaning of penalty provisions, or else those provisions are not sufficiently clear to satisfy due process concerns. It is not enough for the congressional intent to be apparent elsewhere if it is not apparent by examining the language of the statute. No amount of explicit reference in the legislative history of the statute can cure this deficiency.

Id. at 9. This concern that individuals be given unambiguous notice of the boundaries within which they must operate directly contravenes the state's contention that nothing in the spiritual treatment and prayer exception to the child neglect provision reasonably suggests immunity from all prosecution. The exception is broadly worded, stating that a parent may in good faith "select and depend upon" spiritual treatment and prayer, without indicating a point at which doing so will expose the parent to criminal liability. [FN8 *As the court of appeals indicated, at least one other state has attempted to avoid the problem presented in this case by statutorily establishing a point beyond which parents may not rely solely on spiritual means of treatment. Okla.Stat. Tit. 21, § 852 (1988), provides:*

> *Nothing in this section shall be construed to mean a child is endangered for the sole reason the parent or guardian, in good faith, selects and depends upon spiritual means alone through prayer, in accordance with the tenets and practice of a recognized church or religious denomination, for the treatment or cure of disease or remedial care of such child; provided, that medical care shall be provided where permanent physical damage could result to such child * * *.]*

The language of the exception therefore does not satisfy the fair notice requirement inherent to the concept of due process.

Further, the indictments issued against respondents violate the long- established rule that a government may not officially inform an individual that certain conduct is permitted and then prosecute the individual for engaging in that same conduct. *See Cox v. Louisiana*, 379 U.S. 559, 85 S.Ct. 476, 13 L.Ed.2d 487 (1965) (where police official informed protesters they could picket across the street from courthouse, state could not prosecute those protestors for violating a statute prohibiting demonstrations near courthouse); *Raley v. Ohio*, 360 U.S. 423, 79 S.Ct. 1257, 3 L.Ed.2d 1344 (1959) (state could not prosecute individuals for refusing to testify before legislative committee when committee members informed those individuals they could invoke state privilege against self-incrimination).

The spiritual treatment and prayer exception to the child neglect statute expressly provided respondents the right to "depend upon" Christian Science healing methods so long as they did so in good faith. Therefore the state may not now attempt to prosecute them for exercising that right. By virtue of this conclusion, we do not introduce the proposition that conduct complying with one statute *necessarily* complies with all other statutes absent explicit notice to the contrary. Further, we do not here conclude that the state could *never* prosecute an individual whose good faith reliance on spiritual methods of treatment results in the death of a child. Rather, we hold that in this particular instance, where the state has clearly expressed its intention to permit good faith reliance on spiritual treatment and prayer as an alternative to conventional medical treatment, it cannot prosecute respondents for doing so without violating their rights to due process. [FN9 *The Church of Christ, Scientist, as amicus curiae, argues that prosecuting respondents for relying on Christian Science healing methods in the treatment of their son constitutes a violation of the right to freely exercise religious beliefs guaranteed by both the federal and state constitutions. Because of our disposition of this appeal, however, we need not address this issue. Also participating as amicus curiae, the Minnesota Civil Liberties Union contends that the spiritual treatment and prayer exception violates the first amendment's prohibition against state-established religion. Although we find the MCLU's arguments persuasive, our disposition based on due process grounds makes it unnecessary for us to consider the establishment clause issue at this time.*]

We therefore conclude that the indictments issued against respondents, charging them with second degree manslaughter in the death of Ian Lundman, violate the constitutional guarantee of due process of law and must be dismissed. Court of appeals affirmed and indictments dismissed. COYNE, Justice (dissenting) (joined by SIMONETT, Justice).

I respectfully dissent. I fully concur in the majority's determination that nothing in the language of either Minn.Stat. § 609.378 (1988), the child neglect statute, or Minn.Stat. § 609.205 (1988), setting out the crime of second degree manslaughter, suggests they are so closely related as to require them to be interpreted in the light of each other. Having determined that the two statutes, which have quite different purposes, should not be construed together, the majority goes on to hold that the indictments issued here failed to meet constitutional requirements of due process of law because the child neglect statute did not notify them that although depending on "spiritual means or prayer for treatment or care of disease or remedial care of the child" constituted "health care" for purposes of the child neglect statute, that conduct might, under some circumstances, constitute unlawful conduct pursuant to some other statute. This novel proposition, that conduct which complies with the requirements of one statute complies with all other statutes absent notification to the contrary, is in my opinion nothing more than the rejected *in pari materia* argument garbed in the cloak of due process. Inasmuch as defendants do not complain that either the child neglect statute or the manslaughter statute is so vaguely worded that one cannot reasonably discern what conduct each prohibits, the due process argument necessarily depends on construing the two statutes together.

Moreover, the due process argument is defective not only because it depends on construing the two statutes together but also because it depends on misconstruction of a statute and because it rests on an unavailable defense to the charge of manslaughter.

As set forth in Minn.Stat. § 609.205(1) (1988), the offense of second degree culpably negligent manslaughter is "an offense that involves both the objective element of negligence and the subjective element of recklessness, * * * *" *State v. Grover,* 437 N.W.2d 60, 63 (Minn.1989). In order to establish the objective element of negligence the state must prove "a gross deviation from the standard of care that a reasonable person would observe in the actor's situation." *State v. Zupetz,* 322 N.W.2d 730, 733 (Minn.1982) [quoting 2 C. Torcia, *Wharton's Criminal Law* § 168 at 272 (14 ed. 1979]). In order to establish the subjective element of recklessness the state must establish "an actual conscious disregard of the risk created by the conduct." *State v. Frost,* 342 N.W.2d 317, 320 (Minn.1983).

Statutes of this type have regularly and uniformly withstood due process challenges. Indeed, in *State v. Grover,* 437 N.W.2d at 63-64, we upheld against a due process challenge a criminal statute containing only an objective element of negligence. *** In doing this, we quoted Justice Oliver Wendell Holmes, Jr.'s response to a due process challenge to a criminal statute containing a negligence element: "[T]he law is full of instances where a man's fate depends on his estimating rightly, that is, as the jury subsequently estimates it, some matter of degree." *Id.* at 64 [quoting *Nash v. United States,* 229 U.S. 373, 377, 33 S.Ct. 780, 781, 57 L.Ed. 1232 (1913)].

One cannot be convicted of culpably negligent manslaughter simply because one has not "estimated rightly." It is not enough that one has estimated wrongly, even in a grossly deviant sense. The state must also establish that the defendant was aware of the risk created by his or her conduct and actually and consciously disregarded that risk.

The statute on which defendants rely in support of their argument that their prosecution for culpably negligent manslaughter is barred is not the statute dealing with culpably negligent manslaughter, nor is it one of the statutes setting forth the defenses recognized by the legislature as being generally applicable in criminal prosecutions [*See e.g.* Minn.Stat. § 609.08 (1988) (duress)]. Rather, defendants rely on what they characterize as an exception to the statute which makes it a gross misdemeanor to willfully deprive a child of various enumerated necessities, including "health care," if the deprivation "substantially harms the child's physical or emotional health." Minn.Stat. § 609.378 (1988). The relevant statutory language is this definition:

If a parent, guardian or caretaker responsible for the child's care in good faith selects and depends upon spiritual means or prayer for treatment or care of disease or remedial care of the child, this treatment shall constitute "health care" as used in clause (a).

There is no reason to believe that the legislature intended this provision of the child neglect statute to have any effect on a parent's criminal liability for culpably negligent manslaughter. This definitional language does not "except" spiritual means and prayer from operation of the child neglect statute; it simply provides that a parent who "in good faith" selects and depends on spiritual means or prayer for treatment of his or her child is no more--nor less--subject to prosecution for gross misdemeanor child neglect than a parent who furnishes more conventional health care. Whatever kind of health care is selected, one who violates Minn.Stat. § 609.205(1) (1988) has by definition not acted "in good faith" but has both (a) grossly deviated from the standard of care that a reasonable person would observe in the actor's situation and (b) although aware of the risk created by that deviation, callously or consciously disregarded the risk. Whatever kind of health care is selected, due process does not require notification that selection of and reliance on a course of conduct which appears to comply with the requirements of one statute may not meet the requirements of another.

If, for example, a parent selects conventional health care and engages a physician to treat a child, there is no basis for a prosecution for child neglect because the parent has provided necessary health care. If, however, the parent who selects conventional health care knowingly engages a physician whose license has been suspended or revoked because of habitual neglect of patients caused by drug addiction and if the child should die because of the physician's neglect, I think it highly unlikely that anyone would contend that the absence of a warning in the child neglect statute insulated the parent from a charge of manslaughter. Due process does not require notification that selection of a form of treatment acceptable under the child neglect statute does not eliminate all possible criminal responsibility.

Similarly, a parent who provides clothing for a child has not violated the child neglect statute because the parent has not willfully deprived his or her child of necessary clothing. If, however, the parent knowingly clothes the child in pajamas of flammable material with full knowledge that the child's siblings frequently cause fires by playing with matches, and the pajama-clad child is subsequently burned to death in a fire started by the child's brother, the absence of a warning in the child neglect statute could hardly be said to protect the parent from a charge of manslaughter.

I believe that an individual "should be able reasonably to rely upon a statute or other enactment under which his conduct would not be criminal." 1 W. LaFave & A. Scott, *Substantive Criminal Law* § 5.1(2) at 591 (1986). However, I reject the argument that that concept has any application here. In enacting Minn.Stat. § 609.378 (1988), the legislature did not in any way shield parents from prosecution for culpably negligent manslaughter under Minn.Stat. § 609.205(1) (1988). Any mistake by defendants based on the child neglect statute is a mistake of law, which is not recognized as a defense. 1 W. LaFave & A. Scott § 5.1(d).

This is not to say, however, that defendants' belief that prayer is a better cure than medicine is without relevance in a prosecution under Minn.Stat. § 609.205(1) (1988). As stated in 2 W. LaFave & A. Scott § 7.12(a) at 281-82 n. 28:

[I]t is no interference with one's freedom of religion to convict of manslaughter one who, for religious reasons, fails to call a doctor when to fail to do so constitutes criminal negligence. Yet an honest religious belief that prayer is a better cure than medicine, that Providence can heal better than doctors, might serve to negative the awareness of risk which is required for manslaughter in those states which use a subjective test of criminal negligence.

As I stated earlier, there is both an objective element and a subjective element to the offense of second degree culpably negligent manslaughter. Here a grand jury returned an indictment charging the defendants with second degree manslaughter, that is, the grand jury found probable cause to believe that the defendants' conduct met both the objective element (unreasonable risk) and subjective element (consciously disregarded a known risk) of the crime of second degree manslaughter. Nevertheless, the majority simply assumes the defendants acted in good faith. Without intending to address the wisdom of prosecuting these parents or to speak specifically to the various evidentiary issues that might arise at a trial of defendants, I assume as a general matter that a trial court would liberally admit evidence supporting defendants' claim that they acted in good faith in relying on prayer and spiritual means rather than seeking medical care. But in light of the action of the grand jury, whether or not the defendants were culpably negligent--that is, whether they created an unreasonable risk and if so, whether they lacked good faith and consciously disregarded a known risk--is in my opinion a jury question, not a question appropriately decided by this court at the pretrial stage on the basis of a mistaken interpretation of a statute.

b. *Care and Protection of Beth*

Care and Protection of Beth
587 N.E.2d 1377 (Wisc. 1992)

ABRAMS, Justice.

A single justice has reserved and reported the correctness of a substituted judgment determination calling for a "no code" [FN1 *A "no code" order, also referred to as a "DNR" or do-not-resuscitate order, directs a hospital and staff not to employ extraordinary resuscitative measures in the event of cardiac or respiratory failure.****] order to be entered on the medical charts of an incompetent minor ward. A judge of the Holyoke Division of the District Court determined that an infant in a persistent vegetative coma would choose, were she competent, to have the "no code" order entered on her medical charts. For the reasons stated we affirm.

Facts. The child whose treatment is at issue was born on September 30, 1986. Her mother and putative father were both minors at the time. Less than one month after her birth, in response to a petition filed by the Department of Social Services (DSS), a District Court judge found the child to be in need of care and protection. By order of the District Court, DSS gained legal and physical custody of the child. On October 30, 1986, the child's mother was also found in need of care and protection and placed in DSS custody. In December of the same year, DSS returned physical custody of the child to her mother, while retaining legal custody.

Shortly thereafter, the mother and child were involved in an automobile accident. That accident, in which the straps on the child's car seat wrapped around her neck and cut off the supply of oxygen to her brain for a substantial period of time, left the child in an irreversible coma.

As a result of the accident, the child cannot see, hear, or engage in any purposeful movement. Her ability to breathe on her own is extremely limited. A breathing tube has been inserted directly into her lungs through an incision in her trachea, and her rate of breathing is controlled by a machine. She is fed through a feeding tube permanently inserted in her stomach. The child suffered cardiorespiratory arrests as a result of aspirating food regurgitated from her stomach. She was resuscitated on these occasions by extraordinary treatment, including the administration of medication to restart her heart. ****

On July 7, 1987, DSS and the child's mother jointly moved for appointment of a guardian ad litem for the child and entry of a substituted judgment decision as to what further medical care should be given to the child. Because both the child and her parents were minors, as well as under the legal custody of DSS, a guardian was appointed to represent the child.

The primary witness at the hearing for entry of substituted judgment was Dr. Stephen Lieberman, the director of the pediatric intensive care unit at Baystate Medical Center, where the child was hospitalized following the accident. Dr. Lieberman, who has extensive training and experience in treating children with neurological problems, was primarily responsible for the child from the time she was admitted to Baystate. After extensive testing, Dr. Lieberman determined that "there is nothing to indicate that she has any ability to function from her cerebral cortex. But she does function from a brain stem level where things are not under [her conscious] control." He testified that the child is irreversibly in a state of coma from which "she will never regain [consciousness or] be able to function in any way." He testified that "there is really no potential for this condition to be reversed" except through the perfection of a complete brain transplant operation. **** He testified that entry of a "no code" order was completely consistent with medical ethics.

The District Court judge, substituting his judgment for the incompetent child, found that, if competent, the child would choose not to be resuscitated by extraordinary measures. He therefore ordered that "further ventilator treatment and resuscitative measures be withheld" in the event the child "suffers respiratory distress or cardiac arrest in the future." In addition, he ordered that the Nissen fundoplication surgery be performed in order to reduce the likelihood of the child's aspirating regurgitated food.

Pursuant to G.L. c. 211, § 3 (1990 ed.), the child's guardian ad litem sought relief from the District Court's DNR order before a single justice of this court. The single justice reversed and reported the matter after the parties so requested and submitted a statement of agreed facts. The guardian argues that: (1) the judge's factual findings with respect to the effects of full code treatment clearly are erroneous; (2) the judge's determination that the child would choose to decline resuscitative medical treatment in the event of respiratory or cardiac arrest is without support in the record and the judge's findings; and (3) even if the judge's substituted judgment determination were correct, resuscitative treatment should nevertheless be administered because the State's interest in the preservation of life outweighs the child's desire to have a "no code" order entered on her medical charts. The guardian requests that the order placing the child on "no code" status be vacated, and that we enter a judgment that the child would choose to have all extraordinary medical treatment continue in the event of further cardiac or respiratory arrests. ***

Generally, "no code" orders do not require judicial oversight. ***In this case, however, the minor is incompetent by virtue of both her age and irreversible coma. Further, both parents still also minors, and the mother and child were in the legal custody of DSS. The guardian opposes the DNR order. Moreover, as in *Custody of a Minor (No. 1)*, 385 Mass. 697, 709, 434 N.E.2d 601 (1982), "the child already was within the jurisdiction of the court before the question whether a 'no code' order should be made ... arose." In these circumstances, a judicial "no code" determination is appropriate. ***

The right of incompetent individuals to refuse medical treatment is effectuated through the doctrine of substituted judgment. FN10 *Nobody disputes that the child is incompetent and that a substituted judgment decision was necessary in this case.*] *** In making a substituted judgment determination, the court "dons 'the mental mantle of the incompetent' and substitutes itself as nearly as possible for the individual in the decision-making process.... [T]he court does not decide what is necessarily the best decision but rather what decision would be made by the incompetent person if he or she were competent." *Matter of Moe*, 385 Mass. 555, 565, 432 N.E.2d 712 (1982)***
[FN11 *We have noted that, in cases like this one involving incompetent children, "the substituted judgment doctrine is consistent with the 'best interests of the child' test. It is true that, when applying the 'best interests' test, the inquiry is essentially objective in nature, and the decisions are made not by, but on behalf of, the child.... Nevertheless, the best interests analysis, like that of the substituted judgment doctrine, requires a court to focus on the various factors unique to the situation of the individual for whom it must act.... As a practical matter, the criteria to be examined and the basic applicable reasoning are the same."*] In determining what the incompetent person's choice would be, the judge should consider: (1) the patient's expressed preferences, if any; (2) the patient's religious convictions, if any; (3) the impact on the patient's family; (4) the probability of adverse side effects from the treatment; and (5) the prognosis with and without treatment. See *Guardianship of Roe*, 383 Mass. 415, 444, 421 N.E.2d 40 (1981). The judge must also "tak[e] into account the present and future incompetency of the individual as one of the factors which would necessarily enter into the decision-making process of the competent person." *Saikewicz, supra* 373 Mass. at 752-753, 370 N.E.2d 417. The judge should also consider any countervailing State interests, which may include: (1) the preservation of life; (2) the protection of innocent third parties; (3) the prevention of suicide; and (4) the maintenance of the ethical integrity of the medical profession. *** The judge may consider any additional factors which appear to be relevant. ***
[FN12 *The judge did not address two other State interests, the protection of innocent third parties and prevention of suicide, as they are not relevant to this case***The guardian does not contest the fact that these considerations are irrelevant.*]

With respect to the foregoing factors, the judge found the following facts. Because of her infancy, the child had not expressed any wishes from which the judge could draw guidance. "[B]ecause of the absence of natural family involvement there is no information regarding the child's ethical, moral or religious values that the Court could examine." There would be little, if any, impact on the child's family because the family was never intact. "[T]he implications of a full-code effort would involve a substantial degree of bodily invasion." If the infant were to experience cardiac or respiratory arrest, in the absence of extraordinary measures, the child might die. Even with the full-code treatment, "the prognosis for the child ... would remain terminal because of the untreatable 'brain-dead' condition." The child "has made no gains during her long hospitalization;" "at best [she] will live for an indefinite period in a vegetative coma without any real hope of improvement, and as to the brain damage itself the prognosis is hopeless." [FN15 *The judge also found that "there exists a high probability of adverse neurological effects and serious brain damage, were the infant subjected to the vigors of a full-code treatment." This finding is not supported by the evidence. It is not crucial to the judge's substituted judgment determination.*] The judge's findings, excluding the one for which there is no support, *see* note 15, *supra,* are sufficient to support the determination that the child would refuse resuscitative measures in the event of cardiac or respiratory arrest.

Arguing that the child has no dignity interest in being free of bodily invasions, the guardian states that the child "has no cognitive ability and therefore will suffer no 'indignity' that the medical care might be supposed to produce in a conscious person." "Cognitive ability" is not a prerequisite for enjoying basic liberties. In the law of this jurisdiction, incompetent people are entitled to the same respect, dignity and freedom of choice as competent people. ***

The guardian also argues that, in any event, "the necessity for the bodily invasions occasioned by the efforts to resuscitate have been greatly reduced by [the Nissen fundoplication] surgery." The fact that the invasions may be less frequent than before the surgery does not make any particular invasion less likely to offend the child's dignity.

The guardian claims that "treatment would not occasion any financial disruption of the ward's family, nor involve emotional disturbance which the ward would, if competent, find compelling." Although the guardian proposes that lack of financial disruption counsels in favor of continued treatment, we hardly think the guardian would accept the converse proposition. As we recently stated in *Doe, supra* 411 Mass. at 520 n. 15, 583 N.E.2d 1263, "[t]he judge quite properly did not consider whether [the patient's] continued care would pose a burden of any kind on anyone. The cost of care in human or financial terms is irrelevant to the substituted judgment analysis." The guardian's second claim is controverted most strongly by the fact that both the child's mother and father have expressed their desire that extraordinary measures not be used to prolong the child's life. The mother testified: "I don't like to see her going through, suffering that she's going through.... I know what she was like before this accident. She was a very healthy baby, always smiling ... and she's just laying there doing nothing, and it's not like my daughter." Moreover, the emotional disturbance which the ward herself, if competent, would experience as a result of her condition cannot be underestimated. Last, contrary to the guardian's assertions, there is no evidence that the decision to enter the "no code" order reflects the judge's own judgment about the quality of the child's life. [FN16 *The guardian advances as another reason for opposing the "no code" order that "the treatments will keep her alive indefinitely so that should medical advances occur, however unlikely that may at present appear to be, she will be here to take advantage of them." We reject this argument. By this logic, we must mechanically maintain with respirators and ventilators all people whom current medicine classifies as dead, in the hope that one day medical treatment will become available to remedy their condition. We note that the guardian's suggestion is inconsistent with current medical practice.***]*

The guardian alternatively argues that, assuming that the judge was correct in deciding that the child would choose to refuse resuscitation, the State's interest in the preservation of life outweighs the child's wishes. As we have stated on previous occasions, the State's general interest in the preservation of life is not absolute. Here, as in *Saikewicz, supra* 373 Mass. at 742, 370 N.E.2d 417, "[t]he interest of the State in prolonging a life must be reconciled with the interest of an individual to reject the traumatic cost of that prolongation. There is a substantial distinction in the State's insistence that human life be saved where the affliction is curable, as opposed to the

State interest where, as here, the issue is not whether, but when, for how long, and at what cost to the individual that life may be briefly extended."

The substituted judgment decision and the entry of the "do not resuscitate" order are affirmed.
NOLAN, Justice (dissenting).

A person is not obligated to take extraordinary means to prolong his life and, therefore, persons acting in behalf of others who are faced with such a decision, are not required to invoke extraordinary means.

However, the court again has approved application of the doctrine of substituted judgment when there is not a soupcon of evidence to support it. The trial judge did not have a smidgen of evidence on which to conclude that if this child who is now about five and one half years old were competent to decide, she would elect certain death to a life with no cognitive ability. The route by which the court arrives at its conclusion is a cruel charade which is being perpetuated whenever we are faced with a life and death decision of an incompetent person.

c. *Planned Parenthood v. Casey*
Planned Parenthood of Southeastern Pennsylvania v. Casey
505 U.S. 833 (1992)

Justice O'CONNOR, Justice KENNEDY, and Justice SOUTER announced the judgment of the Court and delivered the opinion of the Court with respect to Parts I, II, III, V-A, V-C, and VI, an opinion with respect to Part V-E, in which Justice STEVENS joins, and an opinion with respect to Parts IV, V-B, and -D.
***

We next consider the parental consent provision. Except in a medical emergency, an unemancipated young woman under 18 may not obtain an abortion unless she and one of her parents (or guardian) provides informed consent as defined above. If neither a parent nor a guardian provides consent, a court may authorize the performance of an abortion upon a determination that the young woman is mature and capable of giving informed consent and has in fact given her informed consent, or that an abortion would be in her best interests.

We have been over most of this ground before. Our cases establish, and we reaffirm today, that a State may require a minor seeking an abortion to obtain the consent of a parent or guardian, provided that there is an adequate judicial bypass procedure. *See e.g. Akron II*, *; Hodgson, *; *id.*, at 497-501,; *Akron I*, *;; *Bellotti II*, *. Under these precedents, in our view, the one-parent consent requirement and judicial bypass procedure are constitutional.

The only argument made by petitioners respecting this provision and to which our prior decisions do not speak is the contention that the parental consent requirement is invalid because it requires informed parental consent. For the most part, petitioners' argument is a reprise of their argument with respect to the informed consent requirement in general, and we reject it for the reasons given above. Indeed, some of the provisions regarding informed consent have particular force with respect to minors: the waiting period, for example, may provide the parent or parents of a pregnant young woman the opportunity to consult with her in private, and to discuss the consequences of her decision in the context of the values and moral or religious principles of their family. *
***

Justice STEVENS, concurring in part and dissenting in part [would strike down the informed consent and 24-hour waiting period provisions upheld by the Court and because the parental consent provision included those provisions he would invalidate it] .

Justice BLACKMUN, concurring in part, concurring in the judgment in part, and dissenting in part.
***

Except in the case of a medical emergency, § 3206 requires a physician to obtain the informed consent of a parent or guardian before performing an abortion on an unemancipated minor or an incompetent woman. *** The requirement of an in-person visit would carry with it the risk of a delay of several days or possibly weeks, even where the parent is willing to consent. While the State has an interest in encouraging parental involvement in the minor's abortion decision, § 3206 is not narrowly drawn to serve that interest.

***

Chief Justice REHNQUIST, with whom Justice WHITE, Justice SCALIA, and Justice THOMAS join, concurring in the judgment in part and dissenting in part.

*** We believe that *Roe* was wrongly decided, and that it can and should be overruled consistently with our traditional approach to stare decisis in constitutional cases. We would adopt the approach of the plurality in *Webster v. Reproductive Health Services*, *, and uphold the challenged provisions of the Pennsylvania statute in their entirety.

*** [The dissenters emphasize, *inter alia*, the inconsistencies of the abortion cases.] For example, after *Roe*, many States have sought to protect their young citizens by requiring that a minor seeking an abortion involve her parents in the decision. Some States have simply required notification of the parents, while others have required a minor to obtain the consent of her parents. In a number of decisions, however, the Court has substantially limited the States in their ability to impose such requirements. With regard to parental notice requirements, we initially held that a State could require a minor to notify her parents before proceeding with an abortion. *H. L. v. Matheson*, *. Recently, however, we indicated that a State's ability to impose a notice requirement actually depends on whether it requires notice of one or both parents. We concluded that although the Constitution might allow a State to demand that notice be given to one parent prior to an abortion, it may not require that similar notice be given to two parents, unless the State incorporates a judicial bypass procedure in that two-parent requirement. *Hodgson* *.

We have treated parental consent provisions even more harshly. Three years after *Roe*, we invalidated a Missouri regulation requiring that an unmarried woman under the age of 18 obtain the consent of one of her parents before proceeding with an abortion. We held that our abortion jurisprudence prohibited the State from imposing such a "blanket provision ... requiring the consent of a parent." *Danforth* *. In *Bellotti v. Baird*, *, the Court struck down a similar Massachusetts parental consent statute. A majority of the Court indicated, however, that a State could constitutionally require parental consent, if it alternatively allowed a pregnant minor to obtain an abortion without parental consent by showing either that she was mature enough to make her own decision, or that the abortion would be in her best interests. *. In light of *Bellotti*, we have upheld one parental consent regulation which incorporated a judicial bypass option we viewed as sufficient, see *Planned Parenthood Assn. of Kansas City, Mo., Inc. v. Ashcroft*, *, but have invalidated another because of our belief that the judicial procedure did not satisfy the dictates of *Bellotti*, see *Akron v. Akron Center for Reproductive Health, Inc.*, *. We have never had occasion, as we have in the parental notice context, to further parse our parental consent jurisprudence into one-parent and two-parent components.

***

[The parental consent] provision is entirely consistent with this Court's previous decisions involving parental consent requirements. ***

We think it beyond dispute that a State "has a strong and legitimate interest in the welfare of its young citizens, whose immaturity, inexperience, and lack of judgment may sometimes impair their ability to exercise their rights wisely." *Hodgson*, *. A requirement of parental consent to abortion, like myriad other restrictions placed upon minors in other contexts, is reasonably designed to further this important and legitimate state interest. In our view, it is entirely "rational and fair for the State to conclude that, in most instances, the family will strive to give a lonely or

even terrified minor advice that is both compassionate and mature." *Ohio v. Akron Center for Reproductive Health,* *; *see also Danforth,* * (Stewart, J., concurring) *. We thus conclude that Pennsylvania's parental consent requirement should be upheld.
***

d. Other Supreme Court Cases About Minors' Abortion Decisions

After some initial confusion, the Supreme Court has been quite consistent in upholding laws that mandate some form of parental participation in the abortion decision of a minor, so long as some form of "judicial bypass" of parental participation is allowed in cases of "mature minors" if the abortion is deemed in the best interest of the minor by the judge. Following *Danforth,* in 1979, in *Bellotti v. Baird (II),* 433 U.S. 622 (1979), the Supreme Court invalidated a Massachusetts statute which provided that a minor seeking an abortion had to try to obtain the consent of her parents; if they would not give consent, she could get an abortion by obtaining an approval of a state court judge upon showing that the abortion would be in her best interests. Justice Powell announced the decision of the Court and rendered a plurality opinion for four justices which emphasized that the defect of the Massachusetts law was the requirement that minors notify their parents in all cases; provision for secret, ex-parte proceedings in which minors might be able to convince the court of their maturity or need for a secret abortion was emphasized by this faction of the Court. Four other justices, however, took the position that the defect in the Massachusetts scheme was the requirement of third party *consent* (either parental or judicial) in *all* cases.

The major tack in the development of the minor's abortion doctrine was *H. L. v. Matheson,* 450 U.S. 398 (1981). In that case, the Supreme Court upheld a Utah law that required doctors performing an abortion upon an unmarried minor to notify her parents "if possible" prior to the performance of an abortion. The Court emphasized that the Utah Statute did not authorize parental veto, merely parental notification of the minor's desire for an abortion. The Court further noted that the statute was reasonably flexible (the "if possible" language), and did not preclude the possibility that "mature minors" might obtain abortions without parental notification upon a showing of their emancipation.

In *Planned Parenthood Association of Kansas, Missouri, Inc. v. Ashcroft,* 462 U.S. 476 (1983), the Missouri requirement that minors secure parental consent or judicial consent (based on a finding of maturity or best interests) before obtaining abortions was upheld in as much as it provided an alternative procedure where by a pregnant minor could demonstrate that she was sufficiently mature to make the decision to have an abortion on her own or that the abortion would be in her best interests.

In *Ohio v. Akron Center for Reproductive Health, Inc.,* 497 U.S. 502 (1990) ("*Akron II*"), the Court upheld, by a vote of 6-3, an Ohio law generally requiring that a parent be notified 24-hours before an abortion is performed on a minor child, unless a court order (judicial bypass) was obtained. The same day, in *Hodgson v. Minnesota,* 497 U.S. 417 (1990), the Court struck down a two-parent notification requirement without a judicial bypass provision, but upheld the same requirement with a judicial bypass provision. Four justices indicated that a two-parent notification requirement would be upheld with or without judicial bypass on the ground that parental notification is distinguishable from and less burdensome than a parental consent requirement. Four justices indicated that two-parent notification is so irrational (because of so many divorced, separated and other single-parent families) that it would be unconstitutional even with judicial bypass. One justice (O'Connor) held that with judicial bypass a two-parent requirement is constitutional; without judicial bypass, it is unconstitutional.

In 1992, in *Planned Parenthood v. Casey, supra,* the Court upheld Pennsylvania's parental consent provision by a vote of 4+3+1-1. After *Casey,* there seemed to be a temporary lull in challenges to parental participation laws. Then, in *Lambert v. Wicklund,* 117 S. Ct. 1169 (1997), the Court Per Curiam reversed the Ninth Circuit and a U.S. district court which had invalidated a Montana parental notice law. The law required that one parent must be notified 48 hours before performance of abortion unless a court waived the requirement on showing that (1) the minor was "sufficiently mature," or (2) she had been the victim of a pattern of parental physical, sexual, or emotional abuse, or (3) parental notification was "not in the best interests of the minor." The Supreme Court noted that its prior decisions had never determined whether judicial bypass is necessary when the statute merely requires parental notification (instead of parental consent), and found that the "best interests" exception encompassed both benefit from abortion and harm from notification. Justice Stevens, joined by Ginsburg and Breyer, JJ., concurred because the Montana statute was "essentially identical" to the statute upheld in *Akron II,* but noted that either "best interest" showing would justify judicial bypass, a showing of both was not necessary.

e. Notes and Questions

1) *State v. McKown*
What is the purpose for the spiritual treatment and prayer exception to the child neglect statute? Does this exception adequately protect the well-being of the child?

2) Mature Minors
Many states have codified the common law rule that mature minors may consent to treatment for non-emergency treatment although some states have not adopted the common law rule. Others have extended the mature minors exception to emergency treatment. All states allow minors of a certain age (varies among the states) to consent to treatment for venereal disease, drug and alcohol treatment. For abortion and contraceptive decisions, the United States Supreme Court has addressed the issue. A

state may not prohibit the distribution of contraceptives to minors. *Carey v. Population Service International*, 431 U.S. 678 (1977). If parental consent is required by the state, there must be an alternative procedure to allow the pregnant minor "to show that she is mature enough and well enough informed to make the decision" independently, or if she is not able to make the decision independently, the abortion would be in her best interest. *Bellotti v. Baird*, 43 U.S. 622 (1979); *Planned Parenthood v. Casey*, 505 U.S. 833 (1992). What qualifies a minor to be a "mature minor"? Would a bright line age determination be a more manageable standard? Or, age as a rebuttable presumption of maturity?

3) Mental Health

The United States Supreme Court has recognized that minors have a liberty interest in not being confined in a mental institution and avoiding the stigma of confinement. The minor's liberty interest is, however, not equivalent to that of an adult, including not having all the procedural due process protections in confinement situations. A parent may commit a child to a mental institution as long as there is a pre-commitment investigation by a neutral fact finder. *Parham v. J.R.*, 442 U.S. 584 (1979).

4) *Care and Protection of Beth*

Not all courts would apply the substituted judgment standard in cases of immature minors or persons who have never been competent. They would use the best interests standard. The decision maker determines whether withholding treatment serves the patient's best interests. Typical factors that the decision maker balances are the level of physical, cognitive, and sensory functions, the degree of pain, present life expectancy, prognosis for recovery, etc. Would that standard have satisfied the dissenting judge? Did the majority misapply the substituted judgment standard as the dissent argues?

5) *Danforth* and *Casey*

Was Justice Stevens correct when he suggested that Justice Blackmun's opinion in *Danforth* just substituted one arbitrary measure (ability to ovulate) for an historic-if-arbitrary one (age) as the standard for determining when a minor's constitutional right to have an abortion "springs into being"? Is not abortion a significant moral decision? Should parents be barred from knowing about, advising, counseling their daughters about such a decision? Who will counsel and cope with the consequences of the abortion decision in the life of the teenager? Will the judge who approved her abortion "be there" for her? Will her abortion-clinic counselor?

Why should it be necessary for states specifically to authorize judicial bypass of a parent's participation in such an enormous medical/moral decision of a minor? Why should the state authorize a judge to substitute his or her judgment for that of the parents? Is it any surprise that studies of "judicial bypass" statutes show that courts "rubber stamp" judicial bypass approval (approving the abortion without notification of the parents) in assembly-line, robotic fashion? Is this a form of imperialism of the "elite" judicial class over traditional or poor or ethnic parents who would try to discourage their daughter from having an abortion?

In "judicial bypass" proceedings, the issue is either whether the minor is "mature" enough to make the abortion decision on her own, or whether it would be in her best interests to allow her to have an abortion without notifying her parents. Of course, parents would be very important (in most cases the best) sources of information about both "maturity" and "best interests" issues, including medical best interests. But since the hearing is *ex parte*, they are not even allowed to participate in such hearings. If the decision is of such importance that it merits designation as a constitutionally fundamental right, is it not curious to exclude from the hearing regarding the matter the best sources of factual information upon which to base the decision? The Court acknowledges that parents' interest in knowing of and counseling their pregnant minor daughters regarding a possible abortion decision is rather important. Might it be as important a dimension of parenthood as the right of parents involved in *Meyer v. Nebraska* (to provide education in German for a child under the age of 16)? Yet what procedural protection does the Court provide before that right is taken from the parents? Are they even given notice that a court may take that right away from them? Are they given an opportunity to be heard?

Following *Danforth* and *Casey*, many courts have rejected petitions by the biological fathers of unborn children to give them some voice or right to participate in the abortion decision or to let them protect or take legal custody of their prenatal offspring. *See* Chapter 18.A.2.g, *supra*. Under equal protection doctrine, how is this possible? Could a law give a father the unilateral right to release a child for adoption over the mother's objection? Without even giving her notice? Why/not?

In *Ayotte v. Planned Parenthood*, __ U.S. __, 126 U.S. 961 (2006) the Court unanimously vacated the lower federal courts rulings declaring a New Hampshire parental notification law unconstitutional, and remanded to the First Circuit to determine if a narrower remedy than facial invalidation could be fashioned. The New Hampshire law required parental consent 48 hours before an abortion on a minor, except if the minor's life was endangered by such delay, or if a court found the minor mature or that abortion without notification would be in her best interests, but did not specify an exception for health-endangerment. The state showed that there would be extremely few such situations and the Court ruled that even if the law were unconstitutional in those rare cases, facial invalidation of the law might be inappropriate. If abortion risks serious moral and physical ramifications, under what, if any, circumstances should the persons with the greatest knowledge of the medical history and moral development of the child not be asked to provide such evidence to the court, doctor, or child? Under what, if any, circumstances should the persons legally responsible for the welfare of their child, who will have to help her cope with the consequences (medical, emotional, moral) of such a profound decision as to abort a child) in the months and years following the procedure, be denied notification?

3. Practical and Ethical Consideration

a. Abortion and Mental Health Participation
Why do you think that the Supreme Court differentiates between abortions and mental health confinement in giving parents much more control in the latter and basically none in the former?

b. Mature Minors

Suppose in *State v. McKown*, the child was fifteen years old and consented to the treatment. Would the mature minor exception apply? After his death, how would his parents show he was mature? He consented? Could he be mature but incompetent to make the decision? Are maturity and competency the same?

4. Bibliography

Patricia A. King, *Treatment and Minors: Issues Not Involving Lifesaving Treatment*, 23 J. Fam. L. 241 (1984-85).

Jennifer L. Rosato, *Putting Square Pegs in a Round hole: Procedural Due Process and the Effect of Faith Healing Exemptions on the Prosecution of Faith Healing Parents*, 29 U.S.F. L. Rev. 43 (1994).

Walter Wadlington, *Medical Decisionmaking For and By Children: Tensions Between Parent, State, and Child*, 1994 U. Ill.L. Rev. 311.

B. DISCIPLINE

1. Background

Parents may use reasonable discipline in the care, supervision, and control of their child. On the other hand, parents may not have the legal obligation to support the child if the child wants to avoid parental control and voluntarily abandons the parent's home. Corporal punishment, as a disciplinary practice, has had a long history in this country.

> The right of parents to chastise their refractory and disobedient children is so necessary to the government of families, to the good order of society, that no moralist or lawgiver has ever thought of interfering with its existence or of calling upon them to account for the manner of its exercise, upon light or frivolous pretences. But, at the same time that the law has created and preserved this right, in its regard for the safety of the child it has prescribed bounds beyond which it shall not be carried.
>
> In chastising a child, the parent must be careful that he does not exceed the bounds of moderation and inflict cruel and merciless punishment; if he does, he is a trespasser, and liable to be punished by indictment. It is not, then, the infliction of punishment, but the excess, which constitutes the offence, and what this excess shall be is not a conclusion of law, but a question of fact for the determination of the jury.

Johnson v. State, 21 Tenn. 282, 283 (1840). With the public's growing discomfort about corporal punishment and concerns about child abuse, the line between corporal punishment as a disciplinary measure and child abuse may depend upon the wording of the state's child abuse statute.

2. Statutes, Cases and Doctrines

a. *Petition of Jane Doe*

Petition of Jane Doe
564 A.2D 433 (N.H. 1989)

BATCHELDER, Justice.

Jane Doe petitions this court for a writ of certiorari to reverse a "fair hearing" decision by the New Hampshire Department of Health and Human Services, Division for Children and Youth Services (DCYS), finding that she abused her young son on two separate occasions. On the facts and record of this case, we reverse the decision of the DCYS.

This case requires us to determine whether DCYS proved that Jane Doe committed child abuse, as that term is defined by RSA chapter 169-C, the Child Protection Act and Reporting Law. A brief review of the statute provides the backdrop for this case. The overall purposes of this law are to provide protection to children whose life, health, or welfare may be endangered and to assist parents to contend with, and to correct, family problems in order to avoid having children removed from the family. RSA 169-C:2, I (Supp.1988). To effect the law's purposes, RSA 169-C:29 (Supp.1988) requires that physicians, psychological therapists and teachers, among others, "having reason to suspect that a child has been abused or neglected" report such circumstances to the bureau of child and family services (bureau) within DCYS. Once the DCYS bureau receives a report of abuse or neglect, it must undertake an investigation within seventy-two hours, RSA 169-C:34, I (Supp.1988), to determine: (1) the composition of the child's family or household; (2) whether probable cause exists to believe that any child in the family is abused or neglected, "including a determination of harm or threatened harm to each child, the nature and extent of present or prior injuries, abuse or neglect, and any evidence thereof," as well as a determination of the persons responsible for the abuse; (3) the immediate and long-term risk to the child if he or she remains in the existing home environment; and (4) the protective treatment and ameliorative services necessary to prevent further abuse or neglect, and to improve the home environment and the parents' ability to care for the children, RSA 169-C:34, II (Supp.1988).

One aspect of the bureau's investigation, as noted above, is to decide whether probable cause exists to believe that a child is being abused. The bureau may find probable cause when it possesses knowledge of such "facts and circumstances based upon accurate and reliable information, including hearsay, that would justify a reasonable person to believe that a child ... is abused or neglected." RSA 169-C:3, XXIII (Supp.1988). The statute expansively defines an abused child as one who has been: "(a) Sexually abused; (b) Intentionally physically injured; (c) Psychologically injured ...; or (d) Physically injured by other than accidental means." RSA 169-C:3, II (Supp.1988). Upon finding probable cause that the child has been abused, DCYS may petition the district court, RSA 169-C:7 (Supp.1988), to obtain protective orders for the child, including an order removing the child from the home, RSA 169-C:16, 169-C:19 (Supp.1988). Whether or not probable cause is found, each instance of reported abuse is entered into a central registry. * Unfounded reports, those for which probable cause does not exist, RSA 169-C:3, XXVIII (Supp.1988), are kept in the registry for three years. Founded reports are retained for seven years. *. According to one national study, only forty percent of all child abuse reports are substantiated; the rest are investigated and dismissed.*** When the DCYS finds probable cause to believe abuse has occurred, the alleged child abuser has a due process right to notice of that finding and a hearing to challenge that determination. *** It is from the decision after such a hearing, called a fair hearing by the department of health and human services, that Jane Doe petitions this court. With this statutory and procedural background in mind, we analyze the facts of this case.

Jane Doe is a single, working mother. Her son John was born on March 15, 1984. When John was about twenty-one months old, in December, 1985, his mother hit him in the area of the mouth because, during mealtime, John persisted in throwing food. This punishment cut John's lip, causing it to bleed and swell. The swelling subsided within an hour, according to Jane. Concerned about her actions, Jane told the therapist she was seeing at the time, Sheila Renaud-Finnegan, about the incident. Renaud-Finnegan told Jane that she would have to report the incident to DCYS, and the therapist did so on December 23, 1985. In January, 1986, a DCYS investigating social worker, Judy Malcolm, spoke with Jane about the event. Jane described the circumstances to Malcolm and told her she was working with a counselor. Malcolm determined that the child abuse report was "founded, problem resolved," a designation which resulted in Doe's name being entered into the central registry, but requiring no further intervention by the DCYS because the problem "has been resolved to the Division's satisfaction or a satisfactory referral to another community resource has been made." *N.H.Admin.Rules*, He-C 6426.01(n).

On May 18, 1987, about seventeen months after the first incident, Jane again hit her son. This time, she and John had returned from grocery shopping at 9:00 p.m., after Jane had put in a day's work. Upon being told he had to go to bed, John had a temper tantrum. When Jane instructed him to stop, he swore at her. Jane then slapped John with the back of her hand, hitting him in the temple area. The slap left a bruise on John's temple, which lasted approximately two and one-half days. Jane was wearing a ring at the time, a factor which may have contributed to the bruise.

At John's day-care center the next day, a worker noticed the bruise on his temple. The worker called Jane to discuss the bruise, and Jane admitted striking John. The day-care center notified DCYS's Malcolm of the incident on May 20. That same day, Malcolm interviewed John at the day-care center and photographed his bruise. Malcolm left a message at the day-care center, requesting Jane to call her. Sheryl Fair, Malcolm's supervisor, reviewed notes of the reported abuse and wrote a note to Malcolm. In the note, Fair listed several factors--John's age, the location of the injury, Jane's denial of previous abuse, the failure of "prior safety factors," an "uncontrollable" mother--leading her to conclude that the situation "looks very serious" and instructing Malcolm to "consider placement here."

On May 21, Jane telephoned Malcolm and discussed the incident. In their conversation, Jane claimed it was the first time she had hit John, until Malcolm refreshed her memory about the December, 1985 incident. Jane also said that John was not a behavior problem at home, a fact which contradicted Malcolm's information about John's aggressive behavior at the day-care center. At Malcolm's suggestion, Jane agreed to renew counselling, which she had ended more than a year earlier.

On May 28, 1987, Malcolm met with Jane and told her that she needed counselling to help her deal with her son. On June 12, 1987, Malcolm wrote to Jane, reiterating her concern and offering to help Jane find a therapist. On June 23, 1987, Malcolm again wrote to Jane about obtaining counselling and threatened to take legal action if Jane had not given her the name of her chosen therapist. At some point, Jane contacted a mental health center about its services but was told that weekly sessions would cost forty dollars more than her insurance would cover. Given her weekly net salary of $150, she could not afford such counselling.

On July 8, 1987, Malcolm was informed of another red mark on John's body, this time on his neck. John gave conflicting explanations of how he got the red mark, including that his mother had caused the mark. Jane strongly denied causing the mark on her son's neck. On August 21, 1987, Malcolm designated Jane's case as "opened for protective services," a term which, according to DCYS regulations, is used to refer to all of the social services that can be provided to prevent or remedy, *inter alia*, child abuse. *N.H. Admin. Rules*, He-C 6426.01(z). By letter dated September 8, 1987, sent Jane notice that they had found reason to believe that she had abused her son on both May 18 and on July 7, 1987. The notice also referred to the case of founded abuse involving the December, 1985 incident.

Jane timely requested a fair hearing, *see N.Y.Admin.Rules*, He-C 6201.01(i) (fair hearing is an administrative forum in which impartial decision-maker hears evidence on DCYS action or inaction), on the findings of abuse. The fair hearing was conducted by Dagny Fecht, the hearing officer, and Elizabeth Linsky, the panel expert, on March 24, 1988. In addition to the testimony of Jane Doe and Judy Malcolm, from which the facts recited above were elicited, the hearing officer received a letter from Dr. Thomas C. Bisett, John's pediatrician, describing his October 9, 1987 examination of the boy. Dr. Bisett's letter noted that John's medical record did not indicate a pattern of repeated office visits because of injury, and that regularly scheduled appointments had been kept. In addition, the letter noted that no visible evidence disclosed recent injury, that a series of long bone films ruled out recent and old bone injury, and that John's blood tests, taken because of his mother's claims that he bruised easily, showed results within normal limits. Dr. Bisett concluded his letter by stating that he did "not find a history suggestive of, nor a current situation consistent with, child abuse for John."

Jane Doe also offered the testimony of Dr. Wilfred Derby, a clinical psychologist. Dr. Derby testified to the difficulty in drawing a line between child abuse and acceptable forms of corporal punishment, as well as the differences among various authorities as to what actions constitute abuse. He also testified about two tests, the Adult/Adolescent Parenting Inventory (AAPI) and the Parenting Stress Inventory (PSI), used to assess young parents' inclination toward child abuse. Dr. Derby administered both of the tests to Jane in January, 1988. On the AAPI, Jane scored slightly below the average range on her willingness to consider alternatives to corporal punishment, but not within the range indicating a high potential for abuse. She scored average or above on the other indicators. On the PSI, used to assess the interaction between the parent and the child and the parent's perception of the child, Jane scored within normal ranges for all behaviors, except that she is depressed. Dr. Derby concluded that John was not an abused child, since he found, *inter alia*, that the incidents at issue were isolated and did not require medical attention. According to the definition of abuse he used, if an injury does not require medical attention, the definition is not met.

The other testimony in the fair hearing came from Sheryl Fair, the DCYS supervisor who made the determination of abuse in this case. Fair, who has nearly thirty years experience in dealing with child abuse, stated that John was at moderate risk because of his age, the bruise on his temple, a young single mother who loses control, and the mother's inability to identify precipitating factors. To make a determination of risk, DCYS policy provides for the use of a risk matrix. Fair was unsure whether she relied upon the risk matrix in reaching her conclusion that John was at moderate risk.

At the hearing, the parties agreed that the July, 1987 bruise would not be at issue because the reporter of the alleged abuse may have tainted the investigation by questioning the child improperly. Thus, only the December, 1985 and May, 1987 incidents were relevant; and, as to those, the hearing officer, Dagny Fecht, came to the following conclusions. The testimony of Dr. Bisett was minimized, noting that he had examined John months after the May event had occurred and that the absence of recorded office visits because of injury was negated by Jane's failure to get medical attention for the two incidents at issue. From Dr. Derby's testimony, Fecht concluded that Jane "is depressed, has low attachment, suffers from social isolation and ... is living on [sic] a highly stressful situation...." The officer thus found, despite Jane's argument that she made two mistakes in administering corporal punishment, that the cut lip and temple bruise "were not caused by accidental means but rather the result of a deliberate blow to John on each occasion...." Fecht concluded that these acts constituted physical abuse, threatening harm to the child's health and welfare.

In her petition to this court, Jane contends that the fair hearing officer improperly found child abuse under RSA 169-C:3, II(d) (Supp.1988) because DCYS presented no evidence to show that Jane harmed John's health or welfare. Alternatively, Jane argues that even if the statute was applied properly, such an application violated her constitutional right to privacy under the State and federal due process clauses, and also violated the supremacy clause of the United States Constitution. We agree with the petitioner that a literal reading of RSA 169-C:3, II (Supp.1988) as applied in this case may have constitutional implications, see In re Fay G., 120 N.H. 153, 156, 412 A.2d 1012, 1015 (1980) ("the family and the rights of parents over it are fundamental and inherent within the federal and our own State constitutions"), but we need not address the constitutional issues, as we decide this case on statutory grounds.

Our review on certiorari of the fair hearing decision requires us to determine whether the agency "has acted 'illegally in respect to jurisdiction, authority or observance of the law ... or has abused its discretion or acted arbitrarily or capriciously.' " *** The petitioner's essential argument is that a finding of abuse under the Child Protection Act, RSA chapter 169-C, requires more than a showing that a child has been injured by other than accidental means. Rather, it requires evidence that the child's health or welfare has been or will be harmed. As support for this position, the petitioner notes that the statute's definition of abuse focuses on the child's condition, not the single acts of parents. Further, she points out that for each instance of reported abuse, DCYS's initial investigation must include "a determination of harm or threatened harm to each child" in the family of the person suspected of abusive behavior. RSA 169-C:34, II(ii) (Supp.1988). Unless such a determination is incorporated in the definition of an abused child, she argues, the statute is vague and gives DCYS too much discretion to bring the power of the State to bear on the appropriateness of parental disciplinary choices. Finally, the petitioner asserts that the legislature, by statute, has permitted parents to use reasonable force to control their children without incurring criminal liability, RSA 627:6, and DCYS's interpretation of child abuse conflicts with that statute.

In response, DCYS maintains that the statutory definition of child abuse is clear and should be interpreted according to its plain meaning. DCYS states that John suffered two non-accidental injuries caused by his mother. These injuries thus bring John within the definition of an abused child, which in turn permits DCYS to determine the protective treatment and administrative services necessary to improve the home and prevent further abuse. Further, DCYS contends that its interpretation is entirely consistent with the goals and purposes of the child protection statute, contrary to the petitioner's argument otherwise. Finally, DCYS argues that its interpretation of the definition of child abuse does not conflict with RSA 627:6, because that statute permits only the reasonable use of force, which does not include twice bruising the head of a child under three years of age.

To resolve the statutory arguments, principles of statutory interpretation require us to look first to the statutory language itself, In re John Kevin B., 129 N.H. 286, 288, 525 A.2d 281, 282-83 (1987), and to construe the law in a manner consistent with its plain meaning, when possible, Theresa S. v. Sup't of YDC, 126 N.H. 53, 55, 489 A.2d 592, 593 (1985). To divine the intent of a statute, we will determine its meaning from its construction as a whole, not by examining isolated words and phrases. *** With these canons of statutory interpretation as guides, we address the arguments of the parties.

We agree with the petitioner's argument that RSA 169-C:3, II(d) (Supp.1988) requires more than proof of two incidents, spaced approximately one and one-half years apart, which resulted in a swollen lip and a bruise on the head. Although DCYS is correct in stating that the plain meaning of the statutory definition of child abuse--to be "physically injured by other than accidental means"-- could be interpreted literally to include the minor injuries caused here, such an interpretation is overly broad and could encompass reasonable forms of corporal punishment that do not threaten the well-being of the child. Moreover, such an interpretation conflicts with the language throughout RSA chapter 169-C which emphasizes harm to the health or welfare of the child. E.g., RSA 169-C:2, I (Supp.1988) (purpose of this chapter is "to provide protection to children whose life, health, or welfare is endangered"); RSA 169-C:3, XIX(b) (Supp.1988) (neglected child defined in part as a child without proper parental care or control "necessary for his physical, mental, or emotional health, when it is established that his health has suffered or is likely to suffer serious impairment"); RSA 169-C:3, XXVII-a (Supp.1988) (sexual abuse defined as certain activities under circumstances indicating "that the child's health or welfare is harmed or threatened with harm"); RSA 169-C:34, II (Supp.1988) (child protective investigation must include "a determination of harm or threatened harm to each child"); *see also* 42 U.S.C.A. § 5106g(4) (West Supp.1988) (federal definition of child abuse includes physical injury inflicted "under circumstances which indicate that the child's health or welfare is harmed or threatened thereby").

We do not lightly interpret a statute so as to impose a requirement that does not appear on its face. Nevertheless, given the facts of the case, and reviewing the definition of child abuse in light of the statute as a whole, we conclude that a proper finding of child abuse under RSA 169-C:3, II(d) (Supp.1988) must include a determination of whether the alleged abusive act was committed under circumstances indicating harm or threatened harm to the child's life, health, or welfare. Such harm may be demonstrated by, for example, the severity of the intentionally inflicted injuries; recurring or a threat of recurring injury; or injury when a profile of the child's caretaker indicates a history of, or a propensity for, abuse. These examples are in no way intended to be limiting, as we recognize the myriad situations in which harm or threatened harm may exist.

In reaching the conclusion we do, we emphasize that we are aware of the difficult duties the department of health and human services has in carrying out its responsibilities to protect children in abusive or potentially abusive situations. We are cognizant that there may be instances where two incidents, or even a single one, may properly be considered abuse under the statute. In many cases, the abuse will be all too evident and clear. We are not faced with such a situation in this case, however. The record reveals that Jane Doe struck her child on two occasions, cutting a lip and causing it to swell briefly for an hour, and then, about eighteen months later, striking his head with the back of her hand and leaving a bruise on his temple. DCYS concedes that both injuries were minor. The expert witnesses at the fair hearing concluded that Jane was not an abusive mother, and that John was not an abused child. DCYS presented no evidence, other than evidence concerning the two incidents, to counter the experts' testimony. DCYS failed to offer any facts to show that John's life, health, or welfare was harmed, or would be threatened with harm, by his mother's actions. On such a record, in a case where difficult lines between corporal punishment and child abuse must be drawn, we hold that the findings of abuse must be reversed.

Reversed. All concurred.

b. Notes and Questions

Do you think Jane Doe was an abusive mother or just disciplining her child? There is a growing medical awareness that even shaking a baby moderately may damage the child's brain? Do you think it would be good public policy to mandate all parents attend parenting classes? Often the legal distinction between abuse and discipline depends on the wording of the statute defining abuse and the requirement of "intentionally harming." Do you think the court interpreted the child abuse statute properly in this case? Do you think cases such as *Jane Doe* should be treated civilly and not criminally?

3. Practical and Ethical Considerations

a. Religion and Corporal Punishment

If a state abolished parental corporal punishment, would first amendment issues arise? Some parents believe corporal punishment has a religious basis. "Spare the rod and spoil the child." A number of European countries have outlawed corporal punishment. The trend in many school systems is to abolish corporal punishment even though the Supreme Court in *Ingraham v. Wright*, 430 U.S. 651 (1977), found that corporal punishment did not constitute cruel and unusual punishment.

4. Bibliography

Douglas K. Besharov, *Child Abuse and Neglect Reporting and Investigation: Policy Guidelines for Decision Making,* 22 Family L.Q. 1, 12 (1988).

Kandice K. Johnson, *Crime or Punishment: The Parental Corporal Punishment Defense–Reasonable and Necessary, or Excused Abuse?*, 1998 U. Ill. L. Rev. 413.

Murray A. Straus, *Spanking and the Making of a Violent Society*, 98 Pediatrics 845 (1996).

CHAPTER 23

Quasi-Parental Relations: Grandparents; Stepparents; Foster Families

A. QUASI-PARENTAL RELATIONS

1. Background

a. Family Autonomy

The doctrine of family autonomy (see chapter 2) recognizes the right of parents to have the companionship of, to care for, to supervise, and to control their children without interference from the state or third parties except for specific circumstances. Family autonomy is recognized as part of the fundamental right of family privacy. Often, there are other persons who have develop close relations with the child. For example, extended family members, especially grandparents and stepparents, may also be in a care giving role as well. The state may also assist in the form of providing foster care when parents are not able to provide proper care for their children. Thus, if other persons have developed a quasi-parental relationship with the child, does that relationship rise to an interest that would be protected by the Constitution even if that interest impinges on the parent's liberty interest? At common law the answer was usually no.

b. Grandparents

The law has usually not dealt with the extended family as to their rights and duties except as to incest, succession and inheritance laws. At common law, grandparents had no right to visit with grandchildren. All states have abrogated the common law, granting visitation for grandparents under specific circumstances. In recent years, there has been frequent litigation concerning the constitutionality of these statutes in light of the doctrine of family autonomy. In *Moore v. City of East Cleveland,* 431 U.S. 494 (1977) (Chapter 2), a zoning ordinance was unconstitutional in limiting the right of a grandparent, her grandchild and her son (his uncle) from defining a family other than the nuclear family. The grandparent's interest in that case, however, did not conflict with the parent's interest. It is estimated that 1.2 million children in the United States are being raised by approximately as many grandparents; forty percent (40%) of those arrangements last for five or more years. Knaplund, *infra,* at 2-3.

c. Stepparents

The stepparent-stepchild relationship in and of itself does not confer any rights and duties unless the law has imposed them. In most instances the issue of duties has arisen in the context of child support. During the marriage, stepparents may establish an "*in loco parentis*" relationship with the stepchild by voluntarily and intentionally assuming the role of a parent to the stepchild. During the marriage, some statutes have imposed a child support obligation on stepparents or if the stepparent has established an in loco parentis relationship. Traditionally, stepparents and stepchildren have had no protected liberty interest in their relationship, and stepparents have been treated as third parties in custody cases. Some courts have granted standing to stepparents in custody and visitation cases when the marriage ends, especially if the stepparent has stood "*in loco parentis*" with the stepchild.

> In most American states, there is a policy that encourages stepparents "to be generous and loving with their stepchildren" without the deterrent of a potential duty of support if the marriage breaks down. Consequently, stepparents usually do not have an obligation to support stepchildren. In a few states, however, to prevent a child from becoming a ward of the state, legislatures require stepparents to support stepchildren who live in their household.

Mabry, *infra*, at 25. As of 2001, over ten million American children lived in step- or blended families. U.S. Census Bureau, *infra*.

d. Foster Families

The foster care system has become an important resource in the state's scheme in caring for children when parents are not able to care for them. A child is usually placed in foster care in the adoption process or in cases of child abuse, neglect and dependency. A child may be in foster care for long periods of time and form a strong bond with the foster parents. As of September 2003 there were 523,000 children in state foster care in the United States; approximately 360,000 were in foster homes; 46,000 in group homes; 51,000 in institutions; 25,000 in pre-adoption placement; 36,000 in other situations (including runaways); the mean/median age of the children was 10.2/10.9 years; the mean/median stay in foster care was 31/18 months; the case goals for half of the children was reunification with their parents; for 20% adoption; for 8% long-term foster care, for 6% emancipation; for 5% kinship care; 119,000 children in foster care were waiting to be adopted. USDHHS, *infra*. 68,000 children in foster care have had their parental rights terminated, *id.*, but most are considered hard-to-place because of their age and/or some behavioral characteristics they have acquired - usually in seriously dysfunctional or abusive homes or institutional placements. Foster homes may provide the best option for such children.

e. Former Nonmarital Partners

As nonmarital cohabitation has dramatically increased in recent years, so have the claims to custody and/or visitation by former nonmarital partners. In 2003 it was reported that 1,799,000 children are living with their mother and her unmarried partner (both heterosexual and homosexual), and 1,081,000 children are living with their father and his unmarried partner (both heterosexual and homosexual), for a total of 2,880,000 children being raised by a parent and a nonmarital partner. Fields, *infra*. The 2000 census report revealed that there were a total of 594,392 same-sex couples among the 5,475,768 unmarried partner households; thus, same-sex couples were nearly 11 percent of the nonmarital cohabitants in America. 2002 Statistical Abstract, *infra*. If the ratio of same-sex nonmarital cohabitant couples are raising children is the same as the ratio of heterosexual cohabiting couples that would suggests that perhaps 317,000 children are being raised by same-sex couples. Wardle, *infra*. When the adult relationships end, litigation over the non-biological partner's quasi-parental rights often ensues. Should former partners have standing to claim custody or visitation against the wishes of the biological parent of the child? What (and what extent of) parental rights should such former partners should be allowed to claim, if any? Why/why not? Legislation addresses the issue in only a few states; and increasingly common law doctrines such as *in loco parentis*, and or judicially- or academically-constructed doctrines such as "psychological parent," and "de facto parent" or "parent by estoppel" are being raised in litigation and, to some extent, accepted by courts. *Id.*

2. Statutes, Cases and Doctrines

a. *Troxel v. Granville*

Jenifer Troxel, et vir., Petitioners, v. Tommie Granville
530 U.S. 57 (2000)

Justice O'CONNOR announced the judgment of the Court and delivered an opinion, in which THE CHIEF JUSTICE, Justice GINSBURG, and Justice BREYER join.

Section 26.10.160(3) of the Revised Code of Washington permits "[a]ny person" to petition a superior court for visitation rights "at any time," and authorizes that court to grant such visitation rights whenever "visitation may serve the best interest of the child." Petitioners Jenifer and Gary Troxel petitioned a Washington Superior Court for the right to visit their grandchildren, Isabelle and Natalie Troxel. Respondent Tommie Granville, the mother of Isabelle and Natalie, opposed the petition. The case ultimately reached the Washington Supreme Court, which held that § 26.10.160(3) unconstitutionally interferes with the fundamental right of parents to rear their children.

I

Tommie Granville and Brad Troxel shared a relationship that ended in June 1991. The two never married, but they had two daughters, Isabelle and Natalie. Jenifer and Gary Troxel are Brad's parents, and thus the paternal grandparents of Isabelle and Natalie. After Tommie and Brad separated in 1991, Brad lived with his parents and regularly brought his daughters to his parents' home for weekend visitation. Brad committed suicide in May 1993. Although the Troxels at first continued to see Isabelle and Natalie on a regular basis after their son's death, Tommie Granville informed the Troxels in October 1993 that she wished to limit their visitation with her daughters to one short visit per month. *

In December 1993, the Troxels commenced the present action by filing, in the Washington Superior Court for Skagit County, a petition to obtain visitation rights with Isabelle and Natalie. The Troxels filed their petition under two Washington statutes, Wash. Rev.Code §§ 26.09.240 and 26.10.160(3) (1994). Only the latter statute is at issue in this case. Section 26.10.160(3) provides: "Any person may petition the court for visitation rights at any time including, but not limited to, custody proceedings. The court may order visitation rights for any person when visitation may serve the best interest of the child whether or not there has been any change of circumstances." At trial, the Troxels requested two weekends of overnight visitation per month and two weeks of visitation each summer. Granville did not oppose visitation altogether, but instead asked the court to order one day of visitation per month with no overnight stay. [cit] In 1995, the Superior Court issued an oral ruling and entered a visitation decree ordering visitation one weekend per month, one week during the summer, and four hours on both of the petitioning grandparents' birthdays. [cit]

Granville appealed, during which time she married Kelly Wynn. Before addressing the merits of Granville's appeal, the Washington Court of Appeals remanded the case to the Superior Court for entry of written findings of fact and conclusions of law. [cit] On remand, the Superior Court found that visitation was in Isabelle and Natalie's best interests:

"The Petitioners [the Troxels] are part of a large, central, loving family, all located in this area, and   the Petitioners can provide opportunities for the children in the areas of cousins and music.

"... The court took into consideration all factors regarding the best interest of the children and   considered all the testimony before it. The children would be benefitted from spending quality   time with the Petitioners, provided that that time is balanced with time with the childrens' [sic]   nuclear family. The court finds that the childrens' [sic] best interests are served by spending time   with their mother and stepfather's other six children." App. 70a.

Approximately nine months after the Superior Court entered its order on remand, Granville's husband formally adopted Isabelle and Natalie. *Id.*, at 60a-67a.

The Washington Court of Appeals reversed the lower court's visitation order and dismissed the Troxels' petition for visitation, holding that nonparents lack standing to seek visitation under § 26.10.160(3) unless a custody action is pending. In the Court of Appeals' view, that limitation on nonparental visitation actions was "consistent with the constitutional restrictions on state interference with parents' fundamental liberty interest in the care, custody, and management of their children." [cit]. Having resolved the case on the statutory ground, however, the Court of Appeals did not expressly pass on Granville's constitutional challenge to the visitation statute. [cit]

The Washington Supreme Court granted the Troxels' petition for review and, after consolidating their case with two other visitation cases, affirmed. The court... found that the plain language of § 26.10.160(3) gave the Troxels standing to seek visitation, irrespective of whether a custody action was pending.[cit] The Washington Supreme Court nevertheless agreed with the Court of Appeals' ultimate conclusion that the Troxels could not obtain visitation of Isabelle and Natalie pursuant to § 26.10.160(3). The court rested its decision on the Federal Constitution, holding that § 26.10.160(3) unconstitutionally infringes on the fundamental right of parents to rear their children. In the court's view, there were at least two problems with the nonparental visitation statute. First, according to the Washington Supreme Court, the Constitution permits a State to interfere with the right of parents to rear their children only to prevent harm or potential harm to a child. Section 26.10.160(3) fails that standard because it requires no threshold showing of harm. [cit] Second, by allowing " 'any person' to petition for forced visitation of a child at 'any time' with the only requirement being that the visitation serve the best interest of the child," the Washington visitation statute sweeps too broadly. [cit] *** Four justices dissented from the Washington Supreme Court's holding on the constitutionality of the statute.[cit]

***

II

The demographic changes of the past century make it difficult to speak of an average American family. The composition of families varies greatly from household to household. While many children may have two married parents and grandparents who visit regularly, many other children are raised in single- parent households. In 1996, children living with only one parent accounted for 28 percent of all children under age 18 in the United States.[cit] Understandably, in these single-parent households, persons outside the nuclear family are called upon with increasing frequency to assist in the everyday tasks of child rearing. In many cases, grandparents play an important role. For example, in 1998, approximately 4 million children--or 5.6 percent of all children under age 18--lived in the household of their grandparents.[cit]

The nationwide enactment of nonparental visitation statutes is assuredly due, in some part, to the States' recognition of these changing realities of the American family. Because grandparents and other relatives undertake duties of a parental nature in many households, States have sought to ensure the welfare of the children therein by protecting the relationships those children form with such third parties. The States' nonparental visitation statutes are further supported by a recognition, which varies from State to State, that children should have the opportunity to benefit from relationships with statutorily specified persons--for example, their grandparents. The extension of statutory rights in this area to persons other than a child's parents, however, comes with an obvious cost. For example, the State's recognition of an independent third-party interest in a child can place a substantial burden on the traditional parent-child relationship.***

The Fourteenth Amendment provides that no State shall "deprive any person of life, liberty, or property, without due process of law." *** The Clause also includes a substantive component that "provides heightened protection against government interference with certain fundamental rights and liberty interests."[cit]

The liberty interest at issue in this case--the interest of parents in the care, custody, and control of their children--is perhaps the oldest of the fundamental liberty interests recognized by this Court. More than 75 years ago, in *Meyer v. Nebraska*, 262 U.S. 390, 399 (1923), we held that the "liberty" protected by the Due Process Clause includes the right of parents to "establish a home and bring up children" and "to control the education of their own." Two years later, in *Pierce v. Society of Sisters*, 268 U.S. 510, 534-535 (1925), we again held that the "liberty of parents and guardians" includes the right "to direct the upbringing and education of children under their control." We explained in Pierce that "[t]he child is not the mere creature of the State; those who nurture him and direct his destiny have the right, coupled with the high duty, to recognize and prepare him for additional obligations." *Id.* at 535. We returned to the subject in *Prince v. Massachusetts*, 321 U.S. 158 (1944), and again confirmed that there is a constitutional dimension to the right of parents to direct the upbringing of their children. "It is cardinal with us that the custody, care and nurture of the child reside first in the parents, whose primary function and freedom include preparation for obligations the state can neither supply nor hinder." *Id.* at 166.

In subsequent cases also, we have recognized the fundamental right of parents to make decisions concerning the care, custody, and control of their children. *See e.g. Stanley v. Illinois*, 405 U.S. 645, 651 (1972) ("It is plain that the interest of a parent in the companionship, care, custody, and management of his or her children 'come[s] to this Court with a momentum for respect lacking when appeal is made to liberties which derive merely from shifting economic arrangements' " (citation omitted)); *Wisconsin v. Yoder*, 406 U.S. 205, 232. (1972) ("The history and culture of Western civilization reflect a strong tradition of parental concern for the nurture and upbringing of their children. This primary role of the parents in the upbringing of their children is now established beyond debate as an enduring American tradition"); *Quilloin v. Walcott*, 434 U.S. 246, 255. (1978) ("We have recognized on numerous occasions that the relationship between parent and child is constitutionally protected"); *Parham v. J. R.*, 442 U.S. 584, 602. (1979) ("Our jurisprudence historically has reflected Western civilization concepts of the family as a unit with broad parental authority over minor children. Our cases have consistently followed that course"); *Santosky v. Kramer*, 455 U.S. 745, 753, 102 S.Ct. 1388, 71 L.Ed.2d 599 (1982) (discussing "[t]he fundamental liberty interest of natural parents in the care, custody, and management of their child"); *Glucksberg, supra*, at 720. ("In a long line of cases, we have held that, in addition to the specific freedoms protected by the Bill of Rights, the 'liberty' specially protected by the Due Process Clause includes the righ[t] ... to direct the education and upbringing of one's children" (citing Meyer and Pierce)). In light of this extensive precedent, it cannot now be doubted that the Due Process Clause of the Fourteenth Amendment protects the fundamental right of parents to make decisions concerning the care, custody, and control of their children.

Section 26.10.160(3), as applied to Granville and her family in this case, unconstitutionally infringes on that fundamental parental right. The Washington nonparental visitation statute is breathtakingly broad. According to the statute's text, "[a]ny person may petition the court for visitation rights at any time," and the court may grant such visitation rights whenever "visitation may serve the best interest of the child." § 26.10.160(3) (emphases added). That language effectively permits any third party seeking visitation to subject any decision by a parent concerning visitation of the parent's children to state-court review. Once the visitation petition has been filed in court*** a parent's decision that visitation would not be in the child's best interest is accorded no deference. Section 26.10.160(3) contains no requirement that a court accord the parent's decision any presumption of validity or any weight whatsoever. Instead, the Washington statute places the best-interest determination solely in the hands of the judge. Should the judge disagree with the parent's estimation of the child's best interests, the judge's view necessarily prevails. Thus, in practical effect, in the State of Washington a court can disregard and overturn any decision by a fit custodial parent concerning visitation whenever a third party affected by the decision files a visitation petition, based solely on the judge's determination of the child's best interests. The Washington Supreme Court had the opportunity to give § 26.10.160(3) a narrower reading, but it declined to do so. [cit]

Turning to the facts of this case, the record reveals that the Superior Court's order was based on precisely the type of mere disagreement we have just described and nothing more. The Superior Court's order was not founded on any special factors that might justify the State's interference with Granville's fundamental right to make decisions concerning the rearing of her two daughters. To be sure, this case involves a visitation petition filed by grandparents soon after the death of their son--the father of Isabelle and Natalie--but the combination of several factors here compels our conclusion that § 26.10.160(3), as applied, exceeded the bounds of the Due Process Clause.

First, the Troxels did not allege, and no court has found, that Granville was an unfit parent. That aspect of the case is important, for there is a presumption that fit parents act in the best interests of their children. As this Court explained in *Parham*:

> [O]ur constitutional system long ago rejected any notion that a child is the mere creature of the State and, on the contrary, asserted that parents generally have the right, coupled with the high duty, to recognize and prepare [their children] for additional obligations. ... The law's concept of the family rests on a presumption that parents possess what a child lacks in maturity, experience, and capacity for judgment required for making life's difficult decisions. More important, historically it has recognized that natural bonds of affection lead parents to act in the best interests of their children.[cit]

Accordingly, so long as a parent adequately cares for his or her children (i.e., is fit), there will normally be no reason for the State to inject itself into the private realm of the family to further question the ability of that parent to make the best decisions concerning the rearing of that parent's children.[cit]

The problem here is not that the Washington Superior Court intervened, but that when it did so, it gave no special weight at all to Granville's determination of her daughters' best interests. More importantly, it appears that the Superior Court applied exactly the opposite presumption. ***

The judge's comments suggest that he presumed the grandparents' request should be granted unless the children would be "impact[ed] adversely." In effect, the judge placed on Granville, the fit custodial parent, the burden of disproving that visitation would be in the best interest of her daughters. The judge reiterated moments later: "I think [visitation with the Troxels] would be in the best interest of the children and I haven't been shown it is not in [the] best interest of the children." *Id.* at 214.

The decisional framework employed by the Superior Court directly contravened the traditional presumption that a fit parent will act in the best interest of his or her child.[cit] In that respect, the court's presumption failed to provide any protection for Granville's fundamental constitutional right to make decisions concerning the rearing of her own daughters. Cf., e.g., Cal. Fam.Code Ann. § 3104(e) (West 1994) (rebuttable presumption that grandparent visitation is not in child's best interest if parents agree that visitation rights should not be granted); *** Utah Code Ann. § 30-5-2(2)(e) (1998) [grandparents must rebut parental presumptions by clear and convincing evidence]. In an ideal world, parents might always seek to cultivate the bonds between grandparents and their grandchildren. Needless to say, however, our world is far from perfect, and in it the decision whether such an intergenerational relationship would be beneficial in any specific case is for the parent to make in the first instance. And, if a fit parent's decision of the kind at issue here becomes subject to judicial review, the court must accord at least some special weight to the parent's own determination.

Finally, we note that there is no allegation that Granville ever sought to cut off visitation entirely. Rather, the present dispute originated when Granville informed the Troxels that she would prefer to restrict their visitation with Isabelle and Natalie to one short visit per month and special holidays. ***[T]he Troxels requested two weekends per month and two full weeks in the summer. *** The Superior Court gave no weight to Granville's having assented to visitation even before the filing of any visitation petition or subsequent court intervention. The court instead rejected Granville's proposal and settled on a middle ground, ordering one weekend of visitation per month, one week in the summer, and time on both of the petitioning grandparents' birthdays. [cit] Significantly, many other States expressly provide by statute that courts may not award visitation unless a parent has denied (or unreasonably denied) visitation to the concerned third party. [cit]

Considered together with the Superior Court's reasons for awarding visitation to the Troxels, the combination of these factors demonstrates that the visitation order in this case was an unconstitutional infringement on Granville's fundamental right to make decisions concerning the care, custody, and control of her two daughters. The Washington Superior Court failed to accord the determination of Granville, a fit custodial parent, any material weight. In fact, the Superior Court made only two formal findings in support of its visitation order. First, the Troxels "are part of a large, central, loving family, all located in this area, and the [Troxels] can provide opportunities for the children in the areas of cousins and music." App. 70a. Second, "[t]he children would be benefitted from spending quality time with the [Troxels], provided that that time is balanced with time with the childrens' [sic] nuclear family." *Ibid.* These slender findings, in combination with the court's announced presumption in favor of grandparent visitation and its failure to accord significant weight to Granville's already having offered meaningful visitation to the Troxels, show that this case involves nothing more than a simple disagreement between the Washington Superior Court and Granville concerning her children's best interests. The Superior Court's announced reason for ordering one week of visitation in the summer demonstrates our conclusion well: "I look back on some personal experiences .... We always spen[t] as kids a week with one set of grandparents and another set of grandparents, [and] it happened to work out in our family that [it] turned out to be an enjoyable experience. Maybe that can, in this family, if that is how it works out." Verbatim Report 220-221. As we have explained, the Due Process Clause does not permit a State to infringe on the fundamental right of parents to make childrearing decisions simply because a state judge believes a "better" decision could be made. Neither the Washington nonparental visitation statute generally-- which places no limits on either the persons who may petition for visitation or the circumstances in which such a petition may be granted--nor the Superior Court in this specific case required anything more. Accordingly, we hold that § 26.10.160(3), as applied in this case, is unconstitutional.

Because we rest our decision on the sweeping breadth of § 26.10.160(3) and the application of that broad, unlimited power in this case, we do not consider the primary constitutional question passed on by the Washington Supreme Court-- whether the Due Process Clause requires all nonparental visitation statutes to include a showing of harm or potential harm to the child as a condition precedent to granting visitation. *** Because much state-court adjudication in this context occurs on a case-by-case basis, we would be hesitant to hold that specific nonparental visitation statutes violate the Due Process Clause as a per se matter.

All 50 States have statutes that provide for grandparent visitation in some form.[cit] *** There is no need to hypothesize about how the Washington courts might apply § 26.10.160(3) because the Washington Superior Court did apply the statute in this very case. Like the Washington Supreme Court, then, we are presented with an actual visitation order and the reasons why the Superior Court believed entry of the order was appropriate in this case.***

There is thus no reason to remand the case for further proceedings in the Washington Supreme Court. As Justice KENNEDY recognizes, the burden of litigating a domestic relations proceeding can itself be "so disruptive of the parent-child relationship that the constitutional right of a custodial parent to make certain basic determinations for the child's welfare becomes implicated." Post at ----, 9. In this case, the litigation costs incurred by Granville on her trip through the Washington court system and to this Court are without a doubt already substantial. As we have explained, it is apparent that the entry of the visitation order in this case violated the Constitution. We should say so now, without forcing the parties into additional litigation that would further burden Granville's parental right. We therefore hold that the application of § 26.10.160(3) to Granville and her family violated her due process right to make decisions concerning the care, custody, and control of her daughters.

Accordingly, the judgment of the Washington Supreme Court is affirmed.
Justice SOUTER, concurring in the judgment.

I concur in the judgment affirming the decision of the Supreme Court of Washington, whose facial invalidation of its own state statute is consistent with this Court's prior cases addressing the substantive interests at stake. I would say no more. The issues that might well be presented by reviewing a decision addressing the specific application of the state statute by the trial court, ante, at --- - ----, 9-14, are not before us and do not call for turning any fresh furrows in the "treacherous field" of substantive due process. [cit]

The Supreme Court of Washington invalidated its state statute based on the text of the statute alone, not its application to any particular case. Its ruling rested on two independently sufficient grounds: the failure of the statute to require harm to the child to justify a disputed visitation order, [cit] and the statute's authorization of "any person" at "any time" to petition and to receive visitation rights subject only to a free-ranging best-interests-of-the-child standard. [cit] I see no error in the second reason*** Consequently, there is no need to decide whether harm is required or to consider the precise scope of the parent's right or its necessary protections.
***

*** Although the statute speaks of granting visitation rights whenever "visitation may serve the best interest of the child," Wash. Rev.Code § 26.10.160(3) (1994), the state court authoritatively read this provision as placing hardly any limit on a court's discretion to award visitation rights. As the court understood it, the specific best-interests provision in the statute would allow a court to award visitation whenever it thought it could make a better decision than a child's parent had done.[cit] On that basis in part, the Supreme Court of Washington invalidated the State's own statute: "Parents have a right to limit visitation of their children with third persons."[cit]

Our cases, it is true, have not set out exact metes and bounds to the protected interest of a parent in the relationship with his child, but Meyer's repeatedly recognized right of upbringing would be a sham if it failed to encompass the right to be free of judicially compelled visitation by "any party" at "any time" a judge believed he "could make a 'better' decision" than the objecting parent had done.*** It would be anomalous, then, to subject a parent to any individual judge's choice of a child's associates from out of the general population merely because the judge might think himself more enlightened than the child's parent. To say the least (and as the Court implied in Pierce), parental choice in such matters is not merely a default rule in the absence of either governmental choice or the government's designation of an official with the power to choose for whatever reason and in whatever circumstances.

*** I would simply affirm the decision of the Supreme Court of Washington that its statute, authorizing courts to grant visitation rights to any person at any time, is unconstitutional. I therefore respectfully concur in the judgment.

Justice THOMAS, concurring in the judgment.

I write separately to note that neither party has argued that our substantive due process cases were wrongly decided and that the original understanding of the Due Process Clause precludes judicial enforcement of unenumerated rights under that constitutional provision. As a result, I express no view on the merits of this matter, and I understand the plurality as well to leave the resolution of that issue for another day.*** Consequently, I agree with the plurality that this Court's recognition of a fundamental right of parents to direct the upbringing of their children resolves this case. Our decision in *Pierce v. Society of Sisters*, 268 U.S. 510(1925), holds that parents have a fundamental constitutional right to rear their children, including the right to determine who shall educate and socialize them. The opinions of the plurality, Justice KENNEDY, and Justice SOUTER recognize such a right, but curiously none of them articulates the appropriate standard of review. I would apply strict scrutiny to infringements of fundamental rights. Here, the State of Washington lacks even a legitimate governmental interest--to say nothing of a compelling one--in second-guessing a fit parent's decision regarding visitation with third parties. On this basis, I would affirm the judgment below.

Justice STEVENS, dissenting.

The Court today wisely declines to endorse either the holding or the reasoning of the Supreme Court of Washington. In my opinion, the Court would have been even wiser to deny certiorari.***

***

*** Despite the nature of this judgment, Justice O'CONNOR would hold that the Washington visitation statute violated the Due Process Clause of the Fourteenth Amendment only as applied.[cit] I agree with Justice SOUTER,[cit], that this approach is untenable.

***

While I thus agree with Justice SOUTER in this respect, I do not agree with his conclusion that the State Supreme Court made a definitive construction of the visitation statute that necessitates the constitutional conclusion he would draw.*** *** I believe the Court should identify and correct the two flaws in the reasoning of the state court's majority opinion, and remand for further review of the trial court's disposition of this specific case.

II

In my view, the State Supreme Court erred in its federal constitutional analysis because neither the provision granting "any person" the right to petition the court for visitation,[cit] nor the absence of a provision requiring a "threshold ... finding of harm to the child," *ibid.*, provides a sufficient basis for holding that the statute is invalid in all its applications.*** Even the Court would seem to agree that in many circumstances, it would be constitutionally permissible for a court to award some visitation of a child to a parent or previous caregiver in cases of parental separation or divorce, cases of disputed custody, cases involving temporary foster care or guardianship, and so forth. As the statute plainly sweeps in a great deal of the permissible, the State Supreme Court majority incorrectly concluded that a statute authorizing "any person" to file a petition seeking visitation privileges would invariably run afoul of the Fourteenth Amendment.

The second key aspect of the Washington Supreme Court's holding--that the Federal Constitution requires a showing of actual or potential "harm" to the child before a court may order visitation continued over a parent's objections--finds no support in this Court's case law. *** [W]e have never held that the parent's liberty interest in this relationship is so inflexible as to establish a rigid constitutional shield, protecting every arbitrary parental decision from any challenge absent a threshold finding of harm.***

Cases like this do not present a bipolar struggle between the parents and the State over who has final authority to determine what is in a child's best interests. There is at a minimum a third individual, whose interests are implicated in every case to which the statute applies--the child.

It has become standard practice in our substantive due process jurisprudence to begin our analysis with an identification of the "fundamental" liberty interests implicated by the challenged state action.[cit] My colleagues are of course correct to recognize that the right of a parent to maintain a relationship with his or her child is among the interests included most often in the constellation of liberties protected through the Fourteenth Amendment.[cit] Our cases leave no doubt that parents have a fundamental liberty interest in caring for and guiding their children, and a corresponding privacy interest--absent exceptional circumstances--in doing so without the undue interference of strangers to them and to their child. Moreover, and critical in this case, our cases applying this principle have explained that with this constitutional liberty comes a presumption (albeit a rebuttable one) that "natural bonds of affection lead parents to act in the best interests of their children." *Parham v. J. R.*, 442 U.S. 584, 602, (1979); *see also Casey*, 505 U.S., at 895; *Santosky v. Kramer*, 455 U.S. 745, 759 (1982) (State may not presume, at factfinding stage of parental rights termination proceeding, that interests of parent and child diverge); *see also ante*, at --- - ----, 9-10 (opinion of O'CONNOR, J.).

Despite this Court's repeated recognition of these significant parental liberty interests, these interests have never been seen to be without limits. In *Lehr v. Robertson*, 463 U.S. 248, (1983), for example, this Court held that a putative biological father who had never established an actual relationship with his child did not have a constitutional right to notice of his child's adoption by the man who had married the child's mother. As this Court had recognized in an earlier case, a parent's liberty interests " 'do not spring full-blown from the biological connection between parent and child. They require relationships more enduring.' "[cit]

Conversely, in *Michael H. v. Gerald D.*, 491 U.S. 110, (1989), this Court concluded that despite both biological parenthood and an established relationship with a young child, a father's due process liberty interest in maintaining some connection with that child was not sufficiently powerful to overcome a state statutory presumption that the husband of the child's mother was the child's parent. As a result of the presumption, the biological father could be denied even visitation with the child because, as a matter of state law, he was not a "parent." A plurality of this Court there recognized that the parental liberty interest was a function, not simply of "isolated factors" such as biology and intimate connection, but of the broader and apparently independent interest in family.[cit]

A parent's rights with respect to her child have thus never been regarded as absolute, but rather are limited by the existence of an actual, developed relationship with a child, and are tied to the presence or absence of some embodiment of family. These limitations have arisen, not simply out of the definition of parenthood itself, but because of this Court's assumption that a parent's interests in a child must be balanced against the State's long- recognized interests as parens patriae,[cit] and, critically, the child's own complementary interest in preserving relationships that serve her welfare and protection, *Santosky*, 455 U.S., at 760, 102 S.Ct. 1388.

While this Court has not yet had occasion to elucidate the nature of a child's liberty interests in preserving established familial or family-like bonds,[cit] it seems to me extremely likely that, to the extent parents and families have fundamental liberty interests in preserving such intimate relationships, so, too, do children have these interests, and so, too, must their interests be balanced in the equation. At a minimum, our prior cases recognizing that children are, generally speaking, constitutionally protected actors require that this Court reject any suggestion that when it comes to parental rights, children are so much chattel.[cit] The constitutional protection against arbitrary state interference with parental rights should not be extended to prevent the States from protecting children against the arbitrary exercise of parental authority that is not in fact motivated by an interest in the welfare of the child.

This is not, of course, to suggest that a child's liberty interest in maintaining contact with a particular individual is to be treated invariably as on a par with that child's parents' contrary interests. Because our substantive due process case law includes a strong presumption that a parent will act in the best interest of her child, it would be necessary, were the state appellate courts actually to confront a challenge to the statute as applied, to consider whether the trial court's assessment of the "best interest of the child" incorporated that presumption.*** For the purpose of a facial challenge like this, I think it safe to assume that trial judges usually give great deference to parents' wishes, and I am not persuaded otherwise here.

But presumptions notwithstanding, we should recognize that there may be circumstances in which a child has a stronger interest at stake than mere protection from serious harm caused by the termination of visitation by a "person" other than a parent. The almost infinite variety of family relationships that pervade our ever-changing society strongly counsel against the creation by this Court of a constitutional rule that treats a biological parent's liberty interest in the care and supervision of her child as an isolated right that may be exercised arbitrarily. It is indisputably the business of the States, rather than a federal court employing a national standard, to assess in the first instance the relative importance of the conflicting interests that give rise to disputes such as this. Far from guaranteeing that parents' interests will be trammeled in the sweep of cases arising under the statute, the Washington law merely gives an individual--with whom a child may have an established relationship--the procedural right to ask the State to act as arbiter, through the entirely well-known best-interests standard, between the parent's protected interests and the child's. It seems clear to me that the Due Process Clause of the Fourteenth Amendment leaves room for States to consider the impact on a child of possibly arbitrary parental decisions that neither serve nor are motivated by the best interests of the child.

Accordingly, I respectfully dissent.

Justice SCALIA, dissenting.

*** [W]hile I would think it entirely compatible with the commitment to representative democracy set forth in the founding documents to argue, in legislative chambers or in electoral campaigns, that the state has no power to interfere with parents' authority over the rearing of their children, I do not believe that the power which the Constitution confers upon me as a judge entitles me to deny legal effect to laws that (in my view) infringe upon what is (in my view) that unenumerated right.

Only three holdings of this Court rest in whole or in part upon a substantive constitutional right of parents to direct the upbringing of their children --two of them from an era rich in substantive due process holdings that have since been repudiated. *See Meyer v. Nebraska*, 262 U.S. 390, 399, 401,(1923); *Pierce v. Society of Sisters*, 268 U.S. 510, 534-535, 45 S.Ct. 571, 69 L.Ed. 1070 (1925); *Wisconsin v. Yoder*, 406 U.S. 205, 232-233 (1972); [cit]. The sheer diversity of today's opinions persuades me that the theory of unenumerated parental rights underlying these three cases has small claim to stare decisis protection. A legal principle that can be thought to produce such diverse outcomes in the relatively simple case before us here is not a legal principle that has induced substantial reliance. While I would not now overrule those earlier cases (that has not been urged), neither would I extend the theory upon which they rested to this new context.

*** If we embrace this unenumerated right, I think it obvious--whether we affirm or reverse the judgment here, or remand ***--that we will be ushering in a new regime of judicially prescribed, and federally prescribed, family law. I have no reason to believe that federal judges will be better at this than state legislatures; and state legislatures have the great advantages of doing harm in a more circumscribed area, of being able to correct their mistakes in a flash, and of being removable by the people.

For these reasons, I would reverse the judgment below.

Justice KENNEDY, dissenting.

The first flaw the State Supreme Court found in the statute is that it allows an award of visitation to a non-parent without a finding that harm to the child would result if visitation were withheld; and the second is that the statute allows any person to seek visitation at any time. In my view the first theory is too broad to be correct, as it appears to contemplate that the best interests of the child standard may not be applied in any visitation case. I acknowledge the distinct possibility that visitation cases may arise where, considering the absence of other protection for the parent under state laws and procedures, the best interests of the child standard would give insufficient protection to the parent's constitutional right to raise the child without undue intervention by the state; but it is quite a different matter to say, as I understand the Supreme Court of Washington to have said, that a harm to the child standard is required in every instance.

Given the error I see in the State Supreme Court's central conclusion that the best interests of the child standard is never appropriate in third-party visitation cases, that court should have the first opportunity to reconsider this case. I would remand the case to the state court for further proceedings. ***The judgment now under review should be vacated and remanded on the sole ground that the harm ruling that was so central to the Supreme Court of Washington's decision was error, given its broad formulation.

Turning to the question whether harm to the child must be the controlling standard in every visitation proceeding, there is a beginning point that commands general, perhaps unanimous, agreement in our separate opinions: As our case law has developed, the custodial parent has a constitutional right to determine, without undue interference by the state, how best to raise, nurture, and educate the child. The parental right stems from the liberty protected by the Due Process Clause of the Fourteenth Amendment. [cit] *** The principle exists, then, in broad formulation; yet courts must use considerable restraint, including careful adherence to the incremental instruction given by the precise facts of particular cases, as they seek to give further and more precise definition to the right.

***

On the question whether one standard must always take precedence over the other in order to protect the right of the parent or parents, "[o]ur Nation's history, legal traditions, and practices" do not give us clear or definitive answers. *Washington v. Glucksberg*, 521 U.S. 702, 721, 117 S.Ct. 2258 (1997). The consensus among courts and commentators is that at least through the 19th century there was no legal right of visitation; court-ordered visitation appears to be a 20th-century phenomenon. [cit] A case often cited as one of the earliest visitation decisions, *Succession of Reiss*, 46 La. Ann. 347, 353, 15 So. 151, 152 (1894), explained that "the obligation ordinarily to visit grandparents is moral and not legal"--a conclusion which appears consistent with that of American common law jurisdictions of the time. ***

***

My principal concern is that the holding seems to proceed from the assumption that the parent or parents who resist visitation have always been the child's primary caregivers and that the third parties who seek visitation have no legitimate and established relationship with the child. That idea, in turn, appears influenced by the concept that the conventional nuclear family ought to establish the visitation standard for every domestic relations case. As we all know, this is simply not the structure or prevailing condition in many households. *See e.g. Moore v. East Cleveland*, 431 U.S. 494 (1977). For many boys and girls a traditional family with two or even one permanent and caring parent is simply not the reality of their childhood. This may be so whether their childhood has been marked by tragedy or filled with considerable happiness and fulfillment.

Cases are sure to arise--perhaps a substantial number of cases--in which a third party, by acting in a caregiving role over a significant period of time, has developed a relationship with a child which is not necessarily subject to absolute parental veto.[cit] Some pre-existing relationships, then, serve to identify persons who have a strong attachment to the child with the concomitant motivation to act in a responsible way to ensure the child's welfare. As the State Supreme Court was correct to acknowledge, those relationships can be so enduring that "in certain circumstances where a child has enjoyed a substantial relationship with a third person, arbitrarily depriving the child of the relationship could cause severe psychological harm to the child,"***[cit]

*** Since 1965 all 50 States have enacted a third-party visitation statute of some sort. [cit]. Each of these statutes, save one, permits a court order to issue in certain cases if visitation is found to be in the best interests of the child. While it is unnecessary for us to consider the constitutionality of any particular provision in the case now before us, it can be noted that the statutes also include a variety of methods for limiting parents' exposure to third-party visitation petitions and for ensuring parental decisions are given respect. Many States limit the identity of permissible petitioners by restricting visitation petitions to grandparents, or by requiring petitioners to show a substantial relationship with a child, or both.***

In light of the inconclusive historical record and case law, as well as the almost universal adoption of the best interests standard for visitation disputes, I would be hard pressed to conclude the right to be free of such review in all cases is itself " 'implicit in the concept of ordered liberty.' " Glucksberg, 521 U.S., at 721.[cit] In my view, it would be more appropriate to conclude that the constitutionality of the application of the best interests standard depends on more specific factors. In short, a fit parent's right vis-a-vis a complete stranger is one thing; her right vis-a-vis another parent or a de facto parent may be another. The protection the Constitution requires, then, must be elaborated with care, using the discipline and instruction of the case law system. We must keep in mind that family courts in the 50 States confront these factual variations each day, and are best situated to consider the unpredictable, yet inevitable, issues that arise.[cit]

It must be recognized, of course, that a domestic relations proceeding in and of itself can constitute state intervention that is so disruptive of the parent-child relationship that the constitutional right of a custodial parent to make certain basic determinations for the child's welfare becomes implicated. The best interests of the child standard has at times been criticized as indeterminate, leading to unpredictable results. *See e.g.* American Law Institute, Principles of the Law of Family Dissolution 2, and n. 2 (Tentative Draft No. 3, Mar. 20, 1998). If a single parent who is struggling to raise a child is faced with visitation demands from a third party, the attorney's fees alone might destroy her hopes and plans for the child's future. ***

It should suffice in this case to reverse the holding of the State Supreme Court that the application of the best interests of the child standard is always unconstitutional in third-party visitation cases. ***

In my view the judgment under review should be vacated and the case remanded for further proceedings.

b. *Smith v. Organization of Foster Families*
Henry Smith v. Organization of Foster Families For Equality and Reform et al.
431 U.S. 816 (1977)

Mr. Justice BRENNAN delivered the opinion of the Court.

Appellees, individual foster parents [FN1*] and an organization of foster parents, brought this civil rights class action pursuant to 42 U.S.C. s 1983 in the United States District Court for the Southern District of New York, on their own behalf and on behalf of children for whom they have provided homes for a year or more. They sought declaratory and injunctive relief against New York State and New York City officials, alleging that the procedures governing the removal of foster children from foster homes *** violated the Due Process and Equal Protection Clauses of the Fourteenth Amendment. The District Court appointed independent counsel for the foster children to forestall any possibility of conflict between their interests and the interests asserted by the foster parents. A group of natural mothers of children in foster care were granted leave to intervene on behalf of themselves and others similarly situated.

***

A

The expressed central policy of the New York system is that "it is generally desirable for the child to remain with or be returned to the natural parent because the child's need for a normal family life will usually best be met in the natural home, and . . .parents are entitled to bring up their own children unless the best interests of the child would be thereby endangered," * But the State has opted for foster care as one response to those situations where the natural parents are unable to provide the "positive, nurturing family relationships" and "normal family life in a permanent home" that offer "the best opportunity for children to develop and thrive." ***

Under the New York scheme children may be placed in foster care either by voluntary placement or by court order. Most foster care placements are voluntary. [FN9*] They occur when physical or mental illness, economic problems, or other family crises make it impossible for natural parents, particularly single parents, to provide a stable home life for their children for some limited period. Resort to such placements is almost compelled when it is not possible in such circumstance to place the child with a relative or friend, or to pay for the services of a homemaker or boarding school.

Voluntary placement requires the signing of a written agreement by the natural parent or guardian, transferring the care and custody of the child to an authorized child welfare agency. Although by statute the terms of such agreements are open to negotiation, it is contended that agencies require execution of standardized forms. The agreement may provide for return of the child to the natural parent at a specified date or upon occurrence of a particular event, and if it does not, the child must be returned by the agency, in the absence of a court order, within 20 days of notice from the parent.

The agency may maintain the child in an institutional setting, but more commonly acts under its authority to "place out and board out" children in foster homes. s 374(1). Foster parents, who are licensed by the State or an authorized foster-care agency, §§ 376, 377, provide care under a contractual arrangement with the agency, and are compensated for their services. The typical contract expressly reserves the right of the agency to remove the child on request. Conversely, the foster parent may cancel the agreement at will.

The New York system divides parental functions among agency, foster parents, and natural parents, and the definitions of the respective roles are often complex and often unclear. The law transfers "care and custody" to the agency, but day-to-day supervision of the child and his activities, and most of the functions ordinarily associated with legal custody, are the responsibility of the foster parent. Nevertheless, agency supervision of the performance of the foster parents takes forms indicating that the foster parent does not have the full authority of a legal custodian. Moreover, the natural parent's placement of the child with the agency does not surrender legal guardianship; the parent retains authority to act with respect to the child in certain circumstances. [FN20] The natural parent has not only the right but the obligation to visit the foster child and plan for his future; failure of a parent with capacity to fulfill the obligation for more than a year can result in a court order terminating the parent's rights on the ground of neglect.

Children may also enter foster care by court order. The Family Court may order that a child be placed in the custody of an authorized child-care agency after a full adversary judicial hearing under Art. 10 of the New York Family Court Act, if it is found that the child has been abused or neglected by his natural parents. In addition, a minor adjudicated a juvenile delinquent, or "person in need of supervision" may be placed by the court with an agency. The consequences of foster-care placement by court order do not differ substantially from those for children voluntarily placed, except that the parent is not entitled to return of the child on demand; *** termination of foster care must then be consented to by the court.

B

The provisions of the scheme specifically at issue in this litigation come into play when the agency having legal custody determines to remove the foster child from the foster home, either because it has determined that it would be in the child's best interests to transfer him to some other foster home, or to return the child to his natural parents in accordance with the statute or placement agreement. Most children are removed in order to be transferred to another foster home. The procedures by which foster parents may challenge a removal made for that purpose differ somewhat from those where the removal is made to return the child to his natural parent.

Section 383(2)* provides that the "authorized agency placing out or boarding (a foster) child . . . may in its discretion remove such child from the home where placed or boarded.** The agency is required, except in emergencies, to notify the foster parents in writing 10 days in advance of any removal. * The notice advises the foster parents that if they object to the child's removal they may request a "conference" with the Social Services Department. *Ibid.* The department schedules requested conferences within 10 days of the receipt of the request. The foster parent may appear with counsel at the conference, where he will "be advised of the reasons (for the removal of the child), and be afforded an opportunity to submit reasons why the child should not be removed." The official must render a decision in writing within five days after the close of the conference, and send notice of his decision to the foster parents and the agency. The proposed removal is stayed pending the outcome of the conference.

If the child is removed after the conference, the foster parent may appeal to the Department of Social Services for a "fair hearing," that is, a full adversary administrative,** the determination of which is subject to judicial review ***; however, the removal is not automatically stayed pending the hearing and judicial review.

This statutory and regulatory scheme applies statewide. In addition, regulations promulgated by the New York City Human Resources Administration, Department of Social Services Special Services for Children (SSC) provide even greater procedural safeguards there.**

One further preremoval procedural safeguard is available. Under Soc.Serv.Law s 392, the Family Court has jurisdiction to review, on petition of the foster parent or the agency, the status of any child who has been in foster care for 18 months or longer. ***

C

Foster care of children is a sensitive and emotion-laden subject, and foster- care programs consequently stir strong controversy. The New York regulatory scheme is no exception. New York would have us view the scheme as described in its brief:

> Today New York premises its foster care system on the accepted principle that the placement of a child into foster care is solely a temporary, transitional action intended to lead to the future reunion of the child with his natural parent or parents, or if such a reunion is not possible, to legal adoption and the establishment of a new permanent home for the child. *

Some of the parties and amici argue that this is a misleadingly idealized picture. They contend that a very different perspective is revealed by the empirical criticism of the system presented in the record of this case and confirmed by published studies of foster care.

From the standpoint of natural parents, such as the appellant intervenors here, foster care has been condemned as a class-based intrusion into the family life of the poor.*** It is certainly true that the poor resort to foster care more often than other citizens. For example, over 50% of all children in foster care in New York City are from female- headed families receiving Aid to Families with Dependent Children. Foundation for Child Development, State of the Child: New York City 61 (1976). Minority families are also more likely to turn to foster care; 52.3% of the children in foster care in New York City are black and 25.5% are Puerto Rican.* This disproportionate resort to foster care by the poor and victims of discrimination doubtless reflects in part the greater likelihood of disruption of poverty-stricken families. Commentators have also noted, however, that middle- and upper-income families who need temporary care services for their children have the resources to purchase private care.* The poor have little choice but to submit to state-supervised child care when family crises strike.

The extent to which supposedly "voluntary" placements are in fact voluntary has been questioned on other grounds as well. For example, it has been said that many "voluntary" placements are in fact coerced by threat of neglect proceedings and are not in fact voluntary in the sense of the product of an informed consent.* Studies also suggest that social workers of middle-class backgrounds, perhaps unconsciously, incline to favor continued placement in foster care with a generally higher-status family rather than return the child to his natural family, thus reflecting a bias that treats the natural parents' poverty and lifestyle as prejudicial to the best interests of the child.* This accounts, it has been said, for the hostility of agencies to the efforts of natural parents to obtain the return of their children.

Appellee foster parents as well as natural parents question the accuracy of the idealized picture portrayed by New York. They note that children often stay in "temporary" foster care for much longer than contemplated by the theory of the system. *** The District Court found as a fact that the median time spent in foster care in New York was over four years. Indeed, many children apparently remain in this "limbo" indefinitely. Mnookin II 226, 273. The District Court also found that the longer a child remains in foster care, the more likely it is that he will never leave: "(T)he probability of a foster child being returned to his biological parents declined markedly after the first year in foster care." * It is not surprising then that many children, particularly those that enter foster care at a very early age and have little or no contact with their natural parents during extended stays in fostercare, often develop deep emotional ties with their foster parents.

Yet such ties do not seem to be regarded as obstacles to transfer the child from one foster placement to another. The record in this case indicates that nearly 60% of the children in foster care in New York City have experienced more than one placement, and about 28% have experienced three or more. * The intended stability of the foster-home management is further damaged by the rapid turnover among social work professionals who supervise the foster-care arrangements on behalf of the State. ** Moreover, even when it is clear that a foster child will not be returned to his natural parents, it is rare that he achieves a stable home life through final termination of parental ties and adoption into a new permanent family.*

The parties and amici devote much of their discussion to these criticisms of foster care, and we present this summary in the view that some understanding of those criticisms is necessary for a full appreciation of the complex and controversial system with which this lawsuit is concerned. But the issue presented by the case is a narrow one. Arguments asserting the need for reform of New York's statutory scheme are properly addressed to the New York Legislature. The relief sought in this case is entirely procedural. Our task is only to determine whether the District Court correctly held that the present procedures preceding the removal from a foster home of children resident there a year or more are constitutionally inadequate. To that task we now turn.

II

A

Our first inquiry is whether appellees have asserted interests within the Fourteenth Amendment's protection of "liberty"*** Our inquiry is therefore narrowed to the question whether their asserted interests are within the "liberty" protected by the Fourteenth Amendment.

***

The appellees' basic contention is that when a child has lived in a foster home for a year or more, a psychological tie is created between the child and the foster parents which constitutes the foster family the true "psychological family" of the child. *See* J. Goldstein, A. Freud, & A. Solnit, *Beyond the Best Interests of the Child* (1973). That family, they argue, has a "liberty interest" in its survival as a family protected by the Fourteenth Amendment. Cf. *Moore v. City of East Cleveland,* * Upon this premise they conclude that the foster child cannot be removed without a prior hearing satisfying due process. Appointed counsel for the children, however, disagrees, and has consistently argued that the foster parents have no such liberty interest independent of the interests of the foster children, and that the best interests of the children would not be served by procedural protections beyond those already provided by New York law. The intervening natural parents of children in foster care, also oppose the foster parents, arguing that recognition of the procedural right claimed would undercut both the substantive family law of New York, which favors the return of children to their natural parents as expeditiously as possible, and their constitutionally protected right of family privacy, by forcing them to submit to a hearing and defend their rights to their children before the children could be returned to them.

***

But, to determine whether due process requirements apply in the first place, we must look not to the 'weight' but to the nature of the interest at stake. . . . We must look to see if the interest is within the Fourteenth Amendment's protection of liberty and property."

We therefore turn to appellees' assertion that they have a constitutionally protected liberty interest in the words of the District Court, a "right to familial privacy," in the integrity of their family unit. This assertion clearly presents difficulties.

B

It is, of course, true that "freedom of personal choice in matters of . . . family life is one of the liberties protected by the Due Process Clause of the Fourteenth Amendment." * There does exist a "private realm of family life which the state cannot enter," *Prince v. Massachusetts,* (1944), that has been afforded both substantive and procedural protection. But is the relation of foster parent to foster child sufficiently akin to the concept of "family" recognized in our precedents to merit similar protection? Although considerable difficulty has attended the task of defining "family" for purposes of the Due Process, * we are not without guides to some of the elements that define the concept of "family" and contribute to its place in our society.

First, the usual understanding of "family" implies biological relationships, and most decisions treating the relation between parent and child have stressed this. And *Prince v. Massachusetts,* stated: "It is cardinal with us that the custody, care and nurture of the child reside first in the parents, whose primary function and freedom include preparation for obligations the state can neither supply nor hinder." [FN49 *The scope of these rights extends beyond natural parents. The "parent" in Prince itself, for example, was the child's aunt and legal custodian. 321 U.S., at 159, 64 S.Ct., at 439. And see Moore v. City of East Cleveland, supra, 431 U.S., at 504-506, 97 S.Ct., at 1938-1939 (plurality opinion); 507-511, 97 S.Ct., at 1939-1942 (Brennan, J., concurring)*]

A biological relationship is not present in the case of the usual foster family. But biological relationships are not exclusive determination of the existence of a family. The basic foundation of the family in our society, the marriage relationship, is of course not a matter of blood relation. Yet its importance has been strongly emphasized in our cases:

> We deal with a right of privacy older than the Bill of Rights older than our political parties, older than our school system. Marriage is a coming together for better or for worse, hopefully enduring, and intimate to the degree of being sacred. It is an association that promotes a way of life, not causes; a harmony in living, not political faiths; a bilateral loyalty, not commercial or social projects. Yet it is an association for as noble a purpose as any involved in our prior decisions.

Griswold v. Connecticut.

Thus the importance of the familial relationship, to the individuals involved and to the society, stems from the emotional attachments that derive from the intimacy of daily association, and from the role it plays in "promot(ing) a way of life" through the instruction of children, *Wisconsin v. Yoder*, as well as from the fact of blood relationship. No one would seriously dispute that a deeply loving and interdependent relationship between an adult and a child in his or her care may exist even in the absence of blood relationship. At least where a child has been placed in foster care as an infant, has never known his natural parents, and has remained continuously for several years in the care of the same foster parents, it is natural that the foster family should hold the same place in the emotional life of the foster child, and fulfill the same socializing functions, as a natural family. For this reason, we cannot dismiss the foster family as a mere collection of unrelated individuals. Cf. *Village of Belle Terre v. Boraas* (1974).

But there are also important distinctions between the foster family and the natural family. First, unlike the earlier cases recognizing a right to family privacy, the State here seeks to interfere, not with a relationship having its origins entirely apart from the power of the State, but rather with a foster family which has its source in state law and contractual arrangements. *** Accordingly, unlike the property interests that are also protected by the Fourteenth Amendment,** the liberty interest in family privacy has its source, and its contours are ordinarily to be sought, not in state law, but in intrinsic human rights, as they have been understood in "this Nation's history and tradition." *Moore v. City of East Cleveland.* Here, however, whatever emotional ties may develop between foster parent and foster child have their origins in an arrangement in which the State has been a partner from the outset. While the Court has recognized that liberty interests may in some cases arise from positive-law sources, *see e.g. Wolff v. McDonnell*, 418 U.S. 539, 557 (1974), in such a case, and particularly where, as here, the claimed interest derives from a knowingly assumed contractual relation with the State, it is appropriate to ascertain from state law the expectations and entitlements of the parties. In this case, the limited recognition accorded to the foster family by the New York statutes and the contracts executed by the foster parents argue against any but the most limited constitutional "liberty" in the foster family.

A second consideration related to this is that ordinarily procedural protection may be afforded to a liberty interest of one person without derogating from the substantive liberty of another. Here, however, such a tension is virtually unavoidable. Under New York law, the natural parent of a foster child in voluntary placement has an absolute right to the return of his child in the absence of a court order obtainable only upon compliance with rigorous substantive and procedural standards, which reflect the constitutional protection accorded the natural family. Moreover, the natural parent initially gave up his child to the State only on the express understanding that the child would be returned in those circumstances. These rights are difficult to reconcile with the liberty interest in the foster family relationship claimed by appellees. It is one thing to say that individuals may acquire a liberty interest against arbitrary governmental interference in the family-like associations into which they have freely entered, even in the absence of biological connection or state-law recognition of the relationship. It is quite another to say that one may acquire such an interest in the face of another's constitutionally recognized liberty interest that derives from blood relationship, state-law sanction, and basic human right an interest the foster parent has recognized by contract from the outset. Whatever liberty interest might otherwise exist in the foster family as an institution, that interest must be substantially attenuated where the proposed removal from the foster family is to return the child to his natural parents.

As this discussion suggests, appellees' claim to a constitutionally protected liberty interest raises complex and novel questions. It is unnecessary for us to resolve those questions definitively in this case, however, for like the District Court, we conclude that "narrower grounds exist to support" our reversal. We are persuaded that, even on the assumption that appellees have a protected "liberty interest," the District Court erred in holding that the preremoval procedures presently employed by the State are constitutionally defective.

III

Where procedural due process must be afforded because a "liberty" or "property" interest is within the Fourteenth Amendment's protection, there must be determined "what process is due" in the particular context.***

It is true that "(b)efore a person is deprived of a protected interest, he must be afforded opportunity for some kind of a hearing, 'except for extraordinary situations where some valid governmental interest is at stake that justifies postponing the hearing until after the event.' *** But the hearing required is only one "appropriate to the nature of the case." *** Only last Term, the Court held that "identification of the specific dictates of due process generally requires consideration of three distinct factors: First, the private interest that will be affected by the official action; second, the risk of an erroneous deprivation of such interest through the procedures used, and the probable value, if any, of additional or substitute procedural safeguards; and finally, the Government's interest, including the function involved and the fiscal and administrative burdens that the additional or substitute procedural requirement would entail." *Mathews v. Eldridge*, (1976). Consideration of the procedures employed by the State and New York City in light of these three factors requires the conclusion that those procedures satisfy constitutional standards.

Turning first to the procedure applicable in New York City, SSC Procedure No. 5 provides that before a child is removed from a foster home for transfer to another foster home, the foster parents may request an "independent review."*** Such a procedure would appear to give a more elaborate trial-type hearing to foster families than this Court has found required in other contexts of administrative determinations.* The District Court found the procedure inadequate on four grounds, none of which we find sufficient to justify the holding that the procedure violates due process.

First, the court held that the "independent review" administrative proceeding was insufficient because it was only available on the request of the foster parents. In the view of the District Court, the proceeding should be provided as a matter of course, because the interests of the foster parents and those of the child would not necessarily be coextensive, and it could not be assumed that the foster parents would invoke the hearing procedure in every case in which it was in the child's interest to have a hearing. Since the child is unable to request a hearing on his own, automatic review in every case is necessary. We disagree. As previously noted, the constitutional liberty, if any, sought to be protected by the New York procedures is a right of family privacy or autonomy, and the basis for recognition of any such interest in the foster family must be that close emotional ties analogous to those between parent and child are established when a child resides for a lengthy period with a foster family. If this is so, necessarily we should expect that the foster parents will seek to continue the relationship to preserve the stability of the family; if they do not request a hearing, it is difficult to see what right or interest of the foster child is protected by holding a hearing to determine whether removal would unduly impair his emotional attachments to a foster parent who does not care enough about the child to contest the removal. *** Moreover, automatic provision of hearings as required by the District Court would impose a substantial additional administrative burden on the State. ***

Second, the District Court faulted the city procedure on the ground that participation is limited to the foster parents and the agency and the natural parent and the child are not made parties to the hearing. This is not fatal in light of the nature of the alleged constitutional interests at stake. When the child's transfer from one foster home to another is pending, the interest arguably requiring protection is that of the foster family, not that of the natural parents.

Much the same can be said in response to the District Court's statement:

(I)t may be advisable, under certain circumstances, for the agency to appoint an adult representative better to articulate the interests of the child. In making this determination, the agency should carefully consider the child's age, sophistication and ability effectively to communicate his own true feelings.

But nothing in the New York City procedure prevents consultation of the child's wishes, directly or through an adult intermediary. We assume, moreover, that some such consultation would be among the first steps that a rational factfinder, inquiring into the child's best interests, would pursue. Such consultation, however, does not require that the child or an appointed representative must be a party with full adversary powers in all preremoval hearings.

The other two defects in the city procedure found by the District Court must also be rejected. One is that the procedure does not extend to the removal of a child from foster care to be returned to his natural parent. But as we have already held, whatever liberty interest may be argued to exist in the foster family is significantly weaker in the case of removals preceding return to the natural parent, and the balance of due process interests must accordingly be different. ***

Outside New York City, where only the statewide procedures apply, foster parents are provided not only with the procedures of a preremoval conference and postremoval hearing,*** but also with the preremoval judicial hearing available on request to foster parents who have in their care children who have been in foster care for 18 months or more, Soc.Serv.Law s 392. ***

****We do not think that the 18-month limitation on s 392 actions renders the New York scheme constitutionally inadequate. The assumed liberty interest to be protected in this case is one rooted in the emotional attachments that develop over time between a child and the adults who care for him. But there is no reason to assume that those attachments ripen at less than 18 months or indeed at any precise point. Indeed, testimony in the record, as well as material in published psychological tests, * suggests that the amount of time necessary for the development of the sort of tie appellees seek to protect varies considerably depending on the age and previous attachments of the child. In a matter of such imprecision and delicacy, we see no justification for the District Court's substitution of its view of the appropriate cutoff date for that chosen by the New York Legislature, given that any line is likely to be somewhat arbitrary and fail to protect some families where relationships have developed quickly while protecting others where no such bonds have formed. If New York sees 18 months rather than 12 as the time at which temporary foster care begins to turn into a more permanent and family-like setting requiring procedural protection and/or judicial inquiry into the propriety of continuing foster care, it would take far more than this record provides to justify a finding of constitutional infirmity in New York's choice.

Finally, the s 392 hearing is available to foster parents, both in and outside New York City, even where the removal sought is for the purpose of returning the child to his natural parents. Since this remedy provides a sufficient constitutional preremoval hearing to protect whatever liberty interest might exist in the continued existence of the foster family when the State seeks to transfer the child to another foster home, a fortiori the procedure is adequate to protect the lesser interest of the foster family in remaining together at the expense of the disruption of the natural family.

We deal here with issues of unusual delicacy, in an area where professional judgments regarding desirable procedures are constantly and rapidly changing. In such a context, restraint is appropriate on the part of courts called upon to adjudicate whether a particular procedural scheme is adequate under the Constitution. Since we hold that the procedures provided by New York State in s 392 and by New York City's SSC Procedure No. 5 are adequate to protect whatever liberty interest appellees may have, the judgment of the District Court is Reversed.

Mr. Justice STEWART, with whom THE CHIEF JUSTICE and Mr. Justice REHNQUIST join, concurring in the judgment.

The foster parent-foster child relationship involved in this litigation is, of course, wholly a creation of the State. New York law defines the circumstances under which a child may be placed in foster care, prescribes the obligations of the foster parents, and provides for the removal of the child from the foster home "in (the) discretion" of the agency with custody of the child. * The agency compensates the foster parents, and reserves in its contracts the authority to decide as it sees fit whether and when a child shall be returned to his natural family or placed elsewhere. *See* Part I-A of the Court's opinion. Were it not for the system of foster care that the State maintains, the relationship for which constitutional protection is asserted would not even exist.

The New York Legislature and the New York courts have made it unmistakably clear that foster care is intended only as a temporary way station until a child can be returned to his natural parents or placed for adoption.***

In these circumstances, I cannot understand why the Court thinks itself obliged to decide these cases on the assumption that either foster parents or foster children in New York have some sort of "liberty" interest in the continuation of their relationship. Rather than tiptoeing around this central issue, I would squarely hold that the interests asserted by the appellees are not of a kind that the Due Process Clause of the Fourteenth Amendment protects.

c. Notes and Questions

1) *Troxel* Notes

How helpful is this case to legislatures, courts and attorneys since there is no opinion of the court? Is it helpful in defining the contours of the fundamental liberty interest of parents? Why was the court so fragmented? How do you reconcile *Troxel* with the court-mandated *ex parte* judicial bypass procedure whereby third parties (judges) may authorize secret abortions for minors without parental consent, notice or involvement if they find that to be in the best interests of the minor? *Belotti v. Baird*, 933 US.622 (1979); *Hodgson v Minnesota*, 997 US 417 (1990); *Planned Parenthood v. Casey*, 505 U.S. 833 (1992).

Troxel continues to generate much litigation and many law review articles. One of the issues that court-ordered grandparent visitation raises, which *Troxel* and other grandparent visitation decisions seldom consider, is the practical challenge of visitation. For a detailed analysis of these challenges, *see* Nolan *infra*. It has been argued that *Troxel* did not go far enough to protect parental discretion because judicial review of visitation disputes under a child-welfare standard involves high litigation costs but provides almost no improvement in parental incentives. *See id.*; *see also* Giller, *infra*.

2) Overview of Grandparent Visitation Statutes Before *Troxel*

One reviewer, noting that only the District of Columbia had not enacted a grandparent visitation statute, summarized the grandparent visitation statutes in 1999 as follows:

> All fifty states require a consideration of the "best interest" standard in grandparent visitation cases. Some states articulate specific factors in determining the best interest of grandchildren.

> Some state statutes only allow grandparent visitation in cases of death or divorce of a parent, etc., while other statutes allow grandparent visitation even when the parents are still together. Twenty states only allow grandparent visitation in cases of

death, divorce, or other deprivation of custody. Thirty states allow grandparent
visitation even when parents are still together. The trend is toward more liberal
grandparent visitation rights.

Several states treat post-adoption grandparent visitation rights in different ways.
Five states (Arizona, Colorado, Massachusetts, Maine, and Utah), allow no
grandparent visitation following an adoption. Twenty-two states allow grandparent
visitation, following an adoption, only if the adoption was by a stepparent or other
relative. Three states (Connecticut, Kentucky, and Oklahoma), may allow all
previously determined visitation rights to continue. Two states (Alaska and
Michigan), have broad discretion in allowing visitation rights following adoption.
One state, Wisconsin, allows grandparent visitation to survive an adoption only if
the grandparent's child has died. Seventeen states do not have a provision in their
grandparent visitation statutes which addresses grandparent visitation rights after a
child has been adopted. In these states adoption statutes determine grandparents'
rights.

Averett, *infra* at 371.

3) Judicial Response To *Troxel*

Since *Troxel*, many state supreme courts have examined the constitutionality of
their grandparent visitation statutes, and with predictable inconsistent interpretations
until the U.S. Supreme Court gives further clarity to this decision. Some courts found
their statute or a particular provision in the statute unconstitutional because it failed to
give deference to a fit parent's decision regarding visitation. *See e.g. Santi v. Santi*,
633 N.W.2d 312 (Iowa 2001)(intact families); *In re Marriage of Howard*, 661
N.W.3d (Iowa 2004)(divorced parents); *DeRose v. DeRose*, 666 N.W.2d. 636 (Mich.
2003). Others have found their statute constitutional because they do provide
deference to the parental decision. *See e.g. Rideout v. Riendeau*, 761 A.2d 291 (Me.
2000); *In re Roger D.H.*, 250 Wis 2d 747, 641 N.W. 2d 440 (App. 2002). Other
courts have interpreted the grandparent visitation statute to require a showing of harm
to the child if visitation was denied although *Troxel's* plurality decision expressly left
that issue undecided. *See e.g. Neal v. Lee* 14 P.3d 347 (Okla. 2000); *Roth v. Weston*,
789 A. 2d 431 (Conn. 2002). Still other courts have rejected the harm standard. *See
e.g. Zeman v. Stanford*, 789 So. 2d 798 (Miss. 2001)(use best interest of child
standard if petitioner has established a parent-child like relationship); *State ex. rel
Brandon L. v. Moats*, 551 S.E.2d 674 (W.Va. 2001)(best interest of the child standard
if no substantial interference with parental authority).

4) Legislative Response After *Troxel*

After *Troxel*, several states amended their grandparent visitation statute,
including Washington state. *See e.g.*, Wash. Rev. Code 26.09.240 (requiring the
nonparent seeking visitation show a significant relationship with the child by clear
and convincing evidence, and only in the circumstance that the parent or parents have
already commenced an action for divorce, legal separation, or modification of a
parenting plan); Utah Code Ann. § 30-5-2 (2000)(creating a rebuttable presumption
that the parent's decision is in the best interests of the child and permitting courts to

consider the child wishes); Ore. Rev. Stat. § 109.119 (2001)(permitting any person having a parent-child relationship with a child to be awarded custody, guardianship, or rights of visitation if it is in the best interests of child, but requiring the petitioning party to overcome by clear and convincing evidence the presumption that the legal parent acts in the best interest of the child); S.D. Codified Laws § 25-4-52 (2001)(permitting grandparent visitation if in the best interests of the child if either the visitation would not significantly interfere with the parent-child relationship, or the parent or custodian of the child has unreasonably denied grandparent visitation); N.D. Cen. Code § 14-09-05.1(2002)(permitting visitation if it would be in the child's best interests and would not interfere with the parent-child relationship).

5) ALI Principles

Grandparents would have standing to seek visitation if they qualify as *de facto* parents or parents by estoppel, which means that the grandparents must have resided with the child and performed many parenting functions with the parent's consent in the ALI Principles of the Law of Family Dissolution § 2.03(1) (2002). But the ALI's recommended easy acquisition of parental rights by de facto parents and parents by estoppel has been widely criticized. *See* Loken, *infra* and Wagner, *infra*.

6) *Smith v. OFFER* Notes

What was the liberty interest asserted by the foster parents? What if a family member volunteered to take the child without going through the foster care system? Would that foster parent, under *Smith*, have a better argument for asserting a liberty interest?

3. Practical and Ethical Considerations

a. Legal Representation

In *Smith v. OFFER*, the court appointed independent counsel to represent the children because their interests may conflict with the foster parents. This was a class action suit. Are the duties representing children in a class action suit different from those in non-class action cases? *See* Matthew, *infra*.

b. Mediating Intra-Family Disputes

Might an attorney ethically serve as a mediator to resolve an intrafamily dispute about grandparent visitation? If she is already retained by the parent(s) or the grandparent(s), may she initiate the mediation proposal? What safeguards and restrictions or limits would have to be in place for the attorney to do that? Would there be any potential disadvantages to that proposal for the client(s) or attorney? If so, what?

4. Bibliography

2002 Statistical Abstract of the United States 48, table 49.

Stephen Elmo Averett, *Grandparent Visitation Right Statutes*, 13 BYU J. Pub. L. 355 (1999).

Alison Bell, Note, *Public and Private Child:* Troxel v. Granville *and the Constitutional Rights of Family Members*, 36 Harv. C. R.-C.L. Rev. 225 (2001).

Jason Fields, *Children's Living Arrangements and Characteristics*: March 2002, in Current Population

Reports (June 2003), at 2, Table 1, *Children by Age and Family Structure, March 2002, at* <http://www.census.gov/prod/2003pubs/p20-547.pdf>.

Stephen G. Giller, *Parental (And Grandparental) Rights After* Troxel v. Granville, 9 Supr. Ct. Econ. Rev. No. 69 (2001).

Joseph Goldstein, Anna Freud, & Albert Solnit, Beyond the Best Interests of the Child (1973).

Kristine S. Knaplund, *Grandparents Raising Grandchilden and the Implications for Inheritance,* 48 Ariz. L. Rev. 1 (2006).

Gregory A. Loken, *The New "Extended Family" – "De Facto" Parenthood and Standing Under Chapter 2,* 2001 B.Y.U. L. Rev. 1045.

Cynthia R. Mabry, *"Who Is My Real Father?" The Delicate Task of Identifying A Father and Parenting Children Created from An In Vitro Mix-up,* 18 Nat'l Black L.J. 1 (2004-05).

Margaret Mahoney, Stepfamilies and the Law (1994).

Martha Matthew, *Ten Thousand Tiny Clients: The Ethical Duty of Representation in Children's Class Action Cases,* 64 Fordham Law Review 2485 (1996).

David Meyer, *Lochner Redeemed: Family Privacy After Troxel and Carhart.* 48 U.C.L.A. L R, 1125 (2001).

Laurence C. Nolan, *Beyond Troxel: The Pragmatic Challenges of Grandparent Visitation Continue,* 50 Drake L. R. 267 (2002).

Gabrielle A. Paupeck, Note. *When Grandma Becomes Mom: the Liberty Interests of Kinship Foster Parents,* 70 Fordham L. Rev. 537 (2001).

Michael E. Ratner, Note, *In the Aftermath* Troxel v. Granville*: Is Mediation the Answer?,* 39 Fam. Ct. Rev. 454 (2001).

Symposium: Troxel v. Granville, 32 Rutgers Law Journal (Spring 2001).

U.S. Census Bureau, Children's Living Arrangements and Characteristics (2003), available at http://www.census.gov/population/www/socdemo/children.html.

U.S. Dep't Health & Human Servs [USDHHS], Administration for Children and Families, Administration on Children, Youth and Families, Children's Bureau, AFCARS Report, Current Estimates as of August 2005, available at http://www.acf.hhs.gov/programs/cb/stats_research/afcars/tar/report10.htm.

David M. Wagner, *Balancing "Parnets Are" and "Parents Do" in the Supreme Court's Constitutionalized Family Law: Some Implications for the ALI Proposals on De Facto Parenthood,* 2001 B.Y.U. L. Rev. 1175.

Lynn D. Wardle, *Considering the Impacts on Children and Society of "Lesbigay" Parenting,* 23 Quinnipiac L. Rev. 541 (2004).

Barbara Bennett Woodhouse and Sacha Coupet, Troxel v. Granville*: Implications For At Risk Children and the Amicus Curiae Role of University-Based Interdisciplinary Centers for Children,* 32 Rutgers L J 857 (2001).

Peter A. Zablotsky, *To Grandmother's House We Go: Grandparent Visitation After Stepparent Adoption,* 32 Wayne L. Rev. 1(1985).

CHAPTER 24

Abuse, Neglect and Dependency

A. OVERVIEW OF CHILD ABUSE, NEGLECT AND DEPENDENCY

1. Background

a. Child Abuse/Dependency/Neglect

If parents fail in their duty to protect the child from harm, the doctrine of family autonomy no longer provides them immunity from state intervention. The state, acting under its role as parens patriae, intervenes to protect the child. Much attention, beginning in the latter half of the twentieth century, has been given to child abuse as a national problem. The injury to the child is not accidentally, but purposefully done. The catalyst for the public's recognition of child abuse as a severe, social problem was a 1962 article in the Journal of the American Medical Association that described a medical condition which the authors labeled as the battered child syndrome. This medical condition is "a clinical condition in young children who had received serious physical abuse, generally from a parent or foster parent." Kempe, *infra*.

Dependency and neglect cases differ from abuse cases. In cases of dependency, a child is without proper care through no fault of the parents. The state steps in to protect and care for the child. While in cases of neglect, the state steps in because parents fail to provide the minimum standard of care or control of the child because of negligence or neglect on the part of the parents.

b. Civil Proceedings

Most abuse, neglect and dependency cases are civil proceedings. The civil proceedings usually consist of two parts: adjudicatory and dispositional. The adjudicatory part determines whether or not there is a finding of abuse or neglect or dependency. If there is a finding, the dispositional part follows where the remedy is determined. The juvenile court judge usually has within his or her discretion a wide range of remedies, e.g. "[t]he court may allow the child to remain in the home with court-imposed conditions. The court may remove custody from the parent and give custody to a private person, including a relative, to a child-placing agency, to the county or state welfare department, or to a private agency."Wardle & Nolan, *infra*. The court may terminate parental rights, or a combination of these remedies.

2. Statutes, Cases and Doctrines

a. *Estelle v. McGuire*

Estelle v. Mark Owen McGuire

585

502 U.S. 62 (1991)

Chief JUSTICE REHNQUIST delivered the opinion of the Court.

   *   *   *   *   *

McGuire and his wife brought their 6-month-old daughter, Tori, to a hospital in Hayward, California. The baby was bluish in color and was not breathing. The attending physician noticed a large and relatively recent bruise on Tori's chest with multiple bruises around it, as well as black and blue marks around her ears. Efforts to revive the child were unsuccessful; Tori died 45 minutes after being brought to the hospital. An autopsy revealed 17 contusions on the baby's chest, 29 contusions in her abdominal area, a split liver, a split pancreas, a lacerated large intestine, and damage to her heart and one of her lungs. The autopsy also uncovered evidence of rectal tearing, which was at least six weeks old, and evidence of partially healed rib fractures, which were approximately seven weeks old.

The police questioned McGuire and his wife. McGuire stated his belief that Tori's injuries must have resulted from a fall off the family couch. He told the police that when his wife went out to make a telephone call, he went upstairs, leaving Tori lying on the couch; when he heard the baby cry, he came back downstairs to find her lying on the floor. After a police officer expressed skepticism at this explanation, McGuire replied that "[m]aybe some Mexicans came in" while he was upstairs. During separate questioning, McGuire's wife stated that she had not hit Tori, and that she was unsure whether her husband had done so.

McGuire was charged with second-degree murder. At trial, the prosecution introduced both the statements made by McGuire to police and the medical evidence, including the evidence of prior rectal tearing and fractured ribs. Two physicians testified that Tori was a battered child, relying in part on the prior rib and rectal injuries, as well as on the more recent injuries. McGuire's neighbor testified that she had seen McGuire carry Tori by one of her arms to the car and roughly pinch her cheeks together when she cried. The neighbor added that McGuire's wife had expressed fear in leaving Tori alone with McGuire, because he had been rough with the baby and "did bad things" to her.

In addition, the prosecution called a witness who had overheard a conversation between McGuire and his wife in the hospital emergency room the night of Tori's death. According to the witness, McGuire's wife several times insistently asked, "What really happened?" McGuire replied that he "didn't know," and that he "guessed" the baby fell off the couch. His wife continued to press for an answer, stating, "I am very patient. I can wait a long time. I want to know what really happened." Finally, she told McGuire that "the baby was alright when I left. You are responsible." * McGuire's wife was called by the prosecution to testify at trial, after having been granted transactional immunity from future prosecution. In contrast to her prior statement to the police and her declarations at the hospital, she stated that she had beaten Tori on the day of her death before her husband arrived home. The jury convicted McGuire of second-degree murder.

The California Court of Appeal affirmed McGuire's conviction. The court observed that the evidence of prior rib and rectal injuries was introduced to prove "battered child syndrome." That syndrome exists when a child has sustained repeated and/or serious injuries by nonaccidental means. * After reviewing California authority on the subject, the court concluded that "proof of Tori's 'prior injuries' tending to establish the 'battered child syndrome' was patently proper." * The California Supreme Court denied review.

McGuire then filed a petition for habeas corpus relief in the United States District Court for the Northern District of California. That court denied relief. The Court of Appeals for the Ninth Circuit reversed and granted McGuire's habeas petition. The court ruled that the prior injury evidence was erroneously admitted to establish battered child syndrome, because no evidence linked McGuire to the prior injuries and no claim had been made at trial that the baby died accidentally. In addition, the court believed that the trial court's instruction on the use of prior act evidence allowed a finding of guilt based simply on a judgment that McGuire committed the prior bad acts. [FN1 *The court instructed the jury: "Evidence has been introduced for the purpose of showing that the Defendant committed acts similar to those constituting a crime other than that for which he is on trial. Such evidence, if believed, was not received, and may not be considered by you[,] to prove that he is a person of bad character or that he has a disposition to commit crimes. Such evidence was received and may be considered by you only for the limited purpose of determining if it tends to show three things: "1. The impeachment of Daisy McGuire's testimony that she had no cause to be afraid of the Defendant, 2. To establish the battered child syndrome, and 3. Also a clear connection between the other two offense[s] and the one of which the Defendant is accused, so that it may be logically concluded that if the Defendant committed other offenses, he also committed the crime charged in this case." "For the limited purpose for which you may consider such evidence, you must weigh it in the same manner as you do all other evidence in the case. You are not permitted to consider evidence for any other purpose."*] The court concluded that the admission of the evidence, in conjunction with the prejudicial instruction, "rendered [McGuire's] trial arbitrary and fundamentally unfair" in violation of due process. We hold that none of the alleged errors rise to the level of a due process violation, and so reverse.

I

We first consider whether the admission of the prior injury evidence justified habeas relief. In ruling that McGuire's due process rights were violated by the admission of the evidence, the Court of Appeals relied in part on its conclusion that the evidence was "incorrectly admitted ... pursuant to California law." * Such an inquiry, however, is no part of a federal court's habeas review of a state conviction. We have stated many times that "federal habeas corpus relief does not lie for errors of state law." *** Today, we reemphasize that it is not the province of a federal habeas court to reexamine state-court determinations on state-law questions.

In conducting habeas review, a federal court is limited to deciding whether a conviction violated the Constitution, laws, or treaties of the United States. * [FN2*]

We thus turn to the question whether the admission of the evidence violated McGuire's federal constitutional rights. California law allows the prosecution to introduce expert testimony and evidence related to prior injuries in order to prove "battered child syndrome." *** The demonstration of battered child syndrome "simply indicates that a child found with [serious, repeated injuries] has not suffered those injuries by accidental means." ***. Thus, evidence demonstrating battered child syndrome helps to prove that the child died at the hands of another and not by falling off a couch, for example, it also tends to establish that the "other," whoever it may be, inflicted the injuries intentionally. When offered to show that certain injuries are a product of child abuse, rather than accident, evidence of prior injuries is relevant even though it does not purport to prove the identity of the person who might have inflicted those injuries. *** Because the prosecution had charged McGuire with second-degree murder, it was required to prove that Tori's death was caused by the defendant's intentional act. Proof of Tori's battered child status helped to do just that; although not linked by any direct evidence to McGuire, the evidence demonstrated that Tori's death was the result of an intentional act by *someone*, and not an accident. The Court of Appeals, however, ignored the principle of battered child syndrome evidence in holding that this evidence was incorrectly admitted. For example, the court stated that "[e]vidence cannot have probative value unless a party connects it to the defendant in some meaningful way." *** We conclude that the evidence of prior injuries presented at McGuire's trial, whether it was directly linked to McGuire or not, was probative on the question of the intent with which the person who caused the injuries acted.

In holding the prior injury evidence inadmissible, the Court of Appeals also relied on the theory that, because no claim was made at trial that Tori died accidentally, the battered child syndrome evidence was irrelevant and violative of due process. *** This ruling ignores the fact that the prosecution must prove all the elements of a criminal offense beyond a reasonable doubt. In this second-degree murder case, for example, the prosecution was required to demonstrate that the killing was intentional. * By eliminating the possibility of accident, the evidence regarding battered child syndrome was clearly probative of that essential element, especially in light of the fact that McGuire had claimed prior to trial that Tori had injured herself by falling from the couch. The Court of Appeals, however, ruled that the evidence should have been excluded because McGuire did not raise the defense of accidental death at trial. But the prosecution's burden to prove every element of the crime is not relieved by a defendant's tactical decision not to contest an essential element of the offense. In the federal courts, "[a] simple plea of not guilty ... puts the prosecution to its proof as to all elements of the crime charged." *** Neither the Court of Appeals nor the parties have given us any reason to think that the rule is different in California. The evidence of battered child syndrome was relevant to show intent, and nothing in the Due Process Clause of the Fourteenth Amendment requires the State to refrain from introducing relevant evidence simply because the defense chooses not to contest the point.

Concluding, as we do, that the prior injury evidence was relevant to an issue in the case, we need not explore further the apparent assumption of the Court of Appeals that it is a violation of the due process guaranteed by the Fourteenth Amendment for evidence that is not relevant to be received in a criminal trial. We hold that McGuire's due process rights were not violated by the admission of the evidence.*** ("Cases in this Court have long proceeded on the premise that the Due Process Clause guarantees the fundamental elements of fairness in a criminal trial.... But it has never been thought that such cases establish this Court as a rulemaking organ for the promulgation of state rules of criminal procedure") (citations omitted).

II

The Court of Appeals, however, did not rely solely on a finding that the admission of the evidence was unconstitutional. It based its decision in part on a belief that the instruction given by the trial court, set forth in n. 1, *supra,* allowed the jury to consider the prior injury evidence for more than simply proof of the battered child syndrome, and thereby violated McGuire's due process rights. McGuire focuses on the portion of the instruction explaining to the jury that the prior injury evidence

> was received and may be considered by you only for the limited purpose of determining if it tends to show ... a clear connection between the other two offense[s] and the one of which the Defendant is accused, so that it may be logically concluded that if the Defendant committed other offenses, he also committed the crime charged in this case. *

McGuire argues that, despite the absence of any direct evidence showing that he caused the rib and rectal injuries, the instruction told the jury to find that he had committed those prior offenses. Furthermore, he argues, the instruction left the jury with the mistaken impression that it could base its finding of guilt on the simple fact that he had previously harmed Tori. Under McGuire's reading, the instruction is transformed into a propensity instruction, allowing the jury to consider as evidence of his guilt the fact that his prior acts show a disposition to commit this type of crime. This, he contends, violates the Due Process Clause.

In arguing his point, McGuire makes much of the fact that, in giving its instruction, the trial court deviated in part from standard jury instruction. [FN3 *] As we have stated above, however, the fact that the instruction was allegedly incorrect under state law is not a basis for habeas relief. *"[T]he Due Process Clause does not permit the federal courts to engage in a finely tuned review of the wisdom of state evidentiary rules").

Federal habeas courts therefore do not grant relief, as might a state appellate court, simply because the instruction may have been deficient in comparison to the CALJIC model. Nor do our habeas powers allow us to reverse McGuire's conviction based on a belief that the trial judge incorrectly interpreted the California Evidence Code in ruling that the prior injury evidence was admissible as bad acts evidence in this case. * The only question for us is "whether the ailing instruction by itself so infected the entire trial that the resulting conviction violates due process." *** (" '[I]t must be established not merely that the instruction is undesirable, erroneous, or even "universally condemned," but that it violated some [constitutional right]' "). It is well established that the instruction "may not be judged in artificial isolation," but must be considered in the context of the instructions as a whole and the trial record. *** In addition, in reviewing an ambiguous instruction such as the one at issue here, we inquire "whether there is a reasonable likelihood that the jury has applied the challenged instruction in a way" that violates the Constitution. *** [FN4 *] And we also bear in mind our previous admonition that we "have defined the category of infractions that violate 'fundamental fairness' very narrowly." *** "Beyond the specific guarantees enumerated in the Bill of Rights, the Due Process Clause has limited operation."****

McGuire first claims that the instruction directed the jury to find that he had caused the prior injuries, thereby effectively taking that question from the jury. One might argue that the "two offense[s]" referred to in the instruction were McGuire's pinching of the child's cheeks and the lifting of the child by her arm. When read in context, however, we conclude that the most likely interpretation is that the reference was to the rectal tearing and fractured ribs. McGuire argues that, despite the lack of any direct evidence linking him to those injuries, the instruction directed the jury to find that he had committed them. This claim is clearly foreclosed, however, by the language of the instruction. The challenged portion of the instruction included the words "if the Defendant committed other offenses." * By including this phrase, the trial court unquestionably left it to the jury to determine whether McGuire committed the prior acts; *only if* the jury believed he was the perpetrator could it use the evidence in deciding whether McGuire was guilty of the crime charged. Therefore, if the jury did not believe McGuire caused the prior injuries, he was not harmed by the challenged portion of the instruction. To the extent that the jury may have believed McGuire committed the prior acts and used that as a factor in its deliberation, we observe that there was sufficient evidence to sustain such a jury finding by a preponderance of the evidence. *** The proof of battered child syndrome itself narrowed the group of possible perpetrators to McGuire and his wife, because they were the only two people regularly caring for Tori during her short life. *See People v. Jackson*, 18 Cal.App.3d, at 507, 95 Cal.Rptr., at 921 ("Only someone regularly 'caring' for the child has the continuing opportunity to inflict these types of injuries; an isolated contact with a vicious stranger would not result in this pattern of successive injuries stretching through several months").

A neighbor testified that she had seen McGuire treat Tori roughly on two occasions, and that McGuire's wife was scared to leave Tori alone with McGuire because he "did bad things" to her; the neighbor further testified that she had never seen McGuire's wife abuse the child in any way. Furthermore, when being questioned by the police after Tori died, McGuire's wife stated that she observed bruises on the baby's body when bathing her. When asked by the police for an explanation, she replied, "I don't really know, you know, I am not the only one who is taking care of her." The evidence described, along with other evidence in the record, convinces us that there was sufficient proof for the jury to conclude, if it so desired, that McGuire caused the prior rib and rectal injuries.

McGuire also contends that, even if the determination of the perpetrator was left to the jury, the instruction constituted a "propensity" instruction, allowing the jury to base its determination of guilt in part upon the conclusion that McGuire had committed the prior acts and therefore had a propensity to commit this type of crime. While the instruction was not as clear as it might have been, we find that there is not a "reasonable likelihood" that the jury would have concluded that this instruction, read in the context of other instructions, authorized the use of propensity evidence pure and simple. *** It seems far more likely that the jury understood the instruction, *supra,* at 481, to mean that *if* it found a "clear connection" between the prior injuries and the instant injuries, and *if* it found that McGuire had committed the prior injuries, then it could use that fact in determining that McGuire committed the crime charged. The use of the evidence of prior offenses permitted by this instruction was therefore parallel to the familiar use of evidence of prior acts for the purpose of showing intent, identity, motive, or plan. *See e.g.* Fed.Rule Evid. 404(b). Furthermore, the trial court guarded against possible misuse of the instruction by specifically advising the jury that the "[prior injury] evidence, if believed, was not received, and may not be considered by you[,] to prove that [McGuire] is a person of bad character or that he has a disposition to commit crimes." *See* n. 1, *supra.* Especially in light of this limiting provision, we reject McGuire's claim that the instruction should be viewed as a propensity instruction. [FN5 *Because we need not reach the issue, we express no opinion on whether a state law would violate the Due Process Clause if it permitted the use of "prior crimes" evidence to show propensity to commit a charged crime.*]

We therefore hold that neither the introduction of the challenged evidence, nor the jury instruction as to its use, "so infused the trial with unfairness as to deny due process of law." *** The judgment of the Court of Appeals is therefore *Reversed.*

JUSTICE THOMAS took no part in the consideration or decision of this case.

JUSTICE O'CONNOR, with whom JUSTICE STEVENS joins, concurring in part and dissenting in part.

I agree with the Court that the evidence of battered child syndrome was relevant. The State had to prove that Mark McGuire intended to kill his daughter, and the evidence that Tori was a battered child was probative of causation and intent. I therefore join Part I of the Court's opinion.

I do not join Part II of the opinion because I think there is a reasonable likelihood that the jury misapplied the prior acts instruction. The trial court instructed the jury that evidence of Tori's prior injuries had been admitted to show that McGuire had committed offenses similar to that for which he was on trial, and that, if the jury found a "clear connection" between the prior offenses and the charged offense, "it may be logically concluded that if the Defendant committed other offenses, he also committed the crime charged in this case." In my view, the instruction encouraged the jury to assume that McGuire had inflicted the prior injuries and then directed the jury to conclude that the prior abuser was the murderer. Because the instruction may have relieved the State of its burden of proving the identity of Tori's murderer beyond a reasonable doubt, I would hold that the instruction was error and remand to the Court of Appeals for a determination of whether that error was harmless.

*   *   *   *   *

The trial court's error in implying that McGuire had been identified as the prior abuser was compounded by its further instruction that, if the jury found a "clear connection" between the prior offenses and the charged offense, "it may be logically concluded that if the Defendant committed other offenses, he also committed the crime charged in this case." The Court finds it "likely" that the jury understood the instruction to mean that "*if* it found a 'clear connection' between the prior injuries and the instant injuries, and *if* it found that McGuire had committed the prior injuries, then it could use that fact in determining that McGuire committed the crime charged." *** In my view, there is a reasonable likelihood that the jury did not understand this single sentence to establish a two-step process.

The jury was instructed to "consider" the evidence that McGuire had "committed acts similar" to the crime charged and to "determin[e]" whether there was a "clear connection" between these prior acts and the ones that resulted in Tori's death. The trial court did not instruct the jury that it must first "determine" whether McGuire had in fact inflicted the prior injuries. The part of the instruction relied upon by the Court--"it may be logically concluded that if the defendant committed other offenses, he also committed the crime charged in this case"--does not make clear that it is the jury's role to ascertain whether McGuire was the perpetrator of the prior abuse. Rather, coming as it does in the middle of what appears to be a conclusion of law, it is reasonably likely that the jury understood that such a determination had already been made and that its role was merely to determine if there was a "clear connection" between Tori's prior injuries and the injuries that killed her.

Although we "have defined the category of infractions that violate 'fundamental fairness' very narrowly," ***, it is well established that the fundamental fairness guarantee of the Due Process Clause requires the prosecution to prove beyond a reasonable doubt every element of the offense. *** This constitutional principle "prohibits the State from using evidentiary presumptions in a jury charge that have the effect of relieving the State of its burden of persuasion beyond a reasonable doubt of every essential element of a crime." *** Thus, we have held that mandatory presumptions violate the Due Process Clause if they relieve the State of the burden of persuasion on an element of the offense. *** By contrast, a permissive inference is not a violation of due process because the State still has the burden of persuading the jury that the suggested conclusion should be inferred based on the predicate facts proved. ***

In this case, the instruction perhaps was intended to posit a permissive inference that whoever had inflicted Tori's prior injuries was likely to have inflicted the injuries that caused her death. But the trial court did not make clear that the State first had to prove the predicate facts from which the inference was to be drawn. Furthermore, the wording of the instruction is such that the jury may well have assumed that it had no choice but to "logically conclud[e]" that McGuire was the murderer once it found a "clear connection" between the prior injuries and the fatal ones. [FN***] Because I cannot say with any confidence that the instruction allowed a mere permissive inference drawing from proven facts, I think the instruction should be treated as a mandatory presumption that may have relieved the State of its burden of proving the identity of Tori's killer beyond a reasonable doubt.

Had the instruction been clearly worded, I would agree with the Court that there is sufficient circumstantial evidence in the record to support a finding that McGuire was the perpetrator of the prior injuries. After all, as the Court points out, "[t]he proof of battered child syndrome itself narrowed the group of possible perpetrators to McGuire and his wife, because they were the only two people regularly caring for Tori. In this case, however, it is important to remember that the other person regularly caring for Tori--Daisy McGuire--took the stand and testified, under a grant of immunity, that *she* was the one who inflicted the fatal injuries on the night of July 7, 1981.

McGuire's jury deliberated for three days before returning a verdict of guilty. Any evaluation of the jury instruction must be conducted against the background of Daisy McGuire's surprise testimony and the dilemma it so clearly posed for the jury. In my view, the jury instruction on similar acts was so "ambiguous," * that there was a reasonable likelihood that the jury was encouraged to make assumptions and conclusions about the identity of Tori's murderer that relieved the State of having to prove that element of the offense beyond a reasonable doubt. In cases where the Court has found that jury instructions included mandatory presumptions inconsistent with the guarantees of the Due Process Clause, the Court has remanded to determine whether the erroneous instruction was harmless, which is the course that should be followed here. ***

b. Review *Petition of Jane Doe*, 564 A.2d 433 (N.H. 1989)
    See Chapter 22, *supra*.

c. *Croft v. Westmoreland County Children and Youth Services*

Henry Croft, Jr. and Carol Croft v. Westmoreland County Children and Youth Services
103 F.3d 1123 (3rd Cir 1997)

NYGAARD, Circuit JUDGE.

Plaintiffs-Appellants, Dr. Henry L. Croft, Jr., and Carol Croft, individually and as parents and natural guardians of Chynna Croft, appeal an order of the district court granting summary judgment for defendants-appellees, Carla Danovsky, Westmoreland County Children and Youth Services, and Westmoreland County. We will reverse and remand.

I

On February 1, 1993, Gerald Sopko, Assistant Director of the Westmoreland County Children's Bureau received a call from Childline, informing him that Dr. Croft was sexually abusing his daughter, Chynna. Sopko was further told that the child slept with her parents and that she had recently been out of the house naked, walked to a neighbor's house, knocked on the door, and told the neighbors that she was "sleeping with mommy and daddy."

Barbara Jollie, Program Director for the Assessment Department of the Westminster County Children's Bureau, assigned the matter to Carla Danovsky for investigation. Danovsky, accompanied by State Police Trooper Griffin, went to the Croft home that night. Danovsky told Dr. Croft she was investigating him for possible sexual abuse of his daughter based on the Childline report. Dr. Croft consented to be interviewed.

Dr. Croft explained that Chynna had indeed, in April of 1992, left her bed without waking her parents, gone downstairs and outside, and locked herself out of the house. She then went to the house of her babysitter/nanny, a short distance from the Croft home, wearing her pajama top and holding her pajama bottoms with a soiled diaper inside. He further provided Danovsky with the telephone number of the nanny who could verify his version of events.

Dr. Croft agreed that his daughter had seen him naked and that, in fact, the family vacationed in the French West Indies where nude beaches are routine. Dr. Croft stated that his wife sunbathed nude around Chynna. He explained that Chynna suffered from seizures and, although she regularly slept in her parents' bed so they could be nearby if necessary, she slept naked only rarely. Henry and Carol Croft slept clothed. Dr. Croft told Danovsky that he had applied medicinal creams to her vaginal area when she had a rash. He denied sexually abusing Chynna.

Danovsky gave Dr. Croft an ultimatum: unless he left his home and separated himself from his daughter until the investigation was complete, she would take Chynna physically from the home that night and place her in foster care. Dr. Croft then left the room and Danovsky interviewed Carol Croft while Chynna sat in her lap. Carol Croft confirmed Dr. Croft's version of the April 1992 incident when Chynna locked herself out of the house. Finally, Danovsky questioned Chynna, who also confirmed Dr. Croft's version of the lock-out incident. Chynna provided no indication that she had ever been sexually abused. Danovsky then reiterated her ultimatum, that unless Dr. Croft immediately left his home and had no contact with his daughter, Danovsky would remove Chynna from the home that very night and place her in foster care. Faced with this dilemma, Dr. Croft complied with her ultimatum, and left his home, wife and daughter. [FN1 *Defendants repeatedly have characterized Dr. Croft's decision to leave as "voluntary." This notion we explicitly reject. The threat that unless Dr. Croft left his home, the state would take his four-year-old daughter and place her in foster care was blatantly coercive. The attempt to color his decision in this light is not well taken.*]

Danovsky testified to some inconsistencies between the statements of the Croft parents. She testified that Carol Croft said that Chynna never saw Henry Croft swimming naked, and that she sunbathed topless but not totally nude. One of the parents informed Danovsky that Chynna never slept naked in their bed, while the other said she was not clothed all the time. In sum, however, the differences were insignificant and reasonable under the circumstances. Danovsky also testified that, pursuant to County policy, a parent accused of sexual abuse must prove beyond any certainty that there was no sexual abuse before she would be permitted to leave a child with his or her parents. She further testified that if a County caseworker does not know whether or not the allegation is true, the child will be separated from the alleged perpetrator. Danovsky also testified that at the conclusion of her interview with the Crofts, she was uncertain whether any sexual abuse had occurred.

The Crofts filed a complaint in the federal district court against Westmoreland County Children and Youth Services (WCCYS), Carla Danovsky and Westmoreland County. They alleged that the defendants had impermissibly interfered with their Fourteenth Amendment liberty interest in the companionship of their daughter.

Defendants filed motions to dismiss the complaint, which, since discovery had been completed, were considered as motions for summary judgment. They argued that defendant Danovsky was entitled to qualified immunity for her actions and that the county and WCCYS enjoyed municipal immunity from the charges. The court entered summary judgment against the Crofts on all three counts, asserting that the Crofts would impermissibly have the court elevate their right to freedom of intimate association above Defendants' obligation to protect children. The Crofts timely appealed. [FN2 *We note that the Crofts are appealing the district court's order with respect only to the County and the WCCYS, not as to Carla Danovsky. Furthermore, the Crofts are only appealing the district court's determination of their substantive due process issues.*]

II

We recognize the constitutionally protected liberty interests that parents have in the custody, care and management of their children. *** We also recognize that this interest is not absolute. *** Indeed, this liberty interest in familial integrity is limited by the compelling governmental interest in the protection of children --- particularly where the children need to be protected from their own parents. *** The right to familial integrity, in other words, does not include a right to remain free from child abuse investigations. ***

The Due Process Clause of the Fourteenth Amendment prohibits the government from interfering in familial relationships unless the government adheres to the requirements of procedural and substantive due process. [FN3 *We note here only that the policy of removing the suspected parent from the family home during the pendency of child abuse investigations absent any procedural safeguards raises a procedural due process issue.*] In determining whether the Crofts' constitutionally protected interests were violated, we must balance the fundamental liberty interests of the family unit with the compelling interests of the state in protecting children from abuse. Whatever disruption or disintegration of family life the Croft's may have suffered as a result of the county's child abuse investigation does not, in and of itself, constitute a constitutional deprivation. ***

We realize there may be cases in which a child services bureau may be justified in removing either a child or parent from the home, even where later investigation proves no abuse occurred. However, a state has no interest in protecting children from their parents unless it has some reasonable and articulable evidence giving rise to a reasonable suspicion that a child has been abused or is in imminent danger of abuse. *See Lehr*, 463 U.S. at 254-56, 103 S.Ct. at 2990 (declaring liberty interests in preserving the family unit "are sufficiently vital to merit constitutional protection *in appropriate cases* ") (emphasis added); *accord Myers*, 810 F.2d at 1462-63 (noting parental liberty interest in maintaining integrity of family unit is not a clearly established right where there is a "reasonable suspicion" abuse may have occurred).

Our focus here is whether the information available to the defendants at the time would have created an objectively reasonable suspicion of abuse justifying the degree of interference with the Crofts' rights as Chynna's parents. [FN4] Absent such reasonable grounds, governmental intrusions of this type are arbitrary abuses of power. ***

Before the interviews, Danovsky possessed a six-fold hearsay report by an anonymous informant stating that the mother had told a friend that Dr. Croft had abused Chynna and that Chynna had recently been put out of the house naked, walked several miles, was found by a neighbor, and said she was sleeping with her parents. [FN5 *The anonymous tip reported that "[T]he mother told a friend ..." of sexual abuse. Subsequently, the information went from the informant, to Childline, to Gerald Sopko, to Barbara Jollie, to Danovsky. We recognize that child abuse will often be reported anonymously. We additionally realize that such hearsay may often be the only available evidence to alert the child abuse investigators. Anonymous informants, such as those who report suspected abuse on the Childline, are undoubtedly important in policing "invisible crimes" like child sexual abuse.*]

Dr. Croft confirmed that an incident bearing only the barest resemblance to the anonymous tip had happened. Far from corroborating the anonymous tip, the Crofts' statements raised serious questions about the veracity of the informant. An anonymous tip may justify investigation but will not provide reasonable grounds for removal of a family member absent independent, articulable criteria of reliability; and certainly not when all evidence is to the contrary. ***

Danovsky was entitled to view the statements of an alleged perpetrator skeptically. She was not, however, entitled to rely on the unknown credibility of an anonymous informant unless she could corroborate the information through other sources which would have reduced the chance that the informant was recklessly relating incorrect information or had purposely distorted information. *

Danovsky, in her deposition testimony, pointed to what she called "red flags"--statements given during the interviews which raised questions in her mind about whether the tip was true--as further justification for forcing Henry Croft from his home. The red flags cited by Defendants are incapable of providing the necessary reasonable grounds. For example, at one point during the interview, Dr. Croft told Danovsky that he had applied vaginal creams to Chynna when she had a rash, which Danovsky interpreted to mean that he regularly gave his daughter vaginal exams. Likewise, Danovsky's reliance on supposed inconsistencies between the statements of Carol and Dr. Croft is without foundation. None of the cited inconsistencies is evidence of child sexual abuse, nor did any of the statements in any way confirm the allegations of the anonymous tip. Even considered together, minor inconsistencies which provide no affirmative evidence of sexual abuse cannot alone establish the objectively reasonable grounds necessary to remove a family member from the family unit.

Most damaging to Defendants is Danovsky's deposition testimony that, after the interviews, she had no opinion one way or the other whether sexual abuse had occurred. Alternatively, Danovsky testified that she did not have enough information to make a determination and that further investigation was required. Under either statement, Danovsky did not have reasonable grounds, to *any* degree of certainty, that Chynna was sexually abused or was in imminent danger of abuse. She possessed no evidence of abuse beyond an anonymous tip. Danovsky had no physical evidence of sexual abuse with which to base an opinion. She was merely presented with an anonymous tip relating an incident which was reasonably explained by the accused parents. Record evidence establishes that Danovsky lacked any objective evidence of sexual abuse, and, indeed, that she had no belief that such abuse had occurred.

Considered in light of the circumstances surrounding the ultimatum, Danovsky's conduct was an arbitrary abuse of government power. Based on her lack of an opinion regarding whether sexual abuse had occurred, we hold that she lacked objectively reasonable grounds to believe the child had been sexually abused or was in imminent danger of sexual abuse. Combined with the total absence of objective evidence which would support a belief that sexual abuse had occurred, we hold that Danovsky's conduct will certainly not support the grant of summary judgment in the Defendants' favor. Because the Crofts did not cross-file for summary judgment, we, sitting as a court of review, must remand the cause to the district court for further proceedings.

III

We will reverse the district court's entry of summary judgment.

d. *Commonwealth v. Rapso*

Commonwealth v. Maria Raposo
595 N.E.2d 773 (Mass 1992)

O'CONNOR, JUSTICE.

After a jury-waived trial, a judge in the Superior Court found the defendant guilty of being an accessory before the fact to rape and to indecent assault and battery on a mentally retarded person. After sentencing the defendant to concurrent terms of probation, the judge stayed execution of the sentences and reported the case to the Appeals Court pursuant to Mass.R.Crim.P. 34, 378 Mass. 905 (1979). We transferred the case to this court on our own initiative, and now reverse the convictions and order judgments for the defendant.

Rule 34 states, in relevant part: "If ... with the consent of the defendant, after conviction of the defendant, a question of law arises which the trial judge determines is so important or doubtful as to require the decision of the Appeals Court, the judge may report the case so far as necessary to present the question of law arising therein." Although the record does not disclose that the defendant expressly consented to the report, we infer the defendant's implied consent from the absence of any objection in the trial court or here.

In his report, the judge set forth his findings and a series of questions of law. The significant findings were as follows. The defendant is the mother of a mildly retarded daughter, who was seventeen years old at the time of the incidents described below. The defendant's boy friend, Manuel F. Matos, Jr., lived with the defendant and her daughter for about two months before May 22, 1988. Matos told the defendant that he intended to have sexual intercourse with her daughter. In response, the defendant expressed neither encouragement nor discouragement. On one occasion, Matos told the defendant that he was going to have intercourse with her daughter, stating that "she needs a man." The defendant did not respond, although she knew that her daughter did not want to have intercourse with Matos. Matos had intercourse with the daughter from two to four times by force and against her will. At least once, after Matos had entered the daughter's bedroom, the defendant pounded on the closed, unlocked door and told Matos to stop. On May 22, 1988, the defendant took her daughter to a New Bedford police station, where they gave statements about the sexual activity between Matos and the daughter. Prior to this visit at the police station, the defendant made no effort to enlist outside assistance to prevent Matos from engaging in sexual intercourse with her daughter.

The judge's questions, set forth in his report, are as follows. 1. Does a parent have any duty to take action to prevent harm to his/her child? 2. If such a duty exists, does it include a requirement to take reasonable steps to prevent a sexual assault in the family home on a [seventeen] year old, mildly mentally retarded daughter? 3. If the duty exists, is the failure to fulfill it a crime? 4. If it is a crime, is it a violation of [G.L. c. 274, § 2]?

We need not answer the four questions separately. It is clear that the basic question that prompted the report is whether a person may be found guilty of being an accessory before the fact * to rape * and to indecent assault and battery on a mentally retarded person *, where the victim is a minor, the defendant is the minor's parent, and the defendant failed to take reasonable steps to prevent the sexual attacks by a third person. Stated another way, the question as to each conviction is whether the subsidiary facts found by the judge, on which he clearly based his ultimate guilty findings, support such conclusions.

General Laws c. 274, § 2, provides: "Whoever aids in the commission of a felony, or is accessory thereto before the fact by counselling, hiring or otherwise procuring such felony to be committed, shall be punished in the manner provided for the punishment of the principal felon." The following principles emerge from an examination of our case law in this area. In order to be found guilty as an accessory before the fact, the evidence must prove beyond a reasonable doubt that the defendant must "in some sort associate himself with the venture, that he participate in it as in something that he wishes to bring about, [and] that he seek by his action to make it succeed." *** We have held that the plain language of the statute, involving aiding, counselling, hiring or otherwise procuring a principal to commit the crime, requires "something more than mere acquiescence," although not necessarily physical participation, "if there is association with the criminal venture and any significant participation in it." *** Moreover, "presence at the scene of the [crime], together with the failure to take affirmative steps to prevent it, does not render a person liable as principal." * A person cannot be found guilty as an accessory before the fact simply because she knows a crime is going to be committed, even when this knowledge is coupled with her subsequent concealment of the completed crime. *** Therefore, it is clear that what is required to be convicted as an accessory before the fact is not only knowledge of the crime and a shared intent to bring it about, but also some sort of act that contributes to its happening.

The Commonwealth argues that the case was tried, and the defendant convicted, on the theory that, as the mother of the victim, the defendant had a common law duty to protect her child from harm, and that her failure to take reasonable steps to fulfill this duty is an omission sufficient to make her liable as an accessory.

Putting the Commonwealth's contention another way, it is that, in allowing Matos access to her daughter and failing to take reasonable steps to stop his wrongful actions, the defendant "aided" Matos in committing the crimes and thus became a participant in the criminal activity. The defendant's intent that the underlying crimes be committed, the Commonwealth contends, can be inferred from her knowledge of the crimes and her intentional acts of omission.

Only one case cited by the Commonwealth in support of this theory involves a statute similar to c. 274, § 2. [FN2*] In *State v. Walden*, 306 N.C. 466, 293 S.E.2d 780 (1982), the Supreme Court of North Carolina upheld a mother's conviction of aiding and abetting an assault with a deadly weapon by another person on her child. In general, North Carolina law on aiding and abetting, like our law on accessory before the fact, requires that a person must say or do something that demonstrates consent to the felonious purpose and contributes to the execution of a crime. * In *Walden*, the evidence showed that the mother witnessed, but made no attempt to stop, another person's lengthy beating of her small child with a belt, which resulted in serious injuries to the child. * The *Walden* court created an exception to the general aiding and abetting rule when a parent, who is present, neglects his or her affirmative legal duty to "take all steps reasonably possible to protect the parent's child from an attack by another person" and that such an omission shows the parent's "consent and contribution to the crime being committed." * See *State v. Oliver*, 85 N.C.App. 1, 24, 354 S.E.2d 527 (1987) (evidence sufficient to sustain mother's conviction as aider and abettor to second-degree sexual offense against her child, where mother present in bed while child raped, touched the child during rape, and failed to take any steps to avert assault). The Commonwealth urges this court to follow the Supreme Court of North Carolina in holding that a parent's failure to take reasonable steps to perform his or her affirmative duty to protect his or her child is a form of consent and participation in the commission of a criminal act against the child.

The Commonwealth bolsters its contention that the defendant's conduct was criminal by analogizing this situation to cases in which this court held that a parent's failure to protect his or her child, knowing there was a high degree of likelihood that the child would be substantially harmed, constituted wanton or reckless conduct sufficient to support a manslaughter conviction. In *Commonwealth v. Gallison*, 383 Mass. 659, 665-666, 421 N.E.2d 757 (1981), this court upheld the manslaughter conviction of a mother where the evidence was sufficient for the jury to believe that she made no effort to obtain medical help for her child who had an extreme fever and became unconscious. This court stated, "[a]s a parent ... the defendant had a duty to provide for the care and welfare of her child," and found that the jury could have concluded that her inaction in light of the child's obvious illness was a type of intentional conduct which "involves a high degree of likelihood that substantial harm will result" and thus constituted "wanton or reckless" conduct for the purposes of manslaughter. * See *Commonwealth v. Michaud*, 389 Mass. 491, 499, 451 N.E.2d 396 (involuntary manslaughter convictions of parents reversed where evidence was insufficient to prove that parents' failure to seek medical attention for ailing child was reckless rather than negligent).

Other jurisdictions, referred to by the Commonwealth, have reached similar results. *See State v. Zobel*, 81 S.D. 260, 273, 281, 134 N.W.2d 101 (1965) (father's conviction of second-degree manslaughter upheld where the evidence proved that he knowingly exposed his children to cruel and inhuman beatings by his wife, resulting in their deaths); *State v. Austin*, 84 S.D. 405, 414-415, 172 N.W.2d 284 (1969) (first-degree manslaughter conviction of mother upheld where evidence proved she aided and abetted cruel punishment of child by her companion, resulting in child's death); *Palmer v. State*, 223 Md. 341, 352, 164 A.2d 467 (1960) (involuntary manslaughter conviction of mother upheld where evidence proved she displayed a "wanton or reckless disregard for human life" in failing to remove her child from boy friend who beat the child so severely that it would "put any reasonable person on guard that the child's life was in real and imminent peril").

While it is clear in this and other jurisdictions that a parent's failure to fulfil his or her duty to provide for the safety and welfare of a child may rise to the level of wanton or reckless conduct sufficient to support a manslaughter conviction, we decline to follow the Supreme Court of North Carolina and read into our accessory before the fact law the principle that a mere omission by a parent to take action to protect a child, without more, is the equivalent of intentionally aiding in the commission of a felony against that child. By its very terms, c. 274, § 2, requires more than an omission to act. As our case law makes clear, in order to be punished as an accessory before the fact, the defendant must have actually aided in the commission of the felony or counseled, hired, or otherwise procured someone to commit it. *

Commonwealth v. Hall, 322 Mass. 523, 78 N.E.2d 644 (1948), relied on by the Commonwealth, does not require a different result. In *Hall*, this court affirmed the conviction of murder in the second degree of a mother who, the jury could have found, intentionally placed her baby in the attic of her home and withheld food and liquids from it as a result of which the baby died. * The defendant in *Hall* was not charged as an accessory, as here, and unlike the present case, malicious conduct was involved. For conviction as an accessory before the fact, nothing less than shared intent and significant participation in the underlying crime, neither of which was present here, will suffice.

On the facts reported by the Superior Court judge, the Commonwealth has failed to show beyond a reasonable doubt that the defendant aided, counselled, hired, or procured Matos to commit rape and indecent assault and battery, or that she took any other action which would constitute participation in the commission of these crimes against her daughter. The fact that she knew ahead of time of Matos's intent to commit the criminal acts, and did not report the subsequent crimes to the police immediately, does not make her guilty as an accessory before the fact. ***

We conclude that the convictions must be reversed and that judgments of acquittal are required. So ordered.

ABRAMS, JUSTICE (concurring).

I concur. On the facts of this case, the defendant cannot be convicted as an accessory before the fact pursuant to G.L. c. 274, § 2 (1990 ed.). "[O]rdinary rules of statutory construction require us to construe any criminal statute strictly against the Commonwealth." *** "Plain omissions in the law to provide for exigencies which may arise cannot be supplied by *those charged with administering the law or by the courts in construing and interpreting the statutes* " (emphasis supplied). *** Currently, no criminal statute reaches acts of omission such as the one involved in this case.*** Strong and compelling arguments can be made for and against criminalizing the type of conduct described in the court's opinion. As the court's opinion makes clear, parents have a duty to provide for the safety and welfare of their children. * It is for the Legislature to determine whether expanding that duty by criminalizing acts of omission would better protect the Commonwealth's children.

e. *In the Matter Concerning Baby X, a Minor*

In the Matter Concerning Baby X, a Minor
293 N.W.2d 736 (Mich. Ct. of App. 1980)

RILEY, JUDGE.

On March 30, 1977, the minor child who is the subject of this lawsuit was born in St. Joseph's Hospital of Pontiac, Michigan. Within 24 hours of birth this child, known as Baby X for purposes of these proceedings, began exhibiting symptoms of drug withdrawal, whereupon a petition was filed with the Oakland County Probate Court alleging that appellant, Mother X, had so neglected her child that the court should assert jurisdiction. The probate judge found sufficient evidence of neglect to take temporary custody of Baby X, a decision affirmed by the Oakland County Circuit Court and now appealed by the child's mother.

The Probate Code provides as follows:

> SEC. 2. Except as provided herein, the juvenile division of the probate court shall have:
> (b) Jurisdiction in proceedings concerning any child under 17 years of age found within the county
> (1) Whose parent or other person legally responsible for the care and maintenance of such child, when able to do so, neglects or refuses to provide proper or necessary support, education as required by law, medical, surgical or other care necessary for his health, morals, or who is deprived of emotional well-being, or who is abandoned by his parents, guardian, or other custodian, or who is otherwise without proper custody or guardianship; or "(2) Whose home or environment, by reason of neglect, cruelty, drunkenness, criminality or depravity on the part of a parent, guardian or other custodian, is an unfit place for such child to live in, or whose mother is unmarried and without adequate provision for care and support." M.C.L. § 712A.2; M.S.A. § 27.3178(598.2).

A probate court acting pursuant to this statute must make two determinations. At the adjudicative stage, the court should initially consider whether sufficient facts have been alleged to support assertion of jurisdiction. If sufficient jurisdictional facts exist, for instance, if the facts establish neglect, the court can proceed to the dispositional stage. After considering all the facts and alternatives, the judge should order disposition according to the best interests of the child. ****

In the instant case, it is the adjudicative stage that is currently at issue. Mother X contends that prenatal conduct cannot constitute neglect or abuse under the Probate Code; therefore, the probate court wrongly asserted jurisdiction.

It recently has been held that the probate court may not assert jurisdiction over an unborn person as it is not a "child" under M.C.L. § 712A.2; M.S.A. § 27.3178(598.2). In re Dittrick Infant, 80 Mich.App. 219, 223, 263 N.W.2d 37 (1977). However, since Baby X was born before the instant petition was filed by the Department of Social Services, this aspect of jurisdiction is not properly at issue. The prenatal period is only pertinent because it is the sole asserted basis for establishing jurisdiction based on neglect. The initial question then becomes whether a mother's prenatal behavior is relevant to a determination of a living child's neglect.

While there is no wholesale recognition of fetuses as persons, *Roe v. Wade*, 410 U.S. 113, 162 (1973); *Toth v. Goree*, 65 Mich.App. 296, 303, 237 N.W.2d 297 (1975), fetuses have been accorded rights under certain limited circumstances. *O'Neill v. Morse*, 385 Mich. 130, 188 N.W.2d 785 (1971) (wrongful death action allowable for 8-month- old viable fetus), *Womack v. Buchhorn*,

384 Mich. 718, 187 N.W.2d 218 (1971) (common law action allowable for surviving child injured during the fourth month of pregnancy), *LaBlue v. Specker*, 358 Mich. 558, 100 N.W.2d 445 (1960) (Dramshop action allowable for fetus of dead father). This limited recognition of a child en ventre sa mere as a child in esse is appropriate when it is for the child's best interest. *LaBlue, supra*, at 563, 100 N.W.2d 445. Since a child has a legal right to begin life with a sound mind and body, *Womack, supra*, 384 Mich. at 725, 187 N.W.2d 218, we believe it is within this best interest to examine all prenatal conduct bearing on that right.

It must then be determined whether prenatal conduct specifically, extensive narcotics ingestion by the mother can constitute neglect sufficient for the probate court's assertion of jurisdiction.

Under the Probate Code, a permanent custody order must be based on circumstances which "establish or seriously threaten neglect of the child for the long-run future". The quantum of neglect sufficient for temporary custody or merely establishing jurisdiction implicitly must be less, i. e., temporary neglect. *

In *Dittrick, supra*, this Court recognized that mistreatment of a child is probative of how a parent may treat other soon-to-be-born siblings. It may readily be inferred, then, that such abuse is sufficient to establish jurisdiction.***

Since prior treatment of one child can support neglect allegations regarding another child, we believe that prenatal treatment can be considered probative of a child's neglect as well. We hold that a newborn suffering narcotics withdrawal symptoms as a consequence of prenatal maternal drug addiction may properly be considered a neglected child within the jurisdiction of the probate court. We pass no judgment upon whether such conduct will suffice to permanently deprive a mother of custody. Such custody determinations will be resolved at the dispositional phase where prenatal conduct will be considered along with postnatal conduct.

In addition to the jurisdictional matter, Mother X asserts that her right to confidentiality as a drug abuse patient was impaired by the lower court. Specifically, she contends that a conflict exists between Federal law which protects patients from disclosure of their drug addiction records and state law which mandates disclosure of child abuse and neglect. The probate court rejected Mother X's objections and ruled that hospital records for both her and Baby X were admissible. Although the circuit court did not deal with this issue, we believe that it is of such importance that it must be addressed here. ***

M.C.L. § 722.623; M.S.A. § 25.248(3) provides that certain professionals should report any suspected child abuse to the proper authorities, supplying such information as the child's name, parents' names and a description of the abuse. No privilege (except for that between attorney and client) can constitute grounds for excusing such a report or for excluding evidence in a protective juvenile proceeding. *

These statutes favoring disclosure are diametrically opposed to drug treatment statutes protective of confidentiality. 21 U.S.C. § 1175 [FN3] states that all patient records, which are maintained in connection with drug abuse programs supported by the Federal government, may not be disclosed absent "good cause" and a court order. Interpretative regulations promulgated by the Department of Health, Education and Welfare have extended this confidentiality to information that is in any way related to the diagnosis and treatment of drug abuse. 42 CFR § 2.13 (1979). Thus, the release of the hospital's report and records concerning Baby X's withdrawal symptoms and the information regarding Mother X's drug abuse was allegedly in contravention of the Federal statute as well as possibly a state statute, M.C.L. § 325.728; M.S.A. § 18.1031(28).

Two New York courts have dealt with a similar conflict between the Federal and state law. * In both neglect-proceeding cases, the Social Services Commissioner moved for the production of records on the mothers' drug or alcohol abuse. Production was opposed based on 21 U.S.C. § 1175(a). In both cases, the family courts held that the records should be produced pursuant to orders issued under 21 U.S.C. § 1175(b)(2)(C).

    *   *   *   *   *   *

We too agree that in neglect proceedings confidentiality must give way to the best interests of the child. Where treatment records are found to be "necessary and material",* to the state's proof of neglect, a court of competent jurisdiction may authorize disclosure. Alleged drug or alcohol dependence (here, the alleged heroin addiction of Mother X) which causes a baby's withdrawal and failure to thrive is sufficient "good cause" as required by the Federal statute (and sufficient under the state statute as well) to order production of the records.

While normally, in the absence of this necessary court order, we would be compelled to reverse, we need not do so here. The probate judge conducted a substantial inquiry into the competing concerns and policies inherent in the case sub judice. litem for Baby X and then ultimately limited the records to be produced to "objective data" only. Throughout the proceedings, the court complied with the spirit of the Federal statute that the court weigh "the public interest and the need for disclosure against the injury to the patient, to the physician-patient relationship, and to the treatment services". 21 U.S.C. § 1175(b)(2)(C). In ultimately concluding that the child's best interests must preponderate over the mother's, the judge below did everything but issue the proper court order. In light of his competent balancing, his carefully restrictive admissions and the limited, private nature of the child neglect proceedings, we see no reason to reverse here based on the lack of a proper court order. In future neglect cases, however, any conflict between Federal and state law can be avoided by filing a John or Jane Doe petition with the disclosure of any names and confidential information to follow the issuance of a court order upon "good cause". Affirmed.

f. *Lassiter v. Department of Social Services*
Abby Gail Lassiter v. Department of Social Services of Durham County N.C.
452 U.S. 18 (1981)

In *Lassiter*, the Supreme Court held that indigency alone did not qualify a parent for *per se* appointment of counsel in parental termination cases in order to meet due process requirements. The court must determine on a case-by-case basis whether due process required an appointment of counsel, based on the three factors in *Mathews v. Eldridge*, 424 U.S. 319 (1976): (1) the private interests at stake, (2) the government's interests, and (3) the risk that the procedures used will lead to erroneous decisions.

g. *Santosky v. Kramer*
John Santosky and Annie Santosky v. Bernhardt S. Kramer
455 U.S. 745 (1982)

JUSTICE BLACKMUN delivered the opinion of the Court.

Under New York law, the State may terminate, over parental objection, the rights of parents in their natural child upon a finding that the child is "permanently neglected." N.Y.Soc.Serv.Law ss 384-b.4.(d), 384- b.7. (a) (McKinney Supp.1981-1982) (Soc.Serv.Law). The New York Family Court Act § 622* requires that only a "fair preponderance of the evidence" support that finding. Thus, in New York, the factual certainty required to extinguish the parent-child relationship is no greater than that necessary to award money damages in an ordinary civil action.

Today we hold that the Due Process Clause of the Fourteenth Amendment demands more than this.

Before a State may sever completely and irrevocably the rights of parents in their natural child, due process requires that the State support its allegations by at least clear and convincing evidence.

I.

    *   *   *   *   *   *   *

B

Petitioners John Santosky II and Annie Santosky are the natural parents of Tina and John III. In November 1973, after incidents reflecting parental neglect, respondent Kramer, Commissioner of the Ulster County Department of Social Services, initiated a neglect proceeding under Fam.Ct.Act § 1022 and removed Tina from her natural home. About 10 months later, he removed John III and placed him with foster parents. On the day John was taken, Annie Santosky gave birth to a third child, Jed. When Jed was only three days old, respondent transferred him to a foster home on the ground that immediate removal was necessary to avoid imminent danger to his life or health.

In October 1978, respondent petitioned the Ulster County Family Court to terminate petitioners' parental rights in the three children. [FN4*] Petitioners challenged the constitutionality of the "fair preponderance of the evidence" standard specified in Fam.Ct.Act § 622. The Family Court Judge rejected this constitutional challenge, App. 29-30, and weighed the evidence under the statutory standard. While acknowledging that the Santoskys had maintained contact with their children, the judge found those visits "at best superficial and devoid of any real emotional content." * After deciding that the agency had made " 'diligent efforts' to encourage and strengthen the parental relationship," * he concluded that the Santoskys were incapable, even with public assistance, of planning for the future of their children. * The judge later held a dispositional hearing and ruled that the best interests of the three children required permanent termination of the Santoskys' custody.

Petitioners appealed, again contesting the constitutionality of § 622's standard of proof. [FN6*] The New York Supreme Court, Appellate Division, affirmed, holding application of the preponderance-of-the-evidence standard "proper and constitutional." * That standard, the court reasoned, "recognizes and seeks to balance rights possessed by the child ... with those of the natural parents...." *Ibid.*

The New York Court of Appeals then dismissed petitioners' appeal to that court "upon the ground that no substantial constitutional question is directly involved." * We granted certiorari to consider petitioners' constitutional claim.

II

Last Term in *Lassiter v. Department of Social Services*, 452 U.S. 18, 101 S.Ct. 2153, 68 L.Ed.2d 640 (1981), this Court, by a 5-4 vote, held that the Fourteenth Amendment's Due Process Clause does not require the appointment of counsel for indigent parents in every parental status termination proceeding. The case casts light, however, on the two central questions here--whether process is constitutionally due a natural parent at a State's parental rights termination proceeding, and, if so, what process is due.

In *Lassiter*, it was "not disputed that state intervention to terminate the relationship between [a parent] and [the] child must be accomplished by procedures meeting the requisites of the Due Process Clause." ** The absence of dispute reflected this Court's historical recognition that freedom of personal choice in matters of family life is a fundamental liberty interest protected by the Fourteenth Amendment. (citing cases)

The fundamental liberty interest of natural parents in the care, custody, and **1395 management of their child does not evaporate simply because they have not been model parents or have lost temporary custody of their child to the State. Even when blood relationships are strained, parents retain a vital interest in preventing the irretrievable destruction of their family life. If anything, persons faced with forced dissolution of their parental rights have a more critical need for procedural protections than do those resisting state intervention into ongoing family affairs. When the State moves to destroy weakened familial bonds, it must provide the parents with fundamentally fair procedures.

In *Lassiter*, the Court and three dissenters agreed that the nature of the process due in parental rights termination proceedings turns on a balancing of the "three distinct factors" specified in *Mathews v. Eldridge*, 424 U.S. 319, 335 (1976): the private interests affected by the proceeding; the risk of error created by the State's chosen procedure; and the countervailing governmental interest supporting use of the challenged procedure. * While the respective *Lassiter* opinions disputed whether those factors should be weighed against a presumption disfavoring appointed counsel for one not threatened with loss of physical liberty, * that concern is irrelevant here. Unlike the Court's right-to-counsel rulings, its decisions concerning constitutional burdens of proof have not turned on any presumption favoring any particular standard. To the contrary, the Court has engaged in a straight-forward consideration of the factors identified in *Eldridge* to determine whether a particular standard of proof in a particular proceeding satisfies due process.

In *Addington v. Texas*, 441 U.S. 418, (1979), the Court, by a unanimous vote of the participating Justices, declared: "The function of a standard of proof, as that concept is embodied in the Due Process Clause and in the realm of factfinding, is to 'instruct the factfinder concerning the degree of confidence our society thinks he should have in the correctness of factual conclusions for a particular type of adjudication.' "* *Addington* teaches that, in any given proceeding, the minimum standard of proof tolerated by the due process requirement reflects not only the weight of the private and public interests affected, but also a societal judgment about how the risk of error should be distributed between the litigants.

Thus, while private parties may be interested intensely in a civil dispute over money damages, application of a "fair preponderance of the evidence" standard indicates both society's "minimal concern with the outcome," and a conclusion that the litigants should "share the risk of error in roughly equal fashion." * When the State brings a criminal action to deny a defendant liberty or life, however, "the interests of the defendant are of such magnitude that historically and without any explicit constitutional requirement they have been protected by standards of proof designed to exclude as nearly as possible the likelihood of an erroneous judgment." *Ibid.* The stringency of the "beyond a reasonable doubt" standard bespeaks the "weight and gravity" of the private interest affected, *id.,* *society's interest in avoiding erroneous convictions, and a judgment that those interests together require that "society impos[e] almost the entire risk of error upon itself."*

The "minimum requirements [of procedural due process] being a matter of federal law, they are not diminished by the fact that the State may have specified its own procedures that it may deem adequate for determining the preconditions to adverse official action." *Vitek v. Jones*, 445 U.S. 480, 491, 100 S.Ct. 1254, 1262, 63 L.Ed.2d 552 (1980). * Moreover, the degree of proof required in a particular type of proceeding "is the kind of question which has traditionally been left to the judiciary to resolve." * "In cases involving individual rights, whether criminal or civil, '[t]he standard of proof [at a minimum] reflects the value society places on individual liberty.' " *

This Court has mandated an intermediate standard of proof--"clear and convincing evidence"--when the individual interests at stake in a state proceeding are both "particularly important" and "more substantial than mere loss of money." *Addington v. Texas*, 441U.S., at 424. Notwithstanding "the state's 'civil labels and good intentions,' " *id.*, at 427, 99 S.Ct. at 1810, the Court has deemed this level of certainty necessary to preserve fundamental fairness in a variety of government-initiated proceedings that threaten the individual involved with "a significant deprivation of liberty" or "stigma.". 441 U.S., at 425.

In *Lassiter*, to be sure, the Court held that fundamental fairness may be maintained in parental rights termination proceedings even when some procedures are mandated only on a case-by-case basis, rather than through rules of general application.* But this Court never has approved case-by-case determination of the proper standard of proof for a given proceeding. Standards of proof, like other "procedural due process rules[,] are shaped by the risk of error inherent in the truth-finding process as applied to the generality of cases, not the rare exceptions." *Mathews v. Eldridge*, 424 U.S., at 344. Since the litigants and the factfinder must know at the outset of a given proceeding how the risk of error will be allocated, the standard of proof necessarily must be calibrated in advance. Retrospective case-by-case review cannot preserve fundamental fairness when a class of proceedings is governed by a constitutionally defective evidentiary standard.

As the dissent points out, "the standard of proof is a crucial component of legal process, the primary function of which is 'to minimize the risk of erroneous decisions.' "***But only the standard of proof "instruct[s] the factfinder concerning the degree of confidence our society thinks he should have in the correctness of factual conclusions" he draws from that information. * The statutory provision of right to counsel and multiple hearings before termination cannot suffice to protect a natural parent's fundamental liberty interests if the State is willing to tolerate undue uncertainty in the determination of the dispositive facts.

III

In parental rights termination proceedings, the private interest affected is commanding; the risk of error from using a preponderance standard is substantial; and the countervailing governmental interest favoring that standard is comparatively slight. Evaluation of the three Eldridge factors compels the conclusion that use of a "fair preponderance of the evidence" standard in such proceedings is inconsistent with due process.

A

"The extent to which procedural due process must be afforded the recipient is influenced by the extent to which he may be 'condemned to suffer grievous loss.' " * Whether the loss threatened by a particular type of proceeding is sufficiently grave to warrant more than average certainty on the part of the factfinder turns on both the nature of the private interest threatened and the permanency of the threatened loss.

Lassiter declared it "plain beyond the need for multiple citation" that a natural parent's "desire for and right to 'the companionship, care, custody, and management of his or her children' " is an interest far more precious than any property right. * When the State initiates a parental rights termination proceeding, it seeks not merely to infringe that fundamental liberty interest, but to end it. "If the State prevails, it will have worked a unique kind of deprivation.... A parent's interest in the accuracy and justice of the decision to terminate his or her parental status is, therefore, a commanding one." *

In government-initiated proceedings to determine juvenile delinquency, civil commitment, deportation, and denaturalization, this Court has identified losses of individual liberty sufficiently serious to warrant imposition of an elevated burden of proof. Yet juvenile delinquency adjudications, civil commitment, deportation, and denaturalization, at least to a degree, are all reversible official actions. Once affirmed on appeal, a New York decision terminating parental rights is final and irrevocable. * Few forms of state action are both so severe and so irreversible.

Thus, the first *Eldridge* factor--the private interest affected--weighs heavily against use of the preponderance standard at a state-initiated permanent neglect proceeding. We do not deny that the child and his foster parents are also deeply interested in the outcome of that contest. But at the factfinding stage of the New York proceeding, the focus emphatically is not on them.

The factfinding does not purport--and is not intended--to balance the child's interest in a normal family home against the parents' interest in raising the child. Nor does it purport to determine whether the natural parents or the foster parents would provide the better home. Rather, the factfinding hearing pits the State directly against the parents. The State alleges that the natural parents are at fault.* The questions disputed and decided are what the State did--"made diligent efforts," § 614.1.(c)--and what the natural parents did not do--"maintain contact with or plan for the future of the child." § 614.1.(d). The State marshals an array of public resources to prove its case and disprove the parents' case. Victory by the State not only makes termination of parental rights possible; it entails a judicial determination that the parents are unfit to raise their own children.

At the factfinding, the State cannot presume that a child and his parents are adversaries. After the State has established parental unfitness at that initial proceeding, the court may assume at the dispositional stage that the interests of the child and the natural parents do diverge. See Fam.Ct.Act § 631 (judge shall make his order "solely on the basis of the best interests of the child," and thus has no obligation to consider the natural parents' rights in selecting dispositional alternatives). But until the State proves parental unfitness, the child and his parents share a vital interest in preventing erroneous termination of their natural relationship. [FN11*] Thus, at the factfinding, the interests of the child and his natural parents coincide to favor use of error-reducing procedures.

However substantial the foster parents' interests may be, cf. Smith v. Organization of Foster Families, 431 U.S., at 845-847, 97 S.Ct., at 2110-2111, they are not implicated directly in the factfinding stage of a state-initiated permanent neglect proceeding against the natural parents If authorized, the foster parents may pit their interests directly against those of the natural parents by initiating their own permanent neglect proceeding. * Alternatively, the foster parents can make their case for custody at the dispositional stage of a state-initiated proceeding, where the judge already has decided the issue of permanent neglect and is focusing on the placement that would serve the child's best interests.* For the foster parents, the State's failure to prove permanent neglect may prolong the delay and uncertainty until their foster child is freed for adoption. But for the natural parents, a finding of permanent neglect can cut off forever their rights in their child. Given this disparity of consequence, we have no difficulty finding that the balance of private interests strongly favors heightened procedural protections.

B

Under Mathews v. Eldridge, we next must consider both the risk of erroneous deprivation of private interests resulting from use of a "fair preponderance" standard and the likelihood that a higher evidentiary standard would reduce that risk. * Since the factfinding phase of a permanent neglect proceeding is an adversary contest between the State and the natural parents, the relevant question is whether a preponderance standard fairly allocates the risk of an erroneous factfinding between these two parties.

In New York, the factfinding stage of a state-initiated permanent neglect proceeding bears many of the indicia of a criminal trial. *** The Commissioner of Social Services charges the parents with permanent neglect. They are served by summons. * The factfinding hearing is conducted pursuant to formal rules of evidence. § 624. The State, the parents, and the child are all represented by counsel..* The State seeks to establish a series of historical facts about the intensity of its agency's efforts to reunite the family, the infrequency and insubstantiality of the parents' contacts with their child, and the parents' inability or unwillingness to formulate a plan for the child's future. The attorneys submit documentary evidence, and call witnesses who are subject to cross-examination. Based on all the evidence, the judge then determines whether the State has proved the statutory elements of permanent neglect by a fair preponderance of the evidence.

At such a proceeding, numerous factors combine to magnify the risk of erroneous factfinding. Permanent neglect proceedings employ imprecise substantive standards that leave determinations unusually open to the subjective values of the judge. * In appraising the nature and quality of a complex series of encounters among the agency, the parents, and the child, the court possesses unusual discretion to underweigh probative facts that might favor the parent. Because parents subject to termination proceedings are often poor, uneducated, or members of minority groups, id., at 833-835, such proceedings are often vulnerable to judgments based on cultural or class bias.

The State's ability to assemble its case almost inevitably dwarfs the parents' ability to mount a defense. No predetermined limits restrict the sums an agency may spend in prosecuting a given termination proceeding. The State's attorney usually will be expert on the issues contested and the procedures employed at the factfinding hearing, and enjoys full access to all public records concerning the family. The State may call on experts in family relations, psychology, and medicine to bolster its case. Furthermore, the primary witnesses at the hearing will be the agency's own professional caseworkers whom the State has empowered both to investigate the family situation and to testify against the parents. Indeed, because the child is already in agency custody, the State even has the power to shape the historical events that form the basis for termination.

The disparity between the adversaries' litigation resources is matched by a striking asymmetry in their litigation options. Unlike criminal defendants, natural parents have no "double jeopardy" defense against repeated state termination efforts. If the State initially fails to win termination, as New York did here, *see* n. 4, *supra*, it always can try once again to cut off the parents' rights after gathering more or better evidence. Yet even when the parents have attained the level of fitness required by the State, they have no similar means by which they can forestall future termination efforts.

Coupled with a "fair preponderance of the evidence" standard, these factors create a significant prospect of erroneous termination. A standard of proof that by its very terms demands consideration of the quantity, rather than the quality, of the evidence may misdirect the factfinder in the marginal case.* Given the weight of the private interests at stake, the social cost of even occasional error is sizable.

Raising the standard of proof would have both practical and symbolic consequences. * The Court has long considered the heightened standard of proof used in criminal prosecutions to be "a prime instrument for reducing the risk of convictions resting on factual error." * An elevated standard of proof in a parental rights termination proceeding would alleviate "the possible risk that a factfinder might decide to [deprive] an individual based solely on a few isolated instances of unusual conduct [or] ... idiosyncratic behavior." *Addington v. Texas*, 441 U.S., at 427, 99 S.Ct., at 1810. "Increasing the burden of proof is one way to **1401 impress the factfinder with the importance of the decision and thereby perhaps to reduce the chances that inappropriate" terminations will be ordered.

The Appellate Division approved New York's preponderance standard on the ground that it properly "balanced rights possessed by the child ... with those of the natural parents...." 75 App.Div.2d, at 910, 427 N.Y.S.2d, at 320. By so saying, the court suggested that a preponderance standard properly allocates the risk of error between the parents and the child. That view is fundamentally mistaken.

The court's theory assumes that termination of the natural parents' rights invariably will benefit the child. Yet we have noted above that the parents and the child share an interest in avoiding erroneous termination. Even accepting the court's assumption, we cannot agree with its conclusion that a preponderance standard fairly distributes the risk of error between parent and child. Use of that standard reflects the judgment that society is nearly neutral between erroneous termination of parental rights and erroneous failure to terminate those rights. *** For the child, the likely consequence of an erroneous failure to terminate is preservation of an uneasy status quo. For the natural parents, however, the consequence of an erroneous termination is the unnecessary destruction of their natural family. A standard that allocates the risk of error nearly equally between those two outcomes does not reflect properly their relative severity.

C

Two state interests are at stake in parental rights termination proceedings--a parens patriae interest in preserving and promoting the welfare of the child and a fiscal and administrative interest in reducing the cost and burden of such proceedings. A standard of proof more strict than preponderance of the evidence is consistent with both interests.

"Since the State has an urgent interest in the welfare of the child, it shares the parent's interest in an accurate and just decision" at the factfinding proceeding. * As parens patriae, the

State's goal is to provide the child with a permanent home. * Yet while there is still reason to believe that positive, nurturing parent-child relationships exist, the parens patriae interest favors preservation, not severance, of natural familial bonds. * "[T]he State registers no gain towards its declared goals when it separates children from the custody of fit parents." *

The State's interest in finding the child an alternative permanent home arises only "when it is clear that the natural parent cannot or will not provide a normal family home for the child." Soc.Serv.Law § 384-b.1. (a)(iv) (emphasis added). At the factfinding, that goal is served by procedures that promote an accurate determination of whether the natural parents can and will provide a normal home.

Unlike a constitutional requirement of hearings, * or court-appointed counsel, a stricter standard of proof would reduce factual error without imposing substantial fiscal burdens upon the State. As we have observed, 35 States already have adopted a higher standard by statute or court decision without apparent effect on the speed, form, or cost of their factfinding proceedings.

Nor would an elevated standard of proof create any real administrative burdens for the State's factfinders. New York Family Court judges already are familiar with a higher evidentiary standard in other parental rights termination proceedings not involving permanent neglect. *See* Soc.Serv.Law ss 384-b.3.(g), 384-b.4.(c), and 384-b.4.(e) (requiring "clear and convincing proof" before parental rights may be terminated for reasons of mental illness and mental retardation or severe and repeated child abuse). New York also demands at least clear and convincing evidence in proceedings of far less moment than parental rights termination proceedings.

IV

The logical conclusion of this balancing process is that the "fair preponderance of the evidence" standard prescribed by Fam. Ct. Act § 622 violates the Due Process Clause of the Fourteenth Amendment. The Court noted in *Addington* : "The individual should not be asked to share equally with society the risk of error when the possible injury to the individual is significantly greater than any possible harm to the state." * Thus, at a parental rights termination proceeding, a near-equal allocation of risk between the parents and the State is constitutionally intolerable. The next question, then, is whether a "beyond a reasonable doubt" or a "clear and convincing" standard is constitutionally mandated.

In *Addington*, the Court concluded that application of a reasonable-doubt standard is inappropriate in civil commitment proceedings for two reasons-- because of our hesitation to apply that unique standard "too broadly or casually in noncriminal cases," * and because the psychiatric evidence ordinarily adduced at commitment proceedings is rarely susceptible to proof beyond a reasonable doubt. * To be sure, as has been noted above, in the Indian Child Welfare Act of 1978, Pub.L. 95-608, § 102(f), 92 Stat. 3072, 25 U.S.C. § 1912(f) (1976 ed., Supp.IV), Congress requires "evidence beyond a reasonable doubt" for termination of Indian parental rights, reasoning that "the removal of a child from the parents is a penalty as great [as], if not greater, than a criminal penalty...." Congress did not consider, however, the evidentiary problems that would arise if proof beyond a reasonable doubt were required in all state-initiated parental rights termination hearings.

Like civil commitment hearings, termination proceedings often require the factfinder to evaluate medical and psychiatric testimony, and to decide issues difficult to prove to a level of absolute certainty, such as lack of parental motive, absence of affection between parent and child, and failure of parental foresight and progress. * The substantive standards applied vary from State to State. Although Congress found a "beyond a reasonable doubt" standard proper in one type of parental rights termination case, another legislative body might well conclude that a reasonable-doubt standard would erect an unreasonable barrier to state efforts to free permanently neglected children for adoption. A majority of the States have concluded that a "clear and convincing evidence" standard of proof strikes a fair balance between the rights of the natural parents and the State's legitimate concerns. * We hold that such a standard adequately conveys to the factfinder the level of subjective certainty about his factual conclusions necessary to satisfy due process. We further hold that determination of the precise burden equal to or greater than that standard is a matter of state law properly left to state legislatures and state courts.

We, of course, express no view on the merits of petitioners' claims. At a hearing conducted under a constitutionally proper standard, they may or may not prevail. Without deciding the outcome under any of the standards we have approved, we vacate the judgment of the Appellate Division and remand the case for further proceedings not inconsistent with this opinion.

h. Notes and Questions

1) Battered Child Syndrome

What is the relevancy of the Battered Child Syndrome? In *Estelle v. McQuire*, the dissenting opinion was concerned that a jury may misapply the syndrome because of a faulty jury instruction. How would you draft the instruction to satisfy the dissent's concerns?

2) Child Abuse Reporting Statutes and Registries

All states have enacted child abuse reporting statutes. They mandate certain classes of people who come into contact with children to report suspected child abuse, typically health care providers, child care providers and teachers. They report to a local child protection agency or the police. These classes of people are immune from criminal and civil prosecution if the reports are made in good faith. Congress enacted The Child Abuse Protection and Treatment Act (42 U.S.C.A. §§5101-5117 (West Supp. 1989)) in 1974. The Act created the National Center on Child Abuse and Neglect in the Department of Health and Human Services. It requires, as a condition for states receiving federal funding, they must comply with the Act. Most states maintain a child abuse central registry and require that each report of child abuse be registered as well as when probable cause is found. The length of time a report stays on the register depends on whether it is an unsubstantiated report of abuse (less time) or whether there is probable cause.

3) Immunity

Child Abuse investigation interferes with the parent-child relationship. The state and its subdivisions are, in most circumstances, protected under the doctrine of municipal immunity or a qualified immunity. In the *Croft* case, the court held that the standard for this protection is "whether the information available to the defendants at the time would have created an objectively reasonable suspicion of abuse justifying the degree of interference." What do you think will be the outcome in *Croft*?

4) Criminal Prosecution

Abuse may be tried in the juvenile court as a civil case; or, it may be tried as a criminal case. The Supreme Court has addressed some of the important constitutional issues involving criminal prosecution and Sixth Amendment rights regarding confronting child witnesses. In *Idaho v. Wright*, 497 U.S. 604 (1990), and in *Maryland v. Craig*, 497 U.S. 836 (1990), the Supreme Court addressed the constitutional standard to apply to state statutes that attempt to protect the child from testifying before the accused.

5) Termination of Parental Rights

Termination of parental rights is the most severe dispositional option. Generally, a court will not terminate parental rights unless rehabilitation of the parents is hopeless. The legal consequences of termination of parental rights is that the parent-child relationship is severed, and terminating all legal duties and obligations between the parent and the child. The grounds for termination are determined by the state's statutes. The typical grounds are abuse, dependency, and neglect, together typically with a finding of abandonment or failure to comply with the treatment plan. Before parental rights are termination, the state, typically, attempts to assist in the rehabilitation of the parent(s) through a prescribed treatment plan.

The purpose for terminating parental rights is to allow the child to be adopted. (*See* Chapter 12, *supra*) On the other hand, the policy to preserve the parental-child status and to reunite parent and child has made the process for terminating parental rights slow. Foster care is typically the intermediate step; however, for some children foster care became the permanent arrangement. Congress has tried to address these problems in 1980 and in 1997. One of the major purposes of the Adoption Assistance and Child Welfare Act of 1980 was to have states actively try to reunite families, but if reunification failed to terminate parental rights and place the child in a permanent home. The Adoption and Safe Families Act of 1997 sets deadlines in order to accelerate the termination and placement processes.

6) Guardian Ad Litem (G.A.L.)

The Child Abuse Protection and Treatment Act of 1974 (42 U.S.C.A. §§ 5101-5117) requires States, as a condition of participation in federal funds for foster care, to appoint a guardian at litem to represent each child who is the subject of abuse and neglect proceedings.

7) Neglect and Dependency

Neglect and dependency cases are usually civil cases although they may be tried as criminal cases. They are generally closed to the public and the press and are confidential. Neglect and dependency findings may result in termination of parental rights. In *Calabretta v. Floyd*, 189 F.3d 808 (9th Cir. 1999), the Ninth Circuit held that parents could bring a civil rights claim against a social worker and policeman for their coerced warrantless entry into the parents' home to investigate a days-old report that a neighbor heard a "home-schooled" child of "extremely religious" parents crying "no, daddy, no," at 1:30 a.m., which did not justify immediate intervention to protect children. Also the social worker's insistence that the mother pull down her three-year-old daughter's pants to see if there was any evidence of bruising provided another basis for a civil rights' claim.

8) Foster Care

Children may be placed in the foster care system voluntarily by parents when parents are unable to care for them for a variety of reasons. They may also be placed in the system by court order. The foster care system is an integral part of the child protection and court systems in abuse, neglect and dependency cases. Foster parents enter into an agreement with the State to provide care for these children. Foster care is meant to be a temporary placement of the child until permanent arrangements are arranged. It, however, has become a permanent arrangement for many children, moving from one foster home to another. See chapters 12 and 13 for a discussion of placement in connection with adoption and the note 5 on termination of parental rights, above.

9) *M.J.B. v. S.L.J*

In *M.J.B. v. S.L.J.*, 519 U.S. 102 (1996), the Supreme Court held that under the due process and equal protection clauses an indigent parent has a right to have the state pay for transcript preparation costs when appealing a judgment terminating her parental rights.

10) Juvenile Delinquency and Status Offenses

A *delinquent* act is generally one committed by a minor that would be a crime if committed by an adult. With few exceptions, delinquent acts include all felonies and misdemeanors. Because the emphasis of the juvenile court is focused on treatment and rehabilitation and is civil in nature, its procedure for finding of delinquency was historically informal. Although the child may be institutionalized for long periods of time, the child was not protected by certain constitutional rights that an adult being tried for the same offense would have. Commencing in 1967, the United States Supreme Court has decided a number of cases, resulting in the delinquency proceeding becoming a formal proceeding and extending many of the constitutional protections to the child. Juvenile delinquency proceedings are quasi-criminal in procedure and substance, but the purpose and approach is more rehabilitation-oriented, generally.

All states have enacted transfer statutes that allow the transfer of a minor accused of violating serious criminal laws from the jurisdiction of the juvenile court to that of the adult criminal court. The juvenile is tried as an adult. In recent years, these statutes have been amended so that many more juveniles are tried as adults.

Unlike *delinquent* behavior, a *status* offense would not be an offense if committed by an adult, but is only proscribed if committed by a juvenile. Typical status offenses include incorrigible behavior, truancy, and runaways. Historically, the juvenile court system did not distinguish between delinquent and status offenses. Beginning in the 1960s, they were made separate categories. As a consequence, states refer to status offenders as Persons in Need of Supervision (PINS) or Children in Need of Supervision (CHINS), or Juveniles in Need of Supervision (JINS) or Youth in Need of Supervision (YINS). As a result of the Juvenile Justice and Delinquency Act of 1974 and as amended, in order to receive federal funds, states must remove all status offenders from secured institutions and divert them from the juvenile court to other community programs. A juvenile court judge may order a truant or delinquent child to live away from the parent, perhaps in some secure facility. Under most circumstances, the parent continues to have a duty of support. Should parents who are not indigent be liable for the cost of incarcerating their minor child? Why/why not?

3. Practical and Ethical Considerations

a. Duty to Protect

What was the basic problem facing the prosecutor in *Raposo*? Was it that there was no criminal statute that codified the parent's duty to protect and the prosecutor was trying to fit her conduct under another statute that really did not apply? There is no constitutional violation, however, if the state fails to protect. In *DeShaney v. Winnebago County Department of Social Service*, 489 U.S. 189 (1989), the Supreme Court held that the DSS employees did not violate a child's liberty interest under the Fourteenth Amendment when it negligently failed to take affirmative action to protect him while in his father's custody because that was private action.

b. Child Abuse vs. Child Discipline

Disciplinary methods differ from one region of the country to another, from one class to another, and from one racial or ethnic group to another. Thus, the same actions may constitute abuse before one group of factfinders and constitute discipline before another unless the wording of the statute is not carefully drafted. Compare the child abuse statute of any two states. How would the mother in Petition of Jane Doe likely to fare under each statute?

c. Mandatory Reporting

Mandatory reporting laws clash with professional ethics' codes relating to client confidentiality. Attorneys are typically not included in the classes required to report. (*See In the Matter Concerning Baby X, a Minor, supra*) But, is an attorney required to report suspected abuse that will occur in the future under Rule 1.6 of the ABA Model Rules of Professional Conduct?

d. Separate Representation

In *In re Mary C.*, 48 Cal.Rptr.2d 346 (Ct.App.1995), the child's counsel petitioned the court to appoint separate counsel on appeal from an order terminating parental rights, rather than having the DCFS (Dept. of Child and Family Service) attorney represent both the child and the agency because DCFS had initiated the proceedings against the child's parents. A California court of appeals held that while rules of professional conduct prohibit an attorney from representing adverse interests without the clients' consent, no conflict of interest existed between the child in a TPR (Termination of Parental Rights) action and the DCFS, so separate counsel is not required during the appellate stage to protect child's best interests.

4. Bibliography

Dr. Ray E. Helfer and Dr. C. Henry Kemp (eds.) The Battered Child (1968).

Johnson, *Criminal Liability for Parents Who Fail to Protect*, 5 Law and Ineq. J. 359, 377-390 (1987).

Seth C. Kalichman, Mandated Reporting of Suspected Child Abuse, Ethics, Law and Policy (1993).

Kempe, Silverman, Steele, Droegemuller, and Silver, "The Battered Child Syndrome," 181
    J.A., M.A. 17 1962).

Levine, *Caveat Parens: Demystification of the Child Protection System*, 35 U. Pitt. L. Rev. 1 (1973).

Mason P. Thomas, *Child Abuse and Neglect, Part I: Historical Overview, legal Matrix and Social
    Perspectives*, 50 N.C. L. Rev. 293 (1972).

Robert P. Mosteller, *Child Abuse Reporting Laws and Attorney-Client Confidences: The Reality and the Specter of Lawyer as Informant*, 42 Duke L. J. 203 (1992).

Wardle & Nolan, International Encyclopaedia of Laws, Family and Succession Law, United States of America 159 (Gen. Ed. R. Blanpain, Ed. W. Pintens, Kluwer Law Int'l.1998).

PART VI
TERMINATION OF SPOUSAL RELATIONS

CHAPTER 25

Divorce Jurisdiction and Procedure

A. JURISDICTION FOR DIVORCE

1. Background

a. History of Legislative Divorce

When this country was settled, the power to grant a divorce from the bonds of matrimony was exercised by the Parliament of England. The ecclesiastical courts of that country were limited to the granting of divorces from bed and board. Naturally, the legislative assemblies of the colonies followed the example of Parliament and treated the subject as one within their province. And until a recent period legislative divorces have been granted, with few exceptions, in all the States. Says Bishop, in his Treatise on Marriage and Divorce: "The fact that at the time of the settlement of this country legislative divorces were common, competent, and valid in England, whence our jurisprudence was derived, makes them conclusively so here, except where an invalidity is directly or indirectly created by a written constitution binding the legislative power." § 664. Says Cooley, in his Treatise on Constitutional Limitations: "The granting of divorces from the bonds of matrimony was not confided to the courts in England, and from the earliest days the colonial and state legislatures in this country have assumed to possess the same power over the subject which was possessed by the Parliament, and from time to time they have passed special laws declaring a dissolution of the bonds of matrimony in special cases." p. 110. Says Kent, in his Commentaries: "During the period of our colonial government, for more than one hundred years preceding the Revolution, no divorce took place in the colony of New York, and for many years after New York became an independent state there was not any lawful mode of dissolving a marriage in the lifetime of the parties but by a special act of the legislature." 2 Kent Com. 97. The same fact is stated in numerous decisions of the highest courts of the States. . . .

Maynard v. Hill, 125 U.S. 190, 205 (1888) (upholding legislative divorce granted by Oregon territorial legislature to a man who abandoned his wife and children in Ohio).

b. History of Territorial Jurisdiction

The service of process and matrimonial causes heard in the ecclesiastical courts of England "depended upon the locality of the person cited. Both case and statute law forbade the citing of parties out of their province, diocese, or peculiar jurisdiction. The Statute of Citations, 1531-2, expressly imposed a penalty of forfeiture upon anyone who cited persons out of the diocese where they resided at the time." Rayden, *infra* at 4.

By the nineteenth century, it was well established in Anglo-American law that domicile was required for divorce jurisdiction. 2 J. Bishop, *infra* § 145, at 134-36.

613

The influential nineteenth-century American legal commentator, Professor Joel Bishop, explained:

> The tribunals of a country have no jurisdiction over any cause of divorce, wherever or whenever it arose, if neither of the parties has within its territory an actual, *bona fide* domicile. Nor does it make any difference that both parties are temporarily there, submitting to the jurisdiction.

2 J. Bishop, *infra* § 144, at 132-33; *see id.* § 145 at 134-136.

Originally, married persons could only have one domicile and that was the domicile of the husband because a married woman had no separate legal existence from her husband. English common law adhered to a virtually irrebuttable presumption that the domicile of all members of the family was the domicile of the patriarchal head of the family. But in the nineteenth century most American states enacted Married Women's Property Acts which recognized the separate legal existence of married women, and American courts soon created an exception to the patriarchal domicile role recognizing that a married woman could have a separate domicile of her own if she was not wrongfully living apart from her husband.

By the nineteenth century American courts recognized the doctrine of "divisible divorce." "While a suit for dissolution *in rem*, it is also *in personam*. As to the marriage status, it is the former: as to decrees for alimony and the like, it is the latter." 2 J. Bishop, *infra* § 159, at 148. Jurisdiction to alter domestic status was deemed to be in rem because the marriage was considered to be the "res" or thing that was within the jurisdiction wherever a spouse was domiciled. Thus, in *Pennoyer v. Neff,* 95 U.S. 714 (1877), the Supreme Court noted:

> The jurisdiction which every State possesses to determine the civil *status* and capacities of all its inhabitants involves authority to prescribe the conditions on which proceedings affecting them may be commenced and carried on within its territory. The State, for example, has absolute right to prescribe the conditions upon which the marriage relations between its own citizens shall be created, and the causes for which it may be dissolved. One of the parties was guilty of acts for which, under the law of the State, a dissolution may be granted, may have removed to a State where no dissolution is permitted. The complaining party would, therefore, fail if a divorce were sought in the State of the defendant; and if application could not be made to the tribunals of the complainant's domicile in such case, and proceedings be there instituted without personal service of process or personal notice to the offending party, the injured citizen would be without redress...

Id. at 734-35.

When the United States Supreme Court decided *Haddock v. Haddock*, 261 U.S. 562, (1906), it complicated the rule by holding that a married person who wrongfully had abandoned his or her spouse could not acquire a new matrimonial domicile, and that while a divorce decree entered by a court of the new domicile of the abandoning spouse would be valid within that state, it would have no extraterritorial effect. In that case a wife brought suit for divorce in New York against her husband. The parties had been married in New York and she had continued to reside there, but her husband had moved his domicile to Connecticut. She claimed that her husband had abandoned her.

The husband defended on the basis of a prior Connecticut divorce. The Supreme Court held that the Connecticut divorce was not entitled to Full Faith and Credit because the husband had abandoned his wife in New York; therefore, the marital domicile remained in New York. 201 US at 577.

2. Statutes, Cases and Doctrines

a. *Williams v. North Carolina*

Williams v. State of North Carolina
317 U.S. 287 (1942)

Mr. Justice DOUGLAS delivered the opinion of the Court.

***

Petitioner Williams was married to Carrie Wyke in 1916 in North Carolina and lived with her there until May, 1940. Petitioner Hendrix was married to Thomas Hendrix in 1920 in North Carolina and lived with him there until May, 1940. At that time petitioners went to Las Vegas, Nevada and on June 26, 1940, each filed a divorce action in the Nevada court. The defendants in those divorce actions entered no appearance nor were they served with process in Nevada. In the case of defendant Thomas Hendrix service by publication was had by publication of the summons in a Las Vegas newspaper and by mailing a copy of the summons and complaint to his last post office address. In the case of defendant Carrie Williams a North Carolina sheriff delivered to her in North Carolina a copy of the summons and complaint. A decree of divorce was granted petitioner Williams by the Nevada court on August 26, 1940, on the grounds of extreme cruelty, the court finding that 'the plaintiff has been and now is a bona fide and continuous resident of the County of Clark, State of Nevada, and had been such resident for more than six weeks immediately preceding the commencement of this action in the manner prescribed by law'. The Nevada court granted petitioner Hendrix a divorce on October 4, 1940, on the grounds of wilful neglect and extreme cruelty and made the same finding as to this petitioner's bona fide residence in Nevada as it made in the case of Williams. Petitioners were married to each other in Nevada on October 4, 1940. Thereafter they returned to North Carolina where they lived together until the indictment was returned. Petitioners pleaded not guilty and offered in evidence exemplified copies of the Nevada proceedings, contending that the divorce decrees and the Nevada marriage were valid in North Carolina as well as in Nevada. The State contended that since neither of the defendants in the Nevada actions was served in Nevada nor entered an appearance there, the Nevada decrees would not be recognized as valid in North Carolina. On this issue the court charged the jury in substance that a Nevada divorce decree based on substituted service where the defendant made no appearance would not be recognized in North Carolina ***. The State further contended that petitioners went to Nevada not to establish a bona fide residence but solely for the purpose of taking advantage of the laws of that State to obtain a divorce through fraud upon that court. On that issue the court charged the jury that under the rule of *State v. Herron*, *, the defendants had the burden of satisfying the jury, but not beyond a reasonable doubt, of the bona fides of their residence in Nevada for the required time. Petitioners excepted to these charges. The Supreme Court of North Carolina in affirming the judgment held that North Carolina was not required to recognize the Nevada decrees under the full faith and credit clause of the Constitution (Art. IV, § 1) by reason of *Haddock v. Haddock*, 201 U.S. 562. *** [T]here are two reasons why we do not reach that issue in this case. In the first place, North Carolina does not seek to sustain the judgment below on that ground. Moreover it admits that there probably is enough evidence in the record to require that petitioners be considered 'to have been actually domiciled in Nevada.' In the second place, the verdict against petitioners was a general one. *** Accordingly, we cannot avoid meeting the *Haddock v. Haddock* issue in this case by saying that the petitioners acquired no bona fide domicil in Nevada. *****

Article IV, § 1 of the Constitution not only directs that 'Full Faith and Credit shall be given in each State to the public Acts, Records, and Judicial Proceedings of every other State' but also provides that 'Congress may be general Laws prescribe the Manner in which such Acts, Records and Proceedings shall be proved, and the Effect thereof.' Congress has exercised that power. By the Act of May 26, 1790, c. 11, 28 U.S.C. § 687, Congress has provided that judgments 'shall have such faith and credit given to them in every court within the United States as they have by law or usage in the courts of the State from which they are taken.' Chief Justice Marshall stated in *Hampton v. M'Connel*, 3 Wheat. 234, 235, 4 L.Ed. 378, that 'the judgment of a state court should have the same credit, validity, and effect, in every other court in the United States, which it had in the state where it was pronounced, and that whatever pleas would be good to a suit thereon in such state, and none others, could be pleaded in any other court in the United States.' That view has survived substantially intact. *Fauntleroy v. Lum*, 210 U.S. 230. This Court only recently stated that Art. IV, § 1 and the Act of May 26, 1790 require that 'not some but full' faith and credit be given judgments of a state court. *Davis v. Davis*, 305 U.S. 32, 40. Thus even though the cause of action could not be entertained in the state of the forum either because it had been barred by the local statute of limitations or contravened local policy, the judgment thereon obtained in a sister state is entitled to full faith and credit. * Some exceptions have been engrafted on the rule laid down by Chief Justice Marshall. But as stated by Mr. Justice Brandeis in *Broderick v. Rosner*, 294 U.S. 629, 642, 'the room left for the play of conflicting policies is a narrow one.' So far as judgments are concerned the decisions, as distinguished from dicta, show that the actual exceptions have been few and far between, apart from *Haddock v. Haddock*. For this Court has been reluctant to admit exceptions in case of judgments rendered by the courts of a sister state, since the 'very purpose' of Art. IV, § 1 was 'to alter the status of the several states as independent foreign sovereignties, each free to ignore obligations created under the laws or by the judicial proceedings of the others, and to make them integral parts of a single nation.' *Milwaukee County v. M. E. White Co., supra*, 296 U.S. at pages 276, 277.

This Court, to be sure, has recognized that in case of statutes, 'the extrastate effect of which Congress has not prescribed', some 'accommodation of the conflicting interests of the two states' is necessary. *Alaska Packers Ass'n v. Industrial Accident Comm.*, 294 U.S. 532, 547. But that principle would come into play only in case the Nevada decrees were assailed on the ground that Nevada must give full faith and credit in its divorce proceedings to the divorce statutes of North Carolina. Even then, it would be of no avail here. For as stated in the Alaska Packers case, 'Prima facie every state is entitled to enforce in its own courts its own statutes, lawfully enacted. One who challenges that right, because of the force given to a conflicting statute of another state by the full faith and credit clause, assumes the burden of showing, upon some rational basis, that of the conflicting interests involved those of the foreign state are superior to those of the forum.' *Id.*, 294 U.S. at page 547. It is difficult to perceive how North Carolina could be said to have an interest in Nevada's domiciliaries superior to the interest of Nevada. Nor is there any authority which lends support to the view that the full faith and credit clause compels the courts of one state to subordinate the local policy of that state, as respects its domiciliaries, to the statutes of any other state. Certainly *Bradford Electric Light Co. v. Clapper*, 286 U.S. 145, did not so hold. Indeed, the recent case of *Pacific Employers Ins. Co. v. Industrial Accident Comm.*, 306 U.S. 493, 502, held that in the case of statutes 'the full faith and credit clause does not require one state to substitute for its own statute, applicable to persons and events within it, the conflicting statute of another state, even though that statute is of controlling force in the courts of the state of its enactment with respect to the same persons and events.'

*** [*Haddock*] does not purport to challenge or disturb the rule, earlier established by *Christmas v. Russell, supra*, and subsequently fortified by *Fauntleroy v. Lum, supra*, that even though the cause of action could not have been entertained in the state of the forum, a judgment obtained thereon in a sister state is entitled to full faith and credit. The decisive difference between [*Cheever* and *Atherton*] and *Haddock v. Haddock* was said to be that in the latter the state granting the divorce had no jurisdiction over the absent spouse, since it was not the state of the matrimonial domicil, but the place where the husband had acquired a separate domicil after having wrongfully left his wife. This Court accordingly classified *Haddock v. Haddock* with that group of cases which hold that when the courts of one state do not have jurisdiction either of the subject matter or of the person of the defendant, the courts of another state are not required by virtue of the full faith and credit clause to enforce the judgment. But such differences *** are immaterial, so far as the full faith and credit clause and the supporting legislation are concerned.

The historical view that a proceeding for a divorce was a proceeding in rem * was rejected by the Haddock case. We likewise agree that it does not aid in the solution of the problem presented by this case to label these proceedings as proceedings in rem. Such a suit, however, is not a mere in personam action. Domicil of the plaintiff, immaterial to jurisdiction in a personal action, is recognized in the Haddock case and elsewhere (Beale, Conflict of Laws, § 110.1) as essential in order to give the court jurisdiction which will entitle the divorce decree to extraterritorial effect, at least when the defendant has neither been personally served nor entered an appearance. The findings made in the divorce decrees in the instant case must be treated on the issue before us as meeting those requirements. For it seems clear that the provision of the Nevada statute that a plaintiff in this type of case must 'reside' in the State for the required period requires him to have a domicil as distinguished from a mere residence in the state. * Hence the decrees in this case like other divorce decrees are more than in personam judgments. They involve the marital status of the parties. Domicil creates a relationship to the state which is adequate for numerous exercises of state power. *. Each state as a sovereign has a rightful and legitimate concern in the marital status of persons domiciled within its borders. The marriage relation creates problems of large social importance. Protection of offspring, property interests, and the enforcement of marital responsibilities are but a few of commanding problems in the field of domestic relations with which the state must deal. Thus it is plain that each state by virtue of its command over its domiciliaries and its large interest in the institution of marriage can alter within its own borders the marriage status of the spouse domiciled there, even though the other spouse is absent. *** Accordingly it was admitted in the Haddock case that the divorce decree though not recognized in New York was binding on both spouses in Connecticut where granted. *. And this *Court in Maynard v. Hill*, 125 U.S. 190, upheld the validity within the Territory of Oregon of a divorce decree granted by the legislature to a husband domiciled there, even though the wife resided in Ohio where the husband had deserted her. It therefore follows that, if the Nevada decrees are taken at their full face value (as they must be in the phase of the case with which we are presently concerned), they were wholly effective to change in that state the marital status of the petitioners and each of the other spouses by the North Carolina marriages. Apart from the requirements of procedural due process * not challenged here by North Carolina, no reason based on the Federal Constitution has been advanced for the contrary conclusion. But the concession that the decrees were effective in Nevada makes more compelling the reasons for rejection of the theory and result of the Haddock case.

*** Each would be a bigamist for living in one state with the only one with whom the other state would permit him lawfully to live. Children of the second marriage would be bastards in one state but legitimate in the other. And all that would flow from the legalistic notion that where one spouse is wrongfully deserted he retains power over the matrimonial domicil so that the domicil of the other spouse follows him wherever he may go, while if he is to blame, he retains no such power. *** The existence of the power of a state to alter the marital status of its domiciliaries, as distinguished from the wisdom of its exercise, is not dependent on the underlying causes of the domestic rift. As we have said, it is dependent on the relationship which domicil creates and the pervasive control which a state has over marriage and divorce within its own borders. *** [W] e see no reason, and none has here been advanced, for making the existence of state power [to grant a divorce] depend on an inquiry as to where the fault in each domestic dispute lies. *** It is one thing to say as a matter of state law that jurisdiction to grant a divorce from an absent spouse should depend on whether by consent or by conduct the latter has subjected his interest in the marriage status to the law of the separate domicil acqired by the other spouse. Beale, Conflict of Laws, § 113.11; Restatement, Conflict of Laws, § 113. But where a state adopts, as it has the power to do, a less strict rule, it is quite another thing to say that its decrees affecting the marital status of its domiciliaries are not entitled to full faith and credit in sister states. Certainly if decrees of a state altering the marital status of its domiciliaries are not valid throughout the Union even though the requirements of procedural due process are wholly met, a rule would be fostered which could not help but bring 'considerable disaster to innocent persons' and 'bastardize children hitherto supposed to be the offspring of lawful marriage,' (Mr. Justice Holmes dissenting in Haddock *), or else encourage collusive divorces. * These intensely practical considerations emphasize for us the essential function of the full faith and credit clause in substituting a command for the former principles of comity * and in altering the 'status of the several states as independent foreign sovereignties' by making them 'integral parts of a single nation.' *Milwaukee County v. M. E. White Co.,**.

It is objected, however, that if such divorce decrees must be given full faith and credit, a substantial dilution of the sovereignty of other states will be effected. For it is pointed out that under such a rule one state's policy of strict control over the institution of marriage could be thwarted by the decree of a more lax state. But such an objection goes to the application of the full faith and credit clause to many situations. It is an objection in varying degrees of intensity to the enforcement of a judgment of a sister state based on a cause of action which could not be enforced in the state of the forum. Mississippi's policy against gambling transactions was overriden in *Fauntleroy v. Lum, supra,* when a Missouri judgment based on such a Mississippi contract was enforced by this Court. Such is part of the price of our federal system.

This Court, of course, is the final arbiter when the question is raised as to what is a permissible limitation on the full faith and credit clause. *Alaska Packers Ass'n* *; *Milwaukee County* *. But the question for us is a limited one. In the first place, we repeat that in this case we must assume that petitioners had a bona fide domicil in Nevada, not that the Nevada domicil was a sham. We thus have no question on the present record whether a divorce decree granted by the courts of one state to a resident as distinguished from a domiciliary is entitled to full faith and credit in another state. Nor do we reach here the question as to the power of North Carolina to refuse full faith and credit to Nevada divorce decrees because, contrary to the findings of the Nevada court, North Carolina finds that no bona fide domicil was acquired in Nevada. In the second place, the question as to what is a permissible limiation on the full faith and credit clause does not involve a decision on our part as to which state policy on divorce is the more desirable one. It does not involve selection of a rule which will encourage on the one hand or discourage on the other the practice of divorce. That choice in the realm of morals and religion rests with the legislatures of the states. Our own views as to the marriage institution and the avenues of escape which some states have created are immaterial. It is a Constitution which we are expounding--a Constitution which in no small measure brings separate sovereign states into an integrated whole through the medium of the full faith and credit clause. Within the limits of her political power North Carolina may, of course, enforce her own policy regarding the marriage relation--an institution more basic in our civilization than any other. But society also has an interest in the avoidance of polygamous marriages (*) and in the protection of innocent offspring of marriages deemed legitimate in other jurisdictions. And other states have an equally legitimate concern in the status of persons domiciled there as respects the institution of marriage. So when a court of one state acting in accord with the requirements of procedural due process alters the marital status of one domiciled in that state by granting him a divorce from his absent spouse, we cannot say its decree should be excepted from the full faith and credit clause merely because its enforcement or recognition in another state would conflict with the policy of the latter. Whether Congress has the power to create exceptions (*see Yarborough v. Yarborough,* *) is a question on which we express no view. It is sufficient here to note that Congress in its sweeping requirement that judgments of the courts of one state be given full faith and credit in the courts of another has not done so. And the considerable interests involved and the substantial and far-reaching effects which the allowance of an exception would have on innocent persons indicate that the purpose of the full faith and credit clause and of the supporting legislation would be thwarted to a substantial degree if the rule of *Haddock v. Haddock* were perpetuated.

Haddock v. Haddock is overruled. The judgment is reversed and the cause is remanded to the Supreme Court of North Carolina for proceedings not inconsistent with this opinion. ***

Mr. Justice FRANKFURTER, concurring.

I join in the opinion of the Court but think it appropriate to add a few words.

*** The Constitution of the United States, however, reserves authority over marriage and divorce to each of the forty-eight states. That is our starting-point. In a country like ours where each state has the constitutional power to translate into law its own notions of policy concerning the family institution, and where citizens pass freely from one state to another, tangled marital situations, like the one immediately before us, inevitably arise. ***

We are not authorized nor are we qualified to formulate a national code of domestic relations. *** This Court should abstain from trying to reach the same end by indirection. ***

There is but one respect in which this Court can, within its traditional authority and professional competence, contribute uniformity to the law of marriage and divorce, and that is to enforce respect for the judgment of a state by its sister states when the judgment was rendered in accordance with settled procedural standards. ***

The duty of a state to respect the judgments of a sister state arises only where such judgments meet the tests of justice and fair dealing that are embodied in the historic phrase, 'due process of law'. But in this case all talk about due process is beside the mark. If the actions of the Nevada court had been taken 'without due process of law', the divorces which it purported to decree would have been without legal sanction in every state including Nevada. ***

Mr. Justice MURPHY, dissenting.

I dissent because the Court today introduces an undesirable rigidity in the application of the Full Faith and Credit Clause to a problem which is of acute interest to all the states of the Union and on which they hold varying and sharply divergent views, the problem of how they shall treat the marriage relation.
***

In recognition of the paramount interest of the state of domicile over the marital status of its citizens, this Court has held that actual good faith domicile of at least one party is essential to confer authority and jurisdiction on the courts of a state to render a decree of divorce that will be entitled to extraterritorial effect under the Full Faith and Credit Clause, *, even though both parties personally appear, *. When the doctrine of those cases is applied to the facts of this one, the question becomes a simple one: Did petitioners acquire a bona fide domicil in Nevada? I agree with my brother Jackson that the only proper answer on the record is, no. *** It follows that the Nevada decrees are entitled to no extraterritorial effect when challenged in another state. *Bell v. Bell, supra; Andrews v. Andrews, supra.*
***

Prominent in the residuum of state power, as pointed out above, is the right of a state to deal with the marriage relations of its citizens and to pursue its chosen domestic policy of public morality in that connection. Both Nevada and North Carolina have rights in this regard which are entitled to recognition. The conflict between those rights here should not be resolved by extending into North Carolina the effects of Nevada's action through a perfunctory application of the literal language of the Full Faith and Credit Clause with the result that measures which North Carolina has adopted to safeguard the welfare of her citizens in this area of legitimate governmental concern are undermined. When the interests are considered, those of North Carolina are of sufficient validity that they should as clearly free her of the compulsions of the Full Faith and Credit Clause as did the interest of the state in the devolution of property within its boundaries in *Fall v. Eastin*, *, all of which seem to be matters of far less concern to a state than the untrammeled enforcement within its borders of those standards of public morality with regard to the marriage relation which it considers to be in the best interests of its citizens.

***

Mr. Justice JACKSON, dissenting.

I cannot join in exerting the judicial power of the Federal Government to compel the State of North Carolina to subordinate its own law to the Nevada divorce decrees. *** [The Court's decision] to do so reaches far beyond the immediate case. nullifies the power of each state to protect its own citizens against dissolution of their marriages by the courts of other states which have an easier system of divorce. *** To declare that a state is powerless to protect either its own policy or the family rights of its people against such consequences has serious constitutional implications. It is not an exaggeration to say that this decision repeals the divorce laws of all the states and substitutes the law of Nevada as to all marriages one of the parties to which can afford a short trip there. ***

***

The opinion concedes that Nevada's judgment could not be forced upon North Carolina in absence of personal service if a divorce proceeding were an action in personam. In other words, settled family relationships may be destroyed by a procedure that we would not recognize if the suit were one to collect a grocery bill.

***

To hold that the Nevada judgments were not binding in North Carolina because they were rendered without jurisdiction over the North Carolina spouses, it is not necessary to hold that they were without any conceivable validity. It may be, and probably is, true that Nevada has sufficient interest in the lives of those who sojourn there to free them and their spouses to take new spouses without incurring criminal penalties under Nevada law. I know of nothing in our Constitution that requires Nevada to adhere to traditional concepts of bigamous unions or the legitimacy of the fruit thereof. And the control of a state over property within its borders is so complete that I suppose that Nevada could effectively deal with it in the name of divorce as completely as in any other. But it is quite a different thing to say that Nevada can dissolve the marriages of North Carolinians and dictate the incidence of the bigamy statutes of North Carolina by which North Carolina has sought to protect her own interests as well as theirs. In this case there is no conceivable basis of jurisdiction in the Nevada court over the absent spouses, and, a fortiori, over North Carolina herself. I cannot but think that in its pre-occupation with the full faith and credit clause the Court has slighted the due process clause.

***

The only suggestion of a domicile within Nevada was a stay of about six weeks at the Alamo Auto Court, an address hardly suggestive of permanence. Mrs. Hendrix testified in her case (the evidence in Williams' case is not before us) that her residence in Nevada was 'indefinite permanent' in character. The Nevada court made no finding that the parties had a 'domicile' there. It only found a residence--sometimes, but not necessarily, an equivalent. It is this Court that accepts these facts as enough to establish domicile.

b. *Williams v. North Carolina*
Williams et al. v. State of North Carolina
325 U.S. 226 (1945)

Mr. Justice FRANKFURTER delivered the opinion of the Court.

This case is here to review judgments of the Supreme Court of North Carolina, affirming convictions for bigamous cohabitation, assailed on the ground that full faith and credit, as required by the Constitution of the United States, was not accorded divorces decreed by one of the courts of Nevada. *** [In *Williams (I)*] [t]he record then before us did not present the question whether North Carolina had the power 'to refuse full faith and credit to Nevada divorce decrees because, contrary to the findings of the Nevada court, North Carolina finds that no bona fide domicil was acquired in Nevada.' * This is the precise issue which has emerged after retrial of the cause following our reversal. Its obvious importance brought the case here. *.

The implications of the Full Faith and Credit Clause, Article IV, Section 1 of the Constitution, first received the sharp analysis of this Court in *Thompson v. Whitman*, 18 Wall. 457. Theretofore, uncritical notions about the scope of that Clause had been expressed in the early case of *Mills v. Duryee*, 7 Cranch 481. The 'doctrine' of that case, as restated in another early case, was that 'the judgment of a state court should have the same credit, validity, and effect in every other court in the United States, which it had in the state where it was pronounced.' *Hampton v. McConnel*, 3 Wheat. 234, 235. This utterance, when put to the test, as it was in *Thompson v. Whitman, supra*, was found to be too loose. *Thompson v. Whitman* made it clear that the doctrine of *Mills v. Duryee* comes into operation only when, in the language of Kent, 'the jurisdiction of the court in another state is not impeached, either as to the subject matter or the person.' Only then is 'the record of the judgment * * * entitled to full faith and credit.' 1 Kent, Commentaries (2d Ed., 1832) *261 n.b. ***

But the Clause does not make a sister-State judgment a judgment in another State. The proposal to do so was rejected by the Philadelphia Convention. 2 Farrand, The Records of the Federal Convention of 1787, 447, 448. 'To give it the force of a judgment in another state, it must be made a judgment there.' *McElmoyle v. Cohen*, 13 Pet. 312, 325, 10 L.Ed. 177. It can be made a judgment there only if the court purporting to render the original judgment had power to render such a judgment. A judgment in one States is conclusive upon the merits in every other State, but only if the court of the first State had power to pass on the merits--had jurisdiction, that is, to render the judgment.

'It is too late now to deny the right collaterally to impeach a decree of divorce made in another state, by proof that the court had no jurisdiction, even when the record purports to show jurisdiction
***.

Under our system of law, judicial power to grant a divorce-- jurisdiction, strictly speaking--is founded on domicil. *Bell v. Bell*, 181 U.S. 175; *Andrews v. Andrews*, 188 U.S. 14. The framers of the Constitution were familiar with this jurisdictional prerequisite, and since 1789 neither this Court nor any other court in the English-speaking world has questioned it. Domicil implies a nexus between person and place of such permanence as to control the creation of legal relations and responsibilities of the utmost significance. The domicil of one spouse within a State gives power to that State, we have held, to dissolve a marriage wheresover contracted. In view of *Williams v. North Carolina, supra*, the jurisdictional requirement of domicil is freed from confusing refinements about 'matrimonial domicil', see *Davis v. Davis*, 305 U.S. 32, and the like. Divorce, like marriage, is of concern not merely to the immediate parties. It affects personal rights of the deepest significance. It also touches basic interests of society. Since divorce, like marriage, creates a new status, every consideration of policy makes it desirable that the effect should be the same wherever the question arises.

It is one thing to reopen an issue that has been settled after appropriate opportunity to present their contentions has been afforded to all who had an interest in its adjudication. This applies also to jurisdictional questions. After a contest these cannot be relitigated as between the parties. * But those not parties to a litigation ought not to be foreclosed by the interested actions of others; especially not a State which is concerned with the vindication of its own social policy and has no means, certainly no effective means, to protect that interest against the selfish action of those outside its borders. The State of domiciliary origin should not be bound by an unfounded, even if not collusive, recital in the record of a court of another State. ***

*** This may lead, no doubt, to conflicting determinations of what judicial power is founded upon. Such conflict is inherent in the practical application of the concept of domicil in the context of our federal system. * What was said in *Worcester County Trust Co. v. Riley, supra*, is pertinent here. 'Neither the Fourteenth Amendment nor the full faith and credit clause * * * requires uniformity in the decisions of the courts of different states as to the place of domicil, where the exertion of state power is dependent upon domicil within its boundaries.' * * * If a finding by the court of one State that domicil in another State has been abandoned were conclusive upon the old domiciliary State, the policy of each State in matters of most intimate concern could be subverted by the policy of every other State. This Court has long ago denied the existence of such destructive power. The issue has a far reach. For domicil is the foundation of probate jurisdiction precisely as it is that of divorce. The ruling in *Tilt v. Kelsey*, *, *** [established that] it is open to the courts of any state, in the trial of a collateral issue, to determine, upon the evidence produced, the true domicil of the deceased.' *.

Although it is now settled that a suit for divorce is not an ordinary adversary proceeding, it does not promote analysis, as was recently pointed out, to label divorce proceedings as actions in rem. *Williams v. North Carolina*, *. But insofar as a divorce decree partakes of some of the characteristics of a decree in rem, it is misleading to say that all the world is party to a proceeding in rem. * All the world is not party to a divorce proceeding. *** In short, the decree of divorce is a conclusive adjudication of everything except the jurisdictional facts upon which it is founded, and domicil is a jurisdictional fact. To permit the necessary finding of domicil by one State to foreclose all States in the protection of their social institutions would be intolerable.

*** The necessary accommodation between the right of one State to safeguard its interest in the family relation of its own people and the power of another State to grant divorces can be left to neither State.

The problem is to reconcile the reciprocal respect to be accorded by the members of the Union to their adjudications with due regard for another most important aspect of our federalism whereby 'the domestic relations of husband and wife * * * were matters reserved to the States,' *State of Ohio ex rel. Popovici v. Agler*,*, and do not belong to the United States. *In re Burrus*,*. The rights that belong to all the States and the obligations which membership in the Union imposes upon all, are made effective because this Court is open to consider claims, such as this case presents, that the courts of one State have not given the full faith and credit to the judgment of a sister State that is required by Art. IV, § 1 of the Constitution.
***

*** [S]imply because the Nevada court found that it had power to award a divorce decree cannot, we have seen, foreclose reexamination by another State. Otherwise, as was pointed out long ago, a court's record would establish its power and the power would be proved by the record. Such circular reasoning would give one State a control over all the other States which the Full Faith and Credit Clause certainly did not confer.

*** The judgments of conviction now under review bring before us a record which may be fairly summarized by saying that the petitioners left North Carolina for the purpose of getting divorces from their respective spouses in Nevada and as soon as each had done so and married one another they left Nevada and returned to North Carolina to live there together as man and wife. Against the charge of bigamous cohabitation under § 14-183 of the North Carolina General Statutes, petitioners stood on their Nevada divorces and offered exemplified copies of the Nevada proceedings. The trial judge charged that the State had the burden of proving beyond a reasonable doubt that (1) each petitioner was lawfully married to one person; (2) thereafter each petitioner contracted a second marriage with another person outside North Carolina; (3) the spouses of petitioners were living at the time of this second marriage; (4) petitioners cohabited with one another in North Carolina after the second marriage. The burden, it was charged, then devolved upon petitioners 'to satisfy the trial jury, not beyond a reasonable doubt nor by the greater weight of the evidence, but simply to satisfy' the jury from all the evidence, that petitioners were domiciled in Nevada at the time they obtained their divorces. The court further charged that 'the recitation' of bona fide domicil in the Nevada decree was 'prima facie evidence' sufficient to warrant a finding of domicil in Nevada but not compelling 'such an inference'. If the jury found, as they were told, that petitioners had domicils in North Carolina and went to Nevada 'simply and solely for the purpose of obtaining' divorces, intending to return to North Carolina on obtaining them, they never lost their North Carolina domicils nor acquired new domicils in Nevada. Domicil, the jury was instructed, was that place where a person 'has voluntarily fixed his abode * * * not for a mere special or temporary purpose, but with a present intention of making it his home, either permanently or for an indefinite or unlimited length of time.'

*** There is nothing to suggest that the issue was not fairly submitted to the jury and that it was not fairly assessed on cogent evidence.

[W]e can not say that North Carolina was not entitled to draw the inference that petitioners never abandoned their domicils in North Carolina, particularly since we could not conscientiously prefer, were it our business to do so, the contrary finding of the Nevada court.

[T]he occasional disregard by any one State of the reciprocal obligations of the forty-eight States to respect the constitutional power of each to deal with domestic relations of those domiciled within its borders is hardly an argument for allowing one State to deprive the other forty-seven States of their constitutional rights. ***

In seeking a decree of divorce outside the State in which he has theretofore maintained his marriage, a person is necessarily involved in the legal situation created by our federal system whereby one State can grant a divorce of validity in other States only if the applicant has a bona fide domicil in the State of the court purporting to dissolve a prior legal marriage. The petitioners therefore assumed the risk that this Court would find that North Carolina justifiably concluded that they had not been domiciled in Nevada. Since the divorces which they sought and received in Nevada had no legal validity in North Carolina and their North Carolina spouses were still alive, they subjected themselves to prosecution for bigamous cohabitation under North Carolina law. *** In vindicating its public policy and particularly one so important as that bearing upon the integrity of family life, a State in punishing particular acts may provide that 'he who shall do them shall do them at his peril and will not be heard to plead in defense good faith or ignorance.' *United States v. Balint,**. Mistaken notions about one's legal rights are not sufficient to bar prosecution for crime.

We conclude that North Carolina was not required to yield her State policy because a Nevada court found that petitioners were domiciled in Nevada when it granted them decrees of divorce. North Carolina was entitled to find, as she did, that they did not acquire domicils in Nevada and that the Nevada court was therefore without power to liberate the petitioners from amenability to the laws of North Carolina governing domestic relations. And, as was said in connection with another aspect of the Full Faith and Credit Clause, our conclusion 'is not a matter to arouse the susceptibilities of the states, all of which are equally concerned in the question and equally on both sides.' *Fauntleroy v. Lum,* 210 U.S. 238.

***

Affirmed.

Mr. Justice MURPHY, concurring.

***

The State of Nevada has unquestioned authority, consistent with procedural due process, to grant divorces on whatever basis it sees fit to all who meet its statutory requirements. It is entitled, moreover, to give to its divorce decrees absolute and binding finality within the confines of its borders.

But if Nevada's divorce decrees are to be accorded full faith and credit in the courts of her sister states it is essential that Nevada have proper jurisdiction over the divorce proceedings. This means that at least one of the parties to each ex parte proceeding must have a bona fide domicil within Nevada for whatever length of time Nevada may prescribe.

This elementary principle has been reiterated by this Court many times. In *Bell v. Bell*, *, this Court held that 'because neither party had a domicil in Pennsylvania' the Pennsylvania court had no jurisdiction to grant a divorce and its decree 'was entitled to no faith and credit in New York or in any other state.' The same rule was applied in the companion case of *Streitwolf* * . Referring to these two prior cases as holding that 'domicil was in any event the inherent element upon which the jurisdiction must rest,' the Court in *Andrews v. Andrews*,*, repeated that bona fide domicil in a state is 'essential to give jurisdiction to the courts of such state to render a decree of divorce which would have extraterritorial effect.' The Andrews case made it clear, moreover, that this requirement of domicil is not merely a matter of state law. It was stated specifically that 'without reference to the statute of South Dakota and in any event' domicil in South Dakota was necessary. *. All of the opinions in *Haddock v. Haddock*, *, recognized this principle, with Mr. Justice Brown's dissenting opinion stating that 'the courts of one state may not grant a divorce against an absent defendant to any person who has not acquired a bona fide domicil in that state.' Finally, in *Williams*,*, the Court acknowledged that the plaintiff's domicil in a state 'is recognized in the *Haddock* case and elsewhere (Beale, Conflict of Laws, 110.1) as essential in order to give the court jurisdiction which will entitle the divorce decree to extraterritorial effect, at least when the defendant has neither been personally served nor entered an appearance.' *.

***

The CHIEF JUSTICE and Mr. Justice JACKSON join in these views.

Mr. Justice RUTLEDGE, dissenting.

Once again the ghost of 'unitary domicil' returns on its perpetual round, in the guise of 'jurisdictional fact,' to upset judgments, marriages, divorces, undermine the relations founded upon them, and make this Court the unwilling and uncertain arbiter between the concededly valid laws and decrees of sister states. From *Bell* and *Andrews* to *Davis* to *Haddock* to *Williams* and now back to *Haddock* and *Davis* through *Williams* again the maze the Court has traveled in a domiciliary wilderness, only to come out with no settled constitutional policy where one is needed most.

***

I do not believe the Constitution has thus confided to the caprice of juries the faith and credit due the laws and judgments of sister states. Nor has it thus made that question a local matter for the states themselves to decide. Were all judgments given the same infirmity, the full faith and credit clause would be only a dead constitutional letter.

***

*** The Constitution does not mention domicil. Nowhere does it posit the powers of the states or the nation upon that amorphous, highly variable common-law conception. Judges have imported it. The importation, it should be clear by now, has failed in creating a workable constitutional criterion for this delicate region. In its origin the idea of domicil was stranger to the federal system and the problem of allocating power within it. The principal result of transplanting it to constitutional soil has been to make more complex, variable and confusing than need be inherently the allocation of authority in the federal scheme. The corollary consequence for individuals has been more and more to infuse with uncertainty, confusion, and caprice those human relations which most require stability and depend for it upon how the distribution of power is made.

***

Mr. Justice BLACK, dissenting.

***

Statistics indicate that approximately five million divorced persons are scattered throughout the forty-eight states. More than 85% of these divorces were granted in uncontested proceedings. Not one of this latter group can now retain any feeling of security in his divorce decree. Ever present will be the danger of criminal prosecution and harassment.

All these decrees were granted by state courts. *** Today's opinion, however, undermines and makes uncertain the validity of every uncontested divorce decree. It wipes out every semblance of their finality and decisiveness. It achieves what the Court terms the 'desirable effect' of providing the 'same' quality to every divorce decree,'wherever the question arises'--it endows them all alike with the 'same' instability and precariousness. The result is to classify divorced persons in a distinctive and invidious category. *** Uncontested divorce decrees are thus so degraded that a person who marries in reliance upon them can be sent to jail. ***

***

***

Mr. Justice DOUGLAS joins in this dissent.

c. *Sherrer v. Sherrer*

Sherrer v. Sherrer
334 U.S. 343 (1948)

Mr. Chief Justice VINSON delivered the opinion of the Court.

We granted certiorari in this case and in *Coe v. Coe*, 334 U.S. 378, to consider the contention of petitioners that Massachusetts has failed to accord full faith and credit to decrees of divorce rendered by courts of sister States.

Petitioner Margaret E. Sherrer and the respondent, Edward C. Sherrer, were married in New Jersey in 1930, and from 1932 until April 3, 1944, lived together in Monterey, Massachusetts. Following a long period of marital discord, petitioner, accompanied by the two children of the marriage, left Massachusetts on the latter date, ostensibly for the purpose of spending a vacation in the State of Florida. Shortly after her arrival in Florida, however, petitioner informed her husband that she did not intend to return to him. Petitioner obtained housing accommodations in Florida, placed her older child in school, and secured employment for herself.

On July 6, 1944, a bill of complaint for divorce was filed at petitioner's direction in the Circuit Court of the Sixth Judicial Circuit of the State of Florida. The bill alleged extreme cruelty as grounds for divorce and also alleged that petitioner was a 'bona fide resident of the State of Florida.' The respondent received notice by mail of the pendency of the divorce proceedings. He retained Florida counsel who entered a general appearance and filed an answer denying the allegations of petitioner's complaint, including the allegation as to petitioner's Florida residence.

On November 14, 1944, hearings were held in the divorce proceedings. Respondent appeared personally to testify with respect to a stipulation entered into by the parties relating to the custody of the children. Throughout the entire proceedings respondent was represented by counsel. Petitioner introduced evidence to establish her Florida residence and testified generally to the allegations of her complaint. Counsel for respondent failed to cross- examine or to introduce evidence in rebuttal.

The Florida court on November 29, 1944, entered a decree of divorce after specifically finding 'that petitioner is a bona fide resident of the State of Florida, and that this court has jurisdiction of the parties and the subject matter in said cause; * * *' Respondent failed to challenge the decree by appeal to the Florida Supreme Court.

On December 1, 1944, petitioner was married in Florida to one Henry A. Phelps, whom petitioner had known while both were residing in Massachusetts and who had come to Florida shortly after petitioner's arrival in that State. Phelps and petitioner lived together as husband and wife in Florida, where they were both employed, until February 5, 1945, when they returned to Massachusetts.

In June, 1945, respondent instituted an action in the Probate Court of Berkshire County, Massachusetts, which has given rise to the issues of this case. Respondent alleged that he is the lawful husband of petitioner, that the Florida decree of divorce is invalid, and that petitioner's subsequent marriage is void. Respondent prayed that he might be permitted to convey his real estate as if he were sole and that the court declare that he was living apart from his wife for justifiable cause. Petitioner joined issue on respondent's allegations.

In the proceedings which followed, petitioner gave testimony in defense of the validity of the Florida divorce decree. The Probate Court, however, resolved the issues of fact adversely to petitioner's contentions, found that she was never domiciled in Florida, and granted respondent the relief he had requested. The Supreme Judicial Court of Massachusetts affirmed the decree on the grounds that it was supported by the evidence and that the requirements of full faith and credit did not preclude the Massachusetts courts from reexamining the finding of domicile made by the Florida court.

At the outset, it should be observed that the proceedings in the Florida court prior to the entry of the decree of divorce were in no way inconsistent with the requirements of procedural due process. We do not understand respondent to urge the contrary. The respondent personally appeared in the Florida proceedings. Though his attorney he filed pleadings denying the substantial allegations of petitioner's complaint. It is not suggested that his rights to introduce evidence and otherwise to conduct his defense were in any degree impaired; nor is it suggested that there was not available to him the right to seek review of the decree by appeal to the Florida Supreme Court. It is clear that respondent was afforded his day in court with respect to every issue involved in the litigation, including the jurisdictional issue of petitioner's domicile. Under such circumstances, there is nothing in the concept of due process which demands that a defendant be afforded a second opportunity to litigate the existence of jurisdictional facts. *Chicago Life Insurance Co. v. Cherry,**; *Baldwin v. Iowa State Traveling Men's Association, **.

It should also be observed that there has been no suggestion that under the law of Florida, the decree of divorce in question is in any respect invalid or could successfully be subjected to the type of attack permitted by the Massachusetts court. The implicit assumption underlying the position taken by respondent and the Massachusetts court is that this case involves a decree of divorce valid and final in the State which rendered it; and we so assume.

That the jurisdiction of the Florida court to enter a valid decree of divorce was dependent upon petitioner's domicile in that State is not disputed. This requirement was recognized by the Florida court which rendered the divorce decree, and the principle has been given frequent application in decisions of the State Supreme Court. But whether or not petitioner was domiciled in Florida at the time the divorce was granted was a matter to be resolved by judicial determination. Here, unlike the situation presented in *Williams v. North Carolina,**, the finding of the requisite jurisdictional facts was made in proceedings in which the defendant appeared and participated. The question with which we are confronted, therefore, is whether such a finding made under the circumstances presented by this case may, consistent with the requirements of full faith and credit, be subjected to collateral attack in the courts of a sister State in a suit brought by the defendant in the original proceedings.

This Court has also held that the doctrine of res judicata must be applied to questions of jurisdiction in cases arising instate courts involving the application of the full faith and credit clause where, under the law of the state in which the original judgment was rendered, such adjudications are not susceptible to collateral attack.

In *Davis v. Davis*, 1938, 305 U.S. 32, 59 the courts of the District of Columbia had refused to give effect to a decree of absolute divorce rendered in Virginia, on the ground that the Virginia court had lacked jurisdiction despite the fact that the defendant had appeared in the Virginia proceedings and had fully litigated the issue of the plaintiff's domicile. This Court held that in failing to give recognition to the Virginia decree, the courts of the District had failed to accord the full faith and credit required by the Constitution. During the course of the opinion, this Court stated: 'As to petitioner's domicil for divorce and his standing to invoke jurisdiction of the Virginia court, its finding that he was a bona fide resident of that State for the required time is binding upon respondent in the courts of the District. She may not say that he was not entitled to sue for divorce in the state court, for she appeared there and by plea put in issue his allegation as to domicil, introduced evidence to show it false, took exceptions to the commissioner's report, and sought to have the court sustain them and uphold her plea. Plainly, the determination of the decree upon that point is effective for all purposes in this litigation.'

We believe that the decision of this Court in the *Davis* case and those in related situations are clearly indicative of the result to be reached here. Those cases stand for the proposition that the requirements of full faith and credit bar a defendant from collaterally attacking a divorce decree on jurisdictional grounds in the courts of a sister State where there has been participation by the defendant in the divorce proceedings, where the defendant has been accorded full opportunity to contest the jurisdictional issues, and where the decree is not susceptible to such collateral attack in the courts of the State which rendered the decree.

Applying these principles to this case, we hold that the Massachusetts courts erred in permitting the Florida divorce decree to be subjected to attack on the ground that petitioner was not domiciled in Florida at the time the decree was entered. Respondent participated in the Florida proceedings by entering a general appearance, filing pleadings placing in issue the very matters he sought subsequently to contest in the Massachusetts courts, personally appearing before the Florida court and giving testimony in the case, and by retaining attorneys who represented him throughout the entire proceedings. It has not been contended that respondent was given less than a full opportunity to contest the issue of petitioner's domicile or any other issue relevant to the litigation. There is nothing to indicate that the Florida court would not have evaluated fairly and in good faith all relevant evidence submitted to it. Respondent does not even contend that on the basis of the evidence introduced in the Florida proceedings, that court reached an erroneous result on the issue of petitioner's domicile. If respondent failed to take advantage of the opportunities afforded him, the responsibility is his own. We do not believe that the dereliction of a defendant under such circumstances should be permitted to provide a basis for subsequent attack in the courts of a sister State on a decree valid in the State in which it was rendered.

***

It is urged further, however, that because we are dealing with litigation involving the dissolution of the marital relation, a different result is demanded from that which might properly be reached if this case were concerned with other types of litigation. It is pointed out that under the Constitution, the regulation and control of marital and family relationships are reserved to the States. It is urged, and properly so, that the regulation of the incidents of the marital relation involves the exercise by the States of powers of the most vital importance. Finally, it is contended that a recognition of the importance to the States of such powers demands that the requirements of full faith and credit be viewed in such a light as to permit an attack upon a divorce decree granted by a court of a sister State under the circumstances of this case even where the attack is initiated in a suit brought by the defendant in the original proceedings. But the recognition of the importance of a State's power to determine the incidents of basic social relationships into which its domiciliaries enter does not resolve the issues of this case. This is not a situation in which a State has merely sought to exert such power over a domiciliary. This is, rather, a case involving inconsistent assertions of power by courts of two States of the Federal Union and thus presents considerations which go beyond the interests of local policy, however vital. In resolving the issues here presented, we do not conceive it to be a part of our function to weigh the relative merits of the policies of Florida and Massachusetts with respect to divorce and related matters. Nor do we understand the decisions of this Court to support the proposition that the obligation imposed by Article IV, § 1 of the Constitution and the Act of Congress passed thereunder, amounts to something less than the duty to accord full faith and credit to decrees of divorce entered by courts of sister States. The full faith and credit clause is one of the provisions incorporated into the Constitution by its framers for the purpose of transforming an aggregation of independent, sovereign States into a nation. If in its application local policy must at times be required to give way, such 'is part of the price of our federal system.' *Williams*,*.

This is not to say that in no case may an area be recognized in which reasonable accommodations of interest may properly be made. But as this Court has heretofore made clear, that area is of limited extent. We believe that in permitting an attack on the Florida divorce decree which again put in issue petitioner's Florida domicile and in refusing to recognize the validity of that decree, the Massachusetts courts have asserted a power which cannot be reconciled with the requirements of due faith and credit. We believe that assurances that such a power will be exercised sparingly and wisely render it no less repugnant to the constitutional commands.

It is one thing to recognize as permissible the judicial reexamination of findings of jurisdictional fact where such findings have been made by a court of a sister State which has entered a divorce decree in ex parte proceedings. It is quite another thing to hold that the vital rights and interests involved in divorce litigation may be held in suspense pending the scrutiny by courts of sister States of findings of jurisdictional fact made by a competent court in proceedings conducted in a manner consistent with the highest requirements of due process and in which the defendant has participated. We do not conceive it to be in accord with the purposes of the full faith and credit requirement to hold that a judgment rendered under the circumstances of this case may be required to run the gauntlet of such collateral attack in the courts of sister States before its validity outside of the State which rendered it is established or rejected. That vital interests are involved in divorce litigation indicates to us that it is a matter of greater rather than lesser importance that there should be a place to end such litigation. And where a decree of divorce is rendered by a competent court under the circumstances of this case, the obligation of full faith and credit requires that such litigation should end in the courts of the State in which the judgment was rendered.

Reversed.

Mr. Justice FRANKFURTER, with whom Mr. Justice MURPHY concurs, dissenting.

What Mr. Justice Holmes said of the illstarred *Haddock v. Haddock* may equally be said here: 'I do not suppose that civilization will come to an end whichever way this case is decided.' *. But, believing as I do that the decision just announced is calculated, however unwittingly, to promote perjury without otherwise appreciably affecting the existing disharmonies among the forty-eight States in relation to divorce, I deem it appropriate to state my views.

***

*** [T]here is a consensus of opinion among English-speaking courts the world over that domicile requires some sense of permanence of connection between the individual who claims it and the State which he asks to recognize it.

***

The nub of the *Williams* decision was that the State of domicile has an independent interest in the martial status of its citizens that neither they nor any other State with which they may have a transitory connection may abrogate against its will. Its interest is not less because both parties to the marital relationship instead of one sought to evade its laws. In the *Williams* case, it was not the interest of Mrs. Williams, or that of Mr. Hendryx, that North Carolina asserted. It was the interest of the people of North Carolina. The same is true here of the interest of Massachusetts. While the State's interest may be expressed in criminal prosecutions, with itself formally a party as in the *Williams* case, the State also expresses its sovereign power when it speaks through its courts in a civil litigation between private parties. *Cf. Shelley v. Kraemer,* 334 U.S. 1.

Today's decision may stir hope of contributing toward greater certainty of status of those divorced. But when people choose to avail themselves of laws laxer than those of the State in which they permanently abide, and where, barring only the interlude necessary to get a divorce, they choose to continue to abide, doubts and conflicts are inevitable, so long as the divorce laws of the forty-eight States remain diverse, and so long as we respect the law that a judgment without jurisdictional foundation is not constitutionally entitled to recognition everywhere. These are difficulties, as this Court has often reminded, inherent in our federal system, in which governmental power over domestic relations is not given to the central government. Uniformity regarding divorce is not within the power of this Court to achieve so long as 'the domestic relations of husband and wife * * * were matters reserved to the States.' *State of Ohio ex rel. Popovici v. Agler,**; *In re Burrus,**. *** And so long as the Congress has not exercised its powers under the Full Faith and Credit Clause to meet the special problems raised by divorce decrees, this Court cannot through its adjudications achieve the result sought to be accomplished by a long train of abortive efforts at legislative and constitutional reform. To attempt to shape policy so as to avoid disharmonies in our divorce laws was not a power entrusted to us, nor is the judiciary competent to exercise it. Courts are not equipped to pursue the paths for discovering wise policy. A court is confined within the bounds of a particular record, and it cannot even shape the record. Only fragments of a social problem are seen through the narrow windows of a litigation. Had we innate or acquired understanding of a social problem in its entirety, we would not have at our disposal adequate means for constructive solution. The answer to so tangled a problem as that of our conflicting divorce laws is not to be achieved by the simple judicial resources of either/or--this decree is good and must be respected, that one is bad and may be disregarded. We cannot draw on the available power for social invention afforded by the Constitution for dealing adequately with the problem, because the power belongs to the Congress and not to the Court. The only way in which this Court can achieve uniformity, in the absence of Congressional action or constitutional amendment, is by permitting the States with the laxest divorce laws to impose their policies upon all other States. We cannot as judges be ignorant of that which is common knowledge to all men. We cannot close our eyes to the fact that certain States make an industry of their easy divorce laws, and encourage inhabitants of other States to obtain 'quickie' divorces which their home States deny them. To permit such States to bind all others to their decrees would endow with constitutional sanctity a Gresham's Law of domestic relations.

***

d. *Estin v. Estin*

Estin v. Estin
334 U.S. 541 (1948)

Mr. Justice DOUGLAS delivered the opinion of the Court.

This case, here on certiorari to the Court of Appeals of New York, presents an important question under the Full Faith and Credit Clause of the Constitution. Article IV, § 1. It is whether a New York decree awarding respondent $180 per month for her maintenance and support in a separation proceeding survived a Nevada divorce decree which subsequently was granted petitioner.

The parties were married in 1937 and lived together in New York until 1942 when the husband left the wife. There was no issue of the marriage. In 1943 she brought an action against him for a separation. He entered a general appearance. The court, finding that he had abandoned her, granted her a decree of separation and awarded her $180 per month as permanent alimony. In January 1944 he went to Nevada where in 1945 he instituted an action for divorce. She was notified of the action by constructive service but entered no appearance in it. In May, 1945, the Nevada court, finding that petitioner had been a bona fide resident of Nevada since January 30, 1944, granted him an absolute divorce 'on the ground of three years continual separation, without cohabitation.' The Nevada decree made no provision for alimony, though the Nevada court had been advised of the New York decree.

Prior to that time petitioner had made payments of alimony under the New York decree. After entry of the Nevada decree he ceased paying. Thereupon respondent sued in New York for a supplementary judgment for the amount of the arrears. Petitioner appeared in the action and moved to eliminate the alimony provisions of the separation decree by reason of the Nevada decree. The Supreme Court denied the motion and granted respondent judgment for the arrears. * The judgment was affirmed by the Appellate Division, *, and then by the Court of Appeals. 73 N.E.2d 113.

We held in *Williams v. North Carolina*, *, (I), that a divorce decree granted by a State to one of its domiciliaries is entitled to full faith and credit in a bigamy prosecution brought in another State, even though the other spouse was given notice of the divorce proceeding only through constructive service; and (2) that while the finding of domicile by the court that granted the decree is entitled to prima facie weight, it is not conclusive in a sister State but might be relitigated there. * The latter course was followed in this case, as a consequence of which the Supreme Court of New York found, in accord with the Nevada court, that petitioner is now and since January 1944, has been a bona fide resident of the State of Nevada.' *

Petitioner's argument therefore is that the tail must go with the hide--that since by the Nevada decree, recognized in New York, he and respondent are no longer husband and wife, no legal incidence of the marriage remains. We are given a detailed analysis of New York law to show that the New York courts have no power either by statute or by common law to compel a man to support his ex- wife, that alimony is payable only so long as the relation of husband and wife exists, and that in New York, as in some other states, *see Esenwein v. Pennsylvania*, *, a support order does not survive divorce.

The difficulty with that argument is that the highest court in New York has held in this case that a support order can survive divorce and that this one has survived petitioner's divorce. That conclusion is binding on us, except as it conflicts with the Full Faith and Credit Clause. It is not for us to say whether that ruling squares with what the New York courts said on earlier occasions. It is enough that New York today says that such is her policy. The only question for us is whether New York is powerless to make such a ruling in view of the Nevada decree.

We can put to one side the case where the wife was personally served or where she appears in the divorce proceedings. *Cf. Yarborough v. Yarborough*,*; *Davis v. Davis*,*; *Sherrer v. Sherrer*,*; *Coe v. Coe*,*. The only service on her in this case was by publication and she made no appearance in the Nevada proceeding. The requirements of procedural due process were satisfied and the domicile of the husband in Nevada was foundation for a decree effecting a change in the marital capacity of both parties in all the other States of the Union, as well as in Nevada. *Williams[I]*. But the fact that marital capacity was changed does not mean that every other legal incidence of the marriage was necessarily affected.

Although the point was not adjudicated in *Barber v. Barber*,*, the Court in that case recognized that while a divorce decree obtained in Wisconsin by a husband from his absent wife might dissolve the vinculum of the marriage, it did not mean that he was freed from payment of alimony under an earlier separation decree granted by New York. An absolutist might quarrel with the result and demand a rule that once a divorce is granted, the whole of the marriage relation is dissolved, leaving no roots or tendrils of any kind. But there are few areas of the law in black and white. The greys are dominant and even among them the shades are innumerable. For the eternal problem of the law is one of making accommodations between conflicting interests. This is why most legal problems end as questions of degree. That is true of the present problem under the Full Faith and Credit Clause. The question involves important considerations both of law and of policy which it is essential to state.

The situations where a judgment of one State has been denied full faith and credit in another State, because its enforcement would contravene the latter's policy, have been few and far between. *See Williams v. North Carolina,* *; *Magnolia Petroleum Co. v. Hunt,**, and cases cited; *Sherrer v. Sherrer, supra.* The Full Faith and Credit Clause is not to be applied, accordion-like, to accommodate our personal predilections. It substituted a command for the earlier principles of comity and thus basically altered the status of the States as independent sovereigns. *Williams [I],**; *Sherrer,**. It ordered submission by one State even to hostile policies reflected in the judgment of another State, because the practical operation of the federal system, which the Constitution designed, demanded it. The fact that the requirements of full faith and credit, so far as judgments are concerned, are exacting, if not inexorable (*Sherrer,**), does not mean, however, that the State of the domicile of one spouse may, through the use of constructive service, enter a decree that changes every legal incidence of the marriage relationship.

Marital status involves the regularity and integrity of the marriage relation. It affects the legitimacy of the offspring of marriage. It is the basis of criminal laws, as the bigamy prosecution in *Williams v. North Carolina* dramatically illustrates. The State has a considerable interest in preventing bigamous marriages and in protecting the offspring of marriages from being bastardized. The interest of the State extends to its domiciliaries. The State should have the power to guard its interest in them by changing or altering their marital status and by protecting them in that changed status throughout the farthest reaches of the nation. For a person domiciled in one State should not be allowed to suffer the penalties of bigamy for living outside the State with the only one which the State of his domicile recognizes as his lawful wife. And children born of the only marriage which is lawful in the State of his domicile should not carry the stigma of bastardy when they move elsewhere. These are matters of legitimate concern to the State of the domicile. They entitle the State of the domicile to bring in the absent spouse through constructive service. In no other way could the State of the domicile have and maintain effective control of the marital status of its domiciliaries.

Those are the considerations that have long permitted the State of the matrimonial domicile to change the marital status of the parties by an ex parte divorce proceeding, *Thompson,** ,considerations which in the *Williams* cases we thought were equally applicable to any State in which one spouse had established a bona fide domicile. *. But those considerations have little relevancy here. In this case New York evinced a concern with this broken marriage when both parties were domiciled in New York and before Nevada had any concern with it. New York was rightly concerned lest the abandoned spouse be left impoverished and perhaps become a public charge. The problem of her livelihood and support is plainly a matter in which her community had a legitimate interest. The New York court, having jurisdiction over both parties, undertook to protect her by granting her a judgment of permanent alimony. Nevada, however, apparently follows the rule that dissolution of the marriage puts and end to a support order. *. But the question is whether Nevada could under any circumstances adjudicate rights of respondent under the New York judgment when she was not personally served or did not appear in the proceeding.

Bassett v. Bassett, 9 Cir., 141 F.2d 954, held that Nevada could not. We agree with that view.

The New York judgment is a property interest of respondent, created by New York in a proceeding in which both parties were present. It imposed obligations on petitioner and granted rights to respondent. The property interest which it created was an intangible, jurisdiction over which cannot be exerted through control over a physical thing. Jurisdiction over an intangible can indeed only arise from control or power over the persons whose relationships are the source of the rights and obligations. *

Jurisdiction over a debtor is sufficient to give the State of his domicile some control over the debt which he owes. It can, for example, levy a tax on its transfer by will (*Blackstone v. Miller*, 188 U.S. 189; *State Tax Commission of Utah v. Aldrich*, *) appropriate it through garnishment or attachment (*Sturm*, *; see *Harris v. Balk*, *), collect it and administer it for the benefit of creditors. *Clark v. Williard*, *; *Fischer v. American United Ins. Co.*,*. But we are aware of no power which the State of domicile of the debtor has to determine the personal rights of the creditor in the intangible unless the creditor has been personally served or appears in the proceeding. The existence of any such power has been repeatedly denied. *Pennoyer v. Neff*, *.

We know of no source of power which would take the present case out of that category. The Nevada decree that is said to wipe out respondent's claim for alimony under the New York judgment is nothing less than an attempt by Nevada to restrain respondent from asserting her claim under that judgment. That is an attempt to exercise an in personam jurisdiction over a person not before the court. That may not be done. Since Nevada had no power to adjudicate respondent's rights in the New York judgment, New York need not give full faith and credit to that phase of Nevada's judgment. A judgment of a court having no jurisdiction to render it is not entitled to the full faith and credit which the Constitution and statute of the United States demand. *Hansberry v. Lee*,*; *Williams [II]*, *.

The result in this situation is to make the divorce divisible--to give effect to the Nevada decree insofar as it affects marital status and to make it ineffective on the issue of alimony. It accommodates the interests of both Nevada and New York in this broken marriage by restricting each State to the matters of her dominant concern.

Since Nevada had no jurisdiction to alter respondent's rights in the New York judgment, we do not reach the further question whether in any event that judgment would be entitled to full faith and credit in Nevada. ***. And it will be time enough to consider the effect of any discrimination shown to out-of-state ex parte divorces when a State makes that its policy.

Affirmed.

Mr. Justice FRANKFURTER, dissenting.

The Court's opinion appears to rest on three independent grounds:

(1) New York may, consistently with the Full Faith and Credit Clause, hold that a prior separate maintenance decree of one of its courts survives a decree of divorce within the scope of enforceability of the rule in *Williams v. North Carolina*, 317 U.S. 287 whether such divorce is granted in New York or by a sister State;

(2) By virtue of its interest in preventing its citizens from becoming public charges, New York may constitutionally provide that a domestic separate maintenance decree survives a sister-State divorce decree which must be respected in New York under the rule in the first *Williams* case, *supra*;

(3) A separate maintenance decree creates an obligation which may not, consistently with due process, be extinguished by a court lacking personal jurisdiction of the obligee, though possessed of jurisdiction to terminate her marital status, and any judgment purporting to do so is not entitled to extra- State recognition.

To the first of these grounds I assent, and if such is the law of New York I agree that the decision of the New York Court of Appeals in this case must be upheld. It is for New York to decide whether its decrees for separate maintenance survive divorce or terminate with it, provided, of course, that its decision is not a mere attempt to defeat a federal right, given by the Full Faith and Credit Clause, under the guise of a determination of State law. *

The second ground presents difficulties. I cannot agree that New York's interest in its residents would justify New York in giving less effect to an enforceable Nevada divorce granted to one domiciled in Nevada, against a spouse not personally served, than it would give to a valid New York divorce similarly obtained. As to this, I agree with the views of by brother JACKSON. If, on the other hand, New York does not so discriminate against enforceable 'ex parte' divorce decrees granted by a sister State, no problem under the Full Faith and Credit Clause arises.

***

My difficulty with the third ground of the Court's opinion is that Nevada did not purport, so far as the record discloses, to rule on the survival of the New York separate maintenance decree. Nevada merely established a change in status. It was for New York to determine the effect, with reference to its own law, of that change in status. If it was the law of New York that divorce put an end to its separate maintenance decree, the respondent's decree would have been terminated not by the Nevada divorce but by the consequences, under the New York law, of a change in status, even though brought about by Nevada. Similarly, Nevada could not adjudicate rights in New York realty, but, if New York law provided for dower, a Nevada divorce might or might not terminate a dower interest in New York realty depending on whether or not New York treated dower rights as extinguished by divorce.

***

Mr. Justice JACKSON, dissenting.

If there is one thing that the people are entitled to expect from their lawmakers, it is rules of law that will enable individuals to tell whether they are married and, if so, to whom. Today many people who have simply lived in more than one state do not know, and the most learned lawyer cannot advise them with any confidence. The uncertainties that result are not merely technical, nor are they trivial; they affect fundamental rights and relations such as the lawfulness of their cohabitation, their children's legitimacy, their title to property, and even whether they are law-abiding persons or criminals. In a society as mobile and nomadic as ours, such uncertainties affect large numbers of people and create a social problem of some magnitude. It is therefore important that, whatever we do, we shall not add to the confusion. I think that this decision does just that.

***

The Court reaches the Solomon-like conclusion that the Nevada decree is half good and half bad under the full faith and credit clause. It is good to free the husband from the marriage; it is not good to free him from its incidental obligations. Assuming the judgment to be one which the Constitution requires to be recognized at all, I do not see how we can square this decision with the command that it be given full faith and credit. For reasons which I stated in dissenting in *Williams v. North Carolina*, 317 U.S. 287, I would not give standing under the clause to constructive service divorces obtained on short residence. But if we are to hold this divorce good, I do not see how it can be less good than a divorce would be if rendered by the courts of New York.

***

e. Notes and Questions

1) *Williams (1)* and *Williams (2)*

Williams (1) and *(2)* mark the polar boundaries of divorce jurisdiction and, accordingly, of the duty of sister states to give full faith and credit to such decrees. Try to articulate in black-letter fashion the holding(s) of each case. The clarification of divorce jurisdiction and recognition rules came in the nick of time. *Williams (2)* was decided on May 21, 1945, thirteen days after V-E (Victory in Europe) day, marking the surrender of the German army and cessation of hostilities in the European Theater. Four months later, Japan also surrendered. Upon the return of soldiers from World War II, many hasty war-time marriages ended in divorce and the divorce rate spiked to an unprecedented level that would not be seen for another three decades. Much more confusion would have followed in the wake of that tsunami of divorce decrees had the issues raised in *Williams (1)* and *(2)* not been resolved. The societal "parade of horribles" predicted by the dissenters in *Williams (2)* never occurred. *Williams (1)* and *Williams (2)* have been cited more than 1500 times *each* since they were decided.

Having vindicated its authority to reject transient divorce decrees obtained by its domiciles while temporarily abiding in other states, the state of North Carolina released Mr. Williams and Mrs. Hendrix. The defendants never served a day.

2) More About Divorce Jurisdiction

In *Pennoyer v. Neff,* 95 U.S. (5 Otto) 714 (1877), the well-known jurisdictional decision, the Supreme Court distinguished jurisdiction in ordinary civil proceedings *in personam* from jurisdiction in divorce and related status proceedings. It noted:

> Except in cases affecting the personal *status* of the plaintiff, and cases in which that mode of service may be considered to have been assented to in advance as hereinafter mentioned, the substituted service of process by publication . . . is effectual only where, in connection with the process . . . property in the State is brought under the control of the court, . . . or where the judgment is sought as a means of reaching such property . . .; in other words, where the action is in the nature of a proceeding *in rem.*

95 U.S. at 733-735. In other words, service by process was valid in status and *in rem* cases. Viewing the marriage relationship as an intangible *res* which both spouses carried with them at all times, like a debt carried by the debtor, this treatment made sense.

In *Shaffer v. Heitner*, 433 U.S. 186 (1977), the Supreme Court extended the "minimum contacts" tests for determining the constitutionality of assertion of state court jurisdiction over the interests of non-resident defendants to *all in rem* and *quasi in rem* suits. The logic and sweeping language of that opinion would easily encompass suits to determine family status as well as ordinary commercial in rem and quasi in suits. However, *Shaffer* involved a business suit and the Court did not want to alter prematurely the basis for divorce jurisdiction without first considering that step in the context of the case in which the relevant facts and policy considerations could be carefully assessed. The Court confirmed that the test for divorce jurisdiction allows for jurisdiction over some nonresidents under different standards than applicable in the usual *in personam* civil case. It noted that: "Mr. Justice Field's opinion [in *Pennoyer*] carefully noted that cases involving the personal status of the plaintiff, such as divorce actions, could be adjudicated in the plaintiff's home State even though the defendant could not be served within that State." 433 U.S. at 201. Likewise, in a footnote the Court emphasized that the tests it was requiring for the exercise of *quasi in rem* jurisdiction did not apply to divorce cases. "We do not suggest that jurisdictional doctrines other than those discussed in text, such as the particularized rules governing adjudications of status, are inconsistent with the standard of fairness." 433 U.S. at 209, n. 30.

Since then, the Supreme Court has not had occasion to address the question of what is constitutionally required for divorce jurisdiction. However, just one year after it decided *Shaffer*, the Court held that the "minimum contacts" test for jurisdiction applies to state court actions seeking to modify child support obligations of nonresident defendants. *Kulko v. Superior Court*, 436 U.S. 84 (1978); *Burnham v. Superious Court*, 495 U.S. 604 (1990). The Court's analysis of the jurisdictional question in that domestic relations suit emphasized policy factors that would appear to support a similar conclusion regarding the standard of divorce jurisdiction.

In *Bell v. Bell*, 181 U.S. 175 (1901), the Supreme Court held that "because neither party had a domicil in Pennsylvania" a Pennsylvania court lacked jurisdiction to grant a divorce and its divorce decree "was entitled to no faith and credit in New York or in any other state." Today legal scholars generally believe that domicile of one of the spouses is not constitutionally required for divorce jurisdiction in absolutely all cases. Thus, the *Restatement, Second, Conflicts of Laws* § 72 provides: "A state has power to exercise judicial jurisdiction to dissolve the marriage of spouses, neither of whom is domiciled in the state, if either spouse has such a relationship to the state as would make it reasonable for the state to dissolve the marriage." Likewise, legislators in many states have adopted statutory provisions authorizing state courts to exercise territorial jurisdiction in divorce cases on grounds other than mere domicile. The most prominent kind of exception exists for military personnel, who seldom acquire a new domicile in every posting. The Uniform Marriage and Divorce Act provides the that a state may exercise divorce jurisdiction if (a) one of the spouses is domiciled in the state or stationed on military duty in the state at the time the suit is filed, and (b) for 90 days prior to filing the divorce action. Uniform Marriage and Divorce Act § 302.

In several early decisions, courts refused to give effect to such provisions, based on their belief that domicile was an absolute constitutional prerequisite for jurisdiction. *See e.g. Viernes v District Court*, 509 P.2d 306 (Colo. 1973); *Vollmer v Vollmer*, 371 P.2d 70 (Ore. 1962). One of the leading cases was decided by the Third Circuit Court of Appeals. In *Alton v Alton*, 207 F.2d 667 (3rd Cir. 1953), *vacated as moot*, 347 U.S. 610 (1954), a divided court of appeals held that a Virgin Islands court could not exercise jurisdiction to enter a divorce decree over two nondomiciliaries, even though the islands had a statute authorizing courts to exercise divorce jurisdiction when parties had resided in the place for six weeks. Judge Goodrich explained:

> An attempt by another jurisdiction to affect the relations of a foreign domiciliary as unconstitutional even though both parties are in court and neither one raises the question. The question may well be asked as to what the lack of due process is. The defendant is not complaining. Nevertheless, if the jurisdiction for divorce continues to be based on domicile, as we think it does, we believe it to be lack of due process for one state to take to itself the readjustment of domestic relations between those domiciled elsewhere.

207 F.2d at 676, 77.

However, the trend of later decisions, has been to uphold the exercise of jurisdiction, even when neither party is domiciled in the forum state, if there is some significant connection between the parties or their marriage and the forum. *Lauterbach v Lauterbach*, 392 P.2d 24 (Alaska 1964); *Wallace v Wallace*, 320 P.2d 1020 (N.M. 1958); *Wood v Wood*, 320 S.W.2d 807 (Tex. 1959); *In re Marriage of Ways*, 538 P.2d 1225 (Wash. 1975); *see further In re Marriage of Thorton*, 185 Cal

Rptr 388 (Cal. App. 1982) (residence, not domicile, of husband sufficient basis for California to assert jurisdiction in divorce action filed by Australia-residing wife). *See* Garfield, *infra* at 501.

However, even if a court does not have jurisdiction, the parties may be estopped or precluded from raising that defect in a later proceeding. If both parties have appeared in an action and submitted to jurisdiction, neither party will be permitted to later attack the divorce decree. *Sherrer v Sherrer*, 334 U.S. 343 (1948); *Coe v Coe*, 334 U.S. 378 (1948). *See also Johnson v Muelberger*, 340 U.S. 581 (1951) (a third party also is precluded from attacking jurisdiction of court that rendered divorce decree unless the law of the state that rendered the decree would permit such an attack).

What if neither spouse is domiciled in the jurisdiction but both consent to the jurisdiction of the court? It used to be popular (before ubiquitous no-fault divorce laws) for divorcing parties to agree that one of them would go to a pleasant resort jurisdiction with lax divorce laws, wait the prescribed time, file for divorce, and the other spouse would either default or file a consent. If, later, one of the spouses challenged the jurisdiction of the court issuing a divorce on such basis, how should the court rule? Is domicile merely a waivable personal jurisdiction restriction, or is it also a restriction on subject matter jurisdiction (which generally cannot be waived)? In *Alton v. Alton*, 207 F.2d 667 (3d Cir. 1953), *vacated as moot*, 347 U.S. 610 (1954), the Third Circuit held that a divorce decree obtained by visitors under a Virgin Islands divorce law which, in addition to enacting a no-fault divorce grounds, dispensed with domicile and based divorce jurisdiction on presence alone, violated due process of law.

3) *Sherrer* and *Estin* and Bifurcated Divorce Jurisdiction

Sherrer suggested and *Estin* established the rule of divisible divorce jurisdiction. What is that rule? Were the dissenters who argued that divorce she be treated as a unitary action wiser? Why/why not?

3. Practical and Ethical Considerations

To what extent, if any, should the North Carolina lawyer who suggested that couple go to Nevada and get a divorce be held liable for malpractice? Why?

4. Bibliography

Brian H. Bix, *State of the Union: The States' Interest in the Marital Status of Their Citizens,* 55 U. Miami L. Rev. 1 (2000).

Stanley E. Cox, *Would That Burnham Had Not Come to Be Done Insane! A Critique of Recent Supreme Court Personal Jurisdiction Reasoning, An Explanation of Why Transient Presence Jurisdiction Is Unconstitutional, and Some Thoughts About Divorce Jurisdiction in A Minimum Contacts World,* 58 Tenn. L. Rev. 497, 541 (1991).

Michael J. Oths, *Divorce on the Road, "Going to Gooding,"* Advocate (Idaho), June 2000, at 11.

Lynn D. Wardle, Williams v. North Carolina, *Divorce Recognition, and Same-Sex Marriage Recognition,* 32 Creighton L. Rev. 187 (1998).

Rhonda Wasserman, *Parents, Partners, and Personal Jurisdiction,* 1995 U. Ill. L. Rev. 813.

B. DIVORCE PROCEDURE

1. Background

a. Dissolution of Marriage at Common Law

In 1757, Blackstone explained that marriage could be dissolved in two ways – "by death, or divorce." He elaborated on divorce:

> There are two kinds of divorce, the one total, the other partial; and this is either *a vinculo matrimonii* (from the bond of matrimony), the other mere *a mensa et thoro* (from bed and board). The total divorce, *a vinculo matrimonii*, must be for some of the canonical causes of impediment ***; and those existing *before* the marriage, as is always the case in consanguinity; not supervenient, or arising *afterwards*, as may be the case in affinity or corporal imbecility. For in cases of total divorce, the marriage is declared null, as having been absolutely unlawful *ab initio* (from the beginning); and the parties are therefore separated pro salute animarum (for the welfare of their souls): for which reason, as was before observed, no divorce can be obtained but during the lifetime of the parties. The issue of such marriage as is thus entirely dissolved are bastards.
>
> *** [D]ivorces *a vinculo matrimonii,* for adultery, have of late years been frequently granted by act of parliament.

I William Blackstone, *infra* at *440-441. Divorce *a mensa et thoro* was comparable to what is known today as legal separation.

For four centuries after the Conquest of England, true divorces (*a vinculo matrimonii*) could only be granted by ecclesiastical courts, but in 1670 Parliament began to grant such divorces also. General Intelligence, *infra*. It is reported that "[b]etween 1670 and 1857, only 375 divorces were granted in England. Obtaining a divorce before 1857 required an act of the English Parliament. Most of the divorces were granted for 'great families' and 'special cases.'" Nichols, *infra*, at 55-56.

> As Mr. Justice Maule pointed out to a man convicted of bigamy after his wife had committed adultery and deserted him: 'You should have come to the ecclesiastical court and there obtained against your wife a decree *a mensa et thoro. You should then have brought an action in the court of common law and received *** damages against your wife's paramour. Armed with these decrees, you should have approached the legislature and obtained an Act of Parliament, which would have rendered you free, and legally competent to marry the person whom you have taken upon yourself to marry with no such sanction. It is quite true that these proceedings would have cost you many hundreds of pounds, whereas you probably you have not as many pence. But the law knows no distinction between rich and poor.

General Intelligence, *infra*. In 1857 Parliament passed the Matrimonial Causes Act allowing English courts to grant divorce decrees.

In America, which did not have ecclesiastical courts, the northern states allowed equity courts to grant divorces soon after the Declaration of Independence. In the southern states, the authority to grant divorces was exercised by the legislatures until shortly before the Civil War. Nichol, *infra* at 57. "By 1799, twelve states and the

Northwest Territory had adopted divorce statutes, and by 1860, only South Carolina refused to permit absolute divorce." Kay, *infra*, at 2026.

b. Historical Divorce Pleadings

For a sample of a pleading in the era of fault and in the era before typewriters, *see* J. Clay Smith, Jr., *infra*. The article contains the handwritten petition for a divorce, filed in the District of Columbia in 1875, by one of the early women lawyers admitted to the D.C. Bar.

2. Statutes, Cases and Doctrines

a. Sosna v. Iowa

Carol Maureen Sosna etc., v. State of Iowa et al.
419 U.S. 393 (1975)

Mr. Justice REHNQUIST delivered the opinion of the Court.

Appellant Carol Sosna married Michael Sosna on September 5, 1964, in Michigan. They lived together in New York between October 1967 and August 1971, after which date they separated but continued to live in New York. In August 1972, appellant moved to Iowa with her three children, and the following month she petitioned the District Court of Jackson County, Iowa, for a dissolution of her marriage. Michael Sosna, who had been personally served with notice of the action when he came to Iowa to visit his children, made a special appearance to contest the jurisdiction of the Iowa court. The Iowa court dismissed the petition for lack of jurisdiction, finding that Michael Sosna was not a resident of Iowa and appellant had not been a resident of the State of Iowa for one year preceding the filing of her petition. In so doing the Iowa court applied the provisions of Iowa Code § 598.6 (1973) requiring that the petitioner in such an action be 'for the last year a resident of the state.'

Instead of appealing this ruling to the Iowa appellate courts, appellant filed a complaint in the United States District Court for the Northern District of Iowa asserting that Iowa's durational residency requirement for invoking its divorce jurisdiction violated the United States Constitution. She sought both injunctive and declaratory relief against the appellees in this case, one of whom is the State of Iowa, and the other of which is the judge of the District Court of Jackson County, Iowa, who had previously dismissed her petition.

A three-judge court *** held that the Iowa durational residency requirement was constitutional. * We noted probable jurisdiction, ***. For reasons stated in this opinion, we *** hold that the Iowa durational residency requirement for divorce does not offend the United States Constitution.
***

The durational residency requirement under attack in this case is a part of Iowa's comprehensive statutory regulation of domestic relations, an area that has long been regarded as a virtually exclusive province of the States. Cases decided by this Court over a period of more than a century bear witness to this historical fact. In *Barber v. Barber*, 21 How. 582, 584 (1859), the Court said: 'We disclaim altogether any jurisdiction in the courts of the United States upon the subject of divorce . . . .' In *Pennoyer v. Neff*, 95 U.S. 714, 734--735 (1878), the Court said: 'The State . . . has absolute right to prescribe the conditions upon which the marriage relation between its own citizens shall be created, and the causes for which it may be dissolved,' and the same view was reaffirmed in *Simms v. Simms*, 175 U.S. 162, 167 (1899).

The statutory scheme in Iowa, like those in other States, sets forth in considerable detail the grounds upon which a marriage may be dissolved and the circumstances in which a divorce may be obtained. Jurisdiction over a petition for dissolution is established by statute in 'the county where either party resides,' Iowa Code § 598.2 (1973), and the Iowa courts have construed the term 'resident' to have much the same meaning as is ordinarily associated with the concept of domicile. * Iowa has recently revised its divorce statutes, incorporating the no- fault concept, but it retained the one-year durational residency requirement.

The imposition of a durational residency requirement for divorce is scarcely unique to Iowa, since 48 States impose such a requirement as a condition for maintaining an action for divorce. As might be expected, the periods vary among the States and range from six weeks to two years. The one-year period selected by Iowa is the most common length of time prescribed.

Appellant contends that the Iowa requirement of one year's residence is unconstitutional for two separate reasons: first, because it establishes two classes of persons and discriminates against those who have recently exercised their right to travel to Iowa, *** and, second, because it denies a litigant the opportunity to make an individualized showing of bona fide residence and therefore denies such residents access to the only method of legally dissolving their marriage. *

State statutes imposing durational residency requirements were, of course, invalidated when imposed by States as a qualification for welfare payments, *Shapiro, supra*; for voting, *Dunn, supra*; and for medical care, *Maricopa County, supra*. But none of those cases intimated that the States might never impose durational residency requirements, and such a proposition was in fact expressly disclaimed. What those cases had in common was that the durational residency requirements they struck down were justified on the basis of budgetary or recordkeeping considerations which were held insufficient to outweigh the constitutional claims of the individuals. But Iowa's divorce residency requirement is of a different stripe. Appellant was not irretrievably foreclosed from obtaining some part of what she sought, as was the case with the welfare recipients in *Shapiro*, the voters in *Dunn*, or the indigent patient in *Maricopa County*. She would eventually qualify for the same sort of adjudication which she demanded virtually upon her arrival in the State. Iowa's requirement delayed her access to the courts, but, by fulfilling it, she could ultimately have obtained the same opportunity for adjudication which she asserts ought to have been hers at an earlier point in time.

Iowa's residency requirement may reasonably be justified on grounds other than purely budgetary considerations or administrative convenience. * A decree of divorce is not a matter in which the only interested parties are the State as a sort of 'grantor,' and a divorce petitioner such as appellant in the role of 'grantee.' Both spouses are obviously interested in the proceedings, since it will affect their marital status and very likely their property rights. Where a married couple has minor children, a decree of divorce would usually include provisions for their custody and support. With consequences of such moment riding on a divorce decree issued by its courts, Iowa may insist that one seeking to initiate such a proceeding have the modicum of attachment to the State required here.

Such a requirement additionally furthers the State's parallel interests both in avoiding officious intermeddling in matters in which another State has a paramount interest, and in minimizing the susceptibility of its own divorce decrees to collateral attack. A State such as Iowa may quite reasonably decide that it does not wish to become a divorce mill for unhappy spouses who have lived there as short a time as appellant had when she commenced her action in the state court after having long resided elsewhere. Until such time as Iowa is convinced that appellant intends to remain in the State, it lacks the 'nexus between person and place of such permanence as to control the creation of legal relations and responsibilities of the utmost significance.' *Williams v. North Carolina*, 325 U.S. 226, 229 (1945). Perhaps even more important, Iowa's interests extend beyond its borders and include the recognition of its divorce decrees by other States under the Full Faith and Credit Clause of the Constitution, Art. IV, § 1. For that purpose, this Court has often stated that 'judicial power to grant a divorce-- jurisdiction, strictly speaking--is founded on domicil.' *Williams, supra*; *Andrews v. Andrews*, 188 U.S. 14 (1903); *Bell v. Bell*, 181 U.S. 175 (1901). Where a divorce decree is entered after a finding of domicile in ex parte proceedings, this Court has held that the finding of domicile is not binding upon another State and may be disregarded in the face of 'cogent evidence' to the contrary. *Williams, supra*, 325 U.S. at 236. For that reason, the State asked to enter such a decree is entitled to insist that the putative divorce petitioner satisfy something more than the bare minimum of constitutional requirements before a divorce may be granted. The State's decision to exact a one-year residency requirement as a matter of policy is therefore buttressed by a quite permissible inference that this requirement not only effectuates state substantive policy but likewise provides a greater safeguard against successful collateral attack than would a requirement of bona fide residence alone. This is precisely the sort of determination that a State in the exercise of its domestic relations jurisdiction is entitled to make.

We therefore hold that the state interest in requiring that those who seek a divorce from its courts be genuinely attached to the State, as well as a desire to insulate divorce decrees from the likelihood of collateral attack, requires a different resolution of the constitutional issue presented than was the case in *Shapiro, supra, Dunn, supra*, and *Maricopa County, supra*.

Nor are we of the view that the failure to provide an individualized determination of residency violates the Due Process Clause of the Fourteenth Amendment. *Vlandis v. Kline*, 412 U.S. 441 (1973), relied upon by appellant, held that Connecticut might not arbitrarily invoke a permanent and irrebuttable presumption of non-residence against students who sought to obtain in-state tuition rates when that presumption was not necessarily or universally true in fact. But in *Vlandis* the Court warned that its decision should not 'be construed to deny a State the right to impose on a student, as one element in demonstrating bona fide residence, a reasonable durational residency requirement.' *Id.*, at 452. *. An individualized determination of physical presence plus the intent to remain, which appellant apparently seeks, would not entitle her to a divorce even if she could have made such a showing. For Iowa requires not merely 'domicile' in that sense, but residence in the State for a year in order for its courts to exercise their divorce jurisdiction.

In *Boddie v. Connecticut, supra*, this Court held that Connecticut might not deny access to divorce courts to those persons who could not afford to pay the required fee. Because of the exclusive role played by the State in the termination of marriages, it was held that indigents could not be denied an opportunity to be heard 'absent a countervailing state interest of overriding significance.' *. But the gravamen of appellant Sosna's claim is not total deprivation, as in *Boddie*, but only delay. The operation of the filing fee in *Boddie* served to exclude forever a certain segment of the population from obtaining a divorce in the courts of Connecticut. No similar total deprivation is present in appellant's case, and the delay which attends the enforcement of the one-year durational residency requirement is, for the reasons previously stated, consistent with the provisions of the United States Constitution.

Affirmed.

Mr. Justice WHITE, dissenting.

***

Because I find that the case before the Court has become moot, I must respectfully dissent.

Mr. Justice MARSHALL, with whom Mr. Justice BRENNAN joins, dissenting.

***

The Court omits altogether what should be the first inquiry: whether the right to obtain a divorce is of sufficient importance that its denial to recent immigrants constitutes a penalty on interstate travel. In my view, it clearly meets that standard. The previous decisions of this Court make it plain that the right of marital association is one of the most basic rights conferred on the individual by the State. The interests associated with marriage and divorce have repeatedly been accorded particular deference, and the right to marry has been termed 'one of the vital personal rights essential to the orderly pursuit of happiness by free men.' *Loving v. Virginia*, 388 U.S. 1, 12 (1967). In *Boddie v. Connecticut*, 401 U.S. 371 (1971), we recognized that the right to seek dissolution of the marital relationship was closely related to the right to marry, as both involve the voluntary adjustment of the same fundamental human relationship. *Id.*, at 383. Without further laboring the point, I think it is clear beyond cavil that the right to seek dissolution of the marital relationship is of such fundamental importance that denial of this right to the class of recent interstate travelers penalizes interstate travel within the meaning of Shapiro, Dunn, and Maricopa County.

II

*** I continue to be of the view that the 'rational basis' test has no place in equal protection analysis when important individual interests with constitutional implications are at stake, ***
***

[The Court] ignores the severity of the deprivation suffered by the divorce petitioner who is forced to wait a year for relief. *** The year's wait prevents remarriage and locks both partners into what may be an intolerable, destructive relationship. ***
***

It is not enough to recite the State's traditionally exclusive responsibility for regulating family law matters; some tangible interference with the State's regulatory scheme must be shown. Yet in this case, I fail to see how any legitimate objective of Iowa's divorce regulations would be frustrated by granting equal access to new state residents. ***
***

*** Iowa has a legitimate interest in protecting itself against invasion by those seeking quick divorces in a forum with relatively lax divorce laws, and it may have some interest in avoiding collateral attacks on its decree in other States. These interests, however, would adequately be protected by a simple requirement of domicile--physical presence plus intent to remain--which would remove the rigid one-year barrier while permitting the State to restrict the availability of its divorce process to citizens who are genuinely its own.

b. Homestate Divorce Procedures

Find the statutes that govern proceedings in divorce in your homestate, and find the leading court rules applicable in such cases.

c. Notes and Questions

1) *Sosna* notes

Would the result have been different if the durational residency requirement had been two years? Three years? Five years? Are there any circumstances in which a delay in obtaining a divorce decree might (like a delay in obtaining an abortion) undermine entirely the claim for the relief sought?

In *Boddie v. Connecticut*, 401 U.S. 371 (1971), cited in *Sosna*, the Court held that because of the fundamental importance of marriage in society and because the state had monopolized the means for dissolving marriage, due process of law prevented a state from denying access to that exclusive means of dissolution (judicial divorce), solely because of indigency. Do *Sosna* and *Boddie* protect access to divorce and (re-)marriage, or just divorce? After *Lawrence v. Texas*, 539 U.S. 558 (2003), is marriage still so important? At one time, many states forbade marriage between a divorced adulterer and his or her paramour. Would such laws be valid today under *Sosna? Boddie? Lawrence?*

2) Complex procedures

Divorce cases, historically as well as now, seem to involve especially complex procedures. In addition to jurisdiction, venue, and duration of residency requirements, statutes and court rules may regulate such matters as the labels by which the pleaders are known (for example, petitioner instead of plaintiff, etc.), waiting periods before hearings or final decrees may be entered, periods in which the judgment is interlocutory rather than final, special courts in which the action must be filed, special judicial officers (often a sub-judge or lower-judge called a commissioner, magistrate, etc.) who hears the matter in the first instance, requirements for mediation of certain issues before they can be brought to the court, methods or mandates for sealing court records, rules governing confidentiality of certain proceedings, special procedures for preliminary or interlocutory or pendente lite relief or remedies, special summary procedures applicable only in some cases, separate procedures for protective orders, etc.

3) Bifurcated Divorce Proceedings

In a number of states, divorce statutes authorize the bifurcation of divorce. Typically, these provisions empower a court to enter a divorce final decree terminating the marital relationship before resolving contested issues pertaining to custody, alimony, child support and property division. In many states where no statute explicitly authorizes bifurcated divorce proceedings, divorce courts may exercise their inherent power to manage and administer pending cases to bifurcate divorce cases. The attraction of "bifurcation" of divorce is the separation of the easy from the difficult issues, allowing the uncontested issues to be determined without the delay of waiting for resolution of the contested issues. Perhaps judges (and lawyers) also hope that the parties will come to some agreement on the remaining issues before they come to trial. On the other hand, in some states, statutes explicitly forbid the entry of a divorce decree in some cases before or without including a determination of specific issues (e.g., no divorce decree may be entered in a case involving parents of minor children without specific provision respecting custody and support of the children).

4) Legal Separation and Annulment

A proceeding for divorce or dissolution is separate and different from a proceeding for legal separation or for annulment. A dissolution or divorce proceeding alleges the existence of grounds which give rise to a claim seeking the relief of terminating a marriage. A legal separation proceeding alleges the existence of grounds (usually very similar to divorce grounds) which give rise to a claim for relief seeking the relief of maintaining the legal status and benefits of marriage but entitling the parties to live separate and apart (which otherwise probably would constitute a ground for divorce as abandonment). A proceeding for annulment seeks a declaration nullifying the marriage either prospectively (for defects that render the marriage voidable) or *ab initio* (for defects that render the marriage void *ab initio*. Annulment is discussed *supra* in Part II, generally, and Chapter 3, specifically. Legal Separation is discussed in Chapter 18, *supra* and Chapter 30, *infra*.

5) Divorce Reform Proposals

In recent years there has been growing discussion of proposals for divorce reform to convey the message that other solutions to marital problems should be considered and attempted before seeking divorce, especially if the couple has children. *See* Wardle, *Divorce Reform, infra.* As noted in Chapter 6, *supra*, three states have adopted "covenant marriage" laws giving couples the option of entering a marital regime in which the parties are obligated to seek counseling before filing for divorce, and in which divorce may only be granted in the case of serious marital misconduct or after an extended period of separation. In 2006, the Marriage Movement, a group of clinical marriage professionals (mostly marriage counselors) and academics (including one of the authors of this book), signed a statement calling for divorce law reforms including longer waiting periods (up to two years) for divorce, and additional procedural protections when there are children. Institute, *infra*. What (if any) procedural reforms might help parties unhappy in their marriages explore and find alternatives to marital dissolution? Should it be public policy to discourage divorce in some cases? Are divorce procedures an appropriate tool to promote such a policy? Why/why not?

3. Practical and Ethical Considerations

Perhaps the greatest decision-making influence in divorce cases is money. Lawyers want (and usually need, and sometimes deserve) to be paid. Without the "reality check" of having to pay for legal services, the emotions in the divorce process can drive parties to bitterly contest even the most frivolous matters and to litigate (kicking, spitting, and cussing) until the courts lock the courthouse doors. By charging a reasonable fee, lawyers can help clients realize that despite the disappointment of the failure of their marriage expectations and despite the injuries inflicted by their former spouse, they need to get on with their lives; they cannot afford to obsess on the pains and disappointments of divorce needlessly and endlessly. On the other hand, many clients need the "venting" process afforded by divorce litigation; they yearn for somebody to affirm that they have been "done dirty." Lawyers who are too quick to settle and end the proceedings deprive their clients of the opportunity that a "day in court" provides to come to closure, to properly close that chapter of their lives. What should the lawyer do whose client needs more legal service but cannot afford it (like the poor man who stood before Justice Maule, *supra*)?

4. Bibliography

William Blackstone, Commentaries on the Laws of England *.

General Intelligence, *Marriage and Divorce in Legal History*, 171 The Law Times 462 (London, May 30, 1931).

Herbie DiFonzo, *Customized Marriage*, 75 Ind. L. J. 875 (2000).

Herma Hill Kay, *From the Second Sex to the Joint Venture: An Overview of Women's Rights and Family Law in the United States During the Twentieth Century*, 88 Calif. L. Rev. 2017 (2000).

Institute for American Values, Center for Marriage and Families, Marriage and the Law: A Statement of Principles (2006).

Gary H. Nichols, Note, *Covenant Marriage: Should Tennessee Join the Noble Experiment?* 29 U. Mem. L. Rev. 397 (1999).

Rayden's Practice and Law of Divorce (9th ed., Joseph Jackson, C.F. Turner, & D.R. Ellison eds., 1964)

R. Michael Rogers & John P. Palmer, *A Speaking Analysis of ADR Legislation for the Divorce Neutral,* 31 St. Mary's L.J. 871 (2000).

J .Clay Smith, *Charlotte E.Ray Pleads Before Court,* 43 How. L. J. 121 (2000).

Lynn D. Wardle, *Divorce Reform at the Turn of the Millennium: Certainties and Possibilities,* 33 Fam. L.Q. 783 (1999).

CHAPTER 26

Grounds; Consequences; Reform Movement

A. GROUNDS

1. Background

a. Putting Asunder

3 ¶ The Pharisees also came unto him, tempting him, and saying unto him, Is it lawful for a man to put away his wife for every cause? 4 And he answered and said unto them, Have ye not read, that he which made [them] at the beginning made them male and female, 5 And said, For this cause shall a man leave father and mother, and shall cleave to his wife: and they twain shall be one flesh? 6 Wherefore they are no more twain, but one flesh. What therefore God hath joined together, let not man put asunder.

7 They say unto him, Why did Moses then command to give a writing of divorcement, and to put her away? 8 He saith unto them, Moses because of the hardness of your hearts suffered you to put away your wives: but from the beginning it was not so.

9 And I say unto you, Whosoever shall put away his wife, except [it be] for fornication, and shall marry another, committeth adultery: and whoso marrieth her which is put away doth commit adultery.

10 His disciples say unto him, If the case of the man be so with [his] wife, it is not good to marry.

11 But he said unto them, All [men] cannot receive this saying, save [they] to whom it is given.

12 For there are some eunuchs, which were so born from [their] mother's womb: and there are some eunuchs, which were made eunuchs of men: and there be eunuchs, which have made themselves eunuchs for the kingdom of heaven's sake. He that is able to receive [it], let him receive [it].

-Matthew 19:3-12 (KJV).

b. History of Divorce Grounds and Procedures

Historically, divorce, like marriage, was primarily a matter of ecclesiastical regulation. And during most of Christian-European history, the Church did not generally permit divorce. Marriage was terminable by annulment, on rather narrow grounds; otherwise, most persons who were unhappily yoked only could obtain what today would be called a formal separation (*divoce a mensa et thoro*). Divorce came to Christian Europe with the Protestant Reformation. England was slower than some continental countries to embrace the Reformation, and was likewise slower to permit divorce. Ecclesiastical (canon) law remained in place until Henry VIII's famous break with the Catholic church in 1529 over its refusal to grant him a divorce. Yet even after England separated from the Catholic Church, divorce remained very rare.

645

Blackstone explained that divorce was only granted by ecclesiastical courts or
Parliament upon cause of adultery.

> *** [T]he canon law, which the common law follows in this case, deems so highly
> and with such mysterious reverence of the nuptial tie, that it will not allow it to be
> loosened for any cause whatsoever, that arises after the union is made. And this is said
> to be built on the divine revealed law; though that expressly assigned incontinence as
> a cause, and indeed the only cause, why a man may put away his wife and marry
> another. ***[I]n England adultery is only a cause of separation from bed and board:
> for which the best reason that can be given, is, that if divorces were allowed to depend
> upon a matter within the power of either [of] the parties, they would probably be
> extremely frequent; as was the case when divorces were allowed for canonical
> disabilities, on the mere confession of the parties, which is now prohibited by the
> canons. However, divorces *a vinculo matrimonii,* for adultery, have of late years been
> frequently granted by act of parliament.

I Blackstone, *infra* at *440-441. Parliamentary divorce was rare. Between 1670 and
1857 (when parliament passed a bill allowing judicial divorce) it is estimated that
there were only 375 divorces in all of England. Nichols, *infra,* at 55-56.

> While England had ecclesiastical courts to govern domestic relations prior to the
> mid-nineteenth century, the United States had no comparable mechanism. During this
> period, the state of divorce and divorce law in America differed depending upon the
> geographical area of the country. In New England, the Puritans legalized divorce in
> the mid-1600s. The Puritans viewed marriage as a civil contract that could be
> terminated, rather than a sacrament that could not end except upon a spouse's death.
> Even with divorce a possibility, the states of New England granted no more than
> ninety divorces before 1700. Some of the middle colonies enacted limited divorce
> laws; however, these laws generally only allowed a governor to grant a divorce. The
> Southern colonies remained conservative and did not grant divorces. Divorce during
> the American colonial period was rare, just as it was in England.
> ***
>
> [During the nineteenth century, even though both legislative and judicial divorces
> were available, they were neither common nor popular.] "The [Tennessee]
> Legislature granted only 26% of the legislative divorce petitions. According to
> scholars, Tennessee courts were equally intolerant." Southern judges "looked with
> disfavor upon divorce and often gave conservative readings to general divorce
> statutes."

Nichols, *infra.*

c. Traditional Fault Grounds for and Defenses Against Divorce

By the end of the nineteenth century, all states allowed divorce in cases where one
party's marital conduct fell below minimum standards of social tolerance. Divorce
laws defined the outer boundaries of marital misbehavior that society deemed
necessarily tolerable and provided an aggrieved spouse with an escape hatch to
terminate a marriage to a partner whose misconduct was intolerable. The defendant
spouse had to have breached the core, material terms of the marital contract. The

theory of breach of the marital contract provided a solid paradigm for reconciling the cases and doctrines. The breach had to be substantial because the public policy in favor of upholding marriages was very strong. Brinig, *infra.*

Today, fault grounds for divorce survive in most states, along-side of no-fault divorce grounds. The most common statutory fault grounds for divorce in America are adultery and desertion. Nearly two-thirds of the American states provide for divorce on these grounds. Adultery had to involve consensual sexual intercourse with a person other than the spouse; thus neither rape nor non-intercourse sexual conduct was ground for divorce as adultery. Elaborate rules of proof were developed to protect the defendant (because adultery was also a crime), as well as to avoid collusion. Many cases involved testimony of private investigators, which added an unseemly quality to the judicial proceeding and contributed to the adoption of no-fault divorce. Desertion is the voluntary departure from the marital abode without the other spouse's fault, consent or acquiescence, and the living apart for a specified time. Construction desertion could occur when the parties continued to live together but one refused to perform marital duties, including marital sexual relations, or where the leaving party had been forced out by the deserting party. In some states, nonsupport was also an element of the cause of action. *Id.*

In more than 20 states divorce is available on grounds of separation for a specified period. The length of time required varies from six months to three years. Usually a judicial decree of separation is required. Generally sporadic sex or dating after separation does not defend a claim for divorce on the ground of separation; but resuming husband-wife relations does.

Nearly as many jurisdictions allow divorce on grounds of mental illness or insanity. Usually special procedures must be followed in divorce proceedings alleging this ground. Generally permanent incompetence is necessary, a guardian *ad litem* must be appointed, and the court takes care to see that the estate and interests of the incompetent spouse are fairly treated.

Half of the states allow for divorce on the grounds of inhuman treatment or cruelty. Traditionally, "cruelty" was strictly construed to authorize divorce only for objectively severe mistreatment (originally only physical cruelty), and many cases still distinguish "cruelty" from mere "indignities." But generally cruelty is established if the complainant convinces the court that the defendants conduct has made marriage objectively intolerable for him or her. "Mental cruelty" was adopted expressly by legislation in some states, and by judicial interpretation in others. Over the years, courts became lenient about what constituted sufficient "mental cruelty" to justify a divorce, and in practical effect, "cruelty" became the first "de facto" no-fault divorce grounds in some courts because any subjective designation of cruelty was sufficient.

Nearly half of the states allow divorce for habitual intoxication or addiction to drugs. Usually, however, a time period (to allow rehabilitation) is required for divorce on this ground. The nature of the problem had to be severe, as indicated by the modifier "habitual" used in most statutes.

Conviction of a felony or crime involving moral turpitude is a ground for divorce in about 16 jurisdictions. In another 12 states imprisonment is a ground for divorce.

There are, of course, many other grounds for divorce specified in the divorce statutes the 51 American jurisdictions. In total, there are 32 different grounds for divorce specified in these statutes. In some states particular defects which otherwise might render the marriage invalid are specifically listed as grounds for divorce, giving the offended party the option of suing for annulment or divorce.

Even the old "fault" divorce statutes provided for some no-fault divorces. For example, insanity was one of the traditional grounds for divorce. Most jurisdictions allowed divorce on grounds of insanity of the defendant spouse, even though this was technically not a "fault" ground for divorce, but a no-fault ground (i.e., the defendant did not choose to become insane, but the condition of insanity was deemed to render the marriage intolerable enough to justify divorce and allow the sane spouse to marry another). Likewise, many jurisdictions permitted divorce when the parties had lived separate and apart from each other for a period of time (usually under a decree of separation). Unless the separation decree could only be obtained for reason of fault, this would constitute another "no fault" ground for divorce under traditional fault divorce schemes.

Because the substantive grounds for divorce were specific and substantial, a number of specialized substantive defenses developed as well. These defenses were the source of much consternation and some of the criticism of traditional divorce. As traditional grounds for divorce still survive in many states, many of the traditional defenses also survive. For instance, the traditional defense of *collusion* is still specifically authorized by statute in 10 states, but statutorily abolished in 4 others. Collusion was a defense based on fraud in creating or establishing a ground for divorce and was aimed at preventing agreements by spouses to circumvent strict divorce laws by fabricating the grounds for divorce. The traditional defense of *recrimination* is listed as a defense in statutes in 4 states, but rejected by statute in 12 others. Recrimination was essentially the unclean hands defense. The recrimination defense alleged that the plaintiff was guilty of equally serious grounds for divorce and thus, as a matter of equity, was not entitled to the relief sought. *Provocation* was a related defense. Provocation was based on the notion of retaliation--that the defendant's marital misconduct was provoked by the plaintiff's misconduct. In 5 states *condonation* is still statutorily mentioned as a valid defense (and forgiveness is mentioned in another), while 8 other states specifically abolish condonation as a defense. Condonation was a defense based on forgiveness of the marital offense. Many cases held that sexual intercourse by the offended party with the offending party after the offense and with knowledge of it constituted condonation and prohibited the use of the marital offense as a ground for subsequent divorce. *Connivance* is specifically mentioned as a valid defense in 4 states by statute, and repudiated in 3 others. Connivance was a defense based on the participation of the spouse seeking in divorce and developing grounds for divorce by actually and intentionally creating an opportunity for divorce (e.g., "smoothing the path to the adulterous bed"). *Insanity* is specified as a statutory defense in 1 state, and rejected in 2 others. Delay or inappropriate lapse of time between the marital offense and bringing the action for divorce is specified as a defense in 5 jurisdictions by statute, and abolished in 2 others. Insanity has been traditionally a defense to fault divorce (except to divorce for reason of insanity). The trend ,especially since enactment of "no-fault" divorce, has been to restrict or abolish the traditional divorce defenses.

d. A Short History of the Adoption of No-Fault Divorce Laws in the United States

(The following excerpt is taken from Wardle, *infra*, at 83-96.)

In 1969, California became the first jurisdiction in America (and in the western world) to adopt a modern, purely "no-fault" divorce law when it passed the Family Law Act of 1969, which became effective in 1970. Previously the statutory grounds for divorce in California, as in most other states, consisted of several specific fault grounds, plus insanity. The 1969 Act eliminated all fault grounds for divorce and provided that, apart from the rare case of "incurable insanity," marriage could be terminated only upon the ground of "irreconcilable differences which have caused the irremediable breakdown of the marriage." The statute defined "irreconcilable differences" and "irremediable breakdown" in the broadest terms. The new, simplified judicial procedure was called an action for "dissolution of marriage" instead of an action for divorce, and evidence of marital misconduct was declared to be "improper" and "inadmissible."

The movement to modify California's divorce law actually began in 1963 "as an effort . . . to stem the rising tide of divorce [and] to lessen the very high divorce rate of the state as a whole and of some counties in particular." Legislative hearings in 1964 and an inconclusive legislative report in 1965 focused on "the incidence of family instability" and recommended further study. In 1966, the Governor of California appointed a Governor's Commission on the Family to study the problem and recommend a solution. Some members of the Commission, including Professor Herma Hill Kay of Boalt Hall Law School at the University of California at Berkeley, strongly favored the adoption of no-fault divorce grounds. In December 1966, the Commission submitted its final report recommending the elimination of all fault-grounds for divorce, as well as the adoption of an extensive family court system. Although a bill implementing the recommendations of the Commission was introduced the following year, it lay quietly in the legislature until 1969, when, revised to eliminate the creation of the controversial family court system, it passed with surprisingly little public opposition.

While the California Governor's Commission was meeting in 1966 and preparing its report endorsing no-fault divorce grounds, it received a significant boost from the publication of the widely-heralded report of a group of distinguished individuals appointed by the Archbishop of Canterbury to make recommendations regarding reform of the fault-grounds for divorce in England. Their 1966 report, entitled Putting Asunder: A Divorce Law for Contemporary Society, acknowledged the shortcomings of the existing fault-based divorce system and suggested that divorce morally could be granted when there was such a complete "failure in the marital relationship" that the substance of the relationship had come "unmistakably and irreversibly to an end." However, the Archbishop's group also recommended that a thorough judicial "inquest" be conducted by the courts before granting divorce upon such grounds and rejected the concept of unilateral divorce (or even a right to divorce upon mutual consent). The report of the Archbishop's group was referred to the English Law Commission, which issued another report endorsing the marital breakdown principle and recommending that English divorce law be reformed to permit divorce with "the maximum of fairness, and the minimum of bitterness, distress, and humiliation" when it was determined that a marriage was irretrievably broken. Three years later, the British Parliament passed the Divorce Reform Act, 1969, which provided that divorce could be granted upon one ground only, "irretrievable breakdown." The Act further provided that irretrievable breakdown had to be shown by proof of traditional marital fault, living separate and apart for five years, or living separate and apart with mutual consent for two years. These developments in England did much to legitimize divorce reform in the United States, and while California's no-fault divorce law constituted a much more radical departure from the traditional divorce methods than the English law, the divorce reform movement in England undeniably helped clear the path for California's divorce reform.

The California divorce reform also benefitted from the reform of New York's divorce laws in 1966 and 1968. Before 1966, New York had not significantly reformed its substantive divorce law since it had been drafted by Alexander Hamilton in 1787. Divorce was permitted only upon proof of adultery. In 1965, the state legislature conducted public hearings at which strong support was provided for reforming New York divorce law. After "considerable maneuvering" to defuse any significant opposition, a divorce reform bill was passed in 1966 that added other "fault" grounds for divorce, including cruel and inhuman treatment that threatened the physical or mental well-being of the plaintiff and abandonment for two or more years. The divorce reform law also permitted divorce upon living apart for two years pursuant to a decree of separation or written separation agreement.

***

The no-fault divorce movement was further enhanced when the prestigious National Conference of Commissioners on Uniform State Laws (NCCUSL) endorsed no-fault divorce. By 1966, the NCCUSL had begun its own consideration of divorce law reform. By 1967, Professor Robert J. Levy of the University of Minnesota Law School had been appointed reporter for the drafting committee and had prepared a monograph recommending that irremediable marriage breakdown be adopted as the exclusive ground for divorce. Professor Levy was later joined by Professor Herma Hill Kay, who had been instrumental in California's trail-blazing no-fault reform effort. The proposals Professors Levy and Kay submitted to the NCCUSL committee were "little different from the approach of breakdown pure and simple that was to become the law of California." By the time the NCCUSL debated its committee's proposal, California had already acted. In 1970, shortly after the nation's first modern no-fault divorce law took effect in California, the NCCUSL voted to propose a Uniform Marriage and Divorce Act (UMDA) in which the sole ground for divorce was a modern no-fault ground. While acknowledging "the State's interest in the stability of marriages," the NCCUSL proposed to "totally eliminate[] the traditional concept that divorce is a remedy granted to an innocent spouse." The UMDA draft that was approved by the NCCUSL in 1970 authorized the dissolution of marriage solely upon the ground "that the marriage is irretrievably broken." Moreover, it explicitly provided that property division, spousal maintenance, and child support decisions were to be made "without regard to marital misconduct." Thus, in some respects, it represented a more radical or more complete departure from prior concepts of marriage and divorce than the California law.

For various reasons, the American Bar Association initially declined to endorse the proposed UMDA. Extensive negotiations between the NCCUSL and the ABA followed, and in 1973, the NCCUSL adopted relatively minor revisions to the UMDA. The following year, the ABA approved the revised UMDA.

Altogether, these developments ignited a movement to reform divorce laws that quickly spread throughout the United States. After California adopted its no-fault divorce law in 1969, "[n]o-fault divorce spread like a prairie fire." Between 1971 and 1977, eight states adopted the UMDA at least in part and more than three times that number of states adopted some other form of no-fault divorce. By 1989, forty-nine states and the District of Columbia had explicitly adopted some "modern no-fault" ground for divorce.

Currently, statutes in twenty American jurisdictions provide that divorce is generally available solely upon modern no-fault grounds. In fifteen of these states, "irretrievable breakdown" of the marriage, or "irreconcilable differences" between the spouses is the sole statutory ground for divorce. In two other jurisdictions, the sole ground for divorce is that the parties have lived separate and apart for a short period of time (i.e., not more than one year). In the other three exclusively no-fault states, irretrievable breakdown (or incompatibility) and living separate and apart for a short period of time are alternative grounds for divorce.

In thirty states, the legislatures have added at least one modern no-fault ground for divorce as an alternative to fault-grounds for divorce. Nineteen of these states simply have added marital breakdown, incompatibility, or irreconcilable differences to the traditional grounds for divorce. One state added both a modern breakdown provision and a modern "short separation" provision as alternatives to the traditional fault grounds for divorce. Three others have added a combined requirement of both irretrievable breakdown and a short separation to the traditional grounds for divorce. The remaining seven of these thirty states have added living separate and apart for a short period of time as the sole no-fault ground for divorce to the list of traditional grounds for divorce.

In total, forty-one states have adopted modern no-fault language (breakdown, incompatibility or irreconcilable differences) as the exclusive or an alternative ground for divorce (including seven states that have adopted both modern no-fault terms and short separation periods), and eight other states and the District of Columbia have adopted a short separation period as their modern no-fault ground for divorce. Only one state, Arkansas, does not have a modern no-fault divorce provision of any kind.
***

The pro-no-fault divorce reform legal literature of the 1960s and 1970s asserted four general reasons or arguments for the adoption of no-fault divorce grounds.

First, no-fault divorce grounds were deemed desirable to reduce the hostility and distress of persons involved in divorce. Requiring proof of marital fault in all cases, subject to harsh and antiquated defenses (e.g., recrimination, condonation, collusion, connivance) which historically could preclude divorce even if fault were proven, was widely criticized for breeding costly, bitter, counterproductive litigation that impeded reconciliation. The adversary system and fault-laying substantive grounds proved unworkable. As two advocates of no-fault divorce wrote:
***

Second, advocates of no-fault divorce argued that adoption of no-fault was necessary to protect the integrity of the legal system. There was, in fact, a "tide of discontent" over "the trail of perjury and subterfuge that [traditional fault-based divorce grounds] ha[d] brought into the courts." ***

Thus, advocates of no-fault divorce argued that the integrity and respectability of the legal system and all involved with it would be improved if no-fault divorce grounds were adopted because "sham grounds," "sham residence," "collusion, perjury and hypocrisy" would disappear.

Third, the gap between the law-as-written and the law-as-applied was the focus of another major argument for the adoption of no-fault divorce. Realistically, divorce by mutual consent was generally available without fault before 1970, through collusion or migratory divorce. In states like California, in which mental cruelty was a ground for divorce, ninety-five percent of all divorces were obtained on that ground, which functioned as a de facto no-fault ground. Nationally, unilateral, uncontested, or mutual consent divorces constituted approximately ninety percent of all divorce cases. ***

Moreover, the inability of the law to enforce its policy beyond the realm of formalities was obvious: it could not force an unhappy spouse to live with a despised partner; abandonment--sometimes known as the "poor man's divorce," "common law divorce," or "de facto divorce"--has long been practiced. *** The English Law Commission estimated that nearly 20,000 children were born out of wedlock every year because access to divorce was so restrictive that their parents simply cohabited as lovers without bothering to get a divorce from their legal spouses. ***

The fourth argument asserted that basic notions of marriage and divorce had changed and that no-fault divorce more accurately reflected modern conceptions of terminating marital relations than did the prior laws. The notions that marital breakdown was the "fault" of one spouse entirely and that divorce was both a remedy awarded to the innocent spouse and a judgment imposed against the faulty spouse were widely rejected. *** Thus, by 1960, it was widely believed "that the fault grounds for divorce were usually symptoms rather than causes of the difficulties in marriages" and that the fault-based divorce system was "obsolete and mischievous."

Replacing the old fault-notion of divorce was the assertion that divorce was a private matter that the state had no legitimate interest to restrict when the marriage was irretrievably broken and the parties to the marriage had agreed to terminate the marriage. The thrust of this privacy argument went to protecting parties from unnecessary distress and embarrassing public disclosures. ***

2. Statutes, Cases and Doctrines

a. *Desrochers v. Desrochers*

Dana A. Desrochers v. Real J. Desrochers
347 A.2d 150 (N.H. 1975)

KENISON, Chief Justice.

The parties married in September 1970. Their only child, a daughter, was born in January 1973. The parties separated in May of that year and the wife brought this libel for divorce the following September. A month later the parties agreed to and the court approved arrangements for custody, visitation and support. The defendant did not support his wife and child from the time of separation until the temporary decree. He made the payments called for by the decree from its entry until June 1975. In July 1974, the Hillsborough County Superior Court, Loughlin, J., held a hearing and made certain findings of fact. The critical portion of these findings is: '(T)he action was originally brought because the defendant did not work steadily and stated that he, when he learned that the plaintiff was pregnant, wanted a boy instead of a girl; if the plaintiff bore a girl he would like to put the child up for adoption. After the birth of the child (a daughter) the defendant became very attached to the child, has visited the child weekly except on two occasions, and has been faithfully making support payments under the temporary order of $25.00 a week. The defendant claims that he loves his wife, does not want a divorce. The wife claims that she no longer loves her husband, but since the filing of the divorce he has been an industrious worker and is very attached to the child.' The superior court transferred without ruling the question 'whether, on all the findings of fact, cause exists for granting a divorce under the provisions of RSA 458:7-a.' This appeal was argued in September 1975. At the argument counsel informed the court that the defendant had stopped making support payments and had gone to Nevada in June 1975. At that time he had written to his attorney expressing his desire to remain married.

RSA 458:7-a (Supp.1973) provides: 'A divorce from the bonds of matrimony shall be decreed, irrespective of the fault of either party, on the ground of irreconcilable differences which have caused the irremediable breakdown of the marriage. In any pleading or hearing of a libel for divorce under this section, allegations or evidence of specific acts of misconduct shall be improper and inadmissible, except where child custody is in issue and such evidence is relevant to establish that parental custody would be detrimental to the child or at a hearing where it is determined by the court to be necessary to establish the existence of irreconcilable differences. If, upon hearing of an action for divorce under this section, both parties are found to have committed an act or acts which justify a finding of irreconcilable differences, a divorce shall be decreed and the acts of one party shall not negate the acts of the other nor bar the divorce decree.' This section must be applied in conjunction with RSA 458:7-b (Supp.1973) which precludes divorce when 'there is a likelihood for rehabilitation of the marriage relationship' or when 'there is a reasonable possibility of reconciliation.' *Woodruff v. Woodruff,* 114 N.H. 365, 367-68, 320 A.2d 661, 663 (1974).

RSA 458:7-a (Supp.1973) is the product of a national discussion regarding the proper grounds for divorce. It follows in important respects the California Family Law Act of 1969. That statute, and others following it, have been criticized for vagueness, but have been held to be sufficiently definite to afford due process of law. *Ryan v. Ryan,* 277 So.2d 266 (Fla.1973); *In re Marriage of Walton,* 28 Cal.App.3d 108, 104 Cal.Rptr. 472 (1972). A consensus has emerged that a period of separation due to marital difficulties is strong evidence of the irremediable breakdown of a marriage. Cf. RSA 458:7 VI through XIII. These developments can be traced in the following commentaries: Bodenheimer, Reflections on the Future of Grounds for Divorce, 8 J.Fam.L. 179, 198-207 (1968); Foster and Freed, Divorce Reform: Brakes on Breakdown?, 13 J.Fam.L. 443, 448-453 (1973); Zuckman, The ABA Family Law Section v. The NCCUSL: Alienation, Separation and Forced Reconciliation over the Uniform Marriage and Divorce Act, 24 Cath.U.L.Rev. 61 (1974); and Annot., 55 A.L.R.3d 581 (1974). When asked to interpret a statute similar to RSA 458:7-a, the Florida Court of Appeal stated: 'The Legislature has not seen fit to promulgate guidelines as to what constitutes an 'irretrievably broken' marriage. It is suggested that this lack of definitive direction was deliberate and is desirable in an area as volatile as a proceeding for termination of the marital status. Consideration should be given to each case individually and predetermined policy should not be circumscribed by the appellate courts of this State.

'Thus, we are hesitant to set forth specific circumstances which trial courts could utilize as permissible indices of an irretrievable breakdown of the marital status. Were we to attempt to do so, we feel that the basic purpose of the new dissolution of marriage law would be frustrated. Such proceedings would either again become primarily adversary in nature or persons would again fit themselves into tailor-made categories or circumstances to fit judicially defined breakdown situations. It is our opinion that these two problems are the very ones which the Legislature intended to eliminate.' *Riley v. Riley,* 271 So.2d 181, 183 (Fla.App.1972).

The existence of irreconcilable differences which have caused the irremediable breakdown of the marriage is determined by reference to the subjective state of mind of the parties. *Woodruff v. Woodruff*, 114 N.H. 365, 367, 320 A.2d 661, 663 (1974). While the desire of one spouse to continue the marriage is evidence of 'a reasonable possibility of reconciliation,' it is not a bar to divorce. If one spouse resolutely refuses to continue and it is clear from the passage of time or other circumstances that there is no reasonable possibility of a change of heart, there is an irremediable breakdown of the marriage. H. Clark, Jr., Domestic Relations, s 12.5, at 351 (1968). Comment, Irreconcilable Differences: California Courts Respond to No-fault Dissolutions, 7 Loyola of L.A.L. Rev. 453, 459-60, 466, 485 et seq. (1974). The defendant may attempt to impeach the plaintiff's evidence of his or her state of mind regarding the relationship. If the trial court doubts plaintiff's evidence that the marriage has irremediably broken down, the court may continue the action to determine if reconciliation is possible. However, if the parties do not reconcile, dissolution should be granted.

Knowledge of the sources of marital discord is helpful in determining whether a breakdown is irremediable or whether there is a reasonable possibility of reconciliation. Yet the statutory test is the existing state of the marriage. The statute authorizes the trial court to receive evidence of specific acts of misconduct where it is determined by the court to be necessary to establish the existence of irreconcilable differences. This authority is an exception to the general rule of the statute excluding such evidence, and the intent of the statute to minimize the acrimony attending divorce proceedings.

The question whether a breakdown of a marriage is irremediable is a question to be determined by the trial court. *Woodruff v. Woodruff*, 114 N.H. 365, 367, 320 A.2d 661, 663 (1974). RSA 458:7-a contemplates the introduction of factual testimony sufficient to permit a finding of irreconcilable differences which have caused the irremediable breakdown of the marriage. *Rodrique v. Rodrique*, 113 N.H. 49, 52, 300 A.2d 312, 314 (1973). Nevertheless there are limits to the inquiry. 'In the first place, there is the natural tendency to withhold information of a personal nature from anyone but a trusted and discreet adviser; secondly, any probing into personal matters against the wishes of the party examined would be objectionable . . .; and thirdly, the parties have come to court for a purpose. Their answers, which may be perfectly honest ones, will inevitably be slanted in the direction of their ultimate goal, which is divorce.' *Bodenheimer*, *. Within these limits the trial court must be adequately informed before acting in matters of such importance. But the statute does not contemplate a complete biopsy of the marriage relationship from the beginning to the end in every case. This is a difficult task, but judges face similar problems in other cases. *

The separation of the parties for two and one-half years and the plaintiff's persistence in seeking a divorce during that period is evidence from which the trial court could find that this marriage has irremediably broken down.

Remanded. All concurred.

b. Notes and Questions

1) *Desrochers* Note.

Should "irreconcilable differences which have caused the *irremediable* breakdown of the marriage" necessary and always be judged solely by "reference to the subjective state of mind of the parties," as the court in *Desrochers* indicates? Why/why not? If the parties have made no effort to resolve their differences, are they really *irremediable*? If the differences are objectively trivial, how can they be deemed *irreconcilable*? Could not the terms *irreconcilable* and *irremediable* refer to an objectively discerned "floor" of marital behavior below which there is a strong community consensus that the marital relationship is irremediable? If one party has been saintly in his marital behavior while the other has consistently acted in a manner that would offend even the most hardened person (violence, infidelity, debasing, etc.), should the law prohibit a declaration of relative responsibility for what clearly effects and harms public society (as well as the private parties and their children)?

2) Do No-Fault Divorce Laws Breed Divorce?

The conventional wisdom is that adoption of no-fault grounds for divorce have not caused divorce rates to increase. Professor Jacob noted that "[e]very study of the impact of these [no-fault] laws on divorce rates has concluded that no relationship existed between the introduction of no-fault and the rise in divorce." For decades defenders of no-fault divorce have denied that liberal divorce laws cause any increase in divorce. The main evidence to support this conclusion is that "divorce rates began increasing about eight years before no-fault laws were passed, and that increases in divorce rates were similar for states with and without no-fault statutes . . . ." Dixon, *infra;* Mazur-Hart, *infra*; Schoen, *infra*; Sell, *infra*; and Wright, *infra*.

However, the early studies have been faulted recently for flaws in data used, research design, oversimplicity, and other technical problems. Moreover, even some of the early studies reported a positive correlation between the adoption of no-fault divorce grounds and increases in divorce rates in at least some states. For example, Professor Marvell's comprehensive statistical research has shown a significant causal relationship between adoption of no-fault divorce in individual states and the increase of divorce rates in most states. Of the thirty-five states examined with new no-fault divorce laws effective before 1980, twenty-five experienced higher than average increases in divorce rates when the no-fault laws went into effect, and in eleven states, the increase in the rate of divorce was more than twice the previous rate of increase. Professor Marvell concluded that "[n]o-fault laws, operationalized as a single variable, had a significant impact on divorce rates, with the major thrust delayed for a year."

Moreover, it is apparent that the significant rise in the divorce rate in the United States did not begin until the no-fault divorce reform movement was well-underway. The no-fault divorce movement was well underway by the time the divorce rates for the United States began their significant climb in 1967, from 2.5 divorces per 1000 people (1966) to 5.3 (1979 and 1981). During the years that the legislatures in the American states were adopting no-fault divorce laws, the divorce rates rose abruptly and significantly; and since the no-fault divorce reform movement peaked (leaving virtually every state with some form of no- fault divorce), the divorce rates has stabilized again--at a significantly higher rate of divorce than has ever been recorded, much less maintained, in recorded modern history. (The United States now has the highest rate of divorce of any western nation.) In light of these society-wide trends, it begs the question to argue that because the legislature in a particular state was slower to enact no-fault than in sister states, the adoption of no-fault divorce laws elsewhere did not contribute to the increase in divorce rates inside that state. Thus, it is unsurprising that in a recent study using archival data from the National Center for Health Statistics, researchers at the University of Oklahoma found that no-fault divorce laws had a significant positive effect on the divorce rate across the fifty states. Nakonezny, *infra.*

Of course, it is impossible to determine precisely how much no-fault divorce laws have contributed to the increased divorce rates. Many social forces have apparently contributed to this "boom" in divorce. However, the best evidence indicates that in at least some states the adoption of no-fault divorce was *a* significant factor in increasing divorce rates. Moreover, it seems plausible that no-fault divorce laws in conjunction with other social factors have made divorce an easier and more frequently invoked solution to marital problems than reformers intended.

Both the rise in divorce rates *and* the laws come from the same source, changing values and norms in the larger society, alterations in economic opportunities, political ideologies, even the models presented by the mass media." And as people will try to get divorced, they also will try to liberalize the grounds for divorce, so both developments occur proximately. Goode, *infra* at 322. "The law does have an impact at the margins. Thus those who are not totally determined to divorce [and the poor] are influenced by restrictive laws and administrative hurdles . . . ." *Id,* at 323. Thus, thirty years ago Professor Max Rheinstein noted that a study by a University of Chicago graduate student found that a comparatively high incidence of divorce and breakdown was associated with more liberal divorce laws. However, increased divorce was also associated with other factors including industrialization, economic position of women, religion, urbanization, and the degree of comparative "settledness" or "restlessness" in the area. Rheinstein, *infra* at 306. (Excerpted from Wardle, *infra*).

3) Do Divorce Lawyers and Judges Breed Divorce?

In his review of how legislation in California designed to reduce divorce became the landmark no-fault divorce procedures, Professor Herbie DiFonzo puts substantial responsibility on the divorce bar and local divorce (trial) courts, who wanted divorce reform that would make their practice more convenient, and who insisted on applying the new divorce grounds as eliminating any objective basis for examination of grounds for divorce. DiFonzo, *No-Fault, infra.*

4) Impairment of Contracts?

In *Dartmouth College v. Woodward* 4 Wheat 518 629 (1819) Chief Justice Marshall stated, in pertinent part:

> The [Contracts Clause] of the constitution never has been understood to embrace other contracts, than those which respect property, or some object of value, and confer rights which may be asserted in a court of justice. It never has been understood to restrict the general right of the legislature to legislate on the subject of divorces. Those acts enable some tribunals, not to impair a marriage contract, but to liberate one of the parties, because it has been broken by the other. *When any state legislature shall pass an act annulling all marriage contracts, or allowing either party to annul it, without the consent of the other, it will be time enough to inquire, whether such an act be constitutional. Dartmouth College v. Woodward* (1819) 4 Wheat 518, 629 (emphasis added).

Concurring, Justice Storey explained:

As to the case of the contract of marriage, which the argument supposes not to be within the reach of the prohibitory clause, because it is matter of civil institution, I profess not to feel the weight of the reason assigned for the exception. In a legal sense, all contracts, recognized as valid in any country, may be properly said to be matters of civil institution, since they obtain their obligation and construction *jure loci contractus*. . . . A general law, regulating divorces from the contract of marriage, like a law regulating remedies in other cases of breaches of contracts, is not necessarily a law impairing the obligation of such a contract. (a) It may be the only effectual mode of enforcing the obligations of the contract on both sides. . . . Thus far the contract of marriage has been considered with reference to general laws regulating divorces upon breaches of that contract. *But if the argument means to assert, that the legislative power to dissolve such a contract, without such a breach on either side, against the wishes of the parties, and without any judicial inquiry to ascertain a breach, I certainly am not prepared to admit such a power, or that its exercise would not entrench upon the prohibition of the constitution.*

Dartmouth College v. Woodward (1819) 4 Wheat 518 at 696. (emphasis added). If a couple were married when divorce was only obtainable on "fault" grounds, and now the wife sues for "no-fault" divorce, does the husband have an "impairment of contracts" constitutional objection to application of the no-fault divorce laws to his marriage?

5) Non-substantive Defenses

With the practical elimination of substantive defenses to no-fault divorce, what defenses remain to be invoked by the client who opposes a divorce?

6) Public Policy Against Considering Fault

Some courts have interpreted no-fault divorce laws so broadly as to preclude considering marital misconduct in any proceeding relating to marriage. For example, in *Diosdado v. Diosdado*, 118 Cal.Rptr.2d 494 (Cal.App. 2002), a California appellate panel refused to enforce a liquidated damages provision because it penalized adultery. Five years after the parties married, Wife learned that Husband had an adulterous affair, and the parties separated. They reconciled and signed a Marital Settlement Agreement which contained a fidelity clause in which they agreed not to engage in any physical romantic or sexual contact outside of the marriage. A liquidated damages provision provided that if either party violated the fidelity clause, he would leave the house, pay $50,000 as damages, plus costs and attorneys fees in resulting litigation. That was payable in addition to and "irrespective of, any property settlement and/or support obligation imposed by law as a result of said divorce proceeding." Five years later, H had another adulterous affair. W sued for divorce and to enforce the liquidated damages provision. The trial court declined to enforce the provision, finding it contrary to public policy. The appellate court affirmed, emphasizing that under California's no-fault divorce statute, marital fault is wholly irrelevant to and inadmissible in dissolution proceedings (except rarely relating to child custody). Even though the parties had agreed that a "breach of fidelity by one party hereto may cause serious emotional, physical and financial injury to the other," and W proffered evidence that she experienced such harm and suffering, the court construed the no-fault statutes as absolutely barring consideration of marital fault in dissolution, property division, or alimony.

Is this court's reasoning sound? The court found the liquidated damages provision inconsistent with no-fault dissolution, property division and alimony. However, the contractual obligation was expressly and legally separate, distinct, and severable from those other claims. The court concluded that it violated public policy solely because the payment was based on adultery (marital misconduct). Yet what evidence is there (apart from the Hollywood culture) that adultery is such a favored public policy in California that a freely negotiated contractual restriction of it must be struck down? The court provided no legislative history to support its conclusion that the no-fault divorce statute was intended to make any prohibition of adultery a violation of public policy. If unmarried parties (say a church and a minister) signed a contract with a provision prohibiting and imposing liquidated damages for adultery, would that contract between strangers also be void against public policy? Why/why not? If not, why should strangers be able to so contract, but the persons most directly interested (and at greatest risk of suffering the emotional pain resulting from adultery) not be allowed to so contract? Is it because infidelity really does not hurt the betrayed spouse or children?

3. Practical and Ethical Considerations

(a) Should the strong social interest in marriage influence how a lawyer responds to a client seeking a divorce or how she practices divorce law? Professor DiFonzo makes a strong case that no-fault divorce reform (at least in California) was not intended to become unilateral divorce on demand, and that initially the appellate courts indicated that "irreconcilable" differences and "irretrievable" breakdown" meant that proof that the differences were actually "irreconcilable, and the breakdown truly was "irretrievable." He alleges that it was the trial judges and divorce lawyers who insisted that the no-fault divorce reform law be applied in a "rubber stamp" manner as if it authorized unilateral divorce-on-demand. Difonzo, *infra.*

(b) Should a lawyer try to persuade her client to include "fault" grounds for divorce if they arguably exist, in addition to no-fault, even if the client initially requests a "no-fault" divorce? Should a lawyer try to persuade her client to eliminate "fault" allegations even if they exist, if the client wants to make such allegations, even if it is likely that no-fault grounds will suffice? Why/why not? Should a lawyer try to persuade a divorce client of anything, or should she just be a passive "hired gun" doing the client's bidding? Has a lawyer who fails to refer his client to other professionals who might resolve (more inexpensively, less traumatically, more effectively than divorce) the problems that are driving the client to divorce committed malpractice? Violated professional responsibilities?

(c) Should lawyers be involved in trying to enact divorce reforms? Bar Associations? State Judicial Councils? Why/why not?

(d) Assume that you are practicing in a state in which there are no meaningful substantive defenses to a petition for no-fault divorce, and a woman who has been married for 25 years and has four children hires you to represent her in the divorce action filed by her husband. She does not want a divorce for a lot of very strong personal reasons. She says her husband has been a wonderful husband throughout their marriage, and she does not want to lose him now. She thinks he is going through a "mid-life crisis," and has become temporarily infatuated with his new, 22-year-old secretary. Your client believes that in a few months, at most two years, her husband will snap out of his infantile reversion and she is prepared to patiently endure his faithless mid-life fling for that long, and to forgive him. Apart from nominating your client for sainthood, what legal counsel would you give your client, and why?

4. Bibliography

1 William Blackstone, Commentaries on the Laws of England *.

Contemporary Family Law, vol. 2, Ch. 19 & vol. 3, Ch. 20 (1988).

J. Herbie DiFonzo, *No-Fault Marital Dissolution: The Bitter Triumpth of Naked Divorce*, 31 San Diego L. Rev 519 (1994).

J. Herbie DiFonzo, *Customized Marriage*, 75 Ind. L. J. 875 (2000).

Dixon & Weitzman, *Evaluating the Impact of No-Fault Divorce in California*, 29 Fam Relations 297 (1980).

William J. Goode, World Changes in Divorce Patterns (1993).

Mazur-Hart & Berman, *Changing from Fault to No-Fault Divorce: An Interrupted Time Series Analysis*, 7 J. Applied Soc. Psycho. 300 (1977).

Paul A. Nakonezny, Robert D. Shull, Joseph Lee Rodgers. *The Effect of No-Fault Divorce Law on the Divorce Rate Across the 50 States and Its Relation to Income, Education, and Religiosity*, J. Marr, & Fam., May 1995, at 477 (noted in *http://www.divorcereform.org/stats.html* (Divorce/Marriage Statistics).

Gary H. Nichols, Note, *Covenant Marriage: Should Tennessee Join the Noble Experiment?* 29 U. Mem. L. Rev. 397 (1999).

Rayden's Practice and Law of Divorce (9th ed., Joseph Jackson, C.F. Turner, & D.R. Ellison eds., 1964).

Max Rheinstein, Marriage Stability, Divorce and the Law (1972).

Schoen, Breenblatt, & Meilke, *California's Experience with Nonadversary Divorce*, 12 Demography 223 (1975).

Sell, *Divorce Law Reform and Increasing Divorce Rates* in Current Issues in Marriage and the Family (J. Wells ed. 1979).

Lynn Wardle, *No-Fault Divorce and the Divorce Conundrum*, 1991 B.Y.U.L.Rev. 79.

3 Contemporary Family Law, Chapter 21, No-Fault Divorce (Callaghan 1988).

Wright & Stetson, *The Impact of No-Fault Divorce Law and Reform on Divorce in American States*, 40 J. Marr. & Fam. 575 (1978).

B. Consequences of Divorce

1. Background

a. Personal Consequences of Divorce

Divorce is an economic disaster for most families. The economic security of individuals and society are inextricably linked to the stability and continuity of families. The family is a remarkably efficient economic unit. When that unit is broken and two economic units must subsist instead of one, the overall costs increase. Thus, it should come as no surprise to discover that divorce creates economic distress for most of the individuals affected. In the overwhelming majority of cases divorce *impoverishes* women and children, and often creates economic hardship for men as well. *See* Weitzman, *infra.*

Of course, financial distress is not the only type of personal trauma associated with divorce. Divorce is a traumatic event for individuals and a major cause of psycho-

social disruption. One writer summarized some of the detrimental consequences of
divorce that are identified in professional literature.

> There is now an enormous body of professional literature testifying to the fact that
> marital disruption is a causal factor connected with a wide variety of personal and
> social ills. . .
> Of all the social variables whose relationships with the distribution of
> psychopathology in the population have been studied, none has been more
> consistently and powerfully associated with [mental disorders] than marital status."
> Marital disruption can precipitate intense and complicated emotional responses.
> Heatherington . . . found that divorced parents felt more anxious, depressed, angry,
> rejected, and incompetent that married persons. Divorced men and women both
> experienced changes in self-concept . . . Fathers felt a lack of identity, rootlessness,
> and complained of a lack of structure in their lives . . . Divorced women complained
> of feeling unattractive, helpless, and of having lost their identity as married women.
> The rate of admission to mental institutions for inpatient treatment has been shown
> to be from seven to twenty-two times higher for divorced and separated men than for
> married men, and from three to eight times higher for divorced or separated women
> than married women. Likewise, the rates of admission for outpatient mental health
> treatment are significantly higher for divorced and separated persons than for
> married persons.
> The relationship between stress and physical health has long been known. There is
> growing evidence that the trauma and anxiety of divorce and separation are among
> the most stressful and difficult-to-cope-with human experiences. A seminal study,
> published in 1968, reported that of all major life events, divorce and separation were
> decisively ranked among the most stressful and difficult to cope with (rating 73 and
> 65, respectively, on a 100-point scale), consistently surpassing in intensity and
> difficulty almost all other life crises including such major catastrophes as going to
> jail (rated 63), losing a job (rated 47), personal injury or illness (rated 51), and
> mortgage foreclosure (rated 30). In fact, only the death of a spouse (rated 100) was
> found to be more stressful. . . .
> Thus, it is no surprise that divorced and separated persons have more health
> problems than married individuals. For instance, although married persons suffer
> slightly more chronic diseases than divorced, widowed, and single persons, they
> "have significantly fewer chronic conditions (50% fewer) which limit their
> activities. . . . Although a higher percentage of married than unmarried persons have
> hospital insurance, "the typical single, widowed, or divorced individual remains far
> longer in the hospital for the identical medical problems than do married people. . . .
> The overall death rate for white persons and the death rate for coronary heart
> diseases for all persons are significantly higher for divorced individuals than single,
> widowed, or married persons. The divorced and separated also have a higher
> incidence of high blood pressure, alcoholism, automobile accidents, and suicide than
> married persons. One study concluded that it usually takes from two to four years
> for divorced persons to recover from the emotional distress of divorce.
> ***

Wardle (1983), *infra,* at 30-34.
   More recent research indicates a woman who is aged 48 and married will have an
87% chance of living to age sixty-five, but a divorced woman, only a 67% chance to

do so. There is the same twenty point differential for men: 83% of married men will live to age sixty-five, but only 63% of divorced men. In fact, Waite & Gallagher have compiled an impressive array of data showing that "married people are happier, healthier, and better-off financially" than cohabiting and divorced people. Waite & Gallager, *infra*.

On the other hand, what might be the effects of a law that prohibits divorce upon a woman who is a victim of severe physical abuse? What might be the effect upon the man whose wife is an adulterous alcoholic? Upon the couple who are locked in a decades-long, constant bitter hostility and shouting match?

b. Correcting Dr. Weitzman's Statistics

Dr. Lenore Weitzman reported that, on average, men were 42% better off, and women were 73% worse off a year after divorce than they had been during the marriage. Dr. Wetizman's findings won her a lot of praise and ignited a firestorm of concern about the "feminization of poverty." Weitzman, *infra*. However, when her studies were reexamined and replicated, two things became very clear. First, Weitzan's generalization about no-fault divorce having at least a temporary detrimental effect upon the economic welfare of women and at least a temporary positive effect upon the economic welfare of men is undeniably correct. Second, the amount of that effect is significantly smaller than she calculated. Another scholar reanalyzed Dr. Weitzman's own source data and found mathematical errors; he found that divorced women suffered a 27% decline in the standard of living post-divorce (about 1/3 of what Dr. Weitzman had stated), while men enjoyed a 10% increase in their standard of living (about of 1/4 what Dr. Weitzman had calculated). Peterson, *infra* at 535. Dr. Weitzman has acknowledged the calculation error. Weitzman (1966), *infra* at 538. A more recent study found that women in America experienced a 12% decline in their standard of living after divorce. McKeever, *infra*. In Canada, the government reported in 1997 that women experienced a 23% decline in standard of living after divorce while men experienced a 10% improvement in living standard. Statistics Canada, *infra*. Another study reported an initial average drop in Canadian women's living standard after divorce of 23%, but after five years, that was reduced to only a 5% compared to pre-divorce. Dooley, *infra*. Does this matter? Why/why not?

c. The Social Consequences of Divorce

Divorce constitutes a major social burden as well as a widespread pattern of individual tragedy. The reduced productivity, increased poverty, heightened medical expenses, and lost educational resources directly affect the economic well being of the nation.

Obviously, this personal trauma translates in many respects into significant social burdens. One study of demographic variables found that "disrupted families" correlates more significantly than any other identified variables with a multitude of social problems, including venereal disease rates, rates of referral and treatment of mental retardation and mental illness, infant death rates, and arrest rates. The rate of imprisonment in correctional institutions for divorced men is fifteen times higher than it is for married men; it is five times higher for divorced women than it is for married women. The incidence of antisocial behavior--juvenile delinquency and criminal act--is significantly higher for persons in divorced and separated families than it is for persons living in intact families.

A disproportionate number of divorced families depend upon public welfare. One recent study revealed that approximately 40% of all families headed by a previously-married female had income below the federally-defined poverty level; 24% of such families were receiving public assistance, and 34% of such families with children were receiving public assistance. The lost productivity attributable to the higher rate of disabilities and longer hospital stays of divorced persons also affects the economic health of the country. Moreover, the direct burdens and costs of divorce for the judicial system, which must devote enormous time and resources to resolving divorce-related disputes, are substantial. It has been estimated that more than one-half of all civil filings in state courts are family law matters. The tremendous expenditure of public funds for divorce court administration affects all taxpayers as well as other litigants.

Wardle (1983), *infra*, at 34-35.

The severity of the problem of the instability of marriage in the United States and the gravity of the potential consequences of that phenomenon should not be underestimated. Never before has any society sustained such a high rate of divorce for as long a time as has been sustained in the United States of America. A very sobering study by William J. Goode suggests that the social forces that have combined to generate and support the current unprecedented rate of marital instability, are extremely powerful and socially very (self-) destructive. "[T]he current trend toward a lesser investment of people in the collectivity of the family cannot continue indefinitely; because if the family as a social agency fails to function reasonably well, the economy -- and the society as a whole -- cannot do so either." Goode, *infra*, at 336. He emphasizes *"the magnitude of the social problems created by large increases in marital dissolutions* and the weakening of a commitment to family obligations." *Id.* at 320-321. We cannot separate divorce from its social consequences or reverse the trends in social consequences without changing the social condition; it is not impossible to change those social forces but it is extremely difficult, and such phenomena do not flatten out voluntarily but usually it takes some major external force to produce the change. Goode writes: "I know of no great civilization that at the height of its power and material splendor ever changed its grand onward movement [of forces causing social destabilization], *except by dissolution and military defeat."* *Id.* at 318. "To change all these forces is [very difficult]. It is not impossible, *but no civilization has ever moved in that direction voluntarily." Id.* at 335.

Most divorces occur among middle-class families. And the middle class climate of confidence is extremely important to democratic societies.

People without confidence in a secure tomorrow have no reason to plan or save, invest or organize, vote or obey the more irksome strictures of law. And divorced kids have less confidence than others in social institutions. The one most sacred and precious to them has failed, and this can't help but have an impact on their relationships with other community institutions. If the implied parental promise 'I will always be here to help you, comfort you, support you . . .' can't be trusted, why should these kids believe journalists, teachers, politicians, clergymen? "We're fast approaching the time when half our society will comprise grown-up divorced kids. We need to think about the consequences of that for us all, because people who expect too little aren't much good at contributing, either. Realism and scepticism . . . can be blunted by a false notion that disappointment is the necessary end of every human endeavor. And apathy, a disease which many of our children have caught, can kill the body politic.

Troyer, *infra*, at 174-175.

3. Practical and Ethical Considerations

If a lawyer has strong moral objections to all divorces should he agree to handle a divorce case? Why/why not? Is his "zealous representation" likely to be impaired? If he has strong moral objections to some divorces and is somewhat troubled by the case his client wants him to make or the relief she is seeking, what should he do? If he believes that there are better alternatives than divorce, what should he do? If he believes that divorce will seriously harm the children, what should he do?

4. Bibliography

Contemporary Family Law, vol. 2, Ch. 19 & vol. 3, Ch. 20 (1988).

Martin Dooley, *Lone Mother Families and Social Assistance Policy in Canada* in Family Matters: New Policies for Divorce, Lone Mothers and Child Policy at 48-49 (C. D. Howe Institute, 1995) cited in Moir, *supra.*

William J. Goode, World Changes in Divorce Patterns (1993).

Matthew McKeever & Nicholas Wolfinger, *Reexamining the Economic Costs of Marital Disruption for Women* paper presented July 15, 1997 at the annual meeting of the American Sociological Association, cited in Moir, *infra.*

Donald S. Moir, *A New Class of Disadvantaged Children: Reflections on "Easy" Divorce* in Family Affairs (C. D. Howe Institute 1998) (draft at 11).

Paul A. Nakonezny, Robert D. Shull, Joseph Lee Rodgers, *The Effect of No-Fault Divorce Law on the Divorce Rate Across the 50 States and Its Relation to Income, Education, and Religiosity.* J Marr.& Fam., May 1995, at 477-488 in *http://www.divorcereform.org/stats.html.*

Gary H. Nichols, Note, *Covenant Marriage: Should Tennessee Join the Noble Experiment?* 29 U. Mem. L. Rev. 397 (1999).

Richard R. Peterson, *A Re-Evaluation of the Economic Consequences of Divorce* in 61 Amer. Sociolog. Rev. 528, 535 (1996).

Rayden's Practice and Law of Divorce (9th ed., Joseph Jackson, C.F. Turner, & D.R. Ellison eds., 1964).

Max Rheinstein, Marriage Stability, Divorce and the Law (1972).

Statistics Canada, 1997, *Family Income After Separation*, Cat. 13-588 MPB at 7-11, in *Moir.*

Warner Troyer, Divorced Kids (1979).

Linda J. Waite & Maggie Gallagher, The Case for Marriage (2000).

Lynn D. Wardle, *No-Fault Divorce and the Divorce Conundrum*, 1991 B.Y.U.L.Rev. 79.

Lynn D. Wardle, *Rethinking Marital Age Restrictions*, 22 J. Fam. L. 1 (1983).

Lenore Weitzman, Divorce Revolution: The Unexpected Social and Economic Consequences for Women and Children in America (1987).

Lenore J. Weitzman, *The Economic Consequences of Divorce Are Still Unequal: Comment on Peterson* in 61 Amer. Sociolog. Rev. 537 (1996).

C. Divorce Reform

1. Background

a. The Failure of the No-Fault Divorce Movement

(The following is partially excerpted from Wardle (1991) at 99-112.)

A credible, if not compelling, case can be made that in terms of the four major goals of the no-fault divorce reforms, no-fault divorce has spectacularly failed. The convention wisdom holds that no-fault divorce reform has achieved its first goal of reducing the amount or intensity of hostility, acrimony, and unnecessary adversity in divorce proceedings. But the authors of one study noted that there was a higher percentage of contested cases since the adoption of a no-fault divorce ground in Nebraska and suggested that "[s]ince fighting over who caused the breakup is futile, 'those who want a fight, now use collateral issues as the battle ground.' Fights over custody and support are more prevalent and are often just as acrimonious and humiliating as those over grounds, if not more so." In short, it appears that the hostility has merely shifted from divorce grounds to custody and the economic incidents of divorce. (If a rational person were choosing where to focus the hostility and contention, she might suggest that the grounds for divorce was a pretty innocuous place to lodge such ugliness, and that to transfer it to child custody disputes is not a step forward.)

Anthropologist Paul Bohannon reported similar findings in a survey taken of self-identified "matrimonial lawyers" regarding the effects of no-fault divorce on their own family law practices. Ninety-one percent reported that custody disputes had either increased (53%) or remained the same (38%) as before the adoption of no-fault divorce grounds, and 88% reported increased bitterness (44%) or at least as much bitterness (44%) in custody disputes. In addition, 92% of the attorneys reported that the number of property disputes had either gone up (36%) or remained the same (56%) as before the adoption of no-fault divorce grounds, and 58% reported that there was greater bitterness (35%) or as least as much bitterness (23%) in property disputes as before. Moreover, 90% reported that disputes over spousal support had either increased (34%) or remained the same (56%) as before the adoption of no-fault. Overall, 64% of the respondents reported that the acrimony and hostility of divorce had either increased or remained the same since no-fault divorce laws were introduced.

Second, the "doctoring" of testimony to establish a "fault" ground for divorce was one of the most highly-resented aspects of the old "fault" divorce scheme. Some divorce-seeking clients resented having to publicly charge and prove that their spouses had committed serious marital misconduct. The adoption of no-fault grounds for divorce has provided a way for lawyers and clients to obtain mutual-consent divorces without stooping to such disreputable practices. There is no need to lie or even "finesse" the truth to obtain the termination of an unhappy marriage. Thus, it is fair to assume that no-fault divorce laws have reduced the total amount of perjury in divorce proceedings.

However, the adoption of no-fault grounds for divorce has not eliminated the incentive for parties to stretch the truth to get what they want in divorce proceedings. There is no more judicial scrutiny of no-fault grounds than there was of the fault grounds. It appears that one legal fiction (judicial scrutiny of no-fault grounds) has been substituted for another (judicial scrutiny of fault grounds). Moreover, there are indications that no-fault grounds for divorce have only caused the lying to shift (as did the hostility) from the part of the proceeding dealing with the grounds for divorce to the collateral aspects, especially child custody and visitation disputes. For instance, the practice of one parent (usually the mother) falsely accusing the other parent of child abuse, especially child sexual abuse, appears to have increased since the adoption of no-fault divorce grounds. Getting "control" or asserting "power" or winning custody has assumed even greater emotional significance since the elimination of marital fault has deprived spouses of the opportunity for official vindication of their comparative rectitude. With abandonment of maternal-preference rules the incentive to falsely accuse the ex-husband of serious parental dereliction has increased.

Third, advocates of no-fault divorce argued that adoption of no-fault grounds for divorce would merely codify the existing practice, and bring the written law into harmony with the courtroom practice of permitting divorce upon mutual agreement. However, in many states, the no-fault divorce laws that were enacted have done much more than explicitly authorize divorce by mutual consent. In more than one-third of the states, the only ground for divorce is a no-fault ground. In those states, judicial scrutiny of the causes of marital failure is not permitted. The current law in many states goes further and denies all parties the choice to ask for a judicial determination (no matter how limited) of comparative marital rectitude. Thus, it appears that the no-fault divorce reformers overshot their mark if they really intended to close the gap between law-as-written and law-as- applied.

Finally, reformers were correct when they asserted that ideas about marital relations have changed and that the requirement that "fault" be publicly charged and publicly proven in every case in which divorce is sought no longer reflects modern ideas about marital privacy or marital failure. However, the fact that both spouses share some of the responsibility for marital failure does not mean that spouses will never earnestly desire or (psychologically) need the opportunity for a formal judicial declaration of comparative marital rectitude. Privacy is a powerful component in the modern concepts of marriage and divorce. But, ironically, the adoption of no-fault grounds has led to more, not less, public intrusion into individual and family privacy in regard to divorce. Since the adoption of no-fault divorce grounds there is not only more litigation regarding collateral matters (such as custody and finances) at the time of divorce, but there also is more follow-up litigation. More often, and for longer periods of time, divorced parties are returning to court demanding further judicial scrutiny of the vestiges of a previously-terminated marriage. Consequently, parties under no-fault divorce have ended up opening their private lives to the scrutiny of public (judicial) officials in formal court proceedings many times over prolonged periods of time. Moreover, the type of privacy that supporters of original no-fault reforms promoted was the privacy of couples who had worked out their own differences and were seeking divorce mutually. Yet that mutual privacy is not what has resulted from the adoption of no-fault divorce laws. A more radical notion of individualistic privacy has supplanted the mutual privacy principle. No-fault divorce laws in most American jurisdictions allow any spouse unilaterally to obtain a decree terminating the marriage, without any real judicial examination into the nature of the relationship or cause of breakdown. Modern no-fault divorce laws embody a more atomistic notion of privacy than mainstream advocates of no-fault divorce asserted twenty years ago.

In addition to failing to achieve the four major objectives of no-fault divorce reform, there have been some severe unintended consequences associated with the shift to unilateral no-fault divorce. First, there is some evidence that custodial mothers and their children have suffered more following no-fault divorce than similar mothers and children did before the adoption of no-fault divorce grounds. Second, no-fault divorce appears to have contributed to a dramatic increase in the rate of divorce in the United States.

b. The Divorce Reform Movement

(The following is partly excerpted from Wardle (1999), *infra.*)

There are growing indications that most people in America are very dissatisfied with the current regime of unilateral no-fault divorce laws. [For example, there] is "widespread dissatisfaction with the current social and legal landscape of marriage and divorce, and a sense that marriage itself is threatened under no-fault divorce." Survey after survey of public opinion reports that Americans believe that divorce is too easy, especially divorce of couples with children. For example, Washington Post/Kaiser/Harvard Survey Project American Values: 1998 National Survey of Americans on Values asked whether divorce should be easier, harder or same as it is; respondents saying that divorce should be harder outnumbered those thinking it should be easier nearly three-to-one, and outnumbered those thinking it should be the same or easier nearly two-to-one -- the highest percentage to say they thought divorce is too easy since the pollsters began charting responses to that question 30 years earlier, in 1968. The same survey also reported that 50% of those surveyed believe that divorce is "not acceptable" when the couple has children (compared to 46% who believe that divorce is acceptable then). While seventy-six percent of those polled agree in principle that divorce is acceptable at least sometimes, eighty percent of the respondents indicated that it was not acceptable at least sometimes. A Time/CNN survey May 7-8, 1999, by Yankelovich Partners Inc also reported that fifty percent of those surveyed agreed that "it should be harder than it is not for married couples to get a divorce," while 61% agreed that it should "be harder than it now is for couples with young children to get a divorce," and 64% agreed that people "should be required to take a marriage-education course before they can get a marriage license." Another survey, in 1995, reported by Family Research Council, revealed that thirty-one to fifty-five percent of Americans surveyed favored "divorce reform to strengthen the rights of spouses who want to save the marriage." "Reducing the divorce rate has become a priority in America." The growing public sentiment to do something about the excesses and abuses of unilateral no-fault divorce is beginning to be recognized in many state legislatures. Some commentators refer to the introduction of a bill to replace unilateral no-fault with marital-behavior-based grounds for divorce in the Michigan legislature by Representative Jessie Dalman on Valentines Day, 1996, as the beginning of the "divorce counter-revolution." In three years, bills to [revive] marital-misconduct divorce standards were introduced in at least ten states.

The first legislative reform of the fundamental terms of no-fault divorce was enacted in 1997 by Louisiana. The covenant marriage law enacted by the Louisiana legislature provides that parties may choose to enter a "covenant marriage" by executing a declaration of an intent to contract a covenant marriage and certifying by affidavit that they have undergone premarital counseling regarding the seriousness and nature of covenant marriage and acknowledge that divorce will only be possible where there has been a complete and total breach of the marital covenant. They must attest that full disclosure has been made before marriage of "everything which could adversely affect the decision to enter" covenant marriage. By entering a covenant marriage they commit to take "all reasonable efforts to preserve our marriage, including marital counseling," and commit to remain married "for the rest of our lives." They may file this declaration of intent to contract covenant marriage at the time they apply for a marriage license; previously-married couples may file a declaration to turn their existing marriage into a covenant marriage by filing a declaration and affidavit.

The most controversial difference between covenant marriage and ordinary marriage in Louisiana is that in covenant marriage grounds for divorce are restricted. While ordinary marriages can be terminated by proof of having lived apart for six months (or upon the historical grounds of adultery or conviction for a felony resulting in death or hard labor), covenant marriage cannot be terminated upon six months separation. Rather, covenant marriage may be dissolved only on six grounds: the other spouse has committed adultery, committed a felony resulting in a sentence of death or hard labor, abandoned the matrimonial domicile for one year, has physically or sexually abused the spouse or child of the spouse seeking the divorce, or the spouses have lived separate and apart for *two* years without reconciliation, or one year following a legal separation--(but if there are minor children legal separation must be at least 18 months unless child abuse was the basis for the legal separation). Legal separation is possible on the first five grounds above mentioned or because of the other spouse's habitual intemperance, cruel treatment, or outrages that are "of such a nature as to render their living together insupportable." Actions for legal separation in a covenant marriage are limited by procedures strictly narrowing jurisdiction, strictly limiting venue, and prohibiting summary judgment or judgment on the pleadings.

A year after Louisiana enacted its landmark covenant marriage act, Arizona passed the nation's second covenant marriage law. Since the prior Arizona divorce law provided clearly and exclusively for modern-clean-no-fault divorce, while the prior Louisiana law was only *de facto* no fault, allowing divorce only after six months living apart, or for more traditional grounds, the adoption of covenant marriage in Arizona represented a rather significant, if little-recognized, extension of the divorce reform movement. The Arizona law has been called a "watered down version of the Louisiana law," because if *both* parties to the marriage agree to end the marriage, they may do so without either establishing fault or without living apart for a period of time. Critics of the Arizona covenant marriage amendments have charged that permitting the spouses to end their covenant marriage by mutual agreement practically negates the purpose behind a covenant marriage, and that vulnerable parties might be coerced into agreeing to the dissolution of the marriage. In 2001, Arkansas became the third state to enact a Covenant Marriage law.

In 1998, another dimension of the "shifting paradigm" driving the divorce reform movement was manifest when Florida passed a "Marriage Preservation and Preparation Act" requiring all high school students in the state to be given instruction in "marriage and relationship skills education," offering a reduction in the price of marriage licenses and waiver of the three-day waiting period to couples who undergo at least four hours of training in a "premarital preparation course," and requiring

couples who file for divorce to attend a "Parent Education and Family Stabilization
Course" addressing the legal and emotional impact of divorce on adults and children,
financial responsibility, laws on child abuse or neglect and conflict resolution skills.

At least seven different types of divorce reforms have been proposed to reduce the
high rate of marital breakup. These include proposals to 1) replace no-fault grounds
with marital-misconduct-based divorce laws; 2) require pre-marital and/or pre-
divorce counseling; 3) make fault a more substantial consideration in all economic
aspects of divorce; 4) legalize private contract (precommitment) penalties and
rewards to promote marriage-maintaining behavior; 5) give couples the option to
choose a more committed form of marriage; 6) impose additional divorce procedures
or limitations when children are involved; or 7) marriage education classes in public
schools. Additionally, many proposals, including the covenant marriage laws enacted
in Louisiana and Arizona, contain combinations of several of the foregoing proposals.

The grassroots movement to reform divorce laws appears to be "gaining
momentum . . . across the nation." The intensity and breadth of the dissatisfaction
with the current regime of unilateral no-fault divorce is so great that it has been
described as "a 'counter-revolution' . . . against no-fault divorce . . . ." This
"widespread disillusionment over no-fault divorce," has not escaped the notice of
politicians, who have begun to attempt to capitalize politically upon the groundswell.
"[C]ommentators and politicians across the country decry the loss of 'family values'
and urge legislative and social reform to bring back the traditional family." Concerns
about the disintegration of marriages and the family in general are not just being
expressed by conservatives any more; liberals as well as conservatives have praised
the aims of covenant marriage; even Hillary Rodham Clinton has "expressed support
for the goals of the Louisiana covenant marriage law."

Ironically, it appears that the divorce bar and family law professors are among the
strongest opponents to covenant marriage. Why? What interests (if any) do they have
that might be jeopardized if covenant marriage is widely adopted? *See* DiFonzo (1994
and2000), *infra*. Among the most vehement critics of covenant marriage has been Ira
Ellman, chief Reporter of the American Law Institute's *Principles of the Law of
Family Dissolution*. Chapter 7 of the *Principles* bars enforcement of tie-me-to-the-
mast provisions such as those embodied (modestly) in covenant marriage bills, or any
other contractual arrangements intended to restrict or delay the right of a married
person unilaterally and immediately to dissolve a marriage. What concept of marriage
underlies the insistence that legally any married person must be able at any time
unilaterally and immediately to end the marriage?

c. The Conundrum of Divorce

(The following is partly excerpted from Wardle (1991), *infra*, at 124-136.)

Drafters of divorce laws encounter three dilemmas that constitute what has been
called "the divorce conundrum." The first dilemma of the divorce conundrum arises
from the need to balance two different policy goals: to alleviate the dislocation and
suffering caused by marital failure by making the divorce process easier, and to
promote marital stability and prevent or repair marital disruption. Divorce laws affect
not only people who get divorced; they also affect marriages. Divorce laws affect the
nature, expectations and success of marriages as surely as laws governing breach of
contract affect the nature, success and performance of contracts. In establishing a

divorce law, wise lawmakers must be concerned not only with the effect of the law upon divorcing parties and their children, but also with the impact on ongoing marriages and families in general.

Second, divorce policy also requires consideration of two different notions of fairness: fairness for the divorcing parties and their children, and fairness for spouses in ongoing marriages and their children (especially for families where the marriage may be in difficulty). Fairness for the divorcing parties essentially consists of divisible equality-- i.e., recognizing the equal worth of the contributions of husbands and wives to the marriage and equally dividing their acquisitions. When marriage fails, the principal asset of the marriage that remains--and just about the only aspect of family life with which a court can competently deal--is the material wealth acquired by the parties during the marriage. In an egalitarian society, there is no better model for apportioning such assets than to begin with the premise that the spouses valued equally their own and each others' contributions and to aim for equality in the division of the assets and liabilities of the unsuccessful enterprise.

While the rule of equality is essential to fairness in divorce, a "higher law" governs marriage--the "higher law" of love. The essence of love is sharing and giving, of wanting wholeheartedly to be one (not have one-half). Fairness in marriage is expressed and measured in terms of love. Self-sacrifice, sharing, continuous giving, and continual forgiving are indispensable to any happy marriage. Marriage requires a long view--eternal is the word that lovers like to use--a view that looks beyond the dull daily duties and sometimes-difficult periods of family life.

The language of equality is inadequate to describe the essence of marriage. Marriage is better described in language that is poetic and spiritual--the language of love. The language of equality deals with visible, material things, whereas the essence of marriage is invisible. The problem with the language of equality is that it encourages thinking about an intimate, living relationship in terms that do not fairly characterize it until it is dead.

An accounting mentality, so essential to fairness-as-equality, can canker marital relationships that are striving for fairness-as-love. Any marriage built on the premise that each spouse need only give fifty percent of the time, need carry only fifty percent of the burdens, and should expect to receive a full fifty percent of all the benefits may be headed for a successful divorce, not for marital satisfaction. ***

The critical premise of fairness-as-equality is enforceability. By definition, fairness-as-love (i.e., sharing and giving) cannot be enforced. Love must be offered voluntarily. It can never be coerced or taken away. Additionally, no-fault divorce laws seem to "cultivate a casual commitment to marriage," to foster "the illusion of easy divorce," and to confuse "a cry for help with a demand for divorce."

The third dilemma of divorce law results from the tension between the public and private (or privacy) interests in divorce. That is, by giving absolute priority to the private right of individuals to leave marriage at will, the public interest in the abandonned spouse and in the children of the marriage is shortchanged. Finally, there is a difference between an isolated incident and an epidemic. The law, and society, can accommodate some [marital] instability, but when [marital instability] becomes the [norm], that is a different matter.

d. Divorce Gap Dropping Among Children of No-Fault Divorce

A study by Nicholas Wolfinger for the National Opinion Research Council of nearly 22,000 adults over a 20-year period, presented to the Annual Meeting of the American Sociological Association in Chicago in August, 1999, reportedly suggests that the rate of divorce among the children of divorced parents has fallen. In 1973, the rate of divorce among the children of divorced parents was almost 300% higher than that of children of intact families. Today it is about 50% higher. Several factors may account for this change: children of divorced parents are less likely to marry than children of non-divorced parents; the divorce rate among children from non-broken households has gone up; and divorcing parents may be doing a better job of insulating their children from the worst emotional effects of divorce. Adams, *infra.*

The popular statistic that 50% of all marriages will end in divorce is an exaggeration. This myth probably began when the Census Bureau reported that during one year, there were 2.4 million marriages and 1.2 million divorces. Someone did the math without taking into account the roughly 50 million marriages already in existence, and the myth was born. When divorces are tracked by the year in which the couple married, the divorce rate has risen significantly in the last couple of decades, and persons marrying today have a much higher likelihood of divorce than persons who married thirty or forty years ago. The overall percent of contemporary marriages that are likely to end in divorce is about 40%.

2. Statutes, Cases and Doctrines

a. Arizona Revised Statutes 25-903

Dissolution of a Covenant Marriage; Grounds.

Notwithstanding any law to the contrary, if a husband and wife have entered into a covenant marriage pursuant to this chapter the court shall not enter a decree of dissolution of marriage pursuant to chapter 3, article 2 of this title unless it finds any of the following:

1. The respondent spouse has committed adultery.

2. The respondent spouse has committed a felony and has been sentenced to death or imprisonment in any federal, state, county or municipal correctional facility.

3. The respondent spouse has abandoned the matrimonial domicile for at least one year before the petitioner filed for dissolution of marriage and refuses to return. A party may file a petition based on this ground by alleging that the respondent spouse has left the matrimonial domicile and is expected toremain absent for the required period. If the respondent spouse has not abandoned the matrimonial domicile for the required period at the time of the filing of the petition, the action shall not be dismissed for failure to state sufficient grounds and the action shall be stayed for the period of time remaining to meet the grounds based on abandonment, except that the court may enter and enforce temporary orders pursuant to § 25-315 during the time that the action is pending.

4. The respondent spouse has physically or sexually abused the spouse seeking the dissolution of marriage, a child, a relative of either spouse permanently living in the matrimonial domicile or has committed domestic violence as defined in § 13-3601 or emotional abuse.

5. The spouses have been living separate and apart continuously without reconciliation for at least two years before the petitioner filed for dissolution of marriage. A party may file a petition based on this ground by alleging that it is expected that the parties will be living separate and apart for the required period. If the parties have not been separated for the

required period at the time of the filing of the petition, the action shall not be dismissed for failure to state sufficient grounds and the action shall be stayed for the period of time remaining to meet the grounds based on separation, except that the court may enter and enforce temporary orders pursuant to § 25-315 during the time that the action is pending.

6. The spouses have been living separate and apart continuously without reconciliation for at least one year from the date the decree of legal separation was entered.

7. The respondent spouse has habitually abused drugs or alcohol.

8. The husband and wife both agree to a dissolution of marriage.

b. Notes and Questions

1) Questions about Covenant Marriage?

Do the grounds for divorce in the Arizona Covenant Marriage divorce provision, *supra,* seem terribly strict or onerous? If both parties agreed to such terms, should one be allowed to change his or her mind and get a unilateral no-fault divorce? Will the Arizona covenant marriage regulation of divorce be enforced if one of the parties moves to another state and files for divorce there? *See Spaht, infra.* If the parties "Declaration" of Covenant Marriage is treated as an antenuptial agreement between the parties not to divorce except on such grounds, will it be enforced? Why/why not?

3. Practical and Ethical Considerations

To what extent should a lawyer suggest to her client that her divorce case be used as a "test case" to promote new defense to divorce, new theories of divorce, or otherwise to reform divorce law?

4. Bibliography

David L. Adams, Church & State Update, Lutheran Church-Missouri Synod (Aug., 1999).

Herbie DiFonzo, *Customized Marriage,* 75 Ind. L. J. 875 (2000).

Marygold S. Melli, *Whatever Happened to Divorce?*, 2000 Wis. L. Rev. 637.

Katherine Shaw Spaht & Symeon C. Symeonides, *Covenant Marriage and the Law of Conflicts Laws,* 32 Creighton L. Rev. 1085, 1100 (1999).

Lynn D. Wardle, *Divorce Reform at the Turn of the Millennium: Certainties and Possibilities,* 33 Fam. L. Q. 783 (1999).

Lynn D. Wardle, *No-Fault Divorce and the Divorce Conundrum,* 1991 B.Y.U.L.Rev. 79.

CHAPTER 27

Property Division

A. BASIC PROPERTY DIVISION UPON DIVORCE

1. Background

a. Overview of Marital Property and Equitable Distribution Principles

Property distribution upon divorce has gone through essentially three phases in the United States. The earliest phase was the *title distribution* phase of common law and community property. Most American states inherited their property distribution schemes from English *common law*. Historically, at common law, property was retained after divorce by the party who individually held title to that property. Because the common law suspended the legal personality of women during marriage, and for many other reasons, virtually all property acquired during the marriage (and even some property, personalty, that the wife had brought with her into the marriage) belonged to the husband. Even after the nineteenth century Married Women's Property Acts eliminated many of the legal disabilities of married women, most property acquired during marriage was acquired in the name of the husband. This put the divorced woman at a severe economic disadvantage upon divorce in terms of property ownership. In the absence of statutory authorization to redistribute property (which historically did not exist at common law) courts had little authority to take property from the title owner and give it to another person, even to a former spouse, even to prevent economic injustice upon divorce. Judicial power to redistribute property was not widely authorized until this century.

However, eight states with significant Spanish or French roots historically followed *community property* law rather than common law property law. Under the community property system all property acquired during marriage except that received by gift, devise, bequest or inheritance, was deemed to belong not to either party separately but by both parties together as a community of acquets. (Property acquired before marriage or after the termination of a marriage, and gifts, bequests, devises and inheritances received anytime were deemed the *separate* property of the owning spouse.) The marital community was an entity in which both spouses held equal interests. Upon divorce, both parties traditionally were entitled to all of his or her separate property and an equal share (one-half) of the community property - not as a matter of equity or recognizing a mere inchoate expectancy (as the wife's dower or marital property interest in common law states could be described) but as a matter of recognizing the present, equal community property ownership interest of each spouse. Thus, in the first phase of property division, property went to the title-holder in both common law and community property states, with women getting a much better result in community property states because they were deemed to have equal legal title to the community property.

The second phase can be called the *discretionary distribution phase*. In response to the substantial disparity in economic consequences of divorce for men and women in common law states, legislation authorizing judicial discretion to distribute some part of the property according to principles other than title began to be passed in the twentieth century. While the legislative schemes varied from state to state, typically they gave the divorce court tremendous discretion to divide any property held by either of the divorcing spouses. Often the statutes provided that the court was to make equitable division of property; hence, these property division statutes came to be known as *equitable distribution* laws. Even in community property states, equitable distribution of community property, in lieu of strictly equal division, was adopted by many of the community property states. While this afforded some relief from the inflexibility of the title-distribution system, discretionary distribution had other shortcomings. For example, while the notion of equitable distribution reflected a laudable aspiration for equity, these laws failed to define equity, or to identify the principles which, if followed, would produce equity. Judicial discretion gave room for nonlegal factors to play, including factors such as cultural or personal bias. Also, discretionary distribution could be very unpredictable, and the results could vary dramatically from judge to judge, or even from case to case.

The third and present phase is the *marital property equitable distribution* phase. It functions essentially as a combination of some elements of the community property system and some elements of the equitable property system. Under *marital property* principles, at the time of divorce, property acquired before marriage, or after termination of a marriage, or as gifts, bequests, devises and inheritances received during marriage, is deemed *separate* or *individual* property and is presumably kept by the owner. All other property -- basically all property acquired during marriage except that received by gift, devise, bequest or inheritance, is deemed *marital* property (still called *community* property in community property states). In marital property states, at the time of divorce, marriage is deemed to have created a marital community of acquets, a partnership in which the spouses have interests that are presumed to be equal (at least for purpose of property distribution upon divorce). Upon divorce, the separate property presumably will be awarded to the title-holding spouse, while the marital property will be equitably (re)distributed by the court. Most states (including seven of the nine states that presently adhere to community property law) reportedly permit equitable division of marital (or community) property upon divorce. Two community property states generally require equal distribution instead of equitable distribution, but all others and in all marital common law property states equitable (discretionary) distribution is the standard, although in many states there is an express or tacit rebuttable presumption that absent other factors, an equal division of the marital property would be most equitable. All states allow exceptional redistribution to account for improper dissipation of marital property, and about one-third of the states allow consideration of other kinds of fault generally in making equitable distribution of marital property; a few states allow broader equitable distribution, not limited to marital property. Most states give the court power only to divide and reallocate marital property; the separate property of the parties must be awarded to the owner. A minority of states, however empower the court to dip into separate property if marital assets are insufficient to achieve an equitable property division. In all states the spouses are free to alter their property relations by premarital agreement or by separation agreement.

Property division is one of the most important economic issues decided in most divorce cases. The extraordinary power given to judges to redistribute property upon divorce is one of the most significant legal developments of this century. As Professor Mary Ann Glendon noted: "The wide ranging power recently given to judges in most states to redistribute all the spouses assets (including even premarital and inherited property) in a divorce case is the single most distinctive feature of modern American divorce law." Mary Ann Glendon, The New Family and the New Property 60 (1981). The expansion of the court's discretionary power to divide property stimulated efforts by divorce attorneys for less-propertied spouses to bring within reach of the judicial power of redistribution as many assets as possible. The result has been a remarkable effort to expand the definition of "property" that is divisible upon divorce.

2. Statutes, Cases and Doctrines

a. A typical property division statute: Utah Code Ann. § 30-3-5
The broad terms of Utah's property division statute are typical.

> *Utah Code Ann. § 30-3-5 Disposition of property --Maintenance and health care of parties and children --Division of debts --Court to have continuing jurisdiction -- Custody and visitation --Determination of alimony --Nonmeritorious petition for modification.*
> (1) When a decree of divorce is rendered, the court may include in it equitable orders relating to the children, property, debts or obligations, and parties. ***
> (3) The court has continuing jurisdiction to make subsequent changes or new orders for the custody of the children and their support, maintenance, health, and dental care, and for distribution of the property and obligations for debts as is reasonable and necessary.
> ***

b. A typical property division case – *Newmeyer v. Newmeyer*
The application of the above-quoted provisions in the following case is typical of many state courts' approach to traditional property division issues.

Newmeyer v. Newmeyer
745 P.2d 1276 (Utah 1987)

ZIMMERMAN, Justice:

Plaintiff Kathryn Newmeyer brought this divorce action against her husband, Jeddy Newmeyer. The trial court granted Kathryn custody of the couple's minor child and awarded her the bulk of the property, one dollar per year as alimony, and attorney fees. Jeddy appeals. He contends that the property division was incorrect, that Kathryn should not have been awarded any alimony, and that the evidence is insufficient to support an award of attorney fees. We agree only with the third contention and vacate the award of attorney fees. The judgment is otherwise affirmed.

The Newmeyers were married just over twenty years. During that period, they owned three homes in succession. During the holding periods, each appreciated. The trial court awarded Jeddy an automobile, all rights to his pension plan, miscellaneous household items, his savings of approximately $7,000, and an equitable lien against the couple's current home in the amount of $32,606. The court awarded Kathryn the balance of the equity in the home, valued in excess of $80,000, two automobiles, miscellaneous household items, her savings of approximately $17,000, one dollar per year alimony, and $1,423 in attorney fees. Kathryn also was allowed to take an income tax deduction for the couple's minor child for the tax year 1982. Jeddy was required to pay $200 per month child support and was awarded the tax deduction for the minor child for all the years following 1982.

Jeddy challenges numerous aspects of the property division. However, he concentrates his attention on the division of the equity in the home. He challenges the findings on the relative contribution of each party and the current value of the home. Regarding the first of these issues-- the contribution of each party--he contends that the trial court erred in finding that Kathryn should receive credit for substantial amounts she received from inheritances that were invested in the homes early in the marriage.

In dividing the marital estate, the trial court may make such orders concerning property distribution and alimony as are equitable. Utah Code Ann. § 30-3-5(1) (1984 & Supp.1987). In making such orders, the trial court is permitted broad latitude, and its judgment is not to be lightly disturbed, so long as it exercises its discretion in accordance with the standards set by this Court. *Jones v. Jones,* *; see *Pusey v. Pusey,*.* It is therefore incumbent on the appealing party to prove that the trial court's division violates those standards, *, or that the trial court's factual findings upon which the division is grounded are clearly erroneous under Utah Rule of Civil Procedure 52(a).

Jeddy concedes that Kathryn put money from her inheritances into the homes. However, he argues that because the inheritances received by Kathryn came into the marriage many years ago and were committed to the common venture of purchasing a home, the trial court was bound to divide this contribution equally between both parties. There is nothing in our cases that mandates such a result. The appropriate treatment of property brought into a marriage by one party may vary from case to case. *Compare Workman v. Workman,** (husband's property acquired prior to marriage properly a part of marital assets to be divided upon divorce), and *Jackson v. Jackson,** (title to marital property prior to divorce not binding on trial court's distribution), *with Preston v. Preston,* * (inheritance acquired during marriage properly excluded from valuation of marital assets), and *Jesperson v. Jesperson,* * (not unreasonable for trial court to withdraw from marital property the equivalent of assets brought into marriage). The overriding consideration is that the ultimate division be equitable--that property be fairly divided between the parties, given their contributions during the marriage and their circumstances at the time of the divorce. *See Huck v. Huck,* 734 P.2d 417, 420 (Utah 1986).

In the present case, the circumstances warrant the treatment given the inheritances by the trial court. Under any version of the facts, it is readily apparent that Kathryn paid the lion's share of the cost of the homes from money she received through inheritances. Moreover, the trial court was more than fair to Jeddy by crediting him with an equal share in the appreciation of the value of the homes despite his much lower contribution. Therefore, we conclude that the trial court exercised its discretion within the bounds set by our cases when it credited Kathryn with the inheritances she put into the homes.

Jeddy also disputes the trial court's factual determination of the amount each party contributed toward the purchase of the homes. There was conflicting evidence on this point at trial. Evidence fixed Kathryn's probable contribution at $55,000 to $60,000 and Jeddy's at $7,000 to $12,000. Jeddy's present challenge to the trial court's factual findings as to the relative contributions of the parties amounts to nothing more than an attempt to retry the matter on appeal. There was evidence supporting the positions of both parties. It was for the trial court to resolve the conflicts. We will not overturn such a factual resolution unless the appellant first marshals all the evidence supporting the trial court's finding and then demonstrates that that evidence, when compared to the contrary evidence, is so lacking as to warrant the conclusion that clear error has been committed. ** In the present case, Jeddy has not begun to meet this burden. Therefore, we reject his attack on the trial court's determination of the relative contributions of the parties.

Jeddy next attacks the trial court's findings as to the market value of the current home. Jeddy's expert witness testified that the house was worth $122,000, while Kathryn's testified that the value of the house was $112,000. The trial judge fixed the value of the house at $117,000. Based upon that finding, the appreciation in the value of the couple's successive homes was approximately $50,000. Jeddy argues that in fixing the value at $117,000, the court improperly "split" the difference between the values fixed by the experts. He argues that his expert should have been believed.

This argument, like the one that preceded it, is nothing but an attempt to have this Court substitute its judgment for that of the trial court on a contested factual issue. This we cannot do under Utah Rule of Civil Procedure 52(a). In apparent recognition of this proposition, Jeddy masks this claim as a legal argument by contending that the trial judge acted improperly in splitting the difference between the experts. That argument is, of course, utterly lacking in merit. It is elementary that a judge is not bound to believe one witness's testimony to the total exclusion of that of another witness. When acting as the trier of fact, the trial judge is entitled to give conflicting opinions whatever weight he or she deems appropriate. *See Groen v. Tri-O-Inc.*, *; see also Goodmundson v. Goodmundson*, 201 Mont. 535, 655 P.2d 509, 511 (1982) (in adopting proposed values for marital assets, trial court may average conflicting values given by experts to arrive at an equitable solution). Therefore, we hold that the district court did not abuse its discretion in determining that the value of the home was $117,000.

***

Jeddy's other contentions regarding the trial court's property distribution lack merit. *[FN1. It is worth noting that in attacking the property distribution, Jeddy fails entirely to take account of the fact that Kathryn received an alimony award of only one dollar per year. In determining whether a certain division of property is equitable, neither the trial court nor this Court considers the property division in a vacuum. The amount of alimony awarded and the relative earning capabilities of the parties are also relevant, because the relative abilities of the spouses to support themselves after the divorce are pertinent to an equitable determination of the division of the fixed assets of the marriage.]*

***

The divorce decree is affirmed, but the award of attorney fees to plaintiff is stricken. Costs to respondent.

HALL, C.J., and STEWART, Associate C.J., concur.

HOWE, Justice: (concurring).

I concur. This case presents a recurring issue before this Court, viz., the division of property inherited or received by gift by one spouse from his or her family either before or during marriage. No rules to guide the trial court have been expressed by the legislature or by this Court over the past years except the illusory standard that the ultimate division should be fair and equitable. While I recognize that trial judges must have flexibility and discretion in dividing property, I believe that such inherited or donated property should be dealt with more consistently and according to more definite and meaningful guidelines. Typical of our expressions dealing with inherited property is the following language found in *Burke v. Burke*, 733 P.2d 133, 135 (Utah 1987) (a case in which I concurred), where we said:

[I]n appropriate circumstances equity requires that each party recover the separate property brought into or received during the marriage.

However, no mention was made of what comprise "appropriate circumstances."

From my review of the cases decided by this Court in recent years, many of which are cited in the instant case and in the footnotes to *Burke v. Burke, supra,* no discernible pattern of treating inherited or donated property is apparent. For instance, in *Burke*, Mrs. Burke, ten years into the marriage, inherited from her mother's estate three and one-half acres of unimproved land, then worth less than $5,000. Without any improvements being made to the property or any effort expended by either party, the property appreciated at the time of divorce to $35,000 per acre. The trial court awarded the property solely to Mrs. Burke, giving Mr. Burke no part of the original value ($5,000) or its appreciation during the marriage ($117,500). This Court refused to disturb that award.

Similarly, in *Preston v. Preston*, 646 P.2d 705, 706 (Utah 1982), we affirmed a divorce decree awarding to each party in general the real and personal property he or she brought to the marriage or inherited during the marriage. We there said:

> Following the principle we have approved in cases like *Georgedes v. Georgedes,* *; *Jesperson v. Jesperson,*; and *Humphreys v. Humphreys,* *, the district court concluded that each party should, in general, receive the real and personal property he or she brought to the marriage or inherited during the marriage.

Without any mention or recognition of the principle referred to in the above quotation, we have in other cases approved a division among the parties of property inherited or donated to one party prior to or during the marriage. *Argyle v. Argyle,* *; *Bushell v. Bushell,*;**, No case has been found where we have reversed a trial court's disposition of such property.

A middle approach was taken in the instant case. Mr. Newmeyer was awarded no part of his wife's inheritance, but he was allowed to share equally in the appreciation of the properties in which her inheritance was invested. Yet I am unable to discern why it was "fair and equitable" to deny to Mr. Burke that which was given to Mr. Newmeyer.

While I recognize that each case has its own unique set of circumstances, I am concerned with the lack of consistency in treating inherited and donated property. Without more definite rules, each party takes his or her chances that the particular trial judge assigned to hear the case on that given day will perceive it to be fair and equitable to divide or not to divide such property. I believe that some general rules should at least be articulated and followed.
***

> Legislative guidance would be helpful on this question. ***
> DURHAM, Justice: (concurring and dissenting).
> I concur in the majority opinion except for its vacation of the award of attorney fees. ***

c. *Newmeyer* notes

The traditional approach embodied in the Utah statute represents the "starting point" in property division analysis in most jurisdictions today. Courts have "broad latitude" and use it. Fairness (equity) is the dominant (if subjective) concern. Some courts, like Utah's, have plenary authority to consider and divide all property owned by either spouse, regardless of when or how acquired, but in most states only property acquired during the marriage and not by gift, inheritance, bequest, or judgment for personal injury can be split upon divorce. Note the amount of factual detail that must be examined in reviewing a property division award.

d. Key Issues in Contemporary Property Division

Under prevailing marital property equitable distribution principles, there are four major issues that may arise upon property division: (1) Is the disputed asset "property"? (2) Is it "marital" property? (3) How should it be valued? (4) How should it be distributed.

1) What Assets Are "Property"?

Few if any states' marital property division laws provide a definition of the term *property,* but it is generally understood by the courts to include all assets of value to which a legal ownership interest may attach, including any interest acquired by the parties to the marriage through the use of marital funds or the efforts of the spouses. Transferability, marketability, and capability of valuation are all factors in determining whether an asset is "property" (though none absolutely essential in all cases). Traditional forms of wealth, such as land, money, bank accounts, securities, jewelry, vehicles, etc., are recognized forms of "property" and rarely are questions about their property-status raised. The "new property," however, not infrequently poses definitional dilemmas, as will be noted in the next chapter.

2) Is it "Marital" Property?

Once an asset is determined to be property, it must be classified as marital or separate. Generally, courts only have authority to divide marital property upon divorce. Marital property often is generally defined as all property acquired during marriage that is not separate property, but in a few states the courts have power to treat all property of the parties as "marital" property. This definition give the benefit of doubt in favor of marital property. It is generally presumed that all property acquired during marriage is marital property. *As a general rule, all returns on labor performed by either spouse during marriage are marital property, including deferred returns on labor performed during marriage for which payment or benefit is to be received after marriage.*

3) Valuation of the Property

Finding property to be marital property for purposes of equitable distribution upon divorce leads to the necessity to determine the value of it. Valuation methods can vary and valuation of some forms of property can be extremely complicated and rather subjective. The method of valuation depends upon the kind of property involved. "[F]ew rules of general application can be formulated . . . ." H. Clark, Jr., *op. cit.* § 15.4 at 605. Often the cases turn into contests between competing experts offering widely-varying evaluations of the property.

4) Distribution of the Property

Most equitable distribution statutes require a court to consider a host of factors and to make an "equitable" (that is, a fair) distribution. "One survey lists 38 different factors found in the various state statutes as bearing upon the equitable division of property, but nearly all are a specific application of the need or contribution principle." A.L.I., *infra,*§4.09, Rep. Note a. "Economic circumstances" at time of divorce, "contribution" and "length of the marriage" are the three most commonly listed considerations. *Id.* Marital misconduct ("fault") may affect property distribution amounts in only about fifteen states (apart from exceptional circumstances such as dissipation of the assets, a fault-consideration that all states accept). *Id.* at pp. 43-47. Property division often considers only economic factors in making equitable redistribution. That may operate to the detriment of homemakers, whose major contributions to the marriage may have been non-economic (at least no wage was contributed, though her labor undeniably had economic value to the marriage). Some states have added homemakers non-economic contributions to the list of factors to be considered.

Given the host of potentially relevant factors and the subjectivity of the standard (that is, "equitable" distribution), inconsistency and unpredictability have long been problems with equitable distribution. One solution to that problem is the adoption (formally or informally) of an equal division presumption. Equal distribution is the rule or presumption in most community property states. It is a *de jure* legal presumption in some equitable distribution states, and a *de facto* presumption in many others. The prevailing rule of equitable distribution seems to include a general presumption of equal division of assets, at least in cases of long marriages. The A.L.I.'s *Principles of the Law of Family Dissolution* proposes that "marital property and marital debts [be] divided at dissolution so that the spouses receive net shares equal in value, although necessarily identical in kind." A.L.I., *infra*, at §4.09(1).

Property division traditionally has been seen as a once-and-only, final judicial decision. Thus, when it is possible, the courts prefer a "clean break" result in property division upon divorce. In terms of protection of third parties who may obtain interests in the property and to facilitate alienation, that makes sense. Lump-sum property division awards whereby the employee spouse is awarded the entire marital property and the wife's share is "bought out" by awarding her an offsetting portion of other marital property, or the employee spouse trades some of his separate property to the other spouse to compensate for her share of the particular "new property" asset are preferred. However, in most divorces the parties do not have sufficient other property for the employee to "buy out" the nonemployee's portion of the disputed asset all at once. B. R. Tucker, *infra*, §6.11 at pp. 346-366. Where it is not feasible for one spouse to buy out the other with one lump-sum payment, some courts permit a schedule of payments over a relatively short time period. *Id.* §4.08 at 245.

Thus, deferred distribution or deferred division are often used in cases involving nonwealthy divorcing spouses. For example since most divorces occur within the first six years of marriage, the only valuable asset the parties may own may be the equity in their home. In some cases, the equity may be so great that neither party can "cash out" the other party, both parties may have urgent need for their interest in the property, and a forced sale of the home may be necessary in order to divide the scarce resources of the parties fairly between them.

3. Practical and Ethical Considerations

a. Practical Effect of "Equitable Distribution"

Professor Garrison examined property division in cases before (1978) and after (1984) the adoption of New York's liberal Equitable Distribution law. She expected to find that cases decided after the law was adopted would give a greater share of property to women because the Equitable Distribution law increased (at least in theory) the range of property that could be divided. Her study concluded, however, that this assumption was "highly flawed." Garrison, *infra*, at 667. She found that "[m]ost divorcing husbands did not own significant individual assets" and discovered "the scarcity of marital property and the tendency for it to be in nonliquid assets." *Id.* While liberal equitable distribution of broadly defined property could make a significant difference in rare cases of wealthy divorcing couples, Professor Garrison concluded: "Overall there was little change in the percentage distribution of marital property after the passage of the marital distribution law," and what change she found was not statistically significant. *Id.* at 671.

b. Changing Credit Cards

In *Walker Bank & Trust Co. v. Jones*, 672 P.2d 73 (Utah 1983) a bank sued a married-but-separated woman to recover for charges made by her estranged husband. The woman defended on the ground that she had written and informed the bank of her separation and stated that she would no longer be liable for her separated mate's charges. The Utah Supreme Court upheld judgment for the bank on the ground that the contract between the bank and the woman controlled her liability, and it provided that she could protect herself from his charges only by closing the account or surrendering the credit card. What kind of practical advice should an attorney give his divorce client regarding joint liabilities?

4. Bibliography

American Law Institute, Principles of the Law of Family Dissolution §4.08 (2002).
3 Contemporary Family Law §§ 30:01, et seq. (1988).
Brett R. Turner, Equitable Distribution of Property §2.03 (2d ed. 1994).
Homer H. Clark, Jr., The Law of Domestic Relations in the United States §§7.1, 7.2 (2d ed., 1988).
Marsha Garrison, *Good Intentions Gone Awry: The Impact of New York's Equitable Distribution Law on Divorce Outcomes*, 57 Brooklyn L. Rev. 621 (1991).
Lynn D. Wardle, *Dividing the "New Property" Upon Divorce: The Quest for Economic Equity*, in Law in Motion 678-710 (International Encyclopeadia of Laws, 1997).

B. COMPLEX PROPERTY DIVISION ISSUES

1. Background

a. Complex Property Division Issues in General

Many complex property division issues arise concerning what is called "the new property." The term "new property" comes from a famous 1964 Yale Law Journal article by Professor Charles Reich, in which he suggested that employment income, benefits, and pensions were their primary form of wealth for most people, and for the poor government benefits were the primary form of wealth. Reich, *infra*, at 738-739. Professor Reich proposed that both forms of wealth should be treated like new forms of property and that they "must be surrounded with the kinds of safeguards once reserved for personality." *Id.* In 1981, Professor Mary Ann Glendon explored the implications of "the new property" for family law in a very influential book, *The New Family and the New Property*. She argued that while legal ties between employee and employer are becoming stronger and more permanent, legal relations among family members are becoming looser and more transient, and that employment and government are replacing family as the primary providers of protection for the individual's economic and health security. Mary Ann Glendon, The New Family and the New Property 2 (1981). She also observed that one of the most significant developments in marital property law in the recent decades was the expansion of the definition of property subject to distribution to include these relatively intangible, but highly valuable forms of "new property." Among the most important forms of new property considered upon divorce are pensions, goodwill, educational degrees, professional licenses, workers' compensation, personal injury recovery, and disability benefits.

Historically, most of these assets were not subject to judicial power of redistribution upon divorce. Some of them were not even deemed "property." For instance, educational degrees and professional licenses were personal attributes, not deemed property. Likewise, pensions were considered a gift provided by a generous employer to a loyal servant, terminable at will. However, as courts have acquired power to redistribute property (particularly marital property) upon divorce, lawyers for spouses with less property have sought to have assets characterized in a manner that would give the court power to redistribute it.

2. Statutes, Cases and Doctrines

a. A Typical "New Property" Division Case - *Martinez v. Martinez*
Karen C. Martinez v. Jess M. Martinez
818 P.2d 538 (Utah 1991)

STEWART, Justice:

This case is here on a writ of certiorari to the Utah Court of Appeals to review the single issue of whether that court erred in fashioning a new remedy in divorce cases which it called equitable restitution and which may be awarded in addition to alimony, child support, and property. *

I. FACTS

Karen and Jess Martinez were married in 1968, while Mr. Martinez was serving in the United States Army. Both had high school educations. Mr. Martinez began his college education in 1970. Three children were born to the marriage between 1970 and 1975. While an undergraduate student, Mr. Martinez decided to attend medical school, a decision Mrs. Martinez did not agree with because she thought that medical school would be financially draining and would limit her husband's ability to spend time with the family. Nevertheless, Mr. Martinez entered medical school in 1977 and graduated in 1981. He obtained financial support for his education primarily from his own earnings, student loans, the G.I. Bill, and a bequest from his mother's estate. Mrs. Martinez did not contribute financially to her husband's medical education.

Karen Martinez filed a complaint for divorce in 1983, and a decree of divorce was entered in 1985. The trial court found that Dr. Martinez's gross annual income as a resident was $100,000 and that "[d]uring fourteen years that the parties lived together, [Mrs. Martinez] assisted extensively in [Dr. Martinez's] obtaining a college education, medical degree and internship. In addition, [she] made substantial sacrifices in order to facilitate the completion of [his] medical schooling and internship." Mrs. Martinez also earned a very minor amount of income for a short period which was used for family expenses.

The trial court awarded Mrs. Martinez the house the couple had acquired during the marriage and required her to make the mortgage payments of $309 per month. Dr. Martinez was awarded a lien on that property in the amount of $17,678, which represented half the equity in the home. The court also awarded Mrs. Martinez child support of $300 per month per child, and $400 per month alimony for a period of five years, with the condition that the alimony terminate after three years if she remarried. Dr. Martinez was ordered to provide health, accident, and dental insurance for the children and to maintain a life insurance policy on himself for the benefit of the children. He was also awarded the federal tax exemptions for two of the children. The personal property acquired during the marriage was divided equally. Debts in the amount of approximately $19,000 for student loans were assigned to Dr. Martinez. Finally, the court awarded Mrs. Martinez attorney fees in the amount of $2,500. The trial court ruled that Dr. Martinez's medical degree and training were not a marital asset subject to distribution, but considered his right to practice medicine as it affected his income and ability to pay alimony and child support.

On appeal to the Court of Appeals, Mrs. Martinez contended, inter alia, that the child support, alimony, and attorney fees awarded by the trial court were so inadequate as to constitute an abuse of discretion and that the tax exemptions should not have been awarded to Dr. Martinez. That court awarded the tax exemptions to Mrs. Martinez, increased the child support award to $600 per month per child, and awarded permanent alimony of $750 per month. The court affirmed the trial court's award of only a portion of Mrs. Martinez's attorney fees. *Martinez v. Martinez*, 754 P.2d 69, 72-75 (Utah Ct.App.1988). Relying on its own prior decisions, the Court of Appeals also held that Dr. Martinez's medical degree was not marital property subject to division. *See Martinez*, 754 P.2d at 75-76; *see also Rayburn v. Rayburn*, 738 P.2d 238 (Utah Ct.App.1987); *Petersen v. Petersen*, 737 P.2d 237 (Utah Ct.App.1987).

The court concluded, however, that a means should be devised to compensate Mrs. Martinez for the contribution she had made to the family. The court stated that Mrs. Martinez "has earned an award of some permanent financial benefit, in her own right, that will allow her to share in the economic benefits achieved through their joint efforts" and that Dr. Martinez's earning capacity "must be recognized in fashioning those 'legal and equitable remedies' necessary to assist plaintiff to readjust her life." 754 P.2d at 75, 76. Accordingly, the court created a new type of property interest which it called "equitable restitution," to be awarded Mrs. Martinez in addition to her interest in the home, alimony, and child support. [Fn 1. *The Court of Appeals purported to rely on this Court's opinion in Gardner v. Gardner, 748 P.2d 1076 (Utah 1988), as the starting point to devise the property interest it called "equitable restitution." In Gardner, this Court sidestepped the issue of whether an advanced degree could be valued as a marital asset and made subject to distribution in a property award. We observed that there were sufficient marital assets in that case to distinguish it "from others in which equity and fairness required another solution." 748 P.2d at 1081. That statement, however, did not contemplate any such thing as "equitable restitution."*] Judge Jackson, in dissent, concluded that although Mrs. Martinez was entitled to a "generous but fair distribution of property and award of alimony," the concept of "equitable restitution" was not supportable. 754 P.2d at 82 (Jackson, J., dissenting).

The Court of Appeals listed five factors for trial courts to consider in determining when an award of "equitable restitution" should be made. Those factors are (1) the length of the marriage, (2) financial contributions and personal development sacrifices made by the spouse requesting equitable restitution, (3) the duration of the contributions and sacrifices during the marriage, (4) the disparity in earning capacity between the spouses, and (5) the amount of property accumulated during the marriage. 754 P.2d at 78. Although the court failed to indicate what weight those factors should be accorded or just how equitable restitution should be computed, it remanded the case to the trial court to determine what the amount of equitable restitution should be.

Dr. Martinez filed a petition for a writ of certiorari to this Court. We granted the petition solely on the issue of whether the Court of Appeals erred in devising "equitable restitution" as a new form of property in divorce cases.

Mrs. Martinez argues that the concept of equitable restitution is justified on the ground that the remedies available under current law for the distribution of property and the support of a former spouse are inadequate to provide a fair and equitable result. She contends, in essence, that a new form of property must be recognized by the courts to provide for a just and equitable distribution of the increased earning power which one spouse realizes from an advanced education acquired during the marriage. The "investment" referred to by Mrs. Martinez is whatever effort, support, and sacrifice that is made by the nonadvantaged spouse. (Hereinafter, we refer to the spouse receiving the education as the advantaged spouse and the other spouse as the nonadvantaged spouse.)

The increased earning capacity of the advantaged spouse is, according to Mrs. Martinez, "human capital," which she measures by the discounted present value of the projected increased future earnings of the advantaged spouse during the working life of that spouse. Mrs. Martinez urges us to hold that the nonadvantaged spouse is entitled to financial "reimbursement" for whatever efforts were made in assisting the advantaged spouse to obtain an advanced degree, even when wholly nonfinancial. She candidly admits that the purpose of characterizing that interest as a property interest is to make it a nonterminable interest, unlike alimony, which ordinarily terminates upon remarriage. In other words, the nonadvantaged spouse, even one who remarries, should benefit for life by sharing in his or her former spouse's increased earning capacity.

The Court of Appeals' concept of equitable restitution cannot be sustained for three reasons. First, the concept of equitable restitution is based on the proposition that a failed marriage is a venture akin to a commercial partnership in which the spouses invest their time and effort solely for remunerative activities. Although marriage is a partnership in some respects, a marriage is certainly not comparable to a commercial partnership. The efforts each spouse makes for the other and for their common marital interests cannot be quantified in monetary terms, their respective contributions netted out, and a balance struck at the termination of a marriage. The very idea of marriage contemplates mutual effort and mutual sacrifice. Yet, in this case, Mrs. Martinez would value only her contribution to the marriage and not his. In any event, the spouses' contributions cannot be reduced to a common denominator that allows for a valid comparison in monetary terms. Indeed, the very attempt to do so would interfere with the trial court's ability to achieve an equitable result based on the needs of the spouses in light of the monetary resources available. For example, if a spouse avoids his or her marital responsibilities, the partnership theory might result in denying that spouse any award of support or property at divorce, irrespective of his or her need and the other spouse's ability to pay. That is not the law.

Second, an award of equitable restitution would be extraordinarily speculative. Although the Court of Appeals' opinion is somewhat unclear as to what kind of economic interest it intended to create or just how it should be computed, it did state, "An award of equitable restitution will not terminate upon plaintiff's remarriage, and may be payable in lump sum or periodically over time depending on the circumstances of each case." 754 P.2d at 78-79. Clearly, the Court of Appeals contemplated a substantial award. [FN2] Mrs. Martinez asserts that equitable restitution should be based on the discounted value of Dr. Martinez's earnings as a physician over his remaining working life to age 65, less the amount a high school graduate would have earned over the same time. Based on those calculations, Mrs. Martinez values Dr. Martinez's medical education at $1,555,000. *[Fn 3. Dr. W. Chris Lewis was the expert used by Mrs. Martinez to place a value on the increased "income stream" that Dr. Martinez would have for the remainder of his career. Dr. Lewis had not previously valued a medical degree or medical practice. He calculated the present value of the lifetime earnings of a healthy 38-year-old currently earning $100,000 per year to be $2,482,500. He then deducted what he thought an average high school graduate would earn over the same period of time, or $926,000, and concluded that the value of Dr. Martinez's "medical education and training" based on his increased earning capacity was $1,555,000. On the basis of that amount, Mrs. Martinez would be awarded a substantial sum.]*

Although the Court of Appeals did not specifically adopt this formula for calculating the amount of equitable restitution, neither did it reject it or refer to any formula by which the amount of equitable restitution could be calculated. In any event, any formula which accomplished that court's purpose would necessarily be inherently and highly speculative. If, for example, a court awarded a lump-sum payment, the award would be based upon a wholly false assumption if the payor spouse's working life were cut short by death, illness, change of profession, or early retirement or if the working life were interrupted for any other reason. Furthermore, whether a court awarded a lump sum or periodic payments, the receiving spouse would be given what is tantamount to a lifetime estate in the paying spouse's earnings that have no necessary relationship to the receiving spouse's actual contribution to the enhanced earning power or to that spouse's needs, however broadly defined.

Third, although the Court of Appeals stated that it rejected the proposition that Dr. Martinez's medical degree should be valued as a property interest and Mrs. Martinez given an interest in it, that court's concept of equitable restitution is essentially indistinguishable.

The recipient of an advanced degree obtains that degree on the basis of his or her innate personal talents, capabilities, and acquired skills and knowledge. Such a degree is highly personal to the recipient and has none of the traditional characteristics of property. "It does not have an exchange value or any objective transferable value on an open market. It is personal to the holder. It terminates on death of the holder and is not inheritable. It cannot be assigned, sold, transferred, conveyed, or pledged." In re Marriage of Graham, 194 Colo. 429, 432, 574 P.2d 75, 77 (1978). The time has long since passed when a person's personal attributes and talents were thought to be subject to monetary valuation for commercial purposes. In short, we do not recognize a property interest in personal characteristics of another person such as intelligence, skill, judgment, and temperament, however characterized.

The law accepted in other jurisdictions almost unanimously is that professional degrees are not marital property and are not subject to equitable distribution. Of twenty-four jurisdictions that have considered the issue, all but two have held that a professional degree or license is not marital property subject to equitable distribution. *See Archer v. Archer*, 303 Md. 347, 493 A.2d 1074, 1077 (1985); *see also, In re Marriage of Graham*, 194 Colo. 429, 574 P.2d 75 (1978); *Grosskopf v. Grosskopf*, 677 P.2d 814 (Wyo.1984). *See generally* Annotation, Spouse's Professional Degree or License as Marital Property for Purposes of Alimony, Support, or Property Settlement, 4 A.L.R.4th 1294 (1981 & Supp.1990). [FN4] *See contra O'Brien v. O'Brien*, 114 Misc.2d 233, 452 N.Y.S.2d 801 (N.Y.Sup.Ct.1982), aff'd as modified, 66 N.Y.2d 576, 489 N.E.2d 712, 498 N.Y.S.2d 743 (1985) (holding that a professional degree is a marital asset based on a New York statute unlike Utah's).

Mrs. Martinez's contention that the remedies provided by Utah Code Ann. § 30-3-5 are insufficient is without merit. Those remedies are adequate to fashion an appropriate award that meets the standards to be applied in determining awards of alimony. *Paffel v. Paffel*, 732 P.2d 96, 100-01 (Utah 1986); *Jones v. Jones*, 700 P.2d 1072, 1075 (Utah 1985); *English v. English*, 565 P.2d 409, 410 (Utah 1977). An alimony award should be determined by the receiving spouse's earning capacity, financial condition, and needs and by the ability of the other spouse to provide support. *See Jones*, 700 P.2d at 1075.

Usually the needs of the spouses are assessed in light of the standard of living they had during marriage. *Gardner v. Gardner*, 748 P.2d 1076, 1081 (Utah 1988); Jones, 700 P.2d at 1075. In some circumstances, it may be appropriate to try to equalize the spouses' respective standards of living. *Gardner*, 748 P.2d at 1081; *see also Olson v. Olson*, 704 P.2d 564, 566 (Utah 1985); *Higley v. Higley*, 676 P.2d 379, 381 (Utah 1983). When a marriage of long duration dissolves on the threshold of a major change in the income of one of the spouses due to the collective efforts of both, that change, unless unrelated to the efforts put forward by the spouses during marriage, should be given some weight in fashioning the support award. *Cf. Savage v. Savage*, 658 P.2d 1201, 1205 (Utah 1983). Thus, if one spouse's earning capacity has been greatly enhanced through the efforts of both spouses during the marriage, it may be appropriate for the trial court to make a compensating adjustment in dividing the marital property and awarding alimony. *See e.g. Kerr v. Kerr*, 610 P.2d 1380 (Utah 1980); *Tremayne v. Tremayne*, 116 Utah 483, 211 P.2d 452 (1949).

Here, the trial court found that the parties would have enjoyed a higher family income because of Dr. Martinez's increased income, which was due to some extent to the efforts of both spouses during the marriage. Although Dr. Martinez earned $100,000 a year before the parties divorced, Mrs. Martinez had not enjoyed a higher standard of living as a result of that increased income. The trial court awarded Mrs. Martinez alimony in the amount of $400 per month for a period of five years. That amount was nonterminable for a period of three years even if Mrs. Martinez remarried. The Court of Appeals, relying upon *Jones v. Jones*, 700 P.2d 1072 (Utah 1985), modified that award by increasing it to $750 per month subject to the provisions of Utah Code Ann. § 30-3-5 (1987), which provides for the termination of a permanent alimony award in certain circumstances. That and other modifications made by the Court of Appeals in favor of Mrs. Martinez have not been challenged by either party in this Court.

We granted certiorari solely on the issue of equitable restitution and denied certiorari on all other issues. We therefore express no opinion on the appropriateness of the other modifications made by the Court of Appeals in the divorce decree.

The Court of Appeals' direction to the trial court to devise an award of equitable restitution is reversed, and the case is remanded to the trial court for further proceedings in light of this opinion and the opinion of the Court of Appeals.

HALL, C.J., and HOWE, Associate C.J., concur.

ZIMMERMAN, Justice (concurring and dissenting):

I join Justice Stewart's opinion in its rejection of the equitable restitution doctrine created by the court of appeals. As he states, the trial court has ample power to make alimony and property division awards which will ensure that equity is done to a spouse who is denied an increase in standard of living because a divorce occurs on the threshold of an event that is economically advantageous to the other spouse. There is no reason to create a new and conceptually ill-defined property concept to meet this need.

Justice Durham's dissent deserves some comment. She suggests that we should affirm the court of appeals' adoption of an equitable restitution doctrine because our existing case law on property division and alimony is insufficiently flexible to allow for the fashioning of a remedy for situations of the type presented here. She then suggests that if we are going to rely upon property division and alimony law to deal with these problems, we need to articulate guidelines for the trial courts in dealing with this area.

I disagree with Justice Durham's premise that our cases do not permit the use of alimony and property division to produce a fair result in these cases. It may be that our prior cases have not addressed the issue, but the opinion Justice Stewart has authored today does. The majority specifically states:

> When a marriage of long duration dissolves on the threshold of a major change in the income of one of the spouses due to the collective efforts of both, that change, unless unrelated to the efforts put forward by the spouses during marriage, should be given some weight in fashioning the support award.

At 542.

The majority opinion also makes it clear that the trial court can make such compensating adjustments to both the property division and the alimony award as it deems necessary to make the ultimate decision equitable:

> [I]f one spouse's earning capacity has been greatly enhanced through the efforts of both spouses during the marriage, it may be appropriate for the trial court to make a compensating adjustment in dividing the marital property and awarding alimony.

At 542.

In light of this language, joined in by four members of the court, there can be no doubt that trial judges are empowered and enjoined to take circumstances like those presented here into account in making alimony and property division awards. To the extent that Justice Durham's opinion suggests the contrary, it misstates the law.

As for what appears to be Justice Durham's larger concern--that we have given the trial courts insufficient guidance as to how to make the required adjustments in awards--I agree that over time, we will have to give further shape to the rules governing the division of property and the award of alimony to be sure that both parties in cases like this one are dealt with fairly. However, there seems little need to opt for one theoretical framework now. In this area, law development on a case-by-case basis may be the best approach.

On a separate issue, I dissent from the majority's remand of this matter to the trial court. The court of appeals found that the trial court abused its discretion and attempted to modify the decree to make it sufficiently equitable to pass appellate muster. In doing so, the court of appeals modified the alimony award and the child support award and ordered equitable restitution. We granted certiorari to consider only the equitable restitution portion of that modification of the divorce decree, and we have now said that in making that specific modification, the court of appeals overreached. We have not said that the decree was equitable without some adjustment that would address the problem which motivated the creation of the equitable restitution doctrine. We have only said that the equitable result sought by the court of appeals cannot be achieved that way. In fact, the opinion of Justice Stewart recognizes that the trial court had the power to effect a remedy for the underlying problem.

Under these circumstances, we should remand the matter to the court of appeals for further proceedings. It should be allowed to again address the propriety of the trial court's decree in light of our explication of the law. There is no occasion for us to send this matter back to the trial court. If the court of appeals thinks it needs more information from the trial court, there will be time enough for such a remand.

DURHAM, Justice dissenting:

The majority opinion holds that professional degrees are not marital property and rejects the principle of equitable restitution fashioned by the court of appeals, on the theory that currently recognized rights to alimony, child support, and property distribution are sufficient to solve the complex problems posed by cases like this. I disagree and would argue that if we are going to prohibit the use of the principles relied on by the court of appeals, then we must fashion a new and more flexible theory of alimony.

First, there is insufficient tangible property to compensate the spouse who has been "investing" time, labor, earnings, and postponed improvements in standard of living for the long-term benefit of the marital community when the marriage ends before the investment has "paid off." Second, child support protects the rights of the children of divorcing spouses to share in present and future benefits of earning capacity; it may not legitimately be used to compensate a former spouse for the value of what she has "invested" without return (or lost) as a result of the termination of the marriage. Finally, alimony as currently understood in our law is theoretically inadequate to perform the compensation function that the court of appeals identified as necessary in this case. One need only examine the alimony decisions cited by the majority opinion to ascertain that alimony in this state has depended on (1) the financial conditions and needs of the recipient spouse, (2) the ability of the recipient spouse to produce sufficient income for self-support, and (3) the ability of the payor spouse to provide support. *See e.g. Jones v. Jones*, 700 P.2d 1072, 1075 (Utah 1985). To those fundamental principles, we have added the consideration that "[a]n alimony award should, in as far as possible, equalize the parties' respective standards of living and maintain them at a level as close as possible to the standard of living enjoyed during the marriage." *Higley v.*

Higley, 676 P.2d 379, 381 (Utah 1983) (emphasis added).

I submit that none of the foregoing principles address the specific problem posed by termination of a marriage in which one or both spouses have sacrificed in tangible and intangible ways, foregoing income, accumulation of property, an enhanced standard of living, and the educational and career- development opportunities of one so that the other might acquire a valuable and prestigious professional degree. When the marriage ends before the marital community has enjoyed the benefits expected from that sacrifice, the nonholder of the degree suffers a very real loss. Whether we adopt a doctrine of "equitable restitution" or rethink the theory and function of alimony, we must address the requirements of equity and justice to compensate in some fashion for that loss. As David S. Dolowitz recently noted in the Utah Bar Journal, equitable restitution is a form of alimony "paid to produce an equitable balancing of property and income that cannot be otherwise effected" by the traditional forms of support alimony and rehabilitative alimony. Dolowitz, The Impact of Tax Laws on Divorce, Utah B.J., at 8, 9 (August/September 1991) (emphasis added).

Other commentators have recently devoted a great deal of scholarly attention to the problems of compensating spouses for losses they suffer because of decisions to further the marital enterprise by enhancing the education or career of one spouse at cost to both. In a recent article discussing the question Should "The Theory of Alimony" Include Nonfinancial Losses and Motivations?, 1991 B.Y.U.L.Rev. 259, law professor Ira Ellman (author of The Theory of Alimony, 77 Calif.L.Rev. 1 (1989)) observes:

> [T]he purpose of alimony under "The Theory" is to eliminate the financial disincentives for marital sharing behavior that would be present in the absence of a remedy, rather than to provide positive incentives.... The principle is actually rather modest in scope. The policy upon which it is based would seem, at least at first, to be broadly acceptable: spouses otherwise inclined to conduct themselves during the marriage in a manner that benefits the marital community ought not be discouraged from acting that way for fear that, if the marriage were to dissolve, they would be left with all of the financial loss arising from their decision. This is especially true when, for example, the wife has a loss while her husband has no loss, or even reaps a gain (as would be the case where the wife gives up her employment to advance her husband's).

B.Y.U.L.Rev. at 265.

This approach is connected to an assessment of loss, not one of need, as has traditionally been the case in the theory of alimony. It requires the courts to discover or create means by which a spouse may recover after divorce the value of what he or she lost by reason of investment in the marital enterprise, where that investment has resulted in a net gain to the other spouse.

> Once the spouses' gain or loss from the marriage has been measured, they can be compared against one another to determine if one spouse has a loss that should be reallocated to the other. Clearly all losses cannot be compensable, for the simple reason that the claim is against the other spouse, and both spouses may have suffered a loss from their marriage. A loss is compensable, in whole or part, only if the other spouse's loss is smaller, or if the other spouse has achieved a gain.

Id. at 271. Professor Ellman goes on to describe this as a "reliance measure" of loss, as opposed to the traditional contract damage measure of expectation, and explains its justification at some length. He also suggests several important limitations on his theory of alimony: for example, (1) only residual post-marriage losses are compensable, not inequities in the exchange during marriage; (2) only financial losses are compensable; and (3) only losses arising from marital "sharing behavior" are compensable.

I do not propose that we adopt Professor Ellman's theory wholesale; I only cite it as one example of a thoughtful effort to solve the problems posed by the common circumstances illustrated in this case. My criticism of the majority opinion is that it makes no effort to guide the trial courts in fashioning a realistic remedy for what is a realistic loss. It rejects the effort of the court of appeals to do precisely that and offers no alternative. The legal status quo is unacceptable, in my view, and I hope that the majority will be willing in the future to make good on its representation that the concept of alimony (or property distribution when there is any property) can be accommodated to the need for equity. Unless and until that happens, any woman (or man, for that matter) who sacrifices her own education, earning capacity, or career development so that a spouse may advance and the marriage may prosper as a joint venture will inevitably suffer the full cost of that decision at divorce, while the advantaged spouse will continue to walk away from the marriage with all of the major financial gain. That is unfair, and in this area at least, the responsibility of the law is to seek fairness.

b. Analysis of Complex Property Division Issues

The first question that arises in property distribution disputes is whether an asset is "property." This question seldom arises with regard to traditional forms of property (land, houses, cars, furniture, jewelry, money, stocks, etc.). However, the question has arisen significantly with regard to some forms of the "new property." *The prevailing rule in American law is that skills, earning capacity, and personal attributes are not property.* Rather, skills and earning capacity are personal characteristics inseparable from the core of individual identity protected by the Fourteenth Amendment and over which the state generally has no power to dictate or control. American Law Institute, Principles of the Law of Family Dissolution: Analysis and Recommendations, Preliminary Draft No. 4 (ALI, Philadelphia Sept. 9, 1993) §4.08 at 207-08. As the Colorado Supreme Court stated in *In re Graham*, 194 Colo. 429, 574 P.2d 75, 77 (1978), an asset (in that case an educational degree or professional license) is not "property" if

> [i]t does not have an exchange value or any objective transferable value on an open market. It is personal to the holder. It terminates on death of the holder and is not inheritable. It cannot be assigned, sold, transferred, conveyed, or pledged. An advanced degree is a cumulative product of many years of previous education,˙ combined with diligence and hard work. It may not be acquired by the mere expenditure of money. It is simply an intellectual achievement that may potentially assist in the future acquisition of property. In our view, it has none of the attributes of property in the usual sense of that term.

On the other hand, assets that are transferable generally are deemed to be property. Thus, most courts have concluded that pensions, business and practice goodwill, disability payments, personal injury awards, and workers' compensation awards are "property" for purposes of division upon divorce. These topics are described in further detail below.

With respect to the "new property," the task of separating the "return on labor performed during marriage" from "skills, earning capacity, and personal attributes" may be quite complicated. The "new property" consists primarily of labor-exchange assets, including various forms of protection of the "future" value of labor exchanges. Income-replacement future benefits are a particularly difficult kind of "new property" for courts to characterize.

After an asset is characterized as "property," it must further be characterized as "marital" (or "community") or "separate" property. The currently popular concept of "marital property" is largely borrowed from community property regimes and reflects the community property ideal that during the marriage the parties owe the marital union (themselves together, not individually) their labor and services and the income derived therefrom. It also reflects the default principle that all property acquired during the marriage is presumed to be marital property, unless it is proven to be separate property. Many kinds of valuable assets are acquired in part during marriage and in part before marriage or after divorce. Most states treat these assets as part marital and part separate, in the proportion that they were acquired with labor or resources that were marital or separate. Examples are provided below.

After characterization of the asset (as "property" and "marital" or "separate") the court must determine the present value of the property (called "valuation"). For determining the value of contingent future benefits, there are two prevailing methods of establishing current value. One is to use the amount the earner spouse would get for or from the asset (by sale or withdrawal) at the time of divorce. That is the simplest and clearest, but often the least inclusive. The other method is to determine the value the benefits will have at a later time such as when the pension or benefit is payable (often involving actuarial computation), and reduce that sum to present value by discounting for mortality and vesting. The question may boil down to a contest between appraisal opinions of plaintiff's and defendant's experts.

The final step in the judicial process of property distribution is to distribute the asset. This, too, presents special problems for many forms of "new property." The simplest and historically dominant method of distribution is and was to divide the assets once-for-all at the time of the entry of the decree. With respect to property that will become available or have greater value in the future, this may create problems because it could leave one party penniless for some time. It also puts on the party given the deferred expectancy the risk that the asset will lose its value (stock market crash, devaluation, inability to collect, etc.). Thus, deferred distribution or deferred division are often used in cases involving nonwealthy divorcing spouses with interests in some form of "new property" that will pay potentially valuable sums in the future. For example, the court can order a specific amount to be paid when the benefit is received (for example, upon retirement). Another alternative (apparently now the preferred alternative) is to award the non-employee spouse a percentage of the indefinite future benefits (usually in the form of periodic installments) to be paid whenever the benefits are paid. Another alternative is for the court to simply postpone dividing the "new property" until it begins to pay benefits or a liquid value can be fixed. However, this increases the costs (financial and temporal) to the judiciary, and in the years between divorce and retirement, memories may dim, so this is not the preferred alternative.

c. Examples of How Some Forms of "New Property" Are Analyzed for Equitable Division

Among the most important and contested types of "new property" are pensions, goodwill, degrees and licenses, and recovery for disability, workers' compensation or personal injury awards.

1) Pensions

Historically *pensions* were gratuitous allowances given in recognition of valuable services, bounties which a generous employer might grant to a loyal servant, not as a matter of right but of discretion, and which could be withdrawn and withheld by the grantor at will. Black's Law Dictionary (West Publishing Co., Minneapolis, 1968) p. 1291. Today, a *pension* is usually considered to be a contractual system of deferred compensation for services previously rendered; paid by the employer to the employee after retirement to provide a source of post-retirement income. ERISA, 29 U.S.C.A. §1002(2)(A). It has been said that in many families, the pension and the house are the only assets of substantial value. Since at least two-thirds of all employees in the United States have pensions, the characterization and division of pension benefits upon divorce is a subject of frequent concern in American divorces.

Pension benefits or rights may be *vested* or *nonvested*. They are vested if the employee's right to receive benefits is fixed and would survive termination of employment. Otherwise the pension is deemed "nonvested." It usually takes a substantial period of employment for a pension to vest. A pension is *matured* if the employee has an unconditional right to immediate payment; usually that happens upon retirement. Thus, many pension rights vest after a certain period of employment, but do not mature until retirement and election to begin drawing benefits. For example, under the pension plan offered by the one university, retirement benefits are vested upon completion of certain number of years of service (the number depends upon the age of the employee), but the earliest age at which one may begin to *draw* retirement benefits (early retirement) is 55, and normal retirement with full benefits is at age 65.

The simplest kinds of pensions to value and distribute are called *defined contribution* pension plans. These kinds of pensions consists of contributions made by or on behalf of the employee, plus income from the employer, which are used to purchase an annuity for each covered individual employee. The other kind of pension is a *defined benefit* pension plan, in which there is no separate retirement account for any particular employee and the employees contribute nothing. The employer provides the pension, often establishing a fund from which all employee's pensions are drawn. The pension benefit is determined by a formula (usually a certain amount per period of time) that has no necessary connection to any amounts set aside during employment.

Because pensions historically were matters of discretion, not legal right, early cases declined to treat pensions as property divisible upon divorce. Arguments against treating pensions and retirement benefits as property emphasize their uncertainty (both in ascertaining the scope of benefits to be paid in advance, and in determining how long they will be paid -- death varies) and the nontransferability of the benefits (comparing them to educational degrees or professional licenses). Divorcing employee spouses have argued that they are similar to future inheritances, which are not divisible on divorce. Moreover, pensions are not merely deferred payments for past services, but are intended to replace future [including postdivorce] earnings, which would belong solely to the individual earner after divorce. However, today courts in all states treat *vested* pension or retirement benefits as divisible property upon divorce. Most states view vested pension benefits as deferred compensation -- like money earned during the marriage but put in the bank and saved for retirement -- or note that the financial contributions of the employee spouse that earned the pension benefits were marital property.

Because of contingencies that could prevent realizing any benefits, nonvested pensions were the source of much debate and disparate decisions in the courts for many years. However, today the issue has been resolved in favor treating nonvested pension benefits as marital property in virtually all states. The leading case to establish that nonvested pensions are divisible marital (community) property is *In re Marriage of Brown*, 15 Cal. 3d 838, 544 P.2d 561, 126 Cal. Rptr. 633 (1976), decided by the California Supreme Court in 1976. The California Supreme Court distinguished nonvested pensions from "mere expectancies" such as future inheritances, characterizing pensions instead as "part of the consideration earned by the employee." 544 P.2d at 565. Nonvested pension rights are contractual choses in action, the court reasoned, which are divisible community property. While ripening of nonvested pensions are contingent on continued employment, "when community funds or efforts are expended to acquire a conditional right to future income, the courts do not hesitate to treat that right as a community asset."544 P.2d at 566. If payment is received it is remuneration for serviced performed during marriage by a spouse, and therefore it is community property.

Special mention must be made of the pension and retirement benefits of federal employees. In two significant cases decided in 1979 and 1981 the Supreme Court ruled that federal laws regulating retirement-related benefits, especially those provided by the federal government to certain employees, preempt state property division divorce laws. In *Hisquidero v. Hisquidero*, 439 U.S. 572 (1979), the Supreme Court of the United States held that the federal law preempted state community property and property division law, and that the federal law made railroad employee retirement plan benefits the separate benefits of the employee, exempt from division upon divorce. The Court held that Congress intended to protect such pensions uniformly in all states, considering them to be more like social welfare benefits than private contractual rights, and it interpreted the nonassignment clause of the federal act to override state property division laws. Two years later the U.S. Supreme Court dropped an even bigger bombshell. In *McCarty v. McCarty*, 453 U.S. 210 (1981), the Supreme Court interpreted the federal law regulating military retirement benefits and held, again, that Congress intended that they not be subject to state community property or property division laws. The U.S. Supreme Court found that Congress intended that retirement pay of military service personnel be the personal entitlement of the retiree, free from all claims of creditors and others (except for child support and alimony). That decision meant that state courts could not equitably redistribute or divide as community property military retirement benefits (typically the most substantial benefits acquired by military couples).

Thus, the Court found that when Congress passed the Railroad Retirement Act and the military retirement laws, it did not intend to provide protection for spouses. Indeed, since those laws originated before "marital property" was widely recognized, in the days of the predominance of the title theory of property division upon divorce, the law that such retirement benefits belonged to the earning (title-holding) spouse reflected the prevailing beliefs of the traditional property system of the day. Between passage of those laws and the time *Hisquierdo* and *McCarty* were decided, the property system had substantially changed in most states to reflect partnership (marital property) rather than trusteeship (paternalistic) notions. However, Congress had not revised its statutes to keep up with those changes.

The unpopular Supreme Court rulings in *Hisquierdo* and *McCarty* put pressure on Congress to update these laws. *Hisquierdo* was legislatively overruled when Congress amended the railroad retirement law to create two tiers of railroad retirement benefits. One tier is divisible under state law, the other tier is separate and nondivisible. Likewise, the year after the Supreme Court decided *McCarty*, Congress enacted the Uniformed Services Former Spouses Protection Act of 1982, 10 U.S.C. §1408 (1983 & Supp. 1995), which declared that subject to certain qualifications, state courts "may treat disposable retired or retainer pay [of retired military personnel]. . . either as property solely of the member or as property of the member and his spouse in accordance with the law of the jurisdiction."

Statutes regulating the Federal Employees Retirement System (FERS), 5 U.S.C. §8345(j)(1) et seq. (1980), and Foreign Service Pension System (FSPS), 22 U.S.C. §4054, 4069 (1990), also provide that state courts may treat *federal civil service* and *foreign service* retirement benefits as divisible marital or community property subject to equitable distribution upon divorce. Thus, it is now clear that virtually all federal retirement pension benefits may be (and are) deemed by state courts to be marital property, subject to division or equitable distribution upon divorce.

Pension are among the most difficult of assets to value and distribute upon divorce. The simplest kinds of pensions to value and distribute are *defined contribution* pension plans. The contributions of or for a particular employee are (or easily can be) segregated into a separate retirement account for the specific employee. The value of these kinds of pensions can be computed with accuracy -- the amount contributed (by employer and employee) to the employee's retirement account during the marriage, and the accrued interest, constitutes marital property.

Valuation of *defined contribution plan* pension benefits is relatively simple. The proportion of the pension contributions acquired during marriage (called the *coverture factor*, where the numerator is the years of marriage during employment and the denominator is the total years of employment), is calculated then divided equally (presumably) or equitably. For example, if Husband (H) has been employed for 20 years at Acme Company which has a defined contribution pension plan to which H and Acme have been contributing, and if H was married to Wife (W) during that entire time, the coverture factor would be one (20 over 20), meaning all of the pension would be marital property, and the court would equitably distribute all of it, presumably awarding one-half to W. If H and W had been married only 12 of the 20 years during with the pension was accruing, the coverture factor would be 60%, meaning only 60% of the pension would be marital property, and the court would presumably award one-half of that portion (30% of the total pension) to W.

However, valuation of *defined benefit* pension benefits is much more difficult because in a *defined benefit* pension plan, there is no separate retirement account for any particular employee. The pension benefit is determined by a formula (usually a certain amount per period of time) that has no necessary connection to any amounts set aside during employment. One method of valuation is to use the amount the earner spouse would be entitled to take from the fund at the time of divorce -- the *liquidation value*. That is the simplest and clearest, but least inclusive. The other method is to determined the value the pension will have when payable, and reduce it to *present value* by discounting for mortality and vesting contingencies.

The *present value* of the pension earned to the time of divorce is the preferred method of determining value of a *defined benefit* pension plan. To determine present value, the court must estimate the amount of retirement benefits the owning spouse will receive, discount it to present value taking into account also mortality and forfeiture risks. That dollar amount is split proportionately according to the period of employment during which the parties were married (the *coverture fraction*), and that portion is divided between the parties. However, estimating the value of defined benefit pensions, unlike defined contribution pensions, entails substantial guess-work. The difficulty of estimating life-expectancy, future cost-of-living increases, and selection of retirement payout options makes ascertaining present value very subjective. For these reasons, when large amounts are at stake, future division of defined benefit pensions is preferred. But that creates other problems.

Since 1974, the federal Employees Retirement Income Security Act (ERISA) has regulated employer-sponsored pension and retirement plans in the United States. 29 U.S.C. § 1001 et seq. If an employee benefit plan "qualifies" under ERISA, employer contributions to it are tax deductible, and investment earnings are exempt from immediate taxation. Thus, employers make great effort to see that their pension plans qualify under ERISA. For ten years after ERISA was enacted, the law prohibited the assignment or alienation of an employee's pension benefits. That made it difficult for a divorced spouse of an employee to obtain property division of the pension benefits. Courts and agencies disagreed over whether a state court in a divorce case could divide or offset the pension in the process of dividing marital property.

In 1984 Congress enacted the Retirement Equity Act (REA) to clarify the matter. 29 U.S.C. § 1056 and I.R.C., 26 U.S.C. §401. It authorized the assignment of part or all of an employee's retirement or pension benefits if done under a Qualified Domestic Relations Order, known as a "QDRO." Basically, a QDRO is an order, decree or judgment made pursuant to state domestic relations law that creates or recognizes an alternative payee's right to receive some or all of an employee's benefits under an employee benefit plan. The key requirements of a QDRO are that it clearly

     1) identify the employee,
     2) identify the alternate payee (spouse, former spouse, child, or other dependent),
     3) identify the benefit plan,
     4) identify the amount or percentage of benefits to be paid to the alternate payee,
     5) identify the time period during which the alternate payee is to be paid,
     6) relate to division of marital property, or payment of alimony or child support, and
     7) not alter the amount, form, or benefits payable under the pension plan.

The statute sets forth details of how these requirements are to be fulfilled. Getting QDROs done correctly is of such importance that some family lawyers specialize in QDRO work. An order for property division of pension benefits that complies with the requirement as a QDRO is enforceable against a qualified pension plan, and direct payment of a portion of the pension benefits directly to the ex-spouse of the employee is permitted under the REA for QDROs. The importance of direct payment of retirement benefits to a former spouse can hardly be overstated because it provides increased likelihood that payments will be made. The REA also created two types of survivors benefits for spouses.

Distribution of federal pensions is governed by a different set of federal laws (for the most part) than governs distribution of private (nonfederal) pensions. For *Civil Service*, disability retirement benefits are treated the same as retirement for age and service; no time of service or limit on award is imposed. 5 U.S.C. 8345(j). *Foreign Service* requires marriage for ten years during creditable service for the former spouse to get a share, presumed to be 50% of the retired pay earned during the marriage, but the amount may be lesser or greater by agreement or court decree. 22 U.S.C. 4054(a). *Military* retirement benefits of up to 50% of the member's disposable retirement pay are payable to a former spouse if there was marriage for 10 years during military service. For less than 10 years, direct payment is not authorized, but alimony may be. 10 U.S.C. 1408. The retirement payment stops upon death of either the service member or former spouse.

Social security benefits are a special form of pension or retirement benefit, provided by the federal government as an old-age, retirement survivors, and disability program funded by a special tax. Social security benefits are governed by federal law. Most courts have ruled that social security benefits may not be divided as marital property upon divorce, but there are a few contrary opinions. However, social security benefits are payable to nonearning spouses who were married to an earning spouse for at least 10 years before divorcing (though a spouse or former spouse may not get in full both survivor benefit & social security, to preclude dual payment based on same earnings). The non-earning spouse may get up to one-half of the ex-spouse's benefits unless she would be entitled to more on the basis of her own status as and earner. While social security benefits have been held to be nondivisible, many courts take them into account in awarding other property between the spouses to achieve an overall equal or equitable distribution.

2) Goodwill

Another intangible type of property is the "goodwill" associated with a going economic enterprise. "Goodwill" is commonly defined as "the amount by which the market value of a going concern exceeds the total value of its assets ('asset value'), without regard to the reason for the excess." A.L.I., *op. cit.* §4.07 at 215. "Goodwill reflects the ability of a business to earn a profit that is higher than overage for that industry." Michael E. Kline, "Law Practice Goodwill: an Evolving Concept," in Encyclopedia of Matrimonial Practice 889, 901 (Prentice Hall, Ronald L. Brown, ed., 1993). Goodwill is tied most closely to the expected income flow, and may reflect many variables such as location, reputation, etc. It may reflect the spouse's personal skill, labor, and earning capacity as well as the age, reputation, and location of the enterprise and other business assets. Accounting conventions usually ascribe no goodwill to a business until it is sold. Upon sale, the excess value over tangible assets is listed as goodwill in the buyer's balance sheet. While most going enterprises operating by divorcing parties are not sold at that time, most courts try to ascertain the "goodwill" value of a going business for purposes of property distribution upon divorce.

Since goodwill may derive from both property and nonproperty factors characterization may be complicated; if it results from the spouse's personal skill, labor, and earning capacity, it should not be deemed property; if it results from location, it should be property. The prevailing rule is that, if acquired during marriage goodwill is divisible property to the extent it has value not attributable to the value of the spousal earning capacity and spousal skills. The key to capture and division of goodwill seems to be realizability -- value that can be "realized" on the open market. Thus, the starting point is that goodwill must be transferable (realizable) to be divisible. Proof of the goodwill portion of the sales prices of similar businesses is the key to proving realizabilty. Unrealizable (unsalable) goodwill presents a much more difficult problem, and that is the situation with respect to professional practices. Most professional licenses are heavily regulated by the state and may not be sold. The state courts are split over whether professional goodwill is divisible. Some compare professional goodwill to a professional license itself, which nearly all states have ruled is not divisible property. Others disallow division of professional goodwill on the ground that it may result in double-valuation. On the other hand, some states find that even though professional goodwill may not independently be sold, it has value in conjunction with other assets that can be sold, and it may be treated as divisible property. The prevailing rule appears to be that professional goodwill is divisible property if it has value independent of the reputation of the professional-spouse. Thus, professional goodwill must be separated into two components: practice goodwill and personal/professional goodwill. Generally practice goodwill is deemed divisible property, but the personal/professional goodwill is not.

Valuation of business or practice goodwill is also a matter of conjecture and appraisal. Goodwill is only property to the extent that it is realizable. If the business is not being sold at the time of divorce, proving the amount that would be realized if the business were sold is not a matter of mathematic precision. Actual sales of comparable businesses in the area are the best indicator of the goodwill value, but expert testimony may suffice or buy-out agreements may indicate value.

3) Educational Degrees and Professional Licenses

In 1985, the New York Court of Appeals held in *O'Brien v. O'Brien*, 66 N.Y.2d 576, 498 N.Y.S.2d 743, 489 N.E.2d 712 (1985), that a divorcing man's license to practice medicine, earned while he was largely supported by his wife who sacrificed her own career and educational opportunities to put her husband through medical school, was "property" subject to equitable division upon divorce. The basis for the *O'Brien* holding was very specific language in the New York Equitable Distribution Law declaring that the court must consider in making equitable distribution "contributions [of] . . . a spouse . . . to the career or career potential of the other property" and must ignore the claimed difficulty of valuation of "any interest in a . . . profession." 489 N.E.2d at 716, citing N.Y. Domestic Relations Law §236[B][5][d][6], [9]. Many commentators expected that many other states would follow New York and treat professional licenses and educational degrees as "property" divisible upon divorce. However, only one other appellate court in America followed *O'Brien* (*Daniels v. Daniels*, 418 N.W.2d 924 (Mich. App. 1988)). No other state legislature in America treats a spouse's future enhanced earning capacity as "property" for purposes of equitable distribution. No other state supreme court has followed the *O'Brien* approach. In 1997 the New York bar recommended (unsuccessfully) that the legislature overturn *O'Brien*. Even the ALI *Principles of the Law of Marital Dissolution* reject the *O'Brien* rule treating licenses and degrees as property. *ALI, infra* §4.07.

There are three reasons why the *O'Brien* rule that licenses (and degrees) are property has been so overwhelmingly rejected. The conceptual reason is summarized in *Graham, supra.* A license or degree is quite distinguishable from traditional forms of property, and is much too inseparable from individual talent, skill and effort to be comfortably classified as property. The next reason for the near-unanimous rejection of *O'Brien* has to do with the experience of New York since *O'Brien*. For example, in *Elkus v. Elkus,* 169 A.D.2d 134, 572 N.Y.S.2d 901 (1991), *O'Brien* was applied to the career of an opera singer, awarding her husband a share of her future earning potential because of her career development during marriage. In *Golub v. Golub,* 139 Misc. 2d 440, 527 N.Y.S.2d 946 (Sup. Ct. 1988), the actress-wife's career was deemed marital or community property. In another case a New York court applied *O'Brien* to hold that the value of a divorcing government lawyer's license to practice law included the potential income the attorney-spouse could earn as a private attorney, not just the lower-paying job he had as an attorney employed by a government agency. *Cronin v. Cronin,* 131 Misc.2d 879, 502 N.Y.S.2d 368 (Sup. Ct. 1986). In yet another case, the court applied *O'Brien* to the promotions a husband-policeman had received during marriage after acquiring a college degree. *Alloco v. Alloco,* 578 N.Y.S.2d 995 (Sup. Ct. 1991). Treating professional licenses and educational degrees as property puts the court onto a slippery slope that no other courts have wanted to slalom down. The final reason for rejection of *O'Brien* has to do with valuation of such intangible assets – it is highly speculative. For example, a New York court described valuation as follows:

> In valuing a recently attained advanced degree, an expert will generally calculate the commencement date present value of the difference in the degree holder's earning potential, over his or her lifetime, by comparing the statistical average earnings of persons in the appropriate geographical area who have attained such advanced degree and those who have attained only a bachelor's degree *. Where the degree holder has utilized the degree for a significant period of time, his or her actual earnings are applied to the calculation in lieu of a statistical average *.

Anonymous AB v. Anonymous DB, 9 Misc.3d 1122(A) (N.Y. Sup. Ct. 2005). The contingent nature of such earnings prediction has the potential to turn what seems like a fair division one moment into either an egregious windfall or an inadequate award the next.

While the prevailing rule is that licenses and degrees are not property, that does not mean that there is not remedy for the "degree dilemma" of supporting spouses abandoned by the degree or license acquiring partner. Other remedies for the non-degree supporting spouse include disproportionate distribution of the marital property (if the parties have enough property to make that feasible), award of traditional alimony, reimbursement alimony, restitution alimony, rehabilitative alimony, or equitable restitution. *Hubbard v. Hubbard,* 603 P.2d 747 (Okla. 1979); *Mahoney v.Mahoney,* 91 N.J. 488, 453 A.2d 527 (1982); *In re Marriage of Olar,* 747 P.2d 676

(1987); *Downs v. Downs*, 154 Vt. 161, 574 A.2d 156 (1990). For a thoughtful analysis of marital property from the perspective of marriage as an egalitarian liberal community, *see* Frantz & Dagan, *infra*.

4) Disability Benefits, Workers Compensation, and Personal Injury Awards

Disability pay is an employment (contractual) benefit provided by an employer as a form of private insurance to replace the income a disabled employee may lose as a result of sickness or injury. *Workers' compensation* is a state (statutory) system of no-fault recovery for work-related injuries. The employee gets a certain amount according to a schedule (a scheduled amount for the loss of one finger, another amount for the loss of two fingers, etc.), rather than damages tailored and individualized to his or her specific circumstances and injuries, but the uncertainties and expenses of tort litigation are avoided. *Personal injury* awards are obtained through private settlement or judicial resolution of tort claims for damages suffered as a result of someone's tortious misconduct (often negligence). All of these schemes share at least one common characteristic: Each is intended, at least in part, to compensate an injured worker for damage to or loss of his or her present ability to generate income - a marital property factor. But all also contain an element of recovery for loss of future (including post-divorce) ability, skill, or capacity -- a personal factor. Thus, all of them are hybrid forms of "new property" that may or may not be treated as divisible marital property at the time of divorce.

States are split over whether disability pay is marital or separate property, with some following what has been called a *mechanical* approach, and others following an *analytical* approach. States that follow the mechanical approach look solely to date the right to disability pay acquired. If it was acquired during marriage, since it is not a gift, devise, bequest or inheritance, it is deemed marital property; if it was acquired before or after marriage, it is deemed separate property. States that follow the analytical approach are divided between those that look to the source of the benefit (marital labor) and those that look to the nature of the wages replaced (to the extent the disability recovery replaces postdivorce wages, it is separate). A common judicial tactic is to compare disability awards to personal injury recoveries -- which usually are classified as separate property. That is consistent with how insurance proceeds are characterized. Insurance benefits take the same character as the assets they replace. Since disability pay is really a form of insurance for the earnings of the employee, disability pay should be characterized the same way as earnings -- marital property to the extent it replaces post-marital earnings, and separate to the extent it replaces post-divorce earnings. Disability pay may continue after retirement, if the retiring person so chooses. To avoid double-payment, the retiring employee usually must give up retirement pay equal to the amount of disability pay he receives after retirement. Some states separate retirement-replacement disability pay from true-disability pay, classifying the former as retirement marital property.

Federal law preempts state law regarding whether federal employee disability pay is divisible upon divorce. In 1989, in *Mansell v. Mansell*, 490 U.S. 581 (1989), the U.S. Supreme Court federal disability pay may be divided upon divorce as marital or community property. The case arose (like *Hisquierdo* and *McCarty*) in California, where a state court ordered a retired military man to give his former wife fifty percent of his combined military retirement and disability pay. After *McCarty* was decided, and after Congress passed the USFSPA, the man asked the court to allow him to keep all of his retirement and disability pay. The veteran's disability law contained a broad anti-attachment clause. The California courts ruled that the disability pay was community property. The Supreme Court reversed. The case turned on whether in enacting the USFSPA Congress intended merely to establish that military retirement pay can be treated as divisible marital or community property, or whether it intended broadly that all military benefits, including veterans' disability pay, can be so treated. The Supreme Court opted for the narrow reading, finding no clear congressional intent to do anything other reverse the specific holding of *McCarty* that had forbidden the states to treat retirement pay as marital or community property. While Congress promptly reversed *Hisquierdo* and *McCarty*, it has never overturned the ruling in *Mansell* that veteran's disability may not be treated as marital or community property and divided upon divorce. However, the fact that disability pay itself is not divisible property does not mean that courts may not consider it when dividing other property or setting alimony. In fact, the U.S. Supreme Court has upheld state court jurisdiction to hold a disabled veteran in contempt for failing to pay child support, even though the only income he had from which to pay child support was his exempt veteran's disability pay. *Rose v. Rose,* 481 U.S. 619 (1987).

States are divided between two alternative approaches to categorizing *personal injury* recoveries, also. Under the prevailing replacement (or analytical) approach, personal injury awards are classified according to the nature of the assets they replace. Thus, compensation for wages lost during coverture is marital property, but compensation for wages lost after marriage and for pain and suffering, is separate property A minority of states characterize personal injury recovery on the basis of a mechanical reading of the marital property statutes (the mechanistic view). Since all property that does not fall within the definition of separate property (gift, bequest, devise or inheritance) is marital property, personal injury awards are, mechanically, deemed marital property. The states reportedly are divided over whether pain and suffering awards are marital or separate property. Sometimes the award compensates for joint inconvenience and damage (marital property), sometimes solely for personal pain (separate property), sometimes to cover attorneys fees (presumably marital depending on when the fees were accrued).

Workers' compensation awards are generally classified by the same method of classification as personal injury awards. The states are split between the analytic approach and the mechanistic approach. Since only economic loss is generally covered in workers compensation awards, they are generally treated as marital property in analytical states to the extent the award represents compensation for lost wages during marriage, or reimbursement for medical expenses paid for with marital funds. States following the mechanistic approach focusing on when the injury occurs, as that is when the right to the award is acquired; if the injury occurred during marriage, since it does not fall within the rigid definition of separate property, mechanistic states treat it as marital property. However, some mechanistic states recognize an exception for benefits received after divorce. Thus, under both analytical and mechanistic approaches, workers compensation awards are generally broken into component parts (what the award replaces, what period it covers) and the parts are separately characterized as marital or separate. Some states take a "unitary" approach and characterize the entire workers' compensation award one way of the other, but commentators are generally critical of this minority approach. Some state workers' compensation statutes contain anti-assignment provisions, but they have not been interpreted to prevent classification as marital property and division upon divorce.

d. Recent ERISA Preemption Cases

ERISA (the Employee Retirement Income Security Act of 1974) has been interpreted by the Supreme Court in recent years to overturn state laws concerning control and distribution of pension and insurance benefits. In *Egelhoff v. Egelhoff*, 532 S.Ct. 141 (2001), for example, David was a divorced man with two children from a prior marriage. David then married another woman, Donna, and designated her as his beneficiary of a life insurance policy and pension plan provided by his employer (Boeing Co.) and governed by ERISA. In April 1994 David and Donna also divorced in Washington. A Washington statute provides that: "If a marriage is dissolved . . . a provision made prior to that event that relates to the payment or transfer at death of the decedent's interest in a nonprobate asset in favor of . . . the decedent's former spouse is revoked . . . ." (Wash. Rev. Code § 11.07.010(2)(a). David did not formally remove Donna's name as his insurance and pension beneficiary. Two months later David died. His children by his former marriage (his heirs) sued Donna in state court to get the $46,000 insurance proceeds. The trial court ruled for Donna, ruling that the Washington statute was preempted by ERISA rules requiring pension plan administrators to comply with designation of beneficiaries. The state court of appeals reversed and the Washington Supreme Court agreed that ERISA did not clearly preempt the Washington statute. However, the U.S. Supreme Court reversed (7-2), holding that the state revocation-of-beneficiary-designation-by-divorce statute "directly conflicts by ERISA's requirements that plans be administered, and benefits be paid, in accordance with plan documents," *id.* at 150, and was therefor preempted by ERISA because of the burden upon plan administrators who otherwise would have to comply with varying state rules. The majority opinion (per Thomas) noted:

> [R]espondents emphasize that the Washington statute involves both family law and probate   law, areas of traditional state regulation. There is indeed a presumption against pre-emption in areas of traditional state regulation such as family law. *See e.g. Hisquierdo v. Hisquierdo*, 439 U.S. 572, 581(1979). But that presumption can be overcome where, as here, Congress has made clear its desire for pre-emption. Accordingly, we have not hesitated to find state family law pre-empted when it conflicts with ERISA or relates to ERISA plans. *See e.g. Boggs v. Boggs*, 520 U.S. 833 (1997) (holding that ERISA pre-empts a state   community property law permitting the testamentary transfer of an interest in a spouse's   pension plan benefits).

Id. at 151-52. Justice Breyer, dissenting, emphasized:

> [W]e must remember that petitioner has to overcome a strong presumption *against* pre-emption. That is because the Washington statute governs family property law--a "field of traditional state regulation," where courts will not find federal pre-emption unless such was the " 'clear and manifest purpose of Congress,' " *, or the state statute does " 'major damage' to 'clear and substantial' federal interests," *Hisquierdo*

v. Hisquierdo, 439 U.S. 572, 581 (1979) *. No one can seriously argue that Congress has *clearly* resolved the question before us. And the only damage to federal interests that the Court identifies consists of the added administrative burden the state statute imposes upon ERISA plan administrators.

The Court claims that the Washington statute "interferes with nationally uniform plan administration" by requiring administrators to "familiarize themselves with state statutes." * But administrators have to familiarize themselves with state law in any event when they answer such routine legal questions as whether amounts due are subject to garnishment, *Mackey v. Lanier Collection Agency & Service, Inc.*, 486 U.S. 825, 838 (1988), who is a "spouse," who qualifies as a "child," or when an employee is legally dead. And were that "familiarizing burden" somehow overwhelming, the plan could easily avoid it by resolving the divorce revocation issue in the plan documents themselves, stating expressly that state law does not apply. The "burden" thus reduces to a one-time requirement that would fall primarily upon the few who draft model ERISA documents, not upon the many who administer them. So meager a burden cannot justify pre-empting a state law that enjoys a presumption against pre-emption.

Id. at 157.

Boggs v. Boggs, 520 U.S. 833 (1997) telegraphed the *Egelhoff* decision four years earlier. There, the surviving second wife of deceased pension plan participant brought action against the decedents's sons of a former marriage seeking declaratory judgment that ERISA preempted application of Louisiana's community property laws which would have allowed first wife to transfer to sons, by testamentary instrument, her interest in undistributed pension plan benefits. The federal district court ruled for the sons and the Fifth Circuit affirmed. However, The U.S. Supreme Court, per Justice Kennedy, reversed, holding that ERISA preempted application of Louisiana's community property laws which would have allowed first wife to make testamentary transfer of her interest in survivor's annuity, and her interest in participant's retirement benefits consisting of monthly annuity payments made to participant during his retirement, his individual retirement account (IRA), and his shares of stock pursuant to employee stock ownership plan (ESOP). The majority opinion noted, in part:

Community property laws have, in the past, been pre-empted in order to ensure the implementation of a federal statutory scheme. *See e.g. McCune v. Essig*, 199 U.S. 382 (1905); *Wissner v. Wissner*, 338 U.S. 655 (1950); *Free v. Bland*, 369 U.S. 663 (1962); *Hisquierdo v. Hisquierdo*, 439 U.S. 572 (1979); *McCarty v. McCarty*, 453 U.S. 210 (1981); *Mansell v. Mansell*, 490 U.S. 581 (1989); *cf. Ridgway v. Ridgway*, 454 U.S. 46 (1981). *Free v. Bland, supra*, is of particular relevance here. A husband had purchased United States savings bonds with community funds in the name of both spouses. Under Treasury regulations then in effect, when a co-owner of the bonds died, the surviving co-owner received the entire interest in the bonds. After the wife died, her son--the principal beneficiary of her will--demanded either one-half of the bonds or reimbursement for loss of the community property interest. The Court held that the regulations pre-empted the community property claim . . . *** The obligation to provide an accounting, moreover, as with the probate proceedings referred to in *Free*, is itself a burden of significant proportions. Under respondents' view, a pension plan participant could be forced to make an accounting of a deceased spouse's community property interest years after the date of death. If the couple had lived in several States, the accounting could entail complex, expensive, and time-consuming litigation. Congress could not have intended that pension benefits from pension plans would be given to accountants and attorneys for this purpose.

Id. at 853.

3. Practical and Ethical Considerations

(a) Many lawyers find that they need expert assistance (accountants, appraisers, etc.) in finding, marshaling, evaluating, and properly dividing intangible, deferred and other more complex forms of wealth. Where would you look to find such experts?

(b) If a lawyer with a pending contingency fee agreement gets divorced, should the contingency fee contract be considered a marital asset? *See* Scheiter, *infra*.

4. Bibliography

American Law Institute (ALI), *Principles of the Law of Family Dissolution* (2002).

Craig W. Dallon, The Likely Impact of the ALI Principles of the Law of Family Dissolution on Property Division, 2001 B.Y.U. L. Rev. 891(2001).

Craig W. Dallon, *Reconsidering Property Division in Divorce Under Nebraska's Law In Light of the ALI's Principles of the Law of Family Dissolution: Analysis and Recommendations*, 37 Creighton L. Rev. 1 (2003).

Carolyn J. Frantz & Hannoch Dagan, *Properties of Marriage*, 104 Colum. L. Rev. 75 (2004).

Mary Ann Glendon, *The New Family and the New Property* (1981).

Alicia Brokars Kelly, *Sharing A Piece of the Future Post-Divorce: Toward A More Equitable Distribution of Professional Goodwill*, 51 Rutgers L. Rev. 569 (1999).

Charles P. Kindregan, Jr. & Monroe L. Inker, *A Quarter Century of Allocating Spousal Property Interest: The Massachusetts Experience*, 33 Suffolk U. L. Rev. 11 (1999).

Allen M. Parkman, *Bringing Consistency to the Financial Arrangements at Divorce*, 87 KY. L.J. 51 (1999).

Charles Reich, *The New Property*, 73 Yale L.J. 733 (1964).

Donna A. Scheiter, Note, *Attorneys' Divorces: Are Their Pending Contingency Fee Cases Marital Assets or Not?*, 37 Brandeis L.J. 829 (1998/99).

Alison Thomas, *Pensions: The Long March to Reform*, 34 FAM. L.Q. 209 (Summer 2000).

Brett R. Turner, Equitable Distribution of Property§2.03 (2d ed., 1994).

Lynn D. Wardle, *Dividing the "New Property" Upon Divorce: The Quest for Economic Equity*, in Law in Motion 678 (International Encyclopeadia of Laws, 1997).

David Westfall, *Unprincipled Family Dissolution: The American Law Institute's Recommendations for Spousal Support and Division of Property*, 27 Harv. J. L. & Pub. Pol'y 917 (2004).

CHAPTER 28

Alimony and Other Income Redistribution Schemes

A. ALIMONY

1. Background

a. History of Alimony

The power of courts to award alimony (sometimes called *aliment* or *maintenance*) has long been a part of divorce proceedings, historically traceable to the ecclesiastical courts in England which had authority to award alimony. Two types of alimony were traditionally available: alimony *pendente lite* and *post-divorce (or permanent)* alimony. The former was based upon the fact that marriage still continued until the divorce decree was entered, and the husband had the duty to support the wife during the marriage. Alimony *pendente lite* is theoretically available in all states, though in actual practice it may be difficult to obtain, as some courts are reluctant to assume the ultimate facts in issue, namely, existence of the conditions that support an award of alimony. Originally, *post-divorce* or *permanent* alimony also was based on the fact that the marriage still continued. That is, ecclesiastical courts could only award *divorce a mensa et thoro*, the equivalent of what today would be called legal separation. That divorce decree did not terminate the marriage, and since the marriage still continued the duty of the husband to support his wife remained intact (unless the husband could show some defense that would eliminate his duty to support his wife). Thus the earliest legal justification for alimony was that the marriage still legally existed, and with it the duty of spousal support. Alimony was a gender-based duty; the husband owed the duty of support to the wife (in return for which he was entitled to the domestic services of the wife).

The next stage of alimony law came with the liberalization of grounds for divorce in approximately the nineteenth century. Since divorce was available only for marital misconduct, the duty to pay alimony became tied to fault as well. That is, if the husband had violated the minimum standards of socially tolerable marital behavior, the wife was entitled to a divorce and to alimony (assuming the husband had funds from which the alimony could be paid) because "but for" the husband's extreme misbehavior the marriage (and her right to continued support) would have continued, whereas to terminate alimony because the marriage had ended (due to the husband's misbehavior) would cause the wife to further suffer (and to allow the husband to profit) from his misconduct. On the other hand, if the wife had committed the marital misconduct, by her misbehavior she had forfeited her claim to further support, just as she had forfeited her claim to protection of her status as wife and to the other benefits of marriage. (However, alimony was not often awarded because few parties could afford to pay alimony.)

The next evolution of alimony practice reflected growing ability of spouses to pay alimony. As men's economic opportunities increased so that a real income stream was generated, the awarding of alimony increased and the standards for awarding it became clearer. Alimony was generally awardable upon showing that the wife had a *need* for continued spousal support, and that the husband had the *ability to pay* such support. Of course, "need" is not a very precise standard, and a rough, general reference point was the standard of living the parties enjoyed during marriage, though that was only a general reference point because in most cases it would be impossible for both parties to enjoy the same standard of living after divorce that they enjoyed while living together during marriage. Perhaps it was for that reason that alimony was seldom awarded. For instance, one study of alimony before the time of the no-fault divorce revolution revealed that alimony awards were granted in only 15% of divorce cases. Of course, that figure reflected the fact that most divorces then (as now) occurred early in marriage, (today over half of all divorces occur before six years of marriage).

The award of alimony historically complemented and was supported by the ubiquitous belief that marriage (and the duties of support associated with marriage) was a lifelong commitment. Thus, while misconduct justified termination of the conjugal and legal interrelationship, alimony could be awarded to reflect the economic disadvantages that resulted to the innocent spouse when that lifetime contract was breached and the wife was left without a husband to continue to support her.

While an historical overview of the theory and substance of alimony law is useful, undoubtedly some of the contemporary confusion regarding the principles and grounds for alimony results from the fact that "English law, rather than laying down a general code of financial rights and obligations, usually preferr[ed] to confer rights of access to the courts and to empower the court to exercise very wide discretionary powers in accordance with loosely drawn statutory guidelines." Cretney, *infra* at 323.

2. Statutes, Cases and Doctrines

a. *Orr v. Orr*

William Herbert Orr v. Lillian M. Orr
440 U.S. 268 (1979)

Mr. Justice BRENNAN delivered the opinion of the Court.

The question presented is the constitutionality of Alabama alimony statutes which provide that husbands, but not wives, may be required to pay alimony upon divorce. *[Fn 1:*
The statutes, Ala.Code, Tit. 30 (1975),provide that:

§ 30-251. . . . *If the wife has no separate estate or if it be insufficient for her maintenance, the judge, upon granting a divorce, at his discretion, may order to the wife an allowance out of the estate of the husband, taking into consideration the value thereof and the condition of his family.*

§ 30-2-52. . . . *If the divorce is in favor of the wife for the misconduct of the husband, the judge trying the case shall have the right to make an allowance to the wife out of the husband's estate, or not make her an allowance as the circumstances of the case may justify, and if an allowance is made, it must be as liberal as the estate of the husband will permit, regard being had to the condition of his family and to all the circumstances of the case.*

§ 30-2-53. . . . *If the divorce is in favor of the husband for the misconduct of the wife and if the judge in his discretion deems the wife entitled to an allowance, the allowance must be regulated by the ability of the husband and the nature of the misconduct of the wife.*

The Alabama Supreme Court has held that "there is no authority in this state for awarding alimony against the wife in favor of the husband. . . . The statutory scheme is to provide alimony only in favor of the wife." *Davis v. Davis, 279 Ala. 643, 644, 189 So.2d 158, 160 (1966).]*

On February 26, 1974, a final decree of divorce was entered, dissolving the marriage of William and Lillian Orr. That decree directed appellant, Mr. Orr, to pay appellee, Mrs. Orr, $1,240 per month in alimony. On July 28, 1976, Mrs. Orr initiated a contempt proceeding in the Circuit Court of Lee County, Ala., alleging that Mr. Orr was in arrears in his alimony payments. On August 19, 1976, at the hearing on Mrs. Orr's petition, Mr. Orr submitted in his defense a motion requesting that Alabama's alimony statutes be declared unconstitutional because they authorize courts to place an obligation of alimony upon husbands but never upon wives. The Circuit Court denied Mr. Orr's motion and entered judgment against him for $5,524, covering back alimony and attorney fees. Relying solely upon his federal constitutional claim, Mr. Orr appealed the judgment. On March 16, 1977, the Court of Civil Appeals of Alabama sustained the constitutionality of the Alabama statutes, 351 So.2d 904. On May 24, the Supreme Court of Alabama granted Mr. Orr's petition for a writ of certiorari, but on November 10, without court opinion, quashed the writ as improvidently granted. 351 So.2d 906. We noted probable jurisdiction, *. We now hold the challenged Alabama statutes unconstitutional and reverse.

*** [The Court ruled that Mr. Orr had standing to challenge the alimony law because if his equal protection claim succeeded the state might eliminate alimony, it declined to ask the state court to rule first, and ruled that the wife's potential state law stipulation-to-alimony claim was not before the Court.]

In authorizing the imposition of alimony obligations on husbands, but not on wives, the Alabama statutory scheme "provides that different treatment be accorded . . . on the basis of . . . sex; it thus establishes a classification subject to scrutiny under the Equal Protection Clause," *Reed v. Reed*, 404 U.S. 71, 75 (1971). The fact that the classification expressly discriminates against men rather than women does not protect it from scrutiny. *Craig v. Boren*, 429 U.S. 190 (1976). "To withstand scrutiny" under the Equal Protection Clause, " 'classifications by gender must serve important governmental objectives and must be substantially related to achievement of those objectives.' " *Califano v. Webster*, 430 U.S. 313, 316-317 (1977). We shall, therefore, examine the three governmental objectives that might arguably be served by Alabama's statutory scheme.

Appellant views the Alabama alimony statutes as effectively announcing the State's preference for an allocation of family responsibilities under which the wife plays a dependent role, and as seeking for their objective the reinforcement of that model among the State's citizens. *Cf. Stern v. Stern*, 165 Conn. 190, 332 A.2d 78 (1973). We agree, as he urges, that prior cases settle that this purpose cannot sustain the statutes. *[Fn 9. Appellee attempts to buttress the importance of this objective by arguing that while "[t]he common law stripped the married woman of many of her rights and most of her property, . . . it attempted to partially compensate by giving her the assurance that she would be supported by her husband." Brief for Appellee 11-12. This argument, that the "support obligation was imposed by the common law to compensate the wife for the discrimination she suffered at the hands of the common law," id., at 11, reveals its own weakness. At most it establishes that the alimony statutes were part and parcel of a larger statutory scheme which invidiously discriminated against women, removing them from the world of work and property and "compensating" them by making their designated place "secure." This would be reason to invalidate the entire discriminatory scheme--not a reason to uphold its separate invidious parts. But appellee's argument is even weaker when applied to the facts of this case, as Alabama has long ago removed, by statute, the elements of the common law appellee points to as justifying further discrimination. See Ala.Const., Art. X, § 209 (married women's property rights).] Stanton v.* Stanton, 421 U.S. 7, 10 (1975), held that the "old notio[n]" that "generally it is the man's primary responsibility to provide a home and its essentials," can no longer justify a statute that discriminates on the basis of gender. "No longer is the female destined solely for the home and the rearing of the family, and only the male for the marketplace and the world of ideas," *id.,* at 14-15. *See also Craig v. Boren, supra,* 429 U.S., at 198. If the statute is to survive constitutional attack, therefore, it must be validated on some other basis.

The opinion of the Alabama Court of Civil Appeals suggests other purposes that the statute may serve. Its opinion states that the Alabama statutes were "designed" for "the wife of a broken marriage who needs financial assistance," 351 So.2d, at 905. This may be read as asserting either of two legislative objectives. One is a legislative purpose to provide help for needy spouses, using sex as a proxy for need. The other is a goal of compensating women for past discrimination during marriage, which assertedly has left them unprepared to fend for themselves in the working world following divorce. We concede, of course, that assisting needy spouses is a legitimate and important governmental objective. We have also recognized "[r]eduction of the disparity in economic condition between men and women caused by the long history of discrimination against women . . . as . . . an important governmental objective," *Califano v. Webster, supra,* 430 U.S., at 317, 97 S.Ct., at 1194. It only remains, therefore, to determine whether the classification at issue here is "substantially related to achievement of those objectives." *Ibid.*

Ordinarily, we would begin the analysis of the "needy spouse" objective by considering whether sex is a sufficiently "accurate proxy," *Craig v. Boren, supra,* 429 U.S., at 204, 97 S.Ct., at 460, for dependency to establish that the gender classification rests " 'upon some ground of difference having a fair and substantial relation to the object of the legislation,' " *Reed v. Reed, supra,* 404 U.S., at 76, 92 S.Ct., at 254. Similarly, we would initially approach the "compensation" rationale by asking whether women had in fact been significantly discriminated against in the sphere to which the statute applied a sex-based classification, leaving the sexes "not similarly situated with respect to opportunities" in that sphere, *Schlesinger v. Ballard,* 419 U.S. 498, 508 (1975). Compare *Califano v. Webster, supra,* 430 U.S., at 318, and *Kahn v. Shevin,* 416 U.S. 351, 353 (1974), with *Weinberger v. Wiesenfeld,* 420 U.S. 636, 648 (1975). *[FN11. We would also consider whether the purportedly compensatory "classifications in fact penalized women," and whether "the statutory structure and its legislative history revealed that the classification was not enacted as compensation for past discrimination." Califano v. Webster, 430 U.S., at 317, 97 S.Ct., at 1194.]*

But in this case, even if sex were a reliable proxy for need, and even if the institution of marriage did discriminate against women, these factors still would "not adequately justify the salient features of" Alabama's statutory scheme, *Craig v. Boren, supra,* 429 U.S., at 202-203, 97 S.Ct., at 459-460. Under the statute, individualized hearings at which the parties' relative financial circumstances are considered already occur. *. There is no reason, therefore, to use sex as a proxy for need. Needy males could be helped along with needy females with little if any additional burden on the State. In such circumstances, not even an administrative-convenience rationale exists to justify operating by generalization or proxy. Similarly, since individualized hearings can determine which women were in fact discriminated against vis-a-vis their husbands, as well as which family units defied the stereotype and left the husband dependent on the wife, Alabama's alleged compensatory purpose may be effectuated without placing burdens solely on husbands. Progress toward fulfilling such a purpose would not be hampered, and it would cost the State nothing more, if it were to treat men and women equally by making alimony burdens independent of sex. "Thus, the gender-based distinction is gratuitous; without it, the statutory scheme would only provide benefits to those men who are in fact similarly situated to the women the statute aids," *Weinberger v. Wiesenfeld, supra*, 420 U.S., at 653, 95 S.Ct., at 1236, and the effort to help those women would not in any way be compromised.

Moreover, use of a gender classification actually produces perverse results in this case. As compared to a gender-neutral law placing alimony obligations on the spouse able to pay, the present Alabama statutes give an advantage only to the financially secure wife whose husband is in need. Although such a wife might have to pay alimony under a gender-neutral statute, the present statutes exempt her from that obligation. Thus, "[t]he [wives] who benefit from the disparate treatment are those who were . . . nondependent on their husbands," *Califano v. Goldfarb*, 430 U.S. 199, 221 (1977) (Stevens, J., concurring in judgment). They are precisely those who are not "needy spouses" and who are "least likely to have been victims of . . . discrimination," *ibid.*, by the institution of marriage. A gender-based classification which, as compared to a gender-neutral one, generates additional benefits only for those it has no reason to prefer cannot survive equal protection scrutiny.

Legislative classifications which distribute benefits and burdens on the basis of gender carry the inherent risk of reinforcing the stereotypes about the "proper place" of women and their need for special protection. *Cf. United Jewish Organizations v. Carey*, 430 U.S. 144 (1977) (opinion concurring in part). Thus, even statutes purportedly designed to compensate for and ameliorate the effects of past discrimination must be carefully tailored. Where, as here, the State's compensatory and ameliorative purposes are as well served by a gender-neutral classification as one that gender classifies and therefore carries with it the baggage of sexual stereotypes, the State cannot be permitted to classify on the basis of sex.And this is doubly so where the choice made by the State appears to redound--if only indirectly--to the benefit of those without need for special solicitude.

III

Having found Alabama's alimony statutes unconstitutional, we reverse the judgment below and remand the cause for further proceedings not inconsistent with this opinion. That disposition, of course, leaves the state courts free to decide any questions of substantive state law not yet passed upon in this litigation. * Therefore, it is open to the Alabama courts on remand to consider whether Mr. Orr's stipulated agreement to pay alimony, or other grounds of gender-neutral state law, bind him to continue his alimony payments.

Reversed and remanded.

Mr. Justice BLACKMUN, concurring.

Mr. Justice STEVENS, concurring.

Mr. Justice POWELL, dissenting.

I agree with Mr. Justice REHNQUIST that the Court, in its desire to reach the equal protection issue in this case, has dealt too casually with the difficult Art. III problems which confront us. Rather than assume the answer to questions of state law on which the resolution of the Art. III issue should depend, and which well may moot the equal protection question in this case, I would abstain from reaching either of the constitutional questions at the present time.

This Court repeatedly has observed:

[W]hen a federal constitutional claim is premised on an unsettled question of state law, the federal court should stay its hand in order to provide the state courts an opportunity to settle the underlying state-law question and thus avoid the possibility of unnecessarily deciding a constitutional question.

Harris County Comm'rs Court v. Moore, 420 U.S. 77, 83, 95 S.Ct. 870, 875, 43 L.Ed.2d 32 (1975).

* The Court should follow this principle in the present case.
***

In these circumstances, I find the Court's insistence upon reaching and deciding the merits quite irreconcilable with the long-established doctrine that we abstain from reaching a federal constitutional claim that is premised on unsettled questions of state law without first affording the state courts an opportunity to resolve such questions. I therefore would remand the case to the Supreme Court of Alabama.

Mr. Justice REHNQUIST, with whom THE CHIEF JUSTICE joins, dissenting.

In Alabama only wives may be awarded alimony upon divorce. In Part I of its opinion, the Court holds that Alabama's alimony statutes may be challenged in this Court by a divorced male who has never sought alimony, who is demonstrably not entitled to alimony even if he had, and who contractually bound himself to pay alimony to his former wife and did so without objection for over two years. I think the Court's eagerness to invalidate Alabama's statutes has led it to deal too casually with the "case and controversy" requirement of Art. III of the Constitution.
***

b. *Herndon v. Herndon*

Delores V. Herndon v. Donald L. Herndon
305 N.W.2d 917 (S.D. 1981)

WUEST, Circuit Judge.

This is an appeal from an order denying a reduction in child support payments and termination of alimony. We affirm.

The parties hereto were divorced in 1973 after seventeen years of marriage. There is no transcript of the original trial or any findings of fact and conclusions of law inasmuch as they were waived. It does appear that neither party had much property when they were married. After the marriage, appellant finished his training as a chiropractor and commenced a practice which he maintained with the help of appellee until the divorce. They accumulated property worth $200,000, which the trial court divided nearly equally. The decree further awarded appellee custody of the two sons with child support payments of $250 per child per month, and the additional sum of $600 per month for alimony. In addition, the court ordered a college trust fund of $20,000 per child, which was established. Appellee contributed $26,000 to the trust fund, and appellant contributed $14,000. In 1974 appellant applied for a termination of alimony and reduction in child support. The reduction in alimony was denied; however, the child support for the oldest boy was eliminated because he had married. In 1976 appellant again applied for a termination of alimony and a reduction in child support. Appellant asserted as changed circumstances for termination of alimony and reduction in child support payments appellee's employment income; appreciation of the assets awarded to appellee by the divorce decree; appellant's reduction in income; and appellant's health problems involving the use of his hands.

Appellant has severe osteoarthritic changes at the base of both thumbs at the metacarpal trapezoidal joint which is aggravated by his profession, in which he has to do a great deal of manipulation and massage. The thumbs remain swollen and his work causes increasing pain. X rays show that there has been loss of cartilage so that bone is rubbing on bone at the base of both thumbs. His physician has recommended fusion or locking the joint at the base of the thumb on each hand with two pins, and the building of a bone bridge with bone from another part of the body. This surgery would disable appellant from his profession for at least a year. This condition was urged as a changed circumstance at the 1974 hearing, the 1976 hearing, and at the last hearing now on appeal. As a result of the 1976 hearing, the court reduced the alimony payments to $250 per month but left the child support payment at $250. Neither party appealed.

As changed circumstances since the 1976 hearing, appellant has alleged appreciation of appellee's property awarded in the divorce decree; rental income of appellee's property and employment income of appellee; reduction of appellant's income; and sale of appellant's practice due to the condition of his hands. Appellant now lives in Arizona and no longer practices, although he has Arizona and California licenses. Evidence introduced at the most recent hearing established that there was no change in the condition of appellant's hands since 1974. Appellant maintained his practice until 1979, when it was sold.

The trial court held that there had not been a sufficient change of circumstances since 1976 to justify a reduction in support payments and termination of alimony. This Court has consistently held that there must be a change of circumstances to justify a change in alimony and child support payments. ** This Court does not sit as a trier of fact and will not disturb the decision of the trial court on questions of alimony and child support unless there is an abuse of discretion. **

The term "abuse of discretion" refers to "a discretion exercised to an end or purpose not justified by, and clearly against, reason and evidence." *Root v. Bingham*, 26 S.D. 118, 120, 128 N.W. 132, 133 (1910), quoting from *Murray v. Buell*, 74 Wis. 14, 41 N.W. 1010 (1889).

Applying these principles to the case at bar, we are unable to say that the trial court abused its discretion. The condition of appellant's hands has remained unchanged since the hearings in 1974 and 1976. It is true that appellee's property has appreciated since 1976, but this has resulted largely through inflation, which has also affected the cost of rearing appellant's son. It is true that appellant has sold his practice and that he is not presently practicing his profession, resulting in reduced income; however, appellant has Arizona and California licenses, and there was some testimony that he may re-establish a practice in Sioux Falls. A person cannot voluntarily reduce his income in order to avoid alimony and support payments. *Simmons v. Simmons*, 67 S.D. 145, 290 N.W. 319 (1940). The evidence in this case does not show that appellant is unable to maintain a practice; to the contrary, it shows that appellant did continue practicing from 1974 until 1979.

The order is affirmed. Appellee's motion for attorney fees and costs is denied.

WOLLMAN, C. J., and MORGAN and FOSHEIM, JJ., concur.

WUEST, Circuit Judge, sitting for DUNN, Justice, disqualified.

HENDERSON, Justice (concurring in part, dissenting in part).

I would reverse the trial court's order denying appellant a reduction in alimony. A review of the economic posture of the respective parties clearly indicates that appellee is not a needy recipient of alimony. On the contrary, her monetary status greatly exceeds that of her ex-husband.

First, as the trial court noted, appellant has experienced a "drastic reduction" in income since the 1976 proceedings. This reduction was caused by the necessity of appellant selling his chiropractic practice due to the chronically severe crippling of his hands. Appellant's present income consists of $828 per month from payments received on realty which appellant was forced to sell to support himself, his estranged wife and their child. Appellant also receives $551 as monthly accrued interest on savings accumulated during the years he was able to practice his profession. Between October of 1979 and October of 1980, appellant received one-third of the fees collected from his former patients through the chiropractor who purchased his practice. Currently, appellant is not a practicing chiropractor and, due to the arthritic condition of his hands, appears to have reached the end of his professional career.

In its correspondence to the parties' attorneys in December of 1979, the trial court stated that "it appears (appellant's) income level has dropped below $3,000 per month and on the most conservative basis may have dropped below $2,000 per month. That is a substantial change in circumstances from 1976." I agree that a substantial change in circumstances has occurred since 1976, and point out that a mere change in circumstances is sufficient for a modification of alimony to occur. *Blare v. Blare*, 302 N.W.2d 787 (S.D.1981).

It is true, as the majority points out, that surgery might alleviate much of appellant's discomfort and possibly enable him to resume his chiropractic practice. I find it hard to fathom, however, the "voluntary" nature of appellant's income reduction. Agreed, appellant apparently does not wish to undergo the rather complex surgical procedure and resulting year of incapacitation. But does appellant's decision not to have surgery at the age of sixty necessarily mean he "voluntarily" reduced his income? Did appellant "voluntarily" cause the joints in his trained hands to swell up, thereby inflicting upon himself such pain that work became a painful daily exercise in his profession? The answer to these questions is an obvious "no."

It is absurd to believe that appellant would avoid surgery merely to reduce his income, thereby possibly reducing his alimony obligation. This Court long ago concluded that the ability of the alimony obligor to pay is a paramount consideration in determining whether alimony obligations should be reduced. *Vert v. Vert*, 3 S.D. 619, 54 N.W. 655 (1893). "The fact that the husband has suffered a serious impairment of health or physical condition ... since the entry of a decree for alimony or maintenance may authorize a reduction, suspension, or termination of alimony payments where his condition affects his ability to pay." Annot. 18 A.L.R.2d 45 (1951). ** It is unconscionable to require appellant to ply his profession with proficiency and pain (bone rubbing on bone) so as to enable appellee to enrich her already comfortable economic status.

Coupled with appellant's decreased ability to provide alimony is the fact that appellee cannot realistically be said to require alimony. Appellee is currently employed and grossing approximately $14,560 annually. Furthermore, she owns $209,306 worth of assets, including certificates of deposit which alone total over $100,000. At the hearing on the motion for modification, appellee testified that it cost her $8,336 per year to raise and adequately provide for the parties' son. When appellee's own income is added to appellant's child support obligation of $250 per month, appellee's yearly income comes to $17,560. It is significant that this total does not entail any interest and/or earnings accrued from appellee's stock, certificates of deposit, rental income, savings, or mutual funds. The record simply does not reflect that appellee needs alimony.

As the trial court stated, appellee's income and capital assets have increased since 1976. The trial court also pointed out, however, that inflation has offset this increase. If this be true, would not the same inflationary factors have even more severely eroded appellant's income, in light of the fact that appellant's income had decreased, not increased, over the same period of time? The answer is clearly a resounding "yes."

*** [T]he economic need of an alimony recipient must be considered when reviewing the equity of such an award. * "The fact that the wife has acquired a substantial amount of property, or that her property has increased in value, after the entry of a decree for alimony or maintenance is an important consideration in determining whether and to what extent the decree should be modified." Annot. 18 A.L.R.2d 74 (1951). **

In conclusion, I must agree with the Kentucky Court of Appeals when it stated that "(t)heoretically, alimony or maintenance is based in part on a consideration of the needs of the parties as well as their respective abilities to meet them." *Gann v. Gann*, 347 S.W.2d 540, 542 (Ky.App.1961). Applying this basic theory of equity to the particulars of this case, leads me to the inevitable conclusion that the trial court abused its discretion when it denied appellant's motion for a termination of alimony.

c. Uniform Marriage and Divorce Act, § 308 [Maintenance]

(a) In a proceeding for dissolution of marriage . . . the court may grant a maintenance order for either spouse only if it finds that the spouse seeking maintenance:

(1) lacks sufficient property to provide for his reasonable needs; and (2) is unable to support himself through appropriate employment or is the custodian of a child whose condition or circumstances make it appropriate that they custodian not be required to seek employment outside the home.

(b) The maintenance order shall be in amounts and for periods of time the court deems just, without regard to marital misconduct, and after considering all relevant factors including: (1) the financial resources of the party seeking maintenance, including marital property apportioned to him, his ability to meet his needs independently, and the extent to which a provision for support of a child living with the party includes a sum for that party as custodian; (2) the time necessary to acquire sufficient education or training to enable the party seeking maintenance to find appropriate employment; (3) the standard of living established during the marriage;

(4) the duration of the marriage; (5) the age and the physical and emotional condition of the spouse seeking maintenance; and

(6) the ability of the spouse from whom maintenance is sought to meet his needs while meeting those of the spouse seeking maintenance.

d. Current Status of Alimony in American Law

Today, courts in all American jurisdictions have the power to award "alimony" or "maintenance" to a divorcing spouse at the time of the divorce. Texas was the last state to authorize the award of permanent alimony, though it previously permitted temporary alimony during the pendency of the divorce suit. Tex. Fam. Code Ann § 3.59 (Vernon 1974). Texas is a community property state and the courts considered alimony to be against public policy because it would distort the equal division of community property. However, in 1998, a law permitting permanent alimony became effective in Texas. *See* Tex. Fam. Code Ann. §§ 8.001-.011 (West 1998). (Texas still is one of the strictest states, however, allowing alimony only in cases of marriages that have lasted at least ten years and the applicant lacks the ability to support herself, or when domestic violence has resulted in criminal conviction; there is a minor presumption against alimony; and the duration of alimony is ordinarily no longer than three years at most, or "the shortest reasonable period that allows the spouse seeking maintenance to meet the spouse's minimum reasonable needs"; alimony is capped at the lesser of $2,500 or 20% of gross monthly income; and alimony terminates on remarriage or continuous nonmarital cohabitation. Paulsen, *infra.*) Nearly all states have statutes prescribing a "laundry list" of factors to be considered by the courts when evaluating alimony claims. Elrod, *infra* at 908 (Chart 1). Some of those key factors are reviewed below.

The no-fault divorce revolution has had profound effect upon alimony doctrine and practice. First, as *Orr* demonstrates, the potential liability to pay (and the right to claim) alimony has been gender-neutralized. Second, the prevailing practice of awarding permanent alimony (X dollars per month for life) seems to have given way to common awards of short-term rehabilitative alimony. Third, advocates of greater judicial wealth-redistribution upon divorce have proposed many new theories for awarding alimony, and some courts have experimented with some of these approaches. These theories include restitution, reimbursement, loss, damage, income equalization, and other equitable theories.

e. Notes and Questions

1) *Orr* and Equality

Did the Supreme Court in *Orr* mandate that alimony laws be gender-neutral? Clearly, *formal* equality in the *formal* law is now required. What about *substantive* equality in the law-as-applied? If some study were to confirm (as many divorced men believe) that in 90% or more of the cases when alimony is ordered, a man is ordered to pay and a woman is the recipient, would that raise any concerns? Would it create a *prima facie* case for gender discrimination? Is it justified? Why/why not? What socially desirable consequences of marriage could cause such financial disadvantage to women and create such a huge statistical disparity?

Wanda, a school teacher earning $30,000 per year, married Hal, a lawyer, earning $50,000, and both kept working during the marriage. Ten years later (with two children of the marriage) Wanda files for divorce. (a) If Wanda is then earning $50,000 per year, roughly the same she would have been earning in her chosen profession if she had not married, and Hal is earning $200,000 per year, roughly the same he would have been earning if single, should Wanda be entitled to any alimony? Why/not? If so, how much? (b) A year after the birth of their first child, in response to his family's need for more of his time and help (and his feelings of family duty), Hal quit his demanding large private law firm to take a job with a government agency where the pay is lower but the hours are generally 9-5. At the time of divorce, Wanda was earning $50,000 and Hal was earning $100,000. Wanda gets custody. If Hal can show that "but for" his marriage and family duties, he would have stayed with the private firm and would have been earning $200,000 at the time of divorce, should Hal be entitled to alimony? Why/not? If so, how much?

In *Pfohl v. Pfohl,* 345 So. 2d 371 (1977), an influential case, a Florida appeals court ruled that a house-Husband could obtain alimony upon showing a financial ability by the Wife to pay for such an award coupled with a demonstrated need of H to support, taking into consideration the standard of living shared by the parties to the marriage. W was a multi-millionaire heiress; the husband a toy store salesman who resigned his job after one and a half years of marriage "to satisfy the wife's wishes. She did not like his traveling which was necessary to pursue his line of work, and refused to move to New York with him to accept a promotion." *Id.* at 373. The court rejected W's argument that H's $200,000 in assets "acquired mainly by gift from the wife during the marriage," disqualified H from receiving any alimony. However, the court affirmed the award to H of only $30,000 in lump sum alimony and $5,000 a month rehabilitative alimony for 18 months because "the husband is a relatively young, well-educated man of 37, has excellent physical health although temporarily impaired mental health, has $200,000 in assets of his own, has some employment skills if only limited ones, and lives alone without custody of the parties' two children. We can see no reason why he could not properly rehabilitate himself within eighteen months with the alimony awarded herein." *Id.* at 378. Is it likely that the court would have been more generous if the gender-roles had been reversed?

2) Alimony Theoretical Confusion

There is tremendous confusion in the alimony cases as courts and legislators struggle with the basic question, "why alimony?" The historical justifications for alimony are rarely applicable today. For instance, "fault" as a ground for award of alimony seems inconsistent with, if not eliminated by, the adoption and overwhelming use of no-fault grounds for divorce today. (Yet most states continue to allow consideration of "fault" in alimony awards.) By the same token, unilateral no-fault divorce belies and subverts the assumption that marriage is a lifelong obligation (or even, in some communities, that this is a reasonable expectation). "Need" no longer suffices because social and economic changes in the past thirty years have made it possible (and socially preferred) for women to obtain the same kind of education and jobs that men have. What justification is there for awarding alimony any more?

Of course, this may be an academic question; the practical answer is that it is a long-established historical practice, and courts and legislators are not likely to eliminate such an historic legal doctrine or practice, especially when an active, vocal, and politically influential segment of the population would vigorously object. Aside from the politics of the issue, however, there is a very serious policy dilemma - what is the justification for ordering a man (usually) to continue to pay support to a woman to whom he is no longer married, who has (or is capable of obtaining) an education and a job that will provide her with enough salary to be fully self-sufficient?

One category of answers reflects broad social engineering agendas. For example, Dean Herma Hill Kay has long advocated elimination of alimony (as a goal, at least) in order to force married women to become more self-sufficient (and thus less economically vulnerable in divorce).

> In the long run, however, I do not believe that we should encourage future couples entering marriage to make choices that will be economically disabling for women, thereby perpetuating their traditional financial dependence upon men and contributing to their inequality with men at divorce. I do not mean to suggest that these choices are unjustified. For most couples, they are based on the presence of children in the family. *** Throughout history, the choice of the mother as the primary nurturing parent has been the most common response to the infant's claim. But other choices are possible . ***
>
> [S]ince, . . . Anglo-American family law has traditionally reflected the social division of function by sex within marriage, it will be necessary to withdraw existing legal supports for that arrangement as a cultural norm. ...

Kay, *infra,* at 79-85.

A revolutionary perspective (such as Marxism) might argue for alimony to liberate women from the oppression of marriages to which they might otherwise be bound by virtue of their choices to become mothers. It might be insisted that alimony is a penalty to keep men in marriages to punish them economically for opting to leave marriages or behaving in a way that would cause the wife to want to leave the marriage. *See generally* Olsen, *infra,* and Haddock, *infra.*

However, most of the new alimony theories that have been proposed and attempted rest on notions of contract and equity. They seek to equalize or fairly apportion the economic advantages and disadvantages of the divorce. Thus, they seek to compensate the spouse (usually the wife) who opted to forego market-skill-development or income-development opportunities in order to raise children and/or manage the home; they seek to reimburse the wife who contributed significantly to her husband's acquisition of income-producing non-property assets (like education, degrees, licenses); they attempt to recognize and compensate for the economic value of the contributions of the stay-at-home spouse; they seek restitution for investments in the economic operation that they will not enjoy as a spouse. And they seek to do it by establishing rules that apply in a context of unilateral no-fault divorce, where the wife may be the one leaving her hard-working, faithful high-school-math-teacher-husband to live with her unemployed, paramour poet-lover, as well as in the case where the brain-surgeon husband is leaving the woman who put him through twelve years of medical training so that he can marry his infatuated young lover; as well as in cases of the lazy husband who leaves the 14-hour-per-day working wife; they apply in cases when the husband pressured the wife give up her job to stay home, as well as in cases when he demanded that she work, despite her desires to raise their children; when, despite his pleas and his provision of adequate family income, she left their young children in day care in order to have a career as well, as when she had not children but refused to find employment. They apply to spouses who choose low-paying jobs because they love the work, or because they want to spend more time with family, as well as to spouses who forego those interests in order to maximize income for self or family. Can *any* one-size-fits-all alimony rule work justice in all divorce cases? What principle justifies awarding alimony in any case? How does that principle causally connect to marriage to justify alimony upon divorce?

3) Alimony jurisdiction question

As *Estin v. Estin, supra* Chapter 26, demonstrated, claims for alimony are *in personam*, whereas claims for dissolution of marriage are essentially *quasi in rem*. It is possible for a court to have jurisdiction to dissolve the marriage, but not to award alimony. Consider the following hypothetical.

Alan and Roxanna were married in 1994 in Connecticut. They lived together in Connecticut and their child was born there in 1996. Alan was unemployed most of the time and he received unemployment payments from Connecticut public assistance. In 2000, Alan left his family and Connecticut, returning only occasionally to visit family members. Roxanna and the child continued to receive public assistance. Roxanna last saw Alan in 2001, when he returned to attend his mother's funeral. In 2002, Alan won $16 million (paid in $800,000 annual installments) in a Delaware lottery. In 2006, (six years after Alan left her) Roxanna filed for divorce in Connecticut seeking, *inter alia*, alimony payments based in part on Alan's lottery winnings. Alan was served out of state and objected to the Connecticut court's exercise of jurisdiction over him regarding the alimony claim, arguing that he lacked sufficient contacts with Connecticut for in personam jurisdiction. How should the court rule, and why?

This hypothetical is based loosely on *Panganiban v. Panganiban*, 736 A. 2d 190 (Conn. App.), *app. denied*, 742 A.2d 359 (1999). The Connecticut Appellate Court affirmed the trial court's assertion of jurisdiction over Alan noting that Alan had married in Connecticut, had conducted the daily activities of his marital life there for six years, had enjoyed the benefits of Connecticut law during that time, including welfare benefits, and that those substantial prior contacts were sufficient to justify the assertion of in personam jurisdiction regarding the alimony claim. The court further noted that the assertion of jurisdiction was reasonable because the burden of travel on Alan was minimal, the parties had previously lived in the state together for many years, the state still had an interest in the financial welfare of Roxanna, and she had a legitimate interest in having the issues decided in the same convenient forum that dissolved the marriage, even though it acknowledged that the Interstate Family Support Act provides an interstate process to determine and collect alimony claims. The court also reasoned that to accept Alan's claim would mean that "once a married person left the state, no Connecticut court could exercise in personam jurisdiction over that person in a dissolution action brought by the spouse left behind if the departing spouse had no contact with Connecticut [thereafter]," a position it rejected as "bizarre."

Section 205 of the Uniform Interstate Family Support Act provides, *inter alia*: "(f) A tribunal of this State issuing a support order consistent with the law of this State has continuing, exclusive jurisdiction over a spousal support order throughout the existence of the support obligation." This establishes that the court issuing the alimony order "retains continuing, exclusive jurisdiction over the support except in very narrowly defined circumstances. UIFSA, § 205, *cmnt*. Section 206(c) provides that courts of the state enacting UIFSA "may not serve as a responding tribunal to modify a spousal support order of another state." *Id.*

4) Alimony Factors – Need

The ubiquitous twin considerations in virtually all alimony schemes have been *need* of the party requesting alimony and the *ability of the other party to pay* alimony. Alimony only has been awarded if both elements have been established.

Need is a very subjective term. At one level, i insures that neither spouse will be impoverished and left on welfare (at least so long as the other spouse earns sufficient to keep both off of welfare). That "avoid-disparate-impoverishment" definition of need is seldom at issue in contested alimony disputes. More often, another meaning of "need" is the source of the dispute. As discussed below, the historic base line for measuring *need* has been the standard of living the parties enjoyed during the marriage, which generates many controversies because it commands defiance of simple economic reality. *See infra*, §2.e.5.

"Imputation of income" is the practice of basing alimony calculations upon the amount of income the court reasonably believes the party is able to generate, rather than (in addition to) the actual income the party is receiving. The party objecting to alimony may attempt to show that the party requesting alimony is under-employed and earning less than she could and should earn, and if the court bases the "need" calculation on the amount the requester could earn, then the amount of alimony will be reduced or eliminated. Should the court impute full-time employment income to the woman who chooses to work only part-time in order to be home when the children get home from school? On a woman who wants to return to school for five years to earn a Ph.D? Who applies only for jobs offering 9-5 hours, rather than more lucrative, but time-demanding, positions? Who decided during marriage not to go to business school for an M.B.A. which would have doubled her earning potential, but instead spent the time earning a Master's degree in Humanities (providing marginal or no income enhancement, but great personal satisfaction to her)?

5) Alimony Factors – Standard of Living

The "standard-of-living-during-the-marriage" standard evolved out of historical origins of alimony as a duty to support a wife during the continuation of the marriage, bolstered by a protective concern that women not be dumped penniless on the streets when divorced after a long marriage. Today, do either of these historic concerns still apply in most or a significant number of cases? The "standard of living" standard is meant to provide a baseline for measuring "need."

The "standard of living" standard creates problems in two situations. The first, relatively uncommon but often sensational, is upon the breakup of the marriage of a rich man and a poor woman. The woman has become accustomed to living the jet-set lifestyle, and if awarded an amount of alimony much greater than the amount she was used to living on before her marriage, finds the loss of living style very painful. On the other hand, the very wealthy husband usually has enough money that he can afford to pay his wife enough alimony for her to continue to live a very rich lifestyle; he will still be a very wealthy man. The other situation is much more common and more poignant. That is when a middle-or lower-income couple divorce; while together they were able to enjoy a certain standard of living because of marital economies of scale; after divorce, it is impossible for them to continue to live separately at that level on the limited total income they earn. Typically, the alimony-seeker's attorney presents to the court evidence (always inflated by the "high option" figure) of how much it will cost for divorced wife to continue to live at the same standard of living she enjoyed while married and invariably that amounts to well over one-half (and often closer to 70% or 80%) of the combined disposable income of the parties. Two persons cannot live separately on the same income and at the same standard they enjoyed while living together. If the alimony law (or the judge) requires that alimony recipient to be supported at the same standard of living she enjoyed during marriage, that guarantees the impoverishment (and often the bankruptcy) of the payor. On the other hand, often the alimony-seeker's available income really is not sufficient for her to continue to live at the marital standard of living, while the other spouse's income usually is sufficient for him to approximate that standard of living. Is it fair to just leave the parties in that situation? Why/not?

In the Alan and Roxanna hypothetical (3 *supra),* should Roxanna be entitled to share (via alimony payments) Alan's lottery winnings.? Why/not? This hypothetical is based on *Panganiban v. Panganiban,* 736 A. 2d 190 (Conn. App.), *app. denied,* 742 A.2d 359 (1999). The Connecticut Appellate Court affirmed the trial court's alimony award to Roxanna of $6,000 per month for ten years. Although that would provide Roxanna with a standard of living "far above anything to which she had been accustomed based on her station in life and standard of living," the appellate court affirmed the award noting that what a spouse can afford to pay is a relevant consideration in determining the amount of an alimony award. The moral seems to be that when a man abandon his wife, but does not divorce her, his marital support obligation is not extinguished. Is it fair to take this money away from Alan and give it as a windfall to Roxanna?

6) Alimony Factors – Ability to Pay

Ability to pay, the other universal requirement for an alimony award, is not free from controversy, either. Two major issues are variation of the common theme of "with how much effort." One is the issue of imputing income to the party who has voluntarily chosen a job or profession that does not maximize his earning potential. What about the lawyer who leaves a high-paying job with a very demanding private law firm for a job with a government agency or corporate legal department? What about the man who left an $80,000 a year job as a sporting goods salesman to earn $40,000 a year as a high school teacher? Or the doctor who spends 20 hours per week at a low paying job at a medical clinic for immigrants when he could earn ten times as much if he spent those hours in his suburban hospital or clinic?

The other issue concerns the potential alimony payor who worked a overtime or second job for years to support the family who, upon divorce, decides to give up the second job. Is his ability to provide alimony to be measured against what he is actually earning or what he could be earning, or what he traditionally has been earning? Why? If a man who has planned for years to retire at 62 is divorced at 61, should the court effectively compel him to work longer (to age 65? 67? 70? As long as he is in good health?) by imputing calculating his ability to pay on his full-time employment income, because to retire will voluntarily reduce his "ability to pay" alimony?

7) The "Diploma Dilemma"

The "diploma dilemma" arises when one spouse abandons or refrains from pursuing opportunities for career advancement, training, or educational improvement to support a spouse while he earns are degree or professional license, and the marriage is dissolved shortly after the degree or license is acquired. At that time, the parties may have acquired very little property; most of the income earned during the marriage was "invested" in obtaining the degree or license which generally is considered the personal acquisition of the one holding it. As discussed in another section, recently some states have characterized the degree or license earned under such circumstances as a kind of "marital property" which the courts may divide and apportion upon dissolution.

Another approach, however, which courts in several states have endorsed, is for the trial court to consider the degree or license and the circumstances under which it was acquired among the general equitable considerations affecting the award of alimony. *See e.g. In re Pyeatte*, 135 Ariz. 346, 661 P.2d 196 (1983); *Woodworth v. Woodworth*, 337 N.W.2d 332 (Mich. Ct. App. 1983): *Gebhart v. Gebhart*, 14 Ohio App. 3d 107, 470 N.E.2d 205 (1981). Statutes in several jurisdictions authorize this. *See e.g.* Ind. Code § 31-1-11.5-11(d); Wis. Stat. Ann. §§ 767.36(9), 767.255(5). Some courts have granted "restitutionary alimony" to reimburse a wife for her investment in her husband's acquisition of personal skills, degrees or licenses if he divorces her so soon after the acquisition of that intangible asset that the wife is deprived of any meaningful return on her "investment," but not if the divorce occurs a substantial time afterward. Elrod, *infra* at 618, citing *Jackson v. Jackson*, 995 P.2d 1109 (Okla. 1999) (wife denied restitutionary alimony to reimburse her for contributions to her husband's medical training when the parties divorced more than fifteen years later).

8) Alimony Factors – Marital Misconduct &/or Marital Torts

For many years a debate has raged over whether, in the days of "no-fault" divorce, "marital fault" (such as adultery, domestic violence, incest, etc.) should still be considered in determining whether and/or how much alimony should be awarded. Some leading academics have long rallied to repudiate fault in alimony cases. (*See e.g.* U.M.D.A. § 308(b). For years, there seems to have been a slow trend toward rejecting fault, but the trend is very slight, and it seems to vary depending on the type of fault considered). Even the most ardent opponents of considering "fault" in alimony disputes believe, for example, that "economic fault" (such as the husband, Willy Loman-like, giving expensive gifts to his girl friend purchased with marital assets, or one party going on a huge "fling" resulting in huge debts for the marital community, and other "wasting" activities) should be taken into account in alimony and property division. Today, nearly 60% of the states do consider marital fault in determining alimony; 40% disallow consideration of marital fault. What is the approach in your homestate? "Courts in most states find that the court may award alimony to a "guilty" party if the need is there." Elrod, *infra*, at 618.

In states where marital fault may not be considered (and in other states as well), sometimes claims for "marital torts" have been asserted to provide some economic compensation for the moral element that historically (for at least a century) was part of the alimony award. For example, if a husband contracted a sexually transmitted disease from a prostitute, knew he was infected, and continued to have sex with his wife, causing her to become infected, should the court consider that in connection with her alimony claim? What if the husband beat the wife and left her partially disabled, or unable to work for a few weeks? What if the wife committed adultery and left the husband with deep emotional depression or outrage? Should that affect the wife's alimony claim? Should the injured spouse have a separate claim for marital tort that could be heard (either in the dissolution action or in a separate proceeding)?

The question is complicated by a number of substantive and procedural issues. First, the court must decide whether such an independent claim for marital tort exists at all. Second, it must decide whether such a claim is barred or thwarted by a defense of marital immunity (unlikely if it was an intentional act, but not irrelevant if the claim is for a negligent tort such as negligent infliction of emotional distress). Then the question arises whether the marital tort claim may be asserted in the dissolution proceeding itself (which may be limited to essentially "no-fault" issues in some states). *Windauer v. O'Connor*, 485 P.2d 1157 (Ariz. 1971) (special nature of divorce precludes hearing tort claim by wife against husband in same proceeding); *Walther v. Walther*, 709 P.2d 387 (Utah 1985) (error for court to hear wife's claim for physical assault in the divorce proceeding). Fourth, the question may arise whether it *must* be asserted in the dissolution action (under a rule of mandatory counterclaims or mandatory joinder). Thus, issues such as claim preclusion may arise if the marital tort is asserted after the divorce is entered. *See e.g. Simmons v. Simmons*, 773 P.2d 602 (Colo.App. 1988) (joinder or counterclaim not required; wife recovers $115,000 for physical assaults); *but Tevis v. Tevis*, 400 A.2d 1189 (N.J. 1979) (wife's claim for physical abuse during marriage barred by failure to join). Questions of statutes of limitation may also arise. *See Tevis, supra*. Battering and intentional infliction of emotional distress are two common marital torts, and fraud is increasingly asserted in connection with divorce. For example, " [i]f the defendant knew or should have known that he was unable to marry the plaintiff, there is a claim for misrepresentation. In this particular fact situation, the plaintiff may recover mental distress damages, as well as loss of reputation." Spector, *infra*, at 254. Other marital claims that have been asserted include "tortious infliction of a venereal disease, wiretapping, abuse of process, and tortious interference in custodial relations." Spector, *infra*, at 760-761. As Professor Spector summarized, at the turn of the millennium: "Although there are some courts that have refused to expand the number of claims that can possibly arise out of divorce and some have required that the claims be disposed of in the dissolution proceeding, most courts have allowed the tort claim to proceed in one form or another. Thus it appears from reading appellate reports that tort actions growing out of domestic litigation show no sign of abating, but instead are increasing." *Id.* at 762. *See also* Krohse, *infra*.

9) Alimony Factors – Rehabilitative or Permanent?

The duration of the initial award of alimony is no longer presumably lifetime, as it was at common law. Changed economic conditions and social values now place a premium on economic self-sufficiency of divorced women (including mothers, even of young children). "A new wave of "rehabilitative alimony " statutes restricts the ability of a dependent spouse to collect permanent support under a plethora of circumstances, placing the onus of support on the person who needs support." Morgan, *infra,* at 706, n.4. Courts, as well as legislators, seem to prefer to award alimony now as a means to enable a divorced wife to become economically self-sufficient, at least to a degree comparable to the situation of the husband. Thus, "[w]here the supporting spouse merely postponed her own education, an award of rehabilitative alimony is appropriate." Vicks, *infra* at 2002. Similarly, if the husband was able to get three years of graduate school during the marriage, and the marriage lasted sufficiently long or created economic conditions (such as dependent children) so that some alimony award seems appropriate, it would not be surprising for a court to order a husband to pay alimony long enough to allow the wife to obtain three or four years of graduate school, also. The prevailing rule today seems to be that "[r]ehabilitative alimony is appropriate when a spouse has a degree or job skills that provide the basis for employment in the future but not when rehabilitation is not feasible due to age, lack of job skills, or other factors." Elrod, *infra*, at 618.

Is this fair and appropriate if the husband and wife married with the understanding that wife was to devote her time and talents full-time to being a homemaker? Is it fair and appropriate if the husband was the one to break up the marriage because he became infatuated with and committed adultery with another woman? How long will it take to "rehabilitate" the economic earning position of a responsible mother of four-year old twins, who wants to spend as much time as she can raising them as a stay-at-home-mother, rather than maximizing her income? What about the woman who marries a man primarily to become a stay-at-home-mother, divorces him when the baby is a year old, and wants to remain a full-time (or at least most-time) stay-at-home mother?

10) Termination of Alimony

Since alimony is a personal obligation to provide support for another, alimony should terminate upon death of either the obligor or the recipient. However, the parties can contract otherwise, and it is wise for the obligor's attorney to clearly specify the conditions upon which alimony terminates. A Mississippi court held that the obligor's estate had to provide alimony because the settlement agreement provided that alimony would terminate upon the recipient's death or remarriage but did not mention the obligor's death . *Sheppard v. Pace,* 757 So. 2d 173 (Miss. 2000). However, the general rule seems to be that a clear intent to require payment after death must be expressed to overcome the presumption and termination, at least if based on a statutory death-terminates-alimony provision. *See Diefenbach v. Homberg,* 26 P.3d 1186 (Az. App. 2001) (woman's death ended ex-husband's duty to pay alimony notwithstanding "nonmodifiable" agreement between the parties that he would pay for seven years; lack of unmistakable intent to overcome death-terminates-alimony rule). In *In the Matter of Gonzalez v. The Commissioner,* TC Memo 1999-332, the tax court denied a taxpayer a tax deduction for unallocated alimony payments because no portion of the payment was defined as being terminated by the recipient's death. In order to protect federal income tax benefits, state statutes must and generally do specify that alimony terminates upon death of the recipient.

When the termination of alimony provision was agreed to voluntarily by the parties, rather than dictated by the legislature, even liberal courts are usually willing to enforce them. In *Konzelman v. Konzelman,* the New Jersey Supreme Court upheld a provision terminating alimony upon cohabitation if the provision was voluntary, and fair. *Konzelman v. Konzelman,* 729 A.2d 7, 10 (N.J. 1999). It cuts the other way also. "[P]arties in a consent judgment or property settlement agreement can make even a periodic alimony award nonmodifiable." Elrod, *infra,* at 619.

In most if not all states, alimony terminates upon the remarriage of the recipient. *See generally In re Marriage of Glasser,* 226 Cal.Rptr. 229, 230 (Cal.App.1986) (alimony terminates upon remarriage despite provision making alimony payment for term nonmodifiable because "[a] husband's obligation to his former wife ends by operation of law when she marries another. If the parties intend that support is to be 'nonterminable for any reason whatsoever,' they must say so in their agreement.") Does this create an incentive for the divorced woman to not remarry? To circumvent the alimony-terminating condition, some alimony recipients cohabit with their new de facto husbands. In a state in which common law marriage is permitted, could ex-husband have standing to assert a claim that the ex-wife has contracted a valid common law marriage? Would he be able to prove his case in the face of fervent denials by the ex-wife and her cohabitant that they are merely "shacking up" together, not married? Why/why not?

The increase of nonmarital cohabitation in recent years has created an interesting issue regarding the application of these principles. Divorced alimony recipients who cohabited without marriage technically did not fall within the rule terminating alimony upon remarriage. And their conduct, while reproachable under traditional standards of personal or public morality, occurred after the divorce.

In many states, cohabitation is ground for termination of alimony. (Regardless of the state law, competent attorneys will always include in the divorce decree a provision terminating alimony upon cohabitation, death or remarriage.) Not surprisingly, issue have arisen concerning the meaning and proper application of these provisions authorizing termination of alimony upon cohabitation. For instance, in *Knuteson v. Knuteson,* 619 P.2d 1387 (1980) the Utah Supreme Court held that the stay of a person of the opposite sex for nearly two and one-half months did not amount to residence under a Utah statute which authorized termination of alimony upon proof that the recipient "is residing with a person of the opposite sex, unless it ... is without any sexual contact," Utah Code Ann. § 30-3-5(3). Likewise, in *Haddow v. Haddow*, 707 P.2d 669 (1985), the Utah Supreme Court reversed a trial court's enforcement of an equitable lien which, by the divorce decree, was payable when the wife moved, married, or "cohabited with a male person." Interpreting that language in light of the statute authorizing termination of alimony upon residence with a person of the opposite sex, the Court reasoned that cohabitation required two elements: (1) common residence and (2) sexual contact evidencing conjugal association. Although there was evidence of relatively permanent sexual relations between the alimony recipient and her boyfriend in this case, the evidence of temporary overnight visits did not establish that the boyfriend regarded the home as his principal residence, even though he spent many evenings and some nights each week at the home, left his clothes there, ate some meals there, and reimbursed the alimony recipient for food he ate, but had a permanent home with his parents where he usually resided and received his mail.

In *Gottesegen v. Gottesegen*, N.E.2d (Mass. 1985), the Massachussetts Supreme Judicial Court ruled that it was error to terminate alimony solely upon evidence of cohabitation. The court found that "the statutory authority of a court to award alimony continues to be grounded in the recipient spouse's need for support and the supporting spouse's ability to pay. A court may not limit alimony for reasons unrelated to its statutory base. ... Any event that triggers a change in alimony must bear some relation to the financial circumstances of the parties." *Id.* at . Thus, a court in entering an original alimony award or in modifying a previous alimony award "may not ... order alimony to be terminated on mere cohabitation." *Id.* at . Even though this provision was stipulated by the parties in their separation agreement, that agreement had been merged into the final decree. Concurring, Chief Justice Hennessey opined that if the agreement had not been merged, it would have survived and the termination-for-mere-cohabition provision would have been enforceable as a private contract. In *DeMaria v. DeMaria*, 47 Conn. App. 729 (1998),the Connecticut Court of Appeals reversed a trial court that had confused enforcement of a divorce settlement non-cohabitation clause and the noncohabitation provision ("living together") of Section 46b-86(b) of the Connecticut General Statutes. In *DeMaria*, the divorce judgment provided that "alimony shall terminate upon ... the cohabitation by the plaintiff with an unrelated male." Mr. DeMaria filed a motion to terminate the alimony payments on the ground that Mrs. DeMaria had been cohabiting with a male. The trial court found that she was living with another person, but there was no evidence that cohabitation had altered her financial needs, and denied the defendant's motion to terminate alimony because under the cohabitation provision of the alimony modification statute, that is the ultimate test. On appeal, however, the Appellate Court reversed, explaining that there is a significant difference between a termination of alimony because of operation of a cohabitation clause in a judgment and a modification under the alimony modification cohabitation provision. The latter but not the former requires proof of living together and a resultant change in the alimony recipient's financial circumstances. *See also Dial v. Dial*, 636 N.E.2d 361 (Ohio App. 1993) (heterosexual cohabitation terminates alimony). The general rule now is said to be that "cohabitation may also if the recipient no longer needs support." *Elrod, infra,* at 619.

Will alimony terminate upon cohabitation by the recipient with a same-sex partner? The answer to this question often turns on the specific language used in a statute, settlement or order, as well as on the public policy behind the alimony provisions. For example, in *In re Marriage of Weisbruch*, 710 N.E.2d 439 (Ill. App. 1999) the court explained:

> Petitioner, Carol Weisbruch, appeals the order of the circuit court of McHenry County terminating her right to receive maintenance from respondent, John Weisbruch. Petitioner contends that the court incorrectly found (1) that the settlement agreement permitted maintenance to be terminated and (2) that she was cohabiting with another woman on a continuing, conjugal basis.
>
> . . .
>
> ... The inquiry, as noted by the Missouri court in *Herzog*, is whether the receiving spouse has formed a new relationship wherein the partners look to each other for support, not whether the support provided is in fact adequate to meet the receiving spouse's needs.
>
> The parties have brought to our attention cases from other jurisdictions that have considered this issue, but both parties concede that they are not particularly helpful because of statutory or factual differences. For example, in *Van Dyck v. Van Dyck*, 262 Ga. 720, 425 S.E.2d 853 (1993), the relevant statute provided that maintenance could be terminated only where the receiving spouse was cohabiting with a person of the opposite sex.
>
> Similarly, in *People ex rel. Kenney v. Kenney*, 76 Misc.2d 927, 352 N.Y.S.2d 344 (1974), the statute in question permitted termination where the ex-wife remarried or was habitually living with another "man" and holding herself out as "his" wife. * By contrast, section 510(c) is gender neutral.
>
> In *Taylor v. Taylor*, 17 Conn.App. 291, 293, 551 A.2d 1285, 1286-87 (1989), the statute was gender neutral, but the court affirmed the trial court's factual finding that the relationship could not be considered a substitute for marriage. Finally, in *Gajovski v. Gajovski*, 81 Ohio App.3d 11, 610 N.E.2d 431 (1991), the court held that a homosexual relationship was not "concubinage." The court relied on a Louisiana case that traced the meaning of concubine from the Book of Genesis through the Napoleonic Code, which had been adopted in Louisiana. *Gajovski*, *, citing *Succession of Bacot*, 502 So.2d 1118 (La.Ct.App.1987). The dissent pointed to a dictionary definition of "concubine" as a man living in a state of concubinage with another man or a woman. *. In language more in tune with Illinois' approach to the question, the dissenting judge stated, "It does not seem readily apparent why the parties would have wanted to continue the alimony merely because the paramour is not legally able to marry the former spouse." * (Baird, J., dissenting).
>
> We agree with the *Gajovski* dissent that the focus should be on the fairness to the paying spouse of requiring him or her to continue maintenance payments and on the continuing need of the receiving spouse for the payments, rather than on the moral and legal implications of the receiving spouse's new relationship. This approach is consistent with Illinois cases that have focused on the need for continuing maintenance and the injustice in requiring the former spouse to continue paying when the receiving spouse is being supported by someone else.
>
> . . . .

The trial court's findings here are supported by the evidence. The trial court set forth extensive factual findings in support of its conclusion that petitioner and Diesel were engaged in a conjugal relationship. The evidence recited above demonstrates far more than a casual friendship. The fact that Diesel is the primary beneficiary of petitioner's will, deferred income plan, retirement plan, and life insurance policy demonstrates that she and Diesel are far more than roommates, as petitioner contends, and these actions cannot be explained by considerations of convenience. Although petitioner claims not to understand fully the terms of her will, the fact is that she has chosen specifically to disinherit her two sons--who she testified are the most important people in her life--except for token bequests. If the intention of the will was for Diesel to divide the property between the children, specific bequests would be unnecessary. The trial court's finding was not against the manifest weight of the evidence.

Should voluntariness be a factor? That is, if the party made a voluntary choice that changed the nature of the circumstances, should that be considered? If the nature of the choice or change is moral, rather than economic, should that matter? Why/why not?

11) Enforcement and Modification

It is estimated that approximately one-third of the alimony ordered is not paid. Gregory, *infra* at § 8:01 at 243. In some cases, it is a matter of trying to get green blood from an impoverished financial stone, but in other cases it is a matter of financially able disgruntled obligors refusing to send some or all of the alimony owed to the despised ex-spouse. When public support has been provided to the alimony recipient, state support collection agencies are active (with varying levels of limited success) in seeking recovery. Often those agencies are available (in theory, at least) to assist or seek collection for private alimony obligees who are not receiving public assistance as well.

Because divorce is often followed by a residential move by one or both of the parties, collection often requires interstate actions. The Uniform Interstate Family Support Act, successor to the Uniform (and Revised Uniform) Reciprocal Enforcement of Support Acts, provides mechanism to initiate support enforcement or collection actions (including alimony collection actions) in one state and to have evidence gathered in or the proceeding heard in another state. Radically changing the prior uniform proposed law of URESA and RURESA, UIFSA§§205 & 206 provide that the jurisdiction that issued the alimony award "retains continuing exclusive jurisdiction over an order of spousal support throughout the entire existence of the support obligation." UIFSA, §205, *cmnt.* Thus, "[u]nder UIFSA, modification of spousal support is permitted in the interstate context only if an action is initiated outside of, and modified by the original issuing state." *Id.*

In principle, since alimony is an ongoing support award based upon need and ability to pay, if either the need or the ability to pay drops, the court should have continuing jurisdiction to modify the alimony award. Most alimony statutes or caselaw allow for modification of alimony awards. "Alimony awards may generally be modified even if they are denominated as "permanent" in the decree based upon a substantial change in the financial status or circumstances. Elrod, *infra*, at 618-619.

Courts dislike modification of orders and generally the requirement that the change be
"substantial" generally is emphasized. If the party has voluntarily caused the change
in circumstances, should that effect the modification decision? Why/not?

The alimony modification litigation generally focuses primarily upon the extent
of the changed economic conditions, although any of the alimony factors discussed
above may be raised in motions to modify or terminate alimony. Most states permit
only prospective modification of alimony, but a minority permit retroactive
modification. (If parties are of modest or tight economic means, how realistic is it to
expect them to hire lawyers and return to court modify alimony orders? How wise is
it to have rules that impose accumulating financial burdens -alimony arrearages- upon
them if they cannot do so?)

12) The ALI Family Dissolution Principles

In May 2000, the American Law Institute approved a set of proposed family law
reforms entitled Principles of the Law of Family Dissolution. Among the most
controversial of the many controversial proposals in the ALI's *Principles* are those in
Chapter 5 recommending adoption of a scheme of "compensatory spousal payments"
(the Reporters' euphemism for *alimony*). The ALI proposal rejects all consideration
of "fault" in determining alimony (except for deliberate wasting of assets and the
effects of domestic violence). *Id.* at 42-44. The *Principles* also recommends monetary
compensation for the lower-earning spouse's economic loss or inferior position,
essentially without consideration of causation. The ALI scheme simply assumes that
the loss or lower income a party (typically W) has at the end of a marriage was caused
by marriage, and proof of causation is not required. Of course, assessment of equity
must be made "without regard to marital misconduct." *Id.* §5.02. The goal is to
"allocate equitably . . . financial losses" resulting from divorce including loss of high
living standard, loss of earning capacity resulting from caretaking of children or
elderly or sick relatives, reliance loss from inadequate return on income contributed
or earning power sacrificed to invest in other spouse's earning capacity. *Id.* §5.03.
Compensation for loss of marital living standard or for childcaring as the primary
caretaker (not fulltime, just primary) is by percentage of the difference between
incomes multiplied by a marriage or childcare duration factor. *Id.* §5.06. Modification
of the award is allowed only where "substantial dispar[ity]" or "significant changes"
in economic circumstances occur. The Reporters note that several counties in Kansas
have adopted the following formula for duration of alimony awards: 2.5 years for the
first 5 years of marriage; 1/3 year for every year after 5, up to maximum duration of
alimony award of 10 years. For a general critique of the rejection of fault in alimony
(and other dissolution contexts), *see* Wardle, *Beyond Fault, infra; see also
Reconceiving, infra.*

3. Practical and Ethical Considerations

(a) Because alimony laws vary in detail so profoundly from state, students are
encouraged to look up their home state statutes governing alimony, and to find and at
least quickly skim online some recent appellate court decisions reviewing alimony

awards. How does your homestate alimony law differ from the general principles described above?

(b) Malpractice potential in alimony practice is not insignificant. Mostly it relates to inadequate research, investigation and preparation regarding the facts (deficient discovery) or the law (tax laws, for example), or careless drafting (failure to include termination of alimony upon death, for example). One case, for instance, involved disbarment proceedings for the attorney who prepared the case with the client in the car on the way to the final hearing, *People v. Felker,* 770 P.2d 402 (Colo. 1989). Another case involved failure to do sufficient discovery to determine extent of the other party's assets, *Segall v. Berkson,* 487 N.W.2d 752 (Ill. App. 1985). Even pleading allegations regarding alimony may lead to professional responsibility problems.

> The general rule is that a lawyer is not obligated to vouch for the statements of a client. That rule is altered in states what have rules that treat a lawyer's signing of a pleading as a certification that the allegations were verified by the lawyer. Further, in some states the courts have come to expect that lawyers have at least verified the contents of client's financial affidavits so that the courts can feel comfortable in relying on them for financial orders.

Parley, *infra,* at 34.

4. Bibliography

3 Contemporary Family Law, Chapter 32 (1988).

June Carbone & Margaret F. Brinig, *Rethinking Marriage: Feminist Ideology, Economic Change, and Divorce Reform,* 65 Tulane L. Rev. 953 (1991).

S.M. Cretney & J.M. Masson, Principles of Family Law (5th ed., 1990).

Development 12 Family Law C. *Divorce Decree Amendments: Alimony Termination and its Tax Ramifications,* 1999 Utah L. Rev. 1189.

Linda D. Elrod & Robert G. Spector, *Review of the Year in Family Law: Century Ends with Unresolved Issues,* 33 Fam. L. Q. 865 (2000).

John DeWitt Gregory, Peter N. Swisher, & Sheryl L. Scheible, Understanding Family Law (1993).

David D. Haddock & Daniel D. Polsby, *Family As A Rational Classification,* 74 Wash. U. L. Q. 15 (1996).

Colleen Marie Halloran, Comment, *Petitioning A Court to Modify Alimony When a Client Retires,* 28 U. Balt. L. Rev. 193 (1998).

Herma Hill Kay, *Equality and Difference: A Perspective on No-Fault Divorce and Its Aftermath,* 56 U. Cinn. L. Rev. 1 (1987).

Joan Krauskopf, *Recompense for Financing Spouse's Education: Legal Protection for the Marital Investor in Human Capital,* 28 Kan. L. Rev. 379 (1980).

Kristyn J. Krohse, Note, *No Longer Following The Rule of Thumb – What to do with Domestic Torts and Divorce Claims,* 1997 U. Ill. L. Rev. 923.

Laura W. Morgan, *Family Law at 2000: Private and Public Support of the Family: From Welfare State to Poor Law* 33 Fam. L.Q. 705 (1999).

Frances Olsen, *The Family and the Market: A Study of Ideology and Legal Reform,* 96 Harv. L. Rev. 1497 (1983).

James W. Paulsen, Remarks, *The History of Alimony in Texas and the new "Spousal Maintenance" Statute,* 7 Tex. J. Women & L. 151 (1998).

Louis Parley, The Ethical Family Lawyer (Family Law Section, Amer. Bar. Assn., 1995).

Rayden's Practice and Law of Divorce (9th ed., 1964).

Reconceiving the Family: Critical Reflections on the American Law Institute's Principles of the Law of Family Dissolution (2006).

Robert G. Spector, *Marital Torts: The Current Legal Landscape,* 33 Fam. L.Q. 745 (1999).

Chester G. Vernier & John B. Hurlbut, *The Historical Background of Alimony Law and Its Present Structure,* 6 Law & Contemp. Probs. 197 (1939).

Lynn D. Wardle, *Beyond Fault and No-Fault in the Law of Marital Dissolution,* in Reconceiving the Family: Critical Reflections on the American Law Institute's Principles of the Law of Family Dissolution (2006).

Erik V. Wicks, Note, *Professional Degree Divorces: Of Equity Positions, Equitable Distributions, and Clean Breaks,* 45 Wayne L. Rev. 1975 (2000).

CHAPTER 29

Tax and Bankruptcy Considerations; International and Comparative Divorce Law

A. TAX CONSEQUENCES OF DIVORCE

1. Background

a. Unit of Taxation

In the first half of the twentieth century the individual was the principal unit of federal income taxation, and some argue for a return to that approach. However, differences in state marital property laws resulted in federal income tax disadvantages to married couples in common law property states who could not split the income of one earner-spouse between both spouses, whereas in community property states each spouse had legal co-ownership of the income earned by the other and they could lawfully split the income for tax reporting purposes, get each half taxed at much lower rates, and thus lower their total tax liability. Since at least 1948 the married couple (nuclear family) has been the basic unit of federal income taxation, though individual treatment is possible. That resolves the "income-splitting" differences, but creates a host of other issues including "marriage penalty" (for couples with two significant earners) and "marriage bonus" (for primarily one-earner families) issues noted in Chapter 18.

b. Tax Policy Issues

Today, the "marriage penalty" and "marriage bonus" issues are not the only subjects of family-related federal income tax policy debate. Questions of amount of individual exemptions, definition and allocation of dependency for exemption purposes, child care tax credits, taxation of alimony, child support payments, and tax treatment of children's medical expenses are examples of family-related tax policy issues that are the subject of frequent political wrangling. Because the tax system is progressive, there are advantages when persons with higher incomes are associated with persons with lower incomes, or (upon divorce) potential incentives to transfer income from the higher-earning party to the lower-earning party. Significant tax reforms incorporating changes relevant to family law were passed in 1984, 1986, and 2001. *See* Friske & Pulliam, *infra.*

c. Tax Issues in Divorce

Parties who divorce have rather significant freedom to structure their divorce in ways that will significantly impact the tax burdens of the parties. Decisions that parties may wish to make for non-tax reasons may have very costly tax consequences. Lawyers practicing divorce law must be aware of the tax laws in order to adequately advise clients of the potential tax consequences of the transfers of assets and income and of custody and visitation arrangements so that they can advise their clients of the tax costs and benefits associated with the various alternatives they may be considering.

2. Statutes, Cases and Doctrines

a. Tax Consequences of Property Transfers Related to Divorce

Before 1984, property transfers in the 42 common law states (but not in community property states) from an owner to a non-owning spouse (or ex-spouse) of property that had increased in value since acquisition were taxable transactions, and the owner had to pay tax on the appreciation. *United States v. Davis*, 370 U.S. 65 (1962). Since 1984, §1041 of the Internal Revenue Code (I.R.C.), Title 26 U.S.C., has provided that property transfers to a spouse or former spouse or to an approved third party, "incident to divorce," are not taxable, but the transferee acquires the transferor's basis in the property. A transfer is incident to divorce if made within one year of termination of the marriage or 6 years of termination if made pursuant to a divorce or separation decree. An approved party transfer is one that is required by divorce decree or separation agreement, and pursuant to the written request or consent of the former spouse. Payments under a Qualified Domestic Relations Order (QDRO) including pension division awarded to an ex-spouse are taxable to the recipient - the alternative payee. IRC § 402. *See* Thomas, *infra*. Attorneys' fees for protecting or recovering income-producing property may in some cases be added to the tax basis of the property. Tiso, *infra*.

b. Tax Consequences of Alimony Payments

Under § 215 of the IRC, alimony payments are deductible to the payor and taxable to the payee. Under § 71(b) payments from a spouse to a former spouse are treated as alimony (whether periodic or lump sum) if five conditions are met (unless the divorce decree or separation agreement provides otherwise):
A.   Payments are in cash or equivalent, to or for the benefit of a spouse.
B.   Payments are pursuant to a divorce decree, support decree or written separation agreement.
C.   Parties are not cohabiting with each other (1 month grace period).
D.   Payments must end at payee's death.
E.   Payment may not be treated as child support or be designated that the payment is not includable /deductible as alimony.
However, some front-loading recapture rules apply, such as if alimony declines dramatically during the first three years after divorce in the absence of death, remarriage or some other unusual circumstances. *See* Comeau, *infra*; Thomas, *infra*. "Payment of an award of attorney's fees in a temporary order for support may be taxable/deductible as alimony if it meets the criteria of the Code (as set forth above), the most important of which is that such payments end upon the death of the spouse being benefited. Thus, if the temporary order provides for termination of the liability for the payment of fees or liability ceases by virtue of state law, the cessation on death requirement would be met." Tiso, *infra*, at 40.

c. Tax Consequences of Child Support Payments

Payment of child support is not a taxable transaction. That is, child support is received tax-free by the recipient and is not deductible by the payor. Before 1984, only amounts explicitly identified in court orders as child support were treated by the IRS as such. Since 1984, any amount clearly associated with a child-related contingency is presumed to be child support. IRC § 71(c)(2). The custodial parent may claim certain credits (child care and earned income) and presumably may claim the dependency exemption, but the custodian may by waiver assign the dependency exemption to the other parent, and most courts have held that a court may order the custodial parent to do so. *See* Chapter 37.C., *infra*.

d. *Hoover v. Commissioner of Internal Revenue*

Richard E. Hoover v. Commissioner of Internal Revenue
102 F. 3d 842 (6th Cir. 1996)

Before: SILER, MOORE, and COLE, Circuit Judges.
MOORE, Circuit Judge.

Petitioner-appellant Richard E. Hoover appeals the decision of the United States Tax Court denying him deductions on his federal income taxes for the years 1988 and 1989. Hoover asserts that the Tax Court erred in holding that $72,200 in payments to Hoover's ex-wife were not deductible as alimony pursuant to 26 U.S.C. §§ 215 and 71. For the reasons stated below, we affirm the Tax Court's decision.

I. BACKGROUND

Richard and Linda Hoover obtained a divorce in Ohio in 1988. An Ohio court issued a memorandum in August 1988 announcing that it would grant the divorce, divide the marital property, and, inter alia, award Mrs. Hoover "alimony as division of equity in the amount of $410,000." J.A. at 140. Mr. Hoover was to pay her at least $3000 per month "until said amount is paid in full." Mrs. Hoover was to be granted a lien on Mr. Hoover's shares in Stark Ceramics "as security for said alimony division." *Id*. at 141.

The Hoovers and their attorneys reviewed a draft of a proposed judgment entry and agreed to changes. The draft decree originally provided for an increased amount of "alimony as division of equity" of $521,640 and for termination of "[a]ll payments of alimony" upon Mrs. Hoover's death, remarriage, or cohabitation; the Hoovers, however, at some point deleted the language providing for such termination. J.A. at 144. Mrs. Hoover was still to be granted a lien on the shares as security on payment of that sum, with Mr. Hoover either providing a letter of credit guaranteeing payment or pledging his stockholdings in Stark Ceramics with an escrow agent "until all of the alimony has been paid in full." *Id*. at 145. The decree also stated that Mr. Hoover would provide medical insurance for Mrs. Hoover until her death, remarriage, or cohabitation; the Hoovers did not alter that provision. *Id*. at 145.

The state court entered a final decree on October 19, 1988. The decree did not include a provision for termination of payments of alimony; the security agreement was unchanged. Mr. Hoover was to pay Mrs. Hoover $30,000 within thirty days, and to pay the remainder of the $521,640 in monthly installments of no less than $3000 "until said amount is paid in full." J.A. at 43, 149.

Mrs. Hoover did not include as income on her tax returns the $46,000 Mr. Hoover paid her in 1988 or the $36,200 he paid her in 1989; the Commissioner notified her of a deficiency regarding only the 1988 taxes, which she challenged in the Tax Court. On the other hand, Mr. Hoover claimed deductions for alimony payments for the amounts paid in 1988 and 1989. The Commissioner issued a notice of deficiency to Mr. Hoover disallowing $36,000 of the claimed deduction for 1988 and the entire $36,200 deduction for 1989. Mr. Hoover challenged the

deficiencies in the Tax Court, and his case was consolidated with Mrs. Hoover's. The Tax Court held that the payments did not qualify for treatment as alimony as defined by 26 U.S.C. § 71 and therefore were not includible in Mrs. Hoover's income or deductible from Mr. Hoover's. Richard Hoover appeals this decision.
***

Section 215 of the Tax Code provides for special tax treatment of payments that fall under the definition of "alimony" in § 71. Alimony or separate maintenance payments may be deducted by the payor, but only if they meet the standards set out in the Tax Code. 26 U.S.C. § 215. "Although the property interests of divorcing parties are determined by state law, federal law governs the federal income tax treatment of that property." *Green v. Commissioner*, 855 F.2d 289, 292 (6th Cir.1988). The mere use of the word "alimony" does not affect the tax consequences of payments.
*

Prior to 1984, § 71 required courts to consider a number of factors to determine whether certain transfers of money would be treated as alimony for federal income tax purposes. The Tax Code allowed payments to qualify as alimony if the payments were periodic and were received "in discharge of ... a legal obligation which, because of the marital or family relationship, is imposed on or incurred by the husband under the [divorce] decree or under a written instrument incident to ... divorce or separation." 26 U.S.C. § 71(a)(1) (1982).

Under prior law, payments in discharge of a legal obligation incurred because of the marital relationship "encompass[ed] only payments in the nature of alimony or support, rather than property settlement." *, Whether payments represented support or property settlement was a question of intent. *, Intent was to be ascertained from the agreement itself and from the surrounding facts and circumstances. *; *see also Schatten v. United States*, 746 F.2d 319, 322-23 (6th Cir.1984) (listing seven factors identified by the Tax Court as useful in determining the nature of payments: parties' intent; *).

As part of the Deficit Reduction Act of 1984, Congress rewrote § 71, replacing the previous vague definitions with four requirements intended to cover payments generally considered to be alimony. * (*See also* H.R.Rep. No. 98-432, Part II, 98th Cong., 2d Sess. 1495 (1984): "The committee bill attempts to define alimony in a way that would conform to general notions of what type of payments constitute alimony as distinguished from property settlements and to prevent the deduction of large, one-time lump-sum property settlements." reprinted in 1984 U.S.C.C.A.N. 697, 1137. Section 71(b)(1) as revised defined "alimony or separate maintenance payment" to mean "any payment in cash if--"

(A) such payment is received by (or on behalf of) a spouse under a divorce or separation instrument,

(B) the divorce or separation instrument does not designate such payment as a payment which is not includible in gross income under this section and not allowable as a deduction under section 215,

(C) in the case of an individual legally separated from his spouse under a decree of divorce or of separate maintenance, the payee spouse and the payor spouse are not members of the same household at the time such payment is made, and

(D) there is no liability to make any such payment for any period after the death of the payee spouse and there is no liability to make any payment (in cash or property) as a substitute for such payments after the death of the payee spouse (and the divorce or separation instrument states that there is no such liability).

26 U.S.C. § 71(b)(1)(A)(D) (Supp. III 1985).

With the revision, Congress specifically intended to eliminate the subjective inquiries into intent and the nature of payments that had plagued the courts in favor of a simpler, more objective test. *See* H.R.Rep. No. 98- 432, Part II, at 1495 ("[T]he present law definition of alimony is not sufficiently objective.... [A] uniform Federal standard should be set forth to determine what constitutes alimony for Federal tax purposes."), reprinted in 1984 U.S.C.C.A.N. 697, 1137. Although the revised definition did not require courts to determine the nature of payments, Congress was particularly concerned with excluding property settlements from § 215 treatment. *See generally* H.R.Rep. No. 98-432, Part II, at 1495-97; *.

The requirement that the obligation to make payments terminate immediately upon the death of the recipient is central to Congress's intended distinction between support and property settlements. *See* H.R. Rep. No. 98-432, Part II, at 1496; 1984 U.S.C.C.A.N. at 1138 ("In order to prevent the deduction of amounts which are in effect transfers of property unrelated to the support needs of the recipient, the bill provides that a payment qualifies as alimony only if the payor ... has no liability to make any such payment for any period following the death of the payee spouse."). *See also* Garrison Lepow, Nobody Gets Married for the First Time Anymore--A Primer on the Tax Implications of Support Payments in Divorce, 25 Duq.L.Rev. 43, 53-54 (1986) ("The cash payment of a property settlement is distinguished from a cash payment of alimony under the new statute by the characteristic that alimony payments end on the recipient's death. Whether the cash payment is for the support of the recipient is no longer at issue.") (citing H.R.Rep. No. 98-432).

In the Tax Reform Act of 1986, Congress amended § 71(b)(1)(D) by deleting the parenthetical requirement that the agreement specifically provide for termination upon the death of the payee spouse. *. The requirement that there be no remaining liability after the payee's death survived. The amendment appeared as a "technical correction"; the legislative history explains only that the section was amended "to provide that alimony payments under certain support decrees ... will not be disqualified solely because the decree does not specifically state that the payments will terminate at the payee's death." *. H.R.Rep. No. 99-426,*; S.Rep. No. 99-313, *. Congress made the amendment retroactive to the 1984 revision. *.

The change, which allows state law to "save" alimony arrangements that meet all requirements of § 71(b)(1) except the explicit statement of termination upon death, was apparently intended to mitigate the effects of sloppy lawyering. *. In other words, if payments will necessarily terminate upon the payee's death by operation of state law, the payments can still qualify under § 71 for special tax treatment pursuant to § 215 despite the parties' failure to specify in the divorce instrument that the payments terminate upon the payee's death.

Although the 1986 amendment injected state law into the § 71(b)(1) inquiry, the purpose behind the 1984 revision still stands. A court determining whether payments qualify as alimony as defined in § 71 will turn to state law only to determine whether state law, by requiring that the payments terminate upon the payee's death, ensures that the payments satisfy § 71(b)(1)(D). Congress clearly did not intend courts to engage in the very sort of subjective inquiry that had prompted the 1984 revision. Therefore, when state family law is ambiguous as to the termination of payments upon the death of the payee, a federal court will not engage in complex, subjective inquiries under state law; rather, the court will read the divorce instrument and make its own determination based on the language of the document.

The Hoovers' divorce decree did not explicitly provide that the payments would terminate upon Mrs. Hoover's death. Indeed, such termination language was deleted from the final agreement of the Hoovers. We therefore must determine whether the payments would terminate by operation of Ohio law.

B. Ohio Law

Mr. Hoover argues that "alimony as division of equity" is a term of art under Ohio law, indicating payments that terminate automatically upon the death of the payee spouse. The meaning of "alimony" under then-applicable Ohio law, however, is ambiguous.

At the time of the Hoovers' divorce, the term "alimony" was not clearly defined under Ohio law. The statute providing for alimony did not distinguish between support payments and property settlements. *See* Ohio Rev.Code Ann. § 3105.18 (Anderson 1989) (amended 1991). *[Fn2 The Ohio statute was revised in 1991 to replace "alimony" with specific definitions of "division of marital property" and "spousal support." Ohio Rev.Code Ann. §§ 3105.171, 3105.18 (Banks-Baldwin 1992). Whereas the previous statute was silent with regard to termination of payments upon the payee spouse's death, the revised statute explicitly provides for termination of spousal support payments upon the death of either spouse, unless expressly otherwise provided in the court order containing the award of spousal support. Ohio Rev.Code Ann. §§ 3105.18(B) (Banks-Baldwin 1992).]* As a result, Ohio courts used the term "alimony" to indicate both support payments and property settlements. ***.

The use of the word "alimony" in the Hoovers' divorce decree, therefore, is at best too ambiguous to aid in the § 71 inquiry. *See Yoakum v. Commissioner*, 82 T.C. 128, 136, 1984 WL 15526 (1984) (stating that because "alimony" under Oklahoma law encompassed both support payments and property division, "the Oklahoma trial court's use of the word 'alimony' in this case is not instructive").

If Ohio law did offer any assistance in this court's analysis, however, it probably would not support Mr. Hoover's position that his payment obligation would terminate upon Mrs. Hoover's death. Under Ohio law,

> where an alimony award is for the payment of a sum certain in installments over a definite period of time and is payable without contingencies, that amount is part of the property division, as a matter of law, no matter what the parties or the court actually called the award.

McClusky v. Nelson,*. Payments made pursuant to a division of property do not terminate by operation of Ohio law upon the death of the payee spouse. *See Zimmie v. Zimmie*, * ("Plaintiff is legally entitled to that portion of the award which is classified as a division of marital property. Her eventual remarriage, death, cohabitation or any other contingency is utterly irrelevant to her entitlement to this amount."); *see also McClusky*, * (agreements awarding a definite amount without contingencies "are seen as vesting the obligee's right to receive a sum certain, pursuant to a valid and binding contract between the parties").

The Hoovers' divorce decree ordered Mr. Hoover to pay Mrs. Hoover $521,640 in monthly installments of at least $3000 "until said amount is paid in full " (emphasis added). The final decree included no contingencies on Mrs. Hoover's right to the full amount or on Mr. Hoover's obligation to pay it. Furthermore, the decree described the payments as "alimony as division of equity"; while apparently not a term of art in Ohio, this phrase suggests that the payments reflect a division of marital property. Significantly, an Ohio court refused to modify the divorce decree to accelerate the remaining payments at Mrs. Hoover's request, on the grounds that the court lacked jurisdiction "to modify an award in the nature of a property settlement." J.A. at 194.

Given the ambiguity of the then-applicable state law as to the termination of payments, we hold that Ohio law does not "save" the payments in question for purposes of § 71(b)(1)(D). We therefore must look to the language of the decree itself and make our own determination as to the satisfaction of the § 71(b)(1)(D) requirement.

C. The Divorce Decree

Nothing in the language of the divorce decree itself indicated that the payments to Mrs. Hoover would terminate on her death. In fact, the decree specifically obligated Mr. Hoover to pay her the definite sum of $521,640 in installments "until said amount is paid in full." Such payment was not made contingent on any factor or event. Furthermore, Mrs. Hoover received a lien on Mr. Hoover's shares in Stark Ceramics as security for that payment, with a requirement that Mr. Hoover provide a letter of credit from a bank guaranteeing the payment or that he pledge sufficient stock with an escrow agent, with such pledge to "remain in full force and effect until all of the alimony has been paid in full." We have no reason to conclude that Mr. Hoover's obligation to pay Mrs. Hoover the full amount terminates upon her death.

III. CONCLUSION

The Hoovers' divorce decree contains no provision for termination of the payments at issue upon Mrs. Hoover's death, and Ohio law applicable at the time of the decree did not clearly provide for such termination. The payments therefore fail to meet the definition of alimony set forth in § 71(b)(1), and cannot be deductible under § 215. For these reasons, we AFFIRM the decision of the Tax Court.

e. Notes and Questions

1) *Hoover* notes

Was the problem in Hoover one that the lawyers for the parties or either of them could have remedied? If so, how? While all states apparently have amended their statutes to avoid the *Hoover* problem now, the case indicates the degree of "i"-dotting and "t"-crossing in following the tax rules needed to avoid tax problems.

2) Tax Questions About Property Transfers

Q1. Hal was ordered in the divorce decree to transfer the house (held in his name in a common law state) to Wanda. The house was purchased in 1980 for $80,000; at the time of divorce it was worth $140,000. Wanda lived in the house for three years after divorce, then sold it for $150,000, free of any mortgage. How much taxable income, if any, does she have?

Q2. Hal and Wanda agree in writing upon divorce that Hal will support the children through four years of university education, and when the last child finishes her education, transfer a piece of property Hal bought for $20,000 (that is now worth $50,000) to Wanda. The youngest child is fourteen years old. Is it likely that the property transfer will be taxable to Hal?

Q3. The divorce decree ordered the administrator of Hal's retirement plan to pay 40 percent of the retirement benefits directly to Wanda each month. Hal's retirement plan provides for a monthly retirement benefit of $2000 per month. How much taxable income will (a) Wanda and (b) Hal receive under the retirement plan?

2) Tax Questions About Alimony

Q1. Are Hal's otherwise qualifying payments directly to Wanda's attorney or to Wanda's credit card company taxable to Hal or Wanda?

Q.2 Hal agrees to pay $200 per month (and his estate must pay if he dies) to Wanda until she dies, whichever occurs first. Are the payments deductible to Hal?

Q3. Hal agrees to pay $200 per month to Wanda for 20 years. Are the payments deductible to Hal?

Q4. If the divorce decree orders Hal (who now lives in another city) to pay for the credit card and other outstanding debts the couple accrued during the marriage for some of their living expenses, may Hal treat those payments as alimony or are they just regular (property) debt payments?

3) QDROs

Remember that "qualified domestic relations orders" are critical, *inter alia*, in order to obtain tax benefits from the division of pension, retirement, and benefit plans. *See* Chapter 27, *supra*. Failure to obtain QDRO eligibility can have significant tax consequences. In *Hawkins v. C.I.R.*, 86 F.3d 982 (10th Cir.,1996) a divorce settlement provided that a million-dollar settlement to the wife would be paid from the husband's pension. After divorce, both parties challenged the assessment of income tax deficiencies. Wife claimed and the Tax Court agreed that the distribution should be taxed to the husband. The Tenth Circuit reversed, holding that the marital settlement agreement incorporated into dissolution decree was a qualified domestic relations order that shifted income tax liability to wife.

4) Deductible Attorney's Fees

Payments for an attorney's professional services are deductible to the extent the attorney was providing tax advice relating to the production of taxable income. Alimony that satisfies the requirements of I.R.C. § 71 is taxable income, so attorneys' fees incurred to establish or collect alimony for a client is deductible. But this deduction is part of the miscellaneous itemized deduction that only applies when it exceeds 2 percent of the tax payer's adjusted gross income. Attorneys' services relating to obtaining (or resisting) the divorce, child custody, child support, property division, other non-alimony issues, or to resisting or reducing alimony obligations are not deductible. Tiso, *infra*.

3. Practical and Ethical Considerations

Failure to consider tax consequences of divorce can lead to liability for the attorney, as well as to professional discipline. In some states courts are directed to consider tax consequences, so the attorney's oversight jeopardizes the court's functioning. *See e.g.* Durst, *infra*, at 9-11. Family law cases often raise varied issues that require the skills of experts. For example, few divorce cases are without income tax consequences. Dependency exemptions, recapture of alimony, profit or loss on sale of assets, and transfer and liquidation of retirement accounts are recurring tax issues in the family law setting. Most family law practitioners have at least some ability to identify income tax issues. If they do not, they open themselves to legal liability for failure to do so.
Drew, *infra*, at 9. *See also* Comeau, *infra*; Friske & Pulliam, *infra*.

4. Bibliography

Stephen P. Comeau, *An Overview of Federal Income Tax Provisions Related to Alimony Payments*, 38 Fam. L.Q. 111 (2004).
David S. Dolowitz, *The Impact of Tax Laws on Divorce*, 4 Utah Bar J. 8 (Aug/Sep/ 1991) at 8.
Margaret Drew, *Lawyer Malpractice and Domestic Violence: Are We Revictimizing Our Clients*, 39 Fam. L. Q. 7 (2005).
Robert J. Durst, II, *Taxing Concerns in Matrimonial Law*, N.J. Law. (June 2001), at 9.
Karyn Bybee Friske & Darlene Pulliam, *The Marriage Penalty after the JGTRRA*, 35 Tax Adviser 284 (2004).
C. Garrison Lepow, *Nobody Gets Married for the First Time Anymore – A Primer on the Tax Implications of Support Payments in Divorce*, 25 Duquesne L. Rev. 43 (1986).

Margaret Dee McGarity, *Avoidable Transfers Between Spouses and Former Spouses*, 31 Fam. L. Q. 392 (1997).

Note, *Divorce and Amended Section 152(e) of the Internal Revenue Code: Do State Courts Have the Power to Allocate Dependency Exemptions*, 29 J. Fam. L. 901 (1991).

Lowell S. Thomas, Jr., Tax Consequences of Marriage, Separation and Divorce (3d ed. 1986).

Christopher A. Tiso, *Are Attorney's Fees Deductible?* 27 Fam. Advoc., Winter 2005, at 40.

B. Bankruptcy Consequences of Divorce

1. Background

a. The Acid Test

Bankruptcy is the "acid test" of a settlement agreement negotiated and drafted by a lawyer for a client. The debtor-protective policy behind the Bankruptcy Code is so powerful, the provisions of the Code are so all-encompassing, and the exceptions generally are so strictly construed, that without careful planning and drafting even the most well-conceived schemes for property division, alimony, and child support may be substantially altered or discharged as a result of bankruptcy.

There is some conflict between the policies which underlie bankruptcy law and family law. For example, the primary policy behind Bankruptcy Code is to give the debtor relief from burden of debt and provide a "fresh start" for the debtor. The primary policy behind alimony, support and property division is to provide necessary support for economically dependent family members, and give an economically dependent spouse fair share of assets acquired during the marriage. The Bankruptcy Code emphasizes the priority of bankruptcy court jurisdiction over the property and claims affecting a debtor. But divorce and related matters traditionally have been seen as coming within the virtually exclusive jurisdiction of state divorce courts. Current divorce policies encourage prompt and final disposition of divorce cases, while the Bankrupt Code provides for an automatic stay of all actions involving claims against debtors.

At least five general provisions of the current Bankruptcy Code that may have significant consequences for divorce and post-divorce proceedings and financial relations. These are the *jurisdictional provisions,* the *automatic stay*, the *definition of the estate in bankruptcy,* the *nondischargeable debts* provision, and *Chapter 13* provisions. Questions arise about the authority of federal bankruptcy judges to determine issues ordinarily reserved for family court judges. *See Marshall v. Marshall,_ U.S._, 126 S.Ct. 1735 (2006) (probate exception does not preclude federal bankruptcy court decisions).

2. Statutes, Cases and Doctrines

a. *In re O'Brien*

In re Michael S. O'BRIEN, Debtor
339 B.R. 529 (Bkcy. D. Mass. 2006)

ORDER REGARDING RELIEF FROM STAY

SOMMA, Bankruptcy Judge.

(Carlin and Crowne)

The Debtor's former wife (Paula M. Carlin) ("Carlin") and his former divorce lawyer (Stephen G. Crowne) ("Crowne") filed separate relief from stay motions concerning discrete fee awards issued in favor of each by the Middlesex Probate and Family Court in post-divorce litigation between the Debtor and Carlin occasioned by alleged breaches of their divorce decree ("Motions") ("Fee Awards") ("Probate Court") ("Litigation").

The Movants seek (a) relief from the automatic stay to enforce the Fee Awards (which they label domestic support orders) or (b) alternatively, an order of the Court generally advising Massachusetts state court judges that relief from stay is not necessary for enforcement of such orders. The Debtor opposes the Motions.

The Carlin Fee Award is an award of attorney's fees for services rendered to Carlin by *her* lawyer in the Litigation. The Crowne Fee Award is an order fixing and determining the amount of a Massachusetts attorney's lien asserted by Crowne for services rendered to the Debtor by *his* lawyer in the Litigation.

Although labeled relief from stay, the Motions are more accurately described as requests for determination that (a) the Fee Awards are domestic support obligations under the Bankruptcy Code and (b) thus, the collection of the Fee Awards from non-estate property is not subject to the automatic stay.

Background

The full record of the divorce action and the Litigation is not before the Court. However, the following factual background is derived from the submissions of the parties in connection with the Motions and is not disputed.

Carlin and the Debtor married in May 1981, separated in May 2000 and divorced in March 2001. They have three children. Their divorce judgment issued on March 13, 2001 and incorporated their separation agreement. In late 2004 and early 2005, litigation between them ensued in the Middlesex Probate and Family Court ("Probate Court") involving disputes regarding their obligations with respect to child support, college education funds and certain mandatory reporting ("Litigation"). Crowne represented the Debtor in the Litigation (though he no longer does so).

After trial, the Probate Court (a) modified the divorce judgment by an adjustment to the Debtor's child support obligations favorable to the Debtor; (b) declined to impose upon the Debtor a college education expense obligation thus apparently leaving the divorce judgment unchanged in that regard; (c) found the Debtor guilty of contempt for willful non-payment of child support; and (d) found Carlin guilty of contempt for willful failure to establish college fund accounts and to report to the Debtor regarding the children and these accounts.

In addition, the Probate Court declined to award attorney's fees to the Debtor but did award attorney's fees to Carlin ($15,000) and to Crowne ($18,320.03), directing that they be paid by immediate withdrawal from the Debtor's retirement account(s) established and maintained through his employment at Massachusetts Institute of Technology ("Retirement Account").

On December 7, 2005, the Debtor commenced his Chapter 7 case in which he claims the Retirement Account as exempt under Section 522(d)(10)(E) of the Bankruptcy Code. At that time, the Fee Awards had not been paid by withdrawal from the Retirement Account or otherwise.

On December 23, 2005, the Probate Court held a hearing regarding enforcement of the Fee Awards but apparently declined to act pending a determination by this Court regarding the effect of the within automatic stay on such enforcement.

On January 5, 2006, Carlin filed her Motion, and on January 11, 2006, Crowne filed his Motion.

On February 7, 2006, the Court held a non-evidentiary hearing on the Motions. At that hearing, the Debtor acknowledged that the Retirement Account is not property of the estate. I afforded the parties the opportunity to submit post-hearing briefs regarding whether the Fee Awards constitute domestic support obligations within the contemplation of the Bankruptcy Code, and each party did so. Since then, the matter has been under advisement.

Discussion
1. Framework

The determination of this matter prompts consideration of the interplay between bankruptcy and domestic relations law. The applicable statutory provisions (and their explicating case law) are Section 101 (defined terms), Section 362 (automatic stay) and Section 523 (discharge exceptions).

The term *domestic support obligation* is newly added to the Bankruptcy Code by the Bankruptcy Abuse Prevention and Consumer Protection Act of 2005 ("2005 Amendments"). The definition may be summarized as follows: a *domestic support obligation* is (a) a debt owed to or recoverable by a spouse, former spouse or child of a debtor; (b) in the nature of alimony, maintenance, or support of such spouse, former spouse or child; (c) established under a separation agreement, divorce decree or property settlement agreement, or an order of a court of record; and (d) not assigned other than for collection purposes. 11 U.S.C. § 101(14A). [FN2. The 2005 Amendments also placed this term in Section 362(b)(2)(B) and Section 523(a)(5) in substitution for the phrase alimony, maintenance, and support. Case law construing alimony, maintenance, and support has largely developed in respect of former Section 523(a)(5) whose text is comparable to and largely mirrors Section 101(14)(A).]

The filing of a bankruptcy case does not stay the collection of a domestic support obligation from property that is not property of the estate, 11 U.S.C. § 362(b)(2)(B). A bankruptcy discharge does not discharge an individual debtor (a) from a debt for a domestic support obligation, 11 U.S.C. § 523(a)(5) or (b) from a debt to a spouse, former spouse or child of the Debtor that (i) is not a domestic support obligation and (ii) is incurred in a divorce or divorce-related action, 11 U.S.C. § 523(a)(15).

It is within this framework that the Court considers the Motions and the Fee Awards.

2. Fee Awards

The issue raised in the Motions is this: whether and under what circumstances are debts owed by a debtor to his own lawyer or on account of his former wife's lawyer for services in a divorce-related action domestic support obligations under the Bankruptcy Code. Having considered the Motions, the arguments, the record and applicable law, the Court concludes that there are material factual matters relevant to the determination of the Fee Awards as domestic support obligations requiring an evidentiary hearing. *See In re Rios,* 901 F.2d 71 (7th Cir.1990) and *In re Dean,* 231 B.R. 19 (Bankr.W.D.N.Y.1999) as to the Crowne Fee Award. *See In re Michaels,* 157 B.R. 190 (Bankr.D.Mass.1993) and *In re Hale,* 289 B.R. 788 (1st Cir. BAP 2003) as to the Carlin Fee Award.

The matters for evidentiary hearing include (but are not limited to) the divorce decree, the separation agreement, Crowne's written engagement terms (if any), the intent of the parties regarding support and their financial condition at the time of their divorce, and the scope of services rendered in respect of the Fee Awards. None of these matters is yet (or fully) before the Court. One or more may have some bearing (perhaps dispositive) on the ultimate outcome. The Court is not inclined to make a summary ruling on an incomplete record.

Conclusion

In the foregoing circumstances, the Court will refrain from ruling on the Motions pending the conduct of an evidentiary hearing which will be separately scheduled in accordance with the Court's docket.

b. Notes and Questions

1) *O'Brien* and the Bankruptcy Abuse Prevention and Consumer Protection Act of 2005

In 2005, Congress passed and the President signed the Bankruptcy Abuse Prevention and Consumer Protection Act of 2005 ("BAPCPA"). The amendments, which took effect October 17, 2005, complicate a previously complex set of bankruptcy provisions. The effect of BAPCPA upon divorce, other than making bankruptcy consequences more difficult to ascertain, at least initially, is unclear. To some extent, BAPCPA makes access to bankruptcy more difficult for families and the poor; but among the changes that some will applaud are that

> alimony, maintenance, support and property settlement debts have been given new status as "domestic support obligations;" that these obligations will now receive first-priority for repayment among unsecured creditors; and that the automatic stay has been modified to permit the continuation of many more domestic relations/domestic support actions. Some of the concerns expressed by the bankruptcy community about the dischargeability of marital debts have been addressed in the new law. In addition, the rules relating to the discharge of alimony, maintenance, support and property settlement obligations have been streamlined.

Alexander, *infra*, at 578. On the other hand,

> Before the BAPCPA, a creditor holding a claim had the initial burden of proving that the debt was one under §523(a)(15). If the creditor prevailed, and the court determined that a debt came within the reach of §523(a)(15), the debtor had two affirmative defenses he or she might use to obtain the discharge of such debts--the "ability to pay" test and the "balance of the harms" test.
>
> Under the BAPCPA, Section 523(a)(15) still excludes the same types of debts from discharge, but there are no "ability to pay" or "balance of the harms exceptions. Congress has done away with both of these affirmative defenses. If the debt otherwise comes within the meaning of §523(a)(15), it is nondischargeable.
>
> . . . Before the BAPCPA, a former spouse of the debtor had to file an adversary proceeding (a separate complaint in bankruptcy court) to seek a nondischargeability judgment on a Section 523(a)(15) claim. Section 523(c) mandated that certain debts

would be discharged unless, "on request of a creditor to whom such debt is owed, after notice and a hearing, the court determines such debt to be excepted from discharge." If the former spouse did not pursue the claim, then it was discharged.

In the BAPCPA, Congress removed from Section 523(c) the exception to discharge contained in §523(a)(15). By doing so, Section 523(a)(15) joins those other exceptions to discharge in Section 523(a), which are excepted from discharge without the need for a creditor taking any action. . . .

The full reach of Section 523(a)(15) remains to be determined. The previous version of Section 523(a)(15) excluded from discharge debts "incurred by the debtor in the course of a divorce or separation or in connection with a separation agreement, divorce decree or other order" to the extent that the affirmative defenses identified above did not apply.

. . .

In the BAPCPA, Congress added the phrase "to a spouse, former spouse, or child of the debtor" to define the debt that was excluded from discharge. The question that seems to remain is whether the addition of the phrase "to the former spouse of the debtor" limits the reach of Section 523(a)(15), and if so, how.

French, *infra*, at 18-19.

O'Brien was one of the first cases to apply the BAPCPA in a family law context. Does it shed any light on how BAPCPA will change the bankruptcy effects for parties who are divorcing or who have recently divorced?

2) Anticipating Bankruptcy

As the night follows the day, so bankruptcy seems to follow divorce. This is not surprising; many divorces result from (or at least are hastened by) the strains caused by serious financial problems such as business failure, unemployment, excessive consumer debt, etc. And the relationship between financial problems and marital failure are reciprocal: as marriage relationships fail, the job performance, business judgment, and employment relations of the spouses may be adversely affected. Thus, even when financial problems do not exist before marital breakup they may develop as a result of it.

Since financial distress is often a cause of or consequence of marital failure, every competent lawyer representing clients in dissolution proceedings must be alert to the potential risks and advantages to his client of bankruptcy. The prudent family lawyer will view possible settlements and decrees with an eye toward failure on the part of the client and on the part of the ex-spouse. The thorough lawyer will consider the likely consequences if the former spouse files a petition for bankruptcy, and the likely consequences if the client files for bankruptcy. An understanding of the potential applications of the bankruptcy law can be a powerful tool in negotiating at the time of marital dissolution.

3. Practical and Ethical Considerations

When counseling with a divorce client about his or her post-divorce financial situation, it may be apparent that the party (perhaps both parties) will not be able to service all of the debt incurred during the marriage (and before). Inclusion of indemnification and modification provisions in settlement agreements are two ways to provide a client with some protection against the bankruptcy of the divorcing or ex-spouse. That is a good time to discuss the pros-and-cons of bankruptcy with the client.

Sometimes, it is best for all if both divorcing parties file for bankruptcy together. That results in discharge of liability for most unsecured debt for both parties (not just the one who filed for bankruptcy leaving the other spouse liable for joint debts to unsecured creditors. Usually Chapter 7 is the most useful for divorcing couples, as Chapter 13 requires the parties to work together for three to five years. If the opposing party refuses to file for bankruptcy, your client may file alone. However, that creates significant uncertainties as the effect upon the divorce judge is not predictable, and that makes planning for post-bankruptcy property and debt unclear also. Of course, if one party files for bankruptcy that may force the other party to file also because the repercussions for the non-filing spouse may be great (if any obligations owing to her by the filing spouse are discharged, or obligations to pay joint debt are discharged. *See* Bell, *infra* at 33-36.

Is it fraudulent or unethical for the attorney for husband to negotiate with the other side for husband to assume liability for all of the debt in exchange for keeping all of the retirement, while planning to file for bankruptcy thereby discharging the debt obligation but leaving the creditors free to pursue the wife? Is it malpractice for counsel for the wife to fail to see the risk, if wife remains free to file for bankruptcy also? *See* Bell, *infra* at 33 (suggesting possible violations of Rules of Professional Responsibility 3.4, 4.1, and 8.4).

4. Bibliography

Peter C. Alexander, *"Herstory" Repeats: Bankruptcy Code Harms Women and Children*, 13 Am. Bankr. Inst. L. Rev. 571 (2005).

Brenda J. Bell, Sharon Wright Kellstrom & Anne Burke Miller, *The Effect of Bankruptcy on Divorce Planning*, J. Kan. B.A., Mar. 2001, at 30.

Claude R. Bowles & Jessica B. Allman, *What the Bankruptcy Code Giveth, Congress Taketh Away: The Dischargeability of Domestic Obligations After the Bankruptcy Reform Act of 1994*, 34 Univ. Louis. J. Fam. L. 521 (1995-96).

V. Michael Brigner, *The 1994 Bankruptcy Code Revisions From A Domestic Relations Court Perspective*, 34 J. Fam. L. 643 (1995-96).

Bernice B. Donald & Jennie D. Latta, *The Dischargeability of Property Settlement and Hold Harmless Agreements in Bankruptcy, An Overview of §523(a)(15), 31 Fam.L.Q.* 409 (1997).

Randy French, *The Impact of the New Bankruptcy Code on Divorce, Property Division, and the Allocation of Debt In Divorce*, 49 Advocate (Idaho), January 2006, at 17.

Margaret Howard, *A Bankruptcy Primer for Family Law*, 31 Fam. L. Q. 377 (1997).

Michard H.W. Maloy, *Using Bankruptcy Court to Modify Domestic Relations Decrees: Problems Created by § 523(a)(15)*, 31 Fam. L. Q. 433 (1997).

Margaret Dee McGarity, *Avoidable Transfers Between Spouses and Former Spouses*, 31 Fam. L. Q. 391 (1997).

C. INTERNATIONAL AND COMPARATIVE DIVORCE LAW

1. Background

Although separation agreements are usually associated with the divorce process, they may be used whenever a married couple separates to provide the settlement of the incidents of the marriage contract.

a. Comparative Divorce Grounds

The predominant substantive principle for divorce globally is no-fault divorce (variously phrased). One survey of selected nations revealed that no-fault grounds were available in most of the nations surveyed, though generally no-fault is an optional ground for divorce. The traditional abuses of adultery, extreme cruelty, desertion, and habitual addictions are common grounds for divorce also. The variety of laws governing divorce is tremendous, with some countries still not allowing divorce (e.g., Malta), or making divorce very difficult to obtain (Chile, Philippines), while in other countries divorce is the only legal remedy for a struggling couple as no other legal alternative (such as legal separation) is available.

Of course, the substantive grounds for divorce provide only part of the whole picture of divorce regulation. Often procedures (waiting periods, multiple litigations steps, filing fees, etc.) moderate what appear to be very permissive grounds for divorce, or facilitate what appears to be very restrictive divorce. In few countries are both the grounds and the procedures for divorce as permissive and unrestrained as they are in the United States of America.

Muslim countries provide an exception to the international trend toward marriage terminable at will. Traditionally, Islam allowed non-judicial divorce, including divorce by a unilateral statement of the husband (*talaq*), although there often were powerful cultural constraints against exercise (at least abuse) of the *talaq*. While modernization of legal codes, including family laws, has occurred in most Muslim countries, strong forces in many Muslim cultures have generated powerful opposition to the perceived diminution of the public protection for and status of marriage. In many countries with significant Muslim population, the tension between clerical-regulation of divorce and state-regulation of divorce is notable. One variety of legal pluralism found in many multi-cultural countries with Muslim population is to acceded control of marriage and divorce to certain religious communities. Thus, Islamic family law is the operative family law for Muslim communities in many nations.

b. International Divorce Recognition in General

The law of the forum (*lex fori*) appears to be the predominant choice of law rule in divorce cases. It is especially strongly favored in Anglo-American legal systems. The potential for sharp conflict in a sensitive area of sovereign policy is avoided by this rule, and certainty and predictability enhanced, at the cost of some flexibility and fairness. The next most common choice of law rule is to apply the law of the domicile of the parties; reference to the law of nationality was once popular in continental Europe, but that appears to be waning in the advance of domicile in choice of law regarding personal status.

Of course, the court rendering the divorce must have had jurisdiction to adjudicate the divorce proceeding. "The domicile or the habitual residence of the parties is almost universally accepted as a basis for assuming jurisdiction in divorce and legal separation." However, beyond the broad statement of a general rule, there are vast differences in detail and application of the domicile rule. For instance, there are differences concerning whether the domicile of both parties is required, or the conjugal domicile, or the domicile of either of them, or of only one of them (historically the husband).

Overall, the trend appears to be toward recognition of the foreign divorce if it was valid under the laws of the place it was rendered, or the law of the parties domicile or nationality. This is qualified in some states, however, by the requirement that the divorce was rendered by a judicial tribunal (some countries are hesitant to recognize non-judicial divorces) that had a reasonable basis for jurisdiction (typically domicile or nationality), that accorded the parties basic procedural fairness (notice to all parties of the proceedings, and opportunity to participate), and that the basis for divorce not violate very strong public policy of the forum. In most countries there is a practical (and usually also doctrinal) presumption in favor of recognition of foreign divorce decrees, providing jurisdictional requirements were met in the divorce case.

c. The Connection Between Jurisdiction and Choice of Law

One reason for the popularity of the domicile rule for divorce jurisdiction relates to choice of law. Traditionally states have applied their own law in divorce actions. If at least one of the parties is domiciled in the forum state, there is no question that the forum constitutionally may apply its own divorce law in the action. But if neither party is domiciled in nor has a significant contact with the state, it would violate due process of law or the full faith and credit clause for the forum to apply its own divorce law. And because divorce law reflects so directly deeply held values, the potential for explosive misinterpretation of one state's divorce law by another would cause many courts to be reluctant to assert jurisdiction if it meant they might have to find, interpret and apply the divorce law of a sister state.

2. Statutes, Cases and Doctrines

a. Treaties and Conventions

International recognition and enforcement of decrees relating to divorce are often regulated by multinational agreements, treaties, and conventions. Historically, the United States has avoided getting heavily involved in international treaties and conventions and that applies to those relating to recognition and enforcement of divorce and related decrees. *See* Palsson, *infra*; Wardle (1995), *infra*. However, there now appears to be cautious willingness on the part of American law makers to sign some international conventions and treaties, and within recent years the United States has signed, ratified, and implemented the Hague Convention on International Adoption and the Hague Convention on the Civil Aspects of International Child Abduction, for example. On the other hand, the United States still has not ratified the U.N. Convention on the Rights of the Child and there are some structural as well as substantive controversies about some international family policy proposals and initiatives. *See* Wilkins, *infra*.

b. International Jurisdiction Shopping

There may be very significant economic incentives for a wealthy party to go forum shopping before filing for divorce. For one example of a successful forum shopping case by a wealthy American husband who renounced his U.S. citizenship and filed for divorce in England and got a divorce decree with much more favorable alimony and property division provisions than he likely would have gotten in American courts, which a Michigan court recognized to bar wife's claims filed in the Michigan court, *see Dart v. Dart,* 597 N.W.2d 82 (Mich.,1999); *see also* Burkholder, *infra.*

3. Practical and Ethical Considerations

The risk of foreign decrees (interstate as well as international, but especially international) is the risk of nonrecognition. Conflict of Laws principles allow significant "wiggle room" for courts to massage and manipulate abstract principles to reach the results the judges prefer. To what extent should a divorce lawyer be expected to be familiar with and refer her clients to divorce and related laws of other countries which might be favorable to the client?

4. Bibliography

Karey Burkholder, Notes & Comments, *Darting to England: A Comparison of the United States' and England's Divorce Laws,* 13 Temp. Int'l & Comp. L.J. 163 (1999).

Lennart Pålsson, Marriage in Comparative Conflict of Laws: Substantive Conditions (Martinus Nijhoff Publishers, 1981).

Lynn D. Wardle, *International Marriage Recognition: A World Dilemma,* in Families Across Frontiers 75-88 (Nigel Lowe & Gillian Douglas, eds., The Hague: Martinus Nijhoff Publishers, 1996).

Lynn D. Wardle, *International Marriage and Divorce Regulation and Recognition: A Survey,* 29 Fam. L. Q. 497-517 (Fall 1995).

Richard G. Wilkins & Bradley N. Roylance, *The Impaact of U.N. Conference Declarations on International and Domestic Law.* World Family Policy Center, http://www.worldfamilypolicycenter.org/> (searched 30 July 2001).

CHAPTER 30

Separation Agreements; ADR; Professional Responsibilities and Realities in Divorce Practice; Protective Orders

A. SEPARATION AGREEMENTS

1. Background

At common law, a married couple could not enter into an enforceable contract with one another because of the wife's common law disabilities. Her legal identity merged into that of the husband. With the removal of the disabilities, husband and wife could enter into marital contracts as long as it did not alter the essentials of the marriage or encourage, promote, or facilitate divorce. With the coming of no fault divorce law and the movement toward private ordering in family matters, separation agreements are commonly used in the divorce process.

2. Statutes, Cases and Doctrines

a. Uniform Marriage and Divorce Act

Section 306 [Separation Agreement]
(a) To promote amicable settlement of disputes between parties to a marriage attendant upon their separation or the dissolution of their marriage, the parties may enter into a written separation agreement containing provisions for disposition of any property owned by either of them, maintenance of either of them, and support, custody, and visitation of their children.
(b) In a proceeding for dissolution of marriage or legal separation the terms of the separation agreement, except those providing for the support, custody, and visitation of children, are binding upon the court unless it finds, after considering the economic circumstances of the parties and any other relevant evidence produced by the parties, on their own motion or on request of the court, that the separation agreement is unconscionable.
(c) If the court finds the separation agreement unconscionable, it may request the parties to submit a revised separation agreement or may make orders for the disposition of property, maintenance, and support.
(d) If the court finds that the separation agreement is not unconscionable as to disposition of property or maintenance, and not unsatisfactory as to support:
(1) unless the separation agreement provides to the contrary, its terms shall be set forth in the decree of dissolution or legal separation and the parties shall be ordered to perform them; or
(2) if the separation agreement provides that its terms shall not be set forth in the decree, the decree shall identify the separation agreement and state that the court has found the terms not unconscionable.
(e) Terms of the agreement set forth in the decree are enforceable by all remedies available for enforcement of a judgment, including contempt, and are enforceable as contract terms.

(f) Except for terms concerning support, custody, or visitation of children, the decree may expressly preclude or limit modification of terms set forth in the decree if the separation agreement so provides. Otherwise, terms of a separation agreement set forth in the decree are automatically modified by modification of the decree.

b. *Johnston   Johnston*

J. Edward Johnston, Jr. v. Helen T. Johnston
465 A.2d 436 (Md. 1983)

COUCH, Judge.

Although the parties have raised four issues in this case, the issue, as we see it, is whether a separation agreement approved and incorporated but not merged in a divorce decree may be collaterally attacked. For reasons to be discussed herein, we hold that it may not be where, as here, its validity is conclusively established by the decree which operates as res judicata.

The parties hereto were married in June of 1948 and lived together 23 years prior to separating in June of 1971. During the marriage, four children were born all of whom have now reached their majority. Subsequent to their separation, each party retained counsel and negotiated an agreement the purpose of which was "to effect a final and permanent settlement of their respective property rights." The agreement was executed by the parties in February of 1973 and provided, inter alia, for the support and maintenance of Mrs. Johnston and the four children, the transfer of certain property interests, the execution of testamentary designations, and the creation of various trusts. The agreement was made in contemplation of divorce proceedings and provided:

> This agreement shall be offered in evidence in any such suit, and if acceptable to the court, shall be incorporated by reference in the decree that may be granted therein. *Notwithstanding such incorporation, this agreement shall not be merged in the decree, but shall survive the same and shall be binding and conclusive on the parties for all time.*(Emphasis supplied).

The agreement also provided:

> No modification or waiver of any of the terms of this agreement shall be valid unless in writing and executed with the same formality as this agreement.

Mr. Johnston filed a "Bill of Complaint for Divorce A Vinculo Matrimonii" in the Circuit Court for Baltimore City, specifically requesting "[t]hat the Agreement of the parties dated February 16, 1973 be incorporated by reference in any decree that may be granted herein." A "Decree of Divorce" was entered June 27, 1973, stating in relevant part:

> It is further ADJUDGED, ORDERED AND DECREED that the Plaintiff provide for maintenance, and support of Defendant and of the infant children of the parties, all as provided in the Agreement between the parties dated February 16, 1973 and filed in this cause of action, *said Agreement being hereby approved and made a part hereof as if fully set forth herein....*" (Emphasis added).

In May, 1981, Mr. Johnston filed a "Petition to Set Aside and Void Agreement" on the basis that "consultations [with professionals] ha[d] disclosed that [he] suffered from a mental disease and/or mental defect during the negotiations and subsequent execution of the aforesaid Agreement which severely impaired [his] mental competency at that time." The petition further asserted that Mr. Johnston's mental incompetency justified the voiding of the separation agreement. Mrs. Johnston in turn filed a "Motion to Strike and Motion Raising Preliminary Objection" contending that the four children were necessary parties as they were affected by the agreement, the allegations in the petition were insufficient to advise her of the nature of Mr. Johnston's mental disease or defect, that Mr. Johnston had failed to state whether he is presently mentally competent, and that she and other members of the family have relied upon and continue to rely upon the terms of the agreement. She also asserted that the relief requested should be denied because of laches and public policy. In addition, Mrs. Johnston argued that Mr. Johnston was actually seeking to have the enrolled decree set aside but had failed to allege "fraud, mistake or irregularity" as required by Maryland Rule 625. [FN1 *"For a period of thirty days after the entry of a judgment, or thereafter pursuant to motion filed within such period, the court shall have revisory power and control over such judgment. After the expiration of such period the court shall have revisory power and control over such judgment, only in case of fraud, mistake or irregularity."*]

Following a hearing on the matter, the chancellor granted Mrs. Johnston's motion to strike*** Mrs. Johnston's request for counsel fees was denied. The Court of Special Appeals affirmed the chancellor's ruling***

(1) We believe that the threshold issue, which neither the chancellor nor the intermediate appellate court discussed, is whether the separation agreement merged in the decree so as to be superseded by the decree. [FN3 *"Merger" is defined as the "[s]ubstitution of rights and duties under judgment or decree for those under property settlement agreement." Black's Law Dictionary 892 (5th ed. 1979); Flynn v. Flynn, 42 Cal.2d 55, 265 P.2d 865, 866 (1954) (en banc); Roesbery v. Roesbery, 88 Idaho 514, 401 P.2d 805, 807 (1965)]* The decree expressly approved and incorporated the agreement. However, the agreement explicitly provided that it was not to merge in the decree but was to survive the decree. As observed by the Supreme Court of Arizona in *McNelis v. Bruce*, 90 Ariz. 261, 367 P.2d 625, 631 (1961) (en banc):

> It is the rule that the mere approval of a property settlement in the divorce decree does not operate to make it a part of and enforceable as a decree. If the language of the agreement shows an intent to make it part of the divorce decree and the agreement is actually incorporated in the decree, the provisions of the agreement may be enforced as an order of the court. As soon as a property settlement agreement is incorporated into the decree the agreement is superceded by the decree and the obligations imposed are not those imposed by contract but are those imposed by the decree since the contract is merged in the decree." (Citations omitted).

The language of the agreement in *McNelis* was similar to that in the instant case, providing:

> This agreement shall be offered in evidence in such action and if acceptable to the court shall be incorporated by reference in any decree that may be granted herein. Notwithstanding such incorporation, this agreement shall not be merged in the decree but shall survive the same and shall be binding and conclusive upon the parties for all time.'

Id. 367 P.2d at 631-32.

In determining whether the agreement merged in the decree so as to be modifiable by the court, the court looked to the intent of the parties, stating in pertinent part:

> The foregoing clause manifests the intention of the parties to the agreement. It was not disapproved by the court but rather adopted as part of the agreement; it therefore must be taken as speaking the intention of not only the parties but of the court that the agreement was not to be merged in the judgment.

Id. 367 P.2d at 632.

The Supreme Court of California has also had occasion to discuss the issue of merger:

> Merger is the substitution of rights and duties under the judgment or the decree for those under the agreement or cause of action sued upon. The question as to what extent, if any, a merger has occurred, when a separation agreement has been presented to the court in a divorce action, arises in various situations. Thus, it may be necessary to determine whether or not contempt will lie to enforce the agreement, whether or not other judgment remedies, such as execution or a suit on the judgment, are available, whether or not an action may still be maintained on the agreement itself, and whether or not there is an order of the court that may be modified....
>
> In any of these situations it is first necessary to determine whether the parties and the court intended a merger. If the agreement is expressly set out in the decree, and the court orders that it be performed, it is clear that a merger is intended. On the other hand, the parties may intend only to have the validity of the agreement established, and not to have it become a part of the decree enforceable as such. Whether or not a merger is intended, the agreement may be incorporated into the decree either expressly or by reference. If a merger is not intended, the purpose of incorporation will be only to identify the agreement so as to render its validity res judicata in any subsequent action based upon it. If a merger is intended, the purpose of incorporation is, of course, to make the agreement an operative part of the decree.

Flynn v. Flynn, 42 Cal.2d 55, 265 P.2d 865, 866 (1954) (en banc) *.

The agreement in *Flynn* provided that it could be approved by the court and incorporated in the decree. However, there was no provision, as in the instant case, that it would not merge. The decree ratified, approved, and incorporated the agreement. The court concluded that the parties and the court had clearly intended the agreement to merge in the decree and, accordingly, the court had jurisdiction to modify the provision for monthly payments.

In our view, where, as in the instant case, the agreement provides that it shall be incorporated but not merged in the decree, it is patent that the parties did not intend merger and the agreement survives as a separate and independent contractual arrangement between the parties. *** On the other hand, where, as in *Flynn*, *supra*, the agreement does not include a non-merger clause and it is incorporated in the decree, the agreement is superseded by the decree. *** The agreement, once incorporated and merged in the decree, is enforceable through contempt proceedings and may be modified by the court.*** [W]here the court incorporates the agreement as a whole, including the non-merger clause, the court approves the clause against merger so that the contract survives. ***

It is undisputed that pursuant to Maryland Rule S77 b [FN5 "*A deed, agreement or settlement between husband and wife as described in Art. 16, Sec. 28 of the Annotated Code of Maryland may be received in evidence and made a part of the record in an action for divorce, annulment or alimony and may be incorporated, insofar as the court may deem proper, into the decree.*"] a separation agreement may be incorporated in the divorce decree. Moreover, there are numerous cases previously decided by this Court that firmly establish that once incorporated, the contractual provisions become part of the decree, modifiable by the court where appropriate and enforceable through contempt proceedings. *** It is significant to note that the issue of merger has simply never arisen as none of the incorporated agreements contained a non-merger clause. On the other hand, it appears to be well established that separation agreements not incorporated in divorce decrees remain separate enforceable instruments. For example, we have observed that:

> A support or property agreement is not invalid nor unenforceable merely because it is not embodied in the divorce decree, if not in conflict with such decree. If the divorce decree does not provide for alimony, it does not terminate liability of the husband to make the payments

provided for by a separation agreement. A support or property agreement is not affected by the subsequent decree of divorce, if such settlement is neither incorporated in the decree, disapproved by the decree, nor superseded by provisions of the decree.

Shacter v. Shacter, 247 A.2d 268, 270 (Md. 1968)*. ***

In our view, the cases from other jurisdictions as well as the various treatises concerning the doctrine of merger, as discussed hereinabove at length, are very persuasive. On the basis of such authority, we hold that where the parties intend a separation agreement to be incorporated but not merged in the divorce decree, the agreement remains a separate, enforceable contract and is not superseded by the decree. In the case sub judice, the agreement expressly provided that it was to be incorporated but not merged in the decree. The decree approved the agreement as a whole and made it a part of the decree as if it were fully set forth, thus approving the non-merger clause. Accordingly, the agreement remained an independent contract which in some instances could be attacked separately from the decree and thus the trial judge erred in granting the motion to strike on the basis that the requirements of Md.Rule 625 had not been met.

(2) It has been stated that:

Where there is a valid bilateral divorce--the divorce court having had jurisdiction of the parties and the subject matter--and the court approves the separation agreement, which is then incorporated in the decree, the court will be deemed to have passed on its legality, and subsequent collateral attack on it will not be countenanced. The validity of the agreement is then res judicata; and if the decree approving it is that of a sister state, full faith and credit bars collateral attack on the agreement elsewhere. To put it concretely, the husband cannot in such a case evade his obligations under the agreement by claiming that it is illegal because it was in consideration of divorce, or that it is voidable because it was procured through fraud. Nor can the wife upset the agreement on the ground of misrepresentation or coercion. On the other hand, where the agreement is not approved by or incorporated in an out-of-state decree, the parties are not estopped, as a matter of law, from later challenging its validity elsewhere. And this despite the fact that it may have been brought to the court's attention and may have been referred to in the findings." *** In addition, at least two of our sister jurisdictions have held that where the separation agreement is incorporated in the divorce decree but no merger is intended, the purposes of incorporation are to identify the agreement and to render its validity res judicata. ***

Although the parties in the instant case have not precisely raised the issue of res judicata, [we believe that in the interests of judicial economy it is appropriate for us to address it as it is dispositive of the matter before us. * As Judge Levine stated for this Court in *MPC, Inc. v. Kenny*, 279 Md. 29, 32, 367 A.2d 486, 488-89 (1977):

"The doctrine of res judicata is that a judgment between the same parties and their privies is a final bar to any other suit upon the same cause of action, and is conclusive, not only as to all matters that have been decided in the original suit, but as to all matters which with propriety could have been litigated in the first suit...." ***

In the instant case, the separation agreement was executed "[w]hereas the Husband desire[d] to make provision for the Wife's and children's support and maintenance, and the parties desire[d] to effect a final and permanent settlement of their respective property rights." Both parties were represented by competent counsel at the time of the execution of the agreement as well as during the divorce proceeding. The agreement, consisting of 17 pages and numerous exhibits, was submitted to the court for its approval. By its own terms, it was to be incorporated in the decree only if it were acceptable to the court. Mr. Johnston testified at the divorce hearing and was questioned by the chancellor regarding the separation agreement:

"Q Now, you and your wife have entered into a separation agreement. Is that correct?

A That is correct.

Q And that agreement is dated February 16th, 1973, and you have requested the court to incorporate that agreement into any decree that may be granted in this case. Do you understand what that means?

A Yes, Your Honor.

Q That the agreement will become a part of this decree, and you will be required to comply with the terms and conditions of the agreement. Do you understand that?

A Yes, Your Honor. * * *

Q All right, Mr. Johnston, I show you this agreement and ask whether the agreement is signed by you and your wife?

A Yes, Your Honor."

The divorce decree expressly approved the agreement, which was filed as an exhibit, and ordered, at the request of the parties, that it be sealed due to the confidential nature of various matters and facts contained therein. In our view the property rights of the parties were determined in the divorce proceeding. Moreover, the approval and incorporation of the agreement conclusively established the validity of the agreement and precludes a collateral attack by either party. As stated by the Court of Civil Appeals of Texas, "[u]pon a suit to enforce the terms of the settlement agreement approved [and incorporated] in such judgment, the sanctity and finality of that judgment cannot be collaterally attacked." *** There, as here, the property settlement agreement was approved and incorporated in the divorce decree. ***

For the reasons stated herein, we conclude that where, as in the instant case, the property settlement agreement is presented to the court for approval and is approved by the court and incorporated in the divorce decree, the validity of the agreement is conclusively established and the doctrine of res judicata operates so as to preclude a collateral attack on the agreement.

In accordance with the above, we hold that Mrs. Johnston's motion to strike was properly granted by the chancellor although for reasons different from those assigned by the Court of Special Appeals.

c. *Levine v. Levine*

Myrna P. Levine v. Terry J. Levine
436 N.E. 2d 476 (N.Y. 1982)

JASEN, Judge.

We are asked on this appeal to determine whether the fact that a separation agreement was prepared by one attorney representing both the husband and wife is sufficient, in and of itself, to establish overreaching requiring a rescission of the agreement.

The parties were married on October 18, 1958 and have two children. Due to a variety of differences, the couple separated in 1971. On February 17, 1976, they entered into a separation agreement. At the time, the husband was operating an auto supply parts business and, according to the record, was earning $20,000 per year. The wife was employed as a bookkeeper for her husband's business and earned approximately $170 per week.

The separation agreement provided, among other things, that the wife was to retain custody of the children. The wife was also awarded the right to occupy the marital residence and ownership of all the furniture therein was transferred to her. The husband agreed to pay $125 per week in support for the wife and the two children. In addition, the husband agreed to pay for the children's private education, health insurance, clothing and medical bills. The husband also assumed all carrying charges on the marital residence, including taxes and mortgage interest payments, and agreed to provide the wife with the free use of a Cadillac automobile. For her part, the wife agreed to transfer her half interest in a boat owned by the couple. Although the boat had a market value of between $40,000 and $50,000, it was encumbered by a substantial mortgage.

The separation agreement was prepared by an attorney, related to the husband by marriage, who had previously represented the husband in connection with his business and who had known both parties for a number of years. The husband initially contacted the attorney and informed him that he had discussed the possibility of a separation agreement with his wife and that the couple had agreed on the essential terms. The attorney then arranged to meet with the wife at his office.

At this meeting, the attorney told the wife that he was involved in the matter only because the basic terms of the agreement had already been settled by the parties and that the wife was free to seek the advice of another attorney. Based on conversations with both parties, the attorney prepared a draft agreement. Further negotiations and consultations followed, after which a final agreement was drawn up, thoroughly reviewed by plaintiff, and then signed by her.

On June 14, 1976, the parties executed an amendment to the separation agreement in order to arrange for the sale of the marital residence and the purchase of a second house. A second amendatory agreement, dated November 19, 1976, provided for the transfer of the Cadillac referred to in the original agreement to plaintiff. The husband, based on the 1976 separation agreement, obtained a *** divorce *** on August 23, 1977.

The wife then commenced this action seeking to have the separation agreement and the two subsequent modifications thereof set aside as "inequitable" and "unconscionable". In her complaint, the wife alleged that she "was not represented by counsel of her own choosing, but instead and without her consent was represented by the defendant's attorney" in the execution of the separation agreement and subsequent modifications. The wife further alleged that the husband "coerced and exerted undue influence and overreaching on the plaintiff" such that "plaintiff's use of defendant's attorney was not a choice freely made by plaintiff."

After a nonjury trial, the wife's complaint was dismissed for failure to make out a prima facie case. The court found no evidence of coercion, undue influence or overreaching practiced by the husband. The court also concluded that the agreement was fair, and a specific finding was made that the attorney had "managed to preserve neutrality" throughout his joint representation of the couple.

On appeal, a unanimous Appellate Division reversed, on the law and the facts, and granted the wife judgment setting aside the separation agreement. After noting that the wife was represented by her husband's counsel, the court below stated: "Upon this record, we conclude that the circumstances evince a sufficient degree of overreaching on the part of the husband to require that this separation agreement be set aside." * There should be a reversal.

At the outset, it should be noted that, in the posture in which this case comes before us, the standard of review is rather limited. Where, as here, the Appellate Division reverses "on the law and the facts" and makes new findings, we must examine the record to determine whether the weight of the credible evidence supports the trial court's findings or the new findings made by the Appellate Division. (N.Y.Const., art. VI, s 3, subd. a; CPLR 5501, subd. [b].) In our view, the weight of the evidence supports the finding made by the trial court that the separation agreement was not the product of overreaching by the husband. Moreover--and this would be fatal to the wife's claim, as a matter of law--there was no factual determination at the Appellate Division that the terms of the agreement were unfair to the wife. To establish her entitlement to the relief which she seeks, the wife would have to demonstrate both overreaching and unfairness.

For the most part, a separation agreement which is regular on its face will be recognized and enforced by the courts in much the same manner as an ordinary contract. However, because of the fiduciary relationship between husband and wife, separation agreements generally are closely scrutinized by the courts, and such agreements are more readily set aside in equity under circumstances that would be insufficient to nullify an ordinary contract. *** Although courts may examine the terms of the agreement as well as the surrounding circumstances to ascertain whether there has been overreaching, the general rule is that "[i]f the execution of the agreement *** be fair, no further inquiry will be made." *

Nor does the fact that the same attorney represented both parties in the preparation of the agreement require an automatic nullification of the agreement. While the absence of independent representation is a significant factor to be taken into consideration when determining whether a separation agreement was freely and fairly entered into, the fact that each party retained the same attorney does not, in and of itself, provide a basis for rescission. *** Of course, a claim of overreaching will be subject to a "far more searching scrutiny" and, as a result, is less likely to prevail where the party had the benefit of independent representation during the negotiation and execution of the agreement. *** On the other hand, where one attorney has represented both parties to the agreement, a question of overreaching on the part of the party who is the prime beneficiary of the attorney's assistance may arise. Nevertheless, as long as the attorney fairly advises the parties of both the salient issues and the consequences of joint representation, and the separation agreement arrived at was fair, rescission will not be granted. * While the potential conflict of interests inherent in such joint representation suggests that the husband and wife should retain separate counsel, the parties have an absolute right to be represented by the same attorney provided "there has been full disclosure between the parties, not only of all relevant facts but also of their contextual significance, and there has been an absence of inequitable conduct or other infirmity which might vitiate the execution of the agreement". *

Applying these principles to the case before us, we cannot conclude that it was error for the trial court, as a matter of law, to have found that the separation agreement in this case is fair, both on its face and when considered in light of the parties' circumstances at the time of execution. The husband undertook a variety of financial obligations, all of which were designed to maintain the wife and the two children in the style to which they were accustomed to living. Although the wife has contended throughout this action that the husband earns a far greater income than the record reflects, she has not come forward with an evidentiary showing to support this claim. We agree with the trial court that the wife's bare allegations to the effect that the husband has been "living high on the hog" provide no basis for overturning the parties' agreement.

Contrary to the determination below, the fact that the same attorney represented both parties in the preparation of the separation agreement does not, without more, establish overreaching on the part of the husband. The record discloses that the attorney had been an acquaintance of the husband and wife for a number of years. He agreed to draft the separation agreement only because the parties, prior to consulting him, already had reached an accord on the essential terms. Even then, the attorney told the wife that she could consult with another attorney, but the wife declined to do so. In addition, the wife expressly acknowledged in the separation agreement itself that the attorney had previously represented her husband, that she had "complete faith and trust in him" as her attorney, and that through his representation she was "entering into a better agreement than if she had consulted with independent counsel who tried to bargain for a better agreement". Most importantly, the trial court specifically found that the attorney remained neutral throughout his involvement with the parties, and this particular finding was not disturbed by the Appellate Division. Under these circumstances, any inference of overreaching on the part of the husband arising from the joint representation properly was rejected by the trial court.

Accordingly, the order of the Appellate Division should be reversed, with costs, and the judgment of Supreme Court, Westchester County, reinstated.

d. Notes and Questions

1) Validity Generally

The requirements for the execution of separation agreements, for the most part, are very similar to those for antenuptial agreements. (*See* chapter 7). Husband and wife must be competent to execute a separation agreement. (*See Johnston v. Johnston, supra*) Separation Agreements should be written, signed by the parties, and entered into voluntarily. A finding of overreaching, fraud, undue influence, or duress would invalidate the agreement. In most states, husband and wife are in a confidential relationship although courts may not hold them to the same standard for disclosure as they would an engaged couple, negotiating a prenuptial agreement. Some courts use a version of a fair, just and reasonable standard. The Uniform Marriage and Divorce Act adopts an unconscionability standard. Courts adopting the unconscionability standard vary in defining unconscionability. Separation agreements must not encourage, facilitate or promote divorce although most modern courts narrowly construe the language.

2) Modification and Enforcement

Principles of contract law apply if the separation agreement is not superseded by the divorce decree. The UMDA and most states continue to have jurisdiction over provisions pertaining to child support and custody even if the Agreement is not superseded by the divorce judgment.

3. Practical and Ethical Considerations

a. Legal Representation

Most divorce cases are not litigated. The spouses reach a settlement. The settlement may take the form of a separation agreement or is a provision in the divorce judgment. In either case, more likely than not at least one attorney is involved. Issues involving professional responsibility and ethics are present in divorce cases. What steps should an attorney take to insure that she has met her obligation in advising the client regarding the pros and cons of a proposed settlement? In Levine, was the court too sympathetic to the attorney? Compare the attorney's actions with this version of the Code of Professional Responsibility.

DR 5-105 (A) A lawyer shall decline proffered employment if the exercise of his independent professional judgment in behalf of a client will be or is likely to be adversely affected by the acceptance of the proffered employment, or if it would be likely to involve him in representing different interests, except to the extent permitted under DR 5-105(C).

DR 5-105 (B) A lawyer shall not continue multiple employment if the exercise of his independent professional judgment in behalf of a client will be or is likely to be adversely affected by his representation of another client, or if it would be likely to involve him in representing different interests, except to the extent permitted under DR-105(C).

DR 5-105 (C) If it is obvious that he can adequately represent the interest of each and if each consents to the representation after full disclosure of the possible effect of such representation on the exercise of his independent professional judgment on behalf of each.

4. Bibliography

Homer J. Clark, Jr. The Law of Domestic Relations in the United States (2d ed.1988).

Robert H. Mnookin & Lewis Kornhauser, *Bargaining in the Shadow of the Law: The Case of Divorce*,
      88 Yale L. J. 950 (1979).

Sally Burnett Sharp, *Fairness Standards and Separation Agreements: A Word of Caution on Contractual
      Freedom*, 132 U. Pa. L. Rev. 1399 (1984).

Contemporary Family Law, vol. 3, Chs. 33 (1988).

B. ADR

1. Background

a. Perspectives on Litigation

*"Discourage litigation. Persuade your neighbors to compromise whenever you can.
Point out to them how the nominal winner is often a real loser -- in fees, expenses and
waste of time. As a peacemaker the lawyer has a superior opportunity of being a good
man." --Abraham Lincoln*

> Matthew 5:38-41 (KJV):
> 38 ¶ Ye have heard that it hath been said, An eye for an eye, and a tooth for a
> tooth: 39 But I say unto you, That ye resist not evil: but whosoever shall smite thee
> on thy right cheek, turn to him the other also.
> 40 And if any man will sue thee at the law, and take away thy coat, let him have
> [thy] cloke also.
> 41 And whosoever shall compel thee to go a mile, go with him twain.

> 1 Corinthians 6:1-7:
> 1 Dare any of you, having a matter against another, go to law before the unjust, and
> not before the saints? 2 Do ye not know that the saints shall judge the world? and if
> the world shall be judged by you, are ye unworthy to judge the smallest matters? 3
> Know ye not that we shall judge angels? how much more things that pertain to this
> life? 4 If then ye have judgments of things pertaining to this life, set them to judge
> who are least esteemed in the church. 5 I speak to your shame. Is it so, that there is
> not a wise man among you? no, not one that shall be able to judge between his
> brethren? 6 But brother goeth to law with brother, and that before the unbelievers. 7
> Now therefore there is utterly a fault among you, because ye go to law one with
> another. Why do ye not rather take wrong? why do ye not rather [suffer yourselves
> to] be defrauded?

b. Historical Antecedents for Nonjudicial Resolution of Domestic Disputes

The recent revival of interest in nonlitigational methods of resolving divorce-
related disputes has ancient and honorable origins. For the greater part of western
legal history the regulation of marriage and the resolution of domestic disputes was a
matter primarily within the jurisdiction of the church. Application of church doctrines
and enforcement of canon law was obtained through the institutions of the church, not
the state. Ecclesiastical courts, not royal courts, heard and decided contested marital
causes. Moreover, those courts were a part of a network of church agencies and
agents that provided support for and manifested personal interest in the affected
individuals and their problems. Some modern evangelical lawyers, relying on 1

Corinthians 6:1-7 and Matthew 5:38-41, have revived ADR as a spiritual practice, hearkening to their historic Christian roots.

The current search for alternatives to divorce litigation is, at least in part, a byproduct of the modern "divorce litigation explosion." Not only have the numbers of divorce reached record proportions during the past decade (it now seems to have stabilized at about 1.2 million divorces annually) but the amount of post-divorce litigation between former spouses has increased. Because many divorces involve children or maintenance orders, divorce is seldom the "final" step in a "clean break," but ongoing relations provide occasion for prolonged, subsequent litigation. The large number of divorce cases has created docket backlogs and strained the civil court system. Bahr, *infra* at 39. Approximately one-third of all civil actions filed in state courts of general jurisdiction now are domestic actions. *See* Chapter 1.B.a., *infra*.

c. Types of ADR

There are several different types of ADR. Perhaps the most popular in recent years is *mediation*. "Mediation is a process in which a third party, the mediator, encourages the disputants to find a mutually agreeable settlement by helping them to identify the issues, reduce misunderstandings, vent emotions, clarify priorities, find points of agreement, and explore new areas of compromise and possible solutions." Pearson & Thoennes, *infra*, at 498. The mediator does not decide for the parties, or impose a decision on them, but tries to facilitate their own agreement.

The second type of ADR often discussed is *arbitration*, which involves the resolution of a dispute by a thrid person (usually with special expertise in the area of dispute) selected by the disputing parties, or by a process approved by them. Arbitration is a de-formalized, less adversary form of litigation. The decision of the arbitrator is generally binding, and would be binding in domestic disputes (except for child custody decisions, wherein the court has a nondelegable *parens patriae* duty to decide the issue).

Private negotiation is a third type of ADR. This is the method by which attorneys out-of-court or the parties themselves compromise and settle their claims. Lawyers have an ethical duty to settle a case when the best interest of their client will be subserved, and the Model Rules of Professional Conduct explicitly recognized the role of the attorney in settling cases. However, private negotiation is wholly unstructured; some lawyers do it often, and well; others do it infrequently or poorly.

Two other methods of alternative dispute resolution should be mentioned. *Summary disposition* is the term used to describe procedures which have been adopted in several states allowing for automatic divorce without hearing. Qualified parties (usually short marriages, no children, no real property, and few assets) must agree on the terms of their disillusion; the court rubber stamps their agreement.

Administrative proceedings are becoming more common in domestic cases. Many states have used administrative agencies to insure collection of child support. Often administrative proceedings occur more quickly and informally than in judicial proceedings.

d. The Current Status of ADR in American Law

For the reasons discussed above, there has been a great deal of attention and a trend toward adoption of ADR systems to deal with some divorce issues. The issues most frequently deemed appropriate for non-judicial resolution (the law is subject to judicial review) are custody, child support, visitation, and sometimes property and alimony disputes. In 1977, not a single American jurisdiction required mediation in family law cases; ADR was very uncommon and generally unpopular. By 1990, it was reported that more than 4,500 American courts require mediation in at least some cases (particularly in contested custody and visitation cases). Today, the ADR movement is widespread and growing, especially in family law.

Mediation, the newest of the ADR techniques, has now been approved by legislators or other law makers in nearly a third of the states. In eleven states general statutes authorize the court to divert certain domestic issues to mediation. Local authorities provide for mediation in four other states. Pilot programs have been conducted in several other locales.

All states have statutes which authorize or encourage *arbitration* in some situations. Thirty-one states have adopted the Uniform Arbitration Act. However, only three states have statutes specifically authorizing arbitration of divorce issues. A variation of arbitration that has been successfully done, on a limited basis, in California is private judging. Retired judges are hired, as private arbitrators, to decide disputes generally applying the relevant law.

At one time *conciliation* was a very popular method of ADR. Over half of the states enacted statutes authorizing diversion of some divorce cases into conciliation courts. But the systems generally were too idealistic, often designed to encourage or achieve reconciliation. California appears to be the only state that had significant success with the conciliation court system.

Summary disposition provisions have been adopted by five states. Qualified parties (usually short marriages, no children, no real estate, little and limited assets) may file for summary divorce, if both parties agree to the terms. After the expiration of a certain period of time, if neither party has objected, a final divorce decree is automatically entered. But summary disposition does not really constitute a means of alternative dispute resolution--it presumes that there are no disputes.

Of course, *private negotiation* and out-of-court *settlement* is permitted and encouraged in all courts in all states. But there is no consistency in state encouragement for or control of the method or fairness of private bargaining.

2. Statutes, Cases and Doctrines

a. Cal. Fam. Code § 3170. Setting Matters for Mediation

(a) If it appears on the face of a petition, application, or other pleading to obtain or modify a temporary or permanent custody or visitation order that custody, visitation, or both are contested, the court shall set the contested issues for mediation.

(b) Domestic violence cases shall be handled by Family Court Services in accordance with a separate written protocol approved by the Judicial Council. The Judicial Council shall adopt guidelines for services, other than services provided under this chapter, that counties may offer to parents who have been unable to resolve their disputes. These services may include, but are not limited to, parent education programs, booklets, videotapes, or referrals to additional community resources.

b. Policy Reasons For And Against ADR

If courts were the only institutions that could resolve divorce-related disputes, or if they functioned so much better than other systems, perhaps the ADR movement would not be so powerful. But there has been increasing criticism of the way that courts function. First, courts are not able to (or expected to) directly deal with the nonlegal aspects of marital dissolution; they can only adjust legal (marital and custodial) status, divide property, and order support. Yet often the most important issues, the underlying causal problems, are not legal at all; they are psycho-social issues of personality, interaction, integration, emotion, etc. Often courts deal with the symptoms or consequences of the dilemma, not the basic problems themselves.

Second, the adversary systems seems particularly ill-suited for resolving some emotional, private, family disputes. Forcing the parties to hire competing attorneys, and to deal with each other in a hostility-enhancing win-or-lose contest may be the best way to find a satisfactory solution to the problems of divorcing persons. Rules of procedure and evidence historically fashioned for the resolution of commercial, property or tort disputes may not work well in divorce cases.

Third, most judges are unwilling or unable to devote the time and attention to finding and considering the myriad of details upon which the most rational determinations about such far-reaching issues as custody should be based. As a result the parties are expected to resolve those issues by negotiating "in the shadow of the law." Inequity in bargaining power or skill is seldom considered by the court when it "rubber stamps" the settlement agreement presented by the parties.

Fourth, there is disturbing evidence of a steady erosion of public confidence in the courts and in the judicial system because of dissatisfaction with divorce litigation procedures and outcomes. One evidence of this is reported violence in divorce-related litigation. Another evidence of dissatisfaction is the increased incidence of post-divorce litigation. Not only does the losing party come out of divorce court critical of the judicial system (in a win-lose system one expects the loser to be dissatisfied) but often the winner is equally critical because of the cost, stress, and ultimately unsatisfying result of divorce-related litigation. Nonparties often form negative opinions about the judicial system as a result of the experiences of family or friends, or as a result of participating as a witness in the case.

In addition to these policy reasons, proponents of ADR emphasize that ADR systems seem to cost both the parties and the public less in the long run than formal litigation. Numerous studies have shown that ADR on the whole reduces not only the number of trials (as a certain percentage reach resolution in mediation), but cases that go to trial after mediation are shorter and less expensive (as the parties have narrowed the issues). Likewise, data indicates that the parties are more satisfied with the results of ADR than with the results of litigation. Also, for at least a few, after mediation the parties are less hostile to each other and return to court less frequently than parties who have resolved their disputes judicially without mediation.

While proponents of ADR seem to have caught public attention in recent years, a respectable body of judges, lawyers and scholars have voiced criticisms of the trend toward ADR. It has been noted that all of the benefits of ADR currently are available through private out-of-court negotiations. The ADR industry is relatively new, and there are few professional standards and little regulation. If ADR fails, the parties must litigate anyway. And the results of ADR must ultimately be approved by the court, so ADR does not altogether eliminate the need for court involvement.

Some of the most telling criticisms of ADR have come from feminists who fear that women will be in the weaker bargaining position in any out-of-court system. Some argue that women often do poorly in face-to-face confrontations with men. Others argue that it would be ironic to close the courthouse doors to women soon after the law recognized the equal legal rights of women. Some feminists, however, see ADR as a positive means of avoiding a male-dominated male-methodological legal system. Additionally, some critics raise the issue of whether there is truly a level playing field when there are cultural differences between the parties and the mediator.

Other critics of ADR assert that the public interest in the resolution of divorce and related issues is so compelling that it must be kept a matter of legal resolution. Mediation suggests that the dispute is entirely private, for the parties to resolve privately; whereas the consequences often are very definitely public, and the public picks up the tap for the failures of bad divorces. Some argue that a level playing field does not exist in ADR in some cases in which the parties have different cultural or educational backgrounds. *See* Dominguez, *infra;* Mabry, *infra.*

The claims that ADR is economical and produces more satisfactory results have been challenged. While contrary data has not been produced, critics have noted substantial flaws in the methodology and research designs of some of the studies, and have accused proponents of exaggerating the results.

Finally, one powerful but usually unarticulated reason for opposition by the bar to ADR is the fear that ADR will detrimentally impact the business of lawyers. If a client has only a few hundred dollars to spend on divorce, and he or she is required to spend at least some of it on mandatory ADR, that means the client will not be able to afford or pay as much for legal service. Some lawyers fear that non-lawyer mediators or other ADR personnel will get into the business of practicing law without a license.

c. Notes and Questions

1) Status of Mediation in Divorce Cases

In 1981, California became the first state to mandate mediation of certain issues in divorce cases. It continues to mandate mediation of contested custody and visitation disputes. *See supra,* B.2.a.. (What exception or qualification does it provide?) At least ten other states, or jurisdictions within states, have also mandated mediation in custody cases, including Arizona, Delaware, Florida, Kentucky, Maine, Nevada, North Carolina, Oregon, Utah and Wisconsin). Other states or judicial districts in states permit but do not mandate custody mediation including Alaska, Illinois, Kansas, Illinois, Iowa, Minnesota, Nevada, Rhode Island, and Washington. Hendricks, *infra* at 493; Streeter-Schaeffer, *infra* at 378.

2) Studies of Mediation

Numerous studies have examined mediation in divorce cases in American courts. One of the most exhaustive studies was undertaken in California in the mid-1980s. The Kelly study confirmed that the median costs of cases that went to mediation were about one-third lower than the median cost of non-mediated cases, and the mean costs were less than half as much in mediated cases than in non-mediated cases. Moreover, on nearly every point of qualitative examination, mediation appeared to be more effective, more efficient, and more successful than non-mediated divorce-related dispute resolution. Kelly found that there was less conflict during divorce and for about two years thereafter in mediated cases, there was less intense conflict, there was better communication between the adverse parties, there was more communication between them, there was more cooperation between the parties, there was more contact between the parties, there was a higher rate of compliance with agreements and orders, there was less expense to the parties, there were higher child support awards, the terms of visitation and custody were more specific, and there was more visitation. However, she also reported that "by two years after final divorce, there were no longer any differences attributable to [mediation or adversarial resolution]." *Id.* At 387.

3) Enforcement of Arbitration or Mediation Agreements

Certain issues that may arise in divorce proceedings involve issues that courts may be reluctant to remit to ADR procedures and panels. Child custody and visitation are two particularly sensitive issues because of the strong tradition of exclusive judicial jurisdiction and *parens patriae* responsibilities of the courts. Many courts are reluctant to enforce agreements to mediate or arbitrate custody and visitation issues. For example in *Kelm v. Kelm*, 749 N.E.2d 299 (Ohio 2001), the Ohio Supreme Court flatly held that custody and visitation disputes "cannot be resolved through arbitration. Only the courts are empowered to resolve disputes relating to child custody and visitation." *Id.* at 224. The parties in the highly-contested divorce had negotiated a parenting plan that provided that disputes about custody and visitation would be submitted to arbitration. The trial court approved the parenting plan and neither party objected to the arbitration provision. Several years later the wife filed a motion to modify the parenting plan, and husband responded with a motion to submit the issue to arbitration. The trial court denied the motion to enforce the provision to submit the issue to arbitration and the intermediate court of appeals agreed. The state supreme court affirmed emphasizing the importance of custody and visitation to the life of the child, the *parens patriae* responsibility of the courts, the wastefulness of an arbitration process subject to de novo review, and concluded that arbitration of custody and visitation is contrary to public policy (and, therefore not waivable). While normal principles of preclusion might bar wife raising the issue by her belated collateral attack, the court emphasized that the public interest in the welfare of the child override *res judicata* principles.

Other courts have enforced arbitration agreements regarding custody and visitation but the arbitrators' decision is subject to *de novo* judicial review. *Kovacs v. Kovacs*, 633 A.2d 425 (Md. App. 1993); *Miller v. Miller*, 620 A.2d 1161 (Pa. Super. 1993); *Crutchley v. Crutchley*, 293 S.E.2d 793 (N.C. 1982); *see also Masters v. Masters*, 513 A.2d 104 (Conn., 1986). Some courts have given even greater deference to arbitration decisions about custody and visitation. *Dick v. Dick*, 534 N.W.2d 185 (Mich. App. 1995). What do you think? Should only judges be custody decisionmakers? Why/why not?

3. Practical and Ethical Considerations

a. Mediation Standards

The Association of Family and Conciliation Courts is drafting new Standards applicable to divorce mediation, to replace standards that were drafted in 1984. The current Draft Standards of Practice for Divorce and Family Mediation provide:

> *Standard I*
>
> A family mediator should recognize that mediation is based on the principle of self-determination by the parties
>
> *Standard II*
>
> A family mediator should be qualified by education and training to undertake the mediation.
>
> *Standard III*
>
> A family mediator should define and describe the process of mediation and facilitate the parties' assessment of their capacity and readiness to mediate before the parties reach an agreement to mediate
>
> *Standard IV*
>
> A family mediator should disclose all actual and potential conflicts of interest   reasonably known to the mediator. The parties can choose to retain the mediator by an informed, written waiver of the conflict of interest, unless it so significant that informed waiver offends public policy. The need to protect against conflicts of interest also governs the conduct that occurs during and after the mediation.
>
> *Standard V*
>
> A family mediator should fully disclose and explain the basis of any compensation, fees and charges to the parties.
>
> *Standard VI*
>
> A family mediator should conduct the mediation in an impartial manner.
>
> *Standard VII*
>
> A family mediator should structure the mediation process so that the parties make decisions based on sufficient information and knowledge.
>
> *Standard VIII*
>
> A family mediator should maintain the confidentiality of all information acquired in the mediation process, unless the mediator is permitted or required to reveal the information by law or agreement of the parties.
>
> *Standard IX*
>
> A family mediator should assist parents in determining how to promote the best interests of their children.
>
> *Standard X*
>
> A family mediator should recognize a family situation involving child abuse or neglect, report it to the proper authorities and shape the mediation process accordingly.
>
> *Standard XI*
>
> A family mediator should recognize a family situation involving domestic violence and take appropriate steps to shape the mediation process accordingly.
>
> *Standard XII*
>
> A family mediator should withdraw from further participation in the mediation process when the mediator reasonably believes that further participation will not further the parties' self-determination.
>
> *Standard XIII*
>
> A family mediator should be truthful in the advertisement and solicitation for mediation.
>
> *Standard XIV*

A family mediator should improve the practice of mediation.

The preface and the Standards can be seen in the January 2000 issue of the Family and Conciliation Courts Review and at the AFCC Website at *www.afccnet.org/mediacomit.htm.*

4. Bibliography

Stephen Bahr, *An Evaluation of Court Mediation*, 2 J. Fam. Iss. 39 (1981).

Harriet N. Cohen, *Mediation in Divorce: Boon or Bane,* Women's Advoc., Mar., 1984, at 1.

Contemporary Family Law, vol. 3, Ch. 23 (1988).

Nathan M. Crystal, *Ethical Problems in Marital Practice*, 30 S.C.L.Rev. 323 (1979).

Jessica R. Dominguez, Comment, *The Role of Latina Culture in Mediation of Family Disputes*, 1 J. Legal Advoc. & Prac. 154 (1999).

Harry T. Edwards, *Alternative Dispute Resolution: Panacea or Anathema*, 99 Harv. L. Rev. 668 (1986).

Christy L. Hendricks, Note, *The Trend Toward Mandatory Mediation in Custody and Visitation Disputes of Minor Children: An Overview*, 32 U. Louisville J. Fam. L. 491, 493 (1994).

Joan B. Kelly, *Mediated and Adversarial Divorce Resolution Process, A Comparison of Post-Divorce Outcome*, 32 Fam. L. 382 (G. Br. 1991).

Cynthia R. Mabry, *African Americans "Are Not Carbon Copies" of White Americans – The Role of African Culture in Mediation of Family Disputes*, 13 Ohio St. J. on Disp. Resol. 407 (1998).

Pearson & Thoennes, *Mediating and Litigating Custody Disputes: A Longitudinal Evaluation,* 17 Fam. L. Q. 497 (1984).

Holly A. Streeter-Schaeffer, Note, *A Look at Court-Mandated Civil Mediation*, 49 Drake L. Rev. 367 (2001).

Lynn D. Wardle, *A.D.R. in the U.S.A.,* in Familles et Justice 534 (Bruxelles 1997).

C. PROFESSIONAL RESPONSIBILITIES AND REALITIES IN DIVORCE PRACTICE

1. Background

a. Economics and Passions

Many of the "practical issues" concerning divorce relate to money - i.e., to resources available to pay for the services needed in connection with divorce, including services of an attorney and services necessary for the attorney to do his or her job well, other services the client needs to cope with the trauma of divorce, and to pay for daily living of the client. To deal with these concerns the lawyer must follow rules regulating attorneys fees, attorneys liens, and representation agreements. Most of these subjects are regulated by local law.

Passions are involved because the client in a divorce case is experiencing a profound, personal rejection and yearns to be "validated" as a desirable companion. The lawyer is often cast in the role of the champion or "white knight" galloping forward to defend and protect the client. If they are careless about their lawyer-client relationship, they may be drawn into an illusory, romantic personal relationship founded on temporary roles rather than anything real, permanent or genuine. That relationship risks either exploiting an emotionally vulnerable client, or dealing the emotionally wounded client a deeply painful second personal rejection, and risks the lawyers getting manipulated into the kind of personal relationship with the client that can compromise professional independence, integrity, and trust.

2. Statutes, Cases and Doctrines

a. Model Rules of Professional Conduct 1.5(d)

Rule 1.5(d). A lawyer shall not enter into an arrangement for, charge or collect: (1) any fee in a domestic relations matter, the payment or amount of which is contingent on the securing of a divorce or upon the amount of alimony or support, or property settlement in lieu thereof. *Rule 1.7 (a)*. A lawyer shall not represent a client if the representation of that client will be directly adverse to another client, unless: (1) the lawyer reasonably believes the representation will not adversely affect the relationship wit the other client; and (2) each client consents after consultation.

(B) A lawyer shall not represent a client if the representation of that client may be materially limited by the lawyer's responsibilities to another client or to a third person, or by the lawyer's own interests, unless

(1) the lawyer reasonably believes the representation will not be adversely affected; and (2) the client consents after consultation. When representation of multiple clients in a single matter is undertaken, the consultation shall include explanation of the implications of the common representation and the advantages and risks involved.

b. Notes and Questions

1) Ethical Dilemmas in General

Most ethical problems in family law arise in context of dissolution, because most cases arise in that context. Most ethical problems arise out of or relate to economic dilemmas-- e.g., dual representation (so clients can save money), contingent fees (so clients can save money), inadequate professional service or malpractice (lawyer gave cut-rate service to save client fees). How can a lawyer who represents low and middle-income clients deal with such dilemmas? Most of the ethical problems divorce lawyers encounter involve the seven "C's" – issues of competence, commitment, compensation, conflicts, communications, confidences, and candor.

2) Conflicting Policies re: Dual Representation

There are conflicting policies involved in dual representation rules. The foremost concern of the law is with adequacy of representation for the clients, and with the appearance of impropriety for the profession. Dual representation may impinge upon both of these interests. On the other hand, the bar must be concerned that it does not appear to be featherbedding, running an employment racket for two attorneys when only one is needed. And there are many couples whose economic interests are so small, whose legal entanglements are so simple, and whose mutual interest in ending the marriage on already settled terms are so harmonious that it would involve an unnecessary economic burden to require them to see separate counsel. Generally, dual representation, especially in a divorce proceeding, is viewed suspiciously and is disfavored; however, it is not prohibited in all states in all situations. State rules about dual representation vary significantly. What is the rule regarding dual representation in divorce in your homestate?

3) Contingent Fee Prohibition Policies

For a long time contingent-fee contracts for representing a party in a divorce action have been deemed violative of public policy and void. Basically, five public policy arguments underlie this rule. First, it is believed that contingent fee contracts tend to promote divorce. That is, the attorney has a financial incentive to discourage reconciliation. Second, the contingent fee contract arguably causes the attorney and his or her client to give undue attention to the economic aspects of the divorce action and to aggressively pursue and obtain a large financial recovery for the client, when there are other aspects than financial, and other considerations than large recovery that ought to influence the divorce proceedings. Third, it is believed that statutes authorizing courts to award attorneys fees to needy parties in divorce cases insures that parties will be able to obtain adequate legal representation without the need to give the attorney a share of the recovery. Fourth, there is concern that clients in divorce cases are particularly susceptible to overreaching by overcharging attorneys. Finally, there is the general concern for the reputation of the profession and the appearance of money-grubbing lawyers directly profiting from the misery of others.

However, the first policy has been questioned by many. Not all are convinced that many attorneys would discourage reconciliation to preserve or inflate a fee, and attorneys who would do so would also do so when representing clients on an hourly-fee basis. Moreover, in an era of no-fault divorce, one might wonder whether the rule is straining at a gnat.

The second concern, that lawyers and clients may give too much emphasis to the financial aspect of divorce, may not be directly related to the contract for payment of fees. Indeed, large hourly fees accumulate quickly and by exceeding the reasonable contingent fee percentage may dominate the attention of the client even more than a contingent fee contract. Moreover, while the non-economic aspects of human relationships are extremely significant in divorce, perhaps lawyers do their best work when they focus on matters they (and courts) are best able to deal with, e.g., money and property.

The validity of the third reason for prohibiting contingent fees depends upon the scope of the statutes authorizing attorneys fees awards. In some states those statutes (in derogation of the "American Rule" of common law that attorneys fees will not be awarded in the absence of statute, contract or bad faith) are strictly construed, and a party may not be entitled to an award of attorneys fees for some significant elements of divorce or divorce-related cases. It also depends upon the custom and practice of the courts; as a practical matter some courts' awards of attorneys fees are so inadequate as to make a mockery of the argument that divorcing persons have access to adequate legal assistance because a statute authorizes the court to award attorneys fees.

The argument that lawyers may overreach and overcharge in divorce cases does not logically seem to be limited to lawyers who use contingent fees. Hourly fees may also be excessive. Moreover, courts generally scrutinize contingent fee contracts carefully, and attorneys are ethically prohibited from accepting an excessive fee. There are other ways to protect against excessive fees than to bar all (even reasonable) contingent fee contracts.

Finally, the appearance of professionalism may be more offended by huge hourly fee arrangements than reasonable contingent fee contracts. It is difficult to see how a lawyer may be said to profit more from human misery because he takes a percentage of recovery if successful, but nothing if the claim does not succeed, than if he charges his client an hourly fee regardless of the client benefit.

Contingent fee contracts for representing a client in a divorce case are deemed void as against public policy as a general rule. However, the scope of that rule is shrinking as courts in recent years have fashioned many exceptions to it.

It appears that many courts do not extend the rule against contingent fee contracts in divorce suits to suits (or bifurcated proceedings) to recover separate property or divide marital property, or possibly even to claims for alimony. (Contingent fee contracts in child custody or child support actions are barred under a related rule.) If any part of the contingent fee contract purports to extend to the services done in connection with the divorce action itself, the entire contract may be declared void. *See e.g. In re Cooper*, 344 S.E.2d 27 (N.C. App. 1986) (court refuses to allow attorney to recover under quantum merit theory for services in connection with equitable distribution claim because contract applied to whole divorce claim and thus was void against public policy). Other courts will award quantum merit recovery in lieu of enforcing the contract. Some courts will uphold the contract if it finds that the contract did not actually promote divorce (e.g., the marriage was hopelessly broken, the attorney did not discourage reconciliation, etc.) Despite numerous (often ad hoc) exceptions, however, the general rule remains that contingent fee contracts for representing parties in domestic cases generally and in divorce actions in particular, are against public policy and void. Code of Professional Responsibility Ethical Consideration 2-20. Contingent fees in divorce and divorce-related litigation is generally disfavored and scrutinized closely; however, local professional responsibility rules, ethics opinions, and case law about contingency fees vary from state to state. What is the rule regarding dual representation in divorce in your homestate?

4) Securing Fees

"A lawyer's ability to obtain some form of contractual security interest on a client's property is inhibited by the rules that bar lawyers from acquiring an interest in the property that is the subject of the litigation. In the context of marital matters, that property includes any that might be subject to division or assignment by the courts." Parley, *infra*, at 54.

5) Sexual Relations with Clients

As noted in 32.C.1.a, clients in divorce cases are particularly vulnerable to sexual advances, and lawyers are vulnerable to hero-champion delusions.

> [T]he Rules of Professional Conduct in most states . . . do not prohibit sexual relations between lawyer and client.
> Among other learned professionals, physicians are prohibited by their code of ethics from engaging in sexual relations with current patients or clients. Ethics rules for psychiatrists, psychologists, and other professionals go even further, prohibiting sexual relations not only with present clients or patients, but with former ones as well. Many licensed . . . professionals, including counselors, social workers, and even optometrists, are prohibited by regulation from having sexual relations with clients. For mental health services or health care services providers, sexually

exploiting a patient's or former patient's emotional dependency on the provider is a second degree felony.

Brock, *infra*, at 265-266.

Several state bar associations have adopted rules specifically prohibiting or regulating sexual relations between lawyer and client. California's Ethics Rule 3-120, adopted in 1991, was the first to proscribe most sexual relations between bar members and their clients. It prohibits lawyers from requiring or demanding sex "incident to or as a condition of any professional representation," unless the sexual relations between them "predate the initiation of the lawyer-client relationship," and it provides a rebuttable presumption that any sex between attorney and client violates the rule. New York's rules apply specifically in matrimonial actions (suggesting that the problem is particularly pronounced in that context). In 1999, the Ethics 2000 Commission of the American Bar Association proposed an absolute prohibition against sexual relations between lawyer and client. The proposed rule would change the Title of existing Rule 1.8 of the Model Rules of Professional Conduct from "Prohibited Transactions" to "Conflict of Interest," and would add, *inter alia*, a new subsection: "(j) A lawyer shall not have sexual relations with a client unless a consensual sexual relationship existed between them when the client-lawyer relationship commenced." Model Rules, *infra*, at Proposed Rule 1.8. The Commission suggested the total ban because: "Given the number of complaints of lawyer sexual misconduct that have been filed, the Commission believes that having a specific Rule has the advantage not only of alerting lawyers more effectively to the dangers of sexual relationships with clients but also of alerting clients that the lawyer may have violated ethical obligations in engaging in such conduct." Some lawyers oppose the proposed rule. *See* Mischler, *infra*. What do you think? Why?

6) Counseling and Professional Counseling

One of the most important roles that a lawyer in a divorce has to perform is to counsel the client – to give advice. Lawyers are "counselors" at law, as well as advocates. However, when it comes to some key domestic relations issues (such as, should the client seek a divorce), many lawyers who would not hesitate to advise a client whether or not to seek other legal relief (including whether to sue a debtor, settle a tort claim, waive alimony, or sue for property division) believe that they should not counsel the client about what to do. Some take a primitive "hired gun" approach ("the client tells me what to do, and I just do it"), but many believe that only the client can make that decision because it reflects the kind of values that are so personal. While deciding for the client is clearly inappropriate, should the lawyer decline to offer counsel and make recommendations? Why/why not?

One form of counseling that used to be common but that is often overlooked (in the post-no-fault divorce era) is to counsel the client to carefully consider other remedies, other ways of coping with the difficulties, pains and problems that have led him or her to come to a lawyer to get a divorce. Today society seems to convey the message (through media, movies, songs, and folklore) that when a marriage becomes unhappy, the solution is to end the marriage. So when marital problems arise, the first place that some people turn for help is to a lawyer. It often is not because they want a divorce; the statement "I want a divorce" is often just a cry for help. They are in pain, they know the marriage isn't working the way it should, and they don't know how to fix it or where to turn for help. So, almost by default, they turn to a lawyer and say "I want a divorce.". If the lawyer automatically initiates divorce proceedings, instead of carefully exploring with the client other remedies for the problems, not only may an opportunity to do some good be missed, but the lawyer may leave the client much worse off as a result of turning to the lawyer than he or she would have if they had never entered the lawyer's office. Of course, this means that the competent lawyer must not only be competent about divorce law, property law, alimony law, custody law, etc., but she must also be minimally aware of some variety of potentially useful nonlegal remedies. That requires some interdisciplinary awareness and connection.

Another "counseling" function that lawyers in divorce cases perform is the "listening ear" or "soft shoulder" counseling that lets the client "vent," "unload," "tell his or her story," and seek sympathy. The clients need that – and they need more than most lawyers can provide. First, since the lawyer must bill the client for most of the time he or she spends as the "listening ear," if the lawyer does not monitor it, that can dramatically increase the fees to the client. Second, most lawyers have little training or expertise in performing personal counseling, even of the "listening ear" variety. Third, divorce is very traumatic, and most clients need much more skilled professional attention than even a good lawyer with lots of common sense can provide. Thus, early on (in the first or second meeting with a divorce client) a competent lawyer will generally ask the client about the kind of emotional, psychological, professional or religious counseling his or her clients is receiving. The attorney should be aware of resources that can be recommended to clients who are not receiving such counseling and who do not know where to turn to find good counseling. The lawyer must be aware of the impact that such outside counselors have on the client; sometimes the client may be reflecting and acting upon the bad advice of counselors including not only commercial or ministerial counselors, but also misguided family members and friends.

3. Practical and Ethical Considerations

a. Suggesting Alternatives to Divorce
(a) *See supra* 31.C.A. & B.

(b) Would it be unethical for a lawyer to fail to suggest the client consider other remedies than divorce when the client initially says "I want a divorce"? Would it ever be unethical for a lawyer to suggest that such a client consider other remedies than divorce? Why/why not?

b. Conflict of Interest in Divorce and Bankruptcy
The Maryland State Bar Ethics Committee has ruled that a lawyer who has represented Husband and Wife in preparing and filing their bankruptcy petition may not thereafter represent the Husband in his action for divorce unless the Wife agrees. Maryland State Bar Ass'n Comm. on Ethics, Opin. 02-10 (Dec. 4, 2001). Because the divorce would involve division and distribution of assets, the Committee concluded that the divorce proceeding was "substantially related to" the bankruptcy representation, so representation of the Husband in the divorce proceeding without the consent of the Wife would violate Rule of Professional Conduct 1.9(a).

c. The Stress of Divorce Practice

Let's look in on one matrimonial lawyer--we'll call her "Kathy." As we first meet Kathy, she's engrossed in WordPerfect, putting the finishing keystrokes on a petition for increased support from a hair salon owner who's hidden his assets with a shampoo girl, when her secretary buzzes on the intercom, "Your four o'clock appointment is here."

"Thanks, Gloria," Kathy says, rolling her eyes and thinking, Oh, great, the battling Balabans again! Turning off the computer, Kathy takes a long look out at the soothing greensward passing through the center of town and wishes for just a moment that she hadn't given up cigarettes, and responds, "Please tell her I'll be right out." With a sense of dread rising in her chest and a slowly tightening knot forming in her stomach, Kathy puts on her best smile, opens the door, and wonders what Marvin Mitchelson would do in a case like this.

This--I clearly don't need to tell you--is not a fun way to make a living. But what's happened to make this aspect of Kathy's professional life so painful?

Well, it's as simple as this: Mrs. Helen Simpson Balaban has determined that Katherine Schneider Smith, Esquire is going to be the flaming sword of her own vengeance against husband Bob Balaban--and Kathy's having trouble just being Mrs. Balaban's attorney of record, while not getting enmeshed in their hatreds. Why should this be? Kathy wanted to become a family lawyer to make things easier for people: . . . to help minimize the damage divorce inflicts upon children. But now, she finds herself stuck--at least in the matter of *Balaban v. Balaban.*

Part of the problem is that of boundaries. Mrs. B. isn't sure where she stops, and Kathy begins--this fuzziness of self is part of what destroyed her marriage. And Kathy needs to constantly remember when she is with Mrs. Balaban, that she's her attorney, and not her Siamese twin. Mrs. Balaban has a great deal of emotion--often charismatic anger--at her disposal, and Kathy who has a tendency to intellectualize, can be slightly removed from her own feelings, and thus a little too hungry for some of Mrs. B's. Then, there's the question of identification with people of similar class and background: it's an old saying that in criminal law you see bad people at their best, while in divorce law, good people at their worst. Again, Kathy needs to be able to step back and stay in her role as attorney and not get enmeshed with her client's need to preserve a mutually destructive emotional relationship, no matter how tenuous the legal ties become. Finally, there's the problem of the kids, Natalie and Blaine: the last thing Kathy wanted was for the kids to become pawns in their parents' games of vengeance. And yet she was finding herself occasionally backing Helen's often unrealistic denials of Bob's visitation rights.

Well, that's what was going on superficially. But what was happening on a deeper level, psychologically?

*** [E]ach of us has our most important emotional relationships with the first people we meet in life--our mom, our dad, sisters, brothers. And everyone we meet afterwards--everyone--is measured by the touchstones of our earliest loves and hatreds with this family of origin. Each person we encounter further downstream in life is seen in the light of all those who went before. And, just as our earliest relationships are our most familiar (by the way, take a close look at the root of the word "familiar") we try to engage in similar relationships with others as we go through life. It's not just that we look for people similar to mom and dad, it's also that we often try and coerce people into being like our early family members. One of the jargon words I had warned you about is called "transference," in which we look to see in others the traits of our family members. And another--much more complicated--is called "projective identification," in which we unconsciously try to coerce others into actually being like members of our family. It really shouldn't be all that strange a concept: isn't that what all couples do during their first year or two of marriage? Try to force the spouse into being like their own mother or father. It's only when they finally give up and come to accept the husband or wife for the people they really are that the marriage reaches a mature, less romantic but more adult, stage. As you know, the conflicts around these coercive attempts often result in bread being put on the tables of the families of divorce lawyers.

[N]ot infrequently, in intense relationships, the partner will unconsciously permit themselves to be coerced (our jargon word for this is "counter-transference").

Agar, *infra*, at 7, 8.

4. Bibliography

Steven A. Agar, *Do Divorce Lawyers Really Have More Fun,* Fair$hare, June 1995, at 7.

Ralph H. Brock, *Sex, Clients, & Legal Ethics,* 64 Tex. B.J. 234 (March 2001).

Nathan M. Crystal, *Ethical Problems in Marital Practice,* 30 S.C.L.Rev. 323 (1979).

Linda Fitts Mischler, *Personal Morals Masquerading and Professional Ethics: Regulations Banning Sex Between Domestic Relations Attorneys and Their Clients,* 23 Harv. Women's L.J. 1 (2000).

Model Rules of Professional Conduct, Proposed Rule 1.8 (American Bar Association, Ethics 2000 Commission on the Evaluation of the Rules of Professional Conduct, November, 2000) <http://www.abanet.org/cpr/e2k- rule18.html> .

Louis Parley, The Ethical Family Lawyer (Family Law Section, American Bar Association 1995).

D. PROTECTIVE ORDERS

1. Background

a. Divorce and Violence

Lawyers must be very alert to the risk of domestic violence upon (of by) their clients in divorce cases. In many cases, divorce itself is, in a very real sense, an act of violence, a forcible (albeit lawful) attack upon the integrity of a married individual's familial status and identity. It is often very painful, very unwanted, and very threatening, and some individuals respond with violence. *See* Wardle, *infra*. Not infrequently, that violence is directed not only at the "attacking" spouse, but also at the attorney aiding the opposing party, and even the court. Protective Orders may be of some help and provide some (albeit limited, paper) protection. However, if the restrained party believes that the "system" or the "process" or the law is unfair, the Protective Order (like even criminal arrest and prosecution) may provoke even more anger and trigger rage and violence. Self-violence, including suicide, is also a substantial risk in divorce and divorce-related cases, including suicide. What can a lawyer do to defuse rage and reduce the risk of violence in divorce cases? *See further supra,* § 15.A.1.a.

2. Statutes, Cases and Doctrines

a. *Obermueller v. Obermueller*
Baerbel G. OBERMUELLER v.Reinhard W. OBERMUELLER
24 A.D.3d 641,808 N.Y.S.2d 324 (App. Div. 2005)

STEPHEN G. CRANE, J.P., DANIEL F. LUCIANO, PETER B. SKELOS, and ROBERT A. LIFSON, JJ.

In an action for a divorce and ancillary relief, the defendant husband appeals from an order of the Supreme Court, Suffolk County (Rebolini, J.), dated February 9, 2005, which granted the plaintiff's motion, in effect, for a protective order against the defendant's notice pursuant to CPLR 3121 to the plaintiff to submit to a vocational assessment.

ORDERED that the order is affirmed, with costs.

The Supreme Court providently granted the plaintiff's motion, in effect, for a protective order. Although broad financial disclosure is necessary and required in a matrimonial action, the trial court is also vested with "broad discretion to supervise disclosure to prevent unreasonable annoyance, expense, embarrassment, disadvantage or other prejudice" (*Geller v. Geller*, 240 A.D.2d 539, 660 N.Y.S.2d 21, quoting *Annexstein v. Annexstein*, 202 A.D.2d 1060, 1061, 609 N.Y.S.2d 131). The plaintiff, who is now approximately 60 years of age, never worked outside the home in this more than 28-year marriage. The defendant served a notice pursuant to CPLR 3121 to the plaintiff to submit to a vocational assessment. Under the circumstances of this case, including the fact that the defendant simultaneously sought discovery through other CPLR article 31 devices, which discovery had not been completed when the plaintiff's motion was made, the plaintiff's motion, in effect, for a protective order was appropriately granted to prevent unreasonable annoyance and expense to the plaintiff.

The defendant's remaining contentions are without merit.

b. Notes and Questions

1) *Obermueller* note.
Obermueller illustrates that domestic violence protection laws can protect against not only physical violence but a variety of forms of harassment. Creative lawyering can find useful applications to prevent divorce animosity from being expressed in ways that establishes a pattern of continuing post-marital hostility. Unfortunately, creative lawyering may also find ways to abuse such laws to inflict harassment and humiliation upon the other party (by impeding reasonable contact with children, family, neighbors, interfere with normal life activities, etc.)

2) Modern Domestic Violence Statutes
Statutory provisions designed to provide some protection for victims of domestic violence exist in all states. Most were enacted (or were substantially revised) relatively recently, basically since the women's rights revolution of the 1970s. Virtually all American jurisdictions now have enacted legislation to protect battered women, and most of the laws had been enacted since 1976. *See generally* Lerman,

infra. Initially such laws were call "spouse abuse" laws, but as the incidence of violence among married couples is far lower than among unmarried cohabitants, dating couples, separated parties, and divorced couples, use of the broader term "domestic violence" is both more common and accurate.

To date no "uniform" law on domestic violence has been drafted. However, section 304 of the Uniform Marriage and Divorce Act, 9A Uniform Laws Annotated 91, 128-130 (1979) specifically provides that as a part of an order for temporary maintenance or support, or as an independent order, the court may enjoin any person from, *inter alia*, molesting or disturbing the peace of any party, exclude any party from the family home or from the home of another person, or other similar relief.

Virtually all states have civil laws providing for injunction-like protective orders to issue to protect domestic partners. Lerman, *infra*, at 272. While the terms and provisions vary substantially from state to state, there are several common aspects to them. First, standing is typically clarified; usually only the victim of domestic violence has standing to bring a domestic violence action to enjoin the perpetrator for molesting or disturbing the victim, or entering her residence. Second, the statutes typically provide that some accessible public official (such as the county clerk) must assist complainants in drafting and filing their pleadings seeking relief from domestic violence. Third, the statutes typically require the court to hear the complaint within a very short time. Fourth, the statutes typically authorize the court to enter a temporary restraining order *ex parte*. Fifth, the statutes often provide for police notification of the entry of such orders or other procedures to coordinate law enforcement services which may be necessary to effectuate the order. Sixth, the statutes often refer to or contain provisions for support social services. *See e.g.* Utah Code Ann. § 30-6-1 et seq (1954); *see generally* Lerman, *infra*, at 271-73. Find the statutes governing Protective Orders in your homestate.

In addition to specific Acts designed to provide civil relief to victims of domestic violence, general civil remedies and procedures could be employed by competent and creative counsel to obtain adequate civil protection for client victims of domestic violence where specific domestic violence provisions are inadequate. For instance, ordinary civil actions seeking injunctive relief against further illegal acts causing irreparable injury are possible in all jurisdictions. Temporary restraining orders are available *ex parte* in such actions. The ancient remedy of a bill of peace (or its statutory counterpart) might provide an effective remedy (a bond to keep the peace). Moreover, in most states statutes authorize courts to exercise broad equitable powers in connection with divorce, annulment, or separation actions. *See* Wardle, *Marriage*, *infra*.

3) Criminal Protection Against Domestic Violence

Virtually all states have enacted criminal statutes directly specifically at the problem of domestic violence. Lerman, *infra*, at 273; Waits, *infra*. These acts often describe specific procedures which law enforcement officers must follow when responding to domestic violence incidents, such as advising the victim of her right to seek injunctive relief, restraining or arresting the perpetrator, transporting the victim to a shelter or hospital, filing written reports of the incident, etc. *See e.g.* Utah Code Ann. § 77-36-1 et seq.

Additionally, general criminal provisions concerning assault, mayhem, trespass, criminal mischief, disturbing the peace, stalking, etc. could be applied directly to the perpetrator of domestic violence. However, traditionally law enforcement officers have been reluctant to interfere in domestic quarrels because the complainants subsequently withdraw their complaints, because fault in the quarrel is difficult to assess and victims often forgive their attacker and refuse to prosecute, because officers often become the victims of sudden violence when intervening in family disputes, and because of excessive cultural tolerance for domestic violence. *See generally Bruno v. Codd*, 419 N.Y.S.2d 901(N.Y. 1979)(upholding dismissal of class action by twelve abused wives against probation department and family courts [police department also named defendant but entered consent judgment] alleging refusal to enforce laws and provide legal services to protect battered wives, but thoroughly discussing the problem). *See further Nearing v. Weaver*, 295 Or. 702, 670 P.2d 137 (1983)(police officers who fail to arrest perpetrator of domestic violence may be liable in tort to victims). Find the statutes governing criminal treatment of domestic violence in your homestate.

4) The Violence Against Women Act

In 1994, Congress enacted the Violence Against Women Act of 1994 (VAWA), providing in part that "[a]ll persons within the United States shall have the right to be free from crimes of violence motivated by gender." 42 U.S.C. § 13981(b). To enforce that right, subsection (c) provided a civil cause of action for compensatory and punitive damages, injunctive and declaratory relief for victims of a "crime of violence motivated by gender" against perpetrators of sexual violence. In 1995 Christy Brzonkala brought a VAWA civil action for damages against Antonio Morrison, James Crawford and Virginia Polytechnic Institute. In September, 1994, while she was a student at Virginia Tech she was raped by Morrison and Crawford, Virginia Tech football players, and suffered severe psychological consequences. After she reported the incident to the university, a university panel suspended Morrison for two semesters, but the school's Provost set aside the suspension as being too harsh. Brzonkala then filed a civil suit for damages under VAWA. A federal district court dismissed her claims finding the federal law to be unconstitutional, and a split Fourth Circuit affirmed because Congress lacked the authority to provide a private remedy for such conduct.

In *U.S. v. Morrison*, 529 U.S. 598 (2000), the Supreme Court agreed that Congress lacked constitutional authority to enact 42 U.S.C. § 13981 and affirmed the dismissal by a vote of 5-4. The majority held that: "Every law enacted by Congress must be based on one or more of its powers enumerated in the Constitution." *Id.* at 607. Because this provision of the VAWA did not protect the channels or instruments of interstate commerce, or activities that substantially affect it, it was beyond the constitutional commerce clause power of Congress to enact that provision of VAWA. While numerous studies showed the detrimental effects of gender-related violence, the Court rejected that as justification for Congress to regulate conduct that is not otherwise within federal control, emphasizing that Congress' lack of authority to regulate family relations might be brushed aside if the broad "but for-effects" analysis of the plaintiff to justify VAWA were accepted. "Petitioners' reasoning, moreover, will not limit Congress to regulating violence but may, as we suggested in Lopez, be applied equally as well to family law and other areas of traditional state regulation since the aggregate effect of marriage, divorce, and childrearing on the national economy is undoubtedly significant." *Id.* at 615-616. The dissenters noted that even incidental congressional regulation of family relations is not impermissible if the statute is tied to interstate movement. *Id.* at 659 (Breyer, J., dissenting). Was *Morrison* a sound decision? Why/why not? Is domestic violence, generally, a "federal" problem? Why/why not?

5) Violence During Marriage Distinguished

There may be a significant distinction between the law's response to an incident of domestic abuse during an ongoing marriage and an act or threat of violence at the time of divorce. When a marriage is ongoing and the parties are trying to work out their problems and develop skills of mature problem solving, principles of regard for the family unit and of respect for the individual's (usually wife's) autonomy may counsel significant flexibility, at least when the risk of harm is minimal. On the other hand, because divorce is an excruciatingly painful and wrenching experience, especially for the party opposed to losing his or her spouse, and reflexive violence is how the anguish is not uncommonly expressed by persons with inadequate emotional self-control, especially by those who have a history of violence, there may be greater need for protective intervention at that time. Do most state laws distinguish between these two circumstances? Should they? Why/why not? *See* Wardle, *Divorce Violence, infra.*

3. Practical and Ethical Considerations

Because Protective Orders often are easily obtainable (almost "rubber stamped" by judges on demand in ex parte proceedings), there is a risk that lawyers (perhaps encouraged by or to please their clients) will obtain Protective or Restraining Orders for tactical reasons (such as to get a perceived "leg up" in custody litigation). Surveys in one state revealed that most (in one survey all) the lawyers in small sample surveys were aware of cases in which Protective Orders were sought for tactical or "play hardball" reasons and over three-fourths of the lawyers questioned in one survey reported that they thought Protective Orders were sought for tactical reasons in half or more of the cases. Does this violate the ethical responsibilities of attorneys? Why/why not?

4. Bibliography

Michelle Guido, *Mandatory Reports of Domestic Abuse Worry Victims*, (San Jose) Mercury News, Aug. 1, 2001 <mercurycenter.com/premium/nation/docs/dvstudy0801.htm>.

Lisa Lerman, *Protection of Battered Women: A Survey of State Legislation*, 6 Women's Rts. L. Rptr. 271 (1981).

Lisa G. Lerman, *Statute: A Model State Act: Remedies for Domestic Abuse*, 21 Harv. J. on Legis. 61, 94-97 (1984).

Michael A. Rodriguez, et al, Mandatory Reporting of Domestic Violence to the Police, 286 J.A.M.A. (Aug. 1, 2001) <jama.ama-assn.org/issues/v286n5/rfull/jbr10044.html>.

Kathleen Waits, *The Criminal Justice System's Response to Battering: Understanding the Problem, Forging the Solutions*, 60 Wash. L. Rev. 267 (1985).

Lynn D. Wardle, *Divorce Violence and the No-Fault Divorce Culture*, 1994 Utah L. Rev. 741.

Lynn D. Wardle, *Marriage and Domestic Violence in the United States: New Perspectives About Legal Strategies to Combat Violence,* 15 St. Thomas L. Rev. 791 (2003).

Donna Wills, *Domestic Violence: The Case for Aggressive Prosecution,* 7 UCLA Women's L.J. 173 (1997).

CHAPTER 31

Termination of Quasi-Spousal Relations and Palimony

A. TERMINATION OF QUASI-SPOUSAL RELATIONS AND PALIMONY

1. Background

a. Social Changes

Cohabitation began to jump significantly in the 1970s, and the trend continued through the 1990s. In thirty years, from 1970 to 2000, the total number of nonmarital cohabiting couples increased ten-fold, and the ratio of households comprised of nonmarital couples increase over five-fold. (The rate of increase in couples under age 25 cohabiting nonmaritally increased about fourteen times from 1970 to 1995, and the rate of increase was about 21 times for unmarried couples aged 25-44.)

NON-MARITAL COUPLES (NC) in the USA (by 1,000 couples)

Year	1970	1980	1985	1990	1995	2000
# NC	523	1,589	1,983	2,856	3,668	5,476

(Sources: Statistical Abstracts of the United States 1994at 56 & 58; *id.* 1996 at 56, tables 58, 61, 62, 58 &66; *id.* 1998; Census Bureau, Profile of General Demographic Characteristics, 2000)

Nonmarital couple households now accounts for about four percent (4%) of all households in the United States; the average duration of nonmarital cohabitation is comparatively short, and the incidence of break-up is relatively high (*see* Chapter 8, *supra*). Concomitantly, lawyers are seeing more cases in which one ex-cohabiting party is aggrieved about some aspect of the break-up, often the failure of economic expectations or economic consequences of the break-up.

Some of these cohabiting couples made agreements regarding their economic relations such as agreements regarding support of one partner, or sharing property acquired by one or both of the parties. However, historically, contracts founded upon or in consideration of illicit cohabitation were deemed unenforceable as violative of public policy against extramarital sexual cohabitation. In some cases, that rule was thought to work an economic hardship upon the economically dependant partner, and efforts to modify the traditional rule against enforcement of contracts in derogation of were made by former cohabitants in many states. Those suits have met with a wide variety of results, ranging from outright (or near-total) rejection to very sweeping reform of the former rule. The seminal case to revise the traditional rule against enforcement of such contracts was *Marvin v. Marvin*, 557 P.2d 1006 (Cal. 1976); the decision of the California Supreme Court in that case ignited a wave of copy-cat suits and judicial rulings in other states. The case usually cited as the conceptual counter-point to the *Marvin* decision is *Hewitt v. Hewitt*, 394 N.E.2d 1204 (Ill. 1979). Both *Marvin* and *Hewitt* are included *infra*.

Actions by former nonmarital cohabitants seeking a share of property acquired during or after termination of cohabitation are generally called "palimony" actions. Palimony sounds like "alimony," but conceptually palimony suits usually are closer to property division claims than to claims for maintenance and support (alimony). Factually, it apparently is both uncommon and hard to prove that a nonmarital partner agreed to support a live-in lover after the cohabitation ended, and more common and easier to prove an agreement to share or divide property acquired during the relationship.

2. Statutes, Cases and Doctrines

a. *Marvin v. Marvin*

Michelle Marvin v. Lee Marvin
557 P.2d 106 (Cal. 1976)

TOBRINER, Justice.

During the past 15 years, there has been a substantial increase in the number of couples living together without marrying. [Fn 1. 'The 1970 census figures indicate that today perhaps eight times as many couples are living together without being married as cohabited ten years ago.' (Comment, In re Cary: A Judicial Recognition of Illicit Cohabitation (1974) 25 Hastings L.J. 1226.)] Such nonmarital relationships lead to legal controversy when one partner dies or the couple separates. Courts of Appeal, faced with the task of determining property rights in such cases, have arrived at conflicting positions: two cases (In re Marriage of Cary (1973) 34 Cal.App.3d 345, 109 Cal.Rptr. 862; Estate of Atherley (1975) 44 Cal.App.3d 758, 119 Cal.Rptr. 41) have held that the Family Law Act (Civ.Code, s 4000 et seq.) requires division of the property according to community property principles, and one decision (*Beckman v. Mayhew* (1975) 49 Cal.App.3d 529, 122 Cal.Rptr. 604) has rejected that holding. We take this opportunity to resolve that controversy and to declare the principles which should govern distribution of property acquired in a nonmarital relationship.

We conclude: (1) The provisions of the Family Law Act do not govern the distribution of property acquired during a nonmarital relationship; such a relationship remains subject solely to judicial decision. (2) The courts should enforce express contracts between nonmarital partners except to the extent that the contract is explicitly founded on the consideration of meretricious sexual services. (3) In the absence of an express contract, the courts should inquire into the conduct of the parties to determine whether that conduct demonstrates an implied contract, agreement of partnership or joint venture, or some other tacit understanding between the parties. The courts may also employ the doctrine of quantum meruit, or equitable remedies such as constructive or resulting trusts, when warranted by the facts of the case.

In the instant case plaintiff and defendant lived together for seven years without marrying; all property acquired during this period was taken in defendant's name. When plaintiff sued to enforce a contract under which she was entitled to half the property and to support payments, the trial court granted judgment on the pleadings for defendant, thus leaving him with all property accumulated by the couple during their relationship. Since the trial court denied plaintiff a trial on the merits of her claim, its decision conflicts with the principles stated above, and must be reversed.

1. The factual setting of this appeal.

Since the trial court rendered judgment for defendant on the pleadings, we must accept the allegations of plaintiff's complaint as true, determining whether such allegations state, or can be amended to state, a cause of action. * We turn therefore to the specific allegations of the complaint.

Plaintiff avers that in October of 1964 she and defendant 'entered into an oral agreement' that while 'the parties lived together they would combine their efforts and earnings and would share equally any and all property accumulated as a result of their efforts whether individual or combined.' Furthermore, they agreed to 'hold themselves out to the general public as husband and wife' and that 'plaintiff would further render her services as a companion, homemaker, housekeeper and cook to . . . defendant.'

Shortly thereafter plaintiff agreed to 'give up her lucrative career as an entertainer (and) singer' in order to 'devote her full time to defendant . . . as a companion, homemaker, housekeeper and cook;' in return defendant agreed to 'provide for all of plaintiff's financial support and needs for the rest of her life.'

Plaintiff alleges that she lived with defendant from October of 1964 through May of 1970 and fulfilled her obligations under the agreement. During this period the parties as a result of their efforts and earnings acquired in defendant's name substantial real and personal property, including motion picture rights worth over $1 million. In May of 1970, however, defendant compelled plaintiff to leave his household. He continued to support plaintiff until November of 1971, but thereafter refused to provide further support.

On the basis of these allegations plaintiff asserts two causes of action. The first, for declaratory relief, asks the court to determine her contract and property rights; the second seeds to impose a constructive trust upon one half of the property acquired during the course of the relationship.

Defendant demurred unsuccessfully, and then answered the complaint. Following extensive discovery and pretrial proceedings, the case came to trial. Defendant renewed his attack on the complaint by a motion to dismiss. Since the parties had stipulated that defendant's marriage to Betty Marvin did not terminate until the filing of a final decree of divorce in January 1967, the trial court treated defendant's motion as one for judgment on the pleadings augmented by the stipulation.

After hearing argument the court granted defendant's motion and entered judgment for defendant. Plaintiff moved to set aside the judgment and asked leave to amend her complaint to allege that she and defendant reaffirmed their agreement after defendant's divorce was final. The trial court denied plaintiff's motion, and she appealed from the judgment.

2. Plaintiff's complaint states a cause of action for breach of an express contract.

In *Trutalli v. Meraviglia* (1932) 215 Cal. 698, 12 P.2d 430 we established the principle that nonmarital partners may lawfully contract concerning the ownership of property acquired during the relationship. We reaffirmed this principle in *Vallera v. Vallera* (1943) 21 Cal.2d 681, 685, 134 P.2d 761, 763, stating that 'If a man and woman (who are not married) live together as husband and wife under an agreement to pool their earnings and share equally in their joint accumulations, equity will protect the interests of each in such property.'

In the case before us plaintiff, basing her cause of action in contract upon these precedents, maintains that the trial court erred in denying her a trial on the merits of her contention. Although that court did not specify the ground for its conclusion that plaintiff's contractual allegations stated no cause of action, defendant offers some four theories to sustain the ruling; we proceed to examine them.

Defendant first and principally relies on the contention that the alleged contract is so closely related to the supposed 'immoral' character of the relationship between plaintiff and himself that the enforcement of the contract would violate public policy. *[Fn 4. Defendant also contends that the contract was illegal because it contemplated a violation of former Penal Code section 269a, which prohibited living 'in a state of cohabitation and adultery.' (s 269a was repealed by Stats.1975, ch. 71, eff. Jan. 1, 1976.) Defendant's standing to raise the issue is questionable because he alone was married and thus guilty of violating section 269a. Plaintiff, being unmarried could neither be convicted of adulterous cohabitation nor of aiding and abetting defendant's violation. (See In re*

Cooper (1912) 162 Cal. 81, 85--86, 121 P. 318.) ¶ The numerous cases discussing the contractual rights of unmarried couples have drawn no distinction between illegal relationships and lawful nonmarital relationships. (Cf. Weak v. Weak (1962) 202 Cal.App.2d 632, 639, 21 Cal.Rptr. 9 (bigamous marriage).) Moreover, even if we were to draw such a distinction--a largely academic endeavor in view of the repeal of section 269a--defendant probably would not benefit; his relationship with plaintiff continued long after his divorce became final, and plaintiff sought to amend her complaint to assert that the parties reaffirmed their contract after the divorce.] He points to cases asserting that a contract between nonmarital partners is unenforceable if it is 'involved in' an illicit relationship *, or made in 'contemplation' of such a relationship *. A review of the numerous California decisions concerning contracts between nonmarital partners, however, reveals that the courts have not employed such broad and uncertain standards to strike down contracts. The decisions instead disclose a narrower and more precise standard: a contract between nonmarital partners is unenforceable only to the extent that it explicitly rests upon the immoral and illicit consideration of meretricious sexual services.

In the first case to address this issue, *Trutalli v. Meraviglia, supra,* 215 Cal. 698, 12 P.2d 430, the parties had lived together without marriage for 11 years and had raised two children. The man sued to quiet title to land he had purchased in his own name during this relationship; the woman defended by asserting an agreement to pool earnings and hold all property jointly. Rejecting the assertion of the illegality of the agreement, the court stated that 'The fact that the parties to this action at the time they agreed to invest their earnings in property to be held jointly between them were living together in an unlawful relation did not disqualify them from entering into a lawful agreement with each other, so long as such immoral relation was not made a consideration of their agreement.' (Emphasis added.) (215 Cal. at pp. 701--702, 12 P.2d 430, 431.)

In *Bridges v. Bridges* (1954) 125 Cal.App.2d 359, 270 P.2d 69, both parties were in the process of obtaining divorces from their erstwhile respective spouses. The two parties agreed to live together, to share equally in property acquired, and to marry when their divorces became final. The man worked as a salesman and used his savings to purchase properties. The woman kept house, cared for seven children, three from each former marriage and one from the nonmarital relationship, and helped construct improvements on the properties. When they separated, without marrying, the court awarded the woman one-half the value of the property. Rejecting the man's contention that the contract was illegal, the court stated that: 'Nowhere is it expressly testified to by anyone that there was anything in the agreement for the pooling of assets and the sharing of accumulations that contemplated meretricious relations as any part of the consideration or as any object of the agreement.' (125 Cal.App.2d at p. 363, 270 P.2d at p. 71.)

Croslin v. Scott (1957) 154 Cal.App.2d 767, 316 P.2d 755 reiterates the rule established in *Trutalli* and *Bridges.* In *Croslin* the parties separated following a three-year nonmarital relationship. The woman then phoned the man, asked him to return to her, and suggested that he build them a house on a lot she owned. She agreed in return to place the property in joint ownership. The man built the house, and the parties lived there for several more years. When they separated, he sued to establish his interest in the property. Reversing a nonsuit, the Court of Appeal stated that 'The mere fact that parties agree to live together in meretricious relationship does not necessarily make an agreement for disposition of property between them invalid. It is only when the property agreement is made in connection with the other agreement, or the illicit relationship is made a consideration of the property agreement, that the latter becomes illegal.' (154 Cal.App.2d at p. 771, 316 P.2d at p. 758.)

Numerous other cases have upheld enforcement of agreements between nonmarital partners in factual settings essentially indistinguishable from the present case. * *[FN5. Defendant urges that [nearly] all of the cited cases *** can be distinguished on the ground that the partner seeking to enforce the contract contributed either property or services additional to ordinary homemaking* *services. No case, however, suggests that a pooling agreement in which one partner contributes only homemaking services is invalid * * *.]*

Although the past decisions hover over the issue in the somewhat wispy form of the figures of a Chagall painting, we can abstract from those decisions a clear and simple rule. The fact that a man and woman live together without marriage, and engage in a sexual relationship, does not in itself invalidate agreements between them relating to their earnings, property, or expenses. Neither is such an agreement invalid merely because the parties may have contemplated the creation or continuation of a nonmarital relationship when they entered into it. Agreements between nonmarital partners fail only to the extent that they rest upon a consideration of meretricious sexual services. Thus the rule asserted by defendant, that a contract fails if it is 'involved in' or made 'in contemplation' of a nonmarital relationship, cannot be reconciled with the decisions.

The three cases cited by defendant which have declined to enforce contracts between nonmarital partners involved consideration that was expressly founded upon an illicit sexual services. In *Hill v. Estate of Westbrook, supra*, 95 Cal.App.2d 599, 213 P.2d 727, the woman promised to keep house for the man, to live with him as man and wife, and to bear his children; the man promised to provide for her in his will, but died without doing so. Reversing a judgment for the woman based on the reasonable value of her services, the Court of Appeal stated that 'the action is predicated upon a claim which seeks, among other things, the reasonable value of living with decedent in meretricious relationship and bearing him two children . . . . The law does not award compensation for living with a man as a concubine and bearing him children. . . . As the judgment is, at least in part, for the value of the claimed services for which recovery cannot be had, it must be reversed.' (95 Cal.App.2d at p. 603, 213 P.2d at p. 730.) Upon retrial, the trial court found that it could not sever the contract and place an independent value upon the legitimate services performed by claimant. We therefore affirmed a judgment for the estate. (*Hill v. Estate of Westbrook* (1952) 39 Cal.2d 458, 247 P.2d 19.)

In the only other cited decision refusing to enforce a contract, *Updeck v. Samuel* (1964), 123 Cal.App.2d 264, 266 P.2d 822, the contract 'was based on the consideration that the parties live together as husband and wife.' (123 Cal.App.2d at p. 267, 266 P.2d at p. 824.) Viewing the contract as calling for adultery, the court held it illegal. *[Fn 6. Although not cited by defendant, the only California precedent which supports his position is Heaps v. Toy (1942) 54 Cal.App.2d 178, 128 P.2d 813. In that case the woman promised to leave her job, to refrain from marriage, to be a companion to the man, and to make a permanent home for him; he agreed to support the woman and her child for life. The Court of Appeal held the agreement invalid as a contract in restraint of marriage (Civ.Code, s 1676) and, alternatively, as 'contrary to good morals' (Civ.Code, s 1607). The opinion does not state that sexual relations formed any part of the consideration for the contract, nor explain how-- unless the contract called for sexual relations--the woman's employment as a companion and housekeeper could be contrary to good morals. ¶The alternative holding in Heaps v. Toy, supra, finding the contract in that case contrary to good morals, is inconsistent with the numerous California decisions upholding contracts between nonmarital partners when such contracts are not founded upon an illicit consideration, and is therefore disapproved.]*

The decisions in the *Hill* and *Updeck* cases thus demonstrate that a contract between nonmarital partners, even if expressly made in contemplation of a common living arrangement, is invalid only if sexual acts form an inseparable part of the consideration for the agreement. In sum, a court will not enforce a contract for the pooling of property and earnings if it is explicitly and inseparably based upon services as a paramour. The Court of Appeal opinion in Hill, however, indicates that even if sexual services are part of the contractual consideration, any Severable portion of the contract supported by independent consideration will still be enforced.

The principle that a contract between nonmarital partners will be enforced unless expressly and inseparably based upon an illicit consideration of sexual services not only represents the distillation of the decisional law, but also offers a far more precise and workable standard than that advocated by defendant. Our recent decision in *In re Marriage of Dawley* (1976) 17 Cal.3d 342, 551 P.2d 323, offers a close analogy. Rejecting the contention that an antenuptial agreement is invalid if the parties contemplated a marriage of short duration, we pointed out in *Dawley* that a standard based upon the subjective contemplation of the parties is uncertain and unworkable; such a test, we stated, 'might invalidate virtually all antenuptial agreements of the ground that the parties contemplated dissolution . . . but it provides no principled basis for determining which antenuptial agreements offend public policy and which do not.' (17 Cal.3d 342, 352, 551 P.2d 323, 329.)

Similarly, in the present case a standard which inquires whether an agreement is 'involved' in or 'contemplates' a nonmarital relationship is vague and unworkable. Virtually all agreements between nonmarital partners can be said to be 'involved' in some sense in the fact of their mutual sexual relationship, or to 'contemplate' the existence of that relationship. Thus defendant's proposed standards, if taken literally, might invalidate all agreements between nonmarital partners, a result no one favors. Moreover, those standards offer no basis to distinguish between valid and invalid agreements. By looking not to such uncertain tests, but only to the consideration underlying the agreement, we provide the parties and the courts with a practical guide to determine when an agreement between nonmarital partners should be enforced.

Defendant secondly relies upon the ground suggested by the trial court: that the 1964 contract violated public policy because it impaired the community property rights of Betty Marvin, defendant's lawful wife. Defendant points out that his earnings while living apart from his wife before rendition of the interlocutory decree were community property under 1964 statutory law (former Civ.Code, ss 169, 169.2) and that defendant's agreement with plaintiff purported to transfer to her a half interest in that community property. But whether or not defendant's contract with plaintiff exceeded his authority as manager of the community property (*see* former Civ.Code, s 172), defendant's argument fails for the reason that an inproper transfer of community property is not void ab initio, but merely voidable at the instance of the aggrieved spouse. (*See Ballinger v. Ballinger* (1937) 9 Cal.2d 330, 334, 70 P.2d 629; *Trimble v. Trimble* (1933) 219 Cal. 340, 344, 26 P.2d 477.)

In the present case Betty Marvin, the aggrieved spouse, had the opportunity to assert her community property rights in the divorce action. (*See Babbitt v. Babbitt* (1955) 44 Cal.2d 289, 293, 282 P.2d 1.) The interlocutory and final decrees in that action fix and limit her interest. Enforcement of the contract between plaintiff and defendant against property awarded to defendant by the divorce decree will not impair any right of Betty's, and thus is not on that account violative of public policy. *[FN8. Defendant also contends that the contract is invalid as an agreement to promote or encourage divorce. (See 1 Witkin, Summary of Cal.Law (8th ed.) pp. 390--392 and cases there cited.) The contract between plaintiff and defendant did not, however, by its terms require defendant to divorce Betty, nor reward him for so doing. Moreover, the principle on which defendant relies does not apply when the marriage in question is beyond redemption ***.]*

Defendant's third contention is noteworthy for the lack of authority advanced in its support. He contends that enforcement of the oral agreement between plaintiff and himself is barred by Civil Code section 5134, which provides that 'All contracts for marriage settlements must be in writing . . ..' A marriage settlement, however, is an agreement in contemplation of marriage in which each party agrees to release or modity the property rights which would otherwise arise from the marriage. (*See Corker v. Corker* (1891) 87 Cal. 643, 648, 25 P. 922.) The contract at issue here does not conceivably fall within that definition, and thus is beyond the compass of section 5134. *[Fn 9. Our review of the many cases enforcing agreements between nonmarital partners reveals that the majority of such agreements were oral. In two cases (Ferguson v. Schuenemann, supra, 167 Cal.App.2d 413, 334 P.2d 668; Cline v. Festersen, supra, 128 Cal.App.2d 380, 275 P.2d 149), the court expressly rejected defenses grounded upon the statute of frauds.]*

Defendant finally argues that enforcement of the contract is barred by Civil Code section 43.5, subdivision (d), which provides that 'No cause of action arises for . . . (b)reach of a promise of marriage.' This rather strained contention proceeds from the premise that a promise of marriage impliedly includes a promise to support and to pool property acquired after marriage (*see Boyd v. Boyd* (1964) 228 Cal.App.2d 374, 39 Cal.Rptr. 400) to the conclusion that pooling and support agreements not part of or accompanied by promise of marriage are barred by the section. We conclude that section 43.5 is not reasonably susceptible to the interpretation advanced by defendant, a conclusion demonstrated by the fact that since section 43.5 was enacted in 1939, numerous cases have enforced pooling agreements between nonmarital partners, and in none did court or counsel refer to section 43.5.

In summary, we base our opinion on the principle that adults who voluntarily live together and engage in sexual relations are nonetheless as competent as any other persons to contract respecting their earnings and property rights. Of course, they cannot lawfully contract to pay for the performance of sexual services, for such a contract is, in essence, an agreement for prostitution and unlawful for that reason. But they may agree to pool their earnings and to hold all property acquired during the relationship in accord with the law governing community property; conversely they may agree that each partner's earnings and the property acquired from those earnings remains the separate property of the earning partner. So long as the agreement does not rest upon illicit meretricious consideration, the parties may order their economic affairs as they choose, and no policy precludes the courts from enforcing such agreements.

In the present instance, plaintiff alleges that the parties agreed to pool their earnings, that they contracted to share equally in all property acquired, and that defendant agreed to support plaintiff. The terms of the contract as alleged do not rest upon any unlawful consideration. We therefore conclude that the complaint furnishes a suitable basis upon which the trial court can render declaratory relief. (*See* 3 Witkin, Cal.Procedure (2d ed.) pp. 2335--2336.) The trial court consequently erred in granting defendant's motion for judgment on the pleadings.

3. Plaintiff's complaint can be amended to state a cause of action founded upon theories of implied contract or equitable relief.

As we have noted, both causes of action in plaintiff's complaint allege an express contract; neither assert any basis for relief independent from the contract. In *In re Marriage of Cary, supra,* 34 Cal.App.3d 345, 109 Cal.Rptr. 862, however, the Court of Appeal held that, in view of the policy of the Family Law Act, property accumulated by nonmarital partners in an actual family relationship should be divided equally. Upon examining the Cary opinion, the parties to the present case realized that plaintiff's alleged relationship with defendant might arguably support a cause of action independent of any express contract between the parties. The parties have therefore briefed and discussed the issue of the property rights of a nonmarital partner in the absence of an express contract. Although our conclusion that plaintiff's complaint states a cause of action based on an express contract alone compels us to reverse the judgment for defendant, resolution of the Cary issue will serve both to guide the parties upon retrial and to resolve a conflict presently manifest in published Court of Appeal decisions.

Both plaintiff and defendant stand in broad agreement that the law should be fashioned to carry out the reasonable expectations of the parties. Plaintiff, however, presents the following contentions: that the decisions prior to Cary rest upon implicit and erroneous notions of punishing a party for his or her guilt in entering into a nonmarital relationship, that such decisions result in an inequitable distribution of property accumulated during the relationship, and that Cary correctly held that the enactment of the Family Law Act in 1970 overturned those prior decisions. Defendant in response maintains that the prior decisions merely applied common law principles of contract and property to persons who have deliberately elected to remain outside the bounds of the community property system. *[Fn 11. We note that a deliberate decision to avoid the strictures of the community property system is not the only reason that couples live together without marriage. Some couples may wish to avoid the permanent commitment that marriage implies, yet be willing to share equally any property acquired during the relationship; others may fear the loss of pension, welfare, or tax benefits resulting from marriage (see Beckman v. Mayhew, supra, 49 Cal.App.3d 529, 122 Cal.Rptr. 604). Others may engage in the relationship as a possible prelude to marriage. In lower socio-economic groups the difficulty and expense of dissolving a former marriage often leads couples to choose a nonmarital relationship; many unmarried couples may also incorrectly believe that the doctrine of common law marriage prevails in California, and thus that they are in fact married. Consequently we conclude that the mere fact that a couple have not participated in a valid marriage ceremony cannot serve as a basis for a court's inference that the couple intend to keep their earnings and property separate and independent; the parties' intention can only be ascertained by a more searching inquiry into the nature of their relationship.]* Cary, defendant contends, erred in holding that the Family Law Act vitiated the force of the prior precedents.

As we shall see from examination of the Pre-Cary decisions, the truth lies somewhere between the positions of plaintiff and defendant. The classic opinion on this subject is *Vallera v. Vallera, supra,* 21 Cal.2d 681, 134 P.2d 761. *** In the absence of express contract, *Vallera* concluded, the woman is entitled to share in property jointly accumulated only 'in the proportion that her funds contributed toward its acquisition.' (P. 685, 134 P.2d p. 763.) ***
         ***

This failure of the courts to recognize an action by a nonmarital partner based upon implied contract, or to grant an equitable remedy, contrasts with the judicial treatment of the putative spouse. Prior to the enactment of the Family Law Act, no statute granted rights to a putative spouse. The courts accordingly fashioned a variety of remedies by judicial decision. Some cases permitted the putative spouse to recover half the property on a theory that the conduct of the parties implied an agreement of partnership or joint venture. * Others permitted the spouse to recover the reasonable value of rendered services, less the value of support received. * Finally, decisions affirmed the power of a court to employ equitable principles to achieve a fair division of property acquired during putative marriage. *

Thus in summary, the cases prior to Cary exhibited a schizophrenic inconsistency. By enforcing an express contract between nonmarital partners unless it rested upon an unlawful consideration, the courts applied a common law principle as to contracts. Yet the courts disregarded the common law principle that holds that implied contracts can arise from the conduct of the parties. ***
         ***

Still another inconsistency in the prior cases arises from their treatment of property accumulated through joint effort. To the extent that a partner had contributed Funds or Property, the cases held that the partner obtains a proportionate share in the acquisition, despite the lack of legal standing of the relationship. * Yet courts have refused to recognize just such an interest based upon the contribution of Services. As Justice Curtis points out 'Unless it can be argued that a woman's services as cook, housekeeper, and homemaker are valueless, it would seem logical that if, when she contributes money to the purchase of property, her interest will be protected, then when she contributes her services in the home, her interest in property accumulated should be protected.' *

Thus as of 1973, the time of the filing of *In re Marriage of Cary, supra,* 34 Cal.App.3d 345, 109 Cal.Rptr. 862, the cases apparently held that a nonmarital partner who rendered services in the absence of express contract could assert no right to property acquired during the relationship. The facts of Cary demonstrated the unfairness of that rule.

Janet and Paul Cary had lived together, unmarried, for more than eight years. They held themselves out to friends and family as husband and wife, reared four children, purchased a home and other property, obtained credit, filed joint income tax returns, and otherwise conducted themselves as though they were married. Paul worked outside the home, and Janet generally cared for the house and children.

In 1971 Paul petitioned for 'nullity of the marriage.' Following a hearing on that petition, the trial court awarded Janet half the property acquired during the relationship, although all such property was traceable to Paul's earnings. The Court of Appeal affirmed the award.

Reviewing the prior decisions which had denied relief to the homemaking partner, the Court of Appeal reasoned that those decisions rested upon a policy of punishing persons guilty of cohabitation without marriage. The Family Law Act, the court observed, aimed to eliminate fault or guilt as a basis for dividing marital property. But once fault or guilt is excluded, the court reasoned, nothing distinguishes the property rights of a nonmarital 'spouse' from those of a putative spouse. Since the latter is entitled to half the 'quasi marital property' (Civ.Code, s 4452), the Court of Appeal concluded that, giving effect to the policy of the Family Law Act, a nonmarital cohabitator should also be entitled to half the property accumulated during an 'actual family relationship.' (34 Cal.App.3d at p. 353, 109 Cal.Rptr. 862.)

***

If *Cary* is interpreted as holding that the Family Law Act requires an equal division of property accumulated in nonmarital 'actual family relationships,' then we agree with *Beckman v. Mayhew* that *Cary* distends the act. No language in the Family Law Act addresses the property rights of nonmarital partners, and nothing in the legislative history of the act suggests that the Legislature considered that subject. The delineation of the rights of nonmarital partners before 1970 had been fixed entirely by judicial decision; we see no reason to believe that the Legislature, by enacting the Family Law Act, intended to change that state of affairs.

But although we reject the reasoning of *Cary* and *Atherley*, we share the perception of the *Cary* and *Atherley* courts that the application of former precedent in the factual setting of those cases would work an unfair distribution of the property accumulated by the couple. ***

***

First, we note that the cases denying relief do not rest their refusal upon any theory of 'punishing' a 'guilty' partner. Indeed, to the extent that denial of relief 'punishes' one partner, it necessarily rewards the other by permitting him to retain a disproportionate amount of the property. Concepts of 'guilt' thus cannot justify an unequal division of property between two equally 'guilty' persons.

Other reasons advanced in the decisions fare no better. The principal argument seems to be that '(e)quitable considerations arising from the reasonable expectation of . . . benefits attending the status of marriage . . . are not present (in a nonmarital relationship).' (*Vallera v. Vallera, supra,* 21 Cal.2d at p. 685, 134 P.2d 761, 763.) But, although parties to a nonmarital relationship obviously cannot have based any expectations upon the belief that they were married, other expectations and equitable considerations remain. The parties may well expect that property will be divided in accord with the parties' own tacit understanding and that in the absence of such understanding the courts will fairly apportion property accumulated through mutual effort. We need not treat nonmarital partners as putatively married persons in order to apply principles of implied contract, or extend equitable remedies; we need to treat them only as we do any other unmarried persons.

The remaining arguments advanced from time to time to deny remedies to the nonmarital partners are of less moment. There is no more reason to presume that services are contributed as a gift than to presume that funds are contributed as a gift; in any event the better approach is to presume, as Justice Peters suggested, 'that the parties intend to deal fairly with each other.' *

The argument that granting remedies to the nonmarital partners would discourage marriage must fail; as *Cary* pointed out, 'with equal or greater force the point might be made that the pre-

1970 rule was calculated to cause the income producing partner to avoid marriage and thus retain the benefit of all of his or her accumulated earnings.' (34 Cal.App.3d at p. 353, 109 Cal.Rptr. at p. 866.) Although we recognize the well-established public policy to foster and promote the institution of marriage (see Deyoe v. Superior Court (1903) 140 Cal. 476, 482, 74 P. 28), perpetuation of judicial rules which result in an inequitable distribution of property accumulated during a nonmarital relationship is neither a just nor an effective way of carrying out that policy.

In summary, we believe that the prevalence of nonmarital relationships in modern society and the social acceptance of them, marks this as a time when our courts should by no means apply the doctrine of the unlawfulness of the so- called meretricious relationship to the instant case. As we have explained, the nonenforceability of agreements expressly providing for meretricious conduct rested upon the fact that such conduct, as the word suggests, pertained to and encompassed prostitution. To equate the nonmarital relationship of today to such a subject matter is to do violence to an accepted and wholly different practice.

We are aware that many young couples live together without the solemnization of marriage, in order to make sure that they can successfully later undertake marriage. This trial period, preliminary to marriage, serves as some assurance that the marriage will not subsequently end in dissolution to the harm of both parties. We are aware, as we have stated, of the pervasiveness of nonmarital relationships in other situations.

The mores of the society have indeed changed so radically in regard to cohabitation that we cannot impose a standard based on alleged moral considerations that have apparently been so widely abandoned by so many. Lest we be misunderstood, however, we take this occasion to point out that the structure of society itself largely depends upon the institution of marriage, and nothing we have said in this opinion should be taken to derogate from that institution. The joining of the man and woman in marriage is at once the most socially productive and individually fulfilling relationship that one can enjoy in the course of a lifetime.

We conclude that the judicial barriers that may stand in the way of a policy based upon the fulfillment of the reasonable expectations of the parties to a nonmarital relationship should be removed. As we have explained, the courts now hold that express agreements will be enforced unless they rest on an unlawful meretricious consideration. We add that in the absence of an express agreement, the courts may look to a variety of other remedies in order to protect the parties' lawful expectations. [Fn 24. We do not seek to resurrect the doctrine of common law marriage, which was abolished in California by statute in 1895. * Thus we do not hold that plaintiff and defendant were 'married,' nor do we extend to plaintiff the rights which the Family Law Act grants valid or putative spouses; we hold only that she has the same rights to enforce contracts and to assert her equitable interest in property acquired through her effort as does any other unmarried person.]

The courts may inquire into the conduct of the parties to determine whether that conduct demonstrates an implied contract or implied agreement of partnership or joint venture (see Estate of Thornton (1972) 81 Wash.2d 72, 499 P.2d 864), or some other tacit understanding between the parties. The courts may, when appropriate, employ principles of constructive trust (see Omer v. Omer (1974) 11 Wash.App. 386, 523 P.2d 957) or resulting trust (see Hyman v. Hyman (Tex.Civ.App.1954) 275 S.W.2d 149). Finally, a nonmarital partner may recover in quantum meruit for the reasonable value of household services rendered less the reasonable value of support received if he can show that he rendered services with the expectation of monetary reward. (See Hill v. Estate of Westbrook, supra, 39 Cal.2d 458, 462, 247 P.2d 19.) [Fn 25. Our opinion does not preclude the evolution of additional equitable remedies to protect the expectations of the parties to a nonmarital relationship in cases in which existing remedies prove inadequate; the suitability of such remedies may be determined in later cases in light of the factual setting in which they arise.]

Since we have determined that plaintiff's complaint states a cause of action for breach of an express contract, and, as we have explained, can be amended to state a cause of action independent of allegations of express contract, *[Fn 26. We do not pass upon the question whether, in the absence of an express or implied contractual obligation, a party to a nonmarital relationship is entitled to support payments from the other party after the relationship terminates.]* we must conclude that the trial court erred in granting defendant a judgment on the pleadings.

The judgment is reversed and the cause remanded for further proceedings consistent with the views expressed herein.

WRIGHT, C.J., and McCOMB, MOSK, SULLIVAN and RICHARDSON, JJ., concur.

CLARK, Justice (concurring and dissenting).

The majority opinion properly permits recovery on the basis of either express or implied in fact agreement between the parties. These being the issues presented, their resolution requires reversal of the judgment. Here, the opinion should stop.

This court should not attempt to determine all anticipated rights, duties and remedies within every meretricious relationship--particularly in vague terms. Rather, these complex issues should be determined as each arises in a concrete case.

The majority broadly indicates that a party to a meretricious relationship may recover on the basis of equitable principles and in quantum meruit. However, the majority fails to advise us of the circumstances permitting recovery, limitations on recovery, or whether their numerous remedies are cumulative or exclusive. Conceivably, under the majority opinion a party may recover half of the property acquired during the relationship on the basis of general equitable principles, recover a bonus based on specific equitable considerations, and recover a second bonus in quantum meruit.

The general sweep of the majority opinion raises but fails to answer several questions. First, because the Legislature specifically excluded some parties to a meretricious relationship from the equal division rule of Civil Code section 4452, is this court now free to create an equal division rule? Second, upon termination of the relationship, is it equitable to impose the economic obligations of lawful spouses on meretricious parties when the latter may have rejected matrimony to avoid such obligations? Third, does not application of equitable principles--necessitating examination of the conduct of the parties--violate the spirit of the Family Law Act of 1969, designed to eliminate the bitterness and acrimony resulting from the former fault system in divorce? Fourth, will not application of equitable principles reimpose upon trial courts the unmanageable burden of arbitrating domestic disputes? Fifth, will not a quantum meruit system of compensation for services--discounted by benefits received--place meretricious spouses in a better position than lawful spouses? Sixth, if a quantum meruit system is to be allowed, does fairness not require inclusion of all services and all benefits regardless of how difficult the evaluation?

When the parties to a meretricious relationship show by express or implied in fact agreement they intend to create mutual obligations, the courts should enforce the agreement. However, in the absence of agreement, we should stop and consider the ramifications before creating economic obligations which may violate legislative intent, contravene the intention of the parties, and surely generate undue burdens on our trial courts.

By judicial overreach, the majority perform a nunc pro tunc marriage, dissolve it, and distribute its property on terms never contemplated by the parties, case law or the Legislature.

b. *Victoria L. Hewitt v. Robert M. Hewitt*
Victoria L. Hewitt v. Robert M. Hewitt
394 N.E.2d 1204 (Ill 1979)

UNDERWOOD, Justice:

The issue in this case is whether plaintiff Victoria Hewitt, whose complaint alleges she lived with defendant Robert Hewitt from 1960 to 1975 in an unmarried, family-like relationship to which three children have been born, may recover from him "an equal share of the profits and properties accumulated by the parties" during that period.

Plaintiff initially filed a complaint for divorce, but at a hearing on defendant's motion to dismiss, admitted that no marriage ceremony had taken place and that the parties have never obtained a marriage license. In dismissing that complaint the trial court found that neither a ceremonial nor a common law marriage existed; that since defendant admitted the paternity of the minor children, plaintiff need not bring a separate action under the Paternity Act (Ill.Rev.Stat. 1975, ch. 1063/4, par. 51 Et seq.) to have the question of child support determined; and directed plaintiff to make her complaint more definite as to the nature of the property of which she was seeking division.

Plaintiff thereafter filed an amended complaint alleging the following bases for her claim: (1) that because defendant promised he would "share his life, his future, his earnings and his property" with her and all of defendant's property resulted from the parties' joint endeavors, plaintiff is entitled in equity to a one-half share; (2) that the conduct of the parties evinced an implied contract entitling plaintiff to one-half the property accumulated during their "family relationship"; (3) that because defendant fraudulently assured plaintiff she was his wife in order to secure her services, although he knew they were not legally married, defendant's property should be impressed with a trust for plaintiff's benefit; (4) that because plaintiff has relied to her detriment on defendant's promises and devoted her entire life to him, defendant has been unjustly enriched.

The factual background alleged or testified to is that in June 1960, when she and defendant were students at Grinnell College in Iowa, plaintiff became pregnant; that defendant thereafter told her that they were husband and wife and would live as such, no formal ceremony being necessary, and that he would "share his life, his future, his earnings and his property" with her; that the parties immediately announced to their respective parents that they were married and thereafter held themselves out as husband and wife; that in reliance on defendant's promises she devoted her efforts to his professional education and his establishment in the practice of pedodontia, obtaining financial assistance from her parents for this purpose; that she assisted defendant in his career with her own special skills and although she was given payroll checks for these services she placed them in a common fund; that defendant, who was without funds at the time of the marriage, as a result of her efforts now earns over $80,000 a year and has accumulated large amounts of property, owned either jointly with her or separately; that she has given him every assistance a wife and mother could give, including social activities designed to enhance his social and professional reputation.

The amended complaint was also dismissed, the trial court finding that Illinois law and public policy require such claims to be based on a valid marriage. The appellate court reversed, stating that because the parties had outwardly lived a conventional married life, plaintiff's conduct had not "so affronted public policy that she should be denied any and all relief" (62 Ill.App.3d 861, 869, 20 Ill.Dec. 476, 482, 380 N.E.2d 454, 460), and that plaintiff's complaint stated a cause of action on an express oral contract. We granted leave to appeal. Defendant apparently does not contest his obligation to support the children, and that question is not before us.

The appellate court, in reversing, gave considerable weight to the fact that the parties had held themselves out as husband and wife for over 15 years. The court noted that they lived "a most conventional, respectable and ordinary family life" (62 Ill.App.3d 861, 863, 20 Ill.Dec. 476, 478, 380 N.E.2d 454, 457) that did not openly flout accepted standards, the "single flaw" being the lack of a valid marriage. Indeed the appellate court went so far as to say that the parties had "lived within the legitimate boundaries of a marriage and family relationship of a most conventional sort" (62 Ill.App.3d 861, 864, 20 Ill.Dec. 476, 479, 380 N.E.2d 454, 457), an assertion which that court cannot have intended to be taken literally. Nothing that the Illinois Marriage and Dissolution of Marriage Act (Ill.Rev.Stat.1977, ch. 40, par. 101 Et seq.) does not prohibit nonmarital cohabitation and that the Criminal Code of 1961 (Ill.Rev.Stat.1977, ch. 38, par. 11-8(a)) makes fornication an offense only if the behavior is open and notorious, the appellate court concluded that plaintiff should not be denied relief on public policy grounds.

In finding that plaintiff's complaint stated a cause of action on an express oral contract, the appellate court adopted the reasoning of the California Supreme Court in the widely publicized case of *Marvin v. Marvin* (1976), 18 Cal.3d 660, 134 Cal.Rptr. 815, 557 P.2d 106, quoting extensively therefrom. *** The *[Marvin]* court reached its conclusions because:

> In summary, we believe that the prevalence of nonmarital relationships in modern society and the social acceptance of them, marks this as a time when our courts should by no means apply the doctrine of the unlawfulness of the so- called meretricious relationship to the instant case. * * *
>
> The mores of the society have indeed changed so radically in regard to cohabitation that we cannot impose a standard based on alleged moral considerations that have apparently been so widely abandoned by so many. *

It is apparent that the *Marvin* court adopted a pure contract theory, under which, if the intent of the parties and the terms of their agreement are proved, the pseudo-conventional family relationship which impressed the appellate court here is irrelevant; recovery may be had unless the implicit sexual relationship is made the explicit consideration for the agreement. In contrast, the appellate court here, as we understand its opinion, would apply contract principles only in a setting where the relationship of the parties outwardly resembled that of a traditional family. It seems apparent that the plaintiff in Marvin would not have been entitled to recover in our appellate court because of the absence of that outwardly appearing conventional family relationship.

The issue of whether property rights accrue to unmarried cohabitants can not, however, be regarded realistically as merely a problem in the law of express contracts. Plaintiff argues that because her action is founded on an express contract, her recovery would in no way imply that unmarried cohabitants acquire property rights merely by cohabitation and subsequent separation. However, the Marvin court expressly recognized and the appellate court here seems to agree that if common law principles of express contract govern express agreements between unmarried cohabitants, common law principles of implied contract, equitable relief and constructive trust must govern the parties' relations in the absence of such an agreement. * In all probability the latter case will be much the more common, sinceit is unlikely that most couples who live together will enter into express agreements regulating their property rights. * The increasing incidence of nonmarital cohabitation referred to in Marvin and the variety of legal remedies therein sanctioned seem certain to result in substantial amounts of litigation, in which, whatever the allegations regarding an oral contract, the proof will necessarily involve details of the parties' living arrangements.

Apart, however, from the appellate court's reliance upon Marvin to reach what appears to us to be a significantly different result, we believe there is a more fundamental problem. We are aware, of course, of the increasing judicial attention given the individual claims of unmarried cohabitants to jointly accumulated property, and the fact that the majority of courts considering the question have recognized an equitable or contractual basis for implementing the reasonable expectations of the parties unless sexual services were the explicit consideration. * The issue of unmarried cohabitants' mutual property rights, however, as we earlier noted, cannot appropriately be characterized solely in terms of contract law, nor is it limited to considerations of equity or fairness as between the parties to such relationships. There are major public policy questions involved in determining whether, under what circumstances, and to what extent it is desirable to accord some type of legal status to claims arising from such relationships. Of substantially greater importance than the rights of the immediate parties is the impact of such recognition upon our society and the institution of marriage. Will the fact that legal rights closely resembling those arising from conventional marriages can be acquired by those who deliberately choose to enter into what have heretofore been commonly referred to as "illicit" or "meretricious" relationships encourage formation of such relationships and weaken marriage as the foundation of our family-based society? In the event of death shall the survivor have the status of a surviving spouse for purposes of inheritance, wrongful death actions, workmen's compensation, etc.? And still more importantly: what of the children born of such relationships? What are their support and inheritance rights and by what standards are custody questions resolved? What of the sociological and psychological effects upon them of that type of environment? Does not the recognition of legally enforceable property and custody rights emanating from nonmarital cohabitation in practical effect equate with the legalization of common law marriage at least in the circumstances of this case? And, in summary, have the increasing numbers of unmarried cohabitants and changing mores of our society * reached the point at which the general welfare of the citizens of this State is best served by a return to something resembling the judicially created common law marriage our legislature outlawed in 1905?

Illinois' public policy regarding agreements such as the one alleged here was implemented long ago in *Wallace v. Rappleye* (1882), 103 Ill. 229, 249, where this court said: "An agreement in consideration of future illicit cohabitation between the plaintiffs is void." This is the traditional rule, in force until recent years in all jurisdictions. (See e.g. *Gauthier v. Laing* (1950), 96 N.H. 80, 70 A.2d 207; *Grant v. Butt* (1941), 198 S.C. 298, 17 S.E.2d 689.) Section 589 of the Restatement of Contracts (1932) states, "A bargain in whole or in part for or in consideration of illicit sexual intercourse or of a promise thereof is illegal." *See also* 6A Corbin, Contracts sec. 1476 (1962), and cases cited therein.

It is true, of course, that cohabitation by the parties may not prevent them from forming valid contracts about independent matters, for which it is said the sexual relations do not form part of the consideration. (Restatement of Contracts secs. 589, 597 (1932); 6A Corbin, Contracts sec. 1476 (1962).) Those courts which allow recovery generally have relied on this principle to reduce the scope of the rule of illegality. Thus, California courts long prior to Marvin held that an express agreement to pool earnings is supported by independent consideration and is not invalidated by cohabitation of the parties, the agreements being regarded as simultaneous but separate. (See e.g. *Trutalli v. Meraviglia* (1932), 215 Cal. 698, 12 P.2d 430; *see also* Annot., 31 A.L.R.2d 1255 (1953), and cases cited therein.) More recently, several courts have reasoned that the rendition of housekeeping and homemaking services such as plaintiff alleges here could be regarded as the consideration for a separate contract between the parties, severable from the illegal contract founded on sexual relations. ***

The real thrust of plaintiff's argument here is that we should abandon the rule of illegality because of certain changes in societal norms and attitudes. It is urged that social mores have changed radically in recent years, rendering this principle of law archaic. It is said that because there are so many unmarried cohabitants today the courts must confer a legal status on such relationships. This, of course, is the rationale underlying some of the decisions and commentaries. * If this is to be the result, however, it would seem more candid to acknowledge the return of varying forms of common law marriage than to continue displaying the naivete we believe involved in the assertion that there are involved in these relationships contracts separate and independent from the sexual activity, and the assumption that those contracts would have been entered into or would continue without that activity.

Even if we were to assume some modification of the rule of illegality is appropriate, we return to the fundamental question earlier alluded to: If resolution of this issue rests ultimately on grounds of public policy, by what body should that policy be determined? Marvin, viewing the issue as governed solely by contract law, found judicial policy-making appropriate. Its decision was facilitated by California precedent and that State's no-fault divorce law. In our view, however, the situation alleged here was not the kind of arm's length bargain envisioned by traditional contract principles, but an intimate arrangement of a fundamentally different kind. The issue, realistically, is whether it is appropriate for this court to grant a legal status to a private arrangement substituting for the institution of marriage sanctioned by the State. The question whether change is needed in the law governing the rights of parties in this delicate area of marriage-like relationships involves evaluations of sociological data and alternatives we believe best suited to the superior investigative and fact-finding facilities of the legislative branch in the exercise of its traditional authority to declare public policy in the domestic relations field. * That belief is reinforced by the fact that judicial recognition of mutual property rights between unmarried cohabitants would, in our opinion, clearly violate the policy of our recently enacted Illinois Marriage and Dissolution of Marriage Act. Although the Act does not specifically address the subject of nonmarital cohabitation, we think the legislative policy quite evident from the statutory scheme.

The Act provides:

> This Act shall be liberally construed and applied to promote its underlying purposes, which are to:
> (1) provide adequate procedures for the solemnization and registration of marriage;
> (2) strengthen and preserve the integrity of marriage and safeguard family relationships.

(Ill.Rev.Stat.1977, ch. 40, par. 102.)

We cannot confidently say that judicial recognition of property rights between unmarried cohabitants will not make that alternative to marriage more attractive by allowing the parties to engage in such relationships with greater security. As one commentator has noted, it may make this alternative especially attractive to persons who seek a property arrangement that the law does not permit to marital partners. (Comment, 90 Harv.L.Rev. 1708, 1713 (1977).) This court, for example, has held void agreements releasing husbands from their obligation to support their wives. (*Vock v. Vock* (1937), 365 Ill. 432, 6 N.E.2d 843; *VanKoten v. VanKoten* (1926), 323 Ill. 323, 154 N.E. 146; *see also Rhodes v. Rhodes* (1967), 82 Ill.App.2d 435, 225 N.E.2d 802; Restatement of Contracts sec. 587 (1932); Weitzman, Legal Regulation of Marriage: Tradition and Change, 62 Cal.L.Rev. 1169, 1259-63 (1974).) In thus potentially enhancing the attractiveness of a private arrangement over marriage, we believe that the appellate court decision in this case contravenes the Act's policy of strengthening and preserving the integrity of marriage.

The Act also provides: "Common law marriages contracted in this State after June 30, 1905 are invalid." (Ill.Rev.Stat.1977, ch. 40, par. 214.) The doctrine of common law marriage was a judicially sanctioned alternative to formal marriage designed to apply to cases like the one before us. In *Port v. Port* (1873), 70 Ill. 484, this court reasoned that because the statute governing marriage did not "prohibit or declare void a marriage not solemnized in accordance with its provisions, a marriage without observing the statutory regulations, if made according to the common law, will still be a valid marriage." (70 Ill. 484, 486.) This court held that if the parties declared their present intent to take each other as husband and wife and thereafter did so a valid common law marriage existed. (*Cartwright v. McGown* (1887), 121 Ill. 388, 398, 12 N.E. 737.) Such marriages were legislatively abolished in 1905, presumably because of the problems earlier noted, and the above-quoted language expressly reaffirms that policy.

While the appellate court denied that its decision here served to rehabilitate the doctrine of common law marriage, we are not persuaded. Plaintiff's allegations disclose a relationship that clearly would have constituted a valid common law marriage in this State prior to 1905. The parties expressly manifested their present intent to be husband and wife; immediately thereafter they assumed the marital status; and for many years they consistently held themselves out to their relatives and the public at large as husband and wife. Revealingly, the appellate court relied on the fact that the parties were, to the public, husband and wife in determining that the parties living arrangement did not flout Illinois public policy. It is of course true, as plaintiff argues, that unlike a common law spouse she would not have full marital rights in that she could not, for example, claim her statutory one-third share of defendant's property on his death. The distinction appears unimpressive, however, if she can claim one-half of his property on a theory of express or implied contract.

Further, in enacting the Illinois Marriage and Dissolution of Marriage Act, our legislature considered and rejected the "no-fault" divorce concept that has been adopted in many other jurisdictions, including California. (*See* Uniform Marriage and Divorce Act secs. 302, 305.) Illinois appears to be one of three States retaining fault grounds for dissolution of marriage. (Ill.Rev.Stat.1977, ch. 40, par. 401; Comment, *Hewitt v. Hewitt*, Contract Cohabitation and Equitable Expectations Relief for Meretricious Spouses, 12 J. Mar. J. Prac. & Proc. 435, 452-53 (1979).) Certainly a significantly stronger promarriage policy is manifest in that action, which appears to us to reaffirm the traditional doctrine that marriage is a civil contract between three parties the husband, the wife and the State. (Johnson v. Johnson (1942), 381 Ill. 362, 45 N.E.2d 625; *VanKoten v. VanKoten* (1926), 323 Ill. 323, 154 N.E. 146.) The policy of the Act gives the State a strong continuing interest in the institution of marriage and prevents the marriage relation from becoming in effect a private contract terminable at will. This seems to us another indication that public policy disfavors private contractual alternatives to marriage.

Lastly, in enacting the Illinois Marriage and Dissolution of Marriage Act, the legislature adopted for the first time the civil law concept of the putative spouse. The Act provides that an unmarried person may acquire the rights of a legal spouse only if he goes through a marriage ceremony and cohabits with another in the good-faith belief that he is validly married. When he learns that the marriage is not valid his status as a putative spouse terminates; common law marriages are expressly excluded. (Ill.Rev.Stat.1977, ch. 40, par. 305.) The legislature thus extended legal recognition to a class of nonmarital relationships, but only to the extent of a party's good-faith belief in the existence of a valid marriage. Moreover, during the legislature's deliberations on the Act Marvin was decided and received wide publicity. (*See* Note, 12 J. Mar. J. Prac. & Proc. 435, 450 (1979).) These circumstances in our opinion constitute a recent and unmistakeable legislative judgment disfavoring the grant of mutual property rights to knowingly unmarried cohabitants. We have found no case in which recovery has been allowed in the face of a legislative declaration as recently and clearly enacted as ours. Even if we disagreed with the wisdom of that judgment, it is not for us to overturn or erode it. *Davis v. Commonwealth Edison Co.* (1975), 61 Ill.2d 494, 496-97, 336 N.E.2d 881.

Actually, however, the legislature judgment is in accord with the history of common law marriage in this country. "Despite its judicial acceptance in many states, the doctrine of common-law marriage is generally frowned on in this country, even in some of the states that have accepted it." (52 Am.Jur.2d 902 Marriage sec. 46 (1970).) Its origins, early history and problems are detailed in *In re Estate of Soeder* (1966), 7 Ohio App.2d 271, 220 N.E.2d 547, where that court noted that some 30 States did not authorize common law marriage. Judicial criticism has been widespread even in States recognizing the relationship. (*See e.g. Baker v. Mitchell* (1941), 143 Pa.Super. 50, 54, 17 A.2d 738, 741, "a fruitful source of perjury and fraud * * * "; *Sorensen v. Sorensen* (1904), 68 Neb. 500, 100 N.W. 930.) "It tends to weaken the public estimate of the sanctity of the marriage relation. It puts in doubt the certainty of the rights of inheritance. It opens the door to false pretenses of marriage and the imposition on estates of suppositious heirs." 7 Ohio App.2d 271, 290, 220 N.E.2d 547, 561.

In our judgment the fault in the appellate court holding in this case is that its practical effect is the reinstatement of common law marriage, as we earlier indicated, for there is no doubt that the alleged facts would, if proved, establish such a marriage under our pre-1905 law. (*Cartwright v.*

McGown (1887), 121 Ill. 388, 12 N.E. 737.) The concern of both the *Marvin* court and the appellate court on this score is manifest from the circumstance that both courts found it necessary to emphasize marital values ("the structure of society itself largely depends upon the institution of marriage" (*Marvin v. Marvin* (1976), 18 Cal.3d 660, 684, 134 Cal.Rptr. 815, 831, 557 P.2d 106, 122) and to deny any intent to "derogate from" (18 Cal.3d 660, 684, 134 Cal.Rptr. 815, 831, 557 P.2d 106, 122) or "denigrate" (*Hewitt v. Hewitt* (1978), 62 Ill.App.3d 861, 868, 20 Ill.Dec. 476, 380 N.E.2d 454) that institution. Commentators have expressed greater concern: "(T)he effect of these cases is to reinstitute common-law marriage in California after it has been abolished by the legislature." (Clark, The New Marriage, Williamette L.J. 441, 449 (1976).) "(*Hewitt*) is, if not a direct resurrection of common-law marriage contract principles, at least a large step in that direction." Reiland, *Hewitt v. Hewitt*: Middle America, Marvin and Common-Law Marriage, 60 Chi.B.Rec. 84, 88-90 (1978).

We do not intend to suggest that plaintiff's claims are totally devoid of merit. Rather, we believe that our statement in *Mogged v. Mogged* (1973), 55 Ill.2d 221, 225, 302 N.E.2d 293, 295, made in deciding whether to abolish a judicially created defense to divorce, is appropriate here:

> Whether or not the defense of recrimination should be abolished or modified in Illinois is a question involving complex public-policy considerations as to which compelling arguments may be made on both sides. For the reasons stated hereafter, we believe that these questions are appropriately within the province of the legislature, and that, if there is to be a change in the law of this State on this matter, it is for the legislature and not the courts to bring about that change.

We accordingly hold that plaintiff's claims are unenforceable for the reason that they contravene the public policy, implicit in the statutory scheme of the Illinois Marriage and Dissolution of Marriage Act, disfavoring the grant of mutually enforceable property rights to knowingly unmarried cohabitants. The judgment of the appellate court is reversed and the judgment of the circuit court . . . is affirmed.

Appellate court reversed; circuit court affirmed.

c. Termination of Civil Unions. Vt. Stat. Ann. tit. 15, §1206 provides: "The family court shall have jurisdiction over all proceedings relating to the dissolution of civil unions. The dissolution of civil unions shall follow the same procedures and be subject to the same substantive rights and obligations that are involved in the dissolution of marriage in accordance with chapter 11 of this title, including any residency requirements." And the Family Courts of Vermont have jurisdiction over such actions just as they do over normal divorce, alimony, property division and custody claims. Vt. Stat. Ann. tit. 4, §454(17)).

c. Notes and Questions

1) *Marvin* Notes

On remand the California Superior court found that Michelle was unable to establish any of the grounds for an award of "palimony" listed in the California Supreme Court opinion. Nevertheless, relying on footnotes 25 and 26 that suggested that other equitable remedies might be granted, the trial court awarded her $104,000 in "rehabilitative" palimony to facilitate her economic recovery from seven years of economic dependence upon Lee Marvin. On appeal, however, that award was reversed by the intermediate court of appeals. The appellate court noted that since the trial court had found that "defendant never had any obligation to pay plaintiff . . . for her maintenance and that defendant had not been unjustly enriched by reason of the relationship or its termination" she "suffered no damage resulting from her relationship with defendant," but "actually benefitted economically and socially from the cohabitation of the parties," that "a confidential and fiduciary relationship never existed between the parties with respect to property" of Mr. Marvin, and that "there is nothing in the trial court's findings to suggest that such an award is warranted to protect the expectations of both parties," there was no legal or justifiable equitable basis for the rehabilitative award. *Marvin v. Marvin,* 122 Cal. App. 2d 871, 876, 176 Cal. Rptr. 555, 558 (Cal. App. 1981).

Lee Marvin was married to another woman when he began his cohabitation relationship with Michelle. If that marriage had never been dissolved, would it have changed the outcome? Is it against public policy to allow person who knowingly engages in a polyamorous or concubinage relationship to recover upon a claim of promise to support as a wife? *See generally Kozlowski v. Kozlowski,* 403 A.2d 902 (N.J. 1979).

2) *Hewitt* Notes.

What are the key differences between the analysis of the majority in *Hewitt* and that of the majority in *Marvin*? What was the key dissimilarities in the way the public policy of the states of Illinois and California are described by the courts?

3) Acceptance of the *Marvin* Approach

In *Marvin,* the California Supreme Court held that an unmarried cohabitant might assert basically three types of causes of action for recovery of a share of property from a prior cohabitant: (1) express contract, (2) implied contract, and (3) other equitable theories of recovery. These various theories have received mixed reception in other states.

The most widely accepted of the *Marvin,* rationales has been the express contract theory. Prior to *Marvin,* courts generally refuse to enforce contracts between nonmarried cohabitants under the illegal consideration doctrine, finding the contracts and enforceable as violative of public policy and good morals. *See e.g. In re Greene,* 45 F.2d 428 (S.D.N.Y. 1930); *Rehak v. Mathis,* 238 S.E.2d 81 (Ga. 1977). Since *Marvin,* however, a majority of courts have narrowed the "illegal consideration doctrine" by application of the "severance doctrine" enunciated in *Marvin,*. That is, they find the "illegal" aspect of the contract (illicit cohabitation, fornication, adultery, or prostitution) to be severable from the rest of the agreement to support each other, pool resources, create a partnership, share income, etc. *See generally Koslowski v. Koslowski,* 395 A. 2d 913 (N.J. Super, Ch. Div. 1978) *aff'd* 408. 2d 902 (N.J. 1979) (granting recovery to a woman who lived with a man for fifteen years, performed housekeeping services so he could pursue a business career, because the agreement was not "explicitly and inseparably founded on sexual services" as consideration); *Crowe v. DeGioia,* 495 A. 2d 889 (N.J. super, 1985) (affirming award of more than $155,000 to a woman who was the nonmarital partner for 20 years, because "the sexual services were not explicitly and inseparably the basis of the promise"); *Donovan v. Scuderi,* 443 A. 2d 121 (Md. App. 1982) (no proof that the illicit relationship formed part of the consideration for the nonmarital cohabitation contract); *Kramer v. Kramer,* 478. 2d 553 (Pa. Super. 1983) (the contract will fail only to the extent that it involves payment for sexual services); *Kinnison v. Kinnison,* 627 p. 2d 594 (Wyo. 1981) (enforcing contract between nonmarried cohabitants on the basis that it does not violate public policy unless the sole consideration is maritricious sex). However, some courts have declined to narrow the illegal consideration doctrine as substantially as the California Supreme Court did in *Marvin,.* A leading case to reject *Marvin's* liberal severance doctrine was *Hewitt v. Hewitt,* 394 N.E. 2d 1204 (Ill. 1979). In that case the Illinois Supreme Court viewed separation of the illicit sex component from housekeeping service components, and giving one cohabitant a share of the property of the other as payment for housekeeping, to merely legitimate common law marriage, and declined to do so.

A large number of courts have also embraced the "implied contract" claim for recovery from a former nonmarried cohabitant. Most of these cases, however, have involved nonmarital cohabitation for an extended period of time. *See e.g. Carlson v. Olson,* 256 N.W. 2d 249 (Minn. 1977) (parties lived together for 21 years evidencing implied agreement to share property); *Carrol v. Lee,* 712 p. 2d 923 (Ariz. 1986) (parties cohabited for 14 years jointly acquiring real estate, automobiles, and other property evidencing an intent to share equally their acquisitions). *See also Beal v. Beal,* 577 P.2d 507 (Ore. 1978); *Levar v. Elkins,* 604 P.2d 602 (Alaska 1980); *In re Estate of Steffes,* 290 N.W.2d 697 (Wis. 1981); *Hay v. Hay,* 678 P.2d 672 (Nev. 1984). *See also Estate of Palmen,* 588 N.W.2d 493 (Minn. 1999) (equity claim OK).

However, in several notable decisions other state courts have refused to recognize a cause of action based on implied contract among nonmarried cohabitants. The Minnesota legislature mandated that palimony claims had to be based on a written contract to be enforceable. Minn. Stat. §§ 513.075, .076 (1998), howver the courts found a way to circumvent that restriction. *Estate of Palmen,* 588 N.W.2d 493 (Minn. 1999). A leading case is *Morone v. Morone,* 413 N.E. 2d 1154 (N.Y. 1980), in which a woman alleged for more than 22 years she had performed domestic services and given business assistance to her cohabitant, by whom she bore two children. The parties had filed joint tax returns and held themselves out to be husband and wife to family, friends, and the community. After they separated, she sought recovery of a share of his property on the theory of express (oral) agreement that he would support her in return for her performance of domestic services, and upon theory of implied contract as well. The trial court dismissed the complaint finding that both claims were unenforceable in New York. The Court of Appeals ruled that *express* contracts for economic support between nonmarried cohabitants were enforceable, but affirmed dismissal of the *implied* contract claim emphasizing that "the relationship of the parties makes it natural that the (homemaking and domestic) services were rendered gratuitously" and because of the substantial risks of fraud, misunderstanding or error when attempting to infer what the nature and substance of the agreement between cohabitants after the fact. *See also, Johnston v. Estate of Phillips,* 706 S.W. 2d 554 (Mo. App. 1986) (recovery between nonmarried cohabitants will be allowed only for express contract, not implied contract); *Tapley v. Tapley,* 449 A.2d 1218 (N.H. 1982) (contract based on consideration for domestic services will not be recognized unless it is express because of the risks of fraud and difficulty of determining retrospectively the real intent of the parties). *See also Wilcox v. Trautz,* 693 N.E.2d 141 (Mass. 1998) (recovery on express written contract OK).

Finally, recognition of a cause of action against a prior nonmarried cohabitant based on general equitable principles has not received extensive judicial endorsement. Even in the *Marvin,* case, the Court of Appeals, on remand, reversed an award of $104,000 rehabilatative palimony, based on general equity principles, because there was no specific equitable doctrine to justify such an award. Nonetheless, the inherent power of the court to do equity and avoid injustice has been noted in several decisions by courts upholding claims between former and nonmarried cohabitants. *See e.g. Mason v. Rostat,* 476 A.2d 662 (D.C. 1984) (male cohabitant entitled to recover reasonable value of services and expenditures to improve a home owned by female cohabitant in which they live together in order to prevent unjust enrichment); *Eaton v. Johnson,* 681 p. 2d 606 (Kan. 1984) (upholding power of trial court to equitably distribute property acquired during two and a half years the couple lived together following their divorce; *In re Marriage of Lindsay,* 678 P.2d 328 (Wash. 1984); *See also Gilbert v. Cliche,* 398 A.2d 387 (Me. 1979); *Garr v. Waggoner,* 572 P.2d 405 (Utah 1977); *Karlson v. Olson,* 256 N.W. 2d 249 (Minn. 1977). For an interesting (if rather one-sided) review of the *Marvin* legacy after 25 years, *see Symposium, infra.*

Marvin was cited in about 200 cases and over 300 law review publications in the twenty-five years after it was decided. But, as Professor Ann Laquer Estin succinctly explained, *Marvin* has had inconsistent impact on doctrinal development.

> With all its celebrity, the *Marvin* decision stands more as a cultural icon than as a legal watershed. In the twenty-five years since Lee and Michelle hit the gossip columns, rates of unmarried cohabitation have climbed steadily, and courts have continued to confront the claims of unmarried partners at the end of their relationships. As living together without marriage has become less glamorous, less forbidden, and more ordinary among the middle class, there is more of this legal work for courts and lawyers to do. *But the law governing nonmarital relationships remains largely an ad hoc affair, with tremendous variation between states and from case to case.*
>
> At one end of the spectrum, courts in Illinois and Georgia have refused to embrace the *Marvin* principle and will not enforce even express written "relationship" contracts between unmarried cohabitants. At the other end of the spectrum, courts in Washington and Nevada have begun to apply rules that treat some nonmarital opposite-sex couples as if they were married for purposes of property claims at the end of their cohabitation. In between these extremes, most states' courts routinely enforce express agreements and recognize various equitable claims between unmarried partners, particularly where they share a business or property.

Estin, infra at 1383 (emphasis added).

4) Policy Considerations

The traditional rule prohibiting an action to obtain or recover palimony stems from three public policy concerns: (1) preserving morality, (2) preserving marriage and family institution, and (3) the principle of autonomy, privacy, or judicial prudence that discourages courts from attempting to enforce hard-to-prove agreements (he-said-she-said disputes), especially relating to intimate human relations. Recognition of such an action similarly reflects three other policy considerations: (1) preventing unjust enrichment, (2) enforcing the reasonable expectations of the parties; and (3) legitimating the social morality of nonmarital cohabitation.

Many states have decriminalized fornication, adultery and nonmarital cohabitation. But many states have not. For example, Arizona makes open & notorious cohabitation or adultery a misdemeanor, ARS § 13.1408-09; Utah makes fornication & adultery a misdemeanor, UCA §§ 76-7-103, -104. Is that relevant to the policy question regarding enforcement of alleged "palimony" agreements? Is there some policy inconsistency if a state prohibits fornication and/or adultery, but allows a palimony action, or vice versa? Laws prohibiting prostitution also affect scope of recovery permitted. If a state prohibits prostitution, is it inconsistent to allow recovery for a contract based largely on sexual relations consideration? The oft-cited concurrence of Justice Finley in *West v. Knowles*, 311 P.2d 689, 692 (Wash. 1957)(Finley, J., concurring): declared the old law: "[F]or 10 yrs Bonnie West and Delmer Knowles lived together and were generally accepted as a married couple. However, they had never observed the convention of (a) obtaining a marriage license and (b) formally exchanging marriage vows. Obviously, such a relationship is not generally approved by the mores of our society. It is not a relationship which is encouraged by the courts."

All states favor marriage and the marriage-based family in public policy, at least to some extent. Also, all states have comprehensive schemes re: property rights of married couples. It has been argued that by granting palimony claims, dividing property of unmarried cohabitants, and treating them economically as if they were a marriage unit, the law weakens the economic incentive to marry, and creates an economic incentive for a competing relationship that undermines the marriage-based family. These concerns are offset to some extent by concerns that failure to allow recovery of "palimony" will result in unjust enrichment to the economically well-off nonmarital partner (usually male) and provide him with an economic incentive not to marry, if the unmarried cohabitant is not allowed contract recovery. Prevention of unjust enrichment is the core policy behind the movement toward allowing palimony actions. As the Oregon Supreme Court explained in *Latham v. Latham*, 547 P.2d 144, 147 (1976): "The application of the principle that such a contact will not be enforced has often resulted in the male keeping the assets accumulated in the relationship and the female being deprived of what she accumulated." Other policies used to justify palimony are enforcement of reasonable expectations and performance of freely-made bargains. As the Oregon Supreme court explained in *Beal v. Beal*, 577 P2d 507 (Ore. 1978): "In summary, we hold that courts, when dealing with the property disputes of a man and a woman who have been living together in a nonmarital domestic relationship should distribute the property based upon the expressed or implied intent of the parties." The third concern is harmonizing the law and social customs. This social acceptance of nonmarital cohabitation by the baby boom generation obviously has had an impact on the development of this area of the law. "Changed social conditions" have been identified as contributing justifications *for the recognition of economic rights of unmarried cohabitants in several cases. See Marvin v. Marvin*, 557 P.2d 106 (1976). But how should the changed mores be integrated into the law? When is that an appropriate task for the judiciary? Is that more a legislative than a judicial responsibility?

Criminal laws prohibiting cohabitation are still on the books in a handful of states. Mahoney, *infra*, at 139. Are they unconstitutional under *Lawrence v. Texas*, 539 U.S. 558 (2003) , or does the availability of marriage for such couples distinguish *Lawrence*?

5) Anti-Palimony Statutes

Several states have enacted laws to prevent courts from awarding quasi-marital benefits to nonmarital couples. For example, Tex. Family Code § 8.011 provides: "An order for maintenance is not authorized between unmarried cohabitants under any circumstances." A Nebraska referendum, approved by over sixty percent of the voters in 2000, prohibits recognition not only of same-sex marriage but also recognition of "domestic partnership" or "civil unions" as well. Would that prohibit extending "palimony" to former same-sex couples? To former heterosexual nonmarital cohabitants?

6) ALI *Principles of the Law of Family Dissolution*

Status recognition for nonmarital cohabitation is still rare in the United States. Mahoney, *infra*, at 139-40. However, the American Law Institute's *Principles of the Law of Family Dissolution* recommends, in Chapter 6, that courts extend the same financial consequences upon dissolution to nonmarital cohabitants as the law provides to married couples upon divorce, including property division and alimony awards. Entitlement to such benefits is suggested to flow by presumption after the parties have lived together for a set period of time, or for a shorter time if they have a child together, or upon proof of sufficient cohabitation (considering thirteen factors). The ALI principles are based upon the Reporter's explicit assumption that the relationship between cohabiting couples is basically the same as the relationship that husbands and wives have. However, studies of cohabiting persons reveals that most cohabiting individuals sharply distinguish their cohabitation relationship from marriage, and most keep their finances separate, unlike married couples who usually mix and combine their finances. Thus, the ALI domestic partnership proposal has been criticized because "instead of doing what most parties would want or what is good for broader society, Chapter 6 both over- and undershoots its target." Brinig, *infra*, at 20. *See also* Wardle, *infra*. To date, the ALI proposal has not been widely adopted.

3. Practical and Ethical Considerations

a. Duty to Represent

As the number of nonmarital cohabitants increases, family lawyers can expect to see more clients wishing to assert palimony claims against former partners. Would it be ethically permissible for an attorney to decline to represent a client asserting a palimony claim on grounds of personal moral objections to the nature of the relationship? Why/not? Should palimony claims based on express contract be encouraged or discouraged? Why/not? How would you define the scope of a proper "public policy" exception as it relates to extramarital sexual relations? In the absence of express contract, should palimony claims be favored or discouraged by public policy? Why/not? Should same-sex cohabitants be treated the same as heterosexual nonmarital cohabitants in terms of their ability to assert palimony claims against former partners? Why/why not?

b. Attorney Marvin Mitchelson

Michelle Marvin's attorney, Marvin Mitchelson, remarked that "the day Michelle Marvin was allowed into court was the day marriage and family law changed forever." It was also the day his life changed forever. After the *Marvin* case, Mr. Mitchelson developed a jet set clientele, representing many rich and famous persons in high-profile divorce cases (including Bianca Jagger, Joan Collins and the former wife of arms dealer Adnan Khashoggi). In 1993, however, Mitchelson was convicted of evading taxes. "During the next three years, he fought to stay out of prison while undergoing treatment for skin cancer, heart disease and surgery for crushed spinal disks . . . ." His license to practice was suspended, and in 1996 he began serving more than two years in a federal prison. He later wrote: "'I was led into a yard where other newly arrived prisoners were congregating,' . . . . 'I started to cry, just as I had the day before when I bid my wife and son goodbye, apologizing over and over again for the pain and humiliation I had put us all through.'" In 2000, the California State Bar renewed his license and he later opened a law office in West Hollywood "where wealthy clients are lining up for his special brand of family law." *'Palimony' lawyer, infra* at A10. If such lapses can happen to him, how can a law student prepare to prevent similar problems?

4. Bibliography

American Law Institute, *Principles of the Law of Family Dissolution: Analysis and Recommendations* (2002).

Margaret Brinig, *Domestic Partnership: Missing the Target?*, 4 J. L. & Fam. Studs. 19 (2002).

Brandon Campbell, Comment, *Cohabitation Agreement sin Massachusetts: Wilcox v. Trautz Changes the Rules But Not the Results*, 34 New Eng. L. Rev. 485 (2000).

Ann Laquer Estin, *Ordinary Cohabitation*, 76 Notre Dame L. Rev. 1381 (2001).

Henry Foster & Doris Jonas Freed, *New Wine in Old Bottles*, 5 Fam. L. Reporter 4001 (1979).

David Orgon Coolidge & William C. Duncan, *Reaffirming Marriage: A Presidential Priority*, 24 Harv. J.L. & Pub. Pol'y 623 (2001).

Greg Johnson, *Vermont Civil Unions: The New Language of Marriage*, 25 Vt. L. Rev. 15 (2000).

Kim Kantorowicz, Case Note, *Contracts–Cohabitation in Minnesota: From Love to Contract–Public Policy Gone Awry in re Estate of Palmen*, 26 Wm. Mitchell L. Rev. 213 William (2000).

Margaret M. Mahoney, *Shaping the Law of Cohabitation for Opposite-Sex Couples*, 7 J. L. & Fam. Studs. 135 (2005).

'Palimony' lawyer back at work, Deseret News (Utah) (AP), Aug. 14, 2001, at A10.

Recent Legislation – Domestic Relations – Same-Sex Couples, 114 Harv. L. Rev. 1421 (2001).
  Symposium, Unmarried Partners and the Legacy of Marvin v. Marvin, 76 Notre Dame L. Rev. 1261 *et seq.* (2001).

Lynn D. Wardle, *Deconstructing Family: A Critique of the American Law Institute's "Domestic Partners" Proposal*, 2001 B.Y.U.L. Rev. 1189.

PART VII
TERMINATION AND POST-DISSOLUTION PARENT-CHILD RELATIONS

CHAPTER 32

Custody and Visitation Jurisdiction and Procedure; International Custody Jurisdiction and Procedure

A. CUSTODY AND VISITATION JURISDICTION AND PROCEDURE

1. BACKGROUND

a. Subject Matter Jurisdiction of Custody Disputes

Traditionally, custody judgments were considered not to be final judgments for full faith and credit purposes because they are modifiable. This led to the practice of many parents who were disappointed with the rendering state's custody decision to snatch the child and to go forum shopping to other states because the chances were fair that the new state would not enforce the rendering state's judgment but would modify it under its custody jurisdictional laws.

In 1968, the National Conference of Commissioners on Uniform Laws promulgated the Uniform Child Custody Jurisdiction Act (UCCJA) to encourage states to bring uniformity to the conflicting jurisdictional laws in order to stabilize custody decisions and to discourage child snatching. All states eventually enacted a version of the Act. Total uniformity among the states did not occur because states could have concurrent jurisdiction and were sovereign in their interpretation of the Act.

In 1980, Congress enacted the Federal Parental Kidnapping Prevention Act, 28 U.S.C.A. §1738A (1980), to respond to the findings that the continuing conflict in state custody jurisdiction "contributed to the concealment and interstate transportation of children, the disregard of court orders, [and] excessive relitigation of cases" due to the 'failure of such jurisdictions to give full faith and credit to the judicial proceedings of the other states.' (PL. 96-611 7(a) (1980)) The PKPA establishes constitutional requirements for the enforcement of custody judgments so that the full faith and credit clause of the Constitution applies to custody judgments meeting these constitutional requirements. Therefore, a state must give full faith and credit to such sister states' judgments. Under the Supremacy Clause, the PKPA would preempt conflicting state law.

The Uniform Child Custody Jurisdiction and Enforcement Act, 9 U.L.A. (Pt. 1A) 649 (1999) (herein "UCCJEA") was promulgated in 1997, nearly thirty years after the original UCCJA was drafted, and revises and reorganizes the original uniform act. The UCCJEA incorporates all of the principles of (and largely the same text as) the UCCJA and resolves several issues that have arisen in the last three decades because (a) some states modified the language of the UCCJA before adopting it, (b) several inconsistencies in various state court interpretations of the UCCJA provisions have developed, and (c) some inconsistencies between language or interpretation of the congressional PKPA and the UCCJA have created conflicts and impeded uniformity. However, the UCCJEA retains the core concepts and structure of the UCCJA.

b. Personal Jurisdiction

Traditionally, child custody decisions were treated as a status determination. The court of the child's domicile had jurisdiction to enter the decree. Are "minimum contacts" constitutionally required for a state court to exercise custody jurisdiction involving the custody rights of a nonresident parent? The U.S. Supreme Court has not explicitly answered this question, and while the enactment of the UCCJA and the UCCJEA. have encouraged some state courts to reject any further (e.g., due process) jurisdictional restrictions, the state courts are split on this issue.

The seminal modern Supreme Court decision is *May v. Anderson*, 345 U.S. 528 (1953). In that case, a man and woman were married and domiciled in Wisconsin and had three children there. In December 1946, following marital discord, the wife took the children to her parents' home in Ohio, with her husband's consent. The next month, the husband filed an action in Wisconsin seeking divorce and custody of the children. The wife did not appear (or defend) and the Wisconsin court entered a decree granting the husband divorce and custody by default. Several years later, following custody exchanges and a dispute, he filed an action in Ohio to enforce his Wisconsin custody decree. The Ohio trial court concluded that it had to enforce the Wisconsin decree under the Full Faith and Credit Clause. The Ohio Court of Appeals affirmed and the Ohio Supreme Court denied an appeal.

The U.S. Supreme Court reversed. Writing for the majority of four, Justice Burton concluded that the Wisconsin divorce court lacked "the personal jurisdiction that it must have in order to deprive their mother of her personal right to the[] [children's] immediate possession." *Id.* at 534. He stated:

> [W]e have before us the elemental question whether a court of a state, *where a mother is neither domiciled, resident nor present*, may cut off her immediate right to the care, custody, management and companionship of her minor children without having jurisdiction over her in personam. *Rights far more precious to appellant than property rights will be cut off if she is to be bound by the Wisconsin award of custody.*

345 U.S. at 533 (emphasis added). Thus, the Wisconsin custody decree was not entitled to Full Faith and Credit because the Wisconsin court did not have in personam jurisdiction over the mother (or, at the time, over the children). *Id.*

Justice Frankfurter cast the fifth vote to reverse, but he wrote a separate opinion addressing the full faith and credit issue, solely. The Ohio Supreme Court had indicated that it felt itself bound by the Full Faith and Credit Clause to recognize the custody order in the Wisconsin ex parte divorce decree. Justice Frankfurter agreed with the majority that the Ohio courts were not required by the Full Faith and Credit Clause to recognize the Wisconsin ex parte custody determination, but he emphasized that nothing in the Constitution prevented them from voluntarily choosing to recognize the Wisconsin custody decree if they wanted to do so. Noting that state interests in such cases overrode the national interest in uniformity because "the child's welfare in a custody case has such a claim upon the State that its responsibility is obviously not to be foreclosed by a prior adjudication reflecting another State's discharge of its responsibility at another time." *Id.* at 536. Three additional justices dissented, arguing that the Wisconsin decree was entitled to Full Faith and Credit, and a fourth did not participate in the decision. Thus, four justices found the Wisconsin custody decree based on present domicile of the father and recent domicile of the children, but not in personal jurisdiction over the mother or children, to be constitutional inadequate for inter-state (and arguably even intra-state) recognition, while four other justices (including Frankfurter) found it sufficient to at least allow, if not require, other states to recognize the judgment.

In 1977, the Supreme Court rejected the reliance on labels such as "in rem" or "quasi in rem" to excuse noncompliance with the minimum contacts requirement. In *Shaffer v. Heitner*, 433 U.S. 186 (1977), the Court declared that "all assertions of state court jurisdiction must be evaluated according to the standards set forth in *International Shoe* and its progeny." 433 U.S. at 212. However, in footnote 30, the Court declined to answer the question whether "the particularized rules, governing adjudications of status, are inconsistent with the standard of fairness." *Id.* at 208, n.30. Some people have read this as suggesting that minimum contacts are not required in custody cases. But, it would be strange to read a footnote in the watershed case which *extends* the minimum contacts test to *all* assertions of jurisdiction to silently overturn a decision which extended minimum contacts to custody cases a quarter of a century earlier. The better interpretation of footnote 30 is that the Court's reference to "adjudications of status" meant only to signal that state courts could continue to grant *divorces* based on the *domicile* of either of the parties, thus continuing the *Williams'* Rule. *Williams v. North Carolina*, 317 U.S. 287 (1942); *Williams v. North Carolina*, 325 U.S. 226 (1945). Domicile of a married person is a sufficient contact with the state to grant a divorce because the divorce only affects the *contracted* relationship of two *adult* parties *with each other*. One may argue that custody, on the other hand, is different. Mere domicile of one parent in a jurisdiction is not sufficient contact to justify a court terminating or depriving a nonresident parent of his or her custodial relationship with a child.

The Supreme Court has not addressed the question of the constitutional requirements for child custody jurisdiction since it decided *May v. Anderson*. Although the UCCJA, UCCJEA and the PKPA do not require minimum contacts, a substantial number of state courts have ruled that "minimum contacts" is not required for a state court to assert custody jurisdiction over a nonresident defendant if the statutory requirements of the UCCJA. or UCCJEA are met. *McAtee v. McAtee*, 320 S.E.2d 611 (W.Va. 1984); *In re Marriage of Leonard*, 122 Cal. App. 3rd 443 (1981); *Perry v. Ponder*, 604 S.W. 2d 306 (Ct. Civ. App. Tex. 1980); *Hudson v. Hudson*, 670 P.2d 287 (Wash. App. 1983). *See generally Goldfarb v. Goldfarb*, 268 S.E. 2d 648 (Ga. 1980); *Williams v. Knott*, 690 S.W. 2d 605 (Tex. Ct. App. 1985); *Pratt v. Pratt*, 431 A.2d 405 (R.I. 1981). However, nearly as many state courts have held or assumed that custody jurisdiction must satisfy the minimum contacts test as well as the statutory requirements of the UCCJA before custody jurisdiction may be exercised over nonresident defendants. *Ex parte Dean*, 447 So.2d 733 (A.L.A. 1984); *In re Marriage of Bremer*, 334 N.W.2d 345 (Iowa 1983); *Pasqualone v. Pasqualone*, 406 N.E. 2d 1121 (Ohio 1980); *In re Marriage of Hall*, 607 P.2d 898 (Ct. App. Wash. 1980). *See also C.P. v. District Court*, 696 P.2d 254, 259 n. 7 (Colo. 1985); *In re M.A.C.*, 261 S.E.2d 590 (Ga. 1977); *Neger v. Neger*, 457 A.2d 628 (N.J. 1983). *See further* Coombs, *Interstate Child Custody: Jurisdiction, Recognition and Enforcement*, 66 Minn. L. Rev. 711, 762-64 (1982) (minimum contacts is required).

The question as to whether *May v. Anderson* is still good law remains. In any event, all custody cases require the defendant be given adequate notice and an opportunity to defend.

2. Statutes, Cases and Doctrines

a. Uniform Child Custody Jurisdiction Act

Section 2. [Definitions.]

(5) "home state" means the state in which the child immediately preceding the time involved lived with his parents, a parent, or a person acting as a parent, for at least 6 consecutive months, and in the case of a child less than 6 months the state in which the child lived from birth with any of the persons mentioned. Periods of temporary absence of any of the named persons are counted as part of the 6-month or other period;

(6) "initial decree" means the first custody decree concerning a particular child;

(7) "modification decree" means a custody decree which modifies or replaces a prior decree, whether made by the court which rendered the prior decree or by another court;

Section 3 [Jurisdiction]

(a) A court of this State which is competent to decide child custody matters has jurisdiction to make a child custody determination by initial or modification decree if:

(1) this State (i) is the home State of the child on the date of the commencement of the proceeding, or (ii) had been the child's home State within 6 months before the date of the commencement of the proceeding and the child is absent from such State because of his removal or retention by a person claiming his custody or for other reasons, and a parent or person acting as a parent continues to live in such State; or

(2) it is in the best interest of the child that a court of this State assume jurisdiction because (i) the child and his parents, or the child and at least one contestant, have a significant connection with such State, and (ii) there is available in this State substantial evidence concerning the child's present or future care, protection, training, and personal relationships; or

(3) the child is physically present in such State and (i) the child has been abandoned, or (ii) it is necessary in an emergency to protect the child because he has been subjected to or threatened with mistreatment or abuse; or

(4) (i) it appears that no other State would have jurisdiction under subparagraph (1), (2), (3), or another State has declined to exercise jurisdiction on the ground that the State whose jurisdiction is in issue is the more appropriate forum to determine the custody or visitation of the child, and (ii) it is in the best interest of the child that such court assume jurisdiction.

(b) Except under paragraphs (3) and (4) of subsection (a), physical presence in this State of the child, or of the child and one of th contestants, is not alone sufficient to confer jurisdiction on a court of this State to make a child custody determination.

It is, of course, possible for more than one state to satisfy each of these standards, and since there are four standards, it usually happens in interstate custody disputes that more than one state satisfies the requirements of Section 3.

Section 3, however, is not the only standard for jurisdiction under the UCCJA. It is just the threshold test. There are several other sections that limit or condition UCCJA jurisdiction. "[T]he underlying philosophy of the [UCCJA] is that only the courts of one state should have responsibility for the custody of a particular child . . .

'to eliminate jurisdictional fishing with children as bait.'" *In re Custody of Rector,* 565 P.2d 950, 951 (Colo. App. 1977).

Section 6 is the first qualification of custody jurisdiction. It directs a court not to exercise jurisdiction if, at the time this action was filed "a proceeding concerning the custody of the child was pending in a court of another state exercising jurisdiction substantially in conformity with this act" unless the proceeding in the foreign state is stayed because this state is "a more appropriate forum" or for other reasons. The key phrase used in Section 6 is "jurisdiction substantially in conformity with this Act."

The next qualification for jurisdiction is the forum non conveniens requirement of Section 7 of the UCCJA. It provides that even if a court otherwise has jurisdiction it "may decline to exercise its jurisdiction any time *before making a decree* if it finds that it is an inconvenient forum to make a custody determination . . . and that a court of *another state is a more appropriate forum.*" The Commissioners' Note states:

> The purpose of this provision is to encourage judicial restraint in exercising jurisdiction whenever another state appears to be in a *better position* to determine custody of a child. It serves as a second check on jurisdiction once the test of section 3 or 14 has been met. (Emphasis added.)

Section 7(b) provides that not only may parties object to proceedings on a ground that another state would be more convenient, but that "[a] finding of inconvenient forum may be made upon the court's own motion . . . " Section 7(c) describes five factors which the court must consider in making its determination as to whether it will exercise jurisdiction. They are:

> (1) if another state is or *recently was the child's home state*;
> (2) if another state has a *closer connection with the child and his family or* with the child and one or more of the contestants;
> (3) *if substantial evidence* concerning the child's present or future care, protection, training, and personal relationship *is more readily available in another state*;
> (4) if the parties have agreed on another forum which is no less appropriate; and
> (5) if the exercise of jurisdiction by a court of this state would contravene any of the purposes stated in section 1.

Direct contact (by telephone or mail) between the courts involved is specifically authorized to facilitate this decision.

The next qualification of UCCJA jurisdiction is contained in Section 8. The Commissioners' Note refers to section eight as embodying "the 'clean hands doctrine'." Paragraph (a) of § 8 provides:

> If the petitioner for an initial decree has wrongfully taken the child from another state or has engaged in similar reprehensible conduct the court may decline to exercise jurisdiction if this is just and proper under the circumstances.

The commissioners who drafted the UCCJA commented in their Official Commissioners' Note:

Subsection (a) extends the clean hands principle to cases in which a custody decree has not yet been rendered in any state. For example, if upon a de facto separation the wife returned to her own home with the children without objection by her husband and lived there for two years without hearing from him, and the husband without warning forcibly removes the children one night and brings them to another state, a court in that state although it has jurisdiction after 6 months may decline to hear the husband's custody petition. *"Wrongfully" taking under this subsection does not mean that a "right" has been violated*--both husband and wife as a rule have a right to custody until a court determination is made--*but that one party's conduct is so objectionable that a court in the exercise of its inherent equity powers cannot in good conscience permit that party access to its jurisdiction.* (Emphasis added.)

9A U.L.A. at 526 (1999).

Section 8(b) further provides that a court *shall not* exercise jurisdiction to modify a custody decree entered in another court if the petitioner, like the Coppedges in this case, "has improperly removed the child from the physical custody of the person entitled to custody or *has improperly retained the child after a visit or other temporary relinquishment of physical custody.*" (Emphasis added.) The Commissioners' Notes declare: "In the case of *illegal* removal or *retention refusal of jurisdiction is mandatory* unless the harm done to the child by a denial of jurisdiction outweighs the parental misconduct."

The final qualification on jurisdiction is contained in Section 14. This section forbids a court to modify a custody decree entered previously by a court in another state unless (1) the court that entered the decree would no longer have jurisdiction under the UCCJA standards (e.g., if Colorado entered a custody order four years ago, but all parties have since moved away from Colorado) or if the court that entered the decree would decline to exercise jurisdiction (because of forum non conveniens, child snatchery, etc.), and (2) the forum state court would have jurisdiction under the UCCJA specifically including the clean hands provision.

b. The Uniform Child Custody Jurisdiction and Enforcement Act

Section 102: Definitions

(7) "Home State" means the State in which a child lived with a parent or a person acting as a parent for at least six consecutive months immediately before the commencement of a child-custody proceeding. In the case of a child less than six months of age, the term means the State in which the child lived from birth with any of the persons mentioned. A period of temporary absence of any of the mentioned persons is a part of the period.

Section 201. Initial Child-Custody Jurisdiction

(a) Except as otherwise provided in §204, a court of this State has jurisdiction to make an initial child-custody determination only if:

(1) this State is the home state of the child on the date of the commencement of the proceeding, or was the home State of the child within six months before the commencement of the proceeding and the child is absent from this State but a parent or person acting as a parent continues to live in this State;

(2) a court of another State does not have jurisdiction under paragraph (1), or a court of the home State of the child has declined to exercise jurisdiction on the ground that this State is the more appropriate forum under Section 207 or 208, and:

(A) the child and the child's parents or the child and at least one parent or a person acting as a parent, have a significant connection with this State other than mere physical presence; and

(B) substantial evidence is available in this State concerning the child's care, protection, training, and personal relationships.

(3) all courts having jurisdiction under paragraph (1) or (2) have declined to exercise jurisdiction on the ground that a court of this State is the more appropriate forum to determine the custody of the child under Section 207 or 208; or

(4) no court of any other State would have jurisdiction under the criteria specified in paragraph (1). (2), or (3).

(b) Subsection (a) is the exclusive jurisdictional basis for making a child-custody determination by a court of this State.

(c) Physical presence of, or personal jurisdiction over, a party or a child is not necessary or sufficient to make a child-custody determination.

Section 202. Exclusive Continuing Jurisdiction

(a) Except as otherwise provided in Section 204, a court of this State which has made a child-custody determination consistent with Section 201 or 203 has exclusive, continuing jurisdiction over the determination until:

(1) a court of this State determines that neither the child, nor the child and one parent, nor the child and a person acting as a parent have a significant connection with this State and that substantial evidence is no longer available in this State concerning the child's care, protection, training, and personal relationships; or

(2) a court of this State or a court of another State determines that the child, the child's parents, and any person acting as a parent do not presently reside in this State.

Section 204. Temporary Emergency Jurisdiction

(a) A court of this State has temporary emergency jurisdiction if the child is present in this State and the child has been abandoned or it is necessary in an emergency to protect the child because the child, or a sibling or a parent of the child, is subjected to or threatened with mistreatment or abuse. . . .

Section 206. Simultaneous Proceedings

(a) Except as otherwise provided in §204, a court of this State may not exercise its jurisdiction under this [article] if. at the time of the commencement of the proceeding, a proceeding concerning the custody of the child has been commenced in a court of another State having jurisdiction substantially in conformity with this [Act], unless the proceeding has been terminated or stayed by the court of the other State because a court of this State is a more convenient forum under §207.

Section 207. Inconvenient Forum

(a) A court of this State which has jurisdiction under this [Act} may decline to exercise its jurisdiction at any time if it determines that it is an inconvenient forum under the circumstances and that a court of another State is a more appropriate forum. The issue of inconvenient forum may be raised upon motion of a party, the court's own motion, or a request of another court.

(b) ... the court shall ... consider all relevant factors, including:

(1) whether domestic violence has occurred and is likely to continue in the future and which State could best protect the parties and the child;

(2) the length of time the child has resided outside this State;

(3) the distance between the court of this State and the court in the State that would assume jurisdiction;

(4) the relative financial circumstances of the parties;

(5) any agreement of the parties as to which State should assume jurisdiction;

(6) the nature and location of the evidence required to resolve the pending litigation, including testimony of the child;

(7) the ability of the court of each State to decide the issue expeditiously and the procedures necessary to present the evidence; and

(8) the familiarity of the court of each State with the facts and issues in the pending litigation.

Section 208. Jurisdiction Declined by Reason of Conduct

(a) Except as provided by § 204 [or by other state law], if a court of this State has jurisdiction under this Act because a person seeking to invoke its jurisdiction has engaged in unjustifiable conduct, the court shall decline to exercise its jurisdiction unless:

(1) the parents and all persons acting as parents have acquiesced in the exercise of jurisdiction;

(2) a court of the State otherwise having jurisdiction under §§ 201 through 203 determines that this State is more appropriate forum under §207; or

(3) no court of any other State would have jurisdiction under the criteria specified in §§ 201 through 203.

Section 303. Duty to Enforce.

(a) A court of this State shall recognize and enforce a child-custody determination of a court of another State if the latter court exercised jurisdiction that was in substantial conformity with this [Act] or the determination was made under factual circumstances meeting the jurisdictional standards of this [Act].

Drafters of the UCCJEA identify seven major changes from the original UCCJA. The UCCJEA, (1) like the PKPA and unlike the original UCCJA, provides priority among bases for assertion of jurisdiction, giving top priority to "home state" jurisdiction; (2) clarifies that "emergency jurisdiction" is temporary only, and expands the scope of emergency jurisdiction to include cases when a child, sibling, or parent is subject to or threatened with violence in another jurisdiction; (3) specifies that the court that issued the original custody decree has exclusive continuing jurisdiction; (4) includes an explicit "sweeping definition" of what proceedings are covered that "includes virtually all cases that can involve custody of or visitation with a child . . . ;" (5) eliminates use of the phrase "best interests" to prevent the jurisdictional act from being misused and misinterpreted as providing grounds for awarding custody; (6) harmonizes with the Uniform Interstate Enforcement of Support Act (UIFSA); and (7) adds a new set of provisions to give uniformity to proceedings for interstate enforcement of custody and visitation, including simplified interstate registration, a "swift remedy along the lines of habeas corpus," explicitly limiting the scope of inquiry to whether the decree court had jurisdiction and complied with due process in rendering the original custody decree," allowing a court to take physical custody of a child in cases where there is risk that the parent will flee, and providing for involvement of public authorities in the second state. 9 U.L.A. 649-653 (1999). As of Spring, 2006, 43 states, the District of Colombia, and the Virgin Islands had enacted the UCCJEA, replacing the UCCJA. The remaining states follow their versions of the former UCCJA.

c. Parental Kidnapping Prevention Act

28 U.S.C. § 1738A. Full faith and credit given to child custody determinations (PKPA)
(a) The appropriate authorities of every State shall enforce according to its terms, and shall

not modify except as provided in subsections (f), (g), and (h) of this section, any custody determination or visitation determination made consistently with the provisions of this section by a court of another State.

(b) As used in this section, the term-- (1) "child" means a person under the age of eighteen; (2) "contestant" means a person, including a parent or grandparent, who claims a right to custody or visitation of a child; (3) "custody determination" means a judgment, decree, or other order of a court providing for the custody of a child, and includes permanent and temporary orders, and initial orders and modifications; (4) "home State" means the State in which, immediately preceding the time involved, the child lived with his parents, a parent, or a person acting as parent, for at least six consecutive months, and in the case of a child less than six months old, the State in which the child lived from birth with any of such persons. Periods of temporary absence of any of such persons are counted as part of the six-month or other period; (5) "modification" and "modify" refer to a custody or visitation determination which modifies, replaces, supersedes, or otherwise is made subsequent to, a prior custody or visitation determination concerning the same child, whether made by the same court or not; (6) "person acting as a parent" means a person, other than a parent, who has physical custody of a child and who has either been awarded custody by a court or claims a right to custody; (7) "physical custody" means actual possession and control of a child; (8) "State" means a State of the United States, the District of Columbia, the Commonwealth of Puerto Rico, or a territory or possession of the United States; and (9) "visitation determination" means a judgment, decree, or other order of a court providing for the visitation of a child and includes permanent and temporary orders and initial orders and modifications.

(c) A child custody or visitation determination made by a court of a State is consistent with the provisions of this section only if--

(1) such court has jurisdiction under the law of such State; and

(2) one of the following conditions is met:

(A) such State (i) is the home State of the child on the date of the commencement of the proceeding, or (ii) had been the child's home State within six months before the date of the commencement of the proceeding and the child is absent from such State because of his removal or retention by a contestant or for other reasons, and a contestant continues to live in such State;

(B) (i) it appears that no other State would have jurisdiction under subparagraph (A), and (ii) it is in the best interest of the child that a court of such State assume jurisdiction because (I) the child and his parents, or the child and at least one contestant, have a significant connection with such State other than mere physical presence in such State, and (II) there is available in such State substantial evidence concerning the child's present or future care, protection, training, and personal relationships;

(C) the child is physically present in such State and (i) the child has been abandoned, or (ii) it is necessary in an emergency to protect the child because he has been subjected to or threatened with mistreatment or abuse;

(D) (i) it appears that no other State would have jurisdiction under subparagraph (A), (B), (C), or (E), or another State has declined to exercise jurisdiction on the ground that the State whose jurisdiction is in issue is the more appropriate forum to determine the custody or visitation of the child, and (ii) it is in the best interest of the child that such court assume jurisdiction; or

(E) the court has continuing jurisdiction pursuant to subsection (d) of this section.

(d) The jurisdiction of a court of a State which has made a child custody or visitation determination consistently with the provisions of this section continues as long as the requirement of subsection (c)(1) of this section continues to be met and such State remains the residence of the child or of any contestant.

(e) Before a child custody or visitation determination is made, reasonable notice and opportunity to be heard shall be given to the contestants, any parent whose parental rights have not been previously terminated and any person who has physical custody of a child.

(f) A court of a State may modify a determination of the custody of the same child made by a court of another State, if-- (1) it has jurisdiction to make such a child custody determination; and (2) the court of the other State no longer has jurisdiction, or it has declined to exercise such jurisdiction to modify such determination.

(g) A court of a State shall not exercise jurisdiction in any proceeding for a custody or visitation determination commenced during the pendency of a proceeding in a court of another State where such court of that other State is exercising jurisdiction consistently with the provisions of this section to make a custody or visitation determination.

(h) A court of a State may not modify a visitation determination made by a court of another State unless the court of the other State no longer has jurisdiction to modify such determination or has declined to exercise jurisdiction to modify such determination.

d. *Welch-Doden v. Roberts*
Melissa Marie Welch-Doden v. The Honorable David L. Roberts
202 P.3d 1166 (Ariz. 2002)

BARKER, Judge.

[Case of first impression to resolve a statutory conflict in the meaning of "home state" as that phrase is used in determining initial jurisdiction between competing states in child custody disputes under Arizona's newly adopted Uniform Child Custody Jurisdiction and Enforcement Act (UCCJEA). Melissa Welch-Doden (Mother) married Terry Welch-Doden (Father) in Arizona in November 1996. Later they moved to Oklahoma to secure employment. Their child was born in Oklahoma on April 28, 1999. Mother claims that family eventually intended to resume their residence in Arizona. The child's residences between her birth and January 25, 2001: Oklahoma: April 28,1999 - December 1999 (seven and a half months); Arizona: December 1999 - March 2000 (three months); Oklahoma : March 2000 - September 2000 (six months); Arizona: September 2000 - January 25, 2001 (4 months). The child resided with the mother at all times Mother filed complaint for divorce and custody on January 25, 2001 in Arizona. Father served in Oklahoma. Father filed complaint for divorce and custody in Oklahoma and moved to dismiss custody complaint before the Arizona court, claiming Arizona lacked subject matter jurisdiction for custody because Arizona was not the home state. Arizona trial court dismissed for lack of jurisdiction. Mother appealed.]

*   *   *   *

First does the UCCJEA provide that "home state" jurisdiction is based on a child residing in a state (a) for a six-month period *immediately prior to the filing of a custody petition*, or (b) for a six-month period that is completed *at any time within* six months of the filing?

*   *   *   *   *

[UCCJEA § 201] is the statutory starting place for determining initial jurisdiction. [FN 5: sets forth § 201] In summary, subsection B makes it clear that Arizona *only* has jurisdiction pursuant to subsection A. ("Subsection A of this section is the exclusive jurisdictional basis."). Subsection A, paragraph (1) provides for Arizona to have jurisdiction when Arizona qualifies as a home state. If a state is the 'home state' under this paragraph, it has jurisdiction. There is no further factual inquiry on the *jurisdictional* issue. Paragraphs 2-4 pf subsection A provide the circumstances whereby Arizona may have jurisdiction when it does not qualify as the home state. Paragraph 2, in particular, requires the court to consider whether the child has a significant connection to the state (as well as other factors) before jurisdiction may be found. Subsection C clarifies that the presence of the child is neither necessary nor sufficient to establish jurisdiction.

In considering [§ 201], as it relates to the present case, we must also take into account the statutory definition of "home state." Section 102(7) defines "home state" as follows::

> ...The state in which a child lived with a parent or a person acting as a parent for *at least six consecutive months immediately before the commencement of a child custody proceeding,* including any period during which that person is temporarily absent from that state. (emphasis added).

. . .[This definition of "home state" in [§ 102(7)] conflicts with § 201 which provides that] a state has jurisdiction if [it]

> is the [1] home state of the child on *the date of the commencement of the proceeding,* or [2] was the home state of the child *within six months before the commencement* of the proceeding and the child is absent from this state but a parent or person acting as a parent continues to live in this state.

It is the application of this definition of "home state" to § 201 that creates the statutory conflict. ......
Thus, applying literally the definition of "home state" from Section 102 to element one of [§ 201(a)(1)] renders superfluous the language in [§ 201(a)(1)] that says jurisdiction lies when a state is the home state 'on the commencement of the proceeding." That latter phrase merely restates what is already required by the definition of "home state" in
Section 102.

Element two of [§ 201(a)(1)] poses a more significant problem in statutory construction when the home state definition from Section 102 is applied: the two statutes directly conflict. Element two of [§ 201(a)(1)] provides that a state has jurisdiction if it is the "home state . . *within six months before*" the commencement of the child custody proceeding. Section 102(7) requires that in order to be a "home state" . . . , a child must have lived in a state for six consecutive months "immediately before" the child custody proceeding. Thus, if a child's home state two months before a proceeding was commenced is different from the state to which a child has permanently moved (and in which the proceeding was commenced), Section 102(7) would indicate there is no home state at all. Initial jurisdiction would then be determined based on substantial connections to the state and other factors under [§ 201(A)(2)]. On the other hand, under the same facts, element two of [§ 201(A)(1)] would declare the *prior state* the home state because it was the home state *within* six months of the filing. Initial jurisdiction would then be in the prior state regardless of any significant connections to the state in which the filing was made.

The statutory conflict between element two of [§ 201(A)(1)] and Section 102(7) is directly at issue here. The child lived in Oklahoma for six consecutive months ending in September 2000. The child then resided in Arizona for the next four months, immediately before the petition was filed in January 2001. Thus, under father's (and the trial judge's) reading of the statute, Oklahoma is the home state as a matter of law under element two of [§ 201(A)(1)]. Oklahoma, under this view, was the home state (from March to September 2000) *within* six months of the filing of the petition in January 2001 and thus has initial jurisdiction.

Under mother's reading of the statute, however, neither Oklahoma nor Arizona is the home state as neither meet the requirement of Section 102(7). . . . The trial court would be required to . . . determine whether there were significant connections with Arizona and other factors per [§ 201(A)(2)], to determine whether Arizona should have initial jurisdiction . . .

   *   *   *   *   *

To appropriately resolve the conflict here, it is critical to examine the stated purposes behind the changes in home state jurisdiction brought about by the UCCJEA.

The precursor to the UCCJEA was the . . . [UCCJA]. The stated purposes of the UCCJA were to avoid jurisdictional competition and conflict, to promote cooperation between the states, discourage the use of the interstate system to continue custody controversies, deter abductions, avoid relitigation in different states, and facilitate enforcement of custody decrees between states.

All fifty states, the District of Columbia and the Virgin Islands adopted the UCCJA. 9 U.L.A. 261-62. However, many states departed from its original text, and subsequent litigation produced substantial inconsistencies in interpretation among state courts – defeating the goals of a uniform interstate jurisdictional act. . . .

In particular, prior to the adoption of the UCCJEA, the UCCJA provided four separate bases to take initial jurisdiction in child custody disputes. These bases included (1)home state jurisdiction, (2) significant connections to the state and a consideration of the child's relationships, training, care and protection, (3) the child's best interests, and (4) emergency.

The original drafters of the UCCJA had assumed that home state jurisdiction was the most appropriate factor in demonstrating the best interests of the child. They also thought that a state should be able to proceed without delay and, therefore, should find jurisdiction on any acceptable basis. Thus, the drafters included the four separate bases for jurisdiction. However, state courts were split as to whether the four basis were equal or whether home state was preferred. *** These conflicts created an unworkable and non-uniform interstate act.

Additionally, in 1981 a significant federal statute was passed by the United States Congress. That statute, the Parental Kidnapping Prevention Act ("PKPA"), was aimed at interstate custody problems that continued to exist after the adoption of the UCCJA. It mandated states to apply full faith and credit to interstate custody decisions. Importantly, it did not allow for full faith and credit on the four bases as set forth in the UCCJA. . . Instead, enforceability under the PKPA was based on the priority of home-state jurisdiction: [The Court sets forth (c)(2) of the PKPA].

In 1997, the National Conference of Commissioners on Uniform State Laws, which had authored the UCCJA, drafted the UCCJEA. The main purposes for revising the UCCJA were uniformity and the need to avoid disputes between competing jurisdictions . .. As the drafters of the uniform act noted, lack of uniformity between jurisdictions "increases the costs of the enforcement action; it decreases the lack of certainty of outcome; and it often turns enforcement of a child custody or visitation order into a long and drawn out process." .... Arizona adopted the UCCJEA effective January 1, 2001.

The UCCJEA drafters dealt specifically with the conflict created by differing jurisdictions taking contrary views of the four bases of jurisdiction. They reconciled the jurisdictional provisions of the UCCJA with the PKPA:

> The UCCJA, however, specifically authorizes four independent bases of jurisdiction without prioritization. Under the UCCJA, a significant connection custody determination may have to be enforced even if it would be denied enforcement under the PKPA [which prioritizes home state jurisdiction]. *The UCCJEA prioritizes home state jurisdiction[.]*

9 U.L.A. 650-51 (emphasis added). The drafters made it clear that the new act was to give priority to a finding of home state jurisdiction over any other jurisdictional provisions.

Furthermore, the UCCJEA completely eliminates a determination of "best interests" of a child from the jurisdictional inquiry. These changes advance a more efficient and "bright line" jurisdictional rule consistent with the UCCJEA's purpose. The UCCJEA specifically seeks to avoid a jurisdictional analysis of substantive issues in the determination of jurisdiction. Additionally, as noted above, the statutory text of [§ 201(A)] allows consideration of other substantive factors *only* if no state qualifies as a "home state."

It is clear from the drafters' intent that the UCCJEA should be construed to promote one of its primary purposes: avoiding the jurisdictional competition and conflict that flows from hearings in competing states when each state substantively reviews subjective factors (such as "best interests") for purposes of determinating initial jurisdiction. When this fundamental purpose in mind, when there is a statutory conflict in the application of home state jurisdiction, the conflict should be resolved to strengthen (rather than dilute) the certainty of home state jurisdiction. This is consistent with the UCCJEA's statutory purpose.

Given the fundamental purpose of the UCCJEA to establish the certainty of home state jurisdiction, it is clear to us that [§ 201(A)(1)] acts to enlarge and modify the definition of home state under Section 102(7). We hold that "home state" for purposes of determining initial jurisdiction under [§ 201(A)(1)] is not limited to the time period of "six consecutive months immediately before the commencement of a child custody proceeding[.]" Instead, the applicable time period to determine "home state" in such circumstances is "within six months before the commencement of the [child custody] proceeding." [§ 201]. This interpretation promotes the priority of home state jurisdiction that the drafters specifically intended. To adopt the reading that mother supports would result in narrow home state jurisdiction. It would increase the number of potentially conflicting jurisdictional disputes in competing jurisdictions. This is contrary to the UCCJEA's purpose.

Even though the UCCJEA is a uniform act, which has been adopted in twenty-seven states and introduced in nine states, we have found no cases that construe the statutory conflict at issue. While not discussing the conflict, other states have ruled in a manner that is consistent with the interpretation we adopt. *E.g.*, *In re McCoy*, 52 S.W.3d 297, 303-304 (Tex.App.2001)(finding that Texas was not the children's home state at any time during the six months prior to the filing of the suit; *Nesa v. Baten*, 736 N.Y.S.2d 173, 174 (N.Y.A.D.2002)(New York had not been the children's home state at the time of the commencement of the custody proceeding or within the preceding six months.")

*   *   *   *   *

Thus, we conclude that the trial court did not err in rejecting mother's petition and concluding that Oklahoma had home state jurisdiction.

Mother also contends that even if Oklahoma is the home state according to the foregoing analysis, the trial judge still erred in not conducting a hearing to determine if jurisdiction was in the child's best interests. Mother puts forth two reasons: (1) Arizona's version of UCCJEA requires it, and (2) it would be inequitable and unfair not to consider the child's best interests in a determination of initial jurisdiction. . . .

First, in contending that Arizona's version of the UCCJEA requires a "best interests" hearing even though home state jurisdiction is found elsewhere, mother relies on the prefatory phrase in [§ 201(A)(1)]: *"[A] court of this State has jurisdiction to make an initial child custody determination only if any of the following is true."* Mother argues the phrase "if any of the following is true" allows courts to choose between the four bases of jurisdiction under UCCJEA much as courts chose between the four bases of jurisdiction provided under the UCCJA. This argument is directly contrary to the express language of the statute.

*   *   *   *   *   *

Second, mother argues that the equitable issues presented in a case such as this one (child having always been with mother; mother and child having significant connections with Arizona; mother and child having lived in Arizona for four months prior to filing) or in a hypothetical case (child lives five months and 29 days in one state, but the prior six months in another state resulting in home state jurisdiction in the prior case) require a hearing to consider the child's best interests. Mother's argument does not consider that the UCCJEA expressly provides for a factual hearing *in the home state* in which the state may decline to exercise its jurisdiction and allow another jurisdiction to proceed. [§ 207]. The hearing may include a "best interests" determination.

The drafters . . . expressly recognized – and sought to eliminate – the jurisdictional disputes that resulted when "best interests" was used to determine initial jurisdiction. That language and inquiry, present previously enacted UCCJA, was intentionally omitted from the newly-drafted UCCJEA.. The drafters stated:

> The *"best interest" language* in the jurisdictional sections of the UCCJA was *not intended to be an invitation to address the merits of the custody dispute in the jurisdictional determination* or to otherwise provide that "best interests" considerations should override jurisdictional determinations or provide an additional jurisdictional basis.
> *[This draft eliminates the term "best interests" in order to clearly distinguish between the jurisdictional standards and the substantive standards relating to custody and visitation of children.]*
> 9 U.L.A. at 651-652 (emphasis added.)

Thus, the 'best interests analysis does not take place in determining jurisdiction. "Best interests" may be fully explored and considered in the context of a request under [§207] . . . .
The issue of an inconvenient forum "may be raised on motion of a party, the court's own motion or request of another court." Any such request, however, must be pursued in Oklahoma rather than Arizona, as Oklahoma has home state jurisdiction . . . This is critical: To allow the state without home state jurisdiction to conduct the hearing would lead to the jurisdictional competition the drafters sought to avoid. Thus, the equitable arguments that mother wishes to pursue are not eliminated, but are merely re-directed to the home state . . . [M]other can ask the Oklahoma court to relinquish jurisdiction.
Accordingly, mother's argument that the trial judge erred in not considering the "best interests" of the child . . . is wrong. The trial judge correctly determined that this was an issue for the Oklahoma court.

      *   *   *   *   *   *

Mother also argues, relying on [§ 206(a)] that Arizona should have jurisdiction as her filing was first-in-time. *** What mother ignores is that the first-in-time filing must be in a state 'having jurisdiction substantially in conformity with this chapter." [§ 206(a)]. Because Oklahoma had home state jurisdiction, Arizona did not have jurisdiction "substantially in conformity with this chapter." *Id.* Thus, first-in-time filing granted mother no rights. The trial court did not err by rejecting mother's request that a first-in-time filing conferred initial jurisdiction upon the Arizona Court ......

e. Notes and Questions

1) *Welch-Doden v. Roberts* Note
The Arizona Court determined there was a conflict in the definition of home state in §102(7) and the description of home state jurisdiction in §201(a)(1). Home state jurisdiction apparently is a broader concept than the definition of home state. How does the text of UCCJEA §201(a)(1) differ from UCCJA §3(a)(1) and the PKPA (c)(2)(A)?

2) Federal Jurisdiction
One of the most subtle and intriguing custody issues concerns the extent to which federal courts have subject matter jurisdiction over custody disputes. The judicial power of the federal courts only extends to the kinds of cases which the Constitution enumerates and which Congress has authorized the courts to hear. U.S.

Const., art. III, §§ 1, 2. Most of the cases which federal courts adjudicate come within the diversity jurisdiction or the federal question jurisdiction authorized by statute. 28 U.S.C. §§ 1331, 1332. Although many domestic relations disputes involved citizens of different states and amounts in controversy which exceed [statutory amount], the federal courts have consistently (although not unanimously) declined to exercise diversity jurisdiction in such cases because of the strong tradition of deference to state expertise in matters of domestic relations. Additionally, the use of the phrase "Cases, in Law and Equity" in the Constitution to describe the permissible scope of federal court jurisdiction has been read by some as implicitly excluding most domestic relations cases. The terms "Law" and "Equity" described the jurisdiction exercised by two branches of English courts, the common law courts and the courts of chancery. Another branch of English courts, the ecclesiastical courts, exercised primary jurisdiction over matrimonial causes, probate matters, and other "claims of conscience" at the time the Constitution was drafted. The omission of any reference in the Constitution to "ecclesiastical" cases was taken by some to suggest that the founders of the federal government did not intend the federal courts to hear ecclesiastical causes such as domestic disputes. However, in *Ankenbrandt v. Ankenbrandt*, 504 U.S. 689 (1992), the Supreme Court held that the Constitution does not mandate any domestic relations exception to jurisdiction. Rather, the Court acknowledged that such an exception does exist as a matter of long-accepted statutory construction. Thus, the domestic relations exception was described as divest[ing] the federal courts of power to issue divorce, alimony, and child custody decrees." *Id.* at 703. The Court held in *Ankenbrandt* that the lower federal courts had erred in dismissing a suit by a custodial mother against her divorced husband and his girlfriend seeking damages in tort for alleged sexual and physical abuse of her two daughters, inasmuch as no decree of divorce, custody, or alimony was being sought. The mere fact that facets of domestic relations were involved in the dispute did not deprive the federal court of jurisdiction.

3) The PKPA and Full Faith and Credit

The PKPA does not prevent states from giving greater full faith and credit to child custody judgments under the UCCJEA. It preempts the state's UCCJEA if there is a conflict and the conflict undermines the PKPA.

4) The Parent Locator

The PKPA also provides that the Parent Locator, used in child support enforcement, may be used to locate the person who has violated custody decrees.

5) The PKPA and Federal Courts

The PKPA was enacted as an exercise of Congress' power to determine the rules governing the "full faith and credit" of judicial decrees. U.S. Const., art.IV, § 1. It is codified as an appendage to the general "full faith and credit" statute. 28 U.S.C. § 1738. It does not purport to extend the jurisdiction of the federal courts. Prior to 1988, however, federal courts in several circuits held that if another federal claim is alleged (e.g., violation of the fundamental constitutional rights of individual or parental privacy) that claim plus the indication of federal interest in the matter of orderly custody adjudication justify a federal court to determine which of two conflicting custody decrees or which of two competing custody proceedings is valid under the PKPA. However, in *Thompson v. Thompson*, 484 U.S. 174 (1988), the U.S. Supreme Court ruled unanimously that the PKPA does not confer jurisdiction on federal courts to resolve disputes regarding conflicting state court custody decrees. In that case a mother who had temporary custody under a California decree moved to Louisiana and obtained a Louisiana custody decree awarding her custody. The father later obtained a California decree awarding him custody. The father filed suit in the federal court system to enforce the California decree and to have the Louisiana decree declared invalid. Justice Marshall held that the PKPA does not create an implied federal cause of action, and that Congress did not intend federal courts to play an enforcement role under that Act. Thus, litigants must exhaust the state court system, then appeal by writ of certiorari to the U. S. Supreme Court.

6) Temporary Custody Procedures vs. Permanent Custody
In the majority of custody proceedings, especially in divorce proceedings, the court will enter a temporary custody order until the final disposition of the case. At that time the court will enter a permanent custody order. From a strategic standpoint, the temporary custody order may be beneficial to the party who is granted temporary custody of the child. Frequently, many of the factors that a court may consider and weigh in determining permanent custody are enhanced the longer the period of the time that the child is with the person who has temporary custody.

6) Non-custodial Parents' Standing to Sue for Children or for Violation of Parental Rights
In *Elk Grove Unified School District v. Newdow*, 542 U.S. 1 (2004), Mr. Newdow, a non-custodial father, who had joint physical custody, filed suit for himself and his daughter against a California school district requirement that teachers lead students in a voluntary recitation of the Pledge of Allegiance containing the phrase, "one Nation, under God," arguing that it was an unconstitutional "establishment" of religion. His standing to bring the suit depended on his legal relationship to represent, and to assert his own parental rights regarding, his daughter who attended an elementary school in the district. After the Ninth Circuit ruled for the father, finding that the school district's pledge recitation policy unconstitutional, the girl's mother filed a motion asserting that she had exclusive "legal custody" of the child, and that she did not believe it was in the child's interest to be a party to her father's suit. However, the Ninth Circuit held that, under California law, a noncustodial father retains the right to expose his child to his own religious views even if they contradict her mother's, as well as the right to seek redress for an alleged injury to that parental interests.

The Supreme Court of the United States reversed. Writing for the majority of five justices, Justice Stevens found that California law gives custodial parents the sole right to sue as next friend of their children. Therefore, the majority ruled, Mr. Newdow lacked standing to challenge on behalf of his daughter the school district's pledge of allegiance policy. Mr. Newdow's argument that he as non-custodial father still had standing because of his right to teach his daughter his religious beliefs was rejected because it would negatively impact upon the custodial mother's parental rights as well as the daughter's interests in not being forced into a highly controversial public debate. Under state law, Mr. Newdow's right as a non-custodial parent to share his religious views with his child was not infringed by the pledge policy. He did not have the right to bar his daughter's exposure to religious ideas endorsed by her mother, when he and the mother might disagree. The California non-custodial parent cases do not give Mr. Newdow a right to reach outside the private parent-child sphere to dictate to others what they may and may not say to his child respecting religion. The Court also emphasized that it generally declines to intervene in domestic relations, a traditional subject of state law.

> In our view, it is improper for the federal courts to entertain a claim by a plaintiff whose standing to sue is founded on family law rights that are in dispute when prosecution of the lawsuit may have an adverse effect on the person who is the source of the plaintiff's claimed standing. When hard questions of domestic relations are sure to affect the outcome, the prudent course is for the federal court to stay its hand rather than reach out to resolve a weighty question of federal constitutional law. There is a vast difference between Newdow's right to communicate with his child – which both California law and the First Amendment recognize – and his claimed right to shield his daughter from influences to which she is exposed in school despite the terms of the custody order. We conclude that, having been deprived under California law of the right to sue as next friend, Newdow lacks prudential standing to bring this suit in federal court.

Id. at 17-18.

Three other justice, however, maintained that under California family law, Mr. Newdow still had standing to assert that his own parental rights were infringed by the school district policy. Nonetheless, concluded that the policy did not violate the Establishment Clause.

The *Elk Grove* decision clearly indicates that state law defines the substantive rights of parents and governs their standing to sue for their children or as parents. The majority seemed to favor the convenience of all-or-nothing approach to parental standing to sue for children or as parents. The minority (three justices; there was one abstention in the case) favored an interpretation that recognized broader residual parental rights for non-custodial parents. While some might try to find a gender distinction in the minority and dissenters' views, the two women on the Court split, as did the six men who voted (4-2). Given the public outcry against judicial rejection of the popular Pledge of Allegiance, is it possible that the majority strained the standing issue to avoid having to decide a very divisive and controversial religion issue?

3. Practical and Ethical Considerations

Husband, Wife, and their two children were living in State A when Wife left because of marital difficulties. Two years later, Husband was granted a divorce in State A. He was awarded custody of the children under State A's version of the UCCJEA. Wife was served by publication because she could not be located. Wife is now living in State C. She has reconciled with the children. She has visited them several times in State A. Husband allowed the children to visit Wife in State C on several occasions. On the last visit, Wife did not return the children. Husband has petitioned the court in State C for the return of the children pursuant to his custody decree. Will State C enforce Husband's decree?

4. Bibliography

Contemporary Family Law, vol. 4, Chs. 39 & 40 (1988).
Coombs, *Interstate Child Custody: Jurisdiction, Recognition and Enforcement,* 66 Minn. L. Rev. 711, 762-64 (1982).

B. International Custody Jurisdiction

1. Background

In 1980, The Hague Conference on Private International Law adopted the Hague Convention on the Civil Aspects of International Child Abduction to confront serious problems of international child snatching. The United States is a signatory of the Convention and has implemented the convention by the enabling legislation, the International Child Abduction Remedies Act, 42 U.S.C. §11601-11610 (1994). The purposes of the Convention are to "secure the prompt return of children wrongfully removed or retained in any 'Contracting State' and to ensure that rights of custody and of access under the law of one 'Contracting State' are effectively respected in the other 'Contracting State'. The Convention applies only to a child under the age of 16, who was habitually a resident in a contracting state immediately before any breach of custody or access rights. The Convention gives jurisdiction to the court at the place of the child's habitual residence to decide the merits of the custody case, but it does not define habitual resident.

2. Statutes, Cases and Doctrine

a. *Friedrich v. Friedrich*
Emanuel Friedrich v. Jeana Michele Friedrich
78 F.3d 1060 (Sixth Cir. 1993)
Before:: KEITH, BOGGS, and SILER, Circuit Judges.
BOGGS, Circuit Judge.

For the second time, we address the application of the Hague Convention on the Civil Aspects of International Child Abduction ("the Convention") and its implementing legislation, the International Child Abduction Remedies Act ("the Act"), 42 U.S.C. ss 11601-11610, to the life of Thomas Friedrich, now age six. We affirm the district court's order that Thomas was wrongfully removed from Germany and should be returned.

I

Thomas was born in Bad Aibling, Germany, to Jeana Friedrich, an American servicewoman stationed there, and her husband, Emanuel Friedrich, a German citizen. When Thomas was two years old, his parents separated after an argument on July 27, 1991. Less than a week later, in the early morning of August 2, 1991, Mrs. Friedrich took Thomas from Germany to her family home in

Ironton, Ohio, without informing Mr. Friedrich. Mr. Friedrich sought return of the child in German Family Court, obtaining an order awarding him custody on August 22. He then filed this action for the return of his son in the United States District Court for the Southern District of Ohio on September 23. We first heard this case three years ago. *Friedrich v. Friedrich*, 983 F.2d 1396 (6th Cir.1993) ("*Friedrich I* "). At that time, we reversed the district court's denial of Mr. Friedrich's claim for the return of his son to Germany pursuant to the Convention. We outlined the relevant law on what was then an issue of first impression in the federal appellate courts, and remanded with instructions that the district court determine whether, as a matter of German law, Mr. Friedrich was exercising custody rights to Thomas at the time of removal. We also asked the district court to decide if Mrs. Friedrich could prove any of the four affirmative defenses provided by the Convention and the Act. Thomas, meanwhile, remained with his mother and his mother's parents in Ohio.

On remand, the district court allowed additional discovery and held a new hearing. The court eventually determined that, at the time of Thomas's removal on August 1, 1991, Mr. Friedrich was exercising custody rights to Thomas under German law, or would have been exercising such rights but for the removal. The court then held that Mrs. Friedrich had not established any of the affirmative defenses available to her under the Convention. The court ordered Mrs. Friedrich to return Thomas to Germany "forthwith," but later stayed the order, upon the posting of a bond by Mrs. Friedrich, pending the resolution of this appeal. [FN1*]

Mrs. Friedrich's appeal raises two issues that are central to the young jurisprudence of the Hague Convention. First, what does it mean to "exercise" custody rights? Second, when can a court refuse to return a child who has been wrongfully removed from a country because return of the abducted child would result in a "grave" risk of harm?

In answering both these questions, we keep in mind two general principles inherent in the Convention and the Act, expressed in Friedrich I, and subsequently embraced by unanimous federal authority. First, a court in the abducted-to nation has jurisdiction to decide the merits of an abduction claim, but not the merits of the underlying custody dispute. Hague Convention, Article 19; 42 U.S.C. s 11601(b)(4); Friedrich *1064 I, 983 F.2d at 1400; *Rydder v. Rydder*, 49 F.3d 369, 372 (8th Cir.1995); *Feder v. Evans-Feder*, 63 F.3d 217, 221 (3d Cir.1995); *Journe v. Journe*, 911 F.Supp. 43 (D.P.R.1995). Second, the Hague Convention is generally intended to restore the pre-abduction status quo and to deter parents from crossing borders in search of a more sympathetic court. Pub. Notice 957, 51 Fed.Reg. 10494, 10505 (1986); *Friedrich I*, 983 F.2d at 1400; *Rydder*, 49 F.3d at 372; *Feder*, 63 F.3d at 221; *Wanninger v. Wanninger*, 850 F.Supp. 78, 80 (D.Mass.1994).

II

The removal of a child from the country of its habitual residence is "wrongful" under the Hague Convention if a person in that country is, or would otherwise be, exercising custody rights to the child under that country's law at the moment of removal. Hague Convention, Article 3. The plaintiff in an action for return of the child has the burden of proving the exercise of custody rights by a preponderance of the evidence. 42 U.S.C. s 11603(e)(1)(A). We review the district court's findings of fact for clear error and review its conclusions about American, foreign, and international law de novo. ***

The district court held that a preponderance of the evidence in the record established that Mr. Friedrich was exercising custody rights over Thomas at the time of Thomas's removal. Mrs. Friedrich alleges that the district court improperly applied German law. Reviewing de novo, we find no error in the court's legal analysis. Custody rights "may arise in particular by operation of law or by reason of a judicial or administrative decision, or by reason of an agreement having legal effect under the law of the State." Hague Convention, Article 3. German law gives both parents equal de jure custody of the child, German Civil Code 1626(1), and, with a few exceptions, this de jure custody continues until a competent court says otherwise. *See Currier v. Currier*, 845 F.Supp. 916,

920 (D.N.H.1994) ("under German law both parents retain joint rights of custody until a decree has been entered limiting one parent's rights"); *Wanninger*, 850 F.Supp. at 78 (D.Mass.1994).

Mrs. Friedrich argues that Mr. Friedrich "terminated" his custody rights under German law because, during the argument on the evening of July 27, 1991, he placed Thomas's belongings and hers in the hallway outside of their apartment. The district court properly rejected the claim that these actions could end parental rights as a matter of German law. We agree. After examining the record, we are uncertain as to exactly what happened on the evening of July 27, but we do know that the events of that night were not a judicial abrogation of custody rights. Nor are we persuaded by Mrs. Friedrich's attempts to read the German Civil Code provisions stipulated to by the parties in such a way as to create the ability of one parent to terminate his or her custody rights extrajudicially. [FN2 Mrs. Friedrich cites German Civil Code s 1629, which says that a parent who exercises parental care alone can also represent the child in legal matters alone. Obviously, the ability of one parent to "represent" the child does not imply that the other parent has no custody rights. Mrs. Friedrich also cites German Civil Code s 1631, which says that the Family Court, if petitioned, can assist the parents in providing parental care. We have no idea how this provision, which is essentially no more than a grant of jurisdiction to appoint and direct a family services officer, can support Mrs. Friedrich's claim that "a German parent can certainly relinquish custody or parental rights absent a judicial determination." Defendants-Appellants' Brief at 15.] Mrs. Friedrich also argues that, even if Mr. Friedrich had custody rights under German law, he was not exercising those custody rights as contemplated by the Hague Convention. She argues that, since custody rights include the care for the person and property of the child, Mr. Friedrich was not exercising custody rights because he was not paying for or taking care of the child during the brief period of separation in Germany. The Hague Convention does not define "exercise." As judges in a common law country, we can easily imagine doing so ourselves. One might look to the law of the foreign country to determine if custody rights existed de jure, and then develop a test under the general principles of the Hague Convention to determine what activities--financial support, visitation--constitute sufficient exercise of de jure rights. The question in our immediate case would then be: "was Mr. Friedrich's single visit with Thomas and plans for future visits with Thomas sufficient exercise of custodial rights for us to justify calling the removal of Thomas wrongful?" One might even approach a distinction between the exercise of "custody" rights and the exercise of "access" or "visitation" rights. [FN3 Article 21 of the Hague Convention instructs signatory countries to protect the "rights of access" of non-custodial parents to their children. Courts have yet to address the question whether Article 21 implies that a custodial parent can remove a child from its country of habitual residence without the permission of a parent whose rights that country's courts have expressly limited to "visitation." *See infra* n. 4.] If Mr. Friedrich, who has de jure custody, was not exercising sufficient de facto custody, Thomas's removal would not be wrongful.

We think it unwise to attempt any such project. Enforcement of the Convention should not to be made dependent on the creation of a common law definition of "exercise." The only acceptable solution, in the absence of a ruling from a court in the country of habitual residence, is to liberally find "exercise" whenever a parent with de jure custody rights keeps, or seeks to keep, any sort of regular contact with his or her child.

We see three reasons for this broad definition of "exercise." First, American courts are not well suited to determine the consequences of parental behavior under the law of a foreign country. It is fairly easy for the courts of one country to determine whether a person has custody rights under the law of another country. It is also quite possible for a court to determine if an order by a foreign court awards someone "custody" rights, as opposed to rights of "access." [FN4 For a particularly difficult situation, ably resolved, *see David S. v. Zamira*, 151 Misc.2d 630, 574 N.Y.S.2d 429(Fam.Ct.1991), aff'd *In re Schneir*, 17 F.L.R. 1237 (N.Y.App.Div.2d Dep't). The court here held that an order giving the non-custodial parent visitation rights and restricting the custodial parent from leaving the country constitutes an order granting "custodial" rights to both parents under the Hague Convention.] Far more difficult is the task of deciding, prior to a ruling by a court in the abducted-from country, if a parent's custody rights should be ignored because he or she was not acting sufficiently like a custodial parent. A foreign court, if at all possible, should refrain from making such policy-oriented decisions concerning the application of German law to a child whose habitual residence is, or was, Germany.

Second, an American decision about the adequacy of one parent's exercise of custody rights is dangerously close to forbidden territory: the merits of the custody dispute. The German court in this case is perfectly capable of taking into account Mr. Friedrich's behavior during the August 1991 separation, and the German court presumably will tailor its custody order accordingly.

A decision by an American court to deny return to Germany because Mr. Friedrich did not show sufficient attention or concern for Thomas's welfare would preclude the German court from addressing these issues--and the German court may well resolve them differently.

Third, the confusing dynamics of quarrels and informal separations make it difficult to assess adequately the acts and motivations of a parent. An occasional visit may be all that is available to someone left, by the vagaries of marital discord, temporarily without the child. Often the child may be avoided, not out of a desire to relinquish custody, but out of anger, pride, embarrassment, or fear, vis a vis the other parent. [FN5 When Mrs. Friedrich took Thomas and her belongings from the family apartment on the morning of July 28, she was accompanied by some friends from work: soldiers of the United States Army. Mr. Friedrich testified that he was "intimidated" by the presence of the soldiers, and discouraged from making a stronger objection to the removal of his child.] Reading too much into a parent's behavior during these difficult times could be inaccurate and unfair. Although there may be situations when a long period of unexplainable neglect of the child could constitute non-exercise of otherwise valid custody rights under the Convention, as a general rule, any attempt to maintain a somewhat regular relationship with the child should constitute "exercise." This rule leaves the full resolution of custody issues, as the Convention and common sense indicate, to the courts of the country of habitual residence.

We are well aware that our approach requires a parent, in the event of a separation or custody dispute, to seek permission from the other parent or from the courts before taking a child out of the country of its habitual residence. Any other approach allows a parent to pick a "home court" for the custody dispute ex parte, defeating a primary purpose of the Convention. We believe that, where the reason for removal is legitimate, it will not usually be difficult to obtain approval from either the other parent or a foreign court. Furthermore, as the case for removal of the child in the custody of one parent becomes more compelling, approval (at least the approval of a foreign court) should become easier to secure.

Mrs. Friedrich argues that our approach cannot adequately cope with emergency situations that require the child and parent to leave the country. In her case, for example, Mrs. Friedrich claims that removal of Thomas to Ohio was necessary because she could no longer afford to have the child stay at the army base, and Mr. Friedrich refused to provide shelter. Examining the record, we seriously doubt that Mr. Friedrich would have refused to lodge Thomas at his expense in Germany. In any event, even if an emergency forces a parent to take a child to a foreign country, any such emergency cannot excuse the parent from returning the child to the jurisdiction once return of the child becomes safe. Nor can an emergency justify a parent's refusal to submit the child to the authority of the foreign court for resolution of custody matters, including the question of the appropriate temporary residence of the child. *See Viragh v. Foldes*, 415 Mass. 96, 612 N.E.2d 241 (1993) (child removed to America by one parent without notification to other parent may remain in America in light of decision by Hungarian court in parallel proceeding that best interests of the child require exercise of sole custody by parent in America).

We therefore hold that, if a person has valid custody rights to a child under the law of the country of the child's habitual residence, that person cannot fail to "exercise" those custody rights under the Hague Convention short of acts that constitute clear and unequivocal abandonment of the child. [FN6*] Once it determines that the parent exercised custody rights in any manner, the court should stop—completely avoiding the question whether the parent exercised the custody rights well or badly. These matters go to the merits of the custody dispute and are, therefore, beyond the subject matter jurisdiction of the federal courts. 42 U.S.C. s 11601(b)(4).

In this case, German law gave Mr. Friedrich custody rights to Thomas. The facts before us clearly indicate that he attempted to exercise these rights during the separation from his wife. Mr. and Mrs. Friedrich argued during the evening of July 27, 1991, and separated on the morning of July 28. Mrs. Friedrich left with her belongings and Thomas. She stayed on the army base with the child for four days. Mr. Friedrich telephoned Mrs. Friedrich on July 29 to arrange a visit with Thomas, and spent the afternoon of that day with his son. Mr. and Mrs. Friedrich met on August 1 to talk about Thomas and their separation. The parties dispute the upshot of this conversation. Mrs. Friedrich says that Mr. Friedrich expressed a general willingness that Thomas move to America with his mother. Mr. Friedrich denies this. It is clear, however, that the parties did agree to immediate visitations of Thomas by Mr. Friedrich, scheduling the first such visit for August 3. Shortly after midnight on August 2, Mrs. Friedrich took her son and, without informing her husband, [FN7*] left for America by airplane.

Because Mr. Friedrich had custody rights to Thomas as a matter of German law, and did not clearly abandon those rights prior to August 1, the removal of Thomas without his consent was wrongful under the Convention, regardless of any other considerations about Mr. Friedrich's behavior during the family's separation in Germany.

III

Once a plaintiff establishes that removal was wrongful, the child must be returned unless the defendant can establish one of four defenses. Two of these defenses can be established by a preponderance of the evidence, 42 U.S.C. s 11603(e)(2)(B): the proceeding was commenced more than one year after the removal of the child and the child has become settled in his or her new environment, Hague Convention, Article 12; or, the person seeking return of the child consented to or subsequently acquiesced in the removal or retention, Hague Convention, Article 13a. The other two defenses must be shown by clear and convincing evidence, 42 U.S.C. s 11603(e)(2)(A): there is a grave risk that the return of the child would expose it to physical or psychological harm, Hague Convention, Article 13b; or, the return of the child "would not be permitted by the fundamental principles of the requested State relating to the protection of human rights and fundamental freedoms," Hague Convention, Article 20. [FN8 The situation changes somewhat when the child is older. The Hague Convention allows a court in the abducted-to country to "refuse to order the return of the child if it finds that the child objects to being returned and has attained an age and degree of maturity at which it is appropriate to take account of its views." Hague Convention, Article 13]

All four of these exceptions are "narrow," 42 U.S.C. s 11601(a)(4). They are not a basis for avoiding return of a child merely because an American court believes it can better or more quickly resolve a dispute. See Rydder, 49 F.3d at 372 (citing Friedrich I, 983 F.2d at 1400). In fact, a federal court retains, and should use when appropriate, the discretion to return a child, despite the existence of a defense, if return would further the aims of the Convention. Feder, 63 F.3d at 226 (citing Pub. Notice 957, 51 Fed.Reg. 10494, 10509 (1986)).

Mrs. Friedrich alleges that she proved by clear and convincing evidence in the proceedings below that the return of Thomas to Germany would cause him grave psychological harm. Mrs. Friedrich testified that Thomas has grown attached to family and friends in Ohio. She also hired an expert psychologist who testified that returning Thomas to Germany would be traumatic and difficult for the child, who was currently happy and healthy in America with his mother. [Thomas] definitely would experience the loss of his mother ... if he were to be removed to Germany. That would be a considerable loss. And there then would be the probabilities of anger both towards his mother, who it might appear that she has abandoned him [sic], and towards the father for creating that abandonment. [These feelings] could be plenty enough springboard for other developmental or emotional restrictions which could include nightmares, antisocial behavior, a whole host of anxious-type behavior.

Blaske Deposition at 28-29.

If we are to take the international obligations of American courts with any degree of seriousness, the exception to the Hague Convention for grave harm to the child requires far more than the evidence that Mrs. Friedrich provides. Mrs. Friedrich alleges nothing more than adjustment problems that would attend the relocation of most children. There is no allegation that Mr. Friedrich has ever abused Thomas. The district court found that the home that Mr. Friedrich has prepared for Thomas in Germany appears adequate to the needs of any young child. The father does not work long hours, and the child's German grandmother is ready to care for the child when the father cannot. There is nothing in the record to indicate that life in Germany would result in any permanent harm or unhappiness.

Furthermore, even if the home of Mr. Friedrich were a grim place to raise a child in comparison to the pretty, peaceful streets of Ironton, Ohio, that fact would be irrelevant to a federal court's obligation under the Convention. We are not to debate the relevant virtues of Batman and Max und Moritz, Wheaties and Milchreis. The exception for grave harm to the child is not license for a court in the abducted-to country to speculate on where the child would be happiest. That decision is a custody matter, and reserved to the court in the country of habitual residence.

Mrs. Friedrich advocates a wide interpretation of the grave risk of harm exception that would reward her for violating the Convention. A removing parent must not be allowed to abduct a child and then--when brought to court--complain that the child has grown used to the surroundings to which they were abducted. [FN9*] Under the logic of the Convention, it is the abduction that causes the pangs of subsequent return. The disruption of the usual sense of attachment that arises during most long stays in a single place with a single parent should not be a "grave" risk of harm for the purposes of the Convention.

In thinking about these problems, we acknowledge that courts in the abducted- from country are as ready and able as we are to protect children. If return to a country, or to the custody of a parent in that country, is dangerous, we can expect that country's courts to respond accordingly. Cf. *Nunez- Escudero v. Tice-Menley*, 58 F.3d 374, 377 (8th Cir.1995) (if parent in Mexico is abusive, infant returned to Mexico for custody determination can be institutionalized during pendency of custody proceedings). And if Germany really is a poor place for young Thomas to grow up, as Mrs. Friedrich contends, we can expect the German courts to recognize that and award her custody in America. When we trust the court system in the abducted-from country, the vast majority of claims of harm--those that do not rise to the level of gravity required by the Convention--evaporate.

The international precedent available supports our restrictive reading of the grave harm exception. In *Thomson v. Thomson*, 119 D.L.R.4th 253 (Can.1994), the Supreme Court of Canada held that the exception applies only to harm "that also amounts to an intolerable situation." *Id.* at 286. The Court of Appeal of the United Kingdom has held that the harm required is "something greater than would normally be expected on taking a child away from one parent and passing him to another." *In re A.*, 1 F.L.R. 365, 372 (Eng.C.A.1988). And other circuit courts in America have followed this reasoning in cases decided since *Friedrich I.* ** Finally, we are instructed by the following observation by the United States Department of State concerning the grave risk of harm exception.

This provision was not intended to be used by defendants as a vehicle to litigate (or relitigate) the child's best interests. Only evidence directly establishing the existence of a grave risk that would expose the child to physical or emotional harm or otherwise place the child in an intolerable situation is material to the court's determination. The person opposing the child's return must show that the risk to the child is grave, not merely serious. A review of deliberations on the Convention reveals that "intolerable situation" was not intended to encompass return to a home where money is in short supply, or where educational or other opportunities *1069 are more limited than in the requested State. An example of an "intolerable situation" is one in which a custodial parent sexually abuses the child. If the other parent removes or retains the child to safeguard it against further victimization, and the abusive parent then petitions for the child's return under the Convention, the court may deny the petition. Such action would protect the child from being returned to an "intolerable situation" and subjected to a grave risk of psychological harm. Public Notice 957, 51 FR 10494, 10510 (March 26, 1986) (emphasis added).

For all of these reasons, we hold that the district court did not err by holding that "[t]he record in the instant case does not demonstrate by clear and convincing evidence that Thomas will be exposed to a grave risk of harm." Although it is not necessary to resolve the present appeal, we believe that a grave risk of harm for the purposes of the Convention can exist in only two situations. First, there is a grave risk of harm when return of the child puts the child in imminent danger prior to the resolution of the custody dispute--e.g., returning the child to a zone of war, famine, or disease. Second, there is a grave risk of harm in cases of serious abuse or neglect, or extraordinary emotional dependence, when the court in the country of habitual residence, for whatever reason, may be incapable or unwilling to give the child adequate protection. Psychological evidence of the sort Mrs. Friedrich introduced in the proceeding below is only relevant if it helps prove the existence of one of these two situations. [FN10 The only other circuit addressing the issue had its own doubts about whether a psychological report concerning the difficulty that a child would face when separated from the abducting parent is ever relevant to a Hague Convention action. *Nunez-Escudero*, 58 F.3d at 378 (such reports are not per se irrelevant, but they are rarely dispositive).] ***

b. Notes and Questions

1) *Friedrich* Notes

Friedrich has been a very influential precedent, cited by over 300 courts and commentators. Most, but not all, agree with its high standard of "grave harm." The polymath Judge Posner of the Seventh Circuit distinguished *Friedrich* in *Van de Sande v. Van de Sande*, 431 F.3d 567, 571 (7th Cir. 2005), noting that the characterization of the claim of grave risk as

> "alleg[ing] nothing more than adjustment problems that would attend the relocation of most children" . . . [is dictum] but we do not think it correct. . . . To give a father custody of children who are at great risk of harm from him, on the ground that they will be protected by the police of the father's country, would be to act on an unrealistic premise. The rendering court must satisfy itself that the children will in fact, and not just in legal theory, be protected if returned to their abuser's custody.

2) Other Cases

Recent U. S. cases involve interpreting the Convention's defenses (exceptions) to the return of the child. The courts have usually construed these exceptions narrowly so that most children are returned to the parent in the foreign country. *See* Elrod & Spector, *infra*. There is some concern that the Convention is used by abusers. Women, who are fleeing abuse and take the child with them to another country, often return to the abuser when the child is ordered to be returned. An exception to returning the child if the child would be in grave risk applies only to the child. *Nunez-Escudero v. Tice-Menley*, 58 F.3d 374 (8th Cir. 1995) (mother alleges she was physically, verbally, and sexually abused by the father, but court found no evidence that the child would be placed in grave danger if returned, only the mother would be. The exception of grave risk of harm applies the child.); *Croll v. Croll*, 66 F. Supp. 554 (S.D.N.Y. 1999) (mother alleges being repeatedly assaulted by the father, but court held no evidence that the child would be placed in grave harm if returned); *contra Walsh v. Walsh*, 221 F.3d 201(1st Cir. 2000) (Spousal abuse is a possible grave risk of harm under the Convention; lower court "inappropriately discounted the grave risk of physical and psychological harm to children in cases of spousal abuse. *Id*. at 219.) *See* Nelson and Weiner, *infra*.

3) International Kidnaping Crime Act, 18 U.S.C.A. §1204 (West 1997)

This Act makes the international kidnaping of a child under the age of 16 a crime when a person, with the intent to obstruct the lawful exercise of parental rights, removes a child from the United States or retains a child outside the United States who has been in the United States. There are affirmative defenses including fleeing from domestic violence. Penalties include fines and/or imprisonment for not more than three years.

3. Practical and Ethical Considerations

a. When a Signatory Fails to Abide by the Act

When a signatory fails to abide by the act, what should other signatories do?

4. Bibliography

D. Marianne Blair & Merle H. Weiner, Family Law in the World Community (2003).

Linda D. Elrod & Robert G. Spector, *A Review of the Year in Family Law: Redefining Families, Reforming Custody Jurisdiction, and Refining Support Issues*34 Fam. L. Q. 607 (2001).

Marilyn Freeman, *Rights of Custody and Access Under the Hague Child Abduction Convention–"A Questionable Result?"*, 31 Cal. W. Int'l L. J. 39 (2000).

Rania Nanos, Note, *The Views of a Child: Emerging Interpretation and Significance of the Child's Objection Defense Under the Hague Child Abduction Convention*, 22 Brook. J. Int't L. 437 (1996).

Sharon C. Nelson, Note, *Turning Our Backs on the Children: Implications of Recent Decisions Regarding The Hague Convention on International Child Abduction*2001 U. Ill. L. Rev. 669.

Barbara Stark, International Family Law: An Introduction (2005).

Merle H. Weiner, *International Child Abduction and the Escape from Domestic Violence*, 69 Fordham L. Rev. 593 (2002).

33 N. Y. U. J. Int'l L. & Pol., *Symposium Issue Celebrating Twenty Years: The and Promise of the 1980 Hague Convention on the Civil Aspects of International Child Abduction*(Fall 2000).

CHAPTER 33

The Consequences of Divorce for Children; Historical Child Custody Standards

A. CONSEQUENCES OF DIVORCE FOR CHILDREN

1. Background

Custody issues arise not only in divorce cases but also in paternity cases, guardianship cases, adoption, child abuse, child protection, and child neglect cases. Divorce, however, has had a dramatic effect on the number of custody cases. At common law and during America's colonial period, there were few custody cases because there were few divorces. Unmarried fathers did not have parental rights. With the continuing liberalizing of divorce grounds beginning in the nineteenth century and ending with the present no fault divorce grounds, divorce cases with children have increased. With the increase in divorce, social and psychological studies have begun to focus on the effect of divorce on these children.

a. A Child's Perspective

"My folks didn't like me, so they're getting a divorce" - Devan, age 5.
"I'm trying to be as good as I can. Maybe that will help them be happy with each other." -Emma, age 10.
"I'm scared. I know something is going on, but no one will tell me anything. . . . I feel like a monster is going to jump out of the closet or a bomb is going to drop." - Missy, age 12.
"Mom are Dad are working really hard at making their separation okay for us kids. But it isn't okay. Dad looks lonely in his new apartment. And I don't like taking out the garbage at Mom's house. Dad used to do that." - Hillary, age 14.
"When I was younger, I used to dream that Mom and Dad would get back together again. I remember trying to put their hands together as if that would glue them to each other and, of course, me." -Chelsea, age 15.

Julia Thorne, *infra,* at 8, 10, 21, 26, 46, 51, 61,74, and 132.

b. Snapshots of What Divorce Means for Children

All of the adults I interviewed felt the divorce [of their parents] in their childhoods had altered or atrophied their prospects for full and happy marital relations. Many said they had determined in their youth that they would have no children of their own -- had even made that a condition of marriage in later years. Even at forty or fifty years of age and beyond, these former 'divorced kids' were fearful of commitment, uncertain as to their ability to maintain enduring relationships. Some, divorced themselves, specifically blamed their parents for their own marital failures;

they "rushed into marriage to find the emotional security I missed at home" or they had "been conditioned to believe there was no permanence in marriage."

Not one adult in my sample, at any age, regarded the separation of their parents as irrelevant to their own well-being. Most described the event as the most traumatic of their lives (and, astonishingly for me, the sample included some men and women who'd endured much of the worst that World War II had to offer). Moreover for these adults, memories of the separation and subsequent events were as sharp, clear and painful as yesterday's visit to the dentist

Warner Troyer, Divorced Kids 146 (1979) (based on interviews with kids of divorce).

Most divorces occur among middle-class families. And the middle class climate of confidence is extremely important to democratic societies. "People without confidence in a secure tomorrow have no reason to plan or save, invest or organize, vote or obey the more irksome strictures of law. And divorced kids have less confidence than others in social institutions. The one most sacred and precious to them has failed, and this can't help but have an impact on their relationships with other community institutions. If the implied parental promise 'I will always be here to help you, comfort you, support you . . .' can't be trusted, why should these kids believe journalists, teachers, politicians, clergymen?

We're fast approaching the time when half our society will comprise grown-up divorced kids. We need to think about the consequences of that for us all, because people who expect too little aren't much good at contributing, either. Realism and scepticism . . . can be blunted by a false notion that disappointment is the necessary end of every human endeavor. And apathy, a disease which many of our children have caught, can kill the body politic. Our children need to see our faith in the new beginnings and the endurance of hope. They need, too, an understanding of the continuing dependability of parental love and support.

Divorced kids' faith in other people has been eroded and we have to rebuild it. . . . Divorced kids need demonstrations that marriage can work, that adults often have loving and fulfilling relationships. They need to be persuaded that the failure of a single marriage does not demonstrate the inability of adults to have an enduring and satisfying relationship.

Id. at 174-175 (1979).

In the situation of a broken marriage, the father's visits, no matter how arranged, can never be equivalent to living under the same roof. Nothing can substitute for the daily contact, gestures of affection, firm training, and available attention when the child wants to talk about what he is doing, thinking, and feeling.

Evelyn Miller Berger, Triangle: The Betrayed Wife 144 (1971).

c. Rediscovering the Harm of Divorce and the Advantages of Marriage for Children

As Barbara Dafoe Whitehead has noted in chapter four of her disturbingly insightful book, *The Divorce Culture* (1996), concern about the effects of divorce on the children historically were one of the main reasons for avoiding divorce. People stayed together "for the sake of the children." There was, however, a substantial shift in social attitudes in the 1960s and 1970s. By the 1970s, many commentators, writers and counselors were advocating that divorce was not harmful to children, that children were resilient and would bounce back from any temporary detriment resulting from divorce, and that divorce actually was good for children. At least, they argue that divorce is better for children than for them to grow up in a home where the parents do not fully love each other, are constantly quarreling and unhappy. Some offered what William J. Dougherty called "psychological trickle down" - that if the parents were happier, the children would be happier, therefore divorce to achieve parental happiness was good for children. That kind of advice fit the philosophy of the day and became very popular.

Then, in the 1980s, a wave of empirical research about the effects of divorce on children appeared. The evidence mounted that divorce caused economic deprivation for children of divorce. Studies showed that many children did not just "bounce back". Compared to children in intact families, they did more poorly in school, engaged in higher rates of drug use, alcohol use, premarital sex, and juvenile delinquency. Then psychological studies began to surface showing the tremendous trauma of divorce for children, trauma that did not disappear in some cases. As young adults they were less trusting and more afraid of commitment, more often (than children of intact families) turning to temporary, nonmarital liaisons.

The evidence now is quite compelling that divorce is harmful for children. While children can be, and often are, raised to become wonderful, contributing, exemplary members of society by single parents, the dual-parent family generally provides the most promising environment for healthy emotional and moral development of children. The emotional strain on children of divorce may be severe.

> There is extensive literature testifying to the generally negative consequences of marital disruption for the children of the disrupted family. . . ." The emotional consequences of marital failure for children may include mourning, grief, anger, fantasy, withdrawal, loyalty conflicts, regression, impaired academic functioning, and lowered self-esteem.
>
> [T]he emotional trauma as well as the economic strains of divorce create very dramatic changes in the lives of children. Their custodial mothers are often forced into exhausting schedules which diminish the time and emotional energy available for the children. Contrary to popular myth, rarely do such children receive compensatory care and attention from other adult relatives. Often a divorce is followed by a residential move away from familiar neighborhoods, friends, and schools. These substantial external changes, significant causes of stress in themselves, are exacerbated by the fact that they are occurring simultaneously with the child's emotional separation from one parent. The emotional impact on the child can be overwhelming.   One of the most disturbing consequences of divorce for children is that the resulting interpersonal problems, modeled after the behavior of their stress-ridden parents, are carried into adulthood. "One consequence is readily measured. Children who experience the early disruption of parental contact--whether through divorce, separation, or death--are among the very ones who, upon maturation will contribute in increased numbers to the ranks of those who encounter personal difficulties." And despite their earnest determination not to inflict upon their own children the trauma they underwent when their parents' marriage failed "they may be compelled to repeat it," says Dr. Ner Littner, director of the child

therapy program at the Chicago Institute for Psychoanalysis. Based on his own clinical experience and that of others, he says these children often unconsciously seek out and marry people whom they will subsequently divorce; then, to their horror, they find themselves hurting their own children the same way they were hurt. He believes that fewer than half of the children of divorced parents will be free enough to choose partners who will help them break the cycle.

Lynn D. Wardle, *infra*, 32-34.

Perhaps the first detrimental consequence of divorce for children that researchers have noted was the disastrous economic effects upon children. Numerous studies have shown that children in single-parent families are many times more likely to be living in poverty than children living with both a mother and a father. The National Commission on Children reported in 1992 that "[c]hildren who live with only one parent, usually their mothers, are six times as likely to be poor as children who live with both parents." National Commission at 253. *See also* (66.3% of all children living with mothers who had never married were living below the poverty line, compared to only 10.6% of children living in two-parent families in 1993). ("[A]ccording to William Galston, ... child poverty rates today would be one-third lower if family structure had not changed so dramatically since 1960. Fifty-one percent of the increase in child poverty observed during the 1980's is attributable to changes in family structure during that period."); Eggebeen at 806-07; *id*. (nearly 60% of the rise in child poverty during the 1980s is attributable to the increase in single-parent families).

In addition to the private economic distress for children resulting from divorce are a host of non-economic problems that disproportionately afflict children of divorce. Children from broken homes are two to three times more likely to have behavioral and psychological problems as teenagers than children from intact homes. Zill, *infra*. *See also* Sara McLanahan & Gary Sandefur, *infra*. Separation of children from their fathers (the usual consequence of divorce for children) has been described as "the engine driving our most urgent social problems, from crimes to adolescent pregnancy to child abuse to domestic violence against women." Blankenhorn, *infra* at 1. Children in single-parent families exhibit higher teen-childbirth rates. *See id.* at 66. Children growing up in single-parent households are at a significantly increased risk for drug abuse as teenagers. Denton & Kampfe, *infra*. It has been reported that even after controlling for such factors as low income, "children growing up in single-parent households are at a greater risk for experiencing a variety of behavioral and educations problems, including . . . smoking, drinking, early and frequent sexual experience, and in extreme cases, drugs, suicide, vandalism, violence, and criminal acts." Urie Bronfenbrenner, *infra*. "In New York City, . . . two of every three teen-age suicides are from a broken home. English studies, in 1978, reported children of divorce have shorter life expectancy, higher mortality rates, more illness, and earlier school-leaving than youngsters from intact families." Troyer, at 15. Lack of parental time and direction is a common affliction of children of divorce and out-of-wedlock birth. Children being raised by single parents are at exacerbated risk for "hyperactivity and withdrawal; lack of attentiveness in the classroom; difficulty in deferring gratification; impaired academic achievement; school misbehavior; absenteeism; [and] dropping out of school," to mention just a few problems. Pittman at 265. Parental divorce is associated with many emotional problems for children, including problems with self-esteem and difficulties with social relationships. *See* Furstenburg, *infra*; Amato, *infra*. Moreover, the relationship between juvenile (especially male) criminal behavior and family breakdown of dysfunction has long been known. According to a 1990 study commissioned by the Progressive Policy Institute, the "relationship between crime and one-parent families" is "so strong that controlling for family configuration erases the relationships between race and crime and between low income and crime." *Id.* at 31. The likelihood that a young male "will engage in criminal activity doubles if he is raised without a father, and triples if he lives in a neighborhood with a high concentration of single-parent families." M. Anne Hill & June O'Neill, *infra*. Seventy percent of juveniles and young adults currently serving sentences in long-term correctional facilities did not grow up in a two-parent home. Allen J. Beck et al., U.S. Dep't of Justice, Survey of Youth in Custody, 1987, Bureau of Justice Statistics Special Report (1988).

In a study published in the Journal of Adolescence in 2001, researchers from the University of Utrecht report that family life experience is a more potent predictor of whether young adults can find and hold jobs than formal education. Reviewing data from a national sample of 955 non-school-attending young adults between 18 and 27 years old, the researchers discovered that "family factors are more important of youth employment than are the classic variables," including formal education. Acknowledging several possible explanations, the Utrecht scholars suggested that "parental divorce...may increase the likelihood that children will not learn adaptive interpersonal skills, such as how to reach compromise and communication and communicate effectively. This, in turn, handicaps their job prospects." Martijn de Goede, et al., infra.

In some cases, the ameliorative effects of divorce may outweigh and justify the risk of those serious problems for the children of the divorcing couple. (For example, Paul Amato and Allan Booth estimate that parental divorces end up being better for the children in about 1/4 to 1/3 of the cases, while in 2/3 to 3/4 of the cases the children would be better off if the parents did not divorce.) *See* Amato & Booth, *infra*.

d. Longitudinal Studies

Judith Wallerstein's Longitudinal Studies. Among the most informative and highly-regarded studies of the effects of divorce on children have been performed by Dr. Judith S. Wallerstein, a psychologist in suburban northern California. She began her studies in 1971 by interviewing sixty divorcing families in Marin County, with 131 children and their 120 divorcing parents. The group studied were relatively homogenous, middle-class suburban Americans who had been screened to eliminate persons with pre-existing mental health problems or vulnerabilities. The families were relatively well-off; one-fourth of the fathers were professionals. Her research was originally intended to last for one year. Her assumptions reflected the prevailing beliefs that "normal, healthy people would be able to work out their problems following divorce in about one year's time." Judith S. Wallerstein & Sandra Blakeslee, *Second Chances* x-xxi (1989) (hereinafter "Second Chances").

What Wallerstein discovered, however, was just the opposite of what she had expected. The pain and problems associated with marital failure persisted for many adults and children. Her follow up interviews, twelve-to-eighteen months after divorce, "found most families still in crisis. Their wounds were wide open. . . . Many adults still felt angry, humiliated, and rejected, and most had not gotten their lives back together. An unexpectedly large number of children were on a downward course. Their symptoms were worse than before. Their behavior at school was worse. Their peer relationships were worse." *Id.* She found that "[t]here was a whole group of youngsters who did not believe the divorce was really happening until a year or so later. . . . A third of the younger children did not believe what they were told" *Id.* Only after a year or so did the reality of the divorce sink in, causing these young children tremendous despair.

Wallerstein's initial report of her findings generated a fair amount of hostility and disbelief from lawyers, therapists, and divorced parents who were convinced that divorce did not have significant, long-lasting detrimental effects. *Id.* Nonetheless, Wallerstein extended the study.

After five years Wallerstein interviewed in depth the children and parents again. She found that "[f]ive years after divorce, one-third of the children were clearly doing well and were maintaining good relationships with both parents, who no longer fought with such high intensity. . . . Some were better off than they had been during the failing marriage." But, she also found a larger group of children "well over one-third of the whole group -- who were significantly worse off than before. They were clinically depressed and not doing well in school or with friends. They had deteriorated to the point that some early disturbances, such as sleep problems, poor learning, or acting out, had become chronic." *Id.* They were still "intensely angry" at their parents for divorcing (giving priority to their adult needs over their children's needs). *Id.* Yet, amazingly, she found that after five years, most of children still were hoping that their parents would reconcile.

Wallerstein continued her studies and conducted in-depth follow-up interviews with the 131 children and both of their parents ten years and again fifteen years after divorce. The results, again, were deeply disturbing. Half of the children whose parents had divorced had seen their father or mother get another divorce in the decade following the first divorce. Half of them were living in families where the divorced parents were still angry at each other. One-fourth had experienced a severe and continuing drop in their standard of living. Sixty percent of the children felt rejected by at least one parent. Very few had been helped financially in college by their noncustodial parent. "Many of the children emerged in young adulthood as compassionate, courageous and competent people." *Id.* at 295-398. However, a decade after divorce "almost half of the children entered adulthood as worried, underachieving, self-deprecating, and sometimes angry young men and women." *Id.* Wallerstein found that boys initially had a harder time coping with divorce than girls, "suffering a wide range of difficulties in school achievements, peer relationships, and the handling of aggression, [but] this disparity in overall adjustment eventually dissipated." *Id.* However, for young women there was a very dangerous "'sleeper effect" that manifested itself on the threshold of young adulthood, especially when a serious relationship with a young man was developing. Then "many found themselves struggling with anxiety and guilt" that "led to many maladaptive pathways, including multiple relationships and impulsive marriages that ended in early divorce." *Id.* "[A]s these young men and women faced the development task of establishing love and intimacy, . . . they felt the lack of a template for a loving, enduring, and moral relationship between a man and a woman" and that "threatened to bar the young people's ability to create new, enduring families of their own." A decade after the divorce, close to one-half of the boys (then 19 to 29 years old) were "unhappy, lonely and [had] few if any lasting relationships with women.... One out of three young men and one out of ten young women between the ages 19 and 23 at the ten-year mark [were] delinquent, meaning they act[ed] out their anger in a range of illegal activities, including assault, burglary, arson, drug dealing, theft, drunk driving and prostitution." *Id..*

Wallerstein continued her research, and has now presented the findings of her twenty-five year follow-up interviews with 85% of here original group of 131 children and both parents. As the title of her recently-published report suggests, her study shows convincingly that divorce has long-term detrimental effects, especially for children. Judith S. Wallerstein & Julia Lewis, *infra.* Twenty-five years after divorce, the "core memories" of the youngest children of divorce (approximately 65 children who were 2 ½-to-6 years-old at the time of divorce) are of "an abrupt, sudden diminution of nurturance and protection -- the disappearance of one parent, and the absence of the other over many hours of the day and evening." *Id.* at 370. At the time of divorce these young children had been "terrified that they would be abandoned by both parents. They had concluded that if one parent could leave another, both could surely leave the child." *Id.* Their post-divorce lives had been much as they had feared. "[O]ne after another of these young people," then between 27 and 32 years-old, "spoke sadly of their lost childhood. They described their sadness, their helpless anger, their yearning for someone to take care of them, someone to talk to and play with. This diminished nurturance and protection . . . is their legacy as children of divorce." *Id.* at 370-371. Children who witnessed violence still had "vivid recall" of the violence that had occurred more than a quarter-century earlier. One young woman, 29-years old, still suffers from recurrent nightmares of a violent scene of which she no longer has any conscious memory. *Id.* at 371. The adolescence of these children of divorce had been filled with "emotional hungers, . . . loneliness, . . . lowered expectations" that left them particularly vulnerable during adolescence to the lure of drugs, alcohol and teenage sexual activity. Half of these youth reported being involved in "serious drug and alcohol abuse" as teens, and sexual activity started early, particularly for the girls. *Id.* Some youth ran away or left home because of unfair discipline or neglect resulting from a mother's remarriage to a estranged stepfather. "The intensity of their anger 10 years later was undiminished." *Id.* at 378.

Adulthood "began painfully and precipitously" for these young children of divorce. *Id.* at 372. College education was a strain because less than ten percent received full financial support from their parents or stepparents for college education. One-half of these children ended their educations with less education than their parents had achieved at the same age and only three (less than five percent) had exceeded their parent's education. *Id.* at 373. Forty percent fell below their parents socioeconomic level (for example one 29-year-old college graduate whose mother managed an art gallery and whose father was a lawyer, was a waitress and teacher's aide). *Id.* at 374. These young people "worried . . . almost constantly" about marriage and forming their own families, harboring great fears about their ability to keep a marriage together and about inflicting upon their children what they had suffered. *Id.* at 379. One-fourth of these young adults tried to avoid relationships of intimacy entirely.

Dr. Wallerstein explains that, unlike the adult divorce experience, "the child's suffering does not reach its peak at the breakup and then level off. [Rather, for children], divorce is a cumulative experience . . . . Its impact increases over time. At each developmental stage, the impact is experienced anew and in different ways. . . . the effect of the parents' divorce is played and replayed throughout the first three decades of the children's lives. . . . And many children, who are able to traverse earlier states successfully, go under at a later developmental stage . . . . " *Id.* at 380-81. She notes: "[A]fter 25 years, our jury is no longer out. The children who were rendered mute by the system have returned to give us their verdict." *Id.* at 369. "Many did not feel protected by their parents or by the legal system." *Id.* at 381. "Many felt trapped. . . . They worried themselves sick . . . ." *Id.* at 382.

Dr. Judith S. Wallerstein's most recent work, *The Unexpected Legacy of Divorce: A 25-Year Landmark Study* (Hyperion 2000), with co-authors Dr. Julia M. Lewis and Sandra Blakeslee, focuses on the children as they became adults and were grappling with the negative effects of divorce, such as loneliness and anxiety, especially over love and commitment.

e. Marvis Hetherington's Longitudinal Study

Another recently reported longitudinal study is the 30-year study of 1400 families, roughly half divorced and half not divorced, in the state of Virginia, including 2500 children, by Dr. E. Marvis Hetherington, the distinguished and highly regarded emeritus professor of psychology at the University of Virginia. The findings of this study are reported in *For Better or For Worse: Divorce Reconsidered* (Norton 2002) by Dr. Hetherington and co-author, John Kelly. When this study began, some of these children were in nursery school and are now going through their own divorces. The families in Hetherington's study are similar to those in Dr. Wallerstein's study: mostly white, middle-class families. Dr. Hetherington's methodology of conducting the study differed in some respects. While Dr. Wallerstein personally interviewed all of the children in her study, Dr. Hetherington was assisted by a number of researchers. Dr. Hertherington also ranked damage caused by divorce according to a standardized instrument of social-science pathologies.

Dr. Hetherington's book frames her findings in the positive possibilities of divorce for women, men and children. As to the children of divorce, her findings are, nevertheless, similar to Dr. Wallerstein's findings. Twenty to twenty-five per cent of children from divorced families as compared to 10 per cent from non-divorced families did have serious social, emotional, or psychological problems. Hence, on the positive side, as Dr. Hetherington emphasizes, 75 to 80 per cent of children were functioning normally. The children's divorce rate was about double the rate of divorce of children from low-conflict intact families, but a higher rate than children reared in unhappy intact families. The study also found that 20 years later, about two-third of sons and three-quarters of daughters had poor relations with their fathers as compared to 30 percent of children from intact families.

f. Other Studies Showing Harm to Children

University of Chicago Demographer Linda J. Waite, former President of the Population Association of America, asserts that children of divorce or without fathers in their home are at the greatest risk of crime, child abuse, premarital sex, premarital pregnancy, poverty, lower education and get poorer performance in school and less career success. Waite & Gallagher, *infra*, at 124-134.

Professor Nicholas Wolfinger of the University of Utah reports that "[p]arental divorce affects every important aspect of offspring behavior in intimate relationships: marriage timing; partner selection; the stability of first and subsequent marriages; and behavior in nonmarital cohabiting relationships." Wolfinger, *infra*, at 107. Further: "Parental divorce increases the incidence of premature teenage sexual activity, which in turn leads to teenage marriage. . . . At age eighteen, for instance, 1994 General Social Survey (GSS) respondents from divorced families have marriage rates 27 percent higher than their peers from intact families. . . ." *Id.* at 108. Also, "[i]lf both spouses come from divorced families, the marriage becomes over 200 percent [3x] more likely to fail than a marriage between people who did not grow up in divorced families." *Id.* at 110. "Past age twenty, the children of divorce now have lower overall marriage rates . . . ." *Id.* at 112. And parental divorce even decreases the likelihood that the offspring will marry their cohabiting partners. *Id.* at 115.

Studies of IQ development in children clearly show that family structure is a definite "risk factor" for poor IQ development. "Family status is especially critical . . . because two-parent families are much more likely than single-parent families to have higher income and higher parenting scores." Armon, *infra*, at 92. "[F]amily structure has the largest indirect effect on IQ, 1.7 points through the parenting behaviors. That is, that since family structure has sizable effects on cognitive stimulation and emotional support, and these in turn have strong effects on a child's IQ, the effect of two-parent families in raising parenting scores leads to an additional gain of 1.7 in a child's IQ. . . . [T]he total effect on IQ of two-parent family versus never married single mother including indirect effects . . . is more than three points." *Id.* at 97.

A study of 26 years of scholarly articles published in the prestigious *Journal of Marriage and Family* about the effects of divorce on children "found strong evidence for increased concern about negative family structure effects on children" among family scholars, and the "concerned views clearly became more prevalent" and "outweighed sanguine ones throughout the last 20 years covered by the study." Glenn & Sylvester, *infra*.

Professor Robert Emery reviewing the literature on divorce summarized five major consequences for children:

> First, divorce creates a number of stressors for children and families, such as separation and loss of contact with one parent; potentially troubled relationships with each parent; and involvement in conflict between both parents. Divorce also causes considerable financial hardship for children, families and society . . . .
> Second, the stressors associated with divorce can lead to adjustment problems among children . . . [and] divorce is a risk factor for a number of children's social, psychological, and educational or occupational difficulties. Third, despite the increase in risk, *resilience* is the normative outcome of divorce for children, that is, most children from divorced families function as well as children from married

families . . . . Fourth, there nevertheless appear to be some subtle costs of coping with divorce for children. Most children are resilient, but they experience and express much subclinical distress or "pain" about the past, present, and future in relation to their parents' divorce.

Fifth . . ., there are important individual differences in the psychological adjustment of children following a parental divorce . . . .

Emery, *infra* at 3-4.

In *Between Two Worlds*, Elizabeth Marquardt, a scholar affiliated with the Institute of American Values reports her study of 1500 people ages 18-to-35, all of whose parents divorced before age 14 and had maintained contact with both parents. She concludes that even in a "good" divorce the children faced certain emotional strains that children in

two-parent homes did not. *See* Marquardt, *infra*.

2. Statutes, Cases and Doctrines

Omitted.

3. Practical and Ethical Considerations

Should there be a stricter requirement for divorce when children are involved? Is it accurate that more divorces occur in middle class homes? Or, is it easier to use the middle class for these types of studies? In light of these studies, does the attorney advising a client who has minor children and who is contemplating a divorce, have any obligation to advise the client to seek family counseling?

4. Bibliography

Paul R. Amato, *Children's Adjustment to Divorce: Theories, Hypothesis, and Empirical Support*, 55 J. Marriage and the Family 23 (1993).

Paul Amato & Allan Booth, A Generation at Risk: Growing Up in an Era of Family Upheaval (1997).

David J. Armor, Maximizing Intelligence (2003).

Evelyn Miller Berger, Triangle: The Betrayed Wife (1971).

David Blankenhorn, Fatherless America: Confronting Our Most Urgent Social Problem 1 (1995).

Urie Bronfenbrenner, *Discovering What Families Can Do* in David Blankenhorn,et al. eds., Rebuilding the Nest: A New Commitment to the American Family (1990).

William J. Doherty, *The Best of Times and the Worst of Times: Fathering as a Contested Arena of Academic Discourse*, in Generative Fathering: Beyond Deficit Perspectives 217 (Alan J. Hawkins & David C. Dollahite eds., 1997).

Rhonda E. Denton & Carlene M. Kampfe, *The Relationship Between Family Variable and Adolescent Substance Abuse: A Literature Review*, 114 Adolescence 475 (1994).

Robert E. Emery, *Postdivorce Family Life for Children*, in The Postdivorce Family (Ross A. Thompson & Paul R. Amato, eds., 1999).

Norval Glenn & Thomas Sylvester, *Trends in Scholarly Writing on Family Structure Since 1977 in the* Journal of Marriage and Family, available at http://www.familyscholarslibrary.org/content/readingrooms/shift/.

Martijn de Goede et al., "Family Problems and Youth Unemployment," Adolescence 35 (2000): cited in

David J. Eggebeen & Daniel T. Lichter, Race, Family Structure, and Changing Poverty Among American Children, 56 Am. Soc. Rev. 801 (1991).

Frank F. Furstenburg & Andrew Cherlin, Divided Families: What Happens to Children When Parents Part 56 (Cambridge, MA; Harvard Univ. Press, 1991).

E. Mavis Hetherington & John Kelly, For Better or For Worse: Divorce Reconsidered (Norton 2002).

M. Annie Hill & June O'Neill, Underclass Behaviors in the United States, Measurement and Analysis of Determinants (New York, City University of New York, 1993).

Sara McLanahan & Gary Sandefur, Growing Up with a Single Parent (1994).

Elizabeth Marquardt, Between Two Worlds: The Inner Lives of Children of Divorce (2005).

National Comm'n on Children, Beyond Rhetoric: A New American Agenda for Children and Families (1992).

National Center for Health Statistics, Publication #100, Advance Data (1990).

Frank Pittman, Private Lies, Infidelity and the Betrayal of Intimacy (1989).

Julia Thorne, A Change of Heart, Words of Experience and Hope for the Journey Through Divorce (Harper Perennial 1996).

Warner Troyer, Divorced Kids (1979).

Linda J. Waite & Maggie Gallagher, The Case for Marriage (2000).

Judith S. Wallerstein & Sandra Bladeslee, Second Chances.

Judith S. Wallerstein, Julia Lewis & Sandra Blakesley, The Unexpected Legacy of Divorce (2000).

Judith S. Wallerstein & Julia Lewis, *The Long-Term Impact of Divorce on Children*, 36 Fam. & Concil. Crt. Rev. 368 (1998).

Lynn D. Wardle, *Rethinking Marital Age Restrictions*, 22 J. Fam. L. 1 (1983).

Barbara Dafoe Whitehead, The Divorce Culture (1996).

World Congress of Families, Update Online, July 24, 2001 Vol 2, Issue 29, at <http://www.worldcongress.org/WCF/wcf_update.htm>.

Nicholas H. Wolfinger, Understanding The Divorce Cycle, The Children of Divorce in Their Own Marriages (2005).

Nicholas Zill & Charlotte A. Schoenborn, Developmental, Learning, and Emotional Problems: Health of Our Nation's Children, United States, 1988.

B. HISTORICAL CHILD CUSTODY STANDARDS

1. Background

a. Historical Custody

At common law, the father of a child was legally entitled to custody "for a mother, as such, is entitled to no power, but only to reverence and respect . . . ." 1 W. Blackstone, *infra* at 453. By the eighteenth century the long-established common law right of fathers to custody of their legitimate children began to be challenged. Initially the challenges were from third parties and in most instances the father lost because he was either failing to support his children, had physically abused them, or had voluntarily relinquished their custody to others. Simultaneously, some courts were beginning to recognize the parental rights of mothers of legitimate children, usually in cases against third parties (typically testamentary guardians appointed by deceased fathers). However, when the first custody case between two arguably fit parents of a legitimate child arose, the court affirmed as a rule of law the father's custody right, except in cases where the child was in physical danger. That standard was harsher than the one applied when third parties challenged fathers. One scholar has reviewed the English inter-spousal custody cases between 1804 and 1839 and reports that each time a mother was the plaintiff she lost. The courts created a custody rule that was so rigidly patriarchal that parliament had to step in and establish the custody rights of innocent mothers, though it was two more decades before that rule was judicially supported. *See generally* Danaya C. Wright, *infra*.

b. Tender Years Doctrine

Courts of equity felt obliged to act in fulfillment of their *parens patriae* responsibility to protect the "best interests of the child," and this standard eventually displaced the patriarchal rule. More accurately, the patriarchal rule subsided from a rule to a presumption (that it would be in the best interests of the child to be raised by father). As the Victorian Era progressed, however, the presumption underwent a major shift. In fact, it changed 180 degrees, and by the nineteenth century, courts presumed that it was in the best interests of a child, at least a child of tender years, to be in the custody of its mother. This was the origin of the "tender years" presumption, also known as the maternal preference presumption.

Initially, the maternal preference presumption was very strong. But, it began to change, and by mid-twentieth-century there were at least three variations of the tender years doctrine. The original doctrine provided that the mother of a child of tender years was always to be awarded custody unless the contesting father proved that she was totally unfit to parent. A second variation gave mothers the benefit of a presumption that they would be the best custodian of young children, but allowed the father to rebut the presumption by a substantial showing that he would be the better custodian. A third variation used the tender years presumption as a mere tie-breaker: if the evidence showed that both parents were equally fit, the court was to award custody of young children to the mother. Jones, *infra* at 699-701.

Not surprisingly, under all versions of the tender years presumption mothers were awarded custody in the great majority of the cases. (In all fairness, it should be noted that in many cases custody was essentially uncontested--personally-assumed and culturally-reinforced sex-roles were reflected in the decision of the parties that the mother *should* get custody of young children.) Thus, in the twentieth century, child custody was one area of the law where the legal rights of women were greater than those of men.

Since the gender-equality movement of the 1970's, this has changed. Fathers have claimed equal custodial rights. Today fathers may be winning custody more often than mothers. Jeff Atkin, a noted authority on child custody determinations has stated that his review of child custody reported opinions demonstrates that at least appellate courts in the late 1980's awarded custody to the father more often than to the mother. One recent study showed that West Virginia appellate courts award the mother custody in 46.9% of the reviewed cases and fathers received custody in 30.6% of the cases. To a lesser extent, mediators (but not trial courts, interestingly) "shared this gender bias. They awarded mothers custody in fifty-three percent of the cases, and fathers custody in forty-six percent of the cases." Mercer, *infra* at 132. A similar study of custody decisions in North Dakota found that "[m]others were awarded primary physical custody in 42.8% of those cases. The custody disposition was not appealed in any of those cases. Fathers were awarded custody in 28.5% of the cases. Custody was appealed in three of those cases; two dispositions were reversed and remanded and one was affirmed. Custody was split, appealed, and reversed in one case." Case Comment, *infra*, at 79. "The reported cases also confirm that some trial judges continue to observe the "tender years presumption" or otherwise persist in reflexive maternal custody orders, sometimes in the face of strong evidence of the mother's unsuitability as a custodian." The Missouri Task Force, *infra* at n.287.

2. Statutes, Cases and Doctrines

a. *Shelley v. Westbrooke*

Shelley v. Westbrooke

37 Eng. Rep. 850 (Ch. 1817)

A petition was presented in the name of the infant Plaintiffs, stating the marriage of their father and mother in the year 1811, and that they were the only issue of it; that about three years ago the father deserted his wife, and had since unlawfully cohabited with another woman; that thereupon the mother returned to the house of her father with the eldest of the infants, and the other was soon after born; that they had since that time been maintained by their mother and her father, and that their mother had lately died. It was then stated that the father avowed himself an atheist, and that since his marriage he had written and published a work, in which he blasphemously derided the truth of the Christian revelation, and denied the existence of a God as creator of the universe; and that since the death of his wife, he had demanded that the children should be delivered up to him, and that he intended, if he could, to get possession of their persons, and educate them as he thought proper. Their maternal grandfather had lately transferred £2000 4 *per cents*. Into the names of trustees, upon trust for them on their attaining twenty-one, or marrying with his consent; and in the mean time to apply the dividends for their maintenance and education.

The *Lord Chancellor* gave his judgment in writing. ***

"I have read all the papers left with me, and all the cases cited.
***

"Upon the case, as represented in the affidavits, the exhibits, and the answer, I have formed my opinion, conceiving myself according to the practice of the Court, at liberty so to form it in the case of an infant, whether the petition in its allegations and suggestions has or has not accurately presented that case to the court, and having intimated in the course of the hearing before me that I should so form my judgment.

"There is nothing in evidence before me sufficient to authorize me in thinking that this gentleman has changed, before he arrived at the age of twenty-five, the principles he avowed at nineteen. I think there is ample evidence in the papers and in conduct, that no such change has taken place.
***

"This is a case in which, as the matter appears to me, the father's principles cannot be misunderstood, in which his conduct, which I cannot but consider as highly immoral, has been established in proof, and established as the effect of those principles: conduct nevertheless, which he represents to himself and others, not as conduct to be considered as immoral, but to be recommended and observed in practice, and as worthy of approbation.

"I consider this, therefore, as a case in which the father has demonstrated that he must, and does deem it to be a matter of duty which his principles impose upon him, to recommend to those whose opinions and habits he may take upon himself to form, that conduct in some of the most important relations of life, as moral and virtuous, which the law calls upon me to consider as immoral and vicious - conduct which the law animadverts upon as inconsistent with the duties of persons in such relations of life, and which it considers as injuriously affecting both the interests of such persons and those of the community.

"I cannot, therefore, think that I should be justified in delivering over these children for their education exclusively, to what is called the care to which Mr. *S.* wishes it to be intrusted.
***

"Much has been said upon the fact that these children are of tender years. I have already explained, in the course of the hearing, the grounds upon which I think that circumstance not so material as to require me to pronounce no order.

"I add, that the attention which I have been called upon to give to the consideration, how far the pecuniary interests of these children may be affected, has not been called for in vain. I should deeply regret if any act of mine materially affects those interests. But to such interests I cannot sacrifice what I deem to be interests of greater value and higher importance.

"In what degree and to what extent the Court will interfere in this case against parental authority, cannot be finally determined till after the Master's report.

"In the mean time I pronounce the following order."

[The order restrained the father and his agents from taking possession of the persons of the infants, or intermeddling with them till further order; and it was referred to the Master, to enquire what would be a proper plan for the maintenance and education of the infants; and also to enquire with whom, and under whose care the infants should remain during their minority, or until further order.]

b. Notes

1) *Shelley v. Westbrooke*

This oft-cited case is well-known because of the celebrity status of the losing father (the poet Percy Bysshe Shelley), and the dramatic exception which the court made to the then-powerful rule that a father was entitled to custody of his children. Some people cite the case as the beginning of the erosion of the paternal preference rule in custody law and of the recognition of maternal custodial rights, but that overstates the holding and significance of the case. The custody dispute was not between the two parents but between the father and the maternal grandfather. The children's mother, Harriet Westbrook, Shelley's first wife, had committed suicide about five months earlier (apparently due in part to her husband's notorious and scandalous infidelities). Harriet had married Shelley when she was pregnant and he was only 19; they eloped to Scotland where Lord Hardwicke's Act and its age-restrictions on marriage did not apply. Less than three years later, while Harriet was pregnant with their second child, Shelley began living openly with Mary Wollstonecraft Godwin, whom he married less than two months after Harriet, again pregnant, drowned herself. A few months later in the opinion excerpted above, Chancery denied Percy custody of the two children Harriet had borne him. Just five years after he lost custody, Shelley drowned when the ship on which he was traveling sank. His second wife, Mary, was also a writer; she is best remembered for her novel, *Frankenstein,* published about a year after this case was decided.

3. Practical and Ethical Considerations

a. Tender Years Doctrine as Tie Breaker.

Some courts may still use the "tender years" doctrine as a tie breaker when both parents are equally fit to have custody. Would this application of the doctrine as a tie breaker be constitutional? Why/why not?

4. Bibliography

Case Comment, *Supreme Court Commission on Gender Fairness in the Courts,* 72 N.D. L. Rev. 1115 (1996).

Contemporary Family Law, vol. 4, Ch. 39 (1988).

Joseph Goldstein, Anna Freud and Albert Solnit, Beyond the Best Interests of the Child (1973).

Klaff, *The Tender Years Doctrine: A Defense,* 70 Cal.L.Rev. 335 (1982).

Kathryn L. Mercer, *A Content Analysis of Judicial Decision-Making – How Judges Use the Primary Caretaker Standard to Make Custody Determinations*, 5 Wm. & Mary J. Women & L. 1 (1998).

The Missouri Task Force on Gender and Justice, *1993 Report of the Missouri Task Force on Gender and Justice*, 58 Mo. L. Rev. 485 (1993).

Danaya C. Wright, DeManneville v. DeManneville: *Rethinking the Birth of Custody Law under Patriarchy*, 17 Law and Hist. Rev. 247-307 (1999).

CHAPTER 34

Contemporary Child Custody and Visitation Standards

A. CONTEMPORARY CUSTODY STANDARDS

1. Background

a. Best Interest of the Child

1) Generally

The basic legal doctrine governing child custody determinations plainly reflects the underlying policy of the law. That is, that in awarding custody, visitation, etc., the first responsibility of the court is to make orders that further the "best interests of the child." This policy is of ancient origins, traceable to the time when English courts exercised unwritten parens patriae authority to protect the dependent and vulnerable incompetent subjects of the sovereign. It is unclear in the evolution of the best interest doctrine whether the tender years doctrine evolved as a separate standard for custody or whether it evolved as part of the best interest standard as that standard was evolving in third-party cases. In the nineteenth century, when courts began replacing the paternal preference with the tender years doctrine, courts used "tender years" in terms of best interest. *Commonwealth v. Addicks*, 5 Binn. 520 (Pa. 1813) (children of tender years would be best cared by the mother). *See* L. L. LaFave, *infra*.

A few years ago, the authors of an influential book on child custody emphasized that the phrase "best interests of the child" may be too pretentious and misleading. . J. Goldstein, A. Freud & A. Solnit, *infra*. Divorce itself is rarely "in the best interests" of children, and even the most conscientious courts lack the information and resources to honestly say that their custody determinations are really in the "best interests" of the children involved. With interesting candor, the authors suggested that the standard ought to be the "least detrimental alternative" standard. While other suggestions made by these authors were widely accepted, and this suggestion provoked some discussion, it has had little effect on the language of the law or the practice of the courts. The "best interests of the child" standard not only embodies the ideals of our society for resolving custody disputes, but it still constitutes the express and official rule of decision in most states.

2) Indeterminacy of the Standard

Professor Robert Mnookin has noted the indeterminacy dilemma of the "best interests of the child" standard in the context of determining child custody disputes:

> Assume that a judge must decide whether a child should live with his mother or his father when the parents are in the process of obtaining a divorce. From the perspective of rational choice, the judge would wish to compare the expected utility for the child of living with his mother with that of living with his father. The judge would need considerable information and predictive ability to do this. The judge would also need some source for the values to measure utility for the child. All three are problematic.
>
> a. The Need for Information: Specifying Possible Outcomes
>
> In the example chosen, the judge would require information about how each parent had behaved in the past, how this behavior had affected the child, and the child's present condition. Then the judge would need to predict the future behavior and circumstances of each parent if the child were to remain with that parent and to gauge the effects of this behavior and these circumstances on the child. He would also have to consider the behavior of each parent if the child were to live with the other parent and how this might affect the child. If a custody award to one parent would require removing the child from his present circumstances, school, friends, and familiar surrounding, the judge would necessarily wish to predict the effects these changes would have on the child. These predictions would necessarily involve estimates of not only the child's mutual relationships with the custodial parent, but also his future contacts with the other parent and siblings, the probable number of visits by the noncustodial spouse, the probable financial circumstances of each of the spouses, and a myriad of other factors.
>
> One can question how often, if ever, any judge will have the necessary information. In many instances, a judge lacks adequate information about even the most rudimentary aspects of a child's life with his parents and has still less information available about what either parent plans in the future.
>
> b. Predictions Assessing the Probability of Alternative Outcomes
>
> Obviously, more than one outcome is possible for each course of judicial action, so the judge must assess the probability of various outcomes and evaluate the seriousness of possible benefits and harms associated with each. But even where a judge has substantial information about the child's past home life and the present alternatives, present-day knowledge about human behavior provides no basis for the kind of individualized predictions required by the best-interests standard. There are numerous competing theories of human behavior, based on radically different conceptions of the nature of man, and no consensus exists that any one is correct. No theory at all is considered widely capable of generating reliable predictions about the psychological and behavioral consequences of alternative dispositions for a particular child.
>
> . . . .
>
> c. Values to Inform Choice: Assigning Utilities to Various Outcomes
>
> Even if the various outcomes could be specified and their probability estimated, a fundamental problem would remain unsolved. What set of values should a judge use to determine what is in a child's best interests? If a decision-maker must assign some measure of utility to each possible outcome, how is utility to be determined?

Deciding what is best for a child poses a question no less ultimate than the purposes and values of life itself. Should the judge be primarily concerned with the child's happiness? Or with the child's spiritual and religious training? Should the judge be concerned with the economic "productivity" of the child when he grows up? Are the primary values of life in warm, interpersonal relationships, or in discipline and self-sacrifice? Is stability and security for a child more desirable than intellectual stimulation? These questions could be elaborated endlessly. And yet, where is the judge to look for the set of values that should inform the choice of what is best for the child? Normally, the custody statutes do not themselves give content or relative weights to the pertinent values. And if the judge looks to society at large, he finds neither a clear consensus as to the best child rearing strategies nor an appropriate hierarchy of ultimate values.

Mnookin, *infra*, at 255-68.

b. Presumptions Between Parents

1) Primary Caretaker Presumption

During the early 1980s, as the tender years doctrine came under attack, the primary caretaker presumption evolved to replace the tender years doctrine. The primary caretaker doctrine focuses on specific, physical care taking tasks that each parent has performed to determine which parent is the primary caretaker. Custody is awarded to the parent who has been the primary caretaker. This concept has been more popular with academia than with legislatures and courts.

2) Psychological Parent Doctrine

(*See* discussion at A.1.e.2. *infra*)

c. Joint Custody

With the rise of the no-fault-divorce, the fathers' rights movement not only attacked the tender years doctrine, but advocated that children benefitted from frequent contact with both parents. This movement was behind the passage of joint custody legislation in the 1970s. Herbert Jacob, *infra* at 136-143. Over forty states have enacted joint custody legislation. The legislation varies as to whether joint custody is a presumption, a preference, or an option. Joint custody differs from sole custody in that both parents share custody. Custody, however, involves two dimensions: physical custody and legal custody. Physical custody involves the responsibility of the day-to-day decisions regarding the child's physical care and usually of determining the child's residence. Legal custody involves the responsibility of the major decisions regarding the child. Parents may share both physical and legal custody or legal custody only or physical custody only. Joint custody requires the parents to communicate and cooperate with each other.

d. Preserving Parent-Child Relations

As social attitudes toward divorce have changed during the past 25 years, so have the policies which underlie child custody dispositions changed. When divorce was viewed in moralistic terms, the child custody dispute reflected the moralistic perspective; the contesting parties aimed to portray each other as "bad" or "unfit," and custody awards severely restricted the parental involvement of the noncustodial parent, again reflecting a moralistic-quarantine perspective. (Ironically the "boilerplate" term used to describe the remaining parental rights of the noncustodial parent was "liberal visitation.") Today, the prevailing policy is to perpetuate and encourage parent-child relations after divorce; to emphasize that divorce only means that the parties are no longer spouses, but still are parents. Fostering the parental contacts of the noncustodial parent is usually a delicate matter since it requires support and cooperation from the former marital partner. But, millions of divorced couples are able to overcome their own conflicts and work together to love and raise their children after divorce. That is the current policy and goal of this area of the law.

e. Quasi-Parents: Custody Disputes Between Parents and Nonparents

1) Parental Preference Doctrine
The parental preference doctrine may be also known as the presumption of parental custody. It is a long-established and ubiquitous general principle that the biological parents of a child will be presumed to be the best custodians of their child. Accordingly, in a child custody dispute, a natural parent generally has priority over nonparents who claim custody. The underlying policy of parental preference may emerge in procedural rules as well (e.g., standing). While this presumption or priority is not absolute, it is not lightly dismissed.   Custodial disputes between nonparent relatives and parents seem to be occurring in growing numbers. The contexts in which the disputes arise are many, but frequently the dispute erupts after the death of the parent with whom the children had the closest relationship. For example, it is not unusual after divorce for a parent with custody to return to live with or to establish close relations with his or her parents (the grandparents of the children of the divorce). Accordingly, it is not uncommon for those grandparents to become attached to the grandchildren, and in some cases they may have become significant parental figures, as well. Should the custodial parent die, a custody fight between the grandparents and the surviving noncustodial parent may ensue. Another recent trend in the law is the rising number of custody cases between lesbian partners when their partnership ends and the non-biological mother of the children seeks custody.

2) Psychological Parent Doctrine
The concept of the "psychological parent" was promulgated by the influential book by Joseph Goldstein et al, Beyond the Best Interests of the Child (Free Press 1973). Based on psychoanalytic theory, the authors concluded that young children do not recognize blood ties, but recognize those adults, whether biologically related or not, who regularly meet their emotional needs and give them affection on a day-to-day basis as their caretaker. This person becomes their "psychological parent" and should be granted custody whether that person is a biological parent, adoptive parent, or other caring adult. This concept has been relied upon by nonparents, including biologically unrelated individuals, to justify their claims to custody or visitation "in the best interests of the children." This doctrine may be applied to custody disputes between parents as well.

2. Statutes, Cases and Doctrines

a. Uniform Marriage and Divorce Act

Section 402. [Best Interest of Child]
The court shall determine custody in accordance with the best interest of the child. The court shall consider all relevant factors including:
(1) the wishes of the child's parent or parents as to his custody;
(2) the wishes of the child as to his custodian;
(3) the interaction and interrelationship of the child with his parent or parents, his siblings, and any other person who may significantly affect the child's best interest;
(4) the child's adjustment to his home, school, and community; and
(5) the mental and physical health of all individuals involved.
The court shall not consider conduct of a proposed custodian that does not affect this relationship to the child.

b. *Michael Garska v. Gwendolyn McCoy*

Michael Garska v. Gwendolyn McCoy
278 S.E.2d 357 (W.Va. 1981)

NEELY, Justice:
[Trial court awarded custody to the natural father.]
* * * [I]n the final analysis the entire dispute comes down to a custody fight between the natural father and the natural mother. Although Code, 48-2-15 (1980) is concerned with the award of custody in a divorce proceeding, that section is the preeminent legislative expression of policy concerning custody between natural parents in that it abolishes all gender based presumptions and establishes a "best interest of the child" standard for the award of custody. The final order was entered after the operative date of the 1980 Amendment to W.Va.Code, 48-2-15, the relevant part of which provides:

In making any such order respecting custody of minor children, there shall be no legal presumption that, as between the natural parents, either the father or the mother should be awarded custody of said children, but the court shall make an award of custody solely for the best interest of the children based upon the merits of each case.

Furthermore, the case was tried below on the theory that Code, 48-2-15 (1980) applies to this case to the extent that it obliterates the presumption of *J. B. v. A. B.*, *supra*, that children of tender years should be awarded to the mother. ***
In the case before us the father, by providing fifteen dollars a week child support, probably showed sufficient parental interest to give him standing to object to an adoption. However, there is no evidence before us to indicate that the mother was an unfit parent and, consequently, no justification for the trial court to remove custody from the primary caretaker parent and vest it in a parent who had had no previous emotional interaction with the child.
I
    ***
The loss of children is a terrifying specter to concerned and loving parents; however, it is particularly terrifying to the primary caretaker parent who, by virtue of the caretaking function, was closest to the child before the divorce or other proceedings were initiated. While the primary caretaker parent in most cases in West Virginia is still the mother, nonetheless, now that sex roles are becoming more flexible and high-income jobs are opening to women, it is conceivable that the primary caretaker parent may also be the father. If the primary caretaker parent is, indeed, the

father, then under W.Va.Code, 48-2-15 (1980) he will be entitled to the alimony and support payments exactly as a woman would be in similar circumstances. *Peters v. Narick*, W.Va., 270 S.E.2d 760 (1980).

Since the parent who is not the primary caretaker is usually in the superior financial position, the subsequent welfare of the child depends to a substantial degree upon the level of support payments which are awarded in the course of a divorce. Our experience instructs us that uncertainty about the outcome of custody disputes leads to the irresistible temptation to trade the custody of the child in return for lower alimony and child support payments. Since trial court judges generally approve consensual agreements on child support, underlying economic data which bear upon the equity of settlements are seldom investigated at the time an order is entered. While Code, 48-2-15 (1980) speaks in terms of "the best interest of the children" in every case, the one enormously important function of legal rules is to inspire rational and equitable settlements in cases which never reach adversary status in court.

If every controversy which arose in this society required court resolution, the understaffed judiciary would topple like a house of cards. It is only voluntary compliance with the criminal law and the orderly settlement of private affairs in the civil law which permits the system to function at all. Consequently, anytime a new statute is passed or a new rule of common law developed, both legislators and judges must pay careful attention to interpreting it in a way which is consonant with equity in the area of private settlements.
****

II

In setting the child custody law in domestic relations cases we are concerned with three practical considerations. First, we are concerned to prevent the issue of custody from being used in an abusive way as a coercive weapon to affect the level of support payments and the outcome of other issues in the underlying divorce proceeding. Where a custody fight emanates from this reprehensible motive the children inevitably become pawns to be sacrificed in what ultimately becomes a very cynical game. Second, in the average divorce proceeding intelligent determination of relative degrees of fitness requires a precision of measurement which is not possible given the tools available to judges. Certainly it is no more reprehensible for judges to admit that they cannot measure minute gradations of psychological capacity between two fit parents than it is for a physicist to concede that it is impossible for him to measure the speed of an electron. Third, there is an urgent need in contemporary divorce law for a legal structure upon which a divorcing couple may rely in reaching a settlement.

While recent statutory changes encourage private ordering of divorce upon the "no-fault" ground of "irreconcilable differences," W.Va.Code, 48-2- 4(a)(10) (1977), our legal structure has not simultaneously been tightened to provide a reliable framework within which the divorcing couple can bargain intelligently. Nowhere is the lack of certainty greater than in child custody. Not very long ago, the courts were often intimately involved with all aspects of a divorce. Even an estranged couple who had reached an amicable settlement had to undergo "play-acting" before the court in order to obtain a divorce. Now, however, when divorces are numerous, easy, and routinely concluded out of court intelligible, reliable rules upon which out-of- court bargaining can be based must be an important consideration in the formulation of our rules.

Since the Legislature has concluded that private ordering by divorcing couples is preferable to judicial ordering, we must insure that each spouse is adequately protected during the out-of-court bargaining. Uncertainty of outcome is very destructive of the position of the primary caretaker parent because he or she will be willing to sacrifice everything else in order to avoid the terrible prospect of losing the child in the unpredictable process of litigation. ***

Therefore, in the interest of removing the issue of child custody from the type of acrimonious and counter-productive litigation which a procedure inviting exhaustive evidence will inevitably create, we hold today that there is a presumption in favor of the primary caretaker parent, if he or she meets the minimum, objective standard for being a fit parent as articulated in *J. B. v. A. B.*, *supra,* regardless of sex. Therefore, any custody dispute involving children of tender years it is incumbent upon the circuit court to determine as a threshold question which parent was the primary caretaker parent before the domestic strife giving rise to the proceeding began.

While it is difficult to enumerate all of the factors which will contribute to a conclusion that one or the other parent was the primary caretaker parent, nonetheless, there are certain obvious criteria to which a court must initially look. In establishing which natural or adoptive parent is the primary caretaker, the trial court shall determine which parent has taken primary responsibility for, inter alia, the performance of the following caring and nurturing duties of a parent: (1) preparing and planning of meals; (2) bathing, grooming and dressing; (3) purchasing, cleaning, and care of clothes; (4) medical care, including nursing and trips to physicians; (5) arranging for social interaction among peers after school, i. e. transporting to friends' houses or, for example, to girl or boy scout meetings; (6) arranging alternative care, i. e. babysitting, day-care, etc.; (7) putting child to bed at night, attending to child in the middle of the night, waking child in the morning; (8) disciplining, i.e. teaching general manners and toilet training; (9) educating, i. e. religious, cultural, social, etc.; and, (10) teaching elementary skills, i. e., reading, writing and arithmetic.

In those custody disputes where the facts demonstrate that child care and custody were shared in an entirely equal way, then indeed no presumption arises and the court must proceed to inquire further into relative degrees of parental competence. However, where one parent can demonstrate with regard to a child of tender years that he or she is clearly the primary caretaker parent, then the court must further determine only whether the primary caretaker parent is a fit parent. Where the primary caretaker parent achieves the minimum, objective standard of behavior which qualifies him or her as a fit parent, the trial court must award the child to the primary caretaker parent......

[Ed. note: The West Virginia legislature modified the primary caretaker presumption and replaced it with the ALI Principle of allocation of custodial responsibility. W. Va. Code §48-9-206-207 (2004).]

c. *Ana Marie Burchard v. William Garay*
Ana Marie Burchard v. William Garay
724 P.2d 486 (Ca. 1986)

BROUSSARD, Justice.

This case concerns the custody of William Garay, Jr., age two and one-half at the date of trial. Ana Burchard, his mother, appeals from an order of the superior court awarding custody to the father, William Garay.

As a result of a brief liaison between Ana and William, Ana became pregnant. Early in her term she told William that she was pregnant with his child, but he refused to believe that he was the father. William, Jr., was born on September 18, 1979.

After the birth, Ana undertook the difficult task of caring for her child, with the help of her father and others, while working at two jobs and continuing her training to become a registered nurse. William continued to deny paternity, and did not visit the child or provide any support.

In the spring of 1980 Ana brought a paternity and support action. After court-ordered blood tests established that William was the father, he stipulated to paternity and to support in the amount of $200 a month. Judgment entered accordingly on November 24, 1980. In December of that year William visited his son for the first time. In the next month he moved in with Ana and the child in an attempt to live together as a family; the attempt failed and six weeks later he moved out.

William asked for visitation rights; Ana refused and filed a petition for exclusive custody. William responded, seeking exclusive custody himself. The parties then stipulated that pending the hearing Ana would retain custody, with William having a right to two full days of visitation each week.

[The court ruled that the trial court has applied the correct standard for deciding custody, which was the best interest of the child standard and not changed circumstances. The evidence at the hearing disclosed that William, Jr., was well adjusted, very healthy, well mannered, good natured, and that each parent would be expected to provide him with adequate care.]

Applying the "best interests" test, it awarded custody to William. Its decision appears to be based upon three considerations. The first is that William is financially better off--he has greater job stability, owns his own home, and is "better equipped economically ... to give constant care to the minor child and cope with his continuing needs." The second is that William has remarried, and he "and the stepmother can provide constant care for the minor child and keep him on a regular schedule without resorting to other caretakers"; Ana, on the other hand, must rely upon babysitters and day care centers while she works and studies. Finally, the court referred to William providing the mother with visitation, an indirect reference to Ana's unwillingness to permit William visitation.

Pursuant to the court order William took custody of the child on August 15, 1982. Ana appealed from the order, and sought a writ of supersedeas. The Court of Appeal, however, denied supersedeas and subsequently affirmed the trial court's order. We granted a hearing in August 1984. Ana did not seek supersedeas, and William, Jr., remained in his father's custody pending this appeal.

[The court concluded that the trial court erred in applying the best interests standard.] The court's reliance upon the relative economic position of the parties is impermissible; the purpose of child support awards is to ensure that the spouse otherwise best fit for custody receives adequate funds for the support of the child. Its reliance upon the asserted superiority of William's child care arrangement suggests an insensitivity to the role of working parents. And all of the factors cited by the trial court together weigh less to our mind than a matter it did not discuss--the importance of continuity and stability in custody arrangements. We therefore reverse the order of the trial court.***

We therefore turn to examine the decision of the trial court to determine whether it abused its discretion in deciding that the best interests of the child required it to award custody to William. The trial court's decision referred to William's better economic position, and to matters such as homeownership and ability to provide a more "wholesome environment" which reflect economic advantage. But comparative income or economic advantage is not a permissible basis for a custody award. "[T]here is no basis for assuming a correlation between wealth and good parenting or wealth and happiness." (Klaff, The Tender Years Doctrine: A Defense (1982) 70 Cal.L.Rev. 335, 350; see Mnookin, Child Custody Adjudication: Judicial Function in the Face of Indeterminacy (1975) 39 Law. & Contemp. Problems, 226, 284.) If in fact the custodial parent's income is insufficient to provide a proper care for the child, the remedy is to award child support, not to take away custody The court also referred to the fact that Ana worked and had to place the child in day care, while William's new wife could care for the child in their home. But in an era when over 50 percent of mothers and almost 80 percent of divorced mothers work, the courts must not presume that a working mother is a less satisfactory parent or less fully committed to the care of her child. A custody determination must be based upon a true assessment of the emotional bonds between parent and child, upon an inquiry into "the heart of the parent-child relationship ... the ethical, emotional, and intellectual guidance the parent gives to the child throughout his formative years, and often beyond." (In re Marriage of Carney, supra, 24 Cal.3d 725, 739, 157 Cal.Rptr. 383, 598 P.2d 36.) It must reflect also a factual determination of how best to provide continuity of attention, nurturing, and care. It cannot be based on an assumption, unsupported by scientific evidence, that a working mother cannot provide such care--an assumption particularly unfair when, as here, the mother has in fact been the primary caregiver. We suspect that any presupposition that single working parents provide inferior care to their children will in practice discriminate against women. Divorced men are more likely to remarry than divorced women, and far more likely to marry a nonworking spouse.]

Any actual deficiency in care, whether due to the parent's work or any other cause, would of course be a proper consideration in deciding custody. But the evidence of such deficiencies in the present case is very weak--the testimony of William, disputed by Ana, that on one occasion Ana left the child alone briefly while she cashed a support check, and that sometimes the child was delivered for visitation in clothes that were shabby or too small. But these matters are trivial. The essence of the court's decision is simply that care by a mother who, because of work and study, must entrust the child to daycare centers and babysitters, is per se inferior to care by a father who also works, but can leave the child with a stepmother at home. For the reasons we have explained, this reasoning is not a suitable basis for a custody order.

The trial court recited other grounds for its order. One was that William was "better equipped psychologically" to care for the child. Ana has had emotional problems in the past, and reacted bitterly to the separation, but William's conduct has not been a model of emotional maturity. After they separated, Ana objected to William seeing the child and did not communicate about matters involving the child. But after William obtained custody pursuant to the trial court's order, he proved equally obdurate to Ana's visitation rights, leading the court to amend its order to spell out those rights.

All of these grounds, however, are insignificant compared to the fact that Ana has been the primary caretaker for the child from birth to the date of the trial court hearing, During the six-week period when Ana and William lived together, Ana remained the primary caregiver, and the couple continued the daycare and babysitting arrangements Ana had made.] that no serious deficiency in her care has been proven, and that William, Jr., under her care, has become a happy, healthy, well-adjusted child. We have frequently stressed, in this opinion and others, the importance of stability and continuity in the life of a child, and the harm that may result from disruption of established patterns of care and emotional bonds. The showing made in this case is, we believe, wholly insufficient to justify taking the custody of a child from the mother who has raised him from birth, successfully coping with the many difficulties encountered by single working mothers. We conclude that the trial court abused its discretion in granting custody to William, Sr., and that its order must be reversed.

We acknowledge the anomalous position of an appellate court, especially a supreme court, in child custody appeals. Over four years have passed since the trial court awarded custody to William. Our decision reversing that order returns the case to the trial court which, in deciding the child's future custody, must hold a new hearing and determine what arrangement is in the best interests of the child as of the date of that hearing. *** Thus, the effect of our decision is not to determine finally the custody of William, Jr., but is to relieve Ana of the adverse findings of the trial court and of the burden of proving changed circumstances since the trial court order, and to make clear that in deciding the issue of custody the court cannot base its decision upon the relative economic position of the parties or upon any assumption that the care afforded a child by single, working parents is inferior. The order is reversed.

***

[Chief Justice Bird wrote a concurring opinion to underscore that the trial court's ruling was an abuse of discretion not only in its failure to give due weight to the importance of continuity and stability in custody arrangements but in its assumption that there is a negative relation between a woman's lack of wealth or her need or desire to work and the quality of her parenting.]

d. *Palmore v. Sidoti*

Linda Sidoti Palmore v. Anthony J. Sidoti
466 U.S. 429 (1984)

Chief Justice BURGER delivered the opinion of the Court.

We granted certiorari to review a judgment of a state court divesting a natural mother of the custody of her infant child because of her remarriage to a person of a different race.

I.

When petitioner Linda Sidoti Palmore and respondent Anthony J. Sidoti, both Caucasians, were divorced in May 1980 in Florida, the mother was awarded custody of their 3-year-old daughter.

In September 1981 the father sought custody of the child by filing a petition to modify the prior judgment because of changed conditions. The change was that the child's mother was then cohabiting with a Negro, Clarence Palmore, Jr., whom she married two months later. Additionally, the father made several allegations of instances in which the mother had not properly cared for the child.

After hearing testimony from both parties and considering a court counselor's investigative report, the court noted that the father had made allegations about the child's care, but the court made no findings with respect to these allegations. On the contrary, the court made a finding that "there is no issue as to either party's devotion to the child, adequacy of housing facilities, or respectability of the new spouse of either parent." App. to Pet. for Cert. 24.

The court then addressed the recommendations of the court counselor, who had made an earlier report "in [another] case coming out of this circuit also involving the social consequences of an interracial marriage. *Niles v. Niles*, 299 So.2d 162." *Id.*, at 25. From this vague reference to that earlier case, the court turned to the present case and noted the counselor's recommendation for a change in custody because "[t]he wife [petitioner] has chosen for herself and for her child, a life-style unacceptable to the father and to society.... The child ... is, or at school age will be, subject to environmental pressures not of choice." Record 84 (emphasis added).

The court then concluded that the best interests of the child would be served by awarding custody to the father. The court's rationale is contained in the following:

"The father's evident resentment of the mother's choice of a black partner is not sufficient to wrest custody from the mother. It is of some significance, however, that the mother did see fit to bring a man into her home and carry on a sexual relationship with him without being married to him. Such action tended to place gratification of her own desires ahead of her concern for the child's future welfare. This Court feels that despite the strides that have been made in bettering relations between the races in this country, it is inevitable that Melanie will, if allowed to remain in her present situation and attains school age and thus more vulnerable to peer pressures, suffer from the social stigmatization that is sure to come." App. to Pet. for Cert. 26-27 (emphasis added).

The Second District Court of Appeal affirmed without opinion, 426 So.2d 34 (1982), thus denying the Florida Supreme Court jurisdiction to review the case. *See* Fla. Const., Art. V, § 3(b)(3); *Jenkins v. State*, 385 So.2d 1356 (Fla.1980). We granted certiorari, 464 U.S. 913, 104 S.Ct. 271, 78 L.Ed.2d 253 (1983), and we reverse.

II.

The judgment of a state court determining or reviewing a child custody decision is not ordinarily a likely candidate for review by this Court. However, the court's opinion, after stating that the "father's evident resentment of the mother's choice of a black partner is not sufficient" to deprive her of custody, then turns to what it regarded as the damaging impact on the child from remaining in a racially mixed household. App. to Pet. for Cert. 26. This raises important federal concerns arising from the Constitution's commitment to eradicating discrimination based on race.

The Florida court did not focus directly on the parental qualifications of the natural mother or her present husband, or indeed on the father's qualifications to have custody of the child. The court found that "there is no issue as to either party's devotion to the child, adequacy of housing facilities, or respectability of the new spouse of either parent." *Id.*, at 24. This, taken with the absence of any negative finding as to the quality of the care provided by the mother, constitutes a rejection of any claim of petitioner's unfitness to continue the custody of her child.

The court correctly stated that the child's welfare was the controlling factor. But that court was entirely candid and made no effort to place its holding on any ground other than race. Taking the court's findings and rationale at face value, it is clear that the outcome would have been different had petitioner married a Caucasian male of similar respectability.

A core purpose of the Fourteenth Amendment was to do away with all governmentally imposed discrimination based on race. *See Strauder v. West Virginia,* 100 U.S. 303, 307-308, 310, 25 L.Ed. 664 (1880). Classifying persons according to their race is more likely to reflect racial prejudice than legitimate public concerns; the race, not the person, dictates the category. *See Personnel Administrator of Mass. v. Feeney,* 442 U.S. 256, 272, 99 S.Ct. 2282, 2292, 60 L.Ed.2d 870 (1979). Such classifications are subject to the most exacting scrutiny; to pass constitutional muster, they must be justified by a compelling governmental interest and must be "necessary ... to the accomplishment" of their legitimate purpose, *McLaughlin v. Florida,* 379 U.S. 184, 196 (1967).

The State, of course, has a duty of the highest order to protect the interests of minor children, particularly those of tender years. In common with most states, Florida law mandates that custody determinations be made in the best interests of the children involved. Fla.Stat. § 61.13(2)(b)(1) (1983). The goal of granting custody based on the best interests of the child is indisputably a substantial governmental interest for purposes of the Equal Protection Clause.

It would ignore reality to suggest that racial and ethnic prejudices do not exist or that all manifestations of those prejudices have been eliminated. There is a risk that a child living with a stepparent of a different race may be subject to a variety of pressures and stresses not present if the child were living with parents of the same racial or ethnic origin.

The question, however, is whether the reality of private biases and the possible injury they might inflict are permissible considerations for removal of an infant child from the custody of its natural mother. We have little difficulty concluding that they are not. The Constitution cannot control such prejudices but neither can it tolerate them. Private biases may be outside the reach of the law, but the law cannot, directly or indirectly, give them effect. "Public officials sworn to uphold the Constitution may not avoid a constitutional duty by bowing to the hypothetical effects of private racial prejudice that they assume to be both widely and deeply held." *Palmer v. Thompson,* 403 U.S. 217, 260-261, (1971) (WHITE, J., dissenting).

This is by no means the first time that acknowledged racial prejudice has been invoked to justify racial classifications. In *Buchanan v. Warley,* 245 U.S. 60 (1917), for example, this Court invalidated a Kentucky law forbidding Negroes to buy homes in white neighborhoods.

> It is urged that this proposed segregation will promote the public peace by preventing race conflicts. Desirable as this is, and important as is the preservation of the public peace, this aim cannot be accomplished by laws or ordinances which deny rights created or protected by the Federal Constitution.

Id., at 81, 38 S.Ct., at 20.

Whatever problems racially mixed households may pose for children in 1984 can no more support a denial of constitutional rights than could the stresses that residential integration was thought to entail in 1917. The effects of racial prejudice, however real, cannot justify a racial classification removing an infant child from the custody of its natural mother found to be an appropriate person to have such custody. *[Fn. 3. This conclusion finds support in other cases as well. For instance, in Watson v. Memphis, 373 U.S. 526 (1963), city officials claimed that desegregation of city parks had to proceed slowly to "prevent interracial disturbances, violence, riots, and community confusion and turmoil." Id., at 535. The Court found such predictions no more than "personal speculations or vague disquietudes," id., at 536, and held that "constitutional rights may not be denied simply because of hostility to their assertion or exercise," id., at 535. In Wright v. Georgia, 373 U.S. 284 (1963), the Court reversed a Negro defendant's breach-of-peace conviction, holding that "the possibility of disorder by others cannot justify exclusion of persons from a place if they otherwise have a constitutional right (founded upon the Equal Protection Clause) to be present." Id., at 293.]*

The judgment of the District Court of Appeal is reversed.

e. A Biblical Example of the Dilemma and King Solomon's Solution

16 ¶ Then came there two women, [that were] harlots, unto the king, and stood before him.

17 And the one woman said, O my lord, I and this woman dwell in one house; and I was delivered of a child with her in the house.

18 And it came to pass the third day after that I was delivered, that this woman was delivered also: and we [were] together; [there was] no stranger with us in the house, save we two in the house.

19 And this woman's child died in the night; because she overlaid it.20 And she arose at midnight, and took my son from beside me, while thine handmaid slept, and laid it in her bosom, and laid her dead child in my bosom.

21 And when I rose in the morning to give my child suck, behold, it was dead: but when I had considered it in the morning, behold, it was not my son, which I did bear.

22 And the other woman said, Nay; but the living [is] my son, and the dead [is] thy son. And this said, No; but the dead [is] thy son, and the living [is] my son. Thus they spake before the king.

23 Then said the king, The one saith, This [is] my son that liveth, and thy son [is] the dead: and the other saith, Nay; but thy son [is] the dead, and my son [is] the living.

24 And the king said, Bring me a sword. And they brought a sword before the king.

25 And the king said, Divide the living child in two, and give half to the one, and half to the other.

26 Then spake the woman whose the living child [was] unto the king, for her bowels yearned upon her son, and she said, O my lord, give her the living child, and in no wise slay it. But the other said, Let it be neither mine nor thine, [but] divide [it].

27 Then the king answered and said, Give her the living child, and in no wise slay it: she [is] the mother thereof.

28 And all Israel heard of the judgment which the king had judged; and they feared the king: for they saw that the wisdom of God [was] in him, to do judgment.

1 Kings 3:16-38 (KJV)

f. *Painter v. Bannister*
Mark Wendell Painter, a Minor, by Harold W. Painter, his Father and Next Friend
v. Dwight Bannister and Margaret Bannister
140 N.W.2d 152 (Iowa 1966)

STUART, Justice.

We are here setting the course for Mark Wendell Painter's future. Our decision on the custody of this 7 year old boy will have a marked influence on his whole life. The fact that we are called upon many times a year to determine custody matters does not make the exercising of this awesome responsibility any less difficult. Legal training and experience are of little practical help in solving the complex problems of human relations. However, these problems do arise and under our system of government, the burden of rendering a final decision rests upon us. It is frustrating to know we can only resolve, not solve, these unfortunate situations.

The custody dispute before us in this habeas corpus action is between the father, Harold Painter, and the maternal grandparents, Dwight and Margaret Bannister. Mark's mother and younger sister were killed in an automobile accident on December 6, 1962 near Pullman, Washington. The father, after other arrangements for Mark's care had proved unsatisfactory, asked the Bannisters, to take care of Mark. They went to California and brought Mark to their farm home near Ames in July, 1963. Mr. Painter remarried in November, 1964 and about that time indicated he wanted to take Mark back. The Bannisters refused to let him leave and this action was filed in June, 1965. Since July 1965 he has continued to remain in the Bannister home under an order of this court staying execution of the judgment of the trial court awarding custody to the father until the matter could be determined on appeal. For reasons hereinafter stated, we conclude Mark's better interests will be served if he remains with the Bannisters.

Mark's parents came from highly contrasting backgrounds. His mother was born, raised and educated in rural Iowa. Her parents are college graduates. Her father is agricultural information editor for the Iowa State University Extension Service. The Bannister home is in the Gilbert Community and is well kept, roomy and comfortable. The Bannisters are highly respected members of the community. Mr. Bannister has served on the school board and regularly teaches a Sunday school class at the Gilbert Congregational Church. Mark's mother graduated from Grinnell College. She then went to work for a newspaper in Anchorage, Alaska, where she met Harold Painter.

Mark's father was born in California. When he was 2 1/2 years old, his parents were divorced and he was placed in a foster home. Although he has kept in contact with his natural parents, he considers his foster parents, the McNelly's as his family. He flunked out of a high school and a trade school because of a lack of interest in academic subjects, rather than any lack of ability. He joined the navy at 17. He did not like it. After receiving an honorable discharge, he took examinations and obtained his high school diploma. He lived with the McNelly's and went to college for 2 1/2 years under the G.I. bill. He quit college to take a job on a small newspaper in Ephrata, Washington in November 1955. In May 1956, he went to work for the newspaper in Anchorage which employed Jeanne Bannister.

Harold and Jeanne were married in April, 1957. Although there is a conflict in the evidence on the point, we are convinced the marriage, overall, was a happy one with many ups and downs as could be expected in the uniting of two such opposites.

We are not confronted with a situation where one of the contesting parties is not a fit or proper person. There is no criticism of either the Bannisters or their home. There is no suggestion in the record that Mr. Painter is morally unfit. It is obvious the Bannisters did not approve of their daughter's marriage to Harold Painter and do not want their grandchild raised under his guidance. The philosophies of life are entirely different. As stated by the psychiatrist who examined Mr. Painter at the request of Bannisters' attorneys: 'It is evident that there exists a large difference in ways of life and value systems between the Bannisters and Mr. Painter, but in this case, there is no evidence that psychiatric instability is involved. Rather, these divergent life patterns seem to represent alternative normal adaptations.'

It is not our prerogative to determine custody upon our choice of one of two ways of life within normal and proper limits and we will not do so. However, the philosophies are important as they relate to Mark and his particular needs.

The Bannister home provides Mark with a stable, dependable, conventional, middleclass, middlewest background and an opportunity for a college education and profession, if he desires it.

It provides a solid foundation and secure atmosphere. In the Painter home, Mark would have more freedom of conduct and thought with an opportunity to develop his individual talents. It would be more exciting and challenging in many respects, but romantic, impractical and unstable.

Little additional recitation of evidence is necessary to support our evaluation of the Bannister home. It might be pointed out, however, that Jeanne's three sisters also received college educations and seem to be happily married to college graduates.

Our conclusion as to the type of home Mr. Painter would offer is based upon his Bohemian approach to finances and life in general. We feel there is much evidence which supports this conclusion. His main ambition is to be a free lance writer and photographer. He has had some articles and picture stories published, but the income from these efforts has been negligible. At the time of the accident, Jeanne was willingly working to support the family so Harold could devote more time to his writing and photography. In the 10 years since he left college, he has changed jobs seven times. He was asked to leave two of them; two he quit because he didn't like the work; two because he wanted to devote more time to writing and the rest for better pay. He was contemplating a move to Berkeley at the time of trial. His attitude toward his career is typified by his own comments concerning a job offer:

'About the Portland news job, I hope you understand when I say it took guts not to take it; I had to get behind myself and push. It was very, very tempting to accept a good salary and settle down to a steady, easy routine. As I approached Portland, with the intention of taking the job, I began to ask what, in the long run, would be the good of this job: 1, it was not really what I wanted; 2, Portland is just another big farm town, with none of the stimulation it takes to get my mind sparking. Anyway, I decided Mark and myself would be better off if I went ahead with what I've started and the hell with the rest, sink, swim or starve.'

There is general agreement that Mr. Painter needs help with his finances. Both Jeanne and Marilyn, his present wife, handled most of them. Purchases and sales of books, boats, photographic equipment and houses indicate poor financial judgment and an easy come easy go attitude. He dissipated his wife's estate of about $4300, most of which was a gift from her parents and which she had hoped would be used for the children's education.

The psychiatrist classifies him as 'a romantic and somewhat of a dreamer'. An apt example are the plans he related for himself and Mark in February 1963: 'My thought now is to settle Mark and myself in Sausilito, near San Francisco; this is a retreat for wealthy artists, writers, and such aspiring artists and writers as can fork up the rent money. My plan is to do expensive portraits ($150 and up), sell prints ($15 and up) to the tourists who flock in from all over the world * * *.'

The house in which Mr. Painter and his present wife live, compared with the well kept Bannister home, exemplifies the contrasting ways of life. In his words 'it is a very old and beat up and lovely home * * *'. They live in the rear part. The interior is inexpensively but tastefully decorated. The large yard on a hill in the business district of Walnut Creek, California, is of uncut weeds and wild oats. The house 'is not painted on the outside because I do not want it painted. I am very fond of the wood on the outside of the house.'

The present Mrs. Painter has her master's degree in cinema design and apparently likes and has had considerable contact with children. She is anxious to have Mark in her home. Everything indicates she would provide a leveling influence on Mr. Painter and could ably care for Mark.

Mr. Painter is either an agnostic or atheist and has no concern for formal religious training. He has read a lot of Zen Buddhism and 'has been very much influenced by it'. Mrs. Painter is Roman Catholic. They plan to send Mark to a Congregational Church near the Catholic Church, on an irregular schedule.

He is a political liberal and got into difficulty in a job at the University of Washington for his support of the activities of the American Civil Liberties Union in the university news bulletin.

There were 'two funerals' for his wife. One in the basement of his home in which he alone was present. He conducted the service and wrote her a long letter. The second at a church in Pullman was for the gratification of her friends. He attended in a sport shirt and sweater.

These matters are not related as a criticism of Mr. Painter's conduct, way of life or sense of values. An individual is free to choose his own values, within bounds, which are not exceeded here. They do serve however to support our conclusion as to the kind of life Mark would be exposed to in the Painter household. We believe it would be unstable, unconventional, arty, Bohemian, and probably intellectually stimulating.

Were the question simply which household would be the most suitable in which to raise a child, we would have unhesitatingly chosen the Bannister home. We believe security and stability in the home are more important than intellectual stimulation in the proper development of a child. There are, however, several factors which have made us pause.

First, there is the presumption of parental preference, which though weakened in the past several years, exists by statute. Code of Iowa, Section 668.1; *Finken v. Porter*, 246 Iowa 1345, 72 N.W.2d 445; *Kouris v. Lunn*, Iowa, 136 N.W.2d 502; *Vanden Heuvel v. Vanden Heuvel*, 254 Iowa 1391, 1399, 121 N.W.2d 216. We have a great deal of sympathy for a father, who in the difficult period of adjustment following his wife's death, turns to the maternal grandparents for their help and then finds them unwilling to return the child. There is no merit in the Bannister claim that Mr. Painter permanently relinquished custody. It was intended to be a temporary arrangement. A father should be encouraged to look for help with the children, from those who love them without the risk of thereby losing the custody of the children permanently. This fact must receive consideration in cases of this kind. However, as always, the primary consideration is the best interest of the child and if the return of custody to the father is likely to have a seriously disrupting and disturbing effect upon the child's development, this fact must prevail. *Vanden Heuvel v. Vanden Heuvel, supra; In re Guardianship of Plucar*, 247 Iowa 394, 403, 72 N.W.2d 455; *Carrere v. Prunty*, Iowa, 133 N.W.2d 692, 696; *Finken v. Porter, supra; Kouris v. Lunn, supra*, R.C.P. 344(f) 15.

Second, Jeanne's will named her husband guardian of the children and if he failed to qualify or ceased to act, named her mother. The parent's wishes are entitled to consideration. *Finken v. Porter, supra*.

Third, the Bannister's are 60 years old. By the time Mark graduates from high school they will be over 70 years old. Care of young children is a strain on grandparents and Mrs. Bannister's letters indicate as much.

We have considered all of these factors and have concluded that Mark's best interest demands that his custody remain with the Bannisters. Mark was five when he came to their home. The evidence clearly shows he was not well adjusted at that time. He did not distinguish fact from fiction and was inclined to tell 'tall tales' emphasizing the big 'I'. He was very aggressive toward smaller children, cruel to animals, not liked by his classmates and did not seem to know what was acceptable conduct. As stated by one witness: 'Mark knew where his freedom was and he didn't know where his boundaries were.' In two years he made a great deal of improvement. He now appears to be well disciplined, happy, relatively secure and popular with his classmates, although still subject to more than normal anxiety.

We place a great deal of reliance on the testimony of Dr. Glenn R. Hawks, a child psychologist. The trial court, in effect, disregarded Dr. Hawks' opinions stating: 'The court has given full consideration to the good doctor's testimony, but cannot accept it at full face value because of exaggerated statement and the witness' attitude on the stand.' We, of course, do not have the advantage of viewing the witness' conduct on the stand, but we have carefully reviewed his testimony and find nothing in the written record to justify such a summary dismissal of the opinions of this eminent child psychologist.

Dr. Hawks is head of the Department of Child Development at Iowa State University. However, there is nothing in the record which suggests that his relationship with the Bannisters is such that his professional opinion would be influenced thereby. Child development is his specialty and he has written many articles and a textbook on the subject. He is recognized nationally, having served on the staff of the 1960 White House Conference on Children and Youth and as consultant on a Ford Foundation program concerning youth in India. He is now education consultant on the project 'Head Start'. He has taught and lectured at many universities and belongs to many professional associations. He works with the Iowa Children's Home Society in placement problems. Further detailing of his qualifications is unnecessary.

Between June 15th and the time of trial, he spent approximately 25 hours acquiring information about Mark and the Bannisters, including appropriate testing of and 'depth interviews' with Mark. Dr. Hawks' testimony covers 70 pages of the record and it is difficult to pinpoint any bit of testimony which precisely summarizes his opinion. He places great emphasis on the 'father figure' and discounts the importance of the 'biological father'. 'The father figure is a figure that the child sees as an authority figure, as a helper, he is a nutrient figure, and one who typifies maleness and stands as maleness as far as the child is concerned.'

His investigation revealed: '* * * the strength of the father figure before Mark came to the Bannisters is very unclear. Mark is confused about the father figure prior to his contact with Mr. Bannister.' Now, 'Mark used Mr. Bannister as his father figure. This is very evident. It shows up in the depth interview, and it shows up in the description of Mark's life given by Mark. He has a very warm feeling for Mr. Bannister.'

Dr. Hawks concluded that it was not for Mark's best interest to be removed from the Bannister home. He is criticized for reaching this conclusion without investigating the Painter home or finding out more about Mr. Painter's character. He answered:

'I was most concerned about the welfare of the child, not the welfare of Mr. Painter, not about the welfare of the Bannisters. In as much as Mark has already made an adjustment and sees the Bannisters as his parental figures in his psychological makeup, to me this is the most critical factor. Disruption at this point, I think, would be detrimental to the child even tho Mr. Painter might well be a paragon of virtue. I think this would be a kind of thing which would not be in the best interest of the child. I think knowing something about where the child is at the present time is vital. I think something about where he might go, in my way of thinking is essentially untenable to me, and relatively unimportant. It isn't even helpful. The thing I was most concerned about was Mark's view of his own reality in which he presently lives. If this is destroyed I think it will have rather bad effects on Mark. I think then if one were to make a determination whether it would be to the parents' household, or the McNelly household, or X-household, then I think the further study would be appropriate.'

Dr. Hawks stated: 'I am appalled at the tremendous task Mr. Painter would have if Mark were to return to him because he has got to build the relationship from scratch. There is essentially nothing on which to build at the present time. Mark is aware Mr. Painter is his father, but he is not very clear about what this means. In his own mind the father figure is Mr. Bannister. I think it would take a very strong person with everything in his favor in order to build a relationship as Mr. Painter would have to build at this point with Mark.'

It was Dr. Hawks' opinion 'the chances are very high (Mark) will go wrong if he is returned to his father'. This is based on adoption studies which 'establish that the majority of adoptions in children who are changed, from ages six to eight, will go bad, if they have had a prior history of instability, some history of prior movement. When I refer to instability I am referring to where there has been no attempt to establish a strong relationship.' Although this is not an adoption, the analogy seems appropriate, for Mark who had a history of instability would be removed from the only home in which he has a clearly established 'father figure' and placed with his natural father about whom his feelings are unclear.

We know more of Mr. Painter's way of life than Dr. Hawks. We have concluded that it does not offer as great a stability or security as the Bannister home. Throughout his testimony he emphasized Mark's need at this critical time is stability. He has it in the Bannister home.

Other items of Dr. Hawks' testimony which have a bearing on our decision follow. He did not consider the Bannisters' age anyway disqualifying. He was of the opinion that Mark could adjust to a change more easily later on, if one became necessary, when he would have better control over his environment.

He believes the presence of other children in the home would have a detrimental effect upon Mark's adjustment whether this occurred in the Bannister home or the Painter home.

The trial court does not say which of Dr. Hawks' statements he felt were exaggerated. We were most surprised at the inconsequential position to which he relegated the 'biological father'. He concedes 'child psychologists are less concerned about natural parents than probably other professional groups are.' We are not inclined to so lightly value the role of the natural father, but find much reason for his evaluation of this particular case.

Mark has established a father-son relationship with Mr. Bannister, which he apparently had never had with his natural father. He is happy, well adjusted and progressing nicely in his development. We do not believe it is for Mark's best interest to take him out of this stable atmosphere in the face of warnings of dire consequences from an eminent child psychologist and send him to an uncertain future in his father's home. Regardless of our appreciation of the father's love for his child and his desire to have him with him, we do not believe we have the moral right to gamble with this child's future. He should be encouraged in every way possible to know his father. We are sure there are many ways in which Mr. Painter can enrich Mark's life.

For the reasons stated, we reverse the trial court and remand the case for judgment in accordance herewith.

Reversed and remanded.

g. *V.C. v. M.J.B.*

V.C. v. M.J.B.
748 A.2d 539 (N.J. 2000)

LONG, J.

In this case, we are called on to determine what legal standard applies to a third party's claim to joint custody and visitation of her former domestic partner's biological children, with whom she lived in a familial setting and in respect of whom she claims to have functioned as a psychological parent. Although the case arises in the context of a lesbian couple, the standard we enunciate is applicable to all persons who have willingly, and with the approval of the legal parent, undertaken the duties of a parent to a child not related by blood or adoption. *[FN1 For the purpose of this opinion the term legal parent encompasses biological and adoptive parents.]*

I

The following facts were established at trial. V.C. and M.J.B., who are lesbians, met in 1992 and began dating on July 4, 1993. On July 9, 1993, M.J.B. went to see a fertility specialist to begin artificial insemination procedures. She prepared for that appointment by recording her body temperature for eight to nine months prior for purposes of tracking her ovulation schedule. She had been planning to be artificially inseminated since late 1980. According to M.J.B., she made the final decision to become pregnant independently and before beginning her relationship with V.C. Two individuals who knew M.J.B. before she began dating V.C., confirmed that M.J.B. had been planning to become pregnant through artificial insemination for years prior to the beginning of the parties' relationship.

According to V.C., early in their relationship, the two discussed having children. However, V.C. did not become aware of M.J.B.'s visits with the specialist and her decision to have a baby by artificial insemination until September 1993. In fact, the doctor's records of M.J.B.'s first appointment indicate that M.J.B. was single and that she "desires children."

Nonetheless, V.C. claimed that the parties jointly decided to have children and that she and M.J.B. jointly researched and decided which sperm donor they should use. M.J.B. acknowledged that she consulted V.C. on the issue but maintained that she individually made the final choice about which sperm donor to use.

Between November 1993 and February 1994, M.J.B. underwent several insemination procedures. V.C. attended at least two of those sessions. In December 1993, V.C. moved into M.J.B.'s apartment. Two months later, on February 7, 1994, the doctor informed M.J.B. that she was pregnant. M.J.B. called V.C. at work to tell her the good news. Eventually, M.J.B. was informed that she was having twins.

During M.J.B.'s pregnancy, both M.J.B. and V.C. prepared for the birth of the twins by attending pre-natal and Lamaze classes. In April 1994, the parties moved to a larger apartment to accommodate the pending births. V.C. contended that during that time they jointly decided on the children's names. M.J.B. admitted consulting V.C., but maintained that she made the final decision regarding names.

The children were born on September 29, 1994. V.C. took M.J.B. to the hospital and she was present in the delivery room at the birth of the children. At the hospital, the nurses and staff treated V.C. as if she were a mother. Immediately following the birth, the nurses gave one child to M.J.B. to hold and the other to V.C., and took pictures of the four of them together. After the children were born, M.J.B. took a three-month maternity leave and V.C. took a three-week vacation.

The parties opened joint bank accounts for their household expenses, and prepared wills, powers of attorney, and named each other as the beneficiary for their respective life insurance policies. At some point, the parties also opened savings accounts for the children, and named V.C. as custodian for one account and M.J.B. as custodian for the other.

The parties also decided to have the children call M.J.B. "Mommy" and V.C. "Meema." M.J.B. conceded that she referred V.C. as a "mother" of the children. In addition, M.J.B. supported the notion, both publicly and privately, that during the twenty-three months after the children were born, the parties and the children functioned as a family unit. M.J.B. sent cards and letters to V.C. that referred to V.C. as the children's mother, and indicated that the four of them were a family. The children also gave cards to V.C. that indicated that V.C. was their mother. M.J.B. encouraged a relationship between V.C. and the children and sought to create a "happy, cohesive environment for the children." M.J.B. admitted that, when the parties' relationship was intact, she sometimes thought of the four of them as a family. However, although M.J.B. sometimes considered the children "theirs," other times she considered them "hers".

M.J.B. agreed that both parties cared for the children but insisted that she made substantive decisions regarding their lives. For instance, M.J.B. maintained that she independently researched and made the final decisions regarding the children's pediatrician and day care center. V.C. countered that she was equally involved in all decision-making regarding the children. Specifically, V.C. claimed that she participated in choosing a day care center for the children, and it is clear that M.J.B. brought V.C. to visit the center she selected prior to making a final decision.

M.J.B. acknowledged that V.C. assumed substantial responsibility for the children, but maintained that V.C. was a mere helper and not a co-parent. However, according to V.C., she acted as a co-parent to the children and had equal parenting responsibility. Indeed, M.J.B. listed V.C. as the "other mother" on the children's pediatrician and day care registration forms. M.J.B. also gave V.C. medical power of attorney over the children.

A number of witnesses testified about their observations of the parties' relationship and V.C.'s role in the children's lives. V.C.'s mother testified that M.J.B. told her that V.C. and M.J.B. would be co-parents to the children and that the parties made a joint decision to have children. In addition, she observed that M.J.B., V.C. and the children functioned as a family. Likewise, L.M., a co-worker and friend of M.J.B., testified that she spent time with the parties before, during and after M.J.B.'s pregnancy, and that she regarded the parties as equal co-parents to the children.

Another co-worker and friend of M.J.B., D.B., also testified that V.C. was a co-parent to the children. In addition, D.B. revealed that M.J.B. planned to continue the relationship between V.C. and the children after the breakup, as long as V.C. contributed money toward the children's expenses. However, another witness, A.R., indicated that V.C. was minimally involved in taking care of the children, but acknowledged that V.C. had an important role in the twins' lives. Testifying for M.J.B., both A.R. and M.I. stated that they regarded M.J.B. as the children's primary caretaker.

Together the parties purchased a home in February 1995. Later that year, V.C. asked M.J.B. to marry her, and M.J.B. accepted. In July 1995, the parties held a commitment ceremony where they were "married." At the ceremony, V.C., M.J.B. and the twins were blessed as a "family."

Together, V.C. and M.J.B. joined the Lambda family organization, made up of lesbian and gay parents or expectant parents. The Lambda family organization is a social group in which children become aware of other families that also have gay and lesbian parents. V.C. and M.J.B., together with the children, attended at least ten Lambda functions.

Additionally, as a group, V.C., M.J.B. and the twins attended family functions, holidays, and birthdays. According to V.C., she did not attend family functions with M.J.B.'s family because they were unhappy about M.J.B.'s sexual orientation. However, V.C. claimed that M.J.B. had a very good relationship with V.C.'s mother, S.D., and that the children were very close to V.C.'s family. Apparently, the children referred to S.D. as "Grandma," and to V.C.'s grandmother, as "great-grandma."

During their relationship, the couple discussed both changing the twins' surname to a hyphenated form of the women's names and the possibility of V.C. adopting the children. M.J.B. testified that the parties considered adoption and in June 1996 consulted an attorney on the subject. M.J.B. paid a two thousand dollar retainer, and the attorney advised the parties to get letters from family and friends indicating that the parties and the twins functioned as a family. The parties never actually attempted to get the letters or proceed with the adoption. V.C. alleged that M.J.B. was willing to go through with the adoption even after the parties split.

Just two months later, in August 1996, M.J.B. ended the relationship. The parties then took turns living in the house with the children until November 1996. In December 1996, V.C. moved out. M.J.B. permitted V.C. to visit with the children until May 1997. During that time, V.C. spent approximately every other weekend with the children, and contributed money toward the household expenses.

In May 1997, M.J.B. went away on business and left the children with V.C. for two weeks. However, later that month, M.J.B. refused to continue V.C.'s visitation with the children, and at some point, M.J.B. stopped accepting V.C.'s money. M.J.B. asserted that she did not want to continue the children's contact with V.C. because she believed that V.C. was not properly caring for the children, and that the children were suffering distress from continued contact with V.C. Both parties became involved with new partners after the dissolution of their relationship. Eventually, V.C. filed this complaint for joint legal custody.

At trial, expert witnesses appeared for both parties. Dr. Allwyn J. Levine testified on behalf of V.C., and Dr. David Brodzinsky testified on behalf of M.J.B. Both experts arrived at similar conclusions after having examined the women individually and with the children, and after examining the children separately.

Dr. Levine concluded that both children view V.C. as a maternal figure and that V.C. regards herself as one of the children's mothers. "[B]ecause the children were basically parented from birth" by V.C. and M.J.B. "until they physically separated," Dr. Levine concluded that the children view the parties "as inter-changeable maternal mothering objects" and "have established a maternal bond with both of the women."

Dr. Levine likened the parties' relationship to a heterosexual marriage. Consequently, the children would be affected by the loss of V.C. just as if they had been denied contact with their father after a divorce. Dr. Levine explained that the children would benefit from continued contact with V.C. because they had a bonded relationship with her. Dr. Levine further noted that if the children felt abandoned by V.C., they might also feel unnecessary guilt and assume that they made V.C. angry or somehow caused the parties' separation. Although the doctor believed that the children could adapt to the loss of V.C., he indicated that the long-term effects were unknown. Furthermore, Dr. Levine indicated that the animosity between V.C. and M.J.B. could harm the children, but surmised that counseling could lessen the parties' animosity.

Likewise, Dr. Brodzinsky concluded that V.C. and the children enjoyed a bonded relationship that benefitted both children. Dr. Brodzinsky determined that the children regarded V.C. as a member of their family. The doctor believed that it was normal for young children to feel that way about a person with whom they have spent considerable time. However, Dr. Brodzinsky noted that as children "get older, family becomes more specifically tied ... to biological connections." The doctor's report indicated that, when asked who their mother was, the children did not immediately point to V.C., but upon further inquiry agreed that V.C. was their mother. The doctor further noted that the children viewed M.J.B's new partner as a current member of their family. Dr. Brodzinsky expressed concern that, if visitation were permitted, the parties' animosity would negatively impact the children. The doctor, however, acknowledged that counseling would reduce the level of animosity between the parties. Dr. Brodzinsky further recognized that the children would suffer some short-term stress from the loss of V.C. but would likely recover in time.

In contrast to Dr. Levine's opinion, Dr. Brodzinsky believed that the loss of V.C. was not akin to the loss of a parent in a heterosexual divorce. The doctor explained that societal views foster the expectation that a child and a parent will continue their relationship after a divorce, but that no similar expectation would exist for the children's relationship with V.C. Still, Dr. Brodzinsky testified that "[t]he ideal situation is that [M.J.B.] is allowed to get on with her life as she wants, but to the extent possible that ... these children be able at times to have some contact with [V.C.] who's important to them." Assuming that the parties could maintain a reasonably amicable relationship, Dr. Brodzinsky felt that the children "would probably benefit from ongoing contact [with V.C.] as they would with any person with whom they have a good solid relationship that can nurture them."

[The trial court ordered V.C.'s application for joint legal custody and visitation finding that she was not a "psychological parent," and M.J.B. was not unfit. The Appellate Division affirmed the denial of joint custody but granted visitation with split opinions.]

III

We turn first to M.J.B.'s claim that we lack jurisdiction and that V.C. lacks standing to apply for joint custody and visitation because neither the statutes nor the common law acknowledge the existence of such a cause of action by a third party.

A   There are no statutes explicitly addressing whether a former unmarried domestic partner has standing to seek custody and visitation with her former partner's biological children. That is not to say, however, that the current statutory scheme dealing with issues of custody and visitation does not provide some guiding principles. ****

N.J.S.A. 9:2-13(f) provides that "[t]he word "parent," when not otherwise described by the context, means a natural parent or parent by previous adoption." M.J.B. argues that because V.C. is not a natural or adoptive parent, we lack jurisdiction to consider her claims. That is an incomplete interpretation of the Act. Although the statutory definition of parent focuses on natural and adoptive parents, it also includes the phrase, "when not otherwise described by the context." That language evinces a legislative intent to leave open the possibility that individuals other than natural or adoptive parents may qualify as "parents,"depending on the circumstances.

If a statute is clear and unambiguous on its face, the court must determine the intent of the

Legislature from its plain meaning. *** Moreover, statutory "language must not, if reasonably avoidable, be found to be inoperative, superfluous or meaningless." ***

By including the words "when not otherwise described by the context" in the statute, the Legislature obviously envisioned a case where the specific relationship between a child and a person not specifically denominated by the statute would qualify as "parental" under the scheme of Title 9. Although the Legislature may not have considered the precise case before us, it is hard to imagine what it could have had in mind in adding the "context" language other than a situation such as this, in which a person not related to a child by blood or adoption has stood in a parental role vis-a-vis the child. It is that contention by V.C. that brings this case before the court and affords us jurisdiction over V.C.'s complaint.

B   Separate and apart from the statute, M.J.B. contends that there is no legal precedent for this action by V.C. She asserts, correctly, that a legal parent has a fundamental right to the care, custody and nurturance of his or her child. ***

In general, however, the right of a legal parent to the care and custody of his or her child derives from the notion of privacy. According to M.J.B., that right entitles her to absolute preference over V.C. in connection with custody and visitation of the twins. She argues that V.C., a stranger, has no standing to bring this action. We disagree.

The right of parents to the care and custody of their children is not absolute. *** Likewise, if there is a showing of unfitness, abandonment or gross misconduct, a parent's right to custody of her child may be usurped. ***According to M.J.B., because there is no allegation by V.C. of unfitness, abandonment or gross misconduct, there is no reason advanced to interfere with any of her constitutional prerogatives. What she elides from consideration, however, is the "exceptional circumstances" category (occasionally denominated as extraordinary circumstances) that has been recognized as an alternative basis for a third party to seek custody and visitation of another person's child. *** The "exceptional circumstances" category contemplates the intervention of the Court in the exercise of its parens patriae power to protect a child. ***

Subsumed within that category is the subset known as the psychological parent cases in which a third party has stepped in to assume the role of the legal parent who has been unable or unwilling to undertake the obligations of parenthood. *** At the heart of the psychological parent cases is a recognition that children have a strong interest in maintaining the ties that connect them to adults who love and provide for them.

To be sure, prior cases in New Jersey have arisen in the context of a third party taking over the role of an unwilling, absent or incapacitated parent. The question presented here is different; V.C. did not step into M.J.B.'s shoes, but labored alongside her in their family. However, because we view this issue as falling broadly within the contours we have previously described, and because V.C. invokes the "exceptional circumstances" doctrine based on her claim to be a psychological parent to the twins, she has standing to maintain this action separate and apart from the statute.

IV

The next issue we confront is how a party may establish that he or she has, in fact, become a psychological parent to the child of a fit and involved legal parent. That is a question which many of our sister states have attempted to answer. Some have enacted statutes to address the subject by deconstructing psychological parenthood to its fundamental elements.***

The most thoughtful and inclusive definition of de facto parenthood is the test enunciated in Custody of H.S.H.-K., 193 Wis.2d 649, 533 N.W.2d 419, 421 (1995), and adopted by the Appellate Division majority here. It addresses the main fears and concerns both legislatures and courts have advanced when addressing the notion of psychological parenthood. ***

Recapping, the legal parent must consent to and foster the relationship between the third party and the child; the third party must have lived with the child; the third party must perform parental functions for the child to a significant degree; and most important, a parent-child bond must be forged. We are satisfied that that test provides a good framework for determining psychological parenthood in cases where the third party has lived for a substantial period with the legal parent and her child. *[Obviously, the notion of consent will have different implications in different factual settings. For example, where a legal parent voluntarily absents herself physically or emotionally from her child or is incapable of performing her parental duties, those circumstances may constitute consent to the parental role of a third party who steps into her shoes relative to the child. As in all psychological parent cases, the outcome in such a case will depend on the full factual complex and the existence of the other factors contained in the test.]*

Prong one is critical because it makes the biological or adoptive parent a participant in the creation of the psychological parent's relationship with the child. Without such a requirement, a paid nanny or babysitter could theoretically qualify for parental status. To avoid that result, in order for a third party to be deemed a psychological parent, the legal parent must have fostered the formation of the parental relationship between the third party and the child. By fostered is meant that the legal parent ceded over to the third party a measure of parental authority and autonomy and granted to that third party rights and duties vis-a-vis the child that the third party's status would not otherwise warrant. Ordinarily, a relationship based on payment by the legal parent to the third party will not qualify.

The requirement of cooperation by the legal parent is critical because it places control within his or her hands. That parent has the absolute ability to maintain a zone of autonomous privacy for herself and her child. However, if she wishes to maintain that zone of privacy she cannot invite a third party to function as a parent to her child and cannot cede over to that third party parental authority the exercise of which may create a profound bond with the child.

Two further points concerning the consent requirement need to be clarified. First, a psychological parent-child relationship that is voluntarily created by the legally recognized parent may not be unilaterally terminated after the relationship between the adults ends. Although the intent of the legally recognized parent is critical to the psychological parent analysis, the focus is on that party's intent during the formation and pendency of the parent-child relationship. The reason is that the ending of the relationship between the legal parent and the third party does not end the bond that the legal parent fostered and that actually developed between the child and the psychological parent. Thus, the right of the legal parent [does] not extend to erasing a relationship between her partner and her child which she voluntarily created and actively fostered simply because after the party's separation she regretted having done so.***

In practice, that may mean protecting those relationships despite the later, contrary wishes of the legal parent in order to advance the interests of the child. As long as the legal parent consents to the continuation of the relationship between another adult who is a psychological parent and the child after the termination of the adult parties' relationship, the courts need not be involved. Only when that consent is withdrawn are courts called on to protect the child's relationship with the psychological parent.

The second issue that needs to be clarified is that participation in the decision to have a child is not a prerequisite to a finding that one has become a psychological parent to the child. We make that point because the trial court appeared to view the fact that M.J.B. alone made the decision to have the twins as pivotal to the question of the existence of a psychological parent relationship between V.C. and the children. Although joint participation in the family's decision to have a child is probative evidence of the legally recognized parent's intentions, not having participated in the decision does not preclude a finding of the third party's psychological parenthood. ***

Concerning the remaining prongs of the H.S.H.-K. test, we accept Wisconsin's formulation with these additional comments. The third prong, a finding that a third party assumed the obligations of parenthood, is not contingent on financial contributions made by the third party.

Financial contribution may be considered but should not be given inordinate weight when determining whether a third party has assumed the obligations of parenthood. Obviously, as we have indicated, the assumption of a parental role is much more complex than mere financial support. It is determined by the nature, quality, and extent of the functions undertaken by the third party and the response of the child to that nurturance.

Indeed, we can conceive of a case in which the third party is the stay-at-home mother or father who undertakes all of the daily domestic and child care activities in a household with preschool children while the legal parent is the breadwinner engaged in her occupation or profession.***

It bears repeating that the fourth prong is most important because it requires the existence of a parent-child bond. A necessary corollary is that the third party must have functioned as a parent for a long enough time that such a bond has developed. What is crucial here is not the amount of time but the nature of the relationship. How much time is necessary will turn on the facts of each case including an assessment of exactly what functions the putative parent performed, as well as at what period and stage of the child's life and development such actions were taken. Most importantly, a determination will have to be made about the actuality and strength of the parent-child bond. Generally, that will require expert testimony.

The standards to which we have referred will govern all cases in which a third party asserts psychological parent status as a basis for a custody or visitation action regarding the child of a legal parent, with whom the third party has lived in a familial setting.

V

This opinion should not be viewed as an incursion on the general right of a fit legal parent to raise his or her child without outside interference. What we have addressed here is a specific set of circumstances involving the volitional choice of a legal parent to cede a measure of parental authority to a third party; to allow that party to function as a parent in the day-to-day life of the child; and to foster the forging of a parental bond between the third party and the child. In such circumstances, the legal parent has created a family with the third party and the child, and has invited the third party into the otherwise inviolable realm of family privacy. By virtue of her own actions, the legal parent's expectation of autonomous privacy in her relationship with her child is necessarily reduced from that which would have been the case had she never invited the third party into their lives. Most important, where that invitation and its consequences have altered her child's life by essentially giving him or her another parent, the legal parent's options are constrained. It is the child's best interest that is preeminent as it would be if two legal parents were in a conflict over custody and visitation. **

VI

Once a third party has been determined to be a psychological parent to a child, under the previously described standards, he or she stands in parity with the legal parent. **. Custody and visitation issues between them are to be determined on a best interests standard giving weight to the factors set forth in N.J.S.A. 9:2-4. ***

That is not to suggest that a person's status as a legal parent does not play a part in custody or visitation proceedings in those circumstances. *** The legal parent's status is a significant weight in the best interests balance because eventually, in the search for self-knowledge, the child's interest in his or her roots will emerge. Thus, under ordinary circumstances when the evidence concerning the child's best interests (as between a legal parent and psychological parent) is in equipoise, custody will be awarded to the legal parent. Visitation, however, will be the presumptive rule, subject to the considerations set forth in N.J.S.A. 9:2-4, as would be the case if two natural parents were in conflict.

VII

Ordinarily, when we announce a new standard, we remand the case to the trial court for reconsideration. That is not necessary here. This full record informs us that M.J.B. fostered and cultivated, in every way, the development of a parent-child bond between V.C. and the twins; that they all lived together in the same household as a family; that despite M.J.B.'s after-the-fact characterizations of V.C. as a "stranger" and a "nanny," V.C. assumed many of the day-to-day obligations of parenthood toward the twins, including financial support; and that a bonded relationship developed between V.C. and the twins that is parental in nature. In short, we agree with the Appellate Division that V.C. is a psychological parent to the twins.

That said, the issue is whether V.C. should be granted joint legal custody and visitation. As we have stated, the best interests standard applies and the factors set forth in N.J.S.A. 9:2-4 come into play. Under that statute V.C. and M.J.B. are essentially equal. Each appears to be a fully capable, loving parent committed to the safety and welfare of the twins. Although there is animosity between V.C. and M.J.B., that is not a determinant of whether V.C. can continue in the children's lives.

We note that V.C. is not seeking joint physical custody, but joint legal custody for decision making. However, due to the pendency of this case, V.C. has not been involved in the decision-making for the twins for nearly four years. To interject her into the decisional realm at this point would be unnecessarily disruptive for all involved. We will not, therefore, order joint legal custody in this case.

Visitation, however, is another matter. V.C. and the twins have been visiting during nearly all of the four years since V.C. parted company from M.J.B. Continued visitation in those circumstances is presumed. Nothing suggests that V.C. should be precluded from continuing to see the children on a regular basis. Indeed, it is clear that continued regular visitation is in the twins' best interests because V.C. is their psychological parent. We thus affirm the judgment of the Appellate Division.

h. Notes and Questions

1) Other specific factors and considerations

a. Religion

The issue of religion in custody decisions raises First Amendment issues. Under its free exercise clause, a parent's right to practice his or her religion is protected from court interference. Under its establishment clause, a court cannot weigh the merits of each parent's religion. Many courts follow the rule that unless the religious practice harms the child, religion cannot be considered as a factor. These courts differ as to whether actual harm must be shown or whether potential harm only need to be shown. Other courts consider religion as a factor, but not as the sole factor or dominant factor.

b. Homosexuality

Traditionally, homosexual inclination or activity would completely bar a parent from child custody, and possibly even visitation because of widely-accepted beliefs about the detrimental effects of the "bad" parental example upon (and possible exploitation by the homosexual parent of) minors. Today, those beliefs are not as widely-accepted as they were in past years. The traditional position, that homosexuality by a parent disqualified that parent from custody or even significant visitation rights, is now a minority position. The only state high court to endorse that position in recent years is the Virginia Supreme Court. *Roe v. Roe*, 324 S.E. 2d 691 (Va. 1985). The assumption of potential risk to the child apparently remains in the law in the form of a willingness of some courts to impose restrictions upon overt homosexual activities and associations during periods of custody or visitation. *Pascarella v. Pascarella,* 512 A. 2d 715 (Pa. super 1986). The moderate position taken by some courts in recent years is that homosexuality is not a dispositive consideration, but is a valid consideration in child custody disputes. *Kallas v. Kallas,* 614 P. 2d 641 (Utah 1980). The trend of these cases seems to be following the trend in heterosexual cases. Courts are ruling that sexual behavior of a parent is wholly irrelevant in custody disputes (unless direct evidence of serious harm to the child is shown), and some courts have chastised parents (or indicated that it is a negative factor in custody considerations) for the parents to have expressed to their children their moral or religious criticism of the other parent's homosexual behavior. *See generally* Lynn D. Wardle, *infra.*

c. Child's Preference

Most states now specifically provide for consideration of the child's preference. One study indicates that courts place significant weight on child preference in determining custody. Wallace, *infra.* Some have criticized this because it involves asking a court to choose an alternative that contradicts his or her own perception of what is best, i.e., a home in which both parents are present. Also, to ask a child to express a preference places a huge burden on the child, and professionals have noted that they experience a reduction of stress when they are relieved of the responsibility of making that decision. Shuman, *infra.* Shuman suggests that most children are incapable of making a reasoned choice because of a child's sense of time, manipulation, etc. Another professional notes that "the typical child's choice is actually a nonchoice, based on fears, hostilities, and confusions" and children often express preference for the less affectionate parent because he/she feels secure of the love of the other parent and fears losing the love of the estranged parent. Clawar, One House, Two Cars, Three Kids, 5 Fam Advoc, Fall 1982, at 16. Should the judge ask a child directly which parent he or she would prefer to have custody, or ask mental health professional to evaluate the child? Professionals strongly recommend themselves, emphasizing their superiority in identifying effective parenting, their ability to see through smokescreens, detect alienation, brainwashing, etc.

d. Adultery

Custody determinations are supposed to be based solely on consideration of evidence relating to the welfare of the child; not to reward or punish parents for their conduct unrelated to child welfare. Courts in most states have followed a rebuttable presumption that parental infidelity is not harmful to children because evidence of infidelity by a parent may divert the court's attention from the needs of the child to the misbehavior of the parent. Laura W. Morgan, *infra.* This no-harm presumption is relatively new. Before 1970, evidence of adultery was presumptive (if not proof) of unfitness of a parent to have custody. The sexual revolution, however, changed the old presumption of harm into a new presumption of no-harm.

This rule is not an insignificant rule. The best estimates suggest that about twenty percent of married men and ten percent of married women have committed adultery (and some estimates are higher). Women are disproportionately disadvantaged by this no-harm presumption, as they typically want custody more and are victims of adultery about twice as often as men. The practical effects of the no-harm-from-adultery presumption upon custody litigation are two. First, it means that most courts in most states refuse to admit or consider evidence about parental infidelity in custody cases unless (in most states) the party offering such evidence produces evidence of some significant harm to the child that was directly caused by the parental infidelity. Second, it puts the burden (including the expense and practical difficulties) of obtaining and presenting such evidence to rebut the presumption upon the non-adulterous parent -- the parent/spouse who has been faithful to the marriage commitment.

e. Domestic Abuse

Whether evidence of spousal violence or spousal abuse is admissible in a custody dispute raises an interesting question. On the one hand, it may be argued that violence to an adult by his or her spouse reflects different dynamics and different character flaws than those involved in child abuse. That contention, however, is disputed by many. It can be argued that a parent who has abused his or her spouse has shown such a substantial disregard for the affections and feelings of his or her child for that parent and has traumatized that child by the spousal violence that it should be taken into consideration in determining custody. Thus, the Wisconsin Court of Appeals held that "parental violence and abuse affect 'the interaction entered into a relationship of a child' with the parent and may affect the mental and physical health of the children. The violent and abusive spouse may have the same potential as a parent . . .." *Bertram v. Kilian*, 133 Wis.2d 202, 394 N.W.2d 773 (1986). *See generally*, Family Violence Project, *infra*. (44 states and the District of Columbia consider domestic violence as a factor in custody cases); Khachatorian, *infra*. (reviewing evidence of harm to children from spousal domestic violence).

f. Physical and Mental Disabilities

Most courts have concentrated on whether the disability affects parenting, focusing instead on "the ethical, emotional, and intellectual guidance the parent gives to the child throughout his formative years, and often beyond." *Carney v. Carney*, 598 P.2d 36 (Cal. 1979).

g. Parental Agreements

Custody agreements between parents are not binding on the court. Courts, however, give them great deference because it is presumed parents are acting in the best interest of the child and know better what is best for the child than the court.

2) Experts - Custody Investigations

In most states the court hearing a contested custody case has the authority to order a custody investigation by a state child protection agency. The tremendous influence the investigators have, their questionable methodology, and their subject conclusions are open to abuse. After an exhaustive study of custody investigations in Minnesota, Professor Robert J. Levy concluded that "these investigations make one doubt the wisdom of any participation by an entrenched social service bureaucracy in divorce-custody decision making." Levy, *infra*, at 791. Professor Levy noted that the number of custody investigations performed in Hennepin County, Minnesota had increased from 84 in 1970 to 265 in 1975 to over 700 estimated in 1985. While the caseworkers who performed the investigations were generally highly trained, he criticized their reports as incomplete, idiosyncratic and advocative of the investigator's opinion rather than an objective report on the parents. The investigators were prone to omit facts which seemed to contradict the preference of the investigator. Personal values, particularly regarding the maternal presumption, sexual misconduct (particularly by the mother), and emotional and relational strengths and weaknesses seemed to color the caseworkers' presentation of the facts. Often caseworkers go beyond investigation to engage in mediation and "child saving," in some cases using coercive and punitive manipulations to achieve the objectives. Professor Levy strongly recommends limiting the responsibility of custody investigators by specifying their functions and their report forms. He also encourages the adoption of procedural constraints on child custody investigations and allowing them only when custody is contested and both parents consent to the investigation.

3) *Palmore v. Sidoti*

This case is one of the few Supreme Court decisions regarding substantive custody rules. Why are there so few Supreme Court decisions in this area of law? State the narrow holding of the Court. State the holding broadly. See the huge gap between the two statements. Can you see potential for litigation?

4) *Painter v. Bannister*

This is one of the most well-known custody cases in America. It was the subject of extensive public and professional discussion when it was decided, and by 1999, it had been cited more than 90 times by other courts (mostly in other states) and in numerous law review articles. It is an excellent example of the type of evidence that is critical in custody disputes, and of the influence of psychological experts in custody determinations.

A year after this decision, Mark's father published a touching book about his unsuccessful battle to regain custody of his son entitled "Mark, I Love You." It became a significant publication. A year after the publication of the book, Mark was allowed to visit his father in California for the summer. He decided that he wanted to continue living with his dad. That fall, the Bannisters agreed to let Mark live with his father, who was appointed his guardian.

5) The ALI Family Dissolution Principles

(a) The ALI classify three types of parents: *legal parents* (by law, e.g., by birth, marriage, or acknowledgment or paternity adjudication), *parents by estoppel* (liable for child support, lived with child for two years believing or holding out to be a parent), and *de facto parents* (who for at least two years and performed an equal share of child caretaking duties). American Law Institute, Principles of the Law of Family Dissolution § 2.03 (Tenta. Dr. No. 4, April 10, 2000). All three have standing rights and rights to be notified of and to participate in actions filed by another (but the defacto parent must have lived with the child within the past six months), as well as any other persons with parental duties under a parenting plan. *Id.* at § 2.04.

(b) The ALI Principles also instruct courts to give preponderate weight to "caretaking functions each parent performed for the child before their separation or, if

the child never lived with both parents before the filing of the action." *Id.* at §2.09 (1)(a).

(c) Parenting Plans. The ALI requires all parents to submit an extensive parenting plan. *Id.* at §2.06.

6) Noncustodial Parent and Standing

The Supreme Court held that a noncustodial parent lacked standing to assert a constitutional claim challenging the state law requiring his daughter to recite the pledge allegiance to the flag each school day morning. *Elk Grove Unified School District v. Newdow*, 542 U.S. 1 (2004). "Although we have not exhaustively defined the prudential dimensions of the standing doctrine, we have explained that prudential standing encompasses 'the general prohibition on a litigant's raising another's person's legal rights, the rule barring adjudication of generalized grievances more appropriately addressed in the representative branches, and the requirement that a plaintiff's complaint fall within the zone of interests protected by law invoked."

7) Questions

    a. What makes a parent?
    b. What is King Solomon's view?
    c. What does custody mean?

3. Practical and Ethical Considerations

a. Representation for Children

In every custody dispute, the central figure is the child. Are their due process rights adequately protected through their parents? There is a debate whether there should be mandatory representation for the child through the child's own attorney or through a guardian ad litem or both. Or should representation be discretionary? In most states, representation is discretionary. If there is representation, is the role of the representative as an advocate or as a guardian? If the court appoints an attorney to represent the child, Rules of Professional Conduct must be adhered to, especially Rule 1.2: Scope of Representation ("(a) A lawyer shall abide by a client's decisions concerning the objectives of representation [and] when appropriate, shall conduct with the client as to the means by which they are to be pursued") and Rule 1.14 (sets forth the guidelines for representation of a client under disability).

Who should pay for the child's representation? Parents or the state?

4. Bibliography

Contemporary Family Law, vol. 4, Chs. 39 & 40 (1988).

The Family Violence Project, *Family Violence in Child Custody Statutes: An Analysis of State Codes and Legal Practice,* 29 FAM. L.Q. 197 (1995).

Joseph Goldstein, Anna Freud and Albert Solnit, Beyond the Best Interests of the Child (1973).

Stephen Hellman, *Stepparent Custody Upon the Death of the Custodial Parent,* 14 J. Suffolk Acad. L. 23 (2000).

Herbert Jacob, The Silent Revolution: The Transformation of Divorce Law in the United States (1988).

Lee Khachaturian, Comment, *Domestic Violence and Shared Parental Responsibility: Dangerous Bedfellows,* 44 Wayne L. Rev. 1745 (1999).

L. L. LaFave, *Origins and Evolution of the "Best Interests of the Child" Standard,* 34 S.D. L. Rev. 459

(1989).

Professor Robert Mnookin, *Child Custody Adjudication: Judicial Functions in the Face of Indeterminacy*, 39 Law and Comtemporary Problems 227 (1975).

Laura W. Morgan, *The Relevance of Adultery and Extra-Marital Sexual Conduct in Custody and Visitation Cases*, 9 No. 9 Divorce Litig. 165 (1997).

Jana B. Singer & William L. Reynolds, *A Dissent on Joint Custody*, 47 Md. L. Rev. 497 (1988).

Shuman, *The Unreliability of Children's Expression of Preference in Domestic Relations Litigation: A Psychiatric Approach*, 59 Mass. L .Rev 14, 18 (1984).

Wallace, When the Child Becomes the Prize -- That Child Needs a Lawyer, 9 Barrister, Spring 82, at 16.

Lynn D. Wardle, *The Potential Impact of Homosexual Parenting on Children*, 1997 U. Ill. L. Rev. 833-920 (1997).

Danaya C. Wright, DeManneville v. DeManneville*: Rethinking the Birth of Custody Law under Patriarchy*, 17 Law and Hist. Rev. 247-307 (1999).

B. VISITATION STANDARDS

1. Background

a. Noncustodial Parent

The noncustodial parent continues to have the constitutional right to the parent-child relationship. The law protects this right for noncustodial parent through what is commonly referred to as visitation rights. The standard to guide the court's discretion is the best interests of the child standard. The same factors that influence the custody decision apply to the visitation decision. If it is in the best interest of the child, the court may require supervised or restricted visitation. Courts seldom deny visitation altogether.

b. Quasi-Parents: Third Party

Third party visitation disputes arise either when the third party is seeking custody and in the alternative visitation or when the third party is only seeking visitation. At common law third parties did not have visitation rights. Third party visitation rights may be recognized through legislation or under the court's *parens patriae* prerogative. All fifty states now have enacted some form of grandparent visitation statutes authorizing grandparents (and often other relatives) to sue for, and authorizing courts to grant, visitation in some cases. In a growing number of cases, stepparents and lesbian non-biological mothers are seeking visitation. *See Troxel v. Granville, supra*, Ch. 23.

2. Statutes, Cases and Doctrines

a. Uniform Marriage and Divorce Act

Section 407. [Visitation]

(a) A parent not granted custody of the child is entitled to reasonable visitation rights unless the court finds, after a hearing, that visitation would endanger seriously the child's physical, mental, moral, or emotional health.

(b) The court may modify an order granting or denying visitation rights whenever modification would serve the best interest of the child; but the court shall not restrict a parent's visitation rights unless it finds that the visitation would endanger seriously the child's physical, mental, moral, or emotional health.

b. *Alison D. v. Virginia M.*

In the Matter of Alison D. v. Virginia M.
572 N.E.2d 27 (N.Y. 1991)

PER CURIAM.

At issue in this case is whether petitioner, a biological stranger to a child who is properly in the custody of his biological mother, has standing to seek visitation with the child under Domestic Relations Law s 70. Petitioner relies on both her established relationship with the child and her alleged agreement with the biological mother to support her claim that she has standing. We agree with the Appellate Division, 155 A.D.2d 11, 552 N.Y.S.2d 321, that, although petitioner apparently nurtured a close and loving relationship with the child, she is not a parent within the meaning of Domestic Relations Law s 70. Accordingly, we affirm.

I

Petitioner Alison D. and respondent Virginia M. established a relationship in September 1977 and began living together in March 1978. In March 1980, they decided to have a child and agreed that respondent would be artificially inseminated. Together, they planned for the conception and birth of the child and agreed to share jointly all rights and responsibilities of child-rearing. In July 1981, respondent gave birth to a baby boy, A.D.M., who was given petitioner's last name as his middle name and respondent's last name became his last name. Petitioner shared in all birthing expenses and, after A.D.M.'s birth, continued to provide for his support. During A.D.M.'s first two years, petitioner and respondent jointly cared for and made decisions regarding the child.

In November 1983, when the child was 2 years and 4 months old, petitioner and respondent terminated their relationship and petitioner moved out of the home they jointly owned. Petitioner and respondent agreed to a visitation schedule whereby petitioner continued to see the child a few times a week. Petitioner also agreed to continue to pay one half of the mortgage and major household expenses. By this time, the child had referred to both respondent and petitioner as "mommy". Petitioner's visitation with the child continued until 1986, at which time respondent bought out petitioner's interest in the house and then began to restrict petitioner's visitation with the child. In 1987 petitioner moved to Ireland to pursue career opportunities, but continued her attempts to communicate with the child. Thereafter, respondent terminated all contact between petitioner and
the child, returning all of petitioner's gifts and letters. No dispute exists that respondent is a fit parent. Petitioner commenced this proceeding seeking visitation rights pursuant to Domestic Relations Laws 70. Supreme Court dismissed the proceeding concluding that petitioner is not a parent under Domestic Relations Law s 70 and, given the concession that respondent is a fit parent, petitioner is not entitled to seek visitation pursuant to section 70. The Appellate Division affirmed, with one Justice dissenting, and granted leave to appeal to our Court.

II

Pursuant to Domestic Relations Law s 70 "either parent may apply to the supreme court for a writ of habeas corpus to have such minor child brought before such court; and [the court] may award the natural guardianship, charge and custody of such child to either parent * * * as the case may require". Although the Court is mindful of petitioner's understandable concern for and interest in the child and of her expectation and desire that her contact with the child would continue, she has no right under Domestic Relations Law s 70 to seek visitation and, thereby, limit or diminish the right of the concededly fit biological parent to choose with whom her child associates. She is not a "parent" within the meaning of section 70.

Petitioner concedes that she is not the child's "parent"; that is, she is not the biological mother of the child nor is she a legal parent by virtue of an adoption. Rather she claims to have acted as a "de facto" parent or that she should be viewed as a parent "by estoppel". Therefore, she claims she has standing to seek visitation rights. These claims, however, are insufficient under section 70. Traditionally, in this State it is the child's mother and father who, assuming fitness, have the right to the care and custody of their child, even in situations where the nonparent has exercised some control over the child with the parents' consent *** "It has long been recognized that, as between a parent and a third person, parental custody of a child may not be displaced absent grievous cause or necessity" (*Matter of Ronald FF. v. Cindy GG.*, supra, 70 N.Y.2d at 144, 517 N.Y.S.2d 932, 511 N.E.2d 75; see also *Matter of Bennett v. Jeffreys*, 40 N.Y.2d 543, 549, 387 N.Y.S.2d 821, 356 N.E.2d 277). To allow the courts to award visitation--a limited form of custody--to a third person would necessarily impair the parents' right to custody and control (*id.*). Petitioner concedes that respondent is a fit parent. Therefore she has no right to petition the court to displace the choice made by this fit parent in deciding what is in the child's best interests.

Section 70 gives parents the right to bring proceedings to ensure their proper exercise of their care, custody and control *** Where the Legislature deemed it appropriate, it gave other categories of persons standing to seek visitation and it gave the courts the power to determine whether an award of visitation would be in the child's best interests (see e.g. Domestic Relations Law s 71 [special proceeding or habeas corpus to obtain visitation rights for siblings]; s 72 [special proceeding or habeas corpus to obtain visitation rights for grandparents]; *** We decline petitioner's invitation to read the term parent in section 70 to include categories of nonparents who have developed a relationship with a child or who have had prior relationships with a child's parents and who wish to continue visitation with the child (accord, *Nancy S. v. Michele G.*, 228 Cal.App.3d 831, 279 Cal.Rptr. 212 [1st Dist., 1991]). While one may dispute in an individual case whether it would be beneficial to a child to have continued contact with a nonparent, the Legislature did not in section 70 give such nonparent the opportunity to compel a fit parent to allow them to do so (see *Matter of Ronald FF. v. Cindy GG.*, 70 N.Y.2d 141, 517 N.Y.S.2d 932, 511 N.E.2d 75, supra; compare, Oregon Rev.Stat.Ann. s 109.119[1] [giving "(a)ny person including but not limited to a foster parent, stepparent, grandparent * * * who has established emotional ties creating a child-parent relationship with a child" the right to seek visitation or other right of custody]).

Accordingly, the order of the Appellate Division should be affirmed, with costs.

KAYE, Judge (dissenting).

The Court's decision, fixing biology [*While the opinion speaks of biological and legal parenthood, this Court has not yet passed on the legality of adoption by a second mother.*] as the key to visitation rights, has impact far beyond this particular controversy, one that may affect a wide spectrum of relationships--including those of longtime heterosexual stepparents, "common-law" and nonheterosexual partners such as involved here, and even participants in scientific reproduction procedures. Estimates that more than 15.5 million children do not live with two biological parents, and that as many as 8 to 10 million children are born into families with a gay or lesbian parent, suggest just how widespread the impact may be (see Polikoff, *This Child Does Have Two Mothers: Redefining Parenthood to Meet the Needs of Children in Lesbian-Mother and other Nontraditional Families*, 78 Geo.L.J. 459, 461, n. 2 [1990]; Bartlett, *Rethinking Parenthood as an Exclusive Status: The Need for Legal Alternatives When the Premise of the Nuclear Family has Failed*, 70 Va.L.Rev. 879, 880-881 [1984]; see generally *Developments in the Law--Sexual Orientation and the Law*, 102 Harv.L.Rev. 1508, 1629 [1989]).

But the impact of today's decision falls hardest on the children of those relationships, limiting their opportunity to maintain bonds that may be crucial to their development. The majority's retreat from the courts' proper role-- its tightening of rules that should in visitation petitions, above all, retain the capacity to take the children's interests into account--compels this dissent.

In focusing the difference, it is perhaps helpful to begin with what is not at issue. This is not a custody case, but solely a visitation petition. The issue on this appeal is not whether petitioner should actually have visitation rights. Nor is the issue the relationship between Alison D. and Virginia M. Rather, the sole issue is the relationship between Alison D. and A.D.M., in particular whether Alison D.'s petition for visitation should even be considered on its merits. I would conclude that the trial court had jurisdiction to hear the merits of this petition.

The majority insists, however, that, the word "parent" in this case can only be read to mean biological parent; the response "one fit parent" now forecloses all inquiry into the child's best interest, even in visitation proceedings. We have not previously taken such a hard line in these matters, but in the absence of express legislative direction have attempted to read otherwise undefined words of the statute so as to effectuate the legislative purposes. The Legislature has made plain an objective in section 70 to promote "the best interest of the child" and the child's "welfare and happiness." (Domestic Relations Law s 70.) Those words should not be ignored by us in defining standing for visitation purposes--they have not been in prior case law. Domestic Relations Law s 70 was amended in 1964 to broaden the category of persons entitled to seek habeas corpus relief (L.1964, ch. 564, s 1). Previously, only a husband or wife living within the State, and legally separated from the spouse, had standing to bring such a proceeding. The courts, however, refused to apply the statute so literally. In amending the statute to make domicile of the child the touchstone, and eliminate the separation requirement, the Legislature acted to bring section 70 into conformity with what the courts were already doing (see Mem. of Joint Legis.Comm. on Matrimonial and Family Laws, 1964 McKinney's Session Laws of N.Y., at 1880 [amendment deleted "needless limitations which are not, in fact, observed by the Courts"]).

Apart from imposing upon itself an unnecessarily restrictive definition of "parent," and apart from turning its back on a tradition of reading of section 70 so as to promote the welfare of the children, in accord with the parens patriae power, the Court also overlooks the significant distinction between visitation and custody proceedings.

*** Only recently, we defined the term "family" in the eviction provisions of the rent stabilization laws so as to advance the legislative objective, making abundantly clear that the definition was limited to the statute in issue and did not effect a wholesale change in the law (see Braschi v. Stahl Assocs. Co., 74 N.Y.2d 201, 211-213, 544 N.Y.S.2d 784, 543 N.E.2d 49).

In discharging this responsibility, recent decisions from other jurisdictions, for the most part concerning visitation rights of stepparents, are instructive (see e.g. Gribble v. Gribble, 583 P.2d 64 [Utah]; Spells v. Spells, 250 Pa.Super. 168, 378 A.2d 879). For example in Spells, the court fashioned a test for "parental status" or "in loco parentis" requiring that the petitioner demonstrate actual assumption of the parental role and discharge of parental responsibilities. It should be required that the relationship with the child came into being with the consent of the biological or legal parent, and that the petitioner at least have had joint custody of the child for a significant period of time *** Other factors likely should be added to constitute a test that protects all relevant interests--much as we did in Braschi. Indeed, the criteria described by the Court in Braschi to be applied on a case-by-case basis later became the nucleus of formal standards (see 9 NYCRR 2520.6).

It is not my intention to spell out a definition but only to point out that it is surely within our competence to do so. It is indeed regrettable that we decline to exercise that authority in this visitation matter, given the explicit statutory objectives, the courts' power, and the fact that all consideration of the child's interest is, for the future, otherwise absolutely foreclosed.

I would remand the case to Supreme Court for an exercise of its discretion in determining whether Alison D. stands in loco parentis to A.D.M. and, if so, whether it is in the child's best interest to allow her the visitation rights she claims.

c. *V.C. v. M.J.B.*

V.C. v. M.J.B.
748 A.2d 539 (N.J. 1999)

See *Supra* Chapter 34A.

d. *Troxel v. Granville*
Jennifer Troxel, et vir., Petitioners, v. Tommie Granville
530 U.S. 57 (2000)

See *Supra* Chapter 23

e Notes and questions

1) Alison D. and Standing

Whether a third party has standing to seek custody or visitation is often a procedural defense that a parent raises when there is no specific statute granting the third party visitation rights. How was that issue resolved in *Alison D. v. Virginia M.* and in *V.C. v. M.J.B.*? *Alison D. v. Virginia M.* still appears to be good law in New York, *see Anonymous v. Anonymous*, 797 N.Y.S.2d 754 (App.Div. 2005); *Multari v. Sorrell*, 731 N.Y.S.2d 739 (N.Y. App.Div. 2001), and it also represents the majority view nationwide; but increasingly courts and legislatures are making exceptions for specific groups or circumstances.

2) Grandparents

There has been much litigation since the first grandparent visitation statute appeared in the 1960's, and it has not abated since the ruling in *Troxel v. Granville*. Does *Troxel* contribute to the continued litigation with its six separate opinions? What might these differing opinions reflect? What does *Troxel* add to our understanding of family autonomy from the constitutional perspective? Does it suggest support for more state intervention?

3) Stepparents

What custodial or visitation rights does the spouse of the biological parent of a child have if he or she is not a biological or adoptive parent of the child? The answer depends upon the duration and context of the relationship the spouse has with marriage and the child. For example, during the time he is married to the child's mother, such a man has the status in law of a "stepfather," and under the Uniform Civil Liability for Support Act § 4.2, he is legally obligated to support the child as long as he is married to the child's mother. 9A Uniform Laws Annotated (1954). The acceptance of that duty would appear to give rise to concomitant rights, including quasi-parental rights in the nature of custody or visitation. Would those rights terminate upon the termination of the marriage? Just as the duty to support probably would terminate, so would the quasi-parental rights to custody or visitation terminate since they are derived from the marital relationship. Thus, if the husband had no significant relationship with the child, the mere fact that he was married to the child's mother would not entitle him to any custody or visitation rights. *See J.W.F. v. Schoolcraft*, 763 P.2d 1217 (Utah App. 1988) (husband of woman who had child during marriage by another man denied custody when HLA test confirms, and he concedes, that he was not the biological father, and he was unaware his estranged wife had given birth to the child, he never had a parental relationship with the child, and the parental rights of his wife and the biological father were terminated after they abandoned the child). On the other hand, if he has established over a significant period of time an in loco parentis relationship with the child, from that quasi-parental relationship may arise a legitimate claim to post-divorce visitation, or in an extraordinary case possibly even a claim for custody, in the best interests of the child (N.B.-- a matter of the child's interest not as a matter of the "rights" of the former stepparent). *See Gribble v. Gribble*, 583 P.2d 64 (Utah 1978) (stepfather who lived with child since child was two months old and had established significant in loco parentis relationship with child was entitled to hearing regarding his claim for visitation); *In re Marriage of Allen*, 28 Wash. App. 637, 626 P.2d 16 (1981) (stepmother with substantial in loco parentis relationship considered a "parent" under Washington custody statute).

4) Former Same-Sex Partners

The number of same-sex partners who choose to raise children (often procreated by artificial insemination, or a child of one party by a former heterosexual relationship) has increased significantly in recent years – so much that some describe it as a "gayby" boom. Richman, *infra*, at 287. Census Bureau data in 2002 revealed that 1,799,000 children are living with their mother and her unmarried partner (both heterosexual and homosexual), and 1,081,000 children are living with their father and his unmarried partner (both heterosexual and homosexual), for a total of 2,880,000 children being raised by a parent and a nonmarital partner. Jason Fields, *infra*. Eleven percent (11%) of all nonmarital cohabitant couples are of the same gender. Statistical Abstract, *infra*. That suggests that about 317,000 children are being raised by same-sex couples, if same-sex couples are raising children in the same proportion as unmarried heterosexual couples. However, 2000 Census indicates that only about 20 percent of gay couples and about one-third of lesbian couples are raising children. As the rate of break-up of same-sex couples appears to be at least as high as the rate of breakup of heterosexual couples (married or cohabiting), and since having significant child-rearing responsibility for and an ongoing quasi-parental relationship with children generally are more important to women than men, it is not surprising that fierce litigation over claims for custody or visitation with biologically unrelated children by lesbian former partners of the children's biological mothers (and ex-partners) are occurring with increasing frequency.   Should the fact that a couple were engaged in a relationship that is not formally recognized in a particular jurisdiction be relevant to determining such issues? Should the fact that the biological parent has changed her lifestyle and no longer wants her children to be associated with persons who live a lifestyle she now considers immoral be relevant? Should the fact that the person seeking significant visitation was a former partner of the parent give that ex-partner greater rights or interests than the grandparents had in *Troxel v. Granville*? Should the biological mother's childrearing decision to limit or deny visitation receive less deference and respect than in *Granville* because she formerly lived with the claimant and allowed her to help care for the children? Should former same-sex partners have more/less standing or have claim to greater/fewer custody or visitation rights than former heterosexual partners? Should the standard for determining third-party visitation be higher than the standard applied to claims by biological parents or relatives? In *Troxel*, what standard had the Washington State Supreme Court applied? What standard did the U.S. Supreme Court apply?

3. Practical and Ethical Considerations

a. More Than One Visitation Order

Visitation orders bring many practical problems. One of the most challenging problems for a court is fashioning a third-party visitation order when there is already one for the noncustodial parent. In such a situation, what factors should the court consider in fashioning the order for the third-party? Protection of the parent-child relationship? Best interests of the child?

b. Duty to Visit

Should parents or children be forced to visit one another? Why/why not?

4. Bibliography

Katharine T. Bartlett, *Rethinking Parenthood as an Exclusive Status: The Need for Legal Alternatives When the Premise of the Nuclear Family Has Failed*, 70 Va. L. Rev. 879 (1984).

Joan Catherine Bohl, *Grandparent Visitation Law Grows Up: The Trend Toward Awarding Visitation Only When the Child Would Otherwise Suffer Harm*, 48 Drake L. Rev. 279 (2000).

Jason Fields, Children's Living Arrangements and Characteristics: March 2002, in Current Population Reports (June 2003), at 2, Table 1, Children by Age and Family Structure, March 2002, at http://www.census.gov/prod/2003pubs/p20-547.pdf .

Melanie B. Jacobs, *Micah Has One Mommy and One Legal Stranger: Adjudication Maternity for Nonbiological Lesbian Coparents*, 50 Buff. L. Rev. 341, 342 (2002).

Mark D. Matthew, Note, *Curing the "Every-Other-Weekend Syndrome": Why Visitation Should Be Considered Separate and Apart From Custody*, 5 Wm. & Mary J. Women & L. 411 (199).

Laurence C. Nolan, *Honor Thy Father and Thy Mother: But Court-Ordered Grandparent Visitation in the Intact Family?*, 8 BYU J. Pub. L. 51 (1993).

Nancy Polikoff, *This Child Does Have Two Mothers: Redefining Parenthood to Meet the Needs of Children in Lesbian-Mother and Other Nontraditional Families*, 78 Geo.L.J. 459 (1990).

Kimberly Richman, *Lovers, Legal Strangers, and Parents: Negotiating Parental and Sexual Identity in Family Law*, 36 Law & Soc'y Rev. 285(2002).

Statistical Abstract of the United States, 2002, at 48, table 49.

Lynn D. Wardle, *The Potential Impact of Homosexual Parenting on Children*, 1997 U. Ill. L.Rev. 833.

Lynn D. Wardle, *A Critical Analysis of Interstate Adoption Recognition of Lesbigay Adoptions*, 3 Ave Maria L. Rev. 561-616 (2005).

Lynn D. Wardle, *Considering the Impacts on Children and Society of "Lesbigay" Parenting*, 23 Quinnipiac L. Rev. 541-576 (2004).

CHAPTER 35

Custody and Visitation Modification and Enforcement

A. CUSTODY AND VISITATION MODIFICATION

1. Background

a. Standard for Modification

Custody and visitation orders are not final judgments and may be modified in order to protect the welfare of the child. The majority of courts follow a standard in modification of custody cases that is higher than the best interest of the child standard in order to preserve continuity and stability in the custodial arrangement. Modification of visitation is also within the trial court's discretion. Visitation orders are more apt to be modified because a schedule that is in the best interest of a young child may not be in the child's best interest when that child is older. If visitation is ordered in general terms, such as reasonable visitation, then there is no need for a formal hearing if the parents can reach an agreement as to what is reasonable.

b. Relocation

Relocation cases involving the custodial parent moving to another state have become a large part of recent child custody litigation. Relocation of the custodial parent and the child would interfere with the noncustodial parent's liberty interest in the parent-child relation as well as the child's interest in the parent-child relationship. Although the best interest of the child standard is used, the courts have differed in interpreting that standard in relocation cases. These cases also raise the constitutional issue of the state infringing upon the custodial parent's right to travel. The Supreme Court has not decided a case directly involving a relocation case.

2. Statutes, Cases and Doctrines

a. Uniform Marriage and Divorce Act

Section 409 [Modification]
(a) No motion to modify a custody decree may be made earlier than 2 years after its date, unless the court permits it to be made on the basis of affidavits that there is a reason to believe the child's present environment may endanger seriously his physical, mental, moral, or emotional health.
(b) If a court of this State has jurisdiction pursuant to the Uniform Child Custody Jurisdiction Act, the court shall not modify a prior custody decree or that were unknown to the court at the time of entry of the prior decree, that a change has occurred in the circumstances of the child or his custodian, and that the modification is necessary to serve the best interest of the child.

In applying these standards the court shall retain the custodian appointed pursuant to the prior decree unless:

(1) The custodian agrees to the modification;

(2) the child has been integrated into the family of the petitionor with consent of the custodian; or

(3) the child's present environment endangers seriously his physical, mental, moral, or emotional health, and the harm likely to be caused by a change of environment is outweighed by its advantages to him.

(c) Attorney fees and costs shall be assessed against a party seeking modification if the court finds that the modification action is vexatious and constitutes harassment.

b. *Birnbaum v. Birnbaum*

Lorene Salmen Birnbaum v. Ira Birnbaum
211 Cal. App. 3d 1508 (Cal. App. Ct. 1989)

KING, Associate Justice.

In this case we hold that (1) when parents have joint physical custody of their children, an order modifying the co-parenting residential arrangement does not constitute a change of custody; (2) the standard of appellate review of such an order is whether the trial court has exceeded the bounds of reason and abused the very broad discretion it possesses to make such orders; and (3) there was no abuse of discretion here.

Lorene Salmen Birnbaum appeals from an order modifying the living arrangements of the three daughters whose joint custody she shares with her former husband, Ira Birnbaum. We affirm.

In August 1983, pursuant to an agreement incorporated into their interlocutory judgment of dissolution of marriage, Lorene and Ira Birnbaum received joint legal and physical custody of their three daughters, then aged three, five and seven. One child was given a "primary residence" with her mother, another with her father, and the third to alternate yearly. [FN1*] During the school year all three were to live with Lorene during the week and spend weekends and Wednesday afternoons with Ira.

In September 1983, Lorene moved from the City of San Mateo, where the family had lived and the two older girls attended school, to "the Coast Side" of San Mateo County where the girls were enrolled in the El Granada elementary school.

In August 1986, Lorene filed a motion to modify the existing order for joint physical custody, seeking sole custody and asking that Ira's Wednesday evening visits be eliminated and his school year visitation be limited to alternate weekends. In response, Ira moved for sole physical custody with reasonable visitation rights for Lorene. In his supporting declaration he objected to the existing situation because of the distance between San Mateo and El Granada and because "the schools there are inferior to the San Mateo Schools, especially at the middle and high school levels."

At the initial hearing on the motions, the parties agreed to undergo co-parenting counseling which would result in an evaluation and recommendation by a psychologist they selected. In January 1987, the psychologist submitted a letter in which he praised both Lorene and Ira as parents, analyzed their individual strengths and weaknesses, and reported their continued difficulty in dealing with each other about the children. [*This appears to be one of those rare joint physical and legal custody arrangements which functions by virtue of a highly inflexible schedule because, as the trial court told the parents, "you are so unable to communicate with each other." In its statement of decision the court stated: "Both parents love their children, yet neither can see past their particular egocentric needs to acknowledge the full value of the other parent to the children." One example of the parties' inflexibility is that Ira, because weekends were "his" time, refused to let the girls spend Mother's Day with Lorene. As we will discuss, this form of joint custody might be described as parallel parenting, as contrasted to shared or cooperative parenting.*]

Reluctantly--"much of this falls out of my area of professional expertise"--he proposed a two-year plan allowing each parent "very nearly equal time" with the children, including the opportunity for "quality time" as well as direct involvement in their schooling. In each four-week period Lorene would have the children weekdays and Ira would have them weekends for the first two weeks. Then they would live one week with Lorene, followed by one week with Ira. Wednesday evenings the children would dine with the parent with whom they were not then residing.

At the hearing, the trial court heard testimony from Lorene, Ira and the psychologist. Lorene urged acceptance of the psychologist's proposal. Ira requested that the psychologist's proposal as to the scheduled time with each parent be reversed and the children re-enrolled in the San Mateo City school system.

The court commented at length on the complementary characteristics of Ira and Lorene and fashioned an order "which it believes will allow both these parents to contribute the most positive sides of their personalities to their children in a balanced fashion," adopting, as requested by Ira, "as a general guideline the reverse of the plan set forth by [the psychologist]." For three out of each four weeks the children would reside with Ira during the week and spend weekends and Wednesday nights with Lorene. The fourth week they would reside with Lorene and spend the weekend and one night of her choosing with Ira. During summer vacations the schedule would be reversed. In its statement of decision the trial court incorporated several of the psychologist's written findings and found in addition that "Enrollment in the Schools of the City of San Mateo would provide the children with a greater variety of both educational and enrichment options than they presently enjoy." The provisions of the prior order for joint legal and physical custody of the children remained unchanged. Lorene filed a motion for reconsideration accompanied by declarations from El Granada school personnel about the quality of the school system and the performance of the Birnbaum children therein. Over Ira's objection, the trial court found "the children had not been consulted or in any way had any input with the court," and held a 35-minute reported conference with them in chambers with the attorneys present. The trial court then denied the motion to reconsider and refused to stay its order pending appeal.

I.

In their briefs the parties treat this as an appeal from an order modifying child custody. "An application for modification of an award of custody is addressed to the sound discretion of the trial court, and its discretion will not be disturbed on appeal unless the record presents a clear case of abuse of that discretion." *** "Although precise definition is difficult, it is generally accepted that the appropriate test of abuse of discretion is whether or not the trial court exceeded the bounds of reason, all of the circumstances before it being considered."***

A.

Lorene first asserts that there were no material changed circumstances sufficient to justify a change in custody. "It is settled that to justify ordering a change in custody there must generally be a persuasive showing of changed circumstances affecting the child." *** The basic deficiency in Lorene's contention and her appeal from an order she claims changes custody is, whether there were changed circumstances or not, there has been no change of custody. The trial court ordered, "The parties shall continue to have and share joint legal and joint physical custody of their minor children," just as they did under the prior order. At most there has been a change in what the trial court termed the "co-parenting residential arrangement."

B.

Next, Lorene asserts Ira failed to meet his burden of proof that the children's best interest required a change of custody. *** As pointed out above, there has been no change of custody, just a rearrangement of the children's residential timetable. The thrust of Lorene's argument in this regard seems to be that the trial court based its order on the superiority of the San Mateo school system and on Ira's qualifications to be the "school parent." She contends neither finding is supported by the evidence. "In fact," she suggests, "the evidence is contrary to such findings." "There were, as is not unusual in a proceeding of this nature, conflicts both as to probative facts and as to the proper inferences to be drawn from such facts. But, as is true in all appellate reviews, and most emphatically in this type of controversy, it is not the function of this court to reweigh conflicting evidence and redetermine findings.... Our function has been fully performed when we find in the record substantial evidence which supports the essential findings of the trial court." ***

"Further, the testimony of a single witness, even the party himself may be sufficient." Ira testified as to the relative merits of the two school systems. Recent newspaper articles cited the elementary school his two younger daughters would attend in the City of San Mateo as "one of two schools out of six thousand in the state to be named as an outstanding school." Ira had contacted the schools about extracurricular activities and comparative test scores. He was told that the Cabrillo school district in which the girls had been attending school was comparable to other "somewhat rural" districts, that is, it did not provide the educational diversity and enrichment available in the City of San Mateo school district.

He asked Cabrillo administrators if there were "elective courses and honor courses and special courses, academic mainly, and they said no." He asked "if she'll get music lessons, and things like that, and the answer was no." He offered in evidence four handbooks from San Mateo schools, which he said reported that "these schools are blessed with the adequate resources to provide extensive extracurricular and honor courses and music lessons...." He explained that the availability of extracurricular activities at schools within walking distance of his house would allow the children to spend less time commuting and more time "perform[ing]." Ira mentioned the advantages of a school environment where a large percentage of his daughters' peers would be college bound, and his own commitment to help them get a college education. He described the learning activities he shares with each of them, from playing number and letter Bingo and writing stories, to reading aloud, to composing school papers on his word-processor and discussing "politics and religion." He felt he encouraged academics more aggressively than did Lorene.

According to the psychologist, Ira has been involved in the girls' school work to an appropriate extent, but not so much as he would like to be, because they spend the school week at Lorene's. It has been difficult for him to participate in school functions because the school is so far away. He was concerned about their future education and felt the San Mateo high schools were better than those on the Coast Side.

Clearly, there was sufficient evidence to support the challenged comment and finding.

C.

In its statement of decision, the trial court commented, "It is also troubling that Ms. Salmen unilaterally took the children from the environment where they had started their lives and their school careers without the opportunity for Mr. Birnbaum to have any input. It is hard to imagine an action that could have been more hurtful to Mr. Birnbaum." Lorene maintains this comment shows the purpose of the court's order was to punish her and redress a perceived injury to Ira. In light of the evidence, and the interest and concern displayed by the trial judge throughout this proceeding, and her carefully articulated four-page statement of decision, this allegation is ridiculous.

D.

In actions to dissolve marriages it has become quite common to include requests for joint custody of children. It is doubtful that any two words mean as many different things to as many different people as the words "joint custody." The statutory definition, having to cover the wide variety of arrangements parents make when they have joint custody, is necessarily broad and does not provide much guidance.

There seems to be a popular misconception that joint physical custody means the children spend exactly one-half their time with each parent. Such an arrangement, of course, leaves the child with no time of his or her own to spend with friends. It also elevates parental rights over children's rights and virtually treats the child as the parents' possession. It fails to take into account that the maximum personal growth and development of a child occurs from both a loving and supportive relationship within the family and the development of personal relationships outside the family. Parents' demands for equal amounts of a child's time constitute a disservice to the child, usually creating stress and preventing the child from fully achieving his or her potential. In some cases the nature of the relationship between the parents may necessitate this kind of inflexibility. Usually it is temporary, and when the former spouses have adjusted to their new and limited relationship as parents of the same children, mathematical exactitude of time is no longer necessary. That has not occurred here.

Equal division of a child's time between the parents is not the hallmark of joint custody. After all, Civil Code section 4600, subdivision (b), provides "Custody shall be awarded ... according to the best interests of the child ..." Thus, the primary focus must be what is best for the child, not what is best for the parents. Although time is important to the parents, the determining factor as to whether joint physical custody is in the best interest of the child is the nature of the parenting relationship between the parents.

***

A better public understanding of the nature of joint physical custody is essential. Parents must understand that successful joint physical custody depends upon the quality of the parenting relationship, not the allocation of time. Parents must also understand that it is much harder to be a joint physical custody parent than a sole custody parent. Fully participating with the other parent to share the burden of cooperative or shared parenting for the benefit of the child is much more demanding than having sole physical custody or being a noncustodial parent.

Finally, we cannot conclude without expressing our distress that parents can be as inflexible as Lorene and Ira when it comes to even slight adjustments in the time the children spend with each of them. As this case amply demonstrates, a point can be reached where parents, unwilling or unable to communicate for the best interest of their child, call upon a judge to become super-parent and make parenting decisions the parents themselves cannot agree upon. As a practical matter, if parents with joint physical custody are unable to modify residential arrangements for their children and call upon the court to do so, they have no basis to complain about the decision that is made. In such circumstances the court possesses the broadest possible discretion in adjusting co-parenting residential arrangements involved in joint physical custody. The appellate court certainly cannot second-guess a conscientious and competent trial court, which has had the opportunity to observe the parents and the children personally. Thus a change of the joint custody residential arrangement cannot be reversed on appeal unless the trial judge has abused the very broad discretion it possesses in such cases, that is, has exceeded the bounds of reason.

The judgment is affirmed.

c. *Marriage of Rosenfeld*
In re the Marriage of Beverly Robin Rosenfeld and Martin Sanford Rosenfeld
524 N.W.2d 212 (Iowa App. Ct. 1994)

SACKETT, Presiding Judge.

Respondent-appellant Martin Sanford Rosenfeld brings, with permission of the supreme court, an interlocutory appeal challenging a trial court's temporary order modifying the provision of his dissolution decree to transfer custody of his children, Natalie, born November 20, 1981, and Andrew, born December 27, 1987, to their mother, his former wife, petitioner-appellee Beverly Robin Rosenfeld. Martin contends Beverly has failed to meet the necessary burden for transfer of physical care, and the trial court placed too much emphasis in rendering its decision on the testimony of Dr. Rypma regarding the parental alienation syndrome. Martin contends the theory advanced by Dr. Rypma is not accepted in the field of psychology and his testimony should further be discounted because of what Martin terms an "outrageous" amount being paid for Rypma's testimony and examination of the children. We affirm as modified.

Martin and Beverly, both doctors of osteopathy, were divorced in December 1990. Physical care of the children was awarded to Martin, and Beverly was awarded reasonable visitation and ordered to pay child support of $251 per month per child. As a part of its findings in making the physical care determination, the trial court noted Beverly suffered migraine headaches and was addicted to her medication and had attempted to alienate Natalie from Martin.

Martin remarried in 1991. Beverly, since the dissolution, has obtained employment as an emergency room physician and has expanded her family practice. In July 1992, Beverly filed an application for modification of the original decree contending there had been a substantial change in economic matters. A month later, Beverly amended her petition alleging a substantial change in circumstances as to custody of the children. After an eighteen-day hearing on the issue of child custody, the trial court found Martin had attempted to alienate the children from Beverly; the court found Beverly's drug addiction was traced to a food allergy and she had overcome her addiction and succeeded in establishing a successful medical practice. The trial court granted Beverly physical care.

We are dealing with two well-educated, loving, and caring parents who, despite their many fine characteristics, have been unable to set aside the hostilities and animosities following the dissolution and work collectively for their children's best interests. Martin and Beverly both have much to offer their children. Their children love them both. There is evidence Martin and Beverly have both engaged in childish behavior and, clearly, they both have contributed to the discord. Both attribute outrageous behavior to the other. It is clear to us each has attempted to put circumstances in a light most favorable to them and they have allowed minor incidents to be blown out of proportion. Both parties have focused on building a case against the other.

The children will have a superior upbringing in either their mother's home or their father's home. Other than the attitude both express to the children's other parent, the evidence reveals the best of conditions are available for these children in either home.

This is not an original custody determination. The question, therefore, is not which home is better, but the question is whether Beverly has demonstrated she can offer the children superior care. *** Beverly must show an ability to minister to the child's needs superior to Martin's. *** If both parents are found to be equally competent to minister to the children, custody should not be changed. *** We review de novo. *** The burden for a party petitioning for a change in a dissolution is heavy *** because children deserve the security of knowing where they will grow up, and we recognize the trauma and uncertainty these proceedings cause all children. Custody once fixed should be disturbed only for the most cogent reasons. *** Beverly has the burden to show by the preponderance of evidence that conditions since the dissolution decree was entered have so materially and substantially changed that the children's best interests make it expedient to award custody to her. ***

The trial court spent eighteen days listening to Beverly's twenty-one witnesses, including seven by deposition, and Martin's thirty-five witnesses, including five by deposition. After the evidence was taken, the trial judge made the following ruling and temporary order: Shortly after the divorce, Martin remarried. He, his wife Trudi, Natalie and Andrew all continued to live in the family home on Foster Drive in Des Moines. Beverly has not remarried and lives in a three-bedroom ranch style house in Urbandale. Martin continues in his practice as an orthopedic surgeon. Beverly is presently employed under contract as an emergency room doctor. She is a family practitioner. Both are doctors of osteopathy. Beverly is thirty-eight years of age and Martin is forty-seven.

Two material changes in circumstances have occurred since the decree. At that time, Beverly had a warm and loving reciprocated relationship with her children then ages nine and three. The relationship now cannot be expressed as mutual. Beverly continues trying to be their mother and is devoted to them, but the conduct of the children toward their mother is appalling.

Also, since the decree, Beverly has learned that her migraine headaches were caused by food allergies and has modified her diet and gained control over herself. She no longer uses prescription medication and has fully demonstrated a freedom from prescription medication and continues in a healthy lifestyle.

It is clear both parents can provide for the basic needs of the children. Both parents should be able to support each other in their respective relationships with the children, but in this case that has not happened. While Beverly, either by her nature or her desire to be a mother, may have had some isolated stresses with the children, her conduct simply cannot explain the fact that her children do and say cruel and hurtful things to her. Some of that may be explained by the emergence of a pre-teen adolescent but there simply is no way it can be rationalized on explaining the conduct of a child growing from age three to age six. These children have been turned against Beverly and it has happened by conduct from Martin's household. The only way this most unfortunate situation can be corrected is to place the children in the primary physical care of Beverly.

Following the ruling, Martin requested an interlocutory appeal and a stay of the custody change, both of which were granted.

The trial court then enlarged its findings of fact. In doing so, it found this was a case of parental alienation syndrome and it was severe. The trial court found the course of conduct of Trudi and Martin clearly fit in the pattern of the syndrome. The trial court extracted from the voluminous evidence several specific examples of what it considered conduct on the part of Trudi and Martin to alienate the children from Beverly. The first involved the prior fourth of July weekend. Beverly asked to trade holidays because she had to work a sixty-hour weekend. Martin refused to change the holiday schedule and, although he knew Beverly was working, he got Andrew up to get ready for his mother's visitation and let him sit for two hours with his bag by the window watching for his mother who did not come. When she did not come on Monday, the same scene was reenacted.

The second was an attempt to charge Beverly or someone who cared for Andrew under Beverly's direction with sexually molesting or abusing him. Trudi took Andrew to doctors four times on two separate occasions with her complaints. All medical opinions refuted Trudi's claims but Trudi told others about them, including their Rabbi, and she made her complaints in front of Andrew.

The trial court found, and we agree, Beverly's situation and ability to be a nurturing mother has improved substantially since the dissolution. Beverly has found a reason for her headaches, has remained drug free for a substantial period, and has obtained remunerative and fulfilling employment.

Martin's situation has changed, too. Martin has remarried and his current wife, rather than nannies, assists him with the care of the children.

We recognize both parents have employment that is demanding and requires substantial periods of time away from home. Both have to utilize others to assist with child care. There is considerable animosity between Martin's wife, Trudi, and Beverly and there appears to be little effort to smooth this relationship. We, as did the trial court, find Trudi has contributed substantially to the discord. Disagreements have extended beyond the child custody issue.

The children have seen numerous professionals and statements made to the professionals are in evidence. The children told some professionals their stepmother was mean to them but complained to others about their mother. The children are suffering while their parents are engaged in this warfare. Natalie assumes a mother's position in her relationship with Andrew and Andrew accepts it.

Nearly all experts were of the opinion the children wanted and needed to spend more time with their mother. The guardian ad litem expressed the opinion Beverly and Martin were improving their communication.

Martin complains the trial court improperly considered the parental alienation syndrome and should not have admitted in evidence treatises about the syndrome. Martin argues, and his experts have testified, the parental alienation syndrome is not a reliable theory and should not be considered by this court. Martin contends the amount spent for Dr. Rypma's testimony on the syndrome is outrageous.

We recognize there are situations where one parent will seek to put the other parent in an unfavorable light. Some cases are slight and to be expected in our less than perfect society. Some cases are serious and should not be tolerated. ***

We do not pass upon the issue of whether parental alienation syndrome is a reliable theory. Rather, we look at the evidence induced and draw our own conclusion. Because this is a de novo review, we look only at the evidence we deem admissible. We consider the opinions of all the experts as we do the other testimony. We give opinion testimony the weight we consider it deserves after considering, among other things, the expert's education, experience, familiarity with case, reasons given for the opinion, and interest, if any, in the case. Our major concern focuses on Trudi. Obviously, well-intentioned, she seems to view the children as items to be secreted. She has been manipulative, forbidding Andrew to talk to his mother at school and church functions. The trial court in its findings noted the fact Trudi had alienated her three children from a prior marriage from their father after she divorced him. Martin, too, has failed to be reasonable about Beverly's contact with the children. Beverly volunteered with the school to accompany one of the child's classes on a field trip. After Martin learned about it, he called the school and complained. He also expected Beverly to take the hours she had chaperoned the field trip as her visitation time.

We recognize the attorney for the children has recommended custody remain fixed. We give this opinion considerable weight.

In a trial this long and with this much evidence and with the concern exhibited by the trial judge who listened to all the testimony and viewed the parties, we give considerable weight to the credibility assessments made by the trial court.

We affirm the transfer of physical care to Beverly and we modify only to change the time of transfer. It shall happen after the fall semester of 1994, probably about mid-January of 1995. This will allow Martin to file a petition for further review without requesting another stay order and will allow ample time to arrange the transfer and prepare the children for it.

Beverly and Martin are responsible for their own attorney fees. Costs on appeal are taxed to Martin. Affirmed as modified.

d. *Henry v. Henry*

D. Craig Henry v. Rebecca A. Henry
326 N.W.2d 497 (Mich. Ct. App. 1982)

LAMBROS, Judge.

On November 5, 1980, defendant was awarded a judgment of divorce and custody of her two minor children. That judgment provided that the domicile or residence of said minor children shall not be removed from the State of Michigan without prior approval of the court, as required by GCR 1963, 729.4(1). In addition, the defendant was precluded from changing the domicile or residence of the minor children from the Grand Blanc school district without prior court approval. Defendant filed a petition to obtain the court's approval to move to Minnesota with the children, but this petition was denied. Defendant appeals as of right.

The instant case presents this Court with an opportunity to clarify our position regarding removal of children from this state subsequent to the entry of a judgment of divorce and the award of custody.

M.C.L. s 552.17a; M.S.A. s 25.97(1) provides that our circuit courts shall have the jurisdiction to award custody of minor children in all divorce proceedings. In an attempt to provide guidelines for the resolution of child custody disputes, our Legislature enacted the Child Custody Act of 1970, M.C.L. s 722.21 et seq.; M.S.A. s 25.312(1) et seq. GCR 1963, 729.4 requires that an order or judgment awarding custody, of a child or children shall provide that the domicile or residence of the child shall not be removed from the State of Michigan without the approval of the judge who awarded custody, or his successor. This is the body of codified law which governs our review of the instant inquiry.

Two of our panels have already had an opportunity to examine this issue. In *Hutchins v. Hutchins*, 84 Mich.App. 236, 269 N.W.2d 539 (1978), the Court determined that in attempting to answer removal petitions, the decisions of the lower courts should be based upon the "best interests of the child" standard set out in the Child Custody Act. The Court observed that "[t]his standard applies not only in the original divorce proceeding but also in all actions involving a dispute of custody of a minor child, *see* MCL 722.24; MSA 25.312(4)." *Id.*, 238, 269 N.W.2d 539. This view of the law was adopted by a majority of the Court in *Watters v. Watters*, 112 Mich.App. 1, 314 N.W.2d 778 (1981).

In both of these cases separate opinions were appended by the third judge. Concurring in *Hutchins*, Judge William R. Beasley wrote that "in the absence of compelling reasons to the contrary, permitting a child to be removed from the State of Michigan to a new, satisfactory location, should be routinely granted". (Footnote omitted.) *Hutchins, supra*, 84 Mich.App. 239-240, 269 N.W.2d 539. Dissenting in *Watters*, Judge Kenneth B. Glaser indicated his belief that the criteria for determining the best interest of the child for custody purposes under the Child Custody Act, *322 M.C.L. s 722.23; M.S.A. s 25.312(3), were not intended to, nor should they be, applicable to removal petitions. We agree.

***

To expand the application of the Child Custody Act to include removal petitions does violence to the expressed intention of the Legislature and imposes upon the trial courts the burden to reconsider factors previously before the court in child custody disputes and may be likely to present wholly inappropriate areas of inquiry in removal petitions.

***

We believe the appropriate test to be applied in cases dealing with removal petitions is that articulated by the New Jersey Court in *D'Onofrio v. D'Onofrio*, 144 N.J.Super. 200, 365 A.2d 27 (1976), aff'd. 144 N.J.Super. 352, 365 A.2d 716 (1976), adopted by reference in *Watters v. Watters, supra*, and which recognizes the mutual rights involved:

(1) "It should consider the prospective advantages of the move in terms of its likely capacity for improving the general quality of life for both the custodial parent and the children.

(2) "It must evaluate the integrity of the motives of the custodial parent in seeking the move in order to determine whether the removal is inspired primarily by the desire to defeat or frustrate visitation by the noncustodial parent, and whether the custodial parent is likely to comply with substitute visitation orders when she is no longer subject to the jurisdiction of the courts of this State.

(3) "It must likewise take into account the integrity of the noncustodial parent's motives in resisting the removal and consider the extent to which, if at all, the opposition is intended to secure a financial advantage in respect of continuing support obligations.

(4) "Finally, the court must be satisfied that there will be a realistic opportunity for visitation in lieu of the weekly pattern which can provide an adequate basis for preserving and fostering the parental relationship with the noncustodial parent if removal is allowed." *D'Onofrio v. D'Onofrio, supra.*

The *D'Onofrio* test focuses on what is in the best interest of the new family unit, i.e., custodial parent and child, and not what is in the best interest of the child; the latter having been decided in the earlier custody hearings. Adoption of the *D'Onofrio* test comports with the legislative intent as it is currently expressed and recognizes the increasingly legitimate mobility of our society. Arbitrary imposition of the "best interests of the child" test in all matters concerning children is illogical at best and cruelly insensitive at worst.

For these reasons, the decision of the lower court rejecting defendant's petition to move to another state with the children is reversed and the cause remanded for proceedings consistent with our decision.

e. Notes and questions

1) *Rosenfeld* and the Standard for Modification

In re Marriage of Rosenfeld follows the standard of substantial or material change in circumstances. This standard is followed in most states. A few states will follow the best interest of the child standard. Other states will follow the best interest standard as an exception to the general rule when not all the facts were before the court in the initial hearing (*Simons v. Simons*, 374 A.2d 1040 (Conn. 1977)), or if the custody order was based upon the agreement of the parties or on a default judgment. (*Friederwitzer v. Friederwitzer*, 432 N.E.2d 765 (N.Y. App. Ct. 1982)). What is the UMDA's approach?

How does the UMDA's approach compare with the general rule? What policies might underlie the UMDA's approach? Why should not the best interest standard control in modification cases? Suppose the parties have been separated for a long time and the child has lived with one parent, acting as the primary caregiver. Should this case be treated as an initial custody case or as a change in custody case? *See Burchard v, Garay* 724 P.2d 486 (Ca. 1986).

2) *Henry* and Visitation Issues

It is rare that a court does not allow the noncustodial parent to visit with the child even when visitation must be supervised. Not only this parent's constitutional rights to parent are raised, but the behavioral sciences support that children benefit from contact with both parents Other scientists argue that visitation contact is not just a right of the parent, but a right of the child. Do you agree with *Henry v. Henry's* approach to the relocation issue? Does this approach adequately protect the interests of the noncustodial parent and the children?

Most states continue to disfavor disruption of settled relations between children and their non-custodial parents. *See e.g.* Herbert & Goldberg, *infra*. Several states have enacted statutory guidelines applicable in relocation cases. For example, Michigan Compiled Laws § 722.31 provides, in relevant part:

(4) Before permitting a legal residence change otherwise restricted by subsection (1), the court shall consider each of the following factors, with the child as the primary focus in the court's deliberations:

(a) Whether the legal residence change has the capacity to improve the quality of life for both the child and the relocating parent.

(b) The degree to which each parent has complied with, and utilized his or her time under, a court order governing parenting time with the child, and whether the parent's plan to change the child's legal residence is inspired by that parent's desire to defeat or frustrate the parenting time schedule.

(c) The degree to which the court is satisfied that, if the court permits the legal residence change, it is possible to order a modification of the parenting time schedule and other arrangements governing the child's schedule in a manner that can provide an adequate basis for preserving and fostering the parental relationship between the child and each parent; and whether each parent is likely to comply with the modification.

(d) The extent to which the parent opposing the legal residence change is motivated by a desire to secure a financial advantage with respect to a support obligation.

(e) Domestic violence, regardless of whether the violence was directed against or witnessed by the child.

(5) Each order determining or modifying custody or parenting time of a child shall include a provision stating the parent's agreement as to how a change in either of the child's legal residences will be handled. If such a provision is included in the order and a child's legal residence change is done in compliance with that provision, this section does not apply. If the parents do not agree on such a provision, the court shall include in the order the following provision: "A parent whose custody or parenting time of a child is governed by this order shall not change the legal residence of the child except in compliance with section 11 of the 'Child Custody Act of 1970', 1970 PA 91, MCL 722.31."

With such a laundry list (whether statutory or derived from clear case-law), counsel are better able to advise and prepare clients to deal with relocation issues.

3. Practical and Ethical Considerations

a. Visitation Centers

Many parents find it difficult to communicate and cooperate with one another in order to implement the visitation arrangement. Visitation centers have evolved not only in the United States but in other countries to assist parents with many of the practical problems of visitation. They are frequently involved in providing a place for the parents to pick up and return the child and for a place for supervised visitation. These centers are sponsored by private or public funds or by both. Funding remains a critical issue because of the continuing and growing need for these centers. The federal and state governments have become intimately involved in the collection of child support. Should these governments also show the same involvement in the social part of child's welfare?

4. Bibliography

Debra A. Clement, Note, *A Compelling Need For Mandated Use of Supervised Visitation Programs*, 36 Fam. & Conciliation Cts. Rev. 294 (1998).

Walter A. Herbert, Jr., & Irwin A. Goldberg, *Handling Child Relocation*, 39 Md. Bar J., May/June 2006, at 18.

Judith Wallerstine & Tony J. Tanke, *To Move or Not to Move: Psychological and Legal Considerations in the Relocation of Children After Divorce*, 30 Fam. L. Q. 305 (1996).

Joan Wexler, *Rethinking Modification of Child Custody Decrees*, 94 Yale L. J. 757 (1985).

B. CUSTODY AND VISITATION ENFORCEMENT

1. Background

a. Contempt

Historically, in child custody cases, the courts have used their contempt powers to enforce these orders. Contempt may be either civil or criminal. Most cases involve civil contempt, where the penalty is used to encourage the parent to obey the order. The policies underlying the use of its civil contempt powers are to protect the rights of the non-offending party and the child and to protect the integrity of the judicial system. The most severe penalty for finding a parent in contempt of court is incarceration.

b. Tort and Other Remedies

The tort of intentional interference with the parent-child relationship (or its equivalence) is recognized in many jurisdictions. The action is also brought against third parties who interfere with the parent-child relationship. There are numerous other remedies in enforcing custody and visitation orders. The use of the habeas corpus writ, change of custody to the non-offending party, make-up visitation as well as criminal sanctions are also available.

2 Statutes, Cases and Doctrines

a. Carlson v. Carlson

Glenda Carlson v. Harold Lee Carlson
661 P.2d 833 (Kan.App.Ct. 1983)

SPENCER, Judge.

Plaintiff and defendant, parents of four minor children, were divorced June 18, 1976. They have since been engaged in almost constant litigation relative to child custody and visitation rights.

Under date of February 9, 1981, the trial court, having then entered at least four orders relative to custody exclusive of the original decree, modified its order by placing custody of the children with plaintiff in this manner:

"That the children are placed in the care, custody, and control of the Plaintiff, Glenda Carlson, provided, and when and for so long as, she resides in McPherson County, Kansas; otherwise custody is placed with Defendant."

Under date of January 8, 1982, an evidentiary hearing was conducted and plaintiff was found to be in indirect contempt of an October 16, 1981, order by interfering with defendant's specified rights of visitation. As punishment, the court directed that plaintiff be confined in the McPherson County jail in the custody of the sheriff for a period of 48 hours, scheduled to be served at the rate of 12 hours per day on four specified dates. She was also ordered to pay defendant the sum of $200 for his attorney's fee incurred in that matter. An appeal bond was filed.

[The court's discussion of the removal issue is omitted.]

Plaintiff was found in contempt for failure to have all of the children available for visitation by defendant on two occasions. She was sentenced to serve 48 hours in the county jail and to pay defendant's attorney's fee. Plaintiff challenges the sufficiency of the evidence.

It should suffice to say that we have examined the record before us and find there was sufficient competent evidence that plaintiff had failed on the occasions cited to make all of the children available for visitation by defendant as she had been ordered to do. As was held in *Strecker v. Wilkinson*, 220 Kan. 292, Syl. p 2, 552 P.2d 979 (1976):

> Judgment in a contempt proceeding rests within the sound discretion of the trier of facts and will not be disturbed on appellate review absent a clear showing of abuse of discretion."

We find no abuse of discretion in the determination that plaintiff was guilty of contempt. However, we are concerned with the punishment imposed.

In *Goetz v. Goetz*, 181 Kan. 128, 309 P.2d 655 (1957), we find:

> A proceeding to punish plaintiff for contempt for willfully refusing to comply with an order awarding custody of minor children to plaintiff and granting to defendant visitation rights, is remedial in character and intended to coerce plaintiff to comply with such order for the benefit of the defendant, and is, therefore, civil in nature and one for indirect civil contempt.

Syl. p 2.

> Punishment for indirect civil contempt is ordered where the party in contempt has refused to do an affirmative act required by the provisions of an order, which, either in form or in substance, is mandatory in character. In such a case, imprisonment is not inflicted as punishment but is intended to be remedial by coercing the party in contempt to do what he has refused to do, and the proper sentence is that the party in contempt stand committed unless and until he performs the affirmative act required by the court's order.

Syl. p 3.

> A sentence imposed in an indirect civil contempt proceeding of imprisonment for 90 days in the county jail is wholly punitive and one which may properly be imposed only in a proceeding instituted and tried as for criminal contempt.

Syl. p 4.

Here, as was true in *Goetz*, the jail sentence imposed upon plaintiff was unqualified and contained no provision for her release should she purge herself of contempt. It was not made possible for her to unlock the door of the county jail and to discharge herself by doing that which she had previously failed to do. There was therefore a variance between the indirect civil contempt proceedings adopted and the punishment imposed, which was a punitive sentence appropriate only for criminal contempt. *Goetz*, 181 Kan. at 139, 309 P.2d 655. It follows that the jail sentence imposed upon plaintiff as the result of her indirect civil contempt, as was adjudged by the court, was erroneous and must be set aside.

Finally it is argued the court erred in finding defendant was not in default of child support payments for the period of time custody of the children had been with him. This contention is without merit by reason of the order of the court which provided the child support obligation was to be proportionately suspended during the time the children were with defendant, and by reason of the authority of *Brady v. Brady*, 225 Kan. at 491, 592 P.2d 865.

The jail sentence imposed upon plaintiff under date of January 8, 1982, is set aside and as so modified the judgment is affirmed.

b. *Lombardo v. Lombardo*

Maureen R. Lombardo v. Charles M. Lombardo
507 N.W.2d 788 (Mich. App. Ct. 1993)

HOLBROOK, Judge.

In this child custody dispute, plaintiff appeals as of right the September 24, 1991, Grand Traverse Circuit Court order denying her motion to enroll the parties' minor son, Robert, in a program for gifted and talented children. We vacate the trial court's order and remand.

The parties were divorced on May 14, 1985, and awarded "joint custody, care, control and education" of their children Michael, Erin, and Robert. The original divorce judgment awarded physical custody of the children to plaintiff, but the judgment was amended later to transfer physical custody to defendant. Plaintiff was awarded visitation rights.

On the Traverse City school district's third-grade placement test, the parties' son Robert ranked fourth of nine hundred students. Robert completed a fourth-grade curriculum as a third grader at the Old Mission School. Robert was selected to attend the school district's talented and gifted program, which selects children from home schools and places them with other gifted children for education.

The parties disagree over whether to enroll Robert in the program for gifted children. Plaintiff thinks that Robert's attendance in the program is essential for him to reach his scholastic potential. After watching Robert's brother Michael go through the program, defendant believes that Robert would experience difficulty adjusting to the program and might narrow his focus on academics only. Unable to agree with regard to the issue, plaintiff filed a motion to order Robert into the program.

Following a hearing regarding the matter, the trial court entered its order denying plaintiff's motion. The trial court found that an established educational environment was in place and that Robert was doing well in that environment. The trial court noted the problem of transporting Robert to the school and the segregated nature of the program. In the absence of any law regarding the subject, the trial court determined that the parent who is the primary physical custodian should make the decision. The trial court concluded that if a different standard of review was applicable, then there had not been a showing that keeping Robert at his current school was not in his best interest. ****

Next, plaintiff argues that the trial court erred in determining that the parent who is the primary physical custodian of a child should decide where the child goes to school when the parents are joint custodians of the child and cannot agree concerning that issue. Plaintiff further argues that to the extent that the trial court considered the best interests of the child, it erred in its determination of the best interests of Robert under these circumstances. ****

In *Fletcher v. Fletcher*, 200 Mich.App. 505, 511-512, 504 N.W.2d 684 (1993), this Court recently clarified the standard of review in child custody cases:

> In accord with *Beason* [*v. Beason*, 435 Mich. 791, 460 N.W.2d 207 (1990)], this Court reviews the trial court's findings of fact under the clearly erroneous standard. This review is not de novo. We will not reverse the decision of the trial court if the trial court's view of the evidence is plausible. Otherwise, this Court will review de novo the child custody decision. However, as provided by statute, we will affirm the trial court's decision unless the trial court committed a palpable abuse of discretion or a clear legal error on a major issue. Because child custody decisions are dispositional in nature, the trial court's ultimate disposition is subject to review de novo.

Id.; *Schubring v. Schubring*, 190 Mich.App. 468; 476 N.W.2d 434 (1991).

Defendant has primary physical custody of the children, and plaintiff has physical custody of the children for not less than 128 days each year. When a child resides with a parent, that parent decides all routine matters concerning the child. M.C.L. s 722.26a(4); M.S.A. s 25.312(6a)(4). Because the parties in this case were awarded joint custody of their children, they share the decision-making authority with respect to the "important decisions affecting the welfare of the child." .C.L. s 722.26a(7)(b); .S.A. s 25.312(6a)(7)(b).

This Court has held that a trial court properly denies joint custody in a proceeding to modify the custody portion of a divorce judgment where the parties cannot agree on basic child-rearing issues, in light of the state's interest in protecting the child's best interests. *Fisher v. Fisher*, 118 Mich.App. 227, 324 N.W.2d 582 (1982). Unfortunately, the Legislature has not provided guidance concerning how to resolve disputes involving "important decisions affecting the welfare of the child" that arise between joint custodial parents.

Citing *Griffin v. Griffin*, 699 P.2d 407 (Colo.1985), defendant argues that the parent who has primary physical custody of a child has the power to decide the type of educational program the child will experience. In *Griffin*, the divorce decree awarded custody of the parties' child to the petitioner mother. The petitioner and the respondent agreed in the divorce decree that they were to select jointly the child's schools. When the parties were unable to agree about the choice of schools for their child, the respondent father moved to enforce the education provision of the decree. Noting that the agreement did not provide a means of resolving deadlocks over school selection, the Colorado Supreme Court ruled that the agreement was unenforceable because the court has no power to force the parties to reach agreement. *Id.* at 409. The *Griffin* court determined that "any attempt to enforce the agreement by requiring the parents to negotiate and reach a future agreement would be not only futile, but adverse to the interests of the child as well." *Id.* at 410. The court in Griffin further determined that the power to control the child's education remained with the mother as the custodial parent in accordance with a Colorado statute that authorizes the custodial parent to make child-rearing decisions in the absence of an enforceable agreement concerning the child's education. *Id.* at 411.

Griffin is similar to the present case where the parties have agreed through the use of joint custody to share the decision-making authority with respect to decisions concerning the welfare of the children. However, *Griffin* is distinguishable by the existence of the Colorado statute that authorizes the custodial parent to make child-rearing decisions in the absence of an enforceable agreement concerning the child's education.

We are mindful of the fact that a court is usually ill-equipped to fully comprehend and act with regard to the varied everyday needs of a child in these circumstances, because it is somewhat of a stranger to both the child and the parents in a marital dissolution proceeding. ** We also recognize that requiring the parent to meet and resolve the issue "exposes the child to further discord and surrounds the child with an atmosphere of hostility and insecurity." *Griffin, supra* at 410. However, joint custody in this state by definition means that the parents share the decision-making authority with respect to the important decisions affecting the welfare of the child, and where the parents as joint custodians cannot agree on important matters such as education, it is the court's duty to determine the issue in the best interests of the child. ***

We believe the trial court in this case clearly erred in determining that the parent who is the primary physical custodian has the authority to resolve any disputes concerning the important decisions affecting the welfare of the children. M.C.L. s 722.27(1)(c); M.S.A. s 25.312(7)(1)(c), provides that a court shall change a previous custody order only if there is clear and convincing evidence that it is in the best interests of the children. In allowing the primary physical custodian to resolve the important disputes, a trial court might tacitly violate s 7 of the Child Custody Act.

The controlling consideration in child custody disputes between parents is the best interests of the children. M.C.L. s 722.25; M.S.A. s 25.312(5). Parties to a divorce judgment cannot by agreement usurp the court's authority to determine suitable provisions for the child's best interest. *** Similarly, the court should not relinquish its authority to determine the best interests of the child to the primary physical custodian. Accordingly, we conclude that a trial court must determine the best interests of the child in resolving disputes concerning "important decisions affecting the welfare of the child" that arise between joint custodial parents.

We agree with plaintiff that the trial court did not make specific findings concerning the best interests of Robert. A trial court must consider, evaluate, and determine each of the factors listed at M.C.L. s 722.23; M.S.A. s 25.312(3), in determining the best interests of the child. *** The trial court in this case merely determined that plaintiff had failed to show that keeping Robert at his current school was not in his best interest. Consequently, we remand this case to the trial court to determine the best interests of Robert according to the relevant factors contained in M.C.L. s 722.23; M.S.A. s 25.312(3).

Believing that all relevant evidence should be before the court, we do not preclude the use of Karen McClatchey's testimony at the new hearing in the circuit court if she is properly subpoenaed or if a new deposition is taken and introduced in conformity with the court rules. Vacated and remanded for proceedings consistent with this opinion. We do not retain jurisdiction.

c. Notes and Questions

1) Visitation and Support

As a general rule, child support cannot be withheld as a remedy of violation of a visitation order, and vice versa. This general rule is based on the best interest of the child.

2) Settling Parental Disagreements

Are there advantages to approach parental disagreements in cases like *Lombardo* as that court did or like the court in *Griffin v. Griffin*, 699 P.2d 407 (Col. 1985), discussed in *Lombardo*?

As the use of arbitrators in child custody disputes grows (perhaps as a result often of the use of antenuptial or postnuptial agreements or nonmarital parenting) questions arise about the extent to which courts will enforce such "private" custody arbitration determinations. Some commentators suggest that constitutional values (including respect for parental rights) and prudential considerations (including state respect for intact family decisions and limitations on state intervention) favor judicial deference to arbitral custody decisions. Spitko, *infra* at 1179-1212. Presently, most courts treat such arbitral custody decisions as "valid but voidable" and replace them with judicially-crafted custody decisions rather easily. However, there is authority for the minority position that custody awards by arbitrators acting under parental authorization are binding on the court and must be enforced unless a high standard of harm to the child is shown. Spitko, *infra* at 1162-66.

3) Parental Alienation

In *Schutz v. Schutz*, 581 So.2d 1290, (Fla. 1991), a parental alienation case, the court ordered the offending parent "to do everything in her power to create in the minds of the children a loving, caring feeling toward the father and to convince the children that it is a the mother's desire that they see their father and love their father." What constitutional issues does this order raise?

4) Civil Unions and Visitation Restrictions

In *Burns v. Burns*, 560 Se.2d 47, (Ga. Ct. App. 2d Div. 2002), the divorced parties' consent decree of the visitation agreement provided that neither party would have overnight stays with the children during such times as either of them cohabited with an adult to whom either was not married. Darian Burns had custody of the three children, and Susan Burns had visitation rights. In 2000, Susan and her lesbian partner went to Vermont and registered as a Vermont civil union. On their return to Georgia, Susan began having overnight visitation with the children while her partner was present. Darian moved for an order of contempt for violation of the visitation consent decree. Susan defended on the grounds that the two were legally married. The trial court held a civil union did not make the partner related; hence, Susan was in contempt of the consent decree. On appeal, a panel of the Georgia Court of Appeals unanimously held that a civil union entered into in Vermont was not equivalent to marriage. The court further held that even if a civil union was the equivalent of marriage in Vermont, the State of Georgia did not have to recognize it as such. Georgia's Defense of Marriage Act clearly stated Georgia's public policy that marriage can only be the union of a man and woman. The court held that what constitutes marriage in Georgia was a legislative function, and as judges they were required to follow the clear language of the statute. The court also held that the court was not required to give full faith and credit to same-sex marriages of other states, citing the Federal Defense of Marriage Act. This case is the first case in the country to address the full faith and credit issue as applied to civil unions. Did the court properly apply the law? Is the law sound? Why/why not?

3. Practical and Ethical Considerations

a. Obligations of Attorneys to Clients Who Hide Children

What are the ethical duties of an attorney representing a client who has hidden the child from the other parent? How should the rules governing attorney-client privilege and confidentiality apply?

4. Bibliography

Carol S. Bruch, *Parental Alienation Syndrome and Parental Alienation: Getting It Wrong in Child Custody Cases*, 35 Fam. L. Q. 527 (2001).

Steven L. Novinson, *Post-Divorce Visitation: Untying the Triangular Knot*, 1983 U. Ill. L. Rev. 121.

E. Gary Spitko, *Reclaiming the "Creatures of the State": Contracting for Child Custody Decisionmaking in the Best Interests of the Family*, 57 Wash. & Lee L. Rev. 1139 (2000).

Joan Wexler, *Rethinking Modification of Child Custody Decrees*, 94 Yale L. J. 757 (1985).

CHAPTER 36

Child Support: Jurisdiction;
Procedures; Guidelines; Factors

A. JURISDICTION AND PROCEDURES

1. Background

a. Child Support Jurisdiction

Because child support is paid from the obligor's assets, the court must obtain in personam jurisdiction over the obligor to enter a support order. Obtaining jurisdiction over nonresident obligors may be problematic. If a nonresident obligor is not present in the state when served or does not consent to in personam jurisdiction, the state must rely on its long-arm statute to assert jurisdiction.

The Supreme Court of the United States has twice in recent times addressed the constitutionally-required standards for assertion of jurisdiction to order a defendant to pay child support. The first case was decided just a year after *Shaffer v. Heitner*, 433 U.S. 186 (1977), extended the requirements of minimum contacts to cases involving *quasi in rem* jurisdiction. In *Kulko v. Superior Court*, 436 U.S. 84 (1978), the father and mother of two children, living in New York, obtained a divorce which incorporated a separation agreement which allowed the father to have custody of the two children for nine months of the year in New York, and the mother would have custody for three months. The mother moved to California. A year later, the daughter decided that she wanted to spend nine months with her mother in California, and three months with her father in New York. The father agreed to the arrangement and sent his daughter to California with her belongings. About two years later the other child also decided he wanted to live with his mother and, unbeknownst to his father, had his mother send him a plane ticket which he used to fly to California. After both children were in California, the mother brought an action in California to modify the custody decree to award her full custody of the children, and to increase child support. The father argued that the California court lacked minimum contacts jurisdiction over him. The trial court rejected this claim and the father appealed as to the child support claim (dropping his objection to California's custody modification jurisdiction). California Supreme Court affirmed. The U.S. Supreme Court reversed. Justice Marshall, the author of the *Shaffer* opinion, wrote the opinion for the Court on the appeal which involved only the question of child support. The Court explicitly rejected the argument that the mere act of sending children to reside in another state was enough to subject parents to jurisdiction of the state to determine their custodial rights and duties. To accept that argument, the Court noted:

> would discourage parents from entering into reasonable visitation agreements. Moreover, it could arbitrarily subject one parent to suit in any State of the Union where the other parent chose to spend time while having custody of their offspring pursuant to a separation agreement.

436 U.S. at 93. The Court further held:

> We cannot accept the proposition that appellant's acquiescence in Ilsa's desire to live with her mother conferred jurisdiction over appellant in the California courts in this action. *A father who agrees, in the interests of family harmony and his children's preferences, to allow them to spend more time in California than was required under a separation agreement can hardly be said to have 'purposefully availed himself' of the 'benefits and protections' of California's laws." See Shaffer v. Heitner*, 433 U.S., at 216.

436 U.S. at 94 (emphasis added). Finally, the Court emphasized that minimum contacts in domestic relations cases are more demanding than in ordinary tort or commercial litigation.

> The cause of action herein asserted arises, not from the defendant's commercial transactions in interstate commerce, but rather *from his personal, domestic relations* . . . . [A]ppellant's activities cannot fairly be analogized to an insurer's sending an insurance contract and premium notices into the State to an insured resident of the State. *Cf. McGee v. International Life Insurance Co.*, 355 U.S. 220 (1957). Furthermore, the controversy between the parties arises from a separation that occurred in the State of New York; appellee Horn seeks modification of a contract that was negotiated in New York and that she flew to New York to sign.

Id. at 97 (emphasis added).

Thus, not only did the Court apply the minimum contacts test to child support cases, but it emphasized that certain contacts that would suffice to establish minimum contacts in a commercial context would not be sufficient to establish minimum contacts for a child support claim because of the sensitive nature of the family relationships involved. Public policies favoring contact between parents and children and encouraging cooperation between parents after divorce are so strong that in those preferred activities will not be deemed sufficient contacts for minimum contacts analysis. The inference of the *Kulko* decision is that parenting disputes, like divorce, are "divisible" jurisdictionally, and that the Constitution requires a higher standard for assertion of jurisdiction to impose a support obligation upon an absent parent that to determine and allocate custodial and visitation rights.

Twelve years later, in *Burnham v. Superior Court*, 495 U.S. 604 (1990), the Court tacitly reiterated the status-support distinction. In that case a couple with two children were domiciled in New Jersey; the wife moved to California taking the children with her on the understanding that she would file for divorce. The husband filed for divorce in New Jersey before the wife filed in California, and he refused to cooperate with service by mail in the wife's California divorce case. However, when he was in California on business and stopped to visit the children, she had him served when returning the children from visitation. The husband filed a motion to quash "on the ground that the court lacked personal jurisdiction over him . . . ." California courts refused to quash service of process and U.S. Supreme Court affirmed the assertion of *in personam* jurisdiction. In so doing, the Court emphasized that it was addressing the issue of *in personam* jurisdiction only, and physical presence in the state, even if unrelated to the subject of the action, is sufficient for "gotcha" *in personam* jurisdiction. As in *Kulko* the husband's failure to contest status (child custody) jurisdiction, and the Court's tunnel-vision focus on *in personam* jurisdiction infers a "divisible jurisdiction" rule - that the test for jurisdiction required for imposition of child support obligation upon a nonresident parent is different and higher than the test for assertion of jurisdiction to award custody and visitation. However, *Burnham* may be read as cutting back somewhat on the protection afforded the nonresident parent in child support cases. Mr. Burnham was in Southern California for a brief business trip. Before leaving the state, he took a trip up to the San Francisco area where his wife lived, in order to visit his children. He was served with process when he returned his oldest child to his wife's home after exercising visitation. The fact that the Court upheld the service of process seems to erode somewhat the *Kulko* principle that activities to maintain relations with the children should not be counted as "contacts" in assessing whether minimum contacts exist sufficient to justify the assertion of jurisdiction. (The father had come to the state on business, and the *Burnham* Court did not consider at all the maintain-relations exemption principle of *Kulko*, but focused entirely on whether "gotcha" service in-state is sufficient for assertion of *in personam* jurisdiction generally, even if minimum contacts otherwise do not exist. On the other hand, physical presence in the forum state is the historical basis for *in personam* jurisdiction.)

b. Interstate Jurisdiction

Jurisdiction to enforce child support orders interstate has been problematic because child support orders historically were non-final judgments, and sister states were not obligated to give them full faith and credit as interpreted by decisions of the Supreme Court. In the 1950's, however, states began to respond to these interstate issues by adopting versions of a uniform act (Uniform Reciprocal Enforcement of Support Act (URESA)) and later its revision (Revised Uniform Reciprocal Enforcement of Support Act (RURESA)) in which the states would cooperate in enforcing sister states' child support orders. This Act also provided a means of obtaining an original child support order over a nonresident obligor. By the 1990's, all states had adopted versions of the act. The Uniform Interstate Family Support Act is the latest attempt to address these problems, replacing URESA and RURESA. The Uniform Interstate Family Support Act (UIFSA) was promulgated in 1992 by the National Conference of Commissioners on Uniform State Laws, and approved by the American Bar Association in 1993. In addition, it attempts to clear up many of the inconsistencies among the states under the former uniform acts. In 1996, Congress enacted legislation requiring all states to adopt this Act if they wanted to continue to be eligible for assistance for child support enforcement programs. 42 U.S.C. § 666(f), inserted by Publ. L. No. 104-193, § 321.

In 1994, Congress enacted the Full Faith and Credit Support Orders Act (FFCUSOA), 28 U.S.C. § 1738 B, to address the full faith and credit issue so that states must enforce sister state judgments if they meet the requirement of the statute. Both the FFCUSOA and the UIFSA provide that the state that issues the initial support order retains continuing exclusive jurisdiction over this order as long as that state remains the residence of the child or any party.

2. Statutes , Cases and Doctrines

a. The Uniform Interstate Family Support Act

The Uniform Interstate Family Support Act,"UIFSA," as it is known, provides for broad long-arm jurisdiction to give courts in the home state of the support-receiving family the greatest possible opportunity to obtain personal jurisdiction over the obligor, including if the nonresident parent resided in the State with the child. The UIFSA provides proceedings for support of a child or a spouse (thus, parental support claims are excluded). Modification of child support orders is severely limited, usually to the court that entered it (if it still has jurisdiction). Spousal support is modifiable in an interstate case only after such a request has been made to the original issuing state. The UIFSA provides, generally, that the law of the forum state applies as to procedural matters, except as to certain uniform procedures, but the law and choice of law rules of the state issuing the original order are applied to substantive issues. The UIFSA introduces the principle of continuing, exclusive jurisdiction, so that only one support order will be in effect at any given time. Under the previous uniform acts, it was common to have multiple valid support orders issued by different jurisdictions. Private attorneys as well as attorneys for public agencies may represent parties. Paternity may be adjudicated for the first time, even if support is not sought. However, visitation issues may not be raised in UIFSA proceedings. All enforcement begins with registration of the order in the responding state by means of simplified procedures. Direct enforcement (by mailing a support order to the employer of the obligor) as well as direct administrative enforcement is provided. *See generally Prefatory Note*, Uniform Interstate Family Support Act, 9 (IB) U.L.A. 394-398 (1999); *Uniform Interstate Family Support Act (with Unofficial Annotations by John J. Sampson*, 27 Fam. L.Q. 93, 100-103 (1993).

One question that arose frequently under the various URESA versions is whether the responding court in a URESA action could increase or reduce the amount of support the obligor must pay. Nearly three-fourths of the 25 courts which have addressed this question have answered "yes," noting that the URESA provides for the enforcement of the "duty" of support, not merely the prior support order. *See generally Koon v. Boulder County Department of Social Services*, 494 So.2d 1126 (Fla. 1986) (opinion contains a comprehensive review of case law). However, under UIFSA generally only the issuing court that has continuing jurisdiction may modify a support order.

b. 28 U.S.C. § 1738B. Full faith and Credit for Child Support Orders

(a) General rule.--The appropriate authorities of each State--

(1) shall enforce according to its terms a child support order made consistently with this section by a court of another State; and

(2) shall not seek or make a modification of such an order except in accordance with subsections (e), (f), and (i).

(b) Definitions.--In this section:

"child" means--

(A) a person under 18 years of age; and

(B) a person 18 or more years of age with respect to whom a child support order has been issued pursuant to the laws of a State.

"child's State" means the State in which a child resides.

"child's home State" means the State in which a child lived with a parent or a person acting as parent for at least 6 consecutive months immediately preceding the time of filing of a petition or comparable pleading for support and, if a child is less than 6 months old, the State in which the child lived from birth with any of them. A period of temporary absence of any of them is counted as part of the 6-month period.

"child support" means a payment of money, continuing support, or arrearages or the provision of a benefit (including payment of health insurance, child care, and educational expenses) for the support of a child.

"child support order"--

(A) means a judgment, decree, or order of a court requiring the payment of child support in periodic amounts or in a lump sum; and

(B) includes--

(I) a permanent or temporary order; and

(ii) an initial order or a modification of an order.

"contestant" means--

(A) a person (including a parent) who--

(I) claims a right to receive child support;

(ii) is a party to a proceeding that may result in the issuance of a child support order; or

(iii) is under a child support order; and

(B) a State or political subdivision of a State to which the right to obtain child support has been assigned.

"court" means a court or administrative agency of a State that is authorized by State law to establish the amount of child support payable by a contestant or make a modification of a child support order.

"modification" means a change in a child support order that affects the amount, scope, or duration of the order and modifies, replaces, supersedes, or otherwise is made subsequent to the child support order.

"State" means a State of the United States, the District of Columbia, the Commonwealth of Puerto Rico, the territories and possessions of the United States, and Indian country (as defined in section 1151 of title 18).

(c) Requirements of child support orders.--A child support order made by a court of a State is made consistently with this section if--

(1) a court that makes the order, pursuant to the laws of the State in which the court is located and subsections (e), (f), and (g)--

(A) has subject matter jurisdiction to hear the matter and enter such an order; and

(B) has personal jurisdiction over the contestants; and

(2) reasonable notice and opportunity to be heard is given to the contestants.

(d) Continuing jurisdiction.--A court of a State that has made a child support order consistently with this section has continuing, exclusive jurisdiction over the order if the State is the child's State or the residence of any individual contestant unless the court of another State, acting in accordance with subsections (e) and (f), has made a modification of the order.

(e) Authority to modify orders.--A court of a State may modify a child support order issued by a court of another State if--

(1) the court has jurisdiction to make such a child support order pursuant to subsection (I); and

(2)(A) the court of the other State no longer has continuing, exclusive jurisdiction of the child support order because that State no longer is the child's State or the residence of any individual contestant; or

(B) each individual contestant has filed written consent with the State of continuing, exclusive jurisdiction for a court of another State to modify the order and assume continuing, exclusive jurisdiction over the order.

(f) Recognition of child support orders.--If 1 or more child support orders have been issued with regard to an obligor and a child, a court shall apply the following rules in determining which order to recognize for purposes of continuing, exclusive jurisdiction and enforcement:

(1) If only 1 court has issued a child support order, the order of that court must be recognized.

(2) If 2 or more courts have issued child support orders for the same obligor and child, and only 1 of the courts would have continuing, exclusive jurisdiction under this section, the order of that court must be recognized.

(3) If 2 or more courts have issued child support orders for the same obligor and child, and more than 1 of the courts would have continuing, exclusive jurisdiction under this section, an order issued by a court in the current home State of the child must be recognized, but if an order has not been issued in the current home State of the child, the order most recently issued must be recognized.

(4) If 2 or more courts have issued child support orders for the same obligor and child, and none of the courts would have continuing, exclusive jurisdiction under this section, a court having jurisdiction over the parties shall issue a child support order, which must be recognized.

(5) The court that has issued an order recognized under this subsection is the court having continuing, exclusive jurisdiction under subsection (d).

(g) Enforcement of modified orders.--A court of a State that no longer has continuing, exclusive jurisdiction of a child support order may enforce the order with respect to nonmodifiable obligations and unsatisfied obligations that accrued before the date on which a modification of the order is made under subsections (e) and (f).

(h) Choice of law.--

(1) In general.--In a proceeding to establish, modify, or enforce a child support order, the forum State's law shall apply except as provided in paragraphs (2) and (3).

(2) Law of State of issuance of order.--In interpreting a child support order including the duration of current payments and other obligations of support, a court shall apply the law of the State of the court that issued the order.

(3) Period of limitation.--In an action to enforce arrears under a child support order, a court shall apply the statute of limitation of the forum State or the State of the court that issued the order, whichever statute provides the longer period of limitation.

(i) Registration for modification.--If there is no individual contestant or child residing in the issuing State, the party or support enforcement agency seeking to modify, or to modify and enforce, a child support order issued in another State shall register that order in a State with jurisdiction over the nonmovant for the purpose of modification.

c. Notes and Questions

1) UIFSA, URESA, and RURESA

The UIFSA of 1992 is the latest version of a "uniform" law to facilitate interstate collection of support, including child support. It was intended to replace the Uniform Reciprocal Enforcement of Support Act (URESA) what was been adopted in one version or another by all American states. Actually, however, there were several different versions. The URESA was first proposed in 1950. That version was amended in 1952, and again in 1958. In 1968 a revised version (sometimes referred to as RURESA) was promulgated, and by 1992 thirty-seven (37) states had adopted the RURESA, and seventeen states or other U.S. jurisdictions had adopted one of the versions of the earlier URESA (as all of the versions of the former uniform act are collectively identified). Thus, in terms of multistate acceptance of a uniform procedure for interstate collection of child support, URESA was a great success. URESA provides a dual-court mechanism for the enforcement of child support obligations. It permits the obligee (or state agency subrogee of the obligee) to file an action in his or her homestate (the initiating court) which will be referred to a court in the state in which the obligor resides (the responding court). The proceeding to enforce the support obligation (usually a child support order) continues in the obligor's state court. Thus, the obligor may defend against enforcement of the obligation in a convenient (to him or her) local forum. The obligee is represented in the proceedings at no cost by a public attorney of that state (often a deputy county attorney or similar counsel). URESA also provides for the taking of evidence from the obligee in the initiating state court, which may be used in the proceeding in the responding court. Payment of support is directed to be made to the court of the responding state which transmits it to the initiating court to disburse to the obligee.

With the arrival of the no-fault divorce "revolution" in the 1970s and 1980s, the size of the problem expanded beyond all previous anticipation. Moreover, the government-dependent structure and bureaucratic procedures created by URESA proved to be too cumbersome, too slow, and too unwieldy to efficiently achieve interstate support collection in the days of widespread interstate consequences of a-million-a-year divorces. John J. Sampson & Paul M. Kurtz, *infra*. By the 1990s it was reported that three-quarters of custodial mothers in the United States either lacked a child support order or failed to receive full payment under such orders. Children with nonresiding fathers who live in other states suffer the most. "Interstate child support cases represent approximately 30 percent of the total child support caseload yet only $1 of every $10 collected is from an interstate case. In fact, 34 percent of custodial mothers in interstate cases report that they have never received a dime." Margaret Campbell Haynes, *infra*. In 1990 Congress convened a U.S. Commission on Interstate Child Support which reported and made recommendations regarding the issue. The Commission found, among other problems, that over the 40 years since its initial promulgation, differences in the state-adopted versions of URESA made it "anything but uniform." *Id.* at 11. It also found that too many agencies, departments and personnel were involved, that relevant state doctrines varied significantly, that systems, equipment, and procedures varied from state-to-state, and lack of information was exacerbated in interstate cases. The federal commission made a host of recommendations and proposals including, nor surprisingly, numerous recommendations for much greater direct and collateral federal involvement in addressing the problems of interstate child support. *See Official Recommendations of the United States Commission on Interstate Child Support*, 27 Fam. L.Q. 31-84 (1993). Thus, the (R)URESA was found inadequate for the high volume and complexities of cases generated by state-driven interstate welfare collection litigation, was unsuited for the demands resulting from federal legislation in the 1980s, and was not tailored to take advantage of child support administration in the computer age. In 1992 the UIFSA was completed as an updated replacement for (R)URESA.

2) Retroactive Interstate Child Support Orders

In the majority of states, courts may order child support retroactively, subject to statutes of limitation. A minority of states allows child support to be awarded only prospectively. What happens when the parties move to other states after getting a divorce? If the divorce court entered a support decree, and it still has jurisdiction, the UIFSA seems to require application of the law of the former forum. When a divorce decree is issued in one state which does not address the child support issue, and later a proceeding is filed in another state to which the putative obligor has moved, should that court apply its own law to determine whether a retroactive child support award may be entered, or must it apply the law of the state that entered the divorce decree but did not decide the child support issue? In *Mason v. Cuisenaire*, 128 P.3d 446 (Nev. 2006) the Nevada Supreme Court held that under Full Faith and Credit, it must apply the retroactive support law of North Carolina which entered prior divorce decree. (One wonders whether constitutional preclusion is mandated as to an issue that was neither raised nor decided in the former proceeding.)

3. Practical and Ethical Considerations

Sam and Mary were married in State A and continued to live there until Sam abandoned Mary and their two children, moving to State B, 700 miles away. Mary has obtained an ex parte divorce in State A. What is Mary's best approach to obtain court-ordered support for the children?

4. Bibliography

Official Recommendations of the United States Commission on Interstate Child Support, 27 Fam. L.Q. 31-84 (1993).

Margaret Campbell Haynes, *Supporting Our Children: A Blueprint for Reform*, 27 Fam. L.Q. 7, 7 (1993).

Solangel Maldonado, *Deadbeat or Deadbroke? Redefining Child Support for Poor Fathers*, 39 U.C. Davis 991 (2006).

Jane C. Murphy, *Legal Images of Fatherhood: Welfare Reform, Child Support Enforcement, and Fatherless Children*, 81 Notre Dame L. Rev 325 (2005).

John J. Sampson & Paul M. Kurtz, *UIFSA: An Interstate Support Act for the 21st Century*, 27 Fam. L.Q. 85 (1993).

B. CHILD SUPPORT GUIDELINES AND FACTORS

1. Background

a. Traditional Grounds - Discretionary Standards

Traditionally, the amount ordered for support was within the discretion of the trial court judge. On a case-by-case basis, the trial court used the general principles of the needs of the child and the parent's ability to pay to determine the amount of support. With the introduction of the Uniform Marriage and Divorce Act, many states followed the Uniform Marriage and Divorce and enacted statutes that set forth more specific factors that the court should or might consider in determining the amount of support. Courts in a few states had gone further and had developed guidelines of specific amounts that the court might order. These support guidelines were non-binding and advisory only.

b. Support Guidelines

Beginning in 1975, the federal government has taken an active and influential role in shaping state child support law. That year, the United States Congress enacted legislation requiring states to enact certain legislation regarding child support in order to receive federal funds for their Aid to Families With Dependent Children programs (AFDC), now known as Temporary Assistance to Needy Families program (TANF). This legislation became the framework for child support enforcement in the states. The act established a child support enforcement program under Title IV-D of the Social Security Act. The act required each state to create child support enforcement agencies. In 1984, Congress added the condition that each state develop child support guidelines, which were the numerical amounts of what the child support should be, based on the parents' income. The guidelines were non-binding on the judges. In 1988, Congress enacted the Family Support Act of 1988, that extended the conditions of receipt of federal funds to all families involved in child support enforcement. An important provision of this Act made the child support guidelines presumptive, and not discretionary. The guidelines may be rebutted by a written finding that application of them in a particular case "would be unjust, inappropriate, or not in the best interest of a child . . . ." Most states have enacted legislation setting forth the factors that allow for deviation. There are no national guidelines, however.

State guidelines were initially developed based on research on the cost of rearing children. Economic studies by Thomas Espenshade, *infra*, were influential. The guidelines that each state has developed fall within three categories, although there are variations within categories. The majority of states follow the Income Shares Model. This model bases the amount of child support on the combined incomes of the parents. The state has already determined what the amount of child support should be at the level of the combined incomes. Each parent pays a proportionate share of this amount in proportion to their combined income. The share that the noncustodial parent would pay becomes the amount in the court's order. About sixteen states follow the Percentage of the Noncustodial Parent's Income Model. The percentage varies depending on the number of children. The assumption is that a share of the custodial parent's income is spent on the child.

A few states follow Delaware's Melson Formula. Under this model the non-custodial parent is allowed to keep a basic self-support minimum before more than a token child support payment is required; then he or she is required to contribute to the primary needs of the child, including child care and extraordinary medical expenses, in proportion to his or her income. In addition, a standard of living allowance (SOLA) is added to the basic support amount.

2. Statutes, Cases and Doctrine

a. Uniform Civil Liability for Support Act

The Uniform Civil Liability for Support Act has been widely adopted in the United States. For example, in Utah the provisions are codified at Utah Code Annot. § 78-45-1 to -13, with the Child Support Guideline provisions intermingled. The key provisions of the UCLSA are summarized below.

> Sections 3 and 4 of Title 78, chapter 45, provide that every man and woman shall support his or her child, and also shall support his or her spouse "when he [she] is in need." Both parents are liable for reasonable and necessary medical and dental expenses and other necessities incurred for their children.
> Sections 4.1 -4.3 provides that during their marriage to the parent of a child, stepparents have the same duty to support stepchildren as natural parents, including the right to recover from a natural parent.
> Section 5 predicates duty to support with presence of the obligor (not obligee) in the state.
> Section 6 provides District Courts have jurisdiction.
> Section 7 establishes a list of factors and rules for determining support (which are largely irrelevant since the adoption of the child support guidelines). *(See infra)*.
> Section 8 provides continuing jurisdiction to modify child support awards.
> Section 9 provides enforcement by the "office" for the state and/or the obligee, by the obligee, though the office has no attorney-client relationship with the obligee.
> Section 9.2 provides the county attorney shall assist obligees in specified ways (wage assignment, advice, and some other limited assistance).
> Section 10 provides for ordinary civil appeals.
> Section 11 revokes the marital communications privilege in child support actions.
> Sections 12 & 13 reserve "other rights," and mandate uniform interpretation.

b. Utah Child Support Guidelines Summary

> Utah's child support guidelines, Utah Code Annot. §§ 78-45-7.1 *et seq.*:
> Section 7.1 of title 78, chapter 45, requires inclusion of responsibility for medical expenses, medical insurance and income withholding in child support orders.
> Section 7.2 establishes the child support guidelines as a rebuttable presumption that may be rebutted by a written finding that application of them in a particular case "would be unjust, inappropriate, or not in the best interest of a child . . . ." The presence of non-common, unadopted children in the home of the recipient (wife) may be considered to increase the amount of child support paid to her, but presence of non-common, unadopted children in the home of the payor (husband) may *not* be considered to decrease the amount of child support. A 25% change of support amount due to change in the guidelines is deemed a substantial or material change of circumstances, sufficient to justify modification of child support.
> Section 7.3 governs stipulations (requiring completed guideline worksheets and financial verification).
> Section 7.5 describes what is considered "income." Income equivalent to one 40-hour-per-week job is considered, unless "the parent normally and consistently worked more than 40 hours at his job." Included is gross business income after necessary expenses. Verification of

income yearly is mandated. If a parent is found upon stipulation or after hearing to be voluntarily underemployed income may be imputed based upon employment potential and probable earnings, absent disability, job-training, unusual needs of a child, or the income earnable does not exceed child care costs of a custodial parent. Means-tested welfare benefits are not included as income. Social security benefits from an obligor parent are credited against child support.

Section 7.6 that alimony and child support ordered and paid for others are excluded from income.

Section 7.7 describes how child support is calculated. The child support obligation is apportioned between parents according to their proportionate incomes, unless extremely low. Except in cases of joint physical custody, split custody, or extremely low incomes, the court combines the adjusted gross incomes of the parents, determines the child support amount by the table, calculates each parents proportion of the support amount. Minimum base child support permissible is $20 per month.

Section 7.8 provides that in cases of split custody, the base child support amount is apportioned according to to the number of children in custody of each parent, their respective proportionate income, and the amounts owing each are offset.

Section 7.9 provides that in cases of joint physical custody support is set in proportion to the time the children are in custody of each parent, their respective proportionate income, and the amounts owing each are offset.

Section 7.10 provides that child support for each child terminates upon gradution from high school or becoming 18, whichever first occurs.

Section 7.11 reduces monthly child support by 50% for each child for each time the child is with the obligor parent 25 consecutive days.

Section 7.12 provides that child support for excess income-earning parents is determined case-by-case but not less than the highest level in the guidelines.

Section 7.13 provides for modification of the guidelines every four years by a committee.

Section 7.14 sets forth the child support tables.

Section 7.15 provides additionally that a parent who can obtain medical insurance for the children shall be ordered to do so, and the parents split equally the cost of the insurance and other medical expenses.

Section 7.16 & .17 require both parents to share equally child care expenses presumably if the custodial parent is working, upon proof of need if otherwise.

Section 7.18 provides that the presumption of the guidelines is rebutted if the amount plus either medical or child care exceeds 50% of obligor's adjusted gross income.

Section 7.19 empowers a court or agency to determine liability for medical expenses.

Section 7.20 empowers a court or agency order the obligee to furnish an accounting of child support received.

Section 7.21 provides that if the parties do not stipulate, the court or agency may award the child dependency exemptions for children, considering relative contributions and tax benefits, but an obligor in arrears may not get the exemption.

Excerpt from UCA § 78-45-7.14 Base combined child support obligation table & low income table.

The following includes the Base Combined Child Support Obligation Table and the Low Income Table:

BASE COMBINED CHILD SUPPORT OBLIGATION TABLE
(Both Parents)

Monthly Combined
Adj. Gross Income   Number of Children

From$ - To$	1	2	3	4	5	6
650 - 675	99	184	191	198	200	201
676 - 700	103	190	198	205	207	209
701 - 725	106	197	205	212	214	216
726 - 750	110	204	212	220	221	223
* * * *						
1,401 - 1,450	212	394	463	532	558	580
1,451 - 1,500	220	408	478	549	579	605
1,501 - 1,550	227	421	493	565	600	629
* * * *						
2,001 - 2,100	308	571	643	716	779	833
2,101 - 2,200	319	592	666	741	807	862
2,201 - 2,300	328	608	687	766	835	891
3,001 - 3,100	397	740	851	962	1,048	1,120
* * *						
4,001 - 4,100	472	883	1,050	1,217	1,325	1,415
4,101 - 4,200	479	896	1,069	1,242	1,352	1,444
* * *						
5,901 - 6,000	596	1,122	1,398	1,675	1,826	1,950
6,001 - 6,100	601	1,131	1,414	1,697	1,850	1,976
* * *						
9,901 - 10,000	821	1,392	1,798	2,050	2,257	2,427
10,001 - 10,100	826	1,400	1,808	2,061	2,270	2,441

* * *

[A separate "low income table" that considers the monthly adjusted gross income of the obligor parent only.]

c. *Nash v. Mulle*

Helen Matlock Nash v. Charles Mulle
846 S.W.2d 803 (Tenn. 1993)

DAUGHTREY, Justice.

This child support case presents two principal issues on appeal: (1) the extent to which Tennessee's Child Support Guidelines apply to an obligor's net monthly income in excess of $6,250.00, and (2) the extent to which a trust fund established during the child's minority for her later college education is permitted under Tennessee law. We conclude that the trial judge is not limited to the ordinary schedule in calculating the amount of support to be paid by a wealthy non-custodial parent, and we uphold the use of a trust fund under the circumstances presented here, even though the benefits will be realized after the child reaches the age of majority. Thus, we reverse the judgment of the Court of Appeals and remand the case to the Juvenile Court for the recalculation of an award in accordance with this opinion.

The essential facts in this case are not in dispute. What is contested is the extent of the child support obligation of Charles Mulle, who fathered Melissa Alice Matlock as the result of an extramarital affair with the appellant, Helen Nash, in 1981 but has since had nothing to do with mother or child. After an order was entered establishing his paternity in 1984, the Juvenile Court also ordered him to pay $200.00 each month in child support, in addition to other specified expenses. In 1990, Helen Nash filed this action seeking an increase in the amount of his payments because of Charles Mulle's dramatically increased income. *[FN1 Mr. Mulle's income has risen substantially since the original award, thus justifying this review under T.C.A. s 36-5-101(a), which permits a change in child support only "upon a showing of a substantial and material change of circumstances." Whereas his income when the first award was made was approximately $30,000.00 annually, his gross annual income has risen considerably. In 1988 his gross income was approximately $192,000.00; in 1989, he earned approximately $292,000.00; and in 1990, his income was approximately $260,000.00. These figures contrast with Ms. Nash's 1989 gross annual income of approximately $42,000.00. In its calculation under the guidelines, the Juvenile Court increased Mulle's payments to reflect a more appropriate contribution in light of his present earnings.]* The Juvenile Court then ordered Mulle to pay $3,092.62 per month, with $1,780.17 reserved for a trust fund established for Melissa's college education. The Court of Appeals reversed, limiting the award to $1,312.00 per month, or exactly 21 percent of $6,250.00, the top monthly income to which the child support guidelines explicitly apply. The Court of Appeals also disallowed the trust, finding that it improperly extended the parental duty of support beyond the age of majority. Because the facts are not disputed, we review de novo the questions of law presented on appeal.

Child support in Tennessee is statutorily governed by T.C.A. s 36-5-101. Section 36-5-101(e)(1) provides that "[i]n making its determination concerning the amount of support of any minor child ... of the parties, the court shall apply as a rebuttable presumption the child support guidelines as provided in this subsection." The General Assembly adopted the child support guidelines promulgated by the Tennessee Department of Human Services in order to maintain compliance with the Family Support Act of 1988, codified in various sections of 42 U.S.C. [FN2 Under 42 U.S.C. ss 651, 652, and 654, a "state plan" is essential in order to assure the state's receipt of federal money for child support enforcement. 42 U.S.C. s 667(a) requires that "[e]ach state, as a condition for having its State plan approved ..., must establish guidelines for child support award amounts within the state."] While they add a measure of consistency to child support awards statewide, the guidelines provide more than simple percentages to be applied against the net incomes of non-custodial parents. They also embody "the rules promulgated by the Department of Human Services in compliance with [the] requirements [of the Family Support Act of 1988]." Hence, the purposes, premises, guidelines for compliance, and criteria for deviation from the guidelines carry what amounts to a legislative mandate.

I.

The first issue presented concerns the proper measure of child support to be awarded in this case in view of the fact that Charles Mulle's monthly income exceeds $6,250.00. The guidelines apply in all cases awarding financial support to a custodial parent for the maintenance of a child, whether or not the child is a welfare recipient, and whether or not the child's parents are married. The guidelines are based, however, on several goals; they make many assumptions; and they permit deviation in circumstances that do not always comport with the assumptions. In studying the goals, premises, and criteria for deviation, we are convinced that the guidelines permit a monthly award greater than $1,312.00 without a specific showing of need by the custodial parent.

One major goal expressed in the guidelines is "[t]o ensure that when parents live separately, the economic impact on the child(ren) is minimized and to the extent that either parent enjoys a higher standard of living, the child(ren) share(s) in that higher standard." * This goal becomes significant when, as here, one parent has vastly greater financial resources than the other. It reminds us that Tennessee does not define a child's needs literally, but rather requires an award to reflect both parents' financial circumstances. This goal is consistent with our long-established common law rule, which requires that a parent must provide support "in a manner commensurate with his means and station in life." *

The guidelines are currently structured to require payment by the non-custodial parent of a certain percentage of his or her net income, depending upon the number of children covered by the support order (21 percent for one child, 32 percent for two children, etc.). The statute promulgating the use of the guidelines creates a "rebuttable presumption" that the scheduled percentages will produce the appropriate amounts to be awarded as monthly child support. However, they are subject to deviation upward or downward when the assumptions on which they are based do not pertain to a particular situation. *** Additionally, "[e]xtraordinary educational expenses and extraordinary medical expenses not covered by insurance" are given as reasons for deviation. The guidelines thus recognize that "unique case circumstances will require a court determination on a case-by-case basis."

Among the "unique cases" specifically anticipated in the guidelines are those cases in which the income of the parent paying support exceeds $6,250.00 per month. [FN9 *] In the criteria for deviation the guidelines provide that among the "cases where guidelines are neither appropriate nor equitable" are those in which "the net income of the obligor exceeds $6,250 per month." In the present case, the Juvenile Court calculated Charles Mulle's net monthly income to be $14,726.98, a figure well above the $6,250.00 figure justifying deviation from the guidelines. Yet the total award of $3,092 ordered by the trial judge is exactly 21 percent of Mulle's monthly income.

Obviously, to treat the monthly income figure of $6,250.00 as a cap and automatically to limit the award to 21 percent of that amount for a child whose non-custodial parent makes over $6,250.00 may be "neither appropriate nor equitable." Such an automatic limit fails to take into consideration the extremely high standard of living of a parent such as Charles Mulle, and thus fails to reflect one of the primary goals of the guidelines, i.e., to allow the child of a well-to-do parent to share in that very high standard of living. On the other hand, automatic application of the 21 percent multiplier to every dollar in excess of $6,250.00 would be equally unfair.

We conclude that the courts below found themselves at such polar extremes in this case due to a misreading of the criteria for deviation in the guidelines. The Juvenile Court placed the burden "on Mr. Mulle to convince the Court of the inequity or inappropriateness of the guidelines in this case," i.e., to prove that the court should award less than 21 percent of his income in excess of $6,250.00. That court ultimately found that Mulle had shown no "extraordinary burden" on his budget or other reason justifying deviation downward from the presumptive award of 21 percent, and awarded that amount. The Court of Appeals, on the other hand, held that "to obtain support larger than 21% of $6,250.00 for one child, the [custodial parent] has the burden of showing such need." Thus, to receive more than $1,312.00 per month for the child, Helen Nash would have to demonstrate exactly why the additional money was required. Rather than adopting either of these diametrically opposed approaches, we conclude that the trial court should retain the discretion to determine--as the guidelines provide, "on a case-by-case basis"-- the appropriate amount of child support to be paid when an obligor's net income exceeds $6,250.00 per month, balancing both the child's need and the parents' means. The guidelines' very latitude reflects this need for an exercise of discretion. Twenty-one percent of an enormous monthly income may provide far more money than most reasonable, wealthy parents would allot for the support of one child. However, it would also be unfair to require a custodial parent to prove a specific need before the court will increase an award beyond $1,312.00. At such high income levels, parents are unlikely to be able to "itemize" the cost of living. Moreover, most parents living within their means would not be able to present lists of expenditures made in the mere anticipation of more child support. Until the guidelines more specifically address support awards for the children of high-income parents, we are content to rely on the judgment of the trial courts within the bounds provided them by those guidelines. In this case, although the child support award may be appropriate, we think it expedient to remand this case to the Juvenile Court, thus providing the trial judge an opportunity to reconsider his opinion in light of the fact that he is not limited to the $1,312.00 cap imposed by the Court of Appeals, nor is he bound to award 21 percent of Charles Mulle's full net income, but may exercise his discretion as the facts warrant.

II

. ****Charles Mulle contends that the establishment of an educational trust fund for his daughter unlawfully requires him to support her past her minority. Citing *Garey v. Garey*, 482 S.W.2d 133 (Tenn.1972), and *Whitt v. Whitt*, 490 S.W.2d 159, 160 (Tenn.1973), he argues that the trust fund is incompatible with Tennessee case law. In *Garey*, this Court held that "[b]y lowering the age of majority from 21 to 18 years of age the Legislature has completely emancipated the minor from the control of the parents and relieved the parents of their attendant legal duty to support the child." 482 S.W.2d at 135. Because the trust fund is intended for Melissa's college education, her father insists that it unlawfully requires post-minority support.

We conclude, to the contrary, that the establishment of the trust fund in this case does not conflict with the holding in *Garey*. Although child support payments may not extend beyond the child's minority (except in extraordinary circumstances involving physical or mental disability), the benefits from such payments can. Hence, it is consistent with established rules of Tennessee law to hold, as we do here, that funds ordered to be accumulated during a child's minority that are in excess of the amount needed to supply basic support may be used to the child's advantage past the age of minority.

In reaching this conclusion, we must recognize the obvious fact that responsible parents earning high incomes set aside money for their children's future benefit and often create trusts for that purpose. They save for unforeseen emergencies; they accumulate savings for trips and other luxuries; and they may, and usually do, save for their children's college educations. Melissa's mother has expressed her intention to send her daughter to college. As all parents realize, however, the goal of sending a child to college often requires the wise management of money through savings. For a child of Melissa's age, assumed to begin college in the fall of 2000, it has been estimated that a parent must invest $457.00 per month for a public college education, or $964.00 per month for a private education, in order to save the $61,571.00 or $129,893.00, respectively, that will be required to fund a college education beginning that year. Lacking the resources to write a check for the full amount of college tuition, room, board, and other expenses when that time arrives, Helen Nash must accumulate these savings over the course of the child's minority, or be forced to borrow the money later on. Such savings in this case would inevitably deplete Melissa's child support award. While in many cases parents undergo serious financial sacrifices to make college possible for their children, in this case, as the Juvenile Court found, Charles Mulle's income can afford Melissa a high standard of living that also includes savings for college.

We believe that an approach that refuses to recognize the laudable goal of post-secondary education and instead provides only for the child's immediate needs, would not be a responsible approach. If the most concerned, caring parents do not operate in such a haphazard way, surely the courts cannot be expected to award child support in such a fashion. Thus, we conclude that establishing a program of savings for a college education is a proper element of child support when, as in this case, the resources of the non-custodial parent can provide the necessary funds without hardship to that parent. Moreover, the use of a trust fund for just such a purpose is explicitly approved by the guidelines. *** Thus, the guidelines specifically recommend a trust fund in cases in which a large cash award may be inappropriate. Moreover, the guidelines do not limit expenditures from such trusts to the child's minority. We defer to the policy judgment of the legislature in adopting the guidelines and uphold the use of the trust in this case. ***

We also note the need for a trust as protection for the child of an uncaring non-custodial parent. When the Supreme Court of Washington upheld an order requiring a parent to fund the college education of his three sons, it noted "the long standing special powers the courts have had (in equity, regardless of legislation) over the children of broken homes to assure that their disadvantages are minimized." *Childers v. Childers*, 89 Wash.2d 592, 575 P.2d 201, 207 (1978). *** The Childers court continued, "Parents, when deprived of the custody of their children very often refuse to do for such children what natural instinct would ordinarily prompt them to do." 575 P.2d at 208. When a non-custodial parent has shown normal parental concern for a child, a trust fund may be unnecessary to ensure that his or her feelings are reflected in spending. However, when a non-custodial parent shows a lack of care, the court may step in and require the parent to support his or her child. The establishment of a trust is simply one discretionary mechanism used in the endeavor.

Thus, Charles Mulle's argument that the absence of a relationship with Melissa obviates the need to fund her college education is simply backwards. Child support is designed to prevent a non-custodial parent from shirking responsibility for the child he or she willingly conceived. It is precisely when natural feelings of care and concern are absent, and no parent-child relationship has been developed, that the court must award child support in a manner that best mirrors what an appropriate contribution from an interested parent would be. In fact, at least one court has gone beyond the acknowledgment of this lack of parental interest, and has spoken in terms of compensating the child for the parent's lack of concern. In *Cohen v. Cohen*, * the court stated that the non-custodial parent "should be obliged to make up for his neglect, and to contribute towards his son's education as much as lies within his power." While we do not adhere to this compensatory view of child support, we do believe that an appropriate child support award should reflect an amount that would normally be spent by a concerned parent of similar resources.

We thus find no merit to Charles Mulle's complaint that the order deprives him of the freedom to decide his daughter's educational fate, arguing that a requirement is being imposed upon him that does not exist for married parents. He contends in his brief that "some parents plan for the future education of their children and some do not"; he argues that "[s]urely a divorce decree or a paternity order should not give children rights that children who are living with their parents who are married do not have." This argument overlooks the obvious fact that divorced and unmarried parents face a substantial loss of parental autonomy whenever a court must step in to exercise responsibility for their children in the absence of parental cooperation. Married parents may choose to rear their children in an extravagant or miserly fashion; they may send their children to expensive private schools and universities; or they may require their children to make their ways in the world at age 18. Nevertheless, when children become the subject of litigation, courts must judge the children's needs. Long-standing Tennessee law requires the courts to evaluate children's needs not in terms of life's essentials, but in terms of the parents' "means and station in life." * The guidelines' requirement that child support allow a child to share in the higher standard of living of a high-income parent continues this objective. * Thus, Mulle's complaint about the alleged unfairness of the court's judgment concerning the benefits his standard of living should afford Melissa is misplaced.

Moreover, as the court stated in *Atchley*, "[r]eason, as well as the public policy of this state, favorable as it is to higher learning, permits no other conclusion. The high esteem in which college training is held in this state is unmistakably indicated by the numerous colleges found in the various parts of this state." *** The Washington Supreme Court likewise reasoned in Childers, saying, "[The fact that] it is the public policy of the state that a college education should be had, if possible, by all its citizens, is made manifest by the fact that the state of Washington maintains so many institutions of higher learning at public expense." *Id*. 575 P.2d at 206. Given the public policy favoring higher education in Tennessee, likewise evidenced by our many colleges and universities, it would be highly improper in this case to cast the burden of Melissa's higher education entirely on her mother, or on the "bounty of the state," when her father can provide for her education without unduly burdening himself.

***Moreover the courts and legislatures of many other states have approved the funding of a college education by non-custodial parents who can afford such an expense. Indeed, several courts have done so without explicit statutory permission. *** These courts have used their equitable powers to require wealthy non-custodial parents to fund their children's college educations past the age of majority. ***

In light of the guidelines' explicit provision for the use of trusts in cases involving high-income parents, the goals promoted by the use of a trust in this instance, and the reasoned support of other state courts and legislatures, we find the use of an educational trust in this case to be proper. As noted in Section I, however, there remains the question of the level at which the trust should be funded in this case. We therefore reverse the judgment of the Court of Appeals, and remand the case to the Juvenile Court for calculation of an award in accordance with this opinion.

Finally, we grant the appellant her attorney's fees and all other costs of the appeal, pursuant to T.C.A. s 36-5-101(i).

d. *M.H.B. v. H.T.B.*

M.H.B. v. H.T.B.
498 A.2d 775 (N.J. 1985)

PER CURIAM.

The members of the Court being equally divided, the judgment of the Appellate Division is affirmed.

CONCURRING OPINION

HANDLER, J., concurring.

We have recently recognized that upon a divorce, one spouse may be obligated under principles of equitable estoppel to provide financial support for his or her stepchildren who are the children of the other spouse. *Miller v. Miller*, 97 N.J. 154, 167, 478 A.2d 351 (1984). In this appeal, we consider the circumstances that can give rise to an equitable estoppel forbidding a divorced stepparent from denying the validity of a previous voluntary commitment to provide financial support for a stepchild. The child in this case was born while the defendant was married to the child's mother. However, the defendant knew shortly after the child's birth that he probably was not her natural father. Nevertheless, throughout the marriage and for five years following the divorce, the defendant consistently conducted himself as the child's father, successfully gained the child's love and affection, and established himself as the little girl's parental provider of emotional and material support. Under such circumstances, I believe that the stepfather is obligated to provide continuing financial support for his stepchild.

I.

The parties in this case (referred to by their initials or first names in order to protect the child who is the object of the controversy) were married in 1966. The couple settled in New Jersey where, during their first five years together, they conceived two sons, G.B. and M.B. The marriage turned sour during 1975, however, and sometime thereafter the plaintiff-wife, Marilyn, had a brief extra-marital affair. In 1977, while still married to the defendant-husband, Henry, Marilyn gave birth to a daughter, K.B.

Three months later, Henry first learned that he might not be K.B.'s biological father. He discovered a letter, or a diary entry, implicating Marilyn's former paramour as K.B.'s natural father. Henry then confronted Marilyn with this evidence of her infidelity, and moved out of the family residence. Following this separation, the marriage continued for almost three years. After living for six months in the same town as the rest of his family, however, Henry moved twice, first to California and then to Wisconsin, where he continues to live. During this period of separation, Henry maintained close bonds with all of the children, K.B. as well as the two sons, through phone calls, letters, gifts, and visits.

Marilyn also moved several times with the children. Between March and September 1978, she cohabitated with her erstwhile paramour, K.B.'s purported natural father, whom she briefly considered marrying. In December 1978, however, Marilyn brought herself and the children to Henry's home in Wisconsin, and for six months the parties attempted to reconcile their differences. Henry then professed to Marilyn that he would always love K.B., and that he did not want the child's illegitimacy to interfere with the couple's future together.

The reconciliation attempt failed, however, and, in June 1979, the couple signed a separation agreement covering financial support obligations, child custody, and visitation. Marilyn assumed custody of all three children, then ages 2, 7, and 10, and Henry undertook to pay $600 per month as family support, based on his annual income of over $34,000 at a time when Marilyn had no income.

Marilyn thereafter moved back to New Jersey with all three children. It is undisputed that K.B.'s purported father then lived and still lives nearby to the child and her mother. Marilyn testified, however, that she last saw this man in December 1979, six months after returning to New Jersey, and has not seen him since. Further, although after the separation Marilyn dated several men, none, including the alleged natural father, ever replaced Henry as a father-figure to K.B.

In March 1980, the couple obtained a divorce in Wisconsin under terms established by an extensive written settlement agreement. The parties, Henry as well as Marilyn, stipulated that all three children were born of the marriage. They further agreed that Marilyn would have custody of the children during the school year, and that Henry would get custody during the three summer months.

Although at this point Henry earned about $51,000 each year while Marilyn still had no income, Henry promised only to continue paying $200 per month per child in Marilyn's custody. These payments would have totalled about $5,400 annually if three children had lived with their mother for nine months each year; however, by the parties' agreement, M.B. lived with his father for most of the post-divorce period, and therefore Henry's annual support obligation came to about $3,600. No alimony was awarded, and the couple's remaining, limited assets were divided in half.

All three minor children remained objects of Henry's affection, attention, and solicitude throughout the post-divorce period. In particular, Henry expressed interest in and concern for K.B. As found by the trial judge,

> K.B. bears Henry's surname, is registered on all of her records as bearing his surname, knows no other father, and is ignorant of the facts surrounding her paternity. Henry made innumerable representations to K.B. and to the world that he was her father. * * * The testimony related many tender moments between father and daughter. He sent her roses on her birthdays and comforted her in his bed during thunder and lightening storms.

Thus, Henry treated K.B. exactly as he treated his own son G.B., who was also in Marilyn's custody. Both K.B. and G.B. received Christmas gifts in 1979, 1980, and 1981. Further, Henry willingly provided child support payments on behalf of both children through the end of 1981. Based on all of the evidence, the trial judge concluded that Henry had become K.B.'s "psychological, if not biological parent."

Then, in March of 1981, Henry remarried. The following summer, both K.B. and G.B. visited and remained with Henry. By September 1981, however, Marilyn and Henry's second wife did not get along. The relationship between Marilyn and Henry deteriorated and Henry began withholding child support payments.

In January 1982 Henry petitioned a Wisconsin court to grant him custody of all three children, including K.B. The Wisconsin judge transferred the case to the New Jersey courts based on the children's best interests and the absence of local jurisdictional prerequisites. Marilyn filed a separate complaint, in March 1982, in New Jersey, seeking to retain custody of G.B. and K.B., and to obtain an increase in child support. Consistent with the petition he had filed in Wisconsin, Henry filed a counterclaim requesting custody of these children, K.B. as well as G.B. Later, by a pre-trial motion, Henry amended his counterclaim, claiming, in the alternative, that he should be under no duty to provide child support for K.B., and seeking to litigate the issue of the child's paternity. This was the first time that Henry had ever attempted to repudiate his paternal relationship with K.B. Without conceding Henry's right to contest paternity, Marilyn consented to allow the completion of Human Leucocyte Analysis blood test in December 1982. The results of the test excluded Henry as K.B.'s biological father.

A plenary hearing on the custody and support applications took place over several days in April and May of 1983. In addition to the foregoing facts, including Henry's knowledge in 1977 that he might not be K.B.'s natural father, the trial judge found that [i]t is clear Henry intended to be K.B.'s father and that she relied on that fact. * * * Even Henry's [second] wife * * * described Henry's relationship with K.B. as that of "a loving father-daughter relationship." * * * K.B. relied upon Henry's representations and has treated H.B. as her father, giving to him and receiving back from him all of the love and affection that the parent-child relationship should naturally evoke.

Henry is certainly K.B.'s psychological, if not biological parent. * * * Henry is the only father K.B. knows or has ever known. * * * To permit Henry now to repudiate his intent to support K.B. * * * would cause irreparable harm to the child. Based on these findings, the trial judge concluded that the doctrine of equitable estoppel was applicable to preclude Henry from denying the duty to provide child support on behalf of K.B. This aspect of his decision was affirmed by a divided court in the Appellate Division, and presents the sole issue on the appeal that Henry filed with this Court as of right under R. 2:2- 1(a).

II. The framework for analysis of the issue on this appeal is provided by *Miller v. Miller*, 97 N.J. 154, 478 A.2d 351 (1984). In that case, the Court recognized that the doctrine of equitable estoppel could properly be applied in the context of a matrimonial controversy in which the interests of individual children were at stake. Because we were dealing with responsibilities that may flow from familial relationships that are inherently complicated and subtle, we acknowledged that the application of equitable principles called for great sensitivity, caution, and flexibility.

The *Miller* case involved two girls whose mother remarried after divorcing their father. During the mother's second marriage the defendant, her second husband, assumed sole responsibility for the girls' financial support, as well as other parental privileges and obligations. He also discouraged his wife and stepchildren from maintaining any personal or financial relationship with the children's natural father. The second marriage ended in divorce after seven years, at which time the mother sought to receive continuing child support from the girls' stepfather.

The Court ruled in Miller that, before a duty of child support could be imposed based on equitable considerations, it must first be shown that, by a course of conduct, the stepparent affirmatively encouraged the child to rely and depend on the stepparent for parental nurture and financial support. We specifically recognized that such conduct could interfere with the children's relationship to their natural father. Under the facts, we held that the stepfather would be equitably estopped to deny his duty to continue to provide child support on behalf of his stepchildren, if it could be shown that the children would suffer financial harm if the stepparent were permitted to repudiate the parental obligations he had assumed. We further held the natural father could continue to be liable for the support of these children.***

Applying the principles set forth in Miller, the evidence in this case compels the imposition of equitable estoppel to prevent Henry from denying the duty to provide financial support for K.B. Henry's actions throughout the marriage and following the divorce constituted a continuous course of conduct toward the child that was tantamount to a knowing and affirmative representation that he would support her as would a natural father. By both deed and word, Henry repeatedly and consistently recognized and confirmed the parent-child relationship between himself and K.B. He acted in every way like a father toward his own child. He also stipulated to the child's paternity. At the time of his divorce he promised to pay child support, which obligation was incorporated into the judgment of divorce.

The volitional nature of Henry's conduct is underscored by Henry's persistent attempts to gain custody of K.B., efforts that he continued on appeal from the trial court's award of custody to Marilyn. He thus sought child custody even after blood tests conclusively demonstrated that, biologically, he was not K.B.'s father. Consequently, there can be no suggestion that Henry's prior actions were merely accidental or inadvertent. His actions attest to the previously well-developed father-daughter bond, and convey all possible indicia of an affirmative and purposeful representation of continuing support, which constitutes a primary element of equitable estoppel.

There was clearly reasonable reliance upon Henry's purposeful conduct. The obvious expectations engendered by Henry's conduct were that K.B. fully accepted and reasonably believed Henry to be her father. Significantly, the court found that Henry became K.B.'s psychological father, a finding that imports much more than mere affection. See generally Goldstein, Freud & Solnit, Beyond the Best Interests of the Child 9-28 (1973). The strength and durability of a psychological parent-child relationship is perhaps the most relevant consideration in defining a child's best interests. * Further, it is not disputed that K.B. never knew any person other then Henry to be her natural father. As found by the trial judge, Henry's absorption of the child's time and affection as her father effectively stultified the development of any other filial relationship between K.B. and anyone else.

In these circumstances, Henry's conduct assuredly engendered material and emotional consequences for K.B.--consequences that would be demonstrably adverse to K.B. if Henry were now permitted to repudiate all his prior actions. This becomes understandable upon a consideration of the nature of filial bonding. * This bonding is indispensable in fostering the optimum psychological and emotional development of the child because it is the vehicle of parental love. This love of the parent for the child is a cohesive that binds parent and child and, further, gives unique strength and durability to the natural loyalty that the parent holds for the child. The parent-child bond thus serves to anchor the material and financial, as well as emotional, support that are vital to the well-being of a child. In this frame of reference, the critical factor is K.B.'s total filial dependence on Henry. Were Henry permitted to disavow the parent-child relationship that he created and fostered and to repudiate the parental responsibility that flowed from that relationship, K.B. would suffer demonstrable harm fully commensurate with her dependent condition.

The detrimental character of reliance in such situations has led courts to impose an estoppel against a man whose wife gives birth to another man's child if the husband then knowingly "represents himself to both the child and the community as the natural father." Miller, supra, 97 N.J. at 165, 478 A.2d 351**

In Ross v. Ross, 126 N.J.Super. 394, 314 A.2d 623 (J. & D.R.Ct.1973), aff'd, 135 N.J.Super. 35, 342 A.2d 566 (App.Div.1975), *** the defendant had married the child's mother eighteen months after the birth of her child. During the support hearing following the subsequent breakdown of the marriage, it was established that the child, then seven years old, believed that the defendant was his natural father. The court rejected the husband's argument that he was not obligated to support the child. In applying the doctrine of equitable estoppel, the court stressed that the defendant by his conduct actually represented himself to the child as his father and that the child sincerely believed that defendant was his father. * We pointedly observed in Miller that were the court to have reached any other conclusion, it would result in "irreparable harm and inflict deep injury on the child, the true party in interest."

Similarly in A.S. v. B.S., * the child was raised by the parties as their own from the time he was one month old. The parties separated nine years later, and, in a proceeding by the wife against the husband for support of this child, the court found that the husband was estopped from denying his parental obligation to continue to support the child. We again stated that any result that would have allowed the putative father to repudiate his responsibility "would do irreparable harm to the child," *, and further emphasized this understanding of detrimental reliance by quoting from *A.S. v. B.S.*,*** the following passage:

> [The child] is the real party in interest in this proceeding. To permit defendant to repudiate his intent to support the child and no longer stand in loco parentis to him would cause irreparable harm to the boy. He would be without familial roots, without a known heritage. Equitable estoppel must be applied in this instance to prevent that result. [97 N.J. at 164 (478 A.2d 351)]

***

I am satisfied, as was the trial court, that the evidence in this case establishes that Henry, from the time of K.B.'s birth, engaged in a voluntary and knowing course of conduct with respect to K.B., which constituted in its purpose and effect an affirmative representation that he was her natural father. It is also abundantly clear that the child K.B., as well as her mother Marilyn, relied upon Henry's purposeful conduct and depended upon him for support. Further, it cannot be disputed that the reliance by K.B. was detrimental in the sense of the financial, as well as personal, harm she would suffer if Henry were permitted to disavow his representations, repudiate the expectations he created, and evade the responsibilities he had assumed. Under these circumstances he is equitably estopped from denying a continuing obligation to provide child support on behalf of K.B.

III.

Defendant cites two reasons why he should not be responsible for his stepchild's financial support. He urges that the New Jersey Parentage Act, N.J.S.A. 9:17-38 to -59, requires that if a man is found not to be a child's biological father, then he cannot be held liable to support that child, at least if the biological father may be identified. Defendant also contends that Miller stands for the proposition that Marilyn had a duty to bring the purported natural father into court and that, because she did not, we should remand to consider whether that person should be liable for K.B.'s support. Neither argument is persuasive.

With respect to the argument based on the New Jersey Parentage Act, N.J.S.A. 9:17-45a provides that "a man alleged * * * to be the father [of a child] * * * or any person with an interest recognized as justiciable by the court may bring * * * *578 an action * * * for the purpose of determining the existence or nonexistence of the parent and child relationship." N.J.S.A. 9:17-45d further provides that "[r]egardless of its terms, an agreement, other than an agreement approved by the court in accordance with [N.J.S.A. 9:17-48c] between an alleged or presumed father and the mother of the child, shall not bar an action under this section." Henry alleges that these provisions shield him, as a stepparent, from child support obligations.

The statute, however, draws a distinction between paternity and the duty of support. *** The statute also recognizes the need for flexibility in determining child support. Thus, under N.J.S.A. 9:17-53c, after a court determines paternity and clarifies birth records, "[t]he judgment or order may contain any other provision directed against the appropriate party to the proceeding, concerning the duty of support, the custody * * * of the child, visitation privileges * * *, or any other matter in the best interests of the child." This provision assures that in custody and support cases the children's best interests trump any determination of parentage. * Clearly the Legislature did not intend to preclude the equitable imposition of a duty of child support upon a stepparent when the evidence assessed in accordance with principles of equity demand that result.

With respect to the other contention, in *Miller* there was undisputed evidence of a pre-existing and continuing relationship between the natural father and the daughters prior to the mother's remarriage to the defendant stepfather. There was also considerable testimony regarding the continuing viability of that relationship. In this case, by contrast there is no competent evidence as to K.B.'s actual parentage. Moreover, the uncontroverted testimony revealed no contact whatsoever between K.B. and her alleged natural father, nor any inkling on K.B.'s part that Henry was not her actual father. In addition there was evidence in *Miller* that the natural father had acknowledged in the past his financial ability and willingness to support his daughters. There is no comparable evidence in this case.

We recognized in *Miller* that a natural parent ordinarily is the primary source of financial support of a child, and that such a legal obligation is not abrogated by imposing a current obligation of child support upon a stepparent under principles of equitable estoppel. 97 N.J. at 169, 478 A.2d 351. In that case, the Court felt it would be in the best interests of the child to consider whether the natural father, if available, should be made to honor his legal obligation to support his children. In this case, the circumstances are markedly different because no person, other than Henry, has ever emerged in K.B.'s life as her father.

A determination to affix a present obligation upon a stepfather does not in any way mean that we exonerate or condone a biological father who abdicates his responsibility to support his child. I fully acknowledge the statutory and common law requirement that the primary responsibility of child raising and support is that of the natural parent. Consequently, any decision to impose liability for child support on a stepparent must recognize the exceptional nature of such relief, as we have done in this case. *

Notwithstanding the existence of exceptional circumstances and an equitable basis to impose a child support obligation on a child's stepparent, that relief remains mutable; it is subject to changing circumstances as these may affect the child's best interests. Indeed, in appropriate cases a stepparent, or any other person entitled to represent the interest of the child, may demonstrate the existence of changed circumstances justifying the assumption of liability for child support by the biological parent. That assumption of child support will be required if changed circumstances show that it would be in the best interest of the child, fair to the stepparent, and legally just as to the biological father. The record in this case, however, does not present these issues, and hence we cannot deal with them further.

IV.

For the reasons expressed, I would affirm the judgment below. Chief Justice Wilentz and Justice O'Hern join in this opinion.

POLLOCK, J., concurring in part and dissenting in part.

As Justice Handler's concurrence acknowledges, this case is controlled by our opinion last term in *Miller v. Miller*,* which was published after the judgment of the Appellate Division. *Miller* recognized that the primary duty to support a child rests on the natural parent, but that in certain circumstances a stepparent could be estopped to deny such a duty. Specifically, we stated in *Miller* that it is only when a stepparent "actively interferes with the children's support from their natural parent that he or she may be equitably estopped from denying his or her duty to support the children." * Today's concurring opinion, however, would impose on a stepparent a duty of support not on the basis of estoppel but of a perceived emotional bonding between stepparent and child. From that premise, the opinion then proceeds to force the facts of the present case within its expanded interpretation of *Miller*.

I believe that the expansion of the *Miller* opinion is unwise and unnecessary. I further believe that the better practice would be to remand the matter to the Chancery Division for reconsideration in light of *Miller*. Pending that determination, I would continue to require Henry to support K.B.

*** Significantly, all of the events supporting the "emotional bonding" between K.B. and Henry occurred before confirmation of the fact that Henry was not K.B.'s father.

Furthermore, on learning of Marilyn's liaison with K.B.'s natural father, Henry separated from her. Although he continued to live in the area for six months, Henry moved to California and then to Wisconsin, where he still resides. At one time, in an unsuccessful attempt to save his marriage, he brought his family, including K.B., to Wisconsin for six months. Thereafter, Henry's only contacts with K.B. were for two-month visitation periods in the summer of 1980 and 1981, and a one-month visit in the summer of 1982. Since that time, Henry has ceased all communication with his stepdaughter. In the eight years that have elapsed since K.B.'s birth, Henry has spent a total of only fourteen months with her. Moreover, Henry has since remarried and begun a new family, one in which the trial court found K.B. is not welcome. Thus, Henry's relationship to K.B., which was always ambivalent, is now in tatters. Consequently, I believe that the present case is a poor vehicle to transport into the law the notion that emotional bonding between a stepparent and a child may terminate a natural parent's support obligation.

For her part, Marilyn knows the identity of K.B.'s purported natural father. Furthermore, after K.B.'s birth, Marilyn cohabited with the natural father for about six months. She discussed with the natural father not only his paternity of K.B., but also the prospect of marriage. Ironically, during most of her life, K.B. has lived in closer geographic proximity to the purported father than to Henry. Indeed, the natural father still lives in a neighboring community, where he is engaged in the florist business.

Notwithstanding the contentions of the concurring opinion to the contrary, the record is devoid of any proof that Henry directly interfered with the natural father's relationship with K.B. In this regard, the facts of the present case differ from those in *Miller*, where the stepparent actively interfered with the natural parent's attempt to support his children. For example, the stepfather in *Miller* tore up the natural father's support checks, which eventually induced the natural father to discontinue his support payments.* Here, the natural father has never claimed K.B. as his child and has been content to allow Henry to support her. The tragic fact is that neither Henry nor the natural father has spent much time with K.B.

II

Although the concurrence purports to rely on *Miller v. Miller, supra*, it actually stands the *Miller* opinion on its head. *Miller* recognized "that in appropriate cases, the doctrine of equitable estoppel may be invoked to impose on a stepparent the duty to support a stepchild after a divorce from the child's natural parent." * We admonished, however, that the doctrine was to be invoked "cautiously." *.

Accordingly, we held that a stepparent could be equitably estopped from denying an obligation to support a stepchild on proof of three conditions. First, the stepparent must have made a representation to either the children or the natural parent that he or she would provide support. Second, that representation must have been relied on by either the children or the natural parent. * We declined to rely on these two conditions alone to establish estoppel because such a rule would penalize a "stepparent who tried to create a warm family atmosphere with his or her stepchildren." *Id.* Consistent with that concern, we imposed a third condition, one that required a showing that "the children will suffer future financial detriment as a result of the stepparent's representation or conduct that caused the children to be cut off from their natural parent's financial support." * Such financial detriment could be shown if the custodial parent cannot locate or does not know the whereabouts of the natural parent, or cannot obtain legal jurisdiction over the natural parent, and the natural parent's unavailability is attributable to the actions of the stepparent. Thus, a stepparent is responsible for the unavailability of a natural parent only when he or she takes "positive action interfering with the natural parent's support obligation." * Accordingly, in *Miller*, we remanded the matter to the trial court to determine whether the stepfather had detrimentally affected his stepchildren's ability to obtain future support by interfering with the children's relationship with the natural father.

****Thus, both the majority and separate opinions in *Miller* acknowledged that the primary obligation of support is on the natural parent, and that it is the exceptional case in which the obligation will be transferred to a stepparent

I continue to be counselled by *Miller's* warning not to impose a child- support obligation on a stepfather merely because he developed a close relationship with the stepchildren. Without further proof, I would not alter *Miller's* requirement that when the natural parent can be located and is financially able, he or she remains principally responsible to pay permanent child support. ***

This case stands in stark contrast to *Miller*, where the evidence was that the stepparent actively resisted the natural father's attempt to maintain relations with his children. Here, the whereabouts of the natural father are known; he is in the next town. Most importantly, Henry has not done anything to interfere directly with the natural father's relationship with K.B. On the present record, the absence of financial support from the natural father is as attributable to his insouciance as it is to Henry's conduct.

In seeking an appropriate judicial response, I am guided, as are the concurring justices, by the best interests of the child. Like my colleagues who join in the concurring opinion, I believe that Henry is obliged to provide support for K.B., but I would require Henry to meet that obligation only until such time as a support order may be entered against the natural father. Hence, I would remand the matter to the Chancery Division for reconsideration in light of *Miller*. Of course, support obligations are always subject to modification because of changed circumstances, such as the ability of the natural father to satisfy the child's support needs. *** Because of Henry's previous agreement, included in his divorce decree, to support K.B., I would place the burden upon him to show that it is in the best interest of K.B. to obtain support from the natural father. If for any reason such an order cannot be entered against the natural father, I would continue to require Henry to support K.B.

e Notes and Questions

1) Support Guidelines

While the value of child support guidelines is still being debated, all states have such guidelines as mandated by Congress. Most empirical studies of child support schedules have agreed that each parent should be responsible for the support of children to an amount commensurate with his or her financial situation. Guidelines were initially drafted on the basis of sole custody. A number of states have amended their guidelines to provide for joint and split custody. Most states have codified what deviations may be considered. What pattern does your state's guidelines follow?

2) Use of Child's Trust to Satisfy Support Obligation

The prevailing rule among courts that have addressed the issue is that a parent (or any other person) who is the custodian of the property of minors under the Uniform Transfers to Minors Act or the Uniform Gifts to Minors Act may not use such property to satisfy the child support obligation of a parent. Nor may a court take into account the UGMA assets of the child in setting child support obligations of the parents. *Sutliff v. Sutliff*, 489 A.2d 764 (Pa. Super. 1985); *Newman v. Newman*, 123 Cal. App. 3d 618, 176 Ca. Rptr. 723 (1981); *Weisbaum v. Weisbaum*, 477 A.2d. 690 (Conn. 1984). *But see Lewis v. Lewis*, 708 A.2d 249 (D.C. Ct. App. 1998)(allowing adjustment if child has substantial income that can be used for child support if the child's current and future education would not be impaired.)

3) Support Obligation After the Age of Majority

By statute and common law, the obligation to pay support generally ends when the supported child reaches legal age. Courts, generally, have the authority to order parents to support children only while they are minors, absent additional specific statutory authority. At common law, the parental legal duty of support apparently could not be revived after the child reached majority for any reason. However, many modern courts will require parents to support a disabled child who cannot support himself or herself if the disability exists at the time the child comes of legal age. In some states this exception has been codified. In most states, without explicit statutory direction, the courts have reached the same result on the basis of equity and public policy.

By statute, a minority of states allow courts to order payment of child support after majority if the child is enrolled in college. Other states have reached the same result on the basis of equity and public policy. Critics point out that this subjects divorced parents (at least obligors) to longer and greater support liability than parents in intact families. Proponents of college support point out that children of divorce are in a more precarious position than children in intact families, not only having significant emotional hurdles to overcome to achieve educational success, but typically receiving less support during college from noncustodial parents. Most courts have upheld this different treatment of families as not violating the equal protection clause. *See Curtis v. Klute*, 666 A.2d 265 (Pa. 1995), *contra*.

4) Third Parties

Third Parties are not liable for support of non-biological children unless there is a statute or unless there is a contractual obligation or unless the principles of *loco parentis* or equitable estoppel apply. *See* Nolan, *infra*. A few jurisdictions have statutes that apply to stepparents during the stepparent relationship, which typically may be a codification of the *in loco parentis* status. Stepparent obligations usually cease when the marriage ends unless contract or equitable estoppel principles apply. If, during their marriage, the wife gives birth to an extramarital child, the husband may have a support duty towards that child when the marriage ends under contract or equitable estoppel principles. Not all states recognize the equitable estoppel doctrine in the context of third-party support. The majority of those recognizing the equitable estoppel doctrine would apply it only if the natural parent could not be found. Do you see why Justice Pollock concluded that Justice Handler's opinion was expanding the rationale of *M.H.B. v. H.T.B.*?

5) Nonconforming Support Payment

As a general rule, a parent obligated by judicial decree to make support payments in a specified amount, type, or on a specified schedule or to a specific payee may not vary the terms to suit his or her own convenience. However, where the parties mutually agree to a change of custody whereby the support-obligated parent assumes the full, permanent custody of the children, but no modification of the custody and support decree is obtained, then courts are likely to give the support-obligated parent credit for compliance with the support decree.

6) Imputed Income

Courts may impute income to parents who are unemployed or underemployed. Courts vary as to the approach taken to calculate the imputed amount.

7) Relationship With the Child

The father in *Nash v. Mulle* argues that he should not pay support because he has no relationship with the child. Should this factor be a consideration in ordering support? In determining the amount of support?

8) Parental Agreements

Courts are not bound by agreements made by parents as to the amount and duration of the support. In the past, courts may have given more deference to parental agreements, but child support guidelines are presumptive. Some guidelines may allow parental agreements as one of the deviation considerations.

9) ALI Principles of the Law of Family Dissolution

Chapter 3 of the *Principles of the Law of Family Dissolution* proposed by the American Law Institute contains an extensive commentary on, strong endorsement of, and rather significant extension of child support standards. The ALI recommends that child support guidelines should be based upon not only a share of the obligor's income but also a supplemental amount where the parental earning capacities differ significantly, but the recommendations provide for a cap on the total percentage that can be awarded for compensatory payments of forty percent (40%) of the earning gap. American Law Institute, *infra*, at Chapter 3, Child Support.

3. Practical and Ethical Considerations

a. John thinks that his daughter who is now nine months old is not his biological child because she resembles a neighbor. Several of his relatives have commented directly to him about the resemblance. He has no suspicions that his wife has been unfaithful to him. He wants to know if he finds out later that the child is not his biological child would he have any legal responsibilities towards the child?

b. MHT represented himself pro se in the appellate court. Some local bar associations and courts have pro se litigation clinics in order to provide some training to persons who must represent themselves in family law matters at the trial level. These clinics do not provide legal advice, but provide information on the procedures. Some local courts provide forms in family law cases to assist persons who do not have a lawyer. The Maryland judiciary Web site provides court free forms for divorce, child support, custody, visitation and other domestic cases. (www.courts.state/md.us./family/forms/index.html).

4. Bibliography

American Law Institute, *Principles of the Law of Family Dissolution: Analysis and Recommendations* (2002).

Christopher Blakesley, Child Support in Family Laws in the United States (L. Wardle, C. Blakesley & J. Parker 1987).

Dodson, Child Support Guidelines: Overview of the Alternatives and State Activity to Date, Fair$hare, Sept., 1986, at 3.

Ira Mark Ellman, *Thinking About Custody and Support in Ambiguous-Father Families*, 36 Fam. L.Q. 49 (2002).

Ira Mark Ellman, *Do Americans Play Football*, 19 Int'l J. L, Pol'y, & Fam. 257 (2005).

Thomas Espenshade, Investing in Children: New Estimates of Parental Expenditures (1984).

Laurence C. Nolan, *Legal Strangers and the Duty of Support: Beyond the Biological Tie–But How Far Beyond the Marital Tie?*, 41 Santa Clara L. Rev. 1 (2000).

Thomas Williams, Guidelines for Setting Levels of Child Support Orders, 21 Fam. L. Q. 281 (1987).
Uniform Interstate Family Support Act (with Unofficial Annotations by John J. Sampson, 27 Fam. L.Q. 93, 100-103 (1993).

CHAPTER 37

Child Support: Modification;
Enforcement; Tax Considerations

A. CHILD SUPPORT MODIFICATION

1. Background

In order to protect the welfare of the child, child support orders are modifiable until the child reaches the age of majority on the basis of relevant, substantial change of circumstances. In the past, this discretionary standard allowed the trial court judge to determine how the current order should be changed. Usually, modification cases are initiated by the custodial parent. However, The Family Support Act of 1988 requires states also to set up a process to update child support orders every three years at a minimum.

2. Statutes, Cases and Doctrines

a. *Edwards v. Lowry*

Catherine Munn Edwards v. John Carlton Lowry
348 S.E.2d 259 (Virginia 1986)

Present: All the Justices.

RUSSELL, Justice.

We here consider whether a party whose income has declined as a result of his own misconduct may rely on such diminution of income as ground for a reduction of court-ordered child support payments pursuant to Code s 20-108.

John and Catherine Munn Lowry (now Catherine Munn Edwards) were divorced on no-fault grounds in February 1982. They had earlier entered into a property settlement agreement which provided that Catherine was to have custody of Tabatha, the couple's four-year-old daughter, and that John was to pay $325 per month to Catherine for Tabatha's support. The agreement was filed among the papers in the divorce suit, but was neither ratified by the court nor incorporated into the divorce decree.

A month after the entry of the divorce decree, John petitioned the juvenile and domestic relations (JDR) court for a reduction of child support, alleging changed circumstances. On March 17, 1982, the JDR court entered an order reducing child support to $290 per month. Catherine appealed the ruling to the circuit court, which heard additional evidence and, on June 21, 1982, fixed child support at $300 per month. The case was remanded to the JDR court.

Less than two months later, John filed another petition in the JDR court for a reduction, stating that he had been suspended from his employment on July 1, 1982, and had since been unable to find work. The JDR court denied the petition on the ground that John's loss of employment was a result of his admitted larceny from his employer, a hardware dealer. John appealed to the circuit court.

The appeal was heard on January 24, 1983. John testified that he had been caught stealing from his employer in December 1981 and had been warned that if he stole again he "would be in trouble." When he was accused of pilferage the second time, on June 29, 1982, he was discharged. He had been unable to secure new employment, but was trying, with limited success, to "make ends meet" as a self-employed contractor weatherproofing homes and doing repair work. His financial burdens were greatly increased because of his remarriage in February 1982. His new wife was unemployed and had two children by a prior marriage. John was supporting them. Catherine had also remarried and had a son five months old. The court determined that John's loss of employment, even though caused by his own wrongful activity, should be taken into consideration in fixing the level of child support. Weighing the relative incomes and expenses of the parties in the light of the expenses relating to Tabatha, the court reduced John's support payments to $250 per month plus Tabatha's actual medical and dental insurance premiums.

Neither party was required to pay counsel fees to the other. Catherine appeals, contending that John failed to present evidence justifying a reduction in child support and that she was entitled to an award of counsel fees incurred in the defense of John's petition.

Code s 20-108 gives a divorce court continuing jurisdiction, after a final decree of divorce has been entered, to modify its decree with respect to the custody and maintenance of minor children. The court's power in this respect is unaffected by any contract entered into between husband and wife. Neither ratification nor incorporation of such a contract by the divorce decree affects the court's continuing jurisdiction in this regard. *

In order to invoke the court's continuing jurisdiction to modify its decree, the party seeking a change has the burden of proving, by a preponderance of the evidence, a material change in circumstances justifying a modification of the decree. *Hammers v. Hammers*, 216 Va. 30, 31, 216 S.E.2d 20, 21 (1975); * As we further noted in *Hammers*, a party seeking a reduction in support payments has additional burdens: "[H]e must make a full and clear disclosure relating to his ability to pay. He must also show that his lack of ability to pay is not due to his own voluntary act or * because of his neglect." * In both Hammers and Crosby, the change in circumstances relied on to obtain a reduction in support payments was the former husband's failure to pay his federal income taxes, which were greatly in arrears. Each of those cases, like the case now before us, involved an effort by a former husband to shift to his wife or child the consequences of his own wrongdoing.

In the case before us, it is undisputed that John Lowry's diminution of income was the direct consequence of his voluntary, wrongful act. *[FN We have not been called upon to decide, and do not now decide, the question presented by a voluntarily-incurred reduction of income for a purpose ultimately beneficial to the payee, such as a change to a new occupation offering brighter prospects in the long run, or education and training undertaken to qualify the payor to enter such a new career]* After receiving a direct warning from his employer following a previous theft, he was fired for stealing again. He failed to meet the burden, required by the rule in Hammers, of showing himself free of responsibility for his change in circumstances, and was not entitled to a reduction in support based upon the diminution of income caused by the loss of his job.

A further reason John advanced in favor of a reduction in support payments was that, apart from his loss of income, his expenses had substantially increased since the divorce decree. This was primarily, if not entirely, the result of his remarriage and assumption of responsibility for a new family. But his primary responsibility was to the child of his former marriage. His subsequent, voluntarily-assumed responsibilities should not have been taken into account as a justification for reducing his obligation to support his own child. In reversing a decree reducing a father's child support payments in *Treger v. Treger*, 212 Va. 538, 539, 186 S.E.2d 82, 84 (1972), we said: "His assumption of the responsibility of supporting a new wife and her children is entitled to little, if any, consideration." We find that the evidence fails to support the modification ordered by the trial court, and we will reverse the decree appealed from and reinstate the award of child support in the amount of $300 per month, which was provided by the trial court's order of June 21, 1982.

Undoubtedly, the trial court required each party to bear his or her own counsel fees because there was no great disparity in their respective economic circumstances and because both John's petition and Catherine's defense appeared to the court to have substantial merit. However, after the divorce decree was entered, Catherine was required to engage counsel for four court appearances in less than one year as a result of John's persistent efforts to reduce the level of child support to which he had agreed. Catherine's efforts were necessary for the defense of the child's interests against repeated attacks which we now hold to be meritless.

In *Carswell v. Masterson*, 224 Va. 329, 332, 295 S.E.2d 899 (1982), we held that a court of equity has the power to award counsel fees in aid of contempt proceedings to enforce court orders, particularly where a child's interests are at stake. The same reasoning applies to counsel fees incurred while resisting an attack on a child's interests under a court order. Accordingly, we will award counsel fees for services in this court, and will remand the case to the trial court for the determination of an appropriate award of counsel fees incurred there. Reversed and remanded.

b. *Feltman v. Feltman*

Richard Feltman and Richard Feltman and Paula Feltman, as Guardian for their minor children, G.F. and J.F. v. Sandra Feltman and The State of Dakota, Amicus Curiae
434 N.W.2d 590 (S.D. 1989)

HEEGE, Circuit Judge.

Richard Feltman and Paula Feltman as guardians for their children attack SDCL 25-7-7 (child support guidelines) as violating their constitutional equal protection rights. The trial court held that the Feltmans failed to establish that SDCL 25-7-7 was unconstitutionally discriminatory. We affirm.

FACTS

Richard and Sandra Feltman were married in 1969. They were divorced on March 25, 1974. Two children were born of the marriage. As part of a separation agreement, the parties agreed that Sandra Feltman would have custody and Richard Feltman would pay monthly child support of $75.00 per child, for a total of $150.00 per month for both children. The terms of this agreement were accepted by the court and included in the divorce decree.

Both parties remarried, but Sandra Feltman is now divorced from her second husband. In his second marriage, Richard and his wife, Paula, have two children. These two children are minors and reside with Richard and Paula.

Sandra Feltman petitioned the Department of Social Services to conduct a hearing for the purpose of increasing Richard's monthly child support obligation. In applying SDCL 25-7-7, the Department of Social Services, as affirmed by the circuit court, followed this approach: (1) They determined Richard Feltman's net monthly income to be $1,379.71; (2) They determined that there were two children from the previous marriage; and (3) They then determined the proper support amount as $435 per month as specified for two children in the chart in SDCL 25-7-7.

Both the department and the circuit court considered the children of the second family, but concluded that the guidelines chart amount for two children was proper.

CLAIMS RAISED

In this appeal, the Feltmans raise two claims in their argument that SDCL 25-7-7 violates Article VI, Section 18 of the South Dakota Constitution and the Fourteenth Amendment to the United States Constitution. First, the equal protection rights of their children because the statute gives child support priority to the children of Richard Feltman's first marriage. As a result, the children of Richard Feltman's second marriage may not receive the same amount of economic support as the children of his first marriage. Their second claim is that SDCL 25-7-7 violates the equal protection rights of children in subsequent relationships because their needs are not taken into consideration when determining the amount of child support for children of a prior relationship. We deal with their claims separately.

I.

We apply the rational basis standard of review to Feltman's claim that SDCL 25-7-7 violates

the equal protection rights of children because the statute gives child support priority to the children of the first marriage. No suspect classification nor fundamental right is involved and therefore the strict scrutiny standard is inapplicable. Under the rational basis standard, this court will uphold a statute if the statutory classification bears some rational relationship to a legitimate state purpose.
***

The burden of proving SDCL 25-7-7 unconstitutional rests with the Feltmans. A statute is presumed constitutional and the party attacking its constitutionality "has the burden of proving beyond a reasonable doubt that the classification violates equal protection rights." *

The Feltmans have failed to carry their burden of proving that SDCL 25-7-7 bears no rational relationship to a legitimate state interest. The opposite is true. Every parent is required to support their children. SDCL ch. 25-7, 25-7A. To assure that absent and noncustodial parents contribute to the support of all their children, the legislature passed SDCL 25-7-7. Under this statute, a noncustodial parent's monthly child support payment is determined primarily by his or her net monthly income and the number of children from the prior marriage.

The guidelines used in SDCL 25-7-7 for determining a noncustodial parent's monthly child support obligation reflect this court's policy that "the amount of child support depends on the reasonable expenditures suitable to the child's circumstances at the time of divorce and the payor's financial means and ability to pay."* This state has an interest in protecting the welfare of its children which includes their standard of living. SDCL 25-7- 7 serves to prevent the otherwise often precipitous drop in a child's standard of living when his or her parents divorce and to provide uniform standards for determining the amount of child support each noncustodial parent must pay.

The application of SDCL 25-7-7 may result in the children of a second or third marriage receiving a lesser amount of economic support than the children of the first marriage. This result was clearly considered by the Child Support Commission. In its report to the Governor, the Child Support Commission stated:

> The Commission discussed at length the problem of establishing the support obligation for children of second or third families when the noncustodial parent is responsible for previously existing support obligations. It was concluded that the support obligation for the children of each should be established separately and a deduction from the noncustodial parent's gross income for payments on support obligations for children of previous relationships should be allowed in determining the net income for establishing subsequent obligations.
> As an example, if a noncustodial parent with a net income of $1,200 had two children by marriage and is divorced, the support obligation in accordance with the guidelines if $342. The parent then remarries and has two children by the second marriage and is divorced. The support obligation for the children of the second marriage would be established between $192 and $216 at the net income level of $858. ($1,200 minus $342) for two children.

SDCL 25-7-7 is constitutional even though the children of a first marriage receive priority in child support. Under the rational basis standard, the court accords great deference to the constitutionality of a statute even if imperfect results are achieved. The United States Supreme Court stated:

> In the area of economics and social welfare, a state does not violate the Equal Protection Clause merely because the classifications made by its laws are imperfect. If the classification has some "reasonable basis," it does not offend the Constitution simply because the classification "is not made with mathematical nicety or because in practice it results in some inequality." (citation omitted). "The problems of government are practical ones and may justify, if they do not require, rough accommodations-illogical it may be, and unscientific."

(citation omitted). "A statutory discrimination will not be set aside if any state of facts *593 reasonably may be conceived to justify it." (citation omitted).

Dandridge v. Williams, 397 U.S. 471, 90 S.Ct. 1153, 25 L.Ed.2d 491 (1970).

The support format set forth in SDCL 25-7-7 provides a fair and logical prioritization of claims against a noncustodial parent's income. Without prioritization, the children from the first family might find their standard of living substantially decreased by the voluntary acts of a noncustodial parent. A noncustodial parent who becomes responsible for supporting the children of a second marriage does so with the knowledge of a continuing responsibility to the children of the first marriage. We hold that SDCL 25-7-7 has a rational basis and passes muster under the rational basis standard of review.

II.

The second claim raised by the Feltmans is dealt with separately because it misinterprets SDCL 25-7-7. Equal protection analysis, as a result, is unnecessary. The Feltmans claim that SDCL 25-7-7 does not provide for the needs of subsequent children to be taken into account when determining the amount of child support for children of a prior relationship. This is not the case. SDCL 25-7-7 requires the parents of a child to provide "for the necessary maintenance, education and support of the child in accordance with their respective means."

A parent's "respective means" is one of the factors to be considered in determining the amount of monthly support. * ** If the guidelines operate to deprive children of subsequent families from necessary support, the statute permits deviation from the guidelines upon the entry of specific findings.

The child support enforcement system set forth in SDCL 25-7-7 does not disenfranchise or deny any child the right to the necessary support and maintenance that a child is entitled to from either parent. Appellants have failed to establish that the formula and scheme set forth in SDCL 25-7-7 is unreasonable or discriminatory as to them. The judgment of the circuit court is affirmed.

Sandra Feltman has petitioned this court for an allowance of appellate attorney's fees. That petition is allowed in the amount of $750.00.

HENDERSON, Justice (dissenting)

Are children of a second marriage "children of a lesser god"?

Are children of a second marriage lesser children under the United States Constitution? Are children of a second marriage any less hungry or naked without the support of their father?

Should we weep for children of a second marriage at their birth, rather than at their death?

This decision is reduced to an old adage, "First come, first served." In my judgment, all of God's children, born of the first or second marriage, must be afforded the same consideration under law.

We have, before us, yet another case where the "guidelines chart" is literally supreme. It is further noted, by this minority writer, that the majority suggests, perhaps inferentially, that the priority of the child support for the first marriage results in "imperfect results." Indeed, the law is not, perfect, but as we write it, we should strive for its perfection.

SDCL 25-7-7 is unconstitutional because it discriminates against children of a "noncustodial" parent's second family, denying them equal protection under the law. This statute classifies children by accident of time of birth; a classification that has no rational relationship to any legitimate governmental interest. Conceptually, this discrimination is as irrational, and hence unconstitutional, as discrimination against illegitimate children, decried in *Weber v. Aetna Cas. & Sur. Co.*, 406 U.S. 164, 92 S.Ct. 1400, 31 L.Ed.2d 768 (1972), and *Gomez v. Perez*, 409 U.S. 535, 93 S.Ct. 872, 35 L.Ed.2d 56 (1973). Courts have a very special responsibility for the care and welfare of children. *Houghton v. Houghton*, 37 S.D. 184, 157 N.W. 316 (1916) (children are "wards of the court"). The care and welfare of Richard's youngest children are not furthered by the rigid guidelines set out in SDCL 25-7-7, under the analysis in *Donohue v. Getman*, 432 N.W.2d 281, 283 (S.D.1988) (Henderson, J., specially concurring). This statute also violates the constitutional principle of separation of powers, as discussed in *Sharp v. Sharp*, ***

Even were this statute constitutional, which I do not concede, the needs of Richard's later children were ignored below, requiring reversal for findings of fact and conclusions of law under the holding of the majority opinion in *Bruning v. Jeffries*, 422 N.W.2d at 581, where this Court remanded for "reconsideration and entry of findings regarding the totality of Father's financial condition." Dependent children must be a factor in such "financial condition."

In concluding, reference is made to my minority writing in *Peterson v. Peterson*, 434 N.W.2d 732, 739 (S.D.1989) (Henderson, J., concurring in part and concurring in result in part), wherein I again, as in the past, portray SDCL 25-7-7 as eroding the constitutional power of trial judges in this state and placing their discretion within the rigidity of mathematical analysis of percentages. SDCL 25-7-7 is a legal abomination which, in attempting to achieve a result, shatters due process, the constitutional Doctrine of Separation of Powers and prioritizes children in an amount of support to be received from their father depending upon
when, in point of time, they were birthed. This is an attempt to achieve a social result by prioritizing children of a second or third marriage into second- or third-class citizens. And it is an injustice of mammoth proportion.

c. Notes and Questions

1) Uniform Interstate Family Support Act (UISFA)

Prior to the adoption of UIFSA, states took several approaches as to whether another state had to give full faith and credit to a sister state's judgment and not modify it. Under the UISFA, however, its §205 provides that the original state has continuing, exclusive jurisdiction over the order unless the residence of the obligor, individual obligee, or the child changes or unless each party files consent for another state to have continuing, exclusive jurisdiction. The object of UISFA is that only one state has jurisdiction to modify the child support order. If no state has continuing, exclusive jurisdiction, the child's home state's order takes priority. (*Also see* Chapter 36, *supra*.)

2) Standard for Modification

Edward v. Lowry follows the majority rule. Some states use the term substantial instead of material change. The Uniform Marriage and Divorce Act §316 provides that the change circumstances must be "so substantial and continuing as to be unconscionable." A few states follow a modified rule on "voluntariness" by applying either a good faith rule or a balancing test. If the parent's voluntary change in circumstance is made in good faith and not to avoid paying child support, the change is a modifiable change. In the balancing test, the court balances various factors to determine how the modification will affect the child financially.

3) Subsequent Children

Feltman follows the prevailing view that a subsequent child is not a change of circumstance for modification purposes. A growing number of states, however, do consider the needs of the second family. *See e.g. Martinez v. Martinez*, 660 A.2d 13 (N.J. Ch. Div. 1995).

4) Child Support as Bar to Further Liability

The courts are split on the preclusive effects of a child support order. Courts in several states appear to hold that a child support decree establishes the complete and total liability for child support until it is modified. Other states courts allow recovery of necessaries exceeding the amount of child support ordered. In *Alamance County Hospital, Inc. v. Neighbors*, 338 S.E.2d. 87 (N.C. 1986), the North Carolina Supreme Court held that a hospital could maintain an action against the father of a child to whom it had provided necessary medical services even though there was a valid child support order existing which the father argued included amounts intended to cover the child's medical care. The court was persuaded that the child support provisions entered in connection with a divorce should bind the parents but not the child. The payment of child support would bear on the question whether the father had sufficiently provided for the medical necessaries of the child, but the mere existence of an order did not bar the claim.

5) Death

Most states follow the common law rule that the death of the parent ends the duty of support. Some modern decisions have allowed the duty of support to survive the parent's death and become binding on the parent's estate. *See Kujawinski v. Kujawinski*, 376 NE.2d 1382 (Ill. 1978).

3. Practical and Ethical Considerations

a. Children of a Lesser God

The dissenting opinion in *Feltman* raises the point about second families being the children of a lesser god. That might also happen to other children. Many state guidelines provide that in calculating a parent's income for child support determination in a pending case that the amount of an existing child support order is treated as a deduction. What should be the policy when there is an extramarital child and a paternity case is pending, but there is no existing child support order for the children in the parent's ongoing marriage?

4. Bibliography

Lewis Becker, *Spousal and Child Support and the "Voluntary Reduction of Income" Doctrine*, 29 Conn. L. Rev. 647 (1997).

Contmeporary Family Law, vol. 4, Ch. 38 (1988).

Homer C. Clark, Law of Domestic Relations (1969).

Note, *Making Parents Behave: The Conditioning of Child Support and Visitation Rights*, 84 Colum. L. Rev. 1059 (1984).

B. CHILD SUPPORT ENFORCEMENT

1. Background

The enforcement of child support orders is a national problem. Courts have traditionally used their contempt powers, usually civil contempt, to enforce child support. Since 1975, however, with the influential and continuing involvement of the federal government, other procedures, besides contempt, have become common and effective.

2. Statutes, Cases and Doctrines

a. *Moss v. Superior Court*
Brent N. Moss, Petitioner, v. The Superior Court of Riverside County, Respondent; Tamara
S. Ortiz Real Party in Interest
950 P2d 59 (Cal. 1998)

BAXTER, Justice.

May a parent whose inability to pay court-ordered child support results from a willful failure to seek and obtain employment be adjudged in contempt of court and punished for violation of the order? Concluding that it was bound by this court's decision a century ago in Ex parte Todd (1897) 119 Cal. 57, 50 P. 1071(Todd), which was recognized as binding precedent in In re Jennings (1982) 133 Cal.App.3d 373, 184 Cal.Rptr. 53 (Jennings), the Court of Appeal reluctantly held that to impose a contempt sanction in those circumstances is beyond the power of the court. It therefore annulled the judgment of contempt in issue in this proceeding. Although not expressly articulated in Todd, which, like Jennings, involved spousal support, the apparent basis for the Todd result was either an assumption that employment sought under even an indirect threat of imprisonment for violation of the support order constituted involuntary servitude or a belief that imposition of a contempt or criminal sanction for failure to pay support constituted imprisonment for debt.

We conclude that there is no constitutional impediment to imposition of contempt sanctions on a parent for violation of a judicial child support order when the parent's financial inability to comply with the order is the result of the parent's willful failure to seek and accept available employment that is commensurate with his or her skills and ability. We shall therefore disapprove Todd insofar as it might be read to apply to child support orders. We also address the burden of proof in these contempt proceedings and conclude that inability to comply with a child support order is an affirmative defense. The alleged contemner must prove inability to comply by a preponderance of the evidence, which was not done here.

We shall affirm the judgment of the Court of Appeal, however. We must do so because, in light of the past understanding of Todd, our holding that a willfully unemployed, nonsupporting parent is subject to contempt sanctions if the parent fails to comply with a child support order might be deemed an unanticipated change in the law, and Tamara Ortiz, the custodial parent, did not carry her burden of proof under the existing law by showing that Brent Moss, the alleged contemner, had the actual financial ability to comply with the order.
****

The "Declaration for Contempt" in this matter, [FN1 *A proceeding for the punishment of an indirect contempt is commenced by the presentation of an affidavit setting forth the alleged contemptuous acts. (Code Civ. Proc., § 1211.) The affidavit is in effect a complaint, frames the issues before the court and is a jurisdictional prerequisite to the court's power to punish.*"] executed by Tamara S. Ortiz on June 22, 1995, alleged that a judgment of dissolution filed March 17, 1992, ordered Brent N. Moss to pay $241.50 each, or a total of $483 a month support for the two children of the marriage, one-half due on the first and one-half due on the fifteenth day of each month, commencing on January 15, 1992. The order was modified on November 1, 1994, after which $385 was to be paid monthly, with semimonthly payments of $192.50. The declaration alleged that Brent had knowledge of the order and was able to comply with each order when it was disobeyed. No payments were made from July 1, 1994, through June 15, 1995. A total of $5,210 was due and unpaid.

Brent was unemployed when the support order was made. The amount to be paid was based on his ability to earn $1,671 gross income per month.

The declaration alleged 24 contempt counts and the court treated each of the 24 dates on which a payment had not been made as a separate count. The superior court issued an order to show cause on June 17, 1995, directing Brent to appear and show cause why he should not be found guilty of contempt for willful disobedience of the support order.

At the November 7, 1995, hearing on the order to show cause, Tamara testified that she and Brent, her then husband, were present when the support order was made and that he had not paid any support at all since July 1, 1994.

Brent's counsel assumed that Tamara bore the burden of proof on ability to pay support. On cross-examination Tamara testified that Brent did not have a car and at times had no food in his house. She was not aware of him having a job in the past four years, and did not know if he had any money or any ability to pay.

Betty Lou Moss, Brent's mother, testified that she provided Brent with a home. She paid the utilities expenses most times, but on other times he did so. He worked at odd jobs, and she did not know how much he earned from them. Brent often ate at her home. She did not know if he purchased food on his own. When the children were with him, they slept at his house, but he brought them to Betty Moss's home to eat. Betty Moss did not know if Brent ever fed them at his house. She did not remember how long it had been since Brent had a job. He did not discuss jobs with her. He did odd jobs like lawn mowing once in a while, but she did not know how much he earned. When she asked him about getting a job he said he was trying. He did not tell her what he was trying, however.

No other evidence was presented.

Counsel for Brent did not dispute the existence of a valid order for support, his client's knowledge of that order, and possible " willfulness," but argued that there had been no evidence of ability to comply with the support order. He also argued that in a contempt proceeding to enforce a child support order, the citee need only raise the question of ability to comply, at which point the party seeking the contempt sanction had the burden of proving ability to comply beyond a reasonable doubt. In his view, inability to comply had been adequately raised by the evidence and compelling Brent to work under threat of punishment would constitute involuntary servitude.

Tamara's counsel argued that Brent had the burden of proving inability to comply with the order as an affirmative defense and that ability to comply did not require ability to pay the full amount of support ordered.

The court agreed that the burden of proving inability to comply lay with Brent and observed that there had been no evidence whatsoever that Brent was not able to work. The court found that Brent did have the ability to pay something in child support, as the evidence permitted an inference that he was receiving money from some source other than his mother. In partial explanation of that conclusion, the court stated that Brent was well dressed and had to be doing something to buy his own clothes and feed himself when he did not eat at his mother's home. The court also stated that Brent was "a person who could get a job flipping hamburgers at MacDonald's.... I don't know why he couldn't get a job at minimum wage. He's, in my mind, chosen not to." Brent's attorney then conceded that Brent had the ability to work. When asked later if there was a finding of ability to work, however, the court said only that Brent had "the ability to get money. Now, whether you want to say it's the ability to work, which there is no evidence that he can't, or the ability to get money from his mother, which he apparently freely does as he needs to ... I am left with the inference that he has money from another source." The court also expressed the view that permitting a parent who had the ability to work and support the parent's children, but failed to do so would make a "mockery" of the contempt power.

The court found Brent guilty of 24 counts of contempt, [FN2 *The number of separate* contempt counts appears to exceed the current statutory limit. *Effective January 1, 1995, the statute of limitations for contempt for failure to pay child support is three years from the date that each payment is due and a separate contempt count may be stated for each month for which payment is not made in full. (See Code Civ. Proc., § 1218.5.)]* but delayed imposition of sentence to permit Brent to seek appellate review. The only factual finding set forth in the minute order of November 7, 1995, was that "Respondent has the ability to pay the court ordered support."

After this petition for a writ of mandate was filed, the Court of Appeal noted that no sentence had yet been imposed and held the petition in abeyance pending that action. On March 5, 1996, the superior court imposed a sentence of five days in jail for each of six counts of contempt, and ordered Brent to perform ten hours of community servitude for each of the six counts. [FN3*] Execution of sentence was stayed to permit Brent to purge himself of contempt by making specified payments, and he was placed on three years' informal probation. At that point the Court of Appeal issued its order to show cause in this mandate proceeding.

Brent's petition for a writ of mandate sought to set aside the contempt judgment on the ground that, although he raised the issue of inability to pay, Tamara presented no evidence that he had any resources with which to pay child support and therefore had the ability to comply with the order. Relying on *Todd, supra,* 119 Cal. 57, 50 P. 1071, *Jennings, supra,* 133 Cal.App.3d 373, 184 Cal.Rptr. 53, and *In re Brown* (1955) 136 Cal.App.2d 40, 288 P.2d 27 (*Brown*), he also claimed that, while the amount of support fixed by a child support order may be based on ability to earn, a finding of contempt may not be based on ability to earn. The Court of Appeal set aside the contempt judgment, holding that the evidence was not sufficient to prove that Brent had the ability to pay, and because *Todd* was controlling (*Auto Equity Sales, Inc. v. Superior Court* (1962) 57 Cal.2d 450, 455, 20 Cal.Rptr. 321, 369 P.2d 937), the Court of Appeal reluctantly concluded that he could not be adjudged in contempt based only on ability to earn. The Court of Appeal invited this court to reconsider Todd, at least in the context of child support, and we granted the petition for review of real party in interest for the purpose of doing so.

For the reasons stated below, we conclude that, insofar as *Todd* may apply to child support obligations, it should be disapproved. [FN4 *As this matter involves only a child support obligation, we have no occasion to consider whether Todd should be overruled in toto.*] The duty of a parent to support the parent's child or children is a fundamental parental obligation. We are satisfied that there is no constitutional impediment to use of the contempt power to punish a parent who, otherwise lacking monetary ability to pay child support, willfully fails and refuses to seek and accept available employment commensurate with the parent's skills and abilities.

II

This court's opinion in *Todd, supra,* * is the apparent source of the belief that imposition of a contempt sanction on a parent who willfully disables himself or herself from having the ability to comply with a child support order is constitutionally impermissible. Tamara argues that, regardless of whether *Todd* was based on the constitutional prohibition of slavery and involuntary servitude or on the proscription of imprisonment for debt, it should be disapproved or overruled. Supported by amicus curiae Appellate Committee of the California District Attorneys Association, she asks the court to reconsider Todd.

The one-page Todd opinion offered no explanation for its holding that the court lacked power to punish a person for failing to seek employment in order to pay spousal support. In *Todd* the contemner discontinued making court-ordered alimony payments to his ex-wife. After a hearing on an order to show cause re contempt, the court found that the contemner had no money or other means of payment and had not committed a fraud on his creditors by disposing of property. The court also found that the contemner had been allowed a month within which to seek employment so that he could earn money to make the weekly alimony payments, but had made no effort to obtain employment. He was committed to jail until he paid the $200 then due.

This court held: "This order was clearly in excess of the power of the court, which cannot compel a man to seek employment in order to earn money to pay alimony, and punish him for his failure to do so." (*Todd, supra,* 119 Cal. at p. 58, 50 P. 1071.)

****

III

INVOLUNTARY SERVITUDE

We shall assume, as did the Jennings court, that the Todd holding was based on the constitutional proscriptions of involuntary servitude or imprisonment for debt. We consider each in turn, examining first the circumstances which may constitute involuntary servitude within the meaning of the Thirteenth Amendment of the federal Constitution and article I, section 6 of the California Constitution (article I, section 6).

A. Thirteenth Amendment

Section 1 of the Thirteenth Amendment of the federal Constitution provides: "Neither slavery nor involuntary servitude, except as a punishment for crime whereof the party shall have been duly convicted, shall exist within the United States, or any place subject to their jurisdiction."

The Thirteenth Amendment, unlike the Fourteenth Amendment, prohibits conduct by private persons as well as governmental entities. It has been construed and applied primarily to circumstances in which one individual sought to compel work by another. In its decisions applying the Thirteenth Amendment, the United States Supreme Court has recognized that many fundamental societal obligations involving compelled labor do not violate the proscription of involuntary servitude. It has never held that employment undertaken to comply with a judicially imposed requirement that a party seek and accept employment when necessary to meet a parent's fundamental obligation to support a child is involuntary servitude.

In those decisions in which a Thirteenth Amendment violation has been found on the basis of involuntary servitude, the court has equated the employment condition to peonage, under which a person is bound to the service of a particular employer or master until an obligation to that person is satisfied. A court order that a parent support a child, compliance with which may require that the parent seek and accept employment, does not bind the parent to any particular employer or form of employment or otherwise affect the freedom of the parent. The parent is free to elect the type of employment and the employer, subject only to an expectation that to the extent necessary to meet the familial support obligation, the employment will be commensurate with the education, training, and abilities of the parent.

Because the Jennings court cited *Pollock v. Williams, supra,* 322 U.S. 4, 64 S.Ct. 792 (Pollock), as support for its conclusion, and because in that opinion the Supreme Court observed that its past decisions enforcing the Thirteenth Amendment ban on involuntary servitude had been misunderstood and attempted to clarify that area of constitutional law, our exploration of the scope of "involuntary" servitude necessarily begins with Pollock.

Pollock considered a Florida statute that made it a misdemeanor to induce a monetary advance with intent to defraud by a promise to perform labor. The statute also made failure to perform the labor for which money had been obtained prima facie evidence of intent to defraud. The statute was invalidated under both the Thirteenth Amendment and the Antipeonage Act because it compelled involuntary servitude. **** Whatever of social value there may be, and of course it is great, in enforcing contracts and collection of debts, Congress has put it beyond debate that no indebtedness warrants a suspension of the right to be free from compulsory service. This congressional policy means that no state can make the quitting of work any component of a crime, or make criminal sanctions available for holding unwilling persons to labor. The federal statutory test is a practical inquiry into the utilization of an act as well as its mere form and terms. [§] Where peonage has existed in the United States it has done so chiefly by virtue of laws like the statute in question." (*Pollock, supra,* 322 U.S. at pp. 17-18, 64 S.Ct. at p. 799, fns. omitted.)

The obligation of a parent to support a child, and to become employed if that is necessary to meet the obligation, is in no way comparable or akin to peonage or slavery. It is among the most fundamental obligations recognized by modern society. The duty is not simply one imposed by statute, but "rests on fundamental natural laws and has always been recognized by the courts in the absence of any statute declaring it." * It is an obligation that existed under common law (*In re Ricky H.* (1970) 2 Cal.3d 513, 520, 86 Cal.Rptr. 76, 468 P.2d 204) and has long been recognized in a majority of American jurisdictions as not only a moral obligation, but one that is legally enforceable. (Schuele, *Origins and Development of the Law of Parental Child Support* (1988-1989) 27 J. Fam. L. 807, 814-815.) [FN8 *The state's interest in and public policy mandating parental support of children is so strong that jurisdictions faced with the question hold that it extends even to juvenile fathers who were the victims of statutory rape by adult women.*]

The United States Supreme Court has consistently recognized that the Thirteenth Amendment does not prevent enforced labor as punishment for crime, and does not prevent state or federal governmental entities from compelling the performance of civic duties such as jury service, * military service * and road work * A parent's obligation to support a minor child is a social obligation that is no less important than compulsory military service, road building, jury service and other constitutionally permissible enforced labor. Even if the necessity of accepting employment in order to meet this obligation were somehow analogous to those forms of compelled labor, we have no doubt that this form of labor would be recognized as an exception to the ban on involuntary servitude found in the Thirteenth Amendment. It is clear to us, however, that employment undertaken to meet a child support obligation is not analogous to government- controlled labor and does not otherwise create a condition of peonage or slavery. Unlike those recognized exceptions to the Thirteenth Amendment in which labor is compulsory, undertaking employment because an income is necessary to enable a parent to comply with a valid court order to support a child does not impose on the parent any government control over the type of employment, the employer for whom the parent's labor will be performed, or any other aspect of the parent's individual freedom that might be associated with peonage or slavery.

The Supreme Court's construction and application of the "involuntary servitude" aspect of the Thirteenth Amendment has not changed since the Pollock decision. Involuntary servitude is found only when a person is held to labor under conditions akin to peonage or slavery. ****

Pollock, supra, 322 U.S. 4, 64 S.Ct. 792, and *Bailey v. Alabama, supra,* 219 U.S. 219, 31 S.Ct. 145, in both of which failure to perform services for which money had been advanced was prima facie evidence of intent to defraud and criminal sanctions were imposed for the failure.

The court has also reaffirmed its understanding that the Thirteenth Amendment was not intended to apply to "exceptional cases" in which the right to labor was recognized at common law when the amendment was adopted. Examples given were the right of parents to the custody of children, whose labor could be compelled by the parent, and laws which prevent persons who have contracted to work aboard a ship from deserting the ship. ***

As the authorities reviewed above demonstrate, the court's approach in cases of alleged involuntary servitude has been contextual. No single definition of the term has evolved and each situation must be examined to determine if it bears the indices of peonage or slavery. To date however, neither the Supreme Court nor any state court that has enforced a child support order has suggested that undertaking gainful employment in order to avoid sanctions for violation of a valid child support order is analogous to the peonage or involuntary servitude prohibited by the Thirteenth Amendment. Employment chosen by the employee which the employee is free to leave, either in favor of another employer or if the working conditions are objectively intolerable, is simply not "akin to peonage." It does not become so because a person would prefer not to work but must do so in order to comply with a legal duty to support the person's children. As the court said in

Immediato v. Rye Neck School Dist., supra, 73 F.3d at page 459: "In application, courts have consistently found the involuntary servitude standard is not so rigorous as to prohibit all forms of labor that one person is compelled to perform for the benefit of another. The Thirteenth Amendment does not bar labor that an individual may, at least in some sense, choose not to perform, even where the consequences of that choice are 'exceedingly bad.' " ***[FN12]Some courts have simply dismissed involuntary servitude claims made in the context of support-related orders to find employment as meritless without discussion or analysis. (*See e.g. Freeman v. Freeman* (D.C.1979) 397 A.2d 554, 557, fn. 2 ["This contention has no merit."]; *McKenna v. Steen* (La.Ct.App.1982) 422 So.2d 615, 618 ["These allegations are so ludicrous that they hardly dignify a response.... The [order refusing to reduce child support obligation of dentist who left practice] merely imposes ... [the] inherent obligation to support his minor children.... We find no constitutional impingement."]; *Commonwealth v. Pouliot* (1935) 292 Mass. 229, 231 [198 N.E. 256] ["Manifestly, it is not slavery or involuntary servitude as thus authoritatively defined to sentence this defendant if he fails to perform his duty to support his family.... The statute enforces this duty by appropriate sanctions."]; *In re Marriage of Warwick* (Minn.Ct.App.1989) 438 N.W.2d 673, 679 [order to seek work--rationale of out-of-state cases rejecting Thirteenth Amendment claim consistent with Minnesota law although not previously considered by Minnesota courts].)

When, as here, however, the person claiming involuntary servitude is simply expected to seek and accept employment, if available, and is free to choose the type of employment and the employer, and is also free to resign that employment if the conditions are unsatisfactory or to accept other employment, none of the aspects of "involuntary servitude" which invoke the need to apply a contextual approach to Thirteenth Amendment analysis are present. There is no "servitude" since the worker is not bound to any particular employer and has no restrictions on his freedom other than the need to comply with a lawful order to support a child. Working to earn money to support a child is not involuntary servitude any more than working in order to pay taxes. Failure to do either may subject one to civil and criminal penalties, but that compulsion or incentive to labor does not create a condition of involuntary servitude.

Brent cites no authority and we find none that supports a conclusion that the Thirteenth Amendment precludes imposition of either contempt sanctions or criminal penalties for violation of a criminal child support statute when the violation is the result of a willful failure to seek and/or accept employment when employment is necessary to comply with a support obligation. In *Commonwealth v. Pouliot,* * the Massachusetts Supreme Court rejected a claim like that made here deeming this type of obligation to be one of the exceptional forms of service, and holding that "[t]he obligation of a husband and father to maintain his family, if in any way able to do so, is one of the primary responsibilities established by human nature and by civilized society." Consistent with our understanding of the Thirteenth Amendment and our conclusion that whatever compulsion to labor there may be here it does not create a condition akin to peonage, Professor Alvins comments about that decision: "Of course, this case does not hold that the husband is required to perform any particular kind of work to support his family. He may choose any work and any employer, if able. But if nothing else presents itself, he must work at what he can get." * [FN13 *Cases in which the constitutional argument was not raised reflect a well-established assumption that the defense of inability to comply with a support order may be overcome if the prosecutor proves that a parent or spouse under a support order could have obtained employment.*]

Brent relies on *Todd, Brown, Jennings,* and *Pollock,* but he does not acknowledge that neither *Pollock* nor any other Supreme Court decision holds that a condition of involuntary servitude exists when a person is free to choose and to leave the service of his or her employer, and is bound only to seek and accept employment when necessary to enable that person to fulfill a parental child support obligation. Because Tamara emphasizes the special parental support obligation as a basis for overruling *Todd,* Brent argues that a child support obligation should not be recognized as an exception to a rule otherwise "universally applicable" to the enforcement of monetary obligations. As we have shown, however, the rule is not as broad as Brent would have it. The obligation to support a child is not a contractual obligation entered into with knowledge that neither specific performance of personal services nor payment of a resulting debt may be enforced by imprisonment. Instead, parenthood is a status which is accompanied by a legally enforceable obligation to support one's child or children. The obligation to comply with a child support order and to work if necessary to do so does not constitute involuntary servitude. [FN14 *]

****

IV
IMPRISONMENT FOR DEBT

Tamara also contends that the prohibition of imprisonment for debt found in article I, section 10 of the California Constitution (hereafter article I, section 10) does not support application of the Todd holding to child support obligations. We agree.

Article I, section 10 states in pertinent part: "A person may not be imprisoned in a civil action for debt or tort, or in peacetime for a militia fine."

****

Family support obligations are not ordinary debts subject to the constitutional prohibition of imprisonment for debt. (*Bradley v. Superior Court* (1957) 48 Cal.2d 509, 519, 310 P.2d 634["[A] court may ... punish by imprisonment as a contempt the willful act of a spouse (or former spouse) who, having the ability and opportunity to comply, deliberately refuses to obey a valid order to pay alimony or an allowance for the support of the other spouse (or former other spouse). It is held that the obligation to make such payments is not a 'debt' within the meaning of the constitutional guaranty against imprisonment for debt. * ["The husband is bound to support the wife, yet this duty is an imperfect obligation which is not technically a debt."]*

Even were the obligation considered a debt, however, the *Trombley* rationale would be applicable. Children are dependent on their parents for the necessities of life and it is essential to the public welfare that parents provide support with which to care for their needs. To paraphrase the *Trombley* court, a parent who knows that support is due, has the ability to earn money to pay that support, and still willfully refuses to seek and accept available employment to enable the parent to meet the support obligation acts against fundamental societal norms and fair dealing, and necessarily intentionally does an act which prejudices the rights of his children. This conduct would fall within the fraud exception to the constitutional prohibition of imprisonment for debt. ***

We conclude therefore, that neither the constitutional prohibition of involuntary servitude nor the bar to imprisonment for debt precludes imposition of a contempt or criminal sanction on a parent who, having the ability to do so, willfully fails to pay court-ordered child support, or when necessary to make payment possible willfully fails or refuses to seek and accept available employment for which the parent is suited by virtue of education, experience, and physical ability. To the extent that its application in the enforcement of child support obligations may be inconsistent with this conclusion, *Todd, supra,* is disapproved. ****

VI
BURDEN OF PROOF

As noted earlier, Tamara took the position, and the trial court agreed, that inability to comply with a support order is an affirmative defense. The trial court based its contempt judgment on evidence that the support order had been made, Brent had notice of the order, an inference that Brent must have had some income to meet those needs not met by his mother, and its observation that Brent had the ability to earn money to pay something toward his support obligation. Brent had argued that he needed only to raise the question of ability to comply in order to shift to Tamara the burden of presenting evidence sufficient to prove beyond a reasonable doubt that he had the present financial ability to comply with the order.

Brent's argument reflects a basic misunderstanding of the allocation of burden in support proceedings. Ability to comply with a support order is not an element of the contempt which must be proven beyond a reasonable doubt by the petitioner. Inability to comply is an affirmative defense which must be proven by a preponderance of the evidence by the alleged contemner.

We observe initially that assigning the burden to prove an affirmative defense by a preponderance of the evidence to a defendant in a criminal proceeding, and thus to an alleged contemner in a criminal contempt proceeding, is constitutionally permissible. ***

The California Legislature has made inability to pay--which encompasses both present financial inability and inability to obtain remunerative employment in order to pay--an affirmative defense. Proof of ability to pay is not an element of a contempt based on a failure to comply with a child support order. Code of Civil Procedure section 1209.5, makes this allocation of the burden: "When a court of competent jurisdiction makes an order compelling a parent to furnish support or necessary food, clothing, shelter, medical attendance, or other remedial care for his or her child, proof that the order was made, filed, and served on the parent or proof that the parent was present in court at the time the order was pronounced and proof that the parent did not comply with the order is prima facie evidence of a contempt of court." The United States Supreme Court has confirmed that whether ability to comply is to be an element of the contempt or an affirmative defense, and whether Code of Civil Procedure section 1209.5 shifts the burden of persuasion or simply imposes a burden of producing some evidence showing inability to comply are questions of state law. (*Hicks v. Feiock* (1988) 485 U.S. 624, 629, 108 S.Ct. 1423, 1428, 99 L.Ed.2d 721.)

As the Court of Appeal explained on remand of the Feiock matter from the Supreme Court, ability to pay has traditionally been considered an affirmative defense in contempt proceedings.

"For many years in California ability to pay has been considered, without much analysis, to be a matter of defense in contempt proceedings.

"This approach is consistent with legislative intent, constitutional law, and common sense. When this case was first before this court, the parties and the court all assumed that [Code of Civil Procedure] section 1209.5 dealt with an evidentiary presumption. It does not.

"The section was enacted in response to *Warner v. Superior Court* [(1954)] 126 Cal.App.2d 821, 273 P.2d 89. (Rev. of 1955 Code Legislation (U. of Cal. Ext., 1955) p. 129.) *Warner* held that ability to pay was an element of contempt which had to be alleged in the affidavit and proved by the petitioner in contempt proceedings. The Legislature's purpose in enacting the section was to nullify Warner insofar as it made ability to pay an element.

"The language of the statute strongly suggests this is true. Rather than say that 'ability to pay' shall be presumed from proof of the basic facts, the section states that proof of the order, knowledge of it, and noncompliance 'shall be prima facie evidence of a contempt of court.' ([Code Civ. Proc.,] § 1209.5.) In other words, proof of these basic facts proves the entire contempt. Once the contempt is proved any excuse or justification, such as ability to pay, is a matter of defense. We must adhere to this plain meaning of the statute." (In re Feiock (1989) 215 Cal.App.3d 141, 146-147, 263 Cal.Rptr. 437, fns. omitted.)

We agree with the Feiock court's further observation that this allocation of the burden in a child support contempt proceeding is reasonable.

The Legislature's decision that ability to comply should not be an element of a child support contempt offense and to permit the contemner to escape punishment if inability is established reflects a policy like those underlying the rule of convenience made applicable to many defenses that are dependent on information or evidence accessible to or in the control of the defendant. ***
As the court recognized in Feiock: "The contemner is the person in the best position to know whether inability to pay is even a consideration in the proceeding and also has the best access to evidence on the issue, particularly in cases of self- employment. Considerations of policy and convenience have led courts to sanction placement of the burden of establishing a defense on

defendants under similar circumstances. (*People v. Babbitt* [(1988)] 45 Cal.3d 660, 693, 248 Cal.Rptr. 69, 755 P.2d 253 [unconsciousness]; *People v. Vogel* (1956) 46 Cal.2d 798, 803, 299 P.2d 850 [good faith marriage in bigamy prosecution]**

Although the *Feiock* court correctly recognized that ability to pay is not an element of the contempt offense, it went on to state that the alleged contemner need only raise the issue of ability to pay and that the petitioner must then prove the contempt beyond a reasonable doubt, including ability to pay. *** Because ability to pay is not an element of the child support contempt offense, we do not agree and disapprove *In re Feiock, supra,* 215 Cal.App.3d 141, 263 Cal.Rptr. 437, in that respect. As the court had earlier acknowledged, the elements of this contempt are only a valid court order, the alleged contemner's knowledge of the order, and noncompliance. If the petitioner proves those elements beyond a reasonable doubt the violation is established. He or she need go no farther. To prevail on the affirmative defense of inability to comply with the support order, the contemner must prove such inability by a preponderance of the evidence.

****

VII

DISPOSITION

Nonetheless, the judgment of the Court of Appeal must be affirmed. Our disapproval of Todd insofar as it might apply to child support orders and of In re Feiock insofar as that decision placed the burden on a petitioner to prove that a nonsupporting parent had the ability to pay may reasonably be seen as both an unanticipated expansion of the law of contempt in the child support context and a change in the evidentiary burden of which Brent had no notice at the time of trial. Neither rule may be retroactively applied therefore.

While we sympathize with Justice Kennard's preference for upholding the contempt order in this case, due process concerns preclude adoption of the course she proposes. It is true that Todd dealt with a spousal support order. Nonetheless no basis for distinguishing child support orders was apparent at the time Todd was decided, and the Court of Appeal in this case believed Todd to be controlling and there was no contrary authority from which we could imply that Brent knew otherwise. We are unwilling to assume as Justice Kennard does that because the Legislature has authorized a court to require nonsupporting parents to demonstrate that efforts have been made to find employment, Brent should have known in advance of our decision today, and in a case in which no such order was made, that Todd was inapplicable and that a court does have the authority to hold a nonsupporting parent whose inability to comply with a child support order in contempt because the parent failed to seek employment. [FN16 *We note also the lack of evidence that Brent could have obtained employment. While the trial court found that he had the ability to work and opined that he could have found some employment such as flipping hamburgers we do not deem either employment availability or a person's qualifications for a particular type of employment to be matters subject to judicial notice. Under the rules in place at the time of this proceeding, the evidence was not sufficient to establish ability to comply with the court order on the theory that Brent could have found employment in order to do so.*] The effect would be to make conduct that was not subject to criminal contempt sanctions at the time it was committed contemptuous. This we may not do.

Moreover, Brent reasonably relied on *In re Feiock,* which we disapprove in part only today, for his belief that having raised the issue of inability to pay the burden shifted to Tamara to prove that he could have obtained employment in order to comply with the support order.

Due process precludes retroactive application of either rule. Like retroactive application of an "unforeseeable and retroactive judicial expansion of" a statute (*Bouie v. City of Columbia* (1964) 378 U.S. 347, 352, 84 S.Ct. 1697, 1701, 12 L.Ed.2d 894), retroactive application of a decision disapproving prior authority on which a person may reasonably rely in determining what conduct will subject the person to penalties, denies due process. Brent could reasonably have relied on

Todd for a belief that he could not be compelled to find work in order to make it possible to comply with the child support order. Upholding the contempt sanction here would also have the effect of depriving Brent of an affirmative defense available at the time of the alleged contempt by adding another element--inability to find employment-- thereby expanding the scope of the contempt after its commission. ** This, too, would be forbidden by the ex post facto clause and thus denies due process if accomplished by retroactive application of a new judicial decision.

Moreover, our partial disapproval of *In re Feiock* imposes on the alleged contemner the burden of proof of inability to pay. Under *In re Feiock*, an alleged contemner was only required to offer sufficient evidence to raise the issue of inability to pay. He did not have to prove inability to pay or to find employment in order to do so. The affirmative defense was established once the issue of ability to pay was raised unless the petitioner proved ability to pay. Due process also precludes retroactive application of such a rule. It may be constitutionally permissible to alter the rules of evidence and burdens of proof after the commission of an offense. (*See Collins v. Youngblood, supra*, 497 U.S. at p. 43, fn. 3, 110 S.Ct. at p. 2719, fn. 3.) However, to state a new rule on appeal after trial by holding that a defendant has a burden of proof on the ability-to-pay element of the affirmative defense and to apply the new rule retroactively to a trial at which the defendant did not have notice of the change is not permissible. The judgment of the Court of Appeal is affirmed.

KENNARD, Justice, concurring and dissenting. (omitted)

b. Notes and Questions

1) Civil and Criminal Remedies

All states have both civil and criminal enforcement remedies. Under a court's civil contempt powers, the obligor may be found in contempt of court if he or she has the ability to pay but refuses. Contempt may be civil or criminal. The purpose of civil contempt is to coerce the obligor to pay. One may purge oneself of civil contempt whenever compliance occurs. If the obligor is incarcerated with the finding of civil contempt, the sentence is for an indefinite period in order to allow the obligor to purge himself by compliance. Obligors who willfully disobey the court's order may be found in criminal contempt of court. The purpose of criminal contempt is to punish. It is not remedial as is civil contempt. The inability to pay is usually an affirmative defense and not part of the elements of the prima facie case. In *Moss v. Superior Court*, why was contempt proceedings initiated against Mr. Moss? Were these civil or criminal contempt proceedings?

All states and the federal government have enacted statutes that criminalize the failure to pay support. The Child Support Recovery Act of 1992, 18 U.S.C. §228 (1999) makes the willful failure to pay support for a child, living in a different state from the obligor, a federal crime.

2) Parental Locator Service

In order to facilitate the location of obligors, each state and the federal government have parental locator services. Congress enacted legislation that required the Department of Health and Human Services to create The Parent Locator Service as part of the federal Child Support Enforcement program. Parents, their attorneys, and public attorneys may access the federal service.

3) Tax Intercept

In 1981, Congress created the federal tax refund intercept program. Omnibus Budget Reconciliation Act of 1981, Pub. L. 97-35, § 2331, 95 Stat. 860 (1981). Under this program state agencies administering Aid to Families with Dependent Children (AFDC) programs may notify the Secretary of the Treasury that a particular individual owes past-due child support to a recipient of welfare benefits (who must assign her right to collect child support to the state agency in order to receive these benefits). The Secretary of the Treasury is directed to withhold from any tax refund the delinquent support obligor may be entitled to receive and pay the same to the state agency.. In 1984, this program was expanded to allow states to submit requests for tax intercepts for families not receiving AFDC benefits. Child Support Enforcement Amendments of 1984, Pub. L. 98-378, § 21(e)(1), 98 Stat. 1305, 1325 (1984). *See generally* 45 C.F.R. §§ 301-303 (1985); Note, *Constitutional Implications of the Child Support Enforcement Amendments of 1984*, 24 J. Fam. L. 301 (1986). In 1986 the Supreme Court upheld the application of the refund intercept program to earned-income tax credit refunds. *Sorenson v. Secretary of the Treasury*, 475 U.S. 851 (1986). The tax refund intercept program has been challenged as violating the procedural due process rights of the taxpayer. [**Note**: In 1996, Congress enacted an Act that has substantially revised the AFDC program, which is now called the Temporary Aid to Needy Families (TANF).]

4) Other Common Enforcement Remedies

With the assistance of federal law, including the Personal Responsibility and Work Opportunity Reconciliation Act of 1996, states have enacted statutes authorizing wage assignments (i.e. withholding of wages) as a means to collect child support whether the obligor is delinquent or not, imposing automatic liens on a delinquent obligor's assets, suspending of licenses for delinquent obligors, and the suspension of passports. "Withholding" orders guarantee that child support will be paid because the amount owed is withheld from the obligor's salary before he or she receives (and can spend) it. These work well for salaried obligors, but not so well for self-employed and frequently-job-changing obligors. Licenses often include driver's and professional licenses.

5). Linkage of Support and Visitation

In most cases linkage arises as an issue because a custodial parent has refused to allow the noncustodial parent to exercise visitation rights because the other failed to pay support, or the support-obligated parent has refused to pay support because the custodial parent has denied visitation. Allowing linkage provides an easy and easily abused excuse for noncompliance with support and visitation duties, and it encourages retaliatory misbehavior. The Uniform Interstate Family Support Act prohibits altogether any consideration of visitation in its child support enforcement proceedings. Other rationales for denying linkage are: 1) the support obligation is due the child not the custodian who denies visitation, 2) two wrongs do not make a right, 3) the state has an interest in the recovery of support because if adequate support is not provided by the parents the state will have to provide it, 4) linking is ineffective, and there are less drastic alternatives. These include UCCJA , UCCJEA , and UIFSA actions, contempt, actions for custodial interfere, actions to modify custody, joint custody, etc. *See generally* H. Clark, *infra* at 513.

Most courts follow the general rule prohibiting linkage. Ironically, failure to support a child may appropriately be considered along with other factors to restrict visitation or to justify that termination of visitation is in the best interest of a child. For example, in *Rohr v. Rohr*, 709 P.2d 382 (Utah 1985) the Utah Supreme Court approved the trial court's restriction of a father's visitation rights on the ground of his willful, intentional and contumacious failure to pay child support, as well as his contumacious disregard of the court-ordered visitation schedule and attempt to remove child from the jurisdiction. The lower court had restricted visitation, adding a paragraph that when the father became current in child support, he could apply for revision of the visitation limitations. The Supreme Court struck the latter release-paragraph, because it linked child support and visitation (but left in effect the severely restricted visitation based on the same linkage).

Increasingly, linkage is being approved in court orders. One commentator summarized the status of the law as follows:

> In attempting to fashion sufficiently coercive remedies, some courts have chosen to view the obligations of support and visitation as interdependent and have allowed the willful breach of one provision in a decree to be remedied by the intentional withholding of the other. Recognizing the tendency of divorced parents to privately threaten each other with withholding support or visitation, courts have sanctioned the conditioning of these obligations in the hopes that this threat would be sufficiently coercive to assure the fulfillment of the parents' obligations. Thus they have permitted the noncustodial parent to terminate child support payments when the custodial parent unjustly denies visitation rights. Similarly, when a noncustodial parent fails to make child support payments, some courts have allowed the custodian to cut off visitation rights. Several jurisdictions have enacted statutory provisions authorizing the conditioning of these obligations .... Indeed, the belief among courts is growing that the conditioning of remedies is "one of the better means available" to deter recalcitrant parental behavior and to coerce compliance with postdivorce obligations.

Note, Making Parents Behave, *infra*, at 1061-62 (1984).

Other recent commentary also seem to favor some sort of linkage. Mnookin & Kornhouser, *infra*, conclude that self-help linkage is cheaper and faster than litigation and not as potentially damaging to the child as calling a sheriff to take a child or put mother in jail for contempt. Clark, *infra*, concludes that there may be no prejudice in excusing husband from support payment if the wife has means of supporting the child. Novinson argues that as between denying support payment and denying visitation, the child is harmed more by loss of contact with the noncustodial parent than by the custodial parent being forced onto welfare. *See Hudson v. H*, 412 NYS2d 242 (Sup. Ct 78) and *Szamocki v.S.*, 121 CR 231 (App 75) (where self-help upheld because linkage implicit between mutually dependent obligations).

In another respect custody and support are directly linked. That is, when child custody is changed or modified substantially, the obligation to pay support usually is terminated or reduced proportionately. Thus, a defense against a claim for back support may exist when the parties have between themselves informally modified custody.

6) UIFSA

The enforcement of child support raises additional problems when the obligor moves from the state that rendered the judgment. The UIFSA has attempted to address these problems. It provides a procedure (as did its predecessors URESA and RURESA) for registering the order in the state where the obligor has moved so that this new state may enforce the order in the same manner it enforces its child support orders. The UIFSA also provides an informal procedure so that the obligee can file the order directly with the obligor's employer for immediate withholding of earnings without a hearing unless the employer objects or with an enforcement agency in the new state.

7) **The Economics of Child Support Enforcement**.

In Making Fathers Pay, Professor David Chambers points out that remarriage by a custodial mother provides a very successful and effective safety net against poverty for children of divorced women. He also notes that remarriage decreases the financial welfare of divorce men. Nevertheless, substantially more divorce men than women remarry. Chambers also reluctantly concluded that jailing fathers (for contempt of court in not paying child support) was one of the most effective methods of getting fathers to pay.

8) **Reconsideration of Calculation of Child Support and of Aggressive Enforcement**

Some commentators have expressed concerns that aggressive enforcement of child support obligations may cause some children to lose contact with and support from their biological fathers or *de facto* fathers. Professor Murphy argues:

> State and federal child support and welfare policies that aggressively encourage paternity establishment and focus enforcement efforts on low-income fathers have contributed to a new definition of fatherhood based exclusively on biology and economic support. This definition hurts the state, low-income families, and, most especially, children. Legal fathers may be willing to maintain a formal connection with children who are at risk of becoming fatherless. But current child support policies that privilege the economic function of fatherhood above all others do not permit functional fathers to assume emotional and caretaking responsibilities without assuming full financial responsibilities under a child support regime that hurts low-income fathers. Legal fathers, particularly low-income obligors, must often choose between irreparably harming a child they have called their own for many years or facing financial ruin.

Murphy, *infra*, at 386. Likewise, Professor Solangel Maldonado suggests that informal forms of child support should be counted in assessing child support contributions of poor fathers.

> Studies have found that the majority of deadbroke, never married African-American [non-custodial] fathers make in-kind contributions to their children – buying them diapers, baby formula, and groceries as well as clothing, toys, and baby furniture. Fathers prefer to make in-kind contributions, purchasing "a few symbolically important items" (such as diapers and sneakers), rather than make cash

payments. To a father with limited resources, providing these items may have greater value and significance than giving the custodial mother their cash equivalent. These items are tangible evidence of a father's efforts to support his children despite his economic circumstances.

Maldonado, *infra* at 1004-05.

3. Practical and Ethical Considerations

a. Attorney's Fee

If child support arrearages have been reduced to a money judgment, is it ethical for an attorney to take as her fee a percentage of what is collected? Generally, at least traditionally, contingent fee contracts based upon amount of child support collected are also contrary to public policy. A growing minority of jurisdictions may be loosening the old proscription against attorney's fee contracts providing for payment out of support collected. For instance, District of Columbia Bar Committee on Legal Ethics, Opinion No. 161, as cited in 12 Fam. L. Rptr. (BNA) 1274 (April 8, 1986) found no ethical violation with such a contract. Under the fee agreement, the lawyer was to collect $1300 only if the court awarded child support to his client; 50% of the support collected monthly was to be applied to this bill until it was paid. Noting that some other states would prohibit this arrangement, the D.C. ethics committee concluded that neither the amount was excessive nor was the collection from child support improper; the payment of attorney's fees from wrongful death and malpractice recoveries was cited.

b. Collecting Fees Out of Child Support

Closely related to the proscription against contingent fee contracts based upon divorce is the prohibition of contracts for payment of attorneys fees out of child support collected. It appears to be the generally accepted rule that attorneys fees may not, by contract, be dependant upon the amount of or be payable out of child support collected. The valid policy which underlies this rule seeks to protect child support from diversion into other uses and pockets. Regrettably, however, the rule may do more harm to the child-protective policy than it prevents. Often, the only asset which a support-denied custodial parent can offer to pay an attorney for the professional efforts and expenses he or she will incur to collect unpaid support is part of that support. If that source of funding legal services is denied, the legal services cannot be obtained and the child support goes uncollected. Moreover, many recipients of child support do not segregate their income--they cannot afford to. Whether the attorneys fees are paid out of child support collected, or alimony, or meager earnings, they come out of the same "pot" so to speak -- the family budget. To disallow payment of attorneys fees with dollars that came in a child support payment, but not to disallow payment with dollars that came in through welfare payments, earnings, or alimony makes no sense in these circumstances.

4. Bibliography

Robert Mnookin & Kornhouser, *Bargaining in the Shadow of the Law: The Case of Divorce,* 88 Yale
    L.J. 950 (1979).
Contmeporary Family Law, vol. 4, Ch. 38 (1988).
Note, *Constitutional Implications of the Child Support Enforcement Amendments of 1984,* 24 J. Fam. L.
    301 (1986).
David Chambers, In Making Fathers Pay.
Homer C. Clark, Law of Domestic Relations (1969).
Dodson, Child Support Guidelines: Overview of the Alternatives and State Activity to Date, Fair$hare,
    Sept., 1986, at 3.
Note, *Making Parents Behave: The Conditioning of Child Support and Visitation Rights,* 84 Colum. L.
    Rev. 1059 (1984).
Steven L. Novinson, *Post-Divorce Visitation: Untying the Triangular Knot,* 1983 U. Ill. L. R. 121.

C. TAX CONSIDERATIONS

1. Background

The Internal Revenue Code codifies the tax policies of the federal government.
These policies affect the family. For example, tax policy treats alimony differently
than it treats child support. While alimony payments are taxable to the recipient and
deductible by the obligor, child support payments are taxable neither to the recipient
nor to the children nor deductible by the obligor.

2. Statutes, Cases and Doctrines

a. I.R.C. § 71

The payment of child support is not deductible by the payor, nor is it taxable to
the payee. Since 1984, any amount clearly associated with a child-related contingency
is presumed to be child support, whether clearly defined as child support or not. IRC
§ 71(c)(2). (Still, to clearly define the payment as child support is the most prudent.)
The custodial parent may claim certain credits (child care and earned income) and
also may claim the dependency exemption, but the custodian may assign the
dependency exemption by waiver to the other parent; whether courts can order a
custodial parent to sign such a waiver has split the courts; most court have held that a
court may order the custodial parent to do so. *Compare Soriano v. Soriano,* 400
S.E.2d (W.Va. 1990) (upholding contempt citation of mother for refusing to obey
order to sign waiver of child dependency exemption to ex-husband; listing cases that
agree that "a trial court does have the power to order a custodial parent to execute the
necessary waiver to allocate a dependency exemption to the noncustodial parent.")
with *Voelker v. Voelker,* 520 N.W.2d 903, 909 (S.D. 1994) ("Trial courts do not have
the authority to award dependency exemptions for federal income taxes.") *See
generally* Lepow, *infra* at 164, n. 163.

b. I.R.C. § 152

The custodial parent is allocated the dependency exemption for the child unless
the custodial parent signs a declaration allowing the noncustodial parent to take the
exemption. The Code does not clearly state whether state courts have jurisdiction to
order the custodial parent to execute the declaration in favor of the noncustodial
parent. Many state court decisions, however, support state jurisdiction. In addition to

the dependency exemption, a child care credit is also available. If the parents' adjusted income exceeds $110,00, the credit is phased out.

c. I.R.C. §21; §32

The custodial parent is the only parent who may claim the child care credit and the earned income credit. In joint physical custody cases, the parent who has physical custody longer is designated the custodial parent.

d. I.R.C. § 213

The parent who pays the medical expenses for the child may deduct such expenses.

e. 2001 Tax Reforms for Adoption

The Economic Growth and Tax Relief Reconciliation Act of 2001 increased the adoption tax credit and the income exclusion for employer-paid adoption expenses to $10,000. The breakpoint for the credit phase out is to $150,000, and the credit for non-special needs children was made permanent.

3. Practical and Ethical Considerations

a. Lester Rule

Prior to 1984, in the case, *Commissioner v. Lester*, 366 U.S. 299 (1961), the United States Supreme Court interpreted I.R.C. §71 so that an amount in the court order was treated as alimony even though it was obviously meant to be child support. This became known as the Lester Rule. For example, if in M and F's divorce decree, M was awarded custody of S and D, and F was ordered to pay M $600 as support, which was to be reduced by $200 as each child reached majority, the entire $600 would be treated as alimony. The Tax Reform Act of 1984 reversed the Lester Rule. Under the present rule, only $200 would be treated as alimony. Were there any advantages for the child under the Lester Rule? How would the child support guidelines have affected the Lester Rule?

4. Bibliography

2001 Tax Legislation, Law, Explanation and Analysis, Economic Growth and Tax Relief Reconciliation Act of 2001 (CCH Inc. 2001).

Blake, *The Expanding Tax Implications of Parent's Legal Obligation of Support*, 12 Fam. L. Rptr. 3011 (1986).

Homer C. Clark, Law of Domestic Relations (1969).

C. Garrison Lepow, *The Flimflam Father: Deconstruction Parent-Child Stereotypes in Federal Tax Subsidies*, 5 N.Y.U. J. Leglis. & Pub. Pol'y 129 (2001-02).

TABLE OF AUTHORITIES

TABLE OF CASES

TABLE OF STATUTES

OTHER AUTHORITIES

Cited by Chapter and Section–See Bibliographies in Each Subchapter

2001 Tax Legislation, Law, Explanation and Analysis, Economic Growth and Tax Relief Reconcilation Act of 2001 (CCH Inc. 2001) 17B, 37C

Faith Abbot, *No Bomb, No Book*, The Human Life Rev., Winter 1998, at 31, 43. 8A, 19C

David L. Adams, Church and State Update, an information service of the Office of Government Information of The Lutheran Church--Missouri Synod (Aug. 13, 1999). 26C

Adoption Fact Book III (National Committee For Adoption 1999). 13B

Adoption Fact Book (National Committee For Adoption 1985). 12A, 13B

Steven A. Agar, *Do Divorce Lawyers Really Have More Fun*, Fair$hare, June 1995, at 7. 30C

Peter C. Alexander, *"Herstory" Repeats: Bankruptcy Code Harms Women and Children*, 13 Am Bankcy. Inst. L. Rev. 571 (2005). 30B

Thomas E. Allison, *The Uniform Transfers to Minors Act* New and Improved, But Shortcomings Still Exist*, 10 U. Ark. Little Rock L. J. 339 (1987/1988). 20D

Carol Amandio and Stuart L. Deutsch, *Open Adoption: Allowing Adopted Children to "Stay in Touch" With Blood Relatives*, 22 J. Fam. L. 59 (1983-84). 13B

Paul Amato & Allan Booth, A Generation at Risk: Growing Up in an Era of Family Upheaval (1997). 33A

Paul R. Amato, *Children's Adjustment to Divorce: Theories, Hypothesis, and Empirical Support*, 55 J. Marriage and the Family 23 (1993). 33A

American Bar Association, Commission on Domestic Violence , When Will They Ever   Learn? Educating to End Domestic Violence: A Law School Report (1997). 19A

American Law Institute, Principles of the Law Family Dissolution: Analysis and Recommendations (2002). 6C, 7A, 8A, 22, 23A, 26C, 27A, 28, 34A

American Law Institute, Model Penal Code (1980). 4A, 18C

Americans for Divorce Reform, Review of Current Events in the Marriage Movement: January through August, 1999 < http://www.divorcereform.org> (searched August, 1999). 6C

Aristotle, *Politica* in 10, The Works of Aristotle, 1334-35 (W. Ross ed. 19210, 3A

Lindsay G. Arthur, *Status Offenders Need a Court of Last Resort*, 57 B.U.L.Rev. 631 (1977). 24B

Attorney General's Task Force on Family Violence (1984). 19A

William G. Axinn & Arland Thornton, *The Relationship Between Cohabitation and Divorce: Selectivity or Causal Influence*, 29 Demography 357 (1992). 8A

Stephen Bahr, *An Evaluation of Court Mediation*, 2 J. Fam. Iss. 39 (1981). 30B

J. L. Baier, M.G. Rosenzweig & E.G. Whipple, *Patterns of sexual behavior, coercion, and victimization of university students*, 32 J. College Student Development 310 (1991). 19C

Carlos Ball, *The Positive in the Fundamental Right to Marry: Same-Sex Marriage in the Aftermath of Lawrence v. Texas,* 88 Minn. L. Rev. 1184 (2004). 3B

Mary Jo Bane, Here to Stay (1976), 1A

Elizabeth Bartholet, *International Adoptions: Propriety, Prospects and Pragmatics,* 13 J. Am. Acad. Matrim. Law. 181 (1996). 14A

Katharine T. Bartlett, *Rethinking Parenthood as an Exclusive Status: The Need for Legal Alternatives When the Premise of the Nuclear Family Has Failed,* 70 Va. L. Rev. 879 (1984). 34B

Christine Beasley, *Democracy in the Home* 25 (1954). 1B

Mary Beck, *Toward a Natinal Putative Registry Database,* 25 Harv. J. L. & Pub. Pol'y 1031 (2002). 12A

Lewis Becker, *Spousal and Child Support and the "Voluntary Reduction of Income" Doctrine*, 29 Conn. L. Rev. 647 (1997). 37A

Alison Bell, Note, *Public and Private Child: Troxel v. Granville and the Constitutional Rights of Family Members*, 36 Harv. C. R.-C.L. Rev. 225 (2001). 23A

Brenda J. Bell, Sharon Wright Kellstrom & Anne Burke Miller, *The Effect of Bankruptcy on Divorce Planning*, J. Kan. B.A., Mar. 2001, at 30. 29B

1 Jeremy Benthan, Theory of Legislation 248 (Boston 1840) quoted in Michael Wald, *Children's Rights: A Framework for Analysis,* 12 U.C.D. L.Rev. 255, 256 (1979). 20A

Evelyn Miller Berger, Triangle: The Betrayed Wife (1971). 33A

Douglas K. Besharov, *Child Abuse and Neglect Reporting and Investigation: Policy Guidelines for Decision Making,* 22 Family L.Q. 1, 12 (1988). 22B

J. Bishop, Commentaries on the Law of Marriage and Divorce, vol. 1(6th ed. 1881). 6A

Brian H. Bix, *State of the Union: The States' Interest in the Marital Status of Their Citizens*, 55 U. Miami L. Rev. 1 (2000). 25B

Brian Bix, *Bargaining in the Shadow of Love: The Enforcement of Premarital Agreements and How We Think About Marriage*, 40 Wm. & Mary L. Rev. 145 (1998). 7A

William Blackstone, Commentaries on the Laws of England, *passim.*

D. Marianne Blair & Merle H. Weiner, Family Law in the World Community (2003). 8C

Blake, *The Expanding Tax Implications of Parent's Legal Obligation of Support*, 12 Fam. L. Rptr. 3011 (1986). 37C

Nelson Manfred Blake, The Road to Reno 194 (1962), 5C

Blakesley, Child Support in Family Laws in the United States (L. Wardle, C. Blakesley & J. Parker 1987). 36B

Christophe C. Blakesley & J. Parker eds 1988). 10B

David Blankenhorn, Fatherless America: Confronting Our Most Urgent Social Problem 1 (1995). 33A

Grace Ganz Blumberg, *Legal Recognition of Same-Sex Conuugal Relationships: The 2003 California Domestic Partners Rights and Responsibilities Act in Comparative Civil Rights and Family Law Perspective*, 51 U.L.A.L. Rev. 1555 (2004). 8C

Joan Catherine Bohl, *Grandparent Visitation Law Grows Up: The Trend Toward Awarding Visitation Only When the Child Would Otherwise Suffer Harm*, 48 Drake L. Rev. 279 (2000). 34B

M. J. Bologna, C.K. Waterman & L.J. Dawson, *Violence in Gay Male and Lesbian Relationships: Implications for Practitioner and Policy Makers*, Paper presented at Third National Conference for Family Violence Researchers, Durham, NH (July 1987) 19C

The Book of Mormon, Jacob 2:*passim.* 3D

Patrick J. Borchers, Baker v. General Moters: *Implications for Interjurisdictional Recognition of Non-Traditonal Marriages*, 32 Creighton L. Rev. 147 (1998).8B

Claude R. Bowles & Jessica B. Allman, *What the Bankruptcy Code Giveth, Congress Takety Away: The Dischargeability of Domestic Obligations After the Bankruptcy Reform Act of 1994*, 34 Univ. Louis. J. Fam. L. 521 (1995-96). 29B

Cynthia Grant Bowman, *A Feminist Proposal to Bring Back Common Law Marriage*, 75 Or. L. Rev. 709 (1996). 6A

P.A. Brand & A.H. Kidd, *Frequency of Physical Aggression in Heterosexual and Female Homosexual Dyads*, 59 Psychological Reports 1307 (1986) 19C

Ralph C. Brashier, *Consanguinity, Sibling Relationships, and the Default Rules of Inheritance Law: Reshaping Half-Blood Statutes to Reflect the Evolving Family*, 58 SMU L. Rev. 137 (2005). 4A

Carolyn S. Bratt, *Incest Statutes and the Fundamental Right of Marriage: Is Oedipus Free to Marry*, 18 Fam. L.Q. 257 (1984). 4A

Brigman & Stinnett, *The State of the Family System in America: Perceptions of Family-Life Professionals*, 17 Fam. Perspectives 193 (1983). 1A

V. Michael Brigner, *The 1994 Bankruptcy Code Revisions From A Domestic Relations Court Perspective*, 34 J. Fam. L. 643 (1995-96). 29B

Margaret F. Brinig, *The Supreme Court's Impact on Marriage*, 41 How. L.J. 271 (1998). 3B

Margaret Brinig, *Domestic Partnership: Missing the Target?* 4 J.L.Fam. Studs. 19 (2002) 31.

Broschart, *Gender and the Definition of the Family and Kinship*, 17 Fam. Perspectives 155 (1983). 1A

Ralph H. Brock, *Sex, Clients, & Legal Ethics*, 64 Tex. B.J. 234 (March 2001). 30C

R. Brockelbank, *The Nature of the Promise to Marry–A Study in Comparative Law*, 41 Ill. L. Rev. 1, 3 (1946). 7B

Urie Bronfenbrenner, *Discovering What Families Can Do* in David Blankenhorn, et al, eds., Rebuilding the Nest: A New Commitment to the American Family (1990). 33A

Carol S. Bruch, *Parental Alienation Syndrome and Parental Alienation: Getting It Wrong in Child Custody Cases*, 35 Fam. L. Q. 527 (2001). 35B

W. Buckland, A Textbook of Roman Law From Augustus To Justinian (1921). 1A, 3D, 12A

Karey Burkholder, Notes & Comments, *Darting to England: A Comparison of the United States' and England's Divorce Laws*, 13 Temp. Int'l & Comp. L.J. 163 (1999). 29C

Dean M. Busby, *Violence in the Family* in Family Research, a 60-Year Review, 1930-1990 at 361 (Steven G. Bahr, ed., 1991). 8A, 19C

Naomi Cahn, Perfect Substitutes or the Real Thing?, 52 Duke L. J. 1077 (2003). 12A

Brandon Campbell, Comment, *Cohabitation Agreement sin Massachusetts: Wilcox v. Trautz Changes the Rules But Not the Results*, 34 New Eng. L. Rev. 485 (2000). 31A

June Carbone & Margaret F. Brinig, *Rethinking Marriage: Feminist Ideology, Economic Change, an Divorce Reform*, 65 Tulane L. Rev. 953 (1991).

Richard R. Carlson, *The Emerging Law of Intercountry Adoption: An Analysis of the Hague Conference on Intercountry Adoption*, 30 Tulsa L.J. 243 (1994). 14A

Case Comment, *Supreme Court Commission on Gender Fairness in the Courts*, 72 N.D. L. Rev. 1115 (1996). 33A

Centers for Disease Control and Prevention (CDC), 2003 Assisted Reproduction Technology (ART) Report, available at http://www.cdc.gov/ART/ART2003/nation.htm. 11A

Dan Cere, The Experts' Story of Courtship (Institute for American Values Council on Families, 2000). 3D

David Chambers, In Making Fathers Pay. 37B

Anjani Chandra, et al, *Adoption, Adoption Seeking, and Relinquishment for Adoption in the United States,* in Centers for Disease Control and Prevention/ National Center for Health Statistics, Advance Data, No. 306, May 11, 1999, in Adoption Factbook III, *supra*, at 78. 12A

G. K. Chesterton, in Dale Ahlquist, G. Chesterton's *Uncommonly Sensible Views on the Law,* 3 Ave Maria L. Rev. 685 (2005). 1B

Homer Clark, The Law of Domestic Relations in the United States § 6.1 (1988). 17B, 18C, 20A, 20B, 27A, 30A, 37A

Homer C. Clark, Law of Domestic Relations (1969). 37B, 37C

Homer J. Clark, Jr., Domestic Relations §18.2 (1968). 14A, 20C

Clawar, One House, Two Cars, Three Kids, 5 Fam Advoc, Fall 1982, 34A

Debra A. Clement, Note, *A Compelling Need For Mandated Use of Supervised Visitation Programs*, 36 Fam. & Conciliation Cts. Rev. 294 (1998). 35A

Clive, Eric M., "Marriage: An unnecessary Legal Concept?" In *Marriage and Cohabitation in Contemporary Societies, Areas of Legal, Social and Ethical Change*, edited by John M. Eekelaar & Sanford N. Katz, 71-81. Toronto: Butterworths, 1980 (hereinafter "Cohabitation"). 8B

Harriet N. Cohen, *Mediation in Divorce: Boon or Bane,* Women's Advoc., Mar., 1984, at 1. 30B

Stepehn P. Comeau, An Overview of Federal Income Tax Provisions Related to Alimony Payments, 38 Fam. L.Q. 111 (2004). 29A

Comment, 16 New Eng. L. Rev. 573 (1981). 16C

Contemporary Family Law, Vols. 1,4,(Lynn D. Wardle, Christopher Blakesley & Jacqueline Y. Parker eds., 1988). 2D, 4A, 4B, 4C, 5A, 5B, 5C, 6A, 6B, 6C, 7A,7B, 8A, 9A, 10A, 12A, 13A, 13B, 16B, 16C, 18A, 18B, 18C, 20C 21, 213, 26A, 26B, 30-33, 34A, 37A, 37B

David Orgon Coolidge & William C. Duncan, Beyond Baker: The Case for a Vermont Marriage Amendment, 25 Vt. L. Rev. 61 (2000). 8A.

David Orgon Coolidge & William C. Duncan, Reaffirming Marriage: A Presidential Priority, 24 Harv. J. L. & Pub. Pol'y 623 (2001). 4C, 31A

David Orgon Coolidge & William C. Duncan, Definition or Discrimination? State Marriage Recognition Statutes in the "Same-Sex Marriage" Debate, 32 Creighton L. Rev. 3 (1998). 4C, 8B

David Orgon Coolidge, Playing the Loving Card: Same-Sex Marriage and the Politics of Analogy, 12 J. Pub. L. 201 (1998) 3B

David Orgon Coolidge, Same-Sex Marriage? Baehr v. Mike and the Meaning of Marriage, 38 So. Tex. L. Rev. 1 (1997). 4C

Coombs, Interstate Child Custody: Jurisdiction, Recognition and Enforcement, 66 Minn. L. Rev. 711, 762-64 (1982). 32A

P. Corbett, The Roman Law of Marriage (1930). 3D

Barbara J. Cox, Same-Sex Marriage and Choice of Law: If We Marry in Hawaii , Are We Still Married When We Return Home?, 1994 Wis. L. Rev . 1033, 1062-1118 (1994). 8B

Stanley E. Cox, Would That Burnham Had Not Come to Be Done Insane! A Critique of Recent Supreme Court Personal Jurisdiction Reasoning, An Explanation of Why Transient Presence Jurisdiction Is Unconstitutional, and Some Thoughts About Divorce Jurisdiction in A Minimum Contacts World, 58 Tenn. L. Rev. 497, 541 (1991). 25A

Stephen M Cretney & J.M. Masson, Principles of Family Law (5th ed. 1990). 6A, 12A, 28A

Stephen Cretney, Principles of Family Law (3d ed. 1979). 10A

David B. Cruz, "Just Don't Call It Marriage": The First Amendment and Marriage As An Expressive

Resource, 74 S. Cal. L. Rev. 925 (2001). 17B, 19C

Nathan M. Crystal, *Ethical Problems in Marital Practice,* 30 S.C.L.Rev. 323 (1979). 30B, 30C

Ruth Deech, "The Case Against Legal Recognition of Cohabitation." *Id.* at 300-312. 8B

Defense of Children International, The Hague Convention on Protection of Children in Respect of Intercountry Adoption <http://childhouse.uio.no/childrens_rights/dci_hagu.html>. 14A

Rhonda E. Denton & Carlene M. Kampfe, *The Relationship Between Family Variable and Adolescent Substance Abuse: A Literature Review,* 114 Adolescence 475 (1994). 33A

Robert Destro, *Abortion and the Constitution: The Need for Life-Protective Amendment,* 63 Calif. L. Rev. 1250 (1975). 15A

Alexis deTocqueville, Democracy in America (1945 ed.) 1A

Development 12 Family Law C. *Divorce Decree Amendments: Alimony Termination and its Tax Ramifications,*1999 Utah L. Rev. 1189. 28A

Development in the Law, Statutory Protection for Gays and Lesbians in Private Employment, 109 Harv. L. Rev. 1625 (1996). 1A, 8A

John DeWitt Gregory, Peter N. Swisher, & Sheryl L. Scheible, Understanding Family Law (1993). 20A.

Paula M. DeWitt, Breaking Up is Hard to Do, American Demographics, Oct. 1992, at 53. 1B

Stanley Diamond, *The Rule of Law Versus the Order of Custom,* 38 Soc. Res. 42 (1971). 1A

J. Herbie DiFonzo, *Customized Marriage,* 75 Ind. L. J. 875 (2000). 25B, 26A, 26C

J. Herbie DiFonzo, *No-Fault Marital Dissolution: The Bitter Triumpth of Naked Divorce,* 31 San Diego L. Rev 519 (1994). 26A

Dixon & Weitzman, *Evaluating the Impact of No-Fault Divorce in California,* 29 Fam Relations 297 (1980) 26A

Dodson, Child Support Guidelines: Overview of the Alternatives and State Activity to Date, Fair$hare, Sept., 1986, at 3. 36B, 37B

Dodson, *Legal Rights of Adolescents: Restrictions on Liberty, Emancipation, and Status Offenses* in Legal Rights of Children 114 (R. Horowitz & H. Davidson, eds. 1984). 20A

William J. Doherty, The Best of Times and the Worst of Times: Fathering as a Contested Arena of Academic Discourse, in Generative Fathering: Beyond Deficit Perspectives 217 (Alan J. Hawkins & David C.

Dollahite eds., 1997) 33A

Janet Dolgin, *The Family in Transition: From Griswold to Eisenstadt and Beyond*, 82 Geo. L. J. 1519

(1994). 15A

Janet Dolgin, *Just a Gene: Judicial Assumptions about Parenthood*, 40 UCLA L. Rev. 637 (1993) p. 673-

694. 12A

Dolowitz, *The Impact of Tax Laws on Divorce*, 4 Utah Bar J. 8 (Aug/Sep/1991) at 8. 29A

Jessica R. Dominguez, Comment. *The Role of Latino Culture in Mediation of Family Disputes*, 1 J. Legal

Advoc. & Prac. 154 (1998). 30B

Charles Donahue, Jr., *What Causes Fundamental Legal Ideas? Marital Property in England and France in*

the Thirteenth Century, 78 Mich. L. Rev. 59 (1979). 16B

Bernice B. Donald & Jennie D. Latta, *The Dischargeability of Property Settlement and Hold Harmless*

Agreements in Bankruptcy, An Overview of §523(a)(15), 31 Fam.L.Q. 409 (1997). 29B

Martin Dooley, *Lone Mother Families and Social Assistance Policy in Canada in Family Matters*: New

Policies for Divorce, Lone Mothers and Child Policy at 48-49 (C. D. Howe Institute, 1995) cited in

Moir, *supra.*

Draft Standards of Practice for Divorce and Family Mediation. 30B

D. Duncan, *Prevalence of Sexual Assault Victimization Among Heterosexual and Gay/Lesbian University*

Students, 66 Psychological Reps. 65 (1990). 19C

Robert J. Durst, II, *Taxing Concerns in Matrimonial Law*, N.J. Law. June 2001, at 9. 29A

Harry T. Edwards, *Alternative Dispute Resolution: Panacea or Anathema*, 99 Harv. L. Rev. 668 (1986).

30B

David J. Eggebeen & Daniel T. Lichter, Race, Family Structure, and Changing Poverty Among American

Children, 56 Am. Soc. Rev. 801 (1991). 33A

Ira Ellman, *Survey of Abortion Law*, 1980 Ariz. St. L.J., 67 (1980). 15A

Ira Ellman & Kaye, *Probabilities and Proof: Can HLA and Blood Group Testing Prove Paternity?* 54

N.Y.U.L.Rev. 1131 (1979). 10A

Linda D. Elrod & Robert G. Spector, *A Review of the Year in Family Law; Redefining Families, Reforming*

Custody Jurisdiction, and Refining Support Issues, 34 Fam. L. Q. 607 (2001). 32B

Linda D. Elrod & Robert G. Spector, *Review of the Year in Family Law: Century Ends with Unresolved Issues,* 33 Fam. L. Q. 865 (2000). 28A

Deborah Epstein, *Effective Intervention in Domestic Violence Cases: Rethinking the Roles of Prosecutors, Judges, and the Court System,* 11 Yale J.L. & Feminism 3 (1999). 19A

William Eskridge, The Case for Same-Sex Marriage (1996). 4C

William Eskridge, Jr., *A History of Same-Sex Marriage,* 79 Va. L. Rev. 1419 (1993). 3B, 8B

Thomas Espenshade, Investing in Children: New Estimates of Parental Expenditures (1984). 36B

Ann Laquer Estin, *Ordinary Cohabitation,* 76 Notre Dame L. Rev. 1381 (2001). 31A

The Family Violence Project, *Family Violence in Child Custody Statutes: An Analysis of State Codes and Legal Practice,* 29 FAM. L.Q. 197 (1995) 34A

Mary L. Fasciotti & Luanne Bethke Redmond, *Marriage, Divorce and the Immigration Laws,* 81 Ill. B.J. 644 (1993). 5C

Federalist Papers, 2B

Edwin Brown Firmage & Richard Collin Mangrum, Zion in the Courts: A Legal History of the Church of Jesus Christ of Latter-Day-Saints, 1830-1900 (1988). 3D

Fisher on Matrimonial Property (2d ed., London: 1984) 16B

James S. Fishkin, Justice, Equal Opportunity and the Family (1998). 2D

Fowler, *Adult Adoption: A "New" Legal Tool For Lesbians and Gay Men,* 14 Golden Gate U.L. Rev. 667 (1984). 13A, 13B

Kris Franklin, *"A Family Like Any Other Family:" Alternative Methods of Defining Family Law,* 18 N.Y.U. Rev. L. & Soc. Change 1027 (1990/1991). 1A, 8A

Carolyn J. Frantz and Hannoch Dugan, *Properties of Marriage,* 104 Colum. L. Rev. 75 (2004). 27B

Marilyn Freeman, *Rights of Custody and Access Under the Hague Child Abduction Convention- - "A questionable Result?",* 31 Cal. W. Int'l L. J. 39 (2000). 32B

Karyn Bybee Friske and Darlene Pulliam, *The Marriage Penalty after the JGTRRA,* 35 Tax Advisor 284 (2004). 29A

Lupe Funaki, Kimberly Kennedy Bitner, & Gary Bryner, *Comment on the Indian Child Welfare Act,* Utah Juvenile Court Guidebook 207 (Lynn D. Wardle, Gen. Ed. 1998) (Appendix). 14B.

Frank F. Furstenburg & Andrew Cherlin, Divided Families: What Happens to Children When Parents Part 56

     (Cambridge, MA; Harvard Univ. Press, 1991). 33A

H. Dean Garrett & Bruce A. Chadwick, *Women's Religiosity, Employment, and Mental Illness* in RELIGION,

     MENTAL HEALTH AND THE LATTER-DAY SAINTS at 71 (Daniel K. Judd ed., 1999). 17B

Marsha Garrison, *Law Making for Baby Making: An Interpretive Approach to the Determination of Legal

     Parentage*, 113 Harv. L. Rev. 835 (2000). 11A, 12A.

Marsha Garrison, *Good Intentions Gone Awry: The Impact of New York's Equitable Distribution Law on

     Divorce Outcomes*, 57 Brooklyn L. Rev. 621 (1991). 27A.

Crystal J. Gates, 1999 Immigration Project, *China's Newly Enacted Intercountry Adoption Law: Friend or

     Foe?*, 7 Ind. J. Global Legal Stud. 369 (1999). 12A

George, Robert.P. and Bradley, GerardV., "Marriage and the Liberal Imagination." *Georgetown Law Journal*

     84 (1996): 301-320. 8B

General Intelligence, *Marriage and Divorce in Legal History*, 171 The Law Times 462 (London, May 30,

     1931). 25B.

Janet Gilbert, Richard Grimm, & John Parnham, *Applying Therapeutic Principles to a Family-Focused

     Juvenile Model (Delinquency)*, 52 Ala. L. Rev. 1153 (2000). 24B

Stephen G. Giller, *Parental (And Grandparental) Rights After Troxel v. Granville*, 9 Supr. Ct. Econ. Rev.

     No. 69 (2001). 23A

Carol Gilligan, In a Different Voice (1982). 1A

Mary Ann Glendon, The Transformation of Family Law: State, Law, and family in the United States and

     Western Europe(University of Chicago Press 1989). 4C

Mary Ann Glendon, Abortion and Divorce in Western Law (1988). 4A

Mary Ann Glendon, *The New Marriage and the New Property*. Toronto: Butterworths, 1981. 8B, 27B

Mary Ann Glendon, The New Family and the New Property (1981). 1A, 27B

Martijn de Goede, et al., "Family Problems and Youth Unemployment," Adolescence 35 (2000): cited in

     33A

Carey Goldberg, *Gays and Lesbians Head for Vermont to Make It Legal, but How Legal Is It?*, N.Y.Times,

     June 23, 2000. 8B, 8C

Bernadette W. Hartfield, *The Role of the Interstate Compact on the Placement of Children in Interstate Adoption*, 68 Neb. L. Rev. 292 (1989). 14A

Alan J. Hawkins, *Perspectives on Covenant Marriage*, The Family in America, Nov. 1998, 1-8. 6C

Margaret Campbell Haynes, *Supporting Our Children: A Blueprint for Reform*, 27 Fam. L.Q. 7, 7 (1993). 36A

Dr. Ray E. Helfer and Dr. C. Henry Kemp (eds.) The Battered Child (1968). 24A

Stephen Hellman, *Stepparent Custody Upon the Death of the Custodial Parent*, 14 J. Suffolk Acad. L. 23 (2000). 34A

Christy L. Hendricks, Note, *The Trend Toward Mandatory Mediation in Custody and Visitation Disputes of Minor Children: An Overview*, 32 U. Louisville J. Fam. L. 491, 493 (1994). 30B

Henshaw, *Trends in Abortion*, 1982-84 18 Fam. Plan. Prospectives 34 (1986). 12A, 13B

Henshaw, Forrest, Sullivan & Tietze, *Abortion in the United States, 1979-80*, 14 Fam. Plan. Prospectives 1 (1982). 12A, 13B

E. Mavis Hetherington & John Kelly, for Better or For Worse: Divorce Reconsidered (Norton 2002). 33A

M. Annie Hill & June O,Neill, Underclass Behaviors in the United States, Measurement and Analysis of Determinants (New York, City University of New York, 1993). 33A

Herma Hill Kay, *From the Second Sex to the Joint Venture: An Overview of Women's Rights and Family Law in the United States During the Twentieth Century*, 88 Calif. L. Rev. 2017 (2000). 25B

Herma Hill Kay, *Equality and Difference: A Perspective on No-Fault Divorce and Its Aftermath*, 56 U. Cinn. L. Rev. 1 (1987). 28A

E. Adamson Hoebel. The Law of Primitive Man (1954). 1A

Bert H. Hoff, *The Risk of Serious Physical Injury from Assault by a Woman Intimate: A Re-Examination of National Violence Against Women Survey Data on Type of Assault by an Intimate* <http://www.vix.com/menmag/nvawrisk.htm>. 19A

L. Lynn Hogue, *State Common-Law Choice of Law Doctrine and Same-Sex Marriage: How Will States Enforce the Public Policy Exception*, 32 Creighton L. Rev. 29 (1998). 8B

Joan Heifetz Hollinger, *The Uniform Adoption Act: A Reporter's Ruminations*, 30 Fam. L.Q. 345 (1996). 12A

James A Jones, Comment, *The Immigration Marriage Fraud Amendments: Sham Marriages of Sham Legislation?* 24 Fla. St. U. L. Rev. 679 (1997). 5C

Jill Jones, Comment: *Fanning an Old Flame: Alienation of Affections and Criminal Conversation Revisited*, 26 Pepperdine L. Rev. 61 (1999). 18B

Seth C. Kalichman, Mandated Reporting of Suspected Child Abuse, Ethics, Law and Policy (1993). 24A

Kim Kantorowicz, Case Note, *Contracts–Cohabitation in Minnesota: From Love to Contract–Public Policy Gone Awry in re Estate of Palmen,* 26 Wm. Mitchell L. Rev. 213 William (2000). 31A

Kenneth Karst, *The Freedom of Intimate Association*, 89 Yale L. J. 624 (1980). 15A

Sanford N. Katz & Jeffrey A. Kuhn, Recommendations for A Model Family Court: A Report From the National Family Court Symposium 7 (1991). 2D

Kawashima, *Adoption in Early America*, 20 J. Fam. L. 677 (1982). 12A

Herma Hill Kay, Equality and Differences: A Perspective on No-Fault Divorce and Its Aftermath 56 U. Cinn. L. Rev. 1 (1987). 28A

Alicia Brokars Kelly, *The Marital Partnership Pretense and Career Assets: The Ascendance of Self Over the Marital Community,* 81 B.U. L. Rev. 59 (2001). 16A

Alicia Brokars Kelly, *Sharing A Piece of the Future Post-Divorce: Toward A More Equitable Distribution of Professional Goodwill,* 51 Rutgers L. Rev. 569 (1999). 27B

Joan B. Kelly, *Mediated and Adversarial Divorce Resolution Process, A Comparison of Post-Divorce Outcome,* 32 Fam. L. 382 (G. Br. 1991). 30B

Kempe, Silverman, Steele, Droegemuller, and Silver, "The Battered Child Syndrome," 181 J.A., M.A. 17 1962). 24A

Lee Khachaturian, Comment, *Domestic Violence and Shared Parental Responsibility: Dangerous Bedfellows,* 44 Wayne L. Rev. 1745 (1999). 34A

Charles P. Kindregan, Jr. & Monroe L. Inker, *A Quarter Century of Allocating Spousal Property Interest: The Massachusetts Experience,* 33 Suffolk U. L. Rev. 11 (1999). 27B

Patricia A. King, *Treatment and Minors: Issues Not Involving Lifesaving Treatment*, 23 J. Fam. L. 241 (1984-85). 22A, 27B

Klaff, *The Tender Years Doctrine: A Defense*, 70 Cal.L.Rev. 335 (1982). 33B

Support Payments in Divorce, 25 Duquesne L. Rev. 43 (1986). 29A.

Lisa G. Lerman, *Statute: A Model State Act: Remedies for Domestic Abuse*, 21 Harv. J. on Legis. 61, 94-97 (1984). 30D

Lisa Lerman, *Protection of Battered Women: A Survey of State Legislation*, 6 Women's Rts. L. Rptr. 271 (1981). 30D

Amy B. Levin, Comment, *Chile Witnesses of Domestic Violence: How Should Judges Aply the Best Interests o the Child Standard in Custody and Visitation Cases Involving Domestic Violence?*, 47 UCLA L. Rev. 813 UCLA (2000). 19A

Levine, *Caveat Parens: Demystification of the Child Protection System*, 35 U. Pitt. L. Rev. 1 (1973). 24A

Claude Levi-Strauss, The Elementary Structures of Kinship (James Harle Bell, John Richard von Sturmer & Rodney Needham, transla., 1969). 4A

LexisNexis, The Economic Growth and Tax Relief Reconciliation Act of 2001: An Analysis. 20D

G.W. Lie, R. Schilit, R.J. Bish, M. Montagne & L. Reyes, *Lesbians in currently aggressively relationships: How frequently do they report aggressive past relationships?* 6 Violence and Victims 121 (1991). 19C

G. Lie & S. Gentlewarrior, *Intimate violence in lesbian relationships: Discussion of survey findings and practice implications*, 15 J. Social Serv. Res. 41 (1991). 19C

Orma Linford, *The Mormons and the Law: The Polygamy Cases*, 9 Utah L. Rev. 308 (1964). 3D

Brian J. Linn & Lesly A. Bowers, The Historical Fallacies Behind Legal Prohibitions of Marriages Involving Mentally Retarded Persons – The Eternal Child Grows Up, Gonzaga L. Rev. 625 (1978). 5B

Allan Z. Litovsky & Kirsten Schultz, *Scientific Evidence of Paternity: A survey of State Statutes*, 39 Jurimetrics J. 79 (Fall 1998). 10A

John Locke, Second Treatise of Government (1691). 1A

L.L. Lockhart, B.A. White, V. Causby, & A. Isaaac, *Letting out the secret: Violence in lesbian relationships*, 9 J. Interpersonal Violence 469. 19C

Antoinette Sedillo Lopez, *Evolving Indigenous Law: Navajo Marriage-Cultural Traditions and Modern Challenges*, 17 Ariz. J. Int'l & Comp. L. 283 (2000). 3D, 6A

Kathryn Venturator s Lorio, *Concubinage and Its Alternatives: A Proposal for a More Perfect Union*, 26 Loy. L. Rev. 1 (1980). 8A

Maryland State Bar Ass'n Comm. on Ethics, Opin. 02-10 (Dec. 4, 2001), 30C

W. Somerset Maugham, *The Moon and Sixpence* in Collected Short Stories (1965). 19A

Mazur-Hart & Berman, *Changing from Fault to No-Fault Divorce: An Interrupted Time Series Analysis,* 7 J.
  Applied Soc. Psycho. 300 (1977). 26A

Linda C. McCain, *The Poverty of Privacy,* 3 Colum. J. Gender & L. 119 (1992). 15A

Melanie G. McCulley, *The Male Abortion: The Putative Father's Right to Terminate His Interests in and
  Obligations to the Unborn Child,* 7 J.L. & Pol'y 1, 23 (1998. 18A, 20C

McCurty, *Torts Between Persons in Domestic Relations,* 43 Harv. L. Rev. 1030, 1055 (1930). 16C

Margaret Dee McGarity, *Avoidable Transfers Between Spouses and Former Spouses,* 31 Fam. L. Q. 392
  (1997) 29A, 29B

Matthey McKeever & Nicholas Wolfinger, *Reexamining the Economic Costs of Marital Disruption for
  Women* paper presented July 15, 1997 at the annual meeting of the American Sociological Association,
  cited in Moir, *supra.*

Ross McKenzie, *'This is how a man dies. This is how a man lives,'* Townhall.com (May 23, 2002)
  <http://www.townhall.com/columnists/rossmackenzie/rm20020523.html>. 18A

Sara McLanahan & Gary Sandefur, Growing Up with a Single Parent (1994).
  <http://www.ncsc.dni.us/divisions/research/csp/2001%20Files/Tables5-8.pdf> 1B

Abraham McLaughlin, *Bush's controversial bid to promote marriage,* in The Christian Science Monitor
  (June 4, 2001) in Smart Marriages Archive <http://archives.his.com/smart.marriages/msg01462.html>
  6C

Cyrus Means, *The Phoenix of Abortional Freedom,* 17 N.Y.L.F. 335 (1971). 15A

W. Meezan, S. Cats, & E. Russo, Adoptions Without Agencies: A Study of Independent Adoption. (1978).
  12A, 13A, 13B

Marygold S. Melli, *Whatever Happened to Divorce?,* 2000 Wis. L. Rev. 637. 26C

Kathryn L. Mercer, *A Content Analysis of Judicial Decision-Making – How Judges Use the Primary
  Caretaker Standard to Make Custody Determinations,* 5 Wm. & Mary J. Women & L. 1 (1998). 33B

Steven J. Messinger, *On Moving Toward a Family Court in Georgia Without the Need for Constitutional
  Revision,* 12 Ga. St. U. L. Rev. 667 (1996). 2D

David D. Myer, *Domesticating* Lawrence, 2004 U.Chi. L. Forum 453. 6A

David D. Meyer, Self-Definition in the Constitution of Faith and Family, 56 Minn. L. Rev. 791 (2002). 1A

David D. Meyer, *Self-Definition in the Constitution of Faith and Family,* 86 Minn. L. Rev. 791 (2002). 1A

David Meyer, *Lochner Redeemed: Family Privacy After Troxel and Carhart.* 48 U.C.L.A. L R, 1125 (2001). 23A

John Stewart Mill, On Liberty (1959). 20A

Linda G. Mills, Commentary, *Killing Her Softly: Intimate Abuse and the Violence of State Intervention,* 113 Harv. L. Rev. 550 (1999). 19A

Linda Fitts Mischler, *Personal Morals Masquerading and Professional Ethics: Regulations Banning Sex Between Domestic Relations Attorneys and Their Clients,* 23 Harv. Women's L.J. 1 (2000). 30C

The Missouri Task Force on Gender and Justice, *1993 Report of the Missouri Taks Force on Gender and Justice,* 58 Mo. L. Rev. 485 (1993). 33B

Robert H. Mnookin & Lewis Kornhauser, Bargaining in the Shadow of the Law: The Case of Divorce, 88 Yale L. J. 950 (1979). 30A, 37A

Robert Mnookin, *Child Adjudication: Judicial Functions in the Face of Indeterminancy,* 39 L & Contemp. Prob. 226 (1975). 20A, 34A

Model Rules of Professional Conduct, Proposed Rule 1.8 (American Bar Association, Ethics 2000 Commission on the Evaluation of the Rules of Professional Conduct, November, 2000) <http://www.abanet.org/cpr/e2k- rule18.html> 10A, 24A, 30C

Mohr, *Abortion in America, The Origins and Evolution of Policy,* 1800-1900 (1978). 15B

Richard D. Mohr, *The Case for Gay Marriage,* 9 Notre Dame J.L. Ethics & Pub. Pol'y 215 (1995). 4C

Donald S. Moir, *A New Class of Disadvantaged Children: Reflections on "Easy" Divorce* in Family Affairs __ (C. D. Howe Instutute 1998)

Laura W. Morgan, *It's Ten O'Clock: Do You Know Where Your Sperms Are? Toward a Strict Liability Theory of Parentage,* 11 Divorce Litig. 1 (Jan. 1999). 10A

Laura W. Morgan, *The Relevance of Adultery and Extra-Marital Sexual Conduct in Custody and Visitation Cases,* 9 No. 9 Divorce Litig. 165 (1997). 34A

Robert P. Mosteller, *Child Abuse Reporting Laws and Attorney-Client Confidences: The Reality and the*

Specter of Lawyer as Informant, 42 Duke L. J. 203 (1992). 24A

Jane C. Murphy, *Legal Images of Fatherhood: Welfare Reform, Child Support Enforcement, and Fatherless Children*, 81 Notre Dame L. Rev. 325 (2005). 37B

Richard S. Myers, *Same-Sex "Marriage" and the Public Policy Exception*, 32 Creighton L. Rev. 45 (1998). 8B

Paul A. Nakonezny, Robert D. Shull, Joseph Lee Rodgers. *The Effect of No-Fault Divorce Law on the Divorce Rate Across the 50 States and Its Relation to Income, Education, and Religiosity*, J. Marr, & Fam., May 1995, at 477 (noted in *http://www.divorcereform.org/stats.html* (Divorce/Marriage Statistics). 26A, 26B

Rania Nanos, Note, *The Views of a Child: Emerging Interpretation and Significance of the Child's Objection Defense Under the Hague Child Abduction Convention*, 22 Brook. J. Int't L. 437 (1996). 32B

National Center for State Courts, Examining the Work of State Courts, 1999-2000 – A National Perspective from the Court Statistics Project 42 (Brian J. Ostrom et al. eds. 2001) <http://www.ncsc.dni.us/divisions/research/csp/csp-exam_2001.html>. 1B

National Center for State Courts, National Court Statistics Project, Cases filed in State Courts (2001) <http://www.ncsc.dni.us/divisions/research/csp/csp-stat01.html>. 1B

National Center for State Courts, State Court Caseload Statistics, 2001 (Melissa T. Cantrell, et al. eds 2001)

National Center for Health Statistics, Publication #100, Advance Data (1990). 33A

National Comm'n on Children, Beyond Rhetoric: A New American Agenda for Children and Families (1992). 33A

Nebinger, Criminal Abortion: Its Extent and Prevention, in Abortion in 19th Century America (1974). 15B

Sharon C. Nelson, Note, *Turning Our Backs on the Children: Implications of Recent Decisions Regarding The Hague Convention On International Child Abduction*, 2001 U. Ill. L. Rev. 669. 32B

William E. Nelson, *The Changing Meaning of Equality in Twentieth-Century Constitutional Law*, 52 Wash. & Lee L. Rev. 3 (1995). 5A

B. Nicholas, An Introduction To Roman Law (1962). 1A

Gary H. Nichols, Note, *Covenant Marriage: Should Tennessee Join the Noble Experiment*, 28 U. Memphis L. Rev. 397 (1999). 6C, 25B, 26A, 26B

Note, *Ultimate Weapon?: Demythologizing Spousal Rape and Reconceptualizing Its Prosecution*, 48 Stan.

L. Rev. 677 (1996). 18C

Note, *Will Palmore v. Sidoti Preclude the Use of Race As A Factor In Denying An Adoption?* 24 J. Fam. L.

497 (1985). 12A, 13A

Steven L. Novinson, *Post-Divorce Visitation: Untying the Triangular Knot*, 1983 U. Ill. L. Rev. 121. 35B

Martha C. Nussbaum, *India: Implementing Sex Eauality Through Law*, 2 Chi. J. Int'l L. 35 (2001). 3D

Raymond C. O'Brien, *Domestic Partnership: Recognition and Responsibility*, 32 San Diego L. Rev. 163

(1995). 1A, 8A

Official Recommendations of the United States Commission on Interstate Child Support, 27 Fam. L.Q. 31-84

(1993). 36A

Frances Olsen, *The Family and the Market: A Study of Ideology and Legal Reform*, 96 Harv. L. Rev. 1497

(1983). 28A

Michael J. Oths, *Divorce on the Road, "Going to Gooding,"* Advocate (Idaho), June 2000, at 11. 25A

'Palimony' lawyer back at work, Deseret News (Utah) (AP), Aug. 14, 2001, at A10. 31A

Lennart Pålsson, Marriage in Comparative Conflict of Laws: Substantive Conditions (Martinus Nijhoff

Publishers, 1981). 8C, 29C

Allen M. Parkman, *Bringing Consistency to the Financial Arrangements at Divorce*, 87 KY. L.J. 51 (1999).

27B

Louis Parley, The Ethical Family Lawyer, A Practical Guide to Avoiding Professional Dilemmas (ABA, Fam.

L. Section 1995). 4C, 10A. 10B, 28A, 30C

Jeffrey A. Parness, *Participation of Unwed Biological Fathers in Newborn Adoptions: Achieving Substantive

and Procedural Fairness*, 5 J.L.& Fam. Pol'y 223 (2003). 12A

Jeffrey A. Parness, Old-Fashioned Pregnancy, Newly-Fashioned Paternity, 53 Syracuse L. Rev. 57 (2003).

10A, 10B

James W. Paulsen, Remarks, *The History of Alimony in Texas and the new "Spousal Maintenance" Statute*,

7 Tex. J. Women & L. 151 (1998). 28A

Gabrielle A. Paupeck, Note. *When Grandma Becomes Mom: the Liberty Interests of Kinship Foster Parents*,

70 Fordham L. Rev. 537 (2001). 23A

<http://www.hcch.net/e/status/stat33e.html> (August 17, 2001); Status Sheet, *id.* at

<http://www.hcch.net/e/status/adoshte.html> 14A

Quay, *Justifiable Abortion--Medical and Legal Foundations*, 49 Geo. L.J. 395 (1961). 15B

Michael E. Ratner, Note. *In the Aftermath Troxel v. Granville: Is Mediation the Answer?*, 39 Fam. Ct. Rev.

454 (2001). 23A

Rayden's Practice and Law of Divorce 1-4, 438, 755 (9th ed., Joseph Jackson, C.F. Turner, & D.R. Ellison,

1964). 1A, 4C, 25B, 26A , 26B, 28A

Recent Case, 115 Harv. L. Rev. 1541 (2002), 11A

Recent Legislation – Domestic Relations – Same-Sex Couples, 114 Harv. L. Rev. 1421 (2001). 31A

D. Reed, *Open Adoption Records to Adult Adoptees: Judicial Rejection brings Legislative Favor* (Dec.

1985) (student paper in author's possession). 12A

Sheldon C. Reed, Counseling in Medical Genetics 34-41 (2d ed. 1963). 4A

Charles Reich, *The New Property*, 73 Yale L.J. 733 (19640, 16B, 27B

C. Renzetti, *Violent Betrayal: Partner Abuse in Lesbian Relationships* (Sage 1992) 19C

C. Renzetti, *Building a Second Closet: Third Party Responses to Victims of Lesbian Partner Abuse*, 38 Fam.

Relations 157 (1989) 19C

Report of the (Hawaii) Commission on Sexual Orientation and the Law (Dec. 8, 1995). 17B

Restatement, Second, Conflict of Laws (1971), 4A, 5A, 6A, 8B, 25A

Max Rheinstein, Marriage Stability, Divorce and the Law (1972). 26A, 26B

David G. Richardson, *Family Rights for Unmarried Couples*, 2 Kan. J.L. & Pub. Pol'y 117 (1993). 1A

Michael A. Rodriguez, et al, Mandatory Reporting of Domestic Violence to the Police, 286 J.A.M.A. (Aug.

1, 2001) <http://jama.ama-assn.org/issues/v286n5/rfull/jbr10044.html>. 19A, 30D

R. Michael Rogers & John P. Palmer, *A Speaking Analysis of ADR Legislation for the Divorce Neutral,* 31

St. Mary's L.J. 871 (2000). 25B

Peter F.G. Rook & Robert Ward, Sexual Offenses (1990). 4C

Jennifer L. Rosato, *"A Color of Their Own": Multiracial Children and the Family*, 36 Brandeis J. Fam. L.

41 (1997-98), 13A

Jennifer L. Rosato, *Putting Square Pegs in a Round hole: Procedural Due Process and the Effect of Faith*

Healing Exemptions on the Prosecution of Faith Healing Parents, 29 U.S.F. L. Rev. 43 (1994). 22A

David Rosettenstein, *Transracial Adoption and the Statutory Preference Schemes: Before the "Best Interests" and After the "Melting Pot,'* 68 St. John's L. Rev. 137 (1994) 13A

Sallie L. Rubenzer, *Necessaries and Family Purpose Debts*, Wis. Law. October,1996, at 15. 17A

Eva Rubin, The Supreme Court and the American Family (1986). 1A

David Sampedro, *When Living As Husband and Wife Isn't Enough: Reevaluating Dillon's Close Relationship Test in Light of Dunphy v. Gregor*, 25 Stetson L. Rev. 1085 (1996). 1A

John J. Sampson & Paul M. Kurtz, *UIFSA: An Interstate Support Act for the 21st Century*, 27 Fam. L.Q. 85 (1993). 36A

Elizabeth J. Samuels, *The Idea of Adoption: An Inquiry Into the History of Adult Adoptee Access to Birth Records*, 53 Rutgers L. Rev. 367 (2001). 13B

Scarnecchia, *A Child's Right to Protection from Transfer Trauma in a Contested Adoption Case*, 2 Duke J. Gender L. & Pol'y 41 (1995). 12A

Donna A. Scheiter, Note, *Attorneys' Divorces: Are Their Pending Contingency Fee Cases Marital Assets or Not?*, 37 Brandeis L.J. 829 (1998/99). 27B

Lori L. Schick, Comment, *Breaking the "Rule of Thumb" and Opening the Curtains--Can the Violence Against Women Act Survive Constitutional Scrutiny?*, 28 U. Tol. L. Rev. 887, 887 (1997). 19A

R. Schlit, G. Lie & M. Montagne, *Substance Use as a Correlate of Violence in Intimate Lesbian Relationships*, 19 J. Homosexuality 51 (1990) 19C

Carl E. Schneider & Lynn D. Wardle, *Genetics and Artificial Procreation in the U.S.A.*, in Biomedicine, the Family and Human Rights 55 (2002) 11A

Carl Schneider, *Moral Discourse and the Transformation of American Family Law*, 83 Mich. L. Rev. 1803 (1985). 1A, 2D

Schoen, Breenblatt, & Meilke, *California's Experience with Nonadversary Divorce*, 12 Demography 223 (1975). 26A

Elizabeth Scott and Robert E. Scott, *Marriage As A Relational Contract*, 84 Va. L. Rev. 1225 (1998). 6C

Sell, *Divorce Law Reform and Increasing Divorce Rates* in Current Issues in Marriage and the Family (J. Wells ed. 1979) 26A

William Shakespeare, *King Lear* , Act 1, scene 2, 10B

Mary Shanley, *Unwed Father's Rights, Adoption, and Sex Equality: Gender Neutrality and the Perpetuation of Patriarchy,* 95 Colum. L. Rev. 60 (1995). 12A

Sally Burnett Sharp, *Fairness Standards and Separation Agreements: A Word of Caution on Contractual Freedom,* 132 U. Pa. L. Rev. 1399 (1984). 30A

Andrea M. Sharrin, Note, *Potential Fathers and Abortion: A Woman's Womb is Not a Man's Castle,* 55 Brook. L. Rev. 1359 (1990). 20C

Shuman, The Unreliability of Children's Expression of Preference in Domestic Relations Litigation: A Psychiatric Approach, 59 Mass.L.Rev 14, 18 (1984). 34A

Linda J. Silberman, *Can the Island of Hawaii Bind the World? A Comment on Same-Sex Marriage and Federalism Values,* 16 Quinnipiac L. Rev. 191, 192-203 (1996). 8B

Brett S. Silverman, *The Winds of Change in Adoption Laws: Should Adoptees Have Access to Adoption Records?,* 39 Fam. & Conciliation Courts Rev. 85, 85 (2000). 12A

Anne E. Simerman, Note, *The Right of a Cohabitant to Recover in Tort: Wrongful Death, Negligent Infliction of Emtional Distress and Loss of Consortium,* 32 U. Louisville J. Fam. L. 531 (1993-1994). 1A

Rita J. Simon et al., The Case for Transracial Adoption (1994). 13A

Jana B. Singer, *The Privatization of Family Law,* 1992 Wisc. L. Rev. 1443 (1992). 2D, 13A

Jana B. Singer & William L. Reynolds, *A Dissent on Joint Custody,* 47 Md. L. Rev. 497 (1988). 34A

J .Clay Smith, *Charlotte E.Ray Pleads Before Court,* 43 How. L. J. 121 (2000). 25B

Michael C. Snyder, *An Overview of the Indian Child Welfare Act,* 7 St. Thomas L. Rev. 815 (1995). 14B

Diane Sollee, *Marriage: What's the Buzz,* Smart Marriages newsletter cmfce, in Smart Marriages Archives <http://archives.his.com/smartmarriages/msg01458.html> 6C

South Carolina Marriage Commission: Condon creates panel on family, marriage, faith-based programs, Associated Press (June 19, 2001) in SmartMarriages Archive <http://archives.his.com/smartmarriages/msg01495.html> 6C

Katherine Shaw Spaht and Symeon Symeonides, *Covenant Marriage and the Conflict of Laws,* 32 Creighton L. Rev. 1085 (1999). 6C, 26C

Resurvey and Other Studies in Family Abuse and Its Consequences: New Directions in Research 20 (Hotaling, et al, eds. 1988). 19A

Holly A. Streeter-Schaeffer, Note, *A Look At Court-Mandated Civil Mediation*, 49 Drake L. Rev. 367 (2001). 30B

Charles M. Strom, *Genetic Justice: A Lawyer's Guide to the Science of DNA Testing*, 87 Ill. B.J. 18, 19 (1999). 10A

Study Spotlights Abuse Of Males by Females, USA Today in S.L. Tribune, July 14, 1999 <http://www.sltrib.com/07141999/nation_w/8047.htm> (searched 14 July 99). 19A

Surrogate Parenthood Act, 73 Geo.L.J. 1283 (1985). 13B

Peter N. Swisher, Anthony Miller, and Jana B. Singer, Family Law: Cases, Materials and Problems (1998). Patricia Tjaden & Nancy Thoennes, Full Report of Prevalence, Incidence and Consequences of Violence Against Women: Findings from the National Violence Against Women Survey, U.S. Department of Justice, National Institute of Justice & Centers for Disease Control and   Prevention Research Report, Nov. 2000. NCJ 183781 (2000). <http://www.ncjrs.org/pdffiles1/nij/183781.pdf> 19A

Symposium Issue Celebrating Twenty Years: The and Promise of the 1980 Hague Convention on the Civil Aspects of International Child Abduction. (Fall 2000) 33 N. Y. U. J. Int'l L. & Pol. *passim*, 32B

Symposium: Troxel v. Granville, 32 Rutgers Law Journal (Spring 2001) 23A

Symposium, Unmarried Partners and the Legacy of Marvin v. Marvin, 76 Notre Dame L. Rev. 1261 *et seq.* (2001). 31A

Jay D. Teachman, Jeffrey Thomas, & Kathleen Paasch, *Legal Status and the Stability of Coresidential Unions*, 28 Demography 571, 579 (1991). 8A

Lee E. Teitelbaum, *Family History and Family Law*, 1985 Wisc. L.Rev. 1135 (1985). 2D

Lee E. Teitelbaum, *Foreword: The Meanings of Rights of Children*, 10 New Mex. L. Rev. 235 (1980). 21A

Alison Thomas, *Pensions: The Long March to Reform*, 34 FAM. L.Q. 209 (Summer 2000). 27B

Mason P. Thomas, *Child Abuse and Neglect, Part I: Historical Overview, legal Matrix and Social Perspectives*, 50 N.C. L. Rev. 293 (1972). 24A

Julia Thorne, A Change of Heart, Words of Experience and Hope for the Journey Through Divorce (Harper Perennial 1996). 33A

Information, The Lutheran Church--Missouri Synod), http://WWW.OGI.LCMS.ORG. 4C, 8A

Sol Wachtler, After the Madness: A Judge's Own Prison Memoir (1997). 19A

Walter Wadlington, *Medical Decisionmaking For and By Children: Tensions Between Parent, State, and Child*, 1994 U. Ill.L. Rev. 311. 22A

Linda J. Waite & Maggie Gallagher, The Case for Marriage, Why Married People Are Happier, Healthier, and Better Off Financially (2000). 19C, 26B

Kathleen Waits, *The Criminal Justice System's Response to Battering: Understanding the Problem, Forging the Solutions*, 60 Wash. L. Rev. 267 (1985). 30D

Lisa K. Waldner-Haugrud & Linda Vaden Gratch, *Sexual Coercion in Gay/Lesbian Relationships: Descriptive and Gender Differences*, 12 Violence and Victims 87 (1997). 19C

Lisa K. Waldner-Haugrud, Linda Vaden Gratch & Brian Magruder, *Victimization and Perpetration Rates of Violence in Gay and Lesbian Relationships: Gender Issues Explored*, 12 Violence & Victims 173 (1997). 19C

Wall Street J., Feb. 27, 1987, at 1, col. 1. 12A

Wall St. J., Sep. 25, 1986, at 1, Col. 1, and 26, Col. 1. 1A

Wallace, When the Child becomes the Prize -- That Child Needs a Lawyer, 9 Barrister, Spring 82, at 16. 34A

Judith S. Wallerstein & Sandra Bladeslee, Second Chances. 33A

Judith S. Wallerstein, Julia Lewis, & Sandra Blakesley, The Unexpected Legacy of Divorce (2000). 33A

Judith S. Wallerstein & Julia Lewis, *The Long-Term Impact of Divorce on Children*, 36 Fam. & Concil. Crt. Rev. 368 (1998). 33A

Judith Wallerstein & Tony J. Tanke, *To Move or Not to Move: Psychological and Legal Considerations in the Relocation of Children After Divorce*, 30 Fam. L. Q. 305 (1996). 35A

Want's Federal-State Court Directory. 2A

Lynn D. Wardle, *A.D.R. in the U.S.A.*, in Families et Justice 534 (Bruxelles 1997). 30B

Lynn D. Wardle, The Abortion Privacy Doctrine (1980). 15B

Lynn D. Wardle, *Counting the Costs of Civil Unions: Some Potential Detrimental Effects on Family Law*, 11 Widener J. Pub. L. 401 (2002). 8A

Lynn D. Wardle, *A Critical Analysis of Constitutional Claims for Same-Sex Marriage*, 1996 B.Y.U. L. Rev. 1-101. 4C

Lynn D. Wardle, *Crying Stones: A Comparison of Abortion in Japan and the United States*, 14 N.Y.L. Sch. J. Int'l & Compar. L. 183-259 (1994).

Lynn D. Wardle, *Deconstructing Family: A Critique of The ALI's "Domestic Partners" Proposal*, 2001 B.Y.U. L. Rev. 1189. 1A, 4C, 7A, 8A

Lynn D. Wardle, *Dividing the "New Property" Upon Divorce: The Quest for Economic Equity*, in Law in Motion 678-710 (International Encyclopeadia of Laws, World Law Conference, 1997). 27A, 27B

Lynn D. Wardle, *Divorce Reform at the Turn of the Millenium: Certainties and Possibilities*, 33 Fam.L.Q. 783 (1999). 6C, 26C

Lynn D. Wardle, *Divorce Violence and the No-Fault Divorce Culture*, 1994 Utah L. Rev. 741. 30D

Lynn D. Wardle, *International Marriage Recognition: A World Dilemma*, in FAMILIES ACROSS FRONTIERS 75-88 (Nigel Lowe & Gillian Douglas, eds., The Hague: Martinus Nijhoff Publishers, 1996). 8C, 29C

Lynn D. Wardle, *International Marriage and Divorce Regulation and Recognition: A Survey*, 29 Family Law Q. 497 (Fall 1995). 3D, 6B, 8C, 29C

Lynn D. Wardle, *Is Marriage Obsolete?* 10 Mich. J. Gender & L. 189-135 (2003). 4C

Lynn D. Wardle & Mary Anne Wood, A Lawyer Looks At Abortion (1982). 18A

Lynn D. Wardle, *Legal Claims for Same-Sex Marriage: Efforts to Legitimate a Retreat from Marriage by Redefining Marriage*, 39 So. Tex. L. Rev. 735-768 (1998) 4C, 8A

Lynn D. Wardle, *Liberty Equality & the Quest for Family Justice in the United States* in FAMILLES & JUSTICE 208-229 (Brussels: Bruylant, 1997). 2D

Lynn D. Wardle, *Loving v. Virginia and the Constitutional Right to Marry*, 41 How. L.J. 289. 3B

Lynn D. Wardle, Marriage and Domestic Violence in the United States, 15 St. Shomas L. Rev. 791 (2003). 1A

Lynn Wardle, *No-Fault Divorce and the Divorce Conundrum*, 1991 B.Y.U.L.Rev. 79. 26A, 26B, 26C

Lynn D. Wardle, *Parenting in American Law -- Today and Tomorrow* in The Legal Relationship between Parents and Children 111-147 (Choo Soo Kim ed. 1997). 9A, 11A

Lynn D. Wardle, *Parents' Rights v. Minors' Rights Regarding the Provision of Contraceptives to Minors*, 68 Neb. L. Rev. 216-260 (1989). 15A

Lynn D. Wardle, *The Potential Impact of Homosexual Parenting on Children*, 1997 U. Ill. L. Rev. 833-920 (1997). 34A

Lynn D. Wardle, *The Quandary of Pro-life Free Speech: A Lesson from the Abolitionists*, 62 Albany L. Rev. 853 (1999). 15B, 18A

Lynn D. Wardle, *"Time Enough":* Webster v. Reproductive Health Services *and the Prudent Pace of Justice,* 41 Fla. L. Rev. 881-986 (1989). 15B

Lynn D. Wardle, *Rethinking Roe v. Wade*, 1985 B.Y.U. L. Rev. 231-64. 15B

Lynn D. Wardle, *Rethinking Marital Age Restrictions*, 22 J. Fam. L. 1, 5-7 (1983). 5A, 8B, 26B, 33A

Lynn D. Wardle *State Marriage Amendments; Developments, Precedents, and Significance,* 7 Fla. Coastal L. Rev. 403 (2005). 4C

Lynn D. Wardle, Williams v. North Carolina, *Divorce Recognition, and Same-Sex Marriage Recogniton*, 32 Creighton L. Rev. 187 (1998). 8B, 25A

Rhonda Wasserman, *Parents, Partners, and Personal Jurisdiction*, 1995 U. Ill. L. Rev. 813. 25A

C.K. Waterman, L.J. Dawson & M.J. Bologna, *Sexual coercioin in gay male and lesbian relationships: Predictors and implications for support services*, 26 J. Sex Res. 118 (1989). 19C

A. Watson, The Law of Persons in the Later Roman Republic (1967). 10B

Merle H. Weiner, *International Child Abduction and the Escape From Domestic Violence*, 69 Fordham L. Rev. 593 (2002). 32B

Joseph G. Weis, *Family Violence Research Methodology and Design* in Family Violence 117 (Lloyd Ohlin & Michael Tonry eds. 1989). 19A

Lenore Weitzman, Divorce Revolution: The Unexpected Social and Economic Consequences for Women and Children in America (1987). 26B

Joan Wexler, *Rethinking Modification of Child Custody Decrees*, 94 Yale L. J. 757 (1985). 35A, 35B

Walter Otto Weyrauch, "Metamorphoses of Marriage: Formal and Informal Marriage in the United States," in Cohabitation at 265-281. 8B

Peter A. Zablotsky, *To Grandmother's House We Go: Grandparent Visitation After Stepparent   Adoption*,
    32 Wayne L. Rev. 1(1985). 13B

Teresa A. Zakaria, Note, *By Any Other Name: Defining Male & Female in Marriage Statutes*, Ave Mria L.
    Rev. 349 (2005). 4B

Sanja Zgonjanin, *What Does It Take to be a (Lesbian) Parent? On Intent and Genetics*, 16 Hastings Wo.'s
    L.J. 251 (20050. 4B

Zheng Wu & T.R. Balakrishnan, *Dissolution of Premarital Cohabitation in Canada*, 32 Demography 521,
    526, 529 (1995). 3B, 19C

Angela Zielinski, Comment, *Attorneys Fees as Necessaries of Life: Expanding A Domestic Violence Victim's
    Access to Safety and Justice*, 60 Mont. L. Rev. 201 (1999). 17A

Debbie Zielinski, Note, *Domestic Partnership Benefits: Why Not Offer Them to Same-Sex Partners and
    Unmarried Opposite Sex Partners*, 13 J.L. & Health 281 (1999). 1A, 8A

Nicholas Zill & Charlotte A. Schoenborn, Developmental, Learning, and Emotional Problems: Health of Our
    Nation's Children, United States, 1988. 33A

Index